50 YEARS OF AMERICAN AUTOMOBILES

1939-1989

BEEKMAN HOUSE

Manufactured in Yugoslavia.

h g f e d c b a

This edition published by:
Beekman House
Distributed by Crown Publishers, Inc.
225 Park Avenue South
New York, New York 10003

ISBN: 0-517-68640-6

CREDITS

Photography

The editors gratefully acknowledge the following for their assistance with the photography: Sam Griffith, Bud Juneau, Milton Gene Kieft, Rick Lenz, Doug Mitchel, Richard Spiegelman, Joseph H. Wherry, Nicky Wright.

Owners

Special thanks to the owners of the cars featured in this book for their cooperation: Kirk Alexander, Andrew Alphonso, Mark Alter, A. Boyd Anderson, Roy & Shirley Andrews, Tom Andrews, Eldon Anson, Mark Apel, Ross P. Armijo, Don Armstrong, Ross Arterberry, Jim Ashworth, Les Aubol, Dan & Barbara Baltic, Samuel R. Barone, Dave Bartholomew, Ed Barwick, Chuck Beed, William Benson, George Berg, Cathy & Bill Beutel, Rod & Claudia Bjerke, Jim Blanchard, Pete Bogard, Geoff. Bonebrake, Pete Bose, Bob Botkowsky, James Bottger, Jim Bowersox, Jeff Branson, R. G. Brelsford, Scott Brubaker, Joseph R. Bua, Doug Burnell, Marshall Burton, Kent & Marsha Butterfield, David Cammack, Frank Capolupo, Palmer Carlson, Earl Carpenter, Richard Carpenter, Benjamin R. Caskey Jr., Ron Chamerlik, Mary Lee Cipriano, Al & Irene Coubrough, Mike Cowles, John Cox, Jim K. Craddock, Thomas & Mae Crockatt, Jim Crossen, Phil & Louella Cruz, Keith Cullen, Alan Radtke, Raymond E. Dade, Arthur & Suzanne Dalby, Vincent Daul, Terry S. Davies, Al DeFabrizio, Ray & Nancy Deitke, Harry A. DeMenge, James E. Dinehart, Richard DiVecchi, James L. Dowdy, Dr. Tom Eganhouse, Jerry Emery, Richard Emery, Galen & Fay Erb, Gary L. Faulk, Don & Sue Fennig, Bev Ferreira, Don & Barbara Flinn, Christina Finster, John & Jeanne Finster, John Fitzgerald, Edsel Ford, Robert Fox, Ray Frazier, Kurt Fredericks, Terry Freihage, Bob French, Dave Freiday, Terri Gardner, Charles P. Geissler, Ralph Geissler, Ray Geschke, Glenn A. Gornall, Stephen Gottfried, Robert Graves, Tim Graves, Michael Gray, Joe Greene, Tom Griffith, Bill Groves, Anthony J. Gullatta, Tom Haase, Tim & Sharon Hacker, Robert G. Hall, Tom Hall, Robert Hallada, William K. Hamilton, Earl F. Hansen, Mark Hansen, Bill & Dorothy Harris, Gordon F. Harvey, Roger Hayes, Paul Hem, Jack Henning, Ray Herman, Bud Hicks, Bud Hiler, Bob Hill, Larry Hill, Roger Hill, Donna & Biff Hitzeman, Philip & Nancy Hoffman, Bob Hoffmann, Jane & Eric Hopman, Paul Hostetler, Dick Hoyt, Owen F. Hoyt, Les Huckins, Vern Hunt, Ken Hutchison, Bruce Jacobs, Leroy Janisch, Robert M. Jarrett, Gary Johns, Dennis & Cathy Johnson, Bud Juneau, Gene L. Kappel, Jack Karleskind, Roger Kash, Tom & Arlene Kasper, Jack Kasprzak, John Keck, Winfred & Betty Keep, Joe Kelly, Dan & Karen Kerridge, Gerald King, Michele King, William R. Kipp, Bill Knudson, Tom Korbas, Ken Kowalk, Peter Krakowski, Phil Kuhn, Wesley C. Lantz, Bob & Phyllis Leach, Brad & Reda Leasor, Joseph Leir Memorial Auto Collection, David Lilrich, Lee Lockhart, Andrew & Bonita MacFarland, Cecil S. Madaus, Joe Malta, Duane Mann, Mike Matheson, Don McCormick, Monte McElroy, Ray Menefee, Marty & Itacque Metzgar, Loren E. Miller, S. Ray Miller Jr., George W. Mills, Marvin Minarich, Daniel Mitchell, Ralph Mitchell, Glenn Moist, Bob Montgomery, Jack Moore, Mike Moore, Jordan Morris, Linda Mulligan, Tom Mulligan, Carmel Murray, Randall Mytar, Marvin Nallau, Andrew Nothnagel, Leonard Nowosel, Ben Oliver, Gary Pahee, Richard Panke, Bob Patrick, Steven L. Pegler, Ken Perry, Ed & Vi Pettitt, Robb D. Petty, Thomas & Carol Podemski, John Poochigian, Norman W. Prien, Bill & Lanee Proctor, Mel Quirt, George Randolph, Ken Rathke, Larry Ray, Jim Regnier, William Rehberg, Vera & Glen Reints, Raymond J. Reis, Sr., Raymond J. Reis Jr., Robert F. Richards, George Richardson, Hugh Richardson, John & Janet Ricketts, Joseph H. Risner, Roman Robaszewski, Larry Rohde, Don Ross, Dennis Roxworthy, Eugene Roy, Jim Rudnick, Art Sabin, Col. J.L. Sanders, Rick J. Santelli, Santo Scafide, Walter Schenk, Rick Schick, Lester Schnepen, Jim & Ginger Schoenherr, Stephen Schonegg, Bill Schwanback, Bob Sejnost, Bob & Roni Sue Shapiro, Don Sharp, James & Joan Sharp, M.J. Shelton, Rick Shick, Ray Shinn, Dave Showalter, Jack Shrum, Terry Silcox, Rick Simpson, Sid Slayton, Jack Sltrum, David & Linda Smith, S. Spiegelm, Ronald Smith, Don & Bonnie Snipes, Vince & Helen Springer, Harold Stabe, Tom Stackhouse, Dennis State, Dave Stefun, Danny L. Steine, Kurt Stier, Dan Streick, Roger & Barbara Stroud, Nathan Studer, Chuck Swafford, Robert G. Swanstrom, Ron Szymanowski, Brad & Bev Taffs, Chris Terry, Mike & Yvonne Tifft, William H. Tresize, Phil Troost, David A. Ulrich, Harold Van Brucken, Charles A. Vance, Charles Vickery, Don Vincent, Carlos & Sherry Vivas, Harold Von Brocken, Phil Walker, Ed Wassmann, Al Webster, Alan Wendland, Bob Weggenmann William E. Wetherholt, Ron Wold, Linda Wyatt, Harry Wynn, Andrew & Phyllis Young, Joseph & Glenna Zaborny, Ray Zeman

TABLE OF CONTENTS

SPECIFICATIONS TABLES

INTRODUCTION

Welcome to *50 Years of American Automobiles 1939-1989,* which chronicles the evolution of the American car over those 50 years—a general survey of key developments for major U.S. makes. Historical text and spec tables through 1980 have been adapted from the Auto Editors of CONSUMER GUIDE®'s *Encyclopedia of American Cars 1930-1980,* written by Richard M. Langworth, whose expertise and historical acumen is gratefully acknowledged. Post-1980 material has been prepared especially for this edition and is, we believe, the first attempt to give historical perspective to the tumultuous automotive events of the Eighties.

Notes to the reader

There's very little you need to know in perusing these pages, but a few explanatory words are in order. Unless otherwise stated, production figures cited are always for *model year,* not calendar year. This is because the latter typically involve more than one model year, which can confuse comparisons among makes. By contrast, model year figures include only those cars marketed as 1939, 1949, 1959, etc. models, and are thus more clear-cut and meaningful. Where precise model year tallies were not available, registrations, sales, or calendar year production figures are given and always identified as such.

Some readers may question the inclusion of Avanti, Checker, Excalibur, Shelby, and Tucker, all minor makes with volume representing a mere fraction of the industry total. Our reasoning was partly subjective, tempered by history. Both Avanti and Excalibur are still in business, and though their production isn't ever likely to increase, we felt any postwar make that had managed to survive more than two decades had a place here. Shelby first appeared as a marque in 1965 and expired in 1970 but has recently been reborn. Volume in both incarnations has been considerable for a tiny company and the impact of its cars undeniable. And

A trend-setter from Cadillac: 1941 Sixty Special.

Tucker remains significant, not simply because of the compelling story of its creator, but for its remarkable engineering and safety innovations, many of which are standard features of American automobiles today.

While Canadian and Mexican derivatives of U.S. models are excluded by definition, we made an exception for the Canadian-built 1965-66 Studebakers because that make had been too much a part of the American scene to ignore its final offerings. We had no problem omitting the various late-Eighties Japanese "transplant" models, including the latest Chevy Nova. The reason is that while they may be *built* in the U.S., they are not American designs, though the 1989 Ford Probe, a Mazda MX-6 with Dearborn styling, almost qualifies.

We also decided to treat the Corvair and Corvette apart from Chevrolet and to separate Mustang and Thunderbird from Ford. Reason: All were (are) substantially different in technology and character from the parent make's usual fare. Other sub-models are described in the appropriate entries.

Two more exceptions involve Willys, where postwar coverage is confined to the 1948-51 Jeepster and 1952-55 Aero passenger cars. While some might argue that the 1963-vintage Wagoneer, the late-Sixties Jeepster 2, today's XJ-series Cherokee/Wagoneer and even the civilian Jeep qualify as cars, most industry sources define them as "trucks," while collectors at least consider the original Jeepster a car. We follow their leads, and thus also forego discussion of the Jeep CJ-inspired Chevy Blazer, Ford Bronco, and International Scout sport-utilities, though we recognize that they've long been bought partly for passenger use.

The same could be said for today's minivans, especially the Dodge Caravan/Plymouth Voyager, which some view as successors to the traditional big American station wagon. We tend to see them that way too, and provide appropriate coverage of those trailblazing Chrysler products as well as Ford's Aerostar and Chevy's Astro, in each case emphasizing passenger versions over commercial models.

Industry practice rules in all other cases. The 1956 Clipper gets its own entry because it was registered that year as a make separate from Packard and had its own franchises, though the cars differed little from the '55 models (covered under Packard along with other Clippers). Continental was a distinct Ford Motor Company make in 1956-58 but hasn't been since, and is treated accordingly. The same holds for American Motors, which used the Rambler marque from 1957 through '65, then phased in a new "AMC" brand that replaced Rambler entirely by 1970.

About the text

Automotive historians tend to forget that their subjects are more than mechanical contrivances and do not spring into being by themselves. Cars have ever been created *by* people *for* people, and thus reflect the dreams, dilemmas, passions, and politics we all experience.

Recognizing this simple truth, we cover the whys and wherefores of a make's history as much as the what's and how much's. Because these are basically "people stories," you'll find information about the designers, engineers, and executives who shaped the cars; the reasons they did what they did; alternative plans considered and rejected; and the successes or failures that followed. Each entry is concise yet complete: a quick education for the uninitiated, a solid review for the enthusiast.

You'll also find a good many hoary old myths exploded here—that Ralph Nader torpedoed the Corvair, for instance, or that Studebaker was somehow done in by Ford. So much ignorance has been perpetrated and perpetuated over the years that we couldn't resist setting records straight.

A fascinating 50 years

The automobile and the American auto industry we've come to know had basically evolved by 1939, and it's the cars built since that year which command the greatest interest among enthusiasts today. People generally tend to preserve and collect those things they remember or identify with most strongly from their youth, which is why the focus of the old-car avocation has long since shifted from the antiques and great early-Thirties Classics (ever scarce and, nowadays, largely the province of millionaire entrepreneurs or museums) to newer models that are no less significant and intriguing in their way (with some threatening to become classic-costly, alas).

It was once widely held that Detroit built no collectible automobiles after about 1971, but that view has changed. Though long dismissed as the nadir for American design, the Seventies produced more than a few interesting Detroit cars. The Eighties have given us even more, not least because the industry has learned to live with government mandates and a host of other vexing problems that no one could have predicted 20 years ago.

Twenty years from now, we may well look back on the Eighties as what might be called "The Era of The New Creativity," prompted in part by unprecedented foreign competition and happily symbolized by the return of the factory-built Detroit convertible after a decade's absence. There's little doubt that exciting, sophisticated Eighties cars like the sixth-generation Corvette, Mustang GT, Thunderbird Turbo Coupe and "Super Coupe," the front-drive Dodge Daytona, and the third-series Chevrolet Camaro/Pontiac Firebird will be collectible automobiles in the 21st century.

One writer has characterized the automobile's evolution to date as a three-part drama. In Part I—through World War I—we experimented with all manner of approaches to motive power, including electricity. Part II—WWI to the Depression—saw us settle on the internal-combustion gasoline engine. In Part II— 1930-75—we simply perfected the concepts and components of Part II. One could say the we are now in a Part IV—let's call it "The Age of Efficiency"—that began with GM's first downsized cars of 1977.

In all, the last half-century has been a fascinating and significant period in automotive history. It witnessed the demise of all the late-Twenties/early-Thirties "companion makes" save Pontiac; attempts by prestige producers like Packard to compete in the higher-volume market; the unprecedented cessation of car production during World War II; the postwar decline of the surviving independents; the necessity for mergers and joint ventures; the growing dominance of General Motors through the Seventies and the rise of Ford Motor Company to challenge it in the Eighties; the roller-coaster ride of Chrysler Corporation; the advent of compacts, intermediates, ponycars, muscle cars, and personal-luxury cars; the increasing role of government in automotive design; fuel shortages and rationing; fuel-economy standards; the advent of technical advances such as front drive, turbocharging, electronics; the return of aerodynamics as a major factory in design; periodic challenges from foreign automakers; recessions and energy crises; and—last but not least—extraordinary increases in the cost of buying, owning, and manufacturing cars.

Through it all—and premature notices to the contrary—our national love affair with the automobile has remained abiding and strong. The cars of the USA have always been marvels for the world and, despite prophets of doom, always will be.

This book takes a fond look at the past with high hopes for the future. In that spirit, it is dedicated to every American motorist who has ever loved an automobile.

The Auto Editors of CONSUMER GUIDE®
June 1989

ALLSTATE

In the late '40s, Theodore V. Houser was vice-president of merchandising at Sears, Roebuck but also sat on the board at Kaiser-Frazer. In 1949 he broached the idea of marketing a K-F product under Sears' familiar Allstate name, a complete car to be sold along with parts and accessories for it at the new auto shops then opening up adjacent to Sears' retail stores. A hookup with Kaiser-Frazer was a natural. At the time, Houser was buying Homart enamelware from Kaiser Metals Company in which Sears held a 45-percent share.

The first thought was to simply put Allstate logos on K-F's large 1949 models, but Sears was dubious. Then the compact Henry J came along for 1951, and it was exactly the car T.V. Houser had been looking for: simple, inexpensive, easy to service.

Somehow, K-F president Edgar F. Kaiser managed to convince his dealers to accept a chain department store as a competitor, and the Allstate was announced that November. It was the only new American make for 1952 and the first car Sears had offered since its 1912 high-wheeler. In an apparent attempt to feel out the market, Sears initially concentrated promotion in the Southeast, though the Allstate was ostensibly available nationwide through the 1952 Sears catalog.

It was obviously a Henry J, but sported a distinctive front end designed by Alex Tremulis (lately associated with the Tucker fiasco), plus a major interior upgrade in line with Sears' policy of improving on proprietary products. K-F interior specialist Carleton Spencer used quilted saran plastic combined with a coated paper fiber encapsulated in vinyl, a material he'd discovered in use on the transatlantic telegraph cable. Seemingly impervious to normal wear, it was superior to the upholstery of most Henry Js.

Sears-Allstate batteries, spark plugs, and tube tires were specified, each with the appropriate guarantee: 18 months for tires, 24 months on the battery, and 90 days/4000 miles on the whole car (K-F's standard warranty). Allstates usually had trunklids and dashboard gloveboxes, items found less often on Henry Js, though the basic and standard-trim models lacked the opening trunk. The more expensive Deluxe Six had armrests and a horn ring, which weren't available on the lesser versions even at extra cost.

Otherwise, everything else was the same. This meant KF's pudgy little two-door with fastback styling, 100-inch wheelbase, and choice of two L-head Willys engines: a 134-cubic-inch four-cylinder with 68 horsepower or 161-cid, 80-bhp six. Sears' marketing was more aggressive, though, with five Allstate models to the Henry J's four. The cheapest '52 Allstate, the basic Four, was priced just below the standard Henry J.

There was little change for '53. A full-width rubber-covered pad was added to the instrument panel, taillights were relocated to the rear fenders, and models reduced to two Fours and the Six.

But by then, it was clear that the idea had failed. Whether it was because people didn't take to buying cars in department stores or because of the narrow marketing approach is difficult to determine. Both factors probably contributed. Only 1566 Allstates were built for 1952. The count was 797 when Sears canceled the project in early '53, leaving plans for future models stillborn. Among these were a pair of proposals for a two-door station wagon, one by industrial designer Brooks Stevens, the other by Gordon Tercey of K-F Styling.

Allstates are extremely rare today, and thus more desired than comparable Henry Js by collectors. In 1971, Allstate Insurance purchased one of the Sears cars for historical purposes. In the '60s it would have been hard to convince the folks at Sears parts counters that the car had ever existed.

The '52 Allstate differed from the Henry J mainly in the grille.

Allstate production for the 1952-53 year models totaled 2363 units.

AMERICAN BANTAM

Small cars never made it big in prewar America, but that didn't stop people from pushing them. One was British auto magnate Sir Herbert Austin, who decided in 1929 that what Americans needed was a version of his tiny Austin Seven. He chose to set up in Butler, Pennsylvania, close to vast iron and coal supplies yet not so far from the East Coast as to complicate importing British-built components, and his American Austin Car Company was rolling by May 1930.

Riding a petite 75-inch wheelbase and powered by a 46-cubic-inch L-head four with 13-14 brake horsepower, the American Austin was a simple little car, light (1100-1200 pounds) and attractive (Count Alexis de Sakhnoffsky had a hand in the styling). Roadster, coupe and cabriolet were offered at initial prices of around $450, cut to as low as $330 for 1931 in an effort to improve sales. But Americans were leery of small cars, so sales didn't improve despite Depression-enforced austerity, and the operation was bust by 1934. Production stopped at around 19,700.

The following year, the energetic Roy S. Evans bought American Austin—and its formidable debts: $75,000 in back taxes and interest, plus a $150,000 property mortgage to the Pullman Standard Company. But feeling that Evans might salvage things, the federal court overseeing the bankruptcy proceedings gave him the place for just $5000 cash—only 1/2000 of its appraised valuation. Evans secured a $250,000 loan from the Reconstruction Finance Corporation and hired the necessary talent to help him create a new car to be called American Bantam.

Styling was again assigned to Sakhnoffsky, who created a new front with a smooth hood and rounded grille, and also reworked the fenders and rear deck. His bill was only $300, and Evans was able to retool the entire line for a mere $7000. Indy race-car builder Harry Miller was hired to improve mechanicals, but was confined to a redesigned manifold. Butler's own engineers did most of the engine alterations, replacing the Austin's expensive roller bearings with babbitt bearings; adding full-pressure lubrication, a new three-speed transmission, Hotchkiss final drive, and Ross cam-and-lever steering; devising a heavier frame. Engine size was unchanged, but three main bearings were used instead of two after 1939. Wheel diameter shrank from 18 to 16 inches for '37 and to 15 inches for '38.

Commercial vehicles, like this pickup, were part of the '39 lineup.

The 1939 American Bantam price list ranged from $399 to $565.

American Bantam coupes for '39 came in regular, Special, and DeLuxe.

Even during the depths of the Depression, Americans didn't want little cars. Thus, it's curious that after the American Austin failed in 1934 it would rise again in updated form as the American Bantam. Likewise doomed, it died in 1940.

The 1936 Bantam line comprised a roadster and five coupes in the $295-$385 range. Two roadsters and three coupes were offered for '37 at somewhat higher prices ($385-$492). Several new models arrived for 1938, including a Speedster with pretty "Duesenberg sweep" side panels, and the novel Boulevard Delivery with a rear half-roof. New for 1939 was the smart Riviera convertible, designed by Alex Tremulis, who recalled that it could cruise at 75-80 mph and average 42.5 mpg, through presumably not at the same time.

Bantam production continued into 1941, but not even the dynamic Evans could convince Americans of the value in his tiny package. Output was about 2000 units in 1938, just 1200 the following year, under 1000 in 1940-41, then none at all. The firm found temporary salvation in a contract to design what ultimately became the Army Jeep, which it also briefly manufactured during World War II (along with Ford and Willys-Overland, who built far more). But none of this was sufficient to stave off the inevitable, and American Bantam expired before peace returned.

Only 800 American Bantams were produced in 1940, among them this Foursome Speedster. The wheelbase measured a short 75 inches.

The priciest model offered in '40 was the woody wagon. Price: $565.

This Bantam Riviera was titled as a '41, but output ceased in 1940.

AMC

AMC became a make for 1966 as American Motors applied this badge instead of Rambler nameplates to that year's full-size Ambassador and fastback Marlin. The mid-size Rebel ceased being a Rambler for '68, when the new Javelin ponycar and two-seat AMX arrived. Rambler was last seen on the final, 1969 edition of the 1964-vintage American compact. Hornet and Gremlin replaced it the following year.

The '66 Ambassador was a facelifted version of the redesigned '65 Rambler model, one of the better efforts from the studios of Richard A. Teague, AMC vice-president for styling. Squarish but clean, it spanned a 116-inch wheelbase, four inches longer than the '64 Ambassador's. A new special edition for '66 was the elegantly appointed DPL hardtop coupe, with reclining bucket seats, fold-down center armrests, pile carpeting, and many other standards. This was officially a separate model, not an Ambassador, but became one for '67.

Ranked below it were Ambassador sedans, wagons and hardtops in 880 and 990 trim, plus a 990 convertible. All were offered with the long-running 232-cubic-inch Typhoon six or with optional 287- and 327-cid V8s. Only the 270-horsepower 327 required premium fuel. Although most Ambassadors were ordered with automatic, a few left the factory with three-speed manual transmission or AMC's "Twin-Stick" overdrive. A four-speed synchromesh box was also listed for Ambassador 990s and the DPL.

The big Ambassador evolved nicely through the late '60s. Wheelbase was stretched two inches for '67, when semi-fastback styling with more rounded contours was adopted. The '68s were little changed save a slightly altered hood and a revised model sequence: standard, DPL, and SST. New frontal styling with a more sculpted hood, plastic grille, and horizontal quad headlights marked the '69s, riding a new 122-inch wheelbase and equipped with standard air conditioning. A minor restyle for 1970 brought new rear fenders and taillamps to sedans and hardtops, and new roof panels and taillamps to wagons.

AMC made an unsuccessful try at the booming personal-car market with the radically styled 1965 Rambler Marlin, renamed AMC Marlin for 1966-67. This was a big fastback hardtop coupe, initially based on the mid-size 1965-66 Rambler Classic, with the same 112-inch wheelbase and some of the same front sheetmetal. Teague gave it rakish C-pillars and elliptical rear side windows to help relieve the heavy rear roof quarters, but the overall effect was somewhat clumsy nonetheless. The '66 changed only in detail: revised grille, standard front anti-roll bar for six-cylinder models, and newly optional vinyl roof treatment.

The '67 Marlin was fully restyled, switched to that year's new Ambassador platform and, thanks to the longer wheelbase, much better-looking. Teague helped with handsome lower-body lines of the same hippy sort applied to that year's Ambassador and Rebel. Measuring 6.5 inches longer than previous Marlins, the '67 was perhaps the best of this school, but by then it was too late to save. Sales had been low from the start, and fewer than 5000 and 3000 Marlins were built for 1966 and '67, respectively. Marlin offered

At $2756, the DPL was the top-line Ambassador hardtop in 1966.

The 990 convertible was the most expensive '66 Ambassador: $2968.

The '66 Ambassador came with a 232-cid six; V8s were optional.

Ambassador for 1967 was reskinned and sported vertical headlights.

American Motors, formed via the 1954 Nash-Hudson merger, made its fame with the Rambler. In the early '60s, the "Big Three" brought out their own compacts, so American Motors expanded its lineup and put all of its cars under the AMC umbrella.

The Rebel name reappeared for 1967 on AMC's mid-size cars. SST was the top-line Rebel for '68; the hardtop listed at $2775.

some sports-car features (optional four-speed manual gearbox, tachometer, bucket seats, and engines with up to 280 bhp) but lacked a sports car's taut, precise handling and manageable size.

Replacing it for 1968 was a far more successful sportster: the Javelin, a ponycar in Mustang's image. Beautifully shaped and exciting, it sold like hotcakes. Over 56,000 were built for the model year, helping AMC out of a four-year sales slump. With standard 232 six, a Javelin cruised at 80 mph; with optional 290 V8, it could do 100 mph. An optional "Go Package" offered a 343 V8 with four-barrel carburetor and dual exhausts, plus power front-disc brakes, heavy-duty suspension, and wide tires—good for eight seconds in the 0-60-mph dash and a top speed approaching 120 mph. On its 109-inch wheelbase, Javelin was roomier, larger, and longer than the rival Mustang, Camaro, and Barracuda, and its styling was cleaner.

Javelin was facelifted for 1969, mainly via an altered grille. A "twin-venturi" nose, revised wheel covers, and a new hood with simulated air scoops arrived for 1970. Alas, sales failed to match the first-year total because of tougher ponycar competition, notably a sleek new Chevy Camaro.

An exciting mid-1968 newcomer was the AMX, a two-seat coupe created by sectioning the Javelin bodyshell to a trim 97-inch wheelbase. This car introduced a new 390-cid V8 with forged-steel crankshaft and connecting rods. Output was a healthy 315 bhp and 425 pounds-feet torque. The 290 was standard, a 343 optional. Tight suspension, bucket seats, and extra-cost four-speed gearbox made the AMX a capable semi-sports car; it even did well in competition. As with the Marlin, the handsomest AMX was the last, the 1970 edition looking more integrated and "serious." But demand was always much lower than management hoped for, production for each of these three years failing to top 20,000 units.

As mentioned, Rebel was switched to the AMC line for 1968, though the basic car had appeared the year before as a Rambler, taking over from Classic. It remained the firm's intermediate, however, riding a 114-inch wheelbase and offered with a variety of sixes and V8s. Prices were competitive, starting at around $2500. Sedans, hardtops, wagons, and a convertible were available in three series (550, 770 and SST). Rebel offered AMC's only convertible that year, but few were built: only 377 in the 550 series and another 823 in SST guise. In fact, these would be the last AMC-built drop-tops. The '69 line was trimmed to basic and SST series. A wider track and a new grille plus a restyled rear deck and taillights were the only changes of note.

For 1970, Rebel sedans and hardtops were lengthened two

The '67 Marlin borrowed Ambassador's 118-inch chassis; 2545 were built.

AMX was a two-seater with V8 power and many performance options.

AMC's reply to the Mustang was the 1968 Javelin fastback coupe. It rode a 109-inch wheelbase; 56,462 were built the first year.

inches to accommodate redesigned roof panels and rear fenders, and new taillights appeared. Series stayed the same, but AMC again went after the performance crowd with "The Machine." A Rebel *with* a cause, this hardtop coupe packed the company's most potent V8, plus four-speed manual gearbox with Hurst linkage, and a 3.54:1 rear axle ratio. Providing easy exterior identification were a bold, functional hood air scoop, special red-white-and-blue paint, and 15-inch mag wheels with raised-white-letter tires. An 8000-rpm tachometer, dual exhausts with low-restriction mufflers, and a definite front-end rake completed this expensive package ($3475). The Machine certainly looked the hot performer, but Javelin won the racing honors, Mark Donohue piloting one

The mid-line '68 Ambassador DPL series wagon retailed at $3207.

The '68 Rebel SST hardtop coupe weighed 3348 pounds, cost $2775.

AMC built only 823 Rebel SST convertibles for the 1968 model run.

This '69 Javelin sports optional rally stripes and mag-style wheels.

The use of the AMC logo expanded quickly: Ambassador and Marlin in 1966; Rebel, Javelin, and AMX in 1968; Hornet and Gremlin for 1970. The Rambler badge was retired after 1969 in order to give the last surviving independent a new image.

to win the 1970 Trans-Am road-racing series.

AMC spent $40 million, a million man-hours and three years on a new compact for 1970. It was called Hornet, reviving that time-honored name for the first time since the last Hudsons of 1957. New from the ground up, it came in two- and four-door base and SST sedans on a 108-inch wheelbase, powered by a choice of two sixes. First-year sales were 92,458, a strong showing that helped the company's sagging finances. But on the whole, Kenosha still lost money that year—$58.2 million on sales of over $1 billion.

April 1970 brought the intriguingly named Gremlin, America's first subcompact. With attractive prices and AMC's thriftiest six, this import-fighter initially sold well, over 26,000 moving out before the short model year ended in mid-1970. As the AMX related to Javelin, so Gremlin did to Hornet. Sheetmetal was similar ahead of the B-pillar, but the Gremlin rode an abbreviated 96-inch wheelbase and had a severely truncated tail with lift-up wagon-style rear window. Though Gremlin styling proved controversial, designer Teague insisted it was the only way to go. "Nobody would have paid it any attention if it had looked like one of the Big Three," he said.

With the Hornet and Gremlin, AMC gave up trying to be a "full-line" automaker competing toe-to-toe with the Big Three, and resumed being a "niche" marketer specializing in small cars. But the transition took a long time, and it wasn't until model year '79 that

The '69 Ambassador rode a four-inch-longer wheelbase: 122 inches.

It took $2947 to drive home a brand-new 1969 Rebel SST station wagon.

The 96-inch-wheelbase Gremlin made its debut as a 1970 model.

The 1970 Hornet took over where the 1969 Rambler American left off.

AMC built 40,675 Javelins for '69, among them this $2633 SST. Engine choices ranged from a 232 six to a 390 V8 with 315 bhp.

AMC fully returned to the formula it had found so profitable in the late '50s and early '60s. In a way, it was strange that this tiny outfit would have ever tried to match the giants model-for-model, but Roy Abernethy and even his market-wise successor, Roy D. Chapin, Jr., were somehow persuaded by the AMC board to abandon the course pursued long before by the messianic George Romney.

An important development toward more specialized products was the February 1970 acquisition of Kaiser-Jeep Corporation in Toledo, which instantly made AMC the nation's leading builder of four-wheel-drive vehicles. Though uncharted territory for AMC, Jeep's long experience in the field would ultimately prove valuable, eventually finding its way into the passenger-car line.

Though it took nearly a decade to complete, AMC's market reorientation was evident as early as 1971. The jazzy Rebel Machine and slow-selling AMX were dropped, though the latter's name was applied to a new top-line Javelin. The ponycar was given heavy—and not altogether successful—sheetmetal surgery on a one-inch longer wheelbase, with crisper contours and pronounced bulges over the front wheel openings, the latter aping the contemporary Corvette. Inside was a reworked dash curved inward at the center *a la* Pontiac's then-current Grand Prix so as to bring minor controls closer to the driver.

Javelin stumbled along in this form through 1974, a vestige of

The Ambassador, here a DPL, was extensively restyled for 1970.

AMX was priced at $3395 in 1970, but only 4116 were built that year.

AMX became a top-line Javelin for 1971; only 2054 were produced.

The limited-edition '71 Hornet SC/360 saw only 784 copies built.

Gremlin X for '72 could be had with 232 or 258 sixes or a 304 V8.

AMC's priciest 1972 model was the Ambassador Brougham: $4437.

The '72 Hornet SST four door started at $2265, weighed 2691 pounds.

This '72 Javelin sports a special Pierre Cardin designer interior.

In April 1970, millions of Americans protested pollution via the first Earth Day. That same month, AMC beat Ford and GM to market with a subcompact, the Gremlin. AMC also bought Jeep in 1970, making it number one in four-wheel drive.

past sales tactics. Production never broke 30,000 units for any of these years, reflecting the general decline in ponycar demand after 1970. When it was quietly killed, AMC decided against a direct replacement—reasonable considering the only such cars still selling in decent numbers by then were GM's F-body Chevrolet Camaro/Pontiac Firebird. Even so, Javelin remained faithful to the cause, and a big 401-cid V8, new for '71, was optionally available through the end.

Another AMC nameplate disappeared after 1974: Ambassador. Continued with only minor trim and equipment changes in its final years, the firm's full-size was ultimately done in by lack of interest. Sales had never been great, and though its aging 1967 design was more sensible in some ways than that of early-'70s Big Three rivals, the lack of change increasingly weighed against it. The crowning blow was probably the Middle East oil embargo of 1973-74, which triggered the country's first energy crisis and temporarily crippled sales of all full-size cars.

Another holdover fared only slightly better. This was the Matador, a renamed, restyled version of the mid-size Rebel, appearing for 1971 and basically a continuation of that '67 design. Offered in the same three body styles through 1973, it was pretty ordinary stuff and failed to generate much showroom traffic. In later years, AMC tacitly acknowledged this line's near invisibility with a series of humorous TV commercials that asked "What's a Matador?" Few buyers apparently cared.

An attempt to inject some pizzazz into Matador's staid image arrived for 1974, when the notchback hardtop coupe gave way to a completely different pillared fastback two-door that AMC boldly announced would race in NASCAR. Stylist Teague gave it smooth, curvaceous looks, announced by an unusual front with the hood shaped to form the upper portions of huge headlamp cavities. Despite special "designer" interiors (then a favored AMC marketing ploy) and sporty options like the "X" package, the fastback provided only temporary relief and Matador sales remained underwhelming. Like Ambassador, the intermediate suffered further in the aftermath of the first energy crisis. By 1978 it was quite passe—even the coupes, which had been progressively hoked up in the intervening years—so it was adios, Matador.

Gremlin was one "sow's ear" that Teague made into the proverbial silk purse—generally AMC's number-two seller, behind Hornet. A series of special trim options such as the "X" and "Levi's" packages helped keep interest alive in the little squirt. The former typically comprised special tape striping, black grille, slotted wheels, wider tires, custom bucket-seat interior, sports steering wheel, and similar dressup items. Prices were reasonable, about $300 at first. The Levi's edition, new for 1973, sported seats and door panels done up in blue spun nylon with copper rivets to look just like the genuine cotton denim of Levi Strauss, which happily collaborated on the project, even allowing the use of its distinctive red jeans label for instant identification. This was probably the most winsome and interesting Gremlin, and if anybody ever collects these cars, this one may well be the most popular.

Gremlin vanished for 1979 but lived on in Spirit, essentially the same thing with smoother, more conventional styling. Joining the familiar chopped-tail two-door was a slick new hatchback coupe bearing a particularly graceful superstructure for such a short wheelbase. Both body styles were offered in three trim levels, and the AMX tag was revived for a special "paint-on performance" 1980 coupe. Spirits moved via a standard Pontiac-built 2.5-liter (151-cid) four or the long-lived AMC six. A heavy emphasis on quality meant that Spirits were generally better built than Gremlins, if not always Big Three rivals. But '60s-style specifications betrayed an aging basic design. And while the four was fairly thrifty, it had very little urge; the six was quicker but thirstier.

Shortly before this transformation, Teague similarly reworked the Hornet into the Concord, which bowed for '78. Reflecting the company's limited new-model development funds, it wasn't all that

A Levi's interior was an extra cost option on the 1973 Gremlin X.

Air conditioning came as standard equipment on the '73 Ambassador.

A hatchback joined the 1973 Hornet roster; prices started at $2449.

Javelin's biggest engine option for 1973 was a 255-bhp 401 V8.

Hornet had a good year in '74—a total of 145,458 were produced.

New to the mid-size lineup for '74 was the sleek Matador X coupe. It listed at $3699 with standard 304 V8; about 1500 were built.

The '74 Ambassador Brougham wagon saw production of 7076 units.

Electronic ignition was new to the '75 Gremlin. Base price: $2098.

Pacer debuted for 1975 billed as "The First Wide Small Car." It rode a 100-inch wheelbase and listed at $3299; 72,158 were built.

In the early Seventies, the AMC roster shrank as low sales forced it to drop the AMX, Ambassador, and Javelin. But a widened range of Hornets and Gremlins helped AMC weather the Arab Oil Embargo of 1973-74. The Pacer debuted for 1975.

Among the four 1976 Hornet body styles was the $3199 two-door sedan.

The '76 Gremlin saw only detail changes; prices started at $2889.

different structurally or mechanically, but it looked more "important" and, like other AMC models, benefited from the urgent stress on workmanship prompted by the growing success of Japanese imports. Concord was AMC's volume seller from the time it appeared. By 1980 it boasted a thriftier standard engine, cleaner appearance, more comfort and convenience extras and a broader anti-rust warranty.

Not to be overlooked are three early-'70s Hornet developments. One was the SC/360, a short-lived performance two-door offered only for '71. As its name suggested, it packed AMC's 360 small-block V8, rated at 245 bhp with standard two-barrel carb or 285 bhp with extra-cost four-pot induction. Acceleration was quite vivid, and a large functional hood scoop, heavy-duty suspension, styled wheels, fat tires, and tape striping were all standard. A Hurst four-speed was optional. But as had so often been the case before, AMC was a day late and a dollar short: only 784 were built, making the SC/360 one of the decade's rarest production models and thus something of a collector's item.

A more sensible—and successful—innovation was the Hornet Sportabout, a graceful four-door wagon with one-piece tailgate. New for '71, it would prove uncommonly long-lived. Even lovelier was Teague's new-for-'73 Hornet hatchback coupe. Offering vast load space, it could be quite sporty with the optional "X" package. Unhappily, needless styling gimmickry rendered some versions

Spoilers, rear window louvers, and racy wheels were part of the '77 Hornet AMX package. A 304 V8 was the largest engine offered.

quite tacky by the time the Concord came in, and the hatchback was axed after '79. There was also a special AMX model with this bodyshell, a limited-run 1977-78 offering.

Concord spawned a novel offshoot for 1980, an intriguing and bold product for a small automaker. This was the four-wheel-drive Eagle, reviving a name that AMC owned via the Jeep takeover and, with it, the dregs of Willys-Overland. A natural for a firm with AMC's particular but limited resources, Eagle combined the Concord body/chassis with a new full-time 4WD system called Quadra-Trac, whose transfer case apportioned driving torque between front and rear wheels via a center differential with clutches running in a slip-limiting silicone compound. The result was neither car nor truck but a specialty vehicle with the appeal of both.

Eagle arrived with the three Concord body styles and a nominally longer wheelbase. Its ride height was greater, thanks to larger tires and the required extra ground clearance for the differentials. The drivetrain comprised the firm's well-known 258-cid six mated to Torque Command (actually Chrysler TorqueFlite) three-speed automatic transmission. Power steering and brakes and all-season radial tires were standard. Eagles flew with prominent (and necessary) wheelarch flares made of color-keyed Krayton plastic, and a Sport package option offered black extensions and other trim, plus Goodyear Tiempo tires.

Predictably, the Eagle drove and felt much like any Concord. AMC didn't intend it for off-road use, pitching it instead on the safety advantages of 4WD traction for everyday driving, particularly in the snowbelt. A full range of luxury and convenience features was listed, but there was no V8 option in the interest of fuel economy—and the government's corporate average fuel economy (CAFE) mandates. The Pontiac-built four became available for '81.

AMC's biggest '70s disappointment was the Pacer, announced for 1975 as "the first wide small car." A reply to Chevrolet's Vega and Ford's Pinto in the domestic subcompact stakes, it was conceived around a lightweight Wankel rotary engine that GM was developing in the early '70s but ultimately shelved. Designer Teague penned distinctive lines with acres of glass, a short nose (though sufficient for the compact rotary), and a hatchback body that was almost as wide as it was long.

Unhappily, cancellation of the GM Wankel forced AMC into patchwork engineering alterations that seriously compromised Pacer's original concept. While the rotary would have provided decent performance and fuel economy, AMC had to use its relatively big and weighty six, to the detriment of both as well as handling. With that and its glassy body, the Pacer ended up quite heavy for a 100-inch-wheelbase subcompact, and its styling was frankly odd to many eyes (though doors wrapped into the roof were predictive of '80s design). By 1979, annual sales were down to only 10,000 or so despite the interim addition of wagons and a V8 option, and Pacer was unceremoniously dumped after 1980.

An aging product line that didn't generate sufficient sales for funding development of more modern replacements proved an increasingly vicious cycle for AMC as the '70s wore on. For example, the Eagle owed much to the Concord, which in turn dated from the (by then) decade-old Hornet. Mounting losses were aggravated at decade's end by a deep national recession that cut sales further, and AMC soon found itself the object of a takeover bid by Renault of France, which acquired a controlling interest in the firm by 1982.

Thus was born what some were quick to call "Franco-American Motors." European Renault executives came in to run things alongside AMC officials, and the old Nash factory in Kenosha was retooled at great expense to produce an Americanized version of the European Renault 9 subcompact, aptly renamed Alliance.

Trouble was, acquiring AMC made Renault no wiser about the American market, and it had little more impact as a back-door "domestic" than it had as an outright import. Odd French products

The Gremlin X received revised side striping for the '77 model run.

The Hornet became a Concord in 1978, here a D/L station wagon.

Limited was the top-line Concord in '79, here the $5688 two door.

The Gremlin turned into a Spirit for '79. The D/L sold for $4090.

Sportiest of the '79 Spirits was the hatchback with the AMX package.

America was abuzz in the mid-Seventies with the Watergate scandal and the resignation of President Richard Nixon in 1974. But AMC was still around in 1976 to celebrate the U.S. Bicentennial, mainly because of the popularity of its Hornet.

AMC debuted a line of Concord-based four-wheel-drive Eagles for 1980. They rode a 109.3-inch wheelbase; prices started at $7168.

like the tinny-tiny Le Car and lumpy Fuego coupe didn't help AMC dealers very much. The Alliance did, but not that long. As a car it was no more than adequate, and thus not really up to the formidable task of improving Renault's decidedly second-rate image among U.S. buyers.

Still, Alliance seemed just what the doctor ordered—modern two- and four-door front-drive sedans with a 97.8-inch wheelbase and a thrifty, transverse 85-cid four-cylinder engine—and for a time it sold well: over 142,000 of the debut 1983 models. Bolstered by two- and four-door hatchback derivatives called Encore, sales zoomed to over 208,000 the following year.

But mechanical problems and indifferent workmanship were as evident here as on any French-built Renault. Once word got around, sales tumbled—to 150,000, then to 65,000 for '86 and,

The Pacer wagon bowed in 1977; the '80 model (shown) marked Pacer's last year. The D/L listed at $5558, the Limited at $6182.

Concord listed 18 models for 1980, including the $6394 Limited wagon.

Like so many cars of its era, the '80 Concord sported opera windows.

The '81 Eagle Kammback boasted shift-on-the-fly four-wheel drive.

The '81 Concord Limited measured 185 inches overall, cost $6267.

finally, to some 35,000. AMC tried to stop the slide for '85 by offering an optional 105-cid/78-bhp engine and a brace of new Alliance convertibles—Kenosha's first drop-tops since '68—but to no avail.

By 1987, with AMC's mounting losses and several years of withering home-market sales, Renault was in financial trouble and ready to pull out. Fortunately, Lee Iacocca, the miracle worker who'd lately turned Chrysler Corporation from penniless to prosperous, was willing to take over, mainly to get his hands on AMC's lucrative Jeep business. Thus did America's last sizeable independent automaker pass into history, transmogrified almost overnight into a new Chrysler division called Jeep-Eagle.

AMC's own products departed much earlier, dropped after 1983 in the rush to Renaults. The sole exceptions were the Eagle wag-

This 1982 Eagle SX/4 Liftback features the $499 Sport Package.

AMC referred to the '82 Concord as one of its "Tough Americans."

AMC's alliance with Renault of France resulted in the '83 Alliance.

Alliance was followed up with an '84 hatchback version, the Encore.

Renault of France acquired controlling interest in AMC in 1982 and offered an Americanized version of the Renault 9 in 1983 as the Alliance. Renault's problems back home forced it to sell the U.S. operation to Chrysler Corporation in 1987.

Standard engine on the '84 Eagle was an AMC-built 2.5-liter four.

AMC called the sporty '87 Renault Alliance GTA a "pocket rocket."

on and four-door sedan, which hung on until the Chrysler takeover, then disappeared along with Alliance.

Before the end, AMC slipped the Eagle's full-time 4WD under the Spirit coupe and ex-Gremlin two-door bodies to create a pair of "Eaglets," powered by the same engines. The most interesting of these was the SX/4 Sport, Dick Teague's pretty little fastback with foglights, distinctive striping, rear spoiler, and plush bucket-seat interior. Though pleasant and distinctive, it was no sprinter, and buyers continued to prefer "real" 4WDs.

Still, low production, a drivetrain unique among American cars, and status as AMC's last attempt at something different suggest the short-lived junior Eagles will be minor collector's items one day. Only about 37,500 Eagles in all were sold for 1981 and less than half that number for '82 and '83; exact breakouts aren't available, but the smaller ones probably accounted for no more than a third of each year's total. After 1983, the big Eagles carried on alone, virtually unchanged and garnering some 6000-7000 annual sales—too paltry for industry statisticians to even bother with.

At this writing, Chrysler is hoping that buyers will forget the old 4WDs as it attempts to establish Eagle as a new "upscale" brand. That won't be easy given two of three cars that now wear the name, both inherited from AMC: a competent but dull-looking mid-size sedan, the Premier, and the similar compact Medallion, both front-drivers and just rebadged Renaults. Plans also call for Eagle versions of various Japanese-built Mitsubishis, beginning with the small front-drive Summit sedan, based on the new 1989 Mirage.

Can Chrysler buck postwar history and make a success of this new nameplate? As always, time will render the final verdict.

Priced at $10,295 for the L, the '85 Alliance was the lowest-priced convertible sold in America. The DL version sold for $11,295.

AVANTI II/ AVANTI

Studebaker fled to Canada in late 1963, then left the auto business three years later. By that time, Leo Newman and Nathan Altman, partners in a South Bend, Indiana, Studebaker dealership—one of the oldest—had resurrected the Avanti, Studebaker's greatest car of the '60s.

Designed by a team working under Raymond Loewy, the Avanti had failed Studebaker in the marketplace but succeeded greatly with enthusiasts—the only Studebaker in two generations to inspire so much interest. Before its phaseout on Studebaker's departure from South Bend, the Avanti had broken virtually every major U.S. Auto Club speed record, running a 170.78-mph flying-mile at Bonneville, for example [*see* Studebaker].

Knowing this car was too good to lose, Newman and Altman bought the Avanti name, production rights, and tooling as well as a portion of the century-old South Bend factory where Studebaker had built it. There, in late 1965, they began turning out a revised version called Avanti II. Their goal was 300 a year, a level they'd never reach, though production was always adequate and consistent.

Unlike its predecessor, the Avanti II was a commercial success. Its fiberglass body construction meant there were no expensive sheetmetal dies to maintain, and because Newman and Altman had conceived the II as more exclusive than the original Avanti, it could be built on a miniature assembly line, carefully and largely by hand, and tailored to each customer's personal specifications. Altman, a born salesman, reveled in this business. Visitors to the Avanti factory would frequently find him on the phone talking long-distance to some affluent customer about his or her particular car.

Avanti II production continued through 1982, by which time retail price had risen to just under $30,000. That was a far cry from the mid-'60s, when even the most dedicated sybarite was hard put to push the $6550 base price beyond $10,000—though Newman and Altman did their best to help. Options included Hurst four-speed manual transmission, power steering, air conditioning,

Out of the ashes of Studebaker's departure from South Bend arose the Avanti II, saved by enthusiasts Leo Newman and Nathan Altman.

Studebaker dealers Leo Newman and Nathan Altman resurrected the Avanti in 1965, two years after Studebaker shut down its South Bend assembly plants. Ownership went to entrepreneur Steve Blake in 1982, who set about to update the aging car.

electric window lifts, tinted windshield and rear window, AM/FM radio, Eppe fog or driving lights, limited-slip differential, Magnum 500 chrome wheels, and Firestone bias-ply or Michelin radial tires. Early Avanti IIs had vinyl interiors, but textured "Raphael vinyl" could be ordered for $200 extra. Genuine leather seat and door trim added $300, full leather $500. Paint colors were anything the customer wanted; in later years, so were interior trims. This led to some pretty bizarre individual cars (as Porsche would discover), but it was part of the "custom-built" aura that made the Avanti unique—and helped sales.

Early IIs retained the original Avanti's modified Lark convertible frame, but as the supply of Studebaker V8s dried up once the firm moved to Canada, Newman and Altman followed Studebaker's lead and adopted the same 327-cubic-inch Chevrolet V8—albeit in 300-horsepower Corvette tune. By 1969, the small-block had grown to 350 cid and was duly substituted. Rated power was unchanged. Buyers could choose either a fully synchronized Borg-Warner four-speed manual or a "power-shift" automatic permitting manual hold of first and second gears.

These new mechanicals were installed in a body almost identical with the original Avanti's. The main visual differences were a more level stance (Altman's customers disliked the Studebaker's marked front-end rake), Avanti logos with Roman numeral IIs, and reduced-radius wheel openings.

The Corvette engine made the sleek four-place Avanti a good performer. The typical 0-60-mph time with automatic was under nine seconds; with 3.54:1 rear axle, the II could reach 125 miles per hour. As the Chevy engine was lighter than the old Studebaker V8, front/rear weight distribution improved from the original 59/41 percent to 57/43. Though understeer remained the basic handling trait, final oversteer could now be induced by a judicious poke at the throttle. Assisted front-disc/rear-drum brakes resisted fade while providing excellent deceleration of nearly 1 g in 80-mph panic stops. Obviously, Newman and Altman cared about safety as much as straight-line performance.

Because of the way it was built, the Avanti II necessarily carried a higher price than Studebaker's version, competing in Cadillac Eldorado territory instead of Chrysler country like the $4445 original. Realizing this meant a change in market orientation, Newman and Altman pitched the II more on "personal-luxury" than performance.

And indeed, the car was in its element on the open road. Magazine testers gave it points for safety, quietness, structural rigidity, and its firm but comfortable ride. "In this day of great concern over automotive safety," wrote John R. Bond in 1966, "the Avanti II should make new friends, for obviously there was more thought given to safety in its conception than in most American cars. Good brakes, sensible interior design and decent handling impart security to the driver . . . It's a better car than it was three years ago."

Most Avanti II changes in the '70s were made solely to meet federal safety and emissions regulations. One of the most obvious was an ugly, rubber-tipped "cow catcher" grafted onto the slim original bumpers so as to meet 1973's new five-mph crash standard, although Avanti Motor Corporation was exempted from the required 2½-mph side-impact door beams. Also for '73, the company switched from the 350 small-block to Chevrolet's new detoxed 400 V8. Net horsepower ratings took effect the following year, and this unit came in at a relatively anemic 180 bhp (245 SAE gross). The 350 returned as standard power for '76, and would remain so into the early '80s.

With Nate Altman's untimely death in 1976, Avanti seemed to lose direction, at times appearing halfhearted about its product and its future. Workmanship visibly declined even as prices, partly due to inflationary pressures, scampered upward (breaking $12,000 in '76). Federal rules dictated minor changes to interior fittings (mainly switchgear) that were made with an afterthought carelessness suggesting lack of really thorough engineering and design work. On the plus side, the company reduced the number of outlandish special-order paint jobs and far-out interiors in the interest of standardization, higher build quality and lower inventory costs. But little if any money and effort were put toward updating the original Avanti concept as Altman had done.

After refusing several buyout offers over the years, the Altman family and other Avanti board members gave audience to enthusiast Stephen Blake, a young Washington, D.C., construction magnate. Blake loved his Avanti II and wanted to see its maker move

Stephen Blake took over Avanti in October 1982. One of his first projects was to offer a convertible, first seen in late 1983.

Among the changes instituted under Blake for the '84 Avanti were optional body-color bumpers, black trim, and square headlights.

ahead. Unfortunately, Altman's death came only days after the parties agreed to serious negotiations, and Blake would need another seven years to seal a deal, officially becoming owner, president and CEO of Avanti Motor Corporation in October 1982.

He blew into South Bend like a tornado, rearranging work flow in the crumbling old plant for improved efficiency and quality, resisting UAW organizing efforts, dismissing all the firm's old dealers and inking more businesslike contracts with established Cadillac stores in major markets, bringing in required engineering talent and instituting numerous product updates. The last included tougher paint (DuPont Imron), greater use of GM components throughout the car, optional body-color bumpers and black trim, square headlights, a revamped interior, minor chassis alterations, and availability of the 185-bhp, 302-cid V8 from the latest Camaro Z28 (versus the standard 135-bhp Chevy small-block). Most of these changes came together in a special 20th-anniversary 1983

After Michael Kelly took over the Avanti operation in April 1985, the convertible became a reality, seen here as a 1987 model.

Texan Michael Kelly snapped up the Avanti operation in 1985 and moved it to Youngstown, Ohio, in 1987. He bowed out in 1988, leaving the company in the hands of J.J. Cafaro of the Cafaro Company, a well-known shopping center developer.

Kelly moved Avanti production to Youngstown, Ohio, during 1987.

coupe finished in monochrome black, white, red or silver.

Bolder still were Blake's plans for the first-ever Avanti convertible (unveiled as a prototype in late '83) and an equally new drop-floor chassis with independent rear suspension, designed by Herb Adams and ousting the old live-axle frame at last. There was even a stab at racing, Blake entering a specially prepped Avanti "GT" in the 1983 Pepsi Challenge 24-hour enduro at Daytona. Though it only finished 27th out of 30 survivors from a starting field of 79, its mere appearance was a heartening sign that Avanti was moving forward again.

But Blake tried to do too much, too fast. By early '85 he'd overreached himself into a credit crunch with his prime lender, a South Bend bank, and was forced to declare bankruptcy that June.

Things might have ended right there had it not been for Michael Kelly, a young (then 36) Texas ethanol baron, who snapped up Blake's operation for a mere $725,000 in April 1985. Operating as New Avanti Motor Corporation, his regime began building the promised convertible alongside the familiar coupe, and gave both a more contemporary "cockpit" dash, plus new seats, slightly altered bumpers, and more efficient cooling and climate systems. The coupe remained at about $30,000; the convertible came in some $10,000 higher.

Even more ambitious than Blake, Kelly also announced that Avanti operations would be transferred to modern new facilities in Youngstown, Ohio, starting in 1987, and that annual volume would ultimately swell to an unprecedented 1000 units. To achieve that, the product line would be stretched—literally—with three derivatives: a 117-inch-wheelbase Luxury Sport Coupe, an even longer four-door Luxury Touring Sedan on a 123-inch chassis, and a jumbo limousine on a huge 174-inch span. Purists moaned, though Loewy himself had once proposed Avanti sedans for the '64 Studebaker line, and the LSC didn't look at all bad, a tribute to the basic design's enduring style.

Sadly, Loewy died in late 1987, but at least this part of his legacy lives on. As we write this, the Avanti has just passed its 25th birthday and Kelly's plans are proceeding apace (despite legal hassles from several one-time backers). The firm is now installed at Youngstown (thus closing the old Studebaker factory for good), the planned quadrupling of its work force (to around 400) is on track, and the Luxury Sport Coupe is a reality, priced at $44,000. What's more, the firm's 1987 volume of 300 units (a figure Blake hoped to achieve but didn't) exceeded projections by 50 percent.

Kelly and company have even found time to celebrate, issuing 50 copies of a Silver Anniversary 1988 LSC with Paxton supercharger, still built by the Grantelli brothers as in the Studebaker days. Horsepower wasn't revealed, discretion being the better part of value when it comes to insurance premiums, but was surely 250 at least. Appropriately, exteriors were done exclusively in pearl silver. Interiors featured black or red leather upholstery and a rear "entertainment center" with TV, plus power moonroof, compact-disc player and cellular telephone. Suspension was beefed up, including fat tires on handsome alloy wheels, and there were "ground effects" body addenda—front spoiler with foglamps, rocker-panel skirts, reshaped bumpers—that Loewy never thought of.

This and other recent developments would seem to assure the future for America's only custom-crafted GT—but then, things looked just as rosy after Blake moved in. "The Legacy Continues," promise the latest brochures. "Avanti Still Means Forward!" We sincerely hope so. The Avanti deserves to keep moving ahead.

Among the three Avanti models seen in 1987-88 was the stretched 117-inch-wheelbase Luxury Sport Coupe (*foreground*). Price: $44,000.

BUICK

David Dunbar Buick was a canny Scottish industrialist but an unlikely auto builder. After making his mark with a process for annealing porcelain to steel for bathtubs, he turned to the profit opportunities of the new horseless-carriage phenomenon. His first car, appearing in 1903, was a simple little chain-drive runabout with flat-twin power. One engine feature, overhead valves, was a rarity then but would be a hallmark of all future Buicks.

Soon prosperous, Buick Motor Company was one of the firms William C. Durant brought together to create General Motors in 1908. Six-cylinder engines arrived in 1914, and were the only kind Buick offered through 1930. By then, Buick buyers were mostly upper-class and professional people who'd moved up from a Chevrolet, Oakland or Oldsmobile—hence the "doctor's car" sobriquet of the make's early years—and remain Buick's primary audience to this day. The Depression considerably reduced the size of this clientele—and Buick sales—but the division would bounce back strongly, reaching fourth in industry production by 1938 (from a decade-low seventh in 1934-36).

Buick recovered from "hard times" with a combination of straight-eight power and the same appealing technical advancements applied to its GM contemporaries. Eights ousted sixes across the board for 1931, all "valve-in-head" engines of generally similar design but no shared components. They initially ranged from a 77-horsepower 220.7-cid unit on the bottom-line Series 50 to a 104-bhp 344.8-cid powerplant on the top-echelon Series 80 and 90.

"Silent Second Synchromesh" transmission and more horsepower were the big attractions for '32. Power and wheelbases increased again for '33, but sales didn't as the Depression bottomed out. October 1933 saw installation of Harlow H. Curtice as division general manager, who aimed to offer "more speed for less money." Buick did for 1934, via an even lower-priced new Series 40. Sales moved up, aided by GM's new "Knee Action" independent front suspension and a more modern, streamlined look for all models as Buick shed the last remnants of "Roaring '20s" styling.

The '39 Buicks owed much to the developments of 1936, when bodies adopted GM's new all-steel "Turret Top" construction (no more fabric roof inserts) and were even sleeker, with more rounded lines, massive vertical radiators and integrated luggage compartments (thus dispensing with "trunkback" models). Series numbers gave way to names that would last all the way through 1958—from the bottom, Special, Century, Roadmaster, Limited. Engines were rationalized around a 93-bhp 233-cid Special eight and a new 320-cid design with 120 bhp for other models. The latter would also be a Buick mainstay through the '50s, and putting it in the lighter Special body made the '36 Century a fast car—Detroit's first "factory hot rod."

Several new features marked the mildly facelifted '37s: hypoid final drive, front and rear anti-roll bars, a longer-stroke 248-cid engine for Specials, standard windshield defroster and, a claimed first, steering-wheel horn ring. Appearance was again spruced up for '38, but mechanical changes were more significant: a new all-

The '39 Buick Century touring sedan cost $1246—18,783 were built.

Buick produced only seven 1940 Limited Streamlined Formal Sedans.

The '40 Century sport coupe sold for $1175, but only 96 were built.

An eight-passenger limo was one of eight '41 Limiteds—669 were sold.

John Steinbeck's *Grapes of Wrath* was published in 1939. But Buick wasn't looking back at the "Dustbowl" days of the Depression depicted in the book; it was enjoying a comeback in the marketplace from seventh to fourth place in sales.

The 1941 Buick Century Sedanet fastback weighed in at 3920 pounds and retailed for $1241. Production reached 5547 units.

coil suspension (another industry first), bigger shock absorbers, and domed, high-compression pistons for both engines, now dubbed "Dynaflash."

By this point, Buick covered a very broad model and price spread, ranging from $945 for the basic Special business coupe to near $2500 for the opulent eight-passenger Limited limousine. For really big spenders, Brunn still offered custom bodies for the big Limited chassis, though in greatly reduced numbers compared to the halcyon pre-Depression days.

Buick closed out the '30s with a lower, mildly facelifted lineup for 1939, marked by waterfall-type grilles, "streamboards" (optional concealed running boards), and a sunroof option on some models. Sidemount spares were still available, though they weren't ordered as often as in the past. The Special's 122-inch wheelbase (from 1937-38) shrank two inches. Body choices were as extensive as ever and prices as moderate. The natty Century convertible sport phaeton sold at just $1713, the sport coupe at $1175. Rumble-seat convertibles disappeared this year, but Buick scored a safety innovation with flashing turn signal lights, installed at the rear only and part of the trunk emblem. Also new were column-mounted gearshift and refillable shock absorbers.

In the '40s, Buick was GM's number-two producer after Chevrolet and usually fourth in the industry behind the "Low-Price Three" (Chevy, Ford and Plymouth). The division normally turned out upwards of 300,000 cars a year. GM endured an extended strike after the war and Buick took a while to regain momentum, but was producing nearly 400,000 cars by 1949 and would top half a million the following year.

Buick's largely professional-class buyers were a loyal group, and its '40s slogan "Valve in Head—Ahead in Value" was reflected in the cars: big but reasonably priced and only a bit ostentatious. For those who felt status was everything, there was always Cadillac.

The division's early-'40s lineup was one of the widest in its history, one that wouldn't be matched in scope until well into the '50s. Model groups expanded from four to five for 1940. The Series 40 Special ranged from simple sedans to spectacular open styles. The new Series 50 Super had fewer choices but included a handsome wood-bodied estate wagon. Both lines rode a 121-inch wheelbase and carried Buick's smooth, respected 248-cid five-main-bearing straight eight. Above these, powered by a similar 320.2-cid eight, stood the Series 60 Century and Series 70 Roadmaster on 126-inch chassis, the 133-inch-wheelbase Series 80 Limited, and the 140-inch Series 90 Limited (the last confined to long sedans and limousines).

A number of interesting special bodies were offered for 1940, some for the last time. Low sales had been thinning Buick's crop of '30s convertible sedans. This year brought the final Century model; Super and Roadmaster versions continued for one more season. Streamlined Sedans with fastback styling reminiscent of the Lincoln-Zephyr saw just 14 copies in the Series 80. More popular was the $1952 convertible sedan (phaeton) with conventional styling, though only 250 were called for. Custom styles were still around, but not as regular catalog offerings. Though it wasn't identified as such, one rakish town car done by Brewster on the Series 90 chassis was the first Buick to be honored as a "Classic" by the Classic Car Club of America. Buffalo's Brunn was also still doing customs, including one fairly conventional town car on the Roadmaster chassis.

Buick had a banner 1941 with model year production of 374,000 units. Leading that year's line was a beautiful series of opulent Brunn customs on the Limited chassis. These included a phaeton, town car, landau brougham, and full landau. Most flamboyant was the convertible coupe, offered to dealers for $3500. At that price, only the prototype sold but was significant for a "sweep-spear" side motif that prefigured a postwar Buick styling trademark.

Among production '41s, the two Limiteds were combined into a single Series 90 on a 139-inch wheelbase, while an unchanged Roadmaster series graduated to a 128-inch chassis. Century was shorn of convertible, convertible sedan, and club coupe. The estate wagon shifted to the Special series but sold for about $200 more than the 1940 Super. Specials were split into two sub-series: the 118-inch-wheelbase 40, and the 40A on a 121-inch span. Styling was evolutionary, with a bolder, heavier grille and revised ports on the hood sides. A new idea was the fastback, offered in 40A Special and Century trim as a touring sedan, business coupe, and sedanet. A clean break with the "trunkback" age, it appealed to buyers. The Special fastback touring sedan alone sold over 100,000 units.

The 1941 Special/Super engine gained new-design high-compression pistons for more efficient combustion that boosted horsepower to 115. Available for the 40A Special touring sedan and sedanet was Compound Carburetion, two carburetors with a progressive linkage, which yielded another 10 bhp. Compound Carburetion was standard elsewhere, resulting in 165 bhp for the 320 engine. Chassis were carryovers for all but Limited, which used a new X-member frame.

World War II came at the wrong time for Buick, whose 1942 models were completely restyled along the lines of Harley Earl's Y-Job show car and were much sleeker than previous Buicks. Their wide, low, vertical-bar grille theme would feature on postwar models through 1954, and "torpedo" styling was more popular than ever. The Century, which would be in postwar limbo until 1954, offered only two models, both fastbacks. Counterpart models continued to dominate Special sales, and two-door sedanets were new for Super and Roadmaster. Most '42s featured Earl's new "Airfoil" front fenders, which swept back through almost the entire length of the car to meet the rear-fender leading edges. Limiteds and Specials lacked the full sweep, though their front fenders still extended well back into the doors.

As elsewhere in the industry, Buicks built after January 1, 1942, used painted metal instead of plated parts per government order. Specials and Supers had cast-iron pistons in place of the previous aluminum ones, and this plus lower compression dropped horsepower to 110 (118 with Compound Carburetion). Production ground to a halt in early February after only some 92,000 units, and would not begin again until October 1945.

Thanks to its 1942 redesign, Buick emerged from the war in fine fettle. While nearly all makers were forced to stay with their prewar designs, Flint's styling was technically only one year old in 1945 and thus still fairly fresh. Packard, by contrast, left with a two-year-old design in its very handsome Clipper, felt obliged to undertake a severe facelift by 1948. Buick was able to stretch out its '42 tooling through the 1949 Special, then came back with a brand-new Special for 1950. One year makes a difference. Of course, there were no more exotic customs postwar. But though a mere 2482 Buicks left the line in the closing months of 1945, production picked up the following year to more than 150,000.

While these first postwar models were warmed-over '42s, there were fewer of them: sedans and sedanets in Special, Super, and Roadmaster guise; Super and Roadmaster convertibles; a Super estate wagon; no Centurys or Limiteds. Styling was cleaned via single instead of double side moldings, a simpler grille, and the first of Buick's distinctive "gunsight" hood ornaments. Wheelbases were 121 inches for Special, 124 for Super, and 129 for Roadmaster. Compound Carburetion didn't return either, so Special/Super settled for 110 bhp. This array of models, wheelbases, and engines would endure through 1948 with only minor changes in horsepower.

The '42 Roadmaster rode a 129-inch chassis; 511 soft tops were built.

Flow-through "airflow fenders" were featured on the 1946 Super.

With 40,371 built, Buick was number one in convertibles in 1947.

Styling changes were minimal for 1947-48 as most of GM's first new postwar designs were being readied for '49. The '47 Buicks had a wing-top grille that gave them a very low look; a new, more elaborate crest appeared above it. The only changes for '48 were full-length belt moldings on Specials and chrome fender nameplates on Supers and Roadmasters. Gauges were gold-colored, steering wheels three-spoke, flexible types with semicircular horn rings.

Flint's most important '48 news was Dynaflow, its excellent new automatic transmission, offered as a $244 option for Roadmaster only. Demand for this torque-converter unit proved so strong that the division had to double planned production. By 1951, Dynaflow was being ordered by 85 percent of Buick buyers.

With its all-new '49 design, Buick production surged to 324,276 units, again right behind Chevy-Ford-Plymouth. Its '49s were sleek and graceful next to the 1946-48s, and reviewers agreed they were worth all the attention they got. Harley Earl's Art & Color Studio successfully translated aircraft lines to an automobile, and

Buick's 1941 design was modern and popular, and the '42 introduced the flow-through "airflow" front fenders that would reappear after World War II. Buick's famous "gunsight" hood ornament appeared right after the war.

only a hint of the old separate rear fenders remained on Super and Roadmaster (Special retained its previous styling). Also new was the first of Buick's now-legendary portholes, an idea from Ned Nickles of Earl's staff.

Buick's most eye-catching '49 was the Roadmaster Riviera, introduced at mid-year along with Cadillac's Coupe de Ville and Oldsmobile's Holiday. As Detroit's first modern mass-production hardtop coupes, they began a trend that would eventually render convertibles obsolete. The Roadmaster Riviera was a good-looking, luxurious car with a beautiful pillarless roofline. It was available with either conventional straight side moldings or with sweep-spear trim, the latter soon to be another Buick trademark.

With the emphasis mainly on styling, the '49 Buicks were little different mechanically, though Dynaflow-equipped Supers got higher, 6.9:1 compression that boosted horsepower to 120. The Roadmaster had been similarly raised to 150 bhp in 1948, and continued in that form with Dynaflow standard. Hardtop Riviera aside, body styles remained the same. The woody wagon was reworked to fit the new styling, but though the result was pleasing, it still sold in small numbers. Roadmaster was put on a 126-inch wheelbase and Super reassigned to the 121-inch Special chassis.

Undoubtedly, Buick's production potential went unexploited in the early postwar years. The Special, which would set many '50s records, actually accounted for the smallest number of sales in this period. Supers were the most popular. Special didn't outstrip Super until 1950, when it became Buick's biggest success story. By 1954, it would help the division surpass Plymouth.

Three different styling periods, a 50th anniversary, and the advent of V8 power highlighted Buick in the '50s. Its cars of this decade were always big and powerful, sometimes garish, variously reflecting either the best contemporary thinking or the worst depravity of those glittery years. Yet they were carefully orchestrated to fit the times and the market, maintaining the Buick traditions of quality and high performance for their class.

If '49 was the Year of the Porthole, 1950 was the Year of the Sweep-spear. The Special was restyled to match the bulkier new look of other models and competitively priced to help Buick catch third-place Plymouth, yet was rather utilitarian. But not for long. The pioneering Riviera hardtop, extended to the Super series for 1950, was offered as a Special for '51. The Riviera name was also applied to well proportioned Roadmaster ('50) and Super ('51) four-door sedans on extended wheelbases (130.3 and 125.5 inches respectively). Super and Roadmaster wagons were still around, though with far fewer wood body parts now. All-steel wagons came in for 1954.

All 1950-52 models and the '53 Special continued to rely on Buick's aging but proven valve-in-head straight eight. Displacement, compression, and horsepower varied from model to model. The 1950 Special unit produced 115 bhp (120 bhp with Dynaflow). Supers and 1951-53 Specials offered up to 143 bhp. Roadmasters still used a hefty 320-cid version that put out 170 bhp at 3800 rpm by 1952.

Dynaflow Drive (some called it "Dyna-slush") had become an increasingly popular Super/Special option since 1950. (It remained standard for Roadmaster.) It multiplied torque via a drive turbine induced to rotate through an oil bath by a facing crankshaft-driven turbine. Dynaflow was smooth, but none too exciting for performance. The Twin-Turbine Dynaflow of 1953 was more positive in operation. By decade's end, an even better Triple-Turbine unit was offered across the board as a $296 option. But Dynaflow in any form couldn't deliver acceleration like Hydra-Matic, and was therefore handicapped in an age of horsepower and hot rods.

Golden Anniversary 1953 brought first-time availability of power steering, a 12-volt electrical system, and a fine new overhead-valve V8 for the Super and Roadmaster (the Special retained its straight eight). An oversquare design of 322 cid, the new "Fireball" V8 offered up to 188 bhp on an industry-topping 8.5:1 compression ratio. Roadmasters were demoted to the 121.5-inch wheelbase save the Riviera sedan, which now shared the 125.5-inch chassis of the counterpart Super.

Buick's 50th year also brought a flashy new limited-edition

Along with Cadillac and Olds, Buick debuted the first mass produced hardtop in 1949. A total of 4343 Rivieras were delivered.

Buick built 653 copies of the '49 Roadmaster Estate. Price: $3734.

The '50 Buick wore a toothy smile, here on a Super Riviera hardtop.

sports convertible. Called Skylark, it was perfect for Hollywood types and Texas oil barons. Buick made only 1690 of them, priced at an extraordinary $5000 each.

Another of those Harley Earl styling projects for which GM was already famous, the Skylark was designed for the broadest possible appeal. Instead of being a two-seat sports car—which accounted for only 0.27 percent of the market in 1953—it was a luxurious, sporty "personal" four-seater like Ford's post-1957 Thunderbirds. Like 1953's similar Oldsmobile Fiesta and Cadillac Eldorado, it was basically a chopped-and-sectioned version of the standard ragtop, with a four-inch lower windshield and top. In appearance it was cleaner than other Buicks, bereft of portholes and sporting Kelsey-Hayes chrome wire wheels, then becoming fashionable throughout the industry.

Skylark returned for '54, but was much less radical and sold for only $4483. More Century than Roadmaster, it stood apart with tack-on tailfins; huge, chrome-plated die-cast taillight housings; and fully circular rear wheel cutouts like those of the '54 Wildcat II show car. But apparently, this Skylark was less impressive than the '53, for only 836 were sold and the model was discontinued for '55.

The return of the hot-rod Century highlighted Buick's rebodied 1954 lineup. Bodies were longer and more massively square. An inverted-U grille of fine vertical bars sat below oval nacelles cradling headlamps and parking lamps; windshields were wrapped, and rear fenders were kicked up to mount bullet taillamps high up in their trailing edges. Special received a 264-cid "Fireball" V8 with 143/150 bhp. Other models carried the 322 with power ratings of 177 (manual-shift Century) to 200 (Roadmaster and Skylark). Wheelbases were again realigned: 122 inches for Special/Century/Skylark, 127 inches for Super/Roadmaster.

Much of Buick's 1954 styling was previewed by the XP-300 and 1951 LeSabre show cars, rolling testbeds for a number of new ideas. Both used an experimental 215-cid aluminum V8, not a forerunner of Buick's identically sized early-'60s engine but a very

Like most of the industry, Buick had a record year in 1950 with 667,826 cars built; 10,732 of them were Riviera hardtop coupes.

Along with Olds and Cadillac, Buick was first with the soon-to-be popular "hardtop convertible" body style. Buick called it the Riviera, conjuring up visions of the good life. Not everyone liked the "buck-tooth" grille on the '50 models.

A new grille and restyled ventiports were seen on the '51 Roadmaster.

At $2115, the '52 Special 46S sport coupe was Buick's cheapest model.

Buick celebrated its Fiftieth Anniversary in '53 with the limited-production Skylark. At a lofty $5000, only 1690 were built.

special job. With exactly square dimensions (3.25-inch bore and stroke), 10:1 compression and Roots-type supercharger it produced over 300 bhp—phenomenal for the day. Only trouble was, it had to run on a combination of methanol and gasoline, not exactly common at local filling stations.

Both these showpieces were futuristic. The 116-inch-wheelbase LeSabre sported a wrapped windshield and "Dagmar" bumpers. The XP-300, measuring an inch less between wheel centers, had a concave grille and mesh-backed headlamp nacelles that would be appearing on production '54s.

Speaking of which, Buick had been pushing relentlessly toward the industry's number-three spot. It broke an all-time record in calendar 1950 with more than 550,000 cars. The 1954 tally of 531,000 left Buick trailing only Chevrolet and Ford, a position it hadn't held since 1930. The following year saw output hit 781,000, another record and nearly 50 percent higher than the division's previous best.

This success was based largely on the Special, which had become one of the industry's best-sellers by '54. In 1955, Detroit's banner year of the decade, Specials were everywhere. Over 380,000 were made, including 155,000 Riviera two-door hardtops, Buick's single most popular model. A deft restyle for '55 only kept sales booming, aided by even more potent Fireball V8s delivering 188 bhp on Specials, 236 bhp on other models.

Mid-model year '55 brought four-door Riviera hardtop sedans to the Special and Century series. Super and Roadmaster versions followed for '56. Once more, the rest of the industry had to play

The '54 Century sported four portholes and flashy three-tone paint.

With 100,312 built, the Special four door was 1953's best-seller.

Buick was all-new for '54; the "banker's hot rod" Century reappeared.

Flared fender openings and unique rear styling were '54 Skylark hallmarks. Priced at a hefty $4483, only 836 were produced.

catch-up with a GM innovation (this one initially shared with Oldsmobile).

As elsewhere in Detroit, the '56 Buicks didn't sell as well as the '55s. A mild facelift saw the division add model year designation to exterior nameplates, but this was abandoned after 1957; customers complained that it made each year's car obsolete that much sooner. With the horsepower race in full swing, the '56s were the most powerful Buicks yet. The Special now offered 220 bhp, the rest of the line 255. A Century could leap from 0 to 60 mph in 10.5 seconds and top 110 mph—and every '56 Buick could do 100.

Buick built 85,656 Super Rivieras for 1955. Base price: $2831.

Buyers preferred the Special Riviera in '56—113,861 were produced.

Buick celebrated its Golden Anniversary with the limited-production 1953 Skylark convertible, and built one for 1954, too. It added luster to the Buick image, thereby helping Buick oust Plymouth from third place in sales in 1954.

Buick's 1957 Caballero wagon was a four-door hardtop.

The '57 Century Riviera hardtop coupe listed at $3270.

Buick built 839 Limited convertibles for 1958 at $5125 apiece.

The '61 Invicta hardtop coupe weighed in at 4090 pounds.

The 401 V8 of the posh 1962 Electra 225 churned out 325 bhp.

The '57 line received lower and longer new bodies. Styling was a slightly more exaggerated rendition of '56 themes. Division general manager Ed Ragsdale never said how much the retooling had cost, but it must have run several hundred million. Yet despite the most sweeping alterations since 1949, the '57s didn't sell particularly well, possibly because rivals were pressing hard. Chrysler, where Virgil Exner's tailfinned look was in force, sold almost as many '56s as '55s, and Plymouth was forging back into third with its dramatic '57 styling.

Still, these Buicks were clean, dashing automobiles. Model additions were few but interesting: pillarless Caballero four-door wagons for Century and Special, and new Series 75 Roadmaster Riviera hardtop coupe and sedan. The latter, based on the Series 70, had every possible luxury except air conditioning as standard: Dynaflow, power steering and brakes, dual exhausts, automatic windshield washers, backup lights, clock, special interior with deep-pile carpeting, and a host of others. But though 1957 was a good year for Buick, it was even better for Plymouth, which knocked Flint out of third place for the first time in three years.

Detroit's '50s fondness for chrome produced the ugliest Buicks in history for 1958. From a monstrous grille shell containing 160 shiny little squares to hastily contrived chrome-draped tailfins, it was awful—especially the heroically overdecorated Limited, revived as the new top-line series. None of the "B-58" Buicks sold well, though that year's recession was probably more to blame than the ghastly styling. Production dropped to 240,000 units and the division slipped behind Oldsmobile to fifth place. Air suspension was offered, but seldom ordered. In all, it was a very bad year for Buick.

So was 1959. But if the '58s had been tasteless, the '59s were just the opposite. Though dominated by the omnipresent tailfin, the new design was at least smooth, clean, and fairly dignified, with huge windshields but fewer chrome grille squares. Buick now shared the corporate A-body with other GM lines, but it wasn't obvious.

Series were retitled for the first time in two decades. Special became LeSabre, Century was renamed Invicta, and Super and Roadmaster were dubbed Electra and Electra 225. The last two rode a 126.3-inch wheelbase, trimmed 1.2 inches from 1957-58. LeSabre and Invicta shared a 123-inch chassis and the old Special/Century body styles, though hardtop wagons were dropped due to low sales. Electras were priced down quite a bit from 1958. Buick was called 1959's most changed car, and the changes were definitely for the better.

On the mechanical side, 1959 brought a 401-cid V8 with 325 bhp for the upper three models, a 364 V8 for LeSabre. Power brakes and steering were standard on Electras, a $150 option elsewhere. Air conditioning was $430 across the board. Air suspension, for the rear only, was still nominally available—and almost never ordered.

Significantly, Buick dealers in 1959 sold more Opels than ever. The captive import from GM's German subsidiary had been assigned to Buick in 1958 and promptly grabbed an increasing number of customers growing weary of oversize, overweight automobiles. But Buick was already planning its own compact, and its star would rise again.

In fact, Buick enjoyed great success in the '60s. From about 250,000 cars and ninth place for 1960 it rose to more than 665,000 units and had a tight hold on fifth place by decade's end. This improvement was due in part to the advent of compacts (reviving the Special and Skylark names), in part to increased demand for larger Buicks. For example, only some 56,000 1960 Electras were built but nearly 159,000 of the '69s. Comparable LeSabre figures were some 152,000 and nearly 198,000. Wildcat, which replaced the mid-range Invicta for '63, began at about 35,000 but was almost double that by 1969.

The new 112-inch-wheelbase Special of 1961 was one of GM's

Electra 225 was the top-line 1959 Buick; the ragtop cost $4192. The long, sharp fins were the most noticed styling feature.

Fins were rounded off for 1960, as seen on this Electra 225.

Buick built 11,951 LeSabre convertibles for the 1961 model year.

"second-wave" compacts, the Buick-Oldsmobile-Pontiac models that followed Chevy's first Corvair. It arrived in base and Deluxe coupe, sedan and four-door wagon models priced in the $2300-$2700 range. All were powered by a new 215-cid aluminum-block V8 of 155 bhp—light, smooth-running, efficient, and economical. Amazingly, it's still in production. GM later sold manufacturing rights to British Leyland, which offered somewhat modified versions in various Rover sedans and Land Rover utility vehicles beginning in the late '60s.

Responding quickly to the sporty-car craze begun by the 1960 Corvair Monza, Buick fielded a more special Special Deluxe coupe called Skylark as a mid-'61 entry. Bucket seats, deluxe trim, vinyl roof, and a 185-bhp version of the aluminum V8 helped sell more than 12,000 in its abbreviated debut season. The following year brought Skylark and Deluxe convertibles, an optional Borg-Warner four-speed transmission and sales of more than 42,000 Skylarks.

The big Buicks changed dramatically in the early part of this decade. The 1960 models—LeSabre, Invicta, Electra, and Electra 225 sedans, station wagons, convertibles and hardtops—were basically facelifted '59s. Their 1961 replacements rode the same wheelbases but weighed 100-200 pounds less and were much cleaner in appearance. For 1962, Buick unleashed the Wildcat as a specialty item in the Invicta series. A two-ton, 123-inch-wheelbase luxury hardtop priced close to $4000, it sported bucket seats, vinyl roof, and distinctive exterior trim. First-year sales were so good that the Wildcat name replaced Invicta on all the mid-range Buicks for '63 save a single wagon (fewer than 3500 sold), after which Invicta disappeared.

Production of the top-line Electras increased steadily through the '60s. There were two '61 series—the "basic" Electra and the bigger, more luxurious Electra 225 (named for its overall length in inches and often referred to as the "Deuce-and-a-Quarter"), both on a 126-inch wheelbase. The base series was dropped for '62 and all Electras became "225s"; the division then concentrated on fewer offerings. Electras were powered by Buick's largest 401 V8, which delivered 325 bhp through 1963.

Buick styling was hardly exceptional in these years with the singular exception of the new-for-'63 Riviera, a svelte personal-luxury sports coupe that changed the division's stodgy image almost overnight. Many people felt that GM styling chief William L. Mitchell (who'd succeeded Harley Earl on his retirement back in 1958) had fathered one of the best automotive shapes of all time.

The Riviera originated in a Mitchell project to revive the LaSalle,

Buick had a change of guard in 1959 when it traded Special, Century, Super, and Roadmaster badges for LeSabre, Invicta, Electra, and Electra 225 nameplates. Fins were in in 1959, rounded off for '60, and shorn off completely for 1961.

The Electra 225 soft top found 7181 buyers for 1964; it listed at $4374 and 7181 were built for the model year.

Cadillac's lower-price companion make, which disappeared after 1940. Among the numerous renderings, clay models and full-size mockups completed were an experimental convertible and hardtop sedan shown at the 1955 Motorama featuring LaSalle-type grilles. Both were designed by Buick stylist Ned Nickles and were named LaSalle II. Although neither was planned for production, they encouraged GM to proceed with a "personal-luxury" competitor to Ford's post-1957 Thunderbird. This was ultimately assigned to Buick to give it a much-needed shot in the sales arm. Besides, Cadillac didn't have the facilities, Chevrolet was enjoying record sales, and Oldsmobile and Pontiac were occupied with other things.

LeSabres rode a 123-inch wheelbase in '62, as since 1959.

Buick's compact '62 Special Skylark rode a 112.1-inch wheelbase.

Buick's big news in 1963 was its personal-luxury coupe: Riviera.

Special became an intermediate on a 115-inch wheelbase in 1964.

Riviera, here a Gran Sport, featured hidden headlights for 1965. A total of 37,658 Rivieras were produced that year.

Some of this new Riviera's design elements were borrowed, the razor-edge roof styling, for instance, being inspired by certain English custom coachwork of the '50s. But the finished product was handsome and individual. The final clay model was approved by early 1961, and production of exactly 40,000 was scheduled for model year '63.

Riding a 117-inch wheelbase, Riviera was about 14 inches shorter than other big Buicks and 200-300 pounds lighter. The 325-bhp 401 V8 was standard in its debut year. The '64 graduated to the division's new bored-out 425-cid enlargement with 340 bhp standard, 360 optional. Standard two-speed Turbine Drive automatic was used for '63, three-speed Turbo Hydra-Matic afterwards. Handling was well up to performance. The standing quarter-mile time was 16 seconds at 85 mph with the standard V8; 15.5 seconds and 90-plus mph with the 360-bhp engine.

Buick joined Olds and Pontiac in offering larger, restyled compacts for '64, adopting the new intermediate-size GM A-body also used for Chevy's new Chevelle. Wheelbases lengthened to 115 inches on sedans, 120 inches on wagons. There were new engines, too: a 225-cid V6 with 155 bhp and a cast-iron 300-cid V8 with 210 bhp. In this form, the plush Skylark rapidly became the most popular smaller Buick. Production of Skylarks to Specials was about 9 to 10 for '64, after which Skylark pulled away, reaching a near 5-to-1 ratio by 1969.

The '64 LeSabre, Wildcat and Electra were longer overall but had unchanged wheelbases. The 300 V8 became LeSabre's standard engine that year. Like the old Century, Wildcat was the division's hot rod, carrying the 401 Electra engine in the lighter, shorter LeSabre chassis. Styling was basically the '63 look with corners and edges rounded off. Riviera was basically unchanged except for a larger engine. Production was down by about 2500 units.

By 1965, Buick production had risen 50 percent from the 1960 total, putting the division fifth in the annual industry race. An expanded lineup—and the unique Riviera in particular—played a big part in this, as did a very healthy overall market that bought Detroit cars in record numbers—over 9.3 million for the calendar year, the best since '55.

As elsewhere in Detroit, trim and model variations proliferated for '65, allowing Buick buyers to virtually custom-build their cars. This year's junior line comprised Skylark and standard and Deluxe Specials with V6 or V8 engines priced from about $2350 to $3000,

The '64 Special Skylark Sport Wagon sported a glassy raised roof.

The LeSabre Custom hardtop coupe retailed for $3100 in 1965.

Buick, at low ebb in the early Sixties, was the first GM division to debut a true personal-luxury model to challenge the fast-selling four-seat Thunderbird. The '63 Riviera was quickly acknowledged as a design masterpiece. It still is.

LeSabre four-door sedan output reached 39,146 units for 1966.

The '66 Electra 225 rode Buick's longest wheelbase: 126 inches.

Buick built 41,084 Skylark hardtop coupes for the '67 model run.

The Electra 225 Custom hardtop coupe listed at $4400 in 1968.

The all-new 1968 Skylark coupes rode a 112-inch wheelbase.

and V8 Special Sportwagons in the $3000-$3200 range. Wildcat offered standard, deluxe, and Custom trim packages in sedan, hardtop sedan and hardtop coupe styles, plus deluxe and Custom convertibles. LeSabres and Electra 225s came in standard and Custom versions. At $4440, the Electra 225 Custom convertible was this year's costliest Buick. LeSabres still carried a 300-cid V8 as standard, Wildcats and Electras the big 401. The elegant Riviera received hidden headlights (via "clamshell" sub-grilles in the front fenders) and taillights housed in the rear bumper.

A memorable new performance option for '65 was the Gran Sport package for Riviera and Skylark, some $250 worth of roadability improvements. With oversize tires, Super-Turbine 300 automatic and the Wildcat 401 engine, the Skylark Gran Sport was every inch a grand touring car. The Riviera version was even grander, capable of 125 mph on the straight. *Motor Trend* magazine pronounced it superb in every way: "It goes and handles better than before, and that's quite an improvement."

Buick's main attraction for 1966 was a second-generation Riviera, a cousin to that year's new E-body front-drive Olds Toronado. The Riv retained rear drive and looked much more massive than the crisp 1963-65 original, yet wheelbase was only two inches longer. Curvaceous lower-body contours, wide hidden-headlamp grille, and a sleek semi-fastback profile with vestiges of the previous razor-edge roof made it impressive to the eye. Yet it sold for only about $4400, which seems unbelievably low today.

Other '66 Buicks were mainly carryovers, but a stroked 340-cid version of the 300 V8 was issued as standard power for LeSabre and Skylark sportwagons. Modestly facelifted grilles, side trim and taillights were again the principal alterations for the '67 juniors. That year's senior Buicks were treated to GM's new B- and C-bodies, with sleek semi-fastback roof styling on hardtop coupes and more voluptuous contours for all models. Identifying the '67 Riviera was a horizontal-crossbar grille.

Specials and Skylarks continued with the 225 V6 and 300/340 V8s for '67, but a new 430-cid V8—Buick's biggest engine yet—arrived as standard for Wildcat, Electra, and Riviera. It had no more horsepower than the previous 425 but was smoother and quieter. Also new, as a Special/Skylark option, was a cast-iron 400 V8, a bored-and-stroked 340. This was the heart of a new Skylark sub-series called GS400, offered as a convertible, two-door hardtop and pillared coupe with handling suspension, bucket seats and other sporty touches. A similar hardtop with the 340 engine appeared as the GS340. Sales were excellent. Flint tallied over 560,000 units for the model year.

Skylark sold in record numbers for 1968, partly because Specials were trimmed to just three Deluxe models. In line with other GM intermediates that year, Buick's junior line adopted the new "split-wheelbase" A-body platform: 112 inches on Special/Skylark two-doors, 116 inches on four-doors and Special Deluxe wagons, and 121 inches on Sportwagons (versus 120 inches for the 1964-67 wagons). The attention-getting GS400 returned in hardtop and convertible form. Replacing the GS340 was a GS350 hardtop powered by a new 350-cid V8 with 280 bhp. A 230-bhp version was a new Special/Skylark option and standard for Sportwagon, Skylark Custom and the big LeSabre; all these offered the tuned unit at extra cost. The 225 V6 gave way to a Chevy-built 250 inline six with lower compression, reflecting 1968's new federal emissions rules. The big 430, still pumping out 360 bhp, continued for Wildcat, Electra, and Riviera.

Like the '67s, Buick's '68 seniors had bodyside sculpturing (traced with moldings on some models) that recalled the old '50s sweep-spear, plus divided grilles, big bumpers and, new this season, hidden wipers. The rebodied junior models had similar down-sloped bodyside contour lines, plus new grilles, the hide-away wipers, pointy rear fenders, and big back bumpers containing the taillamps. Riviera got a dubious, heavy-handed divided grille that made it a bit more contrived than in 1966-67. Many Buicks main-

Buick built 6552 Skylark Custom ragtops for the 1969 model run.

tained tradition with stylized front-fender "ventiports," a trademark dating from the '40s, but not Wildcats, GS400s and uplevel Skylark Customs, where rectangular trim was used to suggest air vents of various types.

No engine changes occurred for the record-breaking 1969 model year when Buick produced more than 665,000 cars, its decade high, though it still finished fifth in the industry. Seniors again received new bodies, this time with ventless side glass and a squarer, more "formal" look. The year-old junior line received the expected minor trim shuffles, and Gran Sports and Sportwagons remained separate models as in 1968. LeSabre was still on its 123-inch wheelbase, but Wildcat went back to the Electra chassis.

This hot-selling lineup was unchanged for 1970 except that there were no more Specials (all smaller models were called Skylark) and the big Estate Wagons became a separate series—upper-class two- and three-seat haulers battling the likes of Chrysler's Town & Countrys. Full-size Buicks acquired new grilles, bumpers, and taillights; intermediates a longer hood, bulkier lower-body contours, and different grilles for each series. Riviera also gained a longer hood, reverted to exposed headlamps flanking a new thin-line vertical-bar grille, received a wider rear window and altered bumpers, and sported rear fender skirts for the first time. The result looked more dignified, if a tad stuffy.

Mechanically, Buick's main 1970 development was an enormous 455 V8, supplanting the 430 and an outgrowth of it, which gulped premium gas at the rate of 12 mpg on compression ratios of at least 10:1. The last mammoth V8 Buick would build, it delivered 350, 360, or 370 bhp, and in one of these guises was standard for the GS and LeSabre 455, Riviera, Electra 225, Wildcat, and both Estates.

Buick would be staunchly committed to big cars for the rest of the '70s, but energy economics and government mandates inexorably led to smaller models in an expanding lineup as the decade wore on. Nevertheless, full-size cars would remain the make's bread and butter through 1975, accounting for over 40 percent of total sales that year.

"Wood" trim was part of the '69 Skylark Sport Wagon 400 package.

The '69 Electra 225 sported a sculptured sweepline on its sides.

Massive rioting shook Newark and Detroit in 1967, leaving many dead and thousands homeless, and the U.S. had 475,000 troops in Vietnam. In the auto world, Buick boasted muscle car GS models and debuted a giant 430-cid, 360-bhp V-8.

By 1970, a Riviera cost $4854 and the styling was generally considered more cluttered. Output reached 37,336 units.

The 1970 LeSabre Custom convertible saw only 2487 units produced. It weighed in at 3947 pounds and retailed for $3700.

Buick's performance model in 1970 was the blindingly fast GSX. A huge 455-cid V8 gave it its get up and go.

GM completely redesigned its full-size cars for 1971, and that year's big Buicks were the largest and heaviest yet—as big as American cars would ever get, in fact. Styling was more smoothly rounded, with curved "fuselage" bodysides, massive hoods, and broader expanses of glass. The mid-range Wildcat was retitled Centurion, another name first seen on a mid-'50s Buick show car. This line shared the B-body platform with the popular LeSabre, which grew about an inch in wheelbase. The upmarket Electra remained a C-body cousin to the Olds Ninety-Eight and Cadillac DeVille. Estate Wagons moved up to its 127-inch wheelbase.

The big Buicks continued in this form through 1976, becoming busier and bulkier each year but otherwise little changed except where necessary to meet safety and emissions requirements. All were thirsty. The last 455-cid Electra, for example, was good for only 8.7 mpg in the Environmental Protection Agency's city fuel economy ratings.

Riviera also bulked up for '71, growing two inches longer between wheel centers (to 122 inches) and gaining needless pounds in the process. Dominating its swoopy new Bill Mitchell styling was a dramatic "boattail" rear deck that proved so controversial it had to be toned down the very next year. By 1974 it was gone altogether. The one vestige of sport, the GS option, vanished the year after that, but Buick tried to keep enthusiasts interested with a substitute Rallye package comprising reinforced front stabilizer bar, heavy-duty springs, specially calibrated shocks, and a rear stabilizer bar. It was claimed to deliver even better ride and handling characteristics than the GS, and probably should have been standard to handle the size and weight of these beasts. The oddball styling was partly responsible for sagging sales in this period, which by 1975 were less than half of what they'd been five years earlier.

The last of the 1968-vintage Skylarks appeared for 1971-72. These were still solid, good-looking middleweights, though engines were being emasculated by power-sapping emissions controls and the Gran Sports weren't as hot as they had been. Signalling the imminent demise of mid-size Buick convertibles (ragtop sales were down to a trickle throughout the industry) Skylark hardtop coupes offered a fold-back cloth sunroof as a new '72 option. Trim packages created a plethora of models: base Skylark, Skylark 350, Skylark Custom, Sportwagons and Gran Sports.

Buick's last true muscle cars also appeared in these years, and they've since become coveted collectibles due to minuscule production. The 1970 GS-X, for example, a bespoilered GS455 hardtop with that year's new tuned "Stage I" engine, saw only 875 copies. The GS455 convertible fared little better: 1416. Both were back for '71, the GS-X as a trim package, still with distinctive black tape stripes and hood paint, special grille, chrome wheels and fat tires. Figures aren't available for this one, but only 902 of the '71 GS convertibles were built and just 8268 hardtops, reflecting the big drop in performance-car demand after 1969.

For 1973, Buick revived the respected Century name for a redesigned intermediate line on the same two wheelbases. This was built on a new-generation A-body with so-called "Colonnade" styling that did away with pillarless coupes and sedans as well as convertibles; GM's reaction to a proposed federal rule on rollover crash protection that, ironically, never materialized. Bolstered by spiffy Luxus and Regal sub-models (the latter made a separate series after '74), this Century sold well through 1977, providing an important "safety net" for Buick sales at times when inflation and rising fuel prices sent would-be big-car buyers scurrying for thriftier alternatives.

A compact returned to the Buick line for the first time in 10 years at mid-1973. Called Apollo, it was only a rebadged clone of the 111-inch-wheelbase X-body Chevrolet Nova from 1968, with the same three body styles (two- and four-door sedans plus hatchback two-door) and, initially, the same 250-cid Chevy straight six as standard power. It was a definite asset during the big-car sales

The 1971 GS could be ordered in Stage I tune and with a sunroof.

The Centurion replaced the Wildcat in Buick's 1971 model lineup.

The main difference in the '72 Centurion was a revised grille.

It took $3255 to purchase a 1972 Skylark Custom hardtop coupe.

Styling of the 1972 "boattail" Riviera was controversial to many.

Millions of Americans participated in anti-pollution demonstrations in 1970, marking the first Earth Day. Buick, meanwhile, introduced the largest engine it would ever offer, a 455-cubic-inch V-8 developing a massive 370 horsepower.

Buick returned to the compact field with the 1973 Apollo.

A 231-cid, 110-horsepower V6 powered the '75 Century Special.

By 1975, the Riviera had adopted more formal, upright styling.

The 1976 Century Custom Colonnade Coupe retailed for $4346.

More expensive was the '76 Electra Limited hardtop sedan: $6852.

The 97-inch wheelbase '76 Skyhawk fit into the subcompact class.

The 1977 Riviera was built off the LeSabre's 116-inch platform; 26,138 were produced for the model year.

slump that began with the Middle East oil embargo late that year, but intermediates would prove more important to Buick in the post-energy crisis period.

Confusing buyers for 1975 was the return of the Skylark name at the top of the compact line, where it would eventually supplant Apollo. In common with all X-body variants that year, Buick's version gained heavily revised outer panels that gave it something of a European "sports sedan" flair.

Somewhat of a surprise was the new-for-'75 Skyhawk, the smallest Buick in living memory. A near twin to the Vega-based Chevrolet Monza, this 97-inch-wheelbase subcompact coupe took a bit more than eight percent of total division sales in the first six months of that year. Though not light for its size, Skyhawk offered a decent performance/economy balance thanks to Buick's new 231-cid, 90-degree V6 engine, the only one available. Rated at 110 bhp and adopted as standard power for that year's Skylark, Century and Regal, this V6 would be a significant engine in Buick's immediate future.

Model year 1977 brought the first of GM's downsized cars. Sometime before the first energy crisis, the firm had decided to move to smaller, lighter, more economical models in every size and price category. Its largest cars were the logical starting point, and they were rendered even more timely by the government corporate average fuel economy standards (CAFE) that took effect with model year '78.

The first fruits of this program were dramatically apparent at Buick, where LeSabre and Electra shrank to almost Century size. Wheelbases contracted to 116 and 119 inches respectively (Estate Wagons rode the shorter one) and curb weights dropped several hundred pounds. This made smaller engines feasible, yet interior dimensions were within inches of what they'd been on the old behemoths. Riviera wasn't left out, becoming a high-spec version of the new B-body LeSabre, though it would return to the corporate E-body platform two years later.

Through 1979, all these cars relied on a standard 170-bhp 350 V8; a new 403 with 185 bhp was optional. Convertibles were no more (killed after '75) but two- and four-door sedans were offered in LeSabre, LeSabre Custom, Electra 225 and 225 Limited trim. The following year brought even fancier Electra Park Avenue models. There was also an interesting LeSabre Sport Coupe for '78, powered by that year's new 165-bhp turbocharged version of the Buick V6. But this was really too sporty for a LeSabre and, as sales were always marginal, it was dropped after 1980.

The big Buicks were treated to a facelift for 1980, with sheetmetal subtly restyled to reduce wind resistance as an aid to economy. More extensive use of lightweight materials netted an average 150-pound weight saving, about half that achieved with the '77s. It's odd how perspective changes: these first downsized models initially seemed quite small next to other big cars of the day; now they look just as large as their outsized predecessors.

Intermediates were next on the corporate slenderizing schedule, and a smaller Century bowed for 1978 along with a companion Regal series of personal-luxury coupes, all built on the new 108.1-inch-wheelbase A-body. Regal sold well from the start but Century didn't. Clumsy sloped-roof "aeroback" styling on the two- and four-door sedans was out of phase with buyer tastes, though there was nothing wrong with the handsome wagon. Buick corrected its mistake for 1980 with a more formal-looking notchback four-door bearing a faint resemblance to the first-generation Cadillac Seville, and sales took off. Buick had turbocharged its V6 with the new mid-size line in mind, offering it in sporty Century and Regal Sport Coupe models. But the sales pattern was the same, and the blown Century vanished with the aeroback styling.

Riviera was downsized a second time for '79. Styling was crisper and tighter, and the model at long last fell into line with its Toronado and Cadillac Eldorado cousins by adopting front-wheel drive. A turbo V6 was available here, too, though most buyers

The Electra 225 was all-new for 1977, lighter and smaller.

Buick built just over 100,000 '77 LeSabre Custom four-door sedans.

Buick intermediates were downsized for '78, here a Regal coupe.

The Riviera shrunk for '79, seen here as the sporty S Type.

Sportiest of the '79 subcompact Skylarks was the Road Hawk.

After peddling mainly full-size two-ton cars for most of the decade, Buick began downsizing its fleet in 1977. First came the full-size models and the Riviera, which shed about 800 pounds; they were followed by the intermediates a year later.

opted for the standard powerplants. The blown Riv was a fine performer, though, able to leap 0-60 mph in under 12 seconds while averaging close to 20 mpg in more restrained driving, this despite a still-bulky 3800-pound curb weight. The 1980 follow-up was basically a rerun but introduced a long-time Cadillac feature: "Twilight Sentinel," the automatic on/off headlamp control with delay timer (for keeping the lights on for up to three minutes after switching off the ignition to illuminate your path).

Though it promised much, the little Skyhawk had never been a big seller and was retired after 1980. One interesting 1979-80 variation was the Road Hawk, an option package aimed at younger buyers more interested in sports-car looks than genuine performance. Fore and aft spoilers, special paint and tape stripes, identifying decals, mag-style wheels, and larger tires were included, but there was little action to back up the brag.

An important new Buick arrived in the spring of '79 as an early 1980 entry. This was the front-drive replacement for the long-running rear-drive Skylark, sharing GM's technically advanced

Buick's X-body front-drive compact for 1980 was the Skylark.

The Electra 225 Park Avenue sedan sold for $10,676 in 1980.

Skylark for '81, here a Sport Coupe, received cosmetic changes.

The top-of-the-line Regal coupe for 1981 was the Limited.

One of Buick's front-drive A-body models was the Century Limited.

Buick revived the Skyhawk name for the 1982 J-body lineup.

A limited-production model for '82 was the Riviera convertible.

Buick had great success with the Regal, here an '83 Limited.

new 104.9-inch-wheelbase X-body platform with siblings Chevrolet Citation, Pontiac Phoenix, and Oldsmobile Omega. Buick had learned its styling lesson, so this new smaller compact was offered only in traditional notchback form. Design highlights included rack-and-pinion steering, all-coil suspension, and transversely mounted engines, either 2.5-liter Pontiac-built inline four or an optional 2.8-liter 60-degree V6 from Chevrolet. Skylark performed well with the latter, and tastefully done Sport Coupe and Sport Sedan models offered firmer suspension and sportier appointments for more serious drivers. Likely on the strength of the Buick name, Skylark became the second best-selling X-car after the higher-volume, lower-priced Citation. Unfortunately, execution left much to be desired on all X-cars, which soon supplanted the Dodge Aspen/Plymouth Volaré as the most recalled cars in Detroit.

Yet despite the occasional flawed product and market miscalculation, Buick moved with changing buyer demands in the '70s, reaping the benefit of good sales while some other makes fal-

The '83 Riviera came with a choice of four engines: 4.1-liter V6, 5.0 V8, 5.7 V8 diesel, or 3.8 V6 Turbo.

A 200-bhp turbocharged V6 made the limited-production Grand National one of the fastest cars on the road in 1984.

After two gas crises in the Seventies, Buick in the early Eighties continued to downsize and shift over to front-wheel drive. Diesel engines were also offered, but by the mid-Eighties so was the tire-smoking Regal Grand National.

The 1985 LeSabre Limited two-door coupe retailed for $11,751.

An 88-bhp 2.0-liter four powered the '85 Skyhawk Custom coupe.

The Buick Electra, here a Park Avenue, was downsized for 1985.

Somerset Regal was Buick's '85 offering based on GM's N-body.

The X-body Skylark (Limited shown) was in its last year in 1985.

tered. The division has traditionally been able to anticipate market trends well in advance, and to respond with cars that, if not always on the leading edge of design, are at least in tune with the times. Strong sales year after year are proof positive that Buick not only knows its market, but how to satisfy it.

Flint kept on doing that in the '80s, but again reached out to the younger, more affluent types who'd bought Gran Sports in the "flower power" years. This reflected forward product planning under Lloyd Reuss, former division chief engineer who became Buick general manager in 1980. A genuine "car guy," Reuss wanted at least some Buicks to be rather like American-style BMWs, and he got his way. By 1984 there were sporty T-type editions of every Buick save the plush Electra, with black exterior trim, firmed-up chassis, more potent engines and "driver-oriented" interiors. Buick even mounted an Indy-car racing program for its V6 and offered hop-up components to street racers to cement its new image as a more youthful, performance-oriented outfit.

This strategy worked well for a time but ultimately backfired. Buick jumped to third in industry production for 1982-83 and ran fourth in model years '81 and 1984-86. Even so, '86 volume was well down on '85's, and the slide continued into 1987, when Buick fell back to fifth, behind Oldsmobile. A significant factor was strong new competition from Pontiac, which offered many of the same basic cars but had recently returned to its '60s-style performance theme and was in third place for the first time since 1970. Trying to be all things to all people, Reuss later conceded, only confused Buick's image—and its customers.

But in the end, it didn't matter. Chairman Roger Smith's wholesale corporate reorganization, ordained in 1984 to reverse GM's withering market share and in evidence by '87, called for returning each GM make to its distinct rung on the old price-and-prestige ladder that Al Sloan had fashioned back in the '20s. For Buick this meant a hasty retreat from T-types and turbo V6s, and at decade's end the division was again mostly back to its traditional brand of upper-middle-class luxury—a "doctor's car" once more, GM's "premium" car division.

Buick's generally strong sales in the '80s reflected a consistent model lineup, which evolved in step with those of other GM divisions but was, perhaps, more clear-cut to buyers from year to year. Some individual models certainly seemed ageless. The big 1977-vintage Electra and LeSabre, for example, hardly changed at all after their 1980 update, receiving only minor styling and equipment shuffles through mid-decade while accounting for about a quarter of division output each year.

The full-size Estate Wagons continued in this vein through 1989, garnering fewer sales as time passed, but the old rear-drive coupes and sedans gave way to more efficient and popular front-drive successors beginning with a new C-body Electra for 1985. A similar H-body LeSabre arrived the following year.

Announcing a second wave of GM downsizing, these smaller big Buicks shared a 110.8-inch wheelbase and were some two feet shorter and 400 pounds lighter than the first-wave 1977-84 models. Yet they hardly sacrificed any passenger room and were vastly more pleasurable to drive, more economical, and adequately quick. Transversely mounted V6s were mated to four-speed overdrive automatic transaxles across the board. Initially, 3.0-liter gasoline and 4.3-liter diesel engines were offered, but soon vanished in favor of the old reliable 3.8-liter gas unit, updated with sequential, multi-port electronic fuel injection and, from '86, roller valve lifters. A modified "3800" engine with 165 bhp (versus 150) arrived on certain '88s. Electra coupes disappeared after 1987, when the top-line Park Avenue became a separate model and a laudable new anti-lock brake system (announced for '86) was more widely available for both series. Electra offered a subtly sporty T-type sedan, LeSabre a T-type coupe but, as always, the traditional Custom and Limited offerings sold better by far. And those sales were good: around 100,000-150,000 a year.

The same could not be said for the sixth-generation Riviera. New for '86, the third downsized personal-luxury Buick in 10 years laid a gigantic egg. Sales plunged to an 11-year Riviera low, the '86 tally off a whopping 70 percent from model-year '85. The 1987-88 results were even poorer.

In a way, this was curious. On its tighter, 108-inch wheelbase, the new Riviera was a lot more nimble than the old, and its quiet, well-mannered drivetrain was basically as for the Electra/LeSabre. But it was apparently much too small for the Riv's usual customers. An unfortunate styling resemblance to the N-body Somerset/Skylark didn't help, and hardly anyone liked the gimmicky Graphic Control Center, a touch-sensitive TV-like screen that needlessly complicated even simple driving tasks like changing radio stations.

Hoping to turn things around, Buick made the '89 Riviera look more "important," adding 11 inches to overall length, ladling on chrome, and restyling the tail to resemble that of the 1979-85 models. Did it work? The answer isn't in at this writing, but it certainly couldn't have hurt.

All this must have been a big disappointment to Flint executives, who'd watched the 1981-84 Riviera average 50,000 model-year sales and the '85 over 65,000 (the increase no doubt due to buyers learning of the shrunken '86). Like the last rear-drive Buicks, these cars changed little after 1980. There was a mild facelift for '84 and an optional Olds-built 350 V8 was offered through '82, but turbo and non-turbo V6s were available all along (the latter a new 4.1-liter from '81), as was a 350 Olds diesel V8 (though few were ordered) and a choice of standard and T-type coupes.

But this line's most significant '80s development was undoubtedly the first-ever Riviera convertible, bowing at mid-1982. A coupe conversion performed by an outside contractor, it was a handsome rig, acceptably solid for a drop-top and as luxurious as any Riv. But it was heavier and thus slower with its standard 4.1 V6 (fitted to most examples, though the turbo 3.8 was ostensibly available) and found few takers at $25,000-plus. Production was predictably limited—just 1248, 1750, 500 and 400 respectively for 1982-85—scarcity that guarantees this as at least a minor future collectible. Of course, the ragtop Riv died with the '86 E-body, deemed too small to be a practical four-seater in convertible form, and though Buick has since shown a prototype of such a car, it'll likely never see an assembly line because the Reatta ragtop will fill that slot at Buick.

Two more collectible '80s Buicks are found among the rear-drive Regal coupes, all of which were reskinned for '81 with crisper, more aerodynamic lines that persisted through the end of series production in December 1987. These are the hot turbo-powered T-type and Grand National.

The new-for-'82 Regal T-type, replacing the previous Sport Coupe model, was Flint's standard hot rod, with fat tires, beefier chassis, attention-getting exterior and plush interior. Horsepower was 175-180 at first, boosted to 200 for 1984 via sequential port fuel injection. The GN bowed at mid-'82 as a low-volume commemorative, named for the Chevy-powered Regals then starting to clean up in NASCAR, but mostly it was just a fancy T-type.

After a one-year hiatus, though, the GN returned with a mean all-black exterior and more unique touches than the first iteration. For 1986, an intercooler boosted horsepower by 35 for both T-type and GN. Recalibrated engine electronics gave the '87s 10 bhp more—and truly phenomenal acceleration. In fact, these Buicks bid fair as the fastest cars in the land, able to bound from 0 to 60 in about six seconds.

Most special of all was the 1987-only GNX, a $30,000 end-of-the-line limited edition (500 built, by contractor ASC Corporation) with higher turbo boost, "smarter" electronics, cleaner porting, even bigger tires, still-meaner looks, a claimed 300 bhp and a mighty 355-420 lbs/ft torque. It could turn mid-5-second 0-60-mph

Skylark shifted to the N-body for 1986; the Limited cost $10,290.

At $8971, the T-Type was Skyhawk's sporty model for 1986.

The all-new '86 Riviera lost 19 inches of length and 500 pounds.

LeSabre, also all-new for '86, rode a 110.8-inch wheelbase.

The 1987 Buick Electra Park Avenue sedan listed at $18,769.

In the mid-Eighties, when gas was plentiful and cheap again, Buick brought out smaller, more fuel efficient front-drive LeSabres, Electras, and Rivieras. The public didn't respond to the trimmer Riviera—sales skidded a whopping 66 percent.

times and standing quarter-miles of around 14.5 seconds at 95 mph.

For all this grandstanding, the Regal T-type was always a peripheral seller and the GN almost invisible (only 215 of the '82s, about 2000 for '84, even fewer for 1985-87). Still, they were great fun, even if Buick wasn't the place one expected to find a modern muscle car.

Of far greater importance to Buick's '80s fortunes was the success of its smaller cars, particularly intermediates. For 1981 these comprised the Regal coupes and a mostly carryover group of Century sedans and wagons, all continuations of the 1978 A-body design. This was renamed G-body for '82, when the Centurys became Regals and Buick's 4.1-liter V6 replaced the previous 4.3 V8 option. Respective model year production for this group was some 384,500 and over 328,000, not bad for those two very troubled industry years. Volume eased to some 226,000 for 1983-84, by which time diesels had been dropped as a bad bet and four-speed automatic transmissions adopted as much better for improved mileage.

Meantime, Buick had introduced the first front-drive Century, a notchback coupe and sedan built on the new A-body that also arrived in early '82 at Chevy, Olds and Pontiac. Like its sisters, this Century was basically a higher-priced X-car with more expansive front and rear sheetmetal on the same 104.9-inch wheelbase. Initial engine choices were 2.5-liter Pontiac four; a new destroked, 3.0-liter Buick V6; and a 4.3-liter Olds diesel V6. Euro-style T-type versions were added for '83. The following year brought a 3.8-liter option (standard for T-types) and new five-door Custom and Limited Estate Wagons (replacing the old Regal models).

Though little changed for '85, Century displaced Regal (now down to coupes only) as Buick's most popular model line, production running at over a quarter-million units. The '86s were modestly restyled via a curiously un-aerodynamic undercut nose. The T-type coupe vanished, Chevy's familiar 2.8 V6 ousted Buick's 3.0 as the step-up engine, and the 3.8 was treated to low-friction roller valve lifters, sequential port fuel injection and distributorless triple-coil ignition, gaining 25 horsepower for a total of 150. For 1987, the T-type became a package option and both the four and 2.8 V6 received "Generation II" improvements conferring slightly more power. More standard equipment eased the sticker shock of 1988 prices that were up to the $12,000-$15,000 range (versus $10,000-$12,000 five years before).

A notch below Century stood the compact Skylark, an X-car for 1981-85, an N-body thereafter. For all the recalls and attendant bad publicity that plagued GM's X-body models in these years, the Skylark continued to sell well. Buick built over a quarter-million of the '81s and more than 100,000 a year for 1982-84. The '85s ended the line at around 93,000. Styling, engineering and model changes were strictly evolutionary. There were always 2.5 four and 2.8 V6 coupes and sedans (except '85, sedans only) in base/ Custom and Limited trim. Sport versions through '82 and the two-door 1983-85 T-type could be had with a high-output V6 (with port injection for '85) and came with distinctive exteriors and Buick's firmer "Gran Touring" suspension package. In all, this Skylark served Buick well.

Buick still peddled a subcompact Skyhawk in the '80s, but it was quite different from the late-'70s car of that name. Bowing for '82, it was one of GM's five front-drive J-body clones, riding a 101.2-inch-wheelbase chassis with all-coil suspension via front MacPherson struts and a rear beam axle on trailing arms. Buick hasn't gotten around to a convertible like Chevy and Pontiac, but two- and four-door notchbacks have been available throughout, joined by 5-door wagons for '83 and a fastback hatch coupe for '86. Engines were the familiar four-cylinder fare found at other divisions: Chevy-built overhead-valve 2.0-liter (abandoned after '87) and a Brazilian-built overhead-cam unit. The latter, initially 1.8 liters, was also offered in a more potent turbocharged version from 1984; both grew to 2.0 liters for '87, after which the blown engine was cancelled. Custom and plusher Limited models have been cataloged all along. The inevitable T-types arrived for '83—notchback two-doors at first, later fast/hatch coupes. Styling has changed little since introduction save an optional hidden-headlamp nose for T-types from 1986.

In sales, Skyhawk has typically run in the middle of the J-car pack—behind Chevy Cavalier and Pontiac's 2000/Sunbird but ahead of Olds Firenza and Cadillac Cimarron. While none of these cars have so far proven a match for certain Japanese models in areas like refinement, workmanship and economy, they've been at least competent and usually pleasant. Skyhawk has probably benefitted as much from the Buick tri-shield as any design feature, but would surely have sold better without so much intramural competition. As it was, production peaked with the '84 models—over 145,000 built—after 48,000 and 63,000 for 1982 and '83 respectively. Volume dropped to 82,500 for '85, recovered to about 91,500 the following year, then eased to around 46,600. If not spectacular, Skyhawk sales were likely crucial at times for some Buick dealers.

Much of the J-car's basic engineering appeared in the 1985 Somerset Regal, a notchback two-door heralding the arrival of GM's new N-body. Buick wasn't able to trade on the popular Regal name the way Olds did with Cutlass, so this car soon became just Somerset. Companion N-body four-doors arrived for '86 under the Skylark name to finish off the last X-body Buicks, and Somersets became Skylarks two years later.

Through 1987, Somerset/Skylark engines comprised the familiar 2.5 four (updated to "Generation II" specs that season) and

The T-Type package added $1975 to LeSabre's $13,616 base price.

The '87 Grand National package cost $3574, including turbo V6.

New for 1988 was Buick's two-seater coupe, the Reatta. Based on a shortened Riviera platform, its sticker read $25,000.

extra-cost Buick 3.0 V6. Optional for '88 was Oldsmobile's new "Quad 4," a dual-overhead-cam 2.3-liter four with four-valves-per-cylinder, aluminum head and cast-iron block. With a healthy 150 bhp even in mild initial tune, the Quad-4 promised much. But it wasn't in the same league with similar Japanese engines for smoothness, quietness, and lugging power. Buick was thus wise to retain the V6 option (unlike Pontiac, which dropped it for the '88 Grand Am).

The N-body Buick got off to a good start. Some 86,000 were built for the abbreviated debut model year, followed by nearly 138,000 of the '86s. Like Skyhawk, these compacts are not state-of-the-art competitors, but they've been improving and will no doubt become better still.

Having learned with the J-cars that too many corporate clones spoil the sales broth, GM returned to more individual styling for a trio of 1988 mid-size coupes. At Buick, this new front-drive GM10 or W-body design replaced the veteran rear-drive Regal, retaining traditional Buick appearance "cues" to stand apart more clearly from the related Pontiac Grand Prix and Olds Cutlass Supreme. Significantly, wheelbase was cut just 0.6-inch from the previous Regal's, to the benefit of passenger space, while base curb weight slimmed by some 250 pounds and overall length by 8.4 inches, to the benefit of economy and handling. The usual Custom and Limited versions were on hand, and a sporty appearance option reviving the Gran Sport name was offered, bringing front "bib" spoiler, rocker-panel skirts, black grille, aluminum road wheels, and other "Euro" touches.

Regardless of model you got a transverse, port-injected 2.8

The 1988 Regal boasted an all-new body and front-wheel drive.

Buick's A-body Century was reskinned—and sleeker—for 1989.

In the late Eighties, GM redefined the positioning of all its divisions. Buick was declared to be a "premium" car maker. To enhance that image, Buick introduced the two-seater Reatta in 1988. It will be joined by a convertible in 1990.

The smaller 1986 Riviera sold poorly, so for 1989 it was lengthened and redesigned to look more like the 1979-85 Riv.

Chevy V6 of 125 bhp mated to a four-speed overdrive automatic transaxle, plus all-disc brakes—uncommon in mass-market Detroiters. Equally laudable was an all-independent suspension with the expected front struts and coil springs, plus rear struts on single trailing links and dual lateral links connected by a single transverse plastic leaf spring, as on the big C/H-bodies.

At this writing, the new Regal had just gone on sale in a difficult market, so we don't know whether it'll be a hit. We suspect it will be if GM continues the price moderation chairman Smith has promised in an effort to regain recently lost market share. Initial base sticker prices are certainly attractive: $12,500 for the Custom, another $780 for the Limited. Meantime, we can appreciate this more pleasant and capable Regal while hoping that a very hot version—something like the GNX, perhaps even with a similar engine—materializes soon.

Vying for attention with the '88 Regal was Buick's first production two-seater. Called Reatta (derived from a Spanish-American word for lariat), it was basically a rebodied version of the latest Riviera, riding an abbreviated 98.5-inch chassis but measuring only 4.5 inches shorter overall and weighing about the same (3350 pounds). Powertrain and instrument panel also came from the Riv, but styling was Reatta's own: smooth, rounded and "friendly."

Conceived not as a sports car but a "mature" two-seater, Reatta emphasized luxury, comfort and even practicality. Standard equipment was extensive, options being limited to an electric sliding sunroof and 16 power adjustments for the driver's seat. You had to contend with the dubious Graphic Control Center, but the roomy two-place cabin and a largish trunk with drop-down pass-through panel invited long-distance touring. Even better, Reatta was shrewdly priced: $25,000 basic, about half the cost of Cadillac's slow-selling Italian-bodied Allanté convertible. Speaking of which, an open-air Reatta was envisioned almost from the car's 1982 inception, and was scheduled to arrive during the 1989 model year.

If the Reatta and front-drive Regal are any indication, Buick's prospects are bright. The aging of America's vast baby-boom generation suggests a growing market for the kind of "modern conservatism" long associated with the cars from Flint, so the recent decision by GM planners that Buick move back in this direction seems timely indeed. One thing for sure: There will always be plenty of folks who'd really rather have a Buick.

The Electra Park Avenue added a top-line model for '89: Ultra.

The '89 Century received a Regal nose, as on this Estate wagon.

CADILLAC

Cadillac was founded in late 1902 by Henry Martyn Leland, a brilliant engineer who'd worked at Ford and Oldsmobile. His first cars were simple "one-lung" runabouts, but he soon evolved a far more civilized four-cylinder model, the successful Cadillac 30 of 1909-15. Leland's passion for precision craftsmanship and standardized parts, born of his experience as a gunmaker, was evident early on. In England in 1908, three Cadillacs were disassembled, their components mixed up, then reassembled into three cars that ran perfectly. This feat won Cadillac its first Dewar Trophy and prompted the make's now-familiar slogan, "Standard of the World."

The following year, Cadillac became part of fledgling General Motors. As an upper middle-priced car in those days, it didn't compete directly with Packard or Pierce-Arrow but was always a high-quality item. Cadillac's pioneering 1915 V8 set new standards for smoothness, power, and reliability, and sales increased steadily from the late Teens through the end of the '20s as the make turned to building luxury cars exclusively.

Had it not been part of GM, Cadillac might have perished in the Depression, a time when few could afford—or wanted to be seen in—big, expensive cars no matter how superb. Unlike independent Packard, which was forced to field medium-priced cars to survive, Cadillac was protected by GM's vast size and enormous financial strength. Then too, the division already had a medium-priced car in the companion LaSalle. All this helped Cadillac to endure hard times without squandering its prestige image even as it continued building ultra-luxury cars selling only in small numbers.

Among them were the imposing V16 of 1930 and the lovely V12 of 1931. Both were majestic, carrying some of the era's finest custom coachwork. But they were priced accordingly and thus anachronisms in a decimated market. Only 3250 Sixteens and 5725 Twelves were built for 1930-31, which would be the peak. Yearly volume after 1932 was never more than 300 and 1000 units, respectively. The Twelve was dropped after 1937, but Cadillac managed a new Sixteen for 1938.

V8 cars were Cadillac's bread-and-butter in the '30s (as they still are). Through mid-decade they used a 353-cubic-inch engine derived from a 341-cid unit first offered in 1928. Replacing this from 1936 was an all-new L-head design of 346 cid and 135

The '39 Cadillac Seventy-Five rode a long 141.3-inch wheelbase.

The Depression forced Packard to field a middle-price car in 1935, thus tarnishing its name. Cadillac, with the strength of General Motors behind it, was able to exit the Thirties with its "Standard of the World" reputation fully intact.

Cadillac built 4100 Sixty Specials for the 1941 model run.

The '40 Cadillac-Fleetwood Seventy-Two Formal Sedan cost $3695.

Pontoon fenders were featured on the '42 Series Sixty-Two sedan.

Only 150 Series Seventy-Five touring sedans were built for 1946.

The '47 Series Sixty-Two had "the most modern streamlining."

horsepower. These Cadillac Eights were handsome cars on long, but not unwieldy, wheelbases, and offered a broad selection of body styles, including semi-custom types by Fisher and Fleetwood (built in-house, whereas most luxury rivals relied on outside coachbuilders). Sales were consistent and, for the times, fairly substantial: around 10,000 for 1930-31, a mere 2000-3000 for 1932-33, but back to beyond 10,000 by 1936—helped by that year's new low-priced Series 60. By 1939, V8 volume was up to over 13,000.

Cadillac styling and engineering after 1932 progressed in parallel with that of other GM divisions. The big switch from square to streamlined forms came with the '33s, GM styling director Harley Earl ordaining skirted fenders, vee'd radiators, and less vertical windshields. The fully revised '34s were even sleeker, with pontoon fenders, sloped radiators, bullet headlights, rakish rear decks. The 1935-36 models were relatively dumpy, with roundness prevailing throughout; even door windows were potato-shaped. Everything changed again for 1938 as young William L. Mitchell, an Earl protégé, drew up the Sixty Special four-door sedan as a Series 60 addition. Square yet crisply elegant and quite compact for a Cadillac, it stood apart with chrome-edged side windows, square-back fenders, concealed running boards and a very low profile. It's long been judged one of Detroit's all-time great designs.

The 1930s also saw great technical progress at Cadillac. Having introduced clashless "Syncro-Mesh" transmission in 1929, the division followed up for '32 with "Triple-Silent" Syncro-Mesh (helical-cut gears for all three forward speeds). "No-Draft Ventilation" (door vent windows) and vacuum-assisted brakes appeared for 1933, independent front suspension for '34, and all-steel "Turret Top" construction for 1935. Hydraulic brakes arrived on all but Sixteens for '36. Column gearshift and optional turn signals featured for 1938.

Cadillac scored a production gain of 10,000 units for 1939. There was only a mild facelift and engines were unchanged, but the division now blanketed the luxury market. The new 126-inch-wheelbase Series 61 had four offerings priced from $1610 to $2170, while the Sixty Special returned as a distinct four-model series on its own 127-inch wheelbase, priced from $2090 to $2315. The Series 75 comprised the usual plethora of Fleetwood bodies on a 141-inch wheelbase, Cadillac's longest yet.

Topping the line was the Series 90 Sixteen, revamped for 1938 with a new short-stroke engine that was smaller—431 cid versus 452—but produced the same 185 bhp. Like Cadillac's V8, it was made of cast iron and had dual carburetors but employed nine main bearings and separate manifolds, water pump and distributor for each cylinder bank. The chassis was shared with the 75, as were body styles: two coupes, a convertible, a touring sedan with and without division window, a trunkback convertible sedan, formal sedans for five or seven passengers, and a variety of seven-passenger sedans. The big difference was price. The basic five-passenger sedan of 1940 sold for $2995 with V8 but $5140 with V16—a price premium not really justified, as Cadillac's V8 was one of the smoothest engines anywhere. With sales no better than in 1930-37, the opulent and exotic Sixteen was dropped after 1940—a relic of a grand age we would never see again.

Some of Cadillac's most important engineering developments—and some of its most beautiful cars—appeared in the '40s. Like Buick, the division facelifted for 1940-41, then issued completely new styling for '42, which left it in a good position when civilian car production resumed after World War II. Most 1940 Cadillacs were relatively plain—almost Chevrolet-like up front with their simple bar-type grilles. The exception was the ever-impressive Sixteen, carrying the eggcrate grille theme that had first appeared for 1937 and was destined to be a Cadillac hallmark.

Ranked below the 90 and 75 for 1940 was the new Series 72 on a 138-inch wheelbase, with slightly fewer models and lower prices

Cadillac asked $3442 for a '49 Sixty-Two convertible and built 8000 units. The 160 bhp overhead-valve V8 made history.

($2670-$3695). Though impressive and well-designed, it would be a one-year-only line, sales limited by competition from the more luxurious 75. Yet even counting 75s and Sixteens, Cadillac built only a little over 2500 long-wheelbase 1940 models. In later years, when the 75 was mainly a limousine line, production often neared 5000 units per year.

The crisp Sixty Special returned with minor styling refinements in the four basic models offered for '39. Both the town sedan and Imperial (division-window sedan) could be ordered with a sliding metal sunroof; the town car was available with either painted metal or leather-covered roof. Only 15 town cars were built, the bulk of 1940 production being the basic sedan (4472 units).

The least costly 1940 Cadillacs were the Series 62 coupe, convertible coupe, convertible sedan and touring sedan, spanning a $1685-$2195 range. Mounting a 129-inch wheelbase, the 62 garnered the most sales by far, as it would in later years, and all models were cleanly styled and lushly upholstered. Cadillac's 346-cid, 90-degree L-head V8 retained its unit block and cast-iron crankcase, three main bearings with counterweights, and dual downdraft carburetors. Though heavy, it was reliable and exceptionally smooth. As in '39, it was tuned for 135 horsepower in the 62 and Sixty Special, 140 bhp for the 72 and 75.

A significant and attractive model change occurred for 1941, when the junior LaSalle line was replaced by a new lower-priced Cadillac, the Series 61. This was a marketing decision based on the success of the Lincoln Zephyr and Packard's One Ten/One Twenty, and it worked. While Packard continued to rely on medium-priced cars long after World War II, Cadillac (and Lincoln) had returned to the luxury field exclusively, thus bolstering its "fine car" reputation at Packard's expense.

The '41 Cadillacs wore a fresh face: a complex eggcrate grille with central bulge (carried down from the hood). Taillights were also more prominent, and one concealed the gas filler, another feature that would run long into the future. Higher compression boosted the V8 to 150 bhp, and departure of the Sixteen and Series 72 reduced wheelbases to three: 136 inches for the 75, 138 inches on four new Series 67 sedans, and 126 for others. Three axle ratios were offered: 3.77 and 4.27 standard, a 3.36 for short-wheelbase Hydra-Matic models. The extra horsepower enabled most '41 Cadillacs to achieve a genuine 100 mph; 0-60-mph ac-

Cadillac's lowest priced line for '48 was the Series Sixty-One.

The '48 Sixty-Two touring sedan strutted all-new postwar styling.

The Kinsey Report on *Sexuality in the Human Male* was published in 1948, just as Cadillac introduced its new, more aggressive-looking postwar styling. That was followed up in '49 with a potent—and thoroughly modern—overhead-valve V-8.

A bolder grille and flatter flanks marked the 1950 Cadillacs. A Series Sixty-Two Coupe de Ville hardtop listed for $3523.

celeration averaged around 14 seconds, impressive for the day. A broad price span and V8s only helped Cadillac reach all-time record production for '41—66,130 units. This was only some 6700 short of Packard, which was selling a much higher proportion of less costly cars. Much of the increase, of course, was due to the new 61, which was every inch a Cadillac. The 62 line was also up dramatically, the Sixty Special scored a healthy 4100, and a new Series 63 four-door garnered some 5000 sales. Self-shift Hydra-Matic transmission became an option this year, and would remain so on all Cadillacs through 1949. The 1942 lineup was mostly the same but had a new look, dominated by big bullet-shape fenders front and rear, plus fastback rooflines (first seen on the '41 Series 61) on the Series 62 coupe (named "sedanet"). Alas, this year's Sixty Special was more like other Cadillacs—far less "special." Cadillac built a total 16,511 of its '42s before war halted production in February 1942. The division then turned out tanks, aircraft engines, and munitions until V-J Day.

Resuming civilian operations took several months once peace returned, Cadillac managing only 1000 Series 61 sedans before the end of 1945 and just 31,944 of its 1946 models in all. These were only slightly changed from the '42s, but offerings were greatly reduced. The 63, 67s, and division-window 60 Special were all gone. What remained were fastback 61s, fastback and notchback 62s, a lone Sixty Special, and eight 75s.

The '47s were little changed: round instead of rectangular parking lights, script instead of block-letter fender nameplates. The Sixty Special lacked previous models' trio of vertical chrome louvers behind each rear side window; Series 75s now omitted their stainless-steel-trimmed running boards. Postwar inflation pushed prices up by $150-$200, but production regained its prewar stride, nearing 62,000 units for the model year. As before, the 62 carried most of it, just under 40,000 units.

Then came 1948, The Year of the Tailfin. Before the war, designers Earl, Mitchell, Frank Hershey, and Art Ross had been shown the then-secret Lockheed P-38 "Lightning" pursuit fighter. During the war, a skeleton crew played with ideas for postwar styling that incorporated some of this plane's features: pontoon front fenders, pointed noses, cockpit-like curved windshields—and tailfins. This influence would be seen at other GM divisions. Oldsmobile, for example, adopted the P-38's engine air-scoop motif for the headlamp bezels on its 1948-49 "Futuramic" models. But the fin had the most lasting impact. Said Mitchell: "From a design standpoint the fins gave definition to the rear of the car for the first time. They made the back end as interesting as the front, and established a long-standing Cadillac styling hallmark."

Tailfins were the finishing touch on a magnificent overall design. Cadillac's traditional grille became more aggressive via a larger eggcrate pattern, complemented by a more shapely hood. Roof- and fenderlines were clean, curvaceous, beautiful from every angle. Inside was a new dashboard dominated by a huge, ornate "drum" housing gauges and controls. This lasted only a year, however, as it was complicated and costly to produce. For '49 came a simpler design that duplicated the grille shape, a theme followed closely for the next eight years.

Models, body styles and wheelbases stood pat for '48, but Series 75s wouldn't get the new look until 1950 (low production precluded early amortization of their prewar dies). The '49 line was basically a repeat, except for two stunning developments. One was the Coupe de Ville, a $3497 addition to the 62 series that joined that year's new Oldsmobile 98 Holiday and Buick Roadmaster Riviera as Detroit's first volume hardtop. Cadillac sold 2150 of the '49s, a higher percentage of its total production than either Buick or Olds. Of course, the idea behind all three was the airiness of a convertible combined with the snugness of a closed

The 1951 Caddy began to show evidence of "Dagmar" front bumpers.

The fender vent says this '53 Sixty Special has air conditioning.

Only 532 Eldorados were built for '53. List price: a lofty $7750.

A Series Sixty-Two ragtop retailed for a more reasonable $4144.

car, and they succeeded admirably—the start of a trend that, by the late '50s, would dominate Detroit. (Cadillac also built one '49 Sixty Special Coupe de Ville on the 133-inch wheelbase, strictly as an experiment.)

Equally revolutionary was Cadillac's exciting new 1949 overhead-valve V8, the second punch in a potent one-two combination delivered directly to Packard, Lincoln and Chrysler's Imperial. The product of 10 years' research and experimentation, it was designed by Ed Cole, Jack Gordon and Harry Barr, who aimed for less weight and higher compression (to take advantage of the higher-octane fuels promised after the war). This dictated the valve arrangement, a stroke shorter than bore, wedge-shape combustion chambers and "slipper" pistons. The last, developed by Byron Ellis, traveled low between the crankshaft counterweights, allowing for short connecting rods and low reciprocating mass.

Sized at 331 cid, this new V8 arrived with 160 bhp, 10 bhp more than the old 346 L-head from less displacement, testifying to its efficiency. The ohv had other advantages. Though built of cast iron like the L-head, it weighed nearly 200 pounds less. Compression was just 7.5:1 yet was capable of being pushed as high as 12:1; the L-head wasn't. The ohv also delivered more torque and 14-percent better fuel economy. It was durable, reliable, and capable of being greatly enlarged (as indeed it would be). With it, one of the relatively light 62 models could clock 0-60 mph in around 13 seconds and easily top 100 mph.

Further proof of this V8's prowess was provided by sportsman Briggs Cunningham, who entered a near-stock 1950 Cadillac in that year's Le Mans 24-Hour race in France. Driven by Sam and Miles Collier, it finished 10th overall—an achievement unmatched by any other luxury car. It tore down the Mulsanne Straight at around 120 mph; average speed was 81.5 mph. Cunningham himself drove a streamlined Cadillac-powered special that the French called *Le Monstre.* He went even faster than the Colliers, but lost top gear and finished right behind them.

This brilliant V8 combined with best-in-class styling to put Cadillac firmly atop the luxury heap by 1950. Though the 331-cid size would continue through '55, the V8 gained over 100 bhp in the interim, reaching 270 bhp on that year's Eldorado.

Alas, Cadillac's good styling would gradually give way to chrome-laden glitter. The nadir was the 1958-59 models, though taste soon prevailed again. Still, that 1948 styling was good enough to remain fresh for several years with little facelifting. As Mitchell noted: "A traditional look is always preserved. If a grille is changed, the tail end is left alone; if a fin is changed, the grille is not monkeyed with."

The '54 Coupe de Ville sported a new body, Panoramic windshield.

Some Cadillac fans argue that Cadillac's best-looking postwar cars were built during the era of the Korean conflict. Its level of quality was unmatched, and the exclusive and costly '53 Eldorado only enhanced Cadillac's top-notch reputation.

Styling changes were modest for 1955 (note the side trim). The Coupe de Ville enticed 33,300 buyers that year.

The '56 Coupe de Ville sported altered rear fenders and bumper.

Unique rear fins were a hallmark of the '57 Eldorado Biarritz.

And so it was: a new one-piece windshield and revamped grille for '50, small auxiliary grilles under the headlamps for '51, a winged badge in that spot for '52, one-piece rear windows and suggestive "Dagmar" bumper bullets for '53. The model lineup wasn't changed much either. Still accounting for most sales, the Series 62 offered four-door sedan, coupe, Coupe de Ville hardtop, and convertible in this period. Sixty Special remained a lone sedan on its own 130-inch wheelbase (down from 133 after '49). The Series 75 offered the usual array of limos and long "owner-driver" sedans on a 146.8-inch chassis. The 61 was demoted to a 122-inch wheelbase (from 126 inches) for 1950 and still available in sedan or sedanet (coupe) form. Manual shift was standard on 61s, prices about $575 less than comparable 62s. But the division no longer needed a "price leader" after '51 and this series was dropped, never to appear again. Cadillac observed a milestone the following year: its golden anniversary. For 1953, GM issued a trio of expensive, flashy limited editions, all big convertibles with Motorama-inspired styling features. Buick had its Skylark, Oldsmobile a 98 Fiesta. Cadillac offered Eldorado in the Series 62. Only 532 were built that year, largely because each sold for a towering $7750. Among its attractions: custom interior, special cut-down "Panoramic" wraparound windshield, a sporty "notched" beltline, and a metal lid instead of a canvas boot to cover the lowered top. A striking piece, it was a preview of Cadillacs to come.

Model year 1954 saw a major restyle—longer, lower, and wider Caddys with more power and an all-new GM C-body bearing the trendy wrapped windshield. Wheelbase lengthened to 129 inches on Series 62s and 149.8 on 75s; the V8 was booted to 230 bhp. Eldorado was back, more like the standard 62 convertible but consequently far less expensive ($4738), and Cadillac made more of them: 2150. Volume improved to 3950 units for '55, then doubled for '56, when Eldorados doubled to include a Seville hardtop coupe and Biarritz convertible, each priced at $6556.

After '54, Eldorado was again more distinctive, with sharply pointed "shark" fins above round taillights. The rest of the line continued to use the small taillight-and-fin motif that had become a Cadillac tradition. The basic '54 styling persisted through effective, if evolutionary, facelifts for 1955 and '56. The latter year saw introduction of Cadillac's first four-door hardtop Sedan de Ville, which immediately scored almost as many sales as the Coupe de Ville and 62 standard hardtop combined.

Division sales, which had first topped 100,000 for 1950, continued upward, reaching 140,777 units for '55. But even that was a temporary plateau. Despite occasional challenges—an all-new '56 Lincoln, a revitalized Imperial for '57—Cadillac would never really be threatened as the luxury field's sales leader. In this era, annual Lincoln and Imperial volume never exceeded 40,000 cars; at Cadillac, that was good *quarterly* output.

The line was again rebodied for 1957, emerging with blockier

Cadillac built only 304 Eldorado Broughams for '58. At $13,074, it was Cadillac's response to the $10,000 Continental Mark II.

All Series Seventy-Five models rode a 149.8-inch wheelbase.

Caddys for '58 sported a jeweled grille and reverse-slant fins.

but still evolutionary styling inspired by the Eldorado Brougham and Park Avenue show cars of 1954-55. Reaching into the luxury stratosphere, Cadillac now unveiled a production Eldorado Brougham priced at a princely $13,074. One of the division's most interesting '50s cars, it was a compact, low-slung pillarless sedan on a special 126-inch wheelbase, with center-opening doors and a brushed stainless-steel roof, the latter one of Harley Earl's favorite touches. Standard quad headlights were an industry first shared with Nash and Lincoln that year.

The Brougham's most unique mechanical feature was its air suspension, designed by engineers Lester Milliken and Fred Cowin. Based on systems used for commercial vehicles since 1952, it employed an air "spring" at each wheel comprising a domed air chamber, rubber diaphragm, and pistons. Fed by a central air compressor, the domes were continually adjusted for load and road conditions via valves and solenoids for a smooth, level ride. This system differed from those offered optionally by other GM divisions in being "open" (taking in air from outside) rather than "closed." Unhappily, cost and complexity were too high in relation to benefits. The air domes leaked and dealer replacements were frequent, which led many owners to junk the system in favor of conventional coil springs. Four years later, Cadillac and GM abandoned air suspension altogether.

After two years and 704 units, the Eldorado Brougham was completely restyled and final assembly farmed out to Pininfarina in Italy. Only 99 were built for '59, another 101 of the near-identical '60s. Though clean-looking, these were larger (wheelbase: 130-inches) and heavier cars that weren't put together very well (bodies contained lots of lead filler). They're collector's items now, but restoring one is a chore.

Back to the volume Cadillacs, which were heavily facelifted for 1958 in a manner typical of GM that year. Perhaps the most garish Caddys yet, they were laden with chrome and far less stylish than previous postwar models. Sales were poor, though a nationwide recession was probably more to blame than the styling, which was, after all, in vogue. At 121,778 units, model year production

The '59 Coupe de Ville's fins were some of the wildest ever seen.

Partly because of styling continuity, Cadillac maintained its reputation throughout the Fifties. Although design changes were made yearly—and sometimes extensively—the man on the street *always* knew a Cadillac when he saw one.

Cadillac built 1320 Eldorado Biarritz convertibles for 1959. They listed at $7401 and sat atop a 130-inch wheelbase.

was lower than it had been since 1954. DeVille became a 62 subseries, pillared sedans were temporarily eliminated, and the 62 line gained a hardtop sedan with extended rear deck.

Cadillac's durable V8, which had been bored out to 365 cid for '56, was up to 310 bhp for '58. All models were available with cruise control, high-pressure cooling system, two-speaker radio with automatic signal-seeking, and automatic parking brake release. A special show Eldorado introduced a "thinking" convertible top that raised itself and the side windows when a sensor detected raindrops, but this was another gimmick that came to nothing.

Another body/chassis change for 1959 brought more curvaceous styling marked by soaring tailfins of ridiculous proportions, but there were some suspension changes, a stroked 390-cid V8 and improved power steering. Body styles comprised convertibles, hardtop two-doors, and four- and six-window hardtop sedans. This was the last year for the old 75 chassis, which would be updated for 1960. Prices were generally higher than before, with 62s at around $5000 and Eldorados going for $7400 and up. Still, Cadillac built over 142,000 of its '59s, a fair gain on its 1958 showing. Though not appreciated then, these Caddys are now sought-after as the epitome of '50s kitsch with their massive size, sparkling trim, and especially those overblown fins.

The very next year, Cadillac began backing away from this wretched excess, issuing a more restrained group of 1960 models with cleaner grilles and lower-profile fins. Prices stayed about the same, as did mechanical specifications. Standard horsepower was still 325; Eldorados had 345 bhp. Though Cadillac ran ninth in model year production for 1956-57, it dropped to 10th for '58 and would remain there through 1964, though that was still an impressive position for a luxury make.

Carrying another new GM C-body, the '61s were the cleanest Cadillacs in years, reflecting the influence of Bill Mitchell (installed as GM design chief in 1958), who favored a more chiseled look than Harley Earl and wasn't as enamored of chrome. The grille was reduced to a modest grid, and wrapped windshields were abandoned (except on Series 75s) though Mitchell contrived to improve visibility. The Eldorado Seville and Brougham disappeared, while the remaining Biarritz convertible was downgraded to the standard 325-bhp engine.

With GM settling into a styling groove, the '62 Cadillacs were little changed, basically toned-down '61s. Tailfins were lowered, and front-fender cornering lights were a new option. Detail changes included a slightly flashier grille, a thin bright metal molding low on the bodysides, and rear backup/turn/stop lights com-

The 1961 Coupe de Ville featured sculptured sides and lower fins.

The trend was continued for 1962, as on this Sedan de Ville.

Lowered fins and styling refinements were the order of the day for the 1960 Eldorado Biarritz. Output reached 1275 units.

bined behind a single lens that showed white in daylight. Rooflines were squared up on some models, including a pair of new short-deck four-door hardtops, the 62 Town Sedan and DeVille Park Avenue. A new dual braking system appeared with separate front and rear hydraulic lines. Cadillac produced nearly 161,000 cars for the model year, up by some 23,000 over '61.

The long-running V8 got its first major revision in 14 years for 1963. Bore and stroke were unchanged, as were valves, rocker arms, cylinder heads, compression (still 10.5:1) and conrods. Everything else was different: lighter, stronger crankshaft; a stiffer block weighing 50 pounds less than the previous one; ancillaries relocated to improve service access. The reworked engine did little for performance but was smoother and quieter by far. And performance was already of a high order. The '63s could reach 115-120 mph, do 0-60 mph in 10 seconds, 0-80 mph in 16 seconds, and return about 14 miles per gallon. Most impressive was their near-silence at high speed; many testers held them superior to Rolls-Royce in this respect.

Styling for '63 departed from recent practice. The fins were still there but lower than ever. A bulkier full-width grille put parking lights into extensions under the headlamps. New body panels and side moldings created a more slab-sided effect. The rear was more massive, with elongated vertical taillight/backup-light housings.

Prices rose only slightly for '63, and Cadillac remained an excellent buy for the money. Standard equipment ran to Hydra-Matic, power steering, self-adjusting power brakes, heater, remote-control door mirror, and backup lights. A six-way power seat became standard on Eldorado; power windows were standard for all except Series 62 sedans and coupes. Even power vent windows were offered. So were vinyl roof coverings, a new option. Remarkably, the Series 62 still cost as little as $5026; the Eldo Biarritz was only $6608. Production topped 163,000.

Revisions were minor for '64. Even lower tailfins created an unbroken beltline, accentuating length; grilles got a body-color horizontal divider bar; and taillamp housings were reshaped. A new automatic heating/air-conditioning system maintained a set temperature regardless of outside conditions. It has been on the Cadillac options sheet ever since. Perhaps more significant, the 390 was bored and stroked to 429 cid, yielding 340 bhp. Unit volume improved to near 166,000.

Cadillac had a resounding 1965, producing close to 200,000 cars. But it was a banner year for the rest of the industry too, so that output was only good for 11th place. The Series 62, a fixture

The '63 Series Sixty-Two continued a gradual styling evolution.

A split grille was featured on the 1964 Sedan de Ville.

Stung by Chrysler's styling leadership in 1957, Cadillac responded to that company's lithe, handsome, highly-finned cars with flashy, flamboyant, and even-taller fins of its own in '59. The result has always been highly controversial.

By 1964, the fins on the Coupe de Ville had become quite modest.

The '64 Fleetwood limo sold for $9960; Cadillac built 808 units.

A buyer could choose from 150 interior options on the '65 Calais.

The Seventy-Five for 1966 boasted its first new body since 1959.

It took $6631 to buy an Eldorado convertible in 1966, and 2250 customers did just that. At 4500 pounds, it was no lightweight.

since 1940, was replaced as the "budget" Cadillac by Calais. Eldorado and Sixty Special were now officially Fleetwoods, like the Series 75, bearing the requisite nameplates, wreath-and-crest medallions, broad rocker panel and rear quarter brightwork, and rectangular-pattern rear appliqués. A new Fleetwood Brougham sedan (actually a Sixty Special trim option) offered a vinyl roof and "Brougham" script on the rear pillars.

For 1965, another new body brought a longer, lower silhouette; curved side windows; the return of pillared sedans; and the end of tailfins and six-window four-door hardtops. The Special returned to its old 133-inch wheelbase after riding the standard 129.5-inch chassis for 1959-64. Rear styling featured a straight bumper, vertical lamp clusters and flush-top rear quarter panels. Up front, the headlight pairs switched from side-by-side to vertical, thus making room for an even wider grille.

On the mechanical side, the 340-bhp 429 V8 gave Cadillac the industry's best power-to-weight ratio for '65. "Dual driving range" Turbo Hydra-Matic and full-perimeter frames (replacing the X-type used since '57) were adopted except for 75s. All models came with a new sonically balanced exhaust system. Prices were much the same, having risen only a few dollars since 1961.

Cadillac enjoyed its first 200,000-car year in calendar '66, breaking the barrier by precisely 5001 units. A mild facelift brought a new front bumper and grille, plus more smoothly integrated taillight housings. The perimeter frame was adopted for the 75, now fully restyled for the first time since 1959. Variable-ratio power steering, which "speeded up" the more the wheel was turned from straight-ahead, was a new option along with carbon-cloth seat heating pads. The Fleetwood Brougham became a separate model, more luxuriously trimmed than the plain-roof Sixty Special and priced about $320 higher.

The most significant Cadillac of the decade arrived for 1967: an all-new Eldorado with front-wheel drive. Based on the previous year's new Oldsmobile Toronado, it was a daring concept for the luxury field, with six years of careful planning and research behind it. Front drive gave it outstanding roadability; Bill Mitchell gave it magnificent styling. In effect, it was the spiritual successor to the 1957-60 Eldorado Brougham.

This new Eldorado originated with a 1959 styling exercise code-named XP-727, which underwent several rethinks through early 1962. Management then decided to use front-wheel drive, and further prototypes were evolved with that in mind. For a while, Cadillac considered calling the car LaSalle, but ultimately picked Eldorado, a more current name with greater public recognition. Clay model XP-825, with razor-edge lines and a formal roofline, led directly to the production '67 coupe.

Unlike Toronado, the new Eldorado's introduction was very low-key. This was typical of Cadillac, which used the one-year delay to improve on Oldsmobile's package. The Eldo rode better than the Toronado yet handled at least as well. Its front suspension consisted of torsion bars, A-arms, and telescopic shocks; rear suspension was by semi-elliptic leaf springs with four shock absorbers—two horizontal, two vertical. Self-levelling control and radially vented caliper front disc brakes were also featured.

On its own, relatively compact 120-inch wheelbase, the '67 Eldorado arrived with a $6277 base sticker price. With its traditional precision, Cadillac targeted the model for 10 percent of its total '67 production, about 20,000 units. The final figure was 17,930. For 1968-70, sales ran 23,000-28,000. A technological *tour de force,* the front-drive Eldorado quickly established itself as the ultimate Cadillac. And unlike the old Brougham, it made money from day one.

Cadillac's 1967 "standards" were treated to an extensive restyle announced by a grille and front fenders thrust forward at the top. Line-wide features included mylar printed circuits for the instrument panel, automatic level control (standard on all Fleetwoods), cruise control, and tilt steering wheel. Bolstered by the new Eldorado, also part of the Fleetwood series, Cadillac built precisely 200,000 cars for the model year.

The 1968 spotlight was on motive power: an all-new 472-cid V8 with 375 bhp. Designed to meet the new government emission standards that took effect that year, it was extensively tested, running the equivalent of 500,000 miles in the laboratory. Though not as fuel-efficient as the 429, the 472 could propel a Coupe de Ville from 0 to 100 mph in under half a minute.

Designwise, the '68 Eldorado gained the federally required side marker lights, plus larger taillights, combined turn signal/parking lamps nestled in the front-fender caps, and a hood extended at the rear to conceal the windshield wipers. Standards also got the hidden wipers and side markers, plus a revised grille and a trunklid reshaped for increased cargo space.

Cadillac built a record 266,798 cars for calendar 1969, breezing past Chrysler and American Motors to grab ninth place in the industry rankings. For the model year, though, it was still 11th at a little over 223,000, up some 3000 units from '68.

Eldorado was much as before except that headlights were no longer hidden behind flip-up grille panels. Standards were completely restyled, with a new body and a squarer roofline. Headlamps reverted to horizontal, and parking lights wrapped around at the front to flank a higher grille, still prominently vee'd. A somewhat unpopular change was the elimination of front vent windows. Per Washington edict, no-cost equipment now included front-seat headrests, energy-absorbing steering column, pushbutton seatbelt buckles, ignition-key warning buzzer, and anti-theft steering column/transmission lock. Prices ran from just above $5400 for a Calais to well over $10,000 for the 75 limousine.

Eldorado had a new engine for 1970, and a badge reading "8.2 litres"—a whopping 500 cid—to prove it. The world's largest production-car engine at the time, it developed 400 bhp and 550

Cadillac built 18,202 de Ville soft tops for the '67 model run.

The front-wheel-drive, personal-luxury Eldorado debuted for 1967.

Cadillac touted the "formal roofline" of the '67 Coupe de Ville.

The '68 Eldorado stickered at $6605; output hit 24,528 units.

Names confuse: the '68 Fleetwood Brougham was a Sixty Special.

The '69 Eldorado was powered by a 472-cid V8 developing 375 bhp.

A return to horizontal headlights marked the '69 Sedan de Ville.

A facelifted grille was the major styling change for 1970.

The Sedan de Ville shows off the new 1970 "radial fin" hubcaps.

pounds-feet of torque. Other models retained the 375-bhp 472. New features included integral steering knuckle, fiberglass-belted tires, and a radio antenna imbedded in the windshield.

Senior styling was touched up for 1970: a new grille with bright vertical accents over a cross-hatch pattern, new horizontal chrome trim on parking lights, winged crests instead of V's on DeVille and Calais hoods, new taillamps. Eldorado had a narrowed grille newly separated from the headlamps, and taillamps were more slender than the '69s. Production results were mixed. Model year volume rose to near 239,000 units, though Cadillac again finished 10th, but calendar output dropped by over 100,000 cars, putting the division back in 11th place behind Chrysler and AMC. Still, in a year that was generally quiet for the industry as a whole, Cadillac out-produced Lincoln 3-1 and Imperial by no less than 15-1. The Standard of the World still reigned supreme as America's favorite luxury make.

Cadillac stayed with its successful late-'60s lineup through 1976, though styling didn't change much after 1971 and Calais sales waned each year. Forecasting the '80s was the new compact Seville of 1975, the smallest Cadillac in 50 years, followed by a decisively downsized big-car range for 1977.

Along with its E-body Buick Riviera and Oldsmobile Toronado stablemates, the Eldorado became much heavier and bulkier for '71. It would continue as such through 1978, with few changes apart from government-mandated safety and emissions equipment that, along with inflation, escalated prices each year. Though they accounted for upwards of 40,000 sales annually, these outsized cruisers were hardly the svelte, good-handling cars their predecessors had been.

The first front-drive Eldorado convertible, a body style not offered by its corporate cousins, was introduced with the '71 redesign. By 1976, eroding ragtop sales and high attrition throughout the industry had rendered it the only factory-built convertible on the market. Cadillac made hay with a special run of 2000 all-white "last convertible" commemoratives; snapped up by rabid opportunists despite outrageous prices, and promised to build no more. The division kept its word, but only for a while. As time would prove, the droptop's demise was only temporary, and the '76 Eldos would not be Detroit's "last" convertibles—nor, by the mid-'80s, particularly worth keeping. A busy 1971 also saw a smoother but larger new C-body for the standard Cadillac line, with "fuselage" flanks and softer, more massive contours. Calais remained the latterday equivalent of the old Series 61, though it wasn't that much cheaper than the better-equipped DeVille. Perhaps because of this, volume withered to below 10,000 units by 1974, prompting Calais' cancellation two years later. Only two models were listed in these years: hardtops with two or four doors (a pillared sedan had been offered for 1965-67); the coupe became a fixed-pillar style from 1974 on.

Likewise, the money-spinning DeVille was reduced to just two models for '71, its convertible being judged superfluous with the revived Eldorado ragtop. Considering the history of the name, a pillared Coupe de Ville was a contradiction in terms and, possibly for that reason, proved less popular than the pillarless Sedan de Ville after 1973.

Though still low-volume specialty items, the premium Fleetwoods got a new D-body for '71 and thus fresh styling for the first time since 1966. The Sixty Special remained a four-door sedan on a unique 133-inch wheelbase, but there was only one version now. Called Fleetwood Sixty Special Brougham, it borrowed the 75's new roof styling with more distinctly separate side windows. It, too, would see little appearance change through '76.

The main reason Cadillac styling evolved so slowly in this period is that engineering and design talent was engaged with the more pressing concerns of the day: fuel economy, emissions, occupant crash protection. As it was very difficult to reconcile those last two with the first, Cadillac's engineering emphasis fell on the emissions side with both of its V8s. For example, exhaust-gas recirculation was added for 1973 to reduce oxides of nitrogen (NO_x) emissions, while the air injection reactor pump and engine pulleys were altered to lessen mechanical noise.

Big-car sales slipped badly with the 1973-74 oil embargo. Cadillac was no exception, but it recovered by 1975, when the Eldo's huge 500 V8—by then down to a measly 190 bhp in SAE net measure—became standard for other Cadillacs save one.

And that one marked a big departure from Cadillac tradition: a brand-new four-door sedan that was not only much smaller than anything else in the line but more expensive, outpriced only by the 75. It was christened Seville, recalling the '50s Eldorado model. Cadillac had considered "Leland," to honor its founder, but decid-

Cadillac's Mercedes-size import fighter in 1977 was the Seville. It sold for $13,359 and was a success with 45,060 built.

The 1971 Cadillac Sedan de Ville featured smoother styling.

The side scoop on the '71 Eldorado was like on the 1953 Caddy.

In 1972, the Eldorado boasted a 500 cubic-inch, 235-horse V8.

List price on the '73 Fleetwood Sixty Special Brougham was $7765.

List price on the '73 Fleetwood Eldorado coupe was $7360.

Cadillac built 18,250 Fleetwood Sixty Special Broughams for '74.

The Arab Oil Embargo made fuel economy an important concern to most everyone in late 1973. The inroad of luxury European sedans was also a concern, at least to Cadillac. Its response was a Euro-sedan of its own, the 1975 Seville.

This '75 Coupe de Ville featured the d'Elegance luxury option.

Downsized was the word to describe the new 1977 Sedan de Ville.

The 'international size' Seville had a fuel injected 350 V8.

The '77 Seville rode a 114.3-inch wheelbase, weighed 4192 pounds.

ed most buyers were too young to make the connection. "LaSalle" was also in the running, but was finally rejected because Cadillac's '30s companion make was still felt to have a "loser" image. But this Seville was no loser—carefully planned for the one area of the luxury market that Cadillac had yet to exploit: the quality intermediate typified by Mercedes-Benz.

The Seville bowed to mixed reviews. Clean and trim on its 114.3-inch wheelbase, it compared favorably with German rivals for interior space. But the styling struck some as unimaginative, and it was an open secret that this "baby Cadillac" was actually a heavily reengineered version of GM's workaday X-body compact, a serious deficit in the prestige class.

On the road, though, there was little to criticize. The standard engine, a 350-cid V8 with a new electronic fuel injection system exclusive to this model, delivered brisk, turbinelike performance. Typical 0-60-mph acceleration was in the 10-11-second range,

At 4955 pounds in '77, there would never be a heftier Eldorado.

top speed over 110 mph. The Seville weighed 1000 pounds less and was 27 inches shorter overall than a '75 DeVille, yet its ride was as cloudlike as buyers expected. And it was the best handling Cadillac since the '67 Eldorado—much closer to M-B and BMW than those makers might have liked to admit. To be sure, it wouldn't glide over washboard surfaces with the disdain of a 450SEL—but it didn't cost nearly as much, either. Buyers responded enthusiastically. Seville sales totalled 43,000 in its first full model year, 1976, a healthy 15 percent of division output.

Other Cadillacs were mostly unchanged that season, but a reviving economy meant brisk sales across the board, and the division broke 300,000 units for the first time in history. Things were even better for 1977-78 despite cancellation of the Calais and Eldo convertible—about 335,000 and 350,000 units, respectively. Volume was down for 1979-80, but Cadillac maintained its customary 2-3 percent of total industry production.

Perhaps only Cadillac could so drastically change its cars while setting new sales records. Its 1977 standards were fresh from the ground up—8-12 inches shorter and nearly 1000 pounds lighter on average than the '76s. Wheelbases were now 121.5 inches on DeVilles and the Fleetwood Brougham, 144.5 inches for the Fleetwood limousine. They also had a cleaner, more efficient new engine: a fuel-injected 425-cid V8 with 180 bhp. This was standard across the board. A 195-bhp version was optional except for limos. Upmarket "D'Elegance" trim packages arrived along with pseudo-convertible "Cabriolet" roof coverings for both DeVilles.

The story was much the same for 1979 when Eldorado was downsized, losing 225 pounds, 20 inches of overall length, and 12.3 inches in wheelbase (to 114). An unusual touch for an upmarket domestic was independent rear suspension, more compact than the previous beam axle, which made it possible to reduce wheelbase with little loss of passenger room. Among options for all Cadillacs that year were dual electric remote-control door mirrors, integrated 40-channel CB radio, and "Tripmaster" onboard travel computer. First offered on the '78 DeVille, Tripmaster provided digital readouts for average mpg and speed, miles to destination and estimated arrival time, plus engine rpm, coolant temperature, and electrical system voltage.

Cadillac built 88,951 Sedan de Villes for model year 1978.

Eldorado output was 46,816 for 1978, its last year as a big car.

Fleetwood Brougham for 1978: $14,102. Production: 42,200 units.

The '79 Seville could be equipped with a 350-cid diesel V8.

Attention for 1980 focused on a completely overhauled second-generation Seville. Its most controversial aspect was a sloped "trunkback" rear, conceived by designer Wayne Cady and a sort of valedictory for departing GM styling chief Bill Mitchell. Reminiscent of certain razor-edge Rolls-Royce coachwork done by Hooper and Vanden Plas in the '50s, it made this the most distinctive Cadillac since the first tailfinned '48s, though not everyone liked it. Likely for cost reasons, Seville now shared the latest Eldorado chassis, thus shifting from rear to front drive and gaining the same all-independent suspension with automatic self-leveling. As had been true since 1978, a spiffier Elegante version, usually two-toned, was offered as an alternative to the baseline four-door.

A telling feature of the '80 Seville was its standard engine: a diesel V8 based on Oldsmobile's 350-cid gasoline unit and built in Lansing for use by other GM divisions. Cadillac had first offered this as a 1978 option for all models save Eldorado, which acquired it the following year. Smooth and quiet for a diesel, it gave Cadillac a direct reply to compression-ignition Mercedes models. More importantly, it helped the division contribute to GM's meeting the corporate average fuel economy (CAFE) standards that took effect with model year '78.

As time went on, however, it became clear that most people bought diesel Mercedes not for their economy or longevity but the snob appeal of their three-pointed star. And unhappily for Cadillac's image, the Olds engine suffered early and persistent reliability problems that GM could never seem to fix. By the mid-'80s, however, a glut of cheap gasoline would wash away memories of the second "energy crisis" that played hob with the market in 1979-82. Once buyers began rushing back to big cars and big engines, Cadillac had no trouble abandoning diesels. Neither did most anyone else who'd been peddling them in the U.S.

Although the Sedan de Ville had been downsized in 1977, it still weighed in at 4084 pounds in 1980. A 368-cid V8 was standard.

In its effort to meet late-Seventies federal economy and pollution standards, GM decreed that even Cadillac must reduce the size and weight of its cars. The De Ville shed 900 pounds for 1977, and the Eldorado lost 1100 for '79.

The Seville was completely redesigned for 1980. Its most controversial styling element was the "trunkback" rear end.

Before this came a further blow to the division's quality image: the problematic "V-8-6-4" variable-displacement gasoline engine, a costly stopgap also prompted by CAFE. Displacing 6.0 liters (368 cid) and tuned for a modest 140 bhp, it arrived for 1981 as an option for Seville and was standard elsewhere.

At its heart was an electromechanical system developed by Eaton Corp. that opened and closed the valves on two or four cylinders (hence the name) when signalled by the electronic control module governing the engine's digital fuel injection. The aim, of course, was improved economy, the cylinders shutting down under part-throttle, low-load conditions when you didn't need all eight, such as in medium-speed highway cruising. It was a good

It took $16,141 to purchase a 1980 Eldorado; output hit 52,685.

The '81 Fleetwood had a "modulated-displacement" V8-6-4 engine.

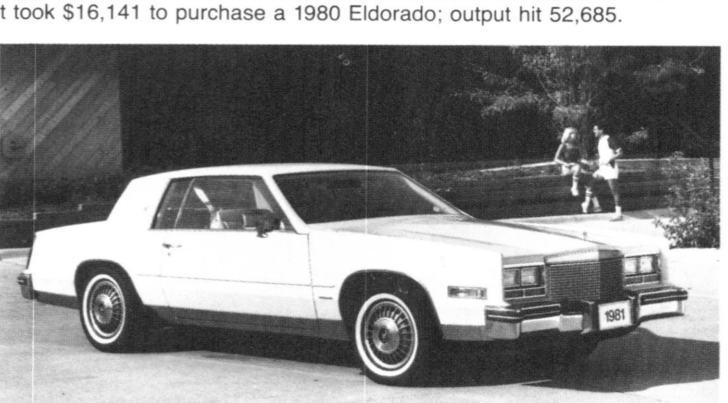

Eldorado horsepower ratings for 1981 were 105, 125, or 140.

Cadillac debuted its own Chevy Cavalier clone in '82: Cimarron.

idea but too complex to be reliable, and Cadillac paid a big price in both image and dollars once angry consumers began suing for redress. Few mourned the V-8-6-4 when it was terminated after just one year (though it persisted a while longer in limos).

A better bet was Buick's 125-bhp 4.1-liter V6, newly optional across the '81 board and the first six in Cadillac history. Another new extra was an electronic "memory" power seat that assumed one of two preset positions at the touch of a button—a flashback to Mercury's mid-'50s "Seat-O-Matic."

There were a couple of new surprises for '82. The biggest one was a Cadillac even smaller than the '75 Seville. Called Cimarron, it was basically a high-zoot version of GM's new 101.2-inch wheelbase J-body subcompact, a four-door loaded to the gills but otherwise much like sister models at every other GM division—except for price: initially $12,000. That looked steep when one of the cheaper versions like a Chevy Cavalier or Pontiac J2000 could be had for less with comparable equipment. True, Cimarron offered a few J-car exclusives like leather upholstery and optional sliding glass "Astroroof," but its humble origins were so obvious that nobody took it for a real Cadillac.

This was a frank embarrassment to division officials who'd been caught with their badge-engineering pants down. Still, Cimmaron was a logical development: intended to boost Cadillac's fleet-average economy until its larger cars could be downsized again while helping dealers stem the rising tide of upscale imports like the BMW 5-Series then beginning to cut into division sales. But the decision to field this gilded J came at the 11th hour and it showed. The resulting criticism stung.

Almost immediately, Cadillac began trying to distance Cimarron from lesser Js—adding more standard features, ringing in a mild facelift and a lush "D'Oro" sub-model for '83, making Chevy's 2.8 V6 an option from mid-'85 and standard for '88 (replacing the original weak and noisy 2.0-liter four), tinkering with the chassis to impart a more "European" feel. But buyers always stayed away in droves, and the division struggled to move an average 20,000 Cimarrons annually through 1986, after which demand slid to less than 15,000.

Not that Cadillac cried much on its way to the bank, because its total sales rose steadily from 1982 through '85—from about 235,500 to nearly 385,000. The Cimarron and troublesome engines may have blotted its once-enviable reputation, but Cadillac still dominated the luxury market.

Which brings us back to 1982's other surprise, yet another new engine. This was a small, 4.1-liter (250-cid) V8 with a cast-iron head atop a lightweight aluminum block, plus digital fuel injection. Dubbed "HT4100," it was standard for all '82s (except Cimarron, of course). Initial rated output was 125 bhp, same as for the Buick 4.1 V6 (probably due to an engineer's pen), which was dropped as an option for that year's Eldorado/Seville, then disappeared entirely. However, the V8 actually produced a bit less torque, so the big Cadillacs were far less rapid than before.

A happier '82 development was a Touring Coupe package for Eldorado with blackout moldings, fatter tires on aluminum wheels, and a standard buckets-and-console interior with unique trim. Traditionalists still had the usual choice of two- and four-door DeVilles and Fleetwoods in plain and D'Elegance trim, plus standard and Biarritz Eldorados and base and Elegante Sevilles— all available with fake wire wheels and convertible-look tops.

The big Caddys changed little over the next two years. HT4100 horsepower and torque rose by 10 each for '83, when Eldo and Seville offered a new acoustically tailored sound system developed by GM's Delco Electronics Division in concert with the Bose speaker people.

All was again mostly quiet for '84 except for the return of an open-air Eldorado, though all that "last convertible" nonsense had already been silenced. In fact, Buick had issued a ragtop Riviera back in '82, which made Cadillac seem rather slow to follow suit with its related Eldo. The reason was certainly not its no-more-

This '82 Fleetwood Brougham d'Elegance started at a cool $19,826.

Eldorado's aluminum 4.1-liter fuel-injected V8 debuted for '82.

Most Fleetwood Brougham buyers shunned the 5.7-liter diesel V8.

The '83 Eldorado Touring Coupe boasted an upgraded suspension.

Rare new, rarer later: the 1984 Eldorado Biarritz convertible.

Cadillac took its knocks in the early '80s. It introduced a "variable-displacement" V-8-6-4 and diesel power, and an aluminum 4.1 V-8. The first two were troublesome, the last underpowered. And nobody liked the Cavalier-clone Cimarron.

The '84 Coupe de Ville had standard electronic level control.

Seville for '84 measured 204.8 inches long, weighed 3804 pounds.

The '85 Fleetwood Brougham d'Elegance with leather: $23,202.

Fleetwood downsized for 1985 and featured front-wheel drive.

Fleetwood for '85: 110.8-inch wheelbase and 195-inch length.

convertibles promise but the Riviera's slow sales, which must have made Cadillac managers hesitate.

But they finally did it, and they did it big. Offered only in uplevel Biarritz trim (a staple option for coupes since the late '70s), the reborn ragtop Eldo was base-priced at $32,105—in raw dollars the most expensive U.S. production convertible ever offered. Like the Riviera, it, too, would die after 1985, though price didn't kill it as much as the advent of a much smaller new E-body and the luxury market's continuing desertion to imports.

Model year '85 was pivotal for Cadillac, as its best-selling DeVille was again downsized and given front-wheel drive for the first time. Sharing GM's new C-body with that year's all-new Buick Electra and Olds Ninety-Eight, it rode the same 110.8-inch-wheelbase chassis with all-independent coil-spring/strut suspension, power rack-and-pinion steering, and assisted front-disc/rear-drum brakes. Dimensionally, it was two feet shorter and some 600 pounds lighter than its rear-drive predecessor. There was also a new Seventy-Five limousine on a 134.4-inch platform. The 4.1 V-8 was turned sideways to provide similar cabin space within the smaller package, but necessary manifolding changes brought horsepower back to 125 and torque to 190 lbs/ft. Still, Cadillac could claim the world's only transverse V8.

Even better, the new Coupe and Sedan de Ville and their lush Fleetwood counterparts quickly outsold the popular rear-drive series. Cadillac built over 197,000 for the first full model year, versus an annual 137,000-175,000 of the 1981-84 C-bodies.

But before buyers had shown their approval, Cadillac had decided to retain some rear-drive models as a hedge. This proved a shrewd move once the market began its strong recovery from the doldrums of '82. Badged Fleetwood Brougham through 1986, then just plain Brougham, these cars continued with few changes through the end of the decade, garnering about 50,000 orders a year, each one pure gravy. We should note the passing of the big Brougham coupe and the diesel V8 option after 1985. The latter wouldn't be missed. Nor was it really needed for CAFE anymore, since the government had relaxed those requirements somewhat.

As planned, the Cadillac line's second wholesale downsizing since '77 was completed with a new-generation Eldorado and Seville for 1986. Remaining twins under the skin, they shared the new 108-inch-wheelbase E-body platform (technically, Seville was still GM's K-body) of that year's Riviera and Olds Toronado. The Cadillac's had the 4.1 V8, of course (now situated transversely rather than longitudinally) instead of the others' Buick V6. Designers again managed similar interior space within much smaller envelopes, trimmed 16 inches in length and 350-plus pounds in curb weight, and Seville shed its controversial "bustle" for a conventional notchback profile. Both had a raft of interesting new features: floor-mounted shifters (for the four-speed overdrive automatic transaxle), flush-mounted "composite" headlamps, and more electronic gadgets than ever.

Sadly, these cars proved even bigger sales disasters than Cimmaron. Seville volume, a strong 40,000 a year for 1984-85, dropped by half; Eldorado, which garnered an annual 76,000-plus orders in the same period, plunged by more than two-thirds.

The reasons were obvious enough: bland styling that was too close to that of GM's much cheaper N-body compacts (which began arriving the previous year) and dimensions that just weren't impressive enough for the cars' regular clientele. (A 1987 *Newsweek* article on GM's declining fortunes graphically highlighted the design problem by picturing a Seville tail-to-tail with an N-body Olds Calais; it was tough to tell them apart.) Worse, workmanship slipped badly due to equipment problems at the highly automated new Detroit-Hamtramck plant dedicated solely to E/K production. (Typical of the woes: robots painting each other instead of cars.)

There was nothing to do but soldier on, so the '87s received only minor suspension tweaks. For 1988, Cadillac tried to rectify its styling mistake via time-honored methods. Seville thus gained a

The 1985 Fleetwood Seventy-Five limousine listed for $32,640.

This 1985 Cimarron is dressed up with the $975 d'Oro package.

The '86 Seville Elegante was mounted on a 108-inch wheelbase.

The Touring Suspension firmed up the '86 Eldorado's handling.

A Touring Coupe package added $2880 to the tab of an '86 DeVille.

Base price for the 1986 Sedan de Ville started at $19,990.

The '86 Sedan de Ville could become a Touring Sedan for $2880.

A 115.8-inch wheelbase marked the '87 Fleetwood Sixty Special.

A restyled rear end was featured on the '87 Sedan de Ville.

The big Brougham lost the Fleetwood part of its name for 1987.

Cadillac began its second round of downsizing as the '85 De Ville/Fleetwood lost another 600 pounds and adopted front drive. The Eldorado and Seville dieted for '86. The former sold well, the latter didn't. The pubic wanted big cars.

Cadillac entered the international ultra-luxury market with the 1987 Allanté. It was to compete with the Mercedes 560 SL.

"power dome" hood and a more "important" grille. Eldorado was similarly treated but also received new squared-up lower-body sheetmetal that stretched overall length by three inches at the rear—shades of the '50s.

Happier developments included first-time availability of anti-lock brakes and a more potent engine. The former was the same laudable option announced for the 1986 DeVille/Fleetwood line (but not readily available until '87), a joint effort between GM and the German firm Alfred Teves (Ate). Stretching bore brought the 4.1 V8 to 4.5 liters (273 cid), and this plus a new two-stage intake manifold, larger throttle bores and other changes lifted horsepower by 25 (to 155 total) and torque by 40 lbs/ft (to 240). The '88 Eldorado and Seville were thus usefully quicker off the line than the 1986-87s—quite punchy in fact—and ABS made panic stops shorter and more controlled. A "touring" suspension package was still available for those seeking crisper handling with little sacrifice in ride comfort.

The bread-winning DeVille/Fleetwood had been improving, too. Besides a slight power increase, the '86 line offered new Touring Coupe and Sedan DeVilles with firm suspension, huskier tires on aluminum wheels, a front air dam with integrated foglights, plus less chrome and special trim inside and out. The '87s lengthened 1.5 inches via extended rear fender caps and got a new grille, while the Sixty Special designation returned for a new stretched,

Eldorado answered its critics in 1987 with more power: a 4.5-liter aluminum V8 that developed 155-bhp and 240 lbs/ft torque.

Seville entered 1989 with cosmetic refinements. Sales of the 1986-88 models had been a disappointment to Cadillac.

115.8-inch-wheelbase Fleetwood four-door, a nod to the "executive car" market. The front-drive Seventy-Five was in its last year. As Chrysler had lately realized, limos were unprofitable and thus better left to aftermarket converters, of which there were plenty. The main changes for '88 involved the more potent 4.5 V8 and standardization of several once-optional features, including Twilight Sentinel, tilt/telescope steering wheel and cruise control.

More drastic steps were taken for 1989, when the DeVille/ Fleetwood was stretched and restyled to look more like its pre-1985 forerunners. Traditional Cadillac styling cues, such as rear fender skirts on the Fleetwood and narrow vertical taillamps on all models, made the 1989 models immediately recognizable. Coupes gained six inches in overall length, while sedans gained three inches in wheelbase (to 113.8) and nine inches overall. The longer wheelbase for the sedans was used to increase rear-seat room, and Cadillac boasted that back-seat passengers now enjoyed more than 43 inches of leg room. Encouraged by increased sales of the 1988 Eldorado after a less dramatic restyling, Cadillac was pinning even greater hopes on the 1989 DeVille/Fleetwood.

Cadillac's most ambitious car of the '80s—certainly its most publicized—was the Allanté, a sharp two-seat convertible aimed squarely at the big-bucks Mercedes 560SL. The first two-seat Caddy since 1941, it bowed with great fanfare for 1987 on a shortened (99.4-inch-wheelbase) Eldorado chassis with modified mechanicals. Power came from a tuned 4.1 V8 with multi-point (instead of single- or dual-point) injection, roller valve lifters, high-flow cylinder heads and tuned intake manifold providing 170 bhp. Italy's renowned Pininfarina was contracted for the styling (more snob appeal that way) and to build the bodywork. Modified Eldo understructures were flown in special 747 jets to a new PF plant set up in Turin especially for Allanté production; fully trimmed shells (galvanized unit steel structures with aluminum hood and trunklid) were then air-shipped back to Detroit-Hamtramck for drivetrain installation and final assembly. Standard equipment was predictably lavish, and included an SL-style lift-off hardtop to supplement the manual soft top. A cellular telephone was the lone option.

Though a pleasant, capable tourer and an entirely new breed of Cadillac, the Allanté initially failed to make the hoped-for impres-

Allanté received the larger 4.5-liter aluminum V8 for 1989.

The Eldorado sailed into model year 1989 largely unchanged.

The late Eighties saw Cadillac desperately trying to regain some of its former luster. Unfortunately, the ultra-luxury '87 Allanté was voted "Flop of the Year" by one magazine, but the enlarged '88 Eldorado and '89 De Ville saw sales go up.

sion. Cadillac predicted 1987 model-year sales of 4000 units but got only 1651; deliveries for the first full production year totaled just 2500 versus a planned 7000. The results: an embarrassing pile-up of unsold cars, rebates to clear it—and a further blow to Cadillac prestige. *Automotive News* went so far as to name Allanté 1987's "Flop of the Year," though division chief John O. Grettenberger dismissed this and wide coverage of the car's slow start as "just the latest round of GM bashing."

Still, for what it was, the Allanté was generally judged too expensive—$54,000 at announcement, $56,500 for the little-changed '88. And it depreciated by a third the minute it left the showroom, whereas a Mercedes SL actually appreciated in value. An assortment of niggling troubles—wind and water leaks, squeaks and rattles, horns that didn't work and heaters that worked too well—only made matters worse.

The Allanté may yet succeed, both as a car and as the image-booster the division so desperately needed by decade's end. Cadillac certainly hasn't given up on it. The '89 was treated to a tuned 4.5 V8 with 200 bhp, plus 16-inch wheels and tires, and a simplified folding soft top that could be raised or lowered by one person in less than 30 seconds.

Still, Allanté may be remembered mainly as a symbol of Cadillac's sad decline in the '80s, marked by a loss of prestige that history will no doubt blame on basically good ideas poorly executed. Fortunately, the signs at this writing are that Cadillac has learned from its mistakes and is willing to do what must be done to regain its former eminence. That won't be easy. As one writer put it: ". . . No matter how rough the sledding, GM has left itself only one option if it is to have any hope of resurrecting the Cadillac name. It must stand and fight."

After downsizing in the mid-Eighties, Cadillac was trying to make its car look more important again, as this '89 model shows.

Anti-lock brakes were a useful option on the '89 Coupe de Ville.

The '89 Fleetwood looked more Cadillac-like with fender skirts.

CHECKER

Checker was long known for taxicabs and airport limousines when it began marketing "civilian" versions in 1960. Initially called Superba, these comprised four-door sedans and wagons in standard and Special trim. The latter were more deluxe inside, but not much. All were the same tanklike affairs familiar to anyone who'd ever hailed a Checker cab. Wheelbase was 120 inches, fairly compact for the day. Curb weights ranged around 3400 pounds for sedans, near 3800 pounds for wagons.

Morris Markin, Checker's founder and president, was steadfast: There'd be no change to this dumpy but practical design as long as there were buyers for reliable, durable "taxi-tough" cars. Not that there'd been many changes before. The Superba design dated back to Checker's A8 taxicab of 1956.

The Checker engine through 1964 came from Continental Motor Company, basically the same 226-cubic-inch L-head six that Kaiser had used. Here it was offered in side- and overhead-valve versions. The former had 7.3:1 compression and produced a mere 80 horsepower at 3100 rpm. The ohv unit had 8.0:1 compression and a more respectable 122 bhp at 4000 rpm. Both cost exactly the same.

True to its taxicab origins, the Superba sedan came with a pair of rear jump seats and could carry up to eight. The wagon's rear seat folded up or down by means of an electronic servo controlled from the dashboard. This gimmick and its different bodywork made the wagon about $350 more expensive.

For 1961, the Superba Special was renamed Marathon, the sedan's 15-inch wheels were replaced by 14-inchers for a slightly lower ride height, and the ohv engine became standard for wagons. Prices stood pat: $2542 for the Superba sedan to $3004 for the Marathon wagon. Air conditioning cost $411 extra, power steering $64. Like Checker cabs, the Superba/Marathon had a full bank of gauges, a spartan but well-padded interior, wide doors, and a spacious rear compartment.

This quartet continued for 1962, the only change being a return to 15-inch wheels for sedans. However, there was now a special Town Custom limousine on a 129-inch wheelbase, optimistically priced at $7500. Vinyl roof and a glassed-in driver's compartment were standard and there was a full range of power options, but production was limited by low demand—understandable, as even the most expensive non-limousine Cadillac cost less. The ohv engine was booted to 141 bhp at 4000 rpm for all '63 models.

Prices rose about $100 across the board for '64 and the Superba name was dropped. Checker switched to Chevrolet engines for 1965: 230-cid, 140-bhp six; 195-bhp 283 V8; 250-bhp 327 V8. The Town Custom limousine was still around, but only on special order. The 283 cost $110 extra, automatic transmission was a $248 option, and overdrive added $108.

For 1966, Checker added a Deluxe sedan and a lower-priced limousine ($4541), thus reestablishing its four-model lineup. Both were dropped the following year, but the Deluxe sedan returned for '68, the limousine for 1969. With their Chevy V8s, the post-1964 Checkers were naturally much faster than the earlier sixes, and they became even more potent as their engines did. The 283 option was dropped for '67 and a 307-cid replacement with 200 bhp arrived the following year. For 1969, the 327 small-block gave way to Chevy's new 350-cid enlargement with 300 bhp. Emissions tuning cut that to 250 bhp for 1970. Prices for the optional engines were usually low: for 1968, $108 for the 307 and $195 for the 327.

Checker sales were always moderate in the '60s, though adequate to sustain the firm's desired annual volume of 6000-7000 units. Checker's best year of the decade was 1962, when it built 8173 cars, though most of these were taxis.

Markin never wavered from his mission of building taxi-tough cars. It isn't widely known, but Nathan Altman once approached Checker about building his Avanti II; Markin replied that the Avanti was too ugly to bother with.

David Markin took over the helm in Kalamazoo on the death of his father in 1970, but there wasn't much change in the company or its products until the mid-'70s. That's when Edward N. Cole, having retired as GM president in 1974, joined Checker to launch a new-model development program. Sadly, he was killed in a plane crash before his efforts reached fruition.

Checker began a long, steady decline in 1970. The main problem was increased competition for fleet sales from the major Detroit automakers, who needed this important outlet when passenger-car sales slowed in the mid-'70s (following the OPEC oil embargo) and again at decade's end. With its low, fixed volume and relatively high overhead, tiny Checker just couldn't compete with the Big Three on price. As a result, its passenger-car volume was dramatically lower after 1969: fewer than 400 for 1970, a more encouraging 600-1000 units a year through 1974, less than 500 thereafter.

Relentless, inflation-fueled price escalation didn't help. The standard sedan was up to $4000 by '73, to near $5400 by '75, over $6000 in '77 and close to $8000 by 1980. That was Chrysler or Buick money, and a lot to ask for such a dull car that really wasn't put together all that well.

These difficulties were reflected in Checker's dwindling number of models and sales as the '70s progressed. The decade began with a four-car lineup on two wheelbases—120 inches for Marathon sedan and wagon, 129 for Marathon Deluxe sedan and limo. The last was dropped as unprofitable after 1971. The Deluxe sedan shifted to the short wheelbase for '75, then disappeared along with the wagon, leaving only the basic sedan. A Chevy six was still standard in these years, the stroked 250-cid version of the 230, adopted for 1971 and rated at 145 bhp through '74, 100-110 thereafter. The 245-bhp 350 V8 remained optional, downrated to 145 bhp SAE net for 1973-76, then retuned for 160-170 bhp. Chevy's 305 small-block with 145 bhp was an additional option from 1977. Meantime, management clung to its extremely dated design, resisting all suggestions that it needed replacing. The addition of federal "crash" bumpers for 1974—big, girder-style lumps of steel—rendered quite ugly a car that had once simply looked old. Ghia came up with a prototype for a handsome new-

Anybody who lives in a big city is familiar with the ubiquitous Checker taxicab, but few people realize that it was also sold as a passenger car. Despite its roominess and heavy construction, only a relative handful were sold.

generation Checker in 1970, but it wasn't adopted. The same fate awaited "Galva II," a 1975 proposal by Autodynamics of Madison Heights, Michigan, which envisioned extremely simple, rectilinear styling to keep tooling costs to an absolute minimum. It likely failed for lack of money, though management stubbornness was still a factor.

But that began to change once the dynamic Ed Cole started planning yet another new Checker soon after he arrived. Targeted for a production start sometime during 1983, this would have been a boxy, square-lined four-door hatchback sedan with front-drive mechanicals borrowed from the GM X-car compacts (which Cole knew were in the works when he joined Checker). A sturdy new box-section chassis of undisclosed design was planned for three models: a 109-inch-wheelbase six-passenger version, a 122-inch eight-seater and a 128-inch nine-seater. A variety of low-cost, easily replaced plastic body panels was contemplated, as was an interesting rear suspension with solid rubber springs, and design work progressed as far as a single full-scale mockup.

But it made no difference in the end. The project lost momentum with Cole's untimely death, by which time even Checker's taxi business had become marginal, and the Kalamazoo company ceased all production in mid-1982.

The 1966 Checker Marathon was available with a Chevy six or eight, here equipped with the extra cost 327-cid 250-bhp V8.

Checker built 6,136 cars for the '65 model run, including taxis.

The '78 Marathon wore clumsy five-mile-per-hour Federal bumpers.

The 1965 Marathon Town Custom eight-passenger limousine weighed in at a hefty 4800 pounds. It listed at $8000.

CHEVROLET

William C. Durant founded General Motors in 1908 but was ousted two years later, so he formed Chevrolet in 1911, intending to make it a powerful lever for regaining control. He did. By 1915, Chevrolet was a force to be reckoned with; by 1919 it was part of General Motors; by the mid-'20s, it was GM's largest volume division—and has been ever since.

Early Chevys were largish medium-price cars with six-cylinder and even V8 engines. The make's historic turn to the low-price field came with the four-cylinder "490" of 1915, named for its advertised list price. It was a big success, outflanking Ford's Model T with more attractive styling and more features. Its closely related successors were Chevy's mainstay into the late '20s.

However, Chevy wouldn't pass Ford in production until 1927, the year Dearborn stopped building the aged T and retooled for the Model A. Chevrolet's strength that year, and throughout the '30s, was its new Stovebolt Six, also called the Cast-Iron Wonder. The nicknames stemmed from the engine's cast-iron pistons and ¼ × 20 slotted-head bolts—not esoteric but wonderfully effective and as reliable as Old Faithful.

The Chevy six was engineered by Ormond E. Hunt from an earlier design by Henry M. Crane that had evolved into the 1926 Pontiac engine. By 1930 it was producing an even 50 horsepower from 194 cubic inches. With various improvements, this solid, overhead-valve engine remained Chevrolet's only powerplant for nearly three decades. For 1933 it gained new combustion chambers and the name "Blue Flame." Two versions were offered through 1935: 60-bhp 181 cid and 80-bhp 206.8 cid. It was then fully redesigned for 1937, made shorter and lighter and given nearly "square" bore/stroke dimensions and four (instead of three) main bearings. The result was 85 bhp from 216.5 cid.

Throughout its history, Chevrolet has usually made the right moves at the right time. To follow the Stovebolt, division general manager William "Big Bill" Knudsen and GM design director Harley Earl cooked up an elegant line of Cadillac-like cars for 1929-32. As ever, Chevy relied on features to win buyers from Ford. Attractions for '33 included "No-Draft" door ventwings, synchromesh transmission, selective free-wheeling, safety plate glass and adjustable driver's seat. Chevy also went to a two-tier lineup that season, which would persist through 1939.

The '30s were good to Chevrolet despite the prevailing Depression. Production outpaced Ford's in 1931-33, bottoming to 313,000 units for '32 but recovering to 486,000 for '33. Volume was up to nearly a million by '36, though Ford's was even nearer.

More streamlined styling and "Knee-Action" independent front suspension made news for 1934. The latter, engineered by Maurice Olley, wasn't universally liked, so solid front axles were retained through 1940, after which Knee-Action became standard throughout the line. Continued modernization occurred for '36 as Chevrolets became even sleeker and adopted Fisher Body's all-steel "Turret Top" construction. Another big plus was hydraulic brakes, which Ford wouldn't offer until 1939, mainly due to old Henry's stubbornness. Chevy was also quicker than Ford to aban-

The Chevy Master 85 Town Sedan was priced at $669 in 1939.

Chevrolet built 40,924 Master DeLuxe Sport Sedans for 1940.

The '42 Special DeLuxe Sport Sedan had "massiveness," said Chevy.

By 1939, Chevrolet was firmly entrenched as "USA-1." It got there on the strength of attractive styling, a bulletproof "Stovebolt" six, and timely updating. Old Henry Ford helped, too, for he was very stubborn about modernizing his cars.

The 1939 Master DeLuxe rode a 112.3-inch wheelbase. It was powered by Chevy's 85-horsepower "Stovebolt" six.

don body styles without roll-up windows, dropping both roadsters and phaetons after 1935.

With its new 85-bhp six, Chevrolet was well equipped for the 1937 sales battle. Styling became rather dull, as for several other GM makes that year, and would remain so through 1939. Despite this, Chevy regained production supremacy for model year 1938 and has rarely surrendered to Ford since.

Renewed competitiveness was evident in an expanded 1940 line with what Chevrolet called "Royal Clipper" styling. Though not a drastic change, this facelift was sufficiently thorough to make the cars look much newer than the '39s. Wheelbase was 113 inches, about what it had been on most models since 1934. Master 85 returned from '39 as the least costly Chevy, with Master DeLuxe above it. Each offered business coupe, two-door Town Sedan and four-door Sport Sedan. Master 85 also listed a woody wagon, Master DeLuxe a sport coupe. A new top-line Special DeLuxe series had all these plus Chevy's first true convertible coupe, which was quite successful (nearly 12,000 sales). Special and Master DeLuxe came with Knee-Action; Master 85 offered Chevy's last solid front axle. Model year production soared from some 577,000 to nearly 765,000 as Chevy bested Ford by over 220,000 cars.

The gap widened to more than 300,000 for 1941 as Chevy enjoyed its first million-car year. Though no one knew it then, this year's substantial redesign would carry the division through 1948: 116-inch wheelbase, Knee-Action on all models, 90-bhp six, and attractive new styling by Harley Earl's Art & Color Studio. Master 85s were dropped, but other models continued. A mid-year Special DeLuxe offering was the sleek Fleetline four-door sedan, which sold 34,000 for the year. It was distinguished by a more formal roofline with closed-in rear quarters *a la* Cadillac 60 Special. The extra horsepower was obtained via higher (6.5:1) compression, new pistons and revised combustion chambers, plus reworked valves, rocker arms and water pump.

Styling refinements were featured for war-shortened '42. Fenders were extended back into the front doors as on costlier GM cars, and a smart, clean grille replaced the somewhat busy '41 rendition. Models stayed the same save substituting five-passenger coupes for business coupes. New series names arrived: Stylemaster for the lower-priced group, Fleetmaster for the upper. The latter now included a Fleetline sub-series comprising a new "torpedo-style" two-door Aerosedan and a conventional four-door Sportmaster, both bearing triple chrome bands on front and rear fenders.

When civilian car production stopped in February 1942, Chevy's model year total was 254,885 units, of which only 45,472 were built in calendar '42. Convertibles and wagons numbered only about 1000 each. Like all of Detroit's '42s, rarity makes any of these Chevys coveted collectors' items today. Strikes and material shortages hampered GM's postwar production startup and enabled Ford to outpace Chevy for '46. But after that, Chevy was again "USA-1" even though its 1946-48 offerings were only slightly

At $628, the Master 85 business coupe was the cheapest '39 model.

For 1941, Chevrolet upped the wheelbase to a full 116 inches.

The Fleetline Aerosedan was a top-of-the-line 1942 offering. It sold for $880; 61,885 were built before World War II interrupted.

modified '42s. Still, differences were apparent in grille treatments, medallions and other exterior trim. Model offerings and mechanical specs stood pat.

Meanwhile, Chevy experimented with a smaller companion model called Cadet. Different configurations were considered, but the final prototype was conventional: a smooth "bathtub-style" four-door sedan with a 108-inch wheelbase and a scaled-down Stovebolt six. After spending a few million dollars on development, management decided there was no need for the Cadet in the booming postwar seller's market, especially as the compact would have cost almost as much to build as a standard Chevy. Ford reached the same conclusions at about the same time. Though stillborn, the Cadet is significant as the first car with engineer Earle S. MacPherson's simple, effective strut-type front suspension, today almost universal among small cars. Ford would be the first to use it in production, however, as MacPherson went to Dearborn soon after Cadet was canceled.

If production Chevys didn't change much in this period, management did, and other new models were being floated for the future: sports cars, hardtop-convertibles, all-steel station wagons. June 1946 saw division chief M.E. Coyle replaced by Cadillac general manager Nick Dreystadt, who encouraged these and other ideas, as well as a forceful engineering program that would ultimately breathe new life into a make that had acquired a respectable, if stodgy, image. But Dreystadt died after just two years in office, and his successor, W.E. Armstrong, resigned early because of illness. Then came Thomas H. Keating, who continued Dreystadt's policies. Soon after he took charge, Edward N. Cole came over from Cadillac to be Chevy chief engineer.

Their first order of business was to make Chevys look more "with it." GM had scheduled its first postwar redesign for 1949, and Chevy's was among the best. Although wheelbase was actually cut an inch, to 115 inches, the '49 was cleanly styled and looked much more streamlined than the 1946-48 Chevys. Its two-piece windshield was curved and two inches lower; fenders swept back smoothly through the cowl and doors; rear fenders rolled gracefully forward. Suspension revisions and a lower center of gravity made it the best-handling Chevy ever—and probably superior to that year's Plymouth and Ford. The '49s were also beautifully put together, testifying that engineers and production people had taken great care to make them "right."

The Chevy model line was again overhauled for '49. The less expensive Special series comprised fastback Fleetline sedans with two and four doors, plus notchback Styleline Town and Sport Sedans, sport coupe and business coupe. All but the last were duplicated in a more luxurious DeLuxe group that added a Styleline convertible and eight-passenger station wagon. There were actually two wagons: an "early" '49 with vestigial wood as a structural material, and a mid-year all-steel replacement. The Fleetlines initially sold well, but the fastback fad soon faded and they were dropped after a lone 1952 Deluxe two-door.

Having regained its production stride in 1947-48, Chevy rolled

It took $845 to purchase a Chevy Special DeLuxe coupe in 1942.

The 1946 Chevy was really a warmed-over '42 with a new grille.

The '41 Chevrolet has long been a favorite with collectors. This Special DeLuxe convertible cost $949 and 15,296 were built.

out a record 1,010,000 cars for '49. Ford, however, rolled out about 108,000 more, thanks to a popular all-new design and an early introduction (in June '48).

No make better reflected the ebullient '50s than Chevrolet, which evolved from family hauler to hot hauler. Again in this decade, Chevy mostly made right moves at the right time. The Bel Air, for example, a single 1950 hardtop that was expanded for '53 into the division's top-line series, came to dominate production by 1957. It was equally right to build the 265- and 283-cid V8s, the engines that forever banished Chevy's staid image almost overnight. And it was right to add strength at the top of the line with the '58 Impala. By 1960, Chevrolet was no longer just one of the "low-priced three" but an alternative for those who usually bought Pontiacs, Dodges, or Mercurys.

The last of the traditional low-cost, low-suds Chevys appeared for 1950-52, with the costlier DeLuxe accounting for 80-85 percent of production. The hoary old 216.5-cid Stovebolt was coaxed up to 92 bhp for 1950, and there was now a 235.5-cid version with 105 bhp for cars equipped with optional two-speed Powerglide, Chevy's new fully automatic transmission. Ford-O-Matic was a year away, and Plymouth wouldn't have a true self-shifter until '55. A torque-converter automatic similar to Buick's Dynaflow, Powerglide was a big reason why Chevy beat Ford in model year car production by no less than 290,000 units with a total of nearly 1.5 million.

Another factor was the new 1950 Bel Air, America's first low-priced hardtop coupe. Again, Chevy led the low-price field by at least a year with an innovation that buyers couldn't get enough of. Like the pioneering Buick, Cadillac and Olds hardtops of 1949, this junior edition was a top-line offering with lush trim that included simulated convertible-top bows on the headliner. It arrived in the Styleline DeLuxe series at $1741, about $100 below the con-

Chevy spruced up the grille for 1947, and raised prices as well.

Chevy wagons were made in wood or steel for 1949, here a woody.

The '49 Fleetline DeLuxe four-door fastback retailed for $1539.

vertible, but outpaced the droptop by better than 2-1 with over 76,000 first-year sales.

Chevy took a breather for the next two years. There were no major mechanical developments, and styling changes were confined to somewhat bulkier sheetmetal for '51 and detail trim revisions for '52. Chevy was first in output both years. The '51 totals were 1.23 million to Ford's 1.013 million. Korean War restrictions forced industry-wide cutbacks for '52, but Chevy's 800,000-plus still beat Ford's 671,000.

Though the Corvette sports car was Chevy's big news for '53 (*see* Chevrolet Corvette), its passenger models got a major facelift. The bottom-end Special series was retitled One-Fifty, the Deluxe became Two-Ten, and the Bel Air name applied to a full range of body styles at the top of the line. Higher compression brought the Blue Flame Six to 105 bhp with manual shift or 115 bhp with Powerglide. The figures were 115 and 125 for 1954, when the '53 became a bit flashier. Chevy continued to set the production pace. With war restrictions over, volume soared to over 1.3 million units for '53 and to near 1.17 million for '54. But though sound and reliable, Chevys still weren't very exciting. All-new styling and Ed Cole's V8 would take care of that.

Without question, the 265 V8 introduced for 1955 was one of the industry's milestone engines. Though designed for efficiency and low unit cost, it was really one of those "blue sky" projects that comes along only once or twice in an engineer's career. As Cole later recalled: "I had worked on V8 engines all my professional life. I had lived and breathed engines. [Motor engineer Harry F.] Barr and I were always saying how we would do it if we could ever design a new engine. You just know you want five main bearings—there's no decision to make. We knew that a certain bore-stroke relationship was the most compact. We knew we'd like a displacement of 265 cubic inches...And we never changed any of this. We released our engine for tooling direct from the drawing boards."

Cole and Barr had reason to be enthusiastic. The 265 had low reciprocating mass that allowed high rpm; die-cast heads with integral, interchangeable valve guides; aluminum "slipper" pistons; and a crankshaft of forged pressed-steel instead of alloy iron—and much more. Best of all, it weighed less than the old six yet was far more potent, initially pumping out 162/170 bhp manual/Powerglide in standard tune or 180 bhp with optional Power-Pak (four-barrel carburetor and dual exhausts).

Of course, it could give a lot more—and did when bored out to 283 cid for 1957 and offered with optional fuel injection. Chevrolet developed a new 348-cid "big-block" V8 for 1958 and beyond. It was a good one, but the original small-block remains the best-known, best-loved engine of its day, earning Chevy a performance reputation the way sixes never could. That reputation has continued to this day, as has the engine itself—still in production for the Corvette, albeit with numerous modifications dictated by the events of nearly 35 intervening years.

At just under $200, Powerglide became an increasingly popular option as the '50s progressed—smooth in operation and well suited to all but the high-powered models. Standard three-speed manual and extra-cost stick-overdrive were offered throughout the decade, and an all-synchromesh four-speed manual came on stream in 1959. Late '57 brought a second automatic option, three-speed Turboglide, but it was complex, costly and short-lived. Powerglide would remain Chevy's principal automatic well into the '60s.

The 1955-57 Chevys are coveted collectibles now, and styling has as much to do with it as engineering. Division designers Clare MacKichan, Chuck Stebbins, Bob Veryzer and Carl Renner, and others worked under Harley Earl's dictum of "Go all the way, then back off." Though the '55 didn't reach showrooms looking like it did in fanciful renderings, it wasn't far off. Its beltline dip and wraparound windshield were Earl hallmarks at the time. Its simple eggcrate grille was inspired by Ferrari and was one of Earl's favorite touches, but became broader, brighter and more conventional for '56 in line with buyer tastes.

There was even more to the winning '55 package: a more capable suspension, bigger brakes, better steering, more interior and trunk room, better visibility—the list goes on and on. Even the old six was better, boosted to 123/136 bhp manual/Powerglide. With all this, plus attractive prices that weren't changed much from '54, Chevy led the industry in a record industry year with over 1.7 million cars, a new high for the marque and a quarter-million units better than Ford.

An interesting '55 newcomer was the Bel Air Nomad, America's first and only "hardtop wagon," a Carl Renner idea first seen on a 1954 Motorama Corvette. The Nomad didn't sell all that well, mainly because two-door wagons were less popular than four-doors, though water leaks were a problem. Then too, it was rela-

A strike by 400,000 miners in 1946 was followed by strikes in other sectors, making it difficult for automakers to reach full production. This at a time when the warmed-over '42s being offered were snapped up as quickly as they were built.

tively expensive—$2600-$2700. Had anybody else built it, the Nomad would probably have seen minuscule production, but a respectable 8386 were built for 1955, 7886 for '56 and 6103 for 1957.

Chevy called its '55 "The Hot One." Ads said the '56 was even hotter. It was. The Stovebolt six, now offered with manual shift only, was now at 140 bhp; the V8 delivered up to 225 bhp with Power-Pak. A $40 million restyle made all models look more like Cadillacs, and four-door hardtop Sport Sedans joined the Two-Ten and Bel Air lines. Despite a broad industry retreat, Chevy managed record market penetration of close to 28 percent on just 88 percent of its '55 volume—about 1.5 million units. Ford repeated at around 1.4 million.

While Ford and Plymouth had all-new '57 styling, Chevy made do with another substantial facelift, though it was a good one and quite popular. In fact, this Chevy has come to be regarded in some quarters as the definitive '50s car. There were now seven engine choices, up two from '56, including no fewer than five 283 V8s with 185 up to 283 bhp. The last was courtesy of "Ramjet" fuel injection, a new option that found few takers among Chevy passenger-car buyers at $500 but enabled the division to claim "1 hp per cu. in." (though Chrysler had achieved that magic figure with its '56 300B). Yet the '57s were fast even without Ramjet. A Bel Air Sport Sedan with the four-barrel 270-bhp setup would do 0-60 mph in 9.9 seconds, the quarter-mile in 17.5 seconds, and over 110 mph flat out.

Properly equipped, the 1955-57 Chevy was a formidable track competitor. Before the Automobile Manufacturers Association recommended that its members withdraw from organized racing in June 1957, Chevy did very well in NASCAR and other stock-car events. At that year's Daytona Speed Weeks, Chevy took the first three places in the two-way flying-mile for Class 4 (213-259 cid); in Class 5 (259-305 cid) it took 33 out of 37 places, the fastest car averaging 131.076 mph. Chevy also won the 1957 Pure Oil Manufacturers Trophy with 574 points against 309 for runner-up Ford.

While the AMA's racing "ban" didn't deter Chevy and others from providing under-the-table racing support, it did affect showroom offerings. Chevy's softer, more luxurious '58s were a case in point. Riding a new 117.5-inch-wheelbase X-member chassis, they were longer, lower, wider and heavier—though not really slower than the lighter and lively '57s. Leading the line was the lush new Impala, a Bel Air sub-series offering convertible and Sport Coupe hardtop with six or V8 in the $2600-$2800 range. The division was now reaching for a buyer group it had never

The '50 Styleline DeLuxe 'bustle-back' was priced at $1529.

After 1952, the fastback would be gone because of lagging sales.

A modest facelift was performed for 1951, here a DeLuxe Styleline.

Chevy was reskinned for 1953, and there were four Bel Airs now.

This DeLuxe Styleline shows the toothy grille adopted for 1952.

A tasteful facelift was undertaken for '54, as on this Bel Air.

sought before: the solid, substantial Pontiac types who cared more about size and comfort than performance or handling. Impala delivered. Despite a rough year for Detroit and the U.S. economy as a whole, Chevy managed over 1.1 million cars, of which 60,000 were Impalas.

Chevy's '58 bodies were all-new: shinier, more "important" and more Cadillac-like than ever. As it turned out, they were one-year-only jobs. Not so the new 348 big-block V8, a modified truck engine (which Chevy understandably failed to mention) offering 250 or 280 bhp. The standard V8 was a lone 185-bhp 283, the standard six a 145-bhp Stovebolt. Below Impala was a rearranged model group. The One-Fifty was now Delray (the name borrowed from a spiffy 1955-57 Two-Ten two-door sedan), Biscayne replaced Two-Ten, and "Station Wagon" was a separate series with no fewer than five models: two-door Yeoman and four-door Yeoman, Brookwood, Nomad, the last with seating for six or nine. Unlike the 1955-57 original, the '58 Nomad was a conventional wagon.

Chevrolet deserved credit for bucking the tailfin trend in 1958, but made up for it the following year with another all-new body bearing huge cat's-eye taillamps and a batwing rear deck that tester Tom McCahill said was "big enough to land a Piper Cub." It could have been worse. Several 1959 proposals envisioned ugly Edsel-like grilles. Ford had shaded Chevy in model year '57 production and came within 12,000 units of doing it again this year. Styling no doubt played a part. The 1960 Chevys would be a lot more subdued now that William L. Mitchell had replaced Harley Earl as GM design chief.

Delray disappeared from the '59 line and a new full-range Impala series displaced Bel Air at the top. All models rode a 119-inch wheelbase, Chevy's longest ever. The growth between 1957 and 1959 was amazing: length up by nearly 11 inches, width by seven inches, weight by 300 pounds. The '59s were the first of the overstuffed "standard" Chevys that would endure for the next 15 years, though they made sense at the time. Buyers demanded ever-bigger cars in the '50s, so even the low-priced three grew to about the size of late-'40s Cadillacs and Lincolns.

In the 1960s, Chevrolet would mostly follow Ford's marketing initiatives but continued its production lead, winning every model year race except 1966. Like its archrival, Chevy expanded into compacts (Corvair and Chevy), intermediates (Chevelle), muscle cars (Malibu SS, Impala SS), full-size luxury-liners (Caprice) and "ponycars" (Camaro). Each was carefully conceived to fill a basic need, and nearly all succeeded.

The '53 Chevy Two-Ten carried less chrome trim than the Bel Air.

Station wagon and hardtop styling were combined on the '55 Nomad.

All-new styling and a magnificent 265-cid overhead-valve V8 made Chevy "The Hot One!" for 1955, seen here as a Bel Air hardtop.

By 1953, a newly aggressive Ford Motor Company was slugging it out with GM for sales leadership. Discount wars erupted, and it looked like Ford might overtake Chevy, but the first of the "classic" Chevys in 1955 kept "USA-1" number one.

The Bel Air Sport Sedan was a new body style for Chevy in 1956.

Chevy's mid-range Two-Ten four-door sedan for 1957: $2174 base.

At $1885, the One-Fifty Utility Sedan was 1957's bargain model.

Such increasing specialization might imply increasing production, but though Chevy did set some records, its 1969 volume was only some 500,000 cars ahead of 1960's despite the introduction of four new model lines. This product proliferation came in response to a market that subdivided, generating more competition than in the '50s. In many cases, Chevy competed less against rivals and more against itself or other GM divisions.

By 1969, the Chevrolet lineup had become exceptionally broad yet spanned just four wheelbases: 108 inches for Corvair and Camaro, 110 for Chevy II/Nova, 115 for Chevelle and 119 for the full-size Chevrolets. The one exception was the post-'67 Chevelle which, like other GM intermediates that year, went to a 112-inch wheelbase on two-door models and 116 on four-doors, an arrangement that would persist through 1977.

The standard Chevrolet progressed from overstyled outrageousness to clean, crisp elegance. As mentioned, the '60 edition was a more subdued '59. Taut new finless styling arrived for '61, followed by a heavily sculptured '63. With no change in wheelbase, the big Chevy became bulkier as the decade progressed but was still deftly styled. Another complete redesign brought more flowing lines for '65, followed by an even curvier all-new '67 body with semi-fastback rooflines on hardtop coupes and more pronounced "Coke bottle" fenders. A bulkier look arrived for 1969 via elliptical wheel openings, emphasized by subtle bulges. This era's prettiest big Chevy might well be the '62, with its straight, correct lines and, again for hardtop coupes, roofline sculpturing like a raised convertible top.

Nineteen sixty-two was also the year that the 283 small-block V8 was enlarged to 327 cid, with an initial 250 or 300 bhp in the full-size cars. The 283 continued. Both would be mainstays throughout the Chevy line through 1968, after which a stroked 350-cid derivative more amenable to emission controls was gradually phased in.

Biscayne remained Chevy's full-size price leader in the '60s, but buyer interest in it fell. The mid-priced Bel Air also waned. But the top-line Impala rapidly became Detroit's single most popular model line. Its best sales year in this decade was 1964, with some 889,600 built.

By far the most collectible Impala is the performance-bred Su-

Chevy built 41,268 Bel Air convertibles for 1956. They listed at $2344, and for a few bucks could be optioned up to 225 bhp.

per Sport, an option package for mid-1961 and 1968-69, an Impala sub-series in other years. Body styles were always limited to convertible and hardtop coupe. The concept was simple: the big, smooth Chevy with sporty styling touches and available performance and handling options. Sixes were offered but not often ordered (only 3600 of the '65s, for instance). Typical features ran to special SS emblems, vinyl bucket seats, central gearshift console and optional tachometer. A variety of V8s was offered, including big-blocks, beginning with the famous 409 of 1961, an enlarged 348 delivering 360 bhp initially and up to 425 bhp by '63.

With options like stiffer springs and shocks, sintered metallic brake linings, four-speed gearbox, and ultra-quick power steering, these were the best-performing big Chevys in history. They wouldn't last, of course. Government regulations and the advent of mid-size muscle cars combined to do in sporty big boats like this. Yet the Impala SS remained exciting right to the end, offering the 427-cid "Mark IV" engine from 1967 with 335-385 bhp.

Meanwhile, Chevrolet uncovered a far more lucrative market by dolling up the Impala with the best grades of upholstery and trim and calling it Caprice. A mid-1965 arrival in response to Ford's LTD, it garnered some 181,000 sales for model year '66, when it became a separate series and the original hardtop sedan was joined by wagons and hardtop coupe. Production through the rest of the decade ranged from 115,500 to nearly 167,000. Obviously, Cadillac luxury at a Chevy price still appealed as much in the '60s as it had in the days of the first Impala.

One rung below Caprice/Impala was the intermediate Chevelle, introduced for 1964 as a reply to Ford's Fairlane. Conventional in design—front engine, rear drive, coil springs in front, leaf springs in back—it offered almost as much interior room as Impala but within more sensible exterior dimensions. In effect, Chevelle was a revival of the ideally proportioned "classic" 1955-57 Chevy. Sales went nowhere but up, from 328,400 units in the first year to nearly 440,000 by 1969. The addition of numerous performance options, including Malibu SS convertible and hardtop, only enhanced Chevelle's appeal.

Third down the size scale was the Chevy II, an orthodox compact rushed out for 1962 to answer Ford's Falcon, which had been handily trimming the radical Corvair (*see* Chevrolet Corvair) since

The '57 Bel Air Nomad is much coveted by car collectors today.

This Biscayne struts Chevy's bigger, heavier look for 1958.

Fins were in in '59, as seen on the all-new Impala Sport Sedan.

The Impala name first appeared on a Chevy in 1958, as an upmarket Bel Air subseries. The V8 Sport Coupe retailed for $2693.

Like Ford and Plymouth, Chevrolet grew bigger and heavier during the Fifties. In Chevy's case, wheelbase had stretched from 115 to 119 inches and it was about 600 pounds heftier. Chevy moved upmarket with the 1958 debut of the Impala.

A Sport Coupe was available in the 1960 Bel Air series for $2596.

Styling of the 1961 Impala Sport Sedan was all-new, cleaner.

For just under $3000, a buyer could choose a '60 Impala ragtop.

A '61 Bel Air two-door sedan with small hubcaps listed for $2491.

The '60 Impala Sport Sedan could be equipped with a 348-cid V8.

The top-of-the-line '61 Nomad wagon seated six or nine people.

Among wagons, the '60 Nomad was trimmed to Impala standards.

New front and rear styling adorned the 1962 Bel Air Sport Coupe.

1960. Initial engine choices were a 90-bhp 153-cid four and a 120-bhp 194-cid six. (Falcon had only sixes through mid-1963, then added a V8 option.) It was a good move, but through 1966 Chevy IIs outnumbered Falcons only once: model year '63. Sales dropped nearly 50 percent for '64, due partly to intramural competition from Chevelle. A spate of Super Sport models didn't help. Nor did heavy facelifts for '65 and '66.

For 1968, Chevy II grew to near intermediate size, switching to GM's all-new 111-inch-wheelbase X-body platform. Convertibles, wagons and hardtop coupes were deleted, leaving four-door sedans and two-door pillared coupes. The latter were available in SS trim, now a package option. Backed by a strong ad campaign and competitive prices, Chevy's compact made a comeback, sales soaring to 201,000 units for '68 and to over a quarter-million by 1970, when the name changed to Nova (originally, the premium Chevy II series).

Adding spice to the line for 1967 was Camaro, which would eventually succeed the ailing Corvair as Chevy's sporty compact. Despite the beautiful styling and impressive performance of the all-new '65 models, Corvair was still no threat to Ford's incredibly successful Mustang in the burgeoning ponycar market. Worse, it was costly to build—entirely different in concept and technology from other Chevrolets. Six months after the '65s debuted, division managers decided Corvair would be allowed to fade away. Camaro would be its replacement—a conventional front-engine sporty car, a direct Mustang-fighter.

Created under the watchful eye of GM design chief Bill Mitchell, Camaro styling was exactly right: long-hood/short-deck proportions; a low, chiseled profile; flowing body lines. Like Mustang, Camaro aimed at those who wanted a sporty four-seater that could be equipped as an economy runabout, vivid straightline performer, or something in between, so there was a Mustang-like plethora of options: some 81 factory items and 41 dealer-installed accessories.

Camaro's 1967 prices started at $2466 for the basic hardtop coupe and $2704 for the convertible with standard 140-bhp 230-cid six. The 155-bhp, 250-cid six cost $26 extra; a 210-bhp 327 V8 listed for $106. Next on the list was a 350-cid V8 with 295 bhp, exclusive to Camaro in '67 (it soon became the most popular Corvette powerplant). To get it, you had to order the $211 Super

The 1963 Impala Sport Coupe featured squarer lines and engines all the way up to 409 cubic inches and 409 horsepower.

Triple taillights were an Impala hallmark in 1963, as since 1958.

The Nova SS Sport Coupe was the sportiest Chevy II sold in 1963.

Ironically, a '65 Impala Super Sport came with a six—or a 409.

The Malibu SS was the sportiest version of the mid-size Chevelle.

Sports package comprising stiffer springs and shocks, D70-14 Firestone Wide Oval tires, modified hood with extra sound insulation, SS emblems, and "bumblebee" nose stripes. A 396 big-block V8 became available during the year at nearly $400.

Also tempting Camaro buyers: custom carpeting, bucket seats, fold-down back seat, luxury interior, full instrumentation, and console shifters for the optional Turbo Hydra-Matic, heavy-duty three-speed manual and four-speed manual. For $105, the Rally Sport package added a hidden-headlight grille, i.d. emblems and other special touches. Other extras ran to tinted glass, radio, heater, air conditioning, clock, cruise control, and a vinyl roof covering for hardtops. Mechanical options included sintered metallic brake linings, ventilated front disc brakes, vacuum brake booster, power steering, fast-ratio manual steering, stiff suspension, Positraction limited-slip differential, and a dozen different axle ratios. With all this, a Camaro could easily be boosted to $5000.

Though two years behind Mustang, Camaro was a big hit. Production topped 220,000 the first year, followed by 235,115 for '68 and another 243,095 for '69. There were no major changes through mid-1970. The '68s were marked by a horizontal grille treatment, ventless side glass and restyled taillights; the '69s had a recontoured lower body with front and rear creaselines atop the wheel openings, plus a vee'd grille and new rear styling.

Available for the street but aimed squarely at the track was Camaro option group Z28, a tailor-made road-racing package announced during 1967. With it, Camaro won 18 of 25 Trans-Am races that year, then the class championship in 1968 and '69. Veteran competition engineer Vincent W. Piggins had convinced management to build a Camaro expressly for the Sports Car Club of America series. To meet its prevailing displacement limit, he combined the 327 block with the 283 crankshaft to produce a high-winding 302.4-cid small-block with a nominal 290 bhp—it was more like 350—and 290 pounds/feet torque. Completing the package were heavy-duty suspension, front disc brakes, metallic rear brake linings, 11-inch-diameter clutch, close-ratio four-speed gearbox, quick steering, wide Corvette wheels, and hood air ducts feeding big carburetors.

At an initial $3300 or so, the Z28 was a whale of high-performance buy. It wasn't for everyone, of course, but production quickly climbed, from 602 of the '67s to 7199 for '68 and 19,014 of the

The big Chevys still ruled the roost in the Sixties, but a changing market brought about the Corvair in 1960, the Chevy II in 1962, and the Chevelle in 1964. Except for the Corvair, Chevy was following Ford's lead with these cars.

'69s. All are now coveted collectibles, not only as the first of a great breed but also because the Z would become less special as time passed.

For 1970, Chevrolet entered the personal-luxury field with the Monte Carlo and fielded an all-new Camaro. A 65-day strike prevented the division from outproducing Ford, but the 12-month total of near 1.5 million cars was hardly bad. For the model year, Chevy built 1.46 million cars to its archrival's two million-plus.

A kissin' cousin of Pontiac's all-new '69 Grand Prix, the cleanly styled Monte Carlo rode the 116-inch Chevelle four-door chassis but came only as a hardtop coupe—with the longest hood ever bolted onto a Chevy. A 250-bhp 350-cid V8 teamed with Turbo-Hydra-Matic as standard, and a variety of luxury options was on hand. Alternative engines ran to a 300-bhp 350 and a new 400 V8 with 330 bhp. Base-priced at just under $3000, the Monte Carlo sold well: over 130,000 copies in its first year (against a mere 40,000 for Ford's considerably costlier Thunderbird). Among them were a mere 3823 equipped with the optional SS454 package—an iron fist in a velvet glove if ever there was one.

Listed as RPO Z20, this package comprised the division's huge new 454 big-block engine, a stroked 427 delivering 360 bhp in this application, plus square-tip dual exhausts and a chassis fortified with automatic-level-control rear shocks, stiffer front shocks, and power front disc brakes. Discreet badges and black rocker panel accents were the only clues to what was under the hood. Acceleration was vivid: 0-60 mph took only about 7.5 seconds. But that

This 1965 Nova SS was powered by Chevy's ubiquitous 283 V8.

The '66 Chevelle Super Sport 396 was a performance buy at $2776.

The Caprice became Chevy's top-line series in '66, here a Custom.

Chevy built approximately 119,300 Impala Super Sports for 1966.

"Formal luxury" was the '66 Caprice Custom's stock in trade.

Chevy's answer to the Mustang: the '67 Camaro, with SS package.

Meaner than a junkyard dog is one way to describe the 1967 Impala Super Sport 427. It was good for an honest 385 horsepower.

wasn't what this new personal Chevy was all about, and it would be years before the Monte would take another run at performance.

With Corvair's demise after 1969, Nova was Chevy's only compact. The 1970 edition was mildly facelifted but saw no substantive change. Chevelle, still with its split-wheelbase 1968 A-body platform, was restyled to look more like the full-size Chevys, gaining a divided grille, bulges around each wheel opening, and a more rounded, massive look. A Super Sport package was still available for both Nova and Chevelle, the former built around the 350 V8, the latter around the big-block 454 and 396 (which was actually a 402 now). None saw very high production with rising fuel prices and insurance rates putting a big damper on muscle-car demand throughout Detroit. The big-car sales emphasis was still on the luxurious Impala and Caprice; Biscayne and Bel Air were reduced to one four-door sedan each.

Announced in the spring of 1970 was a brilliant all-new second-generation Camaro ('69s were sold as '70s through the previous December) with dramatic, European-inspired GT styling. Nearly 125,000 were sold despite the abbreviated model run. The ragtop was no more, another victim of fading demand, but the coupe still offered the usual arm-long list of extras, including two SS packages like Chevelle's plus a separate Rally Sport trim group and the still-formidable Z28 option. Wheelbase was unchanged but most everything else was. If the result was heavier and less efficient, it was also a smoother-riding and better-handling Chevy ponycar.

Chevrolet remained USA-1 throughout the '70s despite a few product blunders and having to contend with the vexing problems that plagued all Detroit in that turbulent decade. In model year production it ran second to Ford only in 1970 and '71. After that, Chevy was the consistent industry leader with at least 2 million cars a year except for troubled '75, when depressed big-car demand in the wake of the 1973-74 energy crisis dropped the tally to about 1.75 million.

Such strength enabled Chevrolet to endure mistakes that would have crippled most any other make save Ford. Even the subcompact Vega, now widely viewed as the division's biggest folly of the decade, remained in the lineup for eight model years and sold respectably in every one.

Vega certainly seemed like a good idea when it bowed for 1971. Riding a 97-inch wheelbase, the shortest in Chevy history, it carried an all-new, all-aluminum 140-cid four with 80 or 90 bhp. Pert styling marked by a Camaro-like front was offered in three practical body styles: two-door notchback sedan, hatchback coupe and a nifty little three-door "Kammback" wagon.

Chevrolet spent vast sums designing, launching and promoting this latterday import (and Ford Pinto) fighter, and on a special factory to build it. But like the Corvair of 10 years before, Vega missed its target—bought not as basic transportation but as a small sporty car (abetted by the presence of a GT coupe and wagon). Worse, it quickly became notorious for early, severe body rust, and the linerless engine suffered persistent oil leaks and cylinder head warping. By 1976 the even smaller Chevette was

Camaro output remained strong for 1968: 235,115 units produced.

The 1967 Chevelle SS 396 Sport Coupe had a prominent hood scoop.

After a 1966 restyle, the '67 Chevy II Nova SS hardly changed.

The 1968 Chevelle SS 396 received all-new styling for 1968.

Camaro was heavily facelifted for 1969, seen here as an SS.

The 1969 Impala Custom Coupe went out the door for only $3085.

Mid-Sixties America was scarred by riots in many big cities. Controversy raged over civil rights and U.S. actions in Vietnam. Chevrolet responded to an increasingly diverse America with five distinct car lines—something for everyone.

The Impala Custom Coupe had escalated in price to $3266 by 1970.

Chevy's first personal-luxury entry was the 1970 Monte Carlo.

A sleek new Camaro Sport Coupe debuted in mid-model-year 1970.

The Caprice Coupe found 46,404 buyers during the '71 model run.

Chevy's import fighter for 1971 was the 97-inch-wheelbase Vega.

A finely textured grille marked the popular 1971 Monte Carlo.

ready, and Vega was being crowded out of contention by a number of domestic and foreign rivals. Though the name was dropped after '77, the basic design (minus the problematic engine) lived on through 1979 in the Monza line.

An intriguing Vega offshoot was the Cosworth-Vega of 1975-76, quite "foreign" for a U.S. car and something of a collectors' item today. Its main attraction was a Vega engine destroked to 122 cid and wearing a special 16-valve twincam aluminum cylinder head designed by England's Cosworth Engineering. Bendix electronic fuel injection fed the cylinders, actuated by a glovebox-mounted computer.

Available only as a hatchback coupe, the "CosVeg" initially came only with black paint and special gold striping and cast-aluminum wheels. Wide radial tires, full instrumentation in an engine-turned dash panel, anti-roll bars at both ends, four-speed gearbox, quick steering, and discreet badges completed the package. Unfortunately, the engine yielded only 111 horsepower with emission controls, so this wasn't the BMW-beater Chevy had planned. The '76 version offered any Vega body color and an optional five-speed gearbox, but many were still unsold at year's end. Respective production was just 2061 and 1447.

Monza proved a far more successful evolution. New for '75, it rode the basic Vega chassis but had handsome 2+2 coupe bodywork with lift-up rear door and a fastback roof reminiscent of certain Ferraris. A notchback "Towne Coupe" was added during the year. The Vega four was base power, but a new 262-cid small-block V8 was optional, mildly tuned for 110 bhp. Enthusiasts could opt for several interesting Regular Production Options such as the Z01 performance and handling package and, for 2+2s, a "Spyder" appearance group.

After 1977, the Vega wagon became a Monza, and all three models got a new standard engine: the 151-cid Pontiac "Iron Duke" four (so named to reassure buyers stung by the Vega unit). That same year, the blunt-front Towne Coupe was offered with the 2+2's "droop snoot" as an option. Monza then saw only minor changes through early 1981, when it departed to make way for an even better small Chevy.

After a mostly stand-pat 1970, the full-size Chevrolets ballooned to as big as they'd ever get, receiving 1971's new "fuselage-style" GM B-body and a longer 121.5-inch wheelbase. As ever, promotion focused on Impala and Caprice. The Biscayne and Bel Air sedans had been relegated to the fleet market, and would be discontinued after 1973 and '76, respectively. Mid-price Impala Custom models, new for '68, continued to find favor among those who liked but couldn't quite afford a Caprice. The Caprice itself was similarly upgraded as more Classic versions were added year by year.

Big Chev engine choices through 1976 revolved around 350, 400 and 454 V8s, though a 145-bhp 305 was rushed out as standard for '76 (except on wagons), a post-oil-embargo economy move. Emissions tuning rendered all decreasingly potent, as did the added weight of federally required "crash" bumpers after 1972 and other equipment. Styling became progressively more ornate and "formal," and threatened rollover standards saw hardtop coupes replaced by "pillared" 1974 models with huge rear side windows. For the same reason, the Caprice convertible (an Impala through '72) disappeared after 1975. Despite their limitations, these big Chevys always sold in large numbers—the essence of middle-class American motoring in this period.

Then, a revolution: the first wave of GM's corporate-wide downsizing program, which saw the 1977 Caprice/Impala trimmed by 5½ inches in wheelbase and 600-800 pounds in gas-wasting bulk. It seemed like a huge gamble then, and Ford tried to take advantage by extolling the "road-hugging weight" of its still-enormous full-size cars. But Chevrolet, as usual, knew exactly what it was doing, and Caprice/Impala sales actually improved (despite the departure of hardtop sedans). And why not? The new models

The 1970 Chevelle SS 396 engine was rated at a whopping 350 bhp. The racing stripes let everyone know this car could *go*!

were not only lighter but more agile, easier on gas and, to some, better looking.

In the intermediate ranks, Chevelle and Monte Carlo were switched to GM's new "Colonnade" A-body for 1973, which meant new styling and no more convertibles or closed pillarless models. The Monte divided into S and more formal Landau models with rather baroque body lines of the "French curve" school. The blockier Chevelles included base, Malibu and ritzy Malibu Classic coupes and sedans plus a plethora of colorfully named wagons (Nomad, Greenbrier and Concours). An interesting cross between luxury tourer and the now-departed SS was the Laguna S-3 coupe of 1974-76, identified by body-color bumpers and grille surround, plus a posh, sporty interior available for a time with optional swivelling front seats, a '50s idea picked up from Chrysler.

When the big Chevys shrank to intermediate stature, it was obvious that the mid-sizers would get smaller too. They did, for 1978. All Chevelles were Malibus now and shared their new 108.1-inch-wheelbase A-body with Monte Carlo. The latter retained its generally florid looks, but the Malibus were crisp and clean. Again, sales didn't suffer—to Chevy's undoubted relief.

A consistently high seller since its '68 overhaul, the compact Nova saw little change through 1973, when a minor facelift occurred and hatchback two-door sedans arrived in the usual base and Custom trim. An extensive reskin for 1975 brought new rooflines and more glass, plus steering and front suspension borrowed from the Camaro and fancy LN ("Luxury Nova") models (renamed Concours for '76). Nova captured 15 percent of Chevy's 1975 sales to become the year's most popular American compact. Engine offerings were simplified for '76. The "performance" option was now a 305 V8, a debored 350 replacing that engine and the little 262. Standard power through 1979 remained the workhorse 250-cid inline six, after which both engine and car were scrubbed in favor of new V6s and "the first Chevy of the '80s," the front-drive X-body Citation. Unveiled in April 1979, the Citation was a runaway success its first year, helped by another fuel crisis. Body styles comprised two- and four-door hatchback sedans and a pillared "slantback" two-door unique among the four versions of this corporate design. The new X-body afforded excellent space utilization at moderate weight, which averaged around 2500 pounds. Pontiac's well-proven 2.5-liter "Iron Duke" four was standard and a new Chevy-built 60-degree 2.8-liter (173-cid) V6 was

Chevy built 4862 hot Camaro Z/28s for the 1971 model year.

The Heavy Chevy was basically a low-buck SS with any V8 engine.

Monte Carlo sported a new body for 1973—and "baroque" styling.

By 1970, imports had gained a strong foothold in the U.S., forcing GM and Ford to compete with their own subcompacts, the Vega and Pinto. Both were flawed, and they didn't drive the imports back to the sea as Henry Ford II had predicted.

optional, both mounted transversely to enhance the space-saving front-drive mechanicals. Four-speed manual transaxle was standard, three-speed automatic optional. For a sporty Citation you ordered either two-door with the X-11 package comprising uprated suspension and other chassis mods, plus brash exterior i.d. Though it had no more power at first, the X-11 was a capable all-rounder with the V6.

Alas, like most new designs, Citation had a hefty helping of engineering and quality-control problems, and would be recalled many times. But overall balance and livability made it a hot number for a while, and Chevy was hard-pressed to meet demand.

Hard to believe, but Camaro almost expired after 1974 as sales sagged in the wake of the first energy crisis. But a determined effort by enthusiastic GMers saved the striking second generation from a premature end, and it enjoyed a remarkable sales resurgence into the '80s.

The 1971-72 Camaros were much like the inaugural "1970½" edition except for minor changes dictated by federal regulations. For '73, the macho SS was replaced by a less pretentious LT (Luxury Touring) model with standard 165-bhp V8, variable-ratio power steering, and appearance touches like hidden wipers, black rockers, Rally wheels and woodgrain dash trim.

Prices started to gallop with the '74s, which were facelifted at each end to meet that year's required 5-mph impact bumpers. A wraparound rear window marked the '75s, which began Camaro's sales revival after a four-year dry spell. Capitalizing on renewed buyer interest in ponycars, Chevy reinstated the Rally Sport package as a mid-season option: matte-black hood and front fender tops, special paint and the further option of color-matched Z28 wheels. The '74 facelift kept going for 1976-77 as Camaro reached, then exceeded, its old '60s sales record.

The big news for '77 was a Z28 revived after a two-year absence—only now the emphasis was on refined road manners instead of just raw acceleration. Chassis engineer Jack Turner took a straightforward approach: tighter springs, a thicker front roll bar, a more flexible rear bar, larger wheels and tires. New exterior graphics and colors were well suited to the smooth lines. Midyear introduction limited sales for '77, but they took off the following year.

Picking up where Vega left off was Chevette, the smallest Chevrolet ever, announced for bicentennial 1976. Derived from the 1974 German Opel Kadett, the first of GM's "world car" T-body models, it rode a 94.3-inch wheelbase, measured 17 inches shorter than a Vega, and weighed in at just under a ton. Its mission, of course, was economy, which it delivered: 35 mpg or so on the highway. Engines were small: initially a 1.4-liter/85-cid overhead-cam four with 52 bhp and a 60-bhp 1.6-liter/98-cid version. The former was gone by '78 and the 1.6 up to a more respectable 63-68 bhp.

Chevette was initially offered as a two-door hatchback sedan; a four-door was added for 1978 on a three-inch-longer wheelbase. Options were numerous, as the car had been built "down" to a low price. Yet like so many Chevys before it, Chevette was exactly right for its time, and far more competitive in the increasingly hard-fought subcompact market.

The entire market would be hard-fought in the 1980s. Detroit found itself battling not only a deep national recession early in the decade but a mighty horde of Japanese competitors, which had already won a lot of U.S. sales territory with low price, top-notch workmanship and superior reliability. Though the economy began recovering after 1982, import penetration reached record levels by mid-decade—some 35-40 percent of the total U.S. car market—despite price increases prompted by a weakening dollar. Much of their gains came at the expense of AMC, Chrysler and Ford, but GM had problems of its own and suffered lower volume too. Chevrolet's withered to about 1.6 million units for 1981, when the market was still relatively good, then to 1.4 million for 1985-87.

At $3203, the Laguna was the top-of-the-line Chevelle for 1973.

The 1975 Monza 2+2 was based on the Vega; it sold for $3953.

Chevy built 55,308 Caprice Sport Sedans for the 1976 model run.

Meantime, the division had decided to switch rather than fight, and began selling a pair of small Japanese models with bow-tie badges. But in domestic production, Chevrolet maintained its traditional number-one rank only through 1985. After that it was overhauled by an increasingly aggressive Ford Division, even as Dearborn as a whole out-earned the General for the first time in 40 years—and on only half the volume.

Chevy's mixed fortunes certainly weren't for lack of product or canny marketing. GM's long-term downsizing effort ushered in a spate of smaller, more efficient new Chevys, yet old standbys were allowed to carry on so long as they sold. Continuing modernization saw fuel injection (both single- and multi-point) replace carburetors on many engines, which increasingly became inline fours and V6s. Yet small-block V8s were still a big part of the picture, as were performance cars once demand for them returned around 1984.

Reflecting these trends are three division staples of the '80s: Monte Carlo, Chevette and Caprice/Impala. The last saw little change following a mild 1980 "aero" reskinning that freshened up the basic '77 styling but did little for mileage. Hoods were lower, rear decks higher, and coupes exchanged their sharply creased wraparound backlights for flat panes. Sedans used 229-cid Chevy

Concours was the luxury Nova in 1976; it retailed for $3995.

The '77 Malibu sported rectangular headlamps and a bluff grille.

Chevy built 9100 Laguna S3 coupes for 1976, priced at $4621.

Camaro's Z/28 sported fender vents for the 1978 model year.

After a two-year absence, the Camaro Z/28 returned for 1977.

The downsized 1978 Malibu was powered by a 3.3-liter V6.

and 231-cid Buick V6s as base power through 1984, a 4.3-liter (262-cid) Chevy V6 thereafter. There was also a diesel V8 option, the trouble-prone 350 Olds engine, cancelled after '85 as Americans bathed again in a sea of cheap gasoline. Most of these big Chevys carried the reliable 305 small-block V8 (usually standard on wagons). Coupes were dropped for '83, revived for '84, then dropped again three years later. The venerable Impala name was gone by '86 as Caprices had proliferated into base, Classic and Classic Brougham models.

Chevy was wise to retain big rear-drive cars after Buick, Olds and, for a time, Pontiac had dropped them, for they were strong sellers even in the worst of times. And when times got better, so did sales, rising from a decade low of about 185,000 units for 1982 to about a quarter-million a year from 1983 on. And Chevy's not through with this platform. An all-new and truly aerodynamic body is scheduled for 1991. Until then, the division will try weaning some buyers away from traditional pillow-soft suspensions by giving the current Caprice more sporting springs, shocks and steering.

The humble Chevette was similarly little changed in this decade, though that was an increasing sales handicap in the fast-moving small-car sector. Model year '81 was the production peak—nearly 454,000 units—after which volume tapered off steadily each year. Still, even the last '86s managed over 100,000 sales, and the lack of change enabled Chevy to keep prices low. Appearance updates were confined to a full-width grille and square headlamps for '79, bigger taillights for '80. Mechanical changes were limited to a five-speed manual option from 1983 and an extra-cost four-cylinder diesel engine that was rarely ordered, probably because it made a slow car even slower. Though few mourned its passing, the Chevette had done an able job for Chevrolet. It was simply time for better things.

The same could be said for the 1978-vintage Monte Carlo, which departed at the end of 1987, though there *was* reason to mourn here. A handsome 1981 facelift similar to the big Chevys' was followed at mid-1983 by a revived Monte Carlo SS, with a smooth raked-back front and a tuned 305 V8 with 180 bhp. You also got a beefy suspension with fat raised-white-letter tires, plus bold i.d. graphics and distinctive trunklid spoiler. Things were pretty plain inside, but comfort and convenience options weren't long in coming.

This new SS was not your typical mid-'80s Monte, but it was the starting point for Chevy's latest racing stockers, which began cleaning up in NASCAR and elsewhere. To help its teams do even

As Viking II settled down on Mars' Utopia Plains in 1976, Chevrolet was grappling with more earthly problems, such as federal safety and emissions standards and upcoming fuel economy regulations. It was a difficult time for automakers.

A 3.8-liter V6 powered the $8802 Caprice Classic for 1983, although the buyer could opt for a 305 V8 or 350 diesel V8.

better, Chevy released an SS "Aerocoupe" at mid-1986 bearing a huge, compound-curve backlight that allegedly added a few more mph on the long supertracks. It only lasted through 1987 and only 2000 or so were built each year—which only makes it a gilt-edged future collectible.

As ever, most Montes sold in these years were the luxury sort; they were even called Luxury Sport from 1986. And sell they did: more than 157,000 for '81, over 188,000 for 1982-83, an average 120,000 a year thereafter. Chevy might well have kept the decade-old coupe going a little longer but, again, it was time to move on.

At the lower end of the Chevy line, "moving on" meant moving to smaller, more efficient front-drive models. The compact Citation X-car had been first. Cavalier and Celebrity would follow for the subcompact and mid-size segments, respectively.

One of four GM A-body lines announced for the '83 model year in early 1982, Celebrity was essentially an X-car in a tailored suit. Inner structure, chassis, even drivetrains were all the same, but squarer, more formal notchback styling contrived to make Celebrity look more expensive than slopeback Citation—which it was, by some $600-$1300. Two- and four-door sedans were the only body styles at first, but an attractive wagon arrived for '84. All could be dressed up via trim packages variously called Custom, CL and Classic. Also new for '84 was the Eurosport option group, available for any model. A gesture to enthusiasts, it comprised Chevy's firmer F41 handling suspension, plus special emblems, less exterior chrome, and sporty accents inside. It gilded a very middle-class lily, but the result was good enough to stand comparison with much costlier European sports sedans. Planned to replace Malibu, Celebrity ran alongside the old rear-drive line through 1983, then soldiered on alone. Not that Chevy needed to worry, for the Celeb handily surpassed Malibu's peak sales in this decade (227,000 for '81) with an average 250,000 a year for 1984-86 and over 290,000 for '87.

Celebrity continued its winning ways through the end of the decade but not the Citation that spawned it. Buyers spurned the first front-drive Chevy in rapidly growing numbers amidst a welter of safety recalls, numerous drivability problems, and damaging publicity about weak brakes that locked up way too early in panic stops. The division tried to stem the tide for '84 with detail changes

Smoother sheetmetal shaping highlighted the '81 Monte Carlo.

and "Citation II" badges, but fooled no one. A high-output, 135-bhp V6 arrived for the 1982 X-11 package, then became optional for any model, but that didn't help either. In unit volume, debut 1980 would be Citation's best year: over 811,000. The tally plunged nearly 50 percent for '81, dropped below 166,000 for '82, then fell to 100,000 and less. It only seemed to prove what some critics had been saying—that GM left final "shakedown" testing to its unwitting customers.

Few complaints attended the front-drive Cavalier subcompact. Replacing Monza for '82, it rode the new 101.2-inch-wheelbase J-body platform, the first ever offered by all five GM divisions, which was basically "right" from the start. Nobody much liked the engine—a new Chevy-built 2.0-liter four with an old-fashioned overhead-valve layout (some called it the "junkyard engine")—and the four-speed manual transaxle wasn't the slickest around, but that was about it. And there were some tangible strengths: decent room for four, neat styling, a choice of four body styles—two- and four-door sedans, five-door wagon and three-door "fasthatch" coupe—and competitive prices, initially less than $6000 basic.

Customers responded strongly to Cavalier, snapping up better than 270,000 for the long '82 model year, over 462,000 of the '84s and some 432,000 of the '86s. And to Chevy's credit, the Cavalier has progressively improved: a five-speed manual option, plus throttle-body fuel injection and more horsepower for '83; a neat convertible and new frontal styling for '84; "mini-muscle" V6-powered Z24 convertible and hatchback for '85; a major facelift for '86; a raft of detail changes each year. In all, the Cavalier has aged well, and seems to have a few more good years ahead of it in the early '90s. It's proof, if any be needed, that no one fights in the sales trenches better than the bow-tie battalion.

Chevy's latest salvos in the compact wars are the Corsica sedan and Beretta coupe, both March 1987 recruits for the '88 campaign. They're built on a new 103.4-inch-wheelbase L-body platform exclusive to Chevrolet, though its engineering borrows heavily from the J-cars as well as the front-drive N-body design at Buick, Olds and Pontiac. Among other things, that means all-independent coil-spring suspension with front MacPherson struts and a beam rear axle on trailing arms, plus rack-and-pinion steering and front-disc/rear-drum brakes. Standard power comes from the latest Cavalier four. The division's fine 2.8 V6 with 130 bhp is optional. Styling is also unique to Chevy and a welcome change from GM's past "corporate-clones" approach: smooth, rounded, and aerodynamically efficient. Best of all, they reflect Chevy's strongest efforts yet to ensure tight, thorough fit and finish.

With all this, Corsica/Beretta got off to a strong sales start, with 225,000 built in calendar '87 alone. The "true" '88s saw only minor running changes. For 1989, Corsica is offered in a second, Euro-style model called LTZ and the base Beretta looks more like the '88 GT. In turn, the '89 GT adopts many features of the racy GTU model introduced at mid-'88, which returns with 16-inch aluminum wheels, "ground effects" rocker skirts, and a tinted upper-windshield band with "Beretta" in big, bold letters. Handling options are available to make both Corsica and Beretta even more capable on winding roads.

For 1985, Chevy launched the Astro into the vast new market for smaller vans uncovered the previous year by Chrysler's "T-wagons." Smooth and functional on a 111-inch wheelbase, it was basically a scaled-down version of Chevy's traditional van, with rear drive (not front drive as on the Chrysler products) and, for passenger models, a standard four-barrel 4.3-liter/262-cid V6 producing 147 bhp. Rear drive and trucklike construction made Astro a better bet than the T-wagons for towing chores, and it could be quite lush inside when equipped with the optional Touring Package. Unfortunately, it drove more like a truck and was a bit pricey, so Chevy wasn't as successful here as Chrysler.

Saving the best for last, we come to Camaro. With another effective facelift for 1978, the durable second generation continued through 1981 in four models: base, Rally Sport, Z28 and new-for-'79 luxury Berlinetta (replacing LT). V6s ousted straight sixes as standard for 1980, when an interim 267-cid V8 option joined the 305 and 350 engines. Sales held up well all things considered: 152,000 for 1980, a bit more than 126,000 for '81.

A smaller new third-generation Camaro was a foregone conclusion by then, and it duly arrived for 1982 on a trim 101-inch wheelbase. Though a traditional rear-drive format was retained, overall length was pared nearly 10 inches, width by nearly three inches, curb weight almost 500 pounds. A more modern all-coil suspension appeared with front MacPherson struts, and rear disc brakes were available at extra cost to complement those up front. Styling, by Chevy design chief Jerry Palmer, was precisely tailored to the smaller package: chiseled yet obviously aerodynamic. A big compound-curve backlight, said to be the largest and most complex piece of glasswork ever used on a car, doubled as a hatch for luggage access.

A new nameplate in '82 was Chevy's A-body, mid-size Celebrity.

The sportiest Celebrity for '84 was the Eurosport; it cost $8116.

A Monte Carlo with go was the '85 SS—it had a 5.0-liter HO V8.

The '85 Cavalier Z24 came with a 125-bhp 2.8-liter V6 standard.

The Rally Sport temporarily departed while the base 1982 Sport Coupe became the first Camaro with a standard four-cylinder engine, the corporate 90-bhp 2.5-liter. Chevy's 2.8 V6 now powered the Berlinetta. As ever, the hunky Z28 garnered the most attention. It arrived with a choice of 305 V8s: a four-barrel 150-bhp engine and a 165-bhp version with "Cross Fire" twin-throttle-body electronic fuel injection, as on that year's Corvette. Four-speed manual gearbox was standard across the board except on the 165-bhp Z28, where it was three-speed automatic only, an option for other models. The base Camaro could be ordered with the V6, Berlinetta with the carbureted 305.

Once more, Chevy scored big with a smaller model as the '82 Camaro immediately garnered 50,000 more model year sales than its immediate predecessor. Two years later it was up to over a quarter-million. But 1985-86 demand eased to the 185,000 level, followed by a further drop of 50,000 for '87. Fast-rising prices and strong performance competition from Ford's reborn V8 Mustang contributed to the decline, though indifferent assembly on early

Chevrolet responded to Federal regulations and a changing marketplace in the early Eighties with a fleet of downsized cars, most of them featuring front-wheel drive. New nameplates included Citation, Cavalier, and Celebrity.

Camaro's go-getter for '86 was the Z/28 IROC with a 215-bhp V8.

Chevy's joint venture car (with Toyota) was Nova, here an '86.

The '86 Chevy Cavalier RS convertible came with a 2.8-liter V6.

The "bubble-back" Monte Carlo SS was intended for NASCAR racing.

The '88 Beretta was aimed at "trend setting young car buyers."

A convertible was part of the Camaro IROC-Z lineup for 1987.

models and another spate of teething troubles that customers shouldn't have encountered also hurt.

Nevertheless, the third-generation Camaro—Z28 especially—was very much in the ponycar spirit of the '60s, and it maintains a wide and loyal following today. Changes through the end of the decade would be evolutionary, but timely. For example, a T-bar roof option appeared for '83, when the Z switched to a fuel-saving four-speed automatic and other engines became available with a five-speed option. The Cross-Fire V8 delivered disappointing performance, so a high-output carbureted version with 190 bhp replaced it for '84. That year's Berlinetta acquired a gimmicky dashboard with hard-to-read electronic digital/graphic instruments and minor controls straight from the Starship *Enterprise*. Thankfully, it didn't last long. More exciting things were in store for 1985 as Chevy unleashed the hot IROC-Z performance package for Z28, named in honor of the Camaros used in the International Race of Champions "top gun" driver's contests. The H.O. V8 was now exclusive to IROC and available with five-speed, which was newly standard with all Camaro engines. More efficient "Tuned Port Injection" (TPI) yielded a new 215-bhp option for all Z28s. IROC hunkered closer to the road on big 16 × 8-in. five-spoke aluminum wheels wearing fat Goodyear Eagle performance rubber, came with its own handling suspension and high-effort power steering, and looked ready to race with its full-perimeter body extensions.

Chevy again turned up the wick for '87. The IROC now carried the TPI V8 and could be ordered with the "big" (how times had changed!) 5.7-liter/350-cid Corvette engine with 225 bhp and a healthy 330 lbs/ft torque (this had been promised for mid-1986, but was delayed). Z28 continued with the 165-bhp four-barrel 305 as standard. The underpowered four was dropped for the base Sport Coupe (few had been sold anyway), and Berlinetta returned to being an LT.

But the real icing on this tasty cake was the return of a Camaro convertible after an 18-year absence. A mid-year announcement, it was a real head-turner in IROC trim, the only way you could get it. A second, tamer-looking version was added the following year. Both were crafted "out of house" to Chevy specs, making these "semi-factory" models, but hardly anybody cared when blasting top-down on a winding two-lane.

Then, suddenly, the Z28 was gone—a big surprise—but the

The '88 Beretta GTU was a limited-production model. It came with the 2.8-liter V6, Z-51 suspension, and boy-racer styling.

Beretta's four-door counterpart was the new-for-'88 Corsica.

Cavalier Z24 received a reskinning and faster roofline for 1988.

1988 Sport Coupe was basically the same thing except for its standard V6. The LT was banished, too. Minor tweaking added five horses to all three Camaro V8s, but you lost 25 bhp on the injected 305 teamed with automatic. Base prices had risen some $2000-$3000 in five years, a rather modest increase really. The ragtop IROC was the costliest '88 Camaro with a starting tariff around 18-grand.

Camaro closed out the '80s with few changes, but the RS designation was revived for a special V6 coupe marketed the previous season only in California. It naturally looked a lot like an IROC, but had its own suspension tuning and a slightly different mix of equipment. The IROC itself could now be had with 16-inch wheels and new Z-rated tires good for over 150 mph.

If Chevy was down by the dawn of the '90s, it most certainly was not out. Due soon is a spiritual successor to the Monte Carlo based on the new front-drive GM10 platform, as well as a four-door version to supplant Celebrity. We can also look forward to that slick new Caprice and a fourth-generation Camaro. Chevrolet may have to fight harder to be "USA-1" in the years ahead, but fight it will.

The Celebrity Eurosport received only minor changes for 1989.

Corsica's '89 Euro-style model—LTZ—was akin to the Beretta GT.

Cheap and plentiful fuel prompted American drivers to demand more performance in the mid-Eighties. Chevy gave it to them with cars such as the Monte Carlo SS, Camaro IROC-Z, Beretta GTU, Celebrity Eurosport, and the Corsica LTZ.

CHEVROLET CORVAIR

Corvair was the most controversial Chevrolet since the abortive "Copper-Cooled" model of 1923. Of course, neither was *supposed* to stir up trouble. Each was merely a response to a particular market situation in its day. The problem with Corvair was a radical design that made it too costly and too "foreign" for its target audience, though it found temporary salvation by opening up an entirely different market, almost by accident. And that's the irony, for it was Corvair's success in that arena that spawned the car that ultimately did it in: the Ford Mustang. A young lawyer-on-the-make named Ralph Nader did the rest.

Chevrolet's interest in a smaller, companion car was evident in the Cadet, a prototype 2200-pound four-door sedan of conventional design begun right after World War II. Powered by a short-stroke 133-cubic-inch six, this 108-inch-wheelbase compact was intended to sell at a rock-bottom price in anticipation of a postwar recession. But instead, the market boomed, rendering the Cadet unnecessary. And as it would have cost about as much to build as a regular Chevy, it was deemed unprofitable at the $1000 target retail price. The project was duly canceled in mid-1947.

Things were far different by the late '50s. Led by Volkswagen and Renault, sales of economy imports were becoming too large to ignore, particularly once a national recession hit in mid-1957. American Motors responded with its compact 1958 American, a warmed-over Nash Rambler. Studebaker chimed in with its similar '59 Lark, which was so successful that it temporarily halted that firm's slide to oblivion. Both cars would soon have rivals. Ford was readying its Falcon and Chrysler its Valiant for model year 1960. General Motors, which in 1958-59 had turned to so-called "captive imports," the British Vauxhall and the German Opel, would rely on Corvair.

Initiated in 1956, the Corvair was largely the product of Chevy chief engineer (and future GM president) Edward N. Cole, who became division general manager in July of that year. It was predictably a technician's car, by far the most radical of the new Big Three compacts. Perhaps inspired by Cole's interest in airplanes (but more likely by the popular VW Beetle) it was planned around a 140-cid air-cooled flat six developing 80 or 95 horsepower in initial form and—just as uncommon—mounted at the rear ("where an engine belongs," Corvair ads would claim). Relatively complicated, it had six separate cylinder barrels and a divided crankcase. Yet despite a lightweight aluminum block, it ended up at 366 pounds, some 78 pounds above the target weight, a miscalculation that would have a negative effect on handling.

All-independent suspension and unit construction were equally unusual for a U.S. car. Corvair's trim 108-inch-wheelbase Y-body platform was all-new, but its all-coil suspension was perhaps too basic: conventional wishbones in front, Beetle-style semi-trailing swing axles in back. Anti-sway bars were omitted to keep retail price as low as possible, but this saved only $4 a car and GM was well aware that they were needed to achieve acceptable handling with rear swing axles and the tail-heavy weight distribution. This decision, as well as management's desire to standardize assembly, precluded more sophisticated chassis components until 1962, when a regular production option including stiffer springs, shorter rear-axle limit straps, and a front sway bar was made available. A major suspension improvement occurred for 1964: a rear transverse camber-compensating spring.

Nevertheless, the original Corvair suspension of 1960-63 did not create a "dangerous, ill-handling car" as later lawsuits claimed. It did oversteer to be sure, but the tail-sliding tendency was not excessive—provided the recommended tire pressures were observed (15 psi front, 26 rear). The problem was that most owners didn't pay attention to that and some got into trouble. When Ralph Nader found out and wrote *Unsafe at Any Speed,* Corvair handling became a *cause celebre* that wasn't settled until a 1972 Congressional investigation cleared the 1960-63 models. But by then, it was too late. Corvair had been laid to rest.

The Corvair's 10-year model run divides into two design generations: 1960-64 and 1965-69. Initial offerings comprised quite spartan four-door sedans in 500 and more deluxe 700 trim selling at $2000-$2100. Three-speed floorshift manual transaxle was standard; Chevy's two-speed Powerglide was optional. Two-door 500 and 700 coupes arrived at mid-season, but the real attention-getter was the new 900 Monza coupe, which boasted an even spiffier interior with bucket seats. For 1961, Chevy offered an optional four-speed gearbox and the Monza caught fire, uncovering a huge latent demand for sporty, fun-to-drive compacts. This was fortunate, because Ford's much simpler and cheaper Falcon was handily outselling other Corvairs in the economy market. With the Monza, Corvair was aimed increasingly at enthusiast drivers.

But it was too late to change some plans, so a brace of Corvair Lakewood station wagons arrived as scheduled for '61, as did a Monza sedan. The Lakewood offered a surprising amount of cargo space—58 cubic feet behind the front seat, 10 more under the front "hood"—more than other compact wagons and even some larger models. It didn't sell well, though, first-year production barely topping 25,000 units. Chevy also issued the interesting Corvair-based Greenbrier window van, Corvan panel and Rampside pickup, all "forward control" models inspired by VW's Type 2 Microbus and forerunners of today's popular minivans. Finally, the flat six was bored out to 145 cid. Standard power remained at 80, but a $27 "Turbo Air" option offered 98.

For 1962 the 500 series was trimmed to a lone coupe and the Monza line expanded with a wagon (no longer called Lakewood) and a new convertible. The Monza wagon was plush, but only about 6000 were built before the body style was dropped entirely to make room on the assembly line for the Chevy II, the resolutely orthodox Falcon-style compact that Chevy rushed out to do what Corvair had failed to in the economy market. Mid-1962 brought what has become the most highly prized first-generation Corvair: the turbocharged Monza Spyder. Initially, this was a $317 option package for Monza two-doors comprising a 150-bhp engine with lots of chrome dressup, a shorter final drive for sprightlier acceleration, heavy-duty suspension, and a multi-gauge instrument

Chevy's first real import fighter was the compact 1960 Corvair.

The '61 Monza was a bucket-seat, four-on-the-floor sport coupe.

Corvair offered station wagons only in 1961-62, here a '62 Monza.

The '63 Monza sported a mildly altered front end, sold for $2272.

The '64 Greenbrier passenger van used the Corvair platform.

Output of the 1964 Monza Spyder soft top reached only 4761 units.

panel with tachometer. The four-speed and sintered-metallic brake linings were "mandatory" options. The Spyder wasn't cheap—a minimum $2600—but it was the next best thing to a Porsche. Annual production ran about 40,000 units through 1964.

Corvair styling saw only minor changes through '64. Most were made at the front. The original winged Chevy bow tie gave way to a smaller emblem on a slim full-width chrome bar for '61. The '62s had simulated air intakes. A wide single chevron appeared for '63, then a double-bar version of the '61 trim. Aside from the aforementioned rear camber-compensator spring, the big news for '64 was a stroked 164-cid engine with 95 or 110 bhp in normally aspirated form. Spyder power was unchanged.

With 1965 came a design revolution. The sleek, second-generation Corvairs looked good even from normally unflattering angles, a tribute to the work of GM Design under chief William L. Mitchell and something an Italian coachbuilder might do. (Pininfarina did, with a specially bodied '64 Corvair of generally similar lines.) It was nicely shaped and not overdone, with just the right amount of trim. Closed models were now pillarless hardtops, and a four-door returned to the 500 series.

The '65s were just as new under the skin. The turbo six was up to 180 bhp at 4000 rpm, but the best all-around engine was the new 140-bhp version, standard for the top-line Corsa coupe and convertible, replacing Monza Spyder. New cylinder heads, redesigned manifolds, and four progressively linked carburetors gave it its extra power. This was an option for lesser Corvairs, which continued with 95 bhp standard and 110 bhp at extra cost.

The 1960 Corvair had been the first mass-produced American car with a swing-axle rear suspension. The '65 was the first with fully independent suspension, not counting the '63 Corvette. The sole difference was that the Corvette linked its rear wheels with a single transverse leaf spring where Corvair had individual coils. Both systems employed upper and lower control arms at each rear wheel. The uppers were actually the axle halfshafts; the lowers were unequal-length nonparallel trailing arms (two per side). Together, these controlled all lateral wheel motion. Small rubber-mounted rods extended from each lower arm to the main rear crossmember to absorb movement at the pivot points.

No question now about tricky behavior "at the limit": Corvair handling was nearly neutral, tending toward mild understeer at

The Corvair was designed to stem the tide of imports, but buyers found the rear-engine compact too radical; it failed as an economy car. It succeeded admirably, however, as the bucket-seat, four-on-the-floor sporty Monza coupe.

This '65 Corsa boasted Corvair's 180-bhp turbocharged flat six.

high speeds. The rear wheels, remaining at a constant angle with the ground, enabled the car to be pushed around corners with fine stability. Attention was also paid to the front suspension, which was tuned to complement the new rear end and provide additional roll stiffness.

Like the Monza Spyder in the first series, the 1965-66 Corsa was the most desirable of the second-generation Corvairs. Base-priced at $2519 for the coupe and $2665 as a convertible, it came with full instrumentation, special exterior trim (including an aluminum rear panel for instant identification), deluxe interior and the 140-bhp engine. The turbo six, a $158 option, put it squarely in the performance league: less than 11 seconds in the 0-60-mph sprint, the standing quarter-mile in 18 seconds at 80 mph. Given enough room, the Corsa could hit 115 mph yet would return more than 20 miles per gallon at moderate speeds.

Unfortunately, the Corsa didn't sell particularly well against Ford's Mustang, which had been introduced about six months before it and which could better the Chevy's performance. More critical was the decline in Monza sales that set in. Though the most popular Corvair rallied slightly for '65, production plunged by some two-thirds the following year. Though *Unsafe at Any Speed* was definitely affecting sales by then, Corvair's fate had already been sealed by an April 1965 GM directive that said in effect, no more development work. Do only enough to meet federal requirements.

When Chevy's true Mustang-fighter, the Camaro, arrived for 1967, the Corvair line was trimmed to just 500 sedan and coupe and Monza sedan, coupe, and convertible. The turbo engine was scratched, too. This would be the last year for the hardtop sedans, all collector's items today.

The 1968-69 Corvairs were the rarest of the breed, available in just three models: 500 and Monza hardtops and Monza convertible. They're readily distinguished by their front side marker lights—clear lenses on the '68s, amber ones for '69. Monza convertibles were the scarcest of all: respectively, just 1386 and 521 built.

With the lack of change and sales falling fast, it was obvious by 1968 that the Corvair was terminal, so many were surprised that Chevy even bothered with the '69 models. Some dealers wouldn't sell them, others refused to service them, so the division offered what few buyers remained a $150 credit on the purchase of another Chevy through 1974. With that, the Corvair was finished.

In retrospect, the rear-engine Chevy died an undeserved death, a victim of its own success. Had it not been for the Monza, we might not have seen the Mustang—and ultimately, the Camaro. Left stillborn by GM's no-more-development edict was project XP-849, which progressed at least as far as a pair of clay mockups, one apparently a rear-engine design, the other with front drive. Intriguingly, both were badged "Corvair 2." A possible prelude to the unfortunate Chevy Vega but more likely for overseas consumption, XP-849 never materialized in these forms, but it showed that at least some GMers hadn't forgotten the adventuresome spirit of the original Corvair despite corporate miscues and years of public controversy.

All 1965-69 Corvairs sported hardtop styling, here a '66 Monza.

The '67 Monza four-door hardtop was changed only in minor detail.

Side marker lights appeared on the '68s, including this Monza.

Corvair made its final appearance in 1969—only 6000 were built.

CHEVROLET CORVETTE

America's first and most enduring sports car debuted in January 1953 as a production-ready Motorama show car culminating a 30-month development effort between Harley Earl's Art & Colour Studio and the Chevrolet Division Engineering Staff. Enthusiastic public response prompted management to okay production of the two-seat roadster—a brave decision, as sales of import sports cars at the time amounted to less than one percent of the market. Production commenced June 30.

Corvette arrived on a 102-inch wheelbase, identical with that of the Jaguar XK120, one of Earl's personal favorites. The chassis was basically a cut-down Chevrolet passenger-car frame with several special touches. Body construction was unique: the first use of fiberglass in a series-production car by a major manufacturer. So was first-generation styling: rounded and rather bulbous through 1955, with extended pod-type taillights, a toothy grille and the then-trendy wraparound windshield—hardly timeless, though it looked great at the time.

Ironically, in view of what lay ahead, Corvette almost expired after 1955 due to disappointing sales. Just 315 were built for '53 (most were reserved for promotion and favored VIPs), followed by 3640 for '54 and a mere 674 of the '55s. Some blamed this on the car's rather odd mix of features. *Boulevardier* types disliked the plastic side curtains, clumsy cloth top and lack of a back seat. Enthusiasts chided the gimmicky styling and plodding drivetrain—two-speed Powerglide automatic and the 235.5-cubic-inch Chevy "Stovebolt" six—though triple carbs, high-lift cam, higher compression and other changes brought the ancient engine to a commendable 150 horsepower.

Thanks to pleas from Earl and Chevy chief engineer Ed Cole, GM decided in late 1954 to give Corvette a second chance. And Cole had what would prove to be its salvation: the brilliant 265-cid overhead-valve V8 he'd designed (with Harry Barr, John Gordon and others) for Chevy's all-new 1955 passenger cars. Rated at 195 bhp, it vastly improved performance, and almost all '55 Corvettes were so equipped. A newly optional three-speed floorshift manual gearbox further shifted the car's image from "plastic bathtub" to genuine sports car.

The all-new second generation announced for '56 did even more. A rounded rump and beautifully sculptured bodysides with curving, concave sections just aft of the front wheel openings were stunning improvements over the stubby, slab-sided original. Proper roll-up door windows and an optional lift-off hardtop (both pre-

The fiberglass-bodied '53 Corvette saw only 315 units produced. It was powered by the old "Stovebolt" six, tweaked to 150 bhp.

The MG may be "The Sports Car America Loved First," but the Corvette is the sports car America loves best. Although it got off to a slow start back in the days of MG TDs and Jaguar XK120s, today it is a respected, world-class sports car.

viewed on a 1954 Motorama Corvette) made motoring more civilized. Dropping the six and tuning the V8 for 210 or 225 bhp (the latter via high-lift cam, twin four-barrel carburetors, and dual exhausts) made for serious performance, as did adept chassis changes wrought by Chevy engineer Zora Arkus-Duntov. The close-ratio three-speed manual replaced Powerglide, which shifted to the options sheet. The most potent '56 could hit 60 mph from rest in just 7.5 seconds and top 120 mph.

There was no need to change the handsome styling for '57, but Chevy upped performance by boring the V8 to 283 cid. This was offered in five versions with 220 bhp up to an amazing 283 bhp, the latter courtesy of new "Ramjet" fuel injection. A four-speed manual transmission arrived in May at $188 extra, and combined with axle ratios as low as 4.11:1 to make "fuelie" '57s thunderingly fast. Published road tests showed 0-60 in 5.7 seconds, 0-100 mph in 16.8 seconds, the standing quarter-mile in 14.3 seconds at 96 mph, and a maximum 132 mph plus. Alas, mechanical bugs and a $500 price limited Ramjet installations to only 240 units that year. Chevy also offered a $725 "heavy-duty racing suspension" package with high-rate springs and shocks, front anti-roll bar, quick steering, and ceramic-metallic brake linings with finned ventilated drums. With one of the high-power engines, a Corvette was virtually ready to race right off the showroom floor.

Indeed, the Corvette now began making its mark in competition. Dr. Richard Thompson won the national Sports Car Club of America C-Production championship in 1956, then took the '57 crown in B-Production, where the 'Vette qualified by dint of its larger engine. John Fitch's '56 was the fastest modified car at that year's Daytona Speed Weeks, a Corvette finished 9th in the gruelling 12 Hours of Sebring in '56, and another came home 2nd at Pebble Beach. Chevy's 1957 Sebring assault saw production Corvettes finish 1-2 in the GT class and 12th and 15th overall.

It was all symbolic of a dramatic metamorphosis. Said one European writer: "Before Sebring . . . the Corvette was regarded as a plastic toy. After Sebring, even the most biased were forced to admit that [it was one] of the world's finest sports cars. . . ." That included buyers, who happily took 3467 of the '56s and 6339 of the '57s. Corvette's future was assured.

Nineteen fifty-eight brought a busier, shinier Corvette that was 10 inches longer, more than two inches wider and some 200 pounds heavier. The basic shape was broadly the same as 1956-57 except for quad headlamps (all the rage that year), a dummy air scoop ahead of each concave bodyside "cove," simulated hood louvers and equally silly longitudinal chrome strips on the trunklid.

Chevy's new 265-cid V8 became available on the 1955 Corvette.

Corvette saw its first restyling in 1956—note the concave sides.

Ramjet fuel injection, a $500 option, helped the '57 Corvette's 283 V8 crank out 283 bhp—one horsepower per cubic inch.

Yet there were genuine improvements, including sturdier bumpers and a redesigned cockpit with a passenger grab bar, locking glovebox, and all instruments directly ahead of the driver. Despite the added heft and hoke, performance remained vivid because the engine lineup was little changed. The top fuel-injected 283 actually gained seven horsepower for a total of 290, thus exceeding the hallowed "1 hp per cu.in." benchmark reached the previous year. Inflation plagued the national economy in '58, yet base price remained reasonable at $3631, up just $118 from '53. Critics generally liked the '58. So did buyers. Model year production gained 2829 units over the '57 tally as Corvette actually turned a profit for the first time.

Volume rose another 500 units for '59, when Chevy smoothed out the hood, deleted the chrome trunk straps, and added trailing radius rods to counteract rear axle windup in hard acceleration, the year's only noteworthy mechanical change. This basic package continued for 1960 as Corvette production broke the magic 10,000-unit barrier for the first time.

That year brought even higher compression on the top fuelie engine (11.0:1) for an incredible 315 bhp, plus aluminum clutch housings for manual-shift models and aluminum radiators for cars with the high-power "Duntov cam" engines. A larger 24-gallon fuel tank was a new extra, and the heavy-duty suspension option was replaced by a larger front anti-roll bar and a new standard rear bar. An extra inch of wheel travel in rebound further contributed to a smoother ride and more neutral handling.

Though Corvette was moving from *pur sang* sports car to plush GT, the third generation was no less a track competitor than the second generation. Highlights include a GT-class win and 12th overall at Sebring '58, national SCCA B-Production championships in 1958-59, fastest sports car at the 1958 Pikes Peak Hill Climb, and a slew of victories by privateers. Thanks to the Automobile Manufacturers Association mid-1957 edict, Chevy was officially "out of racing" now, though not above lending under-the-table support to those campaigning its cars. Among them was sportsman Briggs Cunningham, who gave Corvette one of its finest racing hours when one of his three team cars (driven by John Fitch and Bob Grossman) finished 8th in the 1960 running of the fabled 24 Hours of Le Mans.

The 1960 Corvette might have been very different. Beginning in 1957, Chevy contemplated a smaller, lighter car based on the prototype "Q-model," with rear transaxle, independent rear suspension and inboard brakes. A full-size mockup soon took shape bearing a remarkable resemblance to the production Sting Ray then six years away, but the project was abandoned because of the '58 recession, the time and money being expended to bring out the rear-engine Corvair compact for 1960.

There was nothing to do but soldier on with the existing Corvette while designers and engineers set about creating another, less radical successor. Meantime, GM styling chief Harley Earl had retired in 1958 and his successor, William L. Mitchell, had an idea for breathing new life into the old Corvette.

It took the form of a 1961 model restyled behind the doors along the lines of Mitchell's late-'50s Stingray racer (built on the "mule" chassis salvaged from 1957's unsuccessful Corvette SS effort at Sebring). The flowing "ducktail" not only increased luggage space by some 20 percent but mated handsomely with the 1958-60 frontal styling, which Mitchell simplified by substituting mesh for the familiar chrome grille "teeth." Powerteams again stood pat for '61 as Chevy continued to emphasize refinements: standard sunvisors, higher-capacity aluminum-core radiator, side-mount expansion tanks, a wider choice of axle ratios. Base price was up to $3934, but that dough got you a lot of go. Even the mildest 283 with Powerglide was good for 7.7 seconds 0-60 mph and nearly 110 mph flat out; figures for the optional 315-bhp "fuelie" and four-speed manual were 5.5 seconds and 130-plus mph. In case anyone doubted its prowess, a near-stock '61 finished 11th in that

Dual headlights and a minor restyling marked the 1958 Corvette.

Production of the '59 Corvette reached 9670 units, a record.

The '60 Corvette listed at $3872; horsepower ranged up to 315.

The rear end of the '61 'Vette came from the Stingray racer.

The sides of the '62 'Vette were *not* available with two-toning.

The Corvette received its first V-8, Chevy's high-winding 265-cid powerplant, in 1955 and optional fuel injection in 1957. In between, the Federal-Aid Highway Act put the wheels in motion for the U.S. Interstate highway system.

Although controversial when new, collectors nowadays covet the split-rear-window '63 Sting Ray coupe. Price new: $4252.

year's Sebring 12 Hours against considerably costlier and more exotic machinery.

Refinement was again the keynote for '62, but Chevy gave a hint of things to come by offering the next Corvette's engines in the last of the traditional models. There were four in all—one fuelie and three with carburetors—all 283s bored and stroked to 327 cid and offering from 250 to a thumping 360 bhp. The fuel-injection system was modified, a new 3.08:1 final-drive ratio gave quieter cruising with the two lowest engines, and the heavy-duty suspension option returned from '59. Styling was cleaner than ever. Mitchell eliminated the chrome outline around the bodyside "coves" and their optional two-toning, blacked-in the grille and added ribbed aluminum appliqués to rocker panels and the dummy reverse front-fender scoops.

Corvette continued its winning ways on the track and in the showroom for '62. Dick Thompson, the "flying dentist," won that year's national A-Production crown in SCCA, Don Yenko the B-P title. More important to GM managers, production was still climbing, from 1961's record 10,000-plus to over 14,500. No question now: The 'Vette was here to stay.

And how, for 1963 brought the all-new Sting Ray, the first complete revision of Chevrolet's sports car in 10 years—a revolution and a revelation. Apart from four wheels and two seats, the only things it shared with the '62 were steering, front suspension, the four 327 V-8s, and fiberglass bodywork. Most everything else was changed—definitely for the better.

It began with a slight reduction in overall length, a two-inch narrower rear track and a wheelbase pared four inches (to 98). Curb weight was also reduced, thanks to a new ladder-type box frame (replacing the heavy old X-member affair) and despite a new steel-reinforced "cage" that made for a stronger, safer cockpit. In fact, the Sting Ray had almost twice as much steel support

The largest engine option for the '63 was a 327-cid, 360-bhp V8.

For 1964, the fuel-injected 327 was increased to 395 horsepower.

The '66 'Vette was powered by an optional 390/425-bhp 427-cid V8. Note the side-mounted exhaust system and the bulged hood.

in its main body structure as previous Corvettes and less fiberglass in its body. Brakes remained drums but were now self-adjusting, and the fronts were wider.

The big news was independent rear suspension, a first for a modern U.S. production car. Duntov's clever engineering produced a frame-mounted differential with U-jointed halfshafts acting on a single transverse leaf spring; differential-mounted control arms ran laterally and slightly forward to the hub carriers to limit fore/aft movement, and a pair of trailing radius rods was fitted behind. It was elegantly simple, relatively cheap, and highly effective. Front/rear weight distribution was now 48/52 percent versus the previous 53/47. New recirculating-ball steering combined with a dual-arm, three-link ball-joint front suspension for quicker steering. With all this, Corvette ride and handling were better than they'd ever been.

Though engines were unchanged, there was now an alternator instead of a generator, positive crankcase ventilation and a smaller flywheel. Competition options included stiff suspension, metallic brake linings, handsome cast-aluminum knock-off wheels, and a 36.5-gallon long-distance fuel tank.

Styling was equally new and quite dramatic, evolved from the experimental XP-720 coupe of late 1959. The customary roadster gained a dramatic fastback companion with a rear window split by a vertical divider bar. Duntov lobbied against the last, saying it hampered outward vision. Mitchell huffed that "if you take that off you might as well forget the whole thing." Duntov ultimately won and a one-piece backlight was substituted after '63, leaving the split-window coupe a one-year model—and highly prized because of it.

Shared design highlights comprised hidden headlights (in rotating sections that fit flush with the pointy nose when the lamps were off), an attractive beltline dip at the doors' trailing edges, humped

It cost $4321 to buy a '65 'Vette; 8186 people did just that.

As from 1963, the 1967 Corvette rode a shorter 98-inch wheelbase.

Today, many Corvette aficionados consider the 1963 split-window Sting Ray coupe to be the most collectible Corvette ever built. In 1963, Americans loved it because it was a true go-fast machine and looked supersonic even when parked.

front and rear fenders, slim L-shape half-bumpers at each end, a continuation of the 1961-62 "ducktail," and a sharp full-perimeter "character line" at mid-body height. A new "dual cockpit" dashboard was a fresh approach that worked remarkably well. Doors cut into the roof facilitated cockpit access on the coupe. An optional lift-off hardtop was still available for the roadster.

Work on the stillborn Q-model caused the Sting Ray coupe to be developed first, then the roadster. A four-passenger coupe was considered (progressing as far as a complete full-size mockup) but ultimately rejected as being out of character for a Corvette. Final Sting Ray prototypes were subjected to intense wind tunnel evaluation, resulting in frontal area being reduced by a square foot. Despite the shorter wheelbase, interior space was at least as good as in previous Corvettes.

The Sting Ray quickly proved the fastest and most roadable 'Vette yet. And the most popular: 1963 sales were nearly twice the record '62 total, about 10,000 for each body style. Performance had less to do with this than the wider market appeal of new extra-cost creature comforts: leather upholstery, power steering, power brakes (at last), AM/FM radio, air conditioning and more.

Over the next four years, the Sting Ray was progressively cleaned up, Chevy removing what little nonsense there was or making it functional, as with the fake hood louvers and coupe rear quarter vents for '64. The following year, the sculptured hood was smoothed out and the front-fender slots opened up. The design was virtually perfected by 1967, the only changes being a single oblong backup light above the license plate, bolt-on instead of knock-off aluminum wheels, revised front fender louvers, and an optional vinyl covering for the roadster hardtop.

Naturally, there were important mechanical improvements in these years. The fuelie 327 delivered up to 395 bhp for 1964, while '65 brought optional four-wheel disc brakes (for stopping power to match the steadily escalating performance) and Corvette's first big-block V8, the 425-bhp "Mark IV." This was initially sized at 396 cid, then enlarged to 427 for '66 and beyond. To handle its brute force, Chevy fitted stiffer suspension, extra-heavy-duty clutch, and a larger radiator and fan. With the 4.11:1 rear axle ratio, a '66 Mark IV could do 0-60 mph in less than five seconds and more than 140 mph all out—not bad for a civilized, fully equipped machine selling for around $4500. Fuel injection was dropped for the

Corvette boasted new styling for 1968; the coupe listed at $4663.

smaller-displacement engines after 1965, mainly due to high production costs and low sales.

But Corvette sales as a whole set new records in all but one of the Sting Ray years, peaking at nearly 28,000 for 1966. Horsepower seemed to set yearly records too. That peak came with 1967's stupendous L88, an aluminum-head 427 with 12.5:1 compression, wild cam, and big four-barrel carb, rated at no less than 560 bhp. Only 20 cars were so equipped, but they were symbolic of how far the 'Vette had come.

Of course, many of the high-power Sting Rays went racing, though they often bowed to Carroll Shelby's stark, super-quick Cobras. Still, there were bright spots. Don Yenko was SCCA national B-Production champ in 1963, a Roger Penske car won its class at Nassau '65, and 1966 saw Sting Rays place 12th overall in the Daytona Continental and 9th at Sebring.

The Sting Ray was a tough act to follow, and not everyone liked its 1968 follow-up. Arriving for the first year of federal safety and emissions standards, it combined a new seven-inch-longer body (most of the increase in front overhang) with essentially carryover engines and chassis. Styling, previewed by the 1965 Mako Shark

Output hit 28,566 units for 1968. Roadsters were still more popular than the Corvette coupe, accounting for 18,630 units.

Production soared to 38,762 units for 1969, another record.

II show car, was all humpy and muscular, with fulsome front and rear fenders housing seven-inch-wide wheels for better roadholding. Flip-up headlamps and modest "lip" spoilers at each end were also featured but, like the Sting Rays, there was still no opening trunklid. And the name wasn't Sting Ray anymore, just Corvette. Coupe and convertible returned, the former a new notchback style with an innovative "T-top" whose twin panels could be removed to create a semi-convertible. Mechanical changes were limited to standardizing the previously optional all-disc brakes and substituting General Motors' fine three-speed Turbo Hydra-Matic for the archaic Powerglide.

This fifth-generation design would have bowed for 1967 had Zora Arkus-Duntov not held it up to work out some kinks. Still, the '68s had plenty of problems. The most glaring was poor workmanship, which led one motor-noter to label his press car "unfit to road test." Others judged the new design needlessly gimmicky, its dashboard awash in winking lights, a trouble-prone pop-up cowl panel hiding the wipers. A narrower cockpit, a penalty of the wasp-waisted styling, and less luggage space didn't win any friends. Neither did inadequate cooling on big-block cars nor a 150-pound increase in curb weight. Yet in spite of it all, the '68 set another Corvette sales record: more than 26,500 units.

The tally was nearly 38,800 for '69, when the Stingray name returned (as one word). Duntov did his best to correct flaws, finding a little more cockpit space (smaller steering wheel, slimmer door panels), adding an override so the wiper panel could be left up in freezing weather, reworking other assorted bits. Detail styling changes comprised neater exterior door handles, black instead of chrome grille bars, and backup lights integrated with the inner taillights. Handling improved via wider wheels and the frame was stiffened. Emissions considerations prompted lower compression ratios and a small-block V8 stroked to 350 cid, while a fourth 427 option appeared with 430 bhp and available axle ratios from 4.56:1 to 2.75:1. Even wilder was the all-aluminum ZL-1 big-block, a virtual Can-Am racing engine priced at a formidable $3000. Production? Just two.

Corvette volume plunged some 50 percent for 1970, thanks to an auto workers strike. The main news was a big-block punched out to 454 cid, again to meet emissions standards that were increasingly sapping power from all Detroit engines. Even so, lower compression left the top LS-5 version at 365 bhp, the aluminum-head LS-6 at 425 bhp. (An even more potent 465-bhp version was planned but never actually offered because it couldn't be made "clean" enough.) The rest of the car was again little changed (a finely checked grille and front-fender vents provided i.d.), but Chevy cleaned up more details and offered the 370-bhp solid-lifter LT-1 small-block promised for '69.

Inflation, rising gas prices and soaring insurance rates were putting a big damper on performance-car sales by now. Corvette was no exception, its 1972 volume not even equalling '69's. A switch to more realistic SAE net power ratings made engines seem punier—which they were—and the LS-6 was cancelled along with the fiber-optic exterior light monitors. However, the anti-theft alarm system option was now standard, a belated nod to the 'Vette's high "thievability."

The '73s gained a body-color nose of pliable plastic in line with the government's new 5-mph impact-protection rule, plus more insulation and new chassis mounts for quietness. The coupe's drop-down rear window, a feature since '68, went away. So did all engines save a pair of 350s and one big-block. Rear-impact stan-

Top horsepower option for the '70 Stingray jumped to 460. Coupe sales exceeded those of the roadster, as they first had in 1969.

The humpy and muscular fifth-generation Corvette arrived for 1968, which also happened to be the first year of Federal safety and emissions standards. Though the styling was not to everyone's liking, the '68 'Vette set a new sales record.

The '74 'Vette featured pliable plastic bumpers to meet Federal five-mph crash standards. They were strong *and* attractive.

The '72 Stingray coupe retailed for $5472, weighed 3215 pounds.

A newly styled front end and domed hood were featured for 1973.

Top engine choice for the '74 Stingray was a 270-bhp 454 V8.

The '75 convertible would be Corvette's last for a full decade.

dards dictated a new body-color tail on the '74s, which arrived with the Middle East oil embargo, even higher gas prices, and long lines at the pumps. Yet while other cars suffered sales drops, Corvette kept climbing.

But it kept slipping too. Both the LT-1 and the last big-block options vanished after '74, followed by the roadster after '75, a victim of steadily falling demand. Changes were few through 1977, yet sales continued strong. The '76s broke 1969's record at over 46,550, followed by an improbable 49,000-plus of the '77s.

Clearly, Chevy had made a silk purse of the sow's-ear '68 and reaped the rewards. Government's heavy hand made a change in the car's character inevitable, though that wasn't necessarily bad. By 1975 the Corvette had become more balanced, less outlandish and arguably more pleasant—more high-speed *boulevardier* than straightline screamer.

But enthusiasts were still awaiting an all-new 'Vette. A pair of

1972 rotary-engine show cars strongly hinted it could be a mid-engine design. Perhaps in time for Corvette's 25th birthday in 1978? No, but it came close for 1980. Its basis would have been the Aerovette, the renamed V8-powered iteration of the four-rotor Wankel car. Mitchell lobbied hard for a production derivative, and GM president Tom Murphy actually approved one for 1980. By late '77, Aerovette-based clay models were complete and tooling ready to be ordered. But the project foundered when Mitchell retired that year. Zora Arkus-Duntov, another booster, had retired at the end of '74, and his successor as Corvette chief engineer, David R. McLellan, preferred keeping the "front mid-engine" layout for reasons of packaging, manufacturing, performance, and cost.

Indeed, cost is what ultimately killed the Aerovette—never mind that mid-engine design had not proven to be the wave of the sports-car future that some had predicted in the late '60s. Chevy duly regrouped and, by mid-1978, McLellan and his crew were working on a more conventional new Corvette.

Meantime, the fifth generation would have to hold on awhile—no problem really, what with sales still strong. Still, GM decided to spend some money on rejuvenating the old warrior to mark Corvette's 25th birthday.

The '78 thus received one big change—a new fastback roofline with a huge wraparound rear window—and a host of minor ones (mostly to the cockpit). It was no longer a Stingray but it *was* that year's Indy 500 pace car, and Chevrolet issued 6200 replicas with special paint, leather interior, and owner-applied decals. To the division's chagrin, quick-buck artists were quick to convert standard 'Vettes into bogus replicas, creating no little confusion. There was also a Silver Anniversary edition, actually a trim package and not all that different from stock. Engine choices were down to two 350s: standard 185-bhp L48 and extra-cost 220-bhp L82.

Corvette mostly marked time for '79. It was now quite plush for a sports car. Power windows, air, tilt steering wheel, power door locks, and AM/FM stereo were all included in a base price that inflation swelled from $9645 to $12,313 in just one year. Yet despite that, and poor mileage at a time when gas was again scarcer and costlier, sales leaped to over 50,000.

Corvette finally went on a diet for 1980, shedding some 250 pounds through greater use of plastics and by substituting aluminum for steel in the differential housing and front frame crossmember. Aerodynamics improved via a new sloped nose with integral spoiler, plus a faired-in rear spoiler.

More weight-saving occurred for '81, mostly from a fiberglass rear leaf spring and thinner glass for door windows and the optional see-through T-tops. There was now just one 350, a new L81 version with magnesium rocker covers, stainless-steel exhaust manifold and GM's Computer Command Control engine management system. Horsepower was unchanged. Government fuel-economy mandates dictated a lockup torque converter for the optional automatic transmission. Inflation pushed base price past $15,000, but that included six-way power driver's seat. The year saw the historic transfer of production from St. Louis (where Corvettes had been built since '54) to a new high-tech plant in Bowling Green, Kentucky. With it came promises of improved workmanship.

It also suggested that there really *would* be a new Corvette at last. But first, the fifth generation put in a 15th and final appearance for '82. Previewing the new model's drivetrain was a revised L83 engine with fuel injection for the first time since 1965. And for the first time since 1955, there was no manual gearbox, just a new four-speed automatic with torque-converter lockup on all forward gears save first. But the real kicker was another limited-production job tellingly named "Collector's Edition," with lift-up rear window (belatedly) and unique trim. It was the costliest 'Vette yet at a towering $22,538, a far cry from the $4663 it took to buy a '68.

Historians huffed when the long-awaited sixth generation arrived for 1984 in early '83 (mainly for emissions-certification rea-

Stingray output soared to 46,558 for 1976, all of them coupes.

Chevy built 6200 Official Pace Car (Indy 500) replicas in 1978.

Corvette's most powerful 1979 engine was a 225 bhp (net) 350 V8.

A Computer Command Control emissions system debuted for 1981.

Despite tighter emission regulations and five-mph bumper standards, the Corvette sailed through the Seventies setting one production record after another. Even Big Brother's interference couldn't dampen demand for Chevy's sports car.

After 20 years, fuel injection reappeared on the '82 Corvette.

The sixth-generation '84 Corvette debuted in the spring of 1983.

A roadster rejoined the Corvette roster in mid-model-year 1986. Featured that year was a Bosch-designed anti-lock brake system.

sons), thus depriving them of a 30th-anniversary Corvette. Some observers (former GM styling chief Bill Mitchell among them) criticized appearance as bland, but most liked it. Created under the direction of Jerry Palmer, it was clean, contemporary, recognizably Corvette, and 23.7 percent more aerodynamically efficient—in all, quite a feat. A lift-up hatch window returned from the '82 Collector Edition, but the T-top gave way to a one-piece Targa roof and a new front-hinged "clamshell" hood/fender assembly offered superb engine access.

That engine was still the 205-bhp L83, initially teamed with four-speed converter-lockup Turbo Hydra-Matic. But the autobox ultimately became an optional alternative to a new "4+3 Overdrive" manual. The work of 'Vette specialist Doug Nash, it was basically a normal four-speed with a second planetary gearset actuated by engine electronics to provide gas-saving overdrive ratios in all gears save first.

The rest of the car was equally new, starting with its "uniframe" construction—a Lotus-like backbone chassis welded to an upper "birdcage" for greatly increased rigidity. Front suspension was as before save a single transverse plastic leaf spring instead of individual coils. At the rear was a new five-link setup comprising upper and lower longitudinal links, twin lateral strut rods from differential to hub carriers, and the usual transverse plastic spring, tie rods and halfshafts. Steering switched to rack-and-pinion, and there were new-design disc brakes supplied by the Anglo-American Girlock company. Tires were Goodyear's new ultra-sticky Eagle GTs with unidirectional "gatorback" tread running on wide cast-alloy wheels.

Weight-saving was again a priority, so the '84 had more lightweight materials than any previous Corvette (including beautiful aluminum forgings for suspension components). But though 250 pounds lighter than the '82, it was some 300 pounds heavier than expected despite reductions of two inches in wheelbase (to 96 inches) and 8.8 inches in overall length.

Still, the '84 offered more passenger and cargo space, better outward vision, and all the comfort and luxury expected in a thoroughbred GT. Alas, it also had complicated digital and graphic electronic instruments that were hard to read, especially on a sunny day. A harsh ride—even harsher with the Z51 handling option—emphasized the new structure's surprising flex. A record base price—initially $23,360—also drew barbs. But that was about all anyone could fault. "A world-class sports car with few rivals in performance," was how we described it.

Chevy tended to details for '85, gaining 25 horsepower by switching from twin-throttle-body to "Tuned Port" injection, softening both standard and optional suspensions, adding oil cooler and gas-pressurized shock absorbers. The '86s were even better. The brakes received standard Bosch anti-lock control for stopping

Multi-port fuel injection upped bhp from 205 to 230 for 1985.

By 1986, the Corvette coupe stickered at a pricey $27,027.

An electronic tire pressure monitor cost $325 on the '87 'Vette. Retail prices were $27,999, coupe; $33,172, convertible.

power to match the stupendous cornering power. Though horsepower was unchanged, the evergreen 350 received aluminum cylinder heads, higher compression (9.5:1 versus 9.0) and dual exhausts. But the big event was the mid-season return of the Corvette roadster in time to pace the Indy 500 (which meant another batch of replicas—all '86-model roadsters, in fact). Because the sixth generation had been designed to be topless, structural stiffening was straightforward: an X-member below the floorpan, reinforcements around the cockpit.

The main change for '87 was roller valve lifters that added another 10 horses for a total of 240. Chevrolet also announced an optional in-cockpit tire-pressure monitoring system, similar to that of the otherworldly Porsche 959, but development problems precluded availability until 1989. Still seeking even more cornering power, Chevy offered the '88s with optional 17-inch wheels wearing jumbo P275/40ZR Eagle GT tires. Both of these and the standard 16-inch rims were newly styled. The suspension was slightly modified to better resist rear-end squat in hard acceleration and nosedive in panic braking. Freer-breathing heads and a reprofiled camshaft boosted horsepower to 245.

Another milestone Corvette birthday rolled around in '88—the 35th—and Chevy celebrated with 2000 specially trimmed anniversary coupes (actually, an optional appearance package, Z01). Recalling the '53 original, it was done mostly in white—interior, lower body, wheels, door handles, even nameplates—but black roof pillars and a black-tint glass roof panel made for a strikingly different effect. Automatic climate system, all-leather cockpit trim, power sports seats, heated rear window and door mirrors and a zoomy Delco/Bose sound system were all included. It was a nice way for America's sports car to enter middle age—and to recall that some 900,000 Corvettes had been built before it.

But it was only a warmup to an amazing new "King of the Hill" Corvette, the subject of "buff book" spy reports beginning in late '87. It bowed for 1989 as the ZR1, another Chevy option code destined to make history. Available only in coupe form, it boasted an all-new, all-aluminum V8 designated LT5, still a 350 but with a larger bore and shorter stroke than the existing engine (now called L69)—plus dual overhead camshafts actuating four valves per cylinder.

The LT5's specifications read like a textbook for competition mills: nitrided forged-steel crank, wet-liner block, two-piece crankcase assembly with integral oil pickup, forged-steel conrods with free-floating wrist pins, die-cast pistons, stellate-faced valves, a narrow 22-degree included valve angle, sequential electronic port fuel injection, distributorless ignition (via four direct-firing coils) and high 11.25:1 compression. The result was 385 bhp and an equal amount of torque—astounding for a modern emissions-controlled street engine claimed to deliver up to 22.5 mpg. Per-

Porsche stunned the sports car world with the high-tech 969; Ferrari did likewise with the ferocious F-40. The Corvette's exotic 180-mph ZR1—"The King of the Hill"—was delayed until 1990, but cost only a fraction as much as the other two.

Optional for the 1988 Corvette were P275/40ZR17 149-mph tires.

haps its most unique feature was three-stage throttle control, providing "stepped" power delivery governed by the engine's electronic control module. To keep lesser-skilled—or unauthorized—drivers from getting into trouble, the system included a "power mode" that precluded full power delivery at full throttle without a special key. The LT5 was carefully engineered to fit the existing Corvette engine without alteration, but the ZR1 was easily identified from behind by squared-up taillights and bodywork made subtly wider behind the doors to accommodate even broader tires.

Two more ZR1 innovations were shared with "standard" '89 Corvettes: Selective Ride Control (optional on non-ZR1s) and a new *six*-speed manual gearbox. The latter, designed jointly by Chevy and Germany's ZF, offered vastly better shift quality than the never-liked "4+3" it replaced. One rather odd feature was computer-aided gear selection (CAGS), which automatically shifted from first to fourth on light throttle openings (below 35 percent) at low speeds (12-19 mph). Like the "4+3," CAGS was another subtle extreme dictated by the EPA's fuel-economy test procedures and Chevy's continuing desire that the Corvette avoid the government's dreaded gas guzzler tax, and though it sounded like another way to spoil the fun, it scarcely ever activated in the kind of driving most 'Vette owners do.

Selective Ride Control, option code FX3, was restricted to cars with the new six-speed and the Z51 handling package. Like several similar Japanese setups, this electro-mechanical system offered three driver-selectable levels of shock damping—labelled Touring, Sport and Competition—via electric motors that varied the size of the proportioning-valve orifice in each shock. Two added sophistications were progressively firmer settings for each level, which automatically came into play with increasing speed, and a high-speed override that automatically switched settings for optimum handling. Developed by Bilstein and GM's Delco Division, the system was claimed to improve both ride comfort and cornering power.

Other '89 developments included standardizing the 17-inch wheel/tire combination for all models, plus several items from the former Z52 handling option. These included strengthened front chassis (as introduced with the '86 convertible), faster steering ratio, Delco/Bilstein gas-filled shock absorbers and, for six-speed cars, engine oil cooler, heavy-duty radiator and auxiliary cooling fan. Seats were redesigned, and new leather-covered sport seats, tied to the Z51 option, added full power lumbar adjustment to the usual six-way positioning. Finally, rearranged top latches made the convertible more convenient, and Chevy answered enthusiast demands (while maintaining Corvette tradition) by offering a detachable hardtop for it.

With all this, America's sports car has not only matured into a world-class sports car but ranks as an even better high-performance buy despite higher-than-ever prices. Buyers were quick to recognize this, snapping up close to 50,000 of the '84s and 30,000-40,000 a year in 1985-87—a fair showing, all things considered.

But profits and high volume have never been this car's reason for being. If they had, Chevy would have killed the Corvette back in '55. No, excitement and legendary performance are what it's all about. They're why the 'Vette has survived against all odds for nearly four decades—and why it'll survive another four. And though the car itself may change, its spirit will forever be all-American, and we can all take pride in that.

Corvette sailed into 1989 with detail improvements. The ZR1 performance handling option included 17-inch alloy wheels.

CHRYSLER

Walter Percy Chrysler honed his native mechanical skills on the great Midwestern railroads, then learned about cars by tinkering with a $5000 Locomobile he bought in 1908. Within a few short years he'd become plant manager at Buick under Charles W. Nash, then took over for him as Buick president. But Chrysler didn't get along well with GM's Billy Durant, so he left to form his own car company (as did Nash). By 1924, Chrysler had gained control of faltering Maxwell and Chalmers and had introduced a new car under his own name. With this was born the last of America's "Big Three" automakers.

That first Chrysler was the foundation of the new company's high, early success. Typical of W.P., it was designed with instrumental assistance from three superb engineers: Fred Zeder, Carl Breer and Owen Skelton, the "Three Musketeers" who would dominate the design of Chrysler Corporation products throughout the '30s. Power came from a high-compression 202-cubic-inch L-head six with seven main bearings and 68 horsepower—0.3 bhp per cubic inch, outstanding for the early '20s. Also featured were four-wheel hydraulic brakes, full-pressure lubrication, attractive styling, and competitive prices around $1500. It couldn't miss, and it didn't. By 1927, production had soared from 32,000 to some 182,000 units.

Sixes remained Chrysler's mainstay through 1930, after which it relied chiefly on straight eights. After 1928, when W.P. acquired Dodge and introduced DeSoto and Plymouth, the Chrysler line moved rapidly upmarket in price and prestige, reaching its peak with the 1931-33 Imperial. Powered by the largest version of Chrysler's first eight—a smooth, low-revving 385-cid L-head with nine main bearings and 125 bhp—these majestic 5000-pound luxury cars could do 96 mph and 0-60 mph in 20 seconds. Styling was distinctive and distinguished: long and low, with gracefully curved fenders and a rakish grille resembling Duesenberg's. Depression-limited demand made them rare, but they provided glorious motoring at relatively modest prices and remain among the most beautiful Chryslers ever built.

Meantime, Chrysler cemented its reputation for advanced engineering with "Floating Power" rubber engine mounts and welded steel bodies, both 1931 innovations. Then a setback: the 1934 Airflow, the most radical production design yet attempted by a U.S. producer but the first truly modern car. The name stemmed from wind-tunnel tests that dictated its streamlined shape. An engine placed over the front axle opened up considerable interior space and allowed passengers to sit entirely within the wheelbase for a more comfortable ride. A beam-and-truss body engineered along aircraft lines provided great strength with less weight.

But production delays (due partly to massive retooling) and a smear campaign by jealous competitors (mainly GM) blunted high initial interest and prompted rumors that the Airflow was flawed. The new-fangled styling didn't help. Except for a group of traditional square-rigged Sixes, Chrysler's 1934 offerings were all Airflow, yet sales were underwhelming. While most makes boosted production by up to 60 percent, Chrysler volume rose only 20 percent.

Yet the Airflow wasn't nearly the disaster it's long been portrayed. Chrysler dropped from 8th to 10th in model year output for 1932 but would go no lower through '37, the Airflow's final year, after which it rose to ninth. And though the cars did lose money, the losses were far from crippling. The Airflow's most lasting impact was to discourage Chrysler from fielding anything so adventurous for a very long time. Not until 1955 would the firm again reach for industry styling leadership.

Thus did Chrysler design begin a long conservative period. Planned Airflow-style Dodges and Plymouths were abruptly cancelled, and Chrysler Division regrouped around more conventional "Airstream" Sixes and Eights that literally carried the make through 1935-36. Most 1937 Chryslers and all '38s had transitional styling with barrel grilles, rounded fenders and pod-type headlamps. Eight-cylinder engines were now five-main-bearing side-valve units (the nine-main engine was dropped after '34). Volume recovered from the 1934 low of some 36,000 to over 106,000 by 1937, then dropped by half for recession '38, though the make remained ninth. For 1939, Chrysler fell back to 11th despite building nearly 72,500 cars.

Chrysler had settled on a three-series lineup by that time, but

The New Yorker nameplate first appeared on a Chrysler in 1939.

Base retail price of the 1940 Chrysler Royal coupe was $960.

After the radical Airflow bombed in the mid-Thirties, Chrysler maintained a conservative stance toward styling. The firm was best known for cars with solid, first-class engineering and practical, no-nonsense room and comfort.

Chrysler prices ranged from $995 to $2795 for 1941. Engine offerings were a 241.5-cid six or a 323.5-cid straight eight.

The '41 Crown Imperial rode a long, long 145.5-inch wheelbase.

The '41 Town and Country woody wagon was a one-off prototype.

1939 styling was fully revised by Ray Dietrich, the great coachbuilder who headed the company's design department in the '30s. Headlamps moved stylishly into the fenders, the barrel front gave way to a lower grille composed of vertical bars, and fenders were elongated. Further advancing Chrysler's engineering reputation was "Superfinish," a new process of mirror-finishing engine and chassis components to minimize friction.

Several familiar model names appeared for the first time in the 1939 lineup: Windsor (a Royal sub-series), New Yorker, and Saratoga. The C-22 Royal/Royal Windsor carried the 95/102-bhp six from 1938 and rode a 119-inch wheelbase except for one long sedan and limousine (136 inches). The 125-inch-wheelbase C-23 Imperial series included New Yorker coupes and sedans (inspired by 1938's New York Special four-door) and a brace of Saratogas. Topping the line was the C-24 Custom Imperial, two long sedans and a limo on a 144-inch-wheelbase all of which featured the new Fluid Drive semi-automatic transmission as standard. All eight-cylinder cars used the same 323.5-cid engine this year, rated at 130-138 bhp depending on model. Dating from 1934, it would remain in production until the breakthrough hemi-head V8 of 1951.

Walter Chrysler died in August 1940 after turning over the presidency to his chosen successor, K.T. Keller, in 1935. Engineers would continue to run Chrysler into the '50s. Though appearance remained conservative, its cars of the '40s were soundly built, reasonably well styled and a good value.

The immediate prewar years were good for Chrysler Division. It rose to 10th place on over 92,000 units for 1940, then captured 8th on 1941 volume of nearly 162,000. Much of this stemmed from a broad range of models and prices: for 1940, from $895 for the Royal Six coupe to $2445 for the eight-passenger Crown Imperial limousine.

The 1940 Chryslers had all-new bodies and longer wheelbases but still-orthodox styling: notchback profiles, separate fenders, smooth lines all around. Engineering continued to be emphasized at Keller's wholehearted insistence. The result, as one wag put it, "wouldn't knock your eyes out but wouldn't knock your hat off either." Models again fell into six- and eight-cylinder ranks. Royal and Windsor Sixes rode a 122.5-inch wheelbase (139.5 inches for eight-passenger sedans and limousines). Eights began with Traveler, New Yorker and Saratoga on a 128.5-inch span (the last two also offering formal sedans), while a 145.5-inch chassis carried Crown Imperial sedans and limousine. The eight now delivered 135-143 bhp, the six 108 or 112 bhp.

Two striking show cars from the house of LeBaron appeared during 1940; six of each were built. The Newport, designed by

Ralph Roberts, was a dual-cowl phaeton on the Imperial chassis with a rakish envelope body and smooth fenders. It paced the 1941 Indy 500. The Thunderbolt, designed by Alex Tremulis of Briggs, had even sleeker flush-fender styling, but was a retractable hardtop on the New Yorker chassis with a single bench seat. Both had hidden headlamps.

The most interesting new '41 model was Dave Wallace's unique Town & Country station wagon, Chrysler's first such body style. Unlike other woodies of the day, it had a clean, rounded shape, with "clamshell" center-opening rear doors. Riding the Windsor chassis, it was available with six- or nine-passenger seating and sold for a remarkably low $1412/$1492. A total of 999 were built for '41, mostly the nine-passenger kind. A variation on the familiar four-door was the attractive Town Sedan, available in each series and bearing closed rear roof quarters (*sans* auxiliary rear side windows) plus front- instead of rear-hinged back doors.

Wheelbases were trimmed an inch for all '41s save Crown Imperials. Grille styling was simpler, taillamps more ornate. The Traveler was eliminated and Saratoga offerings expanded to include club and business coupes, two- and four-door sedans and a town sedan. Chrysler offered a variety of interesting upholstery choices: Highlander Plaid, a striking combination of Scots plaid and leatherette; Saran, a woven plastic and leatherette designed for certain open models; and Navajo, a pattern resembling the blankets of the Southwest Indians. The year's main new mechanical feature was optional "Vacamatic" transmission, a self-shifter that operated between the two lower and two higher gears. Manual shifting was still required to go between these ranges.

A significant facelift for 1942 achieved a much smoother appearance by wrapping the grille's chrome bands right around to the front fenders. A sleeker hood opened from the front instead of the sides, and running boards were newly hidden by flared door bottoms. Highlander Plaid returned along with another special upholstery option called Thunderbird, also borrowed from Indian motifs. The Town & Country wagon moved to the Windsor series. Increased bore brought the Chrysler six to 250.6 cid and 120 bhp; the eight was rated at 140 bhp.

Chryslers built after January 1, 1942, used a coating of ivory-coated plastic instead of chrome trim per government order (some other makers used paint). Production ended altogether in early February. Only 5292 Chryslers were built for the calendar year and close to 36,000 for the model year. The division then turned out anti-aircraft guns, Wright Cyclone airplane engines, land mine detectors, radar units, marine engines and Sea Mule harbor tugs; tanks were its most famous wartime product.

Only seven 1946-48 Chrysler Town and Country hardtops were built.

When they could during the war, small teams of designers and engineers would work on ideas for postwar Chryslers—largely smoother versions of the 1940-42 models with fully wrapped bumpers and grilles, thinner A- and B-pillars and skirted rear fenders. But like most everyone else in Detroit, Chrysler needed only warmed-over '42s to satisfy the huge postwar seller's market, and that's what it offered through early 1949.

For 1946, fender brightwork was reduced and the eggcrate grille became one of Detroit's shiniest. All prewar offerings returned save the six- and eight-passenger Crown Imperial sedans, and engines were slightly detuned. A more significant change involved the Town & Country, no longer a wagon but a separate series comprising six- and eight-cylinder sedans and convertibles. Chrysler had promised an array of non-wagon woodies, including two-door brougham sedan, roadster and hardtop coupe, but only a handful of each were built. Hardtops numbered seven, created by grafting an elongated coupe top onto the T&C convertible. The

Chrysler business coupes were a rare sight even in 1948—try to find one now! Base prices ranged from $1819 to $2285.

Chrysler's most interesting models in the 1941-50 era were the Town and Country woodies. Expensive to buy and maintain, and built only in small numbers, they enhanced the entire Chrysler lineup and are avidly collected today.

Chrysler Windsor for 1949: 125.5-inch wheelbase, 116 horsepower.

The '50 Saratoga featured a less-fussy grille and new taillights.

A 180-bhp Hemi V8 powered this 1952 Chrysler Newport hardtop.

A revised grille and greenhouse were seen on the 1953 New Yorker.

eight-cylinder T&C sedan was eliminated after '46 and a run of 100.

Prices were up dramatically due to postwar inflation. For example, the Royal business coupe that had cost a little more than $1000 in 1942 was up to nearly $1500. Prices would continue rising through decade's end, to the point where a Crown Imperial went for nearly double its 1940 tag. Even so, Chrysler was among the top 10 in model year production for 1947-48.

The 1947 line carried only detail alterations to fender trim, hubcaps, colors, carburetion, wheels and instruments; low-pressure Goodyear Super Cushion tires were adopted between August and November. The Traveler name returned on a luxurious Windsor utility sedan with special paint and interior and an attractive wood luggage rack. Unlike the comparable DeSoto Suburban, it lacked fold-down triple seats and wood rear floorboards, having a separate trunk instead. Another revival was an eight-passenger Crown Imperial sedan.

The 1948 models were complete '47 carryovers. The six-cylinder T&C sedan was dropped at mid-year, but the eight-cylinder convertible carried on. Eventually, 8569 would be built from 1946, including a handful reserialed as early '49s.

Chrysler wasn't ready with its redesigned Silver Anniversary 1949 line in late '48, so existing models were sold from December through March, save the Town & Country. Prices were unchanged. None of these "first series" '49s were actually built that year.

While streamlined styling with integral, skirted fenders was considered for the all-new "second series" '49s, Keller insisted on bolt-upright bodies with vast interior space. He got them, but with some loss in sales appeal. Chrysler output thus fell to a bit over 124,000 for model year '49 and the make to 12th place.

Overall, the '49 was ornate, with a massive chrome-laden grille, prominent brightwork elsewhere, and curious vertical taillights (only Crown Imperials were spared these gaudy devices). There was now a host of gimmicky names for certain desirable features: Safety-Level Ride, Hydra-Lizer shock absorbers, Safety-Rim wheels, Full-Flow oil filter, Cycle-Bonded brake linings. Wheelbases were longer and reassigned. Royal and Windsor were up to 125.5 inches, with a 139.5-inch chassis continuing for long models; Saratoga, New Yorker, convertible T&C and a new Imperial sedan rode a 131.5-inch span; Crowns remained at 145.5. Both engines were largely unchanged.

An assortment of Chrysler-based customs were built in the late '40s. Most were by Derham of Pennsylvania, which offered a town limousine and a dual-cowl phaeton in 1946-48 and tried the same padded-top treatment on a '49 New Yorker. Chrysler itself built a custom formal sedan, and A.J. Miller of Ohio did a long-wheelbase limousine/hearse. Wildest of all was a promotional New Yorker with a midsection styled like a giant Zippo lighter.

Chrysler entered the '50s as a high-volume make offering no fewer than seven series and 22 models. By 1959 it was an upper medium-price line with just 15 models in four series (Windsor sixes had been dropped and Imperial made a separate make for '55). But styling and engineering improved rapidly, the dowdy L-head cars of 1950 giving way to exciting, high-style performance machines by mid-decade. Chrysler also had some of the best-looking tailfins of the age.

Those fins, which arrived in grafted-on form for '56, were the work of Virgil M. Exner, who came to Chrysler from Studebaker in 1949. His tastes ran to "classic" themes: upright grilles, circular wheel openings, rakish silhouettes. But the practical, boring boxes of K.T. Keller (then preparing for retirement) weren't selling, and before Exner could get out anything completely new, Chrysler volume was down to barely 100,000 units.

Nineteen-fifty offerings were basically '49 carryovers except for a broad, chrome eggcrate smile and the usual trim shuffles. A Deluxe Imperial sedan with custom interior arrived, but the big news was Chrysler's first volume hardtop coupe, called Newport,

The 1954 Chrysler Custom Imperial Newport weighed 4345 pounds and listed at $4560, but suffered from low sales: only 1249 units.

A splashy paint job marked the '55 New Yorker Deluxe St. Regis.

The Windsor Deluxe four-door was Chrysler's best-seller in 1955.

available as a Windsor, New Yorker and wood-trimmed T&C (the last replacing the previous ragtop).

The six-cylinder Royals, which sold for less than $2200, were in their final year. Ditto the T&C, now with a pioneering four-wheel disc-brake system but no longer needed to glamorize an unglamorous group of cars as it had done in the early postwar years. After '51, the name would apply to station wagons. Saratoga, another peripheral seller, would depart after 1952, as would long-wheelbase Windsor sedans. Standard and Deluxe Windsors and New Yorkers then carried on until 1955's "Hundred Million Dollar Look," when only Deluxes were offered *sans* remaining long models and Imperials.

The 1951-54 Chryslers were much alike. All except Crown Imperials and the long-chassis model rode 125.5- or 131.5-inch wheelbases. Styling wasn't drastically altered. A more conservative three-bar grille arrived for 1951; the '52s were all but identical (the firm didn't even keep separate production figures). Taillights are the only way to tell them apart: the '52s had built-in backup lamps. The '53s gained slightly bulkier lower-body sheetmetal, more chrome, and one-piece windshields. The '54s were "brighter" still. While it lasted, the Saratoga was the quickest Chrysler and a notable stock-car contender, mounting the new-for-'51 hemi-head V8 in the lighter Windsor chassis. New Yorker offered roughly the same models as Windsor DeLuxe but on the 131.5-inch wheelbase. Standard Imperials came as sedans, club coupes, hardtops and convertibles.

Chrysler's plain early-'50s styling may have only emphasized its engineering, which was certainly the firm's great strength at the time. A change in powerplants would emphasize it even more. The Chrysler six had been a dominant seller for years, so its disappearance after 1954 was a surprise to some. But it was all part of a plan partly instigated by Keller's successor, Lester Lum "Tex" Colbert. Then too, the hemi V8 left fewer buyers for the six: close to 100,000 in 1950 but only some 45,000 by '54.

The '49 Chrysler was designed under president K.T. Keller's edict that all of the corporation's cars provide chair-height seats and plenty of headroom. Thus, though it wouldn't knock your eyes out, neither would it knock your hat off.

The '55 C-300 was the first Chrysler "letter series" road burner. It featured an Imperial grille and a 300-bhp Hemi.

Colbert took over as Chrysler Corporation president in 1950 with several goals. The main ones were decentralized division management, a total redesign for all model lines as soon as possible, and an ambitious program of plant expansion and financing. Giving the divisions freer rein meant that those close to retail sales would have more say in mapping policy.

Horsepower shot up to 355 for the '56 300B, which sprouted fins.

The '58 300D boasted 380/390 bhp. Only 618 hardtops were built.

The brilliant hemi-head V8 was unquestionably Chrysler's greatest achievement of this era. First offered for the '51 Saratoga, New Yorker and Imperial, it wasn't really a new idea, but it did have exceptional volumetric efficiency and delivered truly thrilling performance. Lower compression allowed it to run on lower-octane fuel than most other postwar ohv V8s, yet it could produce far more power for a given displacement.

In initial 331-cid form, the hemi had power aplenty. An early demonstration engine recorded 352 bhp on the dynamometer after minor modifications to camshaft, carburetors and exhaust. Drag racers would later extract up to 1000 bhp. However, the hemi was complex and costly to build, requiring twice as many rocker shafts, pushrods, and rockers; its heads were heavy too. It was thus phased out for 1959 in favor of more conventional wedge-head V8s, but would return in Chrysler's great mid-size muscle cars of the '60s.

Yet even in the '50s it made for some very hot Chryslers. A stock Saratoga could do 0-60 mph in as little as 10 seconds and reach close to 110 mph. Bill Sterling won the stock class and ran third overall—behind two Ferraris—in the '51 Mexican Road Race. Chryslers also did well as NASCAR stockers, though they were eclipsed in 1952-54 by the remarkable Hudson Hornets. Briggs Cunningham began running his outstanding Chrysler-powered sports cars in European road races, taking his C-5R to third overall at Le Mans '53 at an average 104.14 mph (against 105.85 mph for the winning Jaguar C-Type). Then came the 1955 Chrysler 300 packing a stock hemi tuned for 300 bhp. It dominated NASCAR in 1955-56, and might have done so longer had the Auto Manufacturers Association not agreed to deemphasize racing in 1957.

The 300 was part of Virgil Exner's all-new '55 line that boosted Chrysler to over 150,000 cars and finally brought styling up to par with performance. An evolution of his long line of Ghia-bodied show cars, they were clean and aggressive-looking on a slightly longer 126-inch wheelbase. Windsor DeLuxe was treated to a standard 301-cid hemi with 188 bhp. New Yorker retained the 331 and was rated at 250 bhp.

The '56s looked even better (rare for a '50s facelift) and offered

A convertible was added to the '57 Chrysler 300C lineup. Prices were $4929, coupe; $5359, ragtop. Production: 1918 and 484.

more power. Windsors moved up to the 331 hemi with 225 bhp standard and 250 optional. New Yorker offered 280 bhp via a newly stroked 354-cid hemi. This year's 300B follow-up to the original C-300 used the same engine tweaked to 340 bhp; with a hot multi-carb option it delivered 355 bhp—making it the first Detroit V8 to break the "1 hp per cubic inch" barrier. Chevy would do the same for '57, but only with fuel injection.

Exner reached his design pinnacle with the '57s: longer, lower, wider and sleeker, with modest grilles and graceful fins. They still look pretty good today. That year's 300C was breathtaking: big

Chrysler produced 8873 New Yorker hardtop coupes for 1957.

The mildly facelifted '58 Windsor saw 6254 hardtop sedans built.

The cheaper '57 Windsor hardtop was more popular with 14,027 made.

Only 690 Chrysler 300Es found owners—the hardtop sold for $5319.

Under Virgil Exner, Chrysler styling became bolder following the 1954 sales disaster. The '55s were lower, longer, and wider. The '56s sprouted modest fins. The high-finned '57s were so stunning they wrested styling leadership from GM.

A 413-cid V8 with 380 bhp motivated the 1959 Chrysler 300E.

The 1959 Chrysler New Yorker featured a two-tone roof treatment.

A 305-bhp "Golden Lion" engine powered the 1959 Chrysler Windsor.

The '60 300F could be had with 400 bhp, and four-speed stick.

Chrysler built 5862 New Yorker four-door hardtops for 1961.

and powerful yet safe and controllable—and offered as a convertible for the first time. A unique trapezoidal grille helped it stand apart from other models.

Supplementing Newport hardtops for 1955-56 were the Windsor Nassau and New Yorker St. Regis, more conservatively two-toned and boasting slightly ritzier interiors. A hastily conceived '56 newcomer, the Newport hardtop sedan, was especially pretty in '57 form, and six- and nine-passenger Town & Country wagons were offered from 1958.

Saratoga returned as Chrysler's mid-range series for '57 and sold over 37,000 copies. It again offered a performance premium in its 295-bhp 354 hemi. That year's Windsors boasted 285 bhp. New Yorkers moved up to a stroked 392 engine with 325 bhp. In the 300C it delivered an incredible 375 or 390 bhp. Nobody ran the "horsepower race" better than Chrysler. PowerFlite two-speed automatic transmission, which had come along in 1954, was joined by three-speed TorqueFlite in mid-'56, one of the finest automatics ever built. At the same time, both automatics gained the now-famous (or infamous) pushbutton controls, mounted in a handy pod to the left of the steering wheel.

Chrysler's 1957 styling was superb, but setting the pace made for sloppy workmanship and a tendency to early body rust. A series of strikes that year hardly helped quality. Even so, Chrysler moved close to 125,000 cars for the model year, down from the 128,000 of 1956 but still good for 10th in the industry.

No discussion of Chrysler in the '50s is complete without a mention of "Torsion-Aire Ride," offered from 1957 on. Torsion bars weren't a new idea—Packard had introduced an excellent four-wheel system for '55—but Torsion-Aire went a long way toward proving big American cars could handle decently. Instead of sending road shocks up into the car like coil or leaf springs, torsion bars absorbed most of them by twisting up against their anchor points. Chrysler used them only at the front—likely for more engine compartment space than improved suspension geometry. Nevertheless, torsion bars must be regarded as a major step toward better handling. Chrysler still uses them today, an indication of how well they work.

A deep national recession and buyer dissatisfaction with assembly quality made 1958 a terrible year for Chrysler. Volume plunged to less than 64,000 units and the make dropped to 11th, still trailing Cadillac (as it had since '56). Styling stood mostly pat, but a convertible was added to the Windsor line, which was put on the 122-inch Dodge/DeSoto wheelbase. Horsepower kept climbing: Windsors now had 290 bhp and Saratogas 310 bhp from their 354 hemis, New Yorkers 345 bhp and the latest 300D a smashing 380/390 from their 392s.

A more substantial restyle marked the "lion-hearted" '59s. Though less graceful, they scored close to 70,000 sales in that year's recovering market. The switch to all-new wedgehead V8s brought a 383-cid unit with 305 bhp for Windsor and 325 for Saratoga: a big-bore 413 gave 350 bhp in New Yorker and 380 bhp in the 300E. Though not as efficient as the hemi, the wedge was much simpler and cheaper to build.

The 300E has been unduly criticized as a performance weakling next to its hemi-powered predecessors, but road tests said it was just as quick as a 300D. With 10.1:1 compression, TorqueFlite, and a 3.31:1 rear axle ratio, the E could run 0-60 mph in less than 8.5 seconds and reach 90 mph by 17.5 seconds. Even so, production was just 550 hardtops and a mere 140 convertibles, a record low that would stand until '63.

The division moved into the '60s with repeated declarations that there would never be a small Chrysler (though there would be, of course, when the time was right and the government would allow little else). Let Buick, Olds and Pontiac rush to compacts. Dodge and Plymouth would field—and sometimes suffer with—smaller cars; Chryslers would continue to be big, brawny and luxurious. And so they were, right through the late '70s.

Output of 576 units makes the '61 New Yorker ragtop rare—then *and* now. The wheelbase stretched 126 inches. Price: $4592.

The 1960-61 models were the last of the outlandishly finned Exner-styled Chryslers and the first to employ unit construction instead of the traditional body on frame. Since "unibodies" were held together more by welds than by nuts and bolts, they weren't as prone to looseness or rattles, though they were more susceptible to rust. Stylewise, the '60s were clean—bereft of excess chrome, fitted with lots of glass and aggressive 300-style inverted-trapezoid grilles. A new option was swiveling front seats that pivoted outward through an automatic latch release when a door was opened, a feature first seen on the 300E and other '59 Chrysler products.

Wheelbases and engines were unchanged for 1960. The Saratoga was in its last year. Windsor would also depart for good, after '61. The larger-engine models comprised six varieties of luxury New Yorker. Through decade's end, New Yorker sold at an annual rate of about 20,000 units, at prices just below Imperial's and about equal to those of the larger Buicks.

As ever, the 300 was the most exciting 1960 Chrysler. Designated 300F, that year's sixth edition of the "letter-series" offered racy styling, a four-place bucket-seat interior, road-hugging suspension and a newly optional French-made Pont-a-Mousson four-speed gearbox. A set of ram-induction manifolds boosted its 413 V8 to 375 or 400 bhp—good for a standing quarter-mile of 16 seconds at 85 mph. The F rode hard but cornered better than any other car of its size. A half-dozen different axle ratios could be ordered. (With the 3.03 gearset plus a tuned engine and some streamlining, Andy Granatelli came close to 190 mph in a flying-mile run.) At $5411 for the hardtop and $5811 for the convertible, the 300F wasn't cheap, but it offered a lot for the money.

The '61 line was mostly a repeat of 1960 except for somewhat more contrived styling. Windsor, still on its 122-inch wheelbase, moved up to replace Saratoga. The base series was downpriced and renamed Newport. It quickly became Chrysler's volume line at very competitive prices starting just below $3000 through 1964, a point emphasized in division advertising. By 1965, Newport sales were exceeding 125,000 units. The '61 carried a 265-bhp 361 V8; Windsor and New Yorker retained their previous engines. That year's 300G didn't offer the four-speed option but returned to 15-inch wheels for the first time since 1956 and continued with 375- or 400-bhp engines, both with ram induction.

The 300H for '62 lost its fins; just 435 hardtops were produced.

Customers had to pay $4263 for a '62 New Yorker hardtop sedan.

Chrysler Corporation entered the Sixties in deep trouble. Sales were down—way down—and so was quality control. Chrysler dropped its flamboyant fins after 1961, and charted a more conservative, middle-of-the-road styling policy.

Only a hardtop was offered for the Chrysler 300J in '63. Output reached only 400 units. The 413 V8 cranked out 390 horses.

The 300J made its debut at an Indianapolis Speedway showing.

The 300L for '65 was the last of the famed Chrysler letter cars.

The '66 New Yorker hardtop sedan found favor with 26,559 buyers.

A semi-fastback roofline was featured on the '67 Newport Custom.

The '67 New Yorker: new grille and altered side sculpturing.

Hidden headlamps were featured on the '68 Chrysler 300 series.

Chrysler Corporation's fortunes were shaky in these years, but Chrysler Division actually improved its volume and industry rank. After sinking to 12th with over 77,000 cars for 1960, it finished 10th on better than 138,000 units for '61.

Nevertheless, the company's general sales difficulties hastened a management shakeup that had an immediate effect on products. At the end of July 1961, "Tex" Colbert retired under fire and turned over the presidency to his chosen successor, William Newberg. But Newberg quit after two months over allegations of having financial interests in several Chrysler suppliers, so he stepped aside for former administrative vice-president Lynn A. Townsend. When Townsend became board chairman in January 1967, Virgil Boyd served as president through early 1970. These changes also prompted Exner to leave in 1962 after shaping the '63 corporate line. His successor was Elwood Engel, recruited from Ford and generally credited for the elegant '61 Lincoln Continental.

The mid-1960s thus saw a new direction for Chrysler styling. For 1962, the division fielded what Exner called the "plucked chicken": a repeat of the '61 *sans* fins. The 1963-64s had "the crisp, clean custom look"—chiseled but chunky. For 1965, Engel unveiled squarish but smooth bodies with fenders edged in bright metal, one of his trademarks.

Among the '62 "plucked chickens" was a four-model group of "non-letter" 300s—hardtop coupe, sedan and hardtop sedan and a convertible—carrying the same engine as the now-departed Windsor. These sporty-looking cars offered fashionable options like center console and front bucket seats, and were quite popular at prices in the $3300-$3800 range. But they hurt that year's 300H, which cost $1200-$1600 more yet looked almost the same. As a result, letter-series volume dropped from about 1530 for '61 to just 558.

New Yorker switched to the 122-inch wheelbase for 1963-64, becoming the same general size as the less costly Chryslers, but sales were strong in both years. Arriving as 1963 "spring specials" were the 300 Pace Setter hardtop and convertible and the New Yorker Salon hardtop sedan. The former, commemorating Chrysler's selection as pace car for that year's Indianapolis 500, was identified by crossed checkered-flag emblems and special trim. The Salon came with such standard luxuries as air conditioning; AM/FM radio; Auto Pilot speed control; power brakes, steering, seats, and windows; TorqueFlite automatic; color-keyed wheel covers and vinyl roof. *Sans* Pace Setters, this lineup returned for '64. Engines and styling were both broadly the same.

The 1963-64 300J/300K (they skipped the letter "I" to avoid confusion with the number "1") were big, burly cars in the letter-series tradition. Only a hardtop J was offered; the convertible was reinstated with the K. Just 400 Js were built—an all-time low—but the K saw a healthy 3600 plus. All ran 413s with 360/390 bhp, down slightly from 300H ratings. The 300L of 1965 was the last of the true letter-series cars. It saw 2845 copies, including a mere 440 convertibles. None of these 300s were quite the performers their predecessors had been, but they remained the most roadable Chryslers. Declining sales with the advent of the non-letter 300s is what killed them, of course.

Chrysler did very well for 1965, selling over 125,000 Newports, nearly 30,000 non-letter 300s and almost 50,000 New Yorkers. Things were even better for '66: the 300 nearly doubled and Newport climbed by 42,000 units.

The post-1964 Engel Chryslers were shorter than their Exner forebears but just as big inside. Wheelbase was 124 inches on all models except wagons (121 inches through '66, then 122 inches). Expanding the '67 line were the Newport Custom two- and four-door hardtop and four-door sedan, tagged some $200 above comparable Newports and promoted as "a giant step in luxury, a tiny step in price." The luxurious New Yorker Town & Country was dropped after 1965 (few were sold that year), but six- and nine-passenger Newport wagons continued through '68, after which T&C became a separate series. Spring 1968 brought the interesting $126 Sportsgrain option—wagon-style simulated wood side paneling for Newport convertible and hardtop coupe—plus Newport Special two- and four-door hardtops with turquoise color schemes (later extended to 300s).

Engine choices for '65 involved 270- and 315-bhp 383s for Newport and 300, and a 413 with 340 or 360 bhp for New Yorkers and 300L. The smaller V8 was detuned slightly for '66, when a huge new 440-cid big-block arrived as either standard or optional, packing 325/350 bhp. A like assortment continued through 1968 offering 270-375 bhp.

These moves and the conservative Engel styling paid off in vastly higher volume: 206,000-plus for '65 and nearly 265,000 the following year. Sales dipped to near 219,000 for '67. Chrysler was 10th in the industry each year, then moved up to ninth with 1968 production that just pipped the '66 record.

The all new "fuselage-styled" '69s did almost as well. If not the most beautiful Chryslers of the decade, they were at least handsome with their big bumper/grille combinations, fulsome bodysides and low rooflines. Newport was brought up to the 124-inch

The bigger '69 Newport Custom sported all-new "fuselage" styling.

Chrysler built 400 units of the 300-H for 1970—H stood for Hurst.

Under the design direction of Elwood Engel, Chryslers from the mid- and late-Sixties featured cleaner, more elegant styling. The public apparently approved—sales improved dramatically, setting a record in 1966 and again in '68.

This 1970 gold Chrysler auto show car was known as the Cordoba.

Newport hardtop coupe output hit 22,049 for the 1971 model run.

Chrysler touted the "fresh appearance" of its 1972 Newport line.

New Yorker Brougham, at $5350, was the new top-line 1972 series.

Safety bumpers and formal grille highlighted the '73 New Yorker.

The 1974 Newport hardtop coupe stickered at $4572, plus options.

All '74 Chryslers had a 124-inch wheelbase, including New Yorker.

The '75 New Yorker Brougham hardtop sedan: $6424, 12,774 built.

Trailer towing was a snap for the 1975 Newport Custom sedan.

Chrysler's first "personal-luxury" offering was the 1975 Cordoba.

wheelbase, and all models were bigger than ever: almost 225 inches long and nearly 80 inches wide.

Predictably, the 1970s changed only in detail, but mid-year introduced the first Cordobas: a Newport hardtop coupe and sedan with paint, vinyl roof, bodyside moldings, wheels and grille all done in gold, plus unique "Aztec Eagle" upholstery. A well-equipped Newport 440 hardtop also arrived with TorqueFlite, vinyl roof and other extras as standard.

A reminder, but not a revival, of the great letter-series in 1970 was the 300-H. The "H" was for Hurst, maker of the floor-mounted shifter used for its automatic gearbox. Performance goodies abounded—special road wheels, white-letter tires, a tuned 440 V8, heavy-duty suspension—set off by a gold-and-white paint job, custom hood, trunklid spoiler, special grille, pinstriping, and unique interior. Only 500 were built. Also appearing for 1970 were Chrysler's last big convertibles, a Newport and 300 that saw respective production of just 1124 and 1077 units. The 300s bid fair as future collector's items.

Vast changes in corporate administration were evident by 1969-70. Quality control had become an end in itself as engineers struggled to correct Chrysler Corporation's poor reputation in that area. Colbert's decentralized structure had been recentralized by Townsend but retained some divisional distinctions between Dodge and Chrysler-Plymouth. Still, the Chrysler marque would face tough sledding in the '70s, partly because it hesitated to bring out a smaller car until it was almost too late.

Chrysler stayed with its basic '69 design through 1973. Style variations through '72 were made via easy-change trim items that became a bit tackier with time. The '73s gained blockier lower-body sheetmetal and a more conventional front with bigger bumpers (per federal requirements).

New for '71 was a lower-priced Newport Royal sub-series with a standard 255-bhp 360 V8, an enlarged corporate small-block. A stroked 400-cid version of the 383 more adaptable to emissions tuning replaced it for '72, then disappeared along with the 360 and all Royal models. Other Chryslers relied on the 440 with added emission controls that sapped horsepower, which was down to 215 bhp by '73 (though that was more realistic SAE net, not gross, horsepower). A popular new addition for '72 was the New Yorker Brougham, two hardtops and a sedan with lusher interiors and a $300-$400 price premium over the standard issue.

Overall, Chrysler did fairly well in this period. Sales fell off to around 177,000 for 1970-71 but recovered to nearly 205,000 for '72, then to 234,000-plus. As ever, though, Chrysler still couldn't seem to surpass Cadillac, trailing GM's flagship every year in 11th place. A milestone was observed on June 27, 1973, when the one-millionth Chrysler, a base Newport sedan, was built at the firm's Jefferson Avenue plant in Detroit.

Sales sank mightily in the wake of the first energy crisis despite a completely redesigned crop of 1974 models, still on a 124-inch wheelbase. Measuring about five inches shorter overall and bearing a crisp new look, both Chryslers and Imperials wore pseudo-classic square grilles of the sort they'd studiously avoided when this fad took hold in the early '70s. Engine options and horsepower were down: 185/205-bhp 400 V8s for Newport and Newport Custom, 230/275-bhp 440s for T&C wagons, New Yorker and New Yorker Brougham. The last was now quite like the Imperial, which was again being marketed as a Chrysler but was still registered as a separate make (and is so treated here). After 1975, the Imperial became a Brougham via the badge-engineering of which Chrysler was fond at the time—to the confusion of customers up and down the corporate line.

Few in Highland Park had foreseen the energy crisis, which only accelerated the buyer resistance to big cars that had been building because of galloping sticker prices. Sales of the record-priced 1974s dropped to 1970 levels and a two-month backlog quickly piled up, yet chairman Townsend refused to slash prices. Instead,

Newport offered "higher appearance levels" for '76, per Chrysler.

The '76 New Yorker Brougham was a '75 Imperial in all but name.

After 150,000 sales in '75, the Cordoba changed little for 1976.

A grille texture change and crown roof set the '77 Cordoba apart.

Chrysler sold 20,738 Newport hardtop sedans in model year '77.

Chrysler's biggest success during the Seventies was its new-for-1975 personal-luxury coupe, the Cordoba. It featured a formal grille, opera windows, and optional Corinthian leather interiors. Output exceeded 150,000 units the first year.

he slashed production. By early November 1974 corporate sales were down 34 percent—not as bad as GM's 43 percent decline but more serious, as Chrysler's fixed costs were spread over much smaller volume. The results were employee layoffs and an unsold inventory of 300,000 units by early 1975.

Finally, Chrysler did something no one in Detroit had ever done before: instituted cash rebates—essentially paying people to buy. Other producers had little choice but to follow. It amounted to throwing money away in an attempt to lose less on the balance sheets, but it was a necessary, if drastic, step: That big inventory was costing Chrysler $300,000 a week.

These sharp reversals prompted a complete rethink that must have seemed quite alien for a make that had solemnly promised never to build a smaller car. But the new philosophy that emerged

LeBaron, a deluxe Plymouth Volaré, made its debut for 1977.

The LeBaron Medallion coupe, with standard 318 V8, cost $5436.

A Town and Country woody wagon joined the 1978 LeBaron lineup.

The Fifth Avenue Edition was the top-line New Yorker for 1979.

All the "big" Chryslers, like this Newport, rode a 118.5-inch wheelbase for '79. The 225-cid, 110-bhp slant-six was standard.

only echoed the 1958 suggestion of then-outgoing president K.T. Keller that Chrysler should "get back to design for function, with more stress on utility."

The most visible evidence of the new order was the 1975 Cordoba. Though this personal-luxury coupe broke new ground for the marque, it wasn't really new, being largely a twin to that year's revamped Dodge Charger with styling that looked like a cross between Jaguar XJ6 and Chevy Monte Carlo. Its 115-inch wheelbase was the shortest of any Chrysler since the war—and only 2.5 inches longer than that of the very first 1924 Six.

Trumpeted as "the new small Chrysler," Cordoba was billed as something of a road car, but it really wasn't, standard anti-roll bars and steel-belted radial tires notwithstanding. Reflecting its true character were optional power seats, windows and door locks, and interiors upholstered in crushed velour or brocade cloth and vinyl. "Fine Corinthian leather," extolled on TV by Ricardo Montalban, cost extra.

The rest of the line was little changed for 1975-76, except for higher prices. The accent was now strictly on luxury with a modicum of "efficiency" thrown in. The opulent New Yorker Brougham boasted standard leather, velour or brocade upholstery, plus shag carpeting, imitation walnut appliqués, and filigree moldings. Economy, such as it was, was boosted with numerically lower final drive ratios and an optional "Fuel Pacer" system, an intake manifold-pressure sensor hooked to a warning light that glowed during heavy-footed moments.

Chrysler fielded something even smaller for 1977: the mid-size, 3500-pound M-body LeBaron. Cleanly styled in the boxy Mercedes idiom on a 112.7-inch wheelbase, it came in standard and upmarket Medallion trim as either a coupe or four-door sedan. Despite its origins in the workaday A-body Dodge Aspen/Plymouth Volaré compacts, it sold extremely well, providing timely sales assistance in a market gone wild for smaller cars. The full-size line was mildly facelifted and lost its Newport Custom series; Cordoba soldiered on in two little-changed versions.

LeBaron got greater emphasis for 1978 with the addition of lower-priced S models and a brace of Town & Country wagons (the big T&Cs were dropped). All offered 90- and 110-bhp slant-six power as an alternative to optional 140- and 155-bhp 318 V8s. The slow-selling full-sizers were further reduced by dropping pillared four-doors. The 440 V8 was still optional for them, but most were ordered with the standard 400. LeBaron had bowed with square headlamps. Cordoba now got them too.

For 1979, Chrysler issued downsized big sedans on a 118.5-inch wheelbase: six and V8 Newport and V8-only New Yorker and New Yorker Fifth Avenue. Built on the firm's 1971-vintage intermediate platform, these R-body models were considerably smaller and lighter (3500-4000 pounds) than the old mastodons but still managed to look big and heavy—which may explain why sales were underwhelming: about 133,000 in a record Detroit year. The LeBaron line now comprised base, Medallion and new mid-range Salon models plus woody-look T&C wagons, none substantially altered. Reviving the spirit of the great letter-series 300 was a mid-year option group for Cordoba comprising unique trim, bucket seats, a crossed-bars grille and a 195-bhp 360 V8 priced at $1600. It looked nice, but looks was about all it had.

Though Chrysler-watchers were now anxiously monitoring the developing business crisis in Highland Park, help was already onboard in the person of newly named chairman Lee A. Iacocca, the recently ousted president of Ford who'd moved into that job at Chrysler in late 1978. He arrived none too soon. Not only was Chrysler near bankruptcy but in "a state of anarchy," as Iaccoca wrote later in his best-selling autobiography. "There was no real committee setup, no cement in the organizational chart, no system of meetings to get people talking to each other. . . . I took one look at the system and I almost threw up. That's when I knew I was in really deep trouble.

"Chrysler had no overall system of financial controls," Iacocca continued. "Nobody in the whole place seemed to fully understand what was going on when it came to financial planning and projecting. I couldn't find out anything. I already knew about the lousy cars, the bad morale, and the deteriorating factories. But I simply had no idea that I wouldn't even be able to get hold of the right numbers so that we could begin to attack some basic problems."

Cordoba was still popular in 1979—88,015 units were built.

The 1980 Cordoba was slightly smaller and 400 pounds lighter.

LeBaron offered 17 models for 1980, including this Medallion V8.

New Yorker for '81: $10,343 plus $1535 for Fifth Avenue package.

Government-mandated safety and emissions regulations put a severe strain on Chrysler Corporation during the '70s. With a much smaller volume over which to spread the enormous cost, Chrysler was facing bankruptcy at the end of the decade.

New products to answer some of those problems were nearing completion when Iaccoca came aboard: others were further away. None would have appeared without the federal loan guarantees he managed to coax from a reluctant Congress by mid-1980.

For the Chrysler line, this dictated a holding action for 1980-81 with a few game attempts at something different. Prime among the latter was a second-generation Cordoba, a crisply reskinned LeBaron coupe on the 112.7-inch wheelbase. It was a fair success in its first year at some 54,000 units, but annual volume then ran at less than half that through '83, when Cordoba said *adios.* A 165-bhp 360 V8 was optional for 1980, after which choices thinned to standard 85-bhp 225-cid slant six or 130-bhp 318 V8. A less expensive LS edition for 1981-83 again tried to evoke letter-series memories, but few were sold.

The big R-body Newport/New Yorker provided little sales help in this period, and was abandoned after much-reduced 1981 volume of fewer than 29,000 (including a high proportion of taxi and police sales). A much happier fate awaited the M-body LeBaron, which seemed destined for extinction at the same time but is with us yet. The line was facelifted for 1980 with bolder grilles, more sharply creased fenders and, on sedans and coupes, blockier rear rooflines. Making room for the downsized Cordoba, LeBaron coupes moved to the 108.7-inch Aspen/Volaré wheelbase and gained a more closely coupled look.

What would ultimately save this design first appeared as a mid-1980 special called the LeBaron Fifth Avenue Edition, a loaded four-door with throwback styling in the image of the like-named R-body New Yorker. When the latter was cancelled and a new front-drive LeBaron instituted for '82, this one model was retained as a badge-engineered "downsized" New Yorker and showed increasing sales strength as the market recovered from its early-decade doldrums. By 1984 it was simply Fifth Avenue and up to over 88,000 sales—which jumped to 120,000-plus the next year. Remarkably, the Fifth Avenue was still bringing in over 100,000 orders as late as 1987.

There was no mystery in this. A lot of folks still craved traditional rear-drive American luxury cars. This one offered plenty of standard amenities at attractive prices that began at around $13,000 and finished the decade only some $5000 higher. Yes, the Fifth Avenue was terribly outmoded by 1989, but as tooling costs had long been amortized, Chrysler could keep prices reasonable (despite pressures to the contrary) and demand healthy. In all, this car was a pleasant surprise success for Chrysler, not least because each one sold was almost pure profit.

Meantime, Chairman Lee had been presiding over a remarkable resurgence that saw Chrysler Corporation solidly back in the black by 1983. The return to prosperity was built almost entirely on clever (if seemingly endless) permutations of the front-drive K-car platform, introduced for 1981 with the compact Dodge Aries/Plymouth Reliant. Chrysler-badged variations followed for '82. By decade's end they'd constitute virtually the entire line.

The first was a smaller LeBaron, base and Medallion coupes and sedans on the 100.1-inch K-car wheelbase. Power came from Chrysler's own newly designed 2.2-liter (135-cid) single-overhead-cam four or an optional 2.6-liter "balancer" four supplied by the firm's long-time Japanese partner, Mitsubishi. A turbocharged 2.2 spinning out 142-146 bhp was also offered and relatively popular. Replacing the old M-body line, these "CV" LeBarons were joined at mid-1982 by a woody-look Town & Country wagon and the first American-made convertibles since the mid-'70s. The latter can be fairly credited to Iacocca and were a brilliant stroke, offered in plain and nostalgic T&C trim.

Iacocca also revived long models in the spirit of the '40s and '50s with a CV-based five-passenger Chrysler Executive Sedan on a stretched 124.3-inch chassis and a seven-seat Limousine on a 131.3-inch wheelbase—the firm's first "carriage trade" cars since the last Stageway Imperial limos of 1970. Both sold in mod-

LeBaron for '82: front drive, 99.6-inch wheelbase, $8155 and up.

A Chrysler 300-style grille adorned the $8365 Cordoba LS for '82.

The '82 Chrysler New Yorker was a disguised 1977-81 LeBaron.

As it turned out, 1983 would be the last year for the Cordoba.

Chrysler revived the ragtop in 1982—here an '83 LeBaron woody.

A stretched '83 LeBaron was transformed into an Executive Sedan.

A slightly stretched LeBaron became the 1984 Chrysler E-Class.

The '85 Chrysler Town and Country woody wagon listed for $10,363.

Chrysler's aero-styled LeBaron GTS bowed for '85. Price: $9024.

The Executive Sedan was gone by '85; seen here the '86 Limousine.

Fifth Avenue for '87 sold for $15,422 plus $500 Gas Guzzler Tax.

Chrysler's sporty coupe entry was the 1984 Laser, a Dodge Daytona twin. The '86 XT stickered at $11,728, plus $993 for the turbo.

Chrysler received federal loan guarantees in mid-1980. New models in the pipeline began appearing for 1981 and even Chrysler began a switch to front-wheel drive with the '82 LeBaron. The company was out of serious trouble by 1983.

The '87 LeBaron Convertible was slotted as a personal-luxury car.

New Yorker for '87 listed at $14,193 with the 2.5-liter four.

The C-body New Yorker Landau debuted for '88 priced at $19,509.

A spring '88 model: LeBaron GTC, all in white, specially priced.

The '89 Chrysler Fifth Avenue came with a driver's side air bag.

LeBaron GTS, suffering poor sales, entered '89 mainly unchanged.

est numbers (mainly to fancy hotels and airport limo services) until Chrysler gave up on them after 1987 as just so much bother.

The CV LeBarons continued through 1986 with only minor styling and mechanical changes. A 2.2 stroked to 2.5 liters (153 cid) and 100 bhp became available that year, TorqueFlite automatic was made standard for all models, and the once-optional five-speed manual transaxle was dropped. The line quickly established itself as Chrysler's top seller, garnering around 100,000 orders annually. The notchback four-door and T&C wagon lasted through 1988.

Next in the line of K-based Chryslers was a stretched four-door, originally named "Gran LeBaron" but announced for 1983 under the prosaic E-Class title, a reference to its E-body platform. Though it spanned a three-inch longer wheelbase, the E-Class was much like the CV LeBaron except for revised rear-quarter styling, a roomier back seat and slightly higher prices, but it failed to catch on—at least as a Chrysler. After 1984 and some 80,000 examples, it was badge-engineered into Plymouth and Dodge models that sold somewhat better as new-age family cars.

A more successful spinoff was the first front-drive New Yorker. Bowing at mid-1983, this was an E-Class with more class—or what passed for it. Taking a cue from Fifth Avenue sales, stylists gave the E-body a blind-quarter padded vinyl roof, a more upright vertical-bar grille, additional chrome accents, even opera lamps (a '70s throwback). There was also a more uptown interior with Mark Cross leather upholstery (introduced with the LeBaron convertible) and high-tech tricks like the irritating Electronic Voice Alert, a "back seat driver" with a synthesized voice that nagged you from within the instrument panel. New Yorker wasn't the only Chrysler afflicted by this ill-conceived device, which was soon dropped. The car itself lasted somewhat longer, generating some 70,000 annual sales through 1987, after which it departed for a more impressive New Yorker.

The two most interesting Chryslers of the '80s were undoubtedly the Laser and LeBaron GTS. The former, new for '84, was a sleek Porsche-like "fasthatch" coupe on an abbreviated 97.1-inch-wheelbase K-car platform. A near-identical twin to the G-24 Dodge Daytona introduced alongside it, the Laser was an exciting, if somewhat crude, performer in turbo form and practical in any guise. But it may have been a little too sporty for most Chrysler buyers, because the Daytona always outsold it. As Dodge was reasserting its claim as the firm's "performance" division, C-P dealers lost the Laser after 1986 but got something more saleable instead.

GTS, a 1985 addition, was a very different LeBaron: a smooth hatchback four-door aimed at America's increasingly affluent baby-boomers and their growing preference for premium European sedans. As usual, there was a duplicate Dodge, the Lancer, sharing the same new H-body and the usual K-car underpinnings on a 103.1-inch wheelbase. Engines were the by-now familiar

Chrysler's TC by Maserati was oft-delayed on its way to market. Last word was that it was to finally appear in late 1988.

assortment of fours teamed with five-speed overdrive manual and TorqueFlite automatic transaxles.

Though no threat to the likes of BMW and Mercedes, the GTS was a competent all-round performer, surprisingly roomy and quite versatile (like Laser, its back seat folded down for extra cargo space). Over 150,000 found buyers in its first two years at starting prices in the \$9000-\$11,000 area. Volume dropped by almost 50 percent for '87, reflecting tough competition from the popular new Ford Taurus/Mercury Sable. For 1989, GTS referred only to a top-spec 2.2 turbo model, the base and mid-range offerings becoming just plain LeBarons.

As if buyers weren't already bewildered by so many LeBarons, Chrysler introduced two more for 1987: a new J-body coupe and convertible to replace the previous CV styles. Chrysler design chief Tom Gale and his staff gave them rounded, GTS-like contours, a clean yet dignified hidden-headlamp nose, and a shapely tail with full-width light panel. From the rear the coupe was nicely reminiscent of Studebaker's Avanti. The convertible looked great from any angle, especially top down.

Though the CV wheelbase was retained, the Js' inner structure related more to Daytona than K-car. By now, corporate planners were seeking to reestablish Chrysler as their premium make, so there were no divisional doubles of these LeBarons. Instead, Chrysler gave up the Laser and the Daytona continued as a Dodge exclusive. This strategy helped the latter less than the LeBaron Js, which got off to a strong sales start at nearly 75,500 units.

New Yorker was the subject of another name game for 1988: fully revised on the 104.3-inch-wheelbase C-body platform shared with Dodge's new Dynasty. At first there were no major chassis innovations, but there was a new engine: a smooth 136-bhp 3.0-liter (181-cid) Mitsubishi V6 with electronic port fuel injection (now almost universal at Highland Park). Styling was clean but archly conservative—really a cautious update of the Fifth Avenue and

A 136-bhp Mitsubishi 3.0-liter V6 powered the '88 New Yorker.

As the Eighties ended, Chrysler had pared its lineup to two basic series, the C-body New Yorker and J-body LeBaron coupe/convertible. However, Chrysler looked forward to entering the '90s with a new front-drive Fifth Avenue and Imperial.

Although based on the Dodge Daytona/Chrysler Laser platform, the '89 LeBaron Coupe really filled in for Chrysler's 1975-83 Cordoba.

said to have been personally dictated by Chairman Lee. Base and better-equipped Landau sedans (the latter with a rear vinyl quarter-roof) were listed from around $17,500. A first for Chrysler was availability of anti-lock brakes—a $1000 option but worth every penny in peace of mind. Handling and performance were nothing special, but these were merely traditional luxury cars of a trimmer, more efficient sort—really, no bad thing to be.

And Chrysler made them better for 1989 with standard all-disc brakes and a new four-speed automatic transaxle that marked an industry first with its fully adaptive electronic shift control. Other new features for the New Yorker nameplate's 50th year included an optional electronic anti-theft alarm system, power front seat-back recliners, two-position "memory" power driver's seat, and a revised electronic instrument cluster.

New in 1988, the '89 Chrysler New Yorker saw only minor changes.

Symbolic of Chrysler's '80s renaissance was its first-ever production two-seater: the TC by Maserati, first shown in mid-1986 but delayed by numerous problems to a late-1988 showroom debut as an '89 model. Maserati, of course, is the well-known Italian sports-car maker in which Chrysler acquired a minority interest earlier in the '80s, but its main role in this joint venture was simply to build Chrysler's design.

Almost too predictably, the TC was yet another K-clone: a shortened 93.3-inch-wheelbase version of that ubiquitous platform topped by a wedgy convertible body looking much like the open LeBaron J (though the TC was actually created first). Powerteams comprised a special 200-bhp turbocharged 2.2 with intercooler, port injection and a new 16-valve twincam cylinder head designed with Maserati's assistance, available only with five-speed manual; and a single-cam 160-bhp Turbo II for buyers preferring three-speed automatic. The customer's only other choice was paint color, the TC being sold as a fully equipped "optionless" model priced at $30,000.

Besides the expected leather upholstery and full power assists, that price included all-disc brakes with anti-lock control, a manually operated soft top with heated glass rear window, and a removable plastic hard top (made of sheet molding compound). The last had a nostalgic styling touch: rear-quarter portholes, recalling the '56 Thunderbird and the earliest days of Iacocca's career at Ford.

Yet for all this, the TC generated little enthusiasm from the automotive press. Its similarity to the much cheaper LeBaron convertible was obvious; handling, refinement and performance undistinguished—all rather unfortunate for a car seeking to carry Chrysler's colors up into the rarefied "ultra-luxury" field. Yet if nothing else, the TC showed that Chrysler was still hanging in there with high hopes for the future—remarkable enough for a make that had almost no future a decade before.

CLIPPER

Marketing wizard James J. Nance became president of Packard in 1952. Immediately, he started to divorce the medium-priced 200 models from Packard's luxury lines, declaring that continued emphasis on cheaper models after World War II had been "bleeding the Packard name white." The 200 duly became the 1953 Packard Clipper. For 1956, Nance registered Clipper as a separate make. There were separate Packard and Clipper dealer signs, and even a new Packard-Clipper Division of Studebaker-Packard Corporation (Packard purchased the debt-ridden South Bend automaker in 1954). The Packard name appeared nowhere on these cars except for a tiny script on decklids. Early examples didn't even have that.

Nance's aim was to distinguish Clipper even further from the senior Packards. Plans for 1957 called for Clipper to use the larger of two new bodyshells proposed for Studebaker, while Packard would continue with its own. But none of these plans materialized because lenders failed to commit sufficient funds for the corporation to finance its all-new 1957 line. Nance resigned in August 1956.

Studebaker-Packard received a temporary reprieve by way of a management agreement with Curtiss-Wright Corporation, which used S-P mainly as a tax write-off. Under this arrangement, the Packard name was applied to a deluxe line of 1957 Studebaker-based cars. But these were called Packard Clippers, so Clipper as a make lasted only a year.

The '56 Clipper line comprised five models: Deluxe, Super and Custom four-door sedans and Super and Custom Constellation hardtop coupes. All shared a 122-inch wheelbase and an overhead-valve Packard V8 of 352 cubic inches producing 275 horsepower for Customs, 240 bhp in other models. Also featured was Packard's innovative Torsion-Level suspension, continued from '55, although a conventional suspension was available on the bottom-line Deluxe. Options included overdrive manual transmission ($110) and Ultramatic automatic transmission ($199).

These Clippers were luxuriously trimmed and nicely styled, though their sales volume wasn't sufficient to help the company. The Deluxe sedan was the best-seller. The handsome Custom Constellation hardtop was rarest, accounting for fewer than 1500 units. As on this year's senior Packards, styling was an evolution of the previous year's heavy facelift on the old 1951 "high pockets" body executed by Richard A. Teague. Though still obvious Packard relatives, Clippers retained their own grille and tail designs, made even more different for '56 in line with Nance's goal.

Making Clipper a separate make was a good idea that came too late. Had the firm taken this approach in the huge seller's market of 1946, Packard might well be with us today.

The Clipper was listed as a separate make for 1956. The Custom Constellation hardtop sold for $3164; only 1466 were built.

Hard-driving Packard president James J. Nance wanted to reestablish Packard as a true luxury make, so he registered the "junior" Packard—the Clipper—as a separate make for 1956. Alas, the change came to late to help Packard *or* Clipper.

CONTINENTAL

Officially, the Continental "Marks" of 1956-58 were not Lincolns but products of a separate Ford division created to establish the firm's dominance in the uppermost reaches of the market—even higher than Cadillac. Only one model was offered for 1956-57: the flawlessly styled, beautifully crafted Mark II. Though priced at a stratospheric $10,000, it was worth every penny. Yet Ford lost about $1000 on every one, because this was primarily an "image" car—more of an ego trip than a calculated profit-maker. An attempt was made to put Continental in the black with a lower-priced 1958-60 line based on the standard Lincoln, but it never sold particularly well.

Ford had been pressured by dealers and customers to build a successor to the original Lincoln Continental ever since its demise in 1948. But there was no money for it until 1953, when profits were looking up and Dearborn management, determined to outflank GM in every market sector, approved a development program to recreate the Continental in the contemporary idiom.

William Clay Ford, the younger brother of company president Henry Ford II, was put in charge of a new Special Products Division to come up with a design. After calling in five outside consultants to submit their ideas for comparison, management reviewed 13 different proposals and unanimously selected the one from . . . Special Products.

It was, nevertheless, an excellent choice. Harley F. Copp, the division's chief engineer, gave it a unique "cowbelly" chassis dipped low between front and rear axles to permit high seating

Continental was listed as a separate make in 1956-57; the Mark II was built by the Continental Division of Ford Motor Company.

The Mark II sold for a breathtaking $10,000 in 1956. Specially assembled Lincoln engines and only the finest cowhide were used.

without a high roofline. The cockpit was starkly simple but richly appointed, the dash inspired by aircraft and locomotive designs. Power would be supplied by Lincoln's new 368-cubic-inch V8 with 285 horsepower, each engine specially selected from the assembly line and individually balanced. They teamed with Multi-Drive, Lincoln's new three-speed automatic transmission, and 3.07:1 rear axles.

Riding a 126-inch wheelbase, the sleek and timeless Mark II measured 218.5 inches overall and weighed close to 4900 pounds. It was offered only as a coupe, though a retractable hardtop-convertible had been proposed (an idea later developed by Ford Division into the 1957-59 Skyliner). The Mark II was greeted with enthusiasm on both sides of the Atlantic, immediately hailed as one of Detroit's all-time design greats.

But the euphoria didn't last. Though Continental Division was hoping to add a beautiful four-door sedan and perhaps a convertible for 1958, word from the sales department deflated those hopes. The Mark II had not had much impact on the luxury market; General Motors was still the leader. A moneyed few were indeed buying Mark IIs, but the car was not convincing those with slightly less cash to buy Lincolns. Production totalled just 1325 of the '56s and a mere 444 of the '57s.

Years later, one Ford executive declared that the Mark II program was, on balance, a big mistake. "For obvious reasons we don't like to talk about it...What we had going for us in the Mark II was literally a revival of the Duesenberg concept. What we ended up with was something much less—and even that didn't last long . . . It was a project that for a time broke Bill Ford's heart, and I guess you could say that in many ways it broke ours too."

In line with an upper management decision, the Mark II's $10,000 price was cut drastically with 1958's "new" Continental, the Mark III. The result of recommendations from a Mercury cost analyst, this square-rigged Lincoln-based giant had a 131-inch wheelbase, elongated fenders, large chrome appliqués, canted quad headlamps, a reverse-slanted roofline and a huge new 430-cid V8 with 375 bhp. Convertible, four-door sedan, hardtop coupe and Landau hardtop sedan were offered in the $5800-$6200 range. A unique feature on all was a rear window that dropped down electrically to improve interior ventilation. Standard luxuries abounded, but the Mark III had been "built to a price" and, at that price, sales improved—a respectable 12,550 for the model year.

For 1959, "Continental" disappeared as a separate marque and became a Lincoln series. Continental Division was absorbed by Lincoln-Mercury, which also acquired the fast-faltering Edsel Division, thus ending Ford's dream of a GM-like hierarchy. The genealogy of the 1968 Mark III, which was given that numeral to emphasize its "official" status as lineal successor to the 1956-57 Mark II, is a bit hazy: To some it is a Lincoln, for others strictly a Continental. Ford Motor Company itself generally includes this Mark III and its successors under the "Lincoln" badge, so we do too (*see* Lincoln).

The '58 Continental Mark III was in reality a deluxe Lincoln.

Mark III prices were more moderate—$6283 for the soft top.

In its quest to surpass Cadillac, Ford debuted a larger, more luxurious Lincoln for 1956 and ushered in the Continental Mark II, an ultra-luxury model priced closer to Rolls-Royce. The Mark II was probably Ford's grandest failure of all time.

CROSLEY

Powel Crosley, Jr., the Cincinnati radio and refrigerator magnate of the '20s and '30s, turned to the auto business in 1939. Deciding that Americans needed something more efficient than Detroit's wares, he proffered a tiny, 80-inch-wheelbase economy car carrying the lowest price in the land: $325-$350. Measuring just 10 feet long and weighing a bit less than half a ton, it garnered a modest 2017 sales its first year. To buy one in 1939, you visited your local hardware store or appliance shop—a novel if short-sighted marketing scheme. Crosley Motors built about 5000 cars by 1942, when the government halted civilian car production for the duration of World War II.

The two-cylinder Crosley wagon sold for a modest $450 in 1940.

A 12-horsepower engine propelled the 925-pound '39 convertible.

Crosley offered just two models for '39: a two-passenger coupe and four-passenger sedan, both with two-door convertible styles. Offerings expanded to five for 1940, priced as low as $299: standard and DeLuxe convertible sedans, wood-body station wagon, a convertible, a "covered wagon" with full canvas top, and several commercial bodies. Styling was basic, dominated by low, free-standing fenders and a prominent hood bulging out ahead of small horizontal grilles built into the front apron. Headlamps attached to the sides of the hood. Interiors were barren—just a central speedometer flanked by fuel and water gauges.

Through 1942, Crosley power came from an air-cooled, two-main-bearing Waukeshaw twin producing just 13½ horsepower from 39.8 cubic inches. Performance wasn't quite as bad as the specifications suggest, since gearing was ultra-low (5.14:1 and 5.57:1). Top speed was about 50 miles an hour, though the factory recommended a cruising velocity of no more than 40 mph. Crosley claimed up to 60 miles per gallon, though few owners likely exceeded 50 mpg.

Completing this bare-bones economy package were unsynchronized three-speed gearbox, cable-operated mechanical brakes, six-gallon fuel tank, sliding (instead of roll-down) door windows, a single hand-operated windshield wiper, and tiny 4.25×12-inch tires on simple disc wheels. The customary universal joints were eliminated as a further aid to rock-bottom price. Flexible rubber engine mounts supposedly made them unnecessary.

But they were necessary, as owners found out. They also discovered that Crosley dealers were better equipped to fix refrigerators than cars. With this, 1940 volume fell by more than three-fourths despite the expanded lineup.

Crosley called in engineer Paul Klotsch, late of the Briggs Manufacturing Company, to fix things up for '41. He redesigned the motor mounts, added U-joints to the driveshaft, revised the lubrication system, shortened stroke and increased main-bearing surface area—the last two to improve engine durability. The revised twin ended up at 35.3 cid and 12 bhp, but it powered a greatly improved Crosley and sales went up—to 2289—despite higher prices ($339-$496). The cars were now sold through separate automobile dealers in addition to Crosley's appliance outlets. There were no technical changes for '42 but prices rose again (to $468-$582) and the "covered wagon" was dropped. Crosley built 1029 cars for the war-shortened model year.

For a wartime U.S. Navy project, Crosley developed an overhead-cam four-cylinder engine using brazed copper and sheet steel for the block. Called "CoBra," it was selected to power Crosley's first postwar cars. This five-main-bearing unit had been fairly successful in a variety of machines from truck refrigerators to Mooney Mite airplanes, but was less than happy in a car. The copper-steel block was subject to electrolysis that caused holes to develop in the cylinders, thus necessitating early rebuilds. Crosley soon rectified the fault by offering a cast-iron version—called CIBA, for Cast-Iron Block Assembly—of the same 44-cid size and

26.5 bhp output. Significantly, used-car price guides of the day gave a higher trade-in value for cars with the cast-iron engine, including retrofitted 1946-48 models.

Production of the '46 Crosleys began in June of that year. A two-door four-seat sedan appeared first, joined later that year by a convertible. A wagon returned for '47; a delivery sedan arrived for '48. Commercial bodies were also offered. Wheelbase was unchanged, but styling now endeavored to make the cars seem more "grown up"—which they were: 28 inches longer than prewar Crosleys. Prices were more than double what they'd been in '39 but, at $888 in 1947, the Crosley was still quite inexpensive.

For a time, things went well. Crosley built almost 5000 1946 models, more than 19,000 for '47 and close to 29,000 of its '48s. Powel Crosley grandly predicted 80,000 a year in the near future, but his firm would never do as well again. New postwar designs from the independents and the Big Three plus Crosley's growing reputation for engine problems drastically lowered 1949 production, the total tumbling to less than 7500.

This was ironic, because the Crosley had become a much better car for '49. There was new styling with a smooth hood and integral front fenders bearing sealed-beam headlights, plus remote-control door handles and turn indicators on sedans and convertibles. In addition, Crosley fielded a smart little "bugeyed" roadster called Hotshot on an 85-inch wheelbase, priced at just $849.

Seeking to turn things around, Crosley offered wagon, convertible, and sedan body styles in standard and Super trim for 1950, plus two roadsters: the doorless Hotshot and the slightly better-trimmed Super Sports, a Hotshot with conventional doors. Crosley was still in a class by itself on price ($872-$984 that year) but its engineering was also unique. Disc brakes, for example, had arrived for 1949-50, a first for series production shared with Chrysler's 1950 Town & Country Newport. Alas, insufficient development led the Crosley brakes to deteriorate quickly when exposed to road salt and grime, thus causing tremendous service woes. Since the firm was still smarting—having recovered from the rash of problems with its unlamented sheetmetal engine—this new problem was the last thing dealers (or customers) needed. Conventional drum brakes were reinstituted for 1951. Though the little roadsters failed to sell, they were tremendous class competitors in racing. They could do up to 90 mph off the showroom floor and offered excellent handling, thanks to their crude but effective semi-elliptic-and-coil-spring front suspension and quarter-elliptic rear suspension. The Hotshot's greatest accomplishment was winning the Index of Performance at Sebring in 1951 after a fine showing in the 12-hour endurance race.

But buyers were unmoved by this or anything Crosley was doing, forcing the firm to give up on cars in July 1952. It was soon acquired by General Tire and Rubber, which quickly disposed of its automotive operations after Powel Crosley had spent about $3 million trying to save them.

The 1947 ragtop weighed in at 1150 pounds, retailed for $949.

By 1949, Crosley weighed 1363 pounds, but had 26.5 bhp to cope.

The SuperSports roadster was added for 1950. It cost but $925.

Crosley's shot at the multi-purpose market was the '50 FarmORoad.

Powell Crosley, Jr., should have looked at the unsuccessful American Austin and American Bantam ventures before launching his tiny Crosley in 1939. Had he done so, he would have learned—for free—that Americans wouldn't buy little cars.

DeSOTO

In the '20s, when prosperity looked like it was going to last forever, Detroit automakers looked on expansion as a way of life, and new makes proliferated. General Motors brought forth the Marquette, Viking, and Pontiac. Chrysler purchased Dodge, then introduced the low-priced Plymouth and medium-priced DeSoto in 1928.

DeSoto's design evolution generally paralleled Chrysler's with one key exception. While Chrysler continued conventionally styled cars for 1934, DeSoto relied exclusively on the radical Airflow. The result was a sales disaster. By mid-decade, it was even money whether DeSoto would survive.

Side-valve L-head sixes were DeSoto's mainstay after 1932: an 82-bhp 217.8-cubic-inch engine for '33, a 100-bhp 241.5-cid unit for 1934-36, thereafter a 228.1 cid with 93 or 100 bhp. All were cast-iron, four-main-bearing engines, smaller versions of their Chrysler counterparts. Styling was related, too: formal, bolt-upright for 1930-31; modified somewhat with barrel-like grilles through '33; the controversial Airflow for '34; the last plus more conventional Airstream models for 1935-36.

All the pros and cons of the Chrysler Airflow held for the DeSoto version. The engine, at least, was a survivor. Destroked for 1937, then enlarged again for 1941 and '51, it remained the division's sole powerplant until the brilliant "FireDome" V8 arrived for 1952. Vice-free and reliable, it would run forever in exchange for an occasional quart of oil and could return good gas mileage—up to 22 mpg.

Late-'30s DeSotos were increasingly larger and duller. Long sedans and limousines on a 130-inch wheelbase were added for

The 1941 DeSoto Custom business coupe weighed in at 3144 pounds, sold for $982, and saw production of just 2033 units.

'36, then went to a 136-inch chassis for '38. Styling, by the great Ray Dietrich of coachbuilding fame, was very conservative, though it matched contemporary tastes. A national recession cut 1938 output and DeSoto ran 12th in volume that year. The industry recovered the following year, but class rivals did much better than DeSoto.

The DeSoto line had settled into a consistent pattern by 1938: DeLuxe and Custom models selling at around $900 and $1000, respectively, sharing the same orthodox chassis with a standard 119-inch wheelbase. Open body styles were conspicuous by their absence for 1939, though a sliding sunroof was offered on selected closed models. Styling still left something to be desired. A '39 DeSoto looked like a Plymouth on steroids. Dumpy appearance would remain one of the make's big sales handicaps until well after World War II.

For 1940, more attractive Dietrich-designed bodywork arrived, the Custom convertible coupe (but not convertible sedan) was reinstated, and wheelbases grew to 122.5 inches standard, 139.5 extended. Though model year production went up by some 11,000 units, DeSoto again finished 13th in the industry race. Like other Chrysler makes, it might have fared better had the company not suffered a crippling strike at the start of 1940 production.

Volume soared with introduction of the '41s, jumping from 65,500 to over 97,000 on the strength of a heavy facelift. These were good-looking cars with lower hoods and bolder front ends. Grilles sported prominent vertical "teeth," which would be a DeSoto hallmark through 1955. Standard models lost an inch in wheelbase but were 5.5 inches longer overall than the '40s, as well as wider and lower. New to DeSoto was Chrysler's semi-automatic Fluid Drive transmission that greatly simplified gear-changing. There was also a new model: the Custom Town Sedan, a formal but pretty adaptation of the standard issue with closed-in ("blind") rear roof quarters and priced about $50 higher. DeSoto wooed buyers with numerous extras including under-seat heater, pushbutton radio and streamlined fender skirts.

A more extensive restyle for 1942 brought "Airfoil" hidden headlamps that remained "out of sight, except at night." While not an industry first (the 1936-37 Cord 810/812 had something similar), they were Detroit's only hidden lamps that year and imparted a cleaner look up front. Emphasizing them was a grille placed entirely on the lower half of the car's "face." A sculpted lady was introduced as a hood mascot.

Offerings were unchanged for '42, but there was a "squarer" six, bored out to 236.6 cid. Somewhat detuned and rated at 115 bhp, it would power all DeSotos for the rest of the decade. There wasn't much time for specials in this war-shortened model year, but DeSoto managed a plush Fifth Avenue version of the Custom Town Sedan. Distinguished outside only by small nameplates, it boasted luxurious leather and Bedford cloth inside and sold for about $75 more than the regular Town Sedan. Production was low everywhere in Detroit, and DeSoto's '42s were no exception: fewer than 25,000 built—fewer than 1000 of some individual models.

DeSoto returned to civilian production with an abbreviated model line, though drivetrain and chassis combinations were the same as '42. Cancellation of the long-wheelbase DeLuxe left only three extended-chassis models, all Customs: limo, seven-passenger sedan, and an intriguing newcomer, the Suburban. The last was designed to provide the ultimate in stylish cargo hauling for hotels, airports and well-heeled individuals. A fold-down rear seat *sans* trunk partition made for a huge cargo hold. A metal-and-wood roof rack and beautifully fitted wood interior panels completed the package. Not surprisingly, the Suburban was the costliest '46 DeSoto: $2093, exactly $200 more than the seven-seat sedan.

As with all Chrysler makes, the 1947-48 DeSotos were largely '46 carryovers; serial numbers are the only guide to model years. All wore a mild facelift of prewar styling with headlamps re-exposed, fenders flowing into the front doors, a heavier and wider

A 100-bhp L-head six powered the 1940 DeLuxe coupe. Price: $845.

The Custom four door was the favored 1941 model: 30,876 built.

Hidden headlights were the big news on the '42 Custom four door.

The Custom two-door sedan sold for $1142; only 913 were produced.

The 1946 eight-passenger Suburban included a luggage roof rack.

Captain Charles A. Lindbergh made the first nonstop solo flight from New York to Paris in May 1928. That same month, Chrysler formed the DeSoto Motor Corporation, named after the Spanish explorer who discovered the Mississippi River.

It took $1761 to purchase a brand-new 1946 Custom convertible.

The 1948 DeLuxe four-door sedan had escalated in price to $1825. It had been $1461. The 236.6-cid six was rated at 109 bhp.

grille, reshuffled medallions and parking lights, and deeper rear fenders. Horsepower was listed at 109 for 1946-48, down 6 bhp from '42, the result of a new rating method, not mechanical alterations. Besides "civilian" cars, DeSoto built 11,600 taxicabs in these years—its fifth best-seller. Suburban production was also quite satisfactory: 7500 for the period.

The 1949 DeSotos were all-new, as were other Chrysler products that year. Standard wheelbase was lengthened four inches (to 125.5 inches) and styling was boxy and upright, typical of the company's new postwar look, but dull compared to Ford and GM. A vertical-bar grille was retained, similar to the 1942-48 design, but the lady mascot was replaced by a bust of Hernando DeSoto. Like many hood ornaments at the time, this one glowed when the parking or headlights were switched on. Horsepower rose by three, to 112. Fluid Drive with "Tip-Toe hydraulic shift" became standard on Customs and a $121 option for DeLuxes.

Appearing in March after a brief run of old-style models to fill the gap, the '49 lineup featured some interesting new utility models. The DeLuxe series included a $2959 woody wagon and the all-steel Carry-All, similar to the Suburban but on the standard chassis. The Suburban itself returned in the Custom line, still on the long wheelbase shared with an eight-passenger sedan (the limo was dropped). As before, the Suburban offered vast cargo space and a roof-top luggage rack, plus rear jump seats that gave it true nine-passenger capacity. The Carry-All handily sold 2690 copies for the model year, but the wagon did only 680, the Suburban a mere 129. The woody lasted only through 1950, the Suburban and Carry-All through '52.

Overall, 1949 was a less-than-spectacular DeSoto year. Volume remained at the '48 level—about 92,500—and the make again finished 12th. However, Customs outsold DeLuxes by 3-1, a sign of growing buyer preference for more luxurious cars. There were few changes for 1950 aside from somewhat sleeker rear ends and the arrival of DeSoto's first hardtop coupe, called Sportsman, in the Custom series. Styling was touched up again for '51, when the venerable L-head six was stroked to 250.6 cid, though that yielded only four extra horsepower. Chrome was much in evidence, perhaps more so than for any other Chrysler product, especially in those toothy fronts. Despite the relative lack of change, model year production leaped to nearly 134,000 units for 1950, a gain of almost 45 percent. The '51 tally eased to 106,000 and DeSoto dropped from 12th to 15th, passed by Kaiser on the strength of its beautiful new '51 design and Hudson with its powerful new six-cylinder Hornets.

DeSoto's first-ever V8 was the major development for '52. Called FireDome, it was a slightly smaller, 276.1-cid version of the brilliant overhead-valve, hemispherical-head Chrysler unit introduced the previous year. With a rated 160 bhp, it put DeSoto firmly in Detroit's escalating "horsepower race."

The FireDome powered a new like-named top-of-the-line series that duplicated Custom offerings save the Suburban. It immediately garnered nearly 50,000 sales, but DeSoto could do no better than 88,000 total for the year, though it moved up a bit in the production stakes, finishing 13th.

For 1953, remaining Custom/DeLuxe models were combined into a new Powermaster Six series that still lagged behind the FireDome in sales, this time by a margin of 2-1. Both groups included Sportsman hardtops, and the growing influence of Virgil Exner was seen in an update of DeSoto's more massive 1952 styling, with new one-piece windshields and more liberal use of bright accents. Model year production jumped back to 130,000 and DeSoto moved up to 11th place, its highest finish in years.

Adding much-needed pizzazz to DeSoto's dour image in 1954 was the interesting Adventurer I show car. This was one in a special series of sporty Virgil Exner designs begun with the Chrysler K-310 of 1951. All were built mainly by Ghia in Italy. Riding a shortened 111-inch wheelbase, Adventurer I was an off-

All-new styling was featured on the 1949 DeSoto, here a Custom.

The 1950 eight-passenger DeLuxe: 139.5-inch wheelbase, 235 built.

A toothy grille and smoother frontal appearance were seen for '51.

A 160-bhp Hemi powered the 1953 FireDome ragtop; 1700 were built.

During most of its existence, DeSoto slotted between Dodge and Chrysler in the corporate hierarchy and sold to a relatively conservative upper-middle class clientele. Sales generally hovered around the 100,000-unit level.

The '55 Fireflite Sportsman listed at $2939; 10,313 were built.

white close-coupled coupe fitted with outside exhausts, wire wheels and full instrumentation. It came close to production—closer than any other Exner special. "Had it been mass-produced," the designer later said, "it would have been the first four-passenger sports car made in this country. It was better than a 2+2, and of course it had the DeSoto Hemi. It was my favorite car." Adventurer II followed in '55, a standard-chassis four-seat coupe designed more by Ghia than Exner. Painted deep red, fitted with wire wheels and lacking bumpers, it was sleek but not quite as integrated as Adventurer I, and wasn't seriously considered for production.

Meantime, the first of Exner's new "Forward Look" production models was due for 1955, so DeSoto's old '49 bodyshell was modestly reworked one last time for '54. The V8 was tweaked to 170 bhp, but the big news came at mid-year with the debut of two-speed PowerFlite, Chrysler's first fully automatic transmission. This would be a DeSoto standard after '54, thus ending the standard three-speed manual. Fluid Drive was still around (at $130 extra), as was overdrive ($96). This would also be the last year for long sedans and the Powermaster Six. Reflecting Chrysler Corporation's 1954 sales nightmare, DeSoto's model year output dropped to below 77,000 and the make slipped to 12th.

Much bolder, fully up-to-date new Exner styling and more powerful engines stood to turn things around for 1955. Firedome now played "second banana" to a new uplevel Fireflite line. Both rode a 126-inch wheelbase and were powered by a hemi V8 bored out to 291 cid. Respective power ratings were 185 and 200 bhp. No '55 Chrysler product was sedate and DeSoto was possibly the most glittery of all—though still attractive, with a much lower silhouettes, wrapped windshield, the ever-toothy front end (though this would be DeSoto's last), "gullwing" dash and broad, optional two-toning. This package appealed to buyers and sold well, boosting division output to nearly 115,000 units, though that was only good for 13th in a year when most every Detroit make did very well.

Firedome offered DeSoto's only '55 wagon, along with a de-trimmed Special hardtop priced some $110 below its Sportsman counterpart. The plush Coronado sedan, an addition to the Firedome line at mid-1954, returned as a "spring special" in the new Fireflite series at a $100 premium over the regular $2800 sedan. It's now a minor collector's item, mainly for having one of the industry's first three-tone paint jobs (turquoise, black and white). Convertibles were available in both '55 DeSoto series but saw minuscule sales: just 625 Firedomes and 775 Fireflites.

For 1956, a longer stroke brought DeSoto's hemi to 330.4 cid, lifting Firedome horsepower to 230 bhp and the Fireflite's to 255. The trademark grille teeth were replaced with wire mesh and unreadable gold-on-white instruments appeared, but the big change, as on other Chrysler lines, was tailfins—still pretty modest and carrying distinctive "tri-tower" taillamps (stacked pairs of round red lenses separated by a matching backup lamp).

Following GM's lead, four-door hardtops arrived in force: a Sportsman in each series and a lower-priced Firedome Seville. A Seville hardtop coupe replaced the previous Firedome Special. (Cadillac's new-for-'56 Eldorado two-door hardtop was also called Seville, but no legal battles ensued.) A mid-season highlight was the limited-edition Adventurer hardtop coupe, a supercar awash in gold anodized aluminum trim. Carrying a new 341-cid, 320-bhp

A spring 1955 model was the three-tone Fireflite Coronado four door. It was DeSoto's most luxurious sedan that year.

The '56 DeSoto sprouted modest fins. The Fireflite Sportsman hardtop listed at $3346 and saw production of 8475 units.

hemi, it was part of an expanded 1956 Highland Park performance squadron that included the Chrysler 300B, Plymouth Fury, and Dodge D-500. DeSoto paced the '56 Indy 500, and the division celebrated by reeling off about 100 "Pacesetter" replicas, all Fireflite convertibles with Adventurer-style trim, priced at $3615 apiece.

DeSoto shared in the industry's general 1956 retreat, building about 4300 fewer cars, but returned to 11th place due to fast-fading sales at Nash and Hudson, Studebaker and Packard. The division finished in that spot again for '57 even though volume jumped to about 110,500—as near as DeSoto ever came to passing Chrysler (ending up about 7200 units behind).

No wonder. The '57s were not only all-new for the second time in three years but superbly engineered and strikingly styled. A low-cost Firesweep series on the 122-inch Dodge wheelbase joined the two existing lines in another effort to extend DeSoto's market territory. It helped. The Firesweep sedan sold for only $2777, whereas the cheapest Firedome was $2958. The line also included two- and four-door hardtops and six-seat Shopper and nine-passenger Explorer four-door wagons. That year's Fireflite series offered all these plus a convertible; Firedome was the same but had no wagons.

All were big, heavy, powerful cars. The two upper series used the 341 V8 from the '56 Adventurer with 270 and 290 bhp, respectively. Firesweeps had the previous year's 330 debored to 325 cid and tuned for 245 bhp standard, 260 bhp optional. Last but not least, a soft-top Adventurer joined the hardtop coupe, both boasting 345 bhp from a modestly bored new 345-cid V8.

Dramatic new Virgil Exner styling made finned fantasies of all '57 Chrysler products. DeSoto's version of this second-generation Forward Look was quite handsome: smooth rear panels, attractively reworked tri-tower taillights, simple but pleasant side moldings, a unique front bumper/grille, acres more glass.

Yet as good as this was, DeSoto could not survive on looks alone. As if on cue, production plunged to 50,000 units the following year—the make's lowest total since 1938. The '58 recession, poor workmanship on the '57s, and unwise marketing decisions all

With 44,090 built, buyers preferred the '56 Firedome four door.

DeSoto exchanged its conservative tailoring for splashy party garb in 1955. The new models were colorful, especially with three-tone paint jobs. The '56 DeSoto added fins and triple taillights, and looked even flashier than the '55 model.

Adventurer was DeSoto's '57 performance model. A 345-bhp V8 made it scat, but only 1650 of the $3995 hardtops were built.

contributed to a downward spiral from which DeSoto would never recover.

Predictably, the '58 DeSotos were basically the same as the '57s save for busier grilles, more ornate trim and standard quad headlights. (Because some states had not approved "quadrilights" for '57, DeSoto front fenders were designed to accept either one or two lamps each, the latter available where law permitted. By '58, four-lamp systems were legal nationwide.) The '57 lineup returned along with a new Firesweep convertible. This year's Adventurer ragtop was the most expensive DeSoto ever ($4272), though Chrysler's corresponding 300D convertible cost $1300 more.

Engines and power ratings grew for '58, but as the hemi was ever complicated and costly to build, Chrysler began switching to wedgehead designs. Among them were two new DeSoto "Turboflash" V8s. Firesweeps had a 350-cid version with 280 bhp standard or 295 optional. Other models used a big-bore 361 that delivered 295 bhp in standard Firedome tune, up to 355 bhp in the Adventurer (with optional fuel injection, expensive and thus rarely ordered).

Even without hemi heads, these DeSotos were quite quick, helped by fast-shifting three-speed TorqueFlite automatic transmission, new for '57. Torsion-bar suspension, another '57 advance, made them among the most roadworthy Detroiters. A Fire-

The '57 Fireflite Sportsman listed at $3614. Output: 7217 units.

Shopper was the '57 Fireflite wagon. At $3982, only 837 were sold.

The 1958 Fireflite convertible has always been rare—only 474 were produced for that recession year. The sticker read $3972.

dome with the optional 305-bhp setup (standard for Fireflite) could scale 0-60 mph in 7.7 seconds, 0-80 mph in 13.5 seconds, and reached 115 mph with little strain.

DeSoto claimed its towering tailfins of this era "added stability at speed," but it was pure propaganda. The fins did little from an aerodynamic standpoint under 80 mph. Their main purpose was to make Chrysler products stand out from the opposition, which they most definitely did.

But fins and flash couldn't keep DeSoto from being squeezed out of the market by Dodge from below and Chrysler from above, and though the same broad lineup returned for another year, 1959 marked the beginning of DeSoto's end. Firesweeps were upgraded to the 361 V8, offered in just one, 295-bhp version. Other models got an even larger new 383 with 305 bhp for Firedome, 325 for Fireflite and 350 bhp on Adventurer. The last saw slightly improved sales, but total model year production of just under 46,000 was hardly the kind of volume that had sustained DeSoto earlier in the decade.

Rumors of DeSoto's imminent demise began cropping up in '59, and naturally affected sales. Although calendar year production was up slightly from '58, volume for both years was less than half that of 1957's near 120,000 units. Though the recession had put DeSoto in the same kind of trouble as Oldsmobile, Buick, and Mercury, those rivals all had higher volume and could thus better withstand the downturn. Furthermore, all were readying smaller models for 1960-61. Although DeSoto's 1962 plans included smaller standard models, there was no program for a compact.

But the real problem was a change in Chrysler's marketing approach. Previously, the company had three types of dealers: Chrysler-Plymouth, DeSoto-Plymouth, and Dodge-Plymouth. The advent of Imperial as a separate make for 1955 prompted Chrysler Division to concentrate on the lower end of its market, while larger and more luxurious Dodges increased that division's spread upward. DeSoto had nowhere to go—except the grave.

At first, Chrysler strongly denied that the make would be terminated, and even staged a 1959 celebration marking production of the two-millionth DeSoto. Press releases noted that almost a million DeSotos were still registered, and the division announced $25 million had been earmarked for future models—$7 million alone for the 1960s. Officials said commitments had been made for '61, and work on the 1962-63 line was in the development stage. It was also pointed out that Chrysler had regularly made a profit on DeSoto.

But then Chrysler merged DeSoto and Plymouth into one division in 1960, with the new compact Valiant an ostensibly separate make. Valiant did very well and Plymouth did fairly well, but DeSoto fared poorly. Sales during the first two months of the year totaled 4746 units or just 0.51 percent of the industry total, down considerably from the same period in '59 (6134 units and 0.72 percent). By the end of the year, the restyled '62s had been shelved and production of the '61 models, announced in October 1960, was halted. Some DeSoto-Plymouth dealers then became Chrysler-Plymouth stores, much to the chagrin of existing C-P agents nearby.

Reflecting these developments was a 1960 DeSoto line reduced to just sedan, hardtop sedan and hardtop coupe in two series. The upper-level group was called Adventurer but sold for a few hundred dollars below the '59 Fireflite and was much less special than previous Adventurers. Fireflite was now in the $3000 area previously occupied by Firesweep. The year's most popular DeSoto was the Fireflite sedan, but even it failed to exceed 10,000 units.

DeSoto jetted into 1957 with higher-flying fins and a 345-bhp Adventurer model. The similar '58 debuted in a recession year, and sales took a severe tumble. While most makes soon recovered, for DeSoto it was the beginning of the end.

DeSoto was reskinned for 1959. The top-line Adventurer boasted 350 bhp from its 383-cid V8, but at $4427 only 590 were sold.

All models now rode the 122-inch wheelbase, shared with the 1960 Chrysler Windsor and Dodge Matador/Polara, and adopted the company's "unibody" construction, new that year. Adventurers used the 305-bhp 383 from the now-departed Firedome, Fireflites the 295-bhp 361 from the '59 Firesweep. Styling was all but identical to the 1960 Chrysler's, dominated by a blunt, trapezoidal grille composed of small horizontal bars and carried over a huge, curved bumper with rubber-capped bumper guards. Fins were as high as they'd ever been, but performance was down. An Adventurer could stay with a Windsor in a drag race, but would lose to a Chrysler Saratoga or the lighter 383 Dodge Phoenix.

DeSoto's appearance for 1961 was brief—token really. Production was predictably low: a mere 3034 units. There was only one nameless series now (the cars were simply "DeSotos") and four-door pillared sedans were eliminated. Publicity concentrated on the individual styling. Odd might be a more apt description. Up

Unibody construction was big news at DeSoto in 1960. So was a sales drop from 45,724 units in 1959 to 25,581 in 1960.

The Adventurer four-door sedan found exactly 5746 buyers in 1960.

DeSoto claimed that the '61 had a "streamlined look of motion."

Swiveling seats were an option on the 1960 Fireflite hardtop.

The $3760 hardtop coupe was one of two '61 models; 911 were built.

front, for example, diagonally stacked quad headlights flanked a curious "double" grille, with a lattice-like lower section topped by a large, blunt oval bearing the DeSoto name in stylized letters against a fine mesh. The rest of the effort was equally uninspired.

DeSoto production ended by Christmas 1960, after which what few orders remained were filled mostly with '61 Chrysler Windsors. It was a sad finale for a marque that had generated considerable business for Chrysler over more than three decades.

And ironically, it was premature. Less than a year later, the last DeSoto was effectively resurrected at Dodge to bolster sales of its unpopular 1962 standard cars, which had been shrunken to near-compact size. Called Custom 880, this reborn full-size Dodge was much like the '61 DeSoto and even cost about the same but sold much better, thanks to smoother styling and more model choices. One suspects, then, that DeSoto's rapid decline, like Edsel's, resulted from a "loser" image as much as a changing market.

Adventurer two-door hardtop output in 1960 reached 3092 units.

For its final year, DeSoto built 3034 cars—a sad ending indeed.

The price of the '61 hardtop sedan slid to $3167, output to 2123.

The good news for 1959 was that Alaska and Hawaii were admitted as the 49th and 50th states. The bad news, at least for DeSoto, was that sales continued to drop—and plummeted in 1960 and '61. DeSoto built its last car in November 1960.

DODGE

The Dodge Brothers Company was 14 years old when Walter Chrysler acquired it in 1928. Dodge built 125,000 cars the following year before the Depression tragically altered the nation's economic climate. Yet while other makes bottomed out in 1933-34, Chrysler's new division averaged 100,000 units a year, running fourth in the industry behind Chevrolet, Ford and sister-make Plymouth.

Brothers John and Horace Dodge were traditionalists who believed in practicality and honest dollar value, so their cars never made any gesture toward sportiness in the early years. Even in the '40s there was little to suggest the high-performance Dodges to come. They were simply solid, reliable, low-to-middle-priced cars, a step up from Plymouth.

Dodge moved around on the Chrysler price ladder in the early '30s, sometimes standing above DeSoto, sometimes below. By 1933, it was decided that Dodge would occupy the attractive territory just above Plymouth and below DeSoto. Because of the Depression, it took Chrysler a good many years to rebuild its new acquisition, but Dodge began surging, reaching 159,000 units by 1935, then soaring to near 264,000 for '36. The prewar record was the 1937 tally of over 295,000 cars. The '38 recession temporarily halted the climb and Dodge almost fell out of the top 10, but by 1941 it was back up to 237,000 units.

Early-'30s Dodges offered a broader range of engines: L-head sixes and eights, the latter built in three displacements through 1933. Dodge then offered nothing but sixes for the next 20 years. This took many forms, with displacements of 190 to 242 cubic inches and horsepower of 60 to 87. Dodge's '30s styling was the most conservative of any Chrysler make, but the division was lucky to escape its planned version of the unfortunate Airflow. The famous ram hood ornament, a manifestation of the Chrysler takeover, appeared in '32. Lines were four-square through 1934, then rounded as part of the company-wide "Airstream" look. By 1939, Dodge had acquired extended pontoon-style fenders, elongated rear decks and a sharp-edge frontal motif under the direction of design chief Ray Dietrich.

Dodge offered numerous body styles in the '30s, including all the popular open types. The latter encompassed a convertible

All 1939 Dodges were called Luxury Liners, here a DeLuxe fastback.

The 1940 Dodge featured a horizontally split grille, ram mascot.

A 217.8-cid six powered the '40 Dodge. Output was 87 horsepower.

Features for '41 included new grille, fender-top lights, 91 bhp.

sedan for most of the decade, absent only for 1935 and finally dropped after '38 due to low demand. A long-wheelbase chassis appeared for 1936 under seven-passenger sedans and limousines, and was stretched to 134 inches for 1939. Dodge also made a strong effort to win custom body business by selling chassis to hearse, ambulance, and station wagon builders.

Nineteen thirty-seven was one of Dodge's more innovative years. Though not vastly altered from the "Air Styled" '36s, these cars introduced non-snag door handles, recessed dash knobs, flush-mount instruments, lower driveshaft tunnels, one-piece steel roof construction and built-in defroster vents. The 1935 D5 series marked a first with its fully insulated rubber body mounts.

Dodge's totally redesigned '39s arrived simultaneously with a futuristic world's fair and the make's Silver Anniversary. In apparent celebration of the twin events, Dodge reinstated a two-series lineup for the first time since 1934: Special and DeLuxe, differing mainly in interior trim. Both rode a 117-inch wheelbase (up two inches from 1937-38) and were badged "Luxury Liner" (reflecting Chrysler's fondness for such sales-boosting names). The cast-iron flathead six, which had originated in 1933 and was enlarged to 217.8 cid the following year, remained at its usual 87 bhp. For 1942 it was stroked for 230.2 cid and exchanged a Carter for the previous Stromberg carburetor. Rated at 105 bhp, it would continue with little change well into the '50s.

Similar continuity attended Dodge bodyshells, the basic new-for-1940 design running all the way through the "first series" 1949 line. Standard wheelbase was 119.5 inches; the long sedan and limousine spanned 139.5 inches for 1940, then 137.5 inches. Styling was typical of Chrysler at the time: separate fenderlines; built-in headlamps; a prominent, peaked grille; low-roofed superstructure; limited glass area.

Dodge's '39 offerings repeated for 1940. The low-priced Special series offered a coupe and two- and four-door sedans. The DeLuxe added a convertible, five-passenger coupe and the aforementioned seven-passenger sedan and limousine (the last costing $1170). The upper series accounted for some 120,000 units—about 60 percent of the division's 1940 production total—though only 1000 were long-wheelbase models. Running boards were on the way out, now a $10 option for all models. Another new 1940 option was two-tone paint, but with fenders, hood, and deck done in a contrasting shade, it gave the cars a taxicab look and was not popular.

A clean facelift greatly improved '41 appearance, announced by parking lights combined with the headlamps in a wider, more horizontal grille. Semi-automatic Fluid Drive transmission became optional, and higher compression booted the old-soldier six to 91 bhp. DeLuxe now designated the inexpensive three-model line, Custom the upper series. The two/four-passenger coupe was replaced by a Town Sedan with more closed-in rear roof quarters, and the two-door sedan was called Brougham. Production divided into 106,000 DeLuxes and 131,000 Customs. The new Town Sedan was a modest success; the long models continued to sell in small numbers. Dodge had moved from ninth to sixth in the industry for 1940, but fell back a spot for '41. The following year it would reclaim sixth from Oldsmobile.

When the federal government terminated civilian production in February 1942, Dodge had built some 68,500 of its redesigned models. These were good-looking cars, not quite as radical as that year's hidden-headlamp DeSotos but nicely done. Front fenders and grille were wider; the latter had a prominent eggcrate texture and bulged center section. Optional fender skirts carried bright moldings to match rear fender trim. A club coupe was added to the DeLuxe line. These Dodges weren't as rare as some other '42s, though they're hard enough to come by now. Of the standard-chassis models, the Custom convertible saw the lowest production: 1185 units.

Wartime studies produced many interesting postwar styling variations on the 1940-42 body: smoother grilles, wraparound

The '42 Custom soft top sold for $1245. A larger 230.2-cid six delivered 105 bhp. Only 1185 were built before war interrupted.

Walter P. Chrysler's acquisition of Dodge on July 31, 1928, marked Chrysler Corporation's historic emergence as a multi-make producer and a new power to rival the "Big Two," Ford and General Motors. Henceforth, it would be the "Big Three."

The 1946-48 Dodges featured a cross-hatch grille and fenders that flowed into the doors. The '48 Custom four-door sold for $1788.

bumpers, thinner door pillars and integral fenders. But body tooling was far from amortized, and Dodge's decision to come back with a mildly facelifted '42 was typical of the postwar industry. The division was especially slow to restart, building only 420 of its 1946 models by the end of 1945. But production zoomed during calendar '46, and Dodge finished the model year in fourth place (behind the low-priced three) with close to 164,000 units. The tally was over 243,000 for '47, but Dodge fell back to fifth behind an equally resurgent Buick. The division regained fourth the following year, again on slightly more than 243,000 cars.

Facelifting for the 1946-48 models—all physically identical except for serial numbers—was created by stylists A.B. "Buzz" Grisinger, John Chika, and Herb Weissinger, a trio later to win fame at Kaiser-Frazer. Allowed bolt-on alterations only, they opted for a new grille with wide horizontal and vertical bars. Square parking lights sat outboard of the bottom grille corners and a prominent Dodge nameplate adorned the hood. Mechanical changes included a dash-mounted pushbutton starter (replacing the previous foot pedal), front brakes with double wheel cylinders, a revised transmission, and a standard in-line fuel filter and full-flow oil filter.

Dodge's first hardtop was the '51 Coronet Diplomat. Cost: $2478.

Semi-automatic Fluid Drive became standard for '47, an important sales point at a time when people were tiring of manual shift. Inaugurated at Chrysler in 1938, it was a complex solution to a simple problem, combining a conventional clutch with a fluid coupling acting as a torque converter; electrical shift circuits added to what one writer called a "full range of potential transmission trouble." The converter performed the usual flywheel functions—storing energy, smoothing power impulses, and carrying the ring gear that meshed with the starter pinion. Lacking a clutch-plate contact, a clutch was mounted in tandem. The coupling itself was a drum filled with low-viscosity mineral oil; as the engine ran, a set of vanes attached to the inner casing rotated, throwing oil outward onto a facing runner that had another set of vanes. The oil turned the runner to provide a smooth flow of power while avoiding any metal-to-metal contact.

Fluid Drive had two gear positions: Low for first and second, High for third and fourth. Low was used mainly for fast starts or towing. For most driving you simply shifted into High and pressed the accelerator; at 14 mph you let up on the gas and a "thump" announced the car shift from third to fourth. Stops and starts required no clutching or shifting, hence Chrysler's claim that Fluid Drive eliminated 95 percent of shift motions. The clutch was there, but was used only to change between Low and High or to back up.

Dodge's first postwar redesign wasn't ready at 1949 announcement time, so '48s were sold through April '49. The "second series" '49s, powered by a 103-bhp version of the 230.2-cid six, were all-new and sold in record numbers: nearly 257,000 for the model year, though that was good for only eighth place.

Model offerings were considerably revised within two series. The inexpensive group was a 115-inch-wheelbase group called Wayfarer, a sedan, coupe, and a novel three-passenger roadster with side curtains. Prices ran $1611-$1738. The volume models

The Wayfarer was Dodge's junior series for 1949. Riding a 115-inch wheelbase, the coupe listed at $1611 and 9342 were built.

were the new Meadowbrook and Coronet on a 123.5-inch chassis offering better trim and equipment in a full range of body styles. The Town Sedan was a luxury trim option with beautiful Bedford cord upholstery that added about $85 to the standard Coronet sedan. The Meadowbrook was a single four-door with simpler trim priced about $75 less than the comparable Coronet.

As with its corporate sisters, Dodge's new '49 styling was very square and slab-sided. A shiny latticework grille bore some resemblance to the 1946-48 affair but was more massive. Bolt-on rear fenders were capped by three-sided taillights. Collectors judge the Wayfarer roadster the most desirable '49 Dodge, and many of these have been restored. This year's Coronet woody wagon was not successful: Only 800 were built. After 600 more for early 1950, it was phased out for an all-steel Sierra wagon.

Unusual for an all-new Detroiter, the '49 Dodge got a heavy facelift for its second year, when a new Diplomat hardtop was added to the Coronet line and the Wayfarer roadster gained roll-down door glass to become the Sportabout convertible (still with a

The '50 Dodge sported a cleaner grille, faired-in taillights. The Coronet four-door sedan was easily the most popular model.

Early postwar Dodges were facelifted '42s. The first all-new design came in 1949. In 1950, while President Harry Truman was approving the production of the H-bomb and sending troops to North Korea, Dodge was kept busy building 341,797 cars.

Highlights for '53 included new styling, more compact dimensions.

single bench seat for three). Other offerings returned from '49, including a seven-passenger Coronet sedan on the 137.5-inch wheelbase. It would continue through 1952, mainly for taxi and limousine use. A new 1950 option was "GyroMatic Drive," an improvement on the standard Fluid Drive that eliminated all gear changing.

Dodge did well in the early '50s despite its dull styling. Production was near 342,000 for 1950 and 290,000 for '51, good for seventh in the industry. The division maintained that rank with only 206,000 cars for '52 and a more satisfying 320,000 for '53, then dropped to eighth on 1954 volume of only 154,000.

Without change in wheelbases, Dodge styling became a little sleeker for 1951-52. All-new styling and a revised lineup appeared for '53, when a lone Meadowbrook Suburban wagon and all two-door models rode the 114-inch Plymouth wheelbase; a 119-inch chassis supported Meadowbrook, Meadowbrook Special and Coronet sedans, all six-cylinder models.

But the big news for '53 was the Coronet Eight—club coupe, sedan, convertible, Diplomat hardtop and two-door Sierra powered by Dodge's first-ever performance engine: the brilliant 241.3-cid Red Ram V8. It arrived with 140 bhp, but was capable of much more. In essence it was a scaled-down version of the new-for-'51 Chrysler 331-cid hemi. Chrysler had long experimented with hemispherical combustion chambers and was now cashing in on what it had learned. The hemi offered advantages in its smoother manifolding and porting, larger valves set farther apart, improved thermal efficiency, ample room for water passages, a nearly central spark plug location, and low heat rejection into coolant. Its main disadvantage was cost: far more expensive to build than, say, Chevy's 265.

The '53 Dodge was one of Chrysler's first production models styled by Virgil Exner, who'd come to Highland Park from Studebaker a few years earlier. Surprisingly light, it handled well and was known for economy as well as performance. A Red Ram Dodge scored 23.4 miles per gallon in the '53 Mobilgas Economy Run; other V8s broke 196 AAA stock-car records at Bonneville that year, and Danny Eames drove one to a record 102.62 mph on California's El Mirage dry lake.

Several interesting show cars also contributed to a more youthful new Dodge image. Like others at Chrysler Corporation in these years, they were designed by Exner and built by Ghia in Italy. The first was the Firearrow, a non-running '53 roadster that was made road-ready the following year. In late 1954 came an evolutionary Firearrow convertible and sport coupe whose lines inspired the limited-production Dual-Ghia of 1956. The coupe was aerodynamically stable and achieved 143.44 mph on the banked oval at the Chrysler Proving Grounds.

Only detail appearance changes were made for the production '54 Dodges, but the lineup was greatly expanded as the Red Ram was newly available for all models, and a luxurious new top-line Royal V8 series arrived with club coupe, sedan, convertible, and Sport hardtop. Dodge paced that year's Indy 500 and duly ran off 701 replica pace-car convertibles called Royal 500. Priced at $2632 each, they sported Kelsey-Hayes chrome wire wheels,

An attempt to hype disastrous '54 sales was this mid-year two-tone paint scheme on the 114-inch-wheelbase Royal hardtop.

Dodge burst out with new "Forward Look" styling and bigger 270.1-cid V8s for '55. The top-line Custom Royal ragtop cost $2913.

This Custom Royal four door has more restrained two-tone paint.

Optional spinner hubcaps grace this '55 Royal Lancer hardtop.

"continental" outside spare tire, special ornamentation and a tuned 150-bhp Red Ram. A dealer-installed four-barrel Offenhauser manifold was also available, which must have made this a screamer, though Chrysler never quoted actual horsepower.

The Royal 500 symbolized Dodge's rapid emergence as Chrysler's "performance" outfit. And indeed, the division was already rolling up the victories. Lincoln is famous for its dominance in the Mexican Road Race of those years. Less widely known is the fact that Dodge overwhelmed the event's Medium Stock class, taking 1-2-3-4-6-9 in 1954.

After suffering in a poor sales year for all Chrysler products, Dodge came back with a bigger and brighter all-new '55 on a 120-inch wheelbase. Styling was flashy but not overdone, the work of Exner staff member Murray Baldwin and part of Chrysler's first-generation "Forward Look." Series comprised six and V8 Coronets and V8-only Royals and Custom Royals. The last, the new line-topper, comprised a basic four-door sedan and three Lancer sub-models: sedan, convertible and hardtop coupe. The old six, upped to 110 bhp for '54, now delivered 123 bhp, and a Red Ram bored out to 270.1 cid offered 175-193 bhp. Dodge prospered with greatly increased '55 volume—nearly 277,000—but rivals also did well in that record industry year and Dodge couldn't budge from eighth place.

An interesting 1955 footnote was La Femme, a Custom Royal Lancer hardtop coupe painted pink and white. As the name implied it featured custom accoutrements for m'lady, including a folding umbrella and a fitted handbag stored in the backs of the front seats. La Femme returned for '56 (the women's movement was still many years away). But though briefly considered for volume production, no more than a handful were produced.

All Chrysler products grew tailfins for '56, and that year's Dodge wore them as well as any. Two-speed PowerFlite, the firm's first

A Dodge for milady: the 1956 La Femme in two-tone lavender.

The new '53 Dodge was chunky and more compact. That approach worked for '53, but sales nosedived in '54. The all-new '55 reversed this trend by being bigger and much flashier—output nearly doubled. The '56 sprouted fins.

The '57 Custom Royal Lancer boasted all-new styling. A 345-cid Hemi produced 340 bhp in D-500 trim—and astounding acceleration.

Like all 1957 Chrysler products, Dodge flouted big, flashy fins.

The Custom Royal Lancer four door rode a 122-inch wheelbase.

fully automatic transmission, had arrived with lever control in '54. Now it had pushbuttons. Revised frontal styling and new interiors were enhanced by a stroked Super Red Ram with 218 bhp, versus 189 for the returning 270 V8 and 131 bhp for that year's six. Available across the board was the first of the D-500 options, basically a multiple carburetor setup that lifted output to a healthy 260 bhp. New Lancer hardtop sedans were added to all three series. In a down year for all Detroit, Dodge built 240,000 cars to again run eighth. Helped by torsion-bar suspension, all-new styling and more power, it would climb to seventh for '57 as volume swelled to nearly 288,000.

Carrying Exner's all-new "second generation" Forward Look, the '57 Dodges were longer, lower, wider and more aggressive-looking, with a massive bumper/grille, lots of glass and high-flying fins. Wheelbase for all models stretched to 122 inches, where it would remain through 1960. The hemi was again enlarged, this time to 325 cid, and delivered 245-310 bhp. The D-500 option was now the 354 engine from the junior Chryslers, tuned for 340 bhp. Even the old six got another seven horses.

The D-500 package was Dodge's alternative to the limited-edition supercars of its sister divisions and could be ordered on any model right down to the plain-Jane Coronet two-door. Shocks, springs and the new-for-'57 front torsion bars were all suitably firmed up for what *Motor Trend* magazine called "close liaison with the road"—handling that put D-500s at the top of their class. Lesser Dodges performed equally well, the typical 245-bhp example scaling 0-60 in about 9.5 seconds. The D-500 continued into 1958-59 but with 361- and 383-cid wedgehead V-8s instead of the expensive hemi. With the fuel injection option offered only for '58, the 361 delivered 333 bhp.

A mild facelift with four headlamps and revised trim arrived for '58. The lineup stayed basically the same until February, when a spiffier Regal Lancer hardtop arrived as one of the "spring specials" favored by Chrysler marketers. Sensibly left alone were Torsion-Aire Ride and optional three-speed TorqueFlite automatic transmission, two new '57 features that had earned near-universal praise—and buyer approval. Both would persist at Dodge and throughout the Chrysler lineup for many years. Now in its final season, the Dodge 325 hemi packed 252/265 bhp. The new 361 wedge delivered 305 or the aforementioned 333 bhp. A smaller

Dodge offered five wagons for 1958: six- and nine-passenger Sierras and Custom Sierras, plus a two-door Suburban.

Dodge for 1958: dual headlamps and compound curved windshield.

350 version offered 285 bhp as standard for Custom Royals and V8 wagons. Though 1958 was a disastrous year for Detroit as a whole, Dodge fared worse than most. Production plunged to 138,000 for the model year as the division barely finished ahead of Cadillac.

Sharing in Detroit's modest 1959 recovery, Dodge built about 156,000 cars and returned from ninth to eighth place in the volume stakes. Contributing to this less-than-sterling performance was a rather heavy-handed facelift with droopy "eyelid" headlamps and misshapen fins above suggestive rear-thrusting taillamps. Revised interiors were newly offered with swivel front seats, semi-bucket affairs that pivoted outward when a door was opened. The venerable flathead six was in its last year. V8s comprised a 255-bhp 326 for Coronets, a 305-bhp 361 for other models, and a 383 with 320/345 bhp—all wedges, of course. The last-named were D-500s and not cheap. The 305-bhp four-barrel unit cost $304 extra; the Super version with twin four-barrel ran $446. Both were thirsty, but it was the age of 30-cent-a-gallon gas and the market still craved performance (if not quite as much as before the '58 recession).

The '60s would see Dodge strengthen its position in the high-performance field, push upward into what had been DeSoto territory and diversify with compacts and intermediates. Volume thus rose rapidly after 1964 to an annual average of over half a million units, and Dodge built a record 634,000 of its '66s. But competitors were up too, so Dodge's standing in the production race varied between fifth or sixth in its best years and eighth or ninth in troubled 1961-63.

Recognizing the growing interest in smaller cars, Dodge entered the '60s with a much broader lineup divided into "junior" and "senior" groups. The former was the new Dart, sixes and V8s on a 118-inch wheelbase for all but wagons, which rode a 122. There were three series: Seneca, Pioneer, and Phoenix. Big Dodges comprised V8 Matadors and Polaras on the 122-inch wheelbase. All employed unit body/chassis construction, new at Chrysler Corporation that year, and bore more sculptured styling announced by bright, blunt, elaborate front ends. Fins were still in evidence, ending ahead of the taillights on Matador/Polara, at the rear on Darts.

Despite appearances, most '60 Dodges were relatively light and offered good performance with reasonable economy. That was especially true of standard-engine Darts, which carried the larger, 225-cid version of that year's new Chrysler Corporation slant six. Initially rated at 145 bhp, this durable new six would continue on into the early '80s. Dart's V8 was the solid, reliable 318 with 230/255 bhp. Matadors used the 295-bhp Chrysler 361; Polaras had a standard 383 (optional for Matador and Dart Phoenix) with 325/330 bhp. After lackluster '59, Dodge scored an impressive sales gain: up over 200,000 for the model year.

For 1961, Dodge was given a twin to the compact 106.5-inch-wheelbase "unibody" Valiant that had bowed the previous year at Chrysler-Plymouth. Called Lancer, it was modestly reworked via a horizontal-bar grille and slightly better trim. There were two series, 170 and 770, each with sedans and wagons. The 770 also had the hardtop coupe new to Valiant for '61. Power came from the smaller, 170-cid slant six with 101 bhp. The Dart's 225 engine was optional.

Jack Kerouac published his beatnik journal, *On the Road*, in 1957. Dodge celebrated with all-new, way-out styling. Longer, lower, wider, it sported an aggressive grille, towering fins, flashy two-toning, and spinner hubcaps.

The heavily facelifted 1959 Dodge, here a Custom Royal, featured a new grille, browed headlights, and modified fins and taillights.

Dodge built 27,908 Matadors ($2996-$3354) for the 1960 model run.

Dodge's 1960 entry in the low-price field: Dart, here a Phoenix.

Dodge featured odd-looking "reverse" fins on the 1961 Polara.

A mid-1962 entry was the full-size Dodge Custom 880—17,505 built.

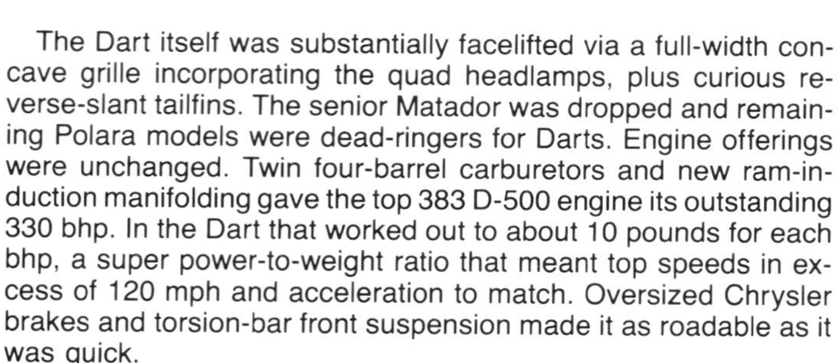

The Dart itself was substantially facelifted via a full-width concave grille incorporating the quad headlamps, plus curious reverse-slant tailfins. The senior Matador was dropped and remaining Polara models were dead-ringers for Darts. Engine offerings were unchanged. Twin four-barrel carburetors and new ram-induction manifolding gave the top 383 D-500 engine its outstanding 330 bhp. In the Dart that worked out to about 10 pounds for each bhp, a super power-to-weight ratio that meant top speeds in excess of 120 mph and acceleration to match. Oversized Chrysler brakes and torsion-bar front suspension made it as roadable as it was quick.

Alas, Dodge sales dropped by over 25 percent for '61, reflecting increased competition and an overall industry downtrend. Lancer didn't sell well, but it was a stopgap anyway. A successor was in the works, so it returned for '62 with a busier grille and a smart bucket-seat GT hardtop as its only significant changes.

Meantime, a brand-new Dart and Polara arrived on a 116-inch wheelbase, measuring 400 pounds lighter and six inches shorter than their '61 predecessors. Virgil Exner thought that if Americans liked compacts, they'd go for downsized "standard" cars, too. But the designer was about 15 years ahead of his time and, aggravated by frankly odd styling, these cars sold as poorly as the Lancer.

As a result, Dodge's total 1962 volume sank to about 240,500, off some 30,000 units in a year when most nameplates scored higher sales. What saved the division was a line of Chrysler-based large cars introduced at mid-year as the Custom 880. Ef-

The 1963 Dodge Polara rode a 119-inch wheelbase, a three-inch stretch from 1962. The hardtop sedan stickered at $2781.

At $3109, the '63 Custom 880 sported a longer 122-inch wheelbase.

The Polara could really be considered Dodge's '64 mid-size car.

The '65 Coronet, here a 500, was Dodge's *real* mid-size offering.

Dart, Dodge's compact since 1963, is shown here in 1965 GT guise.

fectively taking over for DeSoto in the corporate lineup, they looked like the finless '61 Polaras they were, with '62 Chrysler-style "plucked chicken" tails. The year's big performance news was release of two big-block 413-cid wedgehead engines for the mid-size models, offering 410 and 420 bhp. The 318 and 361 V8s returned at their previous power ratings.

While Plymouth struggled on for another year with its shortened '62 design, Dodge increased standard wheelbase to 119 inches for '63 and pushed performance. What had been called Dart was now just "Dodge," comprising 330, 440 and Polara series. As before, the last included a swanky bucket-seat 500 convertible and hardtop coupe. A 413 wedge with 360 bhp was newly available for intermediates, and there was the "Ramcharger" performance version punched out to 426 cid, with aluminum pistons and high-lift cam that helped it develop 415 or 425 bhp. Ramcharger-powered mid-size Dodges had won the 1962 National Hot Rod Association Championship and continued to reign supreme on literally every dragstrip. They were also strong contenders at Daytona.

This year's Dart was an all-new replacement for the compact Lancer. It was basically the redesigned '63 Valiant with more crisply styled exterior sheetmetal and five extra inches in wheelbase (111 total except wagons, still 106 inches). Hardtops, sedans, wagons and convertibles were arrayed in 170, 270 and bucket-seat GT series. Elsewhere, the Custom 880s returned with lower-priced 880 companions, all identified by new grilles with fine verti-

After 1961's odd styling and a smaller than full-size '62, Dodge hurriedly reintroduced a true full-size car in mid-1962. Better styling and a clearly defined lineup of three car sizes boosted 1963 sales a rousing 86 percent.

Under the hood of this '66 Coronet 500 lurks a 425-bhp 426 Hemi.

A 273.5-cid, 235-bhp V8 was optional on the 1966 Dart GT ragtop.

At the top of the Dodge line for '66 was the "distinctive" Monaco.

The Dart was completely restyled for 1967, seen here as a GT.

The '67 Coronet 500 hardtop sported a unique grille and body stripe.

R/T was the sportiest Coronet for 1967, this one Hemi-powered.

The Dodge Coronet 500 convertible retailed for $3036 in 1968.

Note the hood bulge and striping around the tail of the '68 R/T.

The 1968 GTS is probably the most collectible Dart Dodge built.

Hidden headlights and side scoops were unique to the '68 Charger.

cal bars. With so much that was new, Dodge surged past Rambler to grab seventh in the industry standings on record volume of over 446,000 units.

The 1964 lineup was much like '63's, distinguished by facelifts. Darts could be ordered with Valiant's new 273-cid small-block V8 with 180 bhp. This year's Ramcharger was the fabled hemi, making its return to the performance wars in a new 426-cid version with 425 bhp—but only for racers, not production cars. Hemi-powered Dodge and Plymouth intermediates dominated the '64 NASCAR season, sweeping the Daytona 500, for example, 1-2-3. In the production race, Dodge swept back into sixth for the first time since 1960.

For 1965, the Coronet name returned for the first time since 1959 on a revamped mid-size line with more square-cut styling and a 117-inch wheelbase for all models but wagons (116-inch). A much-altered 115-inch-wheelbase Coronet Hemi-Charger two-door sedan weighing just 3165 pounds was offered, but only for off-road drag racing. Base-priced at $3165, it came with heavy-duty springs and shocks, anti-roll bar, four-speed transmission, and strong "police" brakes. Performance was more than ample: 0-60 mph in seven seconds. "Civilians" contented themselves with the more civilized new buckets-and-console Coronet 500 hardtop and convertible.

Capping the '65 line was a completely new group of 121-inch-wheelbase Polaras and Custom 880s, plus a companion sports/luxury hardtop, the $3355 Monaco. All were much like this year's Chryslers, with the same conservatively square Elwood Engel styling differentiated by a "dumbbell" grille and delta taillamps.

Dart was again modestly restyled for '66. Coronets continued in standard, Deluxe, 440, and 500 guise with curvier rear fenders, bolder grilles and wedgy taillights. The big Custom 880 was dropped in favor of a full-line Monaco series, and the top bucket-seat job became a Monaco 500. These plus Polaras got wider taillights and crisper lower-body contours. A bright new addition was the Charger, essentially a fastback Coronet hardtop coupe with hidden headlamps and a sporty interior boasting individual fold-down rear bucket seats. The 318 was standard, but other V8s were available—including the 426 hemi (for both Charger and Coronet). So were manual transmission, "Rallye" suspension, and a long list of luxury equipment. A 383 Charger with TorqueFlite could run 0-60 mph in about nine seconds and hit 110 mph. Polara/Monaco offered Chrysler's new 440-cid big-block at extra cost, rated at 350 bhp. After easing to 489,000 units for '65, volume shot up to its aforementioned decade high as Dodge ran fifth in Detroit production. It has yet to rank as high again.

For 1967, the Dart got an all-new unit structure on the existing wheelbase and dropped wagons. This year's Monaco and Polara, on a new full-size platform shared with Chrysler and the Plymouth Fury, and longer rear decks, a complex grille with a square vertical-bar section between openings divided by horizontal bars, lower profiles and sleeker rooflines. Charger retained its 1966 look, and a facelift made Coronets look more like it.

Also new for '67 were a sporty Coronet R/T (Road/Track) hardtop and convertible with standard 375-bhp 440 "Magnum" V8, heavy-duty suspension, wide tires, and oversize brakes—Dodge's entry in the burgeoning muscle-car market uncovered by Pontiac's GTO. Similar equipment was available for a new Charger R/T. The 426 hemi was again optional for selected intermediates. Despite this appealing lineup, Dodge fell back to seventh on model-year volume of nearly 466,000 units.

Predictably, 1968 brought a facelifted Dart and full-size line, as it was time for Coronet and Charger to be fully revised. They were the best-looking mid-size Dodges yet: long and low, with rounded fuselages, larger windows, and pleasingly simple grilles. Charger again featured hidden headlamps but was now a notchback hardtop with semi-fastback "flying buttress" roofline.

Sporty models continued to proliferate. Dart added a plush GTS

Dodge built 27,846 Coronet Super Bees for the 1969 model year.

Only 505 '69 Charger Daytonas were made, all with NASCAR in mind.

The 1969 Charger received a new grille and minor detail changes.

This 1970 Dart Swinger was powered by the 275-bhp, 340-cid V8.

Dodge finally offered its first ponycar for 1970, the Challenger.

The mid- and late-Sixties saw an intensification of U.S. activities in Vietnam, with troop strength up to 543,000 in 1969. Dodge enjoyed prosperous times during that era, with output hitting 632,658 units in 1966, an all-time record.

A total of 8247 Coronet 500 hardtop coupes were produced for 1970.

For 1970, the Charger sported another new grille. Price: $3001.

Dodge claimed the '70 Monaco was the roomiest car in its class.

The 1971 Charger 500 listed at $3223 and 11,948 were produced.

The Charger S.E. (Special Edition) was a bit pricier at $3422.

hardtop and convertible with a standard 340 V8, an enlarged 273 with 275 bhp. The big 383 with 300 bhp was optional. Coronet offered the new budget-priced Super Bee, a no-frills two-door muscle coupe with a special 335-bhp 383. These and the Coronet and Charger R/Ts made up what Dodge called its "Scat Pack," denoted by bumble-bee stripes. All ranked among 1968's quickest and most roadable performance machines.

Along with Chrysler and Plymouth Fury, the '69 Polara/Monaco arrived with all-new "fuselage" styling but retained a 122-inch wheelbase. Dart, Coronet and Charger wore minor facelifts. Bolstering the Dart line was Swinger, a two-door hardtop with special identifying trim, bright aluminum grille and choice of 318 or 340 V8s.

Pride of the '69 fleet was the Charger Daytona, conceived for long-distance NASCAR races like the Daytona 500 and marked by a unique bullet nose with hidden headlights and "bib" spoiler, plus a flush-window fastback roof and a huge trunklid wing on towering twin stabilizers. The Daytona was about 20 percent more aerodynamic than previous racing Chargers, which gave it an advantage of 500 yards per lap. Dodge built only 505—just enough to qualify as a "production car" for NASCAR purposes—priced at about $8000 apiece. A Daytona won the Talledega 500 in September 1969, though that was partly because the Ford contingent didn't show. In 1970, the Daytonas and Plymouth's similar Superbirds won 38 of 48 major NASCAR races. Dodge also offered a wingless, blunt-nose Charger 500 for '69 at a bit under $3900.

Appearing with Plymouth's third-generation Barracuda for 1970 was a Dodge relative, the division's belated reply to the Mustang, Camaro and other ponycars. Fittingly named Challenger, it was offered with slant-six and V8s, the latter including 318, 383, 440 and even the hemi. Hardtop coupe and convertible were available in plain and sporty R/T trim. The hardtop could also be ordered as a Special Edition with padded vinyl roof and a smaller "formal" rear window. Priced attractively in the $3000-$3500 range and cataloging a broad list of options, Challenger sold very well in its first year, but then tailed off rapidly. In 1970 sales, sixes outpaced V8s, hardtops the convertibles. Only about 10,000 SE coupes were built.

Specifications and dimensions for other 1970 Dodges were largely as for '69, but Coronets, Chargers and Polara/Monaco received large "loop" bumper/grilles. Coronet's divided affair looked a bit swollen. Dart and the big cars gained more massive rear bumpers. Charger was offered in six-cylinder form for the first time, while the exotic Daytona, having proved its point on the track, was dropped (Plymouth picked up the ball with its similar Superbird). Ignition/steering-column locks, fiberglass-belted tires, dual-action wagon tailgates, and a long list of federally mandated safety equipment completed the 1970 story. As in 1969, Dodge remained seventh in industry output, though volume fell from 611,000 to 543,000 for the model year.

Dodge's path through the '70s was strewn with the same obstacles that made life difficult for all U.S. automakers in those years: a growing number of ever-stricter government regulations and a dramatically altered business climate stemming from the OPEC oil embargo of 1973-74. The division was ill prepared for both, its early-decade lines heavy with cars motivated by thirsty V8s and wallowing on overly soft suspensions. Worse, Chrysler's declining fortunes would allow most of these dinosaurs to hang on too long. Indifferent workmanship only further dampened sales, culminating in the corporation's near-demise in 1980. But by that point, Dodge was through its trial by fire and building nothing remotely like its early-'70s dinosaurs save the 118.5-inch-wheelbase St. Regis sedan and the Mirada personal-luxury coupe.

It didn't take much corporate cogitating to dispose of the poor Challenger—clumsy, poorly built and never a serious sales threat to the Camaro/Firebird or even Mustang II (if you call that one a

A 1971 Dodge Challenger paced the 55th Indy 500 on May 29, 1971. Only 2165 Challenger convertibles were assembled that year.

Dodge built 10,098 low-buck, high-performance Demon 340s for '71.

Charger engines for 1972 ranged from a 225-cid six to a 440 V8.

Dodge described the '72 Polara Custom as "economically sound."

The '73 Challenger could be upgraded with an optional Rallye pack.

ponycar). The overweight latecomer was put out to pasture after 1974, when only about 16,000 were sold. Collectors have already noted the end of convertibles, R/Ts and big-inch engines after '71, and have begun gathering in most all Challengers as artifacts of a special era.

With the first energy crisis, the brontosaurus-like Polara/Monaco also seemed headed for the automotive tar pits, but Dodge tried hard to save them via discounts and cash rebates beginning in 1974. Polara vanished after '77, when the Monaco name transferred to the mid-size line, replacing Coronet. A blocky new Monaco arrived for '74, similar to that year's redesigned Chrysler but still on a 122-inch-wheelbase. It then hung on grimly for 1975-78 as the Royal Monaco, selling in decent numbers only by dint of police orders.

Dodge derived its strength in the early Seventies from the successful compact Dart and intermediate Coronet/Charger. Its ponycar, the Challenger, and the full-size models didn't fare as well. The former was gone for good after 1974.

Charger S.E. for '73 sold for $3375. It was Dodge's most popular intermediate-size model that year—61,908 were produced.

Big, black blocks were Polara's answer to 1973 bumper standards.

The top-of-the-line Monaco continued with hidden headlamps for '73.

Challenger was in its last year in 1974; only 16,437 were built.

The Custom four-door sedan was easily the most popular '74 Coronet.

Production plummeted to 36,399 units for the '74 Charger S.E.

The '74 Monaco was all-new, shown here as the top-line Brougham.

The mid-line Monaco was the Custom, which stickered at $4464.

Dodge produced 10,292 Coronet Brougham hardtop coupes for 1975.

Charger moved the S.E. into the personal-luxury market for 1975.

Monaco's top-line model for 1975 was the $5460 Royal Brougham.

Dodge's all-new '76 compact Aspen coupe had a 108.5-inch wheelbase.

The ultra-reliable Dart had been a sales winner for years, but its replacement was a letdown. Introduced for 1976, the Aspen was in essence a slightly larger, roomier and heavier Dart with a wider range of luxury options—much like the Granada was to Maverick at Ford. Alas, it earned the dubious distinction (along with its Plymouth Volaré twin) of being the most recalled car in history, due to poor quality control in general and widespread body rust in particular. (GM's X-cars soon wrested that sorry title.) But performance was good with the extra-cost 360 V8 available through '79, and furnishings were nicer than on late Darts. Aspen also revived a compact Dodge wagon, something Dart had lacked since its '67 redesign, and there were pseudo-muscle R/T coupes and a later "finish it yourself" kit-car racer for the performance crowd.

Despite its problems, Aspen was important for Dodge sales in the late '70s and exemplified one of the few things Detroit began doing well: putting big-car comfort in smaller packages (108.7-inch-wheelbase coupes, 112.7-inch-wheelbase sedans and wagons). Dodge called it the "family car of the future," hyperbole worthy of P.T. Barnum, but it did lead to the genuine article. Dart, meantime, ended its career as just basic transportation aside from the 1974-75 Special Edition sedans.

An unusual Aspen (and Volaré) feature was its front suspension, which had torsion bars per Chrysler tradition but situated crosswise instead of lengthwise. Some critics sneered that this was merely a convoluted gimmick with no real advantage for ride or quietness; a few claimed it actually hampered handling. Regardless, the arrangement did allow for better suspension isolation, which made for smoother going than in the Dart. Aspen's mainstay engines, 225 slant six and 318 V8, were hoary old affairs but proven. And the thrifty six (which could yield up to 25 mpg on the highway with manual shift and a gentle right foot) was about as bulletproof as Detroit engines ever get.

If Aspen didn't realize its sales potential, the larger Dodges fared even worse. The mid-size Coronet/Monaco became more like the equivalent Plymouth Satellite/Fury with each passing year (all were built nose-to-tail at Chrysler's Lynch Road facility in Detroit) and was hardly a bargain at prices averaging $100 higher. It was also thirsty, and styling wasn't memorable. The Charger was simply watered down amidst name shuffles. For 1975 it became a twin to Chrysler's posh Cordoba.

This mid-size generation began with fuselage-style '71 Coronets comprising 114.9-inch-wheelbase coupes and 117.4-inch-wheelbase sedans and wagons. By 1978 they'd been heavily facelifted once (for '75) and trimmed to Charger SE and Magnum XE coupes plus assorted Monacos and Monaco Broughams.

The reason for the thinning of those ranks was Diplomat. Launched for 1977, it was much like the Chrysler LeBaron, built on a stretched Aspen/Volaré platform with sedans and wagons on a 112.7-inch wheelbase, coupes on a 108.7-inch span. Diplomat sold well from the start, and its more sensible design rendered the old-style intermediates superfluous. The Coronet-turned-Monaco was thus transmogrified after 1978 into the St. Regis, all but identical with Chrysler's "downsized" R-body Newport/New Yorker sedan. The Cordoba-like Charger vanished at the same time; the related Magnum hung on through '79.

Then the smooth Mirada took over as the personal-luxury Dodge. Mounting the Diplomat platform, it was a close cousin of 1980's new second-generation Chrysler Cordoba. One of the few true hardtop coupes left by that time, it bore a striking front end recalling the "coffin nose" of the late-'30s Cord 810/812—and the previous Magnum. Good looks won Mirada a lot of good copy in "buff" magazines. And considering how things had changed since the muscle-car days, it was decently quick—if you ordered the optional 185-bhp 360, Dodge's hairiest engine that year. Unhappily, this was another one that was just a shade too late to be of any real value, and annual production averaged less than 7500 units through 1983, Mirada's final year.

In the mid-Seventies, Dodge turned the sporty Charger into a personal-luxury car and debuted a new compact. The Charger was overshadowed by Chrysler's Cordoba and didn't sell well. The Aspen *did*, but suffered because of lousy quality control.

After 14 years, the Dart (here an S.E.) played out its last act in '76.

The Charger lineup encompassed four models for 1976, here the S.E.

The Royal Monaco Brougham was a slow seller in 1976: 4076 units.

Aspen sold well in 1977; the largest engine choice was a 360 V8.

Coronet was gone for '77; Monaco was now the mid-size nameplate.

Capping Dodge's enforced product renewal in the '70s was the L-body Omni, a sensible, front-drive subcompact introduced for 1978 and cut from the trend-setting Volkswagen Rabbit pattern. At first, it was even powered by a special version of VW's overhead-cam four (mounted transversely), though it wasn't quite as much fun to drive as a Rabbit. But it had the same boxy, four-door hatchback styling and high practicality. Along with its Plymouth Horizon twin, Omni was one of the few bright spots in Chrysler's mostly gloomy sales picture at the time.

For 1979, Omni gained a slick companion coupe on a slightly shorter chassis (96.7 inches versus 99.2 inches). Called 024, it won an immediate following, even managing a few conquest sales among import buyers seeking a sporty and nimble 2+2 that was easy on the pocketbook.

After a quiet 1980, Dodge followed Plymouth and Chrysler in beginning another line-wide overhaul, replacing old rear-drive models with smaller, more efficient front-drive designs, most every one derived from the versatile 100.1-inch-wheelbase K-car platform of 1981. Aided by a steadily expanding lineup marketed with renewed emphasis on sporty performance, Dodge reaped the rewards with higher sales. Division volume shot up from 309,000 for 1980 to nearly 341,000 for '81. By 1985, Dodge had achieved its goal of a half-million annual sales.

One model that wouldn't disappear was Diplomat, which got a crisp restyling for 1980, then took over for St. Regis as the traditional full-size Dodge through decade's end. Offered only as a four-door in two trim levels from 1981, it enjoyed steady, if modest, sales (again mainly to police and taxi fleets). The standard slant six was discontinued after '83, leaving only the veteran 318 V8.

Aries-K was the literal foundation of Dodge's 1980's lineup. Replacing Aspen, it was a conventional but well engineered new-wave compact, though no more original than Omni. Design highlights included a choice of two transverse-mounted single-overhead-cam fours—Chrysler 2.2 liter (135 cid) or optional Mitsubishi 2.6 (156 cid)—rack-and-pinion steering, front-disc/rear-drum brakes, and all-coil suspension with front MacPherson struts and a twist-type rear beam axle that doubled as an anti-roll bar.

Most Aries sold with optional TorqueFlite. The standard transaxle was a four-speed manual with floorshift; a five-speed option arrived for 1982, then replaced the four-speed for '86, when a 2.5-liter version of the Chrysler "Trans-4" was added. Coupe, sedan and a neat little five-door wagon were variously available in base, Custom, SE and LE trim at competitive prices identical with those of Plymouth's twin Reliant. A smooth 1985 facelift made all Ks look more grown-up, and coupes could be ordered with sporty options like the turbocharged 2.2 announced for 1982, as well as front bucket seats and center console.

Though Aries consistently lagged behind Reliant in sales, it sold consistently well: nearly 181,000 units for debut '81, between 125,000 and 150,000 a year thereafter. Progressively improved workmanship, longer warranties (up to 7 years/70,000 miles by 1987) and sensible product upgrades helped keep it competitive through decade's end, when the line was trimmed to make room for the new A-body Spirit. By that time, critics had long chided Chrysler for not building anything truly new since 1981, but buyers didn't seem to notice. The K sparked Chrysler's renaissance and no little innovation. Few cars can claim as much, let alone one so humble.

Dodge's first K-car derivatives appeared the year after Aries' launch. This was a personal-luxury duo called 400, a coupe and sedan with a front end like that of the Mirada they replaced, along with plush interiors *a la* Chrysler's new LeBaron with which they shared their basic "CV" platform. A 400 convertible arrived at mid-1982, the first open Dodge since the 1971 Challenger and a deft marketing move by Chrysler chairman Lee Iacocca. Like the LeBaron convertible, the 400 was built by an outside contractor at first but proved so popular that Chrysler took over production

Charger became a one-model series again in '77. Price: $5098.

Dodge built 8665 Monaco Brougham four doors for the '78 model year.

The 1979 Omni 024 hatchback featured four cylinders, front drive.

Dodge's second front-drive platform debuted for '81 as the Aries.

St. Regis was the full-size Dodge for '81. Wheelbase: 118.5 inches.

A four-model Diplomat series bowed for '77, here a $5101 four door.

Charger became Magnum in 1978; Dodge said it had "youth appeal."

The Omni sedan rang up 84,093 sales during the 1979 model year.

Diplomat was Dodge's mid-size 1980 offering, here the "S" Type.

The '81 Diplomat ranged in price from $6495 to $7542, plus options.

By 1980, Dodge production had fallen to less than half of what it had been as late as 1973. Poor quality control, less-than-inspired styling, and Chrysler Corporation's skirmish with bankruptcy had damaged the make's reputation.

The '83 Mirada retailed for $9011, plus $982 for the CMX package.

Mid-1983 saw the debut of the performance-oriented Shelby Charger.

A "cabriolet" roof made the '83 Mirada look like a convertible.

Dodge called its new '84 minivan Caravan a "family wagon."

Boy-racer looks and a 142-bhp turbo motor: 1984 Daytona Turbo Z.

The 400 was a deluxe Aries. The '83 convertible listed for $12,500.

The sportiest 024 for '82 was the 2.2 Charger. List price: $7303.

The '84 Dodge Shelby Charger came only in silver with blue trim.

The '84 600 ES boasted a five-speed stick and handling suspension.

The '85 Shelby Charger became more potent with the 2.2 turbo motor.

itself. Mechanicals and dimensions for all 400s were nearly identical with Aries'.

Arriving for 1983 was a stretched 400 sedan called 600, using the new K-based 103.1-inch-wheelbase corporate E-body. A 400-like front differentiated it from Chrysler's E-Class and New Yorker. A sporty ES version bid for the burgeoning "EuroSedan" market with black exterior trim, handling package and five-speed. It didn't win many buyers from Saab, BMW and Mercedes, but was surprisingly capable all things considered.

Shifting gears for 1984, Dodge dropped the 400 sedan and put 600 badges on the CV coupe and convertible. The latter was also available now in ES trim, tied to the turbo 2.2. It was the raciest Dodge in years, but few were ordered. Still, the new approach helped series sales, which rose from 1983's combined 66,500 to over 72,000 for '84. The following year brought a more prosaic SE sedan, and its strong initial sales pointed the way. After an Aries-like 1986 facelift, the 600 coupe and convertible were cancelled, leaving the SE and a detrimmed base four-door.

Dodge dealers bemoaned losing the 600 convertible, but at least their Daytona sports coupe had no more in-house competition from Chrysler's Laser after 1987. Both models had arrived for '84 on a much-modified 97-inch-wheelbase K-car chassis topped by slick, Porsche-like "fasthatch" styling. Corporate finances at the time dictated they be virtually identical, but the Daytona outsold Laser from the start, perhaps because the product was more appropriate to Dodge than Chrysler. Daytona also had an edge with three models to Laser's two: initially base, Turbo and the racy Turbo Z, the last distinguished by ground-hugging lower-body extensions, discreet hatchlid spoiler, and big wheels and tires.

With the sort of evolutionary improvements found in all Chrysler products in this decade, the Daytona rocked along at around 50,000 units a year through 1986. By that point it was available with a stroked 2.5-liter injected four as base power, plus a T-top option (shared with Laser) and a C/S handling package named for Carroll Shelby, the old friend Iacocca had persuaded to "heat up" certain Dodges the way he'd done with Mustangs when both worked at Ford back in the '60s.

To compensate for the lost convertible, Dodge dealers got a restyled '87 Daytona with a smooth hidden-headlamp "droop-snoot" in base, luxury Pacifica and hot-rod Shelby Z models. Pacifica carried the familiar 146-bhp turbo 2.2, the Z a hot 174-bhp "Turbo II" version; even the base model could be ordered with the 146-bhp engine as part of a new C/S performance package. For 1989, Pacifica was replaced by ES and ES Turbo, the latter powered by that year's new 150-bhp turbocharged 2.5, and the Z was retitled Daytona Shelby. There were several styling and equipment adjustments, including standard four-wheel disc brakes across the board. Of interest to weekend racers was a new C/S Competition Package for the base Daytona—basically the Shelby model with special exterior, 2.2-liter "Turbo II" power and "maximum performance suspension" but few creature comforts so as to realize a 200-pound weight saving.

Though Daytona generated only about a third as many sales as Mustang or Camaro volume, it symbolized Dodge's return to performance better than anything else in the line. And it gave away little in acceleration or handling to its heavier, more powerful rear-drive rivals—proof that Chrysler engineering was as formidable as ever.

Bowing alongside Daytona was a very different '84 Dodge: America's first "garageable" van. Aptly named Caravan, it was essentially a tall K-wagon, riding a special 112-inch wheelbase but having the same overall length. Despite this, it had a very roomy interior that offered seating options for up to eight. Quick-release anchors made for easy removal of the second and third bench seats for cargo-carrying. Front drive and astute packaging conferred a lower ride height than any rear-drive van, which eased entry/exit and contributed to a car-like driving position. In fact,

A sport suspension came with the '85 ES Turbo convertible package.

The '86 Omni GLH was a sleeper. GLH stood for "Goes Like Hell."

The '87 Lancer ES could be best described as Dodge's "Eurosedan."

New front and rear end styling highlighted the '87 Daytona Shelby Z.

The ES package added $2199 to the '87 Shadow's $8075 base price.

Under president Lee Iacocca, Chrysler wrung a lot of mileage out of its K-car chassis. The biggest coup based on it was the compact "garagable" van, the Dodge Caravan (and Plymouth Voyager), an idea Iacocca had taken with him from Ford.

The '88 Dynasty LE shared the Chrysler New Yorker's C-body platform.

Aero exterior treatment was featured on the '88 Daytona Shelby Z.

The '88 Grand Caravan rode a 119.1-inch wheelbase; a V6 was extra.

aside from sitting a little higher and further forward, driving a Caravan was much like driving an Aries wagon.

This as much as attractive pricing made the Caravan (and Plymouth's twin Voyager) an instant hit, generating upwards of 200,000 annual sales. A fair number were windowless Ram Van commercials, but most were passenger models—base, SE and woody-look LE.

Literally extending this line's appeal was the 1988 addition of 14-inch-longer Grand Caravan models on a 119.1-inch wheelbase. At the same time, a new 3.0-liter (187-cid) Mitsubishi V6 option arrived with 144 bhp and 175 pounds-feet torque, bringing a welcome increase in towing capacity over the four-cylinder engines. The main 1989 developments were optional availability of the new 150-bhp turbocharged 2.5 four on standard-wheelbase SE and LE models—something of a surprise for this sort of vehicle—and Chrysler's new electronically controlled four-speed automatic transaxle for V6 LEs and all Grand Caravans.

Unquestionably, Caravan was Chrysler's biggest coup of the '80s. For once, Detroit's perennial number-three outfit had delivered the right product at the right time.

Dodge didn't give up on sport sedans when it cancelled the 600 ES. It merely had something better: the H-body Lancer (reviving the name of the early-'60s compact). This was another new Dodge similar to a new Chrysler, in this case the LeBaron GTS, but it stood apart with the cross-bar grille then being adopted throughout the division (which must have confused Chrysler 300 enthusiasts) and by being offered in a more overtly sporting ES rendition.

All that may be said of the GTS applies equally to Lancer—except sales, about a third less. One suspects the Chrysler name and its luxury aura did more for GTS than the Dodge name did for Lancer despite similar pricing. Perhaps recognizing this, the division issued a bespoilered new Lancer Shelby for 1989, with the 176-bhp "Turbo I" 2.2 and racy body addenda similar to those of the earlier Pacifica and Shelby Lancer limited editions. The '89 ES was sportier, too, gaining the new "Turbo II" 2.5 as standard equipment.

Even more successful was the P-body Shadow, intended to replace the aging Omni but introduced for 1987 as an additional, more ambitious small sedan. Dodge wanted you to think of it as a junior BMW, but it was really more junior Lancer, with the same rounded "aerosedan" styling in three- and five-door notchback body styles on the 97-inch Daytona wheelbase.

K-car heritage was again evident in the Shadow chassis and drivetrains. The latter initially comprised the usual turbocharged and "atmospheric" 2.2-liter fours teamed with manual five-speed and automatic TorqueFlite transaxles. Unlike Plymouth with its similar Sundance, Dodge fielded enthusiast-oriented ES models with uprated suspension and a few "Euro" touches. For 1989, the corporate 2.5-liter balancer-shaft four was a new option for base models in normally aspirated form, and in 150-bhp turbo tune as standard for the ES (replacing the blown 2.2). The turbo 2.5 was also available in a new Daytona-style competition package for three-doors that included performance suspension calibrations, bigger wheels and tires, "aero" body skirting, rear spoiler and performance bucket seats.

Yet for all the emphasis on sport, it was the workaday Shadows that carried the sales load. And that load was considerable: over 93,000 for the first model year. (Plymouth moved a like number of Sundances.)

The reason Omni didn't fade into the Shadow is that it was too good to lose. Despite relatively few changes after 1981, it averaged a remarkable 100,000 sales each year through 1983 and 140,000 or more thereafter. In 1985-87 it actually outsold Aries.

The turning point was 1981, when the K-car's 2.2-liter "Trans-4" became optional for both Omni and the 024 coupe, improving acceleration and quietness with little or no loss in mileage. A smaller Peugeot-built 1.6-liter (replacing the VW 1.7 for '83) was technically standard through 1987, but almost nobody bought it. Likewise the stripped 1981 "Miser" models, which disappeared after just one year.

Sustaining the L-body line through decade's end were an increasingly better-equipped Omni and ever-sportier coupes. The last began at mid-1982 with a rather overdecorated 2.2-powered model reviving the famous Charger name, signalling Dodge's return to interesting cars. The base 024 became a Charger for '83, and the 2.2 was joined at mid-year by a dashing Shelby Charger with a tuned 110-bhp engine, *very* stiff suspension, racy body add-ons, silver paint and big blue stripes evocative of Carroll's late-'60s Mustang GTs. A wider choice of colors was offered for '84, and other Chargers acquired the Shelby's cleaner rear-roof styling. A nose job followed for '85, when the Shelby took on the blown, 146-bhp 2.2 to become the Turbo Charger.

But by 1987, a profusion of sporty Daytonas and Shadows were crowding all Chargers out of the market, so production ceased that March. Incidentally, all L-body Shelbys except for the GLH-S

A revised exterior package came with the high-performance '88 Shadow ES. Also included were turbo motor and a Message Center.

The hottest '88 Shadow was the Shelby CSX: 0-60 in 7.1 seconds, 135 mph top speed, 0.85 g on the skidpad—all for $13,495.

At the close of the Eighties, Dodge offered eight different series in 19 models. It carried the banner as Chrysler's "performance division," an image that was enhanced by Carroll Shelby's hot, low-volume, Dodge-based coupes and sedans.

The '89 Dodge Spirit was designed as a more sophisticated Aries.

Daytona for '89 went largely unchanged, seen here as the ES Turbo.

Assembly of the '89 Omni was moved from Kenosha, WI, to Detroit.

The 1989 Shadow ES sported aero headlights for the first time.

are technically Dodges. (A limited run of highly modified Lancers and Shadows, built at a separate small-scale facility, were sold under the Shelby marque and are covered under that heading.) The Shelby Chargers were fairly rare: about 30,000 for the four years.

Omni, meantime, kept getting better, picking up a more modern dashboard for '84 and additional standard features most every year. Workmanship improved too. The aging 1978 design should have been an increasing liability in the marketplace, but Chrysler took advantage of tooling costs long since amortized to hold keep prices down and sales up.

The company went even further in 1986 by replacing all Omnis with a single fully equipped America model appealingly priced at $5799. A limited number of options was offered to reduce overhead and insure higher, more consistent assembly quality—lessons learned from Europe and Japan. The value-minded rushed to buy, taking over 152,000 of the '87 models—more sales than the entire Omni/Charger line had ever generated in a single year. Chrysler paid heed and put Aries/Reliant on the "America plan" for '88.

A short-lived exception to such crushing sensibility was the GLH, basically the wolfish Shelby Charger in sheepish Omni dress. The initials, which came from Ol' Shel, stood for "Goes Like Hell." It did. The debut '85 was spritely enough with its 110-bhp engine, but the turbocharged 146-bhp GLH was a terror, though it suffered terrible torque-steer (one colleague observed that the accelerator functioned as a "lane-change switch"). Still, like the Shelby Chargers, this Omni was great fun—crude but invigorating in the best muscle-car tradition. And as only a few thousand were built over two years, the GLH and later GLH-S (*see* Shelby) stand as future collector cars.

A new name for 1988 was Dynasty, a sort of latterday Diplomat on the front-drive C-body platform shared with that year's new Chrysler New Yorker. This meant square-lined four-door unibody on a 104.3-inch wheelbase and a choice of two models, here base and uplevel LE. Unlike the Chrysler, however, Dynasty's standard engine was the corporate 2.5-liter four with 96 bhp, a bit weak for the 3000-pound curb weight. Fortunately, the Mitusbishi 3.0-liter V6 was optional. Changes for '89 were confined to a slightly more powerful, 150-bhp V6 teamed with Chrysler's new electronically controlled four-speed overdrive automatic transaxle, plus a newly optional security system, two-position driver's-seat "memory" feature, and all-disc anti-lock brakes (the last phased in during '88).

Billed as a "contemporary family sedan," Dynasty made no gesture toward sport, but it didn't have to. With base prices of $11,500-$12,500, it offered fine value.

Though Aries was down to two- and four-door Americas for 1989, their heir apparent arrived that year as the family Dodge of the '90s. Called Spirit (a name inherited from AMC), this notchback sedan was built on the same 103.3-inch-wheelbase A-body platform as Plymouth's new Acclaim (a name AMC had planned to use) and thus spelled the end for the like-length four-door 600. The now-expected trio of base, luxury LE and sporty ES models was offered, the last with a standard turbocharged 2.5-liter four, the others with the normally aspirated version of same. The Dynasty's V6 was optional only for the ES and also teamed with Chrysler's new four-speed automatic transaxle. Spirit styling was much like Aries' but smoother and more "grown-up." Identifying ES were body-color front and rear end caps and rocker extensions plus integral foglamps.

With the Spirit ended a remarkable decade in which Dodge not only returned to its traditional performance role within Chrysler Corporation but became the firm's only full-line division and thus its best-selling nameplate. In the process, its industry position improved from a lackluster eighth in 1982 to a solid sixth in 1985-87. Assuming it can continue to build on its recent success, Dodge faces a rosy future indeed.

EDSEL

A comedy of errors or a good idea at the wrong time? The Edsel was both—proof that what seems sound today may not be so tomorrow. "Its aim was right," said one prominent historian, "but the target moved."

Edsel was born in the heady climate of 1954, when Ford Motor Company was recovering strongly from its near-collapse of the late '40s. Led by board chairman Ernest R. Breech, optimistic Dearborn managers, determined to match General Motors model for model, laid expansionist plans for a GM-like five-make hierarchy involving a separate new Continental Division (*see* Continental) and a second medium-price make to bolster Mercury. The latter made appealing sense at a time when medium-price car sales were booming. In record-setting 1955, for example, Pontiac, Buick and Dodge built nearly two million cars between them.

But with the industry's usual three-year lead times, Edsel didn't arrive until late 1957, when the entire market was depressed and the medium-price segment had shriveled from 25 percent to about 18 percent. Hoping to sell 100,000 of its first-year '58 models, Edsel Division built only a little over 63,000. From there it was all downhill. After fewer than 45,000 for '59 and a mere 3000 of the token 1960 models, the make was cancelled at the end of November '59.

The name, of course, honored the only son of company founder Henry Ford and the father of then-president Henry Ford II. It wasn't supposed to be the choice, however. Ford solicited monikers from all over—including poetess Marianne Moore, who came up with stunners like "Mongoose Civique," "Turcotinga" and "Utopian Turtletop." Ranger, Pacer, Corsair and Citation were the top finishers among 6000 names considered by the ad agency, and were ultimately adopted as series designations. But Breech didn't like these or any of the other suggestions. While Edsel had popped up as an early prospect, probably because the project was widely known as the "E-car," the Ford family was against it, and even publicly denied it would ever be used. But when a decision lagged, Breech stepped in. "I'll take care of Henry," he declared. He did, and Edsel it was.

Auto buffs will forever argue about *why* the Edsel failed. No matter—the '58 Pacer ragtop, with 1876 built, is desirable *now*.

Some said it looked like an "Oldsmobile sucking a lemon." Others thought the grille looked like a toilet seat. Edsel claimed it was jet-inspired. No matter, the car didn't sell because of its controversial styling and a depressed economy.

The '58 Pacer four-door hardtop cost $2863; just 4959 were built.

The priciest '58 was the Citation ragtop. Production: 930 units.

Bargain hunters purchased the '59 Ranger two-door sedan: $2629.

As the license plate says, this '60 Ranger soft top was "1 of 76."

Though originally conceived as a more expensive and powerful "super Mercury," Edsel was positioned between Ford and Mercury, and was not the radical all-new design rumored for some two years before introduction. The debut '58 line comprised Ranger and Pacer series on the 118-inch wheelbase (wagons: 116 inches) of the 1957-58 Ford; Corsair and Citation rode Mercury's 124-inch chassis. Bodyshells were similarly shared. Ranger offered two- and four-door sedans and hardtops, two-door Roundup wagon, and four-door Villager wagons with seating for six or nine. Pacer deleted the two-door wagon and sedan but added a convertible; its wagons were tagged Bermuda. Corsair was limited to hardtop coupe and sedan; Citation offered these plus a soft-top. Prices were about $500 below comparable Mercurys, in the $2500-$3800 range.

Styling was the '58 Edsel's most unique aspect—and the most controversial, especially its "horse-collar" vertical grille and narrow horizontal taillights (which one cynic termed "ingrown toenails"). But fins were mercifully absent and the package tastefully restrained next to the glittery '58 Buick and Olds. Typical of the day, gadgets abounded: "Teletouch Drive" automatic transmission controlled via pushbuttons in the steering wheel hub; a rotating drum speedometer; power assists for almost everything except the rearview mirror.

Two V8s were offered, both part of Dearborn's new-for-'58 FE-series big-block family. The two lower series carried a 361-cubic-incher with 303 horsepower; a 345-bhp 410 powered Corsair/Citation. Edsels were thus quite rapid, but roadability and braking left much to be desired, typical of the times.

Disappointing first-year sales dictated a slimmed-down lineup for 1959: Corsair, Ranger and Villager on a single 120-inch wheelbase, all basically reskinned Fords. The latter two now carried the Ford 292 V8 with 200 bhp, but a no-charge 145-bhp 223-cid inline six was available in deference to the market's new-found concern for fuel economy that year. Corsairs had a standard 225-bhp 332 V8. The 361 returned as a line-wide option at $58. Rated power was unchanged, but in the lighter '59s it delivered 0-60-mph acceleration of 10 seconds or less. Styling was a toned-down version of the '58 look, marked by grille-mounted headlights, taller windshields, and more conventional taillights moved down into the back panel. Prices were trimmed along with models and weight.

Corsairs and the 361 V8 disappeared for 1960, when the vertical grille gave way to a split horizontal affair looking suspiciously like that of the '59 Pontiac (purely a coincidence). Taillamps were a quartet of vertical ovals, and heavy chrome moldings adorned the upper sides of the body, which was just a mildly restyled version of that year's all-new Ford design. The 292 V8 was detuned to 185 bhp. Two-speed or three-speed automatic transmission, power steering and air conditioning were still available. The Ranger convertible listed at $3000, but could be optioned up to $3800. Only 76 were built. Rarest of all Edsels is this year's three-seat Villager wagon: a mere 59.

The Edsel was Detroit's biggest and most public flop since the Tucker, and the name has since come to be listed in at least one dictionary as a synonym for "loser"—unfortunate considering the great legacy of Edsel Ford. Though the company reportedly lost $250 million on the project, it wasn't all bad. Expanding facilities for Edsel production left Ford with a surplus that came in very handy when its new 1960 Falcon immediately ran away with the compact market.

Had it been a truly different car introduced three to five years either side of 1958, the Edsel might be with us yet. Instead, it stands as a monument to the cynicism of a time when Detroit thought buyers didn't know—or care about—the difference between style and substance.

EXCALIBUR

America's most successful builder of cars fashioned in the image of the great classics is Excalibur, the Milwaukee concern founded by the two sons of industrial designer Brooks Stevens. Fastidiously assembled, the Excalibur is a superb road machine. It's also *very* exclusive.

The Excalibur Series I, introduced in 1964, remained in its original form until it was replaced by the Series II in 1970. Its styling echoed the classic 1928 Mercedes-Benz SSK, and even the firm's sales literature was patterned after that of the prewar Mercedes. Careful engineering and clever design distinguished the Excalibur from a motley group of VW-powered replicas that followed it.

In 1964, Stevens was finishing four years as design consultant to the ill-fated Studebaker Corporation. The old-line automaker had ceased car production at its South Bend, Indiana, plant in late 1963, but continued some operations at its Hamilton, Ontario, factory. Stevens hoped production would go on. But he was unimpressed by the firm's mundane cars at the 1964 Chicago Auto Show, and was determined to build a more exciting Studebaker "special" for the New York show in April. So, he ordered up a Lark Daytona convertible chassis with power disc brakes and a 290-horsepower, supercharged 289-cubic-inch Avanti V8. Company managers tentatively approved his plan to build "a modern classic" for their company's New York display. The prototype Excalibur was created in just six weeks by Stevens' two sons, David and William. No sooner had it left for New York than Studebaker officials changed their minds. A "contemporary classic," they said would conflict with the "common-sense" image they were trying to establish.

More than time and money was at stake, and the Stevenses refused to scrap the project. Through hurried phone calls to the show's management, they arranged to display the Excalibur on a separate stand. The car was a hit, and in August 1964 the sons founded SS Automobiles to manufacture it—with their dad's blessing and assistance. Some 100 copies had been sold by the beginning of 1966.

Studebaker's demise ended the supply of 289 V8s after 1965, so the Stevens brothers went shopping for a new engine. The 327-cid Corvette unit was duly provided by their friends Ed Cole and Semon E. "Bunkie" Knudsen at General Motors. After 1966, Excaliburs were also offered with a Paxton-supercharged V8 rated at 400 bhp, and high-performance Corvette engines. With the standard 3.31:1 rear axle ratio, the car was claimed to have a 0-60 mph time of less than five seconds and a top speed in the area of 160 mph.

The 109-inch-wheelbase Studebaker Daytona convertible chassis was hardly modern, but it offered some advantages. Unlike concurrent torque-box frames, it was quite narrow, as its frame rails were not spread as far apart as on other chassis that had to accommodate more modern, wider body sills. Thus, it was perfectly suited for the Excalibur's narrower, vintage-style body. As a convertible chassis it was firmly X-braced. But it needed considerable re-engineering to insure safe handling in a high-powered car that weighed at least 500 pounds less than a Corvette.

David Stevens was largely responsible for the engineering. The classic-style cowl forced him to lower the Studebaker steering column and control pedals. It was also necessary to alter the suspension geometry drastically by decreasing spring rates and changing caster and camber. This modified Studebaker chassis was retained for all Series I models. Like the Excaliburs that followed them, these cars were fast on both curves and straightaways.

Brooks Stevens was responsible for the styling, which was a surprisingly accurate rendition of the fabulous SSK. He considered outside exhaust pipes mandatory, but no one in the United States could supply them. Ultimately, he bought the flexible tubing from the same German firm that had supplied it to Mercedes back in the Twenties. Bodies on the first few cars were made of hammered aluminum, but the firm soon switched to fiberglass, mainly for reasons of cost and practicality. The radiator was made of sheet brass on the prototype; production radiators were cast aluminum. The Mercedes three-pointed star suggested the hood or-

With less than 100 per year built, the 1965-69 SSK was always rare.

The Series I Phaeton was even rarer, and priced at $10,000 in 1969.

The Excalibur, a Brooks Stevens-designed Studebaker show car that was rejected because it conflicted with Stude's "common-sense" image, was put into production by Stevens' sons. Studebaker's gone, but Excalibur has survived for 25 years.

nament, an Excalibur sword in a circle, which resembled—but not too closely—the symbol jealously protected by the German firm. French-built freestanding headlamps looked very similar to the original SSK units. White-on-black instruments from the Studebaker Hawk were placed in an SSK-like engine-turned dash panel. The seats used were modified Studebaker buckets, covered in expanded vinyl (leather would be used later). The initial price was almost unbelievably low: $7250 for a hand-built car having one of the most competently engineered chassis in the business.

For 1966, the firm changed its name to Excalibur Automobile Corporation and added a more elaborate roadster. Unlike the aggressive-looking SSK, this model had full fenders and running boards. A four-passenger phaeton was offered beginning that same year. Prices began going up, but so did materials, quality and standard equipment. By 1969, the list included air conditioning, heater and defroster, variable-ratio power steering, tilt steering wheel, power front disc brakes, Positraction rear axle, chrome-plated wire wheels, luggage rack, AM/FM stereo, leather seats, Turbo Hydra-Matic transmission, twin side-mounted spare tires, all weather hardtop, air horns, driving lights, steel-belted radial tires, and automatically controlled self-leveling rear shocks.

For 1970, the Series II was introduced on a longer 111-inch wheelbase and powered by a 350-cid Corvette V8. The same body styles were offered, now starting at $12,000, but the old Studebaker frame was replaced by a new box-section chassis designed by David Stevens around Corvette suspension components. GM's four-speed "Muncie" manual gearbox came standard, and the Turbo Hydra-Matic moved to the options list. Independent suspension and four-wheel disc brakes combined with Goodyear Polyglas tires mounted on specially designed wire wheels to offer a fine balance between ride and handling. The factory claimed a Series II would leap from 0 to 60 mph in six seconds flat and reach 150 mph.

Prices and production began taking off with the Series III, announced in 1975 (the firm did not adhere strictly to a model year cycle). Basically, this was the Series II design modified to meet federal safety and emissions regulations, but not so much as to compromise the styling or roadability that were, by this time, traditional for the marque. Besides "shock mounted solid aluminum alloy [bumpers that] meet government standards for absorbing impact," the Series III boasted fuller clamshell-style fenders and standard high-back bucket seats covered in leather and—like most of the rest of the car—made by Excalibur itself. The major mechanical alteration was adoption of Chevy's big-block Mark IV 454-cid V8, an engine more amenable to emissions tuning than the previous unit. Initial prices for the Series III cars were $18,900.

By any standard, Excalibur was still a tiny producer, but the Stevens brothers would not be rushed. Nor did they want to dilute their market with too much of a good thing. As it had since 1969, the more practical four-seat phaeton continued to outsell the two-passenger roadster, but total production was still minuscule even for a specialty maker. A mere 1141 Series III cars were built through 1979, compared with 342 for the Series II and 359 for the Series I.

Excalibur had come a long way since David and William C. "Steve" Stevens had built their first cars (the latter even worked on the assembly line until 1968). Striking evidence of the firm's progress appeared in January 1981 in the elegant new Series IV, which listed at $37,700. More a luxury tourer than a lightweight big-inch sports machine, it was the most radically changed Excalibur in history—and the best yet. Wheelbase was extended to near limousine length (125 inches), and the new model boasted more standard accoutrements than any of its predecessors. Styling remained firmly in the classic tradition, but was smoother, sleeker, and evolutionary in much the same way that the late-'30s Mercedes 500/540K was related to the SS/SSK. The phaeton acquired a new lift-off hardtop plus a fully powered soft top, and the

The Series II Roadster went into production in 1970. Cost: $12,000.

Series III production started in 1975; the Phaeton sold for $18,900.

A long 125-inch wheelbase was featured on the 1980-84 Series IV.

roadster gained a functional rumble seat. Another round of engineering improvements was made in line with federal requirements, and running gear was switched to GM's well-known 5.0-liter (305-cid) V8 and four-speed overdrive automatic transmission.

Appropriately, the Series IV marked the 30th anniversary of the Excalibur marque (Brooks Stevens designed and built the first car to bear the name around Henry J components in 1951).

Unfortunately, the severe economic recession of the early Eighties and the expense of developing the Series V was more than the company could withstand, and it was forced to file for

The 1980 Series IV Phaeton listed at $37,700. Excalibur turned out 93 units that year. A 305-cid Chevy V8 was utilized.

Debuting in early '88 was the 144-inch-wheelbase Sedan, whose overall length measured 224 inches. It was priced at $65,550.

Chapter 11 bankruptcy in early 1986. Later that year, The Acquisition Company of Illinois purchased the assets of Excalibur Automobile Corporation for $2.3 million. Henry A. Warner became president and announced the addition of the Sedan and Limousine to the traditional Roadster and Phaeton.

The Sedan debuted first, in late 1987. Excalibur called it a practical "everyday car," compared to the more specialized Roadster and Phaeton. Up to the cowl, it was the same as other Excaliburs and utilized the same 305-cid GM V8 and four-speed overdrive automatic transmission. However, an extended Phaeton square-tube ladder frame gave it a 20-inch-longer wheelbase (144 inches), allowing for a spacious back seat. Up front, a bench front seat replaced the buckets and console of the Phaeton. Overall, the Sedan measured a whopping 224 inches long, and the curb weight came in at a hefty 4400 pounds. By early 1988, the $65,650 Sedan and the companion Roadster and Phaeton were being produced at a rate of about 150-200 cars per year, a level Warner saw as being profitable.

For 1989, Excalibur planned to officially introduce the limousine, and was working on another new model to debut later in the year. Speculation was that it might be a sportier car offered as an alternative to the Chevrolet Corvette.

Under new management since 1986, Excalibur expanded the Coupe and Phaeton lineup in 1987 with a Sedan and looked to debut a Limousine during 1989. President Henry A. Warner said the firm could be profitable with a volume of 200 cars per year.

FORD

Founded in 1903, Ford Motor Company skyrocketed from obscurity to dominate the American auto industry in less than 12 years. The foundation of this unparalleled success was, of course, the cheap, simple Model T—the world's first mass-produced car, whose lovable quirkiness was matched only by that of Henry Ford, its creator and company founder. Henry's decision to abandon his treasured "Tin Lizzie" only after 19 years and staggering production of over 15-million units—the last car not very different from the first—came almost too late, and his company lost a lot in money and goodwill during the long changeover to the belated new Model A.

Yet despite keen competition from an aggressive Chevrolet and newcomer Plymouth, the A was a success—almost perfectly timed for the Depression that began soon after its 1928 debut. Ford built over 1.1 million cars for 1930—almost twice as many as Chevrolet and more than 11 times as many as Plymouth.

After considerable delay, Ford followed up with an even more attractive innovation for 1932: America's first low-priced V-8 car. It was something of a rush job and early engine problems let Chevrolet take the production lead through '33. But the bugs were quashed fairly quickly and the V8 was another huge Ford success. Equally significant, its basic engineering would survive all the way through 1948.

Reflecting Henry's intransigence, Ford was slower than its rivals to adopt new features and abandon old ones in the years leading up to 1939, but its cars were nevertheless among the most memorable of this era. Among the most universal, too. Aided by pretty styling evolved by E.T. "Bob" Gregorie under the guidance of company president Edsel Ford, Henry's only son, Ford outpaced Chevrolet in 1934-37 production, its volume ranging from a half-million to nearly one million.

Beginning with the '34 line, Ford turned from four-cylinder models to nothing but V-8s—speedy, simple and affordable cars offered with a wide range of body styles in Standard and DeLuxe trim. All were powered by Henry's unassuming cast-iron flathead engine, sized at 221 cubic inches and now developing 90 horse-

Ford built 37,326 DeLuxe five-window coupes for '39. Price: $702.

The DeLuxe Fordor cost $788; buyers took delivery of 90,551 units.

A new grille was the biggest change for '40, here a DeLuxe Tudor.

The '40 DeLuxe coupe is highly desired nowadays by collectors.

power (up from the original 65 bhp). Streamlining, which had arrived for '33, was increasingly evident, culminating with Gregorie's handsome prow-front design for 1937, one of the decade's best.

That same year, Ford abandoned the traditional fabric roof insert on closed bodies for all-steel construction. It also added a companion 60-bhp 136-cid V8 for a group of lower-priced models aimed at Depression-weary buyers interested in greater fuel economy. But poor performance limited sales, especially once war preparations began pulling the national economy out of its prolonged slump, and the V8/60 was discontinued after 1940. Meanwhile, the 221 flathead was re-rated at 85 bhp.

The 1939 Fords originated in a new two-tier 1938 lineup. A low-priced Standard coupe, Tudor sedan and Fordor sedan used a restyled version of the previous body; the costlier DeLuxe models had an all-new design with more fulsome second-generation streamlining. The romantic roadster was gone and the phaeton was making its last stand. Both had long since lost whatever favor they once had, but Ford was far behind its rivals in realizing this (Plymouth's last roadster and phaeton appeared in 1932, Chevrolet's for 1935). Rumble-seat models were in their last year.

DeLuxe models were heavily restyled for 1939, bearing a lower, vee'd vertical-bar grille and clean front fenders with integral headlamps. This year's Standards looked liked '38 DeLuxes. The convertible sedan put in its final appearance, again in the DeLuxe series. Prices were reduced $5 across the board, now covering a $599-$921 spread. Mechanical changes included steering-column instead of floor-mounted gearshift and hydraulic instead of mechanical brakes. Henry had finally given in on the last point—three years after Chevrolet and 11 years after Plymouth. But suspension was still a relic of the Model T days: a solid axle on a transverse leaf spring at each end. Not until 1949 would Ford match the independent front suspension already adopted by its rivals.

Artful refinements made the 1940 Fords even prettier—so much so that the DeLuxes in particular have long since been coveted collectibles. A crisply pointed hood flowed smoothly back to a rakishly angled windshield. Headlamps, sealed beams for the first time, were faired into neat fender nacelles. The fenders themselves were beautifully curved to complement the body contours, and were often skirted at the rear. Standards carried a '39 DeLuxe-style vertical-bar grille. DeLuxes bore a chromed, horizontal-bar center section flanked by painted sub-grilles in the "catwalk" areas twixt nose and fenders.

Wheelbase for 1940 remained at the 112 inches adopted with the 1933 V8 models. Standard coupe, business coupe, Tudor and Fordor sedans were offered for the last time with the little V8/60. The Standard "V8/85" series added a wood-body station wagon of the sort Ford had offered since 1930. These five body types plus a convertible coupe made up the V8/85 DeLuxe line. Despite this wide choice plus the pretty styling and prices in the $620-$950 range, Ford trailed Chevy in model year production by a substantial 222,720 units.

Edsel Ford's new medium-priced Mercury had arrived for 1939, but many dealers were disappointed, feeling a six-cylinder Ford would have been a better idea. Edsel promised them one, but then had to reckon with his father. But Henry approved a six in one of those strange about-faces for which he was noted. Edsel went to work, and a new L-head six bowed for 1941. With 226 cid and 90 bhp, the six had five more cubic inches than the V8 and a like number of extra horsepower, a bit embarrassing.

The lineup expanded to three series: low-priced Special, mid-range DeLuxe and new the Super DeLuxe, all offered with either engine. They were the biggest, flashiest, heaviest Fords yet. Wheelbase stretched two inches, bodysides ballooned outward, and a stouter frame contributed to an average 300-pound gain in curb weight. Styling was evolutionary, with wider, more integrated front fenders; a busy vertical-bar grille with a tall center section

It took $849 to buy a '40 DeLuxe soft top. Try pricing one now.

A '42 Ford DeLuxe Fordor V8 sold for $885 before the war interrupted.

The Super DeLuxe was the top-line '41 Ford. A Tudor cost $818.

Top-down motoring in a '41 Super DeLuxe ragtop came in at $946.

Ford had been the industry giant in the Teens and Twenties, but by 1939 it had relinquished its lead to Chevrolet. A good part of the problem was Henry Ford's stubbornness in bringing out new features such as hydraulic brakes.

The postwar '46 Ford, a warmed-over '42, sported a new grille.

The '47 Super DeLuxe Sportsman listed at $2282. Output: 2250 units.

Ford built 12,249 Super DeLuxe coupes for the 1946 model run.

Ford's Iron Mountain, Michigan, plant built the '48 woody bodies.

and low, flanking sub-grilles; larger rear fenders and more rakish coupe rooflines. Prices ranged from $684 for the six-cylinder Special coupe to $1013 for the V8 DeLuxe woody wagon—the first factory-built Ford to break the $1000 barrier.

But none of this did much for Ford sales. While volume improved to near 691,500, it remained about two-thirds of Chevy's, which went up even more, to slightly over a million.

The 1942 Fords arrived with a lower, wider vertical-bar grille surmounted by rectangular parking lamps in the vestigial catwalks. The V8 returned to its pre-1937 power rating of 90 to match the six (if the V8 had to cost more, it should have at least as much power, even if only on paper). Specials were now sixes only, but the lineup was otherwise unchanged. Prices were hiked about $100 throughout. Ford built just 43,000 cars from January 1 through February 2, when civilian production ended. The model year total was just shy of 160,500, versus Chevy's quarter-million-plus.

A renowned pacifist during World War I, Henry Ford was in his late '70s when the Japanese attacked Pearl Harbor on December 7, 1941. But he realized that World War II was a very different situation and ordered quick conversion to war production. Ford Motor Company duly turned out a variety of military vehicles including Jeeps (with American Bantam and Willys-Overland), and its newly built mile-long plant in Willow Run, near Detroit, produced a variety of bombers through 1945.

With war's end, Henry at last surrendered control of his company—but not to Edsel, who died a broken man in 1943 at age 49. The doddering mogul then stubbornly continued to manage an increasingly troubled Ford Motor Company until his family insisted he step down. In 1945 he did, handing the reigns to grandson Henry Ford II. "HFII" retired in 1980 after 33 years marked by great success. Unlike his grandfather, he consistently sought and encouraged talented managers. However, he just as consistently encouraged their retirement—or fired them—when they attained a certain level of power. Though the family no longer owns a majority of common stock, Ford is still very much a family operation.

Young Henry fast returned Ford to civilian production after V-J day. Ford was again the volume leader for model year '46, but Chevrolet would be back in full swing the following year—and "USA-1" through 1948.

Like most other makes, Ford returned to peacetime with what amounted to restyled '42s. However, the V8 was bored out to 239 cid for an extra 10 bhp. The low-priced Special Sixes were eliminated, leaving six- and eight-cylinder DeLuxe and Super DeLuxe. And there was a second V8 convertible, a novel variation on the standard item called Sportsman.

Developed from Bob Gregorie's wartime sketches, the Sportsman featured white ash and mahogany trim over its doors, rear body panels, and deck like the Chrysler Town & Country. It was an easy way to give an old design new appeal, and it boosted floor traffic at Ford dealers. But a $500 price premium over the all-steel convertible limited sales to just 1209 for '46, 2250 for '47 and just 28 for '48 (the last actually reserialed '47s).

Appearance alterations for 1947 involved shuffled nameplates and lower-mounted round parking lights. No styling changes occurred for '48, but the six was now rated at 95 bhp, up five. Postwar inflation had prices up, the increases averaging about $100 for 1947 and again for '48.

But nothing really new was needed in the car-starved early-postwar market, and Ford output exceeded 429,000 units for 1947. The total was only 236,000 the following year, but that didn't reflect trouble in Dearborn, only an early end to 1948 production. Work on the first all-new postwar Ford had begun in early '46, and it arrived earlier than usual, in June 1948.

Styling for the '49 was a competitive operation, Ford soliciting ideas from freelancers as well as its own designers. Among the

Priciest model in Ford's 1949 lineup was the two-door, eight-passenger woody Custom wagon. Price: $2119. Production: 31,412.

A mild facelift was undertaken for 1950, and quality was improved.

Ford's stopgap reply to Chevy's Bel Air hardtop was the Crestliner.

former was a team headed by George Walker, which developed a slab-sided package with integral fenders. But as the deadline approached, Walker associate Dick Caleal ran into trouble with the front and rear ends. According to Robert Bourke, then chief designer for the Loewy Studios at Studebaker, Caleal asked Bourke and his assistant, Bob Koto, for help. They agreed, working on their own time.

Late-night sessions at the Caleal home in Mishawaka, Indiana, produced a smooth-looking quarter-scale clay model with a bullet or spinner-type grille reminiscent of the 1950 Studebaker then under development. Bourke recalled that Walker put the model under his arm and took it to Dearborn, where it was accepted with only one significant change: The taillights were turned from vertical to horizontal. Of course, the '49 Ford was nowhere near as radical as the Studebaker, but it sold in numbers Ford hadn't seen since 1930: over 1.1 million for the extra-long model year. Reflecting this achievement, Walker became design chief for all of Ford Motor Company in 1955.

The '49 was crucial to Ford's survival. Young Henry II was still scrambling to bring order to the organizational and fiscal chaos he inherited from his grandfather even as the company continued losing money by the bucketful. But the '49 was the most changed Ford since the Model A, and it was much a sensation.

Though wheelbase and engines stayed the same, the '49 was three inches lower, fractionally shorter and usefully lighter than the 1946-48 Fords. Even better, it had a modern ladder-type frame with Dearborn's first fully independent front suspension (via coil springs and upper and lower A-arms) plus a modern rear end with

The Fords of the Forties were still very much old Henry's cars. Although they were V-8 powered, their engineering was dated. The new postwar Fords, the '49s, were Henry II's cars; they boasted modern styling and updated engineering.

Ford debuted its first hardtop after the other '51s appeared. First year output of the Victoria amounted to 110,286 units.

open Hotchkiss drive (replacing torque-tube) and parallel longitudinal leaf springs supporting the live axle. It all added up to a sprightly performer that could run circles around rival Chevys and Plymouths. A '49 Ford couldn't quite reach 100 mph, but hopping up the flathead V8 was still simple, cheap and easy. Multiple carburetors, headers, dual exhausts and other speed equipment were as near as the local auto parts store.

Though Ford briefly considered retaining it, the low-selling Sportsman was dropped for '49 and other offerings regrouped into Standard and Custom series. The former offered a choice of six or V8 Tudor and Fordor sedans and business and club coupes. The better-trimmed V8-only Custom deleted the business coupe but added convertible and a new two-door wood-panelled wagon (replacing the previous four-door style).

Prices increased again, the '49 ranged up to $1333-$2119. Overdrive was optional across the board at $97. Ford wouldn't have its own automatic transmission until 1951, though it tried to get one earlier. Studebaker had developed an excellent automatic

The '51 was Ford's last woody wagon, and the first Country Squire.

The Crestliner was dropped during 1951. Output reached 8703 units.

All-steel wagons arrived for '52, here a mid-range Country Sedan.

The 1952 Crestline series included a convertible called Sunliner.

for 1950, in association with Warner Gear. Ford wanted to buy the rights for use on its own cars, but Studebaker refused—much to its later regret.

The '49 Fords arrived with handling and noise problems stemming from the crash development program, and workmanship was hampered by the rush to production and a 24-day auto workers' strike in May 1948. Nevertheless, they were worthy automobiles, the first tangible evidence that Henry II was at the Dearborn helm—ably assisted by the youthful "Whiz Kid" team of executives and engineers he'd recruited, including one Robert S. McNamara.

And Ford Motor Company would make a smart comeback in the '50s, moving ahead of Chrysler to regain the number-two spot. The reason? Interesting cars that sold well.

A special confection for 1950-51 was the V8 Crestliner, a limited-edition Tudor distinguished by a contrasting bodyside color sweep and padded vinyl top. Only 26,304 were sold. Today, of course, they're collectors' items.

Other 1950s looked much like the '49s except for a crest instead of Ford lettering above the grille, but were vastly improved in handling, quietness and workmanship. Prices held steady. The '51s were attractively facelifted via a new grille with small twin bullets on a thick horizontal bar. The Custom wagon now bore Country Squire script. Arriving with optional three-speed Ford-O-Matic Drive was Ford's first hardtop coupe, the Custom V-8 Victoria. It was a year behind Chevy's Bel Air but no less popular, some 110,000 finding buyers. Ford built over 1.2 million cars for 1950, its highest total since 1930, but Chevrolet built close to 1.5 million, and would remain number-one through 1953.

Model year '52 brought a clean new square-rigged generation with one-piece windshields and a 115-inch wheelbase. Only detail styling changes would occur through 1954. Model offerings were again realigned. At the bottom were Mainline Tudor/Fordor sedans, business coupe and two-door Ranch Wagon. The mid-range Customline offered the sedans, a club coupe and four-door Country Sedan wagon. At the top was the V8 Crestline series comprising Victoria hardtop, newly named Sunliner convertible, and the posh Country Squire four-door wagon. These were Ford's first all-steel wagons, the Squire switching from real wood trim to wood-look decals. A new 101-bhp overhead-valve six of 215.3 cid was standard for the two lower series, and the V8 was tweaked up to 110 bhp.

An outlay of $2043 bought a '53 Sunliner; 40,861 folks did just that.

Ford Motor Company observed its Golden Anniversary in 1953, but that year's Fords had no significant changes in celebration—except for an increase in prices. Ford Division built 1.2 million cars that year, volume shattered in 1955 with nearly 1.5 million cars. Ford was closing in on Chevy, but was straining its dealers. A Ford could be had at "less than cost" in 1953-54 when the "Ford Blitz" reached its peak. Chevrolet was not seriously damaged by the onslaught, but the independents were. Unable to discount as much, Studebaker, American Motors, and Kaiser-Willys were hit hard. The Ford Blitz is generally considered one of the most important factors in the independents' mid-'50s decline.

The venerable flathead was honorably retired for 1954 as Ford

Mainstay of the '53 line was the Customline four door: 374,487 built.

New for '54 was the plastic-top Skyliner; 13,344 were produced.

The "wood" on the '53 Country Squire wasn't real. Output: 11,001.

The Skyliner was in the Crestline series; its ohv V8 was all-new.

Ford pressed Chevrolet in 1952 with all-new styling and, after the Korean conflict was settled, a 1953 sales blitz. In 1954, while the government was launching the Nautilus, the first atomic submarine, Ford launched its all-new ohv V-8.

For $2224, some 49,966 souls thought the '55 Sunliner a good investment for fun-in-the-sun motoring. How right they were!

The Country Sedan weighed in at 3525 pounds and listed at $2451.

New to the '56 Fairlane lineup was a four-door Victoria hardtop.

The '56 Ford received a new grille; the Customline new side trim.

The '57 Custom 300 had a 116-inch wheelbase; here the $2157 four door.

This '56 Fairlane Victoria has the 292 V8; a 312 was optional.

At $2202, the '55 Crown Victoria cost almost as much as a ragtop.

made headlines with its new overhead-valve "Y-block" V8. With 130 bhp, it was easily the hottest engine in the low-price field. Together with ball-joint front suspension, also new that year, it greatly narrowed the engineering gap between expensive and inexpensive cars. Its initial 239 cid was the same as the flathead's displacement, but the ohv V8 had entirely different "oversquare" bore/stroke dimensions. Compression was 7.2:1 in standard trim, but could be upped to 12:1 if required.

The rest of the '54 story was basically a '53 reprise except for a larger, 223-cid ohv six with 115 bhp, plus a novel new hardtop, the Skyliner. This was basically the Crestline Victoria with a see-through green-tinted Plexiglas insert for the front half of its roof, a concept suggested by Dearborn designer Gordon M. Buehrig (of Auburn/Cord/Duesenberg fame) and developed by interior styling director L. David Ash. A forerunner of today's moonroof, it cast a bilious pall over occupants, and heat buildup was a problem. This and a price identical with the convertible's limited '54 Skyliner sales to only 13,344 units. Only the Country Squire and Mainline business coupe fared worse.

Retaining the 1952-54 shell, the '55 Ford was completely reskinned, emerging colorful if chromey, with a rakish look of motion and a modestly wrapped windshield. Styling was handled by Frank Hershey, who also gets most of the credit for this year's new Thunderbird, one of the most important Fords ever (*see* Ford Thunderbird). Club coupes were abandoned, station wagons made a separate series, and the top-shelf Crestline was now Fairlane (the name of Henry Ford's estate). With the "horsepower race" in full swing, Ford ousted the 239 V8 for a 272-cid enlargement with 162/182 bhp as an option. The six gained 5 bhp.

Replacing Skyliner for '55 was the Fairlane Crown Victoria, a hardtop-style two-door with a vee'd chrome band wrapped over the roof from rakishly angled B-posts. The band looked like a roll bar, but added little, if any, strength. The Plexiglas insert rode ahead of it. A full steel-roof model was also offered at a $70 saving and sold much better than the "bubbletopper": 33,000-plus to just 1999. The totals were 9209 and just 603 for '56, after which the Crown Vic was dropped.

A mild facelift and more powerful engines arrived for '56, along with a Customline Victoria and a new Town Victoria hardtop sedan in the Fairlane series. Ford tried selling safety this year, equipping all models with a dished steering wheel, breakaway rearview mirror, and crashproof door locks; padded dash and sunvisors cost $16 extra, factory-installed seatbelts $9. Buyers responded early in the model year, but the rush to seatbelts overtaxed Ford's supplier and only 20 percent of the '56s were so equipped. Ford continued to stress safety for a few more years, but emphasized performance more.

Speaking of which, this year's 272 V8 delivered 173 bhp as a Mainline/Customline option. A new 312 engine with 215/225 was optional across the board, and a mid-range 292 offered 200 bhp.

The 1957 Fords were all-new, offering a vast array of V8s from a 190-bhp 272 on up to a Thunderbird 312 with 245 bhp. The 223-cid was standard for all but one model. There were now two wheelbases and five series: 116 inches for wagons and Custom/Custom 300 sedans, 118 inches for Fairlane and Fairlane 500. All were available with six or V8 power. Styling was particularly simple for the period: a blunt face with a clean, full-width rectangular grille; rakish side moldings; tiny tailfins. This was a good year for the division. Some statisticians put Ford ahead of Chevrolet in calendar year output for the first time since 1935, but the final tabulation showed Chevy ahead by 130 cars. In model year production, though, Ford scored a substantial victory with close to 1.7 million units to Chevy's 1.5 million.

A mid-year addition to the Fairlane 500 line was the unique Skyliner, the first mass-produced retractable hardtop. It stemmed from earlier developmental engineering at Continental Division, where a 1956 Mark II retractable was considered, but not pro-

At $2402, the top-line '57 Fairlane 500 rode a 118-inch wheelbase.

The '57 Fairlane 500 two-door sedan saw output hit 93,756 units.

At $2942, the Skyliner "retractable" cost $437 more than a Sunliner.

Skyliner production slipped from 20,766 in 1957 to 14,713 in '58.

Determined to regain the sales lead, Ford innovated with new body styles in the Fifties. Among them were the '54 Plexiglas-topped Skyliner, the '57 retractable convertible Skyliner, and the '57 Ranchero car-based pickup.

The $2435 Fairlane 500 Victoria found favor with 80,439 buyers in 1958. Ford output in that recession year fell to 987,945 units.

duced. Ford sold 20,766 of the '57 Skyliners, but demand fast tapered off to 14,713 for '58, then to 12,915. The model was duly axed for 1960, a victim of division chief Bob McNamara's no-nonsense approach to marketing and profits. Today the Skyliner is a prime collectible, a monument to an age when Detroit thought it could do anything.

Ford faced the all-new '58 Chevy and a modestly restyled Plymouth with a glittery facelift featuring quad headlamps and taillamps, a '58 T-Bird-like bumper/grille and more anodized aluminum trim. Engine choices expanded via two 332-cid V8s offering 240/265 bhp and new 352-cid big-block, one of company's new FE-series engines, with a rated 300 bhp. A deep national recession cut Ford volume to just under 988,000 units. Chevrolet sold over 1.1 million, but spent much more money to do so.

Chevrolet returned for '59 with an all-new line of radical bat-fin models that enabled Ford to close the model-year gap to less than 12,000 units. A major reskin of the basic '57 platform brought conservative squared-up body lines with simple side moldings, a heavily sculptured back panel and a low, rectangular grille filled with floating star-like ornaments. Mid-season brought a new Galaxie series comprising sedans and Victoria hardtop coupes and sedans with wide-quarter T-Bird-style rooflines. At the same time,

The Custom 300 two-door sedan was a popular '58 model: 137,169 built.

Skyliner production fell to 12,915 units in 1959—its last year.

Country Sedan was Ford's mid-price '59 wagon; 123,412 were built.

Wheelbase grew to 119 inches for 1960, as on this Fairlane 500.

Galaxie was Ford's top series for the all-new 1960 models. The four-door Victoria listed at $2675 and 39,215 were produced.

the Sunliner convertible and Skyliner retrac gained Galaxie rear-fender script but retained Fairlane 500 i.d. at the rear. The 118-inch wheelbase was now used across the board. V8s were down to a 292, 332 and 352 with 200-300 bhp.

For Ford Motor Company as a whole, 1959 justified the strenuous efforts of Henry Ford II and board chairman Ernest Breech. Assuming control of a third-rate company in 1945, they'd turned it into something approaching General Motors in less than 15 years.

Ford's history in the '60s closely parallels Chevrolet's. At decade's end, it was also building about 100,000 more cars each year than in 1960 via expansion into several important new markets, including economy compacts, intermediates, and sportier versions of regular production models. Also like Chevy, Ford built these diverse types on relatively few wheelbases. (Mustang and T-Bird, the two most specialized Fords, are treated separately.)

Key management changes occurred early on. Lee A. Iacocca took charge as Ford Division general manager in 1960. George Walker left the following year and Eugene Bordinat became Dearborn's design chief. Iacocca soon put an end to the mundane people-movers favored by predecessor Robert S. McNamara. By 1970, Ford was offering some of the world's best road cars. In fact, Fords were the cars to beat on the nation's racetracks and drag-

Country Squire continued its winning ways with 81,539 built for 1960.

Ford's compact 1960 Falcon was a smash hit with 435,676 built.

The semi-fastback Starliner cost $2610. Output: 68,461 units.

Falcon was even more popular in '61 as 474,241 went out the door.

Ford marched confidently into the Sixties with larger standard-size cars and the new compact Falcon. The latter had to compete with the established Rambler and the new Chevy Corvair and Chrysler's Valiant. It outdid them all.

Ford assembled 44,614 Sunliners for 1961. Base price: $2849.

Full-size '62 Fords had a more formal look, as on the Galaxie 500.

Bucket seats and four-on-the-floor were '62 Falcon Futura features.

Ford was first to market an intermediate, the '62 Fairlane 500.

The Fairlane 500 Sports Coupe sported bucket seats. Price: $2504.

The most collectible Falcon is the 1963 Sprint—coupe or convertible.

This 1963 Galaxie 500 XL Sunliner boasts a 385/405 bhp 406 V8.

Ford built 21,431 Fairlane 500 Sports Coupes for the '64 model run.

strips for much of the decade. The 1968-69 Dodge Charger program was an all-out effort to halt the Ford superstockers.

The division also evolved from a "Chevy-follower" to "Chevy-leader" in the '60s. Ford's compact Falcon outsold the Corvair, its 1962 mid-size Fairlane was two years ahead of the Chevelle, and its phenomenally successful Mustang sent Chevrolet racing to the drawing boards to develop the Camaro.

The best way to summarize the '60s Ford is by size. The smallest was Falcon, which rode a 109.5-inch wheelbase through 1965, then a 110.9-inch span (113 inches for wagons). Two- and four-door sedans and four-door wagons were always offered, convertibles and hardtop coupes for 1963-65. Falcon production gradually declined, largely because of competition from both inside and outside Ford Division, but the line was always profitable. Falcon's conventional suspension and cast-iron six (mostly a 101-bhp 170-cid unit) were dull next to Corvair engineering, but they made for a simple, roomy little car that rode well and delivered 20-25 mpg.

Replying to the Corvair Monza in spring 1961 was the bucket-seat Futura two-door, which along with other models was reskinned for '64 with a much less distinctive, squared-off shape. The prime collector's Falcon is the mid-1963 Futura Sprint, a convertible and hardtop available with the lively small-block Fairlane V8 with 260 cid and 164 bhp initially, 289 cid and around 200 bhp for '65. It was one fine engine, which helps explain why its later 302-cid derivative is still in production. It completely transformed Falcon performance without greatly affecting mileage.

XL was the sporty big Ford in the Sixties. The '64 Galaxie 500 XL hardtop coupe listed at $3233; output reached 58,306 units.

The 1965 Ford was all-new and featured coil-spring rear suspension.

Like the big Fords, the '65 Falcon took on squarer, bulkier lines.

The 1966 Ford LTD limousine was *not* a production-line model.

The '66 Falcon, here a Futura, was basically a shortened Fairlane.

Sprints had special trim, bucket seats, console, and full instrumentation including a 6000-rpm tachometer. When equipped with the optional four-speed manual transmission, they were great fun to drive.

The 1966 Falcons were basically shortened versions of that year's new Fairlane, with the same sort of curvy styling and long-hood/short-deck proportions *a la* Mustang. It remained in this form through early 1970. In its last year before emission controls, the 289 packed 225 bhp in "Stage 2" tune with four-barrel carburetors and made Falcon Sprints very fast. For 1968 it was detuned to 195 bhp, but its 302 enlargement arrived as an option. With two-barrel carb, the 302 ran on regular gas and delivered 210 bhp. With four barrel, it required premium fuel but developed 230 bhp. Emissions controls then put an end to it.

Mid-1970 brought the final Falcons: a stark wagon and two sedans derived from the intermediate Torino and offered with everything from a 155-bhp 250-cid six to the big-block 429 V8 with 360-370 bhp. But the name had outlived its usefulness and Ford had a new compact that year, the Maverick, so Falcon was consigned to history for '71.

Ford broke new ground for 1962 with the mid-size Fairlane, basically a bigger Falcon on a 115.5-inch wheelbase. Its concept was much like that of Virgil Exner's downsized '62 Plymouths and Dodges. But unlike Chrysler, Ford retained its full-size Customs and Galaxies—a wise move even though Fairlane sold more than 297,000 units its first year and over 300,000 for '63.

Although Chevy widened its sales lead over Ford in the Sixties, Ford continued to innovate. It beat Chevy to market by two years with the intermediate-size Fairlane and Chevy had to respond to the upmarket LTD with the copycat Caprice.

A popular '68 offering was the Torino GT fastback; 74,135 were built that year. This one has a 390 V8, but a 428 was available.

The '66 Country Squire seated six or nine, sold for $3182 or $3265.

A restyled grille marked the '67 Fairlane, here a 500 XL GTA.

Among '66 Fairlane 500s, the hardtop was favored—75,947 were built.

Falcon still offered a Sports Coupe in 1967, but not a hardtop.

The '66 Fairlane 500 had leaf springs in the rear, as seen here.

The reskinned '67 Ford, here a Galaxie 500, took on rounder lines.

The Fairlane was significant for introducing Ford's brilliant small-block V8, the basis for some of its hottest '60s cars. Bored out to 289 cid as a '63 option, it developed 271 bhp, almost one horsepower per cubic inch. Powerful and smooth yet surprisingly economical, it was the definitive small V8. Tuned versions in sports-racers like the Ford GT40 and Shelby Cobra disproved the old saw about there being no substitute for cubic inches. The GT40 nearly took the world GT Manufacturers Trophy away from Ferrari in 1964, its first full season.

Initially, Fairlane offered two- and four-door sedans in base and sportier 500 trim, plus a bucket-seat 500 Sport Coupe. Four-door wagons and a brace of hardtop coupes were added for '63. Beginning with the '64s, Ford offered a growing assortment of handling and performance options, including stiff suspensions and four-speed gearboxes.

Fairlane was completely rebodied for '66 on a 116-inch wheelbase (113 for wagons) and displayed long, sleek styling with curved side glass, stacked quad headlamps and tidy vertical taillights. Heading that year's line was the bucket-seat 500XL hardtop coupe and convertible in base and GT trim. Standard XLs had a standard 120-bhp six, but most were equipped with the optional 289 V8. GTs carried a standard 390 big-block with a potent 335 bhp. This engine could be ordered on any Fairlane, and racers were quick to put it in the lighter two-door sedans, which earned respect for their competitive prowess.

With no change in wheelbases, another body and styling change occurred for 1968, when Fairlane and Fairlane 500 models were joined by a new Torino series as Ford's lushest intermediates. A 115-bhp 200-cid six was standard for all but the Torino GT convertible, hardtop coupe and new fastback hardtop (all duplicated in the 500 line), which came with the 210-bhp 302 V8 as well as buckets-and-console interior, pinstriping, and more performance options than a salesman could memorize.

The '69s were largely unchanged, but new fastback and notchback Torino Cobra hardtops arrived, the name borrowed from Carroll Shelby's muscular Ford-powered sports cars. These came with the 335-cid 428 V8 that had first appeared in the 1968½ Mercury Cyclone as the "Cobra Jet" engine. A $133 option was "Ram-Air," a fiberglass hood scoop with a special air cleaner assembly that ducted incoming air directly into the carburetor through a valve in the air cleaner. Four-speed gearbox, stiff suspension and competition-style hood locks were all standard. One magazine was actually disappointed when its Torino Cobra ran 0-60 mph in 7.2 seconds and the quarter-mile in 15 seconds at 98.3 miles per hour! On the other hand, just about everyone admitted that of all the '69 "supercars"—Plymouth GTX, Dodge Charger R/T, Pontiac GTO, Chevelle 396, and Buick GS400—the Torino Cobra was the tightest, the best built and the quietest.

These Torinos were potent racing machines. Ford discovered that the styling of the counterpart Cyclone was slightly more aerodynamic, and thus usually ran Cyclones in stock-car contests over 250 miles long. Nevertheless, a race-prepped Torino or Cyclone could achieve about 190 mph. Lee Roy Yarborough won the '69 Daytona 500 in a Ford.

With the advent of Thunderbird and then the Falcon, the Custom, pre-1962 Fairlane and Galaxie models became the "standard" or full-size Fords. For 1960 these cars swelled to a 119-inch wheelbase that they would retain through 1968, after which it was stretched two inches. Most big Fords of the '60s were heavy and not particularly exciting to drive on anything other than a superhighway, but certain variations of these 3500-4000-pound cruisers were surprisingly capable on winding roads.

The big 1960 Fords gained an all-new body that would persist through four facelifts: two minor, two major. The '60s were much longer, lower, wider and sleeker than the boxy '59s and even mimicked Chevy's bat-fins a little, but were good-looking cars with their chrome-edged beltlines and bigger glass areas. The Skyliner

Ventless side windows and a 'classic' grille were '69 LTD features.

The '69 Talladega was bred for racing, and named for a NASCAR track.

Only 3939 Torino GT convertibles were built for 1970. Price: $3212.

This 1970 LTD Brougham hardtop sedan is powered by a 320-bhp 429.

Ford's second import fighter was the '70 Maverick, priced at $1999.

All of Ford's cars grew bigger throughout the Sixties, as did most everyone else's. Meanwhile, after the initial assault of the 1960 domestic compacts, imports rebounded and gained strength. The 1970 Maverick was designed to stem the tide.

Torino for '72 was bigger, heavier: 117-inch wheelbase, 3400 pounds.

Ford's third import fighter was the '71 Pinto, priced at $1919.

The '71 Torino GT was aimed at "the sports oriented youth market."

The Galaxie 500 hardtop sedan was one of 19 full-size '72 models.

This '73 Maverick is the highly trimmed LDO—Luxury Decor Option.

was gone, but a sleek semi-fastback Starliner hardtop coupe replaced it in the Galaxie series. Though less popular than the square-roof styles, its slipperier shape was just the thing for NASCAR racing.

Starliner bowed out after 1961, when standard styling was facelifted via a full-width '59-style concave grille and a return to round taillights, capped by discreet blades. That year's top engine option was the new 390-cid version of the FE-series big-block, arriving with 300 bhp and available, on a very limited basis, with 375 and 401 bhp.

A chunkier, more "important" look marked the '62 standards, grouped into Galaxie and Galaxie 500 series with roughly the same body types as before. Reflecting the buckets-and-console craze then sweeping Detroit were the mid-season 500 XL Victoria hardtop coupe and Sunliner convertible. The "500" stood for the 500-mile NASCAR races the division was winning (Ford won every 500 in '63). Though the standard powertrain was a 170-bhp 292 V8 with Cruise-O-Matic, options could turn the big XL into a real fire-breather. There were 300-, 340-, and 375-bhp 390s and a new bored-out 406-cid V8 with 385 and 405 bhp, plus Borg-Warner four-speed gearbox. An even bigger bore for '63 produced a 427-cid powerhouse with 410/425 bhp. High prices—around $400—made these engines uncommon.

New lower-body sheetmetal gave the '63 "Super-Torque" Galaxies a cleaner, leaner look, announced by a simple concave grille. A pair of cheap "300" sedans was added (renamed Custom/Custom 500 for '64), and there was more mid-year excitement in a set of 500 and 500XL sports hardtops with thin-pillar "slantback" rooflines, a bit starchier than the old Starliner but again aimed right at the stock-car ovals.

The final and most substantial restyle on the big 1960 body occurred for '64, bringing heavily sculptured lower-body sheetmetal, a complex grille and slantback rooflines for all closed models. The entire Ford line won *Motor Trend* magazine's "Car of the Year" award, partly because of the division's ever-widening "total performance" campaign. Performance was just what the big Fords had, with available small-block and big-block V8s offering 195 up to a rousing 425 bhp.

Ford had its best NASCAR year ever in 1965, its big cars running for the last time but winning 48 of the 55 events, but luxury got most of the showroom emphasis. All-new except for engines, the '65s were distinguished by simpler, more linear styling announced by stacked quad headlamps. Underneath was a stronger chassis with a completely new front suspension. Arriving at mid-year were the Galaxie 500 LTD hardtop coupe and sedan, the poshest big Fords ever, priced at about $3300. Ford advertising boasted they were as quiet as a Rolls-Royce at speed. Times were changing. With intermediates taking over in competition, the big Fords no longer had to rely on a performance image for sales.

The '65 platform got a minor touchup for '66, and LTDs gained new "7-Litre" companions, powered by the Thunderbird's big 345-bhp 428 engine. The following year brought new outer sheetmetal with more flowing lines and "faster" rooflines on hardtop coupes. LTD became a separate three-model series, adding four-door sedan but losing the slow-selling 7-Litre models. Hidden-headlamp grilles marked the '68 LTDs and Galaxie XLs as part of a lower-body restyle for all models.

A new bodyshell arrived for '69 with a two-inch longer wheelbase, a tunneled backlight for SportsRoof (fastback) models, and ventless door glass on hardtops and convertibles. LTD continued to find increasing favor. Ford had built nearly 139,000 of the '68s. This year it built more than twice that many.

Ford kept pace with Chevrolet in the '60s production race, and actually beat it for model years 1961 and '66. Ford would be number one again for 1970 and '71 at slightly over two-million cars to Chevy's 1.5/1.8 million. Ford enjoyed its first two-million-car year in 1965.

Torino for '73: new grille and five-mph-impact-absorbing bumper.

The '74 Gran Torino received another new grille—and opera windows.

Ford's answer to the Chevy Monte Carlo was the Elite, here a '75.

The '75 Granada was a Mercedes-like, slightly upmarket compact.

A 1976 Maverick with Stallion package: color it silver and black.

The ultimate '76 Granada was a Ghia with the Luxury Decor Option.

Though Ford wouldn't lead Chevy again until the late '80s, it generally fared well in the '70s. However, Dearborn was last of the Big Three to abandon traditional full-size cars—and was the first to suffer for it. In the wake of the OPEC oil embargo and the first energy crisis, Chrysler pushed compacts while GM went forward with plans to downsize its entire fleet. Ford stubbornly resisted the winds of change, instead promoting its aging big cars on the basis of their greater passenger space and the presumed safety of "road-hugging weight." But the public didn't buy this cynical line—or the cars.

In large measure, this reflected the personal view of chairman Henry Ford II, who decreed there would be no rush to smaller cars, no vast capital investment in new technology. As a result, Ford greeted 1980 a critical two to three years behind GM in the fuel efficiency and "space" races—and at a critical sales disadvantage next to its domestic foes and a growing hoard of ever-more-prosperous Japanese companies. The firm would recover, but not before making drastic changes to its products.

Leading the 1970 line were modestly facelifted full-size Fords with "poke-through" center grille sections on LTDs and XLs, plus revamped rear ends on all models. Four series were offered: Custom, Galaxie 500, XL and LTD. The sporty XLs were in their final year, while luxury was further emphasized with a new LTD Brougham hardtop coupe, hardtop sedan and four-door sedan.

Broughams also featured in the 1970 Torino line, which shared new lower-body sheetmetal "shaped by the wind" with a three-model Fairlane 500 series. Wheelbase grew an inch; profiles were lower and five inches longer. The Torino Cobra returned as Ford's "budget muscle car" with a standard 360/375-bhp 429 V8. It was a blistering performer and its new hardtop body with concave backlight was distinctive, but hot-car demand was fast-waning everywhere, and only 7675 were built for the model year.

Ford scored much higher sales with a brand-new compact, the Maverick, a semi-fastback two-door sedan on a 103-inch wheelbase. Introduced in early '69, it was essentially a return to the original Falcon and even used its basic chassis and powertrain. With a price just below $2000 and backed by an aggressive but light-hearted ad campaign, this import-fighter scored an impressive 579,000 sales for the model year. It contributed greatly to Ford's production victory over Chevy.

Bolstering Maverick's appeal for '71 was a new notchback four-door on a 109.9-inch wheelbase (almost the same as the original Falcon's), a sporty two-door called Grabber, and a newly optional 302 V8 as an alternative to the 100-bhp 170 six. With minor changes, Maverick would carry the division's compact sales effort through 1977, which it did tolerably well, though its old-fashioned engineering looked increasingly so with time and the arrival of more capable domestic and foreign competitors.

Of course, there was little here to interest enthusiasts. The Grabber looked jazzy but was pretty tame even with the V8. And

Ford's third import fighter was the 1971 Pinto. It was aimed in part at the youth market, which was perfectly in keeping with the spirit of the times—in 1971 the 26th Amendment to the U.S. Constitution lowered the legal voting age to 18.

certain requisites like decent instruments and front disc brakes were either late in coming or not available (the latter arrived for '76). Maverick's last gesture to the youth market was the Stallion, a 1976 trim package also available for Pinto and Mustang II. The Maverick kit, offered only on the two-door, comprised black paint accents, twin door mirrors, styled steel wheels, raised-white-letter tires, and special i.d. More popular was the Luxury Decor Option (LDO), a 1973 package available for either body style through the end of the line. It comprised upgraded interior appointments color-keyed to a special paint scheme and crowned by a matching vinyl top.

Ford's major 1971 announcement was the four-cylinder Pinto, a 2000-pound, 94.2-inch-wheelbase subcompact with fastback styling in two-door and Runabout three-door hatchback models. A direct reply to Chevrolet's Vega, also new that year, it was smaller, less technically daring and less accommodating, and its performance and fuel economy were nothing special compared to that of many imports. Yet the Pinto usually outsold the trouble-prone Vega as well as many overseas contenders. Offered with 98- and 122-cid engines through 1973, then 122- and 140-cid fours, it was progressively dressed up and civilized with nicer trim and more convenience options. By 1973 there was even a wood-sided Squire wagon, though Pinto remained primarily basic transportation throughout its long 10-year life.

But though Pinto served Ford well in a difficult period, it will forever be remembered mainly as what one wag called "the barbeque that seats four." That's a reference to the dangerously vulnerable fuel tank and filler neck design of the 1971-76 models, implicated in a rash of highly publicized (and fatal) fires following rear-end collisions. Sadly, Ford stonewalled in a number of lawsuits all the way to federal court, which severely tarnished its public image, even if Pinto sales didn't seem to suffer much. What really put Pinto out to pasture after 1980 was not bad publicity but its relative lack of change—and the advent of a much better small Ford.

The mid-size Torino proved exceptionally popular in the early '70s, then fell from favor once fuel economy became a pressing consumer concern. The 14-model 1971 lineup was basically a carryover of the previous year's. The Cobra fastback coupe remained the most exciting of this bunch, though its standard engine was downgraded to a 240-bhp version of the ubiquitous 351 small-block. High-power engines began disappearing at Ford—and elsewhere in Detroit—the following year. By 1980 only a mildly tuned 351 remained, an option for the full-size line.

Except for engines, the 1972 Torino was all-new—and a big disappointment. Like GM's post-1967 intermediates, models now divided along 114-inch-wheelbase two-door hardtops and fastbacks and 118-inch-wheelbase sedans and wagons. Body-on-frame construction was adopted for the first time, and dimensions ballooned close to what the big Galaxies and LTDs had a few years before. Symbolic of most everything wrong with Detroit at the time, these cars were needlessly outsized, overweight and thirsty, with limited interior space and a soggy chassis. Ford tried to make these rigs passably economical, gave up and simply fitted a larger fuel tank. After getting just 13.5 mpg with a '76, CONSUMER GUIDE® magazine decided that "the more buyers learn about the Torino, the more reasons they will find to opt for a Granada."

A tarted-up Torino designed to fend off Chevrolet's highly successful Monte Carlo debuted in mid-1974—the Grand Torino Elite. Sharing Torino's coupe bodyshell and running gear, it leaned on the "Thunderbird tradition" and was fitted with every conceivable personal-luxury car cliché of the era, including long-hood/short-deck proportions, upmarket interior, formal upright grille, vinyl roof, stand-up hood ornament, and *dual* opera windows. Priced initially at $4437, it didn't sell as well as the Monte Carlo, but over 366,000 examples were built before it yielded to the downsized and down-priced 1977 Thunderbird, which rendered it redundant in the Ford lineup.

Granada chased the imports with the '78 ESS: European Sport Sedan.

The compact Fairmont bowed for '78 on a 105.5-inch wheelbase.

The Ford Granada Ghia two-door coupe retailed for $4685 in 1978.

The Fairmont coupe was called Futura—the turbo four cost extra.

A Rallye option was available on the mildly facelifted '79 Pinto.

The all-new '79 big Fords came on the "Panther" platform. They were smaller outside, bigger inside, and 600 pounds lighter.

A Country Squire wagon sold for $5320 in 1980, Pinto's last year.

Ford fiddled with options and two-tone paint on the '80 Granada.

An altogether more rational proposition, the Granada was arguably Ford's best idea of the decade—certainly one of the most timely. Introduced during 1975, it was originally intended as a slightly larger Maverick with the same chassis and drivetrains. When the fuel crunch boosted small-car sales, Ford decided to retain Maverick and launch its erstwhile successor as a more luxurious compact half a step up the price scale. This explains why the Granada appeared on the four-door Maverick's 109.9-inch wheelbase.

Adroitly keyed to the changing market, Granada blended American-style luxury with the mock-Mercedes look then in vogue. Buyers wholeheartedly approved, and the Granada zoomed from nowhere to become Ford Division's top-seller, outdistancing the big Fords and the swollen Torinos by a wide margin. After a year or so, it had achieved all the acceptance and familiarity of a model 20 years old—which it was in some ways, notably its untidy cornering response and a roly-poly ride on rough roads. Nevertheless, it bridged a big market gap at a crucial time, appealing to both compact buyers with upscale aspirations and big-car owners now energy-conscious for the first time.

The Maverick's true successor bowed for 1978 with a name borrowed from Ford's Australian subsidiary: Fairmont. It was undoubtedly the firm's single most significant new product of the decade because, although no one knew it then, its basic engineering would be the foundation for most Ford Motor Company cars introduced through the mid-1980s, including a new-generation Mustang and Thunderbird.

Billed as the first FoMoCo car designed with the aid of computer analysis, the Fairmont (and its Zephyr twin at Mercury) was a common-sense car and pretty conventional. Though conceived around the traditional front-engine/rear-drive layout, it was a big improvement over Maverick: clean-lined; sensibly boxy for good interior space on a shorter 105.5-inch wheelbase; lighter and thus more economical than many expected. Engines were familiar—initially the 140-cid Pinto four, 200-cid six and 302 V8—but there was a new all-coil suspension with modified MacPherson-strut front geometry, with the springs mounted on lower A-arms. Aside from better handling, this arrangement opened up more underhood space for easier servicing. A front stabilizer bar was standard, as was rack-and-pinion steering, offered at extra cost with variable-ratio power assist, a new item shared with several other Ford models that year.

The "Fox" program that produced Fairmont was one of Ford's first projects initiated after the 1973-74 energy crisis. But it wasn't the firm's only attempt at downsizing. For 1977, the old Torino was refurbished with cleaner exterior sheetmetal and "badge engineered" to pass as a new-generation full-size car. Called LTD II, it was only a little lighter than before, and sales went nowhere. One reason was the arrival of a new "downsized" Thunderbird on this basic platform. With much lower prices than before and that magi-

After peddling pretty much the same product line through most of the Seventies, Ford finally began to respond to a changing marketplace and Corporate Average Fuel Economy rules with the 1978 compact Fairmont and the downsized '79 full-size Ford.

The '81 Thunderbird shared its Fox platform with the Fairmont.

The '82 EXP was "the first two-passenger Ford in a quarter century."

The 1981 Granada, here a GLX, also rode atop the Fox platform.

Escort's sporty '83 model was the fuel-injected GT with five speed.

Escort added a five-door hatchback sedan to its 1982 lineup. There were 11 models ranging from $5518 to $7475.

cal name, it swamped the LTD II in sales until both were retired after 1979.

Besides a new Fairmont-based Mustang, 1979 saw the fruition of the "Panther" design project in an LTD that *was* genuinely downsized. Yet it was less successful than the Fairmont or Mustang and that was curious. In size and execution it was fully a match for its GM competition, riding a 114.3-inch wheelbase yet offering more claimed passenger and trunk space than the outsized 1973-78 cars. Styling was boxier and less pretentious, and visibility and fuel economy were better. So were ride and handling, thanks to a new all-coil suspension with more precise four-bar-link location for the live rear axle. With all this, the "New American Road Car" should have scored higher sales, yet model year deliveries actually fell by some 80,000 units compared to 1978. The new LTD thus barely beat out the big Oldsmobiles for second place in full-size sales and ran far behind Chevy's Caprice/Impala.

Two factors seemed to be at work. One was GM's two-year head start. The other was a severe downturn in the national economy—abetted by another fuel crisis—that began in the spring of '79 and put a crimp in all new-car sales. This LTD would enjoy a sales resurgence, but not before Ford and the U.S. industry had passed through three of their bleakest years ever.

Those years—1980-82—saw Ford Division output drop from 1.16 million cars to just under 749,000. But thanks to an improving economy and an ever-changing line of ever-improving Fords, the division went back above the 1.1 million mark—and would stay there through the end of the decade. In the process, Ford overhauled Chevrolet, becoming America's best-seller in 1987.

The most popular '80s Ford by far was the subcompact Escort, the front-drive 1981 replacement for the Pinto. Billed as the first of Ford's "world cars," it was jointly designed by Dearborn and the firm's British and German branches (as the "Erika" project), but the European versions ended up sleeker and faster than their American cousins. No matter. The practical, low-priced Escort set a fast sales pace with 320,000 copies in each of its first two years. Volume declined to below a quarter-million for '83, then returned to 330,000 or better through decade's end. The peak was 1987: over 390,000.

Numerous refinements marked Escort's evolution through 1989. There were always three-door hatchback sedans and five-door wagons, with five-door hatch sedans from 1982. All rode a 94.2-inch wheelbase and employed transverse-mounted four-cylinder engines—a new "CVH" single-overhead-cam design with hemispherical combustion chambers—linked to four-speed overdrive manual or three-speed automatic transaxles. An optional five-speed manual came along for 1983. The same all-coil four-wheel independent suspension persisted throughout, with MacPherson struts and lower control arms fore, modified struts on trailing arms and lower control arms aft. Rack-and-pinion steering and front-disc/rear-drum brakes completed the basic specs.

Escort's original 1.6-liter (98-cid) engine had just 69 bhp but by 1983 was up to 72/80 bhp with two-barrel carb or 88 bhp in optional throttle-body fuel-injected form. The last was standard for a sporty new three-door GT model, which also came with five-speed, special suspension, and black exterior moldings. An optional 2.0-liter (121-cid) 52-bhp diesel four from Mazda in Japan arrived for 1984—just in time for the start of a gas glut that quickly killed most all diesel demand in the U.S. The engine vanished after '87. A more exciting 1984 development was a turbocharged 1.6-liter GT with 120 bhp and suitably uprated suspension. It was fast and fun but crude and not very quiet. A more convenient, restyled dash featured across the line.

A mid-1985 upgrade brought a larger 1.9-liter (116-cid) "CVH" with 86 bhp in standard carbureted form or 108 bhp with port electronic injection. The latter was standard for the GT, which gained its own asymmetric body-color grille, aluminum wheels, bigger tires, rear spoiler and rocker panel "skirts." All Escorts were mildly facelifted with smoother noses in the "aero" idiom pioneered by the '83 Thunderbird, marked by flush headlamps.

By 1987, the previous plethora of alphabet series had been sorted out to encompass a stark three-door called Pony, volume-selling GL (all three body styles) and three-door GT. The base engine was treated to throttle-body injection and moved up to 90 bhp. Styling became smoother at mid-1988: revamped rear quarters for sedans, a new grille and spoiler for GT, and minor clean-ups elsewhere across the board. The GL series was renamed LX, and the dash was restyled a second time. As with Escort's previous mid-year model revisions, this one carried into 1989 practically without change.

Escort's high success was not matched by its interesting sporty coupe offshoot, the EXP. New for 1982, it was Ford's first two-seater since the original Thunderbird, but its "frog-eye" styling wasn't in the same league. And though it was an Escort underneath, it cost considerably more. Just over 113,000 were called for through 1983. The following year, EXP picked up the odd "bubble-back" hatch of its discontinued Mercury twin, the LN7, as well as the new turbo engine. Volume stabilized at about 50,000 units through 1985. Ford suspended production, restyled the front with flush headlamps and a simple slat grille, and reintroduced EXP as part of the Escort line. But it was still unequal to the sales challenge of Japanese two-seaters like the Honda CRX and Toyota MR2. Though volume improved to about 26,500 and held steady, EXP was abandoned after 1988 to free up assembly-line space for regular Escorts.

The other constant of the '80s Ford line was the full-size 1979-vintage LTD, which continued beyond decade's end with only minor interim alterations to equipment, styling and engine specifications. The changes are easy to chart: standard four-speed overdrive automatic transmission and 302-cid V8, a new uplevel series reviving the Crown Victoria name (1980); no more 351 option (1981); standard 302 V8 with throttle-body fuel injection for all models renamed LTD Crown Victoria (1983); sequential port injection for 150 bhp (versus 140), premium LX series added (1986); two-door coupe cancelled, "aero" front and rear styling for remaining four-door and Country Squire wagons (1988). Despite the year-to-year sameness, a lot of buyers still craved big, Detroit-style luxury, and the fact that fewer such cars were available as

An '83 Crown Squire wagon listed at $10,253; a 302 V8 was standard.

The LTD name moved down to the mid-size Fairmont bodyshell for '83.

Only 3260 LTD LXs were built in 1984-85. It had V8 get-up-and-go.

Bowing as an early '84, the Tempo was Ford's new front-drive compact.

LTD, seen here with the Carriage Roof option, was gone after 1985.

After 10 years and over 3,000,000 units, Ford retired the Pinto and replaced it with the lighter front-drive 1981 Escort. Much improved over the years, the first-generation Escort was also destined to last a full decade.

Prices started at $7094 base for the 1985 Tempo two-door coupe.

The '85 EXP coupe was often criticized for its "bug eye" front end.

After much hoopla, the '86 Taurus finally bowed on December 26, 1985.

Taurus rode a 106-inch wheelbase—prices started at $9545 base.

The '87 Escort GT boasted 120 horsepower and listed at $8724.

gas became cheaper again only worked in the Crown Vic's favor. Though sales fluctuated, this line was good for an annual average of well over 100,000 units.

With little change, Fairmont carried Ford's banner in the compact segment into 1983 while two derivatives served as the division's mid-size warrior. First of the latter was a new 1981 Granada, basically the two- and four-door Fairmont sedans with a square eggcrate grille, bulkier sheetmetal and somewhat plusher appointments. Fairmont wagons transferred to this line for '82. This Granada series sold respectably, about 120,000 a year. Engines were the same as Fairmont's: standard 2.3-liter four, optional 200-cid six and 255 V8 (the last eliminated for '82).

For 1983, Granada gave way to a "small" LTD, again Fairmont-based and still somewhat uptown but carrying a sloped nose, an airier "six-light" window treatment and a modestly lipped trunklid—along with Thunderbird, another announcement of Ford's turn to "aero" styling. Granada engines were initially offered along with Ford's new 232-cid V6. By 1985, only this, the four-cylinder and an optional 165-bhp 302 V8 were fielded, the last reserved for a semi-sporting LX sedan that sold only 3260 copies. Undoubtedly helped by image rub-off from the big LTDs, this series sold a lot better than Granada: nearly 156,000 for '83 and over 200,000 in 1984 and '85—Ford's second best-selling line after Escort.

Fairmont, meantime, finished its run after few interim changes from '78. Two sedans, plain and fancy wagons, and the smart "basket-handle-roof" Futura coupe offered through '81 (after which the wagons became Granadas). Engines were the usual Fox assortment: 2.3-liter four, 200-cid straight six and small-block V8s (302 cid 1978-79, 255 cid 1980-81). Sales tapered off along with the economy, dropping from the first-year high of nearly 461,000 to less than 81,000 by swan-song 1983. Still, that was a fine showing in a turbulent period. The Fairmont had more than done its job.

Filling Fairmont's shoes for 1984 was the new front-drive Tempo, a notchback four-door sedan and coupe-like two-door with "jellybean" styling on a 99.9-inch-wheelbase chassis with suspension much like Escort's. Power was supplied by a 2.3-liter four, only it wasn't the Pinto/Fairmont ohc "Lima" unit but a cut-down version of the old overhead-valve Falcon six, rated at 86 bhp. It didn't work that well, but Ford tried to make it better, fitting throttle-body injection and adding a 100-bhp "high-output" option for '85. The latter somehow lost 6 bhp by '87, then returned to its original rating. Several trim levels were offered, including better-equipped Sport versions with the more powerful engine and firmer suspension. Escort's 2.0-liter diesel option was listed through '86, but again generated few sales. Three-speed automatic was available with all engines; the standard manual transaxle shifted from a four- to five-speeder after '84.

A mild flush-headlamp 1986 facelift was followed by an interesting new Tempo option: all-wheel drive, a part-time "shift-on-the-fly" system intended for maximum traction on slippery roads, not dry-pavement driving or off-roading. For 1988, Tempo four-doors were reskinned to look like junior versions of the new Taurus, an effective "nip-and-tuck" operation. A new, rather Japanese-looking dash was shared with the unchanged coupe. Model offerings now comprised base GL, sporty GLS and all-wheel-drive coupe and sedan plus a luxury LX four-door.

Despite prosaic mechanicals and tougher-than-ever compact competition, Tempo proved another fast-selling Ford. It attracted close to 415,000 buyers in its first two seasons and another 343,000 for 1986-87. Dearborn designers and decision-makers evidently had the inside track on what appealed to American buyers.

Yet even they were probably surprised by the success of Taurus, the front-drive 1986 replacement for the junior LTD in the all-important mid-size market. Riding a 106-inch wheelbase, this four-door sedan and five-door wagon were the strongest-ever

Aerostar was Ford's minivan entry; it had a 118.9-inch wheelbase.

Escort EXP carried over its new, smoother 1986½ nose into '87.

The '88 Festiva's wheelbase spanned 90.2 inches; the LX cost $6868.

Styled by Ford, built by Mazda in Flat Rock, Michigan: '89 Probe.

The '89 Ford Probe GT came with a 145-bhp turbo four as standard.

Escort was freshened up for 1988½ with new rear end styling.

The '88½ GT wore spoilers and ground-effects lower body trim.

For 1989, Aerostar came in regular or extended-length models.

Ford's '89 LTD Crown Victoria was built in St. Thomas, Ontario.

The '89 Taurus had a coefficient of drag of 0.35, good for a wagon.

In its quest for improved fuel economy and more distinctive products, Ford turned to aerodynamic—or "jellybean"—styling. This was best seen in the 1986 Taurus, but it actually started with the 1983 Thunderbird and '84 Tempo.

Special lower bodyside cladding and bumpers were SHO features, as were four-wheel disc brakes and suspension mods.

The SHO had a dohc, 24-valve, 3.0-liter V6. 0-60 mph: seven seconds.

Tempo was available with an All Wheel Drive option for 1989.

expressions of Ford's claim to Detroit design leadership: clean, smooth and carefully detailed, yet not lumpy like some other low-drag cars. Dominating the spacious interiors was an obviously European-inspired dashboard.

As expected, Taurus engines mounted transversely in a chassis with all-independent suspension. Sedans used MacPherson struts and coil springs at each corner, supplemented at the rear by parallel control arms. Wagons eschewed rear struts for twin control arms, a system better able to cope with the wider range of load weights wagons often carry.

Initial engine choices began with a 2.5-liter 90-bhp four, an enlarged Tempo unit available with standard five-speed manual or, from late '87, optional four-speed overdrive automatic transaxles. Most Tauruses, though, were ordered with the new port-injected 3.0-liter "Vulcan" V6, a 60-degree overhead-valve design rated at 140 bhp and teamed with automatic only. For 1988, Ford offered a reengineered version of its 90-degree 3.8 V6 as an option. Horsepower was the same, but its extra torque provided usefully quicker acceleration than the 3.0.

With its ultramodern styling, good performance and prices far lower than those of certain coveted German sports sedans, Taurus charged up the sales chart like a bull in a china shop. Ford sold over 236,000 of the '86s and nearly 375,000 of the '87s—astounding for what was, after all, a very daring departure for a middle-class American car.

But there were still those who wanted a Taurus with performance and mechanical specifications as sophisticated as its styling. They got one, for 1989 was showtime—or rather SHO time: a new "Super High Output" version of the 3.0 V6 with overhead-cam cylinder heads and four valves per cylinder (instead of two), plus dual exhausts. Engineered with help from Yamaha, it turned out 220 bhp, good for seven seconds in the 0-60-mph test, according to Ford. It came only in a sedan with standard four-wheel disc brakes and a handling package with larger anti-roll bars and 15-inch aluminum wheels wearing V-rated tires. Added styling distinction was provided by unique lower-body extensions and inboard front foglamps. The interior was special too, boasting multi-adjustable front bucket seats, sport cloth upholstery, center console and an 8000-rpm tachometer.

The SHO and the dramatic new '89 Thunderbird best represent Ford Motor Company's strong resurgence engineered by Donald E. Petersen (president from 1980, chairman from 1987) and his young, enthusiastic executive team. An automaker that was as close to collapse as Chrysler was in 1980 has become a trimmer, more responsive and vastly more efficient one, fielding aggressive new products that have almost always been right on target. Assuming the company doesn't lose its momentum, Ford's 90th anniversary in 1993 should be a happy occasion indeed.

FORD MUSTANG

Mustang, the original ponycar, was Detroit's greatest single success of the '60s. It lifted Ford's 1965 model year volume by well over half a million units and set an all-time record for first-year new-model sales. A total 680,989 were sold between the April 1964 introduction and August 1965 (when production switched to '66 models). Truck drivers drove through showroom windows while staring at them, housewives entered contests to win them, and dealers auctioned them off because demand exceeded supply by 15 to 1. America loved the Mustang.

Spearheading this remarkable achievement was Lee A. Iacocca, the car salesman who worked his way from an obscure position in Pennsylvania to vice-president and general manager of Ford Division in five years. In 1970 he became president of Ford Motor Company and would go on to be chairman of the board at Chrysler Corporation.

The Mustang idea was simplicity itself: a low-cost "personal car." People had been pleading with Ford to revive the two-seat Thunderbird since its demise in 1957. Four years later, Iacocca and company were planning a new young-person's car that would be inexpensive to build, peppy, sporty-looking and priced to sell for less than $2500. Projected volume was 100,000 units a year.

The very first Mustang was a low, two-seat fiberglass roadster with a 90-inch wheelbase and a mid-mounted 2.0-liter V4 developing 90 horsepower. This experimental was pretty but impractical. Iacocca looked at those who flocked to it at shows and concluded, "That's sure not the car we want to build, because it can't be a volume car. It's too far out." But dozens more prototypes followed, culminating in the conventional, four-seat 108-inch-wheelbase production Mustang of "1964½." From a marketing standpoint, it couldn't have been better.

Through 1973, Mustang was offered as a hardtop coupe, convertible, and fastback coupe. Convertible sales started at the 100,000-unit annual level but dropped to less than 15,000 a year by 1969. The crisp notchback hardtop was the sales leader. The coupe, initially a semi-fastback style called 2+2, arrived in autumn 1964 with the rest of the '65 Ford line. It soon overtook the convertible in sales, averaging about 50,000 a year through 1970.

Standard power in the first six months of production came from the 170-cubic-inch Falcon six (101 bhp) and 260-cid V8 (164 bhp). A 200-cid six (120 bhp) and the bored-out 289 small-block V8

The '65 Mustang convertible proved to be a good seller with 101,945 built. Prices started at a modest $2614, plus options.

The 1965 Mustang was inspired by the Corvair Monza, a sporty compact coupe, and was so popular that it forced Chevy to dump the Monza in favor of the Camaro. Not only did Mustang set sales records, it defined what a "ponycar" should be.

Mustang called its fastback coupe a 2 + 2 and built 77,079 of them for the 1965 model run. It stickered at $2589 and up.

The hardtop was the favored '65 Mustang; 501,965 were produced.

A revised grille and new hubcaps and trim marked the '66 Mustang.

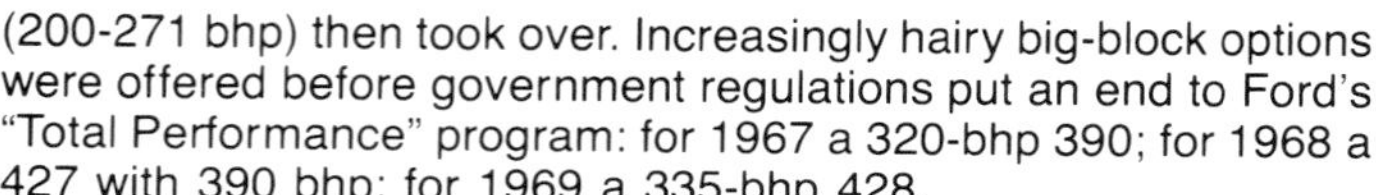

(200-271 bhp) then took over. Increasingly hairy big-block options were offered before government regulations put an end to Ford's "Total Performance" program: for 1967 a 320-bhp 390; for 1968 a 427 with 390 bhp; for 1969 a 335-bhp 428.

Much of Mustang's appeal stemmed from the myriad options that enabled customers to personalize the car. Careful use of the order form could produce a cute economy car, a thunderingly fast drag racer, a deceptively nimble sporty car or a small luxury liner. Transmission choices comprised automatics, three- and four-speed manuals and stick-overdrive. Handling packages, power steering, disc brakes, air conditioning and tachometer were available. A bench seat could be ordered instead of the standard front buckets, though few people did so. A GT package option delivered a pleasant assortment of goodies including front disc brakes, full-gauge instrument panel and special badges. A variety of interior trims was available, as were accent stripes and special moldings for the exterior.

The original Mustang was an inspired piece of design, the work of Joe Oros, L. David Ash and Gayle L. Halderman of the Ford Division styling studio. Its long-hood/short-deck proportions quickly became Detroit *de rigueur*, particularly for the imitators that soon became known, in Mustang's honor, as "ponycars." The basic '65 styling saw careful refinement in the first four years. The '66s changed only in detail. A deeper grille and sculptured side panels ending in twin simulated air scoops marked the '67s; the 2 + 2 adopted a full-fastback roofline. The '68s had a revised grille with a bright inner ring around the galloping-horse emblem.

This relative sameness, plus increasing competition and a steady decline in ponycar demand took its toll in Mustang production. After an impressive 607,500 units for '66, volume dropped to 472,000, then to 317,000 for '68.

The Mustang package was more extensively revised for 1969: lower, longer, wider, more exaggerated. Ventless side glass, quad headlamps and a more imposing dash were featured. A new Mach 1 fastback with firm suspension and a standard 250-bhp 351 V8

The '66 Mustang soft top listed at $2653; output reached 72,199.

Mustang was reskinned for 1967, and a little bit bigger and heavier. The convertible cost $2738 and 44,808 were built.

Mustang GT/A for 1956—the "A" stood for automatic transmission.

The '67 Mustang 2+2 was a true fastback—71,042 were built that year.

joined the line at $3139. It stood apart from the standard "SportsRoof" via a special grille with driving lamps, a matte-black center hood section with functional air scoop, quick-fill gas cap, and black honeycomb rear appliqué. Catering to the luxury market was the new Grande hardtop, priced at $2866/$2971 with standard six/V8 and offering landau-style black or white vinyl roof, racing-type mirrors, special i.d. script and bright wheelwell moldings.

Making an even bigger splash for mid-1969 was the fastback Boss 302, a $3588 roadgoing version of the Mustangs that were cleaning up in the Trans-American racing series. Though its 302 small-block delivered an alleged 290 bhp, estimates pegged output at more like 350. Only 1934 were built for the model year, another 6318 for 1970. All had special striping, front "chin" spoiler, a Mach 1-style rear wing, and distinctive rear window louvers.

A horse of a different color was the big-block Boss 429. Tagged at $4798, it was stuffed full of Ford's Cobra-Jet NASCAR engine

The '67 GT/CS was a California Special with special Shelby touches.

For 1969, Mustang offered a new luxury model, the $2866 Grande.

The Mustang grew a bit bigger and heavier with the restyled 1967 and '69 models. It was rapidly approaching middle age, falling out of step with the 250,000 young anti-Vietnam war demonstrators who marched in Washington, D.C. that year.

The '69 Boss 302 was built with Trans Am racing in mind. It was a bit pricey at $3588, and only 1934 were built that year.

with cast-magnesium head covers and semi-hemispherical combustion chambers. Only 858 were built for '69 and another 498 to 1970 specifications. All were largely custom-crafted, as considerable front metalwork was required to accommodate the bulky 429.

A mild facelift for 1970 brought recessed taillamps and a return to dual headlamps for all Mustangs, as well as standard high-back bucket seats as on the '69 Mach 1. As before, available Mach 1 V8s ran from a 351 to a four-barrel 428 with Ram Air induction. Convertibles were becoming quite scarce by now thanks to the growing buyer preference for air conditioning and closed body styles. This year's total was down by nearly 50 percent from 1969's, dropping from 14,700 to about 7600. Overall Mustang volume was down too. The '69s garnered just under 300,000 sales; the '70s sank to a bit less than 191,000.

The '69 Mach I could be ordered with an optional 335-bhp 428 V8.

The 1969 Shelby GT 500 came with a 360-bhp 428 V8 as standard.

Mach I for 1970 listed at $3271. A 375-bhp 429 V8 was optional.

The '70 convertible sold for $3025. Output was down to 7673 units.

Kar Kraft of Brighton, Michigan, built the '70 Boss 429. Only 499 to 505 were built to homologate the 429 V8 for NASCAR racing.

In late 1970, Ford abandoned most of its Trans-Am, USAC, NASCAR and international competition efforts. Meantime, future Mustangs were being planned with an eye to the plunging market.

But that wasn't evident in the third-generation Mustang of 1971, conceived in the ponycar market's late-'60s heyday. Heavily influenced by Semon E. "Bunkie" Knudsen, the GM executive who served briefly as Ford Motor Company president, it was intended answer a frequent criticism of early ponycars, namely insufficient passenger room. The result was the most changed Mustang yet: larger, heavier, and thirstier—as fat as Mustang would ever get. Though wheelbase grew only an inch, the '71 was eight inches longer overall, six inches wider, and close to 600 pounds heavier than the '65 original. Styling was more massive too, with busier sheetmetal, aggressive noses and a sweeping, near-horizontal roofline on the "SportsRoof" 2+2.

Boss 302 output increased to 6319 units for 1970. Price: $3720.

About 1800 Boss 351s were built for '71, and then it was dropped.

There was now plenty of room for big-block V8s, so the performance-oriented Mach 1 now offered the 429 Cobra Jet as an option, rated at 370 bhp. But with the market's growing preference for luxury and convenience, this engine could now be ordered with air conditioning, power steering, tilt wheel and other niceties. Yet almost any '71 could be blindingly quick. With automatic and 3.25:1 final drive, the 429 Mach 1 could do 0-60 mph in 6.5 seconds and the standing quarter-mile in 14.5 seconds.

A more balanced performer was the new Boss 351 fastback, replacing the previous Bosses but much the same package. Though its efficient, highly tuned small-block delivered 330 bhp and ample go, high price ($4124, more than $1000 above Mach 1) limited sales and the model was dropped after this one year.

Other Mustangs fared little better. Total 1971 production dropped to below 150,000 units, with other Ford products like the compact Maverick cannibalizing some sales. The '72s were little changed, but there were fewer engine options and both horsepower and performance were down. Ford turned to promoting new colors and fabrics as well as the Sprint decor option—white paint set off by broad, blue racing stripes edged in red. Complementary colors were used inside, and mag wheels, raised-white-letter tires, and competition suspension were all available. But nothing seemed to help much, and production bottomed out at a bit over 125,000.

Mustang remained its hefty self for one more year and again saw little change. But Ford was well along on a more practical successor by 1973—and more willing to admit its error. "We started out with a secretary car," said design vice-president Eugene Bordinat, "and all of a sudden we had a behemoth." Most '73 developments were made per federal regulation: 5-mph bumpers (optional color-keyed covers helped to keep them from looking like

Mustang catered to performance-oriented drivers with a large selection of models such as the Mach I, the limited-edition Boss 302 and 351, and the even-more-limited Boss 429. The ultimate Mustangs were the Shelby GTs made from 1965-70.

The 1972 Grande coupe listed at $2915. Output reached 18,045 units.

Red, white, and blue Mustang Sprint models debuted in mid-1972.

The '73 Mach I cost $3674; a 351 V8 was the biggest engine offered.

Mustang was downsized to a short 96.2-inch wheelbase for 1974.

The '78 King Cobra is the most collectible 1974-78 Mustang II.

afterthoughts), rubber-covered control knobs, flame-retardant upholstery, exhaust-gas recirculation to help curb emissions. Volume recovered to nearly 135,000 units, the increase perhaps coming from buyers who'd heard that a "downsized" Mustang was due and feared what it might be like.

Yet the all-new Mustang II, introduced for 1974, was a happy turning point for the original ponycar. Trimmer and thriftier, it couldn't have been better timed, arriving just as the nation experienced its first energy crisis. Sales boomed. With model year production of nearly 400,000 units, the II came within 10 percent of equalling the original Mustang's first-year record.

Taking note of the growing popularity of sporty import coupes, Iacocca had specified that the Mustang II have a wheelbase of 96-100 inches (it ended up at 96.2 inches) plus a scaled-down version of the familiar long-hood/short-deck styling. Compared to the "fat" generation, the II was 20 inches shorter, four inches narrower, an inch lower and 400-500 pounds lighter. Like the subcompact Pinto (which borrowed some Mustang II engineering from 1974), it employed unit construction and a conventional short/long-arm coil-spring front suspension. But instead of being bolted directly to the main structure, the Mustang's lower arms attached to a rubber-mounted subframe that supported the rear of the engine/transmission assembly. This added to production costs but was deemed necessary to provide more precise steering and a smoother, quieter ride than Pinto. Mustang II's rear leaf springs were longer than Pinto's, and its shock absorbers were staggered for better handling and grip.

There was no Mustang II convertible, but notchback and fastback coupe body styles continued, the former now a fixed-pillar style, the latter a hatchback. And for the first time, there was no V8, initial engine offerings being limited to a 2.3-liter inline four of 83-95 bhp and a 2.8-liter V6 with 90-105 bhp. The V6 was standard for the Mach 1 hatchback, which could do 0-60 mph in 13-14 seconds and reach 100 mph with the standard four-speed gearbox.

The Mustang II was built for five years without significant change. The Mach 1 as well as luxury four-cylinder and V6 Ghia notchbacks were available throughout. So were numerous options, per Mustang tradition. Air conditioning, power steering and brakes, a raft of sound equipment, fancier trim, a vinyl top for notchbacks, sunroof and forged-aluminum wheels were among the available items. For 1975 a sliding glass moonroof and a luxury package became optional for the already posh Ghia.

Mustang II sales never came near their 1974 level in subsequent years but were a lot better than 1971-73. The total fell by over half for '75 (to just short of 189,000), then held steady.

Ford made a gesture toward performance by reviving a V8 option for '75. It was, of course, the workhorse 302 small-block, initially rated at 122 bhp. Following at mid-'76 was the Cobra II trim package for hatchbacks, with sports steering wheel, dual remote-control door mirrors, brushed-aluminum dash and door panel appliqués, black grille, styled steel wheels, flip-out rear side windows with add-on louvers, front air dam, rear spoiler and simulated hood scoop. Available at first only in white with blue stripes, Cobra II could be ordered in other colors from 1977. It was flashy, but a far cry from the great Shelby Mustang it tried to ape. Ford again tried "paint-on performance" with the 1978 King Cobra package. This had many of the aforementioned Cobra II items, plus a gaudy snake decal on the hood and tape stripes from stem to stern. You also got the 302, power steering and a handling suspension with 70-series radial tires, all for about $1300. A 17-second quarter-mile time didn't make this a really hot car, but it was decent for its day.

Then came a new-generation Mustang for 1979, in many ways the best car ever to wear the galloping-horse emblem. From some angles it looked vaguely like a BMW—clean, taut and tight—and its surface execution, downswept nose, ample glass area, and lack of superfluous ornamentation combined the best of contemporary American and European design. It was the sort of restrained, efficient and elegant ponycar Ford had built in the first place.

Again, many styling proposals were considered for the '79. The one that went into production originated with a team headed by Jack Telnack, then executive director of Ford North American Light Truck and Car Design. More extensive use of lightweight materials—mainly plastics, low-alloy steel, and aluminum—made the '79 roughly 200 pounds lighter than a comparable Mustang II. A 104.4-inch wheelbase upped rear legroom by five inches. Other interior measurements were up too: for example, shoulder room by 3.5/5.0 inches front/rear, cargo volume by two cubic feet.

The '79's new suspension was borrowed from the compact Fairmont/Zephyr, which meant modified MacPherson-strut geometry in front, four-bar-link live rear axle, anti-sway bars at both ends and coil springs all around. A handling package with higher spring and shock rates plus stiffer bushings was available with mandatory 14-inch tires. There was also a premium setup comprising Michelin TRX tires, specially sized forged-aluminum wheels and appropriately tuned chassis pieces for maximum roadability. The 1978 engine lineup was expanded with a 140-bhp turbocharged version of the standard four, good for 0-60 mph times of 10 seconds or so and fuel economy in the low to mid-20s. Late in the model year, the 200-cid six returned to supplant the V6, which Ford's German subsidiary couldn't supply in adequate numbers.

Mustang paced the 1979 Indianapolis 500, and a pace-car replica was duly issued at mid-year. For 1980, this model's slatted grille showed up on a revived Cobra package offering front and rear spoilers, integral fog lamps, slatted grille, non-functional hood scoop and the TRX suspension. The 302 vanished, but a debored 255 small-block with 118 bhp was optional across the board.

Because the '79 market was strong and Ford's ponycar all-new, Mustang volume was up substantially over 1978, soaring to just over 332,000 units. After easing to 241,000 for 1980, sales sank to average 135,000 or so through 1985, then recovered to near 225,000 for '86. This somewhat disappointing performance can be blamed largely on a very difficult market early in the decade, because Mustang only became more exciting as the '80s progressed, leading the way to the renaissance in Detroit performance we still enjoy at this writing.

Announcing this trend was a revived GT model for 1982, a hatchback packing a reborn 302 small-block with 155 bhp. It looked much like the Cobra it replaced, mostly due to the lack of cartoonish body decoration, and came only with four-speed manual. Arrayed below were L, GL and GLX notchbacks and hatchbacks with the same engine offerings save the turbo-four, which temporarily vanished. A five-speed overdrive manual, announced at mid-1980, was still optional for the normally aspirated four.

Ford turned up the wick again for '83. A pretty facelift brought bigger taillamps and a more aggressive face, but the big news was the first Mustang convertible in 10 years, offered only in top GLX trim. Performance fans applauded a more potent 302 with a big four-barrel carb (instead of two-barrel) that boosted horsepower to 176. An improved blown four offered 145 bhp in a new GT Turbo hatchback, but was nowhere near as satisfying as the smooth, torquey V8 GT, so sales were low. The non-turbo four and a new 232-cid V6 (replacing the old straight six) were offered for slow-laners. Unlike some other reborn ragtops of these years, the Mustang was a "factory" job from the first, built by Ford itself. It was also quite practical for a convertible, with standard features like power top, glass rear window and roll-down rear side windows.

Perhaps as a hedge against another energy crisis, Ford massaged its turbo-four even more for 1984, wrapping the result in a new performance Mustang, the SVO. Named for the company's

A Cobra package and 302 V8 were offered on the all-new '79 Mustang.

Mustang paced the '69 Indy 500; a limited run of replicas was sold.

Engine offerings for 1980 included a 255 V8 and a turbo four.

The 302 V8 reappeared for 1982 on the GT, which stickered at $8308.

The 302 V8 in the '83 Mustang GT cranked out 176 bhp at 4200 rpm.

The 1971-73 Mustangs were as big and heavy as a Mustang would ever be. President Lee Iacocca sensed that the car had gone off course, so he ordered a smaller ponycar for '74. Good thing—it arrived on the eve of the first Arab Oil Embargo.

The four-cylinder turbo motor continued to be offered in 1983.

After a decade's absence, a convertible rejoined the '83 lineup.

A Mustang GT convertible sold for $13,051 for the '84 model year.

The '84 SVO coupe was turbo powered, but sold for a lofty $15,596.

GT for 1985 featured a new grille and a five-speed manual gearbox.

SVO was revitalized for 1985½, but only 9844 were built from 1984-86.

Special Vehicle Operations unit, which engineered it, the SVO boasted 175 bhp via port electronic fuel injection and turbo intercooler, plus standard four-wheel disc brakes—a first for Mustang—and a fortified suspension with 16-inch wheels and meaty 225-section tires. Outside were a special grille-less nose and unique double-wing rear spoiler. But as the SVO was much fussier to drive and a little slower than the V8 GT—and cost over $5000 more—its market was predictably limited. Ford persisted with it through 1986, when the engine was coaxed to an impressive 205 bhp, then gave up on the SVO after building only 9844 units.

The rest of the '84 line was rearranged into two- and three-door L and LX models (the latter merging the previous GL and GLX) plus hatchback and convertible V8 and Turbo GTs. The last, like SVO, succumbed to slow sales, disappearing after 1985. A second 302 with fuel injection and 165 bhp was newly available for non-GTs or with automatic. Ford halfheartedly observed Mustang's 20th anniversary with a modest paint-and-tape special edition called, for no particular reason, GT-350. Carroll Shelby, who by now had joined Lee Iaccoca at Chrysler, had used the title for his first modified Mustang of 1965 and made a fuss over Ford's using it here.

For 1985, the cheap L models were dropped and remaining LX and GT Mustangs acquired new nose styling a la SVO. The high-output GT V8 was booted to 210 bhp via a wilder camshaft profile and low-friction roller valve lifters; similar changes lifted the injected 302 to 180 bhp. The GT remained five-speed only, with revised internal ratios enhancing performance even further. Though the GT now cost some three times more in raw dollars than its predecessor of 20 years before, it was not only a more balanced performer but a better equipped one. This year, for instance, it acquired beefier 60-series "gatorback" tires on seven-inch-wide cast-aluminum wheels as well as gas-pressurized front shock absorbers and an extra pair of rear shocks.

Mustang reached its decade production high for 1986 despite

Sequential multiple-port fuel injection gave the GT 200 bhp for '86.

The '87 Mustang GT featured aero headlights and boy-racer styling.

The Mustang GT galloped into 1989 largely unchanged, but Ford was investing $200 million to upgrade its Dearborn assembly plant.

few changes. The main one was adoption of port fuel injection and lower compression for a single 302 V8 rated at 200 bhp and available with either five-speed or automatic. Ford's continuing attention to details was evident in such practical matters as a longer anti-corrosion warranty, increased sound-deadening, and a more convenient single-key lock system.

The clean fifth-generation Mustang got its first major facelift for 1987 in Ford's now-customary "aero" idiom, announced by new Euro-style flush-mount headlamps. GTs ended up rather busy with their heavily sculptured rocker-panel extensions and multi-slot tail panel. Not everyone liked them, but the more sedate-looking LXs could be ordered with most of the important GT features, including the V8 and handling suspension. The venerable 302 was more potent than ever, new cylinder heads and manifolding bringing an additional 25 horsepower. Strangely, the mid-range V6 option was cancelled, leaving the old four as the only other engine choice. Still standard for LXs, it now had port injection too, but with only 90 bhp the gap with V8 performance was a big one.

Mustang completed the decade with no further changes of consequence, but offerings expanded for '89 with a new "LX 5.0L" series—notchback, hatchback and convertible that amounted to GTs in more conservative LX dress. But wait: 1989 marked Mustang's silver anniversary. Wasn't there any commemorative special? Ford hadn't released one at this writing, but the rumor mill spoke of a hot-rodded GT with 30-50 additional horses (via induction tuning and recalibrated engine electronics) plus unique trim and perhaps the all-disc brakes from the late SVO.

Whatever happens (or doesn't) for Mustang's 25th birthday, you can bet that the original ponycar will continue to be very much a part of Ford's future. Any why not? Despite its older design, the fifth generation is now handily outselling its only surviving ponycar rivals, the Chevy Camaro and Pontiac Firebird—which only goes to show that sometimes, the first shall be first.

The fifth-generation '79 Mustang bowed on the Fairmont "Fox" platform. It has received regular upgrades and added power, and high demand has kept it in production even though it was originally going to be replaced by the Mazda-built Probe.

FORD THUNDERBIRD

Legend says the Thunderbird was born in October 1951, when Ford Division general manager Lewis Crusoe visited the Paris Auto Show with styling consultant George Walker. America had fallen in love with European sports cars in the early postwar years, and both men were taken by the ones they saw there—especially the curvy Jaguar XK-120 and GM's experimental two-seat Le-Sabre. "Why don't we have something like that?" Crusoe asked. Walker replied, "Oh, but we *do!*"—then hurried to phone Dearborn to get his crew cracking.

But like many apocryphal stories, this one isn't true. Frank Hershey, who headed the team that styled the first T-Bird, says Ford had been conjuring two-seaters before this, though there was never a rush to build one because sports-car sales only accounted for a minuscule 0.27 percent of the total U.S. market. But in January 1953, GM threw down a gauntlet Ford couldn't ignore: the Chevrolet Corvette. Barely a month later, Ford was hard at work on the car that would ultimately be named for the god worshipped by America's Southwest Indians as the bringer of rain and prosperity.

First displayed as a wood mockup at the Detroit show in early 1954, the Thunderbird was a "personal" car, not a pure sports car. It rode the same wheelbase as the first-generation Corvette—102 inches—but was far more luxurious and practical. In place of creaking fiberglass and clumsy side curtains was a sturdy steel body with convenient roll-up windows. Instead of an ill-fitting soft top was a snug power top, a detachable hard top, or both. And there was no plodding six-cylinder engine, but a burly 292-cubic-inch Mercury V8 delivering 193 bhp with stickshift or 198 bhp with Ford-O-Matic.

Bill Burnett supervised the engineering, which relied heavily on standard Ford components. Styling, chiefly the work of young Bill Boyer directed by Walker lieutenant Hershey, couldn't have been better: simple and smooth yet clearly Ford, with rakish long-hood/short-deck proportions recalling the classic early-Forties Lincoln Continental.

With European style and American comfort, convenience, and go, Thunderbird proved well-nigh irresistible at just under $3000 without options. It whipped the rival Chevy in 1955 model year production by nearly 24 to 1 with a total 16,155.

You don't mess with success in Detroit, and Ford didn't with the '56 T-Bird. Changes were limited to a larger 312 V8 option with 215/225 bhp (non-overdrive stickshift cars retained the 292, now up to 202 bhp), plus exterior-mount spare (answering cries for more trunk space), softer suspension (for a smoother ride) and no-cost portholes for the hardtop, an idea derived from vintage coachwork by stylist Boyer. Porthole hardtops heavily outsold the non-porthole kind in 1956, and virtually all '57 Thunderbirds had them. Production eased to 15,631 but was still five times Corvette's. Trouble was, Ford wanted much higher volume, and market surveys had indicated much greater demand for a four-seater. For 1958 and beyond, that's what the T-Bird would be.

The '57 was the last two-seat T-Bird—and arguably the best. A handsome facelift brought a prominent bumper/grille and a longer deck (again enclosing the spare) wearing modest blade-like tailfins. There was more power than ever. Stickshift models retained the 292 (now rated at 212 bhp) and there were three 312 V8s offering 245, 270 or 285 bhp, the last being the top twin-four-barrel version with 10.0:1 compression. Ford even built 208 supercharged "F-Birds" with 300/340 bhp courtesy of Paxton-McCulloch blowers, mainly for racing.

And race the early Birds did, albeit with limited success. A '55 sponsored by *Mechanix Illustrated* magazine's Tom McCahill swept the production sports-car class at that year's Daytona Speed Weeks, Joe Ferguson's two-way average of 124.633 mph besting every Austin-Healey, Porsche, and all but one Jaguar XK-120. Chuck Daigh did even better in '56 with a Pete DePaolo-prepped car, running 88.779 mph in the standing mile, though Zora Arkus-Duntov's modified 'Vette was faster (89.735 mph). In '57, Daigh scored 93.312 mph, and a privately entered Bird ran the flying mile at 146.282 mph one way, 138.775 mph both ways. Then the Automobile Manufacturers Association issued its infamous racing "ban" and development stopped.

With a base price still under $3500 for '57, the T-Bird remained an attractive buy. Production ran through the end of the year, so production was the highest for the three two-seater years: 21,380 units.

As expected, the all-new four-seater arrived for 1958, a dramatic design with unibody construction, all-coil suspension, and a low, rakish stance. Its 113-inch wheelbase was compact, yet provided ample interior room. Only one engine was available, a new big-block 352 V8 with 300 bhp. Joining the familiar convertible was a fixed-roof hardtop that popularized the square-cut "formal-look" wide-quarter roofline that would later spread throughout the Ford line—and to other automakers. (A rumored retractable hardtop like the Ford Skyliner was canceled in the design stage, but a similar top-stowing arrangement was applied to the '58 convertible.) A new interior feature, a control console on the transmission tunnel, would also be widely imitated.

With all this, the '58 Thunderbird was a solid hit. Nearly 38,000 were sold for the model year, about twice as many as any of the previous two-seaters. The '59s changed only in detail: a horizontal-bar instead of honeycomb pattern for grille, non-functional hood air scoop and taillight appliqués; "bullet" moldings for the sculptured lower-body "bombs"; reworked Thunderbird script; a bird emblem for the hardtop's rear roof pillar instead of the '58's round emblem. Lincoln's 350-bhp 430 V8, listed the previous year but likely never installed, became a full option. Owing to production over a full model year, the '59 bested the '58 at 67,500 units.

Nineteen-sixty brought last iteration of the three-year "squarebird" styling cycle. Though substantially the same as its predecessor, it had a new grille with a main horizontal bar bisecting three vertical bars ahead of a grid insert, plus new triple taillight clusters and small trim changes. Engines were unchanged. Returning to U.S. production for the first time before World War II was a slide-

Ford debuted the Thunderbird for the 1955 model year. At $2944, it was an instant hit—16,155 were produced for the model year.

The '55 T-Bird was powered by a Mercury 292-cid V8 with 193/198 bhp.

The addition of a continental tire kit was the big change for '56.

Output slipped to 15,631 for 1956, but a 225-bhp 312 V8 was offered. "Portholes" in the hardtop provided better visibility.

Although the Corvette made its debut in 1953, the new-for-'55 two-seater Thunderbird clobbered it in the marketplace. Wisely billed a "personal" car, the T-Bird offered comfort and performance in addition to its stunning good looks.

T-Bird received a new grille and taillights, and finned rear fenders for '57. Production increased to 21,380 units that year.

back metal sunroof, a hardtop option. Volume continued climbing, reaching near 91,000 units. Hardtops outsold convertibles nearly 8-1, indicating that T-Bird buyers wanted luxury first and sportiness second.

A new third-generation design bowed for '61 on the same wheelbase, and would see only detail changes through 1963. Distinctive styling was highlighted by severely pointed front profiles, modest tailfins, big circular taillamps (a Ford tradition) and outward-curving bodysides bereft of sheetmetal sculpturing. There was now just one engine again: the new 390 V8, a stroked 352 but delivering the same rated power. An optional power package offered 40 more bhp for 1962-63. With minor alterations, the 390 would be the basic Thunderbird powerplant through 1968, accompanied by big-block options beginning in '66.

Third-generation engineering was conservative but sound. Ford had considered front-wheel drive but felt it too unorthodox for this market. Instead, engineers stressed quality control, solid construction, high ride comfort, and minimum noise at speed. Extensive use of rubber bushings for the coil-spring independent front and leaf-spring rear suspensions made the 1961-63 Thunderbirds among the best-riding cars of the day.

Two derivative models were added for '62: the Sports Roadster and the Landau. The former was the only production four-seat car to become a two-seater. (There are many examples of the opposite, of course, including the '58 T-Bird.) Ford Division chief Lee A. Iacocca okayed it because dealers had been besieged with requests for a car like the 1955-57 Bird. He concluded there was no significant market for anything like that, but a semi-sports model wouldn't hurt.

The designer most responsible for the Sports Roadster was Bud Kaufman, who developed a fiberglass tonneau for covering the normal convertible's rear seat, thus creating a "two-seater." When fitted, the cover formed twin headrests for the front seats and blended neatly with the rear deck. Kaufman overcame fitting

The '58 T-Bird was completely new, and now carried four passengers.

A horizontal-bar grille and new side trim marked the '59 models.

The Sports Roadster sold for a lofty $5439 in 1962, and only 1427 were built. A removable fiberglass panel covered the rear seat.

problems so that the soft top could be raised and lowered with the tonneau in place. Completing the package were Kelsey-Hayes chrome wire wheels with knock-off hubs that dictated omitting the stock rear fender skirts (due to insufficient clearance).

But stunning though it was, the Sports Roadster didn't sell. The problem was price: about $650 more than the standard convertible. Only 1427 of the '62s were built and just 455 of the '63s, after which the Sports Roadster disappeared. Ford dealers offered a similar tonneau and wire wheels as accessories for the 1964 convertible, but these are even scarcer today.

The Landau was more popular. Priced only $77 above the standard hardtop, it sported a vinyl-covered roof with a fake landau ("S") bar on each rear pillar, plus a slightly spiffier interior. With these touches, buyers flocked to the Landau. By 1966, it was outselling the unadorned hardtop; three years later it was generating the bulk of T-Bird sales. There were also 2000 examples of a Limited Edition 1963 Landau. Introduced in the spring of that year, it came with a special numbered plaque on the console, all-white interior and spinner wheel covers.

Though Thunderbird production was down in these years, it remained far higher than in the two-seater days. The respective totals for model years 1961-63 were 73,000, 78,000 and about 63,300.

Following the usual three-year cycle and with wheelbase again unchanged, the 1964 Thunderbird arrived with completely new sheetmetal—including busy bodyside sculpturing. This design generation would carry on without major change through '66. Quiet, refined luxury got increasing emphasis in these years as convertible sales declined noticeably. The open Thunderbird was thus consigned to history after 1966, when it accounted for only 7.5 percent of production. The '64s set a T-Bird production record at close to 92,500 units. Volume eased to around 75,000 for '65, then to just over 69,000.

Among features introduced with this generation were a cockpit-

Thunderbird production soared 92,843 units for 1960, a record.

The all-new 1961 Thunderbird coupe with a 352 V8 sold for $4172.

Purists have never forgiven Ford for abandoning the two-seater T-Bird after 1957 and replacing it with the 1958-60 "Squarebird." But Ford chief Robert S. McNamara figured a four-seater would sell better, and he was proved right.

Only minor modification attended to the '63 T-Bird. Price: $4445.

T-Bird was extensively restyled for 1964—output hit 92,465 units.

The '64 convertible stickered at $4953—9198 were built that year.

Only 4500 Limited Edition Special Landaus were built for '65 at $4639.

The '66 T-Bird Landau coupe eliminated the rear quarter windows.

Thunderbird for '67 boasted all-new styling and hidden headlights.

style passenger compartment and Silent-Flo ventilation (1964); front disc brakes (1965); full-width taillight housings, including backup lights and sequential turn signals, and a "Town" (formal) roofline for the Landau and hardtop (1966). A popular accessory offered since 1961 was the "Swing-Away" steering wheel. With the transmission in Park it could be shifted about 10 inches inboard to facilitate driver entry/exit. The 300-bhp 390 remained the only engine through 1965, after which it gained 15 horsepower and an optional 428 big-block alternative with a rated 345 bhp.

The pros and cons of offering a Thunderbird sedan were debated by Ford officials throughout the '60s. By mid-decade Iacocca was satisfied that sporty-car buyers were being catered to by other Fords—namely the Mustang and an attractive array of Falcons and Fairlanes. Market surveys indicated that Thunderbird, now firmly entrenched as a personal-luxury car, no longer needed a sporting image.

Reflecting this conclusion was a completely restyled group of 1967 Thunderbirds that included a new four-door Landau on a 117.2-inch wheelbase. The hardtop and two-door Landau continued on a 114.7-inch wheelbase. Front ends featured a deeply recessed honeycomb grille with concealed headlamps and a bumper wrapped underneath. Rear quarter windows on two-doors retracted horizontally into the roof pillars. Engines were unchanged.

This fifth-generation series continued through 1971 despite sales that trended mostly downward. The Landau sedan wasn't very practical—especially its rear-hinged back doors, a throwback to the '30s—and it declined from almost 25,000 sales for '67 to slightly more than 8400 for 1970. Volume as a whole sank from 78,000 to a little more than 49,000 for '69, then recovered to just above the 50,000 mark.

Styling changes were minor through decade's end. The '68s bore narrowed rocker moldings and an eggcrate grille pattern to replace the '67 honeycomb. For '69, horizontal louvers and three vertical dividers made up the grille, divided taillamps replaced the full-width ensemble, and rear quarter windows were eliminated on the Landau coupe. The electric sliding sunroof returned as an option for any vinyl-roof model.

In its first departure from a three-year design cycle, Thunderbird received a heavy facelift of its '67 shell for 1970, marked by a more prominent thrust-forward snout. Radio antenna and windshield wipers were newly concealed (the latter via an extended hood) and two-door models had a "faster" roofline. The customary three-model lineup returned for '71 with wheel covers, grille insert and minor trim the only revisions. However, two-door Landaus were available without the dummy S-bars (a Bird emblem substituted).

Big-block V8s were the order of the day but very mildly tuned, Thunderbird no longer having a performance image to uphold. For 1968, the 428 gave away as the optional engine to Ford's new 429. Rated at 360 bhp, it was more easily adapted for the new emissions standards that took effect that year and would be standard T-Bird power through 1973.

Following a '71 sales decline to some 36,000 units, Thunderbird was completely redesigned for 1972. Riding a new 120.4-inch wheelbase, it was larger and heavier than any generation before—or since. The plain coupe and slow-selling sedans were dropped, leaving a Landau hardtop that shared basic structure with the new Continental Mark IV. Besides list prices starting $2500 below the Lincoln's, a big selling point for this bigger Bird was a new all-coil suspension with four-bar-link location for the live rear axle.

Not surprisingly, greater size and weight conspired with more restrictive emissions tuning to hurt both performance and economy. This explains why a second engine option returned: the big Lincoln 460, though it was scarcely more powerful than the still-standard 429: 224 bhp versus 212, both in newly proscribed SAE net measure. Either way, the '72 Bird needed 12 seconds for the 0-60 mph sprint and returned a dismal 11-12 miles per gallon of increasingly more expensive gas.

Yet buyers apparently didn't care. Perhaps because of its closer similarity with the prestigious Mark, the new model posted a healthy 60-percent sales gain, followed by over 87,000 for '73, the Bird's third-best yearly total yet. Then came the Middle East oil embargo, which put a big dent in big-car sales. Thunderbird was no exception, dropping below 59,000 for '74, then to just under 43,000. A slight recovery—to near 53,000—occurred with the last of this generation, the '76. Disheartening as the figures were, the Bird maintained a solid lead over the rival Buick Riviera and Oldsmobile Toronado.

Relatively few changes attended the heavyweight sixth-generation Bird. Federal bumper standards took effect for 1973, which meant withstanding a 5-mph frontal impact (and a rear shunt the next year) without damage to safety-related components. The Bird met the standard with heavier bumpers that only aggravated the weight problem, boosting the curbside figure to almost 2½ tons. Styling changes comprised headlights set in square chrome bezels, a gaudy eggcrate instead of horizontal bars in the grille, a new stand-up hood ornament and, instead of dummy landau irons, optional "opera" windows, curious little oblong panes in the rear roof quarters.

The '74 had to be the least pleasant of all Birds to live with. The infamous, short-lived seatbelt interlock system mandated by the feds forced you to buckle in a bag of groceries placed on the front seat before the car could be started, and heftier rear bumpers added to overall length with no gain in interior space. With weight up and emissions standards stricter, the whopping 460 became standard equipment this year, along with vinyl roof, opera windows, solid-state ignition, AM radio, air conditioning, power windows and tinted glass. There were eight variations of metalflake paint available, and a glass moonroof appeared as an optional alternative to the steel sunroof.

Aside from details, such as segmented taillights for 1974, this series saw few styling changes after '73. Emissions tuning continued to strangle the 460 V8. Rated horsepower was 194/202 for 1975-76—a ridiculously low level for such a large engine, and this despite adoption of catalytic converter. Ford went all-out to promote the '75 as "the best luxury car buy," trumpeting "new soft-

The Landau sedan, new in '67, continued into 1968. Output: 21,925.

For 1969, T-Bird ads boasted it was "Unique in All the World."

The Landau sedan retailed for $5182 in 1970. Only 8401 were built.

The 1971 formal-roof Landau had "an elegant town car appearance."

Only one model—a hardtop coupe—was offered for 1972. Cost: $5293.

The 1973 Thunderbird rode on a 120.4-inch wheelbase. The price had climbed to $6437, but production jumped to 87,269 anyway.

The '74 T-Bird listed at $7330; output dropped to 58,443 units.

A Copper Luxury Group was an option on the $7701 T-Bird for 1975.

A Creme-and-Gold Luxury Group cost extra on the '76 Thunderbird.

T-Bird lost 900 pounds and 6.4 inches of wheelbase for 1977.

ness, new ease, with ample room for six . . . rich, lavish fabrics . . . 24-oz. cut-pile carpeting . . . woodtone appliqués." More practical options included four-wheel disc brakes (available since '72), Sure-Track anti-lock braking device, and a fuel monitor warning light. The latter was really needed, because these Birds were among the thirstiest cars ever to come from Dearborn.

Ford had long since become a master at keeping interest alive in an aging model via special editions, and the mid-'70s Thunderbird was no exception. An optional gold-tint moonroof was announced at mid-1974, along with Burgundy and White-and-Gold Luxury Groups color-keyed to a fare-thee-well inside and out. There were Copper and Silver Luxury Groups for '75 with either velour or leather upholstery; a Jade LG was added in April. These had a padded vinyl half-roof with opera windows, the latter being deleted when a moonroof was specified. For 1976, the similarly done Creme-and-Gold, Bordeaux, and Lipstick LGs were issued.

For 1977, Thunderbird marked a first in its history by being smaller than it had been the year before. This new "downsized"

The 1979 Thunderbird was basically a carry-over—284,141 were built that year. Prices ranged from $6328 to $11,060.

Thunderbird had a banner year in '78, as 352,751 cars were produced.

For 1980, Thunderbird used a version of the Fox (Fairmont) platform.

A 200-cid six was the base engine for '81; 255 and 302 V8s cost extra.

Model year '82 saw the last of the "baroque" T-Birds produced.

model was nothing more than a derivative of the existing intermediate platform as suggested by the Gran Torino Elite, a 1974 test to see if the public would accept a Monte Carlo-size Thunderbird. Though the Elite sold tolerably well, this "new" Bird would put it in the shade.

Compared to the 1972-76 models, the '77 was lighter and more economical, reflecting big reductions in almost every dimension: nearly 10 inches in overall length, seven inches in wheelbase (to 114.0), three in width—and 1800 pounds of "road-hugging weight." There were big reductions in price, too: nearly $3000 less for the base model. Of course, the old big-blocks were gone. The standard engine was now a 130-bhp version of the trusty 302 V8 except in California, where only a 135-bhp 351 was sold. Optional was a 400 V8, rated at 173 bhp for '77 and 166 bhp the following year, after which it was cancelled.

Downsizing the Bird this way was expedient given the CAFE (corporate average fuel economy) standards that would take effect for '78. But it was that low price and the Thunderbird name

During the '70s, the Thunderbird grew ever bigger, heavier, and thirstier, this caused in part by government-mandated safety and emissions regulations. Ford finally downsized the T-Bird for 1977, cut prices, and watched sales explode.

The '83 Thunderbird emerged with aero styling that would become a Ford hallmark. A 105-bhp 3.8-liter V6 was standard, turbo extra.

that sent sales soaring; better fuel efficiency was merely incidental. Thunderbird thus enjoyed 300,000-unit years for 1977-78—better than three times the previous model year record set in distant 1960. And it easily outsold its sibling LTD II despite far fewer model choices (*see* Ford).

Though the '77 was smaller and less unique than previous Birds, it had many of the same overtones and brash touches. Prices soon started climbing to where they had been. January 1977 brought a new top-line Town Landau with a near $8000 base price and numerous standard luxury features plus a brushed-aluminum "tiara" roof band.

There was little change for 1978, but a Diamond Jubilee edition was issued to commemorate Ford Motor Company's 75th anniversary. Tagged at close to $10,000, it was finished in Diamond Blue Metallic or Ember Metallic and came with the owner's initials on the doors and on a 22-carat-gold dashboard nameplate. This package proved so popular that Ford retained it for 1979 as the Heritage, offered with either special maroon or light blue paint. There were few other changes that year except for volume, which was down again but, at about 284,000 units, hardly bad.

Thunderbird was downsized again and in much the same manner for 1980. Instead of an intermediate, the foundation this time was a compact, the practical "Fox" platform developed for the 1978 Ford Fairmont/Mercury Zephyr. But the size reductions for this eighth generation were just as dramatic as they'd been for the seventh: 16 inches in overall length, 4.5 inches in width, 5.5 inches in wheelbase (now 108.4). Next to the '76, the 1980 looked positively tiny: two feet shorter, eight inches narrower, a foot less between wheel centers, a full half-ton lighter. Yet it was no less comfortable or luxurious than its immediate predecessors.

Adopting the Fox platform returned Thunderbird from body-on-frame to unitized construction for the first time since 1966, which contributed to both weight efficiency and interior space utilization. The interior blended opulence and convenience, and a split front bench seat, buckets and purpose-designed Recaro bucket seats were all available. The 302 V8, now rated at 131 bhp, shifted to the options column and its debored 255-cid relative moved in as standard with 115 bhp. At mid-model year, Ford made its 200-cid six available as a credit option, a first in Thunderbird history.

Other 1980 developments included a new four-speed overdrive automatic transmission, providing OD's traditional economy benefit without the hassle of shifting; rack-and-pinion steering, for precision unknown in previous Birds; and the all-coil suspension system proven in the Fairmont/Zephyr. A mid-year offering expected in the Thunderbird's 25th year was a special Silver Anniversary edition, again featuring a tiara roof appliqué plus standard 302, the overdrive automatic, and gray-and-silver upholstery with complementing paintwork.

This more efficient T-Bird should have sold well, but the market turned sour as another energy crisis began in late '79 and the boxy, overdecorated 1980 styling did not appeal. As a result, production slid to below 157,000, then dropped by 50 percent a year for the 1981s and '82s, which were little changed.

But help was on the way for '83 in the form of a stunning new ninth-generation Bird that announced a new direction for Dearborn styling: the clean, no-frills "aero look." Though still built on the faithful Fox platform, the '83 employed a new 104-inch-wheelbase "S-shell" whose rounded "organic" shape cheated the wind with a drag coefficient of 0.35, a rakish 60-degree windshield angle, and a three-inch reduction in overall width. The only vestige of recent Thunderbirds was a modest eggcrate grille curved snugly on the nose.

This slick new package arrived in base and upmarket Heritage models with a choice of the aluminum-head 232-cid "Essex" V6 or a new 140-bhp version of the 302 V8 with single-point fuel injection. But the real surprise came at mid-year with the Turbo Coupe, the sportiest T-Bird in 20 years. As the name implied, power came from a newly reengineered 145-bhp version of Ford's 2.3-liter turbo four with port fuel injection, linked to a standard five-speed overdrive manual gearbox. A standard handling package, optional for other models, brought high spring and shock rates; a second pair of rear shocks, horizontally mounted to resist axle patter; Traction-Lok limited-slip differential; and beefy performance radials on handsome aluminum wheels. Completing this enthusiasts' T-Bird were black exterior moldings, fog lamps, and a handsomely furnished interior featuring shapely multi-adjustable front bucket seats with variable thigh and lumbar support.

Roundly applauded by "buff books" and even CONSUMER GUIDE® magazine, the Turbo Coupe was a bit crude mechanically but the most roadable T-Bird anyone could remember. It was quick, too: 0-60 mph took 9.6 seconds. Yet it could return an honest 23 mpg in city/suburban driving—impressive for a 3000-pound luxury mid-size. Workmanship was also better than anyone could remember. The '83s were tight and solid, thoroughly detailed and beautifully finished.

Buyers were quick to recognize the excellence of what Ford had wrought, snapping up nearly 122,000 of the '83 Thunderbirds—a sensational 250 percent increase over 1982-model sales. The Turbo Coupe accounted for only about 10 percent but, like T-Birds always have, it undoubtedly lured many people into the showroom who left in one of the tamer versions or another Ford model.

Indeed, the market was fast pulling out of its early-decade slump, and T-Bird shared in the renewed prosperity with some 170,500 sales for 1984. Changes were modest but useful. The V6 discarded its carburetor for throttle-body injection for a slight power increase, and both it and the 302 V8 took on the EEC-IV electronic control system already used for the Turbo Coupe engine. The TC itself was unchanged save newly available three-speed automatic. Heritage was renamed Elan, and a new Fila "designer" model was added with special colors and trim inspired by the Italian sportswear maker.

More refinements followed for '85: a different grille texture, full-width wraparound taillamps, counterbalanced hood (thus banishing the awkward prop-rod), a restyled dashboard with new fully electronic instrumentation (one of the more informative and legible such setups) and wider standard tires (meaty 225/60VR-15s on Turbo Coupe, 205/70-14s on other models). Volume remained healthy at nearly 152,000 units.

Fila fled for '86, but sequential port fuel injection and friction-reducing internal changes lifted the 302 V8 to 150 bhp and a power moonroof became optional. Gas was again plentiful and cheap, so the V8 was specified for the bulk of this year's nearly 164,000 Thunderbirds in spite of its so-so 20-mpg thirst. With judicious use of the options sheet it was possible to order the V8 with most of the Turbo Coupe's features. Many buyers did just that and enjoyed more relaxed performance and far greater refinement. Even in the late '80s there was still no substitute for cubic inches.

Recognizing this trend, Ford issued a rearranged group of '87 Thunderbirds with all-new sheetmetal. The reskin didn't much change silhouette, but it did make an already slick car even slicker. Glass areas were larger (but not the actual window openings) and both headlamps and side glass were now fully flush-mounted to further improve aerodynamics. The Turbo Coupe wore twin functional hood scoops behind a unique grille-less nose. Other models displayed a rather gaudy chrome eggcrate between the headlamps. Replacing Elan were two new offerings: luxury LX and the Sport. The latter combined the V8 with a TC-style chassis, interior and exterior but was otherwise equipped like the base car. At just over $15,000, it cost some $1800 less than the Turbo Coupe, which made it a terrific performance buy—second only perhaps to the Mustang GT.

The '87s had mechanical and equipment improvements aplenty. The TC acquired the intercooled four of the recently departed Mustang SVO, here rated at 190 bhp. Even more laudable

For '84, T-Bird offered a 5.0-liter V8 developing 140 horsepower.

A new grille and full-width taillamps were new to T-Bird for '85.

The '88 Thunderbird sported all-new sheetmetal and aero headlamps.

The '87 Turbo Coupe had a turbocharged four and anti-lock brakes.

After the over-styled and unsuccessful 1980-82 Thunderbirds, Ford give the marque all-new aero-look styling for '83. That proved to be the sales tonic it needed. Another all-new T-Bird, led by the supercharged Super Coupe, bowed for '89.

In addition to all-new, aero styling, the '89 Super Coupe boasted a supercharged V6 and anti-lock four-wheel disc brakes.

were its newly standard four-wheel disc brakes with electronic anti-lock control (developed by Ford with the German Alfred Teves company), plus a new variable shock-absorber damping system (called Automatic Ride Control) and standard 225/60VR-16 unidirectional tires. Air conditioning and tinted glass were standard across the board, and the overdrive automatic took over entirely for the less efficient three-speeder.

The same lineup—V6 base and LX, V8 Sport and four-cylinder Turbo Coupe—returned for '88. The V6 was heavily revised, gaining 20 horsepower via multi-point injection, plus a "balancer" shaft mounted in the vee between cylinder banks to help quell secondary vibrations. TC appointments were upgraded slightly, and the Sport changed from digital/graphic to analog gauges as standard.

A striking new 10th-generation Thunderbird was Ford's big attraction for 1989. And new it was: smoother, slightly wider and lower, and nearly 3.5 inches shorter overall yet with a wheelbase stretched nearly to 113.0—longer than that of even the overblown early-'70s sixth generation. Overall appearance reminded some of BMW's classic 6-Series coupe, but it nevertheless managed to be distinctively Ford—proving perhaps that the '83 Bird and the equally neat '86 Taurus sedan weren't flukes after all.

All 1989 Thunderbirds utilized four-wheel independent suspension.

Surprisingly, both the V8 and turbo four were gone, replaced by a brace of reworked 232 V6s. The familiar 140-bhp unit with sequential port injection returned for the base Thunderbird and luxury LX, offered only with automatic. But all eyes were on the hot new Super Coupe, carrying a supercharged and intercooled V6 packing 210 bhp and teamed with standard five-speed manual (automatic was optional). The engine-driven supercharger was a '30s idea lately revived on several European and Japanese cars. With the SC Bird, Ford also offered its well-known advantages over the exhaust-driven turbocharger—mainly smoother, more progressive power delivery at a slight sacrifice in noise and efficiency.

Chassis engineering was equally new. Though the front suspension retained MacPherson-style coil-over-shock units, geometry now comprised an A-arm at the top of the strut and a transverse arm at the base connected by a long, sickle-shaped member integral with the hub carrier. Rear suspension was fully independent—a first for Thunderbird—and quite compact, with variable-rate coil springs sandwiched between an upper lateral link and a wide H-shaped lower member. Vertical shocks rode ahead of the hub carriers. Steering remained power rack-and-pinion but with a new speed-sensitive variable-assist feature as standard. Base and LX models carried front-disc/rear-drum power brakes, but the SC's standard all-disc system with Teves anti-lock control was optional for the first time. The SC also came with a more sophisticated version of the previous Turbo Coupe's electronically controlled variable-shock-damping system.

Inside was a logically ordered, very European looking instrument panel with digital/graphic or analog instruments (the latter standard on Super Coupe). Maintaining T-Bird tradition was a functional center console on all models. Seats were arguably the best in T-Bird history.

Thunderbird thus entered the '90s in the best shape it had been in for a long time. Its '80s metamorphosis from overdone luxury cruiser to tasteful "personal" performer was gradual but dramatic, and the strong sales upturn that accompanied it showed just how many people hadn't forgotten the special character of the classic little Birds and the early four-seaters. How cheering that Ford hadn't forgotten either. As the T-Bird approached its 35th birthday, it was again a car to fire the imagination and stir the soul, and that's something to cherish.

FRAZER

Joseph Washington Frazer, a descendant of the Virginia Washingtons, was a high-born aristocrat who loved motorcars. Shunning the high society in which he would have blended nicely, he enrolled in a technical college, and learned salesmanship with Packard, Pierce-Arrow and General Motors. He was one of many talented men who helped Walter Percy Chrysler build a great corporation in the 1920s. He even named the Plymouth in 1928. During the late '30s, Frazer breathed new life into Willys-Overland. In the '40s, he and his associates acquired old-line Graham-Paige Motors with the idea of producing a postwar car. The Frazer was the result.

Early in 1945, Frazer was looking for a moneyed partner. Friends introduced him to Henry J. Kaiser, the West Coast sand-and-gravel tycoon and wartime builder of Liberty ships. Kaiser-Frazer Corporation was founded in July 1945.

Initially, Frazers were to be produced by Graham-Paige and Kaisers by Kaiser-Frazer under a joint tenancy agreement at Willow Run, the huge factory 17 miles outside Detroit that once had produced bombers. In early 1947, however, Graham-Paige was unable to sustain plant investment and sold its automotive interests to Kaiser-Frazer. J.W. Frazer was company president from 1945 to early 1949; Henry J. Kaiser was chairman of the board.

During the closing years of the war, Frazer had asked inventor William Stout and custom-car designer Howard Darrin to come up with ideas for the new postwar model. Stout's creation, called Project-Y, was derived from his novel rear-engined Scarab. It was too unorthodox and complicated for G-P to build, and it would have carried a $10,000 price tag. Darrin, however, designed a smooth-looking sedan body with flow-through fenders, a high and blunt hood, and acres of space inside. Although the end result was not all Darrin's work (nor entirely to his satisfaction), it led directly to the production Frazer.

Built initially as a four-door sedan only, the Frazer offered tremendous interior space. At 64 inches, its front seat was one of the widest in the industry; well over 80 percent of its total width was available for passenger room. Frazer's six-cylinder powerplant was derived from the Continental "Red Seal" industrial engine, incorporating improvements for its automotive application. Most of the 226.2-cid, 100-115-bhp engines were built by Kaiser-Frazer; a few were assembled by Continental. Frazer had no automatic transmission until 1951. Up to then, a three-speed manual transmission was offered, with Borg-Warner overdrive an $80 option.

The 1947 Frazer Manhattan listed at $2712 and 32,655 were built. Its wheelbase spanned 123.5 inches and it weighed 3375 pounds.

Starting a new automobile company is not an easy job, even in a sellers' market such as existed after World War II. But that didn't stop Joseph Frazer and Henry Kaiser from trying, even though materials were at first scarce and expensive.

Frazer's 1949 four-door convertible listed at $3295. The side window frames did not retract. Only 70 were made that year.

Interiors of the '48 Frazer were as elegant as anything on the road.

The '49 Frazer facelift featured an attractive new grille.

The 1951 Frazer received new front and rear fenders, grille, and taillights to use up leftover 1949-50 bodies; 10,183 were built.

The box-section chassis was equipped with a conventional suspension—coils and wishbones in front, a beam axle and semi-elliptic leaf springs at the rear.

Production began in June 1946, with a ratio of one Frazer to every two Kaisers. The base sedan was joined by the elegantly upholstered (and usually two-toned) Manhattan, priced about $400 higher.

In a market laden with prewar designs, the all-new Frazer was a refreshing standout. It was extremely clean, with no side trim to speak of and only a modest horizontal grille that was painted at first, but quickly changed to chrome. It demonstrated Darrin's styling ideals in its lack of sheetmetal sculpture or decorative trim. The long 123.5-inch wheelbase provided a smooth ride, and the six-cylinder engine delivered excellent fuel economy. Some people thought these were shortcomings, however, and would have preferred eight cylinders for better performance and more chrome for flashier looks. Frazer ultimately offered optional hood ornaments and more glittery interiors, but was not able to provide an eight-cylinder engine, though several were considered.

The 1948 models were changed only in detail, such as redesigned nameplates. Prices increased to $2483 for the standard model and $2746 for the Manhattan. Despite the relatively tall prices (more than a Buick Roadmaster), Frazer continued to do well in what was a seller's market. A total 48,071 cars were sold for 1948.

Kaiser-Frazer surprised the industry with its volume during those years. Observers had expressed a lack of confidence in the managerial combination. Henry Kaiser was a shipbuilder, they said, and didn't know an automobile from a motorboat. And Frazer had never built cars before; he'd only sold them. Yet, despite postwar material shortages, K-F succeeded. It formed a crack team of expediters who foraged the country for everything from sheetmetal steel to copper wire. They usually got what they wanted—at a price. But that enabled Kaiser-Frazer to reach the highest output of any independent in 1947-48, and a volume sufficient for ninth place in the industry production race.

The situation changed in 1949. Joseph Frazer realized this would be a facelift year for the company, and that its cars would have to sell against all-new designs from the Big Three and Nash. He recommended cutting back on production, but Henry Kaiser wanted even more output. The two were at loggerheads, so Frazer stepped down as president, taking the meaningless position of board vice-chairman. Kaiser's son Edgar assumed the presidency, tooled up for 200,000 cars—and sold less than half that. The firm's downhill slide had begun.

The facelifted 1949 Frazers were well-built, good-looking cars. They adopted an eggcrate grille with prominent rectangular parking lamps and large, vertical, two-lens taillamps. A novel four-door convertible was added to the Manhattan series. It was a makeshift job at best. Engineers John Widman and Ralph Isbrandt, directed to do or die, sheared the top off a sedan, put little glass panes where the door pillars were, and purchased beefed-up X-member frames for an inordinate price. Retailing at over $3000, they simply weren't saleable in large quantities.

Frazer's 1949 sales were generally disappointing. About 5000 leftovers were reserialed for the brief 1950 model run, which ended in the spring of that year.

Model year 1951 was cleanup time for Frazer. At that point, Kaiser had a brand-new body, but the Frazer was merely a heavily facelifted 1949-50 Kaiser. The front and rear end restyling made the Frazers look radically different, however, and 50,000 orders were placed by dealers. Yet, only 10,214 units were delivered because they were built on leftover K-F bodies, and when the bodies were gone, so was the Frazer.

For the abbreviated 1951 model year, the Frazer line used up the remaining Kaiser utility sedan bodies, with rear hatches and folding rear seat; they became Frazer Vagabonds. Former Kaiser Virginian four-door hardtops turned into Manhattan sedans, while pillared sedans were assigned to the standard Frazer series, but were trimmed similarly to the previous year's top-of-the-line Manhattans.

Only 131 Frazer four-door convertibles were produced for 1951.

The '51 Vagabond listed at $2399. Approximately 3000 were sold.

The rear end of the '51 Vagabond opened up for greater versatility.

Kaiser-Frazer's styling department had created numerous renderings for future Frazers, based on the attractive new 1951 Kaiser bodyshell. However, with Joe Frazer out of the corporate picture, the Kaisers were quick to discontinue the Frazer name and concentrate instead on their new—and ill-fated—compact car, the Henry J.

Kaiser-Frazer's early success led to a falling out between Joe Frazer and Henry Kaiser over projected volume for 1949. Frazer was correct to be cautious, but it didn't matter—he stepped down in 1949. His name last adorned the '51 model.

GRAHAM

The three Graham brothers—Joseph, Robert and Ray—purchased the declining Paige Motor Company in 1927 to build their own car, in addition to a line of farm equipment. The car was called Graham-Paige through 1930 and simply Graham afterward, though Paige remained part of the company name. Production reached nearly 80,000 vehicles in 1929. Then came the Depression and company's fortunes plunged. Graham-Paige lost money in every year of the Thirties except 1933. Its attempt to rebound in 1938, dubbed "Spirit of Motion," was too radical a car for the public and was unsuccessful in the marketplace.

The early-Thirties lineup comprised L-head sixes, straight eights, and several body styles arrayed in five or more series. The largest Eight included a beautiful town car by LeBaron on its basic 137-inch-wheelbase chassis. Special Sixes and Eights and Custom Eights all featured Graham-Paige's famous four-speed gearbox. These offerings were continued through early 1932, along with a mid-1931 $785 price leader called the "Prosperity Six." But Graham-Paige didn't prosper. Sales in 1930 were 33,560, only half the previous year's total, and slid to 20,428 in 1931.

Graham dug in for 1932, offering a conventional six-cylinder car and the new Blue Streak Eight. The latter featured magnificent styling with novel skirted fenders that would become a near-universal design element a few years later. Powered by a 245.4-cid straight-eight, it had lots of special engineering: "banjo" frame, outboard springs, aluminum cylinder head. In good times it would have sold well, but 1932 was hardly a good year for anyone.

For 1934, Graham fielded another fine car, the Supercharged Custom Eight. Its blower ran at 23,000 rpm, and boosted rated output to 135 bhp. This was the first moderately priced supercharged car in America, and over the next six years Graham would build more supercharged models than any company before or since. Production rose to 15,745 for model year 1934.

The line was reworked for 1935. Styling was now quite ugly, but sales nevertheless improved and would remain high for two more years. The Eights were dropped for 1936, but Graham-Paige now offered America's first supercharged six, which would be the company's basic engine through 1941. This year's Supercharger and Cavalier series shared their Hayes-built bodies with the Reo Flying Cloud, a result of merger talks between the two automakers during 1935. The marriage was never consummated, though Graham used Reo bodies through 1937, which resulted in some very ordinary-looking cars. The smaller 1936-37 Crusader was based

Graham called the styling of its 1938-40 models "Spirit of Motion." It was controversial, commonly nicknamed "sharknose."

on the 1935 design. Graham sold the tooling for it to Nissan of Japan in 1937 as a way to bolster sagging finances.

There was nothing ordinary about the "Spirit of Motion" design of 1938-40, dominated by a sharply undercut front end that soon earned the nickname "sharknose." Again, Graham was far ahead in styling, and again the public did not respond: production dropped to less than 5000 units.

For 1939, Graham had no choice but to stay with the styling, but a sharknose two-door sedan and club coupe joined the existing four-door sedan and prices were lowered a bit. No matter, Graham output remained about the same as '38, and the Spirit of Motion design was cancelled after 1940.

Company president Joseph Graham had put a half-million dollars of his own money into the firm to keep it afloat. He realized a new model was needed, and quickly. In 1939 he was approached by Norman De Vaux, who'd once built his own cars and later was general manager of Hupmobile. Hupp was in similarly dire financial straits in '39, but De Vaux had an idea. He'd bought the tooling for the discontinued 1936-37 Cord Beverly sedan and wanted to build a Hupp version of it with rear-wheel drive (instead of front drive). Graham said he'd agree to share the project's cost by building the bodies, provided his company could produce its own version with a Graham-Paige engine. The resulting Graham Hollywood had its own special "face" to distinguish it from Hupmobile's car, called the Skylark. But getting the line ready for production took many months, so the sleek new Hollywood sedans didn't roll out of the factory until May 1940.

The 1940 Graham line began with a slightly facelifted "Spirit of Motion" in two series, DeLuxe and Custom, available with or without supercharger. The blower was Graham's own centrifugal type, and was the only such unit available on a popularly priced car. Three body styles were offered: a combination coupe, and sedans with two or four doors. The powerplant, designed by Continental, developed 93 horsepower at 3800 rpm in standard form, or 120 bhp at 4000 rpm with supercharger. A high numerical axle ratio of 4.27:1 gave excellent acceleration. In spite of prices as low as $995, production reached a mere 1000 units.

The Hollywood was first billed as a convertible and sedan, priced at $1380 and $1250. In fact, only one or two convertible prototypes were built. The sedan used the supercharged six and a 115-inch wheelbase, 10 inches shorter than the Cord's. To fit the tall Graham engine into the Beverly's body, engineers had to offset the carburetor and air cleaner to clear the Hollywood's low hoodline. The front end featured a pleasing two-grille combination with freestanding headlamps and delicately curved front fenders.

The big problem in using the old Cord dies was their complexity: it took seven separate pieces of metal to make a top, for example. Joseph Graham had hoped to simplify such matters, but assembly operations were hampered. Perhaps production wouldn't have been high in any case, because the public had lost confidence in Graham by 1940.

For 1941, Graham increased horsepower and sold the Hollywood for $968; the supercharger cost an additional $97. The low prices didn't help, and in November the factory closed for good.

Graham-Paige's departure from the car business a year before U.S. entry into World War II proved to be beneficial. The company received $20 million worth of defense contracts and prospered through the war. Joseph W. Frazer bought the firm in 1944, and built the Frazer as a G-P product in 1946-47 at Kaiser's Willow Run factory rather than G-P's old Detroit plant. In early 1947, Graham-Paige sold its automotive interests to Kaiser-Frazer, and in 1952 quit the farm product field as well. The firm then became a closed investment corporation, dropping the word "Motors" from its title. Later, Graham-Paige operated Madison Square Garden and owned several professional New York athletic teams. All these non-automotive endeavors proved far more profitable than car making had ever been.

The five-passenger coupe was good for 116-bhp when supercharged.

It took $1295 to purchase a 1940 Supercharger Custom four door.

Total production of the 1940-41 Hollywood amounted to 1859 units.

Retail price of the Custom Hollywood ranged from $968 to $1250.

Graham suffered severely throughout the Depression and was lucky to still be alive in 1939. Its radical "sharknose" 1938 models had bombed and would be gone after 1940, while the 1940 Cord-based Hollywood would be gone after 1941.

HENRY J

Kaiser-Frazer was at the crossroads in 1949. The company had degenerated from healthy, record-high production in 1948 to just a skeleton the following year—from ninth place in the industry to fourteenth. Henry J. Kaiser, deciding to press on, borrowed $44 million from the Reconstruction Finance Corporation to maintain inventories, and tooled up for new models. This caused the abrupt departure of co-founder Joseph W. Frazer. Kaiser promised his lenders that part of the loan would go toward a new small car that all Americans could afford to buy: the Henry J.

Designer Howard "Dutch" Darrin had suggested a short-wheelbase compact related to his beautiful 1951 Kaiser, whose design had already been locked up when the Henry J was under development. But Mr. Kaiser wanted something all-new. He settled on a prototype built by American Metal Products, a Detroit supplier of frames and springs for car seats. Darrin reluctantly tried to improve the styling of this ungainly little two-door fastback sedan, applying his trademark "dip" in the beltline and little tailfins. The New York Fashion Academy rewarded his efforts by naming the new Henry J the "Fashion Car of the Year" for 1951.

Henry Js were powered by Willys L-head fours and sixes of 134 and 161 cubic inches and 68 and 80 horsepower, respectively. Incredible economy was promised for the four, while the six-cylinder car turned out to be a little hot rod, giving 0 to 60 times of around 14 seconds thanks to a low 2300-pound curb weight, 800 pounds less than any of the Big Three. Though built on a 100-inch wheelbase, the Henry J could handle four or five passengers and a considerable amount of luggage—51 cubic feet with the rear seat folded down. Overall length, 181.75 inches, measured about a foot and a half less than a Chevrolet. The Standard four-cylinder model cost $1363, about $200 less than a bottom-line Chevy, while the DeLuxe six sold for $1499. Overdrive was a $98 option.

K-F began its 1951 model year early, in March 1950. For a

The 1951 Henry J came as Standard, with a 134.2-cid four, or as a DeLuxe with a 161-cid six. Prices were $1363 and $1499.

Henry J for 1952 featured a new grille. The Corsair cost $1517.

The top-line Corsair DeLuxe sold for $1664; 1952 output totalled 23,500.

while, the Henry J was in demand: 81,942 of the '51s were sold (12,000 more than Nash's Rambler). Unfortunately, that saturated the market and sales were down sharply to 30,585 for 1952, and only 16,672 for 1953.

The 1952-54 models received a mild facelift—a restyled full-width single-bar grille, repositioned taillights and new interiors. An interim model, marketed during the first half of the model year in an effort to use up unwanted '51s, was the 1952 Vagabond. This was merely the previous year's car fitted with a "continental" outside spare tire, identifying script and a black-plastic-and-chrome hood ornament.

By 1954 when the last Henry Js (reserialed '53s) were sold, it was evident the project had failed. Many felt the original approach was wrong. The austere, stripped 1951 models lacked gloveboxes, trunklids and other features normally held essential—they were just too plain for most buyers. "I would have brought it out dressed up," said J.W. Frazer, "and undressed it later." Nash used that approach successfully with the Rambler, and phased in several additional body styles. But in the case of the Henry J, the marque died before plans for hardtops, wagons, four-door sedans and convertibles could be implemented. Total production for its short four-year lifespan came to 130,322 units.

A continental rear tire was featured on the 1952 Vagabond. Only a two-door fastback was seen during the Henry J's short lifetime.

Some say Kaiser would have been smarter spending the money it put into the Henry J on a V-8 engine and hardtop models for the Kaiser. But it didn't, and even though the Henry J won the '51 "Fashion Car of the Year" award, it was gone by 1955.

HUDSON

Founded in 1908, Hudson produced some of America's finest, fleetest automobiles throughout its history, and was usually among the industry production leaders. The low-priced four-cylinder Essex, introduced in 1919, had boosted the company to third place behind Ford and Chevrolet by 1925, and the firm ranked third, fourth, or fifth overall through 1930. Then Hudson began to flounder. From 300,000 units in 1929, production declined to barely 40,000 by 1933 as the firm reeled under the effects of the Depression. Had it not been for the success of the speedy, inexpensive Essex Terraplane, the company might not have survived to see 1940.

Hudson had forged its reputation during the Twenties largely on its Super and Special Sixes—big, smooth-looking, solidly built cars that offered a lot of performance for the money. In 1930, however, Hudson introduced the Great Eight, powered by an engine that was actually smaller than its previous sixes and delivering only 80 horsepower to propel a heavy chassis. Though this powerplant had an integrally cast block and crankcase and the first counterweighted crankshaft ever designed for a straight eight, its splash lubrication system was outmoded. Yet the company stayed with this mill for several more years.

Sadly for Hudson, 1930 saw the closure of the Biddle and Smart coachworks, its long-time supplier of magnificent open bodies. The company turned to Murray and Briggs for phaeton and speedster designs in the early '30s, and a few eight-cylinder chassis were clothed in dashing LeBaron coachwork. Through 1933, the last year for classic four-square styling at Hudson, there were numerous body styles listed on wheelbases from 119 to 132 inches: roadsters, victorias, convertibles, sedans, town sedans, coupes, and broughams. It was an attractive line that would have done justice to many more expensive makes.

Hudson did not field six-cylinder models in 1930-32, selling them instead under the Essex label. It was a mistake. Not only did Hudson sixes have a flawless reputation, but the general economy would have been conducive to sales. To fill the void, the company launched a new Hudson Super Six in 1933, essentially the 193-cid Terraplane engine in the 113-inch-wheelbase Hudson chassis. But the firm hit bottom this year and sales of all models were few. For 1934, Hudson combined its sixes in its new Terraplane junior line.

Along with just about everybody else, Hudson embraced streamlining in the mid-'30s as the old classic look, with its roots in Greek architecture, gradually gave way to the new style. The 1934-35s were transitional designs, still basically boxy but less so than before. Styling was all-new for 1936 and could be compared to the Chrysler and DeSoto Airstreams of a year earlier—not quite Airflow-radical, but much more modern. These Hudsons had skirted fenders, and their rear wheel openings were often covered. They also had tall, rounded, Plymouth-like die-cast grilles and all-steel bodies with rather dowdy appearance.

This move toward the popular "potato shape" came a bit late for Hudson, as its decreased market share during 1935-36 suggests. While 85,000 units had earned it fifth place in production during 1934, its annual volume of more than 100,000 units in 1935-37 was only good for eighth place. There is also evidence the company was cutting prices past the point of profitability, and it continued to lose money despite increased volume. It made less than $1 million profit in 1934 and 1937; with the 1938 recession, it lost close to $5 million. The decline continued through 1940, when defense work helped the company recover.

By 1938, and in the face of that year's economic downturn, Roy D. Chapin reversed his emphasis on performance and concentrated on economy. The Terraplane became a Hudson series that year (rather than a separate make), and there was an all-new big-car entry, the 112 (named for its wheelbase). In performance, the 112 was the complete opposite of the Terraplane: 0-60 mph took 35 seconds and top speed was barely 70 mph. But it did return up to 24 miles per gallon, and prices were as low as $694. All Hudson models had horizontal grilles with thick bars that made for a cleaner frontal appearance than the controversial waterfall grilles of 1936-37.

Hudson celebrated 1939 by completing the consolidation of all of the firm's production under the Hudson name and with extensive restyling. The 112 was reduced to a single group of Deluxe models. With the national economy looking up again, Hudson launched the 118-inch-wheelbase Pacemaker and the 122-inch-wheelbase Country Club Series, both powered by the 212.1-cid, 101-bhp Terraplane engine. Two large, comfortable closed models were offered under the curious Big Boy badge; their wheelbase spanned 119 inches. Topping the lineup was a Country Club Eight series on 122- and 129-inch wheelbases. This year's Hudsons were probably the best looking in some time, thanks to new bodies and some deft design work. The long-wheelbase models were especially graceful, and all models, except for the 112, featured headlights integrated into the fenders.

Hudson had completely restyled its 1939 line, so the 1940 models were merely facelifted. The look was not innovative, but it was pleasing and clean: a rakishly pointed nose, divided horizontal grille, squarer fenders and profile, and little side ornamentation. New also was independent coil spring front suspension. Hudson added another page to its book of endurance runs in 1940 by traveling over 20,000 miles at an average speed of 70.5 miles an hour, setting a new American Automobile Association record in the process.

The 1940 line comprised seven distinct series, three wheelbases, and three different engines with four horsepower ratings (92, 98, 102, 128). On a 113-inch wheelbase were the Traveler and DeLuxe, which included a convertible and convertible sedan powered by Hudson's smaller L-head six. A larger six powered the 118-inch-wheelbase Super, offered in a wide variety of body styles, and the 125-inch-wheelbase "Big Boy" series, made up of a carry-all and a seven-passenger sedan. The L-head eight was available for the 118-inch-wheelbase models, including some deluxe variants. The 125-inch-wheelbase eight-cylinder models formed the Country Club series. This consisted of two six-passenger sedans and one seven-passenger sedan. Registrations in 1940 did not exceed 80,000; the company lost about $1.5 million for the calendar year.

Another facelift was performed for 1941, several new models appeared, and Hudson's unit body was revised for new wheelbases: 116 inches for Traveler and DeLuxe Sixes, 121 and 128 inches for the larger Sixes and Eights. A new Commodore series debuted, listing a wide range of models on the two longer wheelbases. All the '41s had new parking lights mounted in large chrome housings atop the front fenders. Prices this year ranged from $754 for a Traveler coupe to $1537 for a Commodore Eight long-wheelbase sedan. Registrations were almost the same as in 1940, but the company made a profit of nearly $4 million. Credit this to defense contracts, which began materializing in early 1941 and increased the company's total sales by 10 percent.

The defense bonus allowed Hudson a breather. The 1942 line, announced in August 1941, was one of the prettiest of all. Running boards were hidden, the grille was lowered and cleaned up, and optional lights were placed on the fenders. Hudson's famous white triangle logo, placed on either side of the hood, was illuminated to add a touch of distinction after dark. The cars were soundly built and richly appointed. Again, the line began with the series of Travelers and DeLuxes with the small six—coupes, sedans, and convertible sedans. Next was the Super Six, offering the same body choices plus a station wagon. At the top of the line were the Commodore Six and Eight. Most of them rode the 121-inch wheelbase, though one long sedan was offered as well. The war put an end to all car production by February 2, so Hudson output reached only a little over 40,000 cars for model year 1942.

During World War II, Hudson built Helldiver airplanes, Hudson Invader engines for landing craft, sections for B-29 bombers and Aircobras, and a variety of naval munitions. The company made a small profit in the war years, and jumped back into car production quickly after V-J Day. Hudson's output of 4735 cars in 1945 was enough for fifth place in this abbreviated calendar year. The firm hadn't held that slot since 1934—and would not hold it again.

The 1946-47 cars were slightly facelifted prewar models. The engines were still sixes and eights, but only on the 121-inch wheelbase. There were three transmission options: overdrive, priced at $88; Vacumotive Drive, $40; and Drive-Master with Vacumotive Drive, $98. The second automatically engaged and

The 1939 Pacemaker Six weighed 2867 pounds, cost $854.

Concealed running boards were featured on the '42 Commodore Eight.

A new grille was seen on the 1940 Super-Six convertible: $1087.

By 1947, the Commodore Eight had increased in price to $1972.

List prices for the 1941 Hudson Commodore Eight started at $1071.

All '48 Hudsons touted a 124-inch wheelbase and "Step-down" design.

Hudson was a respected automaker, enough so that it managed to weather the Depression. The first postwar models were warmed-over '42s, but Hudson introduced its first postwar design a year earlier than most, the famed 1948 "Step-down."

Hudson built an estimated 595 Commodore Six convertibles for 1949. They rode a 124-inch wheelbase and retailed for $3041.

Four-door sedans were Hudson's mainstay; '49 prices started at $2222.

The grille was slightly modified for 1950, as on this Commodore.

disengaged the clutch; Drive-Master eliminated both clutch and gear lever motion. Hudson built over 90,000 of its 1946 models, two-thirds of which were Super Sixes.

The 1947s were unchanged except in details such as a new chrome nameplate on the trunk, right-hand as well as left-hand door locks, and a small lip around the center grille emblem housing. Again, Hudson produced around 90,000 cars, though its industry ranking changed. Ninth in production for 1946, Hudson dropped to 11th in '47, despite a 10 percent gain in actual volume. Other manufacturers were growing faster as all Detroit responded to the unprecedented seller's market. Hudson sales exceeded $120 million in 1946, and the firm made a profit of over $2.3 million.

For 1948, Hudson had a brand-new car with a new engine, and made more money than it had at any other time after the war, netting $13.2 million on gross sales of $274 million. The "Step-Down" unit-body Hudson of 1948-49 (both models were identical except for serial numbers) was one of the great postwar designs. Low and sleek, it hugged the ground and handled well, thanks to a radically low center of gravity. The design team was led by Frank Spring, a fixture at Hudson and ahead of his time. The Step-Down evolved from wartime doodling—sleek, aerodynamic forms modeled in quarter-scale clay and plaster. Like all Hudsons since 1932, it had a unit body and chassis that was extremely strong and rattle-free. The nickname Step-Down referred to the dropped floorpan, which was completely surrounded by frame girders. It was probably the safest automotive package of its time, and perhaps one of the safest ever.

It was also beautiful in an understated way. The sides were clean, the grille low and horizontal, the taillights modest. The flat dashboard stood positioned upright in front of the driver. It contained a big speedometer and clock, warning lights for battery discharge and low oil pressure, and gauges for fuel and water temperature.

As the new Hudsons debuted in mid-1948, dealers cheered. Here was precisely the formula they needed for good sales in those heady days when lots of eager customers stood in line for a new car. Four series, all riding a new 124-inch wheelbase, were offered: the Super Six and Eight, and the Commodore Six and Eight. The fact that prices were up almost $500, now starting at $2069, didn't seem to hurt a bit, at least at first.

Violating an old Detroit rule about restyling and re-engineering

The NASCAR-winning Hudson Hornet appeared for 1951, along with a new grille. Total production that year was 131,915 units.

Only 2100 Hornet Hollywood hardtops were manufactured for 1951.

Lower-mounted taillights were seen on the '52 Hornet. Price: $2769.

in the same year, Hudson also brought out a new engine for '48: the 262-cid Super Six. It developed 121 bhp at 4000 rpm, only seven horsepower less than the eight. Although it had only four main bearings instead of five like the eight-cylinder unit, the six was a smooth-running, durable engine. By 1951, it had evolved into the 308-cid Hornet powerplant, the largest modern L-head six ever built. The Hornet reigned as king of stock-car racing from 1952 through 1954. Even in 1948 tune, the big six packed surprising power. The car could do 0-40 mph in 12 seconds using Drive-Master. Manual-shift cars were faster. Hudsons had been adequate but not outstanding performers in 1946-47; the gutsy sixes made them some of the quickest, most roadable American cars for 1948-49.

There was one problem. In creating the beautiful Step-Down, Hudson committed itself to a design that would be difficult and costly to change. Unit bodies are almost impossible to rework, and Hudson lacked the financial base to add new Step-Down derivatives such as a station wagon, which probably would have sold well. For too many years, each new Hudson would look too much like last year's model. This, combined with the natural decline of the seller's market after 1950, eventually destroyed the make in the mid-'50s. By 1952, production had dropped to well under 100,000 units. In early 1954, Hudson merged with Nash, forming American Motors. To a large extent, Hudson's problems were common to all independents after the war: they had too little money for really significant production, and too little depth for sufficient change and innovation to keep the public interested.

Roy D. Chapin, Jr., who was a Hudson sales executive in the 1950s, explained the situation this way: "If you don't have enough money to do something and do it right, and if you haven't learned to specialize in a given thing...sooner or later you find you just can't do everything. [Hudson was] usually reacting, rather than anticipating."

Nevertheless, the firm entered the '50s in fine fettle. It sold more than 143,000 cars in 1950, including more than 60,000 of its new 119-inch wheelbase Pacemaker. Generally priced under $2000, the Pacemaker used a destroked version of the flathead Super Six. Performance was as good as that of Nash's top-line Ambassador, and put it well ahead in its price class. The Super Six and Super Eight and the Commodore Six and Commodore Eight were carried over from 1948-49.

All models were available with overdrive, and Drive-Master or

The Step-down was built like a tank and low to the ground. This made it not only one of the strongest cars on the road, but also one of the best handling. The big 308-cubic-inch Hornet six gave it sparkling acceleration and speed.

The '53 Super Wasp four door had a 119-inch wheelbase, cost $2466.

Hudson debuted a compact for '53, seen here as the deluxe Super Jet.

Supermatic Drive—two Hudson semi-automatics of repute. Drive-Master relieved the driver of the need to shift and declutch. The car was started by placing the shift lever in "High" and accelerating. The driver would ease up on the accelerator when the shift to regular drive was desired. With Supermatic, a high cruising gear was added; the shift to high occurred automatically at 22 mph when a dashboard button was engaged. In 1950, overdrive cost $95 extra; Drive-Master cost $105; Supermatic was priced at $199. None of these was a substitute for full automatic transmission, of course. When Hudson offered proprietary Hydra-Matic in '51 (at only $158 extra), Supermatic was dropped.

The Hudson Hornet, with its powerful six, was introduced in 1951 with four body styles, and was priced the same as the Commodore Eight. The Hornet powerplant produced 145 bhp at 3800 rpm in stock form, but was capable of much more than that in the hands of precision tuners. The most famous of these, Marshall Teague, claimed he could get 112 mph from a Hornet certified as stock by AAA or NASCAR. He was helped by an enthusiastic cadre of Hudson engineers who developed "severe usage" options that were really thinly disguised racing parts. Twin H-Power, offered in 1953, consisted of twin carbs and dual manifold induction (the first dual manifold on a six) for greatly improved breath-

The Italian-built Italia was a four-place gran turismo based on the Jet chassis. At $4800 a copy, only 20 units found buyers.

The '54 Hudson Hornet Hollywood two-door hardtop started at $2988.

ing. The "7-X" racing engine, which arrived in late 1953, used .020 overbored cylinders, special cam and head, larger valves, higher compression, Twin H-Power, and headers. Output was about 210 bhp.

The Hornet was invincible in AAA and NASCAR racing during most of 1951-54. Teague finished his 1952 AAA season with a 1000-point lead over his nearest rival after winning 12 of the 13 stock-car events. NASCAR drivers like Herb Thomas, Dick Rathmann, Al Keller, and Frank Mundy drove Hornets to 27 victories in 1952, 21 in 1953, and 17 in 1954. Usually, three out of every four Hornets that entered a race would finish. Even after 1955 when the Step-Down was replaced by the Nash-bodied model, Hornets were still winning races.

But racing success wasn't enough to keep the Hudson ship afloat. Though the company kept adding and subtracting series through 1954, it was unable to add new body styles. The standard Pacemaker and the Super Eight were dropped for '51, when the Hornet and the Hollywood hardtop were added; the Wasp replaced the Super Six for '52. All the Commodores were discontinued for '53, and the line of big cars was cut. A lower-priced Hornet Special for '54 failed to spark sales, even though prices started at $3505. Throughout this period, the big Hudson could offer only two wheelbases and four basic body styles. Production dropped accordingly.

The Step-Down cried for restyling in 1952, but Hudson couldn't afford it. The firm had sunk $12 million into a compact, the ill-fated Jet, in 1953. Using old Commodore Eight tooling (the eight was dropped after 1952), the Jet's 202-cid six produced 104 bhp. Optional Twin H-Power and a high-compression head added 10 horses, and made for a speedy package. The 105-inch-wheelbase Jets were roadable and well-built, but not very pretty. Over the objections of chief designer Spring, management had insisted on bolt-upright, slab-sided styling that failed to impress many customers; only 21,143 Jets found buyers in 1953. Hudson tried hard, adding a very cheap ($1621) Family Club sedan and luxurious Jet-Liner models ($2046 and $2057) in 1954, but the car sold even more poorly—14,224 for the year.

The Jet did spark a project that might have become the long-awaited and much-needed new Hudson: the Italia. This four-place gran turismo on the Jet chassis was designed by Spring and built

Hudson's Step-down design received its first—and last—major facelift for 1954. The rarely seen convertible listed at $3288.

The main drawback to Hudson's Step-down design was that it was almost impossible to facelift. And instead of spending its money on a new big Hudson, it put it into the ill-fated Jet. By 1954, the Step-down was dated and Hudson was broke.

After the 1954 merger with Nash, the Hudson became a "Hash" for 1955. The Wasp had a Hudson-designed 202-cid six with 120 bhp.

by Carrozzeria Touring of Milan. Italias had wraparound windshields, doors cut into the roof, fender scoops that ducted cooling air to the brakes, flow-through ventilation, and form-fitting leather seats. They were 10 inches lower than the production '54 Hornet. Though powered by the 114-bhp Jet engine, the 2710-pound Italias weren't as fast as they looked, and the aluminum body was not very solid. But these were problems that might have been solved if Hudson only had money for a major commitment. The firm's conservative engineers held little hope for the wild European styling anyway. Only 20 "production" Italias, plus the prototype and a four-door derivative called X-161, were built. Roy D. Chapin, Jr., later AMC President, served as Italia sales manager. He shoved them out as fast as he could at $4800 a copy. "I got rid of them," he said, "It wasn't one of my greatest accomplishments."

Late in 1953, rumors began circulating about a Hudson-Nash merger. Nash couldn't have come calling at a better time. Hudson sales were sinking: the books were being written in red ink. Between January 1, 1954, and the end of April when it closed as an independent company, Hudson had lost over $6 million on sales of only $28.7 million. Old-hat styling; the ugly, slow-selling Jet; a weak dealer network; and insufficient capital were the reasons.

In merger talks, George Mason of Nash insisted on one big condition: the Jet had to go. Hudson President A.E. Barit fought this, but not for long. He was in a very poor position to bargain.

The merger was really a Nash takeover. Hudson's Detroit plant was soon shut down, and production was transferred to Kenosha, Wisconsin. Naturally, everybody recognized the all-new 1955 Hudson: it was a restyled Nash. It used Nash's unit-construction sedan and hardtop bodyshell, with a special eggcrate grille, distinct trim, and reworked rear end. The only link to previous Hudsons was the dashboard, which used the old 1954 instruments. Wasps were powered by the former 202 Jet engine; the big six was retained for the Hornet; the Hornet V8 used a 320 Packard mill of 208 bhp. Twin H-Power was available on the sixes, increasing Hornet and Wasp horsepower from 160 to 170. A line of Metropolitans and Ramblers with Hudson emblems was also offered.

American Motors introduced its own 190-bhp V8 for 1956, replacing the Packard unit in mid-season for the Hornet Special.

The '56 Hornet Hollywood boasted a 320-cid, 208-bhp Packard V8.

Three-tone colors were featured on the '56 Hornet Custom. It listed at $2777. The 308-cid Hudson six cranked out 165/175 bhp.

The small Wasp Six remained, as did the Hornet Six, along with the usual assortment of so-called Hudson Ramblers. "V-line Styling" was the way AMC described the horrendous chrome-plated nightmare created by Edmund E. Anderson. It was the ugliest Hudson in a generation. And the AMC V8 was far less powerful than the Packard unit. An anemic engine and terrible styling made for depressing sales. Only 10,671 non-Rambler Hudsons were peddled in '56. In the next year—Hudson's last—styling didn't improve, and only 3876 were sold, all V8s. Rambler was listed as a separate make in 1957, but a rumor that Ramblers would diverge into very different 1958 Hudson and Nash models came to naught. There was no money for that.

AMC's decision to drop Hudson and Nash was only common sense. Said Roy Chapin, "We ran Hudson and Nash Metropolitans and Ramblers—it was a charade. They were basically the exact same automobiles, and the decision really was one that said we've got to spend our money and our effort and our concentration on the Rambler because we haven't got the dough to update the big Nashes and the big Hudsons." Thus expired two once-great marques of the American auto industry, although the newly formed American Motors Corporation would survive for another three decades.

Modified side trim and tacked-on fins were seen on the '57 Hudson.

The '57 Hornet used the brand-new AMC-built 327-cid, 255-bhp V8.

Nash and Hudson merged in 1954. Hudson's plant was shut down and it was decided that the '55 Hudson would be based on the Nash bodyshell. Although the "Hash" got many Hudson touches and engines, it wasn't enough—Hudson was gone after 1957.

HUPMOBILE

The Hupp Motor Car Company came into being on November 8, 1909, a week after Robert C. Hupp completed his Model 20 runabout. The little 16.9-horsepower, four-cylinder car rode an 86-inch wheelbase, and sold for a modest $750, fully $75 less than Henry Ford's recently introduced Model T. With features like a two-speed sliding-gear transmission and high tension magneto, it found immediate acceptance in the marketplace. A total of 1618 cars were sold the first year, and by 1913 production topped 12,000 units.

Hupp left the company in a huff in 1911 (his next venture would be the unsuccessful R.C.H.), but the firm prospered through the Teens and Twenties nonetheless. A straight eight debuted in 1925, and a six replaced the four in 1926. Styling became important to Hupmobile in 1928, which turned out to be its best year ever—the company recorded 55,550 registrations. Unfortunately, from there it was all downhill. After 1932, Hupmobile never produced more than 9500 cars annually. Ironically, the "Aerodynamic" series introduced in 1934 was among the better designs of the period. But buyers just didn't respond. Hupmobile closed down midway through 1936, reopened to produce a handful of 1937-38 models, then struggled on without much success into 1939.

After two record sales years, Hupp watched production plunge to 22,183 for 1930. That year's line comprised the six-cylinder S, a six model series based on a 111-inch wheelbase. Prices ranged from $995 to $1160, placing the S in the mid-price field. Unlike the S, which was assembled in Cleveland at the former Chandler plant, the three straight eight models—C, H, and U—were assembled in Detroit. The S and C were the firm's bread-and-butter cars. The H and U series had a larger 365.6-cubic-inch eight, and included some luxurious limousines on a 137-inch wheelbase.

Hupmobile debuted the 115-inch-wheelbase, $1145 Skylark for 1939.

The next year saw more of the same, plus the new L-series Century with a smaller straight eight. Added to the U series was one of the handsomest Hupmobiles ever, a two-door victoria, and freewheeling was a sales point for all models. Hupp flew buyers to Detroit and Cleveland in a ploy to stimulate sales, but production remained low, totaling 17,456 for the 1931 model year.

Beginning in 1932, Hupp designated model year and wheelbase in its series codes. Thus, the B-216, for example, was a six-cylinder series on a 116-inch wheelbase. This was also the year Hupp acquired the services of designer Raymond Loewy, who styled the F-222 and I-226 eight-cylinder models with tire-hugging cycle-type fenders, vee'd radiator grilles, sloping windshields, and chrome wheel discs. These graceful, handsome cars won Loewy many awards, but Hupmobile production dropped again.

Sales were the worst yet in 1933, just 7316 units. These cars were essentially '32 carryovers, a sloping grille being the only major change. A new cycle-fendered six-cylinder model, the K-321, was followed by a cheaper derivative, the K-321A, with stationary hood louvers and a single windshield wiper and taillight.

For 1934, Hupp released the radical Loewy-designed 421-J and 427T, a six and eight, respectively. Billed under the name "Aerodynamic," they had three-piece wrapped windshields, faired-in headlights and flush-mounted spare tires. Also available was the six-cylinder 417W series with more orthodox looks, thanks to a good many body parts borrowed from Ford. Hupp's sales rose to 9420. The '34s were largely unchanged for 1935, but there were two new entries, the smaller 518-D series Aerodynamic six with flat windshield, and the 121-inch-wheelbase eight-cylinder Model O.

The big news in this period was the fight over company ownership. Archie Andrews, the promoter of the ill-fated front-drive Ruxton, had gained control of Hupp in late 1934, and the firm was in ruins by the time he was forced out a year later. Hupp closed in early 1936, and stayed closed for over 18 months. The company came back in 1938 with the conventional 822-E six and 825-H eight—just in time for a recession. Production totaled just 1020 units.

Meanwhile, Norman De Vaux, Hupmobile's general manager, had bought the body dies for the defunct front-drive 1936-37 Cord 810/812 Beverly sports sedan after Auburn failed. To revive Hupp, De Vaux proposed to build a rear-drive derivation, and reportedly had 6000 orders. But Hupmobile was unable to get the reborn Cord into production beyond 35 handmade prototypes in 1939. So De Vaux approached Graham-Paige, which agreed to manufacture the bodies—provided it could have its own version of the car. The deal gave Hupp a ready supplier and Graham a new model to

The Skylark was based on the 1936-37 Cord, but had rear-wheel drive. It was almost identical to the Graham Hollywood Custom.

supplement its languishing "sharknose" design. This cooperation, said Hupp's president, J.W. Drake, "does not mean a merger of the two corporations. The Hupp-Graham contract is a most favorable one for both of us as careful checking of all production costs demonstrated that great savings could be made." Actually, it was a partnership of desperation.

Hupp's Cord-derived sedan was called the Skylark. Like Graham's Hollywood, it was identical with the Cord from the cowl back, but had a shorter hood and overall length. While the Hollywood used a double grille, the Skylark had a single, horizontal-bar design, not unlike the grille of the legendary Cord itself—except that the headlamps were freestanding, not hidden.

Each company used its own engines. In Hupp's case, this was an L-head six with four main bearings and a displacement of 245 cubic inches and 101 horsepower, as opposed to Graham's 217.8 cid and 93 bhp. The Hupp powerplant was a bit livelier than the regular Graham engine, but Graham's supercharged Hollywood boasted 120 horsepower and was faster.

Bad luck plagued the Hupp-Graham operation from the start. It took Graham nine months to set up the assembly line, so production didn't get underway until May 1940. By that time, most of the advance orders had been canceled, and sales were low for both companies. Graham grabbed the lion's share of publicity with its blown engine, and built six times as many cars as its partner. Hupp gave up in October 1940, only three weeks after 1941 model production had started. Just 319 of the '41 Skylarks had been built. Registrations were equally dismal: 211 in 1940; 103 in 1941—another great American automotive make was gone forever.

The firm recovered slightly during the war by way of defense contracts. After 1945, however, Hupp management elected not to return to the car business. Instead, the firm concentrated on production of accessories for other auto companies, as well as kitchen and electronics equipment.

The Hupp Skylark utilized a 245-cid, 101-bhp six-cylinder engine.

Hupp was still alive at the end of the Thirties—barely. In order to develop a new model, Hupp bought the dies to the defunct Cord 810 and made a deal with Graham to build bodies, but it came to naught. Hupp gave up automaking in late 1940.

IMPERIAL

Imperial became a distinct make for 1955 and remained so for two consecutive decades. The name had been used since the late '20s to denote the most luxurious Chryslers—and that would prove a problem. Somehow, Imperial could never shake its image as a Chrysler, and it was this more than any other handicap that limited sales in the prestige-conscious luxury field.

Nevertheless, some of Imperial's best years were its first. The beautiful 1955 models, based extensively on Virgil Exner's earlier Parade Phaeton show cars and the Ghia-built Chrysler K-310 experimental, are recognized by many as the most desirable Imperials of all. Elegantly trimmed inside and out, these big 130-inch-wheelbase sedans and Newport hardtop coupes wore a distinctive split grille, unique "gunsight" taillights, a modestly wrapped windshield and circular rear wheel openings, making them among the best-looking of Chrysler Corporation's all-new '55 fleet. Chrome was abundant but tastefully applied; two-toning was limited to the roof.

Naturally, the '55s used the brilliant 331-cubic-inch Chrysler hemi-head V8, with 250 bhp for this application, mated to the firm's new fully automatic two-speed PowerFlite transmission. At nearly 11,500 units for the model year, volume was about double that of the 1954 Chrysler Imperial, an auspicious beginning even though Cadillac's output that year was 10 times as great, Lincoln's five times as high.

Wheelbase was stretched three inches for the '56 Imperials, which made them the longest. (It shrank to 129 inches for '57.) The Newport was renamed Southampton and joined by a pillarless four-door. Still topped by "gunsights," rear fenders were raised into fins, but no other Chrysler product that year wore more attractive ones. Frontal styling was unchanged. Following

Up to 1954 the Imperial was a top-of-the-line Chrysler. In 1955 it became a separate make—11,432 were built for the model year.

Chrysler, the hemi was bored out to 354 cid for a gain of 30 bhp, and the transmission gained pushbutton control, a fixture of Chrysler automatics through 1963. Though not in the Chrysler 300's league, the 1955-56 Imperials were lively performers yet surprisingly economical, winning luxury-class laurels in the Mobilgas Economy Runs. The only significant option in these years was air conditioning, priced at $567. List prices ranged from the mid-4000s to just over $5000.

Also available in 1955-56 were long-wheelbase Crown Imperial sedans and limousines. Built in Detroit, they replaced the remaining long Dodge, DeSoto and Chrysler models. Styling and engineering followed that of the standard Imperial, but prices were much higher—$7100-$7700—and availability limited. Just 172 were built for '55, another 226 for '56. Reflecting the industry's general decline from record-setting '55, Imperial's total 1956 volume dropped to just below 11,000 units.

Imperial was all-new for 1957, bearing second-generation "Forward Look" styling marked by huge tailfins (with vestigial gunsights in the trailing edges), airier rooflines with curved side glass (an industry first) and a finely checked full-width grille composed of thick and thin bars. In a push for sales, the lineup added new Crown and LeBaron models more elaborately trimmed than the standard sedan and Southampton hardtops. The Crown duplicated those offerings and added a convertible—the first soft-top Imperial since 1953. LeBaron, arriving in January 1957, offered a pillared sedan and four-door Southampton. Both new series were priced considerably higher: $5400-$5600 for Crown, $5743 for either LeBaron.

All the '57s came with Chrysler's new three-speed TorqueFlite automatic transmission and a hemi enlarged to 392 cid and 325 bhp. As on other Chrysler products that year, new torsion-bar front suspension made for fine roadability—the best in the luxury field. With all this, Imperial showed surprising sales strength. Volume more than tripled from '56, reaching near 38,000 units. That was still far behind Cadillac's 122,000 but enough to best Lincoln, though the difference was less than 1500.

Though the Crown Imperial sedan vanished for '57, the limo returned with a breathtaking $15,075 base price, but that reflected the fact that it was now built by Ghia of Turin, Italy. With such low sales, Chrysler could no longer justify the time and space necessary to build such cars itself, especially with projected tooling costs of some $3.3 million.

Each Ghia Crown limo began as an unfinished two-door hardtop body mounted on the more rigid convertible chassis and shipped with all body panels intact. Ghia cut the car apart, added 20.5 inches to wheelbase, reworked the structure above the beltline, fitted and trimmed the luxurious interior, and finished off the exterior using 150 pounds of lead filler. Construction of each car took a month, and initial delays made the Crown Imperial a very late '57 introduction. Sales were not impressive: only 132 Ghia Crowns had been built by the time this line ended in 1965, but all were impeccably tailored.

A predictably minor facelift was ordained for '58, with circular parking lights, standard quad headlamps (optionally available for '57 where legal) and a simpler grille the main differences. Prices were marginally higher across an unchanged lineup, and the 392 was tweaked to 345 bhp. Reflecting Exner's fondness for "Classic" styling themes was the optional round decklid hump suggesting a spare tire, a '57 option that continued to find favor for '58. But this proved to be a poor year for Chrysler in general and only 16,133 Imperials were built. Imperial would again outsell Lincoln in 1959 and '60, but would never do so again. To the frustration of dealers,

The '55 Imperial Newport hardtop listed at $3418. Output: 3418.

Like other Chrysler products for '56, the Imperial sprouted fins.

Imperial touted all-new styling for '57, plus a new 325-bhp V8.

Prices of the '57 Imperial started at $4838, output reached 37,593.

While America's two largest labor organizations were merging in 1955 to form the AFL-CIO, Chrysler was busy separating the Imperial from Chrysler. Beginning in 1955, the Imperial would stand as a separate make with styling all its own.

Overall length of the '59 Imperial measured a whopping 226.3 inches. Its 413-cubic-inch V8 churned out 350 horsepower.

The 1958 Imperial Crown featured a landau roof and Auto-Pilot.

Wilder fins and another new grille distinguished the '60 Imperial.

people still thought of these cars as "Chrysler Imperials"—and a "Chrysler," though prestigious, didn't have the charisma of a Cadillac.

For 1959 there was a more extensive facelift of the basic '57 styling, with a toothy grille and added brightwork along the sides. The standard series now had its own model name, Custom, for the first time, but the lineup was again unchanged. Along with other Chrysler products, Imperial switched from hemi-head to wedge-head V8s, a 350-bhp 413-cid unit shared with that year's Chrysler New Yorker. It provided comparable performance but was more economical to build and maintain. Production inched up to some 17,270.

After 1960, Imperial was strictly an also-ran among the Big Three's luxury makes. As ever, Cadillac was the overwhelming choice sales leader, Lincoln a distant second, and Imperial an even more distant third.

Though other Chrysler lines adopted "unibody" construction for 1960, Imperial retained a separate body and frame, which was more readily amenable in those days to noise and road shock isolation, necessary for the level of smoothness and silence luxury buyers demanded. The lone 1959 wedge-head, whose 10:1 compression required premium fuel, was unchanged.

So were model offerings, but styling became cartoonish, with swollen fins, a florid grille and an even larger windshield. Interiors were ornate, dominated by an impressively bright and complex-looking dash and an odd squarish steering wheel. Comfort got major emphasis via a new high-back driver's seat padded in thick foam rubber, adjustable "spot" air conditioning, six-way power seat with a single rotary control, Auto-Pilot cruise control and automatic headlamp dimmer. Customs were upholstered in pretty crown-pattern nylon. Crown upholstery was wool, leather or nylon and vinyl. Wool broadcloth was used for LeBarons. Production held at the '59 level.

The new 1960 bodyshell was considerably changed for 1961—and not for the better. Fins were the most blatant ever to appear on an Imperial—high and gull-like, with the trademark gunsight

Free-standing headlights inspired by the classic cars of the Thirties were seen on the 1961-63 Imperials, here a '62.

Standard engine in the 1961 Imperial was a 413-cid, 350-bhp V8.

Imperial lost its "gun sight" taillights for the '63 model run.

taillamps suspended from them. And there was a new gimmick: freestanding headlamps—individual chrome bullets on tiny pedestals, pocketed in severely concave front fenders—another of Exner's "classic" throwbacks. This strange idea would persist through 1963, but rear styling became much more tasteful. Four-door pillared sedans were eliminated for '61, but other offerings returned along with the previous powerteam. The sci-fi styling, Chrysler's now-widespread reputation for indifferent workmanship, and a handsome, more compact new Lincoln Continental conspired to dampen demand, the '61 total falling to around 12,250 units, less than half of Lincoln's.

Exner left Chrysler during 1961, but not before fashioning a completely new, truncated 1962 Imperial as part of an entirely downsized corporate line. It didn't reach production, which is fortunate because his downsized Dodges and Plymouths did—and met a poor reception. Instead, the '61 was reissued but with its ugly fins planed off, leaving straight-top rear fenders capped by cigarlike freestanding taillights. The 413 was detuned and lost 10 bhp, in which form it would continue through 1965. Production rose to a bit over 14,250 but was still only about 50 percent of Lincoln's.

Another facelift gave the '63s a new grille insert made up of elongated rectangles, plus a crisper rear roofline and restyled rear deck. The stylist responsible for much of this revision was Elwood Engel, who'd come over from Ford—where he designed the aforementioned Continental—to replace Exner in mid-1961. The lineup was again unchanged, and production was about the same as for '62.

Clean, all-new Engel styling completely replaced the old Exner silhouette for 1964 as Imperial became very much like his square-lined Continental. Fenderlines were edged in brightwork, a divided grille appeared (recalling 1955), and the freestanding headlamps were replaced by integral units within the grille. One Exner touch remained, however: the simulated trunklid spare tire, though it, too, was now squarish, and carried down into the bumper *a la* the 1956-57 Continental Mark II. A less contrived instrument panel

The '57 Imperial boasted soaring fins, all-new "Forward Look" styling, and record sales of nearly 38,000 units. Imperial's heyday would be short lived, however, as styling became more bizarre through 1963 and sales went up and down like a yo-yo.

The 1964-66 Imperials took on a 1961 Lincoln-look, not surprising since they were designed by the same person—Elwood Engel.

with a strong horizontal format was featured inside. Modelwise, the slow-selling Custom was eliminated along with the Southampton name for pillarless styles, leaving just four offerings (excluding the Ghia Crown limo). Sales were exceedingly good at over 23,000 units for the model year, a level that would not be approached again until 1969.

Good sales and the big '64 redesign dictated a stand-pat 1965 Imperial. The only significant change was a revised grille with glass covers for the headlights, but prices were $100-$200 higher. Displayed at that year's New York Automobile Show was the exotic LeBaron D'Or, a customized hardtop invoking the name of the great LeBaron coachworks of the '30s, headed by Ray Dietrich, which crafted some of its finest creations on the big straight-eight Imperial chassis of the day. D'Or referred to the gold striping

Hardtop sedans were the most popular '65 model with 13,792 built.

Styling was new for 1967—the Crown four door saw 9415 units built.

The '66 Crown Coupe listed at $5887 and 2373 were manufactured.

Imperial for '68: 5000 pounds, 19 feet long, powered by a 440 V8.

and embellishments used, as well as the special Royal Essence Laurel Gold paint.

Ghia stopped building Crown limousines in 1965, but 10 more were constructed in Spain using '66 grilles and rear decks. When Imperial finally went to unit construction for '67, Chrysler worked out a limousine program with Stageway Coaches of Fort Smith, Arkansas. Built through 1971 at the rate of about six per year, these Stageway cars were called LeBarons rather than Crown Imperials. They were much larger, too, riding an unbelievable 163-inch wheelbase, by far the longest in the American industry. Prices ranged from $12,000 to $15,000 depending on equipment.

Once more, the Engel-styled Crowns and LeBarons returned for 1966 with only detail changes. The grille was now an eggcrate affair, with each crate containing tiny elongated rectangles. The rear deck was cleaned up by deleting the fake spare tire. A bore increase brought the wedge-head to 440 cid, and horsepower returned to 350. Model year production went the other way, however, dropping from 1965's 18,500—itself a considerable decline from '64—to fewer than 13,750.

The '67 Imperials were all-new. Chrysler engineers were by now sufficiently experienced with unit construction to use it for their most expensive product. Advancing technology now allowed computerized stress testing of any given shape before it was built. Unibody construction also promised weight savings. And indeed, the '67s were about 100 pounds lighter than comparable '66s.

But the real reason for this switch was Imperial's lackluster sales, which by now had made retaining a completely separate platform just too costly. Thus, as before 1960, Imperial again shared basic architecture with Chrysler in the interest of reduced production costs.

However, this was not apparent from the styling. Up front was a high grille with a prominent nameplate and square-front fenders containing the parking lights. Headlights were still integrated with the grille. The rear bumper was a broad U below a full-width taillamp panel with a large Imperial eagle medallion in a central circle. The sides were still flat, but relieved a little by "character line" moldings. Wheelbase contracted to 127 inches. The four-door pillared sedan returned without a series name. Other models continued as before. Sales moved up to 17,620, still far adrift of Lincoln's, let alone Cadillac's.

Volume dropped below 15,400 the following year and prompted a far-reaching decision: from 1969, Imperial would share Chrysler sheetmetal as well as structure. One casualty of this decision was the Crown convertible, which made its last appearance as a '68. All models were only slightly altered from the '67s. Style changes included a new grille wrapped around the fenders to enclose the parking and cornering lights, plus rear side marker lights as required by Washington. Narrow paint stripes were applied along the beltline on all models. Newly optional dual exhausts and twin-snorkel air cleaner coaxed 360 bhp from the 440 V8.

The Chrysler-like 1969-70 models were certainly the cleanest Imperials in history, their long, low-roof "fuselage styling" announced by a full-width eggcrate grille with concealed headlamps. Ventless side glass featured on air-conditioned coupes. Overall length stretched by five inches with no change in wheelbase, yet curb weights ran about 100 pounds less. Model choices were down to hardtop coupe and sedan in Crown and LeBaron trim, plus a pillared Crown sedan priced identically with the Crown hardtop. LeBaron was no longer the $7000 semi-custom it had been, and its list price was slashed by about $800. Despite fewer models, LeBaron exceeded the Crown in sales for the first time. The overall '69 total was 22,183 units.

Yet the resemblance to Chrysler and the market's steady turn toward more manageable cars contributed to a sales decline and Imperial's ultimate demise. Production for 1970 was only a taste of things to come: down by almost half from '69, to about 11,800.

Imperial retained its basic '69 design through 1973. Styling

The '73 Imperial wore black bumper blocks for 5-mph protection.

Imperial for '69 boasted new "fuselage" styling. Price: $5770.

The '69 LeBaron coupe rode a 127-inch wheelbase, weighed 4555 pounds.

Imperial changed little for 1970; output was only 11,822 units.

Only LeBarons were offered in 1972, here the $6550 hardtop coupe.

Somehow, it seemed as though Chrysler couldn't separate the Imperial name from Chrysler in the pubic's mind. And with low sales the Imperial couldn't justify a separate body, so it moved to the Chrysler shell with modified styling in 1967.

modifications were confined to easy-change items like grilles, taillamps and minor trim, plus modest sheetmetal alterations at each end and year-to-year updates of equipment and prices. The line was pared to just the LeBarons after 1971, but they were down-priced to fill in for the departed Crown. Emissions tuning dropped the 440 V8 to 335 bhp for '71, then to 225 bhp—in newly adopted SAE net measure—and ultimately to 215 bhp. Horsepower recovered to 230 for 1974-75 thanks to the adoption of catalytic converters. A laudable new 1971 option was a Bendix anti-skid brake system, priced at $250, but this Imperial exclusive was extended to the entire Chrysler line for 1972.

Not surprisingly, Imperial suffered more than its rivals from the effects of the first energy crisis. The brand-new 1974 models had crisper lines and bold upright grillework, plus a three-inch shorter wheelbase and about 100 pounds less weight. But these modest reductions had less to do with the fuel shortage—which Chrysler hadn't dreamed of—as the need to realize further economies of scale by even closer sharing with that year's redesigned New Yorker.

The LeBaron hardtop sedan outsold the coupe six-to-one in 1973.

All-new, but more Chrysler-like, styling marked the '74 Imperial.

After building only 8830 units for '75, the Imperial was dropped.

Still, these Imperials were good-looking in their way, and distinctly different from the Chryslers. But with prices rapidly moving upward—now $7700-$7800—they were none too successful. At just over 14,000, model year 1974 volume was the lowest since '71; the following year it was down to fewer than 10,000. Seeking to cut its losses, Chrysler decided it was time to forget Imperial, and the last of the line left the Jefferson Avenue plant in Detroit on June 12, 1975: a LeBaron hardtop sedan bearing serial number YM43-T5C-182947. But only the name vanished immediately, the basic '75 package continuing through 1978 as the Chrysler New Yorker Brougham.

By 1980, however, Chrysler thought it time for another stab at a separate luxury line. Though facing imminent bankruptcy and having staked their future on the sensible front-drive K-car compacts and planned derivatives, Chrysler executives led by president (and soon-to-be-chairman) Lee Iacocca felt a new flagship might just assure the public that Chrysler had a future after all.

The result appeared for 1981 as a revived Imperial that amounted to the world's most expensive Aspen/Volaré. Essentially it was a reskinned version of the new-for-'80 Chrysler Cordoba coupe, built on the same 112.7-inch-wheelbase M-body chassis with its odd transverse-torsion-bar front suspension and an ordinary live rear axle on longitudinal leaf springs. The company's veteran 318 V8 was inevitable, but Imperial received a newly developed fuel-injected version as an exclusive, with mild 8.5:1 compression and a modest 140 bhp. It naturally teamed with TorqueFlite automatic.

Styling was handsome. The front was dominated by a square, Lincoln-like vertical-bar grille flanked by concealed headlamps inboard of sharp-edged front fenders. A distinctive "bustleback" rear evoked thoughts of razor-edge British custom coachwork from the early '50s—and Cadillac's second-generation Seville, introduced the previous year with a similar treatment. There was no way Chrysler could have "borrowed" the idea and the Imp's bustle was arguably more attractive, but the similarity was a bit embarrassing all the same.

Base-priced at $18,311, the revived Imperial was lavishly equipped. Included were clearcoat paint, Mark Cross leather or rich cloth upholstery, electronic digital instrumentation, full power, and a selection of tires and factory sound systems. The only option was an electric sliding sunroof priced at a hefty $1044. Production was assigned to Chrysler's Windsor, Ontario, facility, where special measures were taken to insure that quality would rank with the world's best. Among these were a series of checks, a 5.5-mile road test and a final polish before shipment. Chrysler announced first-year production would be limited to "just" 25,000 units to augment quality—not to mention snob appeal.

Alas, the new Imperial got lost in Chrysler's well-publicized financial crisis and an equal amount of ballyhoo surrounding the make-or-break K-cars, and promotional funds were limited. Frank Sinatra helped his friend Iacocca by singing "It's time for Imperial" in various commercials, but even Ol' Blue Eyes couldn't persuade buyers and model year sales ended up at just 7225 units.

The following year brought no changes save an "FS" package option—special emblems outside, a set of tapes with Frankie's greatest hits inside—and a base price jacked up to nearly $21,000, though the Imperial still cost thousands less than the rival Cadillac Eldorado and Lincoln Mark VI. But neither did anything for sales, and dealers soon resorted to heavy discounts. Even so, production sank to just 2329. The '83s were as little changed—the Sinatra option was dropped, price lowered to $18,688—and fared even worse: just 1427 copies. Having turned the corner by then but in no need of money-losers, Chrysler put Imperial out to pasture a second time.

But this would again be only temporary. As we write, Chrysler is planning yet another new Imperial, this time a four-door sedan—with front drive, of course. Due to appear late in the '89 model year, it shares a new 103.3-inch-wheelbase Y-body platform with

The Imperial was resurrected for 1981 as a personal-luxury coupe, competing with the likes of the Continental Mark VI and Eldorado.

a successor to the rear-drive Chrysler Fifth Avenue. Both are derived from the new-for-'88 C-body New Yorker, with the same basic suspension and inner structure but greater overall length. Styling reportedly involves similarly squarish lines with rounded edges and corners, a raked-back vertical-bar grille, hidden headlamps, and a vinyl rear quarter roof extending down to surround opera windows in the rear doors. Optional all-disc anti-lock brakes, Chrysler's first four-speed automatic and an upgraded version of the C-body's 3.0-liter Mitsubishi V6 are also rumored to be in the cards.

Perhaps this new Imperial will add a happier chapter to the history of Chrysler's premium make. It could certainly use one.

Styling was commendably clean and the quality good, but the 1981-83 Imperial (here an '82) sold poorly—only 10,981 were built.

Chrysler dropped the Imperial after 1975, but revived it for 1981 as a personal-luxury coupe based on the Cordoba. It, too, failed. But Chrysler hasn't given up, for 1990 will witness yet another new Imperial—a stretched C-body model.

KAISER

Henry J. Kaiser and Joseph W. Frazer had a disagreement long before they went into business together. In 1942, Kaiser was experimenting with $400 to $600 plastic cars and suggesting that auto companies announce their postwar plans immediately. Frazer angrily replied: "I resent a West Coast shipbuilder asking us if we have the courage to plan postwar automobiles when the President has asked us to forego all work which would take away from the war effort. Kaiser has done a great job as a shipbuilder . . . but I think his challenge to automobile men is as half-baked as some of his other statements . . . I think the public is being misled by all these pictures of plastic models with glass tops, done by artists who probably wouldn't want to sit under those tops in the summer and sweat."

After the two came together to form Kaiser-Frazer in July 1945, their relationship appeared amicable. Both sides compromised. Henry Kaiser was unable to build his cheap plastic car for the common man, but he had high hopes for a Kaiser with torsion-bar suspension and front-wheel drive.

The proposed front-drive Kaiser K-85 used a unit body/chassis based on the conventional Frazer, but its drivetrain and suspension, conceived by engineer Henry C. McCaslin, were very different. Its 85-horsepower engine, designed by Continental, drove the front wheels. Power was taken through a conventional three-speed transmission, routed to the front wheels by a helical-gear transfer case, and carried to the front-mounted differential by a universal joint. The torsion bar for each wheel was a 1.3-inch steel rod, 44.5 inches long, running the length of the car. The bars twisted to provide the springing. Unit construction was adopted, McCaslin said, because "we needed to use more of the operation in the plant. We had the welding equipment but lacked large dies and cranes. It was a compromise to get the car into production."

But the front-drive Kaiser never saw production. Huge problems developed—hard steering, gear whine, wheel shimmy. With so much weight over the front wheels, the K-85 needed power steering, which would have added $900 to its retail price. In May 1946, the decision was made to drop the project. Instead, K-F would build a conventional, rear-drive Kaiser similar to the Frazer, but priced lower.

This Kaiser Special was introduced for 1947 at $1868, but the price quickly rose to $2104. It shared the Frazer's body, 123.5-inch wheelbase, and 100-bhp six-cylinder engine. Kaiser used a multi-piece grille that was cheaper to produce than the Frazer's because the pieces were smaller. And it was more mundane inside, using conventional pin-striped upholstery. Late in the model year, a fancier model called the Kaiser Custom appeared, priced about $350 higher than the Special, $150 higher than the standard Frazer, and about $250 less than the top-of-the-line Frazer Manhattan. Only 5412 were built, compared to 65,062 Specials.

Willow Run, Ford's ex-bomber plant, was quickly converted for car production, and K-F was turning out finished vehicles by June 1946. The original plan had been to build two Kaisers for every Frazer, but in 1947 the company built about one to one to satisfy initial orders. The cars were basically unchanged for '48, but Custom production skidded to 1263, while Special output increased to 90,558 units. Both 1947 and 1948 were outstanding years for the young corporation; profits were near $20 million in '47 and $10 million in '48. Combined output put K-F ninth in the industry, and, significantly, the best of all the independents.

A facelift in 1949 gave Kaiser a broad horizontal grille and larger taillights. Several new models were added. Henry Kaiser had thought up the Traveler/Vagabond utility car—a conventional sedan with a double-door hatch cut into the rear section and a fold-down rear seat. The economical Traveler and the leather-upholstered Vagabond enabled the company to build a wagon-type model without the tooling expense normally required for a separate wood- or steel-bodied station wagon.

Two other new Kaisers for '49 were the Virginian four-door hardtop and the DeLuxe four-door convertible, the first postwar models to use those body styles. Both were lavishly upholstered, and offered excellent visibility because they had no steel B-pillars, but the window frames and the glass B-pillar did not retract. Unfortunately, they were almost as expensive as Cadillacs, and only a handful were produced. The ones that didn't sell in '49 were given new serial numbers for 1950.

A unique Kaiser-Frazer feature was a wide range of unusual colors, the work of color and fabric designer Carleton Spencer. He and K-F also worked with color research for home interiors with *House & Garden* magazine. The results were hues like Indian Ceramic (a vivid pink), Crystal Green, Caribbean Coral and Arena Yellow. On Kaiser's DeLuxe sedan, the color name was written in chrome script on the front fenders. There were 150 different interior fabrics offered by the automobile industry in 1949, and K-F owned 62 of them. Of the 218 exterior colors offered that year, 37 were Kaiser-Frazer's.

Between 1948 and '49, Kaiser's dashboard changed dramatically. It had been an inexpensive unit with horizontal gauges in 1947-48. In '49, it became more ornate with a giant speedometer in front of the driver and a matching clock on the passenger's side. In Deluxe models, the dash sparkled with chrome, stainless steel, and a massive ivory steering wheel with a big semicircular chrome horn ring. The flashy interior design, colorful paint, and fashion upholstery did much to doll up what was basically an unaltered '47-'48 body.

Kaiser Customs were improved in performance with optional dual intake and exhaust manifolds and a two-barrel carburetor that boosted horsepower to 112. This became standard on the 1949 DeLuxe, Vagabond and Virginian. Kaiser had no automatic; its only transmission alternative was overdrive, priced at $80 extra.

Unfortunately, K-F sales plummeted in 1949. The main reason was the introduction of brand-new postwar designs by GM, Ford and Chrysler, while K-F had only a modest facelift. Joseph Frazer saw the onrush coming and warned against making too many '49s. New K-F designs were scheduled for release in early 1950,

The slab-sided '47 Kaiser was the most modern car on the road.

After a look-alike '48, Kaiser sported a simpler new grille in '49.

Kaiser Vagabond for '49: "Designed for 'play' as well as pay-loads."

The 1949-50 Virginian was a four-door hardtop with a glass center post.

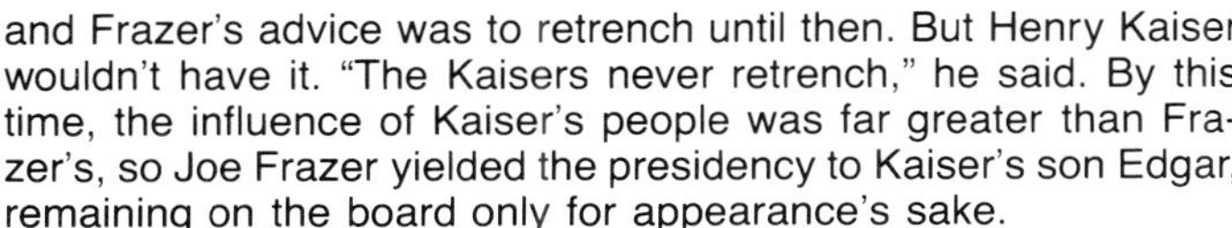

and Frazer's advice was to retrench until then. But Henry Kaiser wouldn't have it. "The Kaisers never retrench," he said. By this time, the influence of Kaiser's people was far greater than Frazer's, so Joe Frazer yielded the presidency to Kaiser's son Edgar, remaining on the board only for appearance's sake.

K-F tooled up for 200,000 units in '49, but built only 101,000. About 20 percent of these couldn't be sold and had to be given 1950 serial numbers. It is impossible to separate 1949 model year production from 1950's except to say that the '49s account for about 84 percent of the total.

By early 1950, the new '51 Kaiser was in production. Its debut was set for March of that year, six months ahead of normal introduction time. Sales rocketed. Close to 140,000 were sold, against about 15,000 of the 1950s. From a dismal 17th place in the industry in '49, Kaiser shot up to 12th—the highest it would ever achieve.

There was reason to be enthusiastic about the '51 Kaiser, which now included two-door models. From every angle it was unlike any other American car of the day. It offered 700 square inches more glass area than its nearest competitor, and a lower beltline than any Detroit car produced through 1956. Unique styling was complemented by an array of bright exterior colors and exciting interiors—again the work of color engineer Spencer.

Kaiser was probably the first company to really push safety. It advertised the new model's padded dash, recessed instruments, narrow windshield corner posts, outstanding visibility and a windshield that popped out if struck with a force of more than 35 pounds per square inch. The engineering, too, was commendable. Engineers John Widman and Ralph Isbrandt shunned unit construction, but designed a very rigid separate body for a 118.5-inch-wheelbase frame that weighed only 200 pounds. A low center of gravity gave Kaiser fine handling, yet curb weight was only about 3100 pounds. Many felt a V8 would have made the car unbeatable in the performance stakes. The lack of one would hurt Kaiser sales as the '50s wore on.

The facelifted '52s weren't quite ready by the end of 1951; in the interim, Kaiser offered the Virginian. About 5500 of these were built. They were nearly identical to the '51 design with similar body style offerings.

A smaller lineup and a mild facelift marked the "regular" 1952 series. The most significant styling changes were "teardrop" taillights and a heavier-looking grille. Kaiser now called its top series Manhattan (the old Frazer model name) and the cheaper Special became the Deluxe. The later '52s are fairly rare: only 7500 Deluxes and 19,000 Manhattans were built in the short production run before the new-model changeover.

The 1953 Kaiser "Hardtop" Dragon four-door sedan was the most luxurious Kaiser of all, inspired by Spencer's Dragon trim option from '51. Distinguished by gold-plated exterior trim (hood ornament, badges, script and keyhole cover) the Dragon featured a padded top, usually made of "bambu" vinyl. This tough, oriental-style material also covered the dash and parts of the seats and door panels. Seat inserts were done in "Laguna" cloth, a fabric with an oblong pattern created by fashion designer Marie Nichols. The Dragon came standard with every possible option: tinted glass, Hydra-Matic drive, whitewalls, dual-speaker radio and Calpoint custom carpeting on the floor and in the trunk. A gold medallion on the dash was engraved with the owner's name. The Dragon was a spectacular car, but its high $3924 list price restricted sales. Only 1277 were built altogether, and the last few were almost given away.

Aside from the Dragon, changes for 1953 were slight. Kaiser

While 400,000 miners and workers in other industries were striking in 1946 and President Harry Truman was handing down the Truman Doctrine in 1947, Kaiser was hustling to set up its auto plant and find the materials to build cars in it.

offered a stripped Carolina model starting at $2313, but sold less than 2000 copies. The company admitted the Carolina's chief purpose was to draw people into the showrooms. The two-door Travelers were eliminated, along with the club coupes. Engine output went up to 118 bhp, and power steering was offered late in the season as a $122 option.

Kaiser sales were plummeting in these years. The make had fallen again to its accustomed low standing in the production race, scoring only 32,000 units for 1952 and just 28,000 for '53. The Toledo-built '54 models were a last-ditch effort, cleverly facelifted by stylist Buzz Grisinger. The front end was much like the Buick XP-300 show car (one of Edgar Kaiser's favorite designs) with a wide, concave grille and "floating" headlights. Rear styling was set off by "Safety-Glo" taillights—big, rounded affairs with a lighted strip running up along the top of the fenders.

In an effort to wring more power out of its 226-cid six, Kaiser bolted a McCulloch centrifugal supercharger to Manhattan engines. Boosting power to 140 bhp, the blower went into full operation only when the accelerator was pressed to the floor. Alongside the two- and four-door Manhattans, K-F sold the unsupercharged Special in two models. The first series was a group of warmed-over 1953 Manhattans with '54 front ends—another effort to use up leftovers. The second was a genuine '54 with a wraparound rear window like the '54 Manhattan's. Neither version did well.

For 1955, Kaiser fielded Manhattans only, distinguished by a

Kaiser received a handsome new body for 1951. It had a large glass area and a windshield that popped out in an accident.

The 1951 Traveler two-door utility sedan listed at $2265 in Special form, $2380 as a Deluxe. About 2500 were produced.

higher fin on the hood scoop and little else. Less than 300 genuine '55s were sold. About 100 were loaded on a ship bound for Argentina, where Kaiser Motors hoped to keep the model in production. It's a tribute to this design's durability that it was built there as the Kaiser Carabella through 1962.

Another memorable but unsuccessful experiment was the Kaiser Darrin sliding-door sports car of 1954, based on the 100-inch-wheelbase Henry J chassis. "Dutch" Darrin designed it in late 1952, and talked Henry Kaiser into marketing it for $3668. Only 435 were built before company operations wound down.

The fiberglass Darrin was beautifully styled, and still looks good today. In addition to the unique sliding doors, it featured a landau top with an intermediate half-up position. Full instrumentation was featured, and the car was usually fitted with a three-speed floor-shift and overdrive, which gave economy of around 30 mpg. Yet, the Darrin could do the 0-60 mph sprint in about 13 seconds, and approach 100 mph flat out. The project was a big disappointment to Dutch Darrin. At the last minute, he bought about 100 leftovers from the factory, fitted some with Cadillac V8s, and sold them for $4350 each at his Los Angeles showroom. The Cadillac-powered cars were potent indeed, capable of about 140 mph at the top end.

The Kaiser itself came to an end in America in 1955, after 10 years and a loss of $100 million. They were usually good cars, offering many innovative features, but they never seemed to make it with the public. Edgar Kaiser liked to say: "Slap a Buick name-plate on it, and it would sell like hotcakes." He was probably right.

The '52 Kaiser sported a heavier grille; the Manhattan cost $2654.

Only 1277 "hardtop" Dragons were sold in 1953—the trim was unique.

Kaiser built approximately 15,450 Manhattan four doors for 1953.

The '54 Kaiser Special sported new, larger "Safety-Glo" taillights.

The grille on the '54 Kaiser looked like the Buick P-300 show car.

The '55 Kaiser can be told by the "bumps" on its hood ornament.

The 1947-50 Kaiser gave way to new-generation models for '51. Alas, the money that could have funded a V-8 and a hardtop was spent on the Henry J instead. Beautiful as the car was, Kaiser moved to a happier home in Argentina after 1955.

LaSALLE

Cadillac's romantic companion make was inspired by the desire of General Motors president Alfred Sloan to offer "a car for every price and pocketbook," the basic philosophy that would make GM the giant it is today. Sloan had detected a gap in the price spread between Buick and Cadillac in the mid-'20s, and assigned the latter to come up with a model line to fill it. The division chose the name LaSalle, honoring another French explorer like Cadillac, and introduced the junior series in 1927 on a wheelbase shorter than that of its senior cars. A big attraction was the new line's elegant body styling created by Harley Earl, the young designer Sloan had hired specifically for this project. LaSalle amply fulfilled its makers' hopes, and launched Earl on his illustrious 30-year career as the company's dean of design. In its first year, it accounted for no less than 25 percent of total division sales, and by 1929 it was outselling Cadillac 11 to 9.

Throughout the 1930s, LaSalle provided the sales volume that helped Cadillac survive. Though the division's total production rarely exceeded Packard's, LaSalle's share was usually substantial—and sometimes crucial. In the hard Depression year of 1933, for example, the division's model year production slid to 6700 units, but LaSalle accounted for half of that. In 1937, when Cadillac built 46,000 cars altogether, fully 32,000 were LaSalles. Yet even with all this, LaSalle sales never really satisfied GM management, who wanted much more.

Cadillac built 10,250 LaSalle 52 Special four-door sedans for 1940. They weighed in at 3900 pounds and retailed for $1440.

In line with general industry thinking at the time, the 1930 LaSalles were longer, heavier and more expensive than the 1929 models, riding a nine-inch-longer wheelbase and available with six luxurious Fleetwood body styles instead of the previous year's two. The Fisher-bodied models—coupes, sedans and a convertible—covered the $2400-$3000 price range, while the Fleetwood line went up to $4000 and included a phaeton, roadster and cabriolet. By comparison, Cadillac prices started at $3295 and went up to about $10,800. Model year production of 15,000 units, three-quarters the level of Cadillac, was respectable in the aftermath of the Great Crash.

Unfortunately, the Depression deepened quickly, and Cadillac was forced to adopt cost-cutting measures for 1931-33. As a result, LaSalle was given the senior line's 353-cid V8 and the 134-inch-wheelbase LaSalle chassis was standardized for the eight-cylinder Cadillacs. Though LaSalle prices were reduced to about $500 under those of comparable Cadillac V8s, the senior models began to look like better buys. Their production matched LaSalle's in these years, and actually exceeded it in 1931.

A new approach was tried for 1934. Abandoning any attempt to win traditional luxury-car buyers, Cadillac gave LaSalle a look all its own and slashed prices to $1000 under those of the least expensive senior V8s. An L-head straight eight from Oldsmobile with aluminum pistons was substituted, GM's new "Knee-Action" front suspension was adopted, and styling was revised with a narrow rounded grille and curious portholes on the hood sides. This basic design and pricing were continued for another two years, although stroke was increased for 1936. Model offerings consisted of coupe, convertible and two- and four-door sedans on 119- and 120-inch wheelbases. However, this formula didn't work well enough, and sales were well below those of rival luxury-class junior editions.

For 1937, wheelbase was stretched and the Oldsmobile engine was ditched in favor of the V8 from the 1936 Cadillac Series 60. The public responded, and LaSalle production rose to 32,000 to set a record. Due mainly to a temporary recession, output for 1938 was down to about half that figure, much to the chagrin of GM accountants. LaSalle was floundering, yet its cars were marvelous bargains.

By 1939, dual-make lineups had long since disappeared from all GM divisions—except Cadillac. In an effort to boost languishing sales, the division completely reworked the LaSalle this year, with new styling, more glass area, a shorter wheelbase and an optional metal sunroof for sedans. Running boards were deleted from all body styles save the convertible (where they were optional). Despite all this, sales again proved disappointing, and only about 23,000 units were built for the model year.

The new styling for 1940 was one of the high points in the marque's 14-year history. Instead of Cadillac's freestanding headlamps, LaSalle's sealed-beams were integrated into the fenders. Lines were gently rounded, functional and clean. Windows were large, and the interior more spacious because of a wheelbase increase from 120 inches in 1939 to 123 for 1940. The trademark LaSalle grille had always been more narrow and delicate than Cadillac's. The 1940 rendition retained these characteristics and was flanked by "catwalk" openings (an idea of Earl's) built into the leading edges of the front fenders.

LaSalles for 1940 came in two series, the 40-50 and the plush 40-52 Special. The Special line was expanded at mid-year by a convertible and convertible sedan, the most elegant LaSalles that final season.

But the marque's exclusive price niche had disappeared by 1940. While the Cadillac nearest in price was the 62 at $1685, Buicks listed from as little as $895 up to $2199. LaSalle's original market position below Cadillac was being covered by a more popular GM make. Cadillac Division did well in 1940. Out of about 37,000 cars, LaSalle accounted for 24,130. But the junior make ranked only slightly ahead of Lincoln, and remained far behind Packard. So, the most romantic of GM's "companion" cars was discontinued for 1941, its place taken by the new lower-priced (but not inexpensive) Cadillac Sixty-One.

In the long run, the decision to drop LaSalle was a correct one. Buyers could have a 1941 Cadillac for about $1300, and the magic of that name was important to dealers. Cadillac continued to price the Sixty-One in luxury territory to prevent cheapening its image. Eventually, this would help Cadillac dominate the fine-car market.

LaSalle never really died in the minds of designers, though. To them it had always stood for distinction, refinement and class. GM Styling had actually prepared a LaSalle design for 1941. A pretty car with the traditional narrow grille and "catwalk" fender inlets, it featured thin horizontal parking lights, spinner hubcaps and a revival of the earlier LaSalle radiator badge—the "LaS" monogram in a circle. In 1955, Harley Earl's studio produced a four-door hardtop sedan and a two-seat roadster, both dubbed LaSalle II, for that year's Motorama. Interestingly, both these cars had grilles composed of vertical slats like that of their 1940 forebear, and the traditional LaSalle badge graced their hoods. In the early 1960s, the name was again considered for what became the Buick Riviera. And only at the last minute was LaSalle dropped in favor of Seville as the moniker for Cadillac's 1976 "compact." But who knows? Perhaps the name may yet be revived someday.

The 1939 LaSalle sported "cat walk" grilles under the headlights.

LaSalle was in its last year in 1940—24,130 units were produced.

The LaSalle had served as Cadillac's companion make since 1927, but it never sold as well as its maker had desired. Of course, it had to contend with the Depression, but when sales remained disappointing in 1939 and '40, it was dropped.

LINCOLN

Lincoln and Cadillac had a common founder: the stern, patrician Henry Martyn Leland—"Master of Precision." Leland and his associates formed Cadillac in 1902 from the remains of the Henry Ford Company (which is why the first Cadillac and production Ford, both named Model A, are so similar). William C. Durant bought Cadillac in 1909 for his burgeoning General Motors. Leland, meantime, went on to build Liberty aero engines during World War I. Then, with son Wilfred, he turned to the car business by forming Lincoln (named for the U.S. president, one of his heroes). When this enterprise ran into financial trouble, he came full circle by selling out to Henry Ford in 1922.

At first, Ford Motor Company did little to alter or update the Lincoln Model L that Leland had designed around 1920. Powered by a comparatively weak 385-cubic-inch V8 rated at 90 horsepower, it was beautifully built and lavishly furnished but an anachronism by 1930: unfashionably upright and quite slow next to contemporary Cadillacs, Packards, and Chrysler Imperials.

Then Henry and son Edsel brought forth the 1931 Model K (why they went backwards in the alphabet remains a mystery). Its massive new 145-inch-wheelbase chassis carried a modernized, 120-bhp V8 that retained the previous engine's "fork-and-blade" rods and three-piece cast-iron block/crankcase assembly, Leland design features that let ads dwell lovingly on its "precision-built" quality.

But the K chassis had really been designed for an all-new V12 that arrived for 1932, a smooth 150-bhp 448-cid unit. The Model KB that resulted was Ford's answer to the twelves and sixteens of Cadillac, Packard and others. Accompanying it was an abbreviated 136-inch-wheelbase V8 chassis that was upgraded the following year to a debored 381.7-cid V12 with 125 bhp for the Model KA. Both series used a single 414-cid twelve of 150 bhp for 1934. After this, they were merged into a single Model K series.

Meantime, the artistic Edsel had been transforming Lincoln styling, updating the standard factory-built bodies and securing a plethora of custom and semi-custom styles from the cream of America's coachbuilders, including Brunn, Dietrich, Judkins, Le-

The 1939 Lincoln Zephyr convertible coupe was rare when new—rarer now—as only 640 were built. They sold for $1747 new.

Lincoln Model K: a 1939 V12 Brunn-bodied non-collapsible cabriolet.

The '41 Zephyr club coupe, Custom *and* base, saw only 178 built.

Baron, Murphy and Willoughby. The result was a line of big, silent, elegant and expensive cars carrying some of the finest expressions of Classic-era design. A cautious evolution toward streamlining began with the 1932s.

The chassis was always a granitic affair, with nine-inch-deep siderails and six cross members with cruciform bracing. Like the old L, the K-series employed torque-tube drive and a floating rear axle. It also had worm-and-roller steering, Houdaille hydraulic shocks and Bendix mechanical brakes. With its progressively more modern styling, the K-series by mid-decade was in the essential form that would carry it through 1940.

But no farther. The strong luxury market of the '20s dried up like an Arizona creek bed in the economic drought of the '30s. Lincoln would not equal its near-9000 unit sales of 1926 until 1935; its best interim total was 5311 in 1931. After 1934, the K-series would see no more than 2000 units in any one year; by 1940 it was available only to special order, built on a chassis completed during 1939. (The largest of these, the 160-inch-wheelbase "Sunshine Special," served as the parade car of presidents Roosevelt and Truman.)

What pulled Lincoln through the Depression was the Zephyr, a medium-price product of the sort Cadillac and Packard also relied on for survival, but far more advanced. Introduced for 1936, it was suggested by a series of radical unit-body prototypes designed by John Tjaarda along aircraft principles and built with help from the Briggs Body Company, eager to win some volume business from Lincoln at last. Tjaarda's original design envisioned a rear-engine layout, but this was switched to a conventional front-engine/rear-drive format.

The rest of the Zephyr was unconventional. Tjaarda claimed it was the first car where aircraft-type stress analysis actually

Squarer lines were seen on the '42 Zephyr. Only 191 ragtops found buyers before World War II halted automobile production.

Like Packard with its One Twenty, Lincoln developed a mid-price model, the '36 Zephyr, to help see it through the Depression. The big 12-cylinder K models were dropped after 1940, leaving the Zephyr to carry the load until 1949.

The 1949 postwar redesign is now known as the "bathtub" Lincoln. The Mercury-based, 121-inch-wheelbase soft top sold for $3116.

The '48 Zephyr four-door sedan with Custom interior sold for $2722.

A '49 Cosmopolitan Sport Sedan cost $3238.

proved the superiority of unit construction. At around 3300 pounds, the Zephyr was lighter than Chrysler's body-on-frame Airflow yet much stiffer. Best of all, unit construction offered important cost savings.

A modified Ford flathead V8 with about 100 bhp was initially slated for Zephyr, but company president Edsel Ford decided that, as a Lincoln, it needed a V12. As Lincoln's existing twelve was too large for this smaller new package, engineer Frank Johnson, one of the ablest in the industry, was directed to add four cylinders to the V8. But because of cost pressures, the result was not outstanding. An L-head four-main-bearing unit of 267 cid, it employed a similar monobloc casting with an exhaust cored between the cylinders and initially developed 110 bhp. The rest of the drivetrain was also derived from Ford V8 components.

Production Zephyr styling was similar to that of Tjaarda's prototypes, but a pointed rear-hinged hood and matching vee'd radiator grafted on by Ford stylist E.T. "Bob" Gregorie made for a much prettier car than the curved-nose Airflow. Briggs actually built most of it; Ford only installed the drivetrain, added front sheetmetal, and took care of trimming and painting. Edsel laughingly told Tjaarda that Briggs might as well build the whole thing, as the Zephyr assembly line was only 40 feet long!

Arriving as a two- and four-door sedan on a 122-inch wheelbase, the Zephyr was a hit. Nearly 15,000 were sold—better than four-fifths of the make's total output for 1936—boosting Lincoln to 18th place in the industry standings, the first time it had ever broken into the top 20. Sales for '37 were near 30,000 despite few changes, though a three-passenger coupe and a division-window Town Limousine were added.

For 1938, wheelbase was stretched three inches and styling extensively revised, with a "mouth organ" grille that beat everyone to the next styling plateau, the horizontal front end. Model offerings again expanded with a convertible coupe and sedan. A Custom interior option provided additional variations for 1939. A deep recession limited 1938 sales to a bit over 19,000—though that was still some 5500 more than Cadillac managed with its LaSalle. At nearly 21,000, the '39 total was more encouraging, but might have been higher had it not been for intramural competition from the new medium-price Mercury.

All these Zephyrs were decent performers, able to do 0-50 mph in about 11 seconds, nearly 90 mph flat out and average 16-18 miles per gallon. Though not styled in the wind tunnel as the Airflow partly was, the Zephyr had a somewhat slipperier shape.

Mechanical alterations followed those of other Ford Motor Company cars. Old Henry's stubbornness precluded hydraulic brakes until 1939. An optional two-speed Columbia rear axle came along, reducing engine speed 28 percent in its higher cruising ratio. Finally, the V12 was modified to cure several problems. Water passages, for example, proved inadequate, leading to overheating, bore warpage and excessive ring wear. Inadequate crankcase ventilation created oil sludge buildup, and oil flow was poor. Yet despite the addition of hydraulic valve lifters for 1938 and cast-iron heads after 1941, this powerplant never shed its poor reliability image. Had World War II not intervened, it might have been completely reengineered. But it wasn't, and many owners of '40s Lincolns have simply replaced it with L-head or later overhead-valve V8s.

With no change in wheelbase or basic appearance, Zephyr was fully rebodied for 1940, with sealed-beam headlamps, larger windows and trunk, bodysides bulged out to cover the old running boards, and a more conventional dash. A bore increase brought the V12 to 292 cid and 120 bhp. The unpopular convertible sedan body style was discarded. Among custom-interior closed models was a special five-passenger "town limousine," a four-door sedan conversion by Briggs. Brunn also built 10 Zephyr town cars in 1940-41 (three of which went to the Ford family), heavy-looking affairs with rooflines that didn't fit the chiseled lower body styling. Total Zephyr production again inched upward for 1940, to just over 21,750.

But Lincoln's big 1940 news was, of course, the Zephyr-based Continental, one of the most stunning automobiles of all time. Styled by Gregorie, it was conceived by Edsel Ford, who directed him to make it "thoroughly continental"—complete with outside spare tire, hence the name. It originated as a one-off convertible that Edsel used on his annual winter vacation in Palm Beach in 1938-39. Everyone who saw it thought it sensational, which encouraged Ford to offer production models scarcely a year later. A coupe and cabriolet debuted at about $2850 a copy and brought customers into dealerships by the thousands.

Continental was thus duly broken out from the '41 Zephyr line and got its own badges. Production increased from 404 to 1250 units. Maintaining a semblance of the K-series' coachbuilt tradition were a new Zephyr-based Custom sedan and limousine on a 138-inch wheelbase. At just under $3000, only 650 were called for. Briggs' town limo was scratched, but other Zephyrs returned with minor mechanical improvements, including power tops for convertibles and optional Borg-Warner overdrive in place of the two-speed rear axle. Styling changes were slight: fender-mounted parking/turn indicator lights and, for Continentals, pushbutton exterior door knobs. Altogether, Lincoln built about 18,250 cars for the last full model year preceeding World War II.

War-shortened 1942 was significant for both styling and engineering. A more reliable V12 bored out to 305 cid arrived with 10 additional horsepower, and there was a flashy facelift that prefigured immediate postwar styling. All models now had longer, higher fenders, a bold two-tier horizontal-bar grille, and headlamps flanked by parking lights on either side. Overall height was a bit lower, curb weights a bit higher. Lincoln built 6547 of these cars before the government-ordered halt in civilian production for the duration.

Despite wartime exigencies, Ford stylists were able to find time for doodling postwar designs. Most involved the "bathtub" look that materialized on several makes for 1948-49. Hundreds of renderings and dozens of scale models were completed. Lincoln concepts were often grotesque, looking as if they'd been "carved out of a bar of soap," as one stylist put it.

Like most other makes, Lincoln returned to civilian production

The 1950 Lincoln featured a new grille and Hydra-Matic transmission.

Lincoln's 1951 answer to the hardtop was the vinyl-topped Capri.

The 125-inch-wheelbase Cosmopolitan ragtop saw only 857 built for '51.

with warmed-over '42 models, which ran unchanged through 1948. The prewar Customs and three-passenger coupe did not return for '46, and the Zephyr name was abandoned for just plain Lincoln. Curiously, the V12 reverted to its pre-1942 displacement but produced 125 bhp. Custom interiors were still available for closed standard models.

The main design difference from 1942 was grillework composed of vertical and horizontal bars, with a Lincoln emblem in the upper segment. A winged globe was adopted for the hood ornament. Continentals carried their name in modest script at the rear edge of the hood. For 1947, "Lincoln" appeared on hubcaps, pull-out door handles were used, interior armrests were "pocket" types, and the hood ornament received a longer "wing." No changes at all occurred when the '47s became the '48s.

Lincoln's first all-new postwar models arrived for 1949, but a Continental was not among them. One had been planned, but was ultimately abandoned due to low projected sales. It would have been ponderous anyway, and some Ford designers, respectful of the late Edsel Ford (who'd died in 1943) were thankful it didn't appear.

The "bathtub" 1949 Lincoln bowed in early 1948, just eight days before the Organization of American States was founded. Like the diplomats forming that group, the Lincoln had an air of dignity about it, but not everyone liked the styling.

Lincoln for 1952 was trimmer, and much faster because of its ohv V8.

Cosmopolitan, shown here, was the base-line Lincoln series in 1952.

Lincoln's 1955 restyling hinted at what would follow for '56.

The '56 Lincoln, here a Premiere, was longer, lower, handsomer.

A longer 126-inch wheelbase and wraparound windshield were features of the '56 Lincoln. A Premiere hardtop listed at $4601.

Concentrating instead on high-volume models, Lincoln issued two series for '49: a 121-inch-wheelbase standard line and the costlier, 125-inch-wheelbase Cosmopolitan. The former, sharing its basic body with that year's Mercury, comprised sedan, coupe, and convertible; the latter added a town sedan, a massive six-window fastback. The aged V12 was replaced at last by a 152-bhp 337-cid L-head V8 originally designed for Ford trucks. Overdrive was a $96 extra.

Ford's original '49 plan called for a 118-inch-wheelbase Ford and a 121-inch-wheelbase Mercury. What emerged as the Lincoln Cosmo was conceived as a Zephyr. At the last minute, Ford's policy committee, led by Ernest Breech and Harold Youngren, mandated a smaller 114-inch-wheelbase Ford, so the proposed Mercury became the '49 standard Lincoln and the 118-inch Ford was made a Mercury—hence the latter's change from "senior Ford" to "junior Lincoln" in this period.

Lincoln's '49 styling was predictably of the "bar-of-soap" school but clean and dignified nonetheless. Fadeaway front fenderlines marked the base models; Cosmos had fully flush fenders plus one-piece (instead of two-piece) windshields, broad chrome gravel deflectors over the front wheel wells, and thin window frames. All models wore conservative grilles, sunken headlights (glass covers were planned) and "frenched" taillights. Model year 1949 volume set a record at 73,507 units.

Lincoln's first all-postwar generation continued with few changes for the next two years. The 1950s had a brand-new dashboard by chief designer Tom Hibbard. An attractive rolled affair with an oblong instrument cluster, its basic format would persist through 1957. Hydra-Matic transmission bought from arch-rival GM arrived as a new option (and would be standard for 1952-54). For 1951 there were elongated rear fenders with upright taillights (versus the previous round units), plus a simpler grille and different wheel covers. Special limited-edition coupes with custom interiors and padded canvas tops were offered in both years: Lido in the base series, Capri in the Cosmopolitan. Few were sold.

While not known for performance, Lincoln had enough of the right stuff to place ninth in the 1950 Mexican Road Race. Lincoln then won the 1951 Mobilgas Economy Run at an average 25.5 mpg. But neither of these feats helped sales, which were well down on record '49. The totals were a bit over 28,000 for 1950 and a more encouraging 32,500 the following year.

All Ford Motor Company cars were completely new for 1952, none more than Lincoln. But though sales rose—up to nearly 41,000 for '53—Lincoln was still miles behind Cadillac. Sedate styling may have been a problem. Ditto dull uniformity, with the same five models offered through 1954. Cosmopolitan was now the lower series and Capri the upper. Both offered a four-door sedan and two-door hardtop (the latter arriving three years behind Cadillac's); Capri added a convertible.

Nevertheless, 1952-54 was a significant period in Lincoln history. The most notable mechanical development was the make's first overhead-valve V8—a new 317.5-cid unit initially producing 160 bhp, then 205 bhp for 1953-54. It was superior in many ways. Its crankshaft, for example, had eight counterweights versus most competitors' six. Intake valves were oversize for better breathing and higher specific output (among '53 engines it produced 0.64 bhp per cubic inch versus 0.63 for Cadillac and 0.54 for the Chrysler hemi). The crankcase extended below the crankshaft centerline to form an extremely stiff shaft support.

Nineteen fifty-two also brought ball-joint front suspension, which together with the new V8s made for taut, powerful road machines that would dominate their class in the Mexican Road Race. Other features included recirculating-ball power steering, oversize drum brakes, liberal sound insulation, optional four-way power seat and, with the extra-cost factory air conditioning, flow-through ventilation when the compressor was turned off. Fabrics and leathers, fit and finish were of a quality that far exceeded conventional Ford products.

Despite a rather short 123-inch wheelbase, the 1952-54s were roomier inside than previous Lincolns—and some later ones. Visibility was better than on any other contemporary U.S. car save Kaiser, and exterior trim was notably free of the era's excesses. Fluted taillights, like those of late-'70s Mercedes, shed water and dirt.

Lincoln turned in some spectacular performances at the *Carrera Panamericana* in Mexico—virtually unrivalled in the International Standard Class. Lincolns took the first five places in 1952, the top four in '53, and first and second in 1954. Major credit for race preparation goes to Clay Smith, a gifted mechanic who was tragically killed in a pit accident in 1954. He had help from publicity-conscious Ford, which supplied stiff "export" suspension components, Ford truck camshafts, mechanical valve lifters, special front spindles and hubs and two rear axle ratios. The higher one enabled a stock Lincoln to top 130 mph. The 1952 race winner, Chuck Stevenson, actually finished the 2000-mile grind from Juarez to the Guatemala border nearly an hour ahead of the Ferrari that had won the year before.

Lincoln wasn't ready with a total redesign for 1955, and its

The '57 Lincoln sported fins borrowed from the '54 Futura dream car.

Lincoln built 3676 Premiere convertibles for the '57 model run.

The all-new 1958 Lincoln stretched an impressive 229 inches overall.

Only 4417 Lincoln Capri four-door hardtops were built for 1959.

The 1952-55 "Road Race Lincolns" won in class in the Mexican *Carrera Panamericana* from 1952-54. The '56 sported an award-winning design, the '57 flaunted fins, and the 1958-60 models ranked as the biggest unit-construction cars ever built.

The 1959 Continental Mark IV spanned a wheelbase of 131 inches and weighed in at 5050 pounds. A total of 6146 were produced.

heavily facelifted cars were Detroit's most conservative that year. Still, their styling was crisp, clean and elegant. The wraparound windshield was being used most everywhere else, but Lincoln didn't have it yet—and was thus more practical. Interiors were luxurious combinations of quality fabrics and top-grain leather. Wheelbase was unchanged, but weight went up 50-100 pounds. Cosmos were redesignated Custom. Lincoln finally offered its own automatic transmission, called Turbo-Drive. But because it didn't look new enough, Lincoln was one of the few makes to do worse in '55 than '54, sales dropping from nearly 37,000 to a bit over 27,000.

The '56s *were* changed—drastically. "Unmistakably Lincoln," read the ads, but there was scarcely a trace of the trim '55s. Wheelbase grew three inches, overall length seven inches, width three inches. Capri became the lower series; the upper was retitled Premiere. Styling, previewed by the Lincoln Futura and Mercury XM-800 show cars, was fully up to date: wrapped windshield, a clean grille, peaked headlights, simple ornamentation, two-toning confined to the roof, and rakish vertical taillights capping long exhaust ports either side of a "grille" motif duplicating the front.

The engine was as new as the styling: a big 368-cid V8 with 285 bhp—"True power," said the ads, "that works for your safety at every speed." Despite the greater bulk, weight wasn't that much higher than on the '55s. As the only make with a major restyle instead of a mere facelift, Lincoln did well for '56, moving over 50,000 cars—though that was still only about a third of Cadillac's total.

For 1957, Lincoln joined a popular Detroit trend by offering its first four-door hardtop, dubbed "Landau," in both Capri and Premiere trim. Huge tailfins sprouted, and the '56 front was modified with four headlamps (stacked in vertical pairs), adopted a bit in advance of most competitors. With 10:1 compression, the 368 V8

Front and rear end styling were new on the '60 Continental Mark V.

A Mark V four-door hardtop set its owner back a hefty $6845 in 1960.

Lincoln aficionados consider the Elwood Engel-designed 1961 Lincoln Continental four-door convertible a modern-day classic.

was rated at 300 bhp. This was a good, but not great, year for Lincoln. Its sales were slightly higher than Imperial's—a bit over 41,000—but only a fourth of Cadillac's. For 1958, Lincoln pinned its hopes on yet another all-new design.

But '58 proved to be a bad year considering the millions invested in new tooling. The economy bottomed out and car sales fell 50 percent or more from 1957 levels. Ford trailed Chevrolet by a quarter-million units, Edsel began its rapid slide to nowhere, and Mercury sales ran 40 percent behind their '57 pace. The new Lincolns were longer, lower and wider at a time when many luxury-car buyers were thinking about more sensible dimensions. Model year production duly tumbled, to about 17,000.

At the bottom of this avalanche was a square-lined giant on a 131-inch wheelbase and measuring six inches longer overall than the '57 Lincoln. It was easily recognized, for there was nothing else like it: heavily sculptured sides, a wide grille flanked by quad headlights in slanted recesses, gigantic flared bumpers. Under a hood not much smaller than a basketball court was 1958's largest American passenger-car engine: a 430-cid V8 of 375 bhp.

Although smaller than the '60, a 1961 Continental weighed 4927 pounds.

Of course, this package had been conceived in the far healthier market of 1955. And, recession or not, most luxury buyers still wanted cars like this. Yet Cadillac attracted more customers with a heavy facelift and Imperial garnered residual sales with its finned wonders. Both rivals had recently expanded with new series and body styles, and Cadillac's comparable models were priced several hundred dollars lower than Lincoln's. But if 1958 was a debacle for Lincoln, it ushered in Elwood Engel and a three-year program that would culminate in a more compact—and far more successful—Lincoln for 1961.

Meantime, there was nothing to do but offer more of the same, so both Lincolns and Continentals were little changed for '59. The Premiere convertible had been transferred to the related but ostensibly separate 1958 Continental Mark III line. Now Continental again became a Lincoln sub-series as the separate Continental Division was combined with Edsel and Lincoln-Mercury to form the one-year-only M-E-L Division. The '59 Mark IV was basically a facelifted Mark III, but offered a new town car and limousine priced about the same as the old Mark II. Likewise, the '59 Lincolns were mainly '58s with less horsepower (350 bhp, as on the Marks). Though the division desperately held prices close to previous levels, Imperial surged ahead in 1959 model year production—and would beat Lincoln again the next year.

Lincoln and Continental styling was again touched up for 1960: revised grilles and front bumpers, the latter's massive guards moving inboard of the canted headlights, plus reworked rear ends and, on Lincolns, a reshaped roof and rear window and new full-length upper bodyside moldings. Though prices stayed much the same and standard equipment was as comprehensive as ever, sales withered from 1959's dismal 15,780 units to just under 14,000.

But the very next year began a happier period in Lincoln history.

The St. Lawrence Seaway opened in 1959, a year when Lincoln rowed upstream trying to sell its huge "ultimate land yachts." Then Lincoln fielded a modern classic for 1961, available as a four-door sedan or four-door convertible.

The 1963 Lincoln Continental wore a new grille. The four-door ragtop weighed 5340 pounds, cost $6916, and 3138 were built.

The reason was an all-new Lincoln Continental. Replacing all the old behemoths, it was offered as a thin-pillar four-door and America's first convertible sedan since the abortive 1951 Frazer Manhattan. Both rode a 123-inch wheelbase, the same as that of the trim mid-'50s models. Classic beauty and superb engineering combined for the most satisfying Lincoln since the prewar K-series and one of this decade's most memorable cars.

Its chiseled good looks were the work of seven Ford stylists—Eugene Bordinat, Don DeLaRossa, Elwood P. Engel, Gail L. Halderman, John Najjar, Robert M. Thomas and George Walker—who were honored with that year's Industrial Designers Institute award. The IDI, which rarely gives prizes to auto designers, called the '61 Lincoln an "outstanding contribution of simplicity and design elegance." Interestingly, basic cowl structure was shared with that year's revamped Thunderbird, which halved tooling costs for these two low-production cars.

The '61 introduced a basic Lincoln look that would continue into the late '80s. The original was naturally the purest: smooth, gently curved bodysides topped by straight-through fenderlines edged in bright metal; a modest grille with horizontal quad headlamps outboard; a simple rear end with a back panel repeating the grille theme and taillamps set in the fender trailing edges. Side windows were curved (inward toward the top) through '63, flat for 1964-69, then curved again. Unlike the old Frazer, the convertible sedan's side glass and window frames slid completely out of sight. So did its top, via 11 relays connecting mechanical and hydraulic linkages.

Aside from styling, these Lincolns were also renowned for quality construction, thanks mostly to Harold C. MacDonald, chief engineer of Ford's Car and Truck Group. The '61s had the most rigid unit body/chassis ever produced, the best sound insulation and shock damping in mass production, extremely close machining tolerances for all mechanical components, an unprecedented number of long-life service components, a completely sealed electrical system, and superior rust and corrosion protection.

They were also the most thoroughly tested cars in Detroit history. Each engine—still the 430 V8, newly rated at 300 bhp—was run on a dynamometer at 3500 rpm (equal to about 98 mph) for three hours, then torn down for inspection and reassembled. Every automatic transmission was tested for 30 minutes before installation. Each finished car was road-checked for 12 miles and nearly 200 individual items. Then an ultraviolet light was used to visualize a fluorescent dye in the cars' lubricants as a check for oil leaks. Backing these measures was a two-year, 24,000-mile warranty.

Response to the '61 line was immediate and satisfying. Sales exceeded 25,000 units and Lincoln went ahead of Imperial for keeps. Styling changes for the second and third year were minimal, Lincoln having stated that it would concentrate mainly on functional improvements. The '62 had a cleaner grille with a narrower central crossbar and headlamps no longer recessed. The '63 had a finely checked grille, matching back-panel appliqué and increased trunk space, plus engine tuning that yielded 20 additional horsepower.

For 1964, wheelbase grew to 126 inches, where it would stay through '69, but basic styling remained the same. A slightly convex vertical-bar grille, a broader rear window and a low-contour convertible top were the only alterations. The '65s had a horizontal grille motif, parking/turn signal lights in the front fenders, and ribbed taillights.

A body change for 1966 ushered in a new two-door hardtop and a more flowing look for all models, helped by a longer hood that added about five inches to overall length. A slight fender hop-up appeared just ahead of larger rear wheel cutouts, the grille acquired fine horizontal bars and a bulged center section (carried through in sheetmetal above), and a front bumper wrapped all the way back to the front wheel openings. The V8 was bored and stroked to 462 cid and 340 bhp.

With all this plus lower prices, Lincoln set a model year sales record for '66: nearly 55,000. Still, that was only 28 percent of

Output hit 27,849 for the '62 Continental four door. Price: $6074.

Production increased to 33,969 units for the '64 Continental sedan.

The '63 Lincoln Continental was motivated by a 430-cid, 320-bhp V8.

The longer 125-inch wheelbase adopted in 1964 carried over to '65.

Cadillac's figure. Another grille-and-taillight shuffle and a spring-loaded hood emblem distinguished the '67s. The convertible sedan put in its final appearance and saw only 2276 copies. Lincoln's total volume remained strong at over 45,500.

One of 1968's more intriguing developments was a new Continental Mark III—not a revival of the 1958 leviathan but a spiritual successor to the matchless 1956-57 Mark II. In large measure it reflected the personal tastes of Henry Ford II, just as his brother William Clay had influenced the Mark II and his father Edsel had sponsored the original 1940 "Mark I." But why use "Mark III" again instead of the more logical "Mark VI?" Because HF II didn't view the heavyweight 1958-60 Mark III/IV/V as true Continentals.

This new one was—conceived beginning in late 1965 as a personal-luxury car with long-hood/short-deck proportions in the Continental tradition. Styling was supervised by design chief Eugene Bordinat. Hermann Brunn, namesake of the great coachbuilder and a member of Bordinat's staff, was largely responsible for the interior. Brunn designed large, comfortable bucket seats and a woodgrained dash with easy-to-reach controls. Henry II selected the final interior and exterior designs from a number of proposals submitted in early 1966.

Because of its late introduction, in April 1968, the Mark III saw only 7770 units that year. But there was no question about its rightness for the market: more than 23,000 would be sold for '69 and another 21,500 of the 1970s.

Initially priced at a reasonable $6585, the Mark III was set on a 117.2-inch wheelbase, some nine inches shorter than the Mark II's. Overall length was the same as that of Cadillac's new-for-'67 front-wheel-drive Eldorado. Though the Eldo was more technically advanced, the Continental seemed to have more magic in its

Continental continued to grow in 1966, stretching now to 220.9 inches.

A two-door hardtop appeared for '66. The '67 version cost $5553.

Continuity keynoted Lincoln styling during the Sixties, which helped to move sales to a higher plateau. Elwood Engel, the '61 Lincoln's chief designer, moved to Chrysler and also gave the 1964-66 Imperial an elegant Lincoln-like look.

By 1967, the Lincoln Continental four-door convertible retailed for $6449. Only 2276 were produced for the model year.

name. It almost matched Eldorado in sales through 1971 and never trailed by more than 2000 units a year. This was a significant achievement considering that Lincoln's annual production had never come close to Cadillac's.

Powering the Mark III was a new 460-cid V8—one of Detroit's largest—with 10.5:1 compression and 365 bhp. Also adopted for the standard '68 Continentals, it would remain Lincoln's mainstay powerplant for the next 10 years.

A good-looking car with America's longest hood—more than six feet—the Mark III offered a wide choice of luxury interiors and 26 exterior colors, including four special "Moondust" metallic paints. The 1969-71 models cost a bit more but were little changed.

Continental's Coupe was in it second year in '67; 11,060 were built.

The Mark III rode a 117.2-inch wheelbase, same as the T-Bird four door.

Lincoln Continental for '69: 224 inches long, 365-bhp 460-cid V8.

Lincoln's Golden Anniversary year was 1971. The sedan cost $7419.

Standard equipment ran to Select-Shift Turbo-Drive automatic, power brakes (discs in front, drums in the rear), concealed headlights, ventless side windows, power seats and windows, flow-through ventilation, and 150 pounds of sound insulation.

Still with their '66 bodyshells, the Continental sedan and hardtop received a new horizontal texture on grille and matching rear bumper appliqué, plus a large Continental star nose ornament (like the one on the trunklid). A multi-function lamp at each corner combined turn signals, side markers (newly required by the government), parking lamps (front), brake and taillights (rear). Volume for this line totaled a bit over 39,000.

Announcing the '69s was a finely checked grille newly separated from the headlamps, still with a raised center section extending into the hood. A new Town Car interior option for the sedan provided "unique, super-puff leather-and-vinyl seats and door panels, luxury wood-tone front seat back and door trim inserts, extra plush carpeting and special napped nylon headlining." Government-required safety equipment included a dual hydraulic brake system with warning light, four-way emergency flasher, day/night rearview mirror, and energy-absorbing steering column and instrument panel. Series production eased once again, settling at about 38,300.

The Continentals were newly rebodied for 1970 on a one-inch longer wheelbase and a new torque-box chassis with coil-spring rear suspension. Styling was updated via hidden headlights, ventless side glass, concealed wipers and full-width taillights, all popular period features. Doors were wider (the sedan's rear ones were newly front-hinged), door glass was frameless, and the fuel tank was made slightly smaller (though still ample at 24.1 gallons). The powertrain, with appropriate emission controls, was carried over with the same rated output.

This heavier, bulkier-looking Lincoln carried on through 1974 with relatively few changes—most dictated by federal, not market, requirements. An even bigger generation arrived for '75 with a fractionally longer wheelbase and some eight inches more overall length, though curb weight was slightly lower than before. Styling remained resolutely blocky and formal throughout the decade as Ford designers sought to establish a closer familial resemblance with the Mark. Sales moved smartly upward for 1972—to nearly 95,000, including Marks—then to a record 128,000-plus for '73. A temporary decline followed in the wake of the OPEC oil embargo. But along with other full-size cars, the big Lincoln rallied beginning in 1975. By 1979, output was close to 190,000 units, another all-time Lincoln high, but still only about half of Cadillac's figure. Another fuel shock occurred in 1979, and volume plunged to just under 75,000 the next year.

Longer-lower-wider was a formula that had traditionally worked well for luxury makes, and it worked well for Lincoln with the Continental Mark IV, introduced for 1972. Sales nearly doubled over those of the last Mark III, and would average 50,000 or so units annually through the final 1976 models. Remarkably, the Mark IV offered less passenger room and was predictably thirstier and less agile. Though it shared basic structure and a 120.4-inch wheelbase with the concurrent Ford Thunderbird, it wasn't immediately apparent.

Lincoln enjoyed good success with the four-door Town Car option. It initially consisted of special leather inserts and vinyl bolsters for the seats, wood-like panels on the backs of the front seats, deeper cut-pile carpeting and soft nylon headliner, all color-keyed in a choice of five hues. For 1971 these were bolstered by special dash and front fender nameplates plus a set of keys and door-mounted owner initials done in 22-carat gold—which made the Golden Anniversary Continental, a commemorative marking Lincoln's 50th birthday. The gold goodies were dropped the following year, by which time the Town Car had become a sub-model. The big two-door got the same treatment for 1973 to become the Town Coupe.

Lincoln marked time for 1974. The only noteworthy news were heavier bumpers at the rear to match the beefier front ones adopted the previous year per federal mandate, plus a brace of Luxury Group interior/exterior packages for the Mark. The revamped big-car line for '75 brought the end of pure "hardtop styling" and the beginning of "opera window" rooflines, with fixed B-posts and heavily padded vinyl coverings. These models continued largely intact through 1979.

For 1977, the Mark IV was restyled inside and out to become the Mark V, distinguished by a crisper, lighter appearance. And appearances were not deceiving. Though it rode the same wheelbase and was little changed mechanically, the V was some 500 pounds lighter at the curb. It also boasted 21 percent more trunk space—which seems a large gain only because the IV had so little. Engineers paid belated attention to fuel economy by standardizing the corporate 400-cid V8 with 179 bhp. The old reliable 460 continued as an option except in California, where it couldn't quite clear that state's tougher emissions hurdles. Output climbed to an impressive 80,321 units.

Model year 1977 also saw Lincoln move into the luxury-compact class, its first response to the radically changed market left behind by the first energy crisis. Called Versailles, this was a hastily contrived reply to Cadillac's remarkably successful Seville, little more than a Ford Granada/Mercury Monarch carrying a Continental-style square grille, stand-up hood ornament and humped trunklid, plus more standard equipment. Established Lincoln buyers looked askance at its plebeian origins (which the press never failed to mention), while buyers balked at the $11,500 price. You can only fool some of the people some of the time, and Lincoln didn't fool many with this one. Versailles' 1977-model sales were a mere 15,434, a fraction of Seville's.

This basic three-car lineup held the fort for 1978-79 while Lincoln prepared a troop of downsized 1980 models. Amazingly, the

The Continental Mark IV bowed in 1972 on a 120.4-inch wheelbase.

Lincoln built 33,513 Continental sedans for the 1975 model run.

As with other makes, model proliferation emerged at Lincoln during the Sixties. A two-door hardtop joined the lineup in 1966 and the Thunderbird-based Continental Mark III arrived for 1968. The latter gave Cadillac a good run for the money.

Lincoln's 'compact' car in 1978 was the Versailles. Price: $12,529.

The 1978 Continental Mark V cost about the same: $12,318 base.

The 4659-pound Town Coupe listed at $10,196 for the '78 model year.

The 1978 edition of the Lincoln Town Car retailed for $10,396.

The Continental Mark VI was all-new and 700 pounds lighter for 1980. Four models ranged in price from $16,291 to $22,243.

big cars continued to sell well, defying the combined threat of further fuel shortages and a fleet of luxury intermediates from Big Three rivals. Part of this was due to circumstance. By 1979, anyone who wanted a truly large luxury liner—a "traditional-size" car, as Lincoln called it—had precious few choices.

One of Lincoln's most successful marketing ploys in this period was its Designer Series. American Motors had tried something similar earlier in the decade with Gucci Hornets and Pierre Cardin Javelins. But, as a luxury make, Lincoln was in a far better position to cash in on the snob appeal of high-fashion names. First seen for 1976, these extra-cost couturier packages were decorated inside and out with colors and materials specified by well-known designers. The schemes varied somewhat from year to year, but the results were invariably striking and usually pleasing. Perhaps the most consistently tasteful was the Bill Blass edition, a nautically inspired blend of navy blue paint and eggshell-white vinyl top outside, and navy velour or dark blue and cream leather upholstery inside. There were also versions by Givenchy (generally turquoise or jade), Emilio Pucci (maroon and gunmetal grey), and Cartier (champagne/grey), the last not a designer per se but, of course, the famous jeweler.

Following a spate of limited-edition 1978 trim packages to mark Ford Motor Company's 75th anniversary, Lincoln came up with its own "Collector Series" option group for the '79 Continental and Mark. These included appropriate nameplates, gold grille accents, special midnight-blue metallic paint, and a host of "custom" accoutrements such as a color-keyed umbrella and leather-bound owner's manual and tool kit. It was a timely offering, for an era was about to end.

The big Continental and the Mark became much more alike—and more sensible—for 1980. Lincoln now adopted the "Panther" platform introduced with the '79 Ford LTD and Mercury Marquis as the basis for a substantially downsized Continental and an upmarket twin, the Mark VI, thus resuming its late-'50s practice of fielding two versions of a single basic design. Compared to their immediate predecessors, these cars were up to 10 inches shorter between wheel centers and significantly lighter yet about as roomy, thanks to only marginal reductions in width plus taller, boxier body styling.

The usual appearance "cues" were retained for each line, but the usual big-block engines weren't. Standard for both was the corporate 302-cid small-block V8 in newly developed, 129-bhp fuel-injected form; a 140-bhp 351 was the only option. It was all for the sake of economy, and Lincoln boasted a further efficiency aid in Ford Motor Company's new four-speed overdrive automatic transmission, basically a three-speed unit with an extra, super-tall (0.67:1) ratio added. There was more competent handling courtesy of a revised suspension with four-bar-link rear geometry and retuned body mounts and suspension bushings, plus standard high-pressure radial tires, which also helped eke out a few more mpg. A four-door Mark bowed for the first time, and the various designer editions were bolstered by a new Signature Series much like the previous Collector option.

A major national recession beginning in the spring of 1979 sent U.S. car sales plunging. Lincoln fared worse than most, its 1980 model year tally down by as much as two-thirds compared to its previous level. The underwhelming Versailles was in its final year and found fewer than 5000 buyers.

The 1981 total was even worse—down to about 69,500—but that would prove the decade low. Lincoln followed the general market in making a strong recovery. By 1985 it was up to some 166,500 cars after building around 157,000 the year before. It would repeat the latter tally for 1986.

Remarkably, the foundation for this success was a single 1980-vintage four-door that saw only one major change all decade: a rounded-corner "aero" facelift for 1985. Officially called Town Car after 1981, it soldiered on alone after cancellation of the 114.3-inch-wheelbase Town Coupe after '81 and the Mark VI duo after '83. The 302 V8 was the only available engine after 1980 and was upgraded twice via different fuel-injection systems: throttle-body in 1983, good for an extra 10 bhp; a more sophisticated multi-point system from 1985, bringing output to 150 bhp. Trim and equipment shuffles were about the only alterations in most years.

The '82 Continental was based on a stretched-wheelbase Fox platform.

Town Cars in '82 came in base, Signature Series, or Cartier Edition.

The Continental, here an '83, was really a Versailles successor.

But it didn't matter: At 50,000-100,000 units annually, this series outsold Lincoln's other Lincolns by margins of 2-1 or greater—sometimes upwards of 5-1. Yes, the Town Car was smaller than its late-'70s predecessor, but it proved that traditional Detroit biggies still had a place in the '80s. Obviously, as Mark Twain would have said, the reports of their demise in the wake of "Energy Crisis II" were greatly exaggerated.

It's interesting that a large, relatively old-fashioned car should carry Lincoln back to prosperity in the '80s. Though Cadillac remained the luxury sales leader by far, an increasing portion of its total volume depended on ever smaller "big" cars that looked too much like cheaper GM products and lacked the Town Car's sheer

Lincoln went a long way in closing the gap with Cadillac during the Seventies. Its only failure was the "compact" Versailles, which looked too much like the Mercury Monarch on which it was based. Downsizing began with the 1980 models.

The '84 Continental came as a base four door, and in Valentino and Givenchy Series. Prices ranged from $21,769 to $24,242.

Mark VII debuted for '84. In addition to the base coupe, Bill Blass and Versace series were offered, as well as a sportier LSC.

An electronic air suspension with Goodyear air springs and automatic three-way leveling was featured on the '85 Mark VII.

Sequential port fuel injection and anti-lock brakes were standard on the '86 Mark VII. The 302 V8 in the LSC developed 200 bhp.

Three models of the '87 Mark VII were sold from $24,216 to $25,863.

The '86 Town Car utilized a 150-horsepower version of the 302 V8.

presence. Lincoln was quick to play up its rival's "lookalike" problem in snobbish TV commercials—and just as quick to cash in with a growing number of "conquest" sales. Chrysler, of course, had nothing remotely like a traditional full-size car after 1981, though its mid-size Fifth Avenue found a steady market for the same reasons the Town Car did: plentiful creature comforts in a package more mature buyers could relate to, all at a reasonable price.

If the Versailles was a hasty reply to Cadillac's Seville, the new compact Continental sedan that arrived for 1982 was a more considered one. It even had "bustleback" styling similar to the 1980 front-drive Seville's, plus a Mark-type grille and the usual base, Signature Series and designer-edition trim and equipment variations.

But underneath it was just a Ford Fairmont, riding an extended 108.6-inch-wheelbase version of the sensible rear-drive "Fox" platform and really none the worse for it—except, perhaps, in rear-seat room, which was limited at best. A 232-cid V6 was originally standard but proved too weak for the 3700-pound curb weight, so most of these Contis left the factory with injected 140- and 150-bhp 302 V8s (the latter from 1986). Front and rear ends were smoothed out for '84 *a la* Town Car, the only appearance change for this series.

A noteworthy mechanical development was anti-lock brakes (ABS), a 1985 option made standard equipment the following year. Developed jointly by Ford and the German Alfred Teves company, ABS greatly improved steering control in panic stops and shortened stopping distances on slick surfaces, a laudable advance for safety.

Lincoln had a bit better luck with this compact, selling an average 20,000-25,000 a year through 1987. If not a vast improvement in appearance over the Versailles, the bustleback Continental was a more roadable and enjoyable car, well put together and as posh as any Lincoln. And at $20,000-$25,000, it was a good luxury buy. But Ford had something even better on the way, more of which shortly.

After years of contrived, overblown elegance, the premium Lincoln took a surprising new direction for 1984 with the dramatic Mark VII. Though built on the same chassis as the bustleback Continental, this swoopy semi-fastback coupe was styled in the image of the new-for-'83 Ford Thunderbird/Mercury Cougar—smooth, distinctive, and much slipperier than any previous Mark.

By 1984, the Lincoln lineup consisted of three basic models: full-size Town Car, a smaller Continental sedan, and the Mark VII personal-luxury coupe. A new front-drive Continental bowed for '88 and a redesigned Town Car was due for 1990.

Front-wheel-drive and a V6 engine were Lincoln firsts for the 1988 Continental, which debuted on December 26, 1987.

A humped trunklid, modest taillights in the rear fender trailing edges and a toned-down Mark grille maintained a link with the past, but this car was clearly aimed at a very different market: the somewhat younger, very affluent buyers who'd been defecting to high-dollar, high-status imports, a group Lincoln had never really courted before. It also represented a timely end-run around Cadillac.

The Mark VII was an instant critical success, especially the performance-oriented LSC (Luxury Sport Coupe)—the fabled "hot rod Lincoln" come to life. Enthusiast magazines fell all over themselves comparing it to the BMW 6-Series and Mercedes SEC. No wonder. Where the base and Designer models offered soft-riding luxury and traditional appointments, the LSC rode a firm suspension with fat performance tires on handsome cast-aluminum wheels and came with multi-adjustable sports bucket seats and Lincoln's best cloth or leather upholstery. For 1985 it adopted the Mustang GT's high-output V8 with 165 bhp (versus 140 for other models). The '86 got an even hotter port-injected version with 200 bhp (versus 150 bhp on other models), plus standard four-wheel disc brakes with anti-lock control and a nice set of analog gauges (replacing the digital/graphic electronic display retained for its linemates). Additional engine tuning gave the '88s another 25 bhp.

With all this, the LSC was the most overtly sporting Lincoln since the first Continental and the most roadable Lincoln since the early-'50s "Mexican Road Race" models. It was also one terrific buy at $23,000-$25,000—about half what its erstwhile German competition cost. Lincoln-Mercury planners thought the lesser VIIs would outsell it, but buyers confounded them by demanding more LSCs—to the point that the division trimmed the original four model variations to two by 1988, Bill Blass and LSC. Overall sales were good: 30,000-plus in the first two seasons, about 20,000 or so thereafter.

Perhaps even more daring than the Mark VII was the all-new Continental sedan that arrived for 1988. Essentially a stretched version of the excellent Ford Taurus/Mercury Sable, it was the first Lincoln with front-wheel drive and the first with all-independent suspension, both of which contributed to a noticeable increase in cabin room despite a wheelbase only half an inch longer than that of its bustleback predecessor. In appearance, which L-M described as "aero limousine" styling, it departed even more sharply from tradition than the Mark VII: squarish but carefully detailed for good air flow "management." The old humped trunklid was abandoned at last, leaving a vertical-bar grille as the sole vestige of the past—and even that was low and smoothly curved to match the nose, flanked by flush-fit Euro-style headlights.

Powering the new Continental was the 140-bhp 3.8-liter V6 made optional for the '88 Taurus/Sable, mounted transversely and teamed with the expected four-speed overdrive automatic transaxle. It didn't provide as much snap in the heavier Conti (which was little lighter than its rear-drive forebear), but performance was at least acceptable and refinement of a high order. The all-MacPherson-strut suspension employed dual-rate shock absorbers and LSC-style air springs, both computer-controlled, but was really too complex to provide a truly outstanding ride/handling balance in the real world. The standard all-disc brakes with ABS were superb, however, and interior decor was a happy blend of Euro modern and American traditional. For 1989 the dash and steering wheel were redesigned to accommodate air bags as mandated under the government's new passive-restraint rule.

Arriving at dealers in December 1987, the front-drive Continental was a quick sellout thanks partly to an attractive $27,000 base price—again, thousands less than similar European cars. Of course, the mere fact that Lincolns could now stand comparison with such high-buck machines spoke volumes about how far the make had come in the '80s and where it would go in the '90s. Lincoln may never outsell Cadillac, but it is again building luxury cars like no other: thoughtfully conceived, sumptuously furnished, and built with precision. Henry Martyn Leland and Edsel Ford would be proud.

MERCURY

Mercury was conceived largely by Edsel Ford, who saw a place for it in the market some time before his father did. Introduced for 1939, it was in the same price league as the eight-cylinder Pontiac but somewhat below Oldsmobile, precisely where Edsel wanted it—and where Ford Motor Company needed it. While it never approached the volume of those GM makes, Mercury averaged about 80,000 cars per year in the early '40s, running 12th or 13th in the industry and bringing Dearborn important new business in the market sector between Lincoln-Zephyr and Ford.

The original Mercury engine would remain in production through 1948. A 239-cubic-inch L-head V8, it was a slightly larger version of the Ford V8/85, having the same stroke but a larger bore. It produced 95 horsepower through 1941, then 100 bhp. Mercury quickly gained a reputation for performance equal to its name (for the winged messenger god of Greek mythology). Well-tuned stock models were quicker than V8 Fords, usually capable of turning close to 100 mph.

Mercury arrived on a 116-inch wheelbase, four inches longer than the '39 Ford's and sufficient to give its similar styling a more "important" look. Its dash and strip-type instruments were also like Ford's, and Mercury's column-mounted gearlever was a talking point at the time. Styling for 1939-40 was marked by crisp, pointed noses, beautifully curved fenders and rounded body lines tapering to beetle backs. Initial offerings comprised two- and four-door fastback sedans, notchback sedan-coupe and convertible coupe, priced from $916 to $957. A $1212 convertible sedan was added for 1940, the heaviest and most expensive model in that year's line. But the body style had waned in popularity, so Mercury's was dropped after 1941 and only about 1150 units.

Offerings expanded to seven for '41 via a two/four-passenger coupe, business coupe and wood-body station wagon. Styling, again in the Ford mold, was chunky and awkward despite a two-inch-longer wheelbase, marked by higher, bulkier fenders, a divider-bar grille and fender-top parking lights.

Mercury tried harder for 1942 with a serious facelift, the aforementioned 100-bhp engine, and a new extra-cost semi-automatic transmission called Liquamatic. America's entry into World War II

Mercury built about 81,000 cars in 1940, its second year on the marketplace. The five models were priced from $946 to $1212.

Throughout the Twenties and into the Thirties, Ford built only the low-price Ford and the ultra-expensive Lincoln. Edsel Ford tried to close the huge gap with the upper-middle-priced 1936 Lincoln Zephyr and the mid-priced 1939 Mercury.

Mercury debuted for '39 with four models; 75,000 units were built.

The '42 Mercury two-door sedan featured rear side vent windows.

A new grille was seen on the '46 Mercury club coupe. Price: $1495.

The '47 station wagon listed at $2207; only 3558 were produced.

limited model year production to less than 23,000 units. Chrome was "in," at least before the government diverted it to war use. This year's Mercs wore a broad, glittery two-section grille composed of massive horizontal bars, plus double chrome bands on each fender and a bright full-perimeter molding at the beltline. Parking lights shifted inboard to flank a still-pointy hood. The general effect was busier than the '41 design.

At war's end, Henry Ford II returned from the Navy to run Ford Motor Company and quickly moved it back to civilian production. Mercury placed 10th in the 1946 production race with 86,608 units. As Dearborn delayed its first new postwar models to 1949, interim Mercurys were quite similar to the '42 design. The inboard parking lights and two-band fender moldings remained, but a reshaped vertical-bar grille appeared with "Mercury Eight" in prominent letters front and center. Mechanicals were unchanged except that the troublesome Liquamatic transmission did not return. Ford's adoption of the 239 V8 for 1946 was hardly to Mercury's advantage.

Mercury's prewar model offerings also carried over into 1946 with a singular exception: the business coupe was replaced by the novel Sportsman convertible. Comparable to the like-named Ford model, it was adorned with maple or yellow birch framing mahogany inserts. The wood was structural, not merely decorative. This created a problem at the rear, where the standard production fenders wouldn't fit. Both Sportsmans thus used 1941 sedan delivery fenders and wood structure shaped to suit. The framing was solid wood, beautifully mitred and finished with multiple coats of varnish. With only 205 called for, the Mercury Sportsman was dropped after '46. The likely reason for its low sales was high price: $2209, some $200 more than the Ford version, which accordingly saw somewhat higher volume and lasted into 1948.

Ford's most important 1947 corporate development was the organization of Lincoln-Mercury Division, Henry Ford II deciding that the two makes could be more competitive as an autonomous operation in the style of the various General Motors divisions. This year's Mercurys used more of the raw materials that had been scarce during the war: mainly aluminum (pistons and hood ornament) and chrome (interior hardware and grille frame). The beltline molding now stopped just ahead of the cowl. Postwar inflation boosted prices about $150 model for model. As Mercury's 1947 production didn't begin until February of that year, output was about the same as for the '46 models.

Except for serial numbers and deletion of the two-door sedan, the '48s were unchanged, sold from November 1947 through mid-April 1948, when the '49s appeared. As a result, production ran to only about 50,250 units.

The '49 Mercurys arrived with flush-fender "inverted bathtub" styling of the sort that had originated in sporadic wartime work. Wheelbase was unchanged, but bodyshells were shared with this year's new standard Lincoln instead of Ford, the result of a last-minute change in postwar plans. Styling was good: clean, massive and streamlined. The grille looked something like the '48 affair but was lower and wider. A single bright molding ran full-length at mid-flank. As before, a single series offered four body styles: coupe, four-door Sport Sedan (with "suicide" rear-hinged back doors), convertible and a new two-door wagon with vestigial wood trim.

Like Ford, the '49 Mercury was treated to a new chassis with fully independent front suspension and a more modern rear end with a live axle on parallel longitudinal leaf springs. Resuming its power lead over Ford, Mercury got a stroked V8 with 255.4 cid, two-barrel downdraft Holley carburetor and 110 bhp to become a genuine 100-mph car for the first time. Also introduced was an automatic overdrive option priced at $97, teamed with a 4.27:1 rear axle ratio instead of the standard 3.90:1.

The 1949 Mercury was an attractive buy with its Lincoln styling, lower prices ($1979-$2716) and a more powerful V8 than Ford's (necessary to offset some 300 extra pounds in curb weight). Buyers responded by taking over 301,000 of the '49s—more than three times the volume of Mercury's previous best year and good for sixth in industry production, another all-time high.

Sales continued strong for the next two seasons—close to 294,000 for 1950 and a record-setting 310,000-plus for '51, when Mercury again claimed sixth—despite few basic changes. The '50s had the Mercury name on a hood chrome strip. The '51s combined this with a large semicircular crest. They also had more prominent grille bars, larger parking light housings (swept back to the front wheel wells), and longer, more upright rear fenders with rounded corners dropping straight down to the bumper. Finally, the '51s offered a nominal two extra horsepower and, more significantly, optional Merc-O-Matic Drive, the new three-speed automatic transmission developed in cooperation with the Warner Gear Division of Borg-Warner.

Mercury added a stripped price-leader coupe for 1950 as well as the more interesting Monterey, a spiffy limited-edition coupe with special trim and a top covered in canvas or leather. At around $2150, it wasn't the costliest 1950-51 model (the wagon was: over $400 more). But like the concurrent Ford Crestliner and Lincoln Lido/Capri, it was merely a stand-in for the new hardtop-convertibles already being offered by GM and Chrysler rivals.

Hardtops arrived in force for 1952, when Ford Motor Company was the only Big Three producer with all-new styling. Mercury got a pair: Sport Coupe and a more deluxe Monterey version (*sans* covered roof). The latter was also offered as a convertible and four-door sedan. Following an industry trend, wagons were now all-steel four-doors with simulated wood trim. Rounding out the line were two- and four-door sedans. Bodyshells were again shared with Ford. So was 1952's tight, clean styling, though some Lincoln resemblance was evident too. Wheelbase was still unchanged. Higher compression boosted the flathead V8 to 125 bhp. The Korean War limited 1952 production throughout Detroit, Mercury built 172,000 cars, finishing eighth in the annual race.

The first two-series Mercury line bowed for 1953: Custom hardtop and two- and four-door sedans; Monterey convertible, hardtop, wagon and four-door sedan. Retained from '52 was a trendy dashboard with aircraft-type toggle controls flanking a large half-moon gauge cluster. Business picked up with the end of Korean War restrictions and Mercury moved nearly 305,000 cars, though it again ran eighth.

Nineteen fifty-four brought a significant engineering change in Mercury's first overhead-valve V8, a bigger version of the new "Y-block" design used on that year's Ford. Though about the same size as Mercury's previous L-head, the ohv had squarer cylinder dimensions, a five-main-bearing crankshaft and much more power: a rated 161 bhp with standard four-barrel carburetor. Teamed with a low 3.9:1 rear axle ratio and standard transmission, it made the '54 a fast car off the line. Equally noteworthy was ball-joint front suspension, another development shared with Ford.

Styling improved via wraparound taillights and a clean but more aggressive grille with larger bullet guards for a more prominent bumper. Joining previous models was a new top-line Sun Valley hardtop that's more famous now than it was in '54. An outgrowth of Dearborn's experiments with plastic-topped cars (as was the companion Ford Skyliner), the Sun Valley was nice in theory: the airiness of a convertible combined with the comfort of a closed hardtop. In practice it was something else. Though the Plexiglas front half-roof was tinted and a shade provided for really hot weather, customers complained the interior heated up like an oven. Predictably, sales weren't impressive: just 9761 of the '54s and a mere 1787 for '55.

At about 260,000 units in all, 1954 wasn't Mercury's greatest sales year, but hopes were high for '55. With colorful new styling on the basic 1952-54 shell, Mercury's first wheelbase increase since 1941 (to 119 inches except on wagons, which remained at 118 inches) and a more potent V8, the '55s couldn't miss. They

Mercury was all-new for 1949; a record 301,319 units were built.

The '51 Merc got a new grille and rear fenders—and Merc-O-Matic.

Mercury was all new for '52. The ragtop cost $2370; 5261 were built.

The '53 was slightly restyled, here a top-line Monterey four door.

The best selling '53 Monterey was the hardtop coupe: 76,119 built.

Except for the 1949-51 models, most people saw the Mercury as a deluxe Ford. Sales in the Forties generally fell into the 80,000-unit range, but the first half of the Fifties saw Mercury's average explode to about 300,000 units per year.

Mercury's new top-of-the-line series for 1955 was the Montclair. The hardtop listed at $2631 and 71,588 were produced that year.

Mercury built 9761 plexiglass-topped Sun Valley hardtops for '54.

A new grille and side chrome trim highlighted the '56 Merc.

A '58 Convertible Cruiser paced the Indy 500; only 1265 were built.

Park Lane became Mercury's new top-of-the-line series in 1958.

didn't: A record 329,000-plus were built.

Topping the '55 line was the new Montclair series comprising four-door sedan, hardtop, convertible, and Sun Valley—all carrying a thin contrast-color panel outlined in bright metal under the side windows. One step below were the Monterey sedan, hardtop and wagon, followed by the Custom series with the same body styles plus a two-door sedan. Mercury's first wrapped windshield, an evolutionary form of the '54 grille, hooded headlamps and eye-catching surface ornamentation were common to all. A Y-block V8 swelled to 292 cid was offered in two forms: 188 bhp for Custom and Monterey, 198 bhp for Montclair and as an option on the lower series, available only with Merc-O-Matic.

Four-door Phaeton hardtops arrived for 1956's "Big M" line, which represented an ambitious expansion into somewhat uncharted territory. To stay competitive in the face of rising prices, Mercury fielded a new cut-rate Medalist series—two- and four-door hardtops and sedans—pitched at the bottom end of the medium-price field. But inflation made these "low-priced" Mercs more expensive than the previous year's Customs and not sufficiently cheaper than the better-trimmed 1956 Customs. Dealers pushed hard with two-door sedans, but only 45,812 of the '56 Medalists were sold. Custom, Monterey, and Montclair all surpassed the price-leader by at least 2-1. The series was dropped after '56, only to resurface for '58, interfering in a market that should have been belonged exclusively to the new Edsel.

Styling for '56 was a good update of '55. All models except Medalists wore bold Z-line bodyside moldings that delineated the contrast color area with optional two-toning (the area below them generally matching the roof). In the Monterey and Montclair lines, the Phaeton hardtop sedans were mid-season replacements for low-roof pillared Sport Sedans, a holdover style from mid-1955. Mercury also offered a second convertible for the first time, in the Custom group. This year's V8 was a 312 offering 210 to 235 bhp, the latter as standard for Monterey and Montclair.

Though 1956 was a downbeat year for the industry as a whole, Mercury was an exception, rolling out some 328,000 cars, only a bit off its '55 pace. An encouraging sign was that the premium Montclair managed to sell almost as well as it had in 1955. The mid-line Monterey was still the breadwinner, though.

The '57 Mercurys were all-new, trumpeted as "a dramatic expression of dream car design." They were, inspired (really previewed) by the XM-Turnpike Cruiser show car of 1956. Its direct production counterparts were the glitzy new top-line Turnpike Cruiser two- and four-door hardtops. Gimmicks abounded: "skylight dual curve windshield," drop-down reverse-slant rear window, dual air intakes over the A-posts housing little horizontal antennae. A new option was the creatively named "Seat-O-Matic" that automatically moved the front seat to one of 49 possible positions at the twist of two dials. Mercury also joined Chrysler in offering pushbutton automatic transmission controls this year. Arriving late in the season was a Convertible Cruiser, similar to the Mercury that paced the '57 Indy 500 and supplied with suitable decal regalia. Yet for all their gadgetry (or maybe because of it) the Cruisers failed miserably—expensive and too far out even for that gilded age.

Nineteen fifty-seven's major redesign gave Mercury its own bodyshells and a new 122-inch-wheelbase chassis—the first time it was neither senior Ford nor junior Lincoln. Like the all-new '57 Ford, this was done partly to prepare for the '58 Edsel line, which borrowed some from both makes. Monterey and Montclair were bereft of station wagons, now a separate series with no fewer than six models: from the top, woody-look Colony Park, a four-door nine-seater; metal-sided two- and four-door Voyagers; and three Commuters with the various seat and door combinations. All had pillarless hardtop styling.

All the '57 Big Ms were a bit heavy-looking, with massive dual-oblong bumpers, available quad headlights and long scallops in the upper rear fenders leading to pie-slice taillamps. A 312 V8 with 255 bhp was standard except on Cruisers, which had a new 290-bhp 368-cid engine, an option for other models.

Mercury did fairly well for '57—but not as well as in '56. Volume dropped to a bit over 286,000 and the make's production rank from seventh to eighth—not encouraging for an all-new design in a fairly strong sales year.

A minor facelift yielded slightly quieter styling for 1958, but the year was a disaster, production falling to 153,000. The Convertible Cruiser was abandoned (after only 1265 of the '57s) and the two hardtops became Montclair sub-models. Lower prices failed to perk up sales. The cheap Medalist returned for a short encore with two- and four-door sedans but, again, proved disappointing: only 18,732 sales. Topping the line was the new Park Lane, two hardtops and a convertible (also offered as Montclairs and Montereys), ostensible Cruiser replacements with less hoke and a standard 430-cid Lincoln V8 with 360 bhp. A new automatic called Multi-Drive debuted along with a 383-cid V8—same displacement as Chrysler's engine but with more oversquare dimensions. Standard for all except Medalist (which came with a 235-bhp 312) and Park Lane, it delivered 312 or 330 bhp depending on model.

Though the bottom dropped out of the medium-price market in

The concave side section was made much larger on the '69 Mercury.

Mercury built 7411 Colony Park nine-passenger wagons for 1960.

Monterey convertible production for 1961 reached 7053 units.

Mercury's new intermediate for 1962 was the Meteor, here a Custom.

Mercury built 73,880 compact Comet two-door sedans for 1962.

Like most of the industry, Mercury enjoyed a banner year in 1955. But by 1958, sales had fallen by half, largely because of questionable styling. Sales didn't improve until compacts and intermediates joined the lineup in 1960 and '62.

Mercury's sportiest full-size model for 1962 was the S-55. The convertible listed at $3738 and only 1315 units found buyers.

'58, Mercury remained in eighth place despite building only 40 percent of its '57 volume. But significantly, Rambler passed it in sales and was fast gaining on Pontiac, Olds and Buick. Mercury would join the rush to compacts and intermediates. In the meantime, it had to make do with more of the old stuff.

More the '59 Mercurys definitely had, with even bigger bodies on a four-inch-longer wheelbase. Styling was still square but more sculptured, marked by a mile-wide grille, huge bumpers at each end, enormous windshields and rear windows, and a more sharply creased version of the odd 1957-58 rear fender motif. The Medalist and Turnpike Cruiser were forgotten and two of the four remaining series were severely cropped, Montclair and wagons each going from six models to four. Engines were detuned as a sop to a newly economy-conscious public. The lineup comprised 210- and optional 280-bhp 312s for Monterey, a 345-bhp 430 for Park Lane, and 280- and 322-bhp 383s for other models.

Despite the retrenchment, 1959 production failed to top 150,000—hardly the hoped-for improvement. But 1960 volume would be up substantially—to 271,000-plus—thanks mainly to the new compact Comet. The four-series big-car line was attractively facelifted with a low-profile concave grille, restyled taillights, single bright bodyside moldings and revised bumpers. Engines were reduced to three: 205-bhp 312 and optional 280-bhp 383 for Commuter wagons and Montereys; 310-bhp 430 for the Colony Park wagon, Montclair and Park Lane.

Mercury then began evolving a plethora of models, sizes and body types, complicated by confusing name changes in some years. The latter is perhaps symbolic of the make's mixed fortunes in the '60s and its struggle to make improvements. Still, many names used at the start of the decade were still around at its end. Comet and Monterey spanned the entire 10 years; Montclair and Park Lane lasted through '68. Meteor, long the brand of a Canadian-made Mercury derivative, was seen on two different U.S. models in 1961-63.

The first American Meteor was the low end of a 1961 full-size line comprising Meteor 600 and 800 series plus Monterey and wagons. In the interest of production economies as well as fuel economy, all rode a 120-inch-wheelbase version of the new-for-'60 big Ford platform. The Big M thus lost its own body and chassis but was lighter, thriftier, and more maneuverable. Meteors came with a standard 135-bhp 223-cid Ford six and outsold Monterey, but were merely a stopgap. The 1962 Meteor was Mercury's version of the intermediate Ford Fairlane and that year's big cars were called Monterey and Monterey Custom.

Most everything said about the 1962-63 Fairlane applies to this Meteor. Its styling was busier and model names were different, but bodies were shared. So were powertrains, including Ford's fine new small-block V8 with 221 cid and 145 bhp or 260 cid and 164 bhp. Custom denoted upmarket models, S-33 the sportier bucket-seaters—a two-door sedan for '62, a hardtop coupe for '63. Wagons—woody-look Country Cruiser and plain-sided Villagers (a name retained from the aborted Edsel line) joined hardtops as

The '63 Meteor S-33 hardtop came with bucket seats. Output: 5900.

Mercury two-door hardtops sported a semi-fastback roofline for '63.

The '65 Comet Caliente convertible rode a 114-inch wheelbase, cost $2664. Output was modest, reaching 6035 units.

1963 arrivals. For all this, the Meteor didn't sell nearly as well as Fairlane, and Mercury dropped it for 1964 in favor of an extensively upgraded Comet.

Once planned as an Edsel, the first Comet was basically Ford's hugely successful 1960 Falcon with squared-up rooflines, a double-row concave grille, and an extended stern with canted fins and oval taillamps. Wheelbase was 114 inches on two- and four-door sedans; wagons used Falcon's 109.5-inch span. It wasn't exciting, but it sold well: over 116,000 for the abbreviated debut 1960 season. Sales set a record for '61 at 197,000 units and were strong for '62, which hurt Meteor. In fact, one reason Meteor didn't sell well is that Comet was comparably sized yet more affordable. The decision to make Comet the only small Mercury after '63 was a good one. Sales jumped by 55,000 units for '64 and remained high into '67.

Though more elaborately trimmed, early Comets ran less than $100 more than comparable Falcons. Mercury responded to the sporty-compact craze for 1961 with the $2300 S-22, a bucket-seat two-door sedan. At the same time, all Comets gained an optional 101-bhp six. Custom sedans and wagons and a posh Villager wagon with imitation tree trim aided 1962 sales. The following year brought Custom and S-22 convertibles and Sportster hard-

The Montclair Marauder four-door hardtop listed at $3181 in 1964.

"Breezeway" rear window styling was featured on the '65 Park Lane.

New taillights were seen on the '66 big Mercs, here a Montclair.

The '67 Comet Cyclone GT hardtop was fairly rare with only 3419 built.

The U.S. space program was beset with problems during the Fifties, but in 1962 John Glenn circled the earth three times in the Mercury capsule Friendship 7. Down on earth, Ford's Mercury also saw its fortunes improve during the Sixties.

This '67 Monterey S-55 ragtop boasts a 428 V8; 570 were produced.

Mercury's entry into the ponycar market was the Cougar, here a '68.

Montego was Mercury's mid-size 1969 offering, here with a 351 V8.

The 1969 Marauder X-100 coupe sold for $4091; 5635 found buyers.

All 1969 Cougars rode a 111-inch wheelbase. With hood scoop and spoiler, the Eliminator 390 GT was the high-performance job.

tops. A squarish facelift arrived for 1964 and S-22 was renamed Caliente. By then, any Comet could be equipped with the outstanding 260 small-block. A mid-season Cyclone hardtop offered even higher performance from a standard 210-bhp 289.

Comet received its first major overhaul for 1966, shifting from compact to intermediate by adopting that year's sleek new Fairlane bodyshell. This underlined a basic marketing decision: Mercury customers were assumed to be wealthier than Ford buyers, and would thus likely be happier with a compact larger than the Falcon.

Comet retained this 116-inch-wheelbase platform through 1969, but sales waned along with the name, which by 1967 applied only to a pair of very basic "202" sedans. The rest of that year's line comprised Capri, Caliente, Cyclone and Station Wagon series. All were replaced for 1968 by a three series Montego line on the same wheelbase. This offered base sedan and hardtop coupe; MX sedan, hardtop coupe, convertible and wagon; and top-line MX Brougham sedan and hardtop. The last was outfitted with high-quality cloth upholstery and other luxury details. The Comet name was retained for a price-leader hardtop, then was temporarily shelved after 1969.

Mercury jumped into the mid-size muscle market with both feet and won more than a few racing laurels. Model year 1966 brought a smooth styled Cyclone GT hardtop coupe and convertible powered by Ford's 335-bhp 390 V8 and offered with a variety of useful suspension upgrades. The '67 was even more thrilling with optional 427 V8s delivering 410-425 bhp.

Similar street racers were available for '68, though the 427 was detuned to 390 bhp. Besides Montego, the mid-size line included new base and GT Cyclone hardtop coupes with the same curvy new lower-body contours and racy, full-fastback rooflines *a la* Ford Mustang. There was also a one-year-only GT notchback hardtop. For 1969, Mercury unleashed the Cyclone CJ with Ford's 428 big-block Cobra Jet mill. GTs and CJs had black grille, special identification, bodyside paint stripes, and unique rear-end and taillight styling. The CJ carried a functional hood scoop when equipped with optional Ram-Air induction. Though Ford won the NASCAR championship in 1968-69, Cyclones turned in many notable performances. A highlight was Cale Yarborough's victory in the '68 Daytona 500 at an average 143.25 mph.

Full-size cars remained Mercury's bread and butter in the '60s. Annual production was usually around 100,000 units except for those back-to-back record years of 1965-66. Of all the big Mercs, only Monterey spanned the entire decade. The upper-echelon Montclair and Park Lane were dropped for '61, revived for 1964-68, then vanished again in favor of a full-range Marquis line.

Moving down into the territory once reserved for Edsel, the '61 big-car line comprised the aforementioned low-priced Meteors plus a separate four-model group of station wagons and a lone Monterey series with a sedan, two hardtops and a convertible. The basic V8 was a 175-bhp 292, with 220-bhp 352 and new 300-bhp 390 engines optional. Styling was conservative—concave grille, rounded sides, vestigial fins—and '50s gimmicks mere memories, but sales were not spectacular.

Meteor became an intermediate for '62, so the standard line was regrouped into Monterey, Monterey Custom and wagons, with the convertible shifting to the upper-priced Custom series. Joining the bucket-seat brigade at mid-year were the S-55 hardtop coupe and convertible. Styling was busier, with tunnelled taillights and a convex grille. All previous V8s returned, and the faithful big six was standard for the base Monterey and Commuter wagons.

A similar array on the same 120-inch wheelbase returned for 1963, when a heavy reskin introduced "Breezeway Styling" for non-wagon closed models—reverse-slant rear windows that dropped down for ventilation as on the old Turnpike Cruiser. Wagons were pared to a pair of Colony Parks. Joining the S-55 sub-series at mid-year was a handsome slantback hardtop like Ford's. Engines now consisted of a 390 V8 with 250-330 bhp and its new 406-cid extension offering 385/405 bhp.

Tradition returned for silver anniversary 1964 in a revived four-series line with Monterey, Montclair, Park Lane, and Commuter/ Colony Park wagons. The first three included Breezeway two- and four-door hardtops and four-door sedans, plus slantback Marauder hardtop coupes and sedans. A toothy convex grille replaced the concave '63 item and trim was shuffled. The previous array of 390 V8s continued, but the optional 406s gave way to bored-out 427s with 410/425 bhp for all models except wagons. Big-inch Marauders were awesome performers.

Record 1965 brought a larger full-size body with crisp, rectilinear styling "in the Lincoln Continental tradition," as well as a new "Torque Box" frame (tuned for each body style to minimize noise, vibration and harshness). Wagons now rode the 119-inch Ford wheelbase; other models were up to 123 inches. Breezeways thinned to a trio of four-door sedans; all hardtops now had slantback roofs and the Marauder name was de-emphasized amidst calls for greater automotive safety. V8s comprised a quartet of 390s and one 427. This basic look carried into 1966 with a new die-cast grille and, on hardtop coupes, a "sweep-style roof" with concave backlight.

More rounded bodysides mixed well with sharp-edged fenders for '67. Sedans adopted conventional roof profiles but still offered the drop-down rear window as an option. Hardtop coupes received "faster" rooflines. Topping the line were the new limited-production Marquis, a two-door hardtop with broad rear roof pillars and vinyl top, and the similar Park Lane Brougham hardtop sedan that expanded into a complete series the following year. Intermediates were waging Mercury's sporty-car campaign by now, so the bucket-seat S-55 convertible and hardtop were in their final year, actually just a Monterey trim package. Respective production was minuscule: just 145 and 570 units.

After a minor '68 facelift, Mercury's standards were fully revised for 1969. Wheelbases grew to 121 inches on wagons and 124 inches for other models, sizes that would persist until the first downsized big Mercs of 1979. Series were realigned around base Monterey, a revived Monterey Custom and the top-line Marquis, which included the Colony Park wagon, a convertible, and standard and Brougham sedans, hardtop coupes and hardtop sedans. Riding the shorter wheelbase was a new Marauder, a high-performance "tunnelback" hardtop that garnered 14,666 sales. Offered

Cyclone "Cale Yarborough Special" honored the famed race driver.

The '70 Mercury Marquis Brougham hardtop sedan sold for $4500.

The 1970 Cyclone Spoiler cost $3759 and only 1631 were produced.

The '70 Cougar XR-7 soft top was rarely seen; only 1977 were built.

Cougar for 1971 was bigger, heavier. Prices started at $3289.

During the late Sixties/early Seventies, performance was in. Mercury jumped on the ponycar bandwagon with the Cougar, and into the sporty-performance sector with models such as the S-55, Marauder X-100, Cyclone Spoiler, and the Eliminator.

At $3238, the Villager was Montego's priciest 1972 offering.

MX Brougham hardtop was Montego's best '73 seller: 40,951 built.

Mercury Marquis' grille looked ever more Lincoln-like for 1974.

Mercury marketed eight Montego models in 1976, here an MX coupe.

Total Monarch Ghia production for 1977 came to 27,596 units.

Monterey front-end styling continued to differ from Marquis in 1972.

The compact '73 Comet came with a 200-cubic-inch six as standard.

Mercury built 62,987 Cougar XR-7 personal-luxury coupes for 1975.

The sportiest Capri II for 1976 wore the black and gold "S" option.

The '77 Cougar lineup included a $5230 Brougham sedan.

in standard and sportier X-100 trim, it shared the Marquis' hidden-headlamp front and the ventless side glass used for most other models. V8s comprised the usual 390s and a new 429 big-block with 420 bhp, the latter standard for Marquis and Marauder X-100.

The 1970s were basically '69 reruns except for minor trim and equipment revisions. Sporty big cars had mostly disappeared by now. Mercury's Marauder would depart after selling just 6043 copies this year.

One of the '60s most interesting and desirable Mercurys was the 111-inch-wheelbase Cougar, premiering for 1967 as a two-door hardtop offered in several versions. Convertibles were added for 1969. Derived from the Mustang but riding a three-inch longer wheelbase, it was a deluxe version of Ford's highly successful "ponycar," priced about $200 higher. Mustang came with a standard six but Cougar's base engine was a 200-bhp 289 V8. The big 335-bhp 428 CJ became an extra-cost option for 1969-70.

The dashing '67 Cougar sported a distinctive "electric-shaver" grille with hidden headlights, as well as sequential turn signals in a matching back panel. Length and width increased on the '69s, which were marked by a Buick-like sweepspear contour line, ventless side glass, new grilles and full-width taillights. The '70s adopted a divided vertical-bar grille with a slightly bulged, separate proboscis.

Early Cougars came in several forms. The most luxurious was the XR-7, boasting a rich interior with leather accents and comprehensive instrumentation set into a simulated walnut dashboard. A separate GT performance package offered a firmed-up suspension for more capable roadholding and a standard 320-bhp 390 V8 for extra go. For 1968 came a GTE edition with several unique appearance features and a 390-bhp 427. The hottest 1969-70 Cougars were called Eliminator, with 428 power and standard rear-deck spoiler. The convertible versions saw very low production, as did all ragtop Cougars.

Though it never approached Mustang's sales, Cougar was a boost to Mercury—more solid and luxurious than Mustang but just as roadable. And though it took awhile, the 1967-70 models have now become collector cars.

Cougar put the finishing touch on a decade that saw Mercury move into luxury cars rivalling Lincoln while returning to the performance image it enjoyed in the late '40s and early '50s. But it wouldn't last. As the '70s progressed the various Mercurys became more like equivalent Fords, while government mandates and the vagaries of petroleum power-politics conspired to sacrifice performance on the twin altars of safety and fuel economy. By 1980, Mercury had more or less resumed its original role as a plusher, pricier and occasionally larger Ford. The only differences were that the parallel model lineups were spread across five or six different size classes instead of one or two, and that styling more often related to Lincoln's than Ford's.

The ponycar field was one area where Ford and L-M parted company in the '70s. Actually, Cougar began diverging from Mustang as early as 1971, when both models were completely redesigned. The Mercury jumped two inches in wheelbase instead of one (to 113 inches) and looked quite a bit bulkier. Standard and XR-7 convertibles remained through the end of this generation in 1973, and have already become minor collectors' items, primarily by dint of low production.

Because ponycar demand fell off abruptly in the early '70s, Mercury took a new course. Where Mustang became a smaller, lighter, Pinto-based sporty car for 1974, Cougar grew into a kind of ersatz Thunderbird, adopting the 114-inch-wheelbase two-door platform from the intermediate Montego line. Oddly enough, L-M had created the design chosen for the production Mustang II. But rather than field a badge-engineered clone of that car, the division opted to continue with the German-built Ford Capri it had been selling successfully since 1970, the same sort of "mini ponycar" but better built and more roadable.

Mercury's subcompact '78 Bobcat Villager wagon listed for $4244.

The '78 Grand Marquis sedan was popular with 37,753 units built.

The '79 Merc was downsized; 32,346 Grand Marquis sedans were sold.

The all-new '80 Cougar XR-7 shared its bodyshell with T-Bird.

Mercury's "Class Cat," the new Cougar, expanded its 1981 lineup.

During the Seventies, performance took a back seat to safety and emissions regulations. Mercury responded with a more upright, formal look. In fact, Mercury lifted many styling cues right off the Lincoln, especially the grillework.

Unlike T-Bird, the all-new '83 Cougar sported a squared-off roofline. Only a 3.8-liter 105-bhp V6 was offered initially.

Like Ford's Escort, Mercury's Lynx added a five-door sedan for '82.

The LN7 was in its second—and last—year of production in 1983.

Cougar continued as Mercury's entry in the mid-size personal-luxury segment through 1976, competing against the likes of Chevrolet's Monte Carlo and Pontiac's Grand Prix. The name was diluted the following year, when it replaced Montego on the entire intermediate line, the XR-7 label being reserved for a single top-shelf coupe. Things were temporarily sorted out again for 1980, only now Cougar really was a Thunderbird, a twin to that year's new downsized model on a special 108.4-inch-wheelbase version of the compact "Fox" platform.

In between, Ford again redesigned the Mustang, and this time Mercury wanted in. The result was a new American-made Capri for 1979. The direct descendent of the genuine Cougar ponycar, it was virtually identical with the new-generation Mustang (*see* Ford Mustang) save slightly busier styling and lacking the Ford's notchback body style. The same four engines were offered in a choice of base and Ghia models, and buyers could opt for the sporty RS package (Mercury never called it "Rally Sport," perhaps out of deference to Chevrolet), which was roughly equivalent to the Mustang Cobra.

One of the last cars with a distinctively Mercury character was the Cyclone, which bowed out after 1971. Offered that year with standard 351 and optional 429 V8s, this muscular mid-size was as impressively fast as ever. Swoopier sheetmetal set it clearly apart from its run-of-the-mill Montego linemates and Ford's corresponding Torino GT and Cobra, particularly the protruding nose and "gunsight" grille appearing with the 1970-71 facelift. Reflecting the muscle-car market's sad state of affairs at the time, Cyclone sold poorly in its farewell season, especially the desirable low-production Spoiler hardtop (just 353 of the '71s were built).

Elsewhere, Mercury's new-model development story in the '70s is primarily one of "badge engineering." It began when the Comet name was revived for a restyled version of the compact Ford Maverick, distinguished mainly by a Montego-style nose. Announced for 1971, this Comet soldiered on through 1974 as the division's sole representative in a size and price sector that took on urgent new importance in the wake of the oil embargo.

Help arrived for 1975 in the form of two new entries. One was the Comet's once-and-future replacement, the slightly larger Granada-based Monarch. The other was Mercury's belated rendition of the subcompact Pinto, bearing the Bobcat name and a pretentious little stand-up grille. Ford replaced Maverick with the more able Fairmont for 1978, and Mercury got a lookalike derivative, the Zephyr. If none of these moves was exactly original, they at least combined to leave Mercury much more competitive in a market that had been forever changed by a combination of forces.

As with Buick and Oldsmobile, intermediate and full-size cars remained Mercury's mainstay through most of the '70s, and it was here that the changes were most dramatic—and most needed. Mercury's mid-size contender wallowed along as a near duplicate of the Ford Torino/LTD II, under the Montego name for 1972-76 and, as noted, with the Cougar badge from 1977 through the last of this body-on-frame design for 1979. Like the Fords, there was little praiseworthy about them, though the Mercurys arguably looked nicer.

In what was loosely called the "standard" class sat the big two-ton Marquis and Monterey. Neither changed much through 1978. Model names centered on Marquis exclusively after 1974, and styling became progressively more like that of the big Lincoln Continental, particularly at the front. These Mercs were mammoths but good ones: smooth and reliable, powered by reasonably potent V8s (400s, 429s and Lincoln 460s), fairly restrained and fully (if not always tastefully) equipped. Pillarless hardtops gave way to pillared styling after 1974. Paralleling Ford's LTD, the Marquis underwent the "big shrink" for '79, losing 10 inches in wheelbase and up to 1200 pounds in curb weight. It was the right move, even if it came about two years too late.

In retrospect, the '70s were not particularly good years for Mercury, which lost its performance reputation only a few years after regaining it. A succession of heavier, clumsier Cougars and confusingly named intermediates hardly helped, while moves into the compact and subcompact arenas were blunted by higher prices on cars that offered little more than the Fords they so obviously were. Meantime, Mercury's traditional big-car foundation was rocked by the new economic order of a more energy-conscious world. Yet by 1980, Mercury was turning the corner with cars like the exciting Capri, the practical Zephyr, and the reborn Cougar and Marquis.

Mercury decisively completed that maneuver in the '80s, benefitting from the same astute management and timely product introductions that made Ford Motor Company the industry's profit leader by 1986. Though no one model line was among Detroit's top-selling nameplates, Mercury's total production rose from a low of 317,500 for 1980 to a decade high of nearly half a million U.S.-built cars for '84—an impressive recovery, if still far below record '79 (669,000-plus). In the model-year production race, Mercury ranked anywhere from sixth to ninth, as it had since the '50s, but managed fifth place for 1983, its best finish ever.

As before, the Mercury line continued to parallel Ford's annual offerings except for somewhat higher prices and different model/equipment mixes. Styling also remained quite similar through 1982, but the following year saw the return of a more distinctive Mercury look, a welcome trend that continues to this day. Much sooner than GM, Dearborn had correctly concluded that too many clones spoil the sales broth. With the '83s, Mercurys again began standing more clearly apart from equivalent Fords—and rival GM cars—to the undoubted benefit of sales.

Still, volume throughout the decade remained much lower than Ford's model-for-model, and Mercury didn't have the same relative success with some of the same products. The Capri ponycar was one. Like Mustang, it received almost annual power increases and higher performance, commencing with 1982's high-output 155-bhp 302 V8. But then Mustang got a handsome facelift and a revived convertible while Capri soldiered on for '83 with just a hatchback coupe and its basic '79 appearance (except for a huge "bubbleback" rear window of dubious esthetic merit). It's almost as if L-M were ashamed of Capri and it showed, half-hearted promotion aggravating the lack of overt change. Production thus steadily waned, from nearly 80,000 for 1980 to only some 18,500 of the '85s (compared with over 156,000 Mustangs). At that level, Capri was too costly to sustain and it was banished after '86.

The same fate awaited another bubbleback Merc: the two-seat LN7, introduced in early 1982 alongside Ford's near-identical EXP. Both were sporty coupe derivatives of the front-drive Ford Escort/Mercury Lynx subcompacts, which had scored big sales since replacing the old Pinto/Bobcat twins the previous season. Unfortunately, the coupes were anything but lovely, and no match for a number of Japanese competitors in performance, refinement and assembly quality. Perhaps buyers didn't expect a two-seater in L-M showrooms, for the LN7 saw only 35,928 copies before being retired after 1983. A facelifted EXP then took on its bulbous backlight and proved somewhat more popular.

Lynx was Mercury's entry in the increasingly tough small-car market, and it sold respectably, racking up over 100,000 units in its first two years and about 65,000 a year thereafter. Like Escort, it began with a three-door hatchback sedan and a neat five-door wagon in trim levels from plain to fancy. These were bolstered for 1982 by five-door sedans and the sporty three-door RS and five-door LTS (Luxury Touring Sedan).

Through mid-'85, Lynx was powered by the Escort's 1.6-liter "CVH" four, also offered in H.O. and turbocharged guises, after

Mercury's new front-drive mid-size Tempo was introduced in May '83.

For 1984, the Capri offered a 205-bhp V8 with 265 lbs/ft torque.

Grand Marquis for '85 came as a two- or four-door sedan or wagon.

Prices for a four-cylinder mid-size '85 Marquis started at $9188.

The German-built Merkur XR4Ti bowed in the U.S. in 1986 at $16,361.

During the Eighties most Mercurys were cloned from Fords, which featured aero-look styling. But Mercury variants were generally squarer, more formal, and differed enough to avoid the look-alike syndrome that was running rampant at GM.

Mercury's Mustang clone, the Capri, was in its last year in 1986.

The 1986 Sable wagon provided a roomy 82-cubic-foot cargo area.

Sable had different sheetmetal than Ford's successful new Taurus.

Mercury's counterpart to the '86 Escort GT was the $8193 Lynx RX3.

Cougar XR-7 for '87 took on new sheetmetal and the 5.0-liter V8.

which the latter were dropped and a normal-tune 1.9-liter enlargement took over. A 2.0-liter diesel four from Mazda in Japan was also offered beginning with the '84s, though it garnered few orders as gas prices fell in an improving national economy. Appearance was cleaned up for "1985½" with a smoother nose and flush headlamps in line with Dearborn's strong turn to "aerodynamic" styling. An even sportier three-door, called XR3, bowed the following year.

But here, too, Ford planners would conclude that one clone was one too many, though a falling dollar and lower "offshore" production costs also figured in their decision to drop Lynx during 1987 in favor of the Mexican-built Tracer, a badge-engineered version of the somewhat smaller Mazda 323. Yet despite generating less than half of Escort's volume in most years, the Lynx must be judged a success, bringing in crucial business for L-M dealers during some very turbulent times.

The same may be said of Mercury's compacts and intermediates. For 1981-82, these comprised the familiar (and largely unchanged) Zephyr line and a new upmarket Cougar sedan series, both built on the proven rear-drive "Fox" platform of 1978. Weighing some 350-400 pounds less the Monarchs they replaced, these Cougars were twins to Ford's reborn '81 Granadas. Styling was similarly squared up and more "important" than Zephyr's, appropriate for the higher prices, and though the origins of these "new" models was obvious, there was evidently still some magic in the Cougar name. Between them, Cougar and Zephyr netted well over 80,000 annual sales in 1981-82, not bad considering the state of the market.

Mercury did even better by replacing the Cougars with a new small Marquis for 1983. This was yet another Fairmont/Zephyr variation, but its simpler, slope-nose styling was a big improvement, even if it looked rather too much like the "downsized" LTD that took over for the Granada that year. Still, the name link with a full-size Merc didn't hurt, and first-year Marquis sales totaled some 108,000, nearly double those of the previous Cougar series.

To avoid confusion, the biggest Mercurys were tagged Grand Marquis after 1982, one of their few important changes in the entire decade. Not that many changes were needed. Roomy, quiet and comfortable, they remained traditional V8 American family cruisers of the sort whose sales bounced back strongly once the economy began recovering and an oil glut pushed gas prices down to more reasonable levels again. And as Chrysler and the B-O-P makes had abandoned most of their old rear-drive biggies by 1985, the full-size Merc was virtually alone in the medium-price field.

Grand Marquis thus evolved through the '80s with only the barest of updates. Two-door coupes were dropped after 1985, the mainstay four-door sedan and wagon gained smoother noses and tails for 1988, and fuel injection replaced carburetors on the 302 V8, but that was about it. Once their original '79 tooling was amortized, the big Mercurys (and Fords) became the darlings of dealers, earning more profit per unit than any other model in the line. Yet buyers kept on buying despite the lack of change. Grand Marquis sales totaled nearly 96,000 for '83, dipped to 90,000 for '84, then soared to better than 120,000 a year in 1986-87. Obviously, they still offered what a lot of folks wanted.

Cougar was Mercury's most dramatic success of these years—not the aforementioned sedan series but L-M's version of the Ford Thunderbird. Blocky and ornate, the downsized 1980 model was little changed through 1982 but laid a gigantic egg, sales dropping below 20,000 units. Then came 1983's handsome "aero-look" reskin and volume more than tripled, reaching nearly 76,000 units. Sales rose by another 60,000 for '84, and would remain at over 100,000 through 1987.

There was a reason, of course: This Cougar had most everything the latest T-Bird did—which was plenty. Aiming for a more conservative clientele, Mercury gave it a more traditional, near-vertical backlight and offered standard 232-cid V6 or optional 302 V8. The basic Fox chassis was retained but more finely tuned for a pleasing ride/handling balance, and interiors could be downright luxurious with just a modicum of options. There was no XR-7 model at first, but it returned for '84 as a counterpart to the Thunderbird Turbo Coupe, with the same hyperaspirated 140-cid four, appropriately beefier suspension, and available five-speed manual transmission, the last an item that hadn't been seen on Cougars since the late '60s.

In all, it was a most pleasing package, made even more so by an interim facelift for '87, Cougar's 20th anniversary year. It involved larger rear quarter windows and shapelier nose bearing flush headlamps and a more rakish grille. At the same time, the XR-7's turbo four was dropped and a new fuel-injected V8 with 155 horses became standard. New for '88 were a hot-looking one-color XR-7 exterior, dual exhausts for the V8, and 20 more horsepower for the base V6 (up to 140 bhp total).

But all this was merely a warmup for the spectacular all-new '89 Cougar. Again, it was based on a new T-Bird, emerging lower and wider but no longer despite a rangier 113-inch wheelbase (previously 104.2). Styling was even more aerodynamic, but the '89 retained the vertical backlight and squarish mini-grille that had set Cougar apart from the Bird since '83.

In something of a surprise, the '89 Cougar forsook V8 and turbo-four power for a pair of 232 fuel-injected V6s: a normally aspirated 140-bhp unit for the LS model and a 210-bhp supercharged version with intercooler for the high-performance XR-7—America's first supercharged six since the 1954-55 Kaiser Manhattan. Underneath was a sophisticated new all-independent suspension system with variable shock-absorber damping and other advances to make this a road car worthy of comparison with premium European models. No doubt about it: Not only had Cougar been completely transformed in the '80s but in an amazingly satisfying way.

Mercury was well represented in the hard-fought late-'80s compact and mid-size fields by the Topaz and Sable, respectively. The former, arriving for 1984 as the front-drive replacement for the Zephyr, was a predictable kissin' cousin of Ford's Tempo and thus evolved in parallel with it. Included in developments through decade's end were the available high-output engine, sporty two-doors, 1987's new all-wheel-drive option, and a stem-to-stern makeover for the 1988 sedan. Dearborn designers tried to downplay similarities by making Topaz look somewhat different from Tempo at each end and by deleting the Tempo sedan's rearmost side window—not huge distinctions, but an encouraging sign that Mercurys were again becoming more individual.

A pleasant and capable compact, though not state-of-the-art, Topaz followed Lynx in generating lower volume than its Ford counterpart: 47,000-62,000 a year, about half of Tempo's sales. But again, that volume was very helpful to L-M dealers.

The Sable was even more helpful, immediately commanding almost 96,000 sales for debut '86 and over 121,000 for 1987. Replacing the little Marquis, this was Mercury's version of the acclaimed front-drive Ford Taurus and thus shared most of its basic design. There were exceptions, though. Where Taurus offered three trim levels, Sable had two: GS and upmarket LS. Mercury also decided it didn't need the Ford's small 2.5-liter four—a wise decision as most Sable buyers would have likely decided they didn't need it either. This left 3.0-liter and, from 1988, 3.8-liter "Vulcan" V6s. Both produced 140 bhp, but the 3.8 was the better choice for all-round performance owing to its larger displacement and commensurately greater torque. Sable also differed in having more simu-wood on dash and door panels.

But the real distinction was exterior styling. Where Taurus sedans had a conventional "six-light" roof treatment, Sable had a rear window wrapped fully around to the rear door trailing edges for a smooth, hidden-pillar effect. Also, its rear wheelarches were flat-topped, versus rounded on Taurus. Even more dramatic was Sable's unique front "light bar," a set of running lights behind a central, white lens that illuminated with the headlamps to make both sedans and wagons unmistakable at night. The net effect of these simple but clever changes was to give Sable an identity quite apart from Taurus's. Seldom in recent times had a Mercury been more its "own car"—or more handsome.

Alas, Sable missed out on a counterpart to the '89 Taurus SHO, but this was a reasonable marketing decision given Mercury's more luxury-oriented clientele. And with a stunning new Cougar to carry the performance banner, plus the updated Topaz and evergreen Grand Marquis, Mercury could take justifiable pride in Golden Anniversary 1989. Despite occasional mistakes and some very rough periods in its first 50 years, Mercury had produced some of America's most memorable automobiles. Now, on the eve of its second half-century, it was doing so again. For enthusiasts, that's something to celebrate—and be grateful for.

Mercury's '88 subcompact was the Mexican-built Mazda-based Tracer.

Merkur Scorpio, here an '88, was Europe's 1986 "Car of the Year."

'89 Cougar XR-7 had a supercharged V6, independent rear suspension.

As Mercury prepared to enter the Nineties, it could claim a well-defined product lineup and better brand identity than it had probably ever known. Key elements were the all-new '89 Cougar and, in mid-1990, a brand-new subcompact Tracer.

NASH

Crusty Charles W. Nash resigned as president of General Motors in 1916, and decided to build a car under his own name. Two years later, he bought the Thomas B. Jeffery Company of Kenosha, Wisconsin, which manufactured the slow-selling Jeffery and had earlier built a car called the Rambler. Now renamed Nash Motors, the firm charged up the sales charts, reaching as high as eighth place in industry production during the 1920s. Along the way, it introduced the low-cost, six-cylinder Ajax, and expanded by absorbing Mitchell and LaFayette. None of these efforts were as successful as the Nash itself, and all were gone by 1930. The firm suffered from the general economic malaise following the stock market crash, but found salvation by merging with the Kelvinator appliance company in 1937. George Mason, Kelvinator's cigar-chomping president, continued in that role with the new combine, while Charles Nash remained chairman of the board. By 1940, the firm had pretty well turned the corner and was profitable once more.

Early-'30s Nashes were sumptuous, beautifully styled automobiles with many special features. A very ordinary side-valve six powered the low-line models through 1933. More interesting were the "Twin Ignition" cars, offered in both six- and eight-cylinder form. The name referred to two sets of spark plugs and points plus dual condensers and coils, all operating from a single distributor. The Twin Ignition six had appeared in 1928; the Eight was new for 1930. Buick, which Charles Nash once headed in his GM days, traditionally espoused overhead valves, so it wasn't surprising that both these engines had them. The eight lasted far longer than the six (gaining power and displacement over time), but cost factors and public demand for greater economy led Nash to drop it. The Twin Ignition Eights of 1935-39 were powered by a smaller-displacement unit first seen in 1932. All Nash eights in these years carried nine main bearings.

Styling on the early Thirties Twin Ignition Nashes was classically upright. The look was retained through 1934 despite a general industry shift to more rounded, streamlined shapes. Seven-passenger sedans and limousines riding long-wheelbase chassis were available in both six- and eight-cylinder series, along with tourers, coupes, cabriolets and Ambassadors in the Eight range. The Ambassadors, luxuriously upholstered for five well-heeled passengers, were nicely proportioned.

Charles Nash believed in offering a lot for the money, and his cars bristled with innovations. Twin Ignition Eights had cowl vents, dashboard starter button, shatterproof glass and automatic radiator vents in 1930; downdraft carburetors and Bijur automatic chassis lubrication for '31; "Syncro-Safety Shift" (with the gearlever sprouting from the dash) and optional freewheeling for 1932; combination ignition and steering wheel locks for '33; and aircraft-type instruments for 1934. Many of these features were shared with the cheaper side-valve eight offered for 1931-33 in the 870/970 Standard series. This engine fell midway between the side-valve six and Twin Ignition eight in displacement and output, and prices were arranged accordingly.

Like most companies, Nash was damaged badly by the Depression. It regularly built over 100,000 cars a year in the late '20s, but wouldn't reach that figure in the 1930s and ranked 11th, 12th or 13th in production. The bottom was 1933, when output totaled less than 15,000 units. Thus, 1934 was clearly a year for new approaches. A planned restyle for the larger models was postponed a year, while resources were put into the LaFayette, Nash's unsuccessful lower-price junior make from 1934-36.

Nash built its one-millionth car in 1934, and looked forward to better times. A severe cropping in the lineup left only three separate series, all with overhead-valve engines. Hydraulic brakes arrived for all 1935 models, but the Ambassador lost its smooth

The '39 Nash Ambassador could be had with an inline six or eight.

It took $1195 to buy a 1940 Nash Ambassador Eight fastback sedan.

322-cubic-inch straight eight and shared the 260.8-cid unit with the Advanced Eight.

The long-awaited restyle (called Aeroform design) appeared for '35, and it was a good one. The fully updated look featured sweeping fastback or curved notchback bodies and skirted fenders, and some sedans were available with swept-down decks and concealed spare tires. Hoods were louvered, radiators vee'd and wheels were all-steel "artillery" types. It was a good year with close to 45,000 cars. Things were even better in 1936, reaching 53,000 units with the help of the low-priced, 117-inch-wheelbase 400 series.

Nash maintained its three-tier lineup for 1937, with the new LaFayette series replacing the 400 on the same chassis. The Ambassador Six rode a 121-inch wheelbase and used the 234.8-cid engine with 105 bhp; the Ambassador Eight, on a 125-inch wheelbase, continued to use the 260.8-cid Twin Ignition eight and had 105 bhp. This spread of engine types and wheelbases would continue throughout the end of the decade, with horsepower gradually increasing. Styling became more conventional as the years passed. The 1937 models bore a distinct resemblance to the Airstream Chryslers, for instance, which seemed to satisfy the public: Nash had its best year of the decade in '37, building 85,949 cars at prices ranging from $740 to $1165.

In 1938, however, Kenosha marched back down the hill it had climbed so laboriously. Production sank to 32,000 units and the new Nash-Kelvinator Corporation lost $7.7 million. The cars received a severe facelift, and now resembled the dumpier GM products, though the major cause of the sales drop was the 1938 recession. Yet despite the unsuccessful appearance changes and a bad year for the economy in general, Nash still had an innovation that year: the "Weather-Eye" combination heating and ventilation system. This pioneering feature was one of the best "climatizers" ever invented, and it remained so for the next 20 years.

A total restyle was deemed necessary for 1939. Fortunately, it was a good one. The ponderous '38 look with its busy front and bustle back was eliminated. Nash now featured a smooth, well-integrated nose with flush-fitting headlamps. A prow-like hood blended with a center grille composed of narrow, vertically stacked bars and flanked either side by chromed catwalk grilles. The result was neat and trim, and combined all the best design elements of the art-deco era. Production, at 66,000 units, was more than double that of 1938. Although Nash-Kelvinator lost $1.6 million this year, the future looked brighter in 1939 than it had for the last 10 years.

For Nash, 1940 marked the end of an era: the last use of the Lafayette name, as well as the phasing out of separate body-and-chassis construction. The line consisted of the Lafayette Six and the Ambassador with six-cylinder or straight eight power. The six was a valve-in-head design, producing 99 horsepower in the Lafayette and 105 bhp in the Ambassador. Having seven main bearings, it was an exceptionally quiet and smooth-running unit, if not exactly speedy off the line. The refined nine-main-bearing Ambassador eight was also a valve-in-head powerplant, with 115 bhp. For about $150 more than the Lafayette, the Ambassador Six offered a four-inch-longer wheelbase and more horsepower. Looks were similar. Both used strong, vertical, peaked grilles and smooth, flowing lines complemented by nicely rounded fenders. Body styles in all three series were exactly the same. Output reached 62,131 units for the model year.

The unit body/chassis 600 for 1941 was an important breakthrough for Nash. (The designation, incidentally, stood for 600 miles to a 20-gallon tankful.) Styling was similar to the 1940 line, but different enough to be accepted as entirely new. It was a handsome package on a 112-inch wheelbase and price was remarkable: just $805 for the Special fastback four-door sedan, less than the price of a Ford Special DeLuxe V-8. *Time* called it "the only completely new car in 1941," and sales were high. The 600 engine was a 172.6-cid six. Eight different models were offered with Special or Deluxe trim, all either sedans or coupes. Cabriolets (two-door convertibles) were listed in the Ambassador Six line, with the 234 engine and a 121-inch wheelbase, and the Ambassador Eight that shared this same body and chassis. Altogether, 1941 proved to be very profitable. Nash-Kelvinator closed the fiscal year with a $4.6 million profit.

Nash built only 31,780 cars for the short 1942 model year. They had distinctive styling, the result of a major facelift. Following a design trend of the day, Nash adopted a low, wraparound grille made up of three horizontal bars. This motif was repeated on the fenders. The tall '41 frontispiece was dropped in favor of a vertical nameplate and small upper grille of horizontal bars. Parking lights appeared atop the front fenders and a larger hood ornament was used. The three-model lineup—600, Ambassador Six and Eight—remained, but fewer body styles were offered and prices were up about ten percent.

During the war, Nash-Kelvinator manufactured $600 million worth of aircraft engines and parts, munitions, cargo trailers and binocular cases.

Nash finished third in the first postwar production race. That was calendar year 1945, which amounted to only four months of civilian car building. But the firm resumed operations earlier than most, and actually built 6148 cars during that period—one Nash for every two Chevrolets. In 1946, the first full postwar model year, Nash produced about 94,000 cars and ranked eighth; in 1947-48, having produced 101,000 and 110,000 units, it ran 10th and 11th.

New front-end styling marked the '41 Nash—84,007 were produced.

Another new grille design distinguished the 1942 Nash Ambassador.

Charles W. Nash resigned the presidency of General Motors in 1916 to start his own auto company. Nash quickly established itself as a quality automaker, introduced a number of innovations, and weathered the Depression better than most.

The '47 Nash was a touched up '42. Prices ranged from $1464 to $2227 and production reached a satisfying 101,000 units.

Nash built a woody in 1946, the Suburban: $1929, 272 produced.

A Custom cabriolet was added for 1948; output came to 1000 units.

These early postwar years were good ones for the company, and profits were high.

In June 1948, Nash president George W. Mason succeeded the venerable Charles W. Nash as chairman of the board. Nash died that month at age 84. During the 1946 celebration of the industry's Golden Jubilee, he'd been one of a dozen industry pioneers still living to share in the honors. Among executives of independent companies, Mason was the most far-seeing. He knew the independents would eventually have to merge to survive, and hoped to put Nash together with Hudson, and ultimately with Studebaker and Packard as well.

Like most other automakers, Nash built slightly renovated versions of its 1942 models for 1946, '47 and '48. Management dropped the eight to concentrate on sixes, increasing the 600's horsepower to 82 and the Ambassador's to 112. Even though alterations were minor, styling appeared quite fresh.

The 600 series comprised three models in 1946-47: a two-door brougham and four-door sedans with trunkback or fastback lines. The Ambassador Six offered those three plus the unique Sedan Suburban. Like the Chrysler Town & Country and Ford/Mercury Sportsman, it was lavishly trimmed with wood. Nash built 272 Sedan Suburbans in 1946; 595 in 1947; 130 in 1948. Because of the handwork involved, they were quite expensive ($2227 in 1947), and were not fast sellers. But they played the same role as their Chrysler and Ford counterparts, attracting buyers to showrooms with the promise of something new. Suburbans were pretty cars, and ultimately became popular with collectors. Unfortunately, only about 10 to 15 are thought to exist today. The 1946 styling was only slightly modified for '47. Nash had used inboard parking lights and a widened upper grille in 1946. For '47, the upper grille was widened again, and new raised-center hubcaps were used. Then in 1948, the side molding below the beltline was eliminated, an inexpensive change that inadvertently made the cars appear higher and less streamlined than before.

The model line was expanded for 1948. Anticipating a significant upsurge in buyer demand, the company made the best of its prewar design, offering three styles of 600 and two of Ambassador. The price leader at $1478 was the 600 DeLuxe business coupe. The usual assortment of sedans and broughams was offered in Super and Custom trim. Similarly, the Ambassador Super and Custom were listed. The Sedan Suburban was continued as a Super. The Custom included a new convertible—the first open Nash since the war. One thousand of these jaunty soft-tops were produced that year. (The company also built a limited number of trucks bearing sedan-type front ends beginning in 1947; most were exported.)

Nash officials knew they'd have to come up with an all-new car for 1949. Most of the company's independent rivals had already restyled by then, and the Big Three were readying all-new designs that year. Nash's answer was the 1949-51 Airflyte. Though some think it looks positively awful now, it was one of the most advanced cars of its day, bristling with unusual features. Its shape was purely aerodynamic, and though most manufacturers had toyed with the "bathtub" look, only Nash actually put it into production. The Airflyte began during World War II. Nils Erik Wahlberg had been a Nash engineer ever since the company was formed in 1916. Ted Ulrich, who'd been a unit-body exponent since the '30s, had helped create the 1941 Nash while he was at Budd Inc., the body builders. The '41 was the first successful mass-produced unit-body car. Its success led to Wahlberg hiring Ulrich.

Actual styling of the Airflyte is claimed with some authority by Holden Koto, who, with partner Ted Pietsch, showed a small scale model very much like the eventual production version to Wahlberg in 1943. Wahlberg must have been interested because he had been experimenting with wind tunnel tests on streamlined bodies. The Airflyte's aerodynamics were superior: only 113 pounds of drag at 60 miles per hour, compared to as much as 171 pounds for the somewhat similarly shaped '48-'50 Packard.

Airflytes were six inches lower, had a one-piece curved windshield, "Uniscope" gauge cluster (a pod mounted atop the steering column), enclosed front and rear wheels, and fully reclining front seatbacks (pneumatic mattresses were sold as accessories). The seats, together with the Nash-Kelvinator Weather-Eye heating and ventilation system, made the new Nash the most habitable long-distance touring car in America.

Nash produced 135,000 cars for the 1949 model year, shooting into the industry's top 10. The Airflyte 600s and Ambassadors used the same wheelbases and powerplants that had been used the year before. Three body types were offered: a two-door sedan, a four-door sedan and a brougham (club coupe). Prices remained competitive: under $2000 for the 600s; about $2200 to $2400 for the Ambassadors.

At the height of the seller's market, these cars did very well: better, in fact, than any big cars in Nash history. For 1950, the figure was 172,000 units—an all-time company record, though it included about 58,000 Ramblers. The Statesman (nee 600) engine at 172.6 cid also powered the Rambler. Respected since its debut as an L-head in 1928, Nash's hardy old seven-main-bearing six had one of the longest production runs in history, and was not dropped until 1956.

Nash called all of its 1949 models Airflyte, here an Ambassador.

Nash invented the postwar compact when it debuted the '50 Rambler.

Riding a 100-inch wheelbase, the little Rambler was the very antithesis of the huge Airflyte. Though there had been smaller cars long before World War II, the Rambler was really the first "compact" to sell in high volume. It was the progenitor of an entirely new breed of American automobiles. Ford and Chevrolet had experimented with (and quickly discarded) compact-car designs

The '51 Nash received a vertical-bar grille and squared-off rear fenders. Seen here are a Statesman Super and Ambassador Custom.

Unlike most independents, Nash waited until 1949 to introduce its new postwar models, which were the most aerodynamic cars on the road. President George Mason knew the independents had to merge to survive, but none of them would listen.

Rambler's hardtop was called the Custom Country Club; it cost $2094.

The '52 Rambler Custom wagon was named Greenbriar. Price: $2119.

The '52 Nash was Pinin Farina-designed, here an Ambassador Super.

Rambler for '53 sported a new grille, here the Custom Country Club.

right after the war, but their concepts were fundamentally different from Nash's. As former AMC President George Romney said, "It's one thing for a small company—a marginal firm—to pioneer a new concept like that and really push it. But it's another thing for people who already have a big slice to begin pushing something that undercuts their basic market."

Small cars fascinated George Mason. In addition to strength-through-mergers, Mason knew that independents needed cars the Big Three didn't offer. Together with chief engineer Meade Moore, Mason kept hammering away until the Rambler—and a little later the Metropolitan—was a reality. It arrived just as the sell-anything era was coming to a close, and held Nash's head above water until the company merged with Hudson to become American Motors in 1954. AMC concentrated on Ramblers after 1957.

The first-generation Rambler spanned model years 1950-52. In its first season, it was sold as a two-door station wagon and an interesting convertible, on which the window frames were permanently fixed and only the top collapsed. A Country Club hardtop was added for '51, but most sales came from the practical, attractive wagons. In those early days of all-steel wagons, Ramblers accounted for 22 percent of total U.S. sales of that body type.

Road tester Tom McCahill admired Mason and Nash tremendously. They were, he said, "busier than a mouse in a barrel of hungry cats" with their many projects. Yet another of these endeavors was the Nash-Healey sports car.

Back where production really counted, Airflyte sales had slowed. Last of that type was the '51, easily recognizable by its prominent rear fenders (1949-50 cars had rounded backs). For his 1952 redesign, Mason went to Pinin Farina and the result was much better looking if less aerodynamic. The new, squared-off line included the 114.3-inch-wheelbase Statesman and the larger 121.3-inch-wheelbase Ambassador, both of course with unit construction. New to the full-size Nashes was the Custom Country Club two-door hardtop.

The story was much the same for the 1953 models, identified by small chrome spacers on the cowl air-scoop. The Statesman engine received a boost in output to 100 bhp. Ambassadors offered a "Le Mans" power option based on the latest Nash-Healey engine: 140 bhp at 4000 rpm through dual carburetors and a high-compression aluminum head.

An attractive new "floating" grille was adopted for 1954. The lineup, however, was much the same as it had been the previous two years. One difference was the deletion of two-door sedans from the two Custom series. Dual carbs and high compression had been successful on the Ambassador, so the Statesman got these modifications in '54. Its six was raised to 110 bhp, and the setup was known (with a furtive look to Chrysler) as "Dual Powerflyte." Nash probably got away with using that name (similar to Chrysler's PowerFlite transmission) only because sales were so dismal. From the heady years of 1950-51, they'd dropped steadily: 154,000 in 1952; 121,000 in 1953; 91,000 in 1954. And a growing portion was accounted for by Rambler. The latter had been facelifted for '53 with a cleaner front end design.

The 1954 model year also saw the introduction of the Nash Metropolitan. Its origins went back to just after World War II, when Nash president George W. Mason and engineer Meade F. Moore accepted a design by independent stylist Bill Flajole. Based on a Fiat 500 chassis/drivetrain, the prototype was named NXI (Nash Experimental International). Mason's top assistant and heir-apparent, George Romney, displayed the NXI at a variety of private showings in 1950, carefully sizing up public reaction before moving ahead with production. Reaction was favorable, but Mason still moved slowly; it wasn't until the end of 1953 that arrangements for volume production were complete. Bodies would be built in England by the well-known Birmingham manufacturers Fisher & Ludlow, Ltd. From there, they would be shipped to Longbridge, where the Austin A40's 1200-cc, 42-horsepower, four-cylinder engines were installed.

The two-passenger, 85-inch-wheelbase Metropolitan debuted in early 1954 in hardtop and convertible styles priced at $1445 and $1469, respectively. The tiny car rode an 85-inch wheelbase and weighed just over 1800 pounds, so gas mileage was good—up to 40 miles per gallon. Sales took off, and Austin shipped 13,905 cars from late 1953 through '54.

For 1955, the big Nash appeared with inboard headlights, an easy way to make the car look different, plus a wraparound wind-

The '53 Nash Ambassador Custom Country Club was priced at $2829.

English bodywork, Nash engine: '53 Nash-Healey—only 162 built.

The big Nash received a new grille for '54, here a Statesman Custom.

Nash debuted a British-built mini for '54, the $1469 Metropolitan.

Nash for '55: wraparound windshield, inboard headlights, V8 power.

Rambler was restyled for '55; the Custom Cross Country sold for $2098.

shield and a V8. Cooperation between newly formed American Motors and Studebaker-Packard put Packard's 320-cid V8 in the Ambassador Eight. It was much quicker than the six and cost $300 more. The Ambassador Six continued to use the six-cylinder engine with optional Le Mans power pack. The Statesman continued with its own L-head six. Each series came in two body styles: four-door sedan and two-door hardtop.

After Hudson joined Nash, 1955-56 Ramblers were distributed to Hudson and Nash dealers alike with the appropriate grille badge. The model lineup grew to include the DeLuxe, Super, and Custom sedans, hardtops, and Cross Country or Suburban wagons. A completely revised model with a 108-inch wheelbase was added for '56. Initially, it was sold as a Nash, but became a separate make the following year. A boxy but practical design, the Rambler line significantly included a novel four-door hardtop (Cross Country) wagon and a hardtop sedan.

With all that, the big Nash was de-emphasized for '56. The last Statesman, a four-door sedan, appeared that year. Ambassadors used the Packard V8 early in the season, then switched to AMC's own 190-bhp, 327-cid V8 in April.

Also in April, American Motors announced the Metropolitan 1500. Badged as a Nash or Hudson, it featured a stronger clutch and an enlarged engine that cranked out 52 horsepower, an increase of 24 percent. Compared to about 70 mph tops for the old model, the 1500 would do close to 80, though not with sports-car efficiency. Styling was updated with loud two-tone paint schemes resembling, as one stylist put it, Neapolitan ice cream. A new oval mesh grille rode up front, while the hood lost its fake airscoop.

For 1957, Nash moved the headlights back out to the fenders and fielded only two Ambassador models, Super and Custom. The latter was heroically overdecorated, and equipped with a more potent 327 V8, developing 255 bhp with the help of four-barrel carburetor, dual exhausts and 9:1 compression ratio. The styling was pretty good by contemporary standards. Nash was among the first to offer four headlights as standard, (vertically stacked, no less), but the make was in its last year, and only about

Although Kaiser, Willys, and Hudson tried, Nash was the only maker in the Fifties to find enduring success with a compact. Rambler gained momentum during that era, and formed the basis for the future success of what had become American Motors.

A glitzier front end was seen on the '56 Nash. The Ambassador Super could be had with either a six or V8, for $2425 or $2716.

The '55 Ambassador Custom Country Club V8 hardtop sold for $3095.

The '56 Ambassador Super sported a flashy three-tone paint job.

Exposed front wheels and wilder three-toning were '57 Nash features.

Nash was in its last year in 1957; about 5000 big cars were built.

5000 were built. AMC was only slowly recovering from the debts forced on it through the Hudson merger and subsequent reorganization. Romney who became company president on Mason's death pinned his hopes for the future on the Rambler.

Meanwhile, the Metropolitan became a separate make from 1958 on. Mid-year 1959 brought more refinements, though the 1500 designation remained. For the first time, the Metropolitan received an opening trunklid; before, cargo had to be pushed into the compartment from behind the seats. More comfortable seats, vent wings and tubeless tires were other improvements. Prices had risen to over $1600, but the Metropolitan nevertheless enjoyed its best year ever: 22,309 were produced. Production ended in mid-1960, though leftovers were sold into 1962. A total of 94,986 units had been built during its nine-year existence. Like many imports, Metropolitan was a victim of the compact onslaught from the Big Three in 1960.

OLDSMOBILE

There was a time when Oldsmobile and not Ford was America's leading car producer. It was 1903-5, when Lansing rolled to success with Ransom Eli Olds' little curved-dash runabout, the world's first series-production automobile. Actually, Olds built his first experimental car in 1891 and had started production by 1897, which made this the industry's second oldest nameplate (after Studebaker) among those that survived into the 1960s.

But age and tradition count for little in this business, and a decline set in soon after Ransom Olds left to form the Reo company in 1904. General Motors bought Olds Motor Works five years later, but even that didn't immediately help sales. It wasn't until the side-valve V8 of 1916 that Oldsmobiles really began to sell well again. Lansing's best years before 1930 were 1921 and 1929, when it finished ninth in sales.

Olds blossomed in the '30s under general manager Charles L. McCuen, featuring synchromesh transmission from 1931, "Knee-Action" independent front suspension from 1934, a semi-automatic transmission in 1937-38, and Hydra-Matic Drive from 1939. The division's worst Depression year was 1932, when it built only 17,500 cars. But Olds recovered rapidly, selling over 191,000 units for 1936. The 1938 recession cut output to only 85,000, but the division again rallied quickly, then reached a new high with 1941 volume of nearly 266,000. It would do even better in the postwar years.

It was in the '30s that Oldsmobile assumed its role as GM's "experimental" division. McCuen had been chief engineer before becoming general manager in 1933. To take his place he recruited Harold T. Youngren, a brilliant innovator. Under him were experimental engineering manager Jack Wolfram and dynamometer wizard Harold Metzel. The last two became divisions chiefs in later years. Youngren left in 1945 to help develop Ford's engineering department.

Oldsmobile suffered less from the Depression than most other makes thanks to conservative but saleable styling and a fairly consistent lineup of six- and eight-cylinder models. The L-head six began the decade at 197.5 cubic inches and 60-65 horsepower. The eight, also a conventional side-valve design, arrived for 1932 with 240 cubic inches and 90 bhp. Both were smooth, quiet and reliable, and both received important improvements as the decade wore on, such as aluminum pistons for 1936. A major redesign the following year brought the six to 230 cid and 95 bhp, the eight to 257 cid and 110 bhp. Other changes included adoption of full-length water jacketing, stiffer piston skirts and crankshaft, stronger cams and valve lifters, and longer valve guides. The eight continued in this form into 1949, when it was honorably retired for the modern high-compression overhead-valve "Rocket" V8. The six ultimately grew to near 260 cid by the time it was phased out in 1950.

Styling followed general industry trends: classically square for 1930-32; slightly streamlined, with angled radiator and skirted fenders for 1933; "potato" shapes for 1934-35, after which the pace of change picked up. Though Olds used the same GM B-body as LaSalle and the smaller Buicks, its cars managed to look individual. More massive fronts with cross-hatched or horizontal-bar grilles appeared for 1936-37; the 1938-39s had Harley Earl's flanking twin "catwalk" auxiliary grilles and headlamp pods partly faired into the front fender aprons. Prices were accurately placed in a competitive market area below Buick and LaSalle and above Pontiac. Aside from choices in wheelbase, engine, and trim, Olds offered styling options such as sidemount spare tires and, toward decade's end, trunkless or "trunkback" sedans. Convertible coupes were always low-production items.

Oldsmobile won its renown as an innovator with two important late-'30s transmission ideas. The first was 1937's "Automatic Safety Transmission," a semi-automatic four-speed unit for eight-cylinder cars that worked like, but was not mechanically identical to, Chrysler's subsequent Fluid Drive. Before moving off, the driv-

Olds' mid-price 1939 series was the 70, here the $891 club coupe.

The 1940 Series 60 wagon listed at $1042. Output was 633 units.

Oldsmobile was already building cars in 1897 and was folded into General Motors in 1909. Over the years, Oldsmobile became known as GM's "experimental" division—its best known innovation was Hydra-Matic Drive, introduced in 1939.

Oldsmobiles for 1940 came on three wheelbases: 116, 120, and 124 inches. A 229.7-cid six yielded 95 bhp, the 257.1-cid eight, 110.

er depressed a conventional clutch pedal and selected Low or High range. The transmission then shifted between first and second in Low or first, third and fourth in High, the changes made automatically via oil pressure and two planetary gearsets, each with one brake and one clutch band. Shift points were preset according to vehicle speed.

Olds claimed AST delivered up to 15 percent better gas mileage, but this was due to the numerically lower rear-axle ratio specified. The "safety" aspect referred to the fact that with less shifting to do, the driver could keep both hands on the wheel more of the time. AST became an $80 option for all 1938 Oldsmobiles and some 28,000 were installed, but its real significance is that it led to Hydra-Matic for '39.

Hydra-Matic also had four speeds but was fully automatic, using a fluid coupling and a complex system of clutches and brake bands. It cost only $57 extra, but that probably didn't reflect its true manufacturing or development costs, though both would be offset by high volume. By the early '50s, Hydra-Matic was being offered by Cadillac and Pontiac as well as independents Nash, Hudson, and Kaiser-Frazer.

Besides Hydra-Matic, Oldsmobile's 1939 line offered newly styled GM B-bodies in three groups: 115-inch-wheelbase Series 60 and a new mid-price, 120-inch-wheelbase Series 70, both powered by the 230-cid six tuned for 90 and 95 bhp respectively; and the eight-cylinder Series 80 with the 110-bhp 257-cid engine in the longer chassis. All listed business and club coupes and two- and four-door sedans, the latter available in the two upper lines with "Sunshine Turret Top," an optional sliding metal sunroof that saw few installations. The 70 and 80 also included a convertible coupe. Prices ranged from $777 to $1119.

This basic lineup returned for 1940 with slightly higher prices, reassigned wheelbases, somewhat smoother looks and two new models. The 60 now rode a 116-inch chassis and included a wood-bodied station wagon built by Hercules. Replacing the 80 was a new 124-inch-wheelbase Series 90 that included Oldsmobile's first convertible sedan (called "phaeton" per GM practice)—an odd latecomer for a body type fast waning elsewhere. At $1570 it was Oldsmobile's costliest 1940 model and production was predictably limited: just 50 in all. Styling was typical of GM that year, with wider grilles and front fenders, semi-faired-in headlights and,

The '41 Series 66 four-door sedan cost $898—30,475 were produced.

A new grille marked the postwar '46 Olds 60 Special club sedan.

on 90s, smoother tails and rear rooflines.

A more massive look arrived for 1941. Headlights were fully enclosed within even wider front fenders that blended more smoothly into the bodysides, and grillework was lower and wider. Series doubled as Olds offered both engines in each trim level for the first time. Series designations reflected the number of cylinders. The low-end 66 and 68 rode a new 119-inch wheelbase, while the Dynamic Cruiser 76 and 78 shared a 125-inch chassis with the top-line Custom Cruiser 96 and 98. The six was bored out to 238.1 cid and 100 bhp. Body styles were as for 1940 and identical with either engine except that the convertible phaeton came only as an eight-cylinder 98. The latter again saw minuscule production: only 119 for the model year, after which Olds followed everyone else by dropping four-door convertibles. Despite record production, the division finished sixth in the annual industry race. Though Olds had risen as high as fifth for '36, it would usually run sixth or seventh into the mid-'50s.

Olds slipped to seventh for war-shortened 1942 but enjoyed respectable volume of just under 68,000 units. Styling for this year's "B-44" line featured "Fuselage Fenders"—elongated pontoon types faired into the front doors—and a busy two-tier grille bisected by a prominent horizontal bar. Longer back fenders tapered beyond the rear deck but were still bolt-on components. Engines stayed the same but not models. The six-cylinder 90 departed and the remaining 98 was cut to three models on a two-inch longer wheelbase. Each series offered a new torpedo-style two-door fastback club sedan, with plain and DeLuxe versions in the 76/78 lines. The 66/68 expanded even further with a four-door Town Sedan, a new notchback style with more closed-in rear roof quarters. Fastback profiles appeared on the standard 76/78 sedans.

During the war, Oldsmobile turned out 350,000 precision aero-engine parts, 175 million pounds of gun forgings, 140,000 machine guns, and millions of rounds of ammunition. It officially became the Oldsmobile Division of General Motors on New Year's Day 1942. Previously it was Olds Motor Works, a name retained from the make's founding in 1896.

Olds returned to peacetime with warmed-over prewar cars that sold close to 118,000 for 1946 and close to 194,000 for '47, though the make remained in seventh place. Most 1942 models immediately returned with no changes in wheelbase, engines and body styles. The exception was the Series 68, which wasn't reinstated until 1947. Styling was cleaned up via a four-bar grille shaped like a wide, upside-down U; a shield-type hood medallion rode above it. Front fender moldings carried the series name, and were enlarged for '47. Strangely, these early-postwar models lacked parking lights. Hydra-Matic was increasingly popular, and Olds began producing more self-shift cars as a percentage of total volume than any other make.

Though called "Dynamic," the '48 Oldsmobiles saw only detail changes: notably a round hood medallion, "Oldsmobile" spelled out in block letters below, and full-length chrome rocker-panel moldings. But in February, Olds got a jump on most competitors with the "Futuramic" 98, arriving simultaneously with similar styling from Cadillac as GM's first all-new postwar body designs. Both were created by Harley Earl's Art & Colour staff with inspiration from the Lockheed P-38 fighter aircraft (well-known for having prompted Cadillac's new '48 tailfins). The beautifully shaped 98s included a convertible, four-door sedan and fastback club sedan on a 125-inch wheelbase. The latter two were offered in standard and deluxe trim. Prices ranged from $2078 for the base two-door to $2624 for the Deluxe-only convertible. The public responded strongly to the new line, particularly the 98s, which saw better than 60,000 sales. Over half were four-door sedans.

Olds followed up with Futuramic styling for all 1949 models and two more innovations. One was the landmark overhead-valve Rocket V8 designed by Gilbert Burrell. Again Olds shared honors

The '48 club coupe could be ordered as a Dynamic 66 or Dynamic 68.

The '49 Oldsmobile Futuramic 98 boasted an all-new overhead-valve V8.

Only 5434 Oldsmobile Futuramic 88 convertibles were built for '49.

The 119.5-inch-wheelbase junior Olds came with six *or* ohv V8 in 1950.

Olds 98 club sedan for 1950 saw 2270 standards built, 9719 Deluxes.

The USSR blockaded the Allied sector of Berlin in April 1948. The U.S. and Britain responded with a massive air-lift of 2,350,000 tons of food and coal by September 1949. During this period, Olds flew high with its new powerful Rocket V-8.

This '50 Olds 88 with a see-through hood showcased the new ohv V8.

The '51 Olds 98 Holiday had a total production run of 17,926 units.

Cheapest model in the '52 Olds lineup was the $2262 88 two door.

The price went unchanged for '53; the V8 was now up to 150 horses.

with Cadillac, which also had a new high-compression V8 that year, though it was developed independently of Lansing's. Both divisions had been encouraged to outdo each other, and Cadillac actually raised its V8 displacement to exceed Oldsmobile's. The Rocket arrived at 303.7 cid; Cadillac had started at 309, then went to 331 cid.

A five-main-bearing unit with oversquare cylinder dimensions, the Rocket was initially rated at 135 bhp. Putting it in the lighter 119.5-inch-wheelbase 76 chassis created a new Futuramic 88 with power-to-weight ratios of about 22.5 pounds/bhp—quite good for the era. Torque was also impressive at 240 foot-pounds. Initial compression was a mild 7.25:1, but the Rocket was designed for ratios as high as 12:1. Engineers had anticipated postwar fuels with ultra-high octane, though levels never became quite high enough to make such ratios practical.

Management had originally planned the Rocket for 98 models only, but dropping it into the smaller B-body Oldsmobiles was a natural move, and the 88 soon began writing stock-car racing history. Meanwhile, the Olds six was enlarged to the old eight's 257.1 cid for 105 bhp. It continued through 1950, after which Olds offered nothing but V8s.

Oldsmobile's other '49 innovation was the 98 Holiday, arriving along with the Buick Riviera and Cadillac Coupe deVille as America's first volume-production pillarless "hardtop convertibles." Also predicting a future trend was Lansing's first all-steel station wagon, offered in 76 and 88 guise. As at Chevy, it bowed at mid-year to replace the initial part-wood wagon, and looked much like it. Not at all predictive was the addition of fastback town sedan four-doors in the 76 and 88 lines. None sold well, and would be dropped after this one year.

With so much new, Olds had a rollicking 1949, production soaring from the previous year's 172,500 to a record 288,000-plus. The 1950 total rose to near 408,000, helped by new 76 and 88 Holiday hardtops.

Weighing 300-500 pounds less than a comparable 98, the Rocket-engine 88 continued wowing race-goers. Oldsmobile claimed the NASCAR championship in 1949. It did so again in 1950 and '51. Of nine 1949 NASCAR Grand National races, 88s won six, with "Red" Byron the national driving champ. In 1950 an 88 broke the class speed record at Daytona with a two-way average of 100.28 mph. That same year, an 88 won the first Mexican Road Race, besting such formidable competitors as Alfa Romeo, Cadillac and Lincoln. On the stock-car ovals Olds won 10 of 19 contests in 1950 and 20 of 41 in '51. Though displaced by the Hudson Hornet in 1952-54, the 88s continued to show their mettle. Paul Frere, for example, drove one to victory in a 1952 stock-car race at Spa in Belgium, and a 1950 model nicknamed "Roarin' Relic" was still winning the occasional modified race as late as 1959.

Such goings-on naturally kept sales going once the seller's market started shrinking around 1950. Olds tapered off to 213,500 for '52 but was back up to 354,000 by 1954, when it reached fifth in

The '54 Olds 98 Deluxe Holiday Coupe—29,688 were built.

Flagship of the '56 Olds line was the Starfire 98 convertible. It retailed for $3740 and saw a production run of 8581 units.

production. It then passed Plymouth to claim fourth for '55. Interestingly, the division managed these triumphs with only three basic series and no station wagons for 1951-56.

Not resting on its styling laurels, GM issued a new C-body for 1950, which gave Oldsmobile's 98 a lower, more massive look, plus a one-piece windshield. Models comprised standard and DeLuxe notchback four-door sedans, fastback club sedans, Holiday hardtops and one convertible. The junior 88 and 76 retained their new '49 styling. Each offered a convertible plus plain and DeLuxe notchback sedans, club coupe, Holiday hardtop, wagon, and two-door club sedans (the last body style now in its final year). Curiously, all three convertibles—76, 88 and 98—were offered only with standard trim.

The big event of 1951 was the new Super 88 with a 120-inch wheelbase and styling much like that of this year's facelifted 98. Cancelling the 76 left the 88 as the base series with just two- and four-door sedans. The 98 was trimmed to a sedan, convertible and Holiday hardtop, the last still available in standard and DeLuxe versions. The Futuramic label was abandoned as styling became more "important," though the grille was formed by simple bars and side decoration was minimal. This basic appearance continued for '52, when the 88 became a detrimmed Super with a new 145-bhp Rocket V8. Horsepower on other models moved up to 160.

Along with the Cadillac Eldorado and Buick Skylark, 1953 brought a limited-production Olds convertible, the Fiesta, a $5717 mid-year addition to the 98 line. Custom leather interior, wraparound "Panoramic" windshield and a special 170-bhp V8 distinguished it from the normal 98 ragtop. Hydra-Matic, power brakes and steering, and hydraulic servos for windows and seats were all standard. So were distinctive spinner wheel covers soon copied by most every accessory house in the business, appearing on hot rods and custom cars from coast to coast. Only 458 Fiestas were built and the model was dropped after '53, but it did serve as a

New to the '55 lineup was the 98 Deluxe Holiday hardtop sedan.

The '55 Starfire 98 listed at $3276. Olds built 9149 examples.

Olds got a jump on most of the industry with an all-new 1954 design that was highlighted by a wraparound "Panoramic" windshield. This enabled Olds to move up to fifth place in the production race and to set a sales record in 1955.

styling preview of the next-generation Olds.

That styling arrived on 1954's new B- and C-bodies bearing squared-up below-the-belt sheetmetal, fully wrapped windshields, wrapped back windows, and distinctive L-shape bodyside moldings that delineated contrast color areas on some two-toned models. This was perhaps the most attractive '50s Olds, and its basic look would persist through 1956.

So would body styles: 88 and Super 88 two- and four-door sedans and hardtop coupe; Super 88 convertible; 98 Holiday, Deluxe Holiday, Deluxe sedan and Starfire convertible. Holiday four-door hardtops arrived at mid-1955, half a year ahead of every other make's save Buick's (which bowed along with Oldsmobile's). Wheelbases shifted to 122 inches for 88/Super 88 and 126 for 98. The Rocket V8 was bored out to 324 cid and delivered 170 bhp in 88s, 185 in Super 88s and 98s. With the horsepower race escalating, the figures were bumped to 185 and 202 for '55, then to 230 and 240 bhp.

Olds set another record by building over 50 percent more cars for '55 than '54—some 553,000—and claimed fourth in the industry. A substantial facelift gave the '55s a bold oval grille and jazzier two-toning. The '56s gained a large, gaping "mouth" front like that of the 1953 Starfire show car. Despite a general industry retreat, the division did quite well to turn out some 485,000 of its '56s, though Plymouth's return to fourth pushed Olds down a spot on the production chart.

Another new B- and C-body arrived for 1957 with sleeker styling and the first Olds wagons since 1950. Called Fiesta, the new haulers comprised a pillared 88 four-door and pillarless 88 and Super 88 models, the latter reflecting the public's passion for hardtop styling. Both 88 series were subtitled Golden Rocket (after a 1956 show car); all 98s gained Starfire as a first name. The Rocket V8 was enlarged to 371.1 cid and 277 bhp, but a new three-by-two-barrel carburetor option lifted that to 300 bhp. The latter, J-2 engine could propel an 88 from 0 to 60 mph in less than eight seconds.

The '57 Olds was rather cleanly styled for a GM car that year. The wide-mouth grille was mildly reshaped; windshield pillars were more rakishly angled; a broad, stainless-steel sweepspear dropped down from the middle of the beltline and shot straight back to the tail to delineate the two-toning area; and there were finless rear fenders ending in peaked, roughly circular taillamps. GM styling was beginning to seem a bit passé next to Virgil Exner's Forward Look at Chrysler, but the age of Harley Earl was coming to an end. Still, Olds built nearly 385,000 cars and again finished fifth.

While most of the industry faltered in recession 1958, Olds reclaimed fourth on production near the 315,000 mark. Model offerings stayed the same except that two-door sedans were now limited to the base series, newly named Dynamic 88. Styling, most observers concluded, was atrocious: Ford's Alex Tremulis satirized Oldsmobile's four horizontal rear-fender chrome strips by drawing in a clef and a few notes of music on a photograph. And indeed, Dearborn's '58s looked better than GM's; Chrysler's products were in another league entirely. But Olds still managed to sell well—aided, no doubt, by more potent 371 V8s, which offered 265 bhp on 88s, 305 bhp on Supers and 312 on 98s (no longer called Starfires).

Meantime, GM had planned a divisional body realignment for 1959, along with crisp new styling marked by vast windshields; curved, non-dogleg A-posts; big rear windows (wrapped fully around on a second hardtop sedan style); thin-section hardtop coupe rooflines; narrow pillars; and lower body sheetmetal that was both more fulsome and sculptured. Chevy and Pontiac would share the corporate A-body, the junior Buick and Oldsmobiles a new B-body, senior models a slightly different C-body with Cadillac. Olds and Buick wheelbases were set at 123 and 126 inches. Pontiac's was slightly shorter, Chevy's shorter still. As ever, styling strived for a distinct divisional look, though the '59 Olds ended up looking more like Pontiac than Olds management would have liked. Aided by a new emphasis on "Wide-Track" handling, Pontiac outpaced Olds in '59 production, something it hadn't done since 1953.

All Ninety-Eights were officially Starfires for the '57 model run.

Whew: '57 Oldsmobile Golden Rocket Super 88 Fiesta hardtop wagon.

Olds produced 3799 chrome-laden Super 88 convertibles for 1958.

Body sharing had other repercussions. Chevrolet, for example, had to drop its all-new '58 platform after only a year. Oldsmobile's previous bodies were just two years old. Still, it was an effective move that held production costs down, thus enabling the company to put more time and money into a squadron of new compacts.

Nevertheless, Oldsmobile's "Linear Look" '59s were big, roomy cars with plenty of power and pizzazz—and a bit thirsty. Engines comprised 270- and 300-bhp 371s for the Dynamic and Super 88s respectively, and a new bored-out 394 for 98s packing 315 bhp with 9.75:1 compression ratio and four-barrel carb. Styling was relatively sedate. The grille was a simple dumbbell shape with four

The '59 Super 88 Fiesta wagon boasted all-new "Linear Look" styling.

Olds' best 1960 seller was the Dynamic 88 Celebrity four-door sedan.

The '61 Dynamic 88 was all-new; 19,878 Holiday coupes were built.

A mid-1961 model was the $4647 Starfire soft top; 7600 were produced.

It wasn't officially listed, but here's a '62 F-85 Jetfire ragtop.

The '62 big Olds looked bulkier; 34,839 Starfire hardtops were made.

widely spaced headlights; rear fenders carried modest fins above oval taillights. All this was good for another fifth-place finish on slightly improved volume of nearly 383,000 units.

Like other makers, Oldsmobile responded to the increasingly segmented market of the '60s with a variety of new models, most of which sold very well. Olds never fell below seventh in industry output and often placed fourth, rising from about 347,000 cars for 1960 to 635,000 at decade's end. Jumping on the 1961 bandwagon for upscale compacts, Olds fielded the F-85, which together with its later Cutlass variations saw progressively higher annual production through 1968. This reflected an astute matching of customer tastes with new products: small V8s for 1961-62, larger compacts with a V6 option for 1964-65, and the high-performance 4-4-2 series from 1964. Each year's junior Olds line was invariably right on the money. The division's standard-size cars also sold consistently well.

The F-85 was one of GM's "second-wave" compacts. Buick, Olds and Pontiac each developed one based on the Y-body 1960 Chevy Corvair, with a common bodyshell and basic dimensions around a conventional front-engine/rear-drive format. Pontiac's Tempest, with its curved driveshaft and rear transaxle, was radical. The F-85 was more conventional. It arrived with a new all-aluminum Buick-built V8 of 215 cid and 155 bhp, which provided reasonable go (0-60 mph in 13 seconds) and economy (18 mpg). In appearance it was a bit less busy than Buick's Special, with a simpler grille but the same sculptured bodysides and crisp roofline.

Naming the F-85 had been a small problem. Starfire was the first choice but seemed to denote a big sporty car. Rockette was suggested, but was thought to project an unwanted image of the Radio City Music Hall dancers. The final choice looked to the Corvette-like F-88 show car of 1954, with "85" selected to avoid

President Eisenhower had to send federal troops to Arkansas in September 1957 to enforce a desegregation order at Little Rock's Central High School. In Lansing, Olds had problems, too, as output fell sharply in 1957 and skidded again in '58.

As in '62, the '63 F-85 Jetfire boasted a turbocharged aluminum V8.

The Starfire soft top was Olds' priciest '63—4401 were produced.

Most popular '64 Ninety-Eight was the Sport Sedan with 24,791 built.

Jetstar 88 was the bargain big Olds for '64; the four door cost $2935.

confusion with big 88s. F-85s were initially offered as standard and Deluxe four-door sedans, pillared club coupes and hatchback four-door wagons, all on a trim 112-inch wheelbase. The Deluxe coupe with bucket seats and luxury trim was called Cutlass, a name that would supplant F-85 entirely after 1972. Plain and Cutlass convertibles arrived in the second year.

Cutlass came with a standard 185-bhp Power-Pack V8 for '62, but greater interest surrounded a new companion model: the turbocharged Jetfire—sharing honors with that year's new Chevy Corvair Monza Spyder as America's first high-volume turbocar. The blower lifted V8 output to 215 bhp—one horsepower per cubic inch—but carbon buildup with certain grades of gas prompted adoption of an unorthodox water injection system (actually, a water/alcohol mix). While the Jetfire was remarkably fast (0-60 mph in about 8.5 seconds, a top speed of 107 mph), the injection system proved unreliable. For 1964, Olds abandoned turbos for a conventional 330-cid V8 of 230-290 bhp and made Buick's new 155-bhp 225-cid V6 the base F-85 engine. The latter ran unchanged until 1966, when an inline six with the same horsepower was substituted.

The junior Oldsmobiles grew larger after 1963 as the public insisted on more impressive compacts. Wheelbase went to 115 inches for '64, when Holiday hardtop coupes were added, then to 112 (two-doors) and 116 inches (four-doors) for 1968. Styling actually improved over time. The original 1961-62 design was made more "important" for '63. The '64 was bulkier but still clean, with a closer resemblance to the big Oldsmobiles. Straight beltlines yielded to more flowing "Coke-bottle" contours for '66, when models expanded once again via hardtop sedans in Cutlass and new F-85 Deluxe trim. Appearance began to be cluttered again after '68, with busier grilles and sometimes clumsy vinyl tops.

The most exciting F-85s were called 4-4-2, which denoted four speeds (400 cubic inches after '65), four-barrel carburetor and dual exhausts. The first 1964 edition was a package option for the Cutlass coupe, convertible and hardtop coupe comprising a 310-bhp 330 V8, heavy-duty suspension and four-speed manual gearbox. The '65 was hotter still with a 345-bhp 400, a debored version of the full-size cars' 425 V8, plus heavy-duty wheels, shocks, springs, rear axle, driveshaft, engine mounts, steering and frame; stabilizer bars front and rear; fat tires; special exterior and interior trim; 11-inch clutch; and a 70-amp battery—all for about $250. Performance was sensational: 0-60 mph in 7.5 seconds, the standing quarter-mile in 17 seconds at 85 mph, top speed of 125 mph. The 4-4-2 proved, as *Motor Trend* magazine said, "that Detroit can build cars that perform, handle and stop, without sacrificing road comfort. . . ."

Each year's 4-4-2 was eagerly awaited. The 400 V8 was never pushed much beyond 350 bhp, but Oldsmobile's mid-size muscle car remained handsome, fast and fun. The '69s had big 4-4-2 numerals on the center grille divider, front fenders, and deck; twin, black horizontal grilles; and a unique bi-level hood with special stripes in contrasting paint. If a bit outlandish, it was no less the performance car it had been in the beginning.

Arriving for 1966 was the most innovative Olds in a generation: the intriguing front-wheel-drive Toronado. Offered only as a hardtop coupe on a 119-inch wheelbase, it represented a clean break with the past—and a commitment to front drive that would become corporate-wide by 1980. It was also a big turnabout for a company that had once panned the front-drive Cord, but GM had planned it well. The Toronado worked, and worked beautifully.

The goal for Toronado was traditional American power combined with outstanding handling and traction. Its 425 V8 was shared with the conventional full-size models but delivered an extra 10 horsepower—385 bhp total—and teamed with a new "split" automatic transmission. A torque converter mounted behind the engine connected via a chain drive and sprocket to a gearbox located remotely under the left cylinder bank. The chain drive, flexible yet virtually unbreakable, saved weight and cut costs. It also resulted in a very compact drivetrain that opened up extra cabin room. Most previous front-drive systems had put the engine behind a front-mounted transmission. Toronado's split transmission allowed the engine to be placed directly over the front wheels for a front/rear weight distribution of 54/46 percent, excellent for a big front-drive car that some said would never work well simply because it was so big.

The '66 4-4-2 convertible retailed for $3118—only 2750 were built. It had a 400-cid, 350-bhp V8 and beefy suspension.

The personal-luxury front-drive Toronado for '66 saw 40,963 built.

Toronado boasted a 425-cid, 385-bhp V8. Prices started at $4617.

The '67 4-4-2 Holiday coupe cost $3015; about 16,500 were built.

Only 515 specially built '68 Hurst/Olds with 455-cid V8 were made.

Toronado styling was as sophisticated as its engineering. The C-pillars fell gently from the roof, there was no beltline aft of the rear windows, the rakish fastback profile terminated in a neatly cropped tail, a curved fuselage was set off by boldly flared wheel-arches, and there was a clean front end with hidden headlamps. Writer Don Vorderman termed the result "logical, imaginative, and totally unique."

That first Toronado was a superb machine. Understeer wasn't excessive for a front-driver, it ran quietly at 100 mph, and top speed was near 135 mph even with the standard final-drive ratio. It was probably the most outstanding single Olds of this decade. Too bad the 1968-70 versions weren't as clean as the 1966-67.

Despite the likes of Toronado and 4-4-2, big cars remained Oldsmobile's stock-in-trade. The 1960-61 line was the usual three series group of price-leader Dynamic 88, extra-performance Super 88, and luxury 98 (increasingly written as "Ninety Eight").

Olds entered the Sixties with 17 models. By 1966, the lineup encompassed 47 models, including two new front-drive personal-luxury Toronados and five muscle-car 4-4-2s. Sales hovered around the 600,000-unit mark in those halcyon days.

The '69 Toronado was 3½ inches longer and had new rear end styling.

Wheelbases remained as introduced for '59: 123 inches for 88s, 126.5 for 98. A smart new bucket-seat Starfire convertible on the Super 88 chassis was added for 1961. The following year it gained a hardtop coupe companion.

The lineup was further expanded for 1964 when the Dynamic series moved up a notch in price to make room for new Jetstar 88s. Among them was a bucket-seat Jetstar I sports coupe with concave backlight, but it lasted only two years. The Super 88 was renamed Delta 88 for 1965; two years later, both Dynamic and Jetstar were replaced by a similar Delmont 88 line, which was then dropped for 1969 in favor of standard, Custom and Royale Deltas on a 124-inch wheelbase. That year's 98 moved up to a 127-inch chassis.

Despite body changes for 1961, '65 and '69, big-Olds styling maintained a consistent look throughout the decade. The "dumbbell" grille shape persisted through 1966, after which the first of Oldsmobile's now-familiar split grilles appeared. Lines were crisp and straight through 1964, then progressively curvier and bulkier. Body styles were the usual assortment through 1963, after which wagons were dropped in deference to new F-85/Cutlass-based Fiesta and Vista Cruiser models, the latter arriving with a raised, glass-in rear superstructure (shared by Buick's contemporary Skylark-based Sportwagons). For 1966, all Olds wagons became Vista Cruisers, a separate series of conventional and high-top models on a special 120-inch wheelbase that grew to 121 inches for 1968.

After a carryover 1960, big-Olds power through 1963 was provided by 394 V8s delivering 250 bhp in the base 88 up to 345 bhp in the '62 Starfire. The low-priced '64 Jetstar shared the F-85's 330 engine. For 1965, the 394 was stroked out to 425 cid, and power gradually rose to 385 bhp for the 1966-67 Toronado. Outputs decreased slightly for 1968-70 with the advent of emission controls. The '67 Delmont was offered with both the 425 and 330 engines. The latter was bored out to 350 cid and 250 bhp for 1968.

Of Oldsmobile's two big bucket-seat performance cars, only the Starfire had any success. Production zoomed from 7600 for debut '61 to over 40,000 for '62. But that would be the peak, output tapering off fast through the end of the series in 1966. Jetstar I was the same idea at a more popular price, but it didn't catch on; only about 22,600 were built over two model years. Though neither was anything like a true sports car (despite Oldsmobile's claims), they were distinctive and handled well for their size.

This '70 Olds 4-4-2 has the W-30 package with 455-cid, 370-bhp V8.

By 1971 the 4-4-2 was a bit tamer because of pollution controls.

The '72 Cutlass Supreme Holiday hardtop was popular: 105,087 units.

Almost 70,000 buyers chose a '72 Ninety-Eight Luxury hardtop sedan.

The '73 Toronado sold for $5441 and Olds dealers sold 55,921 units.

The '72 Toronado Custom boasted a 455-cid V8 with 250 net bhp.

A dollar a pound in '73: the $4221 Delta 88 Royale hardtop coupe.

The all-new '73 Cutlass Supreme Colonnade coupe: 219,857 built.

Like its GM sisters, Oldsmobile's responses to the tumultuous events of the 1970s were quick and usually correct. The 1973-74 OPEC oil embargo and the resulting energy crisis dramatically highlighted the need for smaller, thriftier cars in every size and price range, which Olds needed as much as any medium-price make. At the start of the decade its smallest models were two-door intermediates. Yet by 1980 it was offering no fewer than three model lines on wheelbases of less than 110 inches, plus more sensibly sized full-size cars and the trimmest Toronado ever. It's worth noting, however, that GM's decision to downsize its entire fleet came well in advance of the fuel shortage. That the first of the new breed appeared barely two years after the crisis had passed was merely happy coincidence.

But Oldsmobile's high sales success in the '70s was no coincidence. Instead, it reflected canny marketing. In many years the division ranked number three behind Ford and Chevrolet, remarkable considering its products were basically corporate designs available under other nameplates for the same or less money. What undoubtedly attracted buyers was the extra prestige of the Olds badge on more nicely trimmed cars priced only a little upstream of comparable Chevys and Pontiacs and slightly below equivalent Buicks. The full-size B-body Delta 88 and the mid-size A-body Cutlass were far and away the division's biggest money spinners in these years.

The Cutlass firmly established itself in the '70s as one of America's favorites, often topping the individual model line sales charts. Although it remained essentially an upmarket Chevy Chevelle/Malibu, it always offered a broad range of model and trim choices at competitively attractive prices. Oldsmobile's more "important" styling was another plus.

The posh, top-of-the line Supreme was the most popular of this popular line, having debuted as a single 1966 hardtop sedan that expanded into a full, separate series the following year. By 1973 the two-door alone was accounting for nearly 220,000 sales, greater than the combined total for other Cutlasses and Oldsmobile's compacts. Most buyers specified V8s, especially in the early '70s, though sixes were available beginning with the '75s. Coupes far outsold sedans and wagons in most years.

With all this, the downsized 108.1-inch-wheelbase Cutlass/Cutlass Supreme of 1978 must have seemed very brave, but buyers took to it as enthusiastically as ever. The sole exception was the 1978-79 "aeroback" two- and four-door sedans, which were too dumpy for even Oldsmobile's basically conservative buy-

Oldsmobile's '73 compact was the Nova-based Omega.

The '74 Delta 88 Royale hardtop coupe cost $4584—27,515 were sold.

Despite problems in meeting federal safety and emissions rules, Olds muscled its way into third place for most of the '70s, ousting Pontiac. Olds' success was due to the Cutlass, which was often the best-selling single nameplate in the U.S.

The '75 Hurst/Olds was the most popular up to '75 with 2535 made. Built off the Cutlass Supreme hardtop coupe, it cost $1095 extra.

ers. Conventional notchback styling was thus applied to the four-door for 1980 and found immediate acceptance.

The enthusiast's Cutlass, the 4-4-2, fell on hard times in the '70s, as did every other Detroit muscle machine. The last of the traditional high-power models appeared for 1971, a convertible and Holiday hardtop coupe packing the division's big 455 V8. Sales were meager. GM's redesigned 1973 "Colonnade" intermediates saw the 4-4-2 reduced to a mere option package as Olds tried a new approach with the Salon, an American-style sporty sedan series somewhat akin to Pontiac's Grand Am. It failed to catch on, though the name kept popping up in later years in both the mid-size and compact lines. You could still get the 4-4-2 package as late as 1978, but by then it was more for show than go.

Olds followed Buick back to compacts in 1973—and with basically the same car. Lansing called it Omega, one of three badge-engineered derivatives of the 111-inch-wheelbase X-body platform introduced with the 1968 Chevy Nova. Though it sold a respectable 50,000 units in its first season, Omega was never a big winner. Sales actually fell for 1975 despite a handsome new outer skin and an improved chassis. When the X-bodies were shrunk around more space-efficient front-drive mechanicals for 1980, Omega vied with Pontiac's Phoenix for low spot on the sales totem pole, though a raft of highly publicized reliability and safety problems hardly helped.

A similar fate befell another "company car," the subcompact Starfire. Introduced for 1975, this was Olds's version of the Vega-based Chevrolet Monza, with the same 2+2 hatchback coupe body and the 231-cid V6 found in Buick's near-identical Skyhawk. Though the name was once attached to the largest and most opulent Oldsmobiles, this 97-inch-wheelbase Starfire was the smallest Olds in living memory, and should have done well in the post-energy crisis market. But big-car sales were on the rise again, and Starfire captured a mere six percent of division sales in its first season. It wouldn't do much better in later years.

Upper-middle-class luxury remained Oldsmobile's mainstay in the '70s, and its big cars never strayed from it. What they did stray

Oldsmobile turned out 55,339 Ninety-Eight Regency sedans for '76.

The GT package on the '76 Starfire was mainly an appearance option.

from, eventually, was needless bulk, which became an increasing liability in the more energy-conscious climate of the late-'70s. GM bowed the largest full-size cars in its history for 1971, so Oldsmobile's B-body Delta 88 and C-body Ninety-Eight acquired extra inches and pounds on wheelbases unchanged from '69. Big-block 455 V8s prevailed, but were progressively detuned in line with stricter emissions standards. Wagons in this design generation had an interesting "clamshell" liftgate and tailgate that retracted electrically into the body like a roll-top desk. Olds shared this with the big Chevy, Pontiac and Buick wagons. Unfortunately, it didn't always work well.

As with Cutlass, the full-size Olds lost nothing in sales appeal when downsized for 1977. If anything, they sold even better, no doubt due to improved fuel economy and maneuvering ease with no sacrifice in passenger room and ride comfort. Wheelbases contracted to 116 inches for Delta and the Custom Cruiser wagon and to 119 inches for Ninety-Eight, sizes that would persist into the late '80s. Substantial weight reductions allowed the use of 350- and 403-cid V8s without compromising performance. Diesel V8s and Buick's gas V6 would be offered as standard or optional from 1978. Model choices changed several times through the mid-'80s, but sedans and coupes usually ran to base, Royale and Royale Brougham Deltas and plain, Luxury and Regency Ninety-Eights.

The personal-luxury Toronado evolved through the '70s more or less in parallel with the senior Oldsmobiles. For 1971, it also became as large as it would ever be, changing from mild sportiness to oversized opulence on a 122-inch wheelbase. Styling also changed—mostly for the worse—becoming more contrived and Cadillac-like through the end of this series in 1978.

Two Toronado styling developments bear mention, though. One was a throwback to the early-postwar Studebaker Starlight coupes, a huge rear window that wrapped around to the sides in a near unbroken sweep on the XS and XSR models of 1976-77. More laudable was a second set of brake lights just below the rear window, an item later mandated by the government for all cars sold in the U.S.

Though the Toronado experience probably helped GM in its big switch to front drive that began in the late '70s, the car would probably have sold just as well with rear drive. After 1973, when sales topped 50,000, Toronado volume was never exceptional, with 20,000 units a year considered good. The new downsized generation of 1979 was much closer to the original concept, riding a 114-inch wheelbase and powered by adequately potent small-block V8s. It immediately garnered a bit over 50,000 orders, then around 42,000 a year through 1985.

Oldsmobile's fortunes in the '80s were decidedly mixed. Lansing had sold a record 1.14 million cars for '77 and nearly as many for '78 and '79. With the second energy crisis that began in late '79 came a deep national recession that kept sales well below the million mark through 1983. But then Olds bounced back to set another record: a smashing 1.17 million for 1985. In the yearly production derby the division continued to run its usual third, just ahead of Buick, but it also managed to beat Ford for second spot in 1983 and '85. Yet by 1987, Olds was down to below 671,000 units, its worst total since the mid-'70s, and Pontiac had regained third.

What happened? One problem was that Oldsmobile's image had become confused with Buick's—no surprise given similar model lines that evolved pretty much in lockstep since the mid-'70s at least. Another problem was Pontiac, which in the early '80s began offering the kind of performance-oriented machinery that had served it so well in the '60s. By that point, Oldsmobile's only real marketing asset seemed to be the Cutlass name, and even that had lost a lot of its original panache by being indiscriminately applied to too many models. Olds also suffered from GM's policies of "identicar" styling and divisional duplicates of most every line in the corporate stable.

A W-29 4-4-2 option was available for $169 on the 1977 Cutlass.

At $8134, the '77 Toronado Brougham found favor with 31,371 buyers.

The '77 Toronado XSR was rarer and pricier: $11,132 and 2714 built.

Cutlass Supreme was downsized for '78; output reached 240,917 units.

Oldsmobile continued to expand its lineup in the '70s. The compact Omega arrived for 1973, just ahead of the late-1973 Arab Oil Embargo, and was followed up with the subcompact '75 Starfire. They were based on the Chevy Nova and Monza.

The all-new 1979 Toronado was downsized to a 114-inch wheelbase and weight pared by 900 pounds to 3731. Olds built 50,056 units.

The Delta 88 Royale sedan saw 152,526 units produced for 1979.

A lowered front end and halogen headlamps were '80 Cutlass features.

Oldsmobile's front-wheel-drive compact Omega debuted for 1980. A SportOmega package added $657 to the coupe's $6221 base price.

The Cutlass Supreme received a mid-life facelift for '81, improving aerodynamics by 15 percent. The Brougham listed at $7703.

The '80 Omega, here a Brougham, was 750 pounds lighter than the '79.

After 1980, the Cutlass Salon fastback disappeared due to slow sales.

It took a long time (cynics said too long) but GM finally addressed these problems with the wholesale corporate reorganization hatched by chairman Roger Smith in 1984. Aside from a return to distinct divisional styling identities, its most significant aspect for Olds involved swapping roles with Buick. Flint would return to middle-class luxury while Lansing renewed emphasis on sporting luxury as a sort of GM equivalent to BMW. Evidence of the new order was only beginning to appear at this writing, so it's too soon to say whether things will improve for either division. Still, the return to interesting cars in the great "Rocket Action" tradition of the '50s and '60s must have heartened Lansing loyalists.

They certainly didn't have much to cheer about through 1987. Though Olds made sporadic stabs at sport in this period, workaday intermediates and full-size cars remained its bread and butter.

Surprisingly perhaps, given the difficult early-'80s market, the big rear-drive Delta 88 and Ninety-Eight took over as the division's top-sellers through mid-decade, attracting a quarter-million buyers through 1982 and over 340,000 in 1983 and '84. Both were then put on smaller front-drive platforms (except wagons, which stood pat) as part of GM's second-wave downsizing effort: the Ninety-Eight on 1985's new C-body (shared with Buick Electra), the 88 on the following year's H-body (shared with Buick LeSabre and the '86 Pontiac Bonneville). As with the '77s, these smaller big cars sold just as well as their predecessors. Aside from styling and equipment details, these Oldsmobiles, both front and rear drive, differed little from counterpart Buicks.

Next on the Lansing hit parade was the mid-size Cutlass, which in this period involves two distinct lines: continuations of the 1978-vintage rear-drive series, called Supreme after 1981, and their erstwhile front-drive successor, the A-body Cutlass Ciera, new for '82. Each accounted for upwards of 200,000-300,000 sales in

A new model in the '80 Olds lineup was the Delta 88 Royale Brougham.

President Jimmy Carter created a new Cabinet-level Energy Department in 1977. That was the same year GM started its massive downsizing program. The first to go on a diet were the full-size models, followed by the intermediates in 1978.

Top full-size '82 Olds was the $13,343 Ninety-Eight Regency Brougham.

The '82 Omega featured a new sloping front end for better gas mileage.

most years. Supreme coupes received a sloped-nose "aero" facelift for 1981 (similar to the full-size cars' 1980 redo), then carried on alone after sedans and wagons were dropped for '87 in deference to Ciera models. Only one major appearance change occurred through the end of this series in December 1987: flush-mount "composite" headlamps from '86. Signalling the arrival of a new front-drive Supreme, the last rear-drive '88s were called Supreme Classic (*a la* Coca-Cola).

Of interest to collectors are a trio of low-volume muscle-car revivals based on the rear-drive Supreme coupe: a 15th anniversary Hurst/Olds commemorative for 1983, its similar 1984 follow-up, and a reborn 4-4-2 option package offered for 1985-87. The H/0s wore special i.d. and modest decklid spoilers. All three packed a special four-barrel, 180-bhp version of the 307 Olds small-block V8 and were quite fast all things considered. Their mild engine tuning would have seemed laughable in the '60s, but of course, nobody had to be concerned with corporate average fuel economy in those days.

CAFE was a definite motivation for the Ciera, a smaller mid-size Olds. It was much like Buick's new-wave Century, derived from the front-drive X-car design and initially offered as a notchback coupe and sedan; glass-hatch wagons arrived for 1984. Engines were the same too, including an optional 231-cid Buick V6 that made for much sprightlier performance than the mid-range 173-cid option. For mid-1986, the Ciera coupe gained a measure of distinction over its corporate cousins by taking on a smoother, slightly abbreviated roofline. Sedans got a similarly rounded backlight for 1989, when a new 160-bhp 3.3-liter V6 replaced the 231 option.

Both Supreme and Ciera typically offered a choice of standard and fancy Brougham trim. There were also sporting versions—GT and Euro-style ES Cieras through 1987, Salon and Calais Su-

Toronado for '82 came with a V6, or optional V8 or diesel V8. Retail prices started at $14,462; the ill-fated diesel added $825.

Four-door sedans and a wagon joined the '82 Cutlass Supreme lineup.

There were five Delta 88s for '83, here a Royale Brougham coupe.

The Hurst/Olds for 1983 was based on the Cutlass Supreme Calais two-door coupe. It featured a 180-bhp version of Olds' 307 V8.

Hurst/Olds sported a four-speed automatic with Hurst "Lightning Rod" shifter, special suspension and tires. Only 2500 were made.

Late 1982 saw the U.S. economy reeling under the weight of the highest unemployment rate since 1940, 10.8 percent. Olds, fighting for sales, brought out the mid-size Cutlass Ciera and, in the spring of '82, the subcompact Firenza.

Olds Delta 88 for 1984 ranged in price from $9939 to $10,499.

Oldsmobile's A-body front-drive '85 Cutlass Ciera started at $9307.

The '88 Calais sold for $9283; the GT package cost $1350 extra.

A 2.8-liter V6 and firm suspension were found on the '86 Firenza GT.

The '85 Delta 88, here a Royale Brougham, had V6, V8, or diesel power.

Ninety-Eight was all-new for '85, featuring a front-wheel-drive V6.

The new '86 Delta 88 shrunk 22 inches and shed over 400 pounds.

Toronado for '86 was 18 inches shorter and 550 pounds lighter.

preme coupes—all with fortified suspensions and less traditional interiors. From 1988, the enthusiast's Ciera was retitled International Series but retained the usual black-finish exterior trim, bigger wheel/tire package, and special body addenda (front and rear spoilers, later matched by rocker-panel skirts).

Somehow, Oldsmobile was less successful with small cars than Buick, let alone Chevrolet. Perhaps they weren't sufficiently different enough or maybe Oldsmobile customers just couldn't resist the bigger jobs. Whatever the reason, Lansing's littlest cars were slow movers. The front-drive X-body Omega, for example, peaked at nearly 148,000 for 1981, then tailed off to below 54,000 in two years. Lack of change didn't help, and it was summarily dismissed after 1984.

The Firenza fared even worse. Arriving in March 1982 to replace the Starfire, Lansing's version of GM's front-drive 101.2-inch-wheelbase J-body design failed to attract more than about

45,000 customers in most years (except 1984, a creditable 82,500) even though Olds tried most everything it could think of to sell it. By 1988 the Firenza had offered all the J-body types, sporty GT and ES variants, optional V6 and turbo-four engines, normally aspirated overhead-valve and overhead-cam fours, and a confusing procession of price-leader and luxury models. But nothing seemed to work, and Olds gave up even as other divisions continued their Js.

It was no great loss, though, because 1985 brought a more saleable small Olds in the new N-body Calais, retitled Cutlass Calais from 1988. Sized between Firenza and Omega on a 103.4-inch wheelbase, it bowed as a rounded, short-deck coupe in two versions: base and—just to confuse things—Supreme. Four-door sedans were added for 1986. There was a lot of J-car engineering under the "modern formal" styling, and initial engine choices were the Ciera's familiar 2.5-liter Pontiac-built four and 3.0-liter Buick V6. Even so, customers generally liked this new bottle of old wine, snapping up 100,000-plus in the first year and over 150,000 of the '86s—volume about midway between that of the similar Pontiac Grand Am and Buick Skylark/Somerset.

For 1988, Calais coupes and sedans grouped into base S, luxury SL and sporty International Series models (the last replacing a previous GT package option), but the big news was the first twincam, 16-valve four-cylinder engine in American production, the Quad-4. Designed and built by Olds and offered as an across-the-board Calais option, it delivered 150 slightly rough and noisy horsepower, and was claimed to be capable of much more. Olds proved it by adding a tuned 160-bhp version for 1989, but a more sensible option was that year's new 3.3-liter derivative of the 173-cid Chevy V6. Replacing the 3.0, it produced a still-ample 160 bhp—and more torque than even the high-output Quad-4. As partial fill-ins for the now-departed Firenza, Olds fielded prosaically named Value Leader models with less standard equipment and restricted options but lower prices.

The pioneering Toronado was 20 years old in 1986, and the new fourth-generation E-body design that arrived that model year should have been cause for celebration. In many ways it was: 18 inches trimmer and 550 pounds slimmer on a new 107.5-inch wheelbase; just as quick despite switching from V8s to the Buick 231-cid V6, the first Toro without eight cylinders; clean and contemporary in appearance, with hidden headlamps for the first time since 1969. There was even a second edition aimed straight at enthusiasts: the Trofeo (pronounced tro-FAY-oh, "trophy" in Spanish and Italian), with a more subdued exterior, leather interior, and an uprated "handling" suspension.

Yet for all that, buyers just didn't respond. Toronado had long been eclipsed in sales by its Buick Riviera and Cadillac Eldorado cousins. The '86 was no different, except that sales were only half of what they had been: fewer than 16,000 in the debut season versus 42,000-plus for the last of the third-generation cars. The Riv and Eldo fared little better. Critics blamed this poor performance on styling that was uncomfortably close to that of the much cheaper Calais and a package that had been downsized a little too far for most personal-luxury buyers.

Sadly, there was little Olds could do to improve matters right away. The '87s thus received only new engine mounts plus roller valve lifters that helped lift the V6 from 140 to 150 bhp. A revised "3800" engine gave the '88s another 15 bhp, a new anti-lock brake system (ABS) devised by GM and the German Alfred Teves company became optional, and there were minor mechanical and ergonomic changes. More details were attended to for '89 and the Trofeo came with more standard equipment, including ABS. But while Buick and Cadillac tried to make their E-bodies look more impressive, Olds didn't monkey much with the Toro's clean, taut '86 styling—admirable for aesthetics, if not sales.

But by now, GM had learned the folly of fielding too many cars that looked too much like each other, and the all-new front-drive

Olds showcased its new Quad 4 engine in a few late '87 Calais GTs.

The Grande package added $975 to the $18,388 Brougham coupe.

It took $12,095 to buy an '87 Cutlass Ciera Brougham Cruiser wagon.

The all-new front-drive '88 Cutlass Supreme featured a 2.8-liter V6.

Olds ads in the late '80s said, "This is not your father's Oldsmobile." The all-new '88 Cutlass Supreme looked totally up-to-date and different than its Buick and Pontiac siblings. Olds boasted that future styling would be more unique.

A $24,470 Euro-style Touring Sedan was based on the '88 Ninety-Eight. It had a tighter suspension and the new 165-bhp 3800 V6.

Trofeo was the sportier Toronado for 1988. It listed at $22,695.

This 1989 Cutlass Supreme is the sportier International Series.

The '89 Cutlass Calais boasted a 180-bhp HO version of the Quad 4.

The '89 Cutlass Supreme boasted a 180-bhp HO version of the Quad 4.

Cutlass Supreme that bowed in Oldsmobile's 90th-anniversary year was striking proof. Like the 1988 Buick Regal and Pontiac Grand Prix, it was built on the W-body/GM10 platform but had its own roof styling and outer sheetmetal so that it would never be confused with the others (nor they with the Supreme). Highlights included a low, tapered nose, slim split grille, curvy flanks, large wheel openings, crisply clipped tail, and a glassy notchback superstructure with semi-concealed C-posts and slim pillars.

The front-drive Supreme's initial powerteam was a five-speed manual transaxle driven by the workhorse 173-cid Chevy V6 in 125-bhp port-injected form; for 1989, cars with optional automatic received a 3.1-liter/191-cid enlargement boasting 140 bhp. At the same time, ABS was made optional to fortify the standard all-disc brakes. Model choices comprised Oldsmobile's now-usual range of base, SL and International Series. The last came with quick-ratio power steering, tuned exhaust, full instrumentation and, for '89, cassette tape player, power door mirrors and central locking.

Because buyers had been conditioned by now to expect rebates or low-interest financing offers even on new models, the front-drive Supreme got off to a disappointing start, sales lagging somewhat until Olds offered incentives. Nevertheless, the newest Olds seemed to announce that GM's "innovator" division would again be innovative after too many years of trading on past glories and a few well-known names—happy news indeed.

PACKARD

For many people, Packard was, in its heyday, "the supreme combination of all that is fine in motor-cars." Technologically, it may not have been the "Standard of the World," but sociologically it was the Standard of America—even for the millions of would-be buyers who could never afford one. In 1929, more people owned stock in Packard than any other company save General Motors, and there were far more Packard stockholders than Packard owners.

Packard got its start in Warren, Ohio, in 1899 because James Ward Packard figured he could build a better car than the Winton he had purchased. The first car was a one-cylinder model with automatic ignition advance. James B. Joy took the company over in 1901, and in 1903 he moved it to Detroit. Also that year, Packard debuted its first four. But Packard probably established its great renown with its 48-bhp Six of 1912. Then it leap-frogged Cadillac's new 1915 V8 with a V12, the fabled Twin Six that Packard introduced to an astonished public on May 1, 1915. Over 35,000 Twin Sixes were built through 1923, the year a new straight eight arrived to replace it. Packard did produce a less prestigious Six beginning in 1921, but that disappeared in 1928 and eight-cylinder engines maintained the Packard reputation from then on.

For a builder devoted single-mindedly to luxury cars, Packard compiled a remarkable production record. It had regularly outproduced Cadillac from 1925 on, even though its GM rival had help from LaSalle beginning in 1927. With the exceptions of 1931, 1932, and 1934, Packard volume continued to exceed Cadillac/LaSalle output until World War II. But Packard's post-1934 production rested not on all-out luxury cars, but mainly on middle-priced models, especially the One Twenty, introduced for 1935. It literally saved the company from the Depression.

The 1929-36 lines were composed almost entirely of straight eights. Packard did not observe model years in this period, instead using a "series" number that dated from a practice begun in 1923. Historians have since applied model year designations to each series for ease of recognition, and 1930, for example, coincides with the Seventh Series.

The Seventh Series hierarchy began with the Eight, which had the least pretentious bodies on a relatively short wheelbase. Next came the dashing Speedster Eight, offered as a lithe-looking boattail and standard roadster, as well as phaeton, victoria, and sedan. Speedsters cost the world ($5200 to $6000 in 1930), and only 183 were built in 1929-30. A 385-cubic-inch engine powered the long-wheelbase Custom and Deluxe Eights, generally seen with closed bodies but also available in phaeton, roadster, and convertible styles from Packard and various custom coachbuilders. You can get a better idea of these cars' true cost by considering that $5000 would buy a very nice home in those days.

The 1931 Eighth Series comprised two engines in three model lines, Standard, Custom, and Deluxe Eight. The Eight now includ-

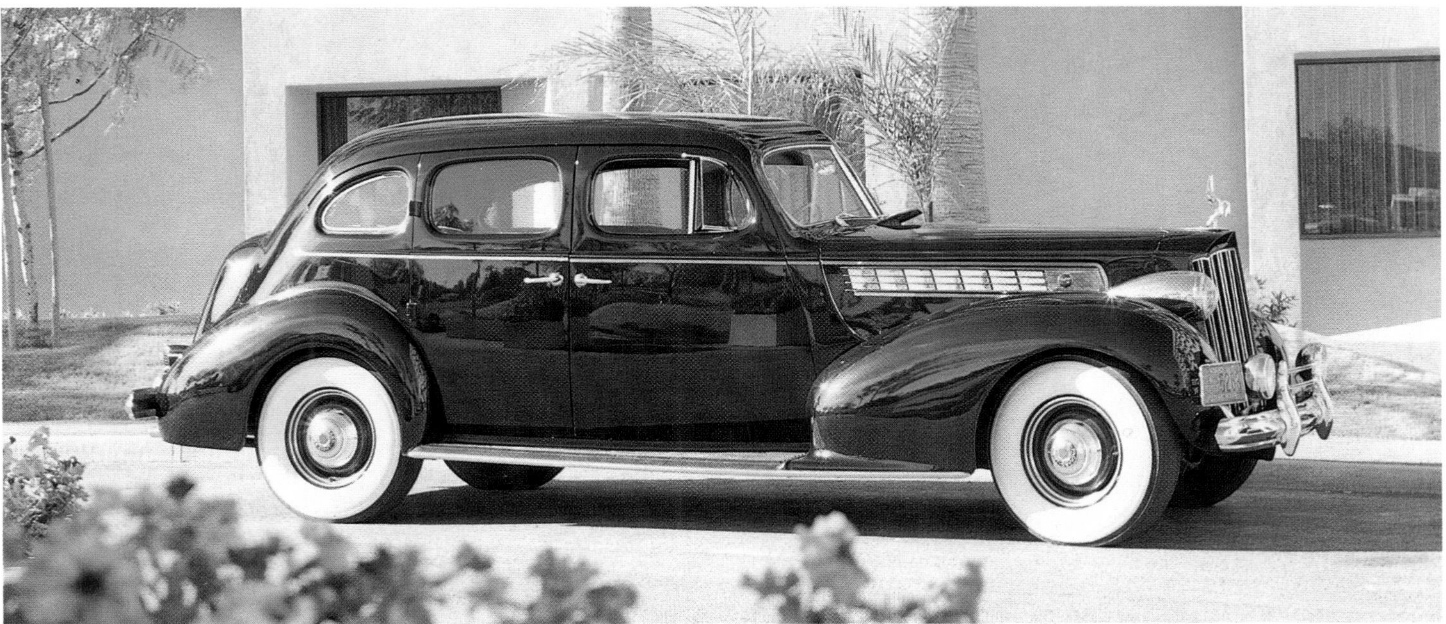

The 1939 Packard Super 8 Touring Sedan weighed 3930 pounds and cost $1732. It was powered by a 130-bhp 320-cid straight eight.

Packard saw output plummet to 4803 units for 1933. Unable to sustain itself on that kind of volume, Packard was forced to enter the medium-price field with the 1935 One Twenty. It saved the company but blemished the exclusivity of its name.

The 1940 Packard sported a narrower grille and lowered headlights.

Packard engines for 1940 came in three sizes: 100, 120, and 160 bhp.

This impressive '40 Custom Super 8 One Eighty was bodied by Rollson.

ed a range of "Individual Custom" models on a 134.5-inch wheelbase with a convertible sedan and victoria by Dietrich plus Packard's own cabriolets, landaulets, and town cars. Mechanically, the Eighth Series gained an automatic Bijur chassis lubrication system and more power via modified intake and exhaust passages similar to those seen on the 1930 Speedster Eight. Packard also designed a quick-shift mechanism for its four-speed gearbox to reduce gear-changing effort, then switched to a three-speed all-synchromesh transmission for 1932.

Styling for 1932 was similar to 1930-31, except that bodies were lower for a more streamlined appearance. Two significant Ninth Series models were the Twin Six and Light Eight. The former bore no relationship to the 1915-23 12-cylinder cars. It had actually been designed for a front-wheel-drive layout that had been shelved before production. Though a fairly low numerical axle ratio was theoretically available, most of the V12 models had numerical ratios of 4.41:1 or higher, intended for smooth, relatively shift-free motoring rather than high performance. Packard claimed a sustained 100 mph was well within the capabilities of the Twin Six engine, but that was under test conditions, and the V12 usually ran out of breath at about 90 mph in stock tune. At 60 or 70 mph, however, it was whisper quiet and highly refined.

Twin Sixes and Twelves of 1932-34 shared bodies and wheelbases with the upper Eight series. Despite their prestige and billing as the ultimate Packards, the factory-bodied V12s were originally only $100-$200 more expensive than the DeLuxe Eights. The price gap grew wider as time went on, however, and custom-bodied Twelves cost considerably more. The 1932 Dietrich sport phaeton body listed for $6500 on the V12 chassis, compared to $5800 on the DeLuxe Eight platform. In 1935, when "senior model" production was consolidated to make space for the high-volume One Twenty, the Twelve shifted to 139- and 144-inch wheelbases. Super Eights were also offered in these sizes and a slightly smaller wheelbase, too, with the same general range of body styles. Custom offerings decreased as coachbuilders went out of business or were bought out by other companies.

As an independent, Packard didn't have the luxury of solid financial backing from a mighty parent like GM or Ford. Therefore, it had to introduce new products more suitable for the Depression-era market somewhat earlier than Cadillac or Lincoln. As a result, the Light Eight—Packard's first car in the medium-price field—arrived two years before Cadillac's smaller, cheaper LaSalle and four years before Lincoln's Zephyr. It used the Eight's 320-cid engine, rated for 1932 at 110 bhp, and had its own 127.6-inch-wheelbase chassis. The Light Eight was a quality product, built with the same meticulous care as other Packards. It was faster than the Eight, owing to its lighter chassis, but it was chunky looking because of its shorter wheelbase. Unfortunately, low prices made this line more minus than plus. It cost almost as much to produce as the Eight yet sold for $500-$850 less, so the factory was lucky to break even on the Light Eight. The range was dropped for 1933, and company president Alvan Macauley began searching the ranks of GM executives for someone wise in the ways of high-volume production who could help the firm develop a profitable middle-priced car.

Packard lost $7 million in 1932, much of it on the Light Eight, then realized a $500,000 profit in 1933. Its proportion of sales in the high-priced field that year was 38 percent, well above Cadillac's share. Trouble was, there was hardly a field left. Macauley's recruiting campaign was vigorous. He ended up with Max Gilman, "that hard-boiled guy in New York," who had started out as a Brooklyn truck salesman in 1919; and George T. Christopher, a production expert enticed out of retirement from General Motors. Gilman astutely built the image of a forthcoming new Packard, while Christopher overhauled most of the factory for high-volume production, modernizing it from end to end. The fruit of their efforts was announced on January 6, 1935: the Packard One Twenty.

The Packard Darrin One Eighty convertible sold for $4593 in 1940. Built in an old Auburn plant, about 50 units were constructed.

The Packard One Eighty Formal Sedan retailed for $3090 in 1941.

At $1753, the '41 One Twenty convertible was good value for money.

The One Twenty was a dramatic departure from Packard tradition. A bit more than half as costly as the unmourned Light Eight, it was aimed precisely at all those people who had always wanted a Packard but had never been able to afford one. As such, it retained traditional Packard hallmarks, like the ox-yoke radiator/hood styling, red hexagon wheel hub emblems, and conservative but elegant body lines. The engine, designed largely by former GM people, was a straightforward L-head eight with five main bearings, a 2.75-inch crankshaft, counterweighted overlapping journals, a heavily ribbed block, ample water jacketing, and individual exhaust ports for each cylinder. It was easy on gas, a smooth performer, and granite strong. The 1936 and later One Twenty models had a longer stroke that yielded more power. Typical performance for these cars was 85 mph top speed and 0-60 mph in less than 20 seconds—pretty decent for any 3500-pound car in the prewar years. In 1936, a convertible sedan bearing "Dietrich" body plates was added to the One Twenty line. (Ray Dietrich personally had nothing to do with it, but his name had been owned by Murray since the early '30s.) A wagon, three DeLuxe closed models, and a long-wheelbase sedan and limousine appeared the next year.

Packard sold One Twentys like nickel hamburgers. The company soared to ninth place in production for calendar year 1935 with over 52,000 units. Output hit about 81,000 in 1936, and 110,000 in 1937. The 1938 recession slowed volume to about 50,000, but production picked up again and remained strong until World War II.

That 1937 production record was also due to the success of another, even less expensive offering, the One Ten, known as the Packard Six in 1938-39. This model had a One Twenty-derived engine and initially rode a 115-inch wheelbase. Displacement was up to 245 cid and wheelbase to 122 inches for 1938-39, although horsepower remained unchanged. The lineup was similar to the One Twenty, but prices were some $150 lower model for model,

Traditional styling was a Packard hallmark before World War II and its yoke-collar grille was known the world over. Packard finally modernized its styling with the sleek mid-1941 Clipper, the only Packard that emerged after the war.

The '47 Custom Super Clipper carried styling similar to the '42.

"Pregnant elephant" is what some critics called the newly styled '48.

and the One Ten outsold the One Twenty by a ratio of 13 to 10 in 1937. Its six was not as smooth or powerful as the eight-cylinder One Twenty engine, but it did offer excellent gas mileage and adequate performance.

With the Fifteenth Series One Ten for 1937, Packard completed its transformation from a builder of exclusive, luxurious, virtually handmade cars to a company with production volume in the industry's top ten. The development most responsible for this change—and the loss of Packard's prestige image—was probably the One Ten. The Light Eight wasn't around long enough to affect anybody's thinking much, and the One Twenty, though priced some $1200 less than a Standard Eight, was still very much a Packard in appearance and road behavior. Indeed, the Eight completely disappeared after 1936 and its 320-cid engine went into the Super Eight, with the 385-cid engine phased out. The One Twenty itself then became simply the Packard Eight. But the small, rather dumpy-looking One Ten/Packard Six was by no stretch of the imagination a Packard in the traditional sense. Perhaps the company had become too greedy for sales, too committed to George Christopher's philosophy of producing more and more cars. At any rate, Cadillac took over as the volume and prestige leader in the high-dollar market by the end of the decade. Many people who would not have been seen in one years before were now buying Cadillacs instead of the big Packards, which had been upstaged by the firm's own Sixes and One Twenty models that looked almost the same, at least from the front.

As Packard entered the 1939 model year, the transformation of the product line was almost complete. The Six started out at an even $1000 for the business coupe (Fords and Chevys were in the $600-$900 price range) while the standard wheelbase One Twentys sold for $1245 to $1700. Further upmarket, the Super Eight blanketed the $1650 to $2294 bracket, while the Twelve topped the line at $4155 to $8355. The last was in its last final year, however, marking the end of the era of truly elegant coachbuilt

Only 230 Custom Eight seven-passenger sedans and limos were built for '48. They rode a 148-inch wheelbase and cost almost $5000.

The '49 Super Eight convertible saw a production run of 1237 units.

Top Packard in 1952 was the $3797 Patrician 400—3975 were built.

Packards. A total of 5744 Twelves were built during its eight-year reign.

The 1940-41 cars were among the most interesting and beautiful in the company's long history. The Packard Six was now designated One Ten and sold in an attractive price range ($867 to $1104). Six body styles were offered including five-passenger club coupe and convertible coupe. The One Twenty series included five deluxe-trim coupes and sedans. One exception to this competitive price structure was the custom-built Darrin Victoria, listed at $3819. An exquisite sporting soft-top with cutdown doors and raked windshield, it was the work of stylist Howard "Dutch" Darrin, and is one of the few One Twentys accorded "Classic" status by the Classic Car Club of America (CCCA). The One Ten was the smallest Packard in a generation, and rode a 122-inch wheelbase. Its 100-horsepower six displaced 245.3 cubic inches. The One Twenty sat on a 127-inch wheelbase and was powered by a 120-bhp, 282-cid straight eight.

Even though Packard dropped the V12 for 1940, it nonetheless retained an impressive line of Super and Custom Eights. Styling remained traditional: an upright, slope-shouldered radiator and chiseled hood. The shortest chassis with a 127-inch wheelbase, was reserved for coupes, convertibles, and sedans. A touring sedan rode a 138-inch stretch, and a long sedan and limousine spanned 148 inches. Custom coachwork was offered for the highest-priced models, two Darrins, a Custom Eight Victoria (priced only about $800 higher than the One Twenty Darrin), and a sleek, four-door convertible sedan priced at $6332, making it the most expensive of all. Other specials were the Rollston all-weather cabriolet, $4473, and town car, $4599. But such exotic models accounted for only a fraction of total output. Of 98,000 cars, only 5662 were Super Eights and just 1900 were Customs. The rest were One Tens and One Twentys. Production was lower for 1941.

Packard's first big departure from traditional square-rigged styling came with the '41 Clipper. Designed by Darrin and modified by Packard's own Werner Gubitz, the Clipper had flowing fenders, hidden running boards, a tapered tail, and a narrow vertical grille. It came in only one body style, a four-door sedan priced at $1420—squarely between the One Twenty and One Sixty. The Clipper used a 127-inch wheelbase and a 125-bhp, 282-cid straight eight.

The same range of One Tens and One Twentys was placed at the lower end of the '41 line, while the Super Eight (now called One Sixty) and Custom Super (One Eighty) were the posher models. Again, Packard offered Darrin, Rollston, and LeBaron custom coachwork. LeBaron built long-wheelbase sedans and limousines and the beautifully formal Sport Brougham. An Electromatic Clutch, which eliminated the need to use the clutch pedal (but did require the driver to shift gears), was offered for only $37.50. Power for Supers and Customs came from a silky smooth straight eight, a 356-cid unit that developed 160 bhp at 3800 rpm. With nine main bearings and a crankshaft that weighed 105 pounds, the 356 was impressively quiet and powerful, capable of propelling some of the lighter models to well over 100 mph. It was used in Supers and Customs through 1947, in the Custom only through 1950, and was then dropped.

The Clipper was popular, and over 16,000 were sold in 1941. Accordingly, Packard converted almost entirely to Clipper styling for 1942. The only exceptions were some One Sixty and One Eighty models, plus convertibles and commercial vehicles.

During the war, Packard built Rolls-Royce Merlin aircraft engines and other power units for military vehicles and PT boats. It was the only independent to emerge from the war completely free of debt. But then a significant decision was made—one that would adversely affect the company's future. Instead of reverting to luxury cars only, Packard continued to sell middle-price models in the One Twenty tradition. While such cars had been necessary before

Packard's sporty 1953 Caribbean was limited to a run of 750 units.

The '53 Patrician four door listed at $3740; 7456 were produced.

Packard's restyled, slabsided 1948 model looked bulbous and ungainly to some; it became known as the "pregnant elephant." Engineering remained top-notch, however—Packard was the only independent to engineer and build an automatic transmission.

Only 400 Caribbean personal-luxury convertibles were sold in '54. They were mounted on a 122-inch wheelbase and sold for $6100.

The '54 Packard convertible listed at $3935, but only 863 were sold.

Output reached 1189 units for the '54 Pacific hardtop. Price: $3827.

the war, they were not afterward and seriously damaged Packard's image. After 1945, Cadillac found it could sell anything on wheels, kept the cheaper LaSalle buried, and built high-priced cars only. Soon, it replaced Packard as the nation's premier luxury make.

The 1946 and '47 models were identical in all respects except for serial numbers. The low-priced '46 Clipper Six sedan ($1730) and coupe ($1680) looked exactly like the Clipper Eight series ($1802 and up), which also included a DeLuxe sedan and club sedan. All used a 120-inch wheelbase. Clipper Supers and Customs—sedans and club sedans—rode the 127-inch wheelbase. The Custom series also included a seven-passenger sedan and a limousine on a 148-inch wheelbase. Eights were equipped with the prewar 282 engine, while Supers and Customs used the 165-bhp 356. Overdrive and Electromatic clutch were available as options. Customs were trimmed with plush broadcloth and leather upholstery, special carpeting, and beautiful imitation wood paneling. Dashboards in these years were symmetrical, as they'd been before the war. The speedometer was located at the left, minor gauges at the far left, clock at the right, and the radio and heater controls in the center. Packard moved out over 30,000 cars in 1946, and over 50,000 in 1947.

But the Clipper design was growing old. Packard replaced it with an extensively facelifted model for '48, similar to a prewar show car known as the Phantom; the results were debatable. Management dictated heavy chunks of sheetmetal for a flow-through-fender effect, but this added about 200 extra pounds and made the new car look fat. "Pregnant elephant" was the term used by many to describe it. The styling wasn't helped by a short, squat grille—an eggcrate style on Customs and a bar-type on other models—that was far less elegant than the tall, narrow 1946-47 grille. Yet the 1948s sold well, and Packard produced some 92,000 of them. In 1949 it did even better, building some 116,000 vehicles.

Chassis assignments were altered slightly for 1948, and the engine lineup was revised. Customs retained the 356 engine, but Supers were fitted with a new 327 straight-eight with five main bearings. Standard Eights received a much squarer 288-cid engine. These powerplants were carried into 1949; horsepower on standards was raised to 135 bhp, Supers to 150.

The 1948 lineup included some familiar models: the standard and DeLuxe Eight in sedan and coupe form, and the sedan and coupe Super and Custom Eights. But some interesting additions were made: a novel Station Sedan in the standard Eight series, priced at $3425, and a pair of convertibles, one with the 127-inch wheelbase. The Station Sedan was made almost entirely of steel; its wooden body work was structural only at the tailgate. The Custom Eight convertible was the most luxurious standard-wheelbase American car and, at $4295, the most expensive. A 141-inch Super Eight wheelbase for two seven-passenger sedans and two limousines was also added, and a few long Custom chassis were created for commercial use. Packard built sixes only for taxi and export markets in 1948.

All Packard offerings were continued unchanged through May 1949, when a new series appeared. These were only slightly facelifted, mainly with a bodyside spear. A new Super Deluxe

The Caribbean was offered as a $5932 convertible for 1955. It had Packard's new torsion bar suspension and 275-bhp 352-cid V8.

Packard built 7206 Four Hundred hardtops for the 1955 model run.

The '56 Caribbean soft top listed at $5995. Only 276 were built.

series, using the Custom's eggcrate grille, was added to the lineup. The late '49s continued unchanged for 1950.

The big news was Ultramatic—the only automatic transmission developed by an independent without help from a transmission manufacturer. This shiftless drive combined a torque converter with multiple-disc and direct-drive clutches and forward/reverse bands. The car started from rest using the torque converter, then shifted into direct mechanical drive at about 15 miles an hour. Compared to Hydra-Matic, it was much smoother, but provided only leisurely acceleration. Frequent use of the low range for faster starts caused premature transmission wear.

Packard finally managed a total restyling for 1951, utilizing designer John Reinhart's praiseworthy shape on 122- and 127-inch wheelbases. But the firm persisted with its less expensive models. Its 200 series even included a business coupe (the cheapest '51 Cadillac was $500 more expensive), plus two- and four-door sedans in basic and DeLuxe trim. The 200 really wasn't a Packard in the traditional sense of the word, and when the seller's market subsided it wasn't able to compete with established middle-priced rivals. Production was 71,000 cars in 1951, and less than 47,000 the following year.

The "real" Packard in 1951-52 was the 250, 300, and 400 line—all well-built, comfortable, high-speed road cars. The 250, on the shorter 122-inch wheelbase, included the Mayfair hardtop and a convertible, luxuriously trimmed, colorful, sporty cars that sold fairly well. The 300s and 400s were sedans, including the Patrician, Packard's highest-priced car in these years. The 356-cid straight eight was considered too expensive to build in light of potential sales, so the top engine for '51 was a 327 eight, also with nine bearings and almost the same output.

The '52 line was basically unchanged, though the 200 business coupe was dropped. Styling changes were minor: the most obvious was a different wing position on the pelican hood ornament. Colorful interiors in high-quality fabric and leather were done up by fashion designer Dorothy Draper. Power brakes were offered for the first time.

At $3560, Executive was Packard's bargain-basement car for 1956.

All-new "contour styling" distinguished the 1951 Packard line. It came in for an extensive facelift for 1955, the year Packard brought out its V-8. Sales picked up, but nosedived in '56, the last year for the "real" Packards.

The '56 Packard Four Hundred had electric pushbutton shift controls.

The '57 Packard Clipper was called a Packardbaker by some wags.

Only 588 Packard hardtop coupes were built for '58. Price: $3262.

Even rarer was the '58 Packard station wagon—only 159 were made.

In May 1952, Packard's aging president, Hugh Ferry, announced the arrival of his successor, James J. Nance, and it was hoped that this market-wise promoter could invigorate the firm. By the time Nance arrived, the plant was working at only 50 percent of capacity. Incredibly, several long-time executives felt this was good enough. But Nance could see Packard was doomed at that level. Aggressively, he sought U.S. military business and laid out a vigorous new auto policy. Nance decreed the cheap 200 would henceforth be called Clipper and would eventually become a separate make. He also said Packard would go back to building nothing but luxury cars, returning to the long-wheelbase formal sedans and limousines it had neglected.

There was no time for a complete line-wide change for '53, but Nance did see to the inclusion of eight-passenger sedans and limousines. He even contracted with the Derham Body Company to build a few formal Patricians with leather-covered tops and tiny rear windows, priced at $6531 apiece. The glamorous Caribbean convertible was introduced, with handsome styling and a 180-bhp engine. Limited to 750 copies, it was well received and outsold Cadillac's comparable Eldorado. A colorful Clipper Sportster coupe was added at the bottom of the line. Production bounced back to over 90,000 units.

Nance had hoped for all-new 1954 models, but time didn't permit this. Instead, a look-alike interim series was offered—outwardly distinguishable from the '53s by horn-rimmed headlamps and backup lights built into the taillight assemblies. The straight eight Patrician engine was enlarged to 359 cid. Packard had been among the first to introduce air conditioning in 1940, and it was back in '54 for the first time since the war. But Packard had a terrible year, producing only about 30,000 cars. A revolutionary new model was on the way, but was delayed, partly because of the hubbub over the so-called Studebaker-Packard merger. Actually, Packard bought Studebaker. What Nance didn't know when he signed the papers was that Studebaker had huge productivity problems in its high-overhead South Bend plant, and that its break-even point was somewhere over 250,000 cars. Contrary to many accounts, Packard was still healthy at this time, but Studebaker was sinking and would drag Packard down with it.

As the '55s neared production, another smoldering problem burst into flame. Packard had given away its body business to Briggs in 1940. Briggs had sold out to Chrysler in 1954. Chrysler told Nance it would not continue Briggs' contract, and Packard had to settle for a cramped body plant on Conner Avenue in Detroit. Never big enough, the plant caused big production line tie-ups and quality control problems. Though Packard built over 55,000 cars in prosperous 1955, the company would have done better to consign body building to its old but adequate main plant on Detroit's East Grand Boulevard.

Despite all these woes, the 1955 Packard was a technological wonder. Leading its list of features was Torsion-Level suspension, an interlinked torsion-bar setup operating on all four wheels. A complicated electrical system allowed the suspension to correct for load weight, and the interlinking of all four wheels provided truly extraordinary ride and handling. And there was more: the old-fashioned straight eights were superseded by powerful new V8s. These oversquare, very powerful engines displaced 320 cubic inches on Clipper DeLuxe and Super, and 352 cid on Clipper Customs and Packards. Ultramatic was also improved to deal better with higher torque outputs. With the V8, Ultramatic, and Torsion-Level suspension, Packard had a fine chassis. Caribbeans sported twin four-barrel Rochester carbs atop the 352, good for 275 bhp. They were impressively fast and roadable cars—real Packards in every sense of the word. Styling also was impressive. A clever facelift of the old 1951 body produced "cathedral" taillights, peaked front fenders, and an ornate grille. The Clipper was given its own special grille and 1954-style taillights.

Some problems at the Conner plant were finally licked, but not

Packard's last gasp came in 1958 when four Studebaker-built models were offered, including this Packard Hawk. List: $3995.

in time to save the 1956 models. Studebaker's desperate struggle was scaring customers away. Also, many people refused to buy a '56 Packard because of the notorious quality and service problems of the '55s. Ironically, the '56s were better built. Ultramatic was given new electronic pushbutton control, and horsepower increased to as high as 310. The Clipper, as a separate make, was given the 352; the Packard engine was bored out to 374 cid. There was a hardtop as well as a convertible Caribbean. Both had unique reversible seat cushions—fabric on one side, leather on the other. In mid-year, an Executive series appeared on the 122-inch wheelbase in sedan and hardtop form, bridging the gap between Packard and Clipper. Executives wore the Clipper's pointed taillights and Packard grilles. But none of this product shuffling helped, and only 10,353 Packards (and 18,482 Clippers) were built for model year 1956.

No financial backer was found for an all-new 1957 line, and in August 1956, Nance resigned. Studebaker-Packard was picked up by Curtiss-Wright Corporation as a dalliance and/or a tax write-off, and C-W's Roy Hurley began directing the firm's fortunes. Late in 1955, S-P decided to leave Detroit and to build Studebaker-based Packards in South Bend.

The 1957 Packard Clipper (or "Packardbaker," as detractors called it) was, despite it all, a very good Studebaker, though hardly in the image of the Packards before it. A sedan and a station wagon were offered. A supercharged Studebaker 289 V8 provided 275 bhp, the same as some previous Packard V8s. Styling evoked Packard themes, and prices were higher than on comparable Studebakers. It was a charade, of course, and the public recognized it: only about 5000 '57 Clippers were built.

A big-Packard revival was still theoretically possible as the '58s were planned, so the firm again tried a holding action. This time, four Studebaker-based cars were marketed at prices up to $3995. On the shorter 116.5-inch wheelbase came a two-door hardtop and wagon; a sedan and the Packard Hawk used the longer 120.5-inch wheelbase. The latter, perhaps the most famous of this generation, was a more luxurious version of the Studebaker Golden Hawk. Featured were an all-leather interior and bizarre styling. In defense of stylist Duncan McRae, the Packard Hawk was really built only because of Roy Hurley, who demanded the long, bolt-on fiberglass nose and gaudy, gold mylar tailfins. McRae, however, takes credit for the car's outside armrests. McRae was also forced to create the other three '58 Packards—garish, finned affairs with hastily contrived four-headlight systems designed to keep up with the competition. Only the Hawk retained the supercharged engine. After '58, Packard vanished from the automotive scene, although the name was continued in the corporation's title until 1962.

A supercharged 289 V8 yielded 275 bhp in the Hawk; 588 were built.

The Studebaker-Packard merger resulted in the closing of Packard's Detroit operations. After 1956, Packard was based on a Studebaker President chassis dressed in Packard trim. It didn't sell—Packard disappeared forever after 1958.

PLYMOUTH

The name for Chrysler's low-priced make was suggested by company sales manager Joseph W. Frazer. It referred, of course, to Plymouth Rock, Massachusetts. Walter Chrysler wasn't sure whether people would make the connection, so Frazer reminded him of a well-known farm product. "Every Goddamn farmer in America's heard of Plymouth Binder Twine," replied ex-farmboy Chrysler—and Plymouth it was.

Plymouth was a success from the day of its 1928 debut. At first it was available only from Chrysler dealers, but demand was high enough by 1930 that the company awarded franchises to Dodge and DeSoto agents, too. It was an excellent strategy, vastly increasing the number of Plymouth outlets while insulating them from the sales declines Chrysler's more expensive lines suffered in the Depression.

Despite hard times—or perhaps because of them—Plymouth prospered in the '30s on a formidable combination of low prices, attractive styling, and engineering that was often more advanced than that of Ford and Chevrolet. Though Plymouth never outproduced these rivals, it was firmly established as America's number-three make as early as 1932, a position it would hold well into the '50s.

Many key features figured in Plymouth's meteoric rise: all-steel construction (per Chrysler practice) in an age of wood-framed bodies; four-wheel hydraulic brakes some years before Ford and Chevy had them; "Floating Power" rubber engine mounts that gave the 1931 models "the smoothness of an eight and the economy of a four"; independent coil-spring front suspension for 1934, again beating Ford; rubber body isolators (1936); standard safety glass, recessed controls, concealed heater blower and defroster vents (1937).

Reflecting these and other pluses, Plymouth was one of the few makes that actually scored higher production in 1930-31. It also gained in 1932-33, two of the roughest Depression years for the industry as a whole. Output peaked at nearly 552,000 for 1937, dropped to about 279,000 for recession 1938, then recovered to beyond the half-million mark by 1941. The foundation for this success were good-looking, well-built, soundly engineered automobiles that offered outstanding value.

That was especially true once Plymouth switched from fours to sixes for 1933. The new engine cost $9 million to develop, but was worth it in added sales. It also delivered more horses for fewer cubic inches. Arriving with 189.8 cid and 70 horsepower, it was stroked to 201.3 cid and 77 bhp for 1934. With an interim increase to 82 bhp for 1935, it continued through 1941, by which time it was spinning out 87 bhp.

Styling in Plymouth's first decade evolved much like Dodge's:

Among the rarest and most desirable of the '39 Plymouths was the DeLuxe convertible sedan. Price: $1150. Production: 387 units.

four-square traditional through 1932; transitional streamlining with skirted fenders and integral trunks for 1933-34; full "potato" streamlining for 1935-38. Like Ford and Chevy, Plymouth offered plain and fancy versions of most body styles, with the more glamorous open types limited to DeLuxe trim only. After a one-year-only trial in 1932, long-wheelbase sedans became regular line items for '36. The 1937 model was the first Plymouth with a list price above $1000.

Arriving for 1938 was Plymouth's first factory-built station wagon, though wagons had been available from independent coachbuilders as early as 1934. Its body, built by U.S. Body & Forge Company of New York and Indiana, was all-wood from the windshield back and demanded a lot of upkeep. Front door windows were standard; glass was optional elsewhere. There was no rear bumper, but the tailgate-mounted spare tire provided some protection.

The 1937-38 Plymouths were lumpy, but Raymond H. Dietrich, the great coachbuilder who headed Chrysler styling at the time, came up with a refreshing new look for 1939. Immediately noticeable was a strongly peaked prow-type front, perhaps inspired by that of the Lincoln Zephyr, plus a vee'd two-piece windshield instead of the previous single pane. Headlights, now rectangular, were flush within the front fenders, and the gearshift moved from floor to steering column. The canvas convertible top could be power-operated for the first time, a definite selling point.

As in 1938, the '39 Plymouth line comprised the spartan Roadking series and a nicer DeLuxe group, both on 114-inch wheelbases; a 134-inch chassis was reserved for the seven-passenger DeLuxe sedan and limousine. Though long models were a Chrysler specialty for many years, even on its lower-priced makes, these Plymouths did not sell well.

A vast array of other body types was available for 1939: coupes with and without rumble-seat, fastback and "trunkback" two- and four-door sedans, utility coupe, commercial sedan and Suburban wagon. The DeLuxe line also included Plymouth's final convertible sedan and rumble-seat convertible coupe sedan (the former the only such body style at Chrysler Corporation that year, revived for a 12-month stand).

The 1940 Plymouths sported all-new bodies with "speedline" fenders, and were better proportioned on three-inch longer wheelbases. Sealed-beam headlamps appeared for the first time, and simple horizontal-bar grilles flanked a less prominent prow. Prices ranged as low as $645 but remained a bit higher than those of equivalent Fords. Rumble seats were consigned to the past, and sedans were now fastback styles but with roomier luggage compartments than even the previous "trunked" models. Despite a slightly more potent four-main-bearing six, Plymouth was still no way a performance threat to the Ford V8, though it did provide reliable cruising at over 65 mph and was well known for economy.

Plymouth model year production jumped from 423,000 to 546,000 for 1941, thanks mainly to heavy output in the closing months of 1940. Calendar year figures reflected the turn toward defense production at the end of '41, running some 50,000 units behind Ford.

The facelifted '41 Plymouths were good-looking cars with simple, almost heart-shaped horizontal grilles, "speedline" fenders and modest bright-metal side embellishments. Series increased to three: standard, DeLuxe, and Special DeLuxe, the last taking over from the 1940 DeLuxe. The slow-selling limousine was dropped after just 24 early examples. Other '41 rarities were the DeLuxe club coupe and the standard coupe, utility sedan and wagon. New for all models was a Chrysler first, the Safety-Rim wheel, designed to prevent tire loss during a blowout. The battery moved under the hood for the first time, and Plymouth offered Powermatic shift, a vacuum transmission assist.

A more massive look arrived for 1942 via a wider grille and front fenders plus door sheetmetal extended to cover the running

Plymouth produced 6986 ragtops for 1940; prices started at $950.

The '41 convertible sold for $1107 and 10,545 were manufactured.

Plymouth's woody wagon listed at $1031 in 1941; 5594 were built.

The 1942 Special DeLuxe coupe was powered by a 217.8-cid, 95-bhp six.

This Plymouth was built in early '42—note the blackout chrome trim.

Plymouth was the success story of the Thirties as it moved from its 1928 introduction to quickly become one of the "Big Three." It featured conservative, though pleasant, styling, a sturdy L-head six, and a competitively low price.

Postwar Plymouths were warmed-over '42s, here a '48 Special DeLuxe.

Output of the 1946-early '49 Special DeLuxe woody was 12,913 units.

The 1949 Special DeLuxe four door cost $1529, weighed 3045 pounds.

Plymouth's 1949 Suburban was one of the earliest all-steel wagons.

The '50s got a new grille and taillights; 12,697 ragtops were built.

boards. The six was bored out to 217.8 cid and 95 bhp; it wouldn't be touched again until 1949. The standard series was cancelled, while the Special DeLuxe line was bolstered by the Town Sedan, a new Chrysler style of the era with more formal, closed-in rear roof quarters.

Nineteen forty-two Plymouth output stopped at close to 152,500 units when the government halted civilian auto production in February for the duration of World War II. While all '42 models are quite scarce today, some of these Plymouths are especially hard to find. For example, only 80 utility sedans, 1136 wagons and 2806 convertibles were built.

Plymouth manufactured munitions and military engines during the war while stylists like A.B. "Buzz" Grisinger, John Chika and Herb Weissinger worked on postwar ideas whenever they could. Typical of Chrysler thinking, they envisioned smooth, flush-fender bodies with thin door pillars and wraparound grilles. But like most everyone else, Plymouth resumed civilian operations with mildly modified '42s, which the booming seller's market happily consumed into model year 1949. The first new postwar Plymouths, bowing in March '49, were squarer and more upright than any wartime study. Plymouth built only 770 cars between V-J Day and December 31, 1945. Output rose quickly, however, reaching close to 265,000 for 1946 and exceeding half a million by '49.

The early-postwar facelift involved a new grille with alternating thick and thin horizontal bars, rectangular parking lights beneath the headlamps, wide front-fender moldings, a new hood ornament and reworked rear fenders. DeLuxe and Special DeLuxe series returned *sans* utility models. No styling or mechanical changes would be made through early '49, so serial numbers are the only clue as to model year.

Postwar inflation boosted 1946 prices by some $270 over 1942. The '47s ran some $250 more than the '46s, and the '48s were up to $300 costlier than the '47s. While Plymouth readied its first all-postwar models for spring introduction, the '48s were sold as "interim" '49s with inch-smaller wheels and tires (6.70 × 15s vs. 6.00 × 16s) and other minor chassis alterations that trimmed weight by about 50 pounds.

When the "real" '49s arrived, Grisinger and Weissinger had departed for Kaiser-Frazer and a new styling philosophy was in force. The latter reflected the tastes of K.T. Keller, who'd taken over as company president when Walter Chrysler died in 1940. No fan of low, "torpedo" shapes, Keller preferred what designers called "three-box styling—one box on top of two others," believing in function over form. "Cars should accommodate people rather than the ideas of far-out designers," he declared. What he didn't appreciate was how much postwar buyers *wanted* the long, low look, never mind that it meant less headroom or ground clearance. In time, Keller's practical bent would severely hurt company sales.

But the seller's market was at its peak in 1949, most everything sold no matter what it looked like, and the new Plymouth was an efficient package—comfortable and roomy with good visibility. Wheelbase was stretched to 118.5 inches for a DeLuxe notchback coupe and sedan priced in the $1500s, and the Special DeLuxe coupe, sedan, convertible and wood-trimmed wagon covering a $1600-$2400 spread. A shorter 111-inch chassis was used for a DeLuxe fastback two-door, business coupe, and the new all-steel Suburban wagon.

Plymouth liked to take credit for this first "modern" wagon, though Chevy, Olds and Pontiac also issued all-steel haulers during 1949. Still, the Suburban cost only $1840, quite a bit less than the GM models, and accordingly sold well. Nearly 20,000 of the '49s were built as buyers realized that wagons didn't have to be made of wood. Within four years, other Chrysler makes and the rest of the industry had followed suit and the "woody" was dead.

Like rival Chevrolet, Plymouth would be transformed from economical, no-nonsense transportation to one of 1955's hottest and best-looking cars. Fading fortunes dictated this revolution.

The '53 Plymouth rode a compact 114-inch wheelbase. The Cranbrook Belvedere hardtop listed at $2064; output hit 35,185 units.

"Saddleback" two-toning was seen on the 1952 Cranbrook Belvedere.

Base price of the '54 Belvedere soft top was $2301—6900 were made.

Though unchallenged since 1932 as the number-three seller, Plymouth built fewer and fewer cars after 1949. By 1954 it had fallen to fifth in calendar year sales.

The 1950-54 Plymouths were well-engineered, solid and reliable but dull and none too fast. All carried the aging L-head six, which produced 97 bhp from 1949 through 1952. Output was raised to 100 bhp for '53 (probably by the stroke of an ad writer's pen). This engine was capable of 20-23 miles per gallon and, if pressed, perhaps 80 mph.

The 1950 line was basically a '49 reprise. An effective facelift brought a simpler square grille with a large horizontal bar, slightly longer rear decks (to relieve the previous stubby look), and taillights placed low within reworked rear fenders. The Special outsold the plain DeLuxe by about seven to five. Two important new innovations for the low-price field were automatic electric choke and combined ignition/starter switch.

After some 611,000 of its 1950s, Plymouth built about the same number of its 1951 models, distinguished by a modified hood and a lower, wider grille that made frontal appearance a little less blunt. New model names accompanied the fresh face. The short-wheelbase DeLuxe was now called Concord, offering business coupe, fastback two-door, and two-door Suburban and Savoy wagons. On the longer DeLuxe/Special DeLuxe chassis were Cambridge and Cranbrook coupes and four-door sedans and a Cranbrook convertible and hardtop coupe. The last, christened Belvedere, was Plymouth's first pillarless style. Arriving a year behind Chevrolet's Bel Air, it also stood apart from other Plymouths via a two-tone paint scheme.

As with all Chrysler makes, Plymouth was essentially unchanged for 1952 save for newly optional overdrive. A small external difference was a rear nameplate integrated with the trunk-handle assembly; the '51s used separate name script. An important 1951-52 improvement was Oriflow shock absorbers, a Chrysler hydraulic type designed to improve ride and handling. Plymouth output sank by about 204,000 cars, but the rest of the industry also cut production due to the Korean War.

Plymouth's conservative styling and engineering were continued through 1954, which was a sales disaster for all Chrysler Corporation makes. But help would soon appear for Plymouth, which lost third place to Buick that year.

New slab-sided styling with flow-through fenderlines and a one-piece windshield marked the 1953 models on a single 114-inch wheelbase. Concord was dropped and the Cambridge line expanded to embrace the business coupe and wagons. A mid-year introduction was Hy-Drive, a manual transmission with torque converter that eliminated shifting between second and third, though you still had to clutch for first-gear starts.

The stubby '53 look continued for 1954, when Plymouth suffered from uninspired styling as much as any Chrysler make. Volume dwindled from over 650,000 to around 463,000, less than half of Ford/Chevy output. Models regrouped into Plaza, Savoy, and Belvedere series covering a $1600-$2300 price spread. Plaza and Savoy each offered a club coupe, sedans with two or four doors and a Suburban wagon; there was also a Plaza business coupe. The top-line Belvedere comprised four-door sedan, convertible, Suburban and Sport Coupe hardtop.

Two important mechanical changes occurred during '54. The old six was enlarged for the first time since 1942, a longer stroke bringing it to 230.2 cid and horsepower to 110. Also at about mid-year, fully automatic two-speed PowerFlite transmission arrived as an option. It would prove very popular.

Plymouth repeated this basic lineup for 1955 but with a dramatic difference: all-new Virgil Exner styling. Suddenly, Plymouth looked exciting. And with brand-new polyspherical-head V8s, it had performance to match.

Called "Hy-Fire," this V8 was an excellent overhead-valve design in the small-displacement tradition begun with Studebaker's 232 of 1951. It arrived in two sizes: a 241-cid unit with 157 bhp, and a 260 delivering 167 bhp "standard" or 177 bhp with four-barrel carb and dual exhausts. Outstanding features ran to lightweight aluminum pistons, aluminum carburetor, and chrome-plated top piston rings for longer life and better oil control. Tuning changes brought the 230.2-cid six to 117 bhp.

Other new mechanical features for '55 included suspended foot pedals, tubeless tires, front shocks enclosed within the coil springs, and dashboard lever control for the PowerFlite automatic. There were also several options new to Plymouth: factory air conditioning, power windows, and power front seat.

But the big attraction was Plymouth's crisp new '55 styling, with pointed front and rear fenders, smooth flanks, a shapely tail and a bright but not gaudy grille. Two-toning was confined to the roof and, via optional moldings, a broad bodyside sweep panel. Four-door wagons were reinstated as Plaza and Belvedere Suburbans. The line-topping Belvedere convertible came only with V8, as it would through the end of the decade.

Ads proclaimed the '55 a "great new car for the young in heart." It was certainly a clean break from Plymouth's plodding past. Customers rushed to buy, production surged, but Plymouth remained in fourth with 704,445 units. And for calendar '55 the division built a record 742,991 cars (including some '56s, of course), a record that would stand into the '60s.

Plymouth again claimed fourth for 1956, which introduced "The Forward Look"—meaning tailfins. Engineers simultaneously brought forth pushbutton PowerFlite, a 12-volt electrical system, and optional Highway Hi-Fi, a record player that used special platters and a tonearm designed to stay in the groove (which it didn't on bumpy roads). Suburbans were now a separate line with two-door Deluxe, two- and four-door Customs and four-door Sport models respectively trimmed like Plaza, Savoy and Belvedere. A Sport Sedan four-door hardtop expanded the Belvedere series, and a Savoy two-door hardtop was added. Both V8s were larger and more potent, comprising a 270-cid base unit with 180 bhp, and a pair of 277s with 187 and 200 bhp.

An even hotter Plymouth arrived at mid-'56: the limited-edition Fury. An attractive hardtop coupe, it came only in white with bodyside sweepspears of gold anodized aluminum. Power was supplied by a special 303-cid V8 with 240 bhp via 9.25:1 compression, solid lifters, stronger valve springs, dual exhausts and Carter four-barrel carb. A stock Fury could do 0-60 mph in about 10 seconds and reach 110 mph, though one modified example approached

This '55 Belvedere had the "Forward Look" and a six under the hood.

Gold side trim marked the high performance Fury hardtop coupe for '56.

Flashy two-tones were popular in '56; 6735 Belvedere ragtops were sold.

Savoy was the mid-line '56 series; 57,927 two doors were produced.

Plymouth advertising for 1957 boasted "Suddenly It's 1960." Styling was sensational; 7438 people bought Fury hardtop coupes.

145 mph on the sands of Daytona Beach. The Fury gave a big boost to Plymouth's growing performance image, and 4485 of the '56s were sold—not bad for the $2866 price, some $600 above the Belvedere hardtop.

After '56 production of nearly 553,000, Plymouth zoomed to better than 762,000 on the strength of its stunning, all-new '57 line. "Suddenly it's 1960," said the ads, and not without justification. Next to its rivals, Plymouth probably was three full years ahead, with the lowest beltline, the cleanest styling and the highest tailfins of the low-price three. Wheelbases stretched to 122 inches on wagons and 118 inches elsewhere. Model offerings were unchanged through mid-year, when a Savoy Sport Sedan hardtop was added.

The old "PowerFlow" six had been coaxed up to 132 bhp by now, and there were no fewer than five V8s: 197- and 235-bhp 277s, new 301s with 215/235 bhp, and the Fury's even larger new

At $2638, the '57 Belvedere convertible was a hit with 9866 buyers.

The carry-over '58 saw 18,194 Belvedere Sport Sedans assembled.

A price-leader spring '58 model was the $1958 Plaza Silver Special.

Sport Fury was Plymouth's top-line '59; 17,867 hardtops were built.

Plymouth burst onto the scene in 1955 with dramatic all-new styling and V-8 power, exactly the tonic it needed. Modest fins sprouted from the rear fenders in 1956. The '57 model was so new that ads proclaimed, "Suddenly it's 1960!"

Total convertible production for the '59 model year was 11,053 units.

Plymouth wagons were called Suburban in 1959—56,997 were produced.

The most popular Fury for '60 was the hardtop sedan: 21,292 built.

Plymouth station wagon output skidded to 34,929 units for 1961.

The most noticed styling feature on the '61 Fury was the lack of fins.

318 with 290 bhp. TorqueFlite, Chrysler's excellent new three-speed automatic, arrived as an optional alternative to PowerFlite. Also shared with other '57 Chrysler cars was torsion-bar front suspension, whose superior geometry made this the best-handling Plymouth in history.

It's hard to remember how truly different Plymouth seemed in '57: low and wide with distinctive shark fins; a graceful grille; a front bumper raised over a central, vertically slotted underpanel; two-toning limited to the roof and tasteful bodyside color panels (sometimes the roof alone); huge glass areas (the convertible windshield curved at the top as well as the sides); a delicate-looking thin-section roofline on hardtop coupes. Suburbans gained load space via an upright spare tire in the right rear fender, an idea borrowed from the 1956 Plymouth Plainsman show car. The '57s were indeed memorable, but their tendency to early rust—reflecting design flaws and the general decline in Chrysler's quality control which began that year—makes good examples fairly rare today.

A predictably mild facelift gave the '58s four headlamps, a horizontal-bar grille insert (repeated in the under-bumper modesty panel), and small round taillights at the base of the fins, the space above filled by bright metal. A trio of 318 V8s offered 225-290 bhp (the latter standard for Fury), and a newly optional 350 "Golden Commando" engine delivered 305 bhp or, with that year's rare fuel injection option, 315 bhp. A deep national recession limited production to just under 444,000, but most everyone else built fewer '58s too.

The '59s were more heavily restyled—and more heavy-handed: longer and higher fins, a garish eggcrate grille, headlamps with odd "siamesed" eyelids, more prominent bumpers, more plentiful bright trim. The Plaza vanished, Savoy and Belvedere moved down a notch, and Fury expanded into a separate top-line series with two hardtops, a four-door sedan and a convertible. This year's high performer was the Sport Fury, a convertible and hardtop coupe priced around $3000 and carrying a 260-bhp 318 V8. The standard 318 delivered 230 bhp. Fuel injection was no more, but a new 305-bhp 361 Golden Commando arrived as an $87 extra. Convertibles and hardtop coupes could be ordered with a simulated spare tire on the decklid, an add-on lump reflecting Virgil Exner's fondness for "classic" design themes.

Several interesting Plymouth show cars appeared in the '50s. Ghia's 1951 XX-500 was a pretty sedan that won Exner's patronage for the Italian coachworks to build various later show cars and limousines. The 1954 Explorer, another Ghia exercise, was a smoothly styled grand tourer. Briggs contributed the 1954 Belmont hoping Plymouth would field a two-seater—with Briggs-supplied body—to answer Corvette and Thunderbird, but minuscule sports-car demand precluded the idea. The glassy '56 Plainsman was followed by the even glassier 1958 Cabana dream wagon, which sported four-door hardtop styling that surfaced on 1960-62 Chrysler wagons, but not Plymouth's.

After '59 volume of more than 458,000, Plymouth eased to just under 448,000 for 1960 despite sales support from the new compact Valiant. By 1962 the make had dropped all the way to eighth, knocked out by Rambler, Pontiac and Oldsmobile as well as its own slow-selling 1962 line of smaller big cars with no full-size alternatives. Plymouth began recovering in '63 but could not dislodge Pontiac from third. These problems reflected management's repeated failure to gauge the market correctly and come up with the right products at the right time.

The difficulties began with 1960's "Unibody" line of garishly styled Savoy, Belvedere, Fury, and Suburban models. Chrysler's new 145-bhp, 225-cid slant six, replacing the old L-head as the standard big-Plymouth six, was a good engine, but Rambler campaigned with conservative styling and more economical sixes to outpace Plymouth by 2000 units for the calendar year. This year's V8s were largely '59 holdovers.

The '62 Plymouth Fury wagon started at $2968; only 4763 were sold.

Sport Fury, Plymouth's top series in 1963, saw 11,483 hardtops built.

Fury became a big car again in '65, here a $3209 Fury III ragtop.

Plymouth produced 64,596 Valiant-based Barracudas, here a Formula S.

The '64 Sport Fury, still on a 116-inch wheelbase, listed at $2864 with standard V8. It had a production run of 23,695 units.

The U.S. launched its first weather satellite, Tiros I, in 1960. Plymouth was somewhere out in space, too, with weird styling that got weirder for '61. The smaller '62 Plymouth also missed the mark, but luckily better days were coming.

Plymouth's answer to Ford's LTD and Chevy's Caprice was the full-size VIP. It carried many luxury trappings and sold for $3069.

The facelifted '56 Barracuda could be ordered with a 235-bhp 273 V8.

Signet was the top-line Valiant in '66. The hardtop sold for $2261.

The drastically restyled '61s were totally devoid of fins and simulated decklid spares, but their pinched grille and ponderous bullet taillights were weird enough. As a result, Rambler claimed third and Plymouth dropped to fourth on volume that just managed to exceed 350,000. The only engine change was optional availability of a new 383 V8 with 330 bhp.

Then, Plymouth's worst mistake of the decade. Anticipating strong demand for smaller "standard" cars, design chief Exner sliced eight inches from wheelbase, trimmed curb weights by 550 pounds and applied Valiant-like styling. With their 318, 361 and 413 V8s, these lighter Plymouths—Savoy, Belvedere, Fury, and new bucket-seat Sport Fury (the last revived after a two-year hiatus)—had fine performance, but, the public was still hungry for large cars and turned to Ford and Chevrolet in droves.

Beating a hasty retreat, Plymouth issued more conservative, squared-up styling for '63, then a Chevy-like '64 facelift (both created under Ford alumnus Elwood Engel, who'd succeeded Exner in 1962). But this didn't help much, either. Plymouth's 1963 rebound to fourth came mainly on continuing strong Valiant sales rather than any increase in demand for its standard models.

But by 1965 a Plymouth renaissance was underway, not least because it returned to the full-size fold that year with a line of big, blocky Furys on a new 119-inch wheelbase (121 inches for wagons). The Fury I and II series comprised two sedans and a wagon; Fury III added two hardtops and a convertible; at the top were a bucket-seat Sport Fury convertible and hardtop coupe. The largest Plymouths ever offered, the '65s were far roomier than the '64s. Unit construction was retained, but a bolt-on subframe carried the engine and front suspension. Powerplants ran from the 145-bhp 225 slant six through 318, 361 and 383 V8s with 230-330 bhp.

Meantime, the advent of intermediates suggested a new role for the 116-inch-wheelbase "standard" Plymouth of 1962-64. Duly reskinned to resemble the big Fury, it was reborn for 1965 as the mid-size Belvedere and met strong buyer approval. Offerings ran to Belvedere I sedans and wagon; Belvedere II four-door sedan, wagon, hardtop coupe and convertible; the bucket-seat V8-only Satellite hardtop and convertible; and a much-altered drag-oriented coupe aptly named Super Stock. Standard on the S/S and

This '67 Satellite hardtop is powered by the 425-bhp 426 Hemi V8.

Sport Fury was still the flashiest big Plymouth in 1968. The semi-fastback hardtop listed at $3225 and 17,073 were produced.

The '67 Barracuda sported all-new styling and its first soft top.

With its 440 V8, the Belvedere GTX was Plymouth's hot rod for 1967.

optional for other Belvederes (and Furys) was a 426-cid wedge-head V8, returning from '64 with 365 or 425 bhp. The S/S rode a special 115-inch chassis and weighed just 3170 pounds, so performance was mighty: 120 mph all out, 0-60 mph in eight seconds. At $4671, it was neither cheap nor readily available. Normal Belvederes offered the same basic engines as Fury, but their base V8 was a new 273-cid small-block rated at 180 bhp.

For 1966, the incredible 425-bhp hemi became available as a limited-production option for Belvedere II/Satellite. The result was the electrifying "Street Hemi," which came with heavy-duty suspension and oversize brakes to cope with its awesome engine. It was first offered with four-speed manual gearbox, later with TorqueFlite automatic. Since the '66 Belvedere was the same size and weight as the '65, the Street Hemi could be a docile tourer at low speeds and a demon when stirred up.

Correctly tuned and with the proper tires and axle ratio, hemi-Belvederes could reach 120 mph in 12-13 seconds, making them prime quarter-mile competitors in A/Stock and AA/Stock, along with Dodge's Coronet-based Hemi-Chargers. These muscle-bound middleweights also ran on NASCAR's shorter circuits—

The '69 Sport Fury boasted new styling. A 318 V8 came standard.

It cost $2907 to buy a '68 Barracuda soft top; only 2840 were sold.

President Johnson ordered continuous bombing of Vietnam below the 20th parallel in early 1965. Plymouth dropped a bomb of its own that year with a neatly styled full-size Fury lineup and attractively restyled compacts and intermediates.

Plymouth's "winged warrior," the 1970 Road Runner Superbird, was designed for NASCAR racing; 1920 were built, listing at $4298.

with predictable results. David Pearson won the '66 championship for Dodge; Richard Petty did the honors for Plymouth the following year. Petty also won the 1964 Daytona 500 in a hemi-powered Plymouth stocker.

With only detail changes, the Belvedere/Satellite's crisp, chiseled styling continued into 1967, the last year for the original '62 platform. Topping the line was the lush new Belvedere GTX, a hardtop coupe and convertible equipped with a standard 375-bhp version of the big-block 440 wedge-head V8 introduced on Chrysler Corporation's full-size '66s. The 1967 hemi option was reserved exclusively for GTX, which was easy to spot with its silver-and-black grille and back panel, simulated hood air intakes, sport striping and dual exhausts.

A new body with no change in wheelbases gave Plymouth's 1968 intermediates a more rounded look that was just as pretty. Belvedere was reduced to a low-line coupe, sedan and wagon. Satellite was now the full-range volume series, and Sport Satellite denoted a top-line wagon, convertible, and hardtop coupe priced just below GTX.

Plymouth scored a marketing coup for '68 with the ingenuous Road Runner, a budget-priced no-frills muscle machine offered as a two-door hardtop and pillared coupe. Exterior i.d. was provided by RR nameplates and cartoon-bird decals on doors and decklid, along with simulated hood scoops and racy wheels. Under the hood was a standard 335-bhp 383 with the 440's intake manifold and heads. The hemi was optional, as were the GTX's beefy

Plymouth had good success with the '69 Road Runner, a bare-bones, low-price, high-performance Belvedere. The coupe sold for $2945.

suspension and four-speed transmission. Dynamite on street or track, this finely tuned package of power and performance cost only $2800-$3100—extraordinary for the day.

The mid-size line continued through 1970 with only minor changes. A convertible and more standard equipment bolstered the Road Runner's appeal for 1969, though higher prices didn't. The ragtop GTX disappeared after '69 and a mere 700 copies.

Following a mild '66 facelift, the big Furys received crisp new lower-body sheetmetal that added inches to length and width. Wheelbases and engines were largely the same. The big-block 440 option returned from '66 with 350 or 375 bhp. The base V8 was a 230-bhp 318. A brace of optional 383s offered 270 or 325 bhp. The 225 slant six was standard for sedans, Fury III hardtops and the Fury I wagon.

Plymouth had joined Ford and Chevy in the move up to medium-price territory with the 1966 Fury VIP, a hardtop coupe and sedan with standard V8, vinyl top and a richly appointed interior. VIP returned as a separate series for '67 with the same two body styles, only the hardtop coupe switched from notchback to "Fast Top" styling, with a slantback profile and very wide C-pillars that also showed up on a second Sport Fury hardtop. Fury hardtop coupes offered the same choice of rooflines for 1968, when another mild facelift occurred.

If not exactly head-turners, the big late-Sixties Furys gave away nothing in appearance to rival Fords and Chevys. The 1965-66 models wore conservative full-width grilles, stacked quad headlamps, minimal side decoration and simple taillights. Sheetmetal was more obviously sculptured on the 1967-68s, crisper yet somehow more imposing.

For 1969, the big Plymouths adopted the smoother, more massive "fuselage look" then favored by Chrysler stylists. Beltlines were higher, windows shorter all around, lower-body contours more flowing but heavier. Squarish fenderlines were a vestige of previous styling, but headlamps reverted to horizontal pairs. Model offerings again stood pat, with non-wagon styles on a one-inch longer wheelbase. Convertibles were waning fast here. The '69 Fury III saw only 4129 copies, the Sport fury a mere 1579. The latter disappeared entirely for 1970, leaving the bench-seat job as Plymouth's last big ragtop; only 1952 were built.

The car that sustained Plymouth during its early-'60s troubles was Valiant. One of the Big Three's original 1960 compacts, it was ostensibly a separate make its first year, but always wore Plymouth badges thereafter. The first design generation ran through 1962—ruggedly built Unibody cars with Virgil Exner styling marked by square grilles, pronounced "blade" fenderlines, and short decks adorned by dummy spare tires, all on a 106-inch wheelbase. A four-door sedan and wagon were initially offered in V100 and V200 trim. A V100 two-door sedan and V200 hardtop coupe arrived for 1961. With bucket seats and spiffy trim, the latter became the 1962 Signet 200, perhaps the most collectible early Valiant.

One of Valiant's strong points was its robust slant six, designed to permit lower hoodlines, though engineers also claimed certain manufacturing and operational efficiencies for the configuration. The initial 170-cid version produced 101 bhp; a 1960-61 four-barrel carburetor option called Hyper-Pack raised that to 148 bhp. The larger 225-cid version from the big Plymouths became optional from 1962. A long-lived design of great durability, the 225 was still being used on some Plymouths as late as the early '80s.

Exner's departure meant Elwood Engel styling for the '63 Valiant, which was clean, if a bit square and stodgy. Bolstered by appealing new Signet and V200 convertibles, Valiant sales picked up. They gained even more momentum for 1964 when Chrysler's new 273 small-block V8 became optional. With 180 bhp, it made these compacts quite sprightly indeed. After two facelift years, Valiant was completely redesigned for 1967, adopting a 108-inch wheelbase and four-square lines reminiscent of some mid-size

Only 1442 Barracuda soft tops were built for '69. List price: $3082.

The 'Cuda AAR (All-American Racer) was a Trans Am racer in spirit.

The 1970 'Cuda convertible saw a production run of only 635 units.

Note the dual exhausts on this '70 Plymouth Sport Fury GT hardtop.

Hidden headlights were a '71 Sport Fury highlight. List: $3677.

Pontiac started the muscle car wars with the GTO, but Plymouth countered with the popular Road Runner and the brash "winged warrior," the 1970 Road Runner Superbird. Barracuda models such as the 'Cuda AAR provided additional ammunition.

At $2547, the '70 Valiant Duster 340 was a bargain; 24,817 were built.

The '71 Road Runner came only as a hardtop; output hit 14,218 units.

Top-of-the-line full-size Plymouth for 1972 was the $3974 Gran Fury.

Scamp was the name given to the '72 Valiant hardtop. List: $2528.

European sedans. Despite the lack of wagons at this point, Valiant remained Detroit's top-selling compact.

The success of Chevy's Corvair Monza prompted Plymouth to refocus its sights on the sporty-compact market. The result was the Barracuda, launched in mid-1964 as a '65 model. Though Ford's Mustang arrived at about the same time, Barracuda was not a direct reply. Instead, a hasty tooling revision of the 106-inch-wheelbase Valiant superstructure resulted in a fastback hardtop coupe with a huge piece of curved glass forming part of a rakish roofline. Despite its obvious workaday origins, the Barracuda offered a pleasing combination of sporty looks, good handling, utility and room for four. Nearly 65,000 were sold for the first full model year—far adrift of Mustang's volume.

Predictably, the 225 slant six was standard for Barracuda. Optional was the new 273-cid derivation of the corporate 318 V8 with 180 bhp in normal tune. A high-performance 235-bhp version was also offered with high-lift, high-overlap camshaft, domed pistons, solid lifters, dual-contact breaker points, unsilenced air cleaner, and a sweet-sounding, low-restriction exhaust system. With Rallye Suspension (heavy-duty front torsion bars and anti-sway bars, stiff rear leaf springs), Firm-Ride shocks, and a four-speed gearbox, the 235-bhp Barracuda would do 0-60 mph in eight seconds flat and the standing quarter-mile in 16 seconds.

Barracuda was facelifted for '66 with an eggcrate grille, then handsomely redesigned for '67. Wheelbase was stretched two inches, overall length five inches, and a shapelier fastback was

Duster was a good seller for Plymouth in the Seventies, here a '72.

Plymouth built 95,203 Sebring hardtops for '73, here a $3258 Plus.

Plymouth billed the 1973 Fury Gran Coupe as "Something of Value."

The '74 full-size Plymouths were all-new, here a Fury Gran Sedan.

joined by a new convertible and notchback hardtop coupe (the latter with a rather odd rear roofline). A newly available four-barrel 383 V8 detuned to 280 bhp provided even better straightline performance, but hurt handling by adding up to 300 extra pounds, mostly up front. The 273 remained a better choice. As for '66, a Formula S package was offered comprising heavy-duty suspension, tachometer, wide-oval tires, and special stripes and badges.

Happily, the '67 Barracuda continued without drastic change through 1969. A vertical-bar grille insert marked the '68s, a checked insert and revamped taillights the '69s. In both years there were muscle-market "'Cuda" models offering a choice of Chrysler's new 340 small-block with 275 bhp or the big-block 383 with 300 bhp for '68 and 330 bhp for '69.

Bowing for 1970 was a completely redesigned third-generation Barracuda that donated its basic structure to a new Dodge double, the Challenger. Compared to previous Barracudas, the '70 was shorter, wider, much heavier and somehow more conventional. Wheelbase remained at 108 inches, but the new "widebody" design had plenty of room for every big-block V8 in the Chrysler stable, up to and including the 426 hemi and a six-barrel 440 with a rated 390 bhp. The latter two were available with a special "shaker" hood, so-called because a functional scoop attached directly to the carb housing poked through the hood and could be seen a-shakin'. The trademark fastback was no more, but hardtop and convertible were offered in three forms: base, performance-oriented 'Cuda, and luxury Gran Coupe (which in ragtop form was thus a Gran Coupe convertible).

Perhaps the most interesting 1970 Barracuda was the racy, mid-year AAR (All-American Racer), inspired by the Dan Gurney team cars that ran in that year's Trans-Am series. Based on the 'Cuda 340 hardtop, it was easily identified by bold bodyside "strobe" stripes, wide tires, matte-black fiberglass hood with functional scoop, rear spoiler, and long exhaust trumpets peeking out from under the rocker panels. A modified 340 V8 carried an Edelbrock intake manifold mounting three two-barrel carbs, plus special heads and a reworked block and valvetrain. Heavy-duty suspension was also included. Only about 2800 were built.

Giving Valiant a lift for 1970 was a new semi-fastback pillared coupe called Duster, a pleasant little car of good quality that sold over 217,000 copies in its debut year. Among them were several thousand equipped with a Gold Duster option package comprising gold accents on grille, body, and interior, plus bucket seats, whitewall tires and special wheel covers. The Duster 340 was a racy derivation with a mechanical package similar to that of the 'Cuda 340. Equipment ran to the 275-bhp small-block, three-speed floorshift, front disc brakes, wide tires and tuned suspension.

Among 1970 Plymouth intermediates was a startling newcomer: the Superbird. Part of the Road Runner series, it was an evolution of Dodge's 1969 Charger Daytona, with a similar hidden-headlamp "droop-snoot" and huge struts carrying a stabilizer wing high above the rear deck. The Superbird looked fast—and was. Racing versions recorded over 220 mph. Street models came with a four-barrel 440 and TorqueFlite automatic, but a six-barrel 440, the 426 hemi and four-speed manual transmission were optional. After Dodge built some 500 Charger Daytonas to qualify it as "production" for NASCAR events, the organization increased its minimum to 1500. That was no problem for Plymouth, which ended up building 1920 Superbirds.

Barracuda was in its last year in 1974. A 318 V8 was standard, a 245-horse 360 optional. Production skidded to 11,734 units.

Emissions regulations and high insurance rates in the early '70s killed off the high-performance Plymouths of the '60s. A waning ponycar market knocked off the Barracuda after '74. In the '70s, Plymouth concentrated mainly on its compacts.

Road Runner had a 318 V8 as standard in 1974; 11,555 were produced.

The '76 Feather Duster was 187 pounds lighter, had special gearing.

It took $4963 to purchase a 1977 Plymouth Gran Fury Brougham coupe.

The optional 360 V8 and spoilers aplenty mark this 1978 Volaré.

The Superbird's great moment came at the 1970 Daytona 500, when Pete Hamilton romped home at an average speed of nearly 150 mph to best every Dodge and every Ford. Superbirds accounted for 21 of Chrysler's 38 Grand National wins that year. But NASCAR changed its rules again for 1971, thus ending the Superbird's dominance on the high-speed ovals.

Even full-size Plymouths got a dose of performance for 1970. Most notable was the new Sport Fury GT, a hardtop coupe carrying a standard 350-bhp 440, heavy-duty suspension and long-legged rear axle ratios (as high as 2.76:1). The Sport Fury line also included a new S/23 hardtop. With its 318 V8, this wasn't in the GT's league, but it did come with a tuned suspension and "strobe" stripes. Other Sport Furys were upgraded to take over for the luxury VIPs. Arriving in February was a plush Gran Coupe pillared two-door boasting most every comfort and convenience feature in the book at $3833 without air conditioning or $4216 with.

For two brief shining moments, 1971 and '74, Plymouth again finished its traditional third in the industry production race. But after this it never ran higher than fourth. By decade's end it had sunk to ninth, even though 1979 was a very healthy Detroit year. By the early '80s, the make was all but invisible.

Several factors contributed to this sad decline: more wrong products at the wrong times, indifferent workmanship on the few that were well timed, dwindling public confidence in Chrysler Corporation as a whole, and an increasing similarity to related Dodges. Plymouth also suffered from a growing dullness that stemmed from the '60s consolidation of Chrysler's five divisions into two—Dodge and Chrysler-Plymouth. Because this obviated the need to put all nameplates on all major platforms, glamour assignments like Cordoba went to Chrysler while Dodge increasingly got sportier models all to itself. By 1978, Plymouth was back to peddling basic family transportation—just as it had started out doing 50 years before.

Yet few could have foreseen this diminished role in 1970, when Plymouth countered Ford and Chevy with five separate car lines spanning 44 individual models and about 70 basic variations (counting trim levels and engines). Valiant, the lone survivor of the original Big Three compacts, dominated its market right on through swan-song '76. A key factor was the Duster coupe, which all by itself chalked up well over a quarter-million 1974 sales. It was conventional but well-engineered and at least as well built as comparable GM and Ford products.

And Plymouth kept sales moving with a stream of extra-cost packages. The 1971-74 "Twister" option included matte-black hood, Duster 340-type black grille, bodyside tape stripes and Rallye wheels. The Gold Duster continued through 1975 with a color-keyed pebble-grain vinyl roof. The "Space Duster" of 1973-74 was Plymouth's equivalent of Dodge's Dart Sport "Convertriple," with a wagon-style fold-down rear seatback that gave a 6½-foot-long carpeted cargo deck. Even at the end of the line there was a special "Silver Duster" (a handsome combination of silver, red and black) as well as a "Feather Duster." The latter, a reply to Ford's "MPG" models, had an economy-tuned 225 six with aluminum intake manifold, plus aluminum instead of steel inner panels on hood and decklid. With the manual-overdrive gearbox, which had an aluminum case, the Feather Duster was surprisingly frugal for its size; a prudent driver could nurse one up to 30 mpg.

Further bolstering the Valiant were the performance-oriented V8 Duster 340/360 (through '75); the 1974-76 Brougham luxury trim option for sedans and two-door hardtops, offering opulence not usually found in compacts; and the Scamp hardtop, which filled the price gap between the basic and high-line offerings. Altogether, the Valiant (and Dodge's Dart) was an impressive seller, in some years giving Chrysler the compact lead.

Unveiled at mid-model year '76 was the Volaré, a more upscale compact that would supersede Valiant entirely for 1977. Though only a bit larger outside, Volaré (and its Dodge Aspen cousin) had been designed for maximum interior space, which was quite good for the day. Workmanship, however, was anything but, though the problems didn't do any immediate sales damage, mainly because they didn't surface for a few years. Trim levels comprised base, mid-range Custom, and high-line Premier, the last offering unexpected luxury for around $4500. Volaré also came as a wagon in addition to the expected coupe and sedan, Plymouth's first compact hauler since 1966.

By 1977, Road Runner was an option package on the compact Volaré. Combined with a Super Pak option it became a "Front Runner."

The Volaré was right on target, racking up almost 400,000 sales for '77. Most examples ran the 225 slant six or 318 V8, both able veterans of some two decades. Though no trend-setter, Volaré appealed mainly for its restrained styling and decent performance/economy compromise.

Compacts were Plymouth's only real success in the '70s, its intermediates and full-size cars faring poorly. So, too, did the Barracuda, which was of no significance in the steadily declining ponycar market. The all-new '70 design was warmed-over for '71, marked by quad headlamps and a vee'd grille with vertical slats. A low-priced pillared hardtop replaced the open Gran Coupe and took the lion's share of drastically reduced sales. Convertibles and

For 1979, Plymouth dusted off the Duster name and put it on a specially trimmed Volaré. Total Volaré output was 209,686 units.

The U.S. celebrated its Bicentennial in 1976. Plymouth celebrated that year with the introduction of its new compact, the Volaré. Although a good seller, it was plagued by poor quality control and a record number of recalls.

Chrysler's 111-bhp 2.2-liter four was optional on the '81 Horizon.

The 1981 Plymouth Reliant Custom four-door sedan started at $6325.

A 225-cid slant six or 318-cid V8 were offered on the '81 Gran Fury.

At $5976, the '82 Plymouth TC3 Miser was a no-frills economy coupe.

The 1982 Gran Fury moved down to Chrysler's M-body platform.

A five-speed overdrive gearbox was a $75 option on the '83 Reliant.

A 110-bhp 2.2-liter four was standard on the '84 Turismo 2.2.

The new-for-1984 Voyager was Plymouth's biggest 1980's success.

Caravelle bowed for '85; it was really a recycled Chrysler E Class.

Woodgrain trim was standard on the '85 Reliant SE and LE wagons.

big-block engines were scrubbed for '72, leaving six and small-block V8 standard and 'Cuda coupes. These carried on for two more seasons before Plymouth gave up.

Consolidated under the Satellite name, the mid-size Plymouths were completely revamped for 1971, shedding their boxy 1968-70 contours for more radically sculptured sheetmetal and large loop bumper/grilles. In line with a Detroit trend, coupes rode a shorter wheelbase than sedans and wagons (115 vs. 117 inches). Convertibles vanished, but Road Runner and GTX were still around, and there was a smart new sports-luxury hardtop called Sebring Plus.

Unfortunately, these cars suffered the same fate as most '70s intermediates, becoming progressively more ponderous, thirsty, and ugly. The GTX was dumped for '72 due to lack of interest, and the Road Runner, still ostensibly a separate model, wasn't nearly as fast on its feet as before. An attempt to regroup for 1975 brought the "small Fury," basically the existing design with squared-up outer sheetmetal and a new name, but sales continued to languish. The last of these cars rolled out the door in 1978.

The big full-size Furys had vanished the year before. Through 1973, these were restyled continuations of the 1969 "fuselage" body/chassis design, with the same four-series lineup of top-drawer Sport Fury and three lower trim levels designated by Roman numerals. C-P began whittling away at this group for '72, with Gran Fury taking over at the top and the economy Fury I offerings cut from four to one. Meanwhile, Chrysler Corporation was preparing a brand-new design for all its full-size lines, scheduled well in advance of the Middle East oil crisis.

Nevertheless, the hulkier new 1974 Fury (and the corresponding Dodge Monaco and Chrysler Newport/New Yorker) seemed incredibly ill-timed. And significantly, sales didn't improve even after gas supplies eased and big-car sales began recovering. The line was called Gran Fury from 1975 to avoid confusion with the newly renamed intermediates, but Chrysler never seemed to understand that badge shifting seldom (if ever) makes any difference in sales. Except for the mid-range Custom sedan, not a single Gran Fury model saw more than 10,000 copies for 1976, and production of some Brougham and wagon models was laughably low for a traditionally high-volume make.

Hoping to cut its losses, Plymouth trimmed its big-car line for '76 and again for '77, deleting mainly hardtop sedans and some trim variations. The losses continued, however, and Plymouth temporarily fled the full-size field. It returned halfheartedly for 1980 with a bargain-basement version of the downsized R-body Chrysler Newport, again bearing the Gran Fury name and intended mainly for the fleet market. But again, sales were disappointing: fewer than 19,000 for the model year.

The shape of Plymouth's future arrived with the all-new 1978 Horizon, a five-door subcompact sedan whose 99.2-inch wheelbase made it the smallest Plymouth since the early '30s. It was virtually identical with Dodge's Omni except for grille insert, taillights and badges, and thus shared the distinction of being America's first domestically produced front-drive small car.

Horizon sold briskly from the start despite ill-founded claims that handling wasn't all it should be. In fact, roadability was one of its strengths. So were fine economy, courtesy of a 70-bhp, Volkswagen-based 104.7-cid four-cylinder engine, and a practical, space-efficient hatchback body. A sleek 2+2 "fasthatch" coupe called TC3 added some spice to the recipe for 1979.

But by that point, Plymouth was a mere shadow of its former self, down to just Horizons, TC3s, and Volarés. Management tried fostering the illusion that this was a still full-line make by slapping Plymouth nameplates on various captive imports from Mitsubishi of Japan. These included the little Arrow hatchback coupe (from 1976), the larger and more luxurious notchback Sapporo (launched for 1978 with a Dodge double called Challenger), and the front-drive Champ economy hatchback (new for '79 and dupli-

The '85 Gran Fury was popular with taxi and police fleet buyers.

The '86 Turismo Duster package included stripes, spoiler, and more.

The rear-drive Gran Fury marched into '86 with only the 318 V8.

The P-body Sundance was Plymouth's new sporty compact for 1987.

The extended body Voyager rode a 119.1-inch wheelbase, had V6 power.

Chrysler's brush with bankruptcy didn't stop Plymouth from fielding a new front-drive subcompact, the Horizon, for '78. The compact Reliant followed for '81, the Caravelle in '85. The Voyager minivan was Plymouth's biggest 1980's success.

A $1400 RS package was available on the '88 Sundance. It added the 2.5-liter engine, premium interior, two-tone paint, more.

cated as the Dodge Colt). It was a good move, providing vital sales support at a crucial time, but it only underscored how far a once-prominent marque had fallen.

Though a raft of more saleable new domestic products appeared soon enough, Plymouth's record in the '80s was pretty sorry for what had been Detroit's third best-seller. After moving slightly more than a half a million American-made cars for 1977 and again for '78, the make wouldn't exceed 400,000 units in any one year through 1986—and was well below 300,000 for 1980, '82 and '83. In industry rank, Plymouth rose to eighth for 1980 and sixth for '81 but was back to ninth by 1983, just ahead of Cadillac and trailing even Chrysler. Only Lincoln and tiny American Motors had lower volume. But an upturn was apparent near decade's end, Plymouth building nearly 444,000 cars and finishing seventh in the 1987 derby. At this writing, it remains to be seen whether the make can sustain that momentum into the '90s.

Though having fewer domestic models was a definite sales handicap, Plymouth's also-ran status in the '80s resulted as much from the conscious decision to change its image and role within the corporate lineup. Planners decreed that Chrysler would cater to the luxury market, per tradition, while Dodge would again go after the performance crowd. This left Plymouth with nothing to emphasize except reliability and value for money in products that duplicated some Dodges but were fewer in number.

The Plymouth product story in the '80s is thus basically the same as for the duller Dodges. And a short one it is, Plymouth missing out on reborn convertibles, luxury models and a latterday ponycar like the Dodge Daytona. As a result, most of Plymouth's sales volume in this decade came from just two model lines: the L-body Horizon and its derivative TC3 coupe (retitled Turismo from 1983), and the seminal K-body Reliant, which ousted Volaré from the line for 1981. Styling and engineering developments paralleled those for Dodge's Omni/Charger and Aries except for minor appearance differences and, in line with Plymouth's solid-citizen role, no Shelby-tuned subcompacts.

In most years, Reliant had the distinction of being Chrysler's best-selling nameplate, generating over 229,000 orders in its debut year, then a steady 150,000-175,000 through 1986. Plymouth's L-bodies also outsold Dodge's, though not by much, averaging 150,000 annual sales except for 1982-83 (about 90,000).

Badge-engineering provided token representation in the full-size and intermediate ranks. For the former, Plymouth got a "downsized" 1982 Gran Fury, a near-identical twin to the 112.7-inch-wheelbase M-body Dodge Diplomat, replacing the slow-sell-

The '88 Horizon America was well equipped for its $5999 base price.

The '89 Voyager could be ordered with a 150-bhp turbocharged 2.5.

The '89 Acclaim was planned as a slightly upmarket Reliant replacement. It was offered with 2.5L, 2.5L turbo, and 3.0L engines.

ing 1980-81 R-body GF. It, too, ran with few year-to-year changes as a single four-door sedan, offered with six and V8 power (V8 only after 1983) and one or two trim levels. Of course, it was nothing like previous Gran Furys, being the original Aspen/Volaré compact as evolved through the mid-size 1977 Diplomat and Chrysler LeBaron. Most sold to police and taxi fleets, where the M-body's aging but proven rear-drive design was an asset.

Canadians had been able to buy an M-body Plymouth before 1982 as the Caravelle. For 1985 this name came to the U.S. on a slightly restyled down-priced version of what had been the Chrysler E-Class. With the same basic design as Dodge's 103.3-inch-wheelbase 600 sedan, this front-drive Caravelle was nominally Plymouth's mid-size family car, and it sold in plain and up-level SE trim at a respectable 45,000-50,000 a year before its 1989 retirement. Unlike Dodge with the 600 ES, Plymouth was never allowed a sportier model or even a five-speed transaxle, but the 146-bhp turbocharged edition of Chrysler's 2.2-liter (135-cid) "Trans-4" engine was optional—and just as out of place here as in the Reliant. Most Caravelles had either a 2.6-liter (156-cid) Mitsubishi "balancer" four or the Chrysler-built 2.5-liter enlargement of the 2.2. All had TorqueFlite automatic.

Like Dodge, Plymouth's other big winner in this decade was the practical K-based T-115 minivan of 1984. The name here was Voyager (retained from Dodge-clone big Plymouth vans of the '70s), but that and a different grille were about all that distinguished it from Dodge's Caravan. It proved just as popular, of course, generating well over 100,000 sales each year, bolstered from 1988 by the addition of extended-body Grand Voyagers on a 119.1-inch wheelbase. Car-like ride, maneuverability and convenience set it apart from trucky rear-drive imitators. Added to the K-cars' success, the fast-selling T-wagons were a big reason why Chrysler Corporation was enjoying record profits by mid-decade, a mere five years or so after nearly tumbling into the financial abyss.

Plymouth naturally got in on the new-for-'87 P-body, the more upscale subcompact originally intended to replace Omni/Horizon. Called Sundance (reviving the name of an early-'70s Satellite trim option), it was much like the Dodge Shadow but initially aimed more at luxury-minded small-car shoppers, offering only one well-equipped trim level and suspension tuned more for ride than handling.

But somebody in Highland Park hadn't forgotten Plymouth's performance past, because 1988 brought a new RS package option with sportier appointments inside and out: integral foglamps, two-tone paint, wider tires on racier wheels, special bucket seats and leather-rim steering wheel. An optional 2.2-liter port-injected turbo-four with 146 bhp backed up this brag through '88, then gave way to a blown 150-bhp 2.5; available through 1989 were a standard 93-bhp 2.2 and optional 100-bhp 2.5, both normally aspirated engines with electronic throttle-body injection. All could be teamed with standard five-speed manual or optional TorqueFlite transaxles.

Like Shadow, the Sundance generated a bit over 93,000 sales in its first year, suggesting that Chrysler could still reach small-car buyers as effectively as ever. Of course, the Sundance was very different from the old Valiant, but arguably just as right for its time and market.

The same might be said of the new-for-'89 Acclaim. Like Sundance, it was conceived to replace an older Plymouth, in this case the remarkable Reliant, but the latter's continuing sales strength prompted corporate planners to let the new and the old run side-by-side for a time, much as Volaré and Valiant did in '76. More immediately, Acclaim replaced the Caravelle as Plymouth's mid-size sedan, riding the same wheelbase but built on the same new A-body platform as Dodge's Spirit. There's still a lot of K-car in Acclaim styling, but the look is more contemporary: formal yet smooth, and carefully detailed for good aerodynamic efficiency.

Here again, Plymouth marketed its version of a shared package less aggressively than Dodge, offering Acclaim in base, mid-range LE and luxury LX models with few overtly sporting touches. Nevertheless, engine choices were the same as Spirit's: blown and unblown 2.5 fours and the new 3.0-liter Mitsubishi V6, the last reserved for LX and teamed with Chrysler's first four-speed overdrive automatic transaxle. And certain sporty features like bucket seats were available, though these were perhaps more expected than sporting by now.

Regardless, the Acclaim offered fresh evidence that "family car" didn't have to mean dull mediocrity, an apt expression of where Plymouth seemed to be headed into the '90s. Though no longer number-three or even known for high-performance, Plymouth was still offering fine value and solid engineering. Some things never change.

The front-drive Reliant served Plymouth through most of the Eighties; its new-for-1989 replacement—the Acclaim—will have to see it through much of the '90s. Indications are that Chrysler will give Plymouth more emphasis in the future.

PONTIAC

Pontiac remains the only General Motors nameplate introduced after the company's founding to survive past 1940. It's also the only survivor among the firm's four companion makes that appeared in the mid-1920s. But Pontiac's future was far from secure in the early Depression years. The first car to bear the name, the Pontiac Six of 1926, quickly proved far more popular than its Oakland parent, pushing total division sales to over 200,000 units by 1929. Then came the Great Crash and, as everywhere else in the industry, Pontiac sales plummeted, hitting rock-bottom in 1932 at a bit over 45,000 units.

What saved the make was the calm, confident policies of GM president Alfred P. Sloan, who combined Pontiac and Chevrolet manufacturing in early 1933, thus saving vast amounts in tooling costs through greater use of shared bodies, chassis and other major components. At the same time, he consolidated Buick, Oldsmobile and Pontiac sales operations, requiring dealers for each make to sell the other two as well. These belt-tightening measures continued through mid-1934, effectively reducing GM to three divisions: Cadillac, Chevrolet, and B-O-P.

The well-styled 1933 Eight turned Pontiac around completely. The division was back over 200,000 by 1937, and would rank among the top five or six producers well into the '50s. A group of highly competent leaders contributed mightily to this recovery. Among the more notable: former Ford executive William S. "Big Bill" Knudsen, division general manager in 1932-33 and GM president in 1937-40; chief engineer Benjamin H. Anibal, father of the Pontiac eight; and studio stylist Frank Hershey, creator of the handsome 1933 and subsequent models.

After two years of all eights, Pontiac revived sixes for 1935 Standard and DeLuxe models on a 112-inch wheelbase. The en-

The DeLuxe Eight, Pontiac's top series for 1939, rode a 120-inch wheelbase and had 100 bhp. The convertible retailed for $1046.

gine was a conventional 208-cubic-inch L-head with 80 bhp. Anibal's 84-bhp 223.4-cid L-head straight eight powered a 116.6-inch-wheelbase line priced about $100 higher, which was a lot in those days. Sixes accordingly outsold Eights by a wide margin through the remainder of the decade.

Having acquired GM's "Knee-Action" independent front suspension for '34, Pontiac inherited its new all-steel "Turret Top" construction for 1935. That same year, Pontiac introduced its distinctive "Silver Streak" trim, which started at the cowl and ran straight forward right over the hood and down the grille. Originated by a young designer named Virgil Exner, who would contribute to the early postwar Studebakers and Chrysler's mid-'50s "Forward Look," Silver Streak ornamentation would be a Pontiac hallmark for the next 20 years.

Pontiac's Depression-era styling evolved along typical lines. The 1930-32s were boxy and undistinguished, but the 1933-34s were among the prettiest medium-price cars of the era. Transitional "potato" shapes prevailed for 1935-36. Thanks partly to longer wheelbases (117/122 inches), the 1937-38 models were better-proportioned, but the vertical streaks on massive horizontal grilles made frontal appearance confused. That was cured for 1939 with Harley Earl's twin "catwalk" grilles twixt fenders and main grille. With mostly vertical facial lines, the '39s looked much better than earlier Pontiacs. Also in evidence that year were wider "pontoon" fenders, lower overall height, larger glass areas, and smaller pod-style headlamps partly faired into the front fenders.

After five years of mostly steady gains, sales fell to just over 97,000 units in recession 1938 as Pontiac dropped from fifth to sixth, behind Dodge. But it built a healthy 144,000 cars for '39 and returned to fifth behind Chevy, Ford, Plymouth and Buick.

The newly rebodied '39 models grouped into three series, one more than for 1937-38. At the bottom was the 115-inch-wheelbase Quality Deluxe comprising coupes, sedans and a wood-body wagon. Priced about $50 higher model for model was a new hybrid offering, the Deluxe 120, which used the six-cylinder engine—enlarged for '37 to 222.7 cid and 85 bhp—in the 120-inch-wheelbase Deluxe Eight chassis. Coupes, sedans, and a convertible made up both DeLuxe lines. The eight had also been uprated for '37, to 248.9 cid and 100 bhp. It would remain there through 1949, and would be the backbone of Pontiac power through 1954. The six was reliable and economical, the eight more refined, a bit

The '47 Streamliner woody could be had with either a six or eight.

As was the custom, the '40 Pontiac shared its body with Chevy.

Pontiac marketed 28 models spread over six series for the '41 season.

Fenders flowed into the doors for '42. The Torpedo Eight cost $1010.

It cost $1538 to buy a brand-new '46 Streamliner Eight four door.

The '47 Pontiac was little changed; soft-top prices started at $1811.

The '48 was mildly restyled. A Streamliner Eight listed at $1775.

The all-new '49 Pontiac came in 32 six- and eight-cylinder models.

The Chieftain Eight sedan coupe retailed for $1779 base in 1949.

thirstier, but powerful enough. An English road test suggested the Pontiac Eight "might be borne along by the wind," so impressive were its quietness and smoothness.

For 1940 there were two lines for each engine: six-cylinder Special and DeLuxe, eight-cylinder DeLuxe and Torpedo. Each offered four-passenger coupes and four-door sedans. The lineup also included a Special business coupe and wagon, DeLuxe Six "cabriolet" convertible, and DeLuxe Eight cabriolet and business coupe. The six was now rated at 87 bhp. Production moved up more substantially, reaching 217,000 for the model year.

In line with a corporate-wide restyle for 1941, Pontiac adopted higher, crisper fenders embellished with additional Silver Streaks. There were now no fewer than six separate series, all called Torpedo: six- and eight-cylinder DeLuxe, Streamliner, and Custom. The DeLuxe, sharing a new 119-inch-wheelbase GM A-body with Chevrolet, offered the most body styles and accounted for 150,000 sales. Among its offerings was the attractive mid-season Metropolitan sedan, with closed-in rear roof quarters that gave it a more formal appearance. Streamliners and Customs rode the 122-inch-wheelbase B-body platform used for junior Buicks and Oldsmobiles, and included new fastback four-door sedans and two-door "sedan coupes." Convertibles, offered only as DeLuxes, appealed for a soft top bereft of rear side windows, a treatment reminiscent of earlier custom-bodied Packards.

Distinguishing all '41 Pontiacs were a new full-width horizontal-bar grille (which mated well with the Silver Streak hood trim), headlamps fully encased within the front fenders, and concealed running boards (via flared door extensions) except on wagons. The six now assumed the form it would retain through 1954, bored out to 239.2 cid and 90 bhp.

As ever, Pontiac was the next step up from Chevy, conservatively trimmed and far less luxurious than Oldsmobile or Buick but carefully built to very competitive prices. The cheapest Pontiac cost just $783 in 1940 and only $828 in '41; the costliest was the $1250 Custom Torpedo station wagon of 1941.

After record volume of over 330,000 units, Pontiac built about 83,500 of its heavily facelifted '42s, all but 15,000 produced in the closing months of 1941. Styling again followed GM practice: a gaudy grille, longer front fenders blended into the front doors, rounded "drop-off" rear fenders. Series thinned to four: 112-inch-wheelbase Streamliner Six and Eight and 119-inch Torpedo Six and Eight. The '41 Streamliners had divided into standard and Super sub-models. The '42s were called standard and Chieftain, each offering fastback sedan coupe, fastback four-door sedan and a woody wagon. Chieftains cost $50 more than standard Streamliners, which ran above corresponding Torpedos. Eights delivered for only $25 more than Sixes, yet production split 50/50.

Like most other makes, Pontiac marked time with warmed-over '42 models for 1946-48, but stylists made each succeeding edition look a little different. The '46s, which began rolling out of the division's Pontiac, Michigan, home plant in September 1945, had triple chrome fender strips and a big bell-shaped grille composed of vertical and horizontal bars. The latter was simplified for '47, then became busy on the '48s, which were the first Pontiacs to carry Silver Streak nameplates.

Otherwise, the 1946-47 Pontiacs were entirely prewar in design and specifications. As before, a three-speed manual was the only transmission available. The '46 lineup was also prewar save the Chieftain sub-models, which did not return. Eights now cost $30 more than Sixes and all prices were higher, rising steadily through '48. A Deluxe Torpedo ragtop was added for 1947.

Though still basically '42s, the 1948 models arrived with some interesting differences. A deluxe trim package was newly available across the line, offering chrome fender moldings, gravel guards, wheel discs and other embellishments for $90-$120 extra. The eight was now inexplicably rated at 104 bhp instead of its usual 103, but the big news was Pontiac's belated introduction of Hydra-Matic Drive as a $185 option.

Hydra-Matic was undoubtedly a factor in the division's near 235,500 model-year '48 sales because of its growing importance to the eight-cylinder buyers then starting to dominate the ranks of Pontiac customers. Eights had first outsold Sixes in 1947 and were far ahead for '48. Only 50 percent of the Sixes were ordered with Hydra-Matic, versus 80 percent of the Eights. All this suggested that Pontiac was moving from its traditional "big Chevy" price

A toothier grille was seen on the '50 Pontiac. A Chieftain Eight convertible listed at $2190. All Pontiacs were Silver Streaks.

All 1950 wagons were Streamliners in 1950, here the $2332 Eight.

The Catalina hardtop debuted for 1951, trimmed as a DeLuxe or Super.

All Pontiacs were Chieftains for '53; all convertibles were DeLuxe.

It's not generally known that Pontiac sold a sedan delivery in '53.

bracket toward the heart of the medium-price field. It was thus understandable that Pontiac dropped sixes after 1954 to concentrate exclusively on overhead-valve V8s through 1960.

Pontiac fared very well in GM's corporate-wide postwar overhaul for 1949, a new 120-inch-wheelbase chassis supporting an equally new A-body created under the watchful eye of company styling chief Harley Earl. Series were named Chieftain and Streamliner, the latter with fastback instead of notchback styling, though it also included wagons. Each line offered the usual choice of six- and eight-cylinder engines and standard and DeLuxe trim. The latter again involved extra chrome (on side and windshield moldings, plus rear fender gravel guards and full wheel covers). Newly optional high-compression heads boosted the six to 93 bhp and the eight to 106.

Pontiac's '49 styling was attractive. A lower, full-width grille was bisected by a single bar above little vertical teeth, a fairly conservative face. Silver Streaks remained on hood and rear deck per tradition, but front fenders were now flush with the bodysides. Though the '49s looked lighter than the '48s, they actually weighed a bit more, so performance was about the same despite the small horsepower increases.

Continuing postwar inflation pushed prices considerably higher

Pontiac's first postwar restyle arrived for 1949. Although lower and sleeker, the new models were very traditionally Pontiac, as evidenced by Chief Pontiac's presence on the hood and by the silver streaks on the hood and decklid.

for '49. The costliest convertible jumped by nearly $200; the woody wagon cost over $2600. As at Chevrolet, the wagon body switched from part-structural wood to more practical all-steel construction at mid-model year, though there was no change in price and very little change in appearance. Despite the heftier price tags, model year volume rose to nearly 305,000, the second highest in Pontiac history.

The 1950 line was predictably much like the '49. Body styles again ran to Chieftain two- and four-door sedans, business and club coupes, and convertibles, plus Streamliner wagons and fastback two- and four-door sedans. As before, there were six- and eight-cylinder standard and DeLuxe versions of each, save the DeLuxe-only ragtop. A significant new arrival was Pontiac's first hardtop-convertible, the Catalina, a Chieftain offered in DeLuxe or new Super trim. By the end of the year, Catalinas were accounting for some nine percent of total sales. A toothy grille and shuffled trim were the main styling changes. The illuminated countenance of Chief Pontiac continued as a hood mascot. On the engine chart, the long-running straight eight was bored out to 268.4 cid, good for 108 bhp standard or 113 with high-compression heads. This year's six was available in only one 90-bhp version.

Production was up again for 1950, smashing the 1941 record at nearly 466,500. Nevertheless, as it had since '48, Pontiac still ranked fifth. It would not finish higher until 1959.

Volume sank to about 370,000 for 1951 as all Detroit began feeling the effects of the Korean War, yet that total was Pontiac's second-best ever. Fastbacks were fading from favor, so the Streamliner four-door was dropped, followed in the spring of '51 by the two-door sedan coupe. The most noticeable styling change was a "gullwing" main grille bar below a prominent medallion. Both engines were tweaked, the six to 102 bhp, the eight to 122 bhp.

A busier grille and deletion of the long-deck Chieftain coupes were the main alterations for 1952. Korean War restrictions and a nationwide steel strike limited model year output to 271,000.

A major reskin of the '49 A-body and a two-inch-longer wheelbase gave 1953's new all-Chieftain line a more "important" look. Sales trends had prompted these and other changes. Catalina hardtops, for example, now regularly took over 20 percent of sales, and Hydra-Matic installations had climbed to 84 percent. The '53s were thus larger in most every dimension, and shinier. Highlighting the new look were kicked-up rear fenders, a lower grille, more prominent bumpers, and a one-piece windshield.

Newly optional power steering made the '53s easier to park: more horsepower made them faster, especially the six. The latter now delivered 115 bhp with manual transmission or 118 with Hydra-Matic; corresponding eight-cylinder outputs were 118/122. A lowish rear axle ratio of 3.03:1 was specified for smooth top-range performance with Hydra-Matic. A mid-1953 fire in the Hydra-Matic plant shortened supplies, however, so about 18,500 Pontiacs were fitted with Chevrolet's Powerglide in 1953-54. Pontiac sold extremely well for 1953: nearly 419,000 units.

Nineteen fifty-four was a facelift year. Revised side moldings and a narrow oval in the central grille bar were the main distinctions. The big news, however, was Star Chief, a top-line eight-cylinder hardtop, convertible and four-door sedan on a new 124-inch wheelbase. They were the plushest Pontiacs yet—and the priciest ($2300-$2600)—another sign of the division's steady drive upmarket. They sold well, but Pontiac's total volume slipped to just below 288,000, suggesting it was time for something new.

That's just what Pontiac delivered for 1955. Among a claimed 109 new features were fully up-to-date styling, an improved chassis and—the really hot item—the make's first modern overhead-valve V8. The last, called "Strato Streak," arrived with 287.2 cid (but would ultimately grow much larger) and 180 bhp standard or 200 bhp with optional four-barrel carburetor. A strong, conventional oversquare design with five main bearings, it somewhat related to Chevy's all-new '55 V8. It wasn't quite as advanced, but it would serve the division admirably for more than a quarter-century.

Pontiac built 19,762 Star Chief soft tops for '55. Cost: $2691.

A new grille and altered two-toning were seen on the 1956 Pontiac.

Pontiac sold 11,536 Chieftain Safari nine-passenger wagons for '57.

As on GM's other '55s, Pontiac styling was somewhat boxier but quite trendy, with wraparound windshield, cowl ventilation, new solid colors and two-tones, and a longer, lower look despite unchanged wheelbases. A blunt face was the one dubious aspect. As before, this completely new A-body was shared with Chevrolet. Pontiac's shorter wheelbase still carried two Chieftain series, only now they were all-V8 models: low-priced 860 sedans and wagons, mid-range 870 sedans, wagons, and Catalina hardtop. Star Chief returned on its extended chassis with a base-trim sedan and convertible and a Custom Catalina and sedan.

Riding the Chieftain wheelbase but officially a Star Chief was the exotic Custom Safari, a new hardtop-styled two-door wagon based on the Chevrolet Nomad. Chevy stylist Carl Renner recalled that "when Pontiac saw [the Nomad] they felt they could do something with it...Management wanted it for the Pontiac line, so it

Under "Bunky" Knudsen, performance moved to the forefront. The fuel-injected '57 Bonneville packed over 300 bhp; 630 were built.

Bonneville became a series in 1958—3096 convertibles were produced.

The '58 Bonneville hardtop saw 9144 units sold at $3481 and up.

worked out." Like Nomad, the original '55 Safari would continue with successive facelifts only through 1957 (after which both names were applied to conventional four-door wagons). It naturally cost more than Nomad, and thus sold in fewer numbers.

On balance, 1955 was a vintage year for Pontiac. Its cars were a solid hit with dealers and public alike, and the division built close to 554,000 of them, a new record. But some rough times lay ahead, and Pontiac wouldn't exceed this figure until 1963, after which it began setting new records. At least three factors accounted for this interim slump. Buick's Special and the base Olds 88 were more aggressively priced; demand for lower-medium cars shrank as import sales expanded in the late '50s; and the 1956-58 Pontiacs weren't that exciting, though they were competitive in most ways and faster than ever.

A mild facelift was ordained for '56, when four-door Catalina hardtops were added to each series. Styling was less distinctive (tester Tom McCahill said the '56 looked like "it had been born on its nose"), and Pontiac had become known as a not-so-easy rider. The V8 grew to 316.6 cid but didn't pack an extraordinary amount of power: only 205 in Chieftains and 227 bhp in Star Chiefs. Like most other makes, Pontiac saw lower '56 output after record-shattering '55, dropping to sixth on volume of 405,500 units.

July 1956 ushered in Semon E. "Bunkie" Knudsen (son of "Big Bill") as Pontiac general manager (the youngest in division history). GM brass told him to do what he could with the existing design, and Knudsen hustled. Among the mechanical changes he instituted for '57: longer rear springs in rubber shackles; 14-inch wheels and tires (replacing 15-inchers); pedal parking brake; optional automatic antenna; and a 347-cid V8 enlargement delivering 252-290 bhp. Stylewise, the grille became a massive bucktooth affair; two-toning switched from its half-car 1955-56 pattern to bodyside sweepspears; and Silver Streak trim was banished as

Pontiac began its transformation from an old man's car to a young man's car in 1955. Styling was bolder, more youthful, and a new ohv V-8 backed up the good looks. The silver streaks disappeared after '56; the Bonneville bowed in 1957.

old-hat. Series were renamed: low-end Chieftain and new mid-price Super Chief on the short wheelbase, Star Chief on the longer chassis.

But where Bunkie really got his way was the fast and flashy Bonneville, a mid-'57 arrival. Delivering 300 bhp via fuel injection, hydraulic lifters and racing cam, this $5782 convertible was the costliest and fastest Pontiac yet—even faster with optional Tri-Power (three two-barrel carbs). A fuel-injected Bonnie was timed at 18 seconds in the standing quarter-mile; a Tri-Power car did it in 16.8.

Because it was basically a promotional piece, the '57 Bonneville saw only 630 copies. But it give Pontiac a whole new performance

Bonneville headed the lineup in '59, the year of the "Wide Track."

The '60 Catalina ragtop listed at $3078 and 17,172 were produced.

Star Chief was the mid-line series in 1960, priced from $2932.

The '62 Catalina seen here had a Jeweltone Morrokide Ventura interior.

The Bonneville two-door hardtop attracted 30,995 customers in 1963.

The Catalina-based $3915 Grand Prix racked up 72,959 sales in 1963.

Ragtops were still popular in '64 as Pontiac built 22,016 Bonnevilles.

Pontiac's hot GTO was just what the younger set wanted in 1964.

image even as the Auto Manufacturers Association came down against factory-sponsored racing. A few '57 Pontiacs raced with distinction in NASCAR, but were strictly private entries. Yet the lack of victories didn't hamper sales. Chevy, Olds and Buick all lost sales to rival Chrysler products, but Pontiac built some 333,500 of its '57 cars to move within 51,000 units of fifth-place Olds.

An all-new body should have made the '58s even more popular, but a recession set in and held output to only 217,000 units. Unlike most GM cars that year, Pontiac was really well-styled, with a simpler, full-width grille, quad headlights, and wider, concave sidespears. Bodies were lower but not much longer or wider; wheelbases were unchanged. Model offerings now ran to no fewer than seven Catalina hardtops with two or four doors. Bonneville became a regular series, and sold about 12,000 convertibles and hardtop coupes. Another bore job took the Pontiac V8 to 370 cid. This year's four "standard" engines ran from 240 bhp for manual-shift Chieftains/Super Chiefs to 285 for automatic Star Chiefs and Bonnevilles. Optional across-the-board were a 300-bhp Tri-Power unit and a 310-bhp fuelie.

The '59s were the first Pontiacs to fully reflect the Bunkie Knudsen touch, and they set the pattern that the division would follow through its glory years of the '60s. Crisp styling on a brand-new A-body brought the split grille theme that remains a Pontiac hallmark to this day, plus modest twin-fin rear fenders and minimal side trim. Wheelbases were again unchanged, but the wheels were set further apart on a new "Wide-Track" chassis that made these some of 1959's most roadable Detroiters.

The V8 was again puffed up, this time to 389 cid, and delivered 315 bhp with Tri-Power down to 245. There was also a detuned 215-bhp "Tempest 420E" for economy-minded buyers, capable of delivering up to 20 mpg in restrained driving. Replacing Chieftain and Super Chief was the new Catalina series on the short wheelbase; Star Chief and Bonneville shared the longer one. Bolstered by wagon and hardtop sedan models, the '59 Bonneville garnered some 82,000 sales. Total volume rose to near 383,000, enough to boost Pontiac into fourth place for the first time.

Pontiac show cars of the '50s were always interesting and often predictive. The smooth 1954 Strato Streak previewed the pillarless four-doors to come for '56. Also shown in '54 was the first Bonneville, a Corvette-like two-seater with canopy-type cockpit on a 100-inch wheelbase. Both cars carried straight eights. The 1955 Strato Star was a two-door, four-seat hardtop that forecast '56 styling. Wildest of all was the 1956 Club de Mer, with "twin pod" seating and dual bubble windshields. Standing only 38.4 inches high, its aluminum body was painted Cerulean blue, Harley Earl's favorite color.

In the '60s, under enthusiast-oriented chiefs like Knudsen and Elliot M. "Pete" Estes (who served as GM president in 1974-81), Pontiac became synonymous with high performance. Much of this can be credited to the compact Tempest and its later mid-size evolutions. The debut '61 was significant for having GM's first postwar four-cylinder engine, a flexible driveshaft, and a rear transaxle (a transmission in unit with the differential, allied to independent link-type suspension).

One buff magazine said the Tempest "sets many new trends and unquestionably is a prototype of the American car for the Sixties." But no U.S. producer ever copied its radical driveline (though Porsche used something similar on its 928 of 1977) and Detroit didn't shift strongly to fours until the early '80s. The 1961-63 Tempests were fairly popular, but their orthodox successors sold far better. The original 110/130-bhp 195-cid four, basically half a 389 V8, was abandoned on the '64s for an inline six—sensibly cost-effective if hardly memorable.

Like a speedometer cable, the Tempest's "rope" driveshaft carried rotary motion through a gentle curve—a long bar that bent slightly beneath the floor, thin but lightly stressed. Carried with a steel case, it was mounted on bearings and permanently lubricated. Its slight sag reduced floor-hump height in front but not in back. It also eliminated universal joints and allowed softer engine mounts for better interior isolation. A first for Detroit if not the world, the transaxle made the Tempest less nose-heavy than its conventional cousins, the Olds F-85 and Buick Special. But though the independent rear suspension was ostensibly superior,

The '64 GTO soft top stickered at $3500 and 6644 were quickly sold.

GTO for 1966 had a larger, curvier body and vertical headlamps.

The hardtop sedan was the favored '66 Bonneville with 68,646 built.

The '67 Catalina 2+2 featured front fender vents and a big 428 V8.

The U.S. launched the first ballistic-missile submarine, the George Washington, in 1959. Pontiac launched its exciting new "Wide Track" models with plenty of emphasis on youth and performance. Pontiac would take over third place in 1962.

Pontiac built 9517 GTO convertibles for 1967. Prices started at $3165 with the standard 335-horsepower 400-cubic-inch V8.

Pontiac's nose became beakier for '68. Bonnevilles started at $3530.

Pontiac joined the ponycar fray in 1967; the '68 lost its vent panes.

it made the car prone to sudden oversteer that could be alarming on wet roads. Still, the Tempest generally handled well.

Tempest's initial 112-inch-wheelbase unit body/chassis structure was the basic B-O-P compact platform of 1961-63. Its standard four teamed with both manual and automatic transaxles and was offered in several stages of tune to suit regular or premium gas. By 1963, horsepower was up to 115-166. Optionally available for 1961-62 was the aluminum 215-cid Buick V8 with 155/185 bhp. This was replaced for '63 by a debored 326-cid version of the Pontiac 389 packing 260 bhp. So equipped, the Tempest was quick: capable of 0-60 mph in 9.5 seconds and a top speed of 115 mph.

Tempest arrived in a single series with two- and four-door sedans and a liftgate four-door Safari wagon. A coupe bowed at mid-season with a choice of standard or sportier bucket-seat interiors, the latter christened LeMans. Deluxe and LeMans convertibles were added for '62 and proved quite popular. LeMans became a separate series for '63. Styling didn't change much in these years.

Output of the '68 Grand Prix fell to 31,701 units. Price: $3697.

Pontiac debuted the Firebird Trans Am at the '69 Chicago Auto Show.

Pontiac moved the 1969 Grand Prix off the Catalina chassis to the mid-size platform. Sales exploded. The '70 model listed at $3985.

The hot car market was waning, but 40,149 GTOs were built for 1970.

The '70 Bonneville was more formal looking. Note the horn ports.

A twin-oval grille was used for '61, a full-width three-section design for '62, a modified twin grille and squarer body lines for '63.

For 1964, GM lengthened its compacts to a 115-inch wheelbase, which made them intermediates. Pontiac issued a redesigned Tempest bearing taut, geometric lines on the accompanying corporate A-body shared with Chevrolet's new Chevelle, the Olds F-85/Cutlass and Buick's Special/Skylark. But the real excitement came with the mid-season debut of the Tempest GTO, the first of the "muscle cars." The nickname was well taken. With the right options, a GTO could deliver unprecedented performance for a six-passenger automobile.

You had to "build" your GTO in '64. Start with a Tempest coupe, hardtop or convertible, then add the GTO package—floorshift, 389 V8, quick steering, stiff shocks, dual exhaust, and premium tires—at about $300. From there you were on your own: four-speed gearbox ($188); metallic brake linings, heavy-duty radiator and limited-slip differential ($75 the lot); 360-bhp engine ($115). Then all you needed was a lead foot and lots of gas.

Sports-car purists took umbrage at Pontiac's use of GTO (*gran turismo omologato*, an Italian term referring to production-based racing cars), but an outspoken enthusiast magazine bravely answered the critics by comparing Pontiac's GTO with Ferrari's. A good Pontiac, they said, would trim the Ferrari in a drag race and lose on a road course. But "with the addition of NASCAR road racing suspension, the Pontiac will take the measure of any Ferrari other than prototype racing cars...The Ferrari costs $20,000. With every conceivable option on a GTO, it would be difficult to spend more than $3800. That's a bargain."

The successful LeMans/Tempest formula saw relatively little change through 1967. Vertical headlights and crisper styling arrived for '65. The '66s had three-inch-longer bodies with smoother contours, including hopped-up "Coke-bottle" rear fenders.

For 1968 came a new GM A-body with dual wheelbase—116 inches for four-doors, 112 inches for two-doors—plus revamped styling that continued to display big-Pontiac elements such as a large bumper/grille and, on hardtop coupes, more rakish fastback rooflines. Standard for GTO was a new 400-cid extension of the 389 V8 pumping out 350 bhp; 360 was optional via a Ram-Air hood scoop. The '68 GTO also featured a neatly integrated energy-absorbing front bumper covered in color-keyed Endura plastic.

The mid-size Pontiacs continued in this basic form through 1972. Among the mildly facelifted '69s was a hotter GTO: "The Judge," with colorful striping, a 366-bhp Ram-Air V8 and three-speed manual gearbox with Hurst shifter. The 1970s received clumsier front ends, bigger rear bumpers, and pronounced longitudinal bodyside bulges above the wheel openings. The result was a heavier-looking Tempest, GTO, LeMans and LeMans Sport. Collectors have since tended to prefer the tidier 1964-69 models.

The base engine on 1964-65 Tempests was a 215-cid inline six from Oldsmobile rated at 140 bhp. For 1966 came a surprise replacement: a European-style overhead-cam six. Sized at 230 cid, it developed 165 bhp standard or 207 bhp in Sprint form (via Rochester Ouadra-Jet carburetor, hotter valve timing and double

Pontiac meant excitement in the Sixties because it was a style and performance leader. One example was the '64 GTO, a hot Pontiac created by dropping a big-block V-8 into a mid-size body. The rest of Detroit was quick to imitate it.

The '71 GTO was available in four models, among them the Judge hardtop coupe. It listed for $3840, and only 357 were produced.

valve springs). The crankshaft had seven main bearings; the camshaft was driven by a fiberglass-reinforced notched belt rather than conventional chain or gear drive.

So equipped, the '66 Tempest was a satisfying performer, if hardly in the GTO's league. The typical Sprint could do 0-60 mph in 10 seconds and reach 115 mph. With options like bucket seats, console and four-speed floorshift, the clean-lined Sprint had the look and feel of a true grand touring car. A longer stroke took the

At $4595 the '71 Trans Am was a bit pricey; only 2116 were built.

The '71 Bonneville had a 455-cubic-inch two-barrel V8 as standard.

ohc engine to 250 cid for 1968, good for 175 bhp or, in Sprint trim, 215 bhp (230 bhp for '69). Sadly, it proved less than reliable and, like the Tempest four before it, departed after 1969 in favor of a conventional overhead-valve Chevy six of the same displacement.

With Pontiac's performance image secure by the mid-'60s, division managers knew that their Firebird "ponycar" had to be something special—especially as it would use the basic 108-inch-wheelbase F-body structure of Chevrolet's new-for-'67 Camaro. But the Firebird was different, sporting a Pontiac-style divided grille and offering an optional 325-bhp 400-cid V8. The base-tune ohc six was initially standard, and the optional Sprint version made for a sprightly yet economical performer.

Debuting about six months behind Camaro, the Firebird wasn't modified much through early 1970. A change of engines made the '67 Firebird 326 a 350 model for '68, when side marker lights were added per federal decree. The '69s were restyled below the belt and gained a host of government-ordered safety features. Convertibles continued until "1970½," when the all-new coupe-only second generation arrived.

Of course, the hottest and most memorable early Firebird was the '69 Trans Am, a $725 option package announced in March and loosely inspired by the Firebirds contesting the Trans-American road-racing series. Special badges, white paint set off by twin dorsal racing stripes, and a decklid spoiler identified it; a 335-bhp Ram Air III 400 gave it great go; a heavily fortified chassis and brakes made for superb roadability. Only 689 of the '69s were built, including a mere eight convertibles and just nine cars with the optional 345-bhp Ram Air IV engine. But the T/A was destined for much greater success, and would earn it soon enough.

Though sometimes overlooked in the excitement surrounding its smaller models, Pontiac built some of Detroit's best-looking, best-handling standard cars in the '60s. The public loved them: Sales jumped from about 400,000 for 1960 to nearly half a million by '69. On a divisional basis, Pontiac ran third to Chevrolet and Ford for 1962-70, and these big cars had a lot to do with it.

They began the decade as facelifted '59s bearing high "twin-tube" taillamps and a vee'd, full-width horizontal-bar grille. A fourth series was added, the Catalina-based Ventura, a hardtop coupe and Vista hardtop sedan priced just below Star Chief. Both were dropped for '62 in favor of the bucket-seat Grand Prix, an elegantly tailored hardtop coupe, also on the Catalina chassis. A fast-riser on the sales charts, the GP finished the decade outdrawing all other full-size Pontiacs save the Catalinas—and with just a single body style. (A GP convertible, offered only for 1967, is now a collector's item as only 5856 were built.)

Big-Pontiac styling kept improving, at least through '66. The distinctive split grille returned for 1961, along with crisp new Bill Mitchell lines on shorter wheelbases: 120 inches for Catalina/Ventura, 123 inches on Star Chief and Bonneville, 119 inches for wagons. Catalina added an inch for '62. Clean machines with stacked quad headlamps and narrow, split grilles appeared for 1963-64. The '65s were well executed, but had a massive, bulging front and billowy bodyside sculpturing, both de-emphasized for '66. Wheelbases lengthened to 121 inches for Catalina/GP/wagons and 124 inches for Star Chief/Bonneville.

Alas, the '67s looked even bulkier, with heavy, curved rear fenders. For 1968 came a huge bumper/grille with prominent vertical center bulge. Both wheelbases tacked on another inch for '69, when the schnoz was toned down. The following year brought an upright twin-element grille that was faintly evocative of the '30s but far less graceful.

Model offerings in this period were remarkably consistent. Bucket-seat "2+2" Catalinas arrived for 1965, an extra-cost trim package for the convertible and hardtop coupe. This became a separate series for 1966, then vanished due to the fast-fading demand for sporty full-size cars. The only other change involved the mid-range Star Chief. It tacked on the name Executive for '66, which then supplanted Star Chief through 1970.

Big-Pontiac engines were also quite consistent in the '60s, with numerous horsepower variations offered in just four basic sizes—two large units and two "small"—all derived from the original 1955 V8. The latter were a 389 through 1966 and a bored-out 400 from '67. Base power for all models, they ranged from 215 to 350 bhp, the latter standard for the 1967-70 Grand Prix. The larger units, optional on most models, were a 421 for 1963-66 and a 428 through '69, after which a 455 took over. Horsepower peaked at 376 for '67, then began declining with federally mandated emission controls. A monster 427-bhp 421 powered a lightweight 1963-64 Catalina drag-racing special featuring aluminum body panels, plastic side windows and a drilled-out frame.

The '70s would prove one of Pontiac's most difficult decades. A decision to outproduce and out-price Chevy (generally credited to John Z. DeLorean, division chief in 1965-69) while simultaneously reaching into Buick/Oldsmobile territory led workmanship to slip badly. It also contributed to a confusing succession of models that left many buyers wondering just what a Pontiac was. Not surprisingly, sales sagged. After slipping to fourth in the 1970 rankings, Pontiac would finish fourth or fifth most every year through 1986, usually behind Olds. Buick was often a threat, closing to within 28,000 units for 1972. By 1980, Pontiac trailed Buick by nearly 84,000 units; the gap with Oldsmobile was 140,000-plus.

But not all was gloom. Given the ponycar market's rapid decline after 1969, Firebird was a surprising bright spot, the Trans Am in particular. The brilliant second-generation design of "1970½" would run all the way through 1981 with just three styling updates (for 1974, '77 and '79), yet always kept Pontiac's "hot car" image simmering—to the point where, as the division later admitted, more people knew what a Trans Am was than what Pontiac stood for.

Like Camaro, Firebird almost died after 1972 due to corporate doubts about the future of performance cars, aggravated by a strike that severely cut volume that year. But Pontiac kept the faith and reaped the rewards. While Chevy dropped its hottest Camaro, the Z28, for 1975-76, Pontiac retained the T/A as the most serious model in the line. As a result, the T/A soon moved from peripheral

The '72 GTO looked much like the '71, but became an option package.

The '72 Luxury LeMans had a distinctive grille and fender skirts.

Ventura II, a Chevy Nova clone, became Pontiac's compact in 1971.

Production figures for the '73 Firebird Trans Am shot up to 4802.

The '73 mid-sizers featured Colonnade styling, here a Luxury LeMans.

Pontiac entered the Seventies in third place, spent most of the decade in fourth, and exited it in fifth. During that long, difficult decade, Pontiac seemed to have lost its magic touch—while Oldsmobile found a new magic sales formula.

Firebirds sported new front-end styling for 1974, here a Trans Am.

The '75 Grand Prix had a catalytic converter; 86,582 were produced.

Dual rectangular headlamps adorned the '76 Bonneville, now $5246.

The Formula was the least popular '76 Firebird with 20,613 built.

Grand LeMans was the grandest '77 LeMans; 7851 two doors were sold.

seller (only 2116 units for '71) to become the most popular Firebird of all (over 93,000 for '78).

Pontiac also helped Firebird sales by fielding the same four models each year—base coupe, luxury Esprit, roadworthy Formula, and T/A (Chevy fiddled with Camaros). Formula and T/A went on a horsepower diet for 1978 in deference to the government's corporate average fuel economy (CAFE) mandates that took effect that year, but they never relinquished their V8s and never failed to provide lively motoring. A turbocharged 301 was issued for 1980, offering a bit less go than the big-blocks of old but somewhat easier on gasoline.

Higher-than-ever fuel prices were but one legacy of the 1973-74 oil embargo, though gas was getting more expensive even before that. Renewed buyer interest in thrifty compacts—and Pontiac's lack of one—prompted the division to graft a different nose onto Chevrolet's 111-inch-wheelbase Nova to create the Ventura II. Launched in March 1971, it evolved in parallel with the Nova through 1979 (minus the Roman numeral after '72) but always saw lower volume. One interesting difference: the hallowed GTO became a Ventura variation for 1974—actually a $195 option package for the workaday pillared two-door comprising hood scoop, different grille, and standard 350 V8. Purists moaned, but Pontiac moved 7058 of these pretenders before ringing the curtain down on a great tradition—a year too late.

Along with GM's other X-body compacts, Ventura adopted a more European look for 1975—and promptly withered on the vine. Inept marketing tactics and mediocre build quality were as much to blame as competition from within the Pontiac line and elsewhere. An upmarket version called Phoenix arrived for mid-1977 with plusher interiors and a busier front end; the Ventura name vanished the following year. Unhappily, Phoenix was another also-ran, and remained so even after it was switched to GM's sprightly front-drive X-body for 1980.

Another "lend-lease" deal with Chevrolet produced the subcompact Astre, arriving in the U.S. for 1975 after being marketed in Canada from mid-1973. This was little more than a modestly restyled twin of the ill-starred Chevy Vega, and thus shared most of its many faults. Pontiac varied the model program a bit with price-leader S and semi-sporty SJ models. There was also a GT package option, combining the low-line interior with the SJ's performance and handling mods. A swan-song 1977 option was Pontiac's then-new 151-cid (2.5-liter) "Iron Duke" four, a nickname chosen partly to counter the horrendous durability reputation of the all-aluminum Vega unit.

Chevy had introduced its Vega-based Monza sporty coupe for 1975, and it was only a matter of time before Pontiac got in on this act too. The time was model year 1976. But unlike other editions of this corporate H-Special design, Pontiac's Sunbird was first offered only as the notchback two-door known at Chevy as the Monza Towne Coupe. The 2+2 fastback was added for 1978 as the Sunbird Sport Hatch, along with the pretty little three-door wagon from the deceased Vega/Astre line. Bolstered by various option groups, including a sporty Formula package, the Sunbird sold respectably but was not the big success the division had hoped for. It carried on with few changes through 1981, the final cars sold actually being 1980 leftovers.

The story of Pontiac's larger cars in the '70s is about as exciting as a dictionary. Basic design was shared with other GM intermediates and standards, but workmanship always seemed half a notch below. By the late-'70s, though, both the LeMans/Grand LeMans and Catalina/Bonneville had evolved into more sensible, better-built and more saleable cars better suited to the times than the aging hulks that Ford and Chrysler still peddled.

The mid-size Pontiacs quickly turned from assured roadability to an emphasis on luxury and convenience, but there was an interesting exception: the Grand Am. Introduced as part of the new 1973 "Colonnade" line, this LeMans-based coupe and sedan

The '78 Firebird Trans Am looked good with a T-Top and a tropical setting. This one was powered by the optional 6.6-liter V8.

were billed as combining Grand Prix luxury with Trans Am performance, hence the name. It was largely the idea of assistant chief engineer Bill Collins, who'd been heavily involved with the original GTO, and chassis wizard John Seaton. The "G/A" aimed at a close approximation of European sports sedans like the Mercedes-Benz 250/280 and BMW Bavaria but selling at a third to one-half their price.

While some features strained at mimicry (a Mercedes-style jumbo-hub steering wheel, for instance), the Grand Am was, on balance, one of the most impressive big Detroiters in this decade. But it failed to make any real impression in a market where most buyers looked for either everyday transportation or as much glitz as their money could buy. The Grand Am thus scored only about 43,000 sales in its debut year (mainly two-doors), then plummeted to 17,000 for '74 and only 11,000 or so for '75. To no one's surprise, Pontiac dropped the model like a hot potato. Curiously, the name reappeared in the downsized LeMans line for '78, but this Grand Am was nowhere near as "special" and would prove similarly short-lived, being dropped after 1980.

Rivalling Firebird's '70s success was the personal-luxury Grand Prix, in some years Pontiac's best-selling single model line. It had been reborn for 1969 as a lighter, quicker mid-size car combining the LeMans hardtop coupe shell with an extended, 118-inch-wheelbase A-body chassis. Powered by 400 and 455 V8s, it was a handsome brute, with short-deck notchback styling, '67 Cadillac Eldorado-style vee'd backlight, and a distinctly Pontiac face ahead of a mile-long hood. Inside was an innovative curved instrument cluster that brought all controls within easier driver reach. Cribbing Duesenberg's Model J and SJ nomenclature was a vain attempt at cachet, but the public applauded this Grand Prix, snapping up nearly 112,500 of the '69s. Sales continued strong through the end of this design in 1972, when just under 92,000 were retailed. Styling didn't change much but horsepower went down a bit after 1970, though big-block performance was still surprisingly good.

Pontiac continued the successful formula through GM's 1973-77 Colonnade intermediates, when the GP adopted the same 116-inch wheelbase as Chevy's imitative Monte Carlo. A vertical grille and a more formal roofline set these GPs apart from the

The all-new '77 Bonneville was downsized to a 115.9-inch chassis.

The all-new '78 Grand Am was downsized to a 108.1-inch wheelbase.

President Jimmy Carter signed the Humphrey-Hawkins full-employment bill in 1978; one of its goals was to reduce unemployment to four percent by 1983. Pontiac did its part—it built 900,000 cars that year, just shy of its 1973 record.

ordinary LeMans, as did more standard amenities and higher prices. Interestingly, the Grand Prix set a new all-time sales record for 1977—close to 288,500 deliveries. The '78 was even more like LeMans, downsized on the same new 108.1-inch wheelbase and less individual in appearance, yet sales weren't affected much—some 228,000 for the model year. Clearly, the GP had succeeded in a way that various gussied-up Luxury and Grand LeMans variations couldn't. Without it, Pontiac wouldn't have weathered the decade's ups and downs nearly as well.

Nevertheless, Pontiac's troubles were far from over as the '80s opened. Workmanship still wasn't what it should have been, and increasing model-sharing with Chevrolet had only made a confused image even fuzzier. Adding insult to these injuries were the deep national recession and an accompanying sharp downturn in auto sales that began in late 1979 when the Shah of Iran was deposed, triggering a second energy crisis. Pontiac suffered as much as any Detroit producer. Volume dropped by almost half for 1981, to around 469,000, then bottomed out at less than 307,000 two years later—a sad state of affairs for a make that had averaged better than 700,000 cars a year since the mid-'60s.

But better times were at hand. Having floundered under four general managers since '69, the division got back on course under William C. Hoglund, who took over the helm in 1980. Taking a cue from history, Hoglund and a bright young team of designers and engineers began steering Pontiac back towards the sort of driver-oriented cars that had been the foundation of its high success in the '60s. Events played right into their hands. The economy recovered, the gas shortage became a gas glut, and the market went crazy again for performance. Under the banner "We Build Excitement," Pontiac turned the corner: By 1984 it was back over the half-million mark. Hoglund left that year to head GM's new Saturn Division, but Pontiac continued picking up steam under new captain J. Michael Losh, breaking 750,000 for 1986, then sailing past Olds to grab third place for the first time in 17 years.

It's thus faintly amazing that Pontiac managed this impressive feat mainly on the strength of just three model lines: compacts, intermediates and the Firebird. Unlike Buick and Olds, big cars were never significant to Pontiac sales in this decade. In fact, for 1982-83 the division offered no traditional full-size cars at all.

Pontiac's Catalina and Bonneville had been redesigned for 1977 as part of GM's pioneering downsizing program, but didn't sell as well as their B-body cousins at Buick, Olds and Chevy. Believing buyers were ready to forsake even these smaller biggies in the midst of another fuel crunch, Pontiac cancelled the line after 1981 and substituted a facelifted LeMans sedan and wagon called Bonneville Model G (the letter denoting a redesignated 108.1-inch-wheelbase A-body platform). But what looked a smart idea in 1980 seemed like just bad timing once big-car sales turned up again, so Pontiac revived the B-body during 1984, giving U.S. dealers the Canadian version (which was never dropped) under its home-market name, Parisienne.

If these moves recalled the great Dodge/Plymouth debacle of 20 years before, they weren't nearly so disastrous. But they weren't that successful either. The Bonneville G peaked in its first year at about 80,500 sales, then tailed off to no more than 50,000 a year through its 1986 demise. Parisienne averaged about 83,000 orders for 1985-86, after which the sedan departed (the B-body two-door hadn't returned) and annual sales ran below 14,000 for the lone Safari wagon marketed through 1988. Design, engineering and yearly changes were virtually the same as for equivalent Chevrolets. Read "Malibu" for the small Bonneville, "Caprice/Impala" for Parisienne and the 1977-81 B-body models.

Another idea from up north was the subcompact T1000, a Chevette-clone inspired by Pontiac Canada's Acadian model. Announced in April 1981, the T1000 immediately attracted 70,000 buyers, but was down to an annual average of 25,000 or so after 1982, when it was called just plain 1000. Black window frames

The Tenth Anniversary of the Trans Am was celebrated in 1980.

Bonneville's top 1979 model was the Brougham, which listed at $7584.

The '80 Grand Prix came in three models; 114,000 were produced.

Pontiac's first front-drive car was the 1980 Phoenix, here an LJ.

The front-drive J2000 debuted in May 1981 with a 1.8-liter inline four.

The mid-size 6000 was built off GM's A-body. It bowed in early '82.

The subcompact T1000, a Chevette twin, came out in February '81.

After an 11-year run, a new generation Firebird roared in for '82.

Bonneville moved down to the old LeMans 108.1-inch chassis for '83.

Pontiac's sporty 6000 model for 1984 was the STE. Price: $14,437.

and a prominent arrowhead grille emblem were its main distinctions from the littlest Chevy. Naturally, the 1000 evolved in parallel with Chevette through 1987, when its place was taken by a new front-drive, Korean-built LeMans. Though the '84s sold unusually well—over 55,000—the 1000 was just a token nod to the subcompact market and never a big money-spinner, but dealers were probably glad to have it.

The second-generation Phoenix was the least popular of GM's front-drive X-body compacts, likely because its basic package was available with more model and trim choices as the Chevy Citation and with higher nameplate prestige as the Buick Skylark and Olds Omega. Pontiac tried hard to set Phoenix apart, offering notchback two-door and four-door hatchback sedans in plain, luxury LJ and sporty SJ trim (the latter two renamed LE and SE after '83). But nothing seemed to work, and demand fell off rapidly when numerous mechanical bugs started surfacing and recalls were announced to fix them. Phoenix never sold better than in its extra-long 1980 debut year—178,000-plus. Volume dipped to less than 50,000 for '82 and was down below 23,000 for the 1984 finale.

But the Phoenix was successful in a sense, leading to a more rational and popular mid-size Pontiac, the front-drive 6000. Arriving in January 1982 as an early '83 model, it was closely related to the new A-body Buick Century, Chevy Celebrity and Oldsmobile Cutlass Ciera, with crisper, more important-looking outer sheetmetal over the 104.9-inch-wheelbase X-car central structure. Initial offerings comprised base and LE coupe and sedan, but Pontiac went a big step further with the STE (Special Touring Edition). Announced for the formal 1983 campaign, this enthusiast-oriented four-door represented a new Pontiac challenge to premium European sports sedans from the likes of Audi, BMW, Mercedes, Saab and Volvo.

And a surprisingly capable challenger it was. Quick-ratio steering and a fortified suspension with air-adjustable rear shocks and upgraded wheels and tires made the STE supremely roadable, appointments were tastefully understated, equipment generous (even running to a leather-bound roadside emergency kit). All it lacked was truly sparkling acceleration, the mandatory three-speed automatic transaxle straining the 135 horses of the standard high-output, 173-cid X/A-car V6. But the STE served notice that Pontiac was not only back to building driver's cars but could compete on a "best-in-class" basis against all comers.

Other 6000s bathed in the STE's glow, and by 1984 this line was Pontiac's best-seller, bolstered by the addition of station wagons that year. Worthy improvements came almost annually: electronic fuel injection for the base 2.5-liter four (throttle-body, 1983) and Chevy-built V6 (multi-point, for all models by 1987); a more versatile and efficient four-speed automatic transaxle for selected models (1986); an S/E sedan and wagon offering much of the STE's sportiness and performance for less money (1987); an all-wheel-drive option with 3.1-liter V6 for an extensively reengineered STE, plus available five-speed manual transaxle (1988). At decade's end, Pontiac dropped two-door 6000s, gave four-doors a curved rear roofline, and offered the STE only with AWD. By that point, the S/E had become what the STE had been, yet was more price-competitive against comparable Japanese sedans.

Vying with the 6000 as the division's '80s sales leader was Pontiac's version of the front-drive J-body subcompact, the 1982 replacement for the old rear-drive Sunbird. Initially, the name seemed to change more than the car, which arrived as the J2000, then evolved as the 2000 (1983), 2000 Sunbird (1984) and finally just Sunbird. Pontiac had gotten into Euro-style "alphamumeric" designations under Hoglund's immediate predecessor, Robert C. Stempel (named GM president in 1987), but quickly backed away from them as confusing to buyers.

There was no confusion about the cars: much like Chevrolet's Cavaliers and offered in the same body styles—including a con-

During the Eighties, Pontiac proclaimed, "We Build Excitement!" It seemed as though Pontiac was reaching back into its past to recapture the glory days of the Sixties. It worked—Pontiac was back in third at decade's end.

Pontiac's bombshell for '84 was the two-passenger mid-engine Fiero.

The 1985 Sunbird could be had as a Turbo convertible with 150 bhp.

Trans Am for '85 listed at $10,699 and had a 205-bhp 5.0-liter V8.

The '86 Pontiac 2 + 2 was built to trounce Ford on NASCAR race tracks.

Grand Am was Pontiac's version of the GM N-body car, here an '86.

vertible from 1983. Though Chevy's overhead-valve four was always available, Pontiac emphasized its Opel-designed overhead-cam engine imported from GM do Brasil. It became standard for 1983, with throttle-body injection and 84 bhp from 1.8 liters (111 cid), followed by a 150-bhp turbocharged option with port injection. Both grew to 2.0 liters for 1987, respective outputs being 96 and 165 bhp.

Three trims levels were offered through 1987: base, plush LE and sporty SE. The LE was cancelled for '86, when turbocharged GT models arrived with a new hidden-headlamp front. The 1988 GTs were trimmed to just convertible and coupe, the latter a restyled slantback two-door also offered in SE form. A new dashboard was the main attraction for '89. With so much variety, plus attractive prices generally a bit above Cavalier's, the 2000/Sunbird garnered well over 100,000 sales in most years, a record 169,000-plus for '84.

As at Buick and Olds, the J-car was the basis for a new compact Pontiac to replace the unloved X-body after 1984. Resurrecting the Grand Am name, Pontiac's rendition of the 103.4-inch-wheelbase N-body design promptly outsold its divisional sisters by emphasizing handling options and sporty appointments in the European mold. Demand was strong: over 82,500 of the debut 1985 coupes, then a stunning 225,000 or so coupes and sedans.

Again seeking individuality, Pontiac offered a more overtly sporting Grand Am SE in addition to the expected plain and luxury trim. The division also varied engines, making the Sunbird turbo-four a 1987 option, then replacing the original 3.0-liter Buick V6 option with GM's new 150-bhp "Quad-4," America's first postwar production engine with dual overhead cams and four valves per cylinder.

Buyers seeking a smaller sports sedan had every reason to look closely at the SE. Its monochrome exterior with color-keyed wheels, front spoiler and perimeter lower-body extensions was aggressive but not loud, its cockpit well-planned and roomy, handling assured, ride comfortable, performance brisk. As with the STE, Pontiac again seemed able to do more with a shared design than either Buick or Olds, at least as far as enthusiasts were concerned.

The same could be said for the first front-drive Bonneville, bowing for 1987 on the 110.8-inch-wheelbase H-body platform introduced with the previous year's new Olds Delta 88 and Buick LeSabre. Pontiac designers strove mightily to make it different, and succeeded handsomely. There wasn't much they could do about the boxy roofline, but much smoother front and rear ends set the Bonneville clearly and cleanly apart from the Delta/LeSabre.

Once more, there was a sporty SE edition *a la* STE, with uprated suspension, larger wheels and tires, mellow-sounding exhaust system, less exterior chrome, console-mount floorshift for the mandatory four-speed automatic transaxle, a shorter final drive for snappier acceleration, and a full set of large, legible instruments including tachometer. All this was enough to make you forget that the SE had the same 150-bhp 3.8-liter (231-cid) V6 as the base and LE sedans.

An improved 165-bhp engine arrived for 1988, when Pontiac went a bit overboard with a new top-line Bonneville SSE. It was faintly contrived, wearing body-color wheels, grille, decklid spoiler and rocker skirting set off by a gaudy grille medallion trimmed in gold. More worthy standards ran to GM/Teves anti-lock brakes (optional on other Bonnevilles for '89), electronically variable shock-absorber damping and a leather-lined interior with multi-adjustable power bucket seats. Still, most critics felt that the SE was the better buy: less expensive, more tasteful and smoother-riding. The public generally agreed but liked all the new Bonnies to the tune of nearly 124,000 debut-year sales—not far adrift of LeSabre and Delta despite lacking their coupe body style.

Firebird showed surprising sales strength in the '80s, averaging

The '87 Firebird with Formula option came with the 5.0-liter four-barrel V8, but the Corvette 210-bhp 5.7 V8 was available.

Bonneville came out as a front-drive V6-powered sedan for 1987.

The '88 GT was the best Fiero yet; alas, it would also be the last.

some 100,000 units a year through 1986. But it was only a reflection of the market's return to performance cars around 1982, the year a totally redesigned Firebird appeared on a new 101-inch-wheelbase F-body platform, shared with Chevy's Camaro. Though GM's latterday ponycars were more alike than ever, division stylists under design director John Schinella maintained a distinctive Pontiac look, marked by a low-riding nose with shallow twin grilles and hidden headlamps—the latter a first for Firebird—and full-width taillamps, with a smoked lens on some models for a custom "blackout" effect.

Initially, the third-generation Firebird was reduced to base, mid-range S/E and the racy Trans Am—all "glassback" hatch coupes—but the Formula was revived as an option package for 1987, along with the "big" 350 V8 of bygone days. The latter powered an even meaner-looking Trans Am, the new GTA. Other technical developments largely paralleled Camaro's except that Pontiac didn't field a convertible like Chevy, and continued to offer somewhat different chassis tuning and trim/equipment combinations. Styling was good enough to last through 1989 with mainly minor alterations. Most applied to the Trans Am. A grille-less "bottom-breather" nose for '84 and revised spoiler and rocker skirts on the new-for-'87 GTA were the most noticeable.

Recalling 1976's Limited-Edition T/A (marking Pontiac's 50th birthday) and 1979's Tenth Anniversary Trans Am was yet another special Firebird for 1989: the 20th Anniversary Trans Am, a 1500-unit run of GTAs powered by the turbocharged 231 V6 from Buick's recently departed Grand National. Available only with four-speed overdrive automatic, it was the most potent T/A in more than a decade, packing a quoted 245 bhp and an imposing 345 pounds-feet torque (versus the V8 GTA's 225 bhp and 330 lbs/ft). You could have any color as long as it was white, just like on the '69 original; no racing stripes, though, just subtle "20th Anniversary" cloisonné emblems and "Turbo Trans Am" badges in the appropriate places. In all, a glorious reminder that nobody in Detroit still cared more about really hot cars than Pontiac—or built them better.

Emblematic of Pontiac's resurgence in this decade was the innovative Fiero, arriving for 1984 as Detroit's first mid-engine production car and only its second volume two-seater since the first Ford Thunderbird. It was broached in 1978 as a low-cost high-mileage "commuter," but that was just a ruse to convince company brass that the car would help GM meet its CAFE requirement. The urge toward something sportier was irresistible, since the plan called for transplanting the front-drive X-body powertrain behind a two-place cockpit to drive the rear wheels.

GM president "Pete" Estes approved the idea in October 1978, perhaps for sentimental reasons. He himself had pleaded for a two-seat Pontiac as division chief in the '60s. Corporate cash-flow problems almost killed the program several times in 1980-82, but director Hulki Aldikacti somehow persuaded management that this new P-car not only made financial sense but was vital for improving Pontiac's image.

What emerged was definitely sporty: a smooth, distinctive notchback coupe on a 93.4-inch wheelbase, evolved under Ron Hill in GM's Advanced Design III section and finalized by John Schinella's production studio. Underneath was a fully driveable steel space-frame chassis, a skeleton to which were attached body panels made of various plastics (but not fiberglass)—con-

Pontiac's excitement theme for the '80s translated into the Firebird Trans Am and the two-seater Fiero. Even many of the more mundane models could be ordered in sportier form, such as the Sunbird GT, Grand Am SE, and Bonneville SSE.

The 1988 Grand Prix was *Motor Trend* magazine's "Car of the Year." It boasted all-new styling, front-wheel drive, and a 2.8-liter V6.

Electronic Ride Control came standard on the '88 Bonneville SSE.

Notchback styling set the '89 GTA apart from lesser Firebirds.

struction that would make style changes cheap, quick and easy. To minimize production costs, steering, front suspension and brakes were borrowed from the humble Chevy Chevette; rear suspension and disc brakes were used as part the X-car power package.

Announced at base prices carefully pitched in $8000-$9600 range, the Fiero predictably generated lots of excitement. The division's Pontiac, Michigan, home plant (fully retooled as the model's exclusive production center) busily turned out more than 134,500 of the '84s. But the Fiero was flawed: heavy and thus slow with the standard 92-bhp, 151-cid four; not much faster with the optional 140-bhp 173-cid V6; low, cramped, noisy and hard to see out of; difficult to shift; stiff-riding; indifferently put together. As it had with the X-cars, GM shot itself in the foot by selling a car before it was fully developed.

It didn't take long for word to get around. Fiero sales crumbled by over 40 percent in the second year, recovered to near 84,000 for '86, then fell by nearly half for '87. A further blow came in September 1987, when a spate of engine fires implicating some 20 percent of 1984 production prompted a government-ordered Fiero recall. With all this, plus a sudden fall-off in two-seater demand prompted by soaring insurance rates, GM announced in early 1988 that the Fiero would not be back for '89, lamely claiming that the car couldn't make a profit at 50,000 units a year. Ironically, the firm had just spent $30 million for an all-new suspension that made the '88 the best-handling Fiero yet. Left stillborn were plans for a 1989 Quad-4 option and the more distant prospect of a pound-paring aluminum space-frame, which would have done wonders for sprinting ability.

As it is, the V6 S/E and GT models stand as the most collectible Fieros. And make no mistake: they will be collected. The GT bowed for 1985 with a snarky new nose inspired by the '84 Indy Fiero pace car (of which a few thousand replicas were sold). Standard rear spoiler, "ground effects" body addenda, uprated suspension and a deep-voiced exhaust system made it a sort of mini-muscle car. *Sans* V6, this package became the mid-range S/E model for 1986, bolstered at mid-season by a restyled GT with modified rear flanks and a "flying buttress" fastback roofline. Arriving in June that year was the five-speed manual transaxle, long promised as an optional alternative to the standard four-speed and extra-cost automatic three-speeder. The main '87 changes involved a reshaped nose for base and S/E models and a larger fuel tank.

Though a compromise in several ways and a relative failure in the marketplace, the Fiero succeeded in best symbolizing Pontiac's renewed commitment to aggressive, exciting automobiles. An equally dramatic expression was the all-new front-drive Grand Prix that replaced one of Detroit's dullest cars for 1988.

Pontiac's personal-luxury coupe had fallen on hard times since its '78 downsizing, limping along after 1981 with somewhat smoother but still uninspired styling that strained at marrying "aero modern" with "middle-class traditional." Engines were equally uninspired: mostly Buick V6s and Chevy small-block V8s, all economy-tuned. The trouble-prone Olds 350 diesel V8 offered through 1984 only aggravated the old-fogey aura of a car that was less visible on the street than on the NASCAR circuit.

But the GP's role as stock-car standard-bearer did lead to one interesting variation: the limited-edition 2+2. Introduced at mid-1986, it boasted a wind-cheating body-color front instead of the usual stand-up brightwork, and a huge compound-curve rear window designed for smoother airflow down to a bespoilered tail. GM Design came up with this configuration to counter Ford's more aerodynamic Thunderbirds in long-distance races. As ever, NASCAR approval hinged on production of a certain number of street models, hence this Pontiac and Chevy's similar Monte Carlo SS Aerocoupe. Showroom 2+2s carried a four-barrel, 165-bhp Olds 307 V8, but all GM stockers in this period ran Chevy engines regardless of bodywork, and the Montes won more races. Still, this is likely to be the only GP built between 1972 and '86 that will interest collectors 20 years from now.

The all-new '88 was a different story. Though built on the same W-body/GM10 platform as the latest Olds Cutlass Supreme and Buick Regal, it could only have been a Pontiac: sleek, purposeful, even menacing from some angles, and obviously much more aerodynamic than its blocky predecessor. More sophisticated, too, with standard all-disc brakes and fully independent suspension. Though a good six inches shorter overall, the '88 rode a wheelbase trimmed only 0.6-inch; this plus adoption of a transverse drivetrain, as had become almost universal with front drive, made for a much roomier interior. *Motor Trend* magazine liked it enough to name it "Car of the Year."

For the base and intermediate LE models, that drivetrain comprised a 130-bhp 173-cid V6 with port fuel injection driving a four-speed automatic transaxle; a five-speed manual designed by Getrag of Germany was optional. The latter was standard on the sporty SE, which came with the usual beefed-up suspension and more comprehensive instrumentation set in a rather busy dash. Automatic GPs were upgraded to a stroked 3.1-liter (191-cid) V6 for 1989½, but the big thrill was a new McLaren Turbo model powered by a blown 3.1 producing some 200 bhp.

Of course, the "Big Mac" was another limited edition, developed in conjunction with ASC/McLaren and planned for only 2000 copies. Available in monochrome red or black, both with gold accents, it rolled on sizeable 16-inch lacy-spoke wheels shod with Z-rated high-performance tires capable of sustained speeds in excess of 150 mph. Wheel openings were suitably flared for clearance via specific lower-body panels with front and rear spats for each wheel, plus a grooved rub strip carried into the bumpers.

Like Ford with its '83 Thunderbird, Pontiac had come up with a car to revitalize a name that had lost all its original magic—and the McLaren Turbo was arguably the best GP ever built for all-around performance. Of course, the '88 Grand Prix—not to mention the reborn Grand Am and Bonneville—are light years from the great '60s Wide-Trackers, the likes of which we'll never see again. But the spirit of those cars still burns bright in Pontiac, Michigan. Who knows? One day soon we might even see a new GTO—a pleasant prospect indeed.

Grand Am, here an SE, received its first major restyling for 1989.

A limited-edition 205-bhp McLaren Turbo Grand Prix debuted for '89.

The '89 Sunbird LE featured a completely redesigned front end.

A new roofline was the most notable change on the '89 Pontiac 6000.

Pontiac debuted an all-new front-drive Grand Prix for 1988. It won *Motor Trend*'s "Car of the Year" award. Pontiac is GM's best-focused division as it leaves the Eighties. If it stays the course, it should enjoy a prosperous Nineties.

RAMBLER

When George Romney succeeded George Mason as president of American Motors, he turned his full attention to the Rambler and soon forgot about Mason's plans (*see* Nash) for a link-up with Studebaker-Packard. The Rambler was AMC's most successful car in the mid-Fifties, and developed a whole new market for "compact" cars. To Romney, Detroit's "bigger is better" philosophy was all wrong; Detroit, he said, was building "gas-guzzling dinosaurs." AMC's compact Rambler, he insisted, meant "More for Americans."

Retaining the 108-inch wheelbase unit body/chassis introduced in '56, AMC removed ostensible Nash and Hudson parentage to make Rambler a separate nameplate for the 1957 model year. The car was solidly built, reliable, and perfectly attuned to the burgeoning market for economy cars. By 1961, its successors had brought Rambler to third place in the industry.

All but forgotten today is the fact that AMC introduced the industry's first four-door hardtop wagon: the 1956 (Nash and Hudson) Rambler Cross Country. This neat, airy, roomy wagon featured a 33 percent increase in cargo space over that of the '55s, and a roll-down tailgate window that eliminated the clumsy upper hatch. "We just rolled with those cars," said former AMC Board Chairman Roy D. Chapin, Jr. "We couldn't get enough." There was nothing like the luxurious little Cross Country, and the public responded accordingly.

In 1957, with the big Hudson and Nash destined for oblivion, American Motors built 118,990 cars, 114,084 of them Ramblers. The overhead-valve six was raised to 135 horsepower, while a lively new oversquare V8 was offered with 190 bhp at 4900 rpm. It was available only on the upper-priced cars—Custom and Super sedan and wagon. An interesting new Custom model was the specially trimmed Rebel, a four-door hardtop announced at mid-year with an even larger V8, the new AMC 327. The Rebel had Gabriel shocks, an anti-roll bar, heavy-duty springs, power steering, and power brakes. All that and 255 bhp from the V8's 9.5:1 compression ratio transformed Rambler's image. During tests at Daytona Beach, a Rebel flew from 0 to 60 mph (and 50 to 80) in scarcely more than seven seconds. Unfortunately, it just didn't appeal to the type of people who bought Ramblers, and only 1500 were built. At $2786, Rebel was the most expensive '57 offering, and that may have contributed to its low sales.

Economy cars were continuing to set sales records, so AMC brought back its old 100-inch-wheelbase '55 two-door model for 1958. Called Rambler American and fitted with a new mesh-type grille and exposed rear wheels, it was priced very low, starting at $1775. It couldn't help but sell, and over 42,000 Americans were registered for the 12 months. Larger Ramblers received more than 100 changes for '58, and were outwardly quite different from their predecessors. The grille was made more massive and square, dual headlamps were used, fashionable little fins appeared at the rear, and a pedal-type parking brake was adopted. The six-cylinder Super Cross Country wagon was the top seller that year. The Rebel name was retained for top-line models powered by the 250-cid V8. But Rambler did not revive its fancy, limited-edition Rebel hardtop. Instead, it created a new 117-inch wheelbase for a separate line powered by the 327 V8. AMC named the new line the Ambassador, a name Nash had used through 1957 for its top-of-the-line models.

Actually, Ambassador styling had been predicted in mid-1957, when it was thought that these cars would bear separate Nash and Hudson identification. In essence, they were stretched versions of the roomy, squarish Rambler unit body/chassis, available as four-door sedans and wagons, with or without roof pillars. The Ambassador hardtop wagon was the only one of its type in the '58 line, and only 294 were sold. In fact, sales overall were quite disappointing—just 1340 for the model year. Ambassador was entering a field of heavy competition and decreasing demand, and AMC did much better with its smaller Ramblers. Registrations of all 1958 AMC models almost doubled to 186,227 units in a year that was generally a disaster for the industry. After four years of losses, AMC turned the corner, making a profit of $26 million on sales of $470 million.

For 1959, it was the same formula again. This time, the company netted $60 million in profits and built nearly 364,000 cars for an all-time record. The same models and powertrains were fielded, but horsepower wasn't raised. Unlike its competitors, AMC had apparently decided enough was enough.

A two-door wagon was revived for the Rambler American DeLuxe and Super lines, helping rack up 90,000 sales for the '59 junior series. The 108-inch-wheelbase cars were mildly facelifted with thin "color sweep" side moldings and simplified grilles. As in 1958, Rambler V8s were called Rebels and used the 250-cid engine. The Ambassador Super and Custom continued as before on the longer wheelbase and with a more ornate grille.

At the beginning of the '60s, everything looked rosy. Led by hard-driving president Romney, Rambler could do no wrong. In 1960, it almost beat Plymouth for third place in production, with nearly half a million cars, and did in 1961. This was the highest sales volume ever recorded for an independent. But Rambler's success triggered an avalanche of compacts from the Big Three—and formidable new competition. A downward slide began in 1962, when Rambler was passed by Pontiac. By 1967, AMC as a whole had fallen all the way to 12th place.

Perhaps Romney saw the handwriting on the wall, because he left the company in 1962 to become the governor of the state of Michigan. Replacing him was Roy Abernethy, who began a program of product diversification that tried to meet the opposition on every front. It didn't work, and Abernethy was succeeded by Roy D. Chapin, Jr., in 1966. Chapin became AMC board chairman in 1967, and William V. Luneberg assumed the presidency. The Chapin-Luneberg administration ordered new makes like the Javelin, and dropped the Rambler name completely after 1969.

For 1960, the 108-inch-wheelbase unibody Rambler acquired less cluttered lines, modified tailfins, and a full-width grille. Facelifts occurred in 1961 and '62 as the cars became known as

The 1956 Rambler Custom four-door hardtop sold for a modest $2224.

A '56 Rambler Custom Cross Country hardtop wagon sold for $2494.

The '57 Rebel boasted a 255-bhp 327-cid V8; only 1500 were built.

Rebel became a six-model series for 1958, all with a 250-cid V8.

The '59 Rebel Custom Country Club hardtop sedan listed at $2588.

At $1781 and up, the American was Rambler's economy series in '59.

This '58 "Hudson" Ambassador is actually a Rambler. Price: $2822.

The '60 Ambassador sported new side trim and a split front bumper.

Rambler Classics. A lower hoodline for '61 was accompanied by an eggcrate grille. In 1962, the crate held larger eggs, the fins were cropped, and the side sweepspear was moved higher. An interesting option was the E-Stick, a combination automatic and clutch transmission that cost $60. But it was too complex to sell really well. It was similar in concept to the twin-stick manual gearbox of the 1979 Dodge Colt FF and Plymouth Champ made by Mitsubishi of Japan.

When Richard A. Teague joined the American Motors design staff in 1961, Edmund Anderson's design for the '63 Classic and Ambassador were already pretty much finalized. The cars featured a longer 112-inch wheelbase, lower silhouette, concave grille, sculptured body panels, and curved side glass to create a smooth new shape. Although still chunky, the new Rambler was at least cleanly styled; in fact, *Motor Trend* magazine was impressed enough with the new design to award the entire AMC lineup its

The Rambler was born in 1950 as a "dressed up" compact convertible. With an expanded model lineup, Rambler accounted for a lion's share of AMC output in the mid-Fifties, and for 1957 Rambler became a separate nameplate.

The '61 Ambassador Custom Cross Country wagon retailed for $3026.

New sheetmetal graced the '61 American; base engine was a 90-hp six.

Base price of the '63 Rambler American 440 convertible was $2344.

The '64 Ambassador 990H weighed 3255 pounds and listed at $2917.

"Car of the Year" award for 1963. The Classic retained this basic bodyshell throughout its life span. Teague was responsible for refining the design over the next few years. The 1964s sported a new flush grille and stainless-steel-trimmed rocker panels. Two hardtop coupes were added to the line, which until then had consisted of two- and four-door sedans and four-door Cross Country station wagons. The 1965s were longer, and received a new grille, squared-off hood, and wraparound taillights. AMC was trying to give them a sportier image, and dubbed them "The Sensible Spectaculars." The '66s featured a new roof with convertible-like accents, a revised roof and tailgate for station wagons, and more sharply creased lines from front to rear.

For 1967, the Classic series was renamed Rebel. From 1968 on, Rebel was listed as a separate make (*see* AMC), the Rambler name reserved only for the smaller American line. The '67 Rebel rode a two-inch longer wheelbase; its all-new styling comprised a

SST was the top-line Rebel for 1967; the ragtop sold for $2604.

floating rectangular grille flanked by horizontal dual headlamps and squarish front fenders that flowed into a curved rear fenderline. The rear end displayed large, canted taillights blended into the fenders.

Rambler started the '60s with two engines, a six and a V8. The six, a holdover from Nash days, developed 127 or 138 bhp, and was standard on Classics through 1964. The V8 had been designed for use by Hudson and Nash in the mid-1950s. In its 1960-61 form, it developed either 200 or 215 bhp.

The '61 Classic V8 scored well for both performance and economy. When equipped with the optional Flash-O-Matic (Borg-Warner) automatic transmission, it could spring from 0 to 60 mph in ten seconds, and delivered 16 to 20 miles per gallon. But the V8 was heavier than the six, so that no less than 57 percent of the car's curb weight was over the front wheels. Sales were not high. When the Ambassador was made smaller for 1962-63, the Classic V8 was temporarily dropped.

In 1964, the Classic returned with a 287-cid, 198 bhp V8 as an option. For 1965, a 270-bhp version of the 327 became available. For the 1967 Rebel, the 287 was stroked slightly to 290 cid for 200 bhp. A larger V8, the Ambassador 327, was also offered for the '66 Classic. For the 1967 Rebel, the top V8 was enlarged by boring and stroking to 343 cid, which gave 235 or 280 bhp, depending on tune.

As an option to the Classic's standard six, Rambler brought out a new oversquare 232-cid six for 1964, the Torque Command or Typhoon six, which yielded 145 bhp. About 2500 special Typhoon hardtops, painted yellow and black, were released to celebrate the occasion.

At the lower end of the size and price scale was the Rambler American. In 1960 form, it was an anachronism with its old Pinin Farina styling and an ancient Nash L-head six, but it sold for as little as $1761. Convinced that the American was marketable, AMC restyled it for 1961. The new model also got a new overhead-valve six that had actually appeared in mid-1960 on the larger Ramblers. With 125 bhp, it gave the American Custom fuel mileage in the middle 20s, plus adequate performance. The styling, created by Edmund Anderson, was something else again: boxy and truncated, with odd, concave side sculpturing. Sedans, business coupes, two- and four-door wagons, and a convertible were offered in three series. Although they were genuine economy cars and provided a fair amount of interior room, they were anything but beautiful. Teague decided to change them for 1964.

The revamped design sat on a longer 106-inch wheelbase, as the Classic had already gone from 108 to 112. It was a clean car with curved glass and modest brightwork—quite in keeping with its function. The styling was so good, in fact, that it wasn't significantly altered for the rest of the decade. By 1968, the American had a specially trimmed hardtop derivative, the $2244 Rogue. In 1969, the base American was still listed under $2000. A post-introduction decision (in mid-1966) was to offer AMC's new 290-cid V8 as an option. This led to a limited-edition Rogue, equipped with an even larger 315-bhp 390 engine and Hurst shifter, called the SC/Rambler. "Scramblers" were sold to a handful of buyers. Though hardly in keeping with the traditional Rambler image, they were impressive performers.

Teague hastily conjured up a bucket-seat fastback for 1965 to do battle with Mustang and Barracuda. The result was the Marlin, a Rambler model in 1965 and a make in its own right for 1966-67. The Marlin was basically a Rambler Classic reworked above the beltline with a sweeping glassed-in greenhouse—a 3+3 fastback. When equipped with the 327 V8, a Marlin would do 0 to 60 mph in 12 seconds and the standing quarter-mile in 18 seconds at 76 mph—not earthshaking, but performance of a sort. And that was the goal: to turn Rambler's image around by making cars that appeared sporty and fun to drive, instead of just dull and economical. The Marlin wasn't popular, however, with only 17,419 built over three years.

The 1960-61 Ambassador was a continuation of the '58 original, with increasingly luxurious interiors and slightly excessive ornamentation. The price leader in both years was the $2395 Deluxe four-door sedan. In addition, there were Super and Custom four-doors, and wagons with either six or eight seats. In 1961, a posh Custom 400 sedan with the highest-quality trim and standard automatic was added. The 327 V8 was standard power. But before the end of the '50s, AMC managers had decided the large Ambassador V8s were not saleable. For 1962, therefore, the 117-inch wheelbase was dropped, and Ambassador shared the Classic's body and 108-inch-wheelbase chassis. The V8 was dropped from the Classic's option list and was restricted to Ambassador only.

For 1963, AMC planned to restyle the Classic, which, of course, meant a restyled Ambassador as well. Again, both cars shared the same wheelbase, now 112 inches. From a distance, Classics and Ambassadors looked almost identical—and they were similar, except for powerplants and trim. For 1964, Classic was offered with an optional 287-cid V8. Ambassador was then restricted to one 327-powered 990 series. There was a sedan, a Cross Country wagon, and two hardtop coupes called the 990 and 990H. The 990H was the only Ambassador with the 270-bhp engine standard.

The 1964 Ambassador lineup wasn't particularly successful, so the game plan was changed again for '65. Ambassador returned to its own (116-inch) wheelbase, and in standard form came with the 232-cid six. There were no major changes for '66, except that the name was registered as a separate make.

The styling of the '65 Rambler Ambassador was probably the best it had ever been. Teague's four-square design resulted in an intermediate comparable in size to the Ford Fairlane, but with distinctive looks and more interior space.

AMC made a play for the soft-top market in 1965: there was a convertible in every line—American, Classic, and Ambassador. Unhappily, they tended to leak because of the curved side windows, and did not sell well. Soft-top production in '65 consisted of 3882 Americans, 4953 Classics, and 3499 Ambassadors. The Ambassador convertible was dropped after 1967.

The Rebel was made a make in its own right for 1968, and the Hornet replaced the Rambler American for 1970. The Rambler name thus disappeared from the roster of American automobile marques after on-and-off use for 70 years.

AMC soft tops for '65: Ambassador 990, American 440, Classic 770.

The '66 Rambler American Rogue sported a unique two-tone paint job.

Ambassador was a separate nameplate in 1967; here a top-line DPL.

The '69 SC/Rambler Hurst had a 315-bhp 390 V8; only 1512 were built.

Rambler steered a conservative course in the early Sixties, but the invasion of the Big Three compacts forced AMC to expand its model lineup. All its nameplates were gradually put under the AMC logo—the Rambler name was gone after 1969.

SHELBY

Carroll Shelby, who retired from racing in 1960 because of a heart ailment, settled down to become America's most charismatic manufacturer of specialty cars. Between 1962 and 1970 he built or contributed to many blindingly fast, raceworthy classics: the AC Cobra, Sunbeam Tiger, Cobra 427, Ford GT40, and Ford Mark IV. He helped bring Ford to its racing pinnacle, the winning of Le Mans.

Shelby's most popular project from the standpoint of sales was the GT-350, a super-tuned version of the Ford Mustang. Built by Shelby American in 1965-66, it was an uncompromising, potent grand touring car equally at home on road or track. Later models, built by Ford from 1967 through 1970, were not quite what their predecessors had been, but were good examples of what talented specialists could do with a stock package like the Mustang.

The 1965 GT-350 was aimed primarily at the B-Production racing class of the Sports Car Club of America (SCCA). (It was B-Production champion in 1965-67.) Shelby began with a blue-striped white Mustang fastback powered by the high-performance version of Ford's 289-cubic-inch V8. He added a high-rise manifold, a big four-barrel carburetor, and free-flow exhaust headers. This brought horsepower up to 306 at 6000 rpm. All Shelbys came with a Borg-Warner T-10 four-speed gearbox, a regular Mustang option. Instead of the Mustang's Falcon-based rear axle, GT-350s used a stronger unit from the Fairlane station wagon. Other significant component revisions included metallic-lined rear brakes, Koni shock absorbers, and extra-heavy-duty front disc brakes with metallic pads. Steering was made quicker by relocating the front suspension mounting points. Connecting the tops of the front shock absorbers to each other with a length of steel tubing prevented shock flex under hard cornering. Shelby used its own 15-inch cast-aluminum road wheels shod with high-performance Goodyear bias-ply tires. The result of all this chassis tuning was nearly neutral handling instead of the stock Mustang's strong understeer.

Externally, the stock Mustang's steel hood was replaced with a fiberglass one containing a prominent scoop and held down by NASCAR hood pins. The galloping horse emblem was removed from the grille, and the simulated side scoops were opened up to admit cool air to the rear brakes. For 1966, the fastback's stock rear-quarter air extractor vents were replaced by plastic windows. Internally, the only changes consisted of competition-style three-inch seatbelts and a mahogany-rimmed steering wheel. GT-350s also came without the stock Mustang's rear seat, with the spare tire lashed down in the vacated space. Shelby offered a kit so the buyer could put the spare back in the trunk and install a new rear seat. The stock front seats were left alone, and all interiors were solid black.

For the racing version of the GT-350, Shelby achieved 350 bhp—an astounding 1.21 horsepower per cubic inch. This engine was basically the same one used in the racing Cobra 289. Its four-

Hertz Rent-A-Car ordered 936 Shelby GT-350Hs in 1966 and rented them for $17 a day and 17 cents a mile. Some of them went racing.

The '65 GT-350 had a high-performance 289 V8; 562 were produced.

Production increased to 2378 for '66. Horsepower was rated at 306.

speed gearbox had an aluminum case to save weight. The interior was stripped and a racing seat was installed along with a roll bar and safety harness. Competition tires and an extra-heavy-duty suspension were fitted. A special fiberglass nose eliminated the front bumper and provided a rudimentary air dam with a central slot as an additional air intake. The ultimate racing GT-350 had four-wheel disc brakes, a 400-bhp engine, and wide tires under flared fenders.

Hertz Rent-A-Car got into the act in 1966 when it ordered 936 Shelbys, most of them painted black with gold stripes. Hertz called it the GT-350H, and would rent one for $17 a day and 17 cents a mile. It was a stock GT-350, aside from the special paint job and a three-speed automatic transmission instead of the stock four-speed manual. Hertz inevitably rented some of these to weekend racers, and a few of them performed successfully on SCCA tracks.

In 1967, when Ford Motor Company offered the Mustang with a 390-cid V8, Shelby went one better and tossed in a huge 428. The result was the GT-500, sold as a linemate to the GT-350. Its advertised horsepower was 335, but the real figure was probably closer to 400. The GT-350 was advertised at its usual 306 bhp, but the actual rating was below 300 because the '67 did not have steel-tube exhaust headers like the '66 model. The '67 Shelby now had its own fiberglass front end to distinguish it from production Mustangs, plus other styling modifications and minor chassis refinements. It also bore a new emblem: a coiled cobra in anodized gold. The interior featured a huge, black-painted roll bar, to which were affixed inertia-reel seatbelts instead of the three-inch harness. Over 3000 cars were built, and they were priced lower than the 1965-66 models.

In 1968, the 350 and 500 were again offered with only a wider hood scoop for identification. Interiors were lifted from the stock

A convertible was added to the '68 Shelby line, here a $4238 GT-350.

Standard engine in the '68 GT-350 was a 250-bhp 302-cubic-inch V8.

The '68 Shelby GT-500KR: 400 horsepower made it "King of the Road."

Output of the '69 GT-500 coupe came to 1536 units. Price: $4709.

Ex-racer Carroll Shelby and Ford division head Lee Iacocca were friends, so it's perhaps not too surprising that they collaborated to create the Shelby Mustangs. Not only were the Shelbys fast, they quickly created an enduring legend.

The '69 GT-500 convertible listed at $5027 and only 335 were made.

Shelby teamed up with Dodge in '83, resulting in the Shelby Charger.

The '85 Dodge Shelby Charger boasted a 146-bhp turbocharged four.

"Sleeper" was the best description for the 1985 Dodge Omni GLH.

The Shelby Lancer did 0-60 mph in 7.7 seconds; only 800 were built.

Mustang with few alterations. A Stewart Warner oil pressure gauge and ammeter were mounted on the central console. A convertible was added to each line, priced about $100 higher than the fast-back. Also new was the GT-500KR ("King of the Road"), which had Ford's Cobra Jet 428 block, extra-large heads and intake manifold, and a Holley 735-cfm four-barrel carburetor. The KR sold for $4473 as a fastback and $4594 as a convertible.

Mechanically, the 1969 GT-350 and GT-500 were more closely related to the production Mustang than their predecessors had been (the Mustang was all-new that year). There were now air scoops in the fiberglass front fenders, and side stripes were relocated midway up the bodysides. Although a few 1969s were re-serialed for 1970, Shelby production effectively ended in '69. A combination of government regulations and spiraling insurance rates (the cars' accident record was staggering) prompted Carroll Shelby to ask president Lee Iacocca to cancel the program.

Shelby then took a 16-year break, turning to other business interests. He revitalized Carroll Shelby Industries (makers of alloy wheels), oversaw the growth of his Goodyear race tire distributorship, got involved in cattle ranching in east Texas, where he resides, and started up a chili company (a hot Texas mix, of course).

Meanwhile, Iacocca remained with Ford Motor Company during the topsy-turvy Seventies—the era when government regulation of the auto industry became a way of life and OPEC temporarily cut off petroleum supplies and raised prices. Then in the summer of 1978, Henry Ford II abruptly fired Iacocca, who then moved over to rapidly failing Chrysler Corporation as president and, soon after, chairman.

Iacocca and Shelby had remained friends during those tumultuous years, and it seemed a natural when the two talked about forming another alliance like the one they had in the Sixties. Chrysler needed to add some pizzazz to its lineup and performance was returning to the marketplace. Thus, in 1982 Chrysler announced that Shelby was working with the corporation as a performance consultant to "bring excitement back to the auto industry."

For the next four years, Shelby recommended high-performance packages to Dodge (Chrysler's "excitement" division) for use in special models. His group, called the Chrysler Shelby California Development Center (CSCDC), also worked with Detroit-based engineers in exploring the use of future products and technology in upcoming production cars. Out of these efforts came the 1983-86 Dodge Shelby Charger coupe and the Dodge Omni GLH ("Goes Like Hell") sedan. Both offered tweaked suspensions, turbo power, and attractive prices.

Taking the relationship one step further, Chrysler Motors' chairman, Gerald Greenwald, and Carroll Shelby announced in February 1986 that Shelby Automobiles, Inc., was being formed to make high-performance, limited-edition vehicles based on Dodge products. On March 1, Shelby Automotive's first car, the Shelby GLH-S—a more powerful and faster adaptation of the GLH—rolled off the firm's Whittier, California, assembly line. Only 500 GLH-S ("Goes Like Hell—Somemore") models were built.

Shelby's second car, the Charger GLH-S coupe, started a run of 1000 units in October of that year. Like the GLH-S sedan, it was a more potent variation of the Shelby Charger.

February 1987 saw the first of 800 Shelby Lancers come off the line. With this car, Shelby changed direction slightly by adding luxury (power everything) to the performance formula. Based on the Dodge Lancer four-door sedan, the Shelby Lancer even came with an integrated Compact Disc stereo system with two 120-watt amplifiers to boost sound to a 10-way speaker system and a remote control for back seat passengers. Other touches included a Carroll Shelby sport steering wheel, special Shelby dash plaque and full analog instrumentation.

Mechanical modifications—plenum chamber, equal-length intake manifold runners, air-to-air intercooler—boosted horsepower

Many auto buffs figure the Shelby Charger is a future collectible.

The '88 Shelby Shadow was closely related to the Shelby Lancer.

The Shelby Shadow carried CSX lettering. It could zip from 0-60 mph in a mere 7.1 seconds and do 90 in the quarter-mile run.

of the 2.2-liter Turbo II four to 176. The Shelby Touring Suspension Package lowered the car by three-quarters of an inch and gave it cornering power equal to 0.85 g on the skidpad, while the four-wheel disc brakes provided added stopping power. Externally, an aero package added a front airdam, side skirts, lower rear panel extension, and a rear spoiler. Only one option was listed, an automatic transmission/leather interior package for $1000.

Shelby's modifications were good for 0-60 mph times of 7.7 seconds and quarter-mile runs of 15.7 seconds with a terminal speed of 89 mph. Top speed, meanwhile, increased from 115 mph with the regular Dodge Lancer Turbo to 135. The Shelby Lancer was aimed directly at the Mercedes 190/16-valve model and the BMW 535i. "Our car does everything that those cars do," Shelby claimed, "plus it goes faster and handles better . . . both [of them are] fine automobiles that cost about twice as much as the $16,995 Shelby Lancer."

Shelby's fourth high-performance Dodge was the CSX, which was based on the subcompact Shadow coupe. It received modifications similar to the Shelby Lancer but was slightly faster because it was smaller and weighed 200 pounds less. It also cost less: $13,495. According to factory test data, it could do 0-60 mph in 7.1 seconds and cover the quarter mile in 15.1 seconds and 90 mph. Like the Shelby Lancer, it topped out at 135 mph and could handle 0.85 g on the skidpad. The stiff suspension, however, gave a rough ride on anything less than perfectly smooth pavement.

Shelby plans to continue its arrangement with Dodge, developing and building affordable high-performance cars capable of challenging the best foreign makes in acceleration, top speed and handling. Production runs will continue to be in the 500-2000 unit range to keep the Shelby name exclusive. The cars are sold through a network of 100-150 selected Dodge dealers. "We're building a limited number of cars for enthusiasts, first-time performance car buyers," Carroll Shelby says, and that's the way he wants to keep it.

After Henry Ford II fired him, Lee Iacocca moved over to Chrysler. Seeking to put some excitement into a bland product lineup, he hired Carroll Shelby as a performance consultant. Now there are Shelby Dodges—and more to come.

STUDEBAKER

America's oldest manufacturer of wheeled vehicles had been around since 1852, when Henry and Clem Studebaker built three covered wagons together. Actually there were five Studebaker brothers, all as bearded as the Brothers Smith, and all participated in the firm's affairs over the years. J.M. "Wheelbarrow Johnny" Studebaker was running the company when it began building automobiles in 1902. At first, these were confined to electrics, as "Mr. J.M." hated gasoline-powered cars, calling them "clumsy, dangerous noisy brutes (that) stink to high heaven, break down at the worst possible moment, and are a public nuisance." But even he was forced to bow to the inevitable, and gas-engine Studebakers appeared beginning in 1911.

J.M. Studebaker relinquished his presidency to Albert Russell Erskine in 1919, and it was this former accountant who took the firm into the '30s. Erskine made a series of serious mistakes, beginning with the short-lived car he named after himself (1927-30), followed by the ill-timed acquisition of Pierce-Arrow in 1928. In the depths of the Depression, he put the company's smallest six-cylinder engine into the Rockne, another short-lived junior make (1932-33). Dictator, another bizarre moniker of the Erskine regime, was a name that seemed downright un-American, with Hitler and Mussolini in power. Yet incredibly, Studebaker stayed with it through 1937.

Studebaker offered no fewer than five or six different engines and seven different series in the early Thirties. Six- and eight-cylinder inline powerplants of similar size and power were featured in the 115-inch-wheelbase Dictator and 120-inch-wheelbase Commander lines. Bracketing these were the short-chassis, low-

The Champion was Studebaker's new economy car for '39. It weighed 2300 pounds, cost $660 to $800, and had a 78-bhp six.

priced Studebaker Six and the magnificent top-line President Eight. The latter were truly memorable cars, the finest automobiles South Bend offered in this decade and perhaps the finest ever. Powered through 1933 by a potent 337-cubic-inch straight eight, the President "finds a parallel in sustained speed only in the light of comets, meteors, and other heavenly bodies," according to company propaganda. Such unabashed hyperbole was hardly unusual, but it did have a basis in fact: two totally stocked President Eight roadsters had each run over 30,000 miles in less than 27,000 minutes back in 1928.

The President of these years sported a pedigree as impressive as its immense proportions. The engineer behind it was the hard-driving Delmar G. "Barney" Roos, formerly of Locomobile, Marmon, and Pierce-Arrow, who designed the model's short-stroke engine with integrally cast block and crankcase. Geared to turn only 2800 rpm at 60 mph, this straight eight was rated at 115 horsepower for 1930. The next year it was given nine (versus the previous five) main bearings, a coated-steel crankshaft, and higher compression, all of which boosted output to 122 bhp, rising to 132 bhp for 1933. The crank was derived from that used in the Liberty aircraft engine, and was largely responsible for the engine's tremendous low-end stamina.

Economic misfortunes spelled the demise of the big-inch Presidents after 1933, but not before they had written a great competition story. Racers based on this platform competed with distinction at Indianapolis, for example, where Russel Snowberger drove to eighth and fifth place finishes in 1930-31, respectively, averaging over 90 mph. The factory sent its own team to Indy in 1932, and Cliff Bergere finished third with an average of 102.66 mph, the first time a semi-stock car had exceeded the magic century mark. Tony Gulotta ended the factory's Indy campaign in 1933 by finishing seventh in the 500 at 99 mph.

Studebaker cut its offerings for 1931, though there were still Dictator, Commander, and President models ranging in output from 70 to 122 bhp and in wheelbase from 114 to 136 inches. The same lineup returned for 1932-33, when the 205-cid six went into the Rockne. Studebaker also retained a six for its senior line, a 230-cid 80-bhp unit for a new 117-inch-wheelbase Dictator chassis. The 205 came back in 1934 for Standard, Special, and Deluxe Dictator models.

Most auto companies suffered greatly in the early Depression years, but Studebaker suffered more than most. One reason was that the successive failures of Erskine, Pierce-Arrow, and Rockne were aggravated by spendthrift financial practices. For instance, the firm continued to pay dividends through 1931, even though they had to come from capital reserves, and a planned merger with White Motors fell through. Meanwhile, sales slowly dwindled. Studebaker went into receivership in 1933 and Erskine resigned; shortly afterwards, he committed suicide.

What saved Studebaker at this point was production vice-president Harold S. Vance and sales vice-president Paul G. Hoffman, who would jointly guide the company's destiny through 1949. They first got rid of Pierce-Arrow, then got South Bend's idle production lines going again. Although the firm realized only a small profit in mid-1934, it was enough to secure a line of credit. The worst was over, and production began inching up: 46,000 units in 1934, 49,000 the next year, and over 80,000 in 1936-37. Part of this success reflected a reversal of Erskine's full-line market approach. Only three series—Dictator Six, Commander Eight, and President Eight—were fielded for 1935, and the firm concentrated on the medium-priced, cleanly styled Dictators and Presidents for 1936-37, both with longer wheelbases and more power.

Studebaker styling in the '30s was usually good and sometimes exceptional. The formal lines of the early years gave way in 1933 to graceful skirted fenders and radiators that curved forward at the bottom. As the streamlining craze got going at mid-decade, Studebaker adopted pontoon fenders and rounded grilles like most other makes, but retained a crisp, individual appearance. And there was considerable technical progress. Along with Warner overdrive for 1935 came Roos' novel "planar" independent front suspension, a successful innovation consisting of a transverse leaf spring with upper and lower links, and rotary (later, telescopic) shocks. The next year, Studebaker trumpeted its new "Hill Holder," a coupling between clutch and brake system that prevented the car from rolling backward down a hill when the clutch was engaged. Other new features in this period were automatic choke, vacuum-powered brakes, rotary door latches, and all-steel bodies. Most of these can be credited to Roos, who left for Britain's Rootes Group in 1936. He later returned to America and Willys-Overland, where he had a hand in designing the World War II Jeep. His post at Studebaker was taken by W.S. James, but the real engineering power after his departure was engineering vice-president Roy Cole.

Hoffmann brought in Raymond Loewy, the brilliant industrial designer who had created the handsome 1932-34 Hupmobiles, to restyle the 1938 Studebakers. He instituted a prow-front motif with flush-mounted headlights a year before most competitors had something similar.

The 1939 front end imitated the streamlined nose of the Lincoln-Zephyr, but it was pretty and distinctive. Production faltered in 1938 due to the national recession, but it improved markedly for the 1939 model year, hitting 106,470 units, a record for the decade and the company's best performance since 1928.

A big reason for this gain was the cleanly styled Champion, a new economy series priced from $660 to $800, about even with Chevy and Ford and slightly below most Plymouths. It was

A "Delux-Tone" paint job adorns this 1941 Studebaker Commander.

The '41 President was powered by a 117-bhp 250.4-cid straight eight.

Studebaker suffered more than most automakers during the Depression. It went into receivership in 1933, but its fortunes improved during the decade and by 1939 it was ready to debut its sensational new economy car, the Champion.

powered by an L-head six that was smaller and less powerful than the "Big Three" engines, but the car weighed 500-700 pounds less than its rivals and thus delivered comparable performance plus fantastic gas mileage—up to 22 mpg. The Champion was no match for the 85-bhp Ford V8, but it would run up to 78 mph, equal to or better than Chevy, Plymouth and the 60-bhp Ford.

Champions came in four body styles for 1940: three- and five-passenger coupes and two- and four-door sedans. Standard and DeLuxe trim were offered. The Champion's price range of $660 to $785 made it a formidable competitor against the Big Three makes, and 1940 volume rose to more than 66,000 units.

The middle-priced 1940 Studebaker was Commander, offered in three body styles on a 116.5-inch wheelbase: a three-passenger coupe, and two- and four-door sedans. Commanders used a 226-cid six with 90 bhp at 3400 rpm, and differed from the Champion in styling. The Commander had a sharply creased nose and a latticework grille, more like Ford's than the Champion's rounded lines.

The company continued to offer the President, equipped with a smooth, nine-main-bearing straight eight delivering 110 bhp at 3600 rpm. Prices—$1025 to $1095—were roughly $125 higher than for the equivalent Commander. Presidents rode a 122-inch wheelbase, were offered in the same three body styles as Commander, and had similar styling.

Raymond Loewy had earned his high standing at Studebaker on the strength of the Champion. For 1941, he reworked the entire line with more formal, elegant styling. A new body style, the Land Cruiser (with closed rear roof quarters), was developed for the Commander and President. Loewy pioneered bodyside two-toning, consisting of a color sweep framed in chrome that ran along the side of the hood and just below the beltline. Engines were reworked. The Champion unit was stroked out to four inches for 169.6 cid and 80 bhp. The Commander powerplant was raised to 94 bhp, while the President's silky straight eight was increased to 117.

The 1941 facelift brought additional trim levels to all three lines. For the Champion, these were Custom, Custom DeLuxe, and Delux-Tone trims available for all body styles. Commanders were offered in Custom, DeLux-Tone, and Skyway versions. The Skyway was a very richly trimmed, fender-skirted series that went into production in March 1941. There was also a top-of-the-line Skyway President Land Cruiser priced at $1260. South Bend had another excellent year in '41: nearly 85,000 Champions and 42,000 Commanders. (Presidents traditionally sold in much smaller quantities.)

Before the war put an end to civilian auto production in 1942, Studebaker built about 50,000 units—sufficient to keep the company in eighth place. Then the factory turned to defense work, building trucks, airplane engines, and Weasel personnel carriers. Styling generally ground to a halt at most auto companies during wartime as skeleton design crews could spend only a fraction of their time on civilian projects. But Studebaker was different since its car styling was being handled by Loewy Associates, an outside consultant firm not entirely occupied with defense contracts. As a result, Studebaker was able to introduce an all-new postwar design in the spring of 1946—well ahead of everyone else except

Studebaker boasted in '47 it was "First by far with a postwar car."

The three-passenger Champion DeLuxe coupe sold for $1378 in 1947.

It took $1902 to buy a '47 Champion Regal DeLuxe convertible coupe.

The 1950 Studebaker featured a controversial "needle-nose" grille.

Kaiser-Frazer.

Earlier that year, the company offered a handful of Skyway Champions, slightly facelifted versions of the 1942 model. The alterations were indeed modest: the upper grille molding was extended under the headlamps, the side hood moldings were eliminated, and optional lamps appeared atop the fenders. The usual four body styles—three- and five-passenger coupes, two- and four-door sedans—were offered. Only 19,275 were built before production changed over.

The appealing new 1947 Studebaker was mainly the product of the Loewy Studios. Virgil M. Exner, who had left Pontiac to join Loewy before the war, had directed the '47 design at first, but split with Loewy before introduction time. Engineer Roy Cole supported Exner with staff and equipment for a home studio outside South Bend. His design was based on shapes that Loewy had developed earlier, and was officially accepted over Loewy's own proposal. Exner's influence on it was mostly from the cowl forward—a shorter hood and a more blunt, very ornate front end. This basic look was retained, except for detail changes, through 1949, followed by Loewy Studio's novel "bullet-nose" facelift for 1950-51.

The Commander and Champion series returned for '47, but the Skyway designation didn't. A special 123-inch wheelbase carried the Commander Land Cruiser, Studebaker's luxury sedan. Among the 119-inch-wheelbase Commanders, the usual four closed body styles were offered in DeLuxe and Regal DeLuxe trim, the latter priced about $120 higher. A new Regal DeLuxe convertible also debuted; at $2236 it was Studebaker's priciest offering. The Champion, which started at $1378, followed the same pattern on a 112-inch wheelbase, and was nearly identical mechanically with its prewar counterpart.

One reason Studebaker styling didn't change much from 1947 to '52 was because the Loewy/Exner design—low profile, large glass area, and flow-through fenders—was so far ahead of the competition. Instant recognition of the '48s was provided by a winged hood medallion. The 1949 Commander was a continuation of the '48, while that year's Champion had a new grille composed of horizontal and vertical louvers forming three rows of rectangular openings. The most significant change in 1947-49 was mechanical. The Commander engine's stroke was lengthened to 4.75 inches for a displacement of 245.6 cubic inches and an even 100 bhp.

Studebaker's model offerings remained the same in 1948-49 as in '47: Commander coupes and sedans in DeLuxe and Regal DeLuxe trim, a Regal DeLuxe convertible, and long-wheelbase Land Cruiser; plus a similar Champion lineup minus the Land Cruiser. The big selling point continued to be styling, despite certain jokes ("Which way is it going?"). The design was innovative, eliminating the bolt-on fenders of prewar models. The envelope body allowed for an increase of six inches in front seat width and 10 in the rear, providing excellent interior room, too. Even after the major manufacturers restyled in 1949, Studebaker's shape remained one of the most advanced on the road.

The company enjoyed its best year ever in 1950 by producing 320,884 cars, and many grand predictions were made about its upcoming "second century." But United States operations came to

Studebaker had a record year in 1950 with 270,604 Champions built. Total production came to 343,166 including Commanders.

The Champion two-door sedan retailed at $1634 to $1800 in 1951.

An 85-bhp 169.6-cid six powered the '51 Champion business coupe.

Studebaker boasted in 1947 that it was "First by far with a postwar car." And aside from Kaiser-Frazer, it was. The new styling evoked a "which way is it going?" reaction, but it proved popular and Studebaker made good money in those days.

Studebaker debuted its first hardtop for 1952, here the Champion Regal Starliner. It weighed 2860 pounds and sold for $2220.

an end some 14 years later, and the Hamilton, Ontario, branch built the last Studebaker automobile two years after that.

The story of how this happened is complex, but it can be summarized as follows: (1) Studebaker's productivity was lower than the rest of the industry, even though its work force was highly paid; (2) the firm's old South Bend plant suffered from high overhead and was more isolated from component suppliers than Detroit factories; and (3) the Big Three, competing with each other, caused casualties among the independents (an example is the Ford and Chevrolet price wars, which Studebaker dealers could not match because of their lower volume).

The product itself probably had less to do with the firm's failures than these commercial factors. Though Studebaker styling was controversial, it usually featured ideas adopted later by other manufacturers. Although the bullet-nose front end of 1950-51 wasn't really copied by anyone else, it did suggest the strong central grille styling that would appear later in different form on Edsels and Pontiacs. The 1950 models also offered Studebaker's excellent automatic transmission, designed in cooperation with the Detroit Gear Division of Borg-Warner.

Studebaker fielded a 113-inch short-wheelbase Champion in three trim variations for 1950. Commanders rode a longer 120-inch stretch and continued to offer a larger 102-bhp six-cylinder engine. The 124-inch-wheelbase Land Cruiser was still part of this series, available as a four-door sedan only.

The Champion 85-bhp engine was continued for 1951, while the Commander received Studebaker's first V8. Displacing 232.6 cubic inches, this new powerplant developed 120 bhp at 4000 rpm. Its engineering was fairly conventional, though overhead cams and hemispherical combustion chambers had been considered. The 232 and its successors have been called heavy for their size, but such statements were made on the basis of comparisons with engines developed much later. In fact, Studebaker's V8 was the first in a long line of robust, efficient small-blocks of less than 300 cid. Those that followed from Dodge, Ford, Chevrolet, and Plymouth certainly benefited from its technology. The 232's greatest contribution, perhaps, was that it closed the power gap between popular-priced cars and luxury machines. As a result, the V8 would become the engine design favored by automakers and buyers alike.

The '51 Studebaker line was essentially the same as in 1950. The main difference was body size: Commanders now shared a

All 1952 Commanders were powered by a 232.6-cid overhead-valve V8.

The '52 Commander Land Cruiser rode an extended 119-inch chassis.

115-inch wheelbase with Champions, while the Land Cruiser shrank from 124 to 119 inches. Prices went up slightly, but buyers seemed happy to pay the difference for the lively V8, which increased Commander sales considerably. The 232 was no powerhouse, but it did give 90-mph performance. As time would tell, it was capable of considerably more displacement and horsepower.

Styling changes for '51 were slight. The bullet-nose was refined with a second chrome ring, the prominent air vents above the grille were deleted, and model names were spelled out on the leading edges of the hood. Whatever can be said about its styling now, the bullet-nose Studebaker was popular when new.

With 222,000 unit sales for calendar 1951, Studebaker fell far below its 1950 record, though this was more a result of Korean War restrictions than decreased demand. The firm's market share actually increased, from 4.02 to 4.17 percent.

The company's centenary was marked in 1952. Though all-new styles weren't ready, that year's facelift was acceptably different. The bullet-nose was replaced by a low, toothy grille that some stylists called the "clam digger." The model lineup stayed the same except for the addition of a new hardtop, the Starliner, available as a Champion or Commander. But production was much lower throughout the industry, and Studebaker built fewer cars: 186,239. Optimistically, management looked on the upcoming '53s with more enthusiasm.

The now-legendary "Loewy coupes"—Commander and Champion Starliner hardtop and Starlight pillar coupe—were actually designed by Robert E. Bourke, chief of the Loewy Studios at South Bend. Originally envisioned only as a special show car, Loewy sold the design as a production model to Studebaker's management. These coupes were truly magnificent. Mounted on the new 120.5-inch Land Cruiser wheelbase rather than the sedans' 116.5-inch span, they were perfect from every angle. Not a line or a detail was out of place. They were hailed at the time as the "new European look." Today, they're considered by many as the finest American automotive styling of the entire decade.

Sadly, the changeover to the new design delayed production, which was disappointingly low at 169,899 units. Further problems surfaced when demand for coupes began running four times higher than for the sedans (which had the same general lines but were shorter, higher, and more ungainly). Management had planned just the reverse, and time and sales were lost in switching around.

The same lineup was offered for 1954 (an eggcrate grille was the most obvious change), but production sank even lower: 81,930 units. By now, the company's weaknesses were becoming painfully apparent: the cost of building each car was frightening. As an experiment, Bourke "priced out" a Commander Starliner using the General Motors cost structure, and found Chevrolet could have sold it for about $1900, compared to the $2502 Studebaker was asking. Meanwhile, the "Ford Blitz" was on, as Dearborn waged a price war with GM. Neither giant damaged the other, but both wreaked havoc on the independents. Just when things looked blackest, Packard bought Studebaker and announced a bold new effort to create "the industry's Big Four."

Unable to justify new styling so soon, Studebaker hung a lot of chrome on the old bodies for '55 and adopted a wraparound windshield in mid-year. The model line was shaken up, with Champions (excluding the coupes) still placed on the shorter wheelbase. The longer 120.5-inch chassis now served a separate series, the revived President. The Champion six was raised to 101 bhp. For more economy, the firm shrank the Commander V8 to 224.3 cid, which resulted in 140 bhp. Presidents, in turn, used a larger V8: 259.2 cid and 175 bhp. The top of the line was the wildly two-toned President Speedster hardtop, with special "quilted" leather seats, tooled metal dash, and color combinations like pink and black or "lemon and lime." At $3253, it was not a big seller (2215 built), and neither were its linemates. In a year when nearly every company was setting new sales records, Studebaker produced only about 116,000 cars. Soon it was determined the company needed to sell about 250,000 cars a year just to break even.

While Studebaker-Packard president James Nance shopped for financing (eventually leading to a takeover by Curtiss-Wright), the firm gamely restyled for 1956. Retaining the old wheelbases and bodyshells, styling became more upright and squared off, with larger, mesh-type grilles. A cheap two-door called the sedanet was offered in the Commander and Champion series. The long-wheelbase chassis was now reserved for the top-line President Classic sedan and the sporty new Hawks.

The Hawks were the last Studebakers of the '50s designed by Loewy's team, and were good-looking, exciting to drive, competent on the curves, and impressive on the straightaways. There were four altogether. The Power (V8) and Flight (six) Hawks were descendants of the pillar-type Starlight coupe. Based on the old Starliner hardtop were the Sky Hawk and Golden Hawk, the latter with the 352-cid Packard engine. Styling was keyed to a square classic-style grille, freestanding parking lights, and deluxe interiors with engine-turned dash like the '55 Speedster's. The Flight Hawk was priced under $2000, while the Golden Hawk listed at only $3061, so they were good buys. Unfortunately, they were all peripheral models that appealed mainly to enthusiasts, while the bread-and-butter family cars continued to sell slowly. Only 70,000 vehicles were turned out at South Bend in 1956, and things would continue to get worse. In 1957 and '58, Studebaker and Packard combined couldn't produce more than 70,000 cars a year.

This was the period when none of the plant's employees knew

The '53 Land Cruiser had a 120.5-inch wheelbase and listed at $2316.

Styling for '56 was squarer, bulkier, as on this President Classic.

Studebaker celebrated its 100th anniversary in 1952 with its first hardtop and a facelift highlighted by a "clam digger" grille. The glamorous Loewy coupes bowed for '53 along with more sedate sedans—Stude's last all-new sedan bodyshells.

Studebaker's sportiest offering for 1955 was the President Speedster. It retailed for $3253 and only 2215 were produced.

from one day to the next whether they were working their last shift. With so little money to alter the '56 design, there was nothing else to do but try a facelift. Accordingly, a full-width grille appeared for 1957, and grew more massive in 1958, when Studebakers also got hastily developed quad headlight systems and ungainly tailfins. The Scotsman—a naked, bargain-priced line of sedans and a station wagon—did not spark sales. Neither did the nice-looking Starlight hardtop with its DeSoto-like roof.

Mechanical changes were beneficial, however. The '56 Golden Hawk's huge Packard engine had made it embarrassingly front-heavy, so the 1957-58 edition used a 289 V8 with Paxton supercharger. This arrangement developed the same 275 bhp, but in a

The Silver Hawk for '57 was a pillared coupe with either the 289-cid V8 or 185.6-cid six. Production reached a modest 9607 units.

more efficient way: the blower free-wheeled economically until the accelerator was floored. The other Hawks were replaced by a single fixed-pillar Silver Hawk with plainer trim and an unblown 289 developing 210 bhp. The Golden Hawk and Silver Hawk were fine road machines, capable of carrying four people comfortably over long distances at high speed in true gran turismo style. As "personal cars," their appeal was limited, however, especially in 1958 when Studebaker hit bottom. Fewer than 45,000 cars were built that year.

The end might have come right there had not the firm succeeded with the compact 1959 Lark. Though the Lark used many body panels and mechanical components from earlier '53-'58 models, stylist Duncan McRae had done enough to the exterior to make it look considerably different. The boxy, practical styling found a market among compact-conscious buyers, and people flocked to Studebaker dealerships in droves. The turnaround was astounding. Compared to 18,850 four-door sedans built for '58, a total of 48,459 four-door '59 Larks rolled off the lines. The Lark was also offered as a two-door sedan, two-door wagon, and two-door hardtop, all on a 108.5-inch wheelbase. Six-cylinder models still used the old 169.6-cid L-head, detuned to 90 bhp. The V8 versions were fitted with the 259, rated at 180 bhp, or 195 with four-barrel carburetor. In V8 form, the Lark was lively, yet surprisingly easy on gas. The Hawk was also continued for '59, but only the Silver Hawk pillared coupe was issued. As a result of all this, Studebaker made its first profit in six years, building 138,858 cars, only 7788 of them Hawks. But the Lark would provide only a temporary reprieve.

For 1960, the year the Big Three introduced their new compacts, Lark was changed only mildly from the introductory model, receiving a new grille composed of thick and thin horizontal bars, and small alterations in script and medallions. The Hawk was carried over virtually unaltered. It sold for $2650 and was worth it. Equipped with functional white-on-black instruments and semi-bucket seats, it was a unique "family sports car" offering good performance. But scant advertising plus emphasis on the Lark hampered its sales, which amounted to only 3939 units. Lark output declined slightly to 127,715.

For 1961, the Lark was modestly facelifted. The six-cylinder engine was finally converted to overhead-valve design, yielding 112 bhp. One new model was the Lark Cruiser, outfitted with rich upholstery and riding the wagon wheelbase for extra rear seat room. It could be ordered with the Hawk's 289 V8, available with a power pack consisting of four-barrel carburetor and dual exhausts that raised output to 225 bhp. The Hawk itself was slightly revised for 1961, receiving two-tone color panels just below the fins and an optional four-speed gearbox.

When Sherwood Egbert became company president in early 1961, he asked Milwaukee stylist Brooks Stevens to help redesign the Lark and Hawk on a six-month crash basis. Randall Faurot, Studebaker's head of styling, willingly stepped back. Stevens adopted the longer 113-inch wheelbase for all four-door models, then developed elongated rear quarters, large round taillights, and a Mercedes-like rectangular grille (Studebaker was distributing Mercedes-Benz cars at the time). A new entry with either six or V8 power was the sporty Lark Daytona hardtop and convertible, which featured bucket seats and an optional 289 engine.

In reworking the Hawk, Stevens reskinned the old Loewy-styled coupe to create a true hardtop with a Thunderbird-like rear roofline. He eliminated the large tailfins, which had become dated by 1960, and restyled the dashboard, which retained its full complement of purposeful gauges. Christened Gran Turismo Hawk, the result was a remarkable piece of expeditious redesign. The GT's optional 225-bhp engine provided a 120-mph top speed and a 0-60 sprint of less than 10 seconds. Although heavy, the 289 V8 was incredibly strong, capable of performance far greater than its displacement suggested. Sales picked up in 1962, when 8388 Gran

The '54 Champion station wagon was a two door called Conestoga.

A 352-cid Packard V8 powered the '56 Golden Hawk; 4071 were built.

It took $2123 to buy a brand-new '57 Champion DeLuxe club sedan.

Studebaker's plushest wagon for 1957 was the four-door Broadmoor.

In the mid- and late-Fifties, Studebaker rode a sales roller coaster mainly downhill—the firm lacked the money to bring out totally new cars to compete with the Big Three. After a dismal 1958, the outlook was bleak indeed in South Bend.

A convertible in Regal trim joined the Lark VIII lineup in 1960. It retailed for $2756 with the standard 195-bhp 259.2-cid V8.

The Hawk came only as a pillared-coupe V8 in '60; 3939 were sold.

Hawk for '61 cost $2650, had rear fender two-toning; 3340 were built.

Turismos were built. Lark production, however, dwindled to 93,004 units.

For 1963, Stevens reworked the Lark's body above the beltline. He improved visibility by using more glass and thinner upper door frames. The grille was revised slightly, but the dashboard was completely new, fitted with needle gauges, rocker-type control switches, and a "vanity" style glove compartment containing a makeup case and pop-up mirror. For utility-car buyers, Stevens came up with a great innovation: the Wagonaire, with a sliding rear roof panel.

Stevens gave the 1963 GT Hawk a new grille similar to the Lark's, round amber parking lights, a wood-like dash, and pleated vinyl seats. Both Lark and Hawk were available by mid-year with the R1 (240 bhp) and R2 (290 bhp) Avanti engines, priced at $210 and $372 respectively. The R2 Super Hawk exceeded 140 mph at Bonneville, and an R2 Super Lark did over 132 mph.

Studebaker's greatest achievement of the decade was undoubtedly the Avanti, introduced for 1963. This brilliantly conceived grand touring car was created by Raymond Loewy and a team of talented designers—John Ebstein, Robert Andrews, and Tom Kellogg. Like Stevens, Loewy had been hired by Sherwood Egbert. While Stevens attended to emergency restyling, Egbert asked Loewy for an exotic sports-type car that would revitalize the company's image. It was the first assignment Loewy had been given by Studebaker since his old contract lapsed following completion of the 1956 Hawks. In haste and in complete secrecy, he gathered his team at a rented house in Palm Springs, California.

The car they developed had a Coke-bottle shape, large rear window, and built-in roll bar. The razor-edged front fenders swept back into curved rear fenders, then flowed into a jacked-up tail.

Avoiding a conventional grille, Loewy designed an air scoop under a thin front bumper. An asymmetrical hump in the hood directed the driver's vision forward and added character to the front-end shape. Inside, ample crash padding was combined with four slim-section vinyl bucket seats and an aircraft-style control panel. The whole design was accepted for production with very little change from Loewy's original small scale model.

Fiberglass was chosen as the body material for reasons of cost and time, and chief engineer Eugene Harding chose a Lark convertible frame, shortened and highly modified, fitted with front and rear anti-sway bars and rear radius rods. The Bendix disc brakes used on the Avanti (as well as on some Larks and Hawks) were the first caliper discs in domestic production. The engine was, of course, the 289 V8. In standard (R1) form, it developed 240 bhp, thanks to a Paxton supercharger, ¾-race high-lift cam, dual-breaker distributor, four-barrel carburetor, and dual exhausts. Andy Granatelli and Paxton also developed a supercharged R2 version with 290 bhp, followed by a bored-out 304.5-cid version in three higher states of tune, the R3, R4, and R5. The experimental R5 had two Paxton superchargers, one for each cylinder bank, along with magneto ignition and Bendix fuel injection. It developed an incredible 575 horsepower, but was not a production option.

The Avanti had a remarkably slippery shape, even though Loewy had not had time for wind tunnel tests—he'd just guessed. In late 1962, Granatelli broke 29 Bonneville speed records with an R3, traveling faster than anyone ever had in an American stock car.

Unfortunately, Studebaker failed to get Avanti production going immediately after announcement. Unexpected distortion during fiberglass curing accounted partly for the delay. As a result, the firm was forced to add its own fiberglass body facility. By the time all the bugs were out, most of the customers who'd placed advance orders had given up on the Avanti and bought Corvettes. Fewer than 4600 were produced during 1963 and 1964. Production had already ceased by the time Studebaker stopped building Larks in South Bend in December 1963.

The car was revived, however, by a pair of South Bend dealers. Equipped with a Corvette engine, it was still being produced in the late 1980s (*see* Avanti II/Avanti).

Despite the Avanti's obvious showroom appeal, Studebaker sales plunged in 1963. Model year output fell short of 70,000 units. The company ranked 12th in production, ahead of only Lincoln and Imperial among the major makes. Egbert, who'd been hospitalized repeatedly, entered the hospital again in November 1963 and did not return to the company. (He died of cancer in 1969.) Byers Burlingame replaced him as president. A month later, after desperate last-ditch attempts to obtain backing for future models, Burlingame announced the closure of the South Bend factory. Operations were transferred to the assembly plant in Hamilton, Ontario, where management hoped to continue production at the rate of 20,000 a year.

The 1964 models were the most attractive of the decade. Brooks Stevens had created more new styling for the bread-and-butter Studebakers, which were now known as the Challenger, Commander, Daytona, Cruiser, and Wagonaire. The Lark name no longer appeared on the car; the only reference to the Lark was in some of the early 1964 sales literature as it pertained to the bottom-of-the-line Challenger and Commander. Stevens designed a crisp, squared-off body, six inches longer than the 1963 version, while a broad, horizontal grille integrated with the headlights and a pointed upper tail section housed backup lights and taillamps. A stripped Challenger line listed at around $2100, while a still more powerful R3 engine was announced for the Super "Lark" and Super Hawk. (The former could do 0 to 60 mph in 7.3 seconds.) The '64 Gran Turismo Hawk had a landau-style roof with partial vinyl top (optional), a smoothed-off deck, and a matte-black dash. A test driver pushed an R2 Hawk to 90 mph in 13.8

Designer Brooks Stevens created the Gran Turismo Hawk for 1962.

The 1963 Lark Daytona hardtop was available with a fabric sunroof.

A sliding roof panel was the '63 Wagonaire's most practical feature.

Raymond Loewy's design team created the stunning '63 Avanti coupe.

The Lark bowed a year before the Big Three compacts, bringing temporary salvation. Clever restyles kept it going; Avanti added a dash of excitement. But the trend was relentlessly downward, and Studebaker built its last car in 1966.

Only 1767 Gran Turismo Hawks were built for 1964 before December 1963, when Studebaker closed its South Bend, Indiana, plant.

The 1964 Daytona convertible sported new front and rear styling.

Studebaker gave up on cars after only 8947 were built for '66.

seconds and estimated its top speed at 150-plus mph. All the high-performance specials were dropped with the move to Canada.

The 1965 models were unchanged in appearance. However, without the South Bend engine plant, Hamilton had to find another powerplant. Ultimately, Chevrolet became the source, providing its solid 120-bhp, 194-cid six and its excellent 283-cid V8 with 195 bhp. A six-cylinder Cruiser was available along with Commander two- and four-door sedans and a four-door Wagonaire (with or without sliding roof). The V8 was offered for Commander sedans and wagon, the Daytona Sport sedan and wagon, and the Cruiser.

The Hamilton plant almost met its 20,000-unit quota for 1965. But the lack of facilities for advanced research and development meant production simply couldn't last, even though the Canadian operation was turning a small profit. The last Studebaker—the '66—had new front-end styling with two dual-beam headlights instead of quads, a revised grille with rectangular panels, new bodyside moldings, and air-extraction ports in the rear panel. But production numbered only 8947 units.

Despite rescue attempts by Stevens and others, auto production by Studebaker was doomed, and the Hamilton plant was duly closed in March 1966. The corporation would survive, however, because it had diversified, owning Paxton (superchargers) and STP, and other enterprises. In mid-1967 Studebaker Corporation purchased the Wagner Electric Corporation and late that year Studebaker combined with Worthington Corporation to form Studebaker-Worthington Corporation. The new firm was bought by the McGraw-Edison Company of Illinois in 1979. At this writing, the Studebaker-Worthington name is retained by McGraw as a division name, although it has no product line.

TUCKER

The backlot of American automotive history is littered with has-beens and never-weres. Some deserved to live—some deserved to die. But what about the Tucker? Here was a car so advanced that many of its features took years to be accepted. Appearing in 1948, it was hailed as "The First Completely New Car in Fifty Years." And to a war-weary America expecting bold new ventures, it did seem like the "car of the future."

Yet the Tucker had no future. Surrounded by controversy that raged for years, it failed before it really had a chance to succeed. Even now, some 40 years later, the question remains: did the Tucker deserve to die?

At the heart of the Tucker story was Preston Thomas Tucker, who for one brief shining moment stood at the forefront of automotive progress. Film director Francis Ford Coppola owned the movie rights to the Tucker saga, and in late 1988—amidst much hoopla—the film made its debut. And as the movie portrays, Tucker cut an impressive figure—six feet tall and 200 pounds.

Veteran designer and one-time Tucker stylist Alex Tremulis remembers him as "an inspiring man. Once he said to me, 'Alex, remember: you and I have a boss that is bigger than both of us and that's the automobile. Whatever you do, make sure it's best for the automobile.' "

Tucker became an "autoholic" at an early age. He started as an office boy for Cadillac Engineering, worked on a Ford assembly line, sold Studebakers and Packards and Dodges, and eventually worked his way up to sales manager for Pierce-Arrow. By the time the war was underway, he had visions of an advanced postwar car to be engineered by Harry Miller, best known as the engine guru for Indy 500 race cars. The shy, retiring Miller could build fast cars, but Tucker could *talk* fast cars and raise fast money. Despite Miller's death in 1943, Tucker forged ahead, with Ben Parsons as chief engineer and announced plans in December 1945 to mass-produce his "car of the future." He then spent the next year securing a plant, lining up suppliers, and hiring talent.

When the Tucker appeared in 1948, it was billed as "The First Completely New Car in Fifty Years"—and for the most part it was.

The Tucker was a radical design that suffered for lack of development money and time. Whether it would have succeeded is doubtful, but a securities and mail fraud trial killed it, even though Preston Tucker was eventually found innocent.

The rear-engine Tucker Torpedo was powered by a lightweight Air-Cooled Motors flat six that had been converted to water cooling.

Ultimately, 51 "production" Tuckers were completed, 37 of which came off the firm's short assembly line at a refurbished wartime plant on the south side of Chicago. Compromises had to be made because the Miller-designed engine couldn't be perfected in time and then-current technology didn't allow for a curved windshield, but what finally emerged was a full-size four-door fastback looking like no other sedan on the road. Built on a 128-inch wheelbase, the Tucker stood just 60 inches high, quite low for the late Forties, and measured 219 inches stem to stern.

Styling features included a pointed nose incorporating a "cyclops-eye" headlamp that turned with the front wheels, low-riding grilles on either side of a small center section just below the center light, and bulged front and rear fenders. Six Chicago Bears football players could sit inside wearing top hats, and front and rear seats were interchangeable so the upholstery could wear more evenly. The car bristled with safety features, including a "Safety Chamber" ahead of the front seat. An all independent suspension and center-point steering allowed for surprisingly good handling and roadholding for a car that weighed over 4200 pounds.

The engine finally chosen was an Air-Cooled Motors flat six that had proved its mettle in World War II. The 335-cid alloy powerplant weighed only 320 pounds, and after being converted to water cooling, boasted the industry's first sealed cooling system. The result was that a Tucker could dash from 0-60 mph in about 10 seconds and top 120 mph. The estimated 0.30 coefficient of drag (Cd)—excellent even today—allowed for an easy cruising speed of 100 mph.

All well and good, except that Tucker was charged with "fast-sell" tactics and Washington became interested. Tucker thus went on trial on a 31-count indictment that included conspiracy and securities and mail fraud. He was eventually exonerated, but his automotive venture died in the process. No one will ever really know the true potential of the Tucker automobile, but the cars that were built prove convincingly that it deserved to live.

A novel "cyclops-eye" center headlight turned with the front wheels.

Tucker acquired a plant in Chicago, but only 51 cars were ever built.

WILLYS

John North Willys was a car dealer in Elmira, New York, with a yen to do more than just sell the things. In 1907 he bought the ailing Overland Company of Indianapolis. A year later he renamed it Willys-Overland, moved into the old Pope plant in Toledo, Ohio, and began rebuilding the firm's fortunes. For most of the Teens, the four-cylinder Overland was second in sales only to the Model T Ford and by 1918, J.N. Willys owned the second largest auto company in the world. The post-World War I recession slowed production, but sales soared with the 1926 introduction of the low-priced Whippet. The all-time record came in 1928, when the company built 315,000 cars and rocketed to third place behind Chevrolet and Ford. Then came the Depression, and Willys-Overland declined to the point of declaring bankruptcy in 1933. It resumed production after reorganization, but built only about 8000 units in calendar 1934.

The Toledo-built cars entered the '30s with a name change, as the Overland badge was dropped in favor of the Willys nameplate. Besides a group of conventionally engined models, the company continued its line of sleeve-valve Willys-Knight offerings through 1933. This engine employed that interesting valve arrangement patented by brilliant inventor Charles Yale Knight. Replacing the usual cam-and-spring actuated poppet valves was a double sliding sleeve that let the fuel/air mixture directly into the cylinders. Although the engines were expensive to build, many makes used the sleeve-valve in the Teens, but Willys built more of them than anybody else and continued them longer.

The rest of the Willys line in this period, comprising conventional L-head sixes and eights, featured attractive styling and competitive prices, which ranged from $500 to $800. The Eight, which rode a longer wheelbase than the Six, was introduced in 1931—an inopportune time for big-engine cars. The 1933 bankruptcy finished off both.

The resulting reorganization saw Willys-Overland put all of its resources into a new small car built on a 100-inch wheelbase, the Willys 77. It continued with little change as the firm's only model from early 1933 through 1936. Powered by an ultra-economical four-cylinder engine developing 48 bhp, the 77 was unique and unmistakable. The radiator was hidden under the hood, and the vertical-bar grille was rounded at the top and tapered at the bottom to a sharp point. This design earned the nickname "potato digger," and the car lived up to that title by digging a financial hole in the ground. The best annual production total it could manage was about 30,000 units. Today, the 77 looks refreshing compared to most of the lumpy cars of this era. But back then—and despite low prices—it just wouldn't sell in volume.

Although retaining the "potato digger" engine and chassis, a complete restyle was undertaken for 1937. The result was, again, less than ideal: a rounded body with pontoon fenders and a wild front not unlike that of the shark-nose Graham. Model offerings were expanded with Standard and Deluxe versions of the basic coupe and sedan. This car was designated Model 37, then Model 38, and finally 38 and 48 for 1939. While this styling was no less bizarre than the 77's, it met with some success, and Willys sales shot up to 63,467 in 1937. But this was a recovery year for the industry as a whole and, despite twice the production, Willys was only able to move from 15th to 14th place in the standings. The 1938 recession put output back to 16,173, and Willys again had to settle for 15th.

For 1939, Toledo fielded the same line it had the previous two years, and it sold just a little better than the '38. Prices started at $499. Some help was provided by a revived Overland nameplate for a new 102-inch-wheelbase entry, the Model 39. Styled differently than the Willys, it also had a Graham-like front end, but with the headlamps carried in fender pods instead of being flush-mounted. Prices were about $100 higher than for the Willys 38, but the extra money bought significantly better performance,

Bumper guards and dual windshield wipers were '39 Willys options.

The '39 Willys Overland had a 102-inch chassis and a 61-bhp four.

Willys-Overland went from 315,000 cars in 1928 to bankruptcy in 1933. From the ashes arose the compact 77, which by World War II had evolved into the slightly larger Americar. Willys gained fame building the tough little Jeep during the war.

Willys cars took on a patriotic air for '41 when the seven-model range was named Americar; 1941-42 output totaled 28,935 units.

thanks to a compression increase and a fixed-jet carburetor that coaxed 62 bhp out of the little four. Calendar year production moved up to 25,383 units.

Joseph W. Frazer left Chrysler Corporation to become president and general manager of Willys-Overland in 1939. He knew how to cut his losses, and decreed much more conventional styling for 1940. However, it's doubtful even he could have saved Willys passenger cars, and the company's ultimate salvation was the wartime Jeep.

The new line, designated Series 440 (four cylinders, 1940) was powered by the firm's 61-bhp L-head four, which displaced 134.2 cubic inches and delivered 25 miles per gallon. It remained the standard Willys powerplant through the decade, though horsepower increased (to 63) in 1941. In 1949 it was converted by engineer Barney Roos to F-head, overhead-valve configuration. The chassis was a conventional ladder design with an X-braced center and a 102-inch wheelbase. There were five body styles in two series, with prices ranging from $529 to $830. Model year production increased modestly to nearly 27,000 for 1940.

For the '41 Series 441, Frazer and his team made further improvements. The new line was named Americar, providing patriotic appeal. It featured more horsepower, a longer 104-inch wheelbase, and prices averaging $100 higher. Three series were offered: Speedway coupe and sedan; DeLuxe coupe, sedan, and wagon; and the top-line Plainsman coupe and sedan. Styling was Ford-like, with faired-in headlamps on the front fenders and a sharply pointed nose over a small vertical-bar grille.

Production for 1942 was cut short earlier than for most automakers since Willys had begun building Jeeps for the Army. The '42 Americars were the same as the '41s—three models and

The 1940 Willys 440 lineup ranged in price from $529 to $830.

Top of the line for '41 was the $916 Americar DeLuxe station wagon.

seven body styles. Prices rose slightly, ranging from $695 to $978. The original Jeep was conceived mainly by American Bantam, but Willys-Overland produced a similar design in vast quantities through 1945.

During the war, Frazer left to take over Graham-Paige, while chairman Ward Canaday planned postwar activities around Jeep-like vehicles.

A truck-type all-steel station wagon using the L-head four and the 104-inch wheelbase was announced for 1946-47. It was significant in that it was the first true all-steel wagon, though for purposes of the industry and this book it was considered more of a truck than a car. It was Willys' main civilian product in those two years, priced at $1495 in 1946 and $1625 in '47.

For 1948, Willys-Overland continued the wagon (now listed at $1645) and added two new vehicles: the four-cylinder Jeepster "phaeton" priced at $1765, and the six-cylinder Station Sedan, which went for $1890. The Jeepster was a pleasant little touring car designed during the war by Brooks Stevens, who borrowed its lines from the Jeep. It had a big open compartment behind the cowl and a mechanically operated soft top. The six-cylinder Station Sedan was a luxury version of the four-cylinder wagon, with a larger body and wider seats. Together with the Jeepster, it helped keep Willys-Overland afloat.

For 1949, Willys offered a new 104.5-inch-wheelbase wagon priced at $1895, plus the regular wagon and two Jeepsters in its four-cylinder lineup. The second series Jeepster appeared in January, powered by the firm's first F-head engine. The company continued to sell the six-cylinder Station Sedan and wagon, and debuted a six-cylinder Jeepster at $1530. Conversion to overhead-valve engines was completed for all models by 1950. Over 10,000 Jeepsters were sold for 1948. In 1950, however, only 4066 fours and 1778 sixes were sold. Some leftovers were registered as '51s.

During this period, Willys was laying the groundwork for a return to passenger-car production. The result was the 1952 Aero-Willys, a lightweight, unit-body, compact weighing 2500-2600 pounds and riding a 108-inch wheelbase. Styled by Phil Wright and engineered by Clyde Paton, the Aero-Willys featured a clean design while providing good comfort and handling. Four separate models were offered. The Aero-Lark used the older 161-cid, 75-bhp L-head six; the Wing, Ace, and Eagle hardtop used the overhead-valve version. The 161 was small, but a good performer, providing economy on the order of 25 mpg. The biggest problem for these cars was their list prices. The Eagle hardtop, for example, carried a $2155 price tag; a Chevrolet Bel Air hardtop cost $150 less. Willys-Overland dealers were hard pressed—not only to explain how builders of Jeeps could produce a smooth, comfortable family car, but also why they had to charge so much for it. Production was good, but not great. For the '52 model year, about 31,000 Aeros were built. About 23 percent were baseline Larks, while seven percent were Eagle hardtops.

Willys reentered the automobile business in 1952 with the Aero.

The 1954 Aero-Ace DeLuxe four door saw production of 1498 units.

Willys expanded the Aero line for 1953 and made only minor appearance changes, including red-painted wheel cover emblems and a gold-plated "W" in the grille to symbolize the firm's 50th anniversary. About 500 Larks were fitted with an F-head four-cylinder engine. The Aero-Wing was replaced by the Aero-Falcon, and a new four-door sedan was developed for the Lark, Falcon, and Ace. Again, the hardtop Eagle was priced on the high side. Willys-Overland had another modestly good year, selling about 42,000 units.

In 1954, Willys-Overland was purchased by Henry Kaiser, who combined it with his ailing Kaiser-Frazer Corporation to form the Toledo-based Kaiser-Willys Sales Corporation. The K-F plant at

The '49 Jeepster "phaeton convertible" sold for $1495 to $1530.

Aero-Lark output for the $1737 two door reached only 1370 units.

Postwar, Willys debuted the Jeepster and the first all-steel wagon. For '52, the year of the first hydrogen explosion in the Pacific's Eniwetok Atoll, Willys exploded with a new car, the Aero. It failed by 1955, but did much better in Brazil.

Willow Run was sold to General Motors, and Kaiser production was shifted to the old Willys plant.

At first, the new '54 Aero appeared to be the same as the '53 with larger taillights and revised interiors. But in March 1954, the company made the 226-cid L-head six available as an option for the Ace and Eagle. To further complicate matters, there were Ace and Eagle Customs—the designation merely indicating the presence of a "continental" spare tire. With the Kaiser 226, the Aero was relatively fast. Though its 85-mph top speed was little higher than the Willys-powered models, it was geared for good acceleration: a typical 0-60 mph sprint took 14 seconds. As an experiment, a few cars were fitted with the 140-bhp supercharged Manhattan engine, which engineers say gave pickup comparable to that of contemporary V8s.

The 1954 Aero also handled much better than before. A new front end was adopted using threaded trunions adjustable for wear. The kingpins and coil springs were longer, shocks and A-arms stronger, and the steering idler arm longer. A cross member connected left and right front suspension assemblies to eliminate lateral torque and reduce tow-in variations. The Aero-Willys was thus one of the best combinations of ride and handling offered by a domestic manufacturer in the '50s. The Eagle hardtop in particular was an attractive car, though price was still a problem: the '54 version sold for close to $2600 with Hydra-Matic. Sales dropped to around 12,000 units.

By early 1955, Kaiser-Willys had decided to abandon passenger cars, but not before selling some 6500 of the '55 models. No longer called Aeros, the line was divided into the Custom two- or four-door sedans and the Bermuda hardtop (plus a handful of Ace sedans). Engine options included 161- and 226-cid sixes. Prices were cut drastically in an effort to spark sales, and the Bermuda, at $1997, was advertised as the nation's lowest-priced hardtop. But only 2215 were built, most powered by the 226 engine.

Styling for '55 was much busier than before, and no designer takes credit for it. A clumsy attempt at two-toning involved complicated side trim; the grille was no longer a simple bar, but a garish expanse of concave, vertical bars. In contrast to this glitter, a neat hardtop wagon had been planned for '55 and a very sleek facelift was also scheduled for 1955. Neither materialized.

The Aero did get a new lease on life in South America. Its dies were shipped to the former Kaiser subsidiary, Willys do Brasil, where a cleaned-up '55 model without the busy side moldings was built with F-head Willys power through 1962. In all, the Aero actually lasted over 10 years—which attests to its good design.

Willys called its '55 hardtop the Bermuda. Still riding a 108-inch wheelbase, it sported a new grille and fancy two-tone paint.

The Aero-Lark DeLuxe was Willys' bottom-of-the-line series in '54.

Willys built 2822 mid-line 1955 Custom four doors. Price: $1795.

TABLES

HOW TO READ THE TABLES

The tables in this book were designed to offer the greatest amount of useful information in a limited space, and make those facts easy to find. Our goal was to provide, at a glance, the data most readers would be likely to need in a hurry: models, wheelbases, body styles, weights, prices, model year production, and engine availability. Over the past half-century, the automobile industry has been marked by constant change, as well as by a lack of uniformity in record-keeping. So when using the tables, please keep the following explanations and qualifications in mind.

Series or Model Codes

Each group of body styles is listed under a series or model heading. This indicates the factory model or series code number (where applicable), name, and wheelbase (in inches). Code numbers posed many problems. On occasion, it was unclear whether a code applied to the series or model line as a whole, to specific body styles, or both. In instances where they were misleading or irrelevant, the code numbers were omitted. Where a code applies to both model/series and body style, the first part is shown with the model/series and the second with the body style. An example is Dodge from 1959 onward. Officially, that year's Coronet six-cylinder club sedan was designated by the factory as MD1-L21, but "MD1-L" applied to all Coronet sixes, and "21" only to the club sedan. The number is divided accordingly.

In the 1960s, some code systems became more complex, so numbers are listed as the situation required. For 1961, for example, codes for the Dodge Lancer followed '59 practice. But the 1961 Dart Six series consisted of Seneca, Pioneer, and Phoenix sub-series. In this case, only the series number "RD3" is shown in the heading; the rest of the designation appears alongside the corresponding body styles. In reality, a 1961 Dart Six Phoenix hardtop coupe went by the code RD3-H434; it is shown as model RD3, body style H434.

Model codes for more recent cars are generally less complex, and in fact are frequently omitted from industry documents. A slash in the code number usually indicates the presence of an option package, identified by the letters and/or numbers to the right of the slash.

Abbreviations

For best readability, it was important to limit each entry, whenever possible, to one line. To do this, the following standard abbreviations were adopted for the body style listings:

abbreviation	meaning
A/S	auxiliary seats
A/W	all-weather
b'ham brgm	brougham (sedan, convertible, etc.)
bkt sts	bucket seats
bus	business (as in coupe)
cab	cabriolet
comm	commercial
conv cpe	two-door convertible
conv sdn	four-door convertible
cpe	coupe
CQ	closed rear roof quarters
d	door (number of doors)
div	division window (limousine)
fstbk	fastback ("torpedo")
form	formal (as in sedan)
FQ	formal rear roof quarters
htchbk	hatchback (three/five-door)
htp cpe	two-door pillarless hardtop
htp sdn	four-door pillarless hardtop
htp wgn	pillarless station wagon
inc	included
J/B	"jet back" (fastback)
lndu, lan	landau
limo	limousine
ntchbk	notchback (coupe or sedan)
phtn	phaeton
proto	prototype
rdstr	two-passenger roadster
R/S	rumble seat (as in roadster)
sdn	sedan
sdnt	sedanette (two-door sedan)
SQ	solid rear roof quarters
spdstr	speedster
spt	sport (as in coupe)
T/B	"trunkback"
tng	touring
util	utility, usually a two-door sedan
wgn	station wagon

Prior to the 1980s, all body styles except sports cars and very small models like American Bantam have five- or six-passenger capacity; exceptions are specified. In some cases, it was necessary to differentiate between otherwise similar types. The abbreviations are:

P (7P, 8P, etc.)	passenger capacity
S (2S, 3S)	number of seats (wagons)
W (4W, 6W)	number of side windows
FW	fixed window

Engine abbreviations also follow a consistent pattern: block configuration is followed by the numbers and, where needed, a suffix letter. The letters are as follows:

L (L6, L8, etc.)	inline or "straight"
V (V6, V8, etc.)	V-block
flat	horizontally opposed
T, turbo	turbocharged
S, schgd	supercharged
D, dsl	diesel

Various abbreviations for model or series are used in the engine listings. Each is derived from a full name in the body style tables above, and should be self-explanatory.

Weight

The column marked "weight" provides the initial advertised curb weight (not including fuel or cargo) for each body style as listed in industry sources, usually National Automobile Dealers Association (NADA) guides. Where curb weights were unavailable, shipping weight was substituted. Weights shown may differ slightly from other published figures, because weights varied depending on equipment fitted or even the scales used—and could change during a model year if standard equipment was revised.

Note that when more than one engine was standard for a given model, and they are not listed separately in the price charts, curb weights shown are averages. For example, the 1955 Chevrolet Bel Air convertible weighed 3315 pounds with the six and 3285 pounds with a V8 engine. Our listed weight is the average: 3300 pounds. Usually, the choice of engine did not change curb weight by more than 100-150 pounds.

Prices

Figures shown in the "price" column are based on initial advertised price (delivered at the factory, not including freight), according to NADA and similar industry sources. Like weights, prices varied during most model years. During inflationary periods such as the late 1970s and early 1980s, several price hikes during a model year were common. When more than one standard engine was available, prices were not averaged. The figure shown is for the "base" or least expensive powerplant, usually a six until the 1980s, when four-cylinder base engines became common.

Model Year Production

The question most often asked about older cars—and one of the most important in a reference work—is "How many did they make?" The answer is not always clear-cut. In some cases, production has been a subject of research—and dispute—among automotive historians for decades. The figures listed are the most recent and accurate available, and have been thoroughly researched and cross-checked.

Note that mainly model year, not calendar year, figures are shown. The reason is that calendar year totals always included some portion of at least two model years, since cars have for decades been introduced sometime in the fall, not in January. That creates confusion when comparing one make or model with another. Model year figures normally represent production of cars marketed as the "1939 model," or "1969 model," etc. For makes and/or years where precise model year totals were not available, registrations or calendar year figures are given, and are always identified as such. Some totals include models produced for export, and are also identified.

Production received long and painstaking analysis in preparing this book. Too often, published totals have been based on company handouts that are often misleading and sometimes inaccurate. The 1953 Buick Skylark, for example, is listed by the Buick division (and at least one other source) as the "Roadmaster Anniversary Convertible." The contradictions and false trails of factory lists were fully explored and compared to other lists from a dozen different sources. Sometimes, it was discovered that cars were built that weren't "officially" listed; in other cases, models were listed that weren't actually produced. Even for recent years, a dismaying number of discrepancies continue to crop up. A uniform and accurate method of gathering and compiling production data never has been adopted by the industry. Instead, each manufacturer "counts" vehicle output in its own way, so figures reported by industry sources frequently differ at least slightly—and all too often, by surprisingly large numbers.

In a few cases, it was possible to go beyond known information by estimating, such as when a company provided only a combined total for two or three model years. Where we felt confident to do so, production was proportioned over individual model years. The usual standard for these breakdowns was calendar year output, in cases where it very nearly coincided with model year output (as when a model year began in January rather than the typical September or October).

In some instances, available factory figures included non-production models—usually styles intended for the market but not produced in volume. These are retained in the charts, where information is available, but clearly labeled as non-production.

There were a few cases where even estimating proved impossible, or where a large group of models or body styles were lumped together. The totals shown reflect the most complete information that's currently available.

Engine

Under each model year roster is a list of standard (S) and optional (O) engines and their model or series availability. Other basic information includes block configuration, number of cylinders, displacement (to the nearest 0.1 cubic inch), bore and stroke (to the nearest .01 inch), and SAE gross horsepower (SAE net after 1972). In cases where there was more than one standard engine, all are shown as "S." For recent models, all extra-cost engines were normally considered options, thus listed after "O."

Manufacturers have differed widely in treating engine options. Some group both standard and extra-cost engines under the same model code; others distinguish between them, and even give them separate model numbers. The charts follow the practice each manufacturer used for a given model year. The Pontiac Six and Eight, for example, were distinct models and are shown as such. Plymouth engines were usually listed as options for a given model and are combined. The difference is emphasized by spelling out and capitalizing the words "Six" and "Eight" in cases like Pontiac, and using the abbreviations "L6" and "V8" in examples like Plymouth.

Where engine choices are combined, prices shown are for base-engine models. In most cases, production figures shown are for the total number of that model built, regardless of engine.

By the 1980s, it had become customary to list the price of the base-engine model only: either a six or, as engines grew smaller, a four-cylinder. The extra-cost V8 (or V6) was just another item on the option list. Where several extra-cost engines are listed as options, the smallest-displacement or lowest-horsepower version is normally the least expensive and may be considered "standard."

1952 Deluxe two-door sedan

1940 Hollywood Convertible

ALLSTATE

1952—1,566 built

A2304 Four (wb 100.0)		Wght	Price	Prod
110	basic sdn 2d	2,300	1,395	200
111	std sdn 2d	2,300	1,486	500
113	Deluxe sdn 2d	2,300	1,539	200
A2404 Six (wb 100.0)				
—	basic sdn 2d	2,325	1,594	200
115	Deluxe sdn 2d	2,325	1,693	466

1952 Engines	bore×stroke	bhp	availability
L4, 134.2	3.11×4.38	68	S-Allstate Four
L6, 161.0	3.13×3.50	80	S-Allstate Six

1953—797 built

A3304 Four (wb 100.0)		Wght	Price	Prod
210	std sdn 2d	2,405	1,528	200
213	Deluxe sdn 2d	2,405	1,589	225
A3404 Six (wb 100.0)				
215	Deluxe sdn 2d	2,455	1,785	372

1953 Engines	bore×stroke	bhp	availability
L4, 134.2	3.11×4.38	68	S-Allstate Four
L6, 161.0	3.13×3.50	80	S-Allstate Six

Note: Model-by-model production totals are estimated.

AMERICAN BANTAM

1939—1,229 built*

Model 62 (wb 75.0)	Wght	Price	Prod
rdstr	1,130	449	—
Special rdstr	1,140	479	—
DeLuxe rdstr	1,160	525	—
cpe 2P	1,230	399	—
Special cpe 2P	1,240	439	—
DeLuxe cpe 2P	1,250	469	—
Sunair cpe 2P	1,250	479	—
Foursome spdstr 4P	1,265	497	—
DeLuxe Foursome spdstr 4P	1,280	549	—
wgn 2d	1,434	565	—

1939 Engine	bore×stroke	bhp	availability
L4, 46.0	2.20×3.00	20	S-all

1940—800 built

Series 65 (wb 75.0)		Wght	Price	Prod
65	cpe	1,261	399	—
65	Master cpe	1,275	449	—
65	conv cpe	1,340	525	—
65	Master rdstr	1,211	449	—
65	conv sdn	1,296	549	—
65	wgn 2d	1,400	565	—

1940 Engine	bore×stroke	bhp	availability
L4, 50.1	2.26×3.13	22	S-all

1941—138 built

Series 65 (wb 75.0)		Wght	Price	Prod
65	cpe	1,261	399	—
65	Master cpe	1,275	449	—
65	conv cpe	1,340	525	—
65	Master rdstr	1,211	449	—
65	conv sdn	1,296	549	—
65	wgn 2d	1,400	565	—

1941 Engine	bore×stroke	bhp	availability
L4, 50.1	2.26×3.13	22	S-all

*Calendar year figures

1940 Speedster

AMC

(also see Rambler)

1966

Marlin (wb 112.0)		Wght	Price	Prod
6659-7	fstbk cpe	3,050	2,601	4,547
Ambassador 880 (wb 116.0)*				
6685-2	sdn 4d	3,006	2,455	—
6686-2	sdn 2d	2,970	2,404	—
6688-2	wgn 4d	3,160	2,759	—
Ambassador 990 (wb 116.0)*				
6685-5	sdn 4d	3,034	2,574	—
6687-5	conv cpe	3,462	2,968	—
6688-5	wgn 4d	3,180	2,880	—
6689-5	htp cpe	3,056	2,600	—
Ambassador DPL (wb 116.0)*				
6689-7	htp cpe	3,090	2,756	—

1966 Engines	bore×stroke	bhp	availability
L6, 232	3.75×3.50	145	S-Marlin
L6, 232	2.75×3.50	155	S-Ambassador
V8, 287	3.75×3.25	198	O-all
V8, 327	4.00×3.25	250/270	O-all

*Total 1966 calendar year 279,225; includes Rambler American and Classic models and early 1967 production.

1967

Marlin (wb 118.0)		Wght	Price	Prod
6759-7	fstbk cpe	3,342	2,963	2,545
Ambassador 880 (wb 118.0)*		**Wght**	**Price**	**Prod**
6785-2	sdn 4d	3,279	2,657	—
6786-2	sdn 4d	3,310	2,519	—
6788-2	wgn 4d	3,486	2,962	—
Ambassador 990 (wb 118.0)*				
6785-5	sdn 4d	3,324	2,776	—
6788-5	wgn 4d	3,545	3,083	—
6789-5	htp cpe	3,376	2,803	—
Ambassador DPL (wb 118.0)*				
6787-7	conv cpe	3,434	3,143	—
6789-7	htp cpe	3,394	2,958	—

1967 Engines	bore×stroke	bhp	availability
L6, 232	3.75×3.50	145	S-Marlin
L6, 232	3.75×3.50	155	S-Ambassador; O-Marlin
V8, 290	3.75×3.28	200	S-Amb. conv; O-others
V8, 343	4.08×3.28	235	O-all
V8, 343	4.08×3.28	280	O-all

*Total Ambassador, 62,839.

1968

Rebel 550 (wb 114.0)*		Wght	Price	Prod
6815	sdn 4d	3,062	2,443	—
6817	conv 2d	3,195	2,736	377
6818	wgn 4d	3,301	2,729	—
6819	htp cpe	3,117	2,454	—
Rebel 770 (wb 114.0)*				
6815-5	sdn 4d	3,074	2,542	—
6818-5	wgn 4d	3,306	2,854	—
6819-5	htp cpe	3,116	2,556	—
Rebel SST (wb 114.0)*		**Wght**	**Price**	**Prod**
6817-7	conv cpe	3,427	2,999	823
6819-7	htp cpe	3,348	2,775	—
AMX (wb 97.0)*				
6839-7	fstbk cpe 2S	3,097	3,245	6,725
Javelin (wb 109.0)—56,462 built				
6879-5	fstbk cpe	2,826	2,482	—
6879-7	SST fstbk cpe	2,836	2,587	—
Ambassador (wb 118.0)*				
6885-2	sdn 4d	3,193	2,820	—
6889-2	htp cpe	3,258	2,892	—
Ambassador DPL (wb 118.0)*				
6885-5	sdn 4d	3,265	2,920	—
6888-5	wgn 4d	3,475	3,207	—
6889-5	htp cpe	3,321	2,947	—
Ambassador SST (wb 118.0)*				
6885-7	sdn 4d	3,496	3,151	—
6889-7	htp cpe	3,530	3,172	—

*Total Rebel, 73,895. Total Ambassador, 54,681.

1968 Engines	bore×stroke	bhp	availability
L6, 232	3.75×3.50	145	S-Javelin, Rebel exc SST
L6, 232	3.75×3.50	155	S-Amb exc SST
V8, 290	3.75×3.28	200	S-Rebel SST, Amb SST; O-all
V8, 290	3.75×3.28	225	S-AMX; O-Javelin
V8, 343	4.08×3.28	235	O-Rebel, Ambassador
V8, 343	4.08×3.28	280	O-AMX Javelin, Rebel, Amb
V8, 390	4.17×3.57	315	O-all

1969

Rebel (wb 114.0)*		Wght	Price	Prod
6915	sdn 4d	3,062	2,484	—
6918	wgn 4d	3,301	2,817	—
6919	htp cpe	3,117	2,496	—
Rebel SST (wb 114.0)*				
6915-7	sdn 4d	3,074	2,584	—
6918-7	wgn 4d	3,306	2,947	—
6919-7	htp cpe	3,140	2,598	—
AMX (wb 97.0)*				
6939-7	fstbk cpe 2S	3,097	3,297	8,293
Javelin (wb 109.0)—40,675 built				
6979-5	fstbk cpe	2,826	2,512	—
6979-7	SST fstbk cpe	2,836	2,633	—

1968 Javelin SST fastback coupe

1969 Ambassador SST four-door sedan

Ambassador (wb 122.0)*		Wght	Price	Prod
6985-2	sdn 4d	3,276	2,914	—
Ambassador DPL (wb 122.0)*				
6985-5	sdn 4d	3,358	3,165	—
6988-5	wgn 4d	3,561	3,504	—
6989-5	htp cpe	3,403	3,182	—
Ambassador SST (wb 122.0)*				
6985-7	sdn 4d	3,508	3,605	—
6988-7	wgn 4d	3,732	3,998	—
6989-7	htp cpe	3,566	3,622	—

*Total 1969 calendar year 242,898; includes Rambler American and early 1970 production. Total model year, 275,350.

1969 Engines	bore×stroke	bhp	availability
L6, 232	3.75×3.50	145	S-Javelin, Rebel
L6, 232	3.75×3.50	155	S-Amb, Amb DPL; O-Rebel
V8, 290	3.75×3.28	200	S-Amb SST; O-Amb, Reb, Jav
V8, 290	3.75×3.28	225	S-AMX; O-Javelin
V8, 343	4.08×3.28	235	O-Rebel, Ambassador
V8, 343	4.08×3.28	280	O-AMX, Jav, Rebel, Amb
V8, 390	4.17×3.57	315	O-AMX, Jav SST, Amb SST

1970*

Hornet (wb 108.0)		Wght	Price	Prod
7005-0	sdn 4d	2,748	2,072	—
7006-0	sdn 2d	2,677	1,994	—
Hornet SST (wb 108.0)				
7005-7	sdn 4d	2,765	2,221	—
7006-7	sdn 2d	2,705	2,144	—
Rebel (wb 114.0)				
7015-0	sdn 4d	3,129	2,636	—
7018-0	wgn 4d	3,356	2,766	—
7019-0	htp cpe	3,148	2,660	—
Rebel SST (wb 114.0)				
7015-7	sdn 4d	3,155	2,684	—
7018-0	wgn 4d	3,375	3,072	—
7019-7	htp cpe	3,206	2,718	—

Rebel Machine (wb 114.0)		Wght	Price	Prod
7019-0	htp cpe	3,650	3,475	2,326
AMX (wb 97.0)—4,116 built				
7039-7	fstbk cpe 2S	3,126	3,395	—
Gremlin (wb 96.0)				
7046-0	sdn 2d	2,497	1,879	—
7046-5	sdn 2d	2,557	1,959	—
Javelin (wb 109.0)—28,210 built				
7079-5	fstbk cpe	2,845	2,720	—
7079-7	SST fstbk cpe	2,863	2,848	—
7079-7	SST/Trans-Am fstbk cpe	3,340	3,995	—
Ambassador (wb 122.0)				
7085-2	sdn 4d	3,328	3,020	—
Ambassador DPL (wb 122.0)				
7085-5	sdn 4d	3,523	3,588	—
7088-5	wgn 4d	3,817	3,946	—
7089-5	htp cpe	3,555	3,605	—

1970 Ambassador SST hardtop coupe

Ambassador SST (wb 122.0)		Wght	Price	Prod
7085-7	sdn 4d	3,557	3,722	—
7088-5	wgn 4d	3,852	4,122	—
7089-5	htp cpe	3,606	3,739	—

*Total 1970 calendar year, 276,110; includes early 1971 production. Total model year, 242,664.

1970 Engines	bore×stroke	bhp	availability
L6, 199	3.75×3.00	128	S-Hornet, Gremlin
L6, 232	3.75×3.50	145	S-Hornet SST, Rebel, Javelin; O-Hornet, Gremlin
L6, 232	3.75×3.50	155	S-Amb; O-Hornet, Rebel
V8, 304	3.75×3.44	210	S-DPL, SST; O-all exc AMX
V8, 360	4.08×3.44	245	O-Rebel, Amb, Jav
V8, 360	4.08×3.44	290	S-AMX; O-Reb, Amb, Jav
V8, 390	4.17×3.57	325	O-AMX, Jav, Reb SST, Amb SST
V8, 390	4.17×3.57	340	S-Rebel Machine; O-all

1971

Gremlin (wb 96.0)		Wght	Price	Prod
7146-0	sdn 2d 2P	2,503	1,899	53,480
7146-5	sdn 2d 4P	2,552	1,999	
Hornet (wb 108.0)—74,685 built				
7105-0	sdn 4d	2,731	2,234	L6: 23,000*
7106-0	sdn 2d	2,654	2,174	V8: 500*
7105-7	SST sdn 4d	2,732	2,334	L6: 40,000*
7106-7	SST sdn 2d	2,691	2,274	V8: 9,500*
7108-7	Sportabout wgn 5d	2,827	2,594	
7106-1	SC/360 sdn 2d	3,057	2,663	784
Javelin (wb 110.0)—29,130 built				
7179-5	htp cpe L6	2,887	2,879	3,500*
7179-7	SST htp cpe 6cyl	2,890	2,999	1,000*
7179-5	htp cpe V8	3,144	2,980	4,000*
7179-7	SST htp cpe V8	3,147	3,100	17,000*
7979-8	AMX htp cpe V8	3,244	3,432	2,054
Matador (wb 118.0)—45,789 built (approx. 30,000 L6)				
7155-7	sdn 4d L6	3,165	2,770	—
7119-7	htp cpe L6	3,201	2,799	—
7118-7	wgn 4d L6	3,437	3,163	6,800
7115-7	sdn 4d V8	3,324	3,100	—
7119-7	htp cpe V8	3,360	3,129	—
7118-7	wgn 4d V8	3,596	3,493	4,200
Ambassador (wb 122.0)—41,674 built				
7185-2	DPL sdn 4d L6	3,315	3,616	650*
7185-2	DPL sdn 4d V8	3,488	3,717	6,000*

		Wght	Price	Prod
7185-5	SST sdn 4d V8	3,520	3,852	7,500*
7189-5	SST htp cpe V8	3,561	3,870	
7188-5	SST wgn 4d V8	3,815	4,253	8,000*
7185-7	Brougham sdn 4d V8	3,541	3,983	10,000*
7189-7	Brougham htp cpe V8	3,580	3,999	
7188-7	Brougham wgn 4d V8	3,862	4,430	10,000*

1971 Engines	bore×stroke	bhp	availability
L6, 232.0	3.75×3.50	135	S-Grem,Hrnt,Jav,Mat
L6, 258.0	3.75×3.90	150	S-Amb; O-Grem,Hrnt, Jav,Mat
V8, 304.0	3.75×3.44	210	S-Jav,Mat,Amb; O-Hrnt
V8, 360.0	4.08×3.44	245	S-Hrnt SC; O-Jav,Mat,Amb
V8, 360.0	4.08×3.44	285	O-Hrnt SC,Jav,Mat,Amb
V8, 401.0	4.17×3.68	330	O-Ambassador

1972

Gremlin (wb 96.0)—61,717 built		Wght	Price	Prod
46-5	sdn 2d L6	2,494	1,999	53,000*
46-5	sdn 2d V8	2,746	2,153	8,500*
Hornet SST (wb 108.0)—71,056 built				
05-7	sdn 4d L6	2,691	2,265	35,000*
06-7	sdn 2d L6	2,627	2,199	
08-7	Sportabout wgn 5d L6	2,769	2,587	30,000*
05-7	sdn 4d V8	2,925	2,403	2,000*
06-7	sdn 2d V8	2,861	2,337	
08-7	Sportabout wgn 5d V8	2,998	2,725	5,000*
Javelin (wb 110.0)				
79-7	SST htp cpe L6	2,876	2,807	23,455
79-7	SST htp cpe V8	3,118	2,901	
79-8	AMX htp cpe V8	3,149	3,109	2,729
Matador (wb 118.0)—54,813 built				
15-7	sdn 4d L6	3,171	2,784	11,000*
19-7	htp cpe L6	3,210	2,818	
18-7	wgn 4d L6	3,480	3,140	3,000*
15-7	sdn 4d V8	3,355	2,883	34,000*
19-7	htp cpe V8	3,394	2,917	
18-7	wgn 4d V8	3,653	3,239	7,500*
Ambassador (wb 122.0)—44,364 built				
85-5	SST sdn 4d	3,537	3,885	18,000*
89-5	SST htp cpe	3,579	3,902	
88-5	SST wgn 4d	3,833	4,270	5,500*
85-7	Brougham sdn 4d	3,551	4,002	15,000*
89-5	Brougham htp cpe	3,581	4,018	
88-5	Brougham wgn 4d	3,857	4,437	5,500*

1971 Gremlin two-door sedan

1972 Matador hardtop coupe

1972 Engines	bore×stroke	bhp	availability
L6, 232.0	3.75×3.50	100	S-Grem,Hrnt,Jav,Mat exc wgn
L6, 258.0	3.75×3.90	110	S-Mat wgn,Grem,Hrnt; O-Jav,Mat
V8, 304.0	3.75×3.44	150	S-all base V8 models
V8, 360.0	4.08×3.44	175	O-all exc Gremlin
V8, 360.0	4.08×3.44	195	O-Jav,Mat,Amb
V8, 401.0	4.17×3.68	225	O-Jav,Mat,Amb

1973

Gremlin (wb 96.0)		Wght	Price	Prod
46-5	sdn 2d L6	2,642	2,098	
46-5	sdn 2d V8	2,867	2,252	
Hornet (wb 108.0)				
05-7	sdn 4d L6	2,854	2,343	
06-7	sdn 2d L6	2,777	2,298	
03-7	htchbk cpe L6	2,818	2,449	
08-7	Sportabout wgn 5d L6	2,921	2,675	
05-7	sdn 4d V8	3,067	2,481	
06-7	sdn 2d V8	2,990	2,436	
03-7	htchbk cpe V8	3,031	2,587	
08-7	Sportabout wgn 5d V8	3,134	2,813	
Javelin (wb 110.0)				
79-7	htp cpe L6	2,868	2,889	22,556
79-7	htp cpe V8	3,104	2,983	
79-8	AMX htp cpe V8	3,170	3,191	4,980
Matador (wb 118.0)				
15-7	sdn 4d L6	3,289	2,853	
19-7	htp cpe L6	3,314	2,887	
18-7	wgn 4d L6	3,627	3,179	
15-7	sdn 4d V8	3,502	2,952	
19-7	htp cpe V8	3,527	2,986	
18-7	wgn 4d V8	3,815	3,278	
Ambassador Brougham (wb 122.0)				
85-7	sdn 4d	3,763	4,461	
89-7	htp cpe	3,774	4,477	
88-7	wgn 4d	4,054	4,861	

1973 Engines	bore×stroke	bhp	availability
L6, 232.0	3.75×3.50	100	S-Grem,Hrnt,Jav,Mat ex wgn
L6, 258.0	3.75×3.90	110	S-Mat wgn; O-Grem,Hrnt, Jav,Mat
V8, 304.0	3.75×3.44	150	S-all base V8 models
V8, 360.0	4.08×3.44	175	O-all exc Gremlin
V8, 360.0	4.08×3.44	195	O-Jav,Mat,Amb
V8, 360.0	4.08×3.44	220	O-Jav,Mat,Amb
V8, 401.0	4.17×3.68	255	O-Jav,Mat,Amb

1974

Gremlin (wb 96.0)		Wght	Price	Prod
46-5	sdn 2d L6	2,649	2,481	119,642
46-5	sdn 2d V8	2,888	2,635	12,263
Hornet (wb 108.0)				
05-7	sdn 4d L6	2,833	2,824	
06-7	sdn 2d L6	2,767	2,774	70,052
03-7	htchbk cpe L6	2,791	2,849	
08-7	Sportabout wgn 5d L6	2,900	3,049	57,414
05-7	sdn 4d V8	3,077	2,962	
06-7	sdn 2d V8	3,011	2,912	7,697
03-7	htchbk cpe V8	3,035	2,987	
08-7	Sportabout wgn 5d V8	3,144	3,187	10,295
Javelin (wb 110.0)				
79-7	htp cpe L6	2,869	2,999	5,036
79-7	htp cpe V8	3,116	3,093	19,520
79-8	AMX htp cpe V8	3,184	3,299	4,980
Matador (wb 118.0; cpe 114.0)—99,922 built				
15-7	sdn 4d L6	3,425	3,052	25,826
16-7	cpe L6	3,437	3,096	
18-7	wgn 4d L6	3,739	3,378	2,975
15-7	sdn 4d V8	3,632	3,151	
16-7	cpe V8	3,634	3,195	35,000*
18-7	wgn 4d V8	3,925	3,477	6,734
16-9	Brougham cpe L6	3,456	3,249	28,000*
16-9	Brougham cpe V8	3,663	3,348	
16-8	"X" htp cpe V8	3,672	3,699	1,500*
Ambassador Brougham (wb 122.0)				
85-7	sdn 4d	3,851	4,559	17,901
88-7	wgn 4d	4,125	4,960	7,070

1974 Engines	bore×stroke	bhp	availability
L6, 232.0	3.75×3.50	100	S-Grem,Hrnt,Jav,Mat wgn
L6, 258.0	3.75×3.90	110	S-Mat wgn; O-Grem,Hrnt, Jav,Mat
V8, 304.0	3.75×3.44	150	S-all base V8 models
V8, 360.0	4.08×3.44	175	O-all exc Gremlin
V8, 360.0	4.08×3.44	195	O-Jav,Mat,Amb
V8, 401.0	4.17×3.68	255	O-Jav,Mat,Amb

1975

Gremlin (wb 96.0)		Wght	Price	Prod
46-5	sdn 2d L6	2,694	2,798	42,630
46-5	sdn 2d V8	2,952	2,952	3,218
Hornet (wb 108.0)				
05-7	sdn 4d L6	2,881	3,124	
06-7	sdn 2d L6	2,815	3,074	36,305
03-7	htchbk cpe L6	2,839	3,174	
08-7	Sportabout wgn 5d L6	2,948	3,374	3,016
05-7	sdn 4d V8	3,127	3,262	
06-7	sdn 2d V8	3,061	3,212	20,369
03-7	htchbk cpe V8	3,085	3,312	
08-7	Sportabout wgn 5d V8	3,194	3,512	4,223
Pacer (wb 100.0)				
66-7	htchbk sdn 3d	2,995	3,299	72,158
Matador (wb 118.0; cpe 114.0)				
85-7	sdn 4d L6	3,586	3,452	9,390
16-7	cpe L6	3,562	3,446	
88-7	wgn 4d L6	3,878	3,844	1,575
85-7	sdn 4d V8	3,746	3,551	40,500
16-7	cpe V8	3,734	3,545	
88-7	wgn 4d V8	4,038	3,943	8,117

1975 Engines	bore×stroke	bhp	availability
L6, 232.0	3.75×3.50	100	S-Grem,Hrnt,Pcr
L6, 258.0	3.75×3.90	110	S-Mat; O-Grem,Hrnt,Pcr
V8, 304.0	3.75×3.44	150	S-Grem,Hrnt,Mat
V8, 360.0	4.08×3.44	175	O-Matador

1973 Hornet Sportabout wagon

1976

Gremlin (wb 96.0)		Wght	Price	Prod
46-3	sdn 2d L6	2,771	2,889	52,115
46-5	Cus sdn 2d L6	2,774	2,998	
46-3	sdn 2d V8	3,020	3,051	826
46-5	Cus sdn 2d V8	3,023	3,160	
Pacer (wb 100.0)				
66-7	htchbk sdn 3d	3,114	3,499	117,244
Hornet (wb 108.0)				
05-7	sdn 4d L6	2,971	3,199	41,025
06-7	sdn 2d L6	2,909	3,199	
03-7	htchbk cpe L6	2,920	3,199	
08-7	Sportabout wgn 5d L6	3,040	3,549	26,787
05-7	sdn 4d V8	3,220	3,344	789
06-7	sdn 2d V8	3,158	3,344	
03-7	htchbk cpe V8	3,169	3,344	
08-7	Sportabout wgn 5d V8	3,289	3,694	2,976
Matador (wb 118.0; cpe 114.0)				
85-7	sdn 4d L6	3,589	3,627	4,993
16-7	cpe L6	3,562	3,621	
85-7	sdn 4d V8	3,838	3,731	25,471
16-7	cpe V8	3,811	3,725	
88-7	wgn 4d V8	4,015	4,373	11,049

1976 Engines	bore×stroke	bhp	availability
L6, 232.0	3.75×3.50	90	S-all exc Mat
L6, 258.0	3.75×3.90	95	S-Mat; O-others
L6, 258.0	3.75×3.90	120	O-Pacer
V8, 304.0	3.75×3.44	120	S-all exc Pcr
V8, 360.0	4.08×3.44	140/180	O-Mat sdn/wgn

1977

Gremlin (wb 96.0)		Wght	Price	Prod
46-4	sdn 2d L4	2,654	3,248	7,558
46-5	sdn 2d L6	2,811	2,995	38,613
36-7	Custom sdn 2d L6	2,824	3,248	
Pacer (wb 100.0)				
66-7	htchbk sdn 3d	3,156	3,649	20,265
68-7	wgn 3d	3,202	3,799	37,999
Hornet (wb 108.0)				
05-7	sdn 4d L6	3,035	2,449	73,752
06-7	sdn 2d L6	2,971	3,399	
03-7	htchbk cpe L6	3,012	3,419	
08-7	wgn 5d L6	3,100	3,699	
05-7	sdn 4d V8	3,268	3,613	4,091
06-7	sdn 2d V8	3,204	3,563	
03-7	htchbk cpe V8	3,245	3,662	
08-7	wgn 5d V8	3,333	3,863	
Matador (wb. 118.0; cpe 114.0)				
85-7	sdn 4d L6	3,713	4,549	2,447
16-7	cpe L6	3,704	4,499	
85-7	sdn 4d V8	3,876	4,669	17,322
16-7	cpe V8	3,872	4,619	
88-7	wgn 4d V8	4,104	4,899	11,078

1977 Engines	bore×stroke	bhp	availability
L4, 121.0	3.41×3.32	80	S-Gremlin
L6, 232.0	3.75×3.50	88	S-all exc Matador
L6, 258.0	3.75×3.90	98	S-Matador
L6, 258.0	3.75×3.90	114	O-all exc Matador
V8, 304.0	3.75×3.44	121	S-Hornet
V8, 304.0	3.75×3.44	126	S-Matador
V8, 360.0	4.08×3.44	129	O-Matador

1978

Gremlin (wb 96.0)		Wght	Price	Prod
46-4	sdn 2d L4	2,656	3,789	6,349
46-5	sdn 2d L6	2,834	3,539	15,755
46-7	Custom sdn 2d L6	2,822	3,789	
Concord (wb 108.0)				
05-7	sdn 4d L6	3,099	3,849	110,972
06-7	sdn 2d L6	3,029	3,749	
03-7	htchbk cpe L6	3,051	3,849	
08-7	wgn 5d L6	3,133	4,049	
05-7	sdn 4d V8	3,332	4,099	6,541
06-7	sdn 2d V8	3,262	3,999	
03-7	htchbk cpe V8	3,284	4,099	
08-7	wgn 5d V8	3,366	4,299	

Note: A total of 3,780 4-cyl. Concords were produced.

Pacer (wb 100.0)		Wght	Price	Prod
66-7	htchbk sdn 3d L6	3,197	4,048	18,717
68-7	wgn 3d L6	3,245	4,193	

1976 Pacer X three-door hatchback sedan

		Wght	Price	Prod
66-7	htchbk sdn 3d V8	3,430	4,298	2,514
68-7	wgn 3d V8	3,478	4,443	
AMX (wb 108.0)				
03-9	htchbk cpe L6	3,159	4,649	2,540
03-9	htchbk cpe V8	3,381	4,899	
Matador (wb 118.0; cpe 114.0)				
85-7	sdn 4d L6	3,718	4,849	23
16-7	cpe L6	3,709	4,799	
85-7	sdn 4d V8	3,921	5,039	6,807
16-7	cpe V8	3,916	4,989	
88-7	wgn 4d V8	4,146	5,299	3,746

1978 Engines	bore×stroke	bhp	availability
L4, 121.0	3.41 × 3.32	80	S-Gremlin, Concord
L6, 232.0	3.75 × 3.50	90	S-all exc Matador, AMX
L6, 258.0	3.75×3.90	120	S-Mat, AMX; O-others
V8, 304.0	3.75×3.44	130	S-Con, Pacer, AMX
V8, 360.0	4.08×3.44	140	S-Mat wgn; O-Matador

1979

Spirit (wb 96.0)		Wght	Price	Prod
43-7	htchbk cpe L4	2,545	3,953	
46-7	sdn 2d L4	2,489	3,853	
43-7	DL htchbk cpe L4	2,635	4,190	
46-7	DL sdn 2d L4	2,579	4,090	16,237
43-7	Limited htchbk cpe L4	2,732	5,190	
46-7	Limited sdn 2d L4	2,676	5,090	
43-7	htchbk cpe L6	2,762	4,133	
46-7	sdn 2d L6	2,706	4,033	
43-7	DL htchbk cpe L6	2,852	4,370	
46-7	DL sdn 2d L6	2,798	4,270	36,241
43-7	Limited htchbk cpe L6	2,949	5,370	
46-7	Limited sdn 2d L6	2,893	5,270	
Concord (wb 108.0)				
05-7	sdn 4d L6	2,939	4,489	
06-7	sdn 2d L6	2,873	4,389	
03-7	htchbk cpe L6	2,888	4,324	
08-7	wgn 5d L6	2,977	4,689	
05-7	DL sdn 4d L6	3,040	4,788	
06-7	DL sdn 2d L6	2,982	4,688	91,842
03-7	DL htchbk cpe L6	3,003	4,623	
08-7	DL wgn 5d L6	3,072	4,988	
05-7	Limited sdn 4d L6	3,146	5,788	
06-7	Limited sdn 2d L6	3,090	5,688	
08-7	Limited wgn 5d L6	3,177	5,988	
05-7	sdn 4d V8	3,146	4,889	
06-7	sdn 2d V8	3,080	4,789	
03-7	htchbk cpe V8	3,095	4,724	
08-7	wgn 5d V8	3,184	5,089	
05-7	DL sdn 4d V8	3,247	5,188	
06-7	DL sdn 2d V8	3,189	5,088	4,656
03-7	DL htchbk cpe V8	3,210	5,023	
08-7	DL wgn 5d V8	3,279	5,388	
05-7	Limited sdn 4d V8	3,353	6,188	
06-7	Limited sdn 2d V8	3,297	6,088	
08-7	Limited wgn 5d V8	3,384	6,888	

Note: 6,355 4-cyl. Concords were produced.

Pacer (wb 100.0)				
66-7	DL htchbk sdn 3d L6	3,133	5,039	
68-7	DL wgn 3d L6	3,170	5,189	
66-7	Limited htchbk sdn 3d L6	3,218	6,039	9,201
68-7	Limited wgn 3d L6	3,255	6,189	
66-7	DL htchbk sdn 3d V8	3,360	5,439	
68-7	DL wgn 3d V8	3,397	5,589	1,014
66-7	Limited htchbk sdn 3d V8	3,445	6,439	
68-7	Limited wgn 3d V8	3,482	6,589	

1979 Spirit AMX hatchback coupe

AMX (wb 96.0)		Wght	Price	Prod
43-9	htchbk cpe L6	2,899	6,090	3,657*
43-9	htchbk cpe V8	3,092	6,465	

*included in Spirit total.

1979 Engines	bore×stroke	bhp	availability
L4, 121.0	3.41 × 3.32	80	S-Spirit; O-Con exc wgn
L6, 232.0	3.75 × 3.50	90	S-Con; O-Spirit
L6, 258.0	3.75×3.90	100	S-Pacer
L6, 258.0	3.75×3.90	110	S-Sprt,AMX; O-Con
V8, 304.0	3.75×3.44	125	S-all V8 models

1980

Spirit (wb 96.0)		Wght	Price	Prod
43-0	htchbk cpe L4	2,556	4,605	
46-0	sdn 2d L4	2,512	4,505	
43-5	DL htchbk cpe L4	2,656	5,004	37,799
46-5	DL sdn 2d L4	2,611	4,904	
43-7	Limited htchbk cpe L4	2,675	5,451	
46-7	Limited sdn 2d L4	2,630	5,351	
43-0	htchbk cpe L6	2,758	4,734	
46-0	sdn 2d L6	2,714	4,634	
43-5	DL htchbk cpe L6	2,858	5,133	
46-5	DL sdn 2d L6	2,813	5,033	33,233
43-7	Limited htchbk cpe L6	2,877	5,580	
46-7	Limited sdn 2d L6	2,832	5,480	
Concord (wb 108.0)				
05-0	sdn 4d L4	2,712	5,219	
06-0	sdn 2d L4	2,646	5,094	
08-0	wgn 5d L4	2,741	5,419	
05-5	DL sdn 4d L4	2,834	5,618	
06-5	DL sdn 2d L4	2,764	5,493	9,949
08-5	DL wgn 5d L4	2,855	5,818	
05-7	Limited sdn 4d L4	2,859	6,065	

1980 Concord DL four-door sedan

		Wght	Price	Prod
06-7	Limited sdn 2d L4	2,789	5,940	
08-7	Limited wgn 5d L4	2,886	6,265	
05-0	sdn 4d L6	2,910	5,348	
06-0	sdn 2d L6	2,844	5,223	
08-0	wgn 5d L6	2,939	5,548	
05-5	DL sdn 4d L6	3,032	5,747	
06-5	DL sdn 2d L6	2,962	5,622	70,507
08-5	DL wgn 5d L6	3,053	5,947	
05-7	Limited sdn 4d L6	3,057	6,194	
06-7	Limited sdn 2d L6	2,987	6,069	
08-7	Limited wgn 5d L6	3,084	6,394	
Pacer (wb 100.0)				
66-5	DL htchbk 2d L6	3,147	5,407	405
68-5	DL wgn 2d L6	3,195	5,558	1,341
66-7	Limited htchbk 2d L6	3,172	6,031	—
68-7	Limited wgn 2d L6	3,220	6,182	—
AMX (wb 96.0)				
43-9	htchbk cpe L4	2,901	5,653	—
Eagle (wb 109.3)				
35-5	sdn 4d L6	3,450	7,418	9,956
36-5	sdn 2d L6	3,382	7,168	10,616
38-5	wgn 5d L6	3,470	7,718	25,807
35-7	Limited sdn 4d L6	3,465	7,815	—
36-7	Limited sdn 2d L6	3,397	7,565	—
38-7	Limited wgn 5d L6	3,491	8,115	—

1980 Engines	bore×stroke	bhp	availability
L4, 151.0	4.00×3.00	90	S-all 4-cyl. models
L6, 258.0	3.75×3.90	110	S-all 6-cyl. models

1981

Spirit (wb 96.0)		Wght	Price	Prod
43-0	htchbk cpe L4	2,587	5,190	
43-0	htchbk cpe L6	2,716	5,326	42,252
43-5	DL htchbk cpe L4	2,673	5,589	
43-5	DL htchbk cpe L6	2,802	5,725	
46-0	sdn 2d L4	2,542	5,090	
46-0	sdn 2d L6	2,671	5,226	2,367
46-5	DL sdn 2d L4	2,627	5,489	
46-5	DL sdn 2d L6	2,756	5,625	
Concord (wb 108.0 in.)				
05-0	sdn 4d L4	2,738	5,944	
05-0	sdn 4d L6	2,864	6,080	
05-5	DL sdn 4d L4	2,837	6,343	24,403
05-5	DL sdn 4d L6	2,963	6,479	
05-7	Limited sdn 4d L4	2,859	6,790	
05-7	Limited sdn 4d L6	2,985	6,926	
06-0	sdn 2d L4	2,672	5,819	

1981 Eagle Limited two-door sedan

1982 Eagle SX/4 hatchback coupe

		Wght	Price	Prod
06-0	sdn 2d L6	2,798	5,955	
06-5	DL sdn 2d L4	2,767	6,218	15,496
06-5	DL sdn 2d L6	2,893	6,354	
06-7	Limited sdn 2d L4	2,789	6,665	
06-7	Limited sdn 2d L6	2,915	6,801	
08-0	wgn 5d L4	2,768	6,144	
08-0	wgn 5d L6	2,894	6,280	
08-5	DL wgn 5d L4	2,852	6,543	15,198
08-5	DL wgn 5d L6	2,978	6,679	
08-7	Limited wgn 5d L4	2,880	6,990	
08-7	Limited wgn 5d L6	3,006	7,126	
Eagle 50 (wb 97.2 in.)				
53-0	SX/4 liftbk cpe 3d L4	2,967	6,717	
53-0	SX/4 liftbk cpe 3d L6	3,123	6,853	17,340
53-5	DL SX/4 liftbk cpe 3d L4	3,040	7,119	
53-5	DL SX/4 liftbk cpe 3d L6	3,196	7,255	
56-0	Kammback sdn 2d L4	2,919	5,995	
56-0	Kammback sdn 2d L6	3,015	6,131	5,603
56-5	DL Kammback sdn 2d L4	2,990	6,515	
56-5	DL Kammback sdn 2d L6	3,146	6,651	
Eagle 30 (wb 109.3 in.)				
35-5	sdn 4d L4	3,172	8,097	
35-5	sdn 4d L6	3,328	8,233	1,737
35-7	Limited sdn 4d L4	3,180	8,494	
35-7	Limited sdn 4d L6	3,336	8,630	
36-5	sdn 2d L4	3,104	7,847	
36-5	sdn 2d L6	3,260	7,983	2,378
36-7	Limited sdn 2d L4	3,114	8,244	
36-7	Limited sdn 2d L6	3,270	8,380	
38-5	wgn 5d L4	3,184	8,397	
38-5	wgn 5d L6	3,340	8,533	10,371
38-7	Limited wgn 5d L4	3,198	8,794	
38-7	Limited wgn 5d L6	3,354	8,930	

1981 Engines	bore × stroke	bhp	availability
L4, 151.0	4.00 × 3.00	82	S-all 4-cyl. models
L6, 258.0	3.75 × 3.90	110	S-all 6-cyl. models

1982

Spirit (wb 96.0)		Wght	Price	Prod
43-0	htchbk cpe L4	2,588	5,576	
43-0	htchbk cpe L6	2,687	5,726	20,063
43-5	DL htchbk cpe L4	2,666	5,959	
43-5	DL htchbk cpe L6	2,765	6,109	
46-0	sdn 2d L4	2,538	5,476	
46-0	sdn 2d L6	2,637	5,626	119
46-5	DL sdn 2d L4	2,614	5,859	
46-5	DL sdn 2d L6	2,713	6,009	

1982 Concord DL four-door sedan

1983 Renault Fuego hatchback coupe

Concord (wb 108.0 in.)		Wght	Price	Prod
05-0	sdn 4d L4	2,752	6,254	
05-0	sdn 4d L6	2,842	6,404	
05-5	DL sdn 4d L4	2,841	6,761	25,572
05-5	DL sdn 4d L6	2,931	6,911	
05-7	Limited sdn 4d L4	2,862	7,258	
05-7	Limited sdn 4d L6	2,952	7,408	
06-0	sdn 2d L4	2,683	5,954	
06-0	sdn 2d L6	2,773	6,104	
06-5	DL sdn 2d L4	2,768	6,716	6,132
06-5	DL sdn 2d L6	2,858	6,866	
06-7	Limited sdn 2d L4	2,790	7,213	
06-7	Limited sdn 2d L6	2,880	7,363	
08-0	wgn 5d L4	2,786	7,013	
08-0	wgn 5d L6	2,876	7,163	
08-5	DL wgn 5d L4	2,940	7,462	12,106
08-5	DL wgn 5d L6	3,030	7,612	
08-7	Limited wgn 5d L4	2,892	7,959	
08-7	Limited wgn 5d L6	2,982	8,109	
Eagle 50 (wb 97.2 in.)				
53-0	SX/4 liftbk cpe 3d L4	2,972	7,451	
53-0	SX/4 liftbk cpe 3d L6	3,100	7,601	10,445
53-5	DL SX/4 liftbk cpe 3d L4	3,041	7,903	
53-5	DL SX/4 liftbk cpe 3d L6	3,169	8,053	
56-0	Kammback sdn 2d L4	2,933	6,799	
56-0	Kammback sdn 2d L6	3,061	6,949	520
56-5	DL Kammback sdn 2d L4	3,000	7,369	
56-5	DL Kammback sdn 2d L6	3,128	7,519	
Eagle 30 (wb 109.3 in.)				
35-5	sdn 4d L4	3,172	8,869	
35-5	sdn 4d L6	3,310	9,019	4,091
35-7	Limited sdn 4d L4	3,180	9,316	
35-7	Limited sdn 4d L6	3,308	9,466	
36-5	sdn 2d L4	3,107	8,719	
36-5	sdn 2d L6	3,235	8,869	1,968
36-7	Limited sdn 2d L4	3,115	9,166	
36-7	Limited sdn 2d L6	3,243	9,316	
38-5	wgn 5d L4	3,299	9,566	
38-5	wgn 5d L6	3,327	9,716	20,899
38-7	Limited wgn 5d L4	3,213	10,013	
38-7	Limited wgn 5d L6	3,341	10,163	

1982 Engines	bore × stroke	bhp	availability
L4, 151.0	4.00 × 3.00	82	S-all 4-cyl. models
L6, 258.0	3.75 × 3.90	110	S-all 6-cyl. models

1983

Alliance (wb 97.8)		Wght	Price	Prod
96-0	sdn 2d	1,945	5,595	
96-3	L sdn 2d	1,945	6,020	55,556
96-6	DL sdn 2d	1,945	6,655	
96-6	MT sdn 2d	—	7,450	
95-3	L sdn 4d	1,980	6,270	
95-6	DL sdn 4d	1,980	6,905	86,649
95-8	Limited sdn 4d	1,980	7,470	
95-6	MT sdn 4d	—	7,700	
Spirit (wb 96.0)				
43-5	DL htchbk cpe L6	2,810	5,995	3,491
43-9	GT htchbk cpe L6	2,817	6,495	
Concord (wb 108.0 in.)				
05-0	sdn 4d L6	2,904	6,724	4,433
05-5	DL sdn 4d L6	2,999	6,995	
08-0	wgn 5d L6	2,948	7,449	
08-5	DL wgn 5d L6	3,037	7,730	867
08-7	Limited wgn 5d L6	3,061	8,117	
Eagle 50 (wb 97.2 in.)				
53-0	SX/4 liftbk cpe 3d L4	3,034	7,697	
53-0	SX/4 liftbk cpe 3d L6	3,165	7,852	2,259
53-5	DL SX/4 liftbk cpe 3d L4	3,094	8,164	
53-5	DL SX/4 liftbk cpe 3d L6	3,225	8,319	
Eagle 30 (wb 109.3 in.)				
35-5	sdn 4d L4	3,265	9,162	3,093
35-5	sdn 4d L6	3,396	9,317	
38-5	wgn 5d L4	3,285	9,882	
38-5	wgn 5d L6	3,416	10,037	12,378
38-7	Limited wgn 5d L4	3,301	10,343	
38-7	Limited wgn 5d L6	3,432	10,498	

1983 Engines	bore × stroke	bhp	availability
L4, 85.2	2.99 × 3.03	56	S-Alliance
L4, 151.0	4.00 × 3.00	84	S-early Eagle
L4, 150.0	3.88 × 3.19	—	S-late Eagle
L6, 258.0	3.75 × 3.90	110	S-Spirit, Conc; O-Eagle

1984

Encore (wb 97.8)		Wght	Price	Prod
93-0	htchbk sdn 3d	2,010	5,755	
93-3	S htchbk sdn 3d	2,021	6,365	
93-6	LS htchbk sdn 3d	2,069	6,995	55,343
93-9	GS htchbk sdn 3d	2,079	7,547	
93-6	Diamond Ed htchbk sdn 3d	—	7,570	
99-3	S htchbk sdn 5d	2,044	6,615	
99-6	LS htchbk sdn 5d	2,095	7,195	32,266
99-6	Diamond Ed htchbk sdn 5d	—	7,770	
Alliance (wb 97.8)				
96-0	sdn 2d	1,970	5,959	

1984 Eagle wagon

		Wght	Price	Prod
96-3	L sdn 2d	1,972	6,465	50,978
96-6	DL sdn 2d	2,011	7,065	
96-6	Diamond Ed sdn 2d	—	7,715	
95-3	L sdn 4d	2,000	6,715	
95-6	DL sdn 4d	2,038	7,365	70,037
95-8	Limited sdn 4d	2,055	8,027	
95-6	Diamond Ed sdn 4d	—	8,015	
Eagle 30 (wb 109.3 in.)				
35-5	sdn 4d L4	3,273	9,495	4,241
35-5	sdn 4d L6	3.391	9,666	
38-5	wgn 5d L4	3,304	10,225	
38-5	wgn 5d L6	3,422	10,396	21,294
38-7	Limited wgn 5d L4	3,320	10,695	
38-7	Limited wgn 5d L6	3,438	10,866	

1984 Engines	bore × stroke	bhp	availability
L4, 85.2	2.99 × 3.03	56	S-Alliance, Encore
L4, 150.0	3.88 × 3.19	—	S-Eagle
L6, 258.0	3.75 × 3.90	110	O-Eagle

1985

Encore (wb 97.8)		Wght	Price	Prod
93-0	htchbk sdn 3d	1,982	5,895	
93-3	S htchbk sdn 3d	2,021	6,360	
93-6	LS htchbk sdn 3d	2,069	7,060	38,623
93-9	GS htchbk sdn 3d	2,079	7,560	
99-3	S htchbk sdn 5d	2,044	6,610	19,902
99-6	LS htchbk sdn 5d	2,095	7,310	
Alliance (wb 97.8)				
96-0	sdn 2d	1,958	5,995	
96-3	L sdn 2d	1,965	6,400	33,617
96-6	DL sdn 2d	1,998	7,000	
95-3	L sdn 4d	2,000	6,650	
95-6	DL sdn 4d	2.037	7,250	50,906
95-8	Limited sdn 4d	2,087	7,750	
97-3	L conv cpe	2,189	10,295	7,141
97-6	DL conv cpe	2,226	11,295	

1985 Eagle Limited wagon

Eagle 30 (wb 109.3 in.)		Wght	Price	Prod
35-5	sdn 4d L6	3,390	10,457	2,655
38-5	wgn 5d L6	3,421	11,217	13,535
38-7	Limited wgn 5d L6	3,452	11,893	

1985 Engines	bore × stroke	bhp	availability
L4, 85.2	2.99 × 3.03	56	S-Alliance, Encore
L4, 105.0	3.19 × 3.29	77	S-Alliance, conv, Encore GS; O-Alliance, Encore
L6, 258.0	3.75 × 3.90	110	S-Eagle

1986

Encore (wb 97.8)		Wght	Price	Prod
93-3	S htchbk sdn 3d	2,006	6,710	
93-6	LS htchbk sdn 3d	2,010	7,310	
93-9	GS htchbk sdn 3d	2.013	7,968	12,239
93-4	Electronic htchbk sdn 3d	2,051	7,498	
99-3	S htchbk sdn 5d	2,039	6,960	6,870
99-6	LS htchbk sdn 5d	2,043	7,560	

Alliance (wb 97.8)		Wght	Price	Prod
96-0	sdn 2d	1,959	5,999	
96-3	L sdn 2d	1,964	6,510	23,204
96-6	DL sdn 2d	1,971	7,110	
95-0	sdn 4d	1,993	6,199	
95-3	L sdn 4d	1,998	6,760	42,891
95-6	DL sdn 4d	2,005	7,360	
97-3	L conv cpe	2,222	10,557	2,015
97-6	DL conv cpe	2,228	11,557	

Eagle 30 (wb 109.3)		Wght	Price	Prod
35-5	sdn 4d L6	3,391	10,719	1,274
38-5	wgn 5d L6	3,425	11,489	6,943
38-7	Limited wgn 5d L6	3,456	12,179	

1986 Engines	bore × stroke	bhp	availability
L4, 85.2	2.99 × 3.03	56	S-Alliance, Encore
L4, 105.0	3.19 × 3.29	77	S-Alliance, conv, Encore Elect/GS; O-Alliance, Encore
L6, 258.0	3.75 × 3.90	110	S-Eagle

1987

Alliance (wb 97.8)		Wght	Price	Prod
96-0	sdn 2d	1,959	6,399	
96-3	L sdn 2d	1,965	6,925	
96-6	DL sdn 2d	2,000	7,625	13,132
96-7	GTA sdn 2d	2,104	8,999	
95-0	sdn 4d	1,997	6,599	
95-3	L sdn 4d	2,003	7,200	16,214
95-8	DL sdn 4d	2,038	7,900	
97-3	L conv cpe	2,206	11,099	
97-6	DL conv cpe	2,239	12,099	1,991
97-7	GTA conv cpe	2,298	12,899	
93-0	htchbk sdn 3d	1,985	6,599	
93-3	L htchbk sdn 3d	1,991	6,975	2,857
93-6	DL htchbk sdn 3d	2,028	7,675	
93-9	GS htchbk sdn 3d	2,057	8,499	
99-3	L htchbk sdn 5d	2,039	7,250	2,142
99-6	DL htchbk sdn 5d	2,081	7,950	

Eagle (wb 109.3 in.)		Wght	Price	Prod
35-5	sdn 4d L6	3,383	11,150	751
38-5	wgn 5d L6	3,417	11,943	4,452
38-7	Limited wgn 5d L6	3,431	12,653	

1987 Engines	bore × stroke	bhp	availability
L4, 85.2	2.99 × 3.03	56	S-Alliance
L4, 105.0	3.19 × 3.29	77	S-Alliance Conv; O-Alliance
L4, 120.0	3.23 × 3.66	95	S-Alliance GTA
L6, 258.0	3.75 × 3.90	112	S-Eagle

Note: Production totals that were unavailable from AMC have been compiled from industry sources.

1987 Eagle wagon

AVANTI II/AVANTI

1965

(wb 109.0)	Wght	Price	Prod
spt cpe	3,217	6,550	21

1965 Engine	bore×stroke	bhp	availability
V8, 327.0	4.00×3.25	300	S-all

1966

(wb 109.0)	Wght	Price	Prod
spt cpe	3,181	7,200	98

1966 Engine	bore×stroke	bhp	availability
V8, 327.0	4.00×3.25	300	S-all

1967

(wb 109.0)	Wght	Price	Prod
spt cpe	3,217	7,200	60

1967 Engine	bore×stroke	bhp	availability
V8, 327.0	4.00×3.25	300	S-all

1968

(wb 109.0)	Wght	Price	Prod
spt cpe	3,217	6,645	89

1968 Engine	bore×stroke	bhp	availability
V8, 327.0	4.00 × 3.25	300	S-all

1969

(wb 109.0)	Wght	Price	Prod
spt cpe	3,217	7,145	103

1969 Engine	bore×stroke	bhp	availability
V8, 327.0	4.00×3.25	300	S-all
V8, 350.0	4.00×3.48	300	O-all

1970

(wb 109.0)	Wght	Price	Prod
spt cpe	3,342	7,500	111

1970 Engine	bore×stroke	bhp	availability
V8, 350.0	4.00×3.48	300	S-all

1971

(wb 109.0)	Wght	Price	Prod
spt cpe	3,217	7,645	107

1971 Engine	bore×stroke	bhp	availability
V8, 350.0	4.00×3.48	270	S-all

1972

(wb 109.0)	Wght	Price	Prod
spt cpe	3,217	8,145	127

1972 Engine	bore×stroke	bhp	availability
V8,350.0	4.00×3.48	270	S-all

1973

(wb 109.0)	Wght	Price	Prod
spt cpe	3,250	8,145	106

1973 Engine	bore×stroke	bhp	availability
V8, 400.0	4.13×3.75	245	S-all

1974

(wb 109.0)	Wght	Price	Prod
spt cpe	3,250	8,645	123

1974 Engine	bore×stroke	bhp	availability
V8, 400.0	4.13×3.75	180	S-all

1975

(wb 109.0)	Wght	Price	Prod
spt cpe	3,250	9,945	125

1975 Engine	bore×stroke	bhp	availability
V8, 400.0	4.13×3.75	180	S-all

1976

(wb 109.0)	Wght	Price	Prod
spt cpe	3,500	12,195	156

1976 Engine	bore×stroke	bhp	availability
V8, 400.0	4.13 × 3.75	180	S-all

1977

(wb 109.0)	Wght	Price	Prod
spt cpe	3,500	13,195	146

1977 Engine	bore×stroke	bhp	availability
V8, 350.0	4.00×3.48	180	S-all

1978

(wb 109.0)	Wght	Price	Prod
spt cpe	3,500	15,980	165

1978 Engine	bore×stroke	bhp	availability
V8, 350.0	4.00×3.48	180	S-all

1979

(wb 109.0)	Wght	Price	Prod
spt cpe	3,570	17,670	142

1982 Avanti II sport coupe

1979 Engine	bore×stroke	bhp	availability
V8, 350.0	4.00×3.48	185	S-all

1980

(wb 109.0)	Wght	Price	Prod
spt cpe	3,570	18,995	168

1980 Engine	bore×stroke	bhp	availability
V8, 350.0	4.00×3.48	190	S-all

1981

(wb 109.0)	Wght	Price	Prod*
spt cpe	3,570	20,495	200

1981 Engine	bore × stroke	bhp	availability
V8, 305.0	3.74 × 3.48	155	S-all

1982

(wb 109.0)	Wght	Price	Prod*
spt cpe	3,570	22,995	200

1982 Engine	bore × stroke	bhp	availability
V8, 305.0	3.74 × 3.48	155	S-all

*Calendar year figures (estimated)
Note: The "II" was dropped from Avanti's name after 1981.

1983

(wb 109.0)	Wght	Price	Prod
spt cpe	3,690	24,995	—

1983 Engine	bore × stroke	bhp	availability
V8, 305.0	3.74 × 3.48	155	S-all

1987 Avanti II sport coupe

1984

(wb 109.0)	Wght	Price	Prod
spt cpe	3,680	31,860	287

1984 Engine	bore × stroke	bhp	availability
V8, 305.0	3.74 × 3.48	190	S-all

1985

(wb 109.0)	Wght	Price	Prod
spt cpe	3,680	37,995	—
GT cpe	3,210	37,995	—

1985 Engines	bore × stroke	bhp	availability
V8, 305.0	3.74 × 3.48	190	S-cpe
V8, 305.0	3.74 × 3.48	205	S-GT

1986

Due to bankruptcy, there were no 1986 Avantis; but the company re-emerged to produce a series of 1987 models.

1984 Avanti II sport coupe

1987

(wb 109.0)		Wght	Price	Prod
	spt cpe	NA	29,995	—
	conv cpe	NA	39,995	—
	luxury spt cpe	NA	55,900	—

1987 Engines	bore × stroke	bhp	availability
V8, 305.0	3.74 × 3.48	185	S-all
V8, 305.0	3.74 × 3.48	215	O-all

1988

(wb 109.0)		Wght	Price	Prod
	spt cpe	3,750	35,000	—
	conv cpe	NA	45,000	—
	luxury cpe	NA	53,000	—

1988 Engine	bore × stroke	bhp	availability
V8, 305.0	3.74 × 3.48	NA	S-all

1989

(wb 109.0)		Wght	Price	Prod
	spt cpe	NA	NA	—
	conv cpe	NA	NA	—
	luxury cpe	NA	NA	—

1989 Engine	bore × stroke	bhp	availability
V8, 305.0	3.74 × 3.48	NA	S-all

BUICK

1939

Series 40 Special (wb 120.0)		Wght	Price	Prod
41	tng sdn T/B 4d	3,482	966	111,473
41C	spt phtn T/B 5P	3,642	1,406	830
46	bus cpe	3,322	894	14,609
46C	conv cpe T/B 4P	3,452	1,077	4,809
46S	spt cpe T/B 4P	3,372	950	10,276
48	tng sdn T/B 2d	3,417	955	27,290
—	chassis	—	—	6,281
Series 60 Century (wb 126.0)				
61	tng sdn T/B 4d	3,782	1,246	18,783
61C	spt phtn T/B 5P	3,917	1,713	269
66C	conv cpe T/B 4P	3,712	1,343	850
66S	spt cpe T/B 4P	3,637	1,175	3,470
—	chassis	—	—	518
Series 80 Roadmaster (wb 133.0)				
80C	spt phtn 4d 6P	4,237	1,983	3
81	tng sdn T/B 4d	4,247	1,543	5,619
81C	spt phtn T/B 4d	4,392	1,983	364
81F	form sdn T/B 6P	4,312	1,758	340
87	spt sdn 6P	4,262	1,543	20
—	chassis	—	—	143
Series 90 Limited (wb 140.0)				
90	tng sdn T/B 8P	4,608	2,350	686
90L	limo T/B 8P	4,653	2,453	543
91	tng sdn T/B 4d	4,568	2,074	382
—	chassis	—	—	176

1939 Engines	bore×stroke	bhp	availability
L8, 248.0	3.09×4.13	107	S-40
L8, 320.2	3.44×4.31	141	S-60, 80, 90

1940

Series 40 Special (wb 121.0)		Wght	Price	Prod
41	sdn 4d	3,660	996	68,816
41C	spt phtn	3,755	1,355	597
41T	taxi	3,700	1,000	48
46	bus cpe	3,505	895	12,382
46C	conv cpe	3,665	1,077	3,763
46S	spt cpe	3,540	950	8,401
48	sdn 2d	3,605	955	20,768
Series 50 Super (wb 121.0)				
51	sdn 4d	3,790	1,109	97,226
51C	spt phtn	3,895	1,549	534
56C	conv cpe	3,785	1,211	4,804
56S	spt cpe	3,735	1,058	26,462
59	wgn 4d	3,870	1,242	501
Series 60 Century (wb 126.0)				
61	sdn 4d	3,935	1,210	8,708
61C	spt phtn	4,050	1,620	203
66	bus cpe	3,800	1,128	44
66C	conv cpe	3,915	1,343	550
66S	spt cpe	3,765	1,175	96
Series 70 Roadmaster (wb 126.0)				
71	sdn 4d	4,045	1,359	13,733
71C	spt phtn	4,195	1,768	238
76C	conv cpe	4,055	1,431	612
76S	spt cpe	3,990	1,277	3,972
Series 80 Limited (wb 133.0)				
80C	Streamlined spt phtn	4,540	1,952	7
81	sdn 4d	4,440	1,553	3,898
81C	T/B spt phtn	4,540	1,952	250
81F	T/B form sdn	4,455	1,727	270
87	Streamlined spt sdn 4d	4,380	1,553	14
87F	Streamlined form sdn	4,455	1,727	7
Series 90 Limited (wb 140.0)				
90	sdn 4d, 8P, A/S	4,645	2,096	828
90L	limo 8P, A/S	4,705	2,199	634
91	sdn 4d	4,590	1,942	418

1940 Engines	bore×stroke	bhp	availability
L8, 248.0	3.09×4.13	107	S-40, 50
L8, 320.2	3.44×4.31	141	S-60, 80, 90

1940 Century convertible coupe

1941 Century sedanet

1941

Series 40 Special (wb 121.0)		Wght	Price	Prod
41	sdn 4d	3,730	1,052	92,528
41SE	sdn 4d	3,790	1,134	13,402
46	bus cpe	3,630	935	9,201
46S	sedanet	3,700	1,006	88,148
46SSE	sedanet	3,690	1,063	9,614
49	wgn 4d	3,980	1,463	850
Series 40A Special (wb 118.0)				
44	bus cpe	3,530	915	3,261
44C	conv cpe	3,780	1,138	4,309
44S	spt cpe	3,590	980	5,290
47	sdn 4d	3,670	1,021	14,139
Series 50 Super (wb 121.0)				
51	sdn 4d	3,770	1,185	58,638

1941 Century fastback four-door sedan

		Wght	Price	Prod
51C	conv phtn	4,014	1,555	508
56	bus cpe	3,620	1,031	2,452
56C	conv cpe	3,810	1,267	12,391
56S	spt cpe	3,670	1,113	19,876
Series 60 Century (wb 126.0)		**Wght**	**Price**	**Prod**
61	sdn 4d	4,025	1,288	15,136
66	bus cpe	3,870	1,195	222
66S	sedanet	3,920	1,241	5,547
Series 70 Roadmaster (wb 128.0)				
71	sdn 4d	4,010	1,364	10,553
71C	conv phtn	4,469	1,775	326
76C	conv cpe	4,045	1,457	1,869
76S	spt cpe	3,920	1,282	2,834
Series 90 Limited (wb 139.0)				
90	sdn 4d, 8P, A/S	4,680	2,360	906
90L	limo 8P, A/S	4,760	2,465	669
91	sdn 4d	4,575	2,155	1,231
91F	form sdn, A/S	4,665	2,310	296

1941 Engines	bore×stroke	bhp	availability
L8, 248.0	3.09×4.13	115	S-40A, 40 exc SE
L8, 248.0	3.09×4.13	125	S-50, 41SE, 46SSE
L8, 320.2	3.44×4.31	165	S-60, 70, 90

1942

Series 40A Special (wb 118.0)		Wght	Price	Prod
44	util cpe	3,510	990	461
44C	conv cpe	3,790	1,260	1,788
47	sdn 4d	3,650	1,080	1,652
48	bus sedanet	3,555	1,010	559
48S	fam sedanet	3,610	1,045	5,990
Series 40B Special (wb 121.0)				
41	sdn 4d	3,760	1,120	17,497
41SE	sdn 4d	3,785	1,200	2,288

1942 Roadmaster convertible two-door

		Wght	Price	Prod
46	bus sedanet	3,650	1,020	1,408
46S	fam sedanet	3,705	1,075	11,856
46SSE	fam sedanet	3,725	1,130	1,809
49	wgn 4d	3,925	1,450	327
Series 50 Super (wb 124.0)				
51	sdn 4d	3,890	1,280	16,265
56C	conv cpe	4,025	1,450	2,489
56S	sedanet	3,800	1,230	14,629
Series 60 Century (wb 126.0)				
61	sdn 4d	4,065	1,350	3,319
66S	sedanet	3,985	1,300	1,232
Series 70 Roadmaster (wb 129.0)				
71	sdn 4d	4,150	1,465	5,418
76C	conv cpe	4,300	1,675	511
76S	sedanet	4,075	1,395	2,475
Series 90 Limited (wb 139.0)				
90	sdn 4d, 8P, A/S	4,710	2,445	150
90L	limo 8P, A/S	4,765	2,545	250
91	sdn 4d	4,665	2,245	215
91F	form sdn	4,695	2,395	85

1942 Engines	bore×stroke	bhp	availability
L8, 248.0	3.09×4.13	110	S-40A, 40B exc SE
L8, 248.0	3.09×4.13	118	S-50, 46SSE, 41SE
L8, 320.2	3.44×4.31	165	S-60, 70, 90

1946

Series 40 Special (121.0)		Wght	Price	Prod
41	sdn 4d	3,720	1,580	1,650
46S	sedanet	3,670	1,522	1,350
Series 50 Super (wb 124.0)				
51	sdn 4d	3,935	1,822	77,724
56C	conv cpe	4,050	2,046	5,987
56S	sedanet	3,795	1,741	34,425
59	wgn 4d	4,170	2,594	798
Series 70 Roadmaster (wb 129.0)				
71	sdn 4d	4,165	2,110	20,864
76C	conv cpe	4,345	2,347	2,587
76S	sedanet	4,095	2,014	8,292

1946 Engines	bore×stroke	bhp	availability
L8, 248.0	3.09×4.13	110	S-40, 50
L8, 320.2	3.44×4.31	144	S-70

1947

Series 40 Special (wb 121.0)		Wght	Price	Prod
41	sdn 4d	3,720	1,623	18,431
46S	sedanet	3,760	1,611	14,603
Series 50 Super (wb 124.0)				
51	sdn 4d	3,910	1,929	83,576

		Wght	Price	Prod
56C	conv cpe	4,050	2,333	28,297
56S	sedanet	3,795	1,843	46,917
59	wgn 4d	4,170	2,940	2,036
Series 70 Roadmaster (wb 129.0)				
71	sdn 4d	4,190	2,232	47,152
76C	conv cpe	4,345	2,651	12,074
76S	sedanet	4,095	2,131	19,212
79	wgn 4d	4,445	3,249	300

1947 Engines	bore×stroke	bhp	availability
L8, 248.0	3.09×4.13	110	S-40, 50
L8, 320.2	3.44×4.31	144	S-70

1948

Series 40 Special (wb 121.0)		Wght	Price	Prod
41	sdn 4d	3,705	1,809	14,051
46S	sedanet	3,635	1,735	11,176
Series 50 Super (wb 124.0)				
51	sdn 4d	3,855	2,087	53,447
56C	conv cpe	4,020	2,518	19,017
56S	sedanet	3,770	1,987	33,819
59	wgn 4d	4,170	3,127	2,018
Series 70 Roadmaster (wb 129.0)				
71	sedan 4d	4,160	2,418	47,569
76C	conv cpe	4,315	2,837	11,503
76S	sedanet	4,065	2,297	20,649
79	wgn 4d	4,460	3,433	350

1948 Engines	bore×stroke	bhp	availability
L8, 248.0	3.09×4.13	110	S-40
L8, 248.0	3.09×4.13	115	S-50
L8, 320.2	3.44×4.31	144	S-70

1949

Series 40 Special (wb 121.0)		Wght	Price	Prod
41	sdn 4d	3,695	1,861	5,940
46S	sedanet	3,625	1,787	4,687
Series 50 Super (wb 121.0)				
51	sedan 4d	3,835	2,157	136,423

1947 Super convertible two-door

		Wght	Price	Prod
56C	conv cpe	3,985	2,583	22,110
56S	sedanet	3,735	2,059	66,260
59	wgn 4d	4,100	3,178	1,847
Series 70 Roadmaster (wb 126.0)				
71	sdn 4d	4,205	2,735	55,242
76C	conv cpe	4,370	3,150	8,244
76R	Riviera htp cpe	4,420	3,203	4,343
76S	sedanet	4,115	2,618	18,537
79	wgn 4d	4,490	3,734	653

1949 Engines	bore×stroke	bhp	availability
L8, 248.0	3.09×4.13	110	S-40
L8, 348.0	3.09×4.13	115/120	S-50
L8, 320.2	3.44×4.31	150	S-70

1950

Series 40 Special (wb 121.5)		Wght	Price	Prod
41	sdn 4d	3,710	1,941	1,141
41D	DeLuxe sdn	3,735	1,983	141,396
43	J/B sdn 4d	3,715	1,809	58,700
43D	DeLuxe J/B sdn, 4d	3,720	1,952	14,335
46	J/B cpe	3,615	1,803	2,500
46D	DeLuxe J/B cpe	3,665	1,899	76,902
46S	J/B sedanet	3,655	1,856	42,935

1949 Roadmaster four-door wagon

Series 50 Super (wb 121.5)		Wght	Price	Prod
51	sdn 4d	3,745	2,139	55,672
56C	conv cpe	3,965	2,476	12,259
56R	Riviera htp cpe	3,790	2,139	56,030
56S	J/B sedanet	3,645	2,041	10,697
59	wgn 4d	4,115	2,844	2,480
Series 50 Super (wb 125.5)				
52	sdn 4d	3,870	2,212	114,745
Series 70 Roadmaster (wb 126.3; 72-130.3)				
71	sdn 4d	4,135	2,633	6,738
72	Riviera sdn 4d	4,220	2,738	54,212
75R	Riviera htp cpe	4,135	2,633	2,300
76R	Riv DeLuxe htp cpe	4,245	2,854	8,432
76C	conv cpe	4,345	2,981	2,964
76S	J/B sedanet	4,025	2,528	2,968
79	wgn 4d	4,470	3,407	420

1950 Engines	bore×stroke	bhp	availability
L8, 248.0	3.09×4.13	115/120	S-40
L8, 263.3	3.19×4.13	124/128	S-50
L8, 320.2	3.44×4.31	152	S-70

1951

Series 40 Special (wb 121.5)		Wght	Price	Prod
41	sdn 4d	3,605	2,139	999
41D	DeLuxe sdn 4d	3,680	2,185	87,848
45R	Riviera sdn 2d	3,645	2,225	16,491
46C	conv cpe	3,830	2,561	2,099
46S	spt cpe	3,600	2,046	2,700
48D	DeLuxe sdn 2d	3,615	2,127	54,311
Series 50 Super (wb 121.5; 52-125.5)				
51	sdn 4d	3,755	2,356	10,000
52	Riviera sdn 4d	3,845	2,437	92,886
56C	conv cpe	3,965	2,728	8,116
56R	Riviera sdn 2d	3,765	2,356	54,512
56S	DeLuxe sdn 2d	3,685	2,248	1,500
59	wgn 4d	4,100	3,133	2,212
Series 70 Roadmaster (wb 126.3; 72R-130.3)				
72R	Riviera sdn 4d	4,240	3,044	48,758
76C	conv cpe	4,355	3,283	2,911
76MR	Riviera htp cpe	4,185	3,051	809
76R	Riv htp cpe, hydraulic controls	4,235	3,143	12,901
79R	wgn 4d	4,470	3,780	679

1951 Engines	bore×stroke	bhp	availability
L8, 263.3	3.19×4.13	120/128	S-40
L8, 263.3	3.19×4.13	124/128	S-50
L8, 320.2	3.44×4.31	152	S-70

1952

Series 40 Special (wb 121.5)		Wght	Price	Prod
41	sdn 4d	3,650	2,209	137
41D	DeLuxe sdn 4d	3,665	2,255	63,346
45R	Riviera htp cpe	3,665	2,295	21,180
46C	conv cpe	3,850	2,634	600
46S	spt cpe	3,605	2,115	2,206
48D	sdn 2d	3,620	2,197	32,684
Series 50 Super (wb 121.5; 52-125.5)				
52	sdn 4d	3,825	2,563	71,387
56C	conv cpe	3,970	2,869	6,904
56R	Riviera htp cpe	3,775	2,478	55,400
59	wgn 4d	4,105	3,296	1,641
Series 70 Roadmaster (wb 126.3;72R-130.3)				
72R	sdn 4d	4,285	3,200	32,069
76C	conv cpe	4,395	3,453	2,402

1950 Super Estate Wagon four-door

1950 Super convertible two-door

		Wght	Price	Prod
76R	Riviera htp cpe	4,235	3,306	11,387
79R	wgn 4d	4,505	3,977	359

1952 Engines	bore×stroke	bhp	availability
L8, 263.3	3.19×4.13	120/128	S-40
L8, 263.3	3.19×4.13	124/128	S-50
L8, 320.2	3.44×4.31	170	S-70

1953

Series 40 Special (wb 121.5)		Wght	Price	Prod
41D	DeLuxe sdn 4d	3,710	2,255	100,312
45R	Riviera htp cpe	3,705	2,295	58,780
46C	conv cpe	3,815	2,553	4,282
48D	DeLuxe sdn	3,675	2,197	53,796
Series 50 Super (wb 121.5; 52-125.5)				
52	Riviera sdn 4d	3,905	2,696	90,685
56C	conv cpe	4,035	3,002	6,701
56R	Riviera htp cpe	3,845	2,611	91,298
59	wgn 4d	4,150	3,430	1,830
Series 70 Roadmaster (wb 121.5; 72R-125.5)				
72R	Riviera sdn 4d	4,100	3,254	50,523
76C	conv cpe	4,250	3,506	3,318
76R	Riviera htp cpe	4,125	3,358	22,927
76X	Skylark conv cpe	4,315	5,000	1,690
79R	wgn 4d	4,315	4,031	670

1953 Engines	bore×stroke	bhp	availability
L8, 263.3	3.19×4.13	125/130	S-40
V8, 322.0	4.00×3.20	164/170	S-50
V8, 322.0	4.00×3.20	188	S-70

1953 Super convertible two-door

1954

Series 40 Special (wb 122.0)		Wght	Price	Prod
41D	DeLuxe sdn 4d	3,735	2,265	70,356
46C	conv cpe	3,810	2,563	6,135
46R	Riviera htp cpe	3,740	2,305	71,186
48D	DeLuxe sdn 2d	3,690	2,207	41,557
49	DeLuxe wgn 4d	3,905	3,163	1,650
Series 50 Super (wb 127.0)				
52	Riviera sdn 4d	4,105	2,711	41,756
56C	conv cpe	4,145	2,964	3,343
56R	Riviera htp cpe	4,035	2,626	73,531
Series 60 Century (wb 122.0)				
61	sdn 4d	3,805	2,520	31,919
66C	conv cpe	3,950	2,963	2,790
66R	Riviera htp cpe	3,795	2,534	45,710
69	wgn 4d	3,975	3,470	1,563
Series 70 Roadmaster (wb 127.0)				
72R	Riviera sdn 4d	4,250	3,269	26,862
76C	conv cpe	4,355	3,521	20,404
76R	Riviera htp cpe	4,215	3,373	3,305
Series 100 Skylark (wb 122.0)				
100M	conv cpe	4,260	4,483	836

1954 Engines	bore×stroke	bhp	availability
V8, 264.0	3.63×3.20	143/150	S-40
V8, 322.0	4.00×3.20	177/182	S-50
V8, 322.0	4.00×3.20	195/200	S-60
V8, 322.0	4.00×3.20	200	S-70, 100

1955

Series 40 Special (wb 122.0)		Wght	Price	Prod
41	sdn 4d	3,745	2,291	84,182
43	Riviera htp sdn	3,820	2,409	66,409
46C	conv cpe	3,825	2,590	10,009
46R	Riviera htp cpe	3,720	2,332	155,818
48	sdn 2d	3,715	2,233	61,879
49	wgn 4d	3,940	2,974	2,952
Series 50 Super (wb 127.0)				
52	sdn 4d	4,140	2,876	43,280
56C	conv cpe	4,280	3,225	3,527
56R	Riviera htp cpe	4,075	2,831	85,656

1955 Special four-door sedan

Series 60 Century (wb 122.0)		Wght	Price	Prod
61	sdn 4d	3,825	2,548	13,269
63	Riviera htp sdn	3,900	2,733	55,088
66C	conv cpe	3,950	2,991	5,588
66R	Riviera htp cpe	3,805	2,601	80,338
68	sdn 2d	3,795	2,490	270
69	wgn 4d	3,995	3,175	4,243
Series 70 Roadmaster (wb 127.0)				
72	sdn 4d	4,300	3,349	31,717
76C	conv cpe	4,415	3,552	4,739
76R	Riviera htp cpe	4,270	3,453	28,071

1955 Engines	bore×stroke	bhp	availability
V8, 264.0	3.63×3.20	188	S-40
V8, 322.0	4.00×3.20	236	S-50, 60, 70

1956

Series 40 Special (wb 122.0)		Wght	Price	Prod
41	sdn 4d	3,790	2,416	66,977
43	Riviera htp sdn	3,860	2,528	91,025
46C	conv cpe	3,880	2,740	9,712
46R	Riviera htp cpe	3,775	2,457	113,861
48	sdn 2d	3,750	2,357	38,672
49	wgn 4d	3,945	2,775	13,770
Series 50 Super (wb 127.0)				
52	sdn 4d	4,200	3,250	14,940
53	Riviera htp sdn	4,265	3,340	34,029
56C	conv cpe	4,340	3,544	2,489
56R	Riviera htp cpe	4,140	3,204	29,540
Series 60 Century (wb 122.0)				
61	sdn 4d	3,930	exp	1
63	Riviera htp sdn	4,000	3,025	20,891

1956 Special Riviera hardtop coupe

		Wght	Price	Prod
63D	Riviera DeLuxe htp sdn	4,000	3,041	35,082
66C	conv cpe	4,045	3,306	4,721
66R	Riviera htp cpe	3,890	2,963	33,334
69	wgn 4d	4,080	3,256	8,160
Series 70 Roadmaster (wb 127.0)				
72	sdn 4d	4,280	3,503	11,804
73	Riviera htp sdn	4,355	3,692	24,779
76C	conv cpe	4,395	3,704	4,354
76R	Riviera htp cpe	4,235	3,591	12,490

1956 Engines	bore×stroke	bhp	availability
V8, 322.0	4.00×3.20	220	S-40
V8, 322.0	4.00×3.20	255	S-50, 60, 70

1955 Century Riviera hardtop coupe

1957 Century Caballero wagon four-door

1958 Limited convertible two-door

1957

Series 40 Special (wb 122.0)		Wght	Price	Prod
41	sdn 4d	4,012	2,660	59,739
43	Riviera htp sdn	4,041	2,780	50,563
46C	conv cpe	4,082	2,987	8,505
46R	Riviera htp cpe	3,956	2,704	64,425
48	sdn 2d	2,596	2,596	23,180
49	wgn 4d	4,292	3,047	7,013
49D	Caballero wgn 4d	4,309	3,167	6,817
Series 50 Super (wb 127.5)				
53	Riviera htp sdn	4,356	3,681	41,665
56C	conv cpe	4,414	3,981	2,065
56R	Riviera htp cpe	4,271	3,536	26,529
Series 60 Century (wb 122.0)				
61	sdn 4d	4,137	3,234	8,075
63	Riviera htp sdn	4,163	3,354	26,589
66C	conv cpe	4,234	3,598	4,085
66R	Riviera htp cpe	4,081	3,270	17,029
68	sdn 2d	4,080	exp	2
69	Caballero wgn 4d	4,423	3,706	10,186
Series 70 Roadmaster (wb 127.5)				
73	Riviera htp sdn	4,469	4,053	11,401
73A	Riviera htp sdn, 1-piece backlight	4,455	4,066	10,526
76C	conv cpe	4,500	4,066	4,363
76R	Riviera htp sdn	4,374	3,944	3,826
76A	Riviera htp sdn, 1-piece backlight	4,370	3,944	2,812
Series 75 Roadmaster (wb 127.5)				
75	Riviera htp sdn	4,539	4,483	12,250
75R	Riviera htp cpe	4,427	4,373	2,404

1957 Engines	bore×stroke	bhp	availability
V8, 364.0	4.13×3.40	250	S-40
V8, 364.0	4.13×3.40	300	S-50, 60, 70, 75

1958

Series 40 Special (wb 122.0)		Wght	Price	Prod
41	sdn 4d	4,115	2,700	48,238
43	Riviera htp sdn	4,180	2,820	31,921
46C	conv cpe	4,165	3,041	5,502
46R	Riviera htp cpe	4,058	2,744	34,903
48	sdn 2d	4,063	2,636	11,566
49	wgn 4d	4,396	3,154	3,663
49D	Caballero htp wgn 4d	4,408	3,261	3,420
Series 50 Super (wb 127.5)				
53	Riviera htp sdn	4,500	3,789	28,460
56R	Riviera htp cpe	4,392	3,644	13,928
Series 60 Century (wb 122.0)				
61	sdn 4d	4,241	3,316	7,241
63	Riviera htp sdn	4,267	3,436	15,171
66C	conv cpe	4,302	3,680	2,588
66R	Riviera htp cpe	4,182	3,368	8,110
68	sdn 2d	4,189	exp	2
69	Caballero htp wgn 4d	4,498	3,831	4,456
Series 75 Roadmaster (wb 127.5)				
75	Riviera htp sdn	4,668	4,667	10,505
75C	conv cpe	4,676	4,680	1,181
75R	Riviera htp cpe	4,568	4,557	2,368
Series 700 Limited (wb 127.5)				
750	Riviera htp sdn	4,710	5,112	5,571
755	Riviera htp cpe	4,691	5,002	1,026
756	conv cpe	4,603	5,125	839

1958 Engines	bore×stroke	bhp	availability
V8, 364.0	4.13×3.40	250	S-40
V8, 364.0	4.13×3.40	300	S-50, 60, 75, 700

1959

4400 LeSabre (wb 123.0)		Wght	Price	Prod
4411	sdn 2d	4,159	2,740	13,492
4419	sdn 4d	4,229	2,804	51,379
4435	wgn 4d	4,565	3,320	8,286
4437	htp cpe	4,188	2,849	35,189
4439	htp sdn	4,266	2,925	46,069
4467	conv cpe	4,216	3,129	10,489
4600 Invicta (wb 123.0)				
4619	sdn 4d	4,331	3,357	10,566
4635	wgn 4d	4,660	3,841	5,231

1958 Limited Riviera hardtop sedan

1959 Electra 225 convertible

		Wght	Price	Prod
4637	htp cpe	4,274	3,447	11,451
4639	htp sdn	4,373	3,515	20,156
4667	conv cpe	4,317	3,620	5,447
4700 Electra (wb 126.3)				
4719	sdn 4d	4,557	3,856	12,357
4737	htp cpe	4,465	3,818	11,216
4739	htp sdn	4,573	3,963	20,612
4800 Electra 225 (wb 126.3)				
4829	Riviera htp sdn	4,632	4,300	6,324
4839	htp sdn	4,641	4,300	10,491
4867	conv cpe	4,562	4,192	5,493

1959 Engines	bore×stroke	bhp	availability
V8, 364.0	4.13×3.40	250	S-LeSabre
V8, 401.0	4.19×3.64	325	S-others

1960

4400 LeSabre (wb 123.0)		Wght	Price	Prod
4411	sdn 2d	4,139	2,756	14,388
4419	sdn 4d	4,219	2,870	54,033
4435	wgn 4d, 2S	4,568	3,386	5,331
4437	htp cpe	4,163	2,915	26,521
4439	htp sdn	4,269	2,991	35,999
4445	wgn 4d, 3S	4,574	3,493	2,222
4467	conv cpe	4,233	3,145	13,588
4600 Invicta (wb 123.0)				
4619	sdn 4d	4,324	3,357	10,839
4635	wgn 4d, 2S	4,644	3,841	3,471
4637	htp cpe	4,255	3,447	8,960
4639	htp sdn	4,365	3,515	15,300
4645	wgn 4d, 3S	4,679	3,948	1,605
4667	conv cpe	4,347	3,620	5,236
4700 Electra (wb 126.3)				
4719	sdn 4d	4,544	3,856	13,794
4737	htp cpe	4,453	3,818	7,416
4739	htp sdn	4,554	3,963	14,488

4800 Electra 225 (wb 126.3)		Wght	Price	Prod
4829	Riviera htp sdn	4,653	4,300	8,029
4839	htp sdn	4,650	4,300	5,841
4867	conv cpe	4,571	4,192	6,746

1960 Engines	bore×stroke	bhp	availability
V8, 364.0	4.13×3.40	235/250	S-LeSabre
V8, 364.0	4.13×3.40	300	O-LeSabre
V8, 401.0	4.19×3.40	325	S-others

1961

4000 Special (wb 112.0)		Wght	Price	Prod
4019	sdn 4d	2,610	2,384	18,339
4027	spt cpe	2,579	2,330	4,232
4035	wgn 4d	2,775	2,681	6,101
4045	wgn 4d, 3S	2,844	2,762	798
4119	Deluxe sdn 4d	2,632	2,519	32,986
4135	Deluxe wgn 4d	2,794	2,816	11,729
4317	Skylark spt cpe	2,687	2,621	12,683

1960 Electra 225 convertible

1961 Electra four-door sedan

4400 LeSabre (wb 123.0)		Wght	Price	Prod
4411	sdn 2d	4,033	2,993	5,959
4435	wgn 4d	4,450	3,623	5,628
4437	htp cpe	4,054	3,152	14,474
4439	htp sdn	4,129	3,228	37,790
4445	wgn 4d, 3S	4,483	3,730	2,423
4467	conv cpe	4,186	3,382	11,951
4469	sdn 4d	4,102	3,107	35,005
4600 Invicta (wb 123.0)				
4637	htp cpe	4,090	3,447	6,382
4639	htp sdn	4,179	3,515	18,398
4667	conv cpe	4,206	3,620	3,953
4700 Electra (wb 126.0)				
4719	sdn 4d	4,298	3,825	13,818
4737	htp cpe	4,260	3,818	4,250
4739	htp sdn	4,333	3,932	8,978

4800 Electra 225 (wb 126.0)		Wght	Price	Prod
4829	Riviera htp sdn	4,417	4,350	13,719
4867	conv cpe	4,441	4,192	7,158

1961 Engines	bore×stroke	bhp	availability
V8, 215.0	3.50×2.80	155	S-Special (Skylark 185 bhp)
V8, 364.0	4.13×3.40	235/250	S-LeSabre
V8, 401.0	4.19×3.64	325	S-others

1962

Special (wb 112.1)		Wght	Price	Prod
4019	sdn 4d	2,666	2,358	23,249
4027	cpe	2,638	2,304	19,135
4035	wgn 4d	2,876	2,655	7,382
4045	wgn 4d, 3S	2,896	2,736	2,814
4067	conv cpe	2,858	2,587	7,918
4119	Del sdn 4d	2,648	2,593	31,660
4135	Del wgn 4d	2,845	2,890	10,380

1962 LeSabre hardtop coupe

1962 Invicta convertible

		Wght	Price	Prod
4167	Del conv cpe	2,820	2,879	8,332
4347	Skylark htp cpe	2,707	2,787	34,060
4367	Skylark conv cpe	2,871	3,012	8,913
LeSabre (wb 123.0)				
4411	sdn 2d	4,041	3,091	7,418
4439	stp sdn	4,156	3,369	37,518
4447	htp cpe	4,054	3,293	25,479
4469	sdn 4d	4,104	3,227	56,783
Invicta (wb 123.0)				
4435	wgn 4d	4,471	3,836	9,131
4639	htp sdn	4,159	3,667	16,443
4645	wgn 4d, 3S	4,505	3,917	4,617
4647	spt cpe	4,077	3,733	10,335
4647	Wildcat spt cpe	4,150	3,927	2,000
4667	conv cpe	4,217	3,617	13,471
Electra 225 (wb 126.0)				
4819	sdn 4d	4,304	4,051	13,523
4829	Riviera htp sdn 6W	4,390	4,448	15,395
4839	htp sdn	4,309	4,186	16,734
4847	htp cpe	4,235	4,062	8,922
4867	conv cpe	4,396	4,366	7,894

1962 Engines	bore×stroke	bhp	availability
V6, 198.0	3.63×3.20	135	S-Special
V8, 215.0	3.50×2.80	155	S-Special Deluxe
V8, 215.0	3.50×2.80	190	S-Skylark; O-Special
V8, 401.0	4.19×3.64	265/280	S-LeSabre
V8, 401.0	4.19×3.64	325	S-Invicta, Electra

1963

Special (wb 112.1)		Wght	Price	Prod
4019	sdn 4d	2,696	2,363	21,733
4027	cpe	2,661	2,309	21,886
4035	wgn 4d	2,866	2,659	5,867
4045	wgn 4d, 3S	2,903	2,740	2,415
4067	conv cpe	2,768	2,591	8,082
4119	Del sdn 4d	2,720	2,521	37,695
4135	Del wgn 4d	2,854	2,818	8,771
4347	Skylark spt cpe	2,757	2,857	32,109
4367	Skylark conv cpe	2,810	3,011	10,212
LeSabre (wb 123.0)				
4411	sdn 2d	3,905	2,869	8,328
4435	wgn 4d	4,320	3,526	5,566
4439	htp sdn	4,007	3,146	50,420
4445	wgn 4d, 3S	4,340	3,606	3,922
4447	htp cpe	3,924	3,070	27,977
4467	conv cpe	4,052	3,339	9,975
4469	sdn 4d	3,970	3,004	64,995
Wildcat (wb 123.0)				
4639	htp sdn	4,222	3,871	17,519
4647	htp cpe	4,123	3,849	12,185
4667	conv cpe	4,228	3,961	6,021
Invicta (wb 123.0)				
4635	wgn 4d	4,397	3,969	3,495
Electra 225 (wb 126.0)				
4819	sdn 4d	4,241	4,051	14,268
4829	pillarless sdn	4,284	4,254	11,468
4839	htp sdn	4,272	4,186	19,714
4847	htp cpe	4,153	4,062	6,848
4867	conv cpe	4,297	4,365	6,367
Riviera (wb 117.0)				
4747	htp cpe	3,988	4,333	40,000

1963 Engines	bore×stroke	bhp	availability
V6, 198.0	3.63×3.20	135	S-Special, Special Deluxe
V8, 215.0	3.50×2.80	155	O-Special Deluxe, Skylark
V8, 215.0	3.50×2.80	200	S-Skylark, O-all Specials
V8, 401.0	4.19×3.64	265/280	S-LeSabre
V8, 401.0	4.19×3.64	325	S-Invicta, Wildcat, Electra, Riviera
V8, 425.0	4.31×3.64	340	O-Riviera

1964

Special (wb 115.0; wgns-120.0)		Wght	Price	Prod
4027	cpe	2,991	2,343	15,030
4035	wgn	3,266	2,689	6,270

1963 Electra 225 convertible

1964 Special convertible

		Wght	Price	Prod
4067	conv cpe	3,108	2,605	6,308
4069	sdn 4d	3,008	2,397	17,983
4127	Del cpe	3,006	2,457	11,962
4135	Del wgn 4d	3,285	2,787	9,467
4169	Del sdn 4d	3,026	2,490	31,742
4337	Skylark spt cpe	3,057	2,680	42,356
4367	Skylark conv cpe	3,175	2,834	10,225
4369	Skylark sdn 4d	3,070	2,669	19,635
4255	Skylark Spt Wgn	3,557	2,989	2,709
4355	Skylark Custom Spt Wgn	3,595	3,161	3,913
4265	Skylark Spt Wgn 4d 3S	3,689	3,124	2,586
4365	Skylark Custom Spt Wgn	3,727	3,286	4,446
LeSabre (wb 123.0)				
4439	htp sdn	3,730	3,122	37,052
4447	htp cpe	3,629	3,061	24,177
4467	conv cpe	3,787	3,314	6,685
4469	sdn 4d	3,693	2,980	56,729
4635	wgn 4d	4,352	3,554	6,517
4645	wgn 4d, 3S	4,362	3,635	4,003
Wildcat (wb 123.0)				
4639	htp sdn	4,058	3,327	33,358
4647	htp cpe	4,003	3,267	22,893

		Wght	Price	Prod
4667	conv cpe	4,076	3,455	7,850
4669	sdn	4,021	3,164	20,144
Electra 225 (wb 126.0)				
4819	sdn 4d	4,212	4,059	15,968
4829	pillarless sdn	4,238	4,261	11,663
4839	htp sdn	4,229	4,194	24,935
4847	htp cpe	4,149	4,070	9,045
4867	conv cpe	4,280	4,374	7,181
Riviera (wb 117.0)				
4747	htp cpe	3,951	4,385	37,658

1964 Engines	bore×stroke	bhp	availability
V6, 225.0	3.75×3.40	155	S-Special
V8, 300.0	3.75×3.40	210/250	S-LeSabre 4400; O-Special
V8, 401.0	4.19×3.64	325	S-LeS 4600, Wildcat, Elec
V8, 425.0	4.31×3.64	340(O-360)	S-Riv; O-LeS 4600, Wldct, Elec

1965

Special (wb 115.0)		Wght	Price	Prod
43327	cpe	2,977	2,343	12,945
43335	wgn 4d	3,258	2,688	2,868
43367	conv cpe	3,087	2,605	3,357
43369	sdn 4d	3,010	2,397	13,828
43427	cpe V8	3,080	2,414	5,309
43435	wgn 4d V8	3,365	2,759	3,676
43467	conv cpe V8	3,197	2,676	3,365
43469	sdn 4d V8	3,117	2,468	8,121
43535	Del wgn 4d	3,242	2,787	1,677
43569	Del sdn 4d	3,016	2,669	11,033
43635	Del wgn 4d	3,369	2,858	9,123
43669	Del sdn 4d	3,143	2,561	26,299
Skylark (wb 115.0; wgns-120.0)				
44255	wgn 4d	3,642	2,989	4,226
44265	wgn 4d, 3S	3,750	3,123	4,664
44327	cpe	3,035	2,537	4,195
44337	htp cpe	3,057	2,680	4,549
44367	conv cpe	3,149	2,834	1,181
44369	sdn 4d	3,086	2,669	3,385
44427	GS cpe	3,146	2,608	11,877

1965 Electra 225 hardtop coupe

		Wght	Price	Prod
44437	GS htp cpe	3,198	2,751	47,034
44455	Cus wgn 4d	3,690	3,160	8,300
44465	Cus wgn 3S	3,802	3,285	11,166
44467	GS conv cpe	3,294	2,905	10,456
44469	sdn 4d	3,194	2,740	22,335
LeSabre (wb 123.0)				
45237	htp cpe	3,753	3,030	15,786
45239	htp sdn	3,809	3,090	18,384
45269	sdn 4d	3,788	2,948	37,788
45437	Cus htp cpe	3,724	3,100	21,049
45439	Cus htp sdn	3,811	3,166	23,394
45467	Cus conv cpe	3,812	3,325	6,543
45469	Cus sdn 4d	3,777	3,024	22,052
Wildcat (wb 126.0)				
46237	htp cpe	3,988	3,286	6,031
46239	htp sdn	4,089	3,346	7,499
46269	sdn 4d	4,058	3,182	10,184
46437	Del htp cpe	4,014	3,340	11,617
46439	Del htp sdn	4,075	3,407	13,903
46467	Del conv cpe	4,069	3,502	4,616
46469	Del sdn 4d	4,046	3,285	9,765
46637	Cus htp cpe	4,047	3,566	15,896
46639	Cus htp sdn	4,160	3,626	14,878
46667	Cus conv cpe	4,087	3,727	4,398
Electra 225 (wb 126.0)				
48237	htp cpe	4,208	4,082	6,302
48239	htp sdn	4,284	4,206	12,842
48269	sdn 4d	4,261	4,071	12,459
48437	Cus htp cpe	4,228	4,265	9,570
48439	Cus htp sdn	4,344	4,389	29,932
48467	Cus conv cpe	4,325	4,440	8,505
48469	Cus sdn 4d	4,272	4,254	7,197
Riviera (wb 117.0)				
49447	htp cpe	4,036	4,408	34,586

1965 Engines	bore×stroke	bhp	availability
V6, 225.0	3.75×3.40	155	S-Special, Skylark
V8, 300.0	3.75×3.40	210/250	S-LeS; O-Special, Skylark
V8, 401.0	4.19×3.64	325	S-Wildcat, Electra, Riviera; O-LeS
V8, 425.0	4.31×3.64	340/360	O-Wildcat, Electra Riviera

1966

Special (wb 115.0; wgns-120.0)		Wght	Price	Prod
43307	cpe	3,009	2,348	9,322
43335	wgn 4d	3,296	2,695	1,451
43367	conv cpe	3,092	2,604	1,357
43369	sdn 4d	3,046	2,401	8,797
43407	cpe V8	3,091	2,418	5,719
43435	wgn 4d V8	3,399	2,764	3,038
43467	conv cpe V8	3,223	2,671	2,036
43469	sdn 4d V8	3,148	2,471	9,355
43507	Del cpe	3,009	2,432	2,359
43517	Del htp cpe	3,038	2,504	2,507
43535	Del wgn 4d	3,290	2,783	824
43569	Del sdn 4d	3,045	2,485	5,573
43607	Del cpe V8	3,112	2,502	4,908
43617	Del htp cpe V8	3,130	2,574	10,350
43635	Del wgn 4d V8	3,427	2,853	7,592
43669	Del sdn 4d V8	3,156	2,555	27,909
Skylark (wb 115.0; wgns -120.0)				
44255	wgn 4d	3,713	3,025	2,469
44265	wgn 4d, 3S	3,811	3,173	2,667
44307	cpe V6	3,034	2,624	1,454
44317	htp cpe	3,069	2,687	2,552
44339	htp sdn	3,172	2,846	1,422
44367	conv cpe	3,158	2,837	608
44407	cpe V8	3,145	2,694	6,427
44417	htp cpe V8	3,152	2,757	33,326
44439	htp sdn V8	3,285	2,916	18,873
44455	Cus wgn 4d	3,720	3,155	6,964
44465	Cus wgn 4d, 3S	3,844	3,293	9,510
44467	conv cpe V8	3,259	2,904	6,129
44607	GS cpe	3,479	2,956	1,835
44617	GS htp cpe	3,428	3,019	9,934
44667	GS conv cpe	3,532	3,167	2,047
LeSabre (wb 123.0)				
45237	htp cpe	3,751	3,022	13,843
45239	htp sdn	3,828	3,081	17,740
45269	sdn 4d	3,796	2,942	39,146
45437	Cus htp cpe	3,746	3,109	18,830
45439	Cus htp sdn	3,824	3,174	21,914
45467	Cus conv cpe	3,833	3,326	4,994
45469	Cus sdn 4d	3,788	3,035	25,932
Wildcat (wb 126.0)				
46437	htp cpe	4,003	3,326	3,774
46439	htp sdn	4,108	3,391	15,081
46467	conv cpe	4,065	3,480	2,690
46469	sdn 4d	4,070	3,233	14,389
46637	Cus htp cpe	4,018	3,547	10,800
46639	Cus htp sdn	4,176	3,606	13,060
46667	Cus conv cpe	4,079	3,701	2,790
Electra 225 (wb 126.0)				
48237	htp cpe	4,176	4,032	4,882
48239	htp sdn	4,271	4,153	10,792
48269	sdn 4d	4,255	4,022	11,740
48437	Cus htp cpe	4,230	4,211	10,119
48439	Cus htp sdn	4,323	4,332	34,149
48467	Cus conv cpe	4,298	4,378	7,175
48469	Cus sdn 4d	4,292	4,201	9,368
Riviera (wb 119.0)				
49487	htp cpe	4,180	4,424	45,348

1965 Riviera hardtop coupe

1966 Engines	bore×stroke	bhp	availability
V6, 225.0	3.75×3.40	160	S-Special, Skylark
V8, 300.0	3.75×3.40	210	O-Special, Skylark
V8, 340.0	3.75×3.85	220	S-4440 wagon, LeSabre
V8, 401.0	4.19×3.64	325	S-Skylark GS, Wildcat, Electra
V8, 425.0	4.31×3.64	340	S-Riviera; O-Wildcat, Electra

1967

Special (wb 115.0; wgns-120.0)		Wght	Price	Prod
43307	cpe	3,071	2,411	6,989
43335	wgn 4d	3,343	2,742	908
43369	sdn 4d	3,077	2,462	4,711
43407	cpe	3,173	2,481	8,937
43435	wgn 4d	3,425	2,812	1,688

1966 Riviera hardtop coupe

		Wght	Price	Prod
43469	sdn 4d	3,196	2,532	5,793
43517	Del htp cpe	3,127	2,566	2,357
43569	Del sdn 4d	3,142	2,545	3,650
43617	Del htp cpe	3,202	2,636	14,408
43635	Del wgn 4d	3,317	2,901	6,851
43669	Del sdn 4d	3,205	2,615	26,057
Skylark (wb 115.0; wgns-120.0)				
34017	GS340 htp cpe	3,283	2,845	3,692
44307	cpe V6	3,137	2,665	894
44407	cpe V8	3,229	2,735	3,165
44417	htp cpe	3,199	2,796	41,084
44439	htp sdn	3,373	2,950	13,721
44455	wgn 4d	3,713	3,025	5,440
44465	wgn 4d, 3S	3,811	3,173	5,970
44855	Cust wgn 4d	3,772	3,202	3,114
44865	Cust wgn 4d, 3S	3,876	3,340	4,559
44467	conv cpe	3,335	2,945	6,319
44469	sdn 4d	3,324	2,767	9,213
44607	GS400 cpe	3,439	2,956	1,014
44617	GS400 htp cpe	3,500	3,019	10,659
44667	GS400 conv cpe	3,505	3,167	2,140
LeSabre (wb 123.0)				
45239	htp sdn	3,878	3,142	17,464
45269	sdn 4d	3,847	3,002	36,220
45287	htp cpe	3,819	3,084	13,760
45439	Cus htp sdn	3,873	3,236	32,526
45467	Cus conv cpe	3,890	3,388	4,624
45469	Cus sdn 4d	3,855	3,096	27,930
45487	Cus htp cpe	3,853	3,172	22,666
Wildcat (wb 126.0)				
46439	htp sdn	4,069	3,437	15,110
46467	conv cpe	4,064	3,536	2,276
46469	sdn 4d	4,008	3,277	14,579
46487	htp cpe	4,021	3,382	10,585
46639	Cus htp sdn	4,119	3,652	13,547
46667	Cus conv cpe	4,046	3,757	2,913
46687	Cus htp cpe	4,055	3,603	11,871

Electra 225 (wb 126.0)		Wght	Price	Prod
48239	htp sdn	4,293	4,184	12,491
48257	htp cpe	4,197	4,075	6,845
48269	sdn 4d	4,246	4,054	10,787
48439	Cus htp sdn	4,336	4,363	40,978
48457	Cus htp cpe	4,242	4,254	12,156
48467	Cus conv cpe	4,304	4,421	6,941
48469	Cus sdn 4d	4,312	4,270	10,106
Riviera (wb 119.0)				
49487	htp cpe	4,189	4,469	42,799

1967 Engines	bore×stroke	bhp	availability
V6, 225.0	3.75×3.40	160	S-Special, Skylark
V8, 300.0	3.75×3.40	210	O-Special, Skylark
V8, 340.0	3.75×3.85	220/260	S-4400 wgn, LeS; O-Skyl
V8, 401.0	4.19×3.64	340	S-GS400
V8, 430.0	4.19×3.90	360	S-Wildcat, Electra, Riviera

1967 Skylark GS400 hardtop coupe

1968

Special Deluxe (wb 116.0; 2d-112.0)		Wght	Price	Prod
43327	cpe	3,185	2,513	21,988
43369	sdn 4d	3,277	2,564	16,571
43435	wgn 4d	3,670	3,001	10,916
Skylark (wb 116.0; 2d-112.0)				
43537	htp cpe	3,240	2,688	32,795
43569	sdn 4d	3,278	2,666	27,387
44437	Cus htp cpe	3,344	2,956	44,143
44439	Cus htp sdn	3,481	3,108	12,984
44467	Cus conv cpe	3,394	3,098	8,188
44469	Cus sdn 4d	3,377	2,924	8,066
Sportwagon (wb 121.0)				
44455	wgn 4d	3,975	3,341	10,530
44465	wgn 4d, 3S	4,118	3,499	12,378

Note: Sportwagon production includes 10,909 series 48000 woodgrain models.

Gran Sport (wb 112.0)		Wght	Price	Prod
43437	GS350 htp cpe	3,375	2,926	8,317
44637	GS400 htp cpe	3,514	3,127	10,743
44667	GS400 conv cpe	3,547	3,271	2,454
LeSabre (wb 123.0)				
45239	htp sdn	3,980	3,281	18,058
45269	sdn 4d	3,946	3,141	37,433
45287	htp cpe	3,923	3,223	14,922
45439	Cus htp sdn	4,007	3,375	40,370
45467	Cus conv cpe	3,966	3,504	5,257
45469	Cus sdn 4d	3,950	3,235	34,112
45487	Cus htp cpe	3,932	3,311	29,596
Wildcat (wb 126.0)				
46439	htp sdn	4,133	3,576	15,153
46469	sdn 4d	4,076	3,416	15,201
46487	htp cpe	4,065	3,521	10,708
46639	Cus htp sdn	4,162	3,791	14,059
46667	Cus conv cpe	4,118	3,873	3,572
46687	Cus htp cpe	4,082	3,742	11,276
Electra 225 (wb (126.0)				
48239	htp sdn	4,270	4,330	15,376
48257	htp cpe	4,180	4,221	10,705
48269	sdn 4d	4,253	4,200	12,723
48439	Cus htp sdn	4,314	4,509	50,846
48457	Cus htp cpe	4,223	4,400	16,826
48467	Cus conv cpe	4,285	4,541	7,976
48469	Cus sdn 4d	4,304	4,415	10,910
Riviera (wb 119.0)				
49487	htp cpe	4,222	4,615	49,284

1968 Engines	bore×stroke	bhp	availability
L6, 250.0	3.88×3.53	155	S-Special Del, Skylark
V8, 350.0	3.80×3.85	230	S-Swgn, Sky Cus, LeS; O-Spec, Sky
V8, 350.0	3.80×3.85	280	S-GS350; O-Sp Del, Sky, LeS, Swgn
V8, 401.0	4.19×3.64	340	S-GS400, Sportwagon 400
V8, 430.0	4.19×3.90	360	S-Wildcat, Electra, Riviera

1969

Special Deluxe (wb 116.0; 2d-112.0)		Wght	Price	Prod
43327	cpe	3,216	2,562	15,268
43369	sdn 4d	3,182	2,613	11,113
43435	wgn 4d	3,736	3,092	2,590
43436	luxury wgn 4d	3,783	3,124	6,677
Skylark (wb 116.0; 2d-112.0)				
43537	htp cpe	3,240	2,736	38,658
43569	sdn 4d	3,270	2,715	22,349
44437	Cus htp cpe	3,341	3,009	35,639
44439	Cus htp sdn	3,477	3,151	9,609
44467	Cus conv cpe	3,398	3,152	6,552
44469	Cus sdn 4d	3,397	2,978	6,423
Sportwagon (wb 121.0)				
44456	wgn 4d	4,106	3,465	9,157
44466	wgn 4d, 3S	4,321	3,621	11,513

1968 Electra 225 hardtop sedan four-door

Gran Sport (wb 112.0)		Wght	Price	Prod
43437	GS350 htp cpe	3,406	2,980	4,933
44637	GS400 htp cpe	3,549	3,181	6,356
44667	GS400 conv cpe	3,594	3,325	1,776
LeSabre (wb 123.2)				
45237	htp cpe	3,936	3,298	16,201
45239	htp sdn	3,983	3,356	17,235
45269	sdn 4d	3,966	3,216	36,664
45437	Cus htp cpe	4,018	3,386	38,887
45439	Cus htp sdn	4,073	3,450	48,123
45467	Cus conv cpe	3,958	3,579	3,620
45469	Cus sdn 4d	3,941	3,310	37,136
Wildcat (wb 123.2)				
46437	htp cpe	3,926	3,596	12,416
46439	htp sdn	4,304	3,651	13,805
46469	sdn 4d	4,102	3,491	13,126
46637	Cus htp cpe	4,134	3,817	12,136
46639	Cus htp sdn	4,220	3,866	13,596
46667	Cus conv cpe	4,152	3,948	2,374
Electra 225 (wb 126.2)				
48239	htp sdn	4,294	4,432	15,983
48257	htp cpe	4,203	4,323	13,128
48269	sdn 4d	4,238	4,302	14,521
48439	Cus htp sdn	4,328	4,611	65,240
48457	Cus htp cpe	4,222	4,502	27,018
48467	Cus conv cpe	4,309	4,643	8,294
48469	Cus sdn 4d	4,281	4,517	14,434
Riviera (wb 119.0)				
49487	htp cpe	4,199	4,701	52,872

1969 Engines	bore×stroke	bhp	availability
L6, 250.0	3.88×3.53	155	S-SD cpe & sdn, Skylark
V8, 350.0	3.80×3.85	230	S-SD wgn, Sky Cus, Swgn LeS
V8, 350.0	3.80×3.85	280	S-GS350; O-LeS, SW, SD, Sky
V8, 401.0	4.19×3.64	340	S-GS400; O-Sportwagen, LeS
V8, 430.0	4.19×3.90	360	S-Riviera, Electra, Wildcat

1970

Skylark (wb 116.0; 2d-112.0)		Wght	Price	Prod
43327	cpe	3,250	2,685	18,620
43369	sdn 4d	3,311	2,736	13,420
43537	350 htp cpe	3,277	2,859	70,918
43569	350 sdn 4d	3,320	2,838	30,281
44437	Cus htp cpe	3,435	3,132	36,367
44439	Cus htp sdn	3,565	3,220	12,411
44467	Cus conv cpe	3,499	3,275	4,954
44469	Cus sdn 4d	3,499	3,101	7,113
Sportwagon (wb 116.0)				
43435	wgn 4d	3,775	3,210	2,239
43436	luxury wgn 4d	3,898	3,242	10,002
Gran Sport (wb 112.0)				
43437	htp cpe	3,434	3,098	9,948
44637	455 htp cpe	3,562	3,283	8,732
44667	455 conv cpe	3,619	3,469	1,416
LeSabre (wb 124.0)				
45237	htp cpe	3,866	3,419	14,163
45239	htp sdn	4,018	3,477	14,817
45269	sdn 4d	3,970	3,337	35,404
45437	Cus htp cpe	3,921	3,507	35,641
45439	Cus htp sdn	3,988	3,571	43,863
45467	Cus conv cpe	3,947	3,700	2,487
45469	Cus sdn 4d	3,950	3,431	36,682
46437	Cus 455 htp cpe	4,066	3,675	5,469
46439	Cus 455 htp sdn	4,143	3,739	6,541
46469	Cus 455 sdn 4d	4,107	3,599	5,555
Estate Wagon (wb 124.0)				
46036	wgn 4d	4,691	3,923	11,427
46046	wgn 4d, 3S	4,779	4,068	16,879
Wildcat Custom (wb 124.0)				
46637	htp cpe	4,099	3,949	9,447

1969 Riviera hardtop coupe

1970 Estate wagon

		Wght	Price	Prod
46639	htp sdn	4,187	3,997	12,924
46667	conv cpe	4,214	4,079	1,244
Electra 225 (wb 127.0)				
48239	htp sdn	4,296	4,592	14,338
48257	htp cpe	4,214	4,482	12,013
48269	sdn 4d	4,274	4,461	12,580
48439	Cus htp sdn	4,385	4,771	65,114
48457	Cus stp cpe	4,297	4,661	26,002
48467	Cus conv cpe	4,341	4,802	6,045
48469	Cus sdn 4d	4,283	4,677	14,109
Riviera (wb 119.0)				
49487	htp cpe	4,216	4,854	37,336

1970 Engines	bore×stroke	bhp	availability
L6, 250.0	3.88×3.53	155	S-Skylark, Skylark 350
V8, 350.0	3.80×3.85	260	S-LeS, Sky Cus, SW; O-Sky
V8, 350.0	3.80×3.85	285	O-LeS, Sky, Sportwagon
V8, 350.0	3.80×3.85	315	S-GS; O-LeS, Sky, Swgn
V8, 455.0	4.31×3.90	350/360	S-GS455
V8, 455.0	4.31×3.90	370	S-Wldct, Est Wgn, LeS 455, Elec, Riv

1971

Skylark (wb 116.0; 2d 112.0)		Wght	Price	Prod
43327	cpe	3,254	2,847	14,500
43337	htp cpe	3,272	2,918	61,201
43369	sdn 4d	3,326	2,897	34,037
44437	Custom htp cpe	3,391	2,317	29,536
44439	Custom htp sdn	3,547	3,397	10,814
44467	Custom conv cpe	3,431	3,462	3,993
44469	Custom sdn 4d	3,455	3,288	8,299
Sportwagon (wb 116.0)				
43436	wgn 4d	3,928	3,515	12,525
Gran Sport (wb 112.0)				
43437	htp cpe	3,461	3,285	8,268
43467	conv cpe	3,497	3,476	902
LeSabre (wb 124.0)				
45239	htp sdn 4d	4,109	4,119	14,234
45257	htp cpe	4,049	4,061	13,385
46269	sdn 4d	4,078	3,992	26,348
45439	Custom htp sdn	4,147	4,213	41,098
45457	Custom htp cpe	4,095	4,149	29,944
45467	Custom conv cpe	4,086	4,342	1,856
45469	Custom sdn 4d	4,107	4,085	26,970
Estate Wagon (wb 127.0)				
46035	wgn 4d 2S	4,906	4,640	8,699
46045	wgn 4d 3S	4,965	4,786	15,335

1971 Skylark GS455

Centurion (wb 124.0)		Wght	Price	Prod
46639	htp sdn	4,307	4,564	15,345
46647	htp cpe	4,195	4,678	11,892
46667	conv cpe	4,227	4,678	2,161
Electra 225 (wb 127.0)				
48237	htp cpe	4,345	4,801	8,662
48239	htp sdn	4,381	4,915	17,589
48437	Custom htp cpe	4,359	4,980	26,831
48439	Custom htp sdn	4,421	5,093	72,954
Riviera (wb 122.0)				
49487	htp cpe	4,325	5,253	33,810

1971 Engines	bore×stroke	bhp	availability
L6, 250.0	3.88×3.53	145	S-Skylark
V8, 350.0	3.80×3.85	230	S-SW, LeS, O-Sky
V8, 350.0	3.80×3.85	260	S-Sky GS; O-Sky, LeS
V8, 455.0	4.31×3.90	315	S-Cent,Elec,EWgn; Riv,O-Sky,LeS
V8, 455.0	4.31×3.90	330	O-Cent,Riv
V8, 455.0	4.31×3.90	345	O-Sky,LeS

1972

Skylark (wb 116.0; 2d 112.0)		Wght	Price	Prod
4D69	sdn 4d	3,475	2,973	42,206
4D69	350 sdn 4d	3,600	3,104	
4D27	cpe	3,420	2,925	14,552
4D37	htp cpe	3,426	2,993	84,868
4D37	350 htp cpe	3,600	3,124	
4G37	GS htp cpe	3,471	3,225	7,723
4G67	GS conv cpe	3,525	3,406	852
4H69	Custom sdn 4d	3,516	3,228	9,924

1972 Electra Limited hardtop sedan

		Wght	Price	Prod
4H39	Custom htp sdn	3,609	3,331	12,925
4H37	Custom htp cpe	3,477	3,255	34,271
4H67	Custom conv cpe	3,534	3,393	3,608
4F36	Sportwagon 4d 2S	3,987	3,444	14,417
LeSabre (wb 124.0)				
4L69	sdn 4d	4,201	3,958	29,505
4L39	htp sdn	4,211	4,079	15,160
4L57	htp cpe	4,166	4,024	14,011
4N69	Custom sdn 4d	4,221	4,047	35,295
4N39	Custom htp sdn	4,226	4,168	50,804
4N57	Custom htp cpe	4,181	4,107	36,510
4N67	Custom conv cpe	4,235	4,291	2,037
Estate Wagon (wb 127.0)				
4R45	wgn 4d 3S	5,060	4,728	18,793
4R35	wgn 4d 2S	4,975	4,589	10,175
Centurion (wb 124.0)				
4P39	htp sdn	4,406	4,508	19,852
4P47	htp cpe	4,336	4,579	14,187
4P67	conv cpe	4,396	4,616	2,396
Electra 225 (wb 127.0)				
4U39	htp sdn	4,515	4,890	19,433
4U37	htp cpe	4,445	4,782	9,961
4V39	Custom sdn 4d	4,530	5,060	104,754
4V37	Custom htp cpe	4,455	4,952	37,974
Riviera (wb 122.0)				
4Y87	htp cpe	4,343	5,149	33,728

1972 Engines	bore×stroke	bhp	availability
V8, 350.0	3.80×3.85	150	S-Skylark,LeSabre
V8, 350.0	3.80×3.85	190	S-GS,O-Sky,LeS
V8, 455.0	4.31×3.90	225	S-Cent,Elec,EWgn; O-Sky,GS,LeS
V8, 455.0	4.31×3.90	250	S-Riviera; O-Cent, LeS

1973

Apollo (wb 111.0)		Wght	Price	Prod
B69	sdn 4d	3,239	2,628	8,450
B27	sdn 2d	3,195	2,605	14,475
B17	htchbk sdn 3d	3,297	2,754	9,868
Century (wb 116.0; 2d 112.0)				
D29	Colonnade sdn 4d	3,780	3,057	38,202
D37	Colonnade cpe	3,713	3,057	56,154
F35/45	wgn 4d 2S/3S	4,156*	3,486*	7,760*
H29	Luxus Colonnade sdn 4d	3,797	3,326	22,438
H57	Luxus Colonnade cpe	3,718	3,331	71,712
K35/45	Luxus wgn 4d 2S/3S	4,190*	3,652*	10,645*
J57	Regal Colonnade cpe	3,743	3,470	91,557
LeSabre (wb 124.0)				
L69	sdn 4d	4,234	3,998	29,649
L39	htp sdn	4,259	4,125	13,413
L57	htp cpe	4,210	4,067	14,061
N69	Custom sdn 4d	4,264	4,091	42,854
N39	Custom htp sdn	4,284	4,217	55,879
N57	Custom htp cpe	4,225	4,154	41,425
Centurion (wb 124.0)				
P39	htp sdn	4,329	4,390	22,354
P57	htp cpe	4,260	3,336	16,883
P67	conv cpe	4,316	4,534	5,739
Estate Wagon (wb 127.0)				
R35	wgn 4d 2S	4,952	4,645	12,282
R45	wgn 4d 3S	5,021	4,790	23,513

1973 Century Colonade coupe

Electra 225 (wb 127.0)		Wght	Price	Prod
T39	htp sdn	4,581	4,928	17,189
T37	htp cpe	4,488	4,815	9,224
V39	Custom htp sdn	4,603	5,105	107,031
V37	Custom htp cpe	4,505	4,993	44,328
Riviera (wb 122.0)				
Y87	htp cpe	4,486	5,221	34,080

1973 Engines	bore×stroke	bhp	availability
L6, 250.0	3.87×3.50	100	S-Apollo
V8, 350.0	3.80×3.85	150	S-Apollo, Cnty, LeS
V8, 350.0	3.80×3.85	175	S-Cnty; O-Ap, LeS
V8, 455.0	4.31×3.90	225	S-EWgn,Elec; O-Cnty,LeS
V8, 455.0	4.31×3.90	250	S-Riv; O-LeS,EWgn,Elec
V8, 455.0	4.31×3.90	260/270	O-Riviera

*figures for 2S wgns shown; for 3S wgns add approx. 40 lbs and $125. Production combined.

1974

Apollo (wb 111.0)		Wght	Price	Prod
B69	sdn 4d	3,362	3,060	16,779
B27	sdn 2d	3,322	3,037	28,286
B17	htchbk sdn 3d	3,428	3,160	11,644
Century (wb 116.0; 2d 112.0)				
D29	350 Colonnade sdn 4d	3,890	3,836	22,856
D37	350 Colonnade cpe	3,845	3,790	33,166
D37	Grand Sport Colonnade cpe	3,937	3,904	
F35/45	wgn 4d 2S/3S	4,272*	4,205*	4,860*
H29	Luxus Colonnade sdn 4d	3,910	4,109	11,159
H57	Luxus Colonnade cpe	3,835	4,089	44,930
K35/45	Luxus wgn 4d 2S/3S	4,312*	4,371*	6,791*
J29	Regal Colonnade htp sdn	3,930	4,221	9,333
J57	Regal Colonnade htp cpe	3,900	4,201	57,512

1973 Apollo two-door hatchback

LeSabre (wb 124.0)		Wght	Price	Prod
N69	sdn 4d	4,337	4,355	18,572
N39	htp sdn	4,387	4,482	11,879
N57	htp cpe	4,297	4,424	12,522
P69	Luxus sdn 4d	4,352	4,466	16,039
P39	Luxus htp sdn	4,397	4,629	23,910
P57	Luxus htp cpe	4,307	4,575	27,243
P67	Luxus conv cpe	4,372	4,696	3,627
Estate Wagon (wb 127.0)				
R35	wgn 4d 2S	5,082	5,019	4,581
R45	wgn 4d 3S	5,182	5,163	9,831
Electra 225 (wb 127.0)				
T39	htp sdn	4,682	5,373	5,750
T37	htp cpe	4,607	5,260	3,339
V39	Custom htp sdn	4,702	5,550	29,089
V37	Custom htp cpe	4,627	5,438	15,099
X39	Limited htp sdn	4,732	5,921	30,051
X37	Limited htp cpe	4,682	5,886	16,086
Riviera (wb 122.0)				
Y87	htp cpe	4,572	5,678	20,129

1974 Engines	bore×stroke	bhp	availability
L6, 250.0	3.87×3.50	100	S-Apollo
V8, 350.0	3.80×3.85	150	S-Ap,Cnty,LeS
V8, 350.0	3.80×3.85	175	O-Ap,Cnty,LeS
V8, 455.0	4.31×3.90	175	O-Cnty,EWgn
V8, 455.0	4.31×3.90	210	S-EWgn,Elec,Riv; O-Cnty
V8, 455.0	4.31×3.90	245	O-EWgn,Elec,Riv,Cnty

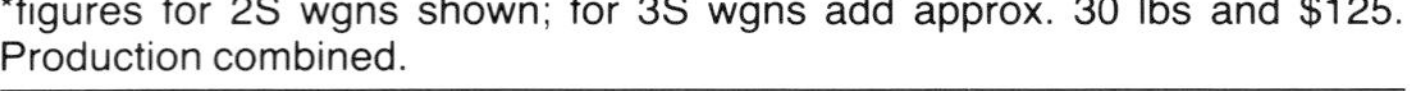

*figures for 2S wgns shown; for 3S wgns add approx. 30 lbs and $125. Production combined.

1975

Skyhawk (wb 97.0)		Wght	Price	Prod
S07	htchbk cpe 3d	2,891	4,173	29,448 (S07 and T07 combined)
T07	S htchbk cpe 3d	2,851	3,860	
Apollo/Skylark (wb 111.0)*				
B69	Apollo sdn 4d L6	3,438	3,436	21,138
W27	Skylark "S" cpe V6	3,405	3,234	27,689 (W27 and B27 combined)
B27	Skylark cpe V6	3,438	3,463	

1975 Skyhawk hatchback coupe

		Wght	Price	Prod
B17	Skylark htchbk sdn 3d V6	3,512	3,586	6,814
C69	Apollo S/R sdn 4d L6	3,478	4,092	2,241
C27	Skylark S/R cpe V6	3,404	4,136	3,746
C17	Skylark S/R htchbk V6	3,514	4,253	1,505
Century (wb 116.0; 2d 112.0)*				
D37	Colonnade cpe	3,762	3,894	39,556 (D37 and E37 combined)
E37	Special Colonnade cpe V6	3,613	3,815	
D29	Colonnade sdn 4d	3,818	3,944	22,075
F35	wgn 4d 2S V8	4,320	4,636	4,416 (F35 and F45 combined)
F45	wgn 4d 3S V8	4,370	4,751	
H29	Custom Colonnade sdn 4d	3,851	4,211	9,995
H57	Custom Colonnade cpe	3,759	4,154	32,966
K35	Custom wgn 4d 2S	4,350	4,802	7,078 (K35 and K45 combined)
K45	Custom wgn 4d 3S	4,400	4,917	
Regal (wb 116.0; 2d 112.0)*				
J29	Colonnade sdn 4d V6	3,888	4,311	10,726
J57	Colonnade cpe V6	3,821	4,257	56,646
LeSabre (wb 123.5)				
N69	sdn 4d	4,355	4,771	14,088
N39	htp sdn	4,411	4,898	9,119
N57	htp cpe	4,294	4,840	8,647

1976 Skyhawk hatchback coupe

		Wght	Price	Prod
P69	Custom sdn 4d	4,388	4,934	17,026
P39	Custom htp sdn	4,439	5,061	30,005
P57	Custom htp cpe	4,316	5,007	25,016
P67	Custom conv cpe	4,392	5,133	5,300
Estate Wagon (wb 127.0)				
R35	wgn 4d 2S	5,055	5,447	4,128
R45	wgn 4d 3S	5,135	5,591	9,612
Electra 225 (wb 127.0)				
V39	Custom htp sdn	4,706	6,201	27,357
V37	Custom htp cpe	4,582	6,041	16,145
X39	Limited htp sdn	4,762	6,516	33,778
X37	Limited htep cpe	4,633	6,352	17,650
Riviera (wb 122.0)				
Z87	htp cpe	4,539	6,420	17,306

1975 Engines	bore×stroke	bhp	availability
V6, 231.0	3.80×3.40	110	S-Skh,Skl,Cnty,Rgl
L6, 250.0	3.87×3.50	105	S-Apollo
V8, 260.0	3.50×3.39	110	S-Apollo, Skylark
V8, 350.0	3.80×3.85	145	S-Cnty exc wgns
V8, 350.0	3.80×3.85	165	S-Cnty wgns,Les; O-Cnty, Rgl
V8, 400.0	4.12×3.75	185	S-LeSabre (Cal.)
V8, 455.0	4.31×3.90	205	S-EWgn,Elec,Riv; O-LeS

*Six & V8 weights averaged. Prices for sixes shown; for V8s add approx. $80 to L6 or $20-30 to V6 models.

1976

Skyhawk (wb 97.0)		Wght	Price	Prod
S07	htchbk cpe 3d	2,889	4,216	15,768
T07	S htchbk cpe 3d	2,857	3,903	
Skylark (wb 111.0)				
W27	S cpe	3,416	3,435	51,260
B27	cpe	3,426	3,549	
B69	sdn 4d	3,384	3,609	48,157
B17	htchbk cpe 3d	3,494	3,687	6,703
C69	S/R sdn 4d	3,406	4,324	3,243
C27	S/R cpe	3,410	4,281	3,880
C17	S/R htchbk cpe 3d	3,430	4,398	1,248

1978 Century Custom wagon

Century (wb 116.0; 2d 112.0)		Wght	Price	Prod
D37	Colonnade cpe	3,748	4,070	59,448
E37	Special Colonnade cpe V6	3,508	3,935	
D29	Colonnade sdn 4d	3,567	4,105	33,632
H29	Custom Colonnade sdn 4d	3,817	4,424	19,728
H57	Custom Colonnade cpe	3,705	4,346	34,036
K35	Custom wgn 4d 2S V8	4,363	4,987	16,625
K45	Custom wgn 4d 3S V8	4,413	5,099	
Regal (wb 116.0; 2d 112.0)				
J29	Colonnade sdn 4d V8	4,104	4,825	17,118
J57	Colonnade cpe V6	3,866	4,465	124,498
LeSabre (wb 124.0)				
N69	sdn 4d V6	4,170	4,747	4,315
N39	htp sdn V6	4,059	4,871	2,312
N57	htp cpe V6	4,129	4,815	3,861
P69	Custom sdn 4d V8	4,328	5,046	34,841
P39	Custom htp sdn V8	4,386	5,166	46,109
P57	Custom htp cpe V8	4,275	5,144	45,669
Estate Wagon (wb 127.0)				
R35	wgn 4d 2S	5,013	5,591	5,990
R45	wgn 4d 3S	5,139	5,731	14,384
Electra 225 (wb 127.0)				
V39	htp sdn	4,641	6,527	26,655
V37	htp cpe	4,502	6,367	18,442

1978 Century Sport Coupe

1978 Riviera Anniversary Edition two-door coupe

		Wght	Price	Prod
X39	Limited htp sdn	4,709	6,852	51,067
X37	Limited htp cpe	4,521	6,689	28,395
Riviera (wb 122.0)				
Z87	htp cpe	4,531	6,798	20,082

1976 Engines	bore×stroke	bhp	availability
V6, 231.0	3.80×3.40	110	S-Skh,Skl,Cnty,Rgl,LeS
V8, 260.0	3.50×3.39	110	S-Skylark
V8, 350.0	3.80×3.85	145	S-Rgl,Cnty exc wgn; O-Skl
V8, 350.0	3.80×3.85	165	S-Cnty wgn,LeS Cus; O-Skl,Cnty,Rgl
V8, 455.0	4.31×3.90	205	S-EWgn,Elec,Riv; O-LeS Cus

1977

Skyhawk (wb 97.0)		Wght	Price	Prod
S07	htchbk cpe 3d	2,817	4,294	12,345
T07	S htchbk cpe 3d	2,805	3,981	
Skylark (wb 111.0)*				
W27	S cpe	3,286	3,642	49,858
B27	cpe	3,286	3,765	
B69	sdn 4d	3,324	3,825	48,121
B17	htchbk cpe 3d	3,408	3,942	5,316
C69	S/R sdn 4d	3,324	4,587	4,000
C27	S/R cpe	3,330	4,527	5,023
C17	S/R htchbk cpe	3,358	4,695	1,154
Century (wb 116.0; 2d 112.0)*				
D37	cpe	3,582	4,304	52,864
E37	Special cpe	3,590	4,170	
D29	sdn 4d	3,754	4,364	29,065
H29	Custom sdn 4d	3,750	4,688	13,645
H57	Custom htp cpe	3,610	4,628	20,834
K35	Custom wgn 4d 2S V8	4,260	5,219	19,282
K45	Custom wgn 4d 3S V8	4,310	5,271	
Regal (wb 116.0; 2d 112.0)*				
J29	sdn 4d V8	3,928	5,244	17,946
J57	cpe V6	3,612	4,713	174,560
LeSabre (wb 115.9)*				
N69	sdn 4d	3,560	5,093	19,827
N37	cpe	3,522	5,033	8,455
P69	Custom sdn 4d	3,572	5,382	103.855
P37	Custom htp cpe	3,530	5,322	58,589
F37	Custom htp cpe V8	3,634	5,819	
Estate Wagon (115.9)				
R35	wgn 4d 2S	4,015	5,903	25,075
R45	wgn 4d 3S	4,141	6,078	
Electra 225 (wb 119.0)				
V69	sdn	3,814	6,866	25,633
V37	cpe	3,761	6,673	15,762
X69	Limited htp sdn	3,839	7,226	82,361
X37	Limited htp cpe	3,785	7,033	37,871
Riviera (wb 116.0)				
Z37	htp cpe	3,784	7,385	26,138

1977 Engines	bore×stroke	bhp	availability
V6, 231.0	3.80×3.40	105	S-Skh,Skl,Cnty,Regl,LeS
V8, 301.0	4.00×3.00	135	S-Skl,LeS
V8, 305.0	3.74×3.48	145	O-Skl,Cnty wgn
V8, 350.0	3.80×3.85	140	S-Cnty exc wgn,Rgl; O-Skl
V8, 350.0	3.80×3.85	155	S-Cnty wgn,Elec,Riv; O-Skl,Cnty,Rgl
V8, 350.0	4.06×3.39	170	S-EWgn; O-Les,Elec,Riv
V8, 403.0	4.35×3.38	185	O-Cnty ,LeS,E, Elec,Riv

*Six & V8 weights averaged. Prices for sixes shown; for V8s add $150

1978

Skyhawk (wb 97.0)		Wght	Price	Prod
S07	htchbk cpe 3d	2,707	4,414	24,589
T07	S htchbk cpe 3d	2,678	4,146	
Skylark (wb 111.0)*				
W27	S cpe	3,285	3,911	42,087
B27	cpe	3,287	4,035	
B69	sdn 4d	3,318	4,120	40,951
B17	htchbk cpe 3d	3,397	4,217	2,642
C69	Custom sdn 4d	3,303	4,367	14,523
C27	Custom cpe	3,270	4,282	12,740
C17	Custom htchbk cpe 3d	3,369	4,464	1,277
Century (wb 108.1)*				
E09	Special sdn 4d	3,087	4,520	12,533
E87	Special sdn 2d	3,096	4,413	10,818
E37	Special wgn 4d 2S	3,231	5,021	9,586
H09	Custom sdn 4d	3,111	4,768	18,361
H87	Custom sdn 2d	3,084	4,658	12,434
H35	Custom wgn 4d 2S	3,265	5,233	24,014
G87	Sport Coupe sdn 2d	3,124	5,051	NA
L09	Limited sdn 4d	3,148	5,127	NA
L87	Limited sdn 2d	3,171	4,017	NA
Regal (wb 108.1)*				
J47	cpe	3,065	4,885	236,652
M47	Limited cpe	3,114	5,268	NA
K47	Sport Coupe turbo V6	3,153	5,958	NA
LeSabre (wb 115.9)*				
N69	sdn 4d	3,522	5,536	23,354
N37	cpe	3,531	5,451	8,265
P69	Custom sdn 4d	3,534	6,045	86,638
P37	Custom cpe	3,496	5,727	53,675
F37	Sport Coupe turbo V6	3,559	6,346	NA
Estate Wagon (wb 115.9)				
R35	wgn 4d 2S V8	4,063	6,394	25,964
Electra 225 (wb 119.0)				
V69	sdn 4d	3,730	7,431	14,590
V37	cpe	3,682	7,252	8,259
X69	Limited sdn 4d	3,757	7,817	65,335
X37	Limited cpe	3,710	7,638	33,365
U69	Park Avenue sdn 4d	3,777	8,208	NA
U37	Park Avenue cpe	3,730	7,952	NA
Riviera (wb 116.0)				
Z37	cpe	3,701	9,224	20,535

1979 Le Sabre Sport Coupe

1978 Engines	bore×stroke	bhp	availability
V6, 196.0	3.50×3.40	90	S-Cnty exc wgn,Rgl exc S/C
V6, 231.0	3.80×3.40	105	S-Skh,Skl,Cnty wgn,LeS; O-Rgl exc S/C, Century
V6T, 231.0	3.80×3.40	150	S-Rgl & LeS S/Cs; O-Rgl
V6T, 231.0	3.80×3.40	165	O-Rgl & LeS S/Cs
V8, 301.0	4.00×3.00	140	S-LeS exc wgn
V8, 305.0	3.74×3.48	145	S-Skl,Cnty wgn,Rgl exc S/C,O-Cnty
V8, 305.0	3.74×3.48	160	O-Cnty,Rgl exc S/C
V8, 350.0	3.80×3.85	155	S-EWgn,Elec,Riv O-LeS
V8, 350.0	4.00×3.48	170	O-Skl,Cnty
V8, 403.0	4.35×3.38	185	O-LeS,Elec,Riv

*Six & V8 weights averaged. Prices for sixes shown; for V8s add $175.

1979

Skyhawk (wb 97.0)		Wght	Price	Prod
S07	htchbk cpe 3d	2,740	4,778	23,139
T07	S htchbk cpe 3d	2,724	4,560	
Skylark (wb 111.0)				
W27	S cpe	3,164	4,082	10,201
B27	cpe	3,174	4,208	
B69	sdn 4d	3,218	4,308	10,849
B17	htchbk cpe 3d	3,254	4,357	608
C69	Custom sdn 4d	3,226	4,562	3,822
C27	Custom cpe	3,182	4,462	3,546
Century (wb 108.1)				
E09	Special sdn 4d	3,105	5,021	7,363
E87	Special sdn 2d	3,090	4,921	4,805
E35	Special wgn 4d 2S	3,222	5,492	10,413
H09	Custom sdn 4d	3,123	5,290	9,681
H87	Custom sdn 2d	3,103	5,165	2,474
H37	Custom wgn 4d 2S	3,258	5,806	21,100
G87	Sport Coupe sdn 2d	3,099	5,473	1,653
L09	Limited sdn 4d	3,156	5,658	2,694
Regal (wb 108.1)				
J47	cpe	3,081	5,407	157,228
M47	Limited cpe	3,123	5,814	94,748
K47	Sport Coupe turbo V6	3,190	6,497	21,389
LeSabre (wb 115.9)				
N69	sdn 4d	3,523	6,110	25,431
N37	cpe	3,492	6,010	7,542
P69	Limited sdn 4d	3,567	6,620	75,939
P37	Limited cpe	3,518	6,495	38,290
F37	Sport Coupe turbo V6	3,545	6,953	3,582
Estate Wagon (wb 115.9)				
R35	wgn 4d 2S V8	4,021	7,169	21,312

1979 Electra Limited Coupe

Electra 225 (wb 119.0)		Wght	Price	Prod
V69	sdn 4d	3,831	8,878	11,055
V37	cpe	3,767	8,703	5,358
X69	Limited sdn 4d	3,853	9,278	76,340
X37	Limited cpe	3,789	9,103	28,878
U69	Park Avenue sdn 4d	3,860	9,959	NA
U37	Park Avenue cpe	3,794	9,784	NA
Riviera (wb 114.0)				
Z57	cpe V8	3,759	10,684	52,181
Y57	S-Type cpe	3,774	10,960	

1979 Engines	bore×stroke	bhp	availability
V6, 196.0	3.50.×3.40	105	S-Cnty exc wgn,Rgl exc S/C
V6, 231.0	3.80×3.40	115	S-Skh,Skl,Cnty wgn,LeS; O-Cnty,Rgl
V6T, 231.0	3.80×3.40	170-185	S-Riv S; O-Cnty/Rgl/LeS Spt
V8, 301.0	4.00×3.00	140	S-Cnty,Rgl,LeS
V8, 301.0	4.00×3.00	150	O-Cnty,Rgl
V8, 305.0	3.74×3.48	130	S-Skl
V8, 305.0	3.74×3.48	155	O-Cnty, Rgl
V8, 350.0	3.80×3.85	155	S-EWgn, Elec; O-LeS
V8, 350.0	4.00×3.48	165	O-Sky, Cent wgn
V8, 350.0	4.06×3.39	170	S-Riv; O-Riv S
V8, 403.0	4.35×3.38	185	O-EWgn, Elec

1980

Skyhawk (wb 97.0)		Wght	Price	Prod
S07	htchbk cpe 3d	2,754	5,211	8,322
T07	S htchbk cpe 3d	2,754	4,993	
Skylark (wb 104.9)				
B69	sdn 4d	2,458	5,488	80,940
B37	sdn 2d	2,430	5,342	55,114
C69	Limited sdn 4d	2,498	5,912	86,948
C37	Limited sdn 2d	2,458	5,765	42,652
D69	Sport Sedan 4d	2,490	6,102	—
D37	Sport Coupe 2d L4/V6	2,450	5,955	—
Century (wb 108.1)**				
H69	sdn 4d	3,158	5,858	129,740
L69	Limited sdn 4d	3,202	6,344	—
H87	sdn 2d	3,138	5,758	1,074
G87	Sport Coupe sdn 2d	3,202	6,275	—
H35	Estate wgn 4d 2S	3,311	6,432	11,122
E35	wgn 4d 2S	3,300	6,134	6,493
Regal (wb 108.1)**				
J47	cpe 2d	3,179	6,506	214,735
M47	Limited cpe 2d	3,282	6,925	
K47	Sport Coupe turbo V6 2d	3,194	7,203	

LeSabre (wb 115.9)**		Wght	Price	Prod
N69	sdn 4d	3,433	6,940	23,873
N37	cpe 2d	3,380	6,845	8,342
P69	Limited sdn 4d	3,439	7,242	37,676
P37	Limited cpe 2d	3,391	7,100	20,561
F37	Sport Coupe turbo V6	3,430	8,003	—
R35	wgn 4d 2S V8	3,898	7,844	9,318
R35	wgn 4d 3S V8	3,928	8,037	
Electra 225 (wb 119.0; wgns 115.9)**				
X69	Limited sdn 4d	3,670	9,580	54,422
W69	Park Avenue sdn 4d	3,670	10,676	—
X37	Limited cpe 2d	3,664	9,425	14,058
W37	Park Avenue cpe 2d	3,692	10,537	—
V35	Estate wgn 4d 2S V8	4,105	10,806	—
V35	Estate wgn 4d 3S V8	4,135	10,999	—
Riviera (wb 114.0)				
Z57	cpe V8	3,633	11,640	48,621
Y57	S-Type cpe	3,734	12,151	

1980 Engines	bore×stroke	bhp	availability
L4, 151.0	4.00×3.00	90	S-Skylark
V6, 173.0	3.50×3.00	115	O-Skyhawk
V6, 231.0	3.80×3.40	110	S-Skyhawk, Cnty, Rgl, LeS
V6T, 231.0	3.80×3.40	170	S-Rgl S/C,LeS S/C; O-Cnty
V6T, 231.0	3.80×3.40	175	S-Cnty S/C
V6T, 231.0	3.80×3.40	185	S-Riv"S"; O-Riv
V6, 252.0	3.97×3.40	125	S-Elec; O-LeS
V8, 265.0	3.75×3.00	120	S-Cnty,Rgl
V8, 301.0	4.00×3.00	140	S-LeS,Elec,EWgn, O-Cnty,Rgl
V8, 305.0	3.74×3.48	155	O-Cnty,Rgl
V8, 350.0	3.80×3.85	155	O-LeS,Elec,EWgn
V8, 350.0	4.06×3.39	160	S-Elec,Riv; O-LeS, Riv S,EWgn
V8D, 350.0	3.88×3.53	105	O-EWgn,Elec

*L4 & V6 weights averaged. Prices are for L4s; V6s add $225
**V6 & V8 weights averaged. Prices are for V6s; V8s add $105

1981

Skylark (wb 104.9)		Wght	Price	Prod
B69	sdn 4d	2,479	6,551	104,091
B37	sdn 2d	2,453	6,405	46,515
C69	Limited sdn 4d	2,513	7,007	81,642
C37	Limited sdn 2d	2,482	6,860	30,080
D69	Sport Sedan 4d	2,512	7,186	—
D37	Sport Coupe 2d	2,486	7,040	—

1980 Skylark Sport Coupe

Century (wb 108.1)		Wght	Price	Prod
H69	sdn 4d	3,224	7,094	127,119
L69	Limited sdn 4d	3,249	7,999	
H35	Estate wgn 4d 2S	3,368	7,735	11,659
E35	wgn 4d 2S	3,321	7,391	5,489
Regal (wb 108.1)				
J47	cpe 2d	3,245	7,555	123,848
K47	Sport Coupe turbo V6 2d	3,261	8,528	
M47	Limited cpe 2d	3,382	8,024	116,352
LeSabre (wb 115.9)				
N69	sdn 4d	3,573	7,805	19,166
N37	cpe 2d	3,544	7,715	4,909
P69	Limited sdn 4d	3,595	8,101	39,006
P37	Limited cpe 2d	3,562	7,966	14,862
R35	Estate wgn 4d 2S V8	4,118	8,722	4,934
Electra (wb 118.9; wgn 115.9)				
X69	Limited sdn 4d	3,802	10,368	58,832
W69	Park Avenue sdn 4d	3,818	11,396	
X37	Limited cpe 2d	3,686	10,237	10,151
W37	Park Avenue cpe 2d	3,808	11,267	
V35	Estate wgn 4d 2S V8	4,290	11,291	6,334
Riviera (wb 114.0)				
Z57	cpe 2d	3,643	12,147	52,007
Y57	T Type cpe turbo V6	3,651	13,091	

1981 Engines	bore × stroke	bhp	availability
L4, 151.0	4.00 × 3.00	90	S-Skylark
V6, 173.0	3.50 × 3.00	115	O-Skylark
V6, 231.0	3.80 × 3.40	110	S-Cnty, Rgl, LeS
V6T, 231.0	3.80 × 3.40	170	S-Rgl S/C
V6T, 231.0	3.80 × 3.40	180	S-Riv T; O-Riv
V6, 252.0	3.97 × 3.40	125	S-Elec, Riv; O-LeS, Riv T
V8, 265.0	3.75 × 3.00	119	O-Cnty, Rgl
V8, 307.0	3.80 × 3.39	140	S-EWgn; O-LeS, Elec, Riv
V8D, 350.0	4.06 × 3.39	105	O-LeS, Elec, EWgn, Riv

1982

Skyhawk (wb 101.2)		Wght	Price	Prod
S69	Custom sdn 4d	2,385	7,489	22,540
T69	Limited sdn 4d	2,411	7,931	
S27	Custom cpe 2d	2,327	7,297	25,378
T27	Limited cpe 2d	2,349	7,739	
Skylark (wb 104.9)				
B69	sdn 4d	2,521	7,647	65,541
B37	cpe 2d	2,490	7,477	21,017
C69	Limited sdn 4d	2,547	8,079	44,290
C37	Limited cpe 2d	2,517	7,917	13,712
D69	Sport Sedan 4d	2,552	8,219	1,295*
D37	Sport Coupe 2d	2,522	8,048	
Century (wb 104.9)				
H19	Custom sdn 4d	2,671	9,141	83,250
L19	Limited sdn 4d	2,683	9,581	
H27	Custom cpe 2d	2,643	8,980	19,715
L27	Limited cpe 2d	2,654	9,417	
Regal (wb 108.1)				
J47	cpe 2d	3,152	8,712	134,237
M47	Limited cpe 2d	3,192	9,266	
K47	Sport Coupe turbo V6 2d	3,265	9,738	2,022
J69	sdn 4d	3,167	8,862	74,428
M69	Limited sdn 4d	3,205	9,364	
J35	wgn 4d	3,410	9,058	14,732
LeSabre (wb 115.9)				
N69	Custom sdn 4d	3,594	8,876	23,220
N37	Custom cpe 2d	3,565	8,774	5,165
P69	Limited sdn 4d	3,666	9,331	47,224
P37	Limited cpe 2d	3,583	9,177	16,062

1981 Regal Sport Coupe

1982 Riviera coupe

1982 Electra Estate wagon

		Wght	Price	Prod
R35	Estate wgn 4d 2s V8	4,228	10,668	7,149
Electra (wb 118.9; wgn 115.9)				
X69	Limited sdn 4d	3,807	11,884	59,601
W69	Park Avenue sdn 4d	3,888	13,559	
X37	Limited cpe 2d	3,747	11,713	8,449
W37	Park Avenue cpe 2d	3,824	13,408	
V35	Estate wgn 4d 2s V8	4,299	12,911	8,182
Riviera (wb 114.0)				
Z57	cpe 2d	3,680	14,272	42,823
Y57	T Type cpe turbo V6	—	14,940	
Z67	conv cpe	—	23,994	1,248

1982 Engines	bore × stroke	bhp	availability
L4, 112.0	3.50 × 2.91	88	S-Skyhawk
L4, 112.0	3.33 × 3.12	80	O-Skyhawk

	bore×stroke	bhp	availability
L4, 121.0	3.50×3.15	90	O-Skyhawk
L4, 151.0	4.00×3.00	90	S-Skylark, Century
V6, 173.0	3.50×3.00	112	O-Skylark
V6, 173.0	3.50×3.00	135	O-Skylark
V6, 181.0	3.80×2.66	110	O-Century
V6, 231.0	3.80×3.40	110	S-Rgl, LeS
V6T, 231.0	3.80×3.40	175/180	S-Rgl S/C, Riv T
V6, 252.0	3.96×3.40	125	S-Elec, Riv; O-Regal, LeS
V8D, 262.5	4.06×3.39	85	O-Cnty, Rgl
V8, 307.0	3.80×3.38	140	S-EWgn; O-LeS, Elec, Riv
V8D, 350.0	4.06×3.39	105	O-Rgl, LeS, Elec, EWgn, Riv

*Sport model production included in basic Skylark totals.

1983

Skyhawk (wb 101.2)		Wght	Price	Prod
S69	Custom sdn 4d	2,369	7,166	19,847
T69	Limited sdn 4d	2,411	7,649	
S27	Custom cpe 2d	2,316	6,958	27,557
T27	Limited cpe 2d	2,333	7,457	
S35	Custom wgn 5d	2,439	7,492	10,653
T35	Limited wgn 5d	2,462	7,934	
E27	T Type cpe 2d	2,336	7,961	5,095
Skylark (wb 104.9)				
B69	Custom sdn 4d	2,521	7,718	51,950
B37	Custom cpe 2d	2,492	7,548	11,671
C69	Limited sdn 4d	2,549	8,150	30,674
C37	Limited cpe 2d	2,519	7,988	7,863
D37	T Type cpe 2d V6	2,608	9,337	2,489
Century (wb 104.9)				
H19	Custom sdn 4d	2,692	9,002	50,296
H27	Custom cpe 2d	2,644	8,841	
L19	Limited sdn 4d	2,705	9,425	73,030
L27	Limited cpe 2d	2,662	9,261	
G27	T Type cpe 2d V6	2,749	10,017	4,600*
G19	T Type sdn 4d V6	2,801	10,178	
Regal (wb 108.1)				
J47	cpe 2d	3,123	9,100	147,935
M47	Limited cpe 2d	3,164	9,722	
K47	T Type turbo V6 cpe 2d	3,194	10,366	3,732
J69	sdn 4d	3,139	9,279	61,285
M69	Limited sdn 4d	3,177	9,856	
J35	wgn 4d	3,289	9,550	15,287
LeSabre (wb 115.9)				
N69	Custom sdn 4d	3,574	9,394	31,196
N37	Custom cpe 2d	3,545	9,292	6,974
P69	Limited sdn 4d	3,613	9,990	66,547
P37	Limited cpe 2d	3,579	9,836	22,029
R35	Estate wgn 4d 2S V8	4,105	11,187	9,306
Electra (wb 118.9; wgn 115.9)				
X69	Limited sdn 4d	3,794	12,586	79,700
W69	Park Avenue sdn 4d	3,871	14,245	
X37	Limited cpe 2d	3,734	12,415	8,885
W37	Park Avenue cpe 2d	3,806	14,094	
V35	Estate wgn 4d 2S V8	4,175	13,638	9,581
Riviera (wb 114.0)				
Z57	cpe 2d	3,689	15,238	47,153
Y57	T Type cpe turbo V6	3,593	15,906	1,331
Z67	conv cpe	3,875	24,960	1,750

1983 Engines	bore×stroke	bhp	availability
L4, 112.0	3.34×3.13	84	O-Skyhawk
L4, 121.0	3.50×3.15	86	S-Skyhawk
L4, 151.0	4.00×3.00	90	S-Skylark, Century
V6, 173.0	3.50×2.99	112	O-Skylark
V6, 173.0	3.50×2.99	135	S-Skylark T; O-Skylark
V6, 181.0	3.80×2.66	110	O-Century
V6, 231.0	3.80×3.40	110	S-Rgl, LeS
V6T, 231.0	3.80×3.40	180	S-Rgl T, Riv T

1983 Century T Type four-door sedan

	bore × stroke	bhp	availability
V6, 252.0	3.97 × 3.40	125	S-Elec, Riv; O-Regal, LeS
V8D, 262.5	4.06 × 3.39	85	O-Cnty, Rgl
V8, 307.0	3.80 × 3.39	140	S-EWgn; O-LeS, Elec, Riv
V8D, 350.0	4.06 × 3.39	105	O-Rgl, LeS, Elec, EWgn, Riv

*T Type production included in basic totals.

1984

Skyhawk (wb 101.2)		Wght	Price	Prod
S69	Custom sdn 4d	2,436	7,345	45,648
T69	Limited sdn 4d	2,471	7,837	
S27	Custom cpe 2d	2,383	7,133	74,760
T27	Limited cpe 2d	2,424	7,641	
S35	Custom wgn 5d	2,507	7,677	13,668
T35	Limited wgn 5d	2,536	8,127	
E27	T Type cpe 2d	2,399	8,152	11,317
Skylark (wb 104.9)				
B69	Custom sdn 4d	2,593	7,707	56,495
B37	Custom cpe 2d	2,561	7,545	12,377
C69	Limited sdn 4d	2,618	8,283	33,795
C37	Limited cpe 2d	2,587	8,119	7,621
D37	T Type cpe 2d V6	2,676	9,557	923
Century (wb 104.9)				
H19	Custom sdn 4d	2,790	9,274	178,454
L19	Limited sdn 4d	2,811	9,729	
H27	Custom cpe 2d	2,742	9,110	15,429
L27	Limited cpe 2d	2,763	9,562	
H35	Custom wgn 5d	2,958	9,660	25,975
L35	Limited wgn 5d	2,976	10,087	
G27	T Type cpe 2d V6	2,855	10,510	3,477*
G19	T Type sdn 4d V6	2,903	10,674	
Regal (wb 108.1)				
J47	cpe 2d	3,172	9,487	160,638
M47	Limited cpe 2d	3,210	10,125	

1984 Skyhawk T Type two-door coupe

		Wght	Price	Prod
K47	T Type turbo V6 cpe 2d	3,254	12,118	5,401
J69	sdn 4d	3,219	9,671	58,715
M69	Limited sdn 4d	3,254	10,263	
LeSabre (wb 115.9)				
N69	Custom sdn 4d	3,717	10,129	36,072
N37	Custom cpe 2d	3,684	9,984	3,890
P69	Limited sdn 4d	3,763	10,940	86,418
P37	Limited cpe 2d	3,730	10,780	28,332
Electra (wb 118.9; wgn 115.9)				
R69	Limited sdn 4d	3,944	13,332	52,551
U69	Park Avenue sdn 4d	3,994	15,044	
R37	Limited cpe 2d	3,884	13,155	4,075
U37	Park Avenue cpe 2d	3,928	14,888	
V35	Estate wgn 4d 2s V8	4,295	14,483	17,563

1984 Regal Grand National two-door

Riviera (wb 114.0)		Wght	Price	Prod
Z57	cpe 2d	3,766	15,967	56,210
Y57	T Type cpe turbo V6	3,666	17,050	1,153
Z67	conv cpe	3,873	25,832	500

1984 Engines	bore × stroke	bhp	availability
L4, 112.0	3.34 × 3.13	84	O-Skyhawk
L4T, 112.0	3.34 × 3.13	150	S-Skyhawk T; O-Skyhawk
L4, 121.0	3.50 × 3.15	86	S-Skyhawk
L4, 151.0	4.00 × 3.00	92	S-Skylark, Century
V6, 173.0	3.50 × 2.99	112	O-Skylark
V6, 173.0	3.50 × 2.99	135	S-Skylark T; O-Skylark
V6, 181.0	3.80 × 2.66	110	O-Century
V6, 231.0	3.80 × 3.40	110	S-Rgl, LeS
V6, 231.0	3.80 × 3.40	125	S-Century T; O-Century
V6T, 231.0	3.80 × 3.40	200	S-Rgl T
V6T, 231.0	3.80 × 3.40	190	S-Riv T
V6, 252.0	3.97 × 3.40	125	S-Elec, Riv; O-Regal, LeS
V8D, 262.5	4.06 × 3.39	85	O-Cnty, Rgl
V8, 307.0	3.80 × 3.39	140	S-EWgn; O-LeS, Elec, Riv
V8D, 350.0	4.06 × 3.39	105	O-LeS, EWgn, Riv

*T Type production included in basic totals.

1985

Skyhawk (wb 101.2)		Wght	Price	Prod
S69	Custom sdn 4d	2,392	7,581	27,906
T69	Limited sdn 4d	2,424	8,083	
S27	Custom cpe 2d	2,347	7,365	44,804
T27	Limited cpe 2d	2,380	7,883	
S35	Custom wgn 5d	2,469	7,919	5,285
T35	Limited wgn 5d	2,496	8,379	
E27	T Type cpe 2d	2,362	8,437	4,521

1984 Skylark Limited two-door

1985 Century Estate wagon

1985 LeSabre Limited four-door sedan

Skylark (wb 104.9)		Wght	Price	Prod
B69	Custom sdn 4d	2,618	7,707	65,667
C69	Limited sdn 4d	2,655	8,283	27,490
Somerset Regal (wb 103.4)				
J27	Custom cpe 2d	2,567	8,857	48,470
M27	Limited cpe 2d	2,571	9,466	37,601
Century (wb 104.9)				
H19	Custom sdn 4d	2,790	9,545	215,928
L19	Limited sdn 4d	2,812	10,012	
H27	Custom cpe 2d	2,742	9,377	13,043
L27	Limited cpe 2d	2,764	9,841	
H35	Custom wgn 5d	2,958	9,941	28,221
L35	Limited wgn 5d	2,975	10,379	
G27	T Type cpe 2d V6	2,881	11,249	4,043*
G19	T Type sdn 4d V6	2,930	11,418	
Regal (wb 108.1)				
J47	cpe 2d	3,172	9,928	60,597
M47	Limited cpe 2d	3,199	10,585	59,780
K47	T Type turbo V6 cpe 2d	3,349	12,640	2,067
K47	Grand National V6 cpe 2d	NA	13,315	2,102
LeSabre (wb 115.9)				
N69	Custom sdn 4d	3,683	10,603	32,091
N37	Custom cpe 2d	3,672	10,455	5,156
P69	Limited sdn 4d	3,729	11,916	84,432
P37	Limited cpe 2d	3,696	11,751	22,211
R35	Estate wgn 5d	4,153	12,704	5,597
Electra (wb 110.8; wgn 115.9)				
X69	sdn 4d	3,250	14,331	131,011
W69	Park Avenue sdn 4d	3,269	16,240	
X11	cpe 2d	3,205	14,149	5,852
W11	Park Avenue cpe 2d	3,223	16,080	
F69	T Type sdn 4d V6	3,261	15,568	4,644*
F11	T Type cpe 2d V6	3,216	15,386	
V35	Estate wgn 4d 2s V8	4,231	15,323	7,769
Riviera (wb 114.0)				
Z57	cpe 2d	3,857	16,710	63,836
Y57	T Type cpe turbo V6	3,668	17,654	1,069
Z67	conv cpe	3,977	26,797	400

1985 Engines	bore × stroke	bhp	availability
L4, 112.0	3.34 × 3.13	84	S-Skyhawk T; O-Skyhawk
L4T, 112.0	3.34 × 3.13	150	O-Skyhawk T
L4, 121.0	3.50 × 3.15	86	S-Skyhawk

1986 LeSabre Limited Coupe

	bore×stroke	bhp	availability
L4, 151.0	4.00×3.00	92	S-Skylark, Cnty, Somerset
V6, 173.0	3.50×2.99	112	O-Skylark, Century
V6, 173.0	3.50×2.99	125	O-Skylark
V6, 181.0	3.80×2.66	110	S-Electra; O-Century
V6, 181.0	3.80×2.66	125	O-Somerset
V6, 231.0	3.80×3.40	110	S-Rgl, LeS
V6, 231.0	3.80×3.40	125	S-Century T, Electra T/Park; O-Century, Electra
V6T, 231.0	3.80×3.40	200	S-Rgl T
V6T, 231.0	3.80×3.40	190	S-Riv T
V8D, 262.5	4.06×3.39	85	O-Cnty, Rgl, Elec
V8, 307.0	3.80×3.39	140	S-EWgn, Riv; O-LeS
V8D, 350.0	4.06×3.39	105	O-LeS, EWgn, Riv

*T Type production included in basic totals.

1986

Skyhawk (wb 101.2)		Wght	Price	Prod
S69	Custom sdn 4d	2,392	8,073	29,959
T69	Limited sdn 4d	2,425	8,598	
S27	Custom cpe 2d	2,343	7,844	45,884
T27	Limited cpe 2d	2,381	8,388	
S35	Custom wgn 5d	2,469	8,426	6,079
T35	Limited wgn 5d	2,498	8,910	
E27	T Type cpe 2d	2,440	8,971	6,071
E77	T Type htchbk 3d	2,526	9,414	
S77	Sport htchbk 3d	2,433	8,184	—
Skylark (wb 103.4)				
J69	Custom sdn 4d	2,601	9,620	62,235
M69	Limited sdn 4d	2,608	10,290	
Somerset (wb 103.4)				
J27	Custom cpe 2d	2,557	9,425	72,062
M27	Limited cpe 2d	2,577	10,095	
K27	T Type cpe 2d	2,562	11,390	3,558
Century (wb 104.9)				
H19	Custom sdn 4d	2,773	10,228	229,066
L19	Limited sdn 4d	2,795	10,729	
H27	Custom cpe 2d	2,726	10,052	13,752
L27	Limited cpe 2d	2,748	10,544	
NA	Gran Sport cpe 2d	NA	NA	1,029
H35	Custom wgn 5d	2,938	10,648	25,374
L35	Limited wgn 5d	2,955	11,109	
G19	T Type sdn 4d V6	2,941	12,223	5,286
Regal (wb 108.1)				
J47	cpe 2d	3,289	10,654	39,734
M47	Limited cpe 2d	3,315	11,347	43,599
K47	T Type turbo V6 cpe 2d	3,380	13,714	7,896
K47	Grand National V6 cpe 2d	NA	14,349	5,512*

LeSabre (wb 110.8; wgn 115.9)		Wght	Price	Prod
P69	Custom sdn 4d	3,150	12,511	30,235
P37	Custom cpe 2d	3,108	12,511	7,191
R69	Limited sdn 4d	3,161	13,633	43,215
R37	Limited cpe 2d	3,119	13,633	14,331
R35	Estate wgn 5d	4,206	13,597	7,755
Electra (wb 110.8; wgn 115.9)				
X69	sdn 4d	3,256	15,588	109,042
W69	Park Avenue sdn 4d	3,305	17,338	
X11	cpe 2d	3,205	15,396	4,996
W11	Park Avenue cpe 2d	3,250	17,158	
F69	T Type sdn 4d V6	3,278	16,826	5,816
V35	Estate wgn 5d 2s V8	4,242	16,402	10,371
Riviera (wb 108.0)				
Z57	cpe 2d	3,298	19,831	20,096
Y57	T Type cpe	3,329	21,577	2,042

1986 Engines	bore×stroke	bhp	availability
L4, 112.0	3.34×3.13	88	S-Skyhawk T; O-Skyhawk
L4T, 112.0	3.34×3.13	150	O-Skyhawk T
L4, 121.0	3.50×3.15	88	S-Skyhawk
L4, 151.0	4.00×3.00	92	S-Skylark, Cnty, Somerset
V6, 173.0	3.50×2.99	112	O-Century
V6, 181.0	3.80×2.66	125	S-Smrst T, LeS; O-Smrst, Sky
V6, 231.0	3.80×3.40	110	S-Rgl
V6, 231.0	3.80×3.40	140	S-Elec, Riv
V6, 231.0	3.80×3.40	150	S-Century T; O-Century, LeS

1986 Skyhawk T Type hatchback coupe

1987 Riviera T Type coupe

1987 Electra T Type four-door sedan

	bore×stroke	bhp	availability
V6T, 231.0	3.80×3.40	235	S-Rgl T
V8, 307.0	3.80×3.39	140	S-EWgn; O-Regal

*Production included in basic Regal total.

1987

Skyhawk (wb 101.2)		Wght	Price	Prod
S69	Custom sdn 4d	2,385	8,559	15,778
T69	Limited sdn 4d	2,423	9,503	2,200
S27	Custom cpe 2d	2,336	8,522	19,814
T27	Limited cpe 2d	2,345	9,445	1,556
S35	Custom wgn 5d	2,463	9,249	3,061
T35	Limited wgn 5d	2,498	9,841	498
S77	Sport htchbk 3d	2,396	8,965	3,757
Skylark (wb 103.4)				
J69	Custom sdn 4d	2,535	9,915	26,173
M69	Limited sdn 4d	2,609	11,003	7,532
Somerset (wb 103.4)				
J27	Custom cpe 2d	2,489	9,957	34,916
M27	Limited cpe 2d	2,574	11,003	11,585
Century (wb 104.9)				
H19	Custom sdn 4d	2,783	10,989	88,445
L19	Limited sdn 4d	2,811	11,593	71,340
H27	Custom cpe 2d	2,736	10,844	2,878
L27	Limited cpe 2d	2,765	11,397	4,384
H35	Custom wgn 5d	2,866	11,478	10,141
L35	Limited Estate wgn 5d	2,886	11,998	6,990
Regal (wb 108.1)				
J47	cpe 2d	3,286	11,562	44,844
M47	Limited cpe 2d	3,315	12,303	20,441
J47/Y56	T Type V6 cpe 2d	NA	14,857	8,541*
J47/WE2	Grand National V6 cpe 2d	NA	15,136	20,193*
J47/T26	GNX cpe	NA	NA	547*
LeSabre (wb 110.8)				
H69	sdn 4d	3,141	13,438	6,243
P69	Custom sdn 4d	3,140	13,616	60,392
R69	Limited sdn 4d	3,171	14,918	70,797

		Wght	Price	Prod
P37	Custom cpe 2d	3,104	13,616	5,035
R37	Limited cpe 2d	3,137	14,918	7,741
L37	T Type cpe 2d	NA	15,521	4,123
Electra (wb 110.8)				
X69	sdn 4d	3,269	16,902	7,787
W69	Park Avenue sdn 4d	3,338	18,769	75,600
W11	Park Avenue cpe 2d	3,236	18,577	4,084
F69	T Type sdn 4d	3,278	18,224	2,570
Estate Wagons (wb 115.9)				
R35	LeSabre wgn 5d	4,160	14,724	5,251
V35	Electra wgn 5d	4,239	17,697	7,508
Riviera (wb 108.0)				
Z57	cpe 2d	3,320	20,337	12,636
Z57/Y50	T Type cpe	3,360	22,181	2,587

1987 Engines	bore×stroke	bhp	availability
L4, 121.0	3.50×3.15	90	S-Skyhawk
L4, 121.0	3.39×3.39	96	O-Skyhawk

1988 Reatta coupe

	bore×stroke	bhp	availability
L4T, 121.0	3.39×3.39	165	O-Skyhawk
L4, 151.0	4.00×3.00	98	S-Skylark, Cnty, Somerset
V6, 173.0	3.50×2.99	125	O-Century
V6, 181.0	3.80×2.66	125	O-Somerset, Skylark
V6, 231.0	3.80×3.40	110	S-Regal
V6, 231.0	3.80×3.40	1540	S-LeS, Elec, Riv; O-Cnty
V6T, 231.0	3.80×3.40	245	S-Rgl Grand Nat'l; O-Regal
V8, 307.0	3.80×3.39	140	S-EWgn; O-Regal

*Production included in basic Regal total.

1988

Skyhawk (wb 101.2)		Wght	Price	Prod
S69	sdn 4d	2,396	8,884	14,271
S27	cpe 2d	2,336	8,884	9,857
S35	wgn 5d	2,474	9,797	1,707
S27/WN2	S/E cpe 2d	NA	9,979	3,299
Skylark (wb 103.4)				
C69	Custom sdn 4d	2,601	10,399	24,940
D69	Limited sdn 4d	2,622	11,721	5,316
J27	Custom cpe 2d	2,555	10,684	19,590
M27	Limited cpe 2d	2,576	11,791	4,946
Century (wb 104.9)				
H19	Custom sdn 4d	2,796	11,793	62,214
L19	Limited sdn 4d	2,803	12,613	39,137
H27	Custom cpe 2d	2,725	11,643	1,322
L27	Limited cpe 2d	2,732	12,410	1,127
H35	Custom wgn 5d	2,945	12,345	5,312
L35	Limited Estate wgn 5d	2,949	13,077	4,146
Reatta (wb 98.5)				
C97	cpe 2d	3,350	25,000	4,708
Regal (wb 107.5)				
B57	Custom cpe 2d	2,953	12,449	64,773
D57	Limited cpe 2d	2,972	12,782	65,224
LeSabre (wb 110.8)				
P37	cpe 2d	3,192	14,560	2,403
P69	Custom sdn 4d	3,239	14,405	67,213
R69	Limited sdn 4d	3,291	15,745	57,524
R37	Limited cpe 2d	3,242	16,350	2,474
P37/WE2	T Type cpe 2d	NA	16,518	6,426
Electra (wb 110.8)				
X69	Limited sdn 4d	3,288	17,479	5,791
W69	Park Avenue sdn 4d	3,326	19,464	84,853
F69	T Type sdn 4d	3,333	20,229	1,869
Estate Wagons (wb 115.9)				
R35	LeSabre wgn 3S 5d	4,156	16,040	3,723
V35	Electra wgn 3S 5d	4,217	18,954	5,901
Riviera (wb 108.0)				
Z57	cpe 2d	3,364	21,615	6,560
Z57/Y50	T Type cpe	NA	23,380	2,065

1988 Engines	bore×stroke	bhp	availability
L4, 121.0	3.39×3.39	96	S-Skyhawk
L4, 138.0	3.62×3.35	150	O-Skylark (dohc)
L4, 151.0	4.00×3.00	98	S-Skylark, Century
V6, 173.0	3.50×2.99	125	O-Century, Regal
V6, 181.0	3.80×2.66	125	O-Skylark
V6, 231.0	3.80×3.40	50	S-LeS; O-Cnty
V6, 231.0	3.80×3.40	165	S-LeS T, Elec, Riv; O-LeS
V6T, 231.0	3.80×3.40	245	S-Regal Grand Nat'l
V8, 307.0	3.80×3.39	140	S-Estate Wgn

1989

Skyhawk (wb 101.2)		Wght	Price	Prod
S69	sdn 4d	2,469	9,285	—
S27	cpe 2d	2,420	9,285	—
S35	wgn 5d	2,551	10,230	—
Skylark (wb 103.4)				
C69	Custom sdn 4d	2,640	11,115	—
D69	Limited sdn 4d	NA	12,345	—
J27	Custom cpe 2d	2,583	11,115	—
M27	Limited cpe 2d	NA	12,345	—
Century (wb 104.9)				
H69	Custom sdn 4d	2,769	12,429	—
L69	Limited sdn 4d	NA	13,356	—
H37	Custom cpe 2d	2,725	12,199	—
H35	Custom wgn 5d	2,905	13,156	—
L35	Limited Estate wgn 5d	NA	13,956	—
Reatta (wb 98.5)				
C97	cpe 2d	3,394	26,700	—
Regal (wb 107.5)				
B57	Custom cpe 2d	3,144	14,214	—
D57	Limited cpe 2d	NA	14,739	—
LeSabre (wb 110.8)				
P37	cpe 2d	3,227	15,425	—
P69	Custom sdn 4d	3,267	15,330	—
R69	Limited sdn 4d	NA	16,730	—
R37	Limited cpe 2d	NA	16,630	—

1988 Regal Limited with Gran Touring package

1989 Century Custom four-door sedan

Electra (wb 110.8)		Wght	Price	Prod
X69	Limited sdn 4d	3,289	18,525	—
W69	Park Avenue sdn 4d	NA	20,460	—
U69	Park Avenue Ultra sdn 4d	NA	NA	—
F69	T Type sdn 4d	NA	21,325	—
Estate Wagons (wb 115.9)				
R35	LeSabre wgn 3S 5d	4,209	16,770	—
V35	Electra wgn 3S 5d	4,273	19,860	—
Riviera (wb 108.0)				
Z57	cpe 2d	3,436	22,540	—

1989 Engines	bore × stroke	bhp	availability
L4, 121.0	3.50 × 3.15	90	S-Skyhawk
L4, 138.0	3.62 × 3.35	150	O-Skylark (dohc)
L4, 151.0	4.00 × 3.00	98	S-Century
L4, 151.0	4.00 × 3.00	110	S-Skylark
V6, 173.0	3.50 × 2.99	130	S-Regal
V6, 191.0	3.50 × 3.31	140	S-late Regal
V6, 204.0	3.70 × 3.16	160	O-Skylark, Century
V6, 191.0	3.50 × 3.31	140	S-late Regal
V6, 231.0	3.80 × 3.40	165	S-LeS, Elec, Reatta, Riv
V8, 307.0	3.80 × 3.39	140	S-Estate Wgn

CADILLAC

1939

Series 61 (wb 126.0)		Wght	Price	Prod
6119	sdn 4d	3,770	1,680	3,955
6119	sdn 4d CKD	—	—	196
6119A	sunroof sdn 4d	NA	NA	43
6119F	Imperial sdn 5P	NA	NA	30
6127	cpe 2-4P	3,685	1,610	1,023
6129	conv sdn 5P	3,810	2,170	140
6167	conv cpe 2-4P	3,765	1,770	350
—	comm chassis (wb 156.0)	—	—	237
Series 60 Special (wb 127.0)				
6019S	sdn 4d	4,110	2,090	5,135
6019S	sdn 4d CKD	—	—	84
6019SA	sunroof sdn 4d	NA	NA	225
6019SAF	Imperial sunroof sdn 4d	NA	NA	55
—	chassis	—	—	7
Series 75 (wb 141.3)				
7519	sdn 5P	4,785	2,995	543
7519F	Imperial div sdn 5P	4,845	3,155	53
7523	sdn 7P	4,865	3,210	412
7523L	bus sdn 7P	4,865	3,105	33
7529	conv sdn 5P	5,030	3,945	36
7533	Imperial sdn 7P	5,025	3,360	638
7533	Imperial sdn 7P CKD	—	—	60
7533F	formal sdn 7P	5,025	3,995	44
7533L	Imperial bus sdn 7P	5,025	3,260	2
7539	Town sdn 5P	4,820	3,635	51
7553	town car 7P	5,095	5,115	13
7557	cpe 2P	4,595	3,280	36
7557B	cpe 5P	4,695	3,380	23
7559	formal sdn 5P	4,785	3,995	53
7567	conv cpe 2P	4,675	3,380	27
—	chassis	—	—	13
—	comm chassis (wb 161.0)	—	—	28
Series 90 (wb 141.3)				
9019	sdn 5P	5,190	5,140	13
9019F	Imperial sdn 5P	5,265	5,215	2
9023	sdn 7P	5,215	5,270	18
9029	conv sdn 5P	5,220	6,000	4
9033	Imperial sdn 7P	5,260	5,345	60
9033F	formal sdn 7P	5,260	6,055	8
9039	Town sdn 5P	5,230	5,695	2
9053	town car 7P	5,330	7,175	5
9057	cpe 2P	4,830	5,340	6
9057B	cpe 5P	4,930	5,440	5
9059	formal sdn 5P	5,190	6,055	4
9067	conv cpe 2P	4,970	5,440	7
—	chassis	—	—	2

1939 Engines	bore×stroke	bhp	availability
V8, 346.0	3.50×4.50	135	S-60,61
V8, 346.0	3.50×4.50	140	S-75
V16, 431.0	3.25×3.25	185	S-90

1940

Series 62 (wb 129.0)		Wght	Price	Prod
6219	sdn 4d	4,065	1,745	4,302
6227	cpe 2-4P	3,975	1,685	1,322
6229	conv sdn	4,265	2,195	75
6267	conv cpe	4,080	1,795	200
62	chassis	—	—	1
Series 60 Special (wb 127.0)				
6019F	division sdn	4,110	2,230	110
6019S	sdn 4d	4,070	2,090	4,472
6053LB	town car-leather back	4,365	3,820	6
6053MB	town car-metal back	4,365	3,465	9
Series 72 (wb 138.0)				
7219	sdn 4d	4,670	2,670	455
7219F	division sdn	4,710	2,740	100
7223	sdn 4d, 7P	4,700	2,785	305
7223L	livery sdn 7P	4,700	2,690	25
7233	imperial sdn 7P	4,740	2,915	292
7233F	formal sdn 7P	4,780	3,695	20
7233L	livery imp sdn 7P	4,740	2,825	36
7259	formal sdn	4,670	3,695	18
72	comm chassis (wb 165.0)	—	—	275
Series 75 (wb 141.3)				
7519	sdn 4d	4,900	2,995	155
7419F	division sdn	4,940	3,155	25
7523	sdn 4d, 7P	4,930	3,210	166
7529	conv sdn 7P, T/B	5,110	3,945	45
7533	imperial sdn 7P	4,970	3,360	338
7533F	formal sdn 7P	4,970	3,995	42
7539	town sdn	4,935	3,635	14
7553	town car 7P	5,195	5,115	14
7557	cpe 2-4P	4,785	3,280	15
7557B	cpe	4,810	3,380	12
7559	formal sdn, T/B	4,900	3,995	48
7567	conv cpe	4,915	3,380	30
75	chassis	—	—	3
75	comm chassis (wb 161.0)	—	—	52
Series 90 Sixteen (wb 141.3)				
9019	sdn 4d	5,190	5,140	4
9023	sdn 4d, 7P	5,215	5,270	4
9029	conv sdn, T/B	5,265	6,000	2
9033	imperial sdn 7P	5,260	5,420	20
9033F	formal sdn 7P, T/B	5,260	6,055	20
9039	town sdn, T/B	5,220	5,695	1
9053	town car 7P, T/B	5,330	7,175	2
9057	cpe 2-4P	4,830	5,340	2
9057B	cpe	4,930	5,440	1
9059	formal sdn, T/B	5,190	6,055	2
9067	conv cpe 2-4P	4,970	5,440	2
90	chassis	—	—	1

1940 Sixty-Special four-door sedan

1940 Engines	bore×stroke	bhp	availability
V8, 346.0	3.50×4.50	135	S-62, 60S
V8, 346.0	3.50×4.50	140	S-72, 75
V16, 431.0	3.25×3.25	185	S-Sixteen

1941

Series 61 (wb 126.0)		Wght	Price	Prod
6109	sdn 4d	4,065	1,445	10,925
6109D	del sdn 4d	4,085	1,535	3,495
6127	cpe	3,985	1,345	11,812
6127D	del cpe	4,005	1,435	3,015
61	chassis	—	—	3
Series 62 (wb 126.0)				
6219	sdn 4d	4,030	1,495	8,012
6219D	del sdn 4d	4,050	1,585	7,850
6227	cpe 2-4P	3,950	1,420	1,985
6227D	del cpe 2-4P	3,970	1,510	1,900
6229D	conv sdn	4,230	1,965	400
6267D	conv cpe	4,055	1,645	3,100
62	chassis	—	—	4
62	comm chassis (wb 163.0)	—	—	1,475
Series 63 (wb 126.0)				
6319	sdn 4d	4,140	1,695	5,050
Series 60 Special (wb 126.0)				
6019	sdn 4d	4,230	2,195	3,878
6019F	division sdn	4,290	2,345	220
6053LB	town car	4,485	—	1
60	chassis	—	—	1
Series 67 (wb 139.0)				
6719	sdn 4d	4,555	2,595	315
6719F	division sdn	4,615	2,745	95
6723	sdn 4d, 7P	4,630	2,735	280
6733	imperial sdn 7P	4,705	2,890	210

Series 75 (wb 136.0)		Wght	Price	Prod
7519	sdn 4d	4,750	2,995	422
7519F	division sdn	4,810	3,150	132
7523	sdn 4d, 7P	4,800	3,140	405
7523L	business sdn 9P	4,750	2,895	54
7533	imperial sdn 7P	4,860	3,295	757
7533F	formal sdn 7P	4,915	4,045	98
7533L	business imperial sdn 7P	4,810	3,050	6
7559	formal sdn	4,900	3,920	75
75	chassis	—	—	5
75	comm chassis (wb 163.0)	—	—	150

1941 Engine	bore×stroke	bhp	availability
V8, 346.0	3.50×4.50	150	S-all

1942

Series 61 (wb 126.0)		Wght	Price	Prod
6107	club cpe	4,035	1,450	2,482
6109	sdn 4d	4,115	1,530	3,218

1941 Sixty-Special four-door sedan

1942 Series 61 Sedanet

Series 62 (wb 129.0)		Wght	Price	Prod
6207	club cpe	4,105	1,545	515
6207D	club cpe	4,125	1,630	530
6267D	conv cpe	4,365	1,880	308
6269	sdn 4d	4,185	1,630	1,780
6269D	sdn 4d	4,205	1,705	1,827
Series 63 (wb 126.0)				
6319	sdn 4d	4,115	1,745	1,750
Series 60 Special (wb 133.0)				
6069	sdn 4d	4,310	2,265	1,684
6069F	division sdn	4,365	2,415	190
60	chassis	—	—	1
Series 67 (wb 139.0)				
6719	sdn 4d	4,605	2,700	200
6719F	division sdn	4,665	2,845	50
6723	sdn 7P	4,680	2,845	260
6733	imperial sdn 7P	4,755	2,995	190
Series 75 (wb 136.0)				
7519	sdn 4d	4,750	3,080	205
7519F	division sdn	4,810	3,230	65
7523	sdn 4d, 7P	4,800	3,230	225
7523L	business sdn 9P	4,750	2,935	29
7533	imperial sdn 7P	4,860	3,375	430
7533F	formal sdn 7P	4,915	4,215	80
7533L	business imperial sdn 9P	4,860	3,080	6
7559	formal sdn	4,900	4,060	60
75	chassis	—	—	1
75	comm chassis (wb 163.0)	—	—	425

1942 Engine	bore×stroke	bhp	availability
V8, 346.0	3.50×4.50	150	S-all

1946

Series 61 (wb 126.0)		Wght	Price	Prod
6107	club cpe	4,145	2,052	800
6109	sdn 4d	4,225	2,176	2,200
61	chassis	—	—	1
Series 62 (wb 129.0)				
6207	club cpe	4,215	2,284	2,323
6267D	conv cpe	4,475	2,556	1,342
6269	sdn 4d	4,295	2,359	14,900
62	chassis	—	—	1
Series 60 Special (wb 133.0)				
6069	sdn 4d	4,420	3,095	5,700
Series 75 (wb 136.0)				
7519	sdn 4d	4,860	4,298	150
7523	sdn 4d, 7P	4,905	4,475	225
7523L	business sdn 9P	4,920	4,153	22
7533	imperial sdn 7P	4,925	4,669	221
7533L	business imperial sdn 9P	4,925	4,346	17
75	comm chassis (wb 163.0)	—	—	1,292

1946 Engine	bore×stroke	bhp	availability
V8, 346.0	3.50×4.50	150	S-all

1947

Series 61 (wb 126.0)		Wght	Price	Prod
6107	club cpe	4,080	2,200	3,395
6109	sdn 4d	4,165	2,324	5,160
Series 62 (wb 129.0)				
6207	club cpe	4,145	2,446	7,245
6267	conv cpe	4,455	2,902	6,755
6269	sdn 4d	4,235	2,523	25,834
62	chassis	—	—	1
Series 60 Special (wb 133.0)				
6069	sdn 4d	4,370	3,195	8,500
Series 75 (wb 136.0)				
7519	sdn 4d	4,875	4,471	300

		Wght	Price	Prod
7523	sdn 4d, 7P	4,895	4,686	890
7523L	business sdn 9P	4,790	4,368	135
7533	imperial sdn 7P	4,930	4,887	1,005
7533L	business imperial sdn 9P	4,800	4,560	80
75	chassis	—	—	3
75	comm & bus chassis (wb 163.0)	—	—	2,623

1947 Engine	bore×stroke	bhp	availability
V8, 346.0	3.50×4.50	150	S-all

1948

Series 61 (wb 126.0)		Wght	Price	Prod
6107	club cpe	4,068	2,728	3,521
6169	sdn 4d	4,150	2,833	5,081
61	chassis	—	—	1
Series 62 (wb 126.0)				
6207	club cpe	4,125	2,912	4,764
6267	conv cpe	4,449	3,442	5,450
6259	sdn 4d	4,179	2,996	23,997
62	chassis	—	—	2
Series 60 Special (wb 133.0)				
6069	sdn 4d	4,356	3,820	6,561
Series 75 (wb 136.0)				
7519	sdn 4d	4,875	4,779	225
7523	sdn 4d, 7P	4,878	4,999	499
7523L	business sdn 9P	4,780	4,679	90
7533	imperial sdn 7P	4,959	5,199	382
7533L	bus imperial sdn 9P	—	—	64
75	chassis	—	—	2
75	comm chassis (wb 163.0)	—	—	2,067

1948 Engine	bore×stroke	bhp	availability
V8, 346.0	3.50×4.50	150	S-all

1949

Series 61 (wb 126.0)		Wght	Price	Prod
6107	club cpe	3,838	2,788	6,409
6169	sdn 4d	3,915	2,893	15,738
61	chassis	—	—	1
Series 62 (wb 126.0)				
6207	club cpe	3,862	2,966	7,515
6237	Coupe de Ville htp cpe	4,033	3,497	2,150
6267	conv cpe	4,218	3,442	8,000
6269	sdn 4d	3,956	3,050	37,977
62	chassis	—	—	1
Series 60 Special (wb 133.0)				
6037	Coupe de Ville htp cpe	4,200	exp	1
6069	sdn 4d	4,129	3,828	11,399
Series 75 (wb 136.0)				
7519	sdn 4d	4,579	4,750	220
7523	sdn 4d, 7P	4,626	4,970	595
7523L	business sdn 9P	4,522	4,650	35
7533	imperial sdn 7P	4,648	5,170	626
7533L	business imperial sdn 9P	4,573	4,839	25
75	chassis	—	—	1
86	comm chassis (wb 163.0)	—	—	1,861

1949 Engine	bore×stroke	bhp	availability
V8, 331.0	3.81×3.63	160	S-all

1950

Series 61 (wb 122.0)		Wght	Price	Prod
6137	club cpe	3,829	2,761	11,839
6169	sdn 4d	3,822	2,866	14,931
61	chassis	—	—	2
Series 62 (wb 126.0)				
6219	sdn 4d	4,012	3,234	41,890
6237	club cpe	3,993	3,150	6,434
6237D	Coupe de Ville htp cpe	4,074	3,523	4,507
6267	conv cpe	4,316	3,654	6,986
62	chassis	—	—	1
Series 60 Special (wb 130.0)				
6019	sdn 4d	4,136	3,797	13,755
Series 75 (wb 146.8)				
7523	sdn 4d, 7P	4,555	4,770	716
7523L	business sdn 9P	4,235	exp	1
7533	imperial sdn 7P	4,586	4,959	743
86	comm chassis (wb 157.0)	—	—	2,052

1950 Engine	bore×stroke	bhp	availability
V8, 331.0	3.81×3.63	160	S-all

1951

Series 61 (wb 122.0)		Wght	Price	Prod
6137	club cpe	3,829	2,810	2,400
6169	sdn 4d	3,827	2,917	2,300

1948 Series 60 Special four-door sedan

1949 Coupe deVille hardtop coupe

1950 Coupe deVille hardtop coupe

1953 Eldorado convertible coupe

1954 Eldorado convertible coupe

1955 Eldorado convertible coupe

Series 62 (wb 126.0)		Wght	Price	Prod
6219	sdn 4d	4,062	3,528	55,352
6237	cpe	4,081	3,436	10,132
6237D	Coupe De Ville htp cpe	4,156	3,843	10,241
6267	conv cpe	4,377	3,987	6,117
62-126	chassis	—	—	2
Series 60 Special (wb 130.0)				
6019	sdn 4d	4,234	4,142	18,631
Series 75 (wb 146.8)				
7523	sdn 4d, 8P	4,621	5,200	1,090
7523L	business sdn 9P	4,300	exp	30
7533	imperial sdn 8P	4,652	5,405	1,085
86	comm chassis (wb 157.0)	—	—	2,960

1951 Engine	bore×stroke	bhp	availability
V8, 331.0	3.81×3.63	160	S-all

1952

Series 62 (wb 126.0)		Wght	Price	Prod
6219	sdn 4d	4,140	3,684	42,625
6237	cpe	4,173	3,587	10,065
6237D	Coupe de Ville htp cpe	4,203	4,013	11,165
6267	conv cpe	4,416	4,163	6,400
Series 60 Special (wb 130.0)				
6019	sdn 4d	4,255	4,323	16,110
Series 75 (wb 146.8)				
7523	sdn 4d, 8P	4,698	5,428	1,400
7533	imperial sdn 8P	4,733	5,643	800
8680S	comm chassis (wb 157.0)	—	—	1,694

1952 Engine	bore×stroke	bhp	availability
V8, 331.0	3.81×3.63	190	S-all

1953

Series 62 (wb 126.0)		Wght	Price	Prod
6219	sdn 4d	4,225	3,666	47,640
6237	cpe	4,320	3,571	14,353
6237D	Coupe de Ville htp cpe	4,320	3,995	14,550
6267	conv cpe	4,500	4,144	8,367
6267S	Eldorado conv cpe	4,800	7,750	532
62	chassis	—	—	4
Series 60 Special (wb 130.0)				
6019	sdn 4d	4,415	4,305	20,000
Series 75 (wb 146.8)				
7523	sdn 4d, 8P	4,830	5,408	1,435
7533	imperial sdn 8P	4,850	5,621	765
8680S	comm chassis (wb 157.0)	—	—	2,005

1953 Engine	bore×stroke	bhp	availability
V8, 331.0	3.81×3.63	210	S-all

1954

Series 62 (wb 129.0)		Wght	Price	Prod
6219	sdn 4d	4,370	3,933	34,252
6219S	DeVille htp sdn	—	proto	1
6237	htp cpe	4,365	3,838	17,460
6237D	Coupe de Ville htp cpe	4,405	4,261	17,170
6267	conv cpe	4,610	4,404	6,310
6267S	Eldorado conv cpe	4,815	5,738	2,150
62	chassis	—	—	1

Series 60 Special (wb 133.0)		Wght	Price	Prod
6019	sdn 4d	4,500	4,863	16,200
Series 75 (wb 149.8)				
7523	sdn 4d, 8P	5,055	5,875	889
7533	imperial sdn 8P	5,105	6,090	611
8680S	comm chassis (wb 158.0)	—	—	1,635

1954 Engine	bore×stroke	bhp	availability
V8, 331.0	3.81×3.63	230	S-all

1955

Series 62 (wb 129.0)		Wght	Price	Prod
6219	sdn 4d	4,370	3,977	45,300
6237	htp cpe	4,358	3,882	27,879
6237D	Coupe de Ville htp cpe	4,424	4,305	33,300
6267	conv cpe	4,627	4,448	8,150
6267S	Eldorado conv cpe	4,809	6,286	3,950
62	chassis	—	—	7
Series 60 Special (wb 133.0)		**Wght**	**Price**	**Prod**
6019	sdn 4d	4,540	4,728	18,300
Series 75 (wb 149.8)				
7523	sdn 4d, 8P	5,020	6,187	1,075
7533	limo 8P	5,113	6,402	841
8680S	comm chassis (wb 158.0)	—	—	1,975

1955 Engines	bore×stroke	bhp	availability
V8, 331.0	3.81×3.63	250	S-62, 60S, 75
V8, 331.0	3.81×3.63	270	S-Eldorado

1956

Series 62 (wb 129.0)		Wght	Price	Prod
6219	sdn 4d	4,430	4,296	26,666
6237	htp cpe	4,420	4,201	26,649
6237D	Coupe de Ville htp cpe	4,445	4,624	24,086
6237S	Eldorado Seville htp cpe	4,665	6,556	3,900
6239D	Sedan de Ville htp cpe	4,550	4,753	41,732
6267	conv cpe	4,645	4,766	8,300
6267S	Eldorado Biarritz conv cpe	4,880	6,556	2,150
62	chassis	—	—	19

Series 60 Special (wb 133.0)		Wght	Price	Prod
6019	sdn 4d	4,610	5,047	17,000
Series 75 (wb 149.8)				
7523	sdn 4d, 8P	5,050	6,613	1,095
7533	limo 8P	5,130	6,828	955
8680S	comm chassis (wb 158.0)	—	—	2,025

1956 Engines	bore×stroke	bhp	availability
V8, 365.0	4.00×3.63	285	S-62, 60S, 75
V8, 365.0	4.00×3.63	305	S-Eldorado

1957

Series 62 (wb 129.5)		Wght	Price	Prod
6237	htp cpe	4,565	4,677	25,120
6237D	Coupe de Ville htp cpe	4,620	5,116	23,813
6237S	Eldorado Seville htp cpe	4,810	7,286	2,100
6239	htp sdn	4,595	4,781	32,342
6239D	Sedan de Ville htp sdn	4,655	5,256	23,808
6239S	Eldorado Seville htp sdn	4,810	7,286	4
6267	conv cpe	4,730	5,293	9,000
6267S	Eldorado Biarritz conv cpe	4,930	7,286	1,800
62	chassis & export sdn	—	—	385
Series 60 Special (wb 133.0)				
6039	htp sdn	4,735	5,614	24,000
Series 70 Eldorado Brougham (wb 129.0)				
7059	htp sdn	5,315	13,074	400
Series 75 (wb 149.8)				
7523	sdn 4d, 8P	5,340	7,440	1,010
7533	limo 8P	5,390	7,678	890
8680S	comm chassis (wb 156.0)	—	—	2,169

1957 Engines	bore×stroke	bhp	availability
V8, 365.0	4.00×3.63	300	S-62, 60S, 70
V8, 365.0	4.00×3.63	325	S-Eldorado

1958

Series 62 (wb 129.5)		Wght	Price	Prod
6237	htp cpe	4,630	4,784	18,736

1957 Series 62 hardtop sedan

		Wght	Price	Prod
6237D	Coupe de Ville htp cpe	4,705	5,251	18,414
6237S	Eldorado Seville htp cpe	4,910	7,500	855
6239	htp sdn	4,675	4,891	13,335
6239E	htp sdn (ext. deck)	4,770	5,079	20,952
6239	Sedan de Ville htp sdn	4,855	5,497	23,989
6267	conv cpe	4,856	5,454	7,825
6267S	Eldorado Biarritz conv cpe	5,070	7,500	815
62	chassis & exp sdn	—	—	206
Series 60 Special (wb 133.0)				
6039	htp sdn	4,930	6,232	12,900
Series 70 Eldorado Brougham (wb 126.0)				
7059	htp sdn	5,315	13,074	304
Series 75 (wb 149.8)				
7523	sdn 4d, 9P	5,360	8,460	802
7533	limo 9P	5,425	8,675	730
8680S	comm chassis (wb 156.0)	—	—	1,915

1958 Engines	bore×stroke	bhp	availability
V8, 365.0	4.00 × 3.63	310	S-all exc Eldorado
V8, 365.0	4.00 × 3.63	365	S-Eldo; O-all

1959

Series 62 (wb 130.0)		Wght	Price	Prod
6229	htp sdn 6W	4,770	5,080	23,461
6237	htp cpe	4,690	4,892	21,947
6239	htp sdn 9W	4,835	5,080	14,138
6267	conv cpe	4,855	5,455	11,130
62	export sdn	—	—	60
De Ville (wb 130.0)				
6329	htp sdn 6W	4,850	5,498	19,158
6337	htp cpe	4,720	5,252	21,924
6339	htp sdn 4W	4,825	5,498	12,308
Eldorado (wb 130.0)				
6437	Seville htp cpe	—	7,401	975
6467	Biarritz conv cpe	—	7,401	1,320
6929	Brougham htp sdn	—	13,075	99
Series 60 Special (wb 130.0)				
6039	htp sdn	4,890	6,233	12,250
Series 75 (wb 149.8)				
6723	sdn 4d, 9P	5,490	9,533	710
6733	limo 9P	5,570	9,748	690
6890	comm chassis (wb 156.0)	—	—	2,102

1959 Engines	bore×stroke	bhp	availability
V8, 390.0	4.00×3.88	325	S-62, DeVille, 60S, 75
V8, 390.0	4.00×3.88	345	S-Eldorado

1960

Series 62 (wb 130.0)		Wght	Price	Prod
6229	htp sdn 6W	4,805	5,080	26,824
6237	htp cpe	4,670	4,892	19,978
6239	htp sdn 4W	4,775	5,080	9,984
6267	conv cpe	4,850	5,455	14,000
62	chassis & export sdn	—	—	38
DeVille (wb 130.0)				
6329	htp sdn 6W	4,835	5,498	22,579
6337	htp cpe	4,705	5,252	21,585
6339	htp sdn 4W	4,815	5,498	9,225
Eldorado (wb 130.0)				
6437	Seville htp cpe	—	7,401	1,075
6467	Biarritz conv cpe	—	7,401	1,285
6929	Brougham htp sdn	—	13,075	101
Series 60 Special (wb 130.0)				
6039	htp sdn	4,880	6,233	11,800
Series 75 (wb 149.8)				
6723	sdn 4d, 9P	5,475	9,533	718
6733	limo 9P	5,560	9,748	832
6890	comm chassis (wb 156.0)	—	—	2,160

1960 Engines	bore×stroke	bhp	availability
V8, 390.0	4.00×3.88	325	S-62, DeVille, 60S, 75
V8, 390.0	4.00×3.88	345	S-Eldorado

1961

Series 62 (wb 129.5)		Wght	Price	Prod
6229	htp sdn 6W	4,680	5,080	26,216
6237	htp cpe	4,560	4,892	16,005
6239	htp sdn 4W	4,660	5,080	4,700
6267	conv	4,720	5,455	15,500
62	chassis	—	—	5
DeVille (wb 129.5)				
6239	htp sdn 6W	4,710	5,498	26,415
6337	htp cpe	4,595	5,252	20,156
6339	htp sdn 4W	4,715	5,498	4,847
6399	Town Sedan htp 6W	—	5,498	3,756
Eldorado (wb 129.5)				
6367	Biarritz conv cpe	—	6,477	1,450
Series 60 Special (wb 129.5)				
6039	htp sdn	4,770	6,233	15,500
Series 75 (wb 149.8)				
6723	sdn 4d, 9P	5,390	9,533	699
6733	limo 9P	5,420	9,748	926
6890	comm chassis (wb 156.0)	—	—	2,204

1961 Engine	bore×stroke	bhp	availability
V8, 390.0	4.00×3.88	325	S-all

1962

Series 62 (wb 129.5)		Wght	Price	Prod
6229	htp sdn 6W	4,640	5,213	16,730
6239	htp sdn 4W	4,645	5,213	17,314
6247	htp cpe	4,530	5,025	16,833
6267	conv cpe	4,630	5,588	16,800
6289	Town Sedan htp sdn	4,590	5,213	2,600
DeVille (wb 129.5)				
6329	htp sdn 6W	4,660	5,631	16,230

1959 Series 62 six-window hardtop sedan

1959 Series 62 convertible

1959 Eldorado Biarritz convertible

		Wght	Price	Prod
6339	htp sdn 4W	4,675	5,631	27,378
6347	htp cpe	4,595	5,385	25,675
6389	Park Avenue htp sdn	4,655	5,631	2,600
Eldorado (wb 129.5)				
6367	Biarritz conv cpe	4,620	6,610	1,450
Series 60 Special (wb 129.5)				
6039	htp sdn 6W	4,710	6,366	13,350
Series 75 (wb 149.8)				
6723	sdn 4d, 9P	5,325	9,722	696
6733	limo 9P	5,390	9,937	904
6890	comm chassis (wb 156.0)	—	—	2,280

1962 Engine	bore×stroke	bhp	availability
V8, 390.0	4.00×3.88	325	S-all

1963

Series 62 (wb 129.5)		Wght	Price	Prod
6229	htp sdn 6W	4,610	5,214	12,929
6239	htp sdn 4W	4,595	5,214	16,980
6257	htp cpe	4,505	5,026	16,786
6267	conv cpe	4,545	5,590	17,600
62	chassis	—	—	3
DeVille (wb 129.5)				
6329	htp sdn 6W	4,650	5,633	15,146
6339	htp sdn 4W	4,605	5,633	30,579
6357	htp cpe	4,520	5,386	31,749
6389	Park Avenue htp sdn	4,590	5,633	1,575
Eldorado (wb 129.5)				
6367	Biarritz conv cpe	4,640	6,608	1,825
Series 60 Special (wb 129.5)				
6039	htp sdn	4,690	6,366	14,000
Series 75 (wb 149.8)				
6723	sdn 4d, 9P	5,240	9,724	680
6733	limo 9P	5,300	9,939	795
6890	comm chassis (wb 156.0)	—	—	2,527

1963 Engine	bore×stroke	bhp	availability
V8, 390.0	4.00×3.88	325	S-all

1962 Series 62 convertible coupe

1964

Series 62 (wb 129.5)		Wght	Price	Prod
6229	htp sdn 6W	4,575	5,236	9,243
6239	htp sdn 4W	4,550	5,236	13,670
6257	htp cpe	4,475	5,048	12,166
6267	conv cpe	4,545	5,612	17,900
DeVille (wb 129.5)				
6329	htp sdn 6W	4,600	5,655	14,627
6339	htp cpe 4W	4,575	5,655	39,674
6357	htp cpe	4,495	5,408	38,195
Eldorado (wb 129.5)				
6367	Biarritz conv cpe	4,605	6,630	1,870
Series 60 Special (wb 129.5)				
6039	htp sdn	4,680	6,388	14,550
Series 75 (wb 149.8)				
6723	sdn 4d, 9P	5,215	9,746	617
6733	limo 9P	5,300	9,960	808
6890	comm chassis (wb 156.0)	—	—	2,639

1964 Engine	bore×stroke	bhp	availability
V8, 429.0	4.13×4.00	340	S-all

1965

Calais (wb 129.5)		Wght	Price	Prod
68239	htp sdn	4,500	5,247	13,975
68257	htp cpe	4,435	5,059	12,515
68269	sdn 4d	4,490	5,247	7,721
DeVille (wb 129.5)				
68339	htp sdn	4,560	5,666	45,535
68357	htp cpe	4,480	5,419	43,345
68367	conv cpe	4,690	5,639	19,200
68369	sdn 4d	4,555	5,666	15,000
Eldorado (wb 129.5)				
68467	conv cpe	4,660	6,738	2,125

Sixty Special (wb 133.0)		Wght	Price	Prod
68069	sdn 4d	4,670	6,479	18,100

Seventy-Five (wb 149.8)		Wght	Price	Prod
69723	sdn 4d, 9P	5,190	9,746	455
69733	limo 9P	5,260	9,960	795
69890	comm chassis (wb 156.0)	—	—	2,669

1965 Engine	bore×stroke	bhp	availability
V8, 429.0	4.13×4.00	340	S-all

1966

Calais (wb 129.5)		Wght	Price	Prod
68239	htp sdn	4,465	5,171	13,025
68257	htp cpe	4,390	4,986	11,080
68269	sdn 4d	4,460	5,171	4,575
DeVille (wb 129.5)				
68339	htp sdn	4,515	5,581	60,550
68357	htp cpe	4,460	5,339	50,580
68367	conv cpe	4,445	5,555	19,200
68369	sdn 4d	4,535	5,581	11,860
Eldorado (wb 129.5)				
68467	conv cpe	4,500	6,631	2,250
Sixty Special (wb 133.0)				
68069	sdn 4d	4,615	6,378	5,455
68169	Fleetwood Brougham sdn 4d	4,665	6,695	13,630
Seventy-Five (wb 149.8)				
69723	sdn 4d, 9P	5,320	10,312	980
69733	limo 9P	5,435	10,521	1,037
69890	comm chassis (wb 156.0)	—	—	2,463

1966 Engine	bore×stroke	bhp	availability
V8, 429.0	4.13×4.00	340	S-all

1967

Calais (wb 129.5)		Wght	Price	Prod
68247	htp cpe	4,447	5,040	9,085
68249	htp sdn	4,495	5,215	9,880
68269	sdn 4d	4,499	5,215	2,865
DeVille (wb 129.5)				
68347	htp cpe	4,486	5,392	52,905
68349	htp sdn	4,532	5,625	59,902
68367	conv cpe	4,479	5,608	18,202
68369	sdn 4d	4,534	5,625	8,800
Eldorado (wb 120.0)				
69347	htp cpe	4,500	6,277	17,930
Sixty Special (wb 133.0)				
68069	sdn 4d	4,678	6,423	3,550
68169	Fleetwood Brougham sdn 4d	4,715	6,739	12,750
Seventy-Five (wb 149.8)				
69723	sdn 4d, 9P	5,344	10,360	835
69733	limo 9P	5,436	10,571	965
68490	comm chassis (wb 156.0)	—	—	2,333

1967 Engine	bore×stroke	bhp	availability
V8, 429.0	4.13×4.00	340	S-all

1968

Calais (wb 129.5)		Wght	Price	Prod
68247	htp cpe	4,570	5,315	8,165
68249	htp sdn	4,640	5,491	10,025
DeVille (wb 129.5)				
68347	htp cpe	4,595	5,552	63,935
68349	htp sdn	4,675	5,785	72,662
68367	conv cpe	4,600	5,736	18,025
68369	sdn 4d	4,680	5,785	9,850
Eldorado (wb 120.0)				
69347	htp cpe	4,580	6,605	24,528
Sixty Special (wb 133.0)				
68069	sdn 4d	4,795	6,583	3,300
68169	Fleetwood Brougham sdn 4d	4,805	6,899	15,300
Seventy-Five (wb 149.8)				
69723	sdn 4d, 9P	5,300	10,629	805
69733	limo 9P	5,385	10,768	995
69890	comm chassis (wb 156.0)	—	—	2,413

1968 Engine	bore×stroke	bhp	availability
V8, 472.0	4.30×4.06	375	S-all

1969

Calais (wb 129.5)		Wght	Price	Prod
68247	htp cpe	4,555	5,484	5,600
68349	htp sdn	4,630	5,660	6,825
DeVille (wb 129.5)				
68347	htp cpe	4,595	5,721	65,755
68349	htp sdn	4,660	5,954	72,958
68367	conv cpe	4,590	5,905	16,445
68369	sdn 4d	4,640	5,954	7,890
Eldorado (wb 120.0)				
69347	htp cpe	4,550	6,711	23,333
Sixty Special (wb 133.0)				
68069	sdn 4d	4,765	6,779	2,545
68169	Fleetwood Brougham sdn 4d	4,770	7,110	17,300

1964 Series 62 convertible coupe

1966 Eldorado convertible coupe

Seventy-Five (wb 149.8)		Wght	Price	Prod
69723	sdn 4d, 9P	5,430	10,841	880
69733	limo 9P	5,555	10,979	1,156
69890	comm chassis (wb 156.0)	—	—	2,550

1969 Engine	bore×stroke	bhp	availability
V8, 472.0	4.30×4.06	375	S-all

1970

Calais (wb 129.5)		Wght	Price	Prod
68247	htp cpe	4,620	5,637	4,724
68249	htp sdn	4,680	5,813	5,187
DeVille (wb 129.5)				
68347	htp cpe	4,650	5,884	76,043
68349	htp sdn	4,725	6,118	83,274
68367	conv cpe	4,660	6,068	15,172
68369	sdn 4d	4,690	6,118	7,230
Eldorado (wb 120.0)				
69347	htp cpe	4,630	6,903	28,842
Sixty Special (wb 133.0)				
68089	sdn 4d	4,830	6,953	1,738
68189	Fleetwood Brougham sdn 4d	4,835	7,284	16,913
Seventy-Five (wb 149.8)				
69723	sdn 4d, 9P	5,530	11,039	876
69733	limo 9P	5,630	11,178	1,240
69890	comm chassis (wb 156.0)	—	—	2,506

1970 Engines	bore×stroke	bhp	availability
V8, 472.0	4.30×4.06	375	S-all exc Eldorado
V8, 500.0	4.30×4.30	400	S-Eldorado

1971

Calais (wb 130.0)		Wght	Price	Prod
68247	htp cpe	4,635	5,899	3,360
68249	htp sdn	4,710	6,075	3,569
DeVille (wb 130.0)				
68347	htp cpe	4,685	6,264	66,081
68349	htp sdn	4,730	6,498	69,345
Eldorado (wb 120.0)				
69346	htp cpe	4,675	7,383	20,568
69367	conv	4,730	7,751	6,800
Sixty Special Brougham (wb 133.0)				
68169	Fleetwood sdn 4d	4,815	7,763	15,200
Seventy-Five (wb 151.5)				
69723	sdn 4d	5,510	11,869	752
69733	limo 9P	5,570	12,008	848
69890	comm chassis (wb 157.5)	—	—	2,014

1971 Engines	bore×stroke	bhp	availability
V8, 472.0	4.30×4.06	345	S-all exc Eldorado
V8, 500.0	4.30×4.30	365	S-Eldorado

1972

Calais (wb 130.0)		Wght	Price	Prod
68247	htp cpe	4,642	5,771	3,900
68249	htp sdn	4,698	5,938	3,875
DeVille (wb 130.0)				
68347	htp cpe	4,682	6,168	95,280
68349	htp sdn	4,762	6,390	99,531
Eldorado (wb 126.3)				
69347	htp cpe	4,682	7,230	32,099

1971 Fleetwood Sixty Special Brougham four-door sedan

		Wght	Price	Prod
69367	conv	4,772	7,546	7,975
Sixty Special Brougham (wb 133.0)				
68169	Fleetwood sdn 4d	4,858	7,637	20,750
Seventy-Five (wb 151.5)				
69723	sdn 4d	5,515	11,748	955
69733	limo 9P	5,637	11,880	960
69890	comm chassis (wb 157.5)	—	—	2,462

1972 Engines	bore×stroke	bhp	availability
V8, 472.0	4.30×4.06	220	S-all exc Eldorado
V8, 500.0	4.30×4.30	235	S-Eldorado

1973

Calais (wb 130.0)		Wght	Price	Prod
68247	htp cpe	4,900	5,866	4,275
68249	htp sdn	4,953	6,038	3,798
DeVille (wb 130.0)				
68347	htp cpe	4,925	6,268	112,849
68349	htp sdn	4,985	6,500	103,394
Eldorado (wb 126.3)				
69347	htp cpe	4,880	7,360	42,136
69367	conv	4,966	7,681	9,315
Sixty Special Brougham (wb 133.0)				
68169	Fleetwood sdn 4d	5,102	7,765	24,800
Seventy-Five (wb 151.5)				
69723	sdn 4d	5,620	11,948	1,043
69733	limo 9P	5,742	12,080	1,017
69890	comm chassis (wb 157.5)	—	—	2,212

1973 Engines	bore×stroke	bhp	availability
V8, 472.0	4.30×4.06	220	S-all exc Eldorado
V8, 500.0	4.30×4.30	235	S-Eldorado

1974

Calais (wb 130.0)		Wght	Price	Prod
68247	cpe	4,900	7,371	4,559
68249	sdn 4d	4,979	7,545	2,324
DeVille (wb 130.0)				
68347	cpe	4,924	7,867	112,201
68349	sdn 4d	5,032	8,100	60,419
Eldorado (wb 126.3)				
69347	htp cpe	4,960	9,110	32,812
69367	conv	5,019	9,437	7,600
Sixty Special Brougham (wb 133.0)				
68169	Fleetwood sdn 4d	5,143	9,537	18,250

Seventy-Five (wb 151.5)		Wght	Price	Prod
69723	sdn 4d	5,719	13,120	895
69733	limo 9P	5,883	13,254	1,005
69890	comm chassis (wb 157.5)	—	—	2,265

1974 Engines	bore×stroke	bhp	availability
V8, 472.0	4.30×4.06	205	S-all exc Eldorado
V8, 500.0	4.30×4.30	210	S-Eldorado

1975

Seville (wb 114.3)		Wght	Price	Prod
S69	sdn 4d	4,232	12,479	16,355
Calais (wb 130.0)				
68247	cpe	5,003	8,184	5,800
68249	sdn 4d	5,087	8,377	2,500
DeVille (wb 130.0)				
68347	cpe	5,049	8,600	110,218
68349	sdn 4d	5,146	8,801	63,352
Eldorado (wb 126.3)				
69347	cpe	5,108	9,935	35,802
69367	conv	5,167	10,354	8,950
Sixty Special Brougham (wb 133.0)				
68169	Fleetwood sdn 4d	5,242	10,414	18,755
Seventy-Five (wb 151.5)				
69723	sdn 4d	5,720	14,218	876
69733	limo 9P	5,862	14,557	795
69890	comm chassis (wb 157.5)	—	—	1,329

1975 Engines	bore×stroke	bhp	availability
V8, 350.0	4.06×3.39	180	S-Seville
V8, 500.0	4.30×4.30	190	S-all exc Seville

1976

Seville (wb 114.3)		Wght	Price	Prod
S69	sdn 4d	4,232	12,479	43,772
Calais (wb 130.0)				
68247	cpe	4,989	8,629	4,500
68249	sdn 4d	5,083	8,825	1,700
DeVille (wb 130.0)				
68347	cpe	5,025	9,067	114,482
68349	sdn 4d	5,127	9,265	67,677
Eldorado (wb 126.3)				
69347	cpe	5,085	10,586	35,184
69367	conv	5,153	11,049	14,000
Sixty Special Brougham (wb 133.0)				
68169	Fleetwood sdn 4d	5,213	10,935	24,500
Seventy-Five (wb 151.5)				
69723	sdn 4d	5,746	14,889	981
69733	limo 9P	5,889	15,239	834
69890	comm chassis (wb 157.5)	—	—	1,509

1976 Engines	bore×stroke	bhp	availability
V8, 350.0	4.06×3.39	180	S-Seville
V8, 500.0	4.30×4.30	190	S-all exc Seville
V8, 500.0	4.30×4.30	215	O-all exc Seville

1977

Seville (wb 114.3)		Wght	Price	Prod
S69	sdn 4d	4,192	13,359	45,060
De Ville (wb 121.5)				
68347	cpe	4,186	9,810	138,750
68349	sdn 4d	4,222	10,020	95,421
Eldorado (wb 126.3)				
69347	cpe	4,955	11,187	47,344
Fleetwood Brougham (wb 121.5)				
68169	sdn 4d	4,340	11,546	28,000
Fleetwood limousine (wb 144.5)				
69723	sdn 4d	4,738	18,349	1,582
69773	formal sdn 4d	4,806	19,014	1,032
69890	comm chassis (wb 157.5)	—	—	1,299

1977 Engines	bore×stroke	bhp	availability
V8, 350.0	4.06×3.39	180	S-Seville
V8, 425.0	4.08×4.06	180	S-all exc Seville
V8, 425.0	4.08×4.06	195	O-Brgm,DeVille,Eldo

1978

Seville (wb 114.3)		Wght	Price	Prod
S69	sdn 4d	4,179	14,710	56,985
DeVille (wb 121.5)				
68347	cpe	4,163	10,584	117,750

1973 Coupe deVille

1977 Fleetwood Brougham D'Elegance four-door sedan

		Wght	Price	Prod
68349	sdn 4d	4,236	10,924	88,951
Eldorado (wb 126.3)				
69347	cpe	4,906	12,401	46,816
Fleetwood Brougham (wb 121.5)				
68169	sdn 4d	4,314	12,842	36,800
Fleetwood limousine (wb 144.5)				
69723	sdn 4d	4,772	20,007	848
69773	formal sdn 4d	4,858	10,742	682
69890	comm chassis (wb 157.5)	—	—	852

1978 Engines	bore×stroke	bhp	availability
V8, 350.0	4.06×3.39	170	S-Seville
V8, 350.0 Dsl	4.06×3.39	120	0-Seville
V8, 425.0	4.08×4.06	180	S-all exc Seville
V8, 425.0	4.08×4.06	195	S-Brgm,DeVille,Eldo

1979

Seville (wb 114.3)		Wght	Price	Prod
S69	sdn 4d	4,179	14,710	53,487
Eldorado (wb 113.9)				
L57	cpe	3,792	14,668	67,436
DeVille (wb 121.5)				
D47	cpe	4,143	11,728	121,890
D69	sdn 4d	4,212	12,093	93,211
Fleetwood Brougham (wb 121.5)				
B69	sdn 4d	4,250	14,102	42,200
Fleetwood limousine (wb 144.5)				
F23	sdn 4d	4,782	21,869	2,025 (F23 and F33)
F33	formal sdn 4d	4,866	22,640	
—	comm chassis (wb 157.5)	—	—	864

1979 Engines	bore×stroke	bhp	availability
V8, 350.0	4.06×3.39	170	S-Seville,Eldo
V8, 350.0 Dsl	4.06×3.39	125	O-all
V8, 425.0	4.08×4.06	180	S-all exc Seville
V8, 425.0	4.08×4.06	195	O-Brgm,DeVille

1980

Eldorado (wb 113.9)		Wght	Price	Prod
L57	cpe	3,806	16,141	52,685
DeVille (wb 121.5)				
D47	cpe	4,048	12,899	55,490
D69	sdn 4d	4,084	13,282	49,188
Fleetwood Brougham (wb 121.5)				
B47	cpe	4,025	15,307	2,300
B69	sdn 4d	4,092	15,564	29,659
Fleetwood limousine (wb 144.5)				
F23	sdn 4d	4,629	23,509	1,612
F33	formal sdn 4d	4,718	24,343	—
—	comm chassis (wb 157.5)	—	—	750
Seville (wb 114.3)				
S69	sdn 4d	3,911	20,477	39,344

1980 Engines	bore×stroke	bhp	availability
V8, 350.0 Dsl	4.06×3.39	105	S-Seville O-Flt/Brgm,Eldo
V8, 350.0	4.06×3.39	160	O-Seville,Eldo
V8, 368.0	3.80×4.06	150	S-DeV,Fltwd
V8, 368.0	3.80×4.06	145	S-Eldo; O-Seville

1981

Seville (wb 114.0)		Wght	Price	Prod
S69	sdn 4d	4,167	21,088	28,631
Eldorado (wb 114.0)				
L57	cpe	3,930	16,492	60,643
DeVille (wb 121.4)				
D47	cpe	4,151	13,450	54,145
D69	sdn 4d	4,202	13,847	55,100
Fleetwood Brougham (wb 121.4)				
B47	cpe	4,204	15,942	8,300
B69	sdn 4d	4,250	16,365	31,500
Fleetwood limousine (wb 144.5)				
F23	sdn 4d	4,629	24,464	610
F33	formal sdn 4d	4,717	25,323	590
	commercial chassis	—	—	670

1981 Engines	bore × stroke	bhp	availability
V6, 252.0	3.97 × 3.40	125	O-all except limos
V8, 350.0 Dsl	4.06 × 3.39	105	S-Seville; O-DeV, Brgm, Eldo
V8-6-4, 368.0	3.80 × 4.06	140	S-DeV, Brgm, Eldo; O-Seville
V8, 368.0	3.80 × 4.06	150	S-comm chassis

1978 Coupe deVille

1980 Coupe deVille

1983 Cimarron four-door sedan

1982

Cimarron (wb 101.2)		Wght	Price	Prod
G69	sdn 4d	2,594	12,131	25,968
Seville (wb 114.0)				
S69	sdn 4d	4,167	23,433	19,998
Eldorado (wb 114.0)				
L57	cpe	3,930	18,716	52,018
DeVille (wb 121.4)				
D47	cpe	3,923	15,249	44,950
D69	sdn 4d	3,979	15,699	53,870
Fleetwood Brougham (wb 121.4)				
B47	cpe	3,965	18,096	5,180
B69	sdn 4d	4,006	18,567	32,150
Fleetwood limousine (wb 144.5)				
F23	sdn 4d	4,628	27,961	514
F33	formal sdn 4d	4,718	28,941	486
	commercial chassis	—	—	450

1982 Engines	bore × stroke	bhp	availability
L4, 112.0	3.50 × 2.90	88	S-Cimarron
V8, 249.0	3.46 × 3.31	125	S-Sev, Eldo, DeV, Fltwd
V6, 252.0	3.97 × 3.40	125	O-Sev, Eldo, DeV, Fltwd
V8, 350.0 Dsl	4.06 × 3.39	105	O-Seville, Eldo, DeV, Fltwd
V8-6-4, 368.0	3.80 × 4.06	140	S-limousines
V8, 368.0	3.80 × 4.06	150	S-comm chassis

1983

Cimarron (wb 101.2)		Wght	Price	Prod
G69	sdn 4d	2,639	12,215	19,294
Seville (wb 114.0)				
S69	sdn 4d	3,844	21,440	30,430
Eldorado (wb 114.0)				
L57	cpe	3,748	19,334	67,416
DeVille (wb 121.5)				
D47	cpe	3,935	15,970	60,300
D69	sdn 4d	3,993	16,441	70,423
Fleetwood Brougham (wb 121.5)				
B47	cpe	3,986	18,688	5,200
B69	sdn 4d	4,029	19,182	38,300
Fleetwood limousine (wb 144.5)				
F23	sdn 4d	4,765	29,323	492
F33	formal sdn 4d	4,852	30,349	508
	commercial chassis	—	—	451

1983 Engines	bore × stroke	bhp	availability
L4, 121.0	3.50 × 3.15	88	S-Cimarron
V8, 249.0	3.46 × 3.30	135	S-Sev, Eldo, DeV, Fltwd
V8, 350.0 Dsl	4.06 × 3.39	105	O-Seville, Eldo, DeV, Fltwd
V8-6-4, 368.0	3.80 × 4.06	140	S-limousines
V8, 368.0	3.80 × 4.06	150	S-comm chassis

1984

Cimarron (wb 101.2)		Wght	Price	Prod
G69	sdn 4d	2,583	12,614	21,898
Seville (wb 114.0)				
S69	sdn 4d	3,804	22,468	39,997
Eldorado (wb 114.0)				
L57	cpe	3,734	20,342	74,506
L67	Biarritz conv cpe	3,926	31,286	3,300
DeVille (wb 121.5)				
M47	cpe	3,940	17,140	46,340
M69	sdn 4d	3,981	17,625	68,270
Fleetwood Brougham (wb 121.5)				
W47	cpe	3,990	19,942	4,500
W69	sdn 4d	4,034	20,451	39,650
Fleetwood limousine (wb 144.5)				
F23	sdn 4d	4,765	30,454	462

		Wght	Price	Prod
F33	formal sdn 4d	4,855	31,512	631
	commercial chassis	—	—	746

1984 Engines	bore × stroke	bhp	availability
L4, 121.0	3.50 × 3.15	88	S-Cimarron
V8, 249.0	3.46 × 3.30	135	S-Sev, Eldo, DeV, Fltwd
V8, 350.0 Dsl	4.06 × 3.39	105	O-Seville, Eldo, DeV, Fltwd
V8-6-4, 368.0	3.80 × 4.06	140	S-limousines

1985

Cimarron (wb 101.2)		Wght	Price	Prod
G69	sdn 4d	2,583	12,962	19,890
Seville (wb 114.0)				
S69	sdn 4d	3,803	23,259	39,755
Eldorado (wb 114.0)				
L57	cpe	3,724	20,931	74,101
L67	conv cpe	3,915	22,105	2,300
Note: Production total includes 2,463 Commemorative Edition models.				
DeVille (wb 110.8)				
D47	cpe	3,324	17,990	39,500*
D69	sdn 4d	3,396	18,571	101,366*
Fleetwood (wb 110.8)				
B47	cpe	3,346	21,069	*
B69	sdn 4d	3,422	21,040	*
*Fleetwood production included in DeVille coupe and sedan totals.				
Fleetwood Brougham RWD (wb 121.5)				
W47	cpe	3,977	20,798	3,000
W69	sdn 4d	4,020	21,402	52,450
Fleetwood limousine (wb 134.4)				
H23	sdn 4d	3,583	32,640	405
H33	formal sdn 4d	3,642	NA	—

1985 Engines	bore × stroke	bhp	availability
L4, 121.0	3.50 × 3.15	88	S-Cimarron
V6, 173.0	3.50 × 2.99	125	O-Cimarron
V8, 249.0	3.46 × 3.30	125	S-DeV, Fltwd, limo
V8, 249.0	3.46 × 3.30	135	S-Sev, Eldo, Brgm
V6, 262.0 Dsl	4.06 × 3.39	85	O-DeV, Fltwd
V8, 350.0 Dsl	4.06 × 3.39	105	O-Seville, Eldo, Brgm

1986

Cimarron (wb 101.2)		Wght	Price	Prod
G69	sdn 4d	2,583	13,128	24,534
Seville (wb 108.0)				
S69	sdn 4d	3,428	26,756	19,098
Eldorado (wb 108.0)				
L57	cpe	3,365	24,251	21,342
	American II cpe	—	—	1,500
DeVille (wb 110.8)				
D47	cpe	3,319	19,669	36,350*
D69	sdn 4d	3,378	19,990	129,857*
Fleetwood (wb 110.8)				
	cpe	NA	23,443	*
	sdn 4d	NA	23,764	*
*Fleetwood (option package) production included in DeVille coupe and sedan totals.				
Fleetwood Brougham RWD (wb 121.5)				
W69	sdn 4d	4,020	21,265	49,137
Fleetwood Seventy-Five limousine (wb 134.4)				
H23	sdn 4d	3,637	33,895	650
H33	formal sdn 4d	3,736	35,895	350
	commercial chassis	—	—	365

1986 Engines	bore × stroke	bhp	availability
L4, 121.0	3.50 × 3.15	85	S-Cimarron
V6, 173.0	3.50 × 2.99	120	O-Cimarron
V8, 249.0	3.46 × 3.30	130/135	S-Sev, Eldo, DeV, Fltwd
V8, 249.0	3.46 × 3.30	135	S-limo
V8, 307.0	3.80 × 3.39	140	S-Brgm

1987

Cimarron (wb 101.2)		Wght	Price	Prod
G69	sdn 4d	2,659	15,032	14,561
Allante (wb 99.4)				
R67	cpe	3,494	54,700	3,363
Seville (wb 108.0)				
S69	sdn 4d	3,420	26,326	18,578
Eldorado (wb 108.0)				
L57	cpe	3,360	23,740	17,775

1984 Sedan deVille

1985 Seville Elegante 4-door sedan

DeVille (wb 110.8)		Wght	Price	Prod
D47	cpe	3,312	21,316	32,700
D69	sdn 4d	3,370	21,659	129,521
Fleetwood d'Elegance (wb 110.8)				
B69	sdn 4d	3,421	26,104	—
Fleetwood Sixty Special (wb 115.8)				
S19	sdn 4d	3,408	34,850	—
Fleetwood Brougham RWD (wb 121.5)				
W69	sdn 4d	4,046	22,637	65,504
Fleetwood Seventy-Five limousine (wb 134.4)				
H23	sdn 4d	3,678	36,510	302
H33	formal sdn 4d	3,798	38,580	
	commercial chassis	—	—	577

1987 Engines	bore × stroke	bhp	availability
V6, 173.0	3.50 × 2.99	125	S-Cimarron
V8, 249.0	3.46 × 3.30	130	S-Sev, Eldo, DeV, Fltwd, limo
V8, 249.0	3.46 × 3.30	170	S-Allante
V8, 307.0	3.80 × 3.39	140	S-Brgm

1988

Cimarron (wb 101.2)		Wght	Price	Prod
G69	sdn 4d	2,756	16,071	6,454
Allante (wb 99.4)				
R67	cpe	3,489	56,533	2,569
Seville (wb 108.0)				
S69	sdn 4d	3,449	27,627	22,968
Eldorado (wb 108.0)				
L57	cpe	3,399	24,891	33,210
DeVille (wb 110.8)				
D47	cpe	3,397	23,049	152,513
D69	sdn 4d	3,437	23,404	
Fleetwood d'Elegance (wb 110.8)				
B69	sdn 4d	3,463	28,024	—
Fleetwood Sixty Special (wb 115.8)				
S19	sdn 4d	3,547	34,750	—
Fleetwood Brougham RWD (wb 121.5)				
W69	sdn 4d	4,156	23,846	53,130

1988 Engines	bore × stroke	bhp	availability
V6, 173.0	3.50 × 2.99	125	S-Cimarron
V8, 249.0	3.46 × 3.30	170	S-Allante
V8, 273.0	3.62 × 3.31	155	S-Sev, Eldo, DeV, Fltwd
V8, 307.0	3.80 × 3.39	140	S-Brgm

1989

Allante (wb 99.4)		Wght	Price	Prod
R67	conv cpe	3,492	57,183	—
Seville (wb 108.0)				
S69	sdn 4d	3,422	29,750	—
Eldorado (wb 108.0)				
L57	cpe	3,422	26,738	—
DeVille (wb 110.8; sdn 113.8)				
D47	cpe	3,397	24,960	—
D69	sdn 4d	3,470	25,435	—
Fleetwood (wb 110.8; sdn 113.8)				
847	cpe	3,459	29,825	—
869	sdn 4d	3,545	30,300	—
Fleetwood Sixty Special (wb 113.8)				
S69	sdn 4d	3,598	34,230	—
Fleetwood Brougham RWD (wb 121.5)				
W69	sdn 4d	4,190	25,699	—

1989 Engines	bore × stroke	bhp	availability
V8, 273.0	3.62 × 3.31	155	S-Sev, Eldo, DeV, Fltwd
V8, 273.0	3.62 × 3.31	200	S-Allante
V8, 307.0	3.80 × 3.39	140	S-Brgm

1989 Coupe deVille

CHECKER

1960—6,980 built, inc taxis

Superba (wb 120.0)		Wght	Price	Prod
	sdn 4d	3,410	2,542	—
	Special sdn 4d	3,410	2,650	—
	wgn 4d	3,780	2,896	—
	Special wgn 4d	3,780	3,004	—

1960 Engines	bore×stroke	bhp	availability
L6, 226.0	3.31×4.38	80	S-all
L6, 226.0	3.31×4.38	122	O-all

1961—5,683 built, inc taxis

Superba (wb 120.0)		Wght	Price	Prod
	sdn 4d	3,320	2,542	—
	wgn 4d	3,570	2,896	—
Marathon (wb 120.0)				
	sdn 4d	3,345	2,650	—
	wgn 4d	3,615	3,004	—

1961 Engines	bore×stroke	bhp	availability
L6, 226.0	3.31×4.38	80	S-all
L6, 226.0	3.31×4.38	122	S-wgn; O-sdn

1962—8,173 built, inc taxis

Superba (wb 120.0)		Wght	Price	Prod
	sdn 4d	3,320	2,642	—
	wgn 4d	3,570	2,991	—
Marathon (wb 120.0)				
	sdn 4d	3,345	2,793	—
	wgn 4d	3,615	3,140	—
Town Custom (wb 129.0)				
	limo 8P	5,000	7,500	—

1962 Engines	bore×stroke	bhp	availability
L6, 226.0	3.31×4.38	80	S-all
L6, 226.0	3.31×4.38	122	O-all

1963—7,050 built, inc taxis

Superba (wb 120.0)		Wght	Price	Prod
	sdn 4d	3,485	2,642	—
	wgn 4d	3,625	2,991	—
Marathon (wb 120.0)				
	sdn 4d	3,485	2,773	—
	wgn 4d	3,625	3,140	—
Town Custom (wb 129.0)				
	limo 8P	5,000	7,500	—

1963 Engines	bore×stroke	bhp	availability
L6, 226.0	3.31×4.38	80	S-all
L6, 226.0	3.31×4.38	141	O-all

1964—6,310 built, inc taxis

Marathon (wb 120.0)		Wght	Price	Prod
	sdn 4d	3,625	2,814	—
	wgn 4d	3,720	3,160	—
Town Custom (wb 129.0)				
	limo 8P	5,000	8,000	—

1964 Engines	bore×stroke	bhp	availability
L6, 226.0	3.31×4.38	80	S-all
L6, 226.0	3.31×4.38	141	O-all

1965—6,136 built, inc taxis

Marathon (wb 120.0)		Wght	Price	Prod
A12	sdn 4d	3,360	2,793	—
A12W	wgn 4d	3,450	3,140	—
Town Custom (wb 129.0)				
A12E	limo 8P	4,800	8,000	—

1965 Engines	bore×stroke	bhp	availability
L6, 230.0	3.88×3.25	140	S-all
V8, 283.0	3.88×3.00	195	O-all
V8, 327.0	4.00×3.25	250	O-all

1966—1,056 built; 5,761 inc taxis

Marathon (wb 120.0)		Wght	Price	Prod
A12	sdn 4d	3,400	2,874	—
A12E	Deluxe sdn 4d	3,800	3,567	—
A12E	limo 8P	3,800	4,541	—
A12W	wgn 4d	3,500	3,500	—

1966 Engines	bore×stroke	bhp	availability
L6, 230.0	3.88×3.25	140	S-all
V8, 283.0	3.88×3.00	195	O-all
V8, 327.0	4.00×3.25	250	O-all

1967—935 built; 5,822 inc taxis

Marathon (wb 120.0)		Wght	Price	Prod
A12	sdn 4d	3,400	2,874	—
A12W	wgn 4d	3,500	3,075	—

1967 Engines	bore×stroke	bhp	availability
L6, 230.0	3.88×3.25	140	S-all
V8, 327.0	4.00×3.25	250	O-all

1968—992 built; 5,477 inc taxis

Marathon (wb 120.0)		Wght	Price	Prod
A12	sdn 4d	3,390	3,221	—
A12E	Deluxe sdn 4d	3,590	3,913	—
A12W	wgn 4d	3,480	3,491	—

1968 Engines	bore×stroke	bhp	availability
L6, 230.0	3.88×3.25	140	S-all
V8, 307.0	3.88×3.25	200	O-all
V8, 327.0	4.00×3.25	275	O-all

1969—760 built; 5,417 inc taxis

Marathon (wb 120.0)		Wght	Price	Prod
A12	sdn 4d	3,390	3,290	—
A12W	wgn 4d	3,480	3,560	—
DeLuxe (wb 129.0)				
A12E	sdn 4d	3,590	3,984	—
A12E	limo 8P	3,802	4,969	—

1969 Engines	bore×stroke	bhp	availability
L6, 230.0	3.88×3.25	155	S-all
V8, 327.0	4.00×3.25	235	O-all
V8, 350.0	4.00×3.48	300	O-all

1970—397 built

Marathon (wb 120.0)		Wght	Price	Prod
A12	sdn 4d	3,268	3,671	—
A12W	wgn 4d	3,470	3,941	—

Marathon DeLuxe (wb 129.0)		Wght	Price	Prod
A12E	sdn 4d	3,378	4,364	—
A12E	limo 8P	3,578	5,338	—

1970 Engines	bore×stroke	bhp	availability
L6, 230.0	3.88×3.25	155	S-all
V8, 350.0	4.00×3.48	250	O-all

1971

Marathon (wb 120.0)		Wght*	Price*	Prod*
A12	sdn 4d	3,400	3,843	500
A12W	wgn 4d	3,600	4,113	
Marathon DeLuxe (wb 129.0)				
A12E	sdn 4d	3,700	4,536	100
A12E	limo 8P	3,975	5,510	

1971 Engines	bore×stroke	bhp	availability
L6, 250.0	3.88×3.53	145	S-all
V8, 350.0	4.00×3.48	245	O-all

*L6 weight/price given; V8 adds 100 lbs & $110. Production estimated.

1972

Marathon (wb 120.0)		Wght*	Price*	Prod*
A12	sdn 4d	3,400	3,654	750
A12W	wgn 4d	3,600	3,910	
Marathon DeLuxe (wb 129.0)				
A12E	sdn 4d	3,700	4,312	100

1972 Engines	bore×stroke	bhp	availability
L6, 250.0	3.88×3.53	145	S-all
V8, 350.0	4.00×3.48	245	O-all

*L6 weight/price given; V8 adds 100 lbs & $250. Production estimated.

1973

Marathon (wb 120.0)		Wght*	Price*	Prod*
A12	sdn 4d	3,622	3,955	800
A12W	wgn 4d	3,825	4,211	
Marathon DeLuxe (wb 129.0)				
A12E	sdn 4d 8P L6	3,822	4,612	100
A12E	sdn 4d 8P V8	3,923	4,727	

1973 Engines	bore×stroke	bhp	availability
L6, 250.0	3.88×3.53	145	S-all
V8, 350.0	4.00×3.48	245	O-Marathon

*L6 weight/price given; V8 adds 100 lbs & $115. Production estimated.

1974

Marathon (wb 120.0)		Wght*	Price*	Prod*
A12	sdn 4d	3,720	4,453	900
A12W	wgn 4d	3,925	4,710	
Marathon DeLuxe (wb 129.0)				
A12E	sdn 4d 8P	3,920	5,394	50

1974 Engines	bore×stroke	bhp	availability
L6, 250.0	3.88×3.53	100	S-all
V8, 350.0	4.00×3.48	145	O-all

*L6 weight/price given; V8 adds 100 lbs & $150. Production estimated.

1975

Marathon (wb 120.0; DeL 129.0)		Wght	Price	Prod*
A12	sdn 4d L6	3,774	5,394	450
A12	sdn 4d V8	3,839	5,539	
A12E	DeLuxe sdn 4d V8	4,137	6,216	

1975 Engines	bore×stroke	bhp	availability
L6, 250.0	3.88×3.53	100	S-sixes
V8, 350.0	4.00×3.48	145	S-V8s

*Production estimated.

1976

Marathon (wb 120.0)		Wght	Price	Prod*
A12	sdn 4d L6	3,774	5,749	400
A12	sdn 4d V8	3,839	5,894	
Marathon DeLuxe (wb 129.0)				
A12E	sdn 4d V8	4,137	6,736	—

1976 Engines	bore×stroke	bhp	availability
L6, 250.0	3.88×3.53	105	S-sixes
V8, 350.0	4.00×3.48	145	S-V8s

1977

Marathon (wb 120.0)		Wght	Price	Prod*
A12	sdn 4d L6	3,765	6,156	300
A12	sdn 4d V8	3,830	6,301	
Marathon DeLuxe (wb 129.0)				
A12E	sdn 4d V8	4,137	NA	—

1977 Engines	bore×stroke	bhp	availability
L6, 250.0	3.88×3.53	110	S-sixes
V8, 305.0	3.74×3.48	145	S-V8s
V8, 305.0	4.00×3.48	170	O-V8s

1978

Marathon (wb 120.0)		Wght	Price	Prod*
A12	sdn 4d L6	3,765	6,814	300
A12	sdn 4d V8	3,830	6,959	
Marathon DeLuxe (wb 129.0)				
A12E	sdn 4d V8	4,062	7,867	—

1978 Engines	bore×stroke	bhp	availability
L6, 250.0	3.88×3.53	110	S-sixes
V8, 305.0	3.74×3.53	145	S-V8s
V8, 350.0	4.00×3.48	170	O-V8s

1979

Marathon (wb 120.0)		Wght	Price	Prod*
A12	sdn 4d L6	3,765	7,314	200
A12	sdn 4d V8	3,830	7,515	
Marathon DeLuxe (wb 129.0)				
A12E	sdn 4d V8	3,999	8,389	—

1979 Engines	bore×stroke	bhp	availability
L6, 250.0	3.88×3.53	110	S-sixes
V8, 305.0	3.74×3.48	145	S-V8s
V8, 350.0	4.00×3.48	160	O-V8s

1980

Marathon (wb 120.0)		Wght	Price	Prod*
A12	sdn 4d L6	3,765	7,800	250
A12	sdn 4d V8	3,830	8,000	
Marathon DeLuxe (wb 129.0)				
A12E	sdn 4d V8	3,999	9,192	—

1980 Engines	bore×stroke	bhp	availability
V6, 229.0	3.74×3.48	115	S-sixes
V8, 267.0	3.50×3.48	120	S-DeL; O-all

	bore×stroke	bhp	availability
V8, 305.0	3.74×3.48	155	O-V8s
V8D, 350.0	4.06×3.39	125	O-V8s

*Production estimated

1981—2,950 built, inc taxis

Marathon (wb 120.0)		Wght	Price	Prod
A12	sdn 4d V6	3,680	9,632	—
A12	sdn 4d V8	—	9,869	—
Marathon DeLuxe (wb 129.0)				
A12E	sdn 4d V8	3,999	10,706	—

1981 Engines	bore×stroke	bhp	availability
V6, 229.0	3.73×3.48	110	S-sixes
V8, 267.0	3.50×3.48	115	S-V8s
V8, 305.0	3.74×3.48	150	O-V8s
V8D, 350.0	4.06×3.39	105	O-V8s

1982—2,000 built, inc taxis

Marathon (wb 120.0)		Wght	Price	Prod
A12	sdn 4d V6	3,680	10,950	—
A12	sdn 4d V8	—	11,187	—
Marathon DeLuxe (wb 129.0)				
A12E	sdn 4d V8	3,839	12,025	—

1982 Engines	bore×stroke	bhp	availability
V6, 229.0	3.73×3.48	110	S-sixes
V8, 267.0	3.50×3.48	115	S-V8s
V8D, 350.0	4.06×3.39	105	O-V8s

CHEVROLET

1939

JB Master 85 (wb 112.3)	Wght	Price	Prod
cpe 2P	2,780	628	41,770
coach 5P	2,795	648	1,404
Town sdn 2d T/B	2,820	669	124,059
sdn 4d	2,805	689	336
spt sdn 4d T/B	2,845	710	22,623
wgn 4d	3,010	848	430*

*229 with folding end gates, 201 with rear door

JA Master DeLuxe (wb 112.3)	Wght	Price	Prod
bus cpe 2P	2,845	684	33,809
spt cpe 4P	2,845	715	20,908
coach 5P	2,865	699	180
Town sdn 2d T/B	2,875	720	220,181
sdn 4d	2,875	745	68
spt sdn 4d T/B	2,910	766	110,521
wgn 4d	3,060	883	989

1939 Engine	bore×stroke	bhp	availability
L6, 216.5	3.50×3.75	85	S-all

1940

KB Master 85 (wb 113.0)	Wght	Price	Prod
bus cpe	2,865	659	25,734
Town Sedan 2d, T/B	2,915	699	66,431
Sport Sedan 4d, T/B	2,930	740	11,468
wgn 4d, 8P	3,106	903	411
KH Master DeLuxe (wb 113.0)			
bus cpe	2,920	684	28,090
Sport Coupe	2,925	715	17,234
Town Sedan 2d, T/B	2,965	725	143,125

1939 Master DeLuxe

	Wght	Price	Prod
Sport Sedan 4d, T/B	2,990	766	40,924
KA Special DeLuxe			
bus cpe	2,930	720	25,537
Sport Coupe	2,945	750	46,628
conv cpe	3,160	898	11,820
Town Sedan 2d, T/B	2,980	761	205,910
Sport Sedan 4d, T/B	3,010	802	138,811
wgn 4d, 8P	3,158	934	2,493*

*367 with double rear doors

1940 Engine	bore×stroke	bhp	availability
L6, 216.5	3.50×3.75	85	S-all

1941

AG Master DeLuxe (wb 116.0)	Wght	Price	Prod
bus cpe	3,020	712	48,763
cpe	3,025	743	79,124
Town Sedan 2d	3,050	754	219,438
Sport Sedan 4d	3,090	795	59,538
AH Special DeLuxe (wb 116.0)			
bus cpe	3,040	769	17,602
cpe	3,050	800	155,889
conv cpe	3,285	949	15,296
Town Sedan 2d	3,095	810	228,458
Sport Sedan 4d	3,127	851	148,661
wgn 4d, 8P	3,410	995	2,045
Fleetline sdn 4d	3,130	877	34,162

1941 Engine	bore×stroke	bhp	availability
L6, 216.5	3.50×3.75	90	S-all

1942

BG Stylemaster (wb 116.0)	Wght	Price	Prod
cpe 2P	3,055	760	8,089
cpe 5P	3,060	790	17,442
Town Sedan 2d	3,090	800	41,872
Sport Sedan 4d	3,110	840	14,093
BH Fleetmaster (wb 116.0)			
cpe 2P	3,070	815	1,716
cpe 5p	3,085	845	22,187
conv cpe	3,385	1,080	1,182
Town Sedan 2d	3,120	855	39,421
Sport Sedan 4d	3,145	895	31,441
wgn 4d, 8P	3,425	1,095	1,057

1941 Coupe Pickup

BH Fleetline (wb 116.0)		Wght	Price	Prod
	Aerosedan 2d	3,105	880	61,855
	Sportmaster sdn 4d	3,165	920	14,530

1942 Engine	bore×stroke	bhp	availability
L6, 216.5	3.50×3.75	90	S-all

1946

DJ Stylemaster (wb 116.0)		Wght	Price	Prod
	Sport Sedan 4d	3,175	1,205	75,349
	Town Sedan 2d	3,170	1,152	61,104
	spt cpe	3,130	1,137	19,243
	bus cpe	3,105	1,098	14,267
DK Fleetmaster (wb 116.0)				
	Sport Sedan 4d	3,225	1,280	73,746
	Town Sedan 2d	3,190	1,225	56,538
	spt cpe	3,145	1,212	27,036
	conv cpe	3,445	1,476	4,508
	wgn 4d, 8P	3,465	1,712	804
DK Fleetline (wb 116.0)				
	Sportmaster sdn 4d	3,240	1,309	7,501
	Aerosedan 2d	3,165	1,249	57,932

1946 Engine	bore×stroke	bhp	availability
L6, 216.5	3.50×3.75	90	S-all

1947

EJ Stylemaster (wb 116.0)		Wght	Price	Prod
1503	Sport Sedan 4d	3,130	1,276	42,571
1502	Town Sedan 2d	3,075	1,219	88,534
1524	spt cpe	3,060	1,202	34,513
1504	bus cpe	3,050	1,160	27,403
EK Fleetmaster (wb 116.0)				
2103	Sport Sedan 4d	3,185	1,345	91,440
2102	Town Sedan 2d	3,125	1,286	80,128
2124	spt cpe	3,090	1,281	59,661
2134	conv cpe	3,390	1,628	28,443
2109	wgn 4d, 8P	3,465	1,893	4,912
EK Fleetline (wb 116.0)				
2113	Sportmaster sdn 4d	3,150	1,371	54,531
2144	Aerosedan 2d	3,125	1,313	159,407

1947 Engine	bore×stroke	bhp	availability
L6, 216.5	3.50×3.75	90	S-all

1948

FJ Stylemaster (wb 116.0)		Wght	Price	Prod
1502	Town Sedan 2d	3,095	1,313	70,228
1503	Sport Sedan 4d	3,115	1,371	48,456
1504	bus cpe	3,045	1,244	18,396
1524	spt cpe	3,020	1,323	34,513
FK Fleetmaster (wb 116.0)				
2102	Town Sedan 2d	3,110	1,381	66,208
2103	Sport Sedan 4d	3,150	1,439	93,142
2109	wgn 4d, 8P	3,430	2,013	10,171
2124	spt cpe	3,050	1,402	58,786
2134	conv cpe	3,340	1,750	20,471
FK Fleetline (wb 116.0)				
2113	Sportmaster sdn 4d	3,150	1,492	64,217

		Wght	Price	Prod
2144	Aerosedan 2d	3,100	1,434	211,861

1948 Engine	bore×stroke	bhp	availability
L6, 216.5	3.50×3.75	90	S-all

1949

GJ Styleline Special (wb 115.0)		Wght	Price	Prod
1502	Town Sedan 2d	3,070	1,413	69,398
1503	Sport Sedan 4d	3,090	1,460	46,334
1504	bus cpe	3,015	1,339	20,337
1524	spt cpe	3,030	1,418	27,497
GJ Fleetline Special (wb 115.0)				
1552	sdn 2d	3,060	1,413	58,514
1553	sdn 4d	3,095	1,460	36,317
GK Styleline DeLuxe (wb 115.0)				
2102	Town Sedan 2d	3,100	1,492	147,347
2103	Sport Sedan 4d	3,125	1,539	191,357
2109	wgn 4d, wood body	3,485	2,267	3,342
2119	wgn 4d, steel body	3,465	2,267	2,664
2124	spt cpe	3,065	1,508	78,785
2134	conv cpe	3,375	1,857	32,392
GK Fleetline DeLuxe (wb 115.0)				
2152	sdn 2d	3,100	1,492	180,251
2153	sdn 4d	3,135	1,539	130,323

1949 Engine	bore×stroke	bhp	availability
L6, 216.5	3.50×3.75	90	S-all

1950

HJ Styleline Special (wb 115.0)		Wght	Price	Prod
1502	Town Sedan 2d	3,085	1,403	89,897
1503	Sport Sedan 4d	3,120	1,450	55,644
1504	bus cpe	3,025	1,329	20,984
1524	spt cpe	3,050	1,408	28,328
HJ Fleetline Special (wb 115.0)				
1552	sdn 2d	3,080	1,403	43,682
1553	sdn 4d	3,115	1,450	23,277
HK Styleline DeLuxe (wb 115.0)				
2102	Town Sedan 2d	3,100	1,482	248,567
2103	Sport Sedan 4d	3,150	1,529	316,412
2119	wgn 4d, steel body	3,460	1,994	166,995
2124	spt cpe	3,090	1,498	81,536
2134	conv cpe	3,380	1,847	32,810
2154	Bel Air htp cpe	3,225	1,741	76,662
HK DeLuxe Fleetline (wb 115.0)				
2152	sdn 2d	3,115	1,482	189,509
2153	sdn 4d	3,145	1,529	124,287

1950 Engine	bore×stroke	bhp	availability
L6, 216.5	3.50×3.75	92	S-all
L6, 235.5	3.56×3.94	105	S-Powerglide

1951

JJ Styleline Special (wb 115.0)		Wght	Price	Prod
1502	sdn 2d	3,095	1,540	75,566
1503	sdn 4d	3,130	1,595	63,718
1504	bus cpe	3,040	1,460	17,020
1524	spt cpe	3,060	1,545	18,981
JJ Fleetline Special (wb 115.0)				
1552	sdn 2d	3,090	1,540	6,441
1553	sdn 4d	3,130	1,594	3,364

1949 Styleline DeLuxe wood-body 4-door wagon

1953 Two-Ten four-door sedan

JK Styleline DeLuxe (wb 115.0)		Wght	Price	Prod
2102	sdn 2d	3,110	1,629	262,933
2103	sdn 4d	3,140	1,680	380,270
2119	wgn 4d	3,470	2,191	23,586
2124	spt cpe	3,115	1,647	64,976
2134	conv cpe	3,380	2,030	20,172
2154	Bel Air htp cpe	3,225	1,914	103,356
JK Fleetline DeLuxe (wb 115.0)				
2152	sdn 2d	3,125	1,629	131,910
2153	sdn 4d	3,155	1,680	57,693

1951 Engine	bore×stroke	bhp	availability
L6, 216.5	3.50×3.75	92	S-all
L6, 235.5	3.56×3.94	105	S-Powerglide

1952

KJ Styleline Special (wb 115.0)		Wght	Price	Prod
1502	sdn 2d	3,085	1,614	54,781
1503	sdn 4d	3,115	1,670	35,460
1504	bus cpe	3,045	1,530	10,359
1524	spt cpe	3,050	1,620	8,906
KK Styleline DeLuxe (wb 115.0)				
2102	sdn 2d	3,110	1,707	215,417
2103	sdn 4d	3,145	1,761	319,736
2119	wgn 4d	3,475	2,297	12,756
2124	spt cpe	3,100	1,726	36,954
2134	conv cpe	3,380	2,128	11,975
2154	Bel Air htp cpe	3,215	2,006	74,634
KK Fleetline DeLuxe (wb 115.0)				
2152	sdn 2d	3,110	1,707	37,164

1952 Engines	bore×stroke	bhp	availability
L6, 216.5	3.50×3.75	92	S-manual shift

	bore×stroke	bhp	availability
L6, 235.5	3.56×3.94	105	S-Powerglide

1953

150 Special (wb 115.0)		Wght	Price	Prod
1502	sdn 2d	3,180	1,613	79,416
1503	sdn 4d	3,215	1,670	54,207
1504	bus cpe	3,140	1,524	13,555
1509	Handyman wgn 4d	3,420	2,010	22,408
1524	club cpe	3,140	1,620	6,993
210 DeLuxe (wb 115.0)				
2102	sdn 2d	3,215	1,707	247,455
2103	sdn 4d	3,250	1,761	332,497
2109	Handyman wgn 4d	3,450	2,123	18,258
2119	Townsman wgn 4d, 8P	3,495	2,273	7,988
2124	club cpe	3,190	1,726	23,961
2134	conv cpe	3,435	2,093	5,617
2154	htp cpe	3,295	1,967	14,045
240 Bel Air (wb 115.0)				
2402	sdn 2d	3,230	1,820	144,401
2403	sdn 4d	3,275	1,874	247,284
2434	conv cpe	3,470	2,175	24,047
2454	htp cpe	3,310	2,051	99,028

1953 Engines	bore×stroke	bhp	availability
L6, 235.5	3.56×3.94	108	S-manual shift
L6, 235.5	3.56×3.94	115	S-Powerglide

1954

150 Special (wb 115.0)		Wght	Price	Prod
1502	sdn 2d	3,165	1,680	64,855
1503	sdn 4d	3,210	1,623	32,430
1509	Handyman wgn 4d	3,455	2,020	21,404
1512	Utility sdn 2d, 3P	3,145	1,539	10,770
210 DeLuxe (wb (115.0)				
2102	sdn 2d	3,185	1,717	195,498
2103	sdn 4d	3,230	1,771	235,146
2109	Handyman wgn 4d	3,470	2,133	27,175
2124	Delray cpe	3,185	1,782	66,403
240 Bel Air (wb 115.0)				
2402	sdn 2d	3,220	1,830	143,573
2403	sdn 4d	3,255	1,884	248,750
2419	Townsman wgn 4d, 8P	3,540	2,283	8,156
2434	conv cpe	3,445	2,185	19,383
2454	Sport Coupe htp cpe	3,300	2,061	66,378

1954 Engines	bore×stroke	bhp	availability
L6, 235.5	3.56×3.94	115	S-manual
L6, 235.5	3.56×3.94	125	S-Powerglide

1955

150 (wb 115.0)		Wght	Price	Prod
1502	sdn 2d	3,145	1,685	66,416
1503	sdn 4d	3,150	1,728	29,898
1512	Util sdn	3,070	1,593	11,196
1529	Handyman wgn 4d	3,275	2,030	17,936
210 (wb 115.0)				
2102	sdn 2d	3,130	1,775	249,105
2103	sdn 4d	3,165	1,819	317,724
2109	Townsman wgn 4d	3,355	2,127	82,303
2124	Delray cpe	3,130	1,835	115,584
2129	Handyman wgn 2d	3,315	2,079	28,918
2154	htp cpe	3,158	1,959	11,675
Bel Air (wb 115.0)				
2402	sdn 2d	3,140	1,888	168,313
2403	sdn 4d	3,185	1,932	345,372
2409	Beauville wgn 4d	3,370	2,262	24,313
2429	Nomad wgn 2d	3,285	2,571	8,386
2434	conv cpe	3,300	2,206	41,292
2454	Sport Coupe htp cpe	3,180	2,067	185,562

1955 Engines	bore×stroke	bhp	availability
L6, 235.5	3.56×3.94	123/136	S-manual/Powerglide
V8, 265.0	3.75×3.00	162/170	O-manual/Powerglide
V8, 265.0	3.75×3.00	180	O-all

1956

150 (wb 115.0)		Wght	Price	Prod
1502	sdn 2d	3,154	1,826	82,384
1503	sdn 4d	3,196	1,869	51,544

1955 Bel Air Sport Coupe

		Wght	Price	Prod
1512	Util sdn	3,117	1,734	9,879
1529	Handyman wgn 2d	3,299	2,171	13,487
210 (wb 115.0)				
2102	sdn 2d	3,167	1,912	205,545
2103	sdn 4d	3,202	1,955	283,125
2109	Townsman wgn 4d	3,371	2,263	113,656
2113	Sport htp sdn	3,252	2,117	20,021
2119	Beauville wgn 4d, 9P	3,490	2,348	17,988
2124	Delray cpe	3,172	1,971	56,382
2129	Handyman wgn 2d	3,334	2,215	22,038
2154	Sport htp cpe	3,194	2,063	18,616
Bel Air (wb 115.0)				
2402	sdn 2d	3,187	2,025	104,849
2403	sdn 4d	3,221	2,068	269,798
2413	Sport htp sdn	3,270	2,230	103,602
2419	Beauville wgn 4d, 9P	3,506	2,482	13,279
2429	Nomad wgn 2d	3,352	2,608	7,886
2434	conv cpe	3,330	2,344	41,268
2454	Sport htp cpe	3,222	2,176	128,382

1956 Engines	bore×stroke	bhp	availability
L6, 235.5	3.56×3.94	140	S-all
V8, 265.0	3.75×3.00	162/170	O-manual/Powerglide
V8, 265.0	3.75×3.00	205/225	O-all

1957

150 (wb 115.0)		Wght	Price	Prod
1502	sdn 2d	3,211	1,996	70,774
1503	sdn 4d	3,236	2,048	52,266
1512	Util sdn 2d	3,163	1,885	8,300
1529	Handyman wgn 2d	3,406	2,307	14,740
210 (wb 115.0)				
2102	sdn 2d	3,225	2,122	160,090
2103	sdn 4d	3,270	2,174	260,401
2109	Townsman wgn 4d	3,461	2,456	127,803
2113	Sport htp sdn	3,320	2,270	16,178
2119	Beauville wgn 4d	3,561	2,563	21,083
2124	Delray cpe	3,220	2,162	25,644
2129	Handyman wgn 2d	3,406	2,402	17,528
2154	Sport htp cpe	3,260	2,204	22,631
Bel Air (wb 115.0)				
2402	sdn 2d	3,232	2,238	62,751
2403	sdn 4d	3,276	2,290	254,331
2409	Townsman wgn 4d	3,460	2,580	27,375
2413	Sport htp sdn	3,340	2,364	137,672
2429	Nomad wgn 2d	3,465	2,757	6,103
2434	conv cpe	3,409	2,511	47,562
2454	Sport htp cpe	3,278	2,299	166,426

1957 Engines	bore×stroke	bhp	availability
L6, 235.5	3.56×3.94	140	S-all
V8, 265.0	3.75×3.00	162	O-all w/manual shift
V8, 283.0	3.88×3.00	185	S-all w/automatic
V8, 283.0	3.68×3.00	220	O-all
V8, 283.0	3.88×3.00	245/250	O-all
V8, 283.0	3.88×3.00	270/283	O-manual shift

1958

Delray (wb 117.5)—178,000* built		Wght	Price	Prod
1121	Util sdn 2d, L6	3,351	2,013	—
1141	sdn 2d, L6	3,396	2,101	—
1149	sdn 4d, L6	3,439	2,155	—
1221	Util sdn 2d, V8	3,156	2,120	—

1956 Bel Air four-door sedan

1957 Bel Air convertible coupe

1958 Delray two-door sedan

		Wght	Price	Prod
1241	sdn 2d, V8	3,399	2,208	—
1249	sdn 4d, V8	3,442	2,262	—
Biscayne (wb 117.5)—100,000* built exc 1541				
1541	sdn 2d, L6	3,404	2,236	76,229
1549	sdn 4d, L6	3,447	2,290	—
1641	sdn 2d, V8	3,407	2,343	—
1649	sdn 4d, V8	3,450	2,397	—
Bel Air (wb 117.5)—592,000* built				
1731	Sport htp cpe, L6	3,455	2,447	—
1739	Sport htp sdn, L6	3,511	2,511	—
1741	sdn 2d, L6	3,424	2,386	—
1747	Impala htp cpe, L6	3,458	2,586	—
1749	sdn 4d, L6	3,467	2,440	—
1767	Impala conv cpe, L6	3,522	2,734	—
1831	Sport htp cpe, V8	3,458	2,554	—
1839	Sport htp sdn, V8	3,514	2,618	—
1841	sdn 2d, V8	3,427	2,493	—

		Wght	Price	Prod
1847	Impala htp cpe,V8	3,459	2,693	—
1849	sdn 4d, V8	3,470	2,547	—
1867	Impala conv cpe, V8	3,523	2,841	—
Station Wagon (wb 117.5)—187,063 built				
1191	Yeoman 2d, L6	3,693	2,413	—
1193	Yeoman 4d, L6	3,740	2,467	—
1291	Yeoman 2d, V8	3,696	2,520	—
1293	Yeoman 4d, V8	3,743	2,574	—
1593	Brookwood 4d, 6P, L6	3,748	2,571	—
1594	Brookwood 4d, 9P, L6	3,837	2,678	—
1693	Brookwood 4d, 6P, V8	3,751	2,678	—
1694	Brookwood 4d, 9P, V8	3,839	2,785	—
1793	Nomad 4d, L6	3,768	2,728	—
1893	Nomad 4d, V8	3,771	2,835	—

*To nearest 100. Impalas approximately 60,000.

1958 Engines	bore×stroke	bhp	availability
L6, 235.5	3.56×3.94	145	S-six
V8, 283.0	3.88×3.00	185	S-V8
V8, 283.0	3.88×3.00	230/250	O-all
V8, 283.0	3.88×3.00	290	O-all w/manual shift
V8, 348.0	4.13×3.25	250	O-all
V8, 348.0	4.13×3.25	280/315	O-all

1959

Biscayne (wb 119.0)—311,800* built		Wght	Price	Prod
1111	sdn 2d, L6	3,535	2,247	—
1119	sdn 4d, L6	3,605	2,301	—
1121	Util sdn 2d, L6	3,480	2,160	—
1211	sdn 2d, V8	3,530	2,365	—
1219	sdn 4d, V8	3,600	2,419	—
1221	Util sdn 2d, V8	3,490	2,278	—
Bel Air (wb 119.0)—447,100* built				
1511	sdn 2d, L6	3,515	2,386	—
1519	sdn 4d, L6	3,600	2,440	—
1539	Sport htp sdn, L6	3,660	2,556	—
1611	sdn 2d, V8	3,510	2,504	—
1619	sdn 4d, V8	3,615	2,558	—
1639	Sport htp sdn, V8	3,630	2,674	—
Impala (wb 119.0)—407,200* built exc 1867				
1719	sdn 4d, L6	3,625	2,592	—
1737	Sport htp cpe, L6	3,570	2,599	—
1739	Sport htp sdn, L6	3,665	2,664	—
1767	conv cpe, L6	3,660	2,849	—
1819	sdn 4d, V8	3,620	2,710	—
1837	Sport htp cpe, V8	3,580	2,717	—
1839	Sport htp sdn, V8	3,670	2,782	—
1867	conv cpe, V8	3,650	2,967	65,800
Station Wagon (wb 119.0)—195,583 built exc 1215				
1115	Brookwood 2d, L6	3,870	2,571	—
1135	Brookwood 4d, L6	3,955	2,638	—
1215	Brookwood, 2d, V8	3,860	2,689	18,800
1235	Brookwood, 4d, V8	3,955	2,756	—
1535	Parkwood 4d, L6	3,965	2,749	—
1545	Kingswood, 4d, 9P, L6	4,020	2,852	—
1635	Parkwood 4d, V8	3,970	2,867	—
1645	Kingswood 4d, 9P, V8	4,015	2,970	—
1735	Nomad 4d, L6	3,980	2,891	—
1835	Nomad 4d, V8	3,975	3,009	—

*To nearest 100.

1959 Engines	bore×stroke	bhp	availability
L6, 235.5	3.56×3.94	135	S-six
V8, 283.0	3.88×3.00	185	S-V8
V8, 280.0	3.88×3.00	230-290	O-all
V8, 348.0	4.13×3.25	250-315	O-all

1960

Biscayne (wb 119.0)—287,700* built		Wght	Price	Prod
1111	sdn 2d, L6	3,485	2,262	—
1119	sdn 4d, L6	3,555	2,316	—
1121	Util sdn 2d, L6	3,455	2,175	—
1211	sdn 2d, V8	3,500	2,369	—
1219	sdn 4d, V8	3,570	2,423	—
1221	Util sdn 2d, V8	3,470	2,282	—
Biscayne Fleetmaster (wb 119.0)—prod included with Biscayne				
1311	sdn 2d, L6	3,480	2,230	—
1319	sdn 4d, L6	3,545	2,284	—
1411	sdn 2d, V8	3,495	2,337	—
1419	sdn 4d, V8	3,560	2,391	—
Bel Air (wb 119.0)—381,500* built				
1511	sdn 2d, L6	3,490	2,384	—
1519	sdn 4d, L6	3,565	2,438	—

1959 Impala convertible coupe

1960 Impala convertible coupe

		Wght	Price	Prod
1537	Sport htp cpe, L6	3,515	2,489	—
1539	Sport htp sdn, L6	3,605	2,554	—
1611	sdn 2d, V8	3,505	2,491	—
1619	sdn 4d, V8	3,500	2,545	—
1637	Sport htp cpe, L6	3,530	2,596	—
1639	Sport htp sdn, V8	3,620	2,661	—
Impala (wb 119.0)—411,000* built exc 1867				
1719	sdn 4d, L6	3,575	2,590	—
1737	Sport htp cpe, L6	3,530	2,597	—
1739	Sport htp sdn, L6	3,625	2,662	—
1767	conv cpe, L6	3,625	2,847	—
1819	sdn 4d, V8	3,580	2,697	—
1837	Sport htp cpe, V8	3,540	2,704	—
1839	Sport htp sdn, V8	3,625	2,769	—
1867	conv cpe, V8	3,635	2,954	79,903
Station Wagon (wb 119.0)—212,700* built				
1115	Brookwood 2d, L6	3,845	2,586	—
1135	Brookwood 4d, L6	3,935	2,653	—
1215	Brookwood 2d, V8	3,855	2,693	—
1235	Brookwood 4d, V8	3,935	2,760	—
1535	Parkwood 4d, L6	3,945	2,747	—
1545	Kingswood, 4d, 9P, L6	3,990	2,850	—
1635	Parkwood 4d, V8	3,950	2,854	—
1645	Kingswood 4d, 9P, V8	4,000	2,957	—
1735	Nomad 4d, L6	3,955	2,889	—
1835	Nomad 4d, V8	3,960	2,996	—

*To nearest 100

1960 Engines	bore×stroke	bhp	availability
L6, 235.5	3.56×3.94	135	S-six
V8, 283.0	3.88×3.00	170	S-V8
V8, 283.0	3.88×3.00	230	O-all
V8, 348.0	4.13×3.25	250–335	O-all

1961

Biscayne (wb 119.0)—201,000* built		Wght	Price	Prod
1111	sdn 2d, L6	3,415	2,262	—
1121	Util sdn 2d, L6	3,390	2,175	—
1169	sdn 4d, L6	3,500	2,316	—
1211	sdn 2d, V8	3,425	2,369	—
1221	Util sdn 2d, V8	3,395	2,282	—
1269	sdn 4d, V8	3,505	2,423	—
Biscayne Fleetmaster (wb 119.0)				
1311	sdn 2d, L6	3,410	2,230	3,000* (1311–1469)
1369	sdn 4d, L6	3,495	2,284	
1411	sdn 2d, V8	3,415	2,337	
1469	sdn 4d, V8	3,500	2,391	
Bel Air (wb 119.0)—330,000* built				
1511	sdn 2d, L6	3,430	2,384	—
1537	Sport htp cpe, L6	3,475	2,489	—
1539	Sport htp sdn, L6	3,550	2,554	—
1569	sdn 4d, L6	3,515	2,438	—
1611	sdn 2d, V8	3,435	2,491	—
1637	Sport htp cpe, V8	3,480	2,596	—
1639	Sport htp sdn, V8	3,555	2,661	—
1669	sdn 4d, V8	3,520	2,545	—
Impala (wb 119.0)—426,400* built exc 1867				
1711	sdn 2d, L6	3,445	2,536	—
1737	Sport htp cpe, L6	3,485	2,597	—
1739	Sport htp sdn, L6	3,575	2,662	—
1767	conv cpe, L6	3,605	2,847	—
1769	sdn 4d, L6	3,530	2,590	—
1811	sdn 2d, V8	3,440	2,643	—
1837	Sport htp cpe, V8	3,480	2,704	—
1839	Sport htp sdn, V8	3,570	2,769	—
1867	conv cpe, V8	3,600	2,954	64,600
1869	sdn 4d, V8	3,525	2,697	—
Station Wagon (wb 119.0) —168,900 built**				
1135	Brookwood 4d, L6	3,850	2,653	—
1145	Brookwood 4d, 9P, L6	3,900	2,756	—
1235	Brookwood 4d, V8	3,845	2,760	—

1961 Impala Sport Coupe

		Wght	Price	Prod
1245	Brookwood 4d, 9P, V8	3,895	2,864	—
1535	Parkwood 4d, L6	3,865	2,747	—
1545	Parkwood 4d, 9P, L6	3,910	2,850	—
1635	Parkwood 4d, V8	3,860	2,854	—
1645	Parkwood 4d, 9P, V8	3,905	2,957	—
1735	Nomad 4d, L6	3,885	2,889	—
1745	Nomad 4d, 9P, L6	3,935	2,992	—
1835	Nomad 4d, V8	3,880	2,996	—
1845	Nomad 4d, 9P, V8	3,930	3,099	—

*To nearest 100.
**Included with models above.

1961 Engines	bore×stroke	bhp	availability
L6, 235.5	3.56×3.94	135	S-six
V8, 283.0	3.88×3.00	170	S-V8
V8, 283.0	3.88×3.00	230	O-all
V8, 348.0	4.13×3.25	250-350	O-all
V8, 409.0	4.31×3.50	360	O-Impala SS

1962

Chevy II 100 (wb 110.0)		Wght	Price	Prod
0111	sdn 2d, L4	2,410	2,003	
0135	wgn 4d, L4	2,665	2,399	11,500*
0169	sdn 4d, L4	2,445	2,041	
0211	sdn 2d, L6	2,500	2,063	
0235	wgn 4d, L6	2,755	2,399	35,500*
0269	sdn 4d, L6	2,535	2,101	
Chevy II 300 (wb 110.0)				
0311	sdn 2d, L4	2,425	2,084	—
0345	wgn 4d, 9P, L4	2,765	2,517	—
0369	sdn 4d, L4	2,460	2,122	—
0411	sdn 2d, L6	2,515	2,144	
0445	wgn 4d, 9P, L6	2,855	2,577	92,800*
0469	sdn 4d, L6	2,550	2,182	
Chevy II Nova 400, L6 (wb 110.0)				
0435	wgn 4d	2,775	2,497	—
0437	Sport htp cpe	2,550	2,254	59,586
0441	sdn 2d	2,540	2,198	44,390
0449	sdn 4d	2,575	2,336	139,004
0467	conv cpe	2,745	2,475	23,741
Biscayne (wb 119.0)—160,000 built**				
1111	sdn 2d, L6	3,405	2,324	—
1135	wgn 4d, L6	3,845	2,725	—
1169	sdn 4d, L6	3,480	2,378	—
1211	sdn 2d, V8	3,400	2,431	—
1235	wgn 4d, V8	3,840	2,832	—
1269	sdn 4d, V8	3,475	2,485	—
Bel Air (wb 119.0)—365,000 built**				
1511	sdn 2d, L6	3,410	2,456	—
1535	wgn 4d, L6	3,845	2,819	—
1537	Sport htp cpe, L6	3,445	2,561	—
1545	wgn 4d, 9P, L6	3,895	2,922	—
1569	sdn 4d, L6	3,480	2,510	—
1611	sdn 2d, V8	3,405	2,563	—
1635	wgn 4d, V8	3,840	2,926	—
1637	Sport htp cpe, V8	3,440	2,668	—
1645	wgn 4d, 9P, V8	3,890	3,029	—
1669	sdn 4d, V8	3,475	2,617	—
Impala (wb 119.0)—704,900 built (includes SS models)**				
1735	wgn 4d, L6	3,870	2,961	—
1739	Sport htp sdn, L6	3,540	2,734	—
1745	wgn 4d, 9P, L6	3,925	3,064	—
1747	Sport htp cpe, L6	3,455	2,669	—
1767	conv cpe, L6	3,565	2,919	—
1769	sdn 4d, L6	3,510	2,662	—

1962 Bel Air Sport Hardtop Coupe

1963 Impala convertible coupe

1964 Impala Sport hardtop sedan

		Wght	Price	Prod
1835	wgn 4d, V8	3,865	3,068	—
1839	Sport htp sdn, V8	3,535	2,841	—
1845	wgn 4d, 9P, V8	3,920	3,171	—
1847	Sport htp cpe, V8	3,450	2,776	—
1867	conv cpe, V8	3,560	3,026	—
1869	sdn 4d, V8	3,505	2,769	—

*To nearest 100.
**Does not include wagons (187,600 built).

1962 Engines	bore×stroke	bhp	availability
L4, 153.0	3.88×3.25	90	S-Chevy II 100, 300
L6, 194.0	3.56×3.25	120	S-Chevy II all
L6, 235.5	3.56×3.94	135	S-Chevrolet
V8, 283.0	3.88×3.00	170	S-Chevrolet
V8, 327.0	4.00×3.25	250/300	O-V8-all Chev
V8, 409.0	4.31×3.50	380/409	O-V8-all Chev

1963

Chevy II 100 (wb 110.0)—50,400* built		Wght	Price	Prod
0111	sdn 2d, L4	2,430	2,003	—
0135	wgn 4d, L4	2,725	2,338	—
0169	sdn 4d, L4	2,455	2,040	—
0211	sdn 2d, L6	2,520	2,062	—
0235	wgn 4d, L6	2,810	2,397	—
0269	sdn 4d, L6	2,545	2,099	
Chevy II 300 (wb 110.0)—78,800* built				
0311	sdn 2d, L4	2,440	2,084	—
0345	wgn 4d, 9P, L4	2,810	2,516	—
0369	sdn 4d, L4	2,470	2,121	—
0411	sdn 2d, L6	2,530	2,143	
0445	wgn 4d, 9P, L6	2,900	2,575	—
0469	sdn 4d, L6	2,560	2,180	
Chevy II Nova 400, L6 (wb 110.0)				
0435	wgn 4d	2,835	2,494	—
0437	Sport htp cpe	2,590	2,267	87,415
0449	sdn 4d	2,590	2,235	58,862
0467	conv cpe	2,760	2,472	24,823
Biscayne (wb 119.0)—186,500* built				
1111	sdn 2d, L6	3,205	2,322	—
1135	wgn 4d, L6	3,685	2,723	—
1169	sdn 4d, L6	3,280	2,376	—
1211	sdn 2d, V8	3,340	2,429	—
1235	wgn 4d, V8	3,810	2,830	—
1269	sdn 4d, V8	3,415	2,483	—
Bel Air (wb 119.0)—354,100* built				
1511	sdn 2d, L6	3,215	2,454	—
1535	wgn 4d, L6	3,685	2,818	—
1545	wgn 4d, 9P, L6	3,720	2,921	—
1569	sdn 4d, L6	3,280	2,508	—
1611	sdn 2d, V8	3,345	2,561	—
1635	wgn 4d, V8	3,810	2,925	—
1645	wgn 4d, 9P, V8	3,850	3,028	—
1669	sdn 4d, V8	3,415	2,615	—
Impala (wb 119.0) —832,600* built (includes 153,271 SS models)				
1735	wgn 4d, L6	3,705	2,960	—
1739	Sport htp sdn, L6	3,350	2,732	—
1745	wgn 4d, 9P, L6	3,745	3,063	—
1747	Sport htp cpe, L6	3,265	2,667	—
1767	conv cpe, L6	3,400	2,917	—
1769	sdn 4d, L6	3,310	2,661	—
1835	wgn 4d, V8	3,835	3,067	—
1839	Sport htp sdn, V8	3,475	2,839	—
1845	wgn 4d, 9P, V8	3,870	3,170	—
1847	Sport htp cpe, V8	3,390	2,774	—
1867	conv cpe, V8	3,525	3,024	—
1869	sdn 4d, V8	3,435	2,768	—

*To nearest 100; does not include wagons. Total wagons 198,542; Chevy II wagons 75,274.

1963 Engines	bore×stroke	bhp	availability
L4, 153.0	3.88×3.25	90	S-Chevy II
L6, 194.0	3.56×3.25	120	S-Chevy II
L6, 230.0	3.87×3.25	140	S-Chevrolet
V8, 283.0	3.88×3.00	195	S-Chevrolet
V8, 327.0	4.00×3.25	250-340	O-Chevrolet
V8, 409.0	4.31×3.50	340–425	O-Chevrolet

1964

Chevy II 100 (wb 110.0)—53,100 built*		Wght	Price	Prod
0111	sdn 2d, L4	2,455	2,011	—
0169	sdn, L4	2,495	2,048	—
0211	sdn 2d, L6	2,540	2,070	—
0235	wgn 4d, L6	2,840	2,406	—
0269	sdn 4d, L6	2,580	2,108	—

Chevy II Nova 400, L6 (wb 110.0)—102,900* built (includes SS)		Wght	Price	Prod
0411	sdn 2d	2,560	2,206	—
0435	wgn 4d	2,860	2,503	—
0437	Sport htp cpe	2,660	2,271	—
0469	sdn 4d	2,595	2,243	—
Chevy II Nova SS, L6 (wb 110.0)				
0447	Sport htp cpe	2,675	2,433	10,576
Chevelle 300 (wb 115.0)—68,300* built				
5311	sdn 2d, L6	2,825	2,231	—
5315	wgn 2d, L6	3,050	2,528	—
5335	wgn 4d, L6	3,130	2,566	—
5369	sdn 4d, L6	2,850	2,268	—
5411	sdn 2d, V8	2,995	2,339	—
5415	wgn 2d, V8	3,170	2,636	—
5435	wgn 4d, V8	2,250	2,674	—
5469	sdn 4d, V8	2,980	2,376	—
Chevelle Malibu (wb 115.0) 149,000* built				
5535	wgn 4d, L6	3,140	2,647	—
5537	Sport htp cpe, L6	2,850	2,376	—
5545	wgn 4d, 9P, L6	3,240	2,744	—
5567	conv cpe, L6	2,995	2,587	—
5569	sdn 4d, L6	2,870	2,349	—
5635	wgn 4d, V8	3,265	2,755	—
5637	Sport htp cpe, V8	2,975	2,484	—
5645	wgn 4d, 9P, V8	3,365	2,852	—
5667	conv cpe, V8	3,120	2,695	—
5669	sdn 4d, V8	2,996	2,457	—
Chevelle Malibu SS (wb 115.0)—76,860 built				
5737	Sport htp cpe, L6	2,875	2,538	—
5767	conv cpe, L6	3,020	2,749	—
5837	Sport htp cpe, V8	3,000	2,646	—
5867	conv cpe, V8	3,145	2,857	—
Biscayne (wb 119.0)—173,900* built				
1111	sdn 2d, L6	3,230	2,363	—
1135	wgn 4d, L6	3,700	2,763	—
1169	sdn 4d, L6	3,300	2,417	—
1211	sdn 2d, V8	3,365	2,471	—
1235	wgn 4d, V8	3,820	2,871	—
1269	sdn 4d, V8	3,430	2,524	—
Bel Air (wb 119.0)—318,100* built				
1511	sdn 2d, L6	3,235	2,465	—
1535	wgn 4d, L6	3,745	2,828	—
1545	wgn 4d, 9P, L6	3,705	2,931	—
1569	sdn 4d, L6	3,305	2,519	—
1611	sdn 2d, V8	3,370	2,573	—
1635	wgn 4d, V8	3,825	2,935	—
1645	wgn 4d, 9P, V8	3,865	3,039	—
1669	sdn 4d, V8	3,440	2,626	—

1964 Impala SS Sport hardtop coupe

Impala (wb 119.0) —889,600* built (includes 185,325 SS)		Wght	Price	Prod
1735	wgn 4d, L6	3,725	2,970	—
1739	Sport htp sdn, L6	3,370	2,742	—
1745	wgn 4d, 9P, L6	3,770	3,073	—
1767	conv cpe, L6	3,400	2,927	—
1769	sdn 4d, L6	3,340	2,671	—
1835	wgn 4d, V8	3,850	3,077	—
1839	Sport htp sdn, V8	3,490	2,850	—
1845	wgn 4d, 9P, V8	3,895	3,181	—
1847	Sport htp cpe, V8	3,415	2,786	—
1867	conv cpe, V8	3,525	3,035	—
1869	sdn 4d, V8	3,460	2,779	—
Impala SS (wb 119.0)				
1347	htp cpe, L6	3,325	2,839	—
1367	conv cpe, L6	3,435	3,088	—
1447	Sport htp cpe,V8	3,450	2,947	—
1467	conv cpe, V8	3,555	3,196	—

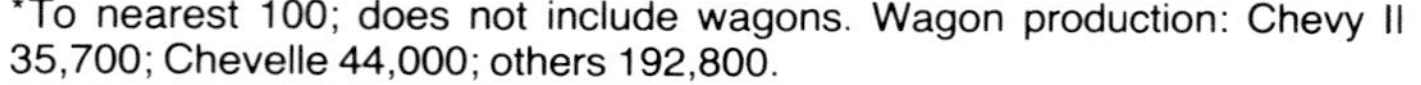
*To nearest 100; does not include wagons. Wagon production: Chevy II 35,700; Chevelle 44,000; others 192,800.

1964 Engines	bore×stroke	bhp	availability
L4, 153.0	3.88×3.25	90	S-Chevy II 100
L6, 194.0	3.56×3.25	120	S-Chevy II 100/400, Chevelle
L6, 230.0	3.87×3.25	140	S-Chevrolet; O-others
L6, 230.0	3.87×3.25	155	O-all
V8, 283.0	3.88×3.00	195	S-V8 Chvlle, Chvrlet; O-Chevy II
V8, 283.0	3.88×3.00	220	O-Chevelle
V8, 327.0	4.00×3.25	250/300	O-Chevrolet, Chevelle
V8, 409.0	4.31×3.50	340-425	O-Chevrolet

1965 Impala 4-door 9-passenger wagon

1965 Chevy II Nova SS hardtop coupe

1965

Chevy II 100 (wb 110.0)		Wght	Price	Prod
11111	sdn 2d, L4	2,505	2,011	1,300*
11169	sdn 4d, L4	2,520	2,048	
11311	sdn 2d, L6	2,605	2,077	
11335	wgn 4d, L6	2,875	2,413	39,200*
11369	sdn 4d, L6	2,620	2,115	
Chevy II Nova 400, L6 (wb 110.0)—51,700* built				
11535	wgn 4d	2,880	2,510	—
11537	htp cpe	2,645	2,270	—
11569	sdn 4d	2,645	2,243	—
Chevy II Nova SS, L6 (wb 110.0)				
11737	htp cpe	2,690	2,433	9,100
Chevelle 300 (wb 115.0) —31,600* built (plus 41,600* DeLuxe)				
13111	sdn 2d, L6	2,870	2,156	—
13115	wgn 2d, L6	3,140	2,453	—
13169	sdn 4d, L6	2,900	2,193	—
13211	sdn 2d, V8	3,010	2,262	—
13215	wgn 2d, V8	3,275	2,561	—
13269	sdn 4d, V8	3,035	2,301	—
13311	Del sdn 2d, L6	2,870	2,231	—
13335	Del wgn 4d, L6	3,185	2,567	—
13369	Del sdn 4d, L6	2,910	2,269	—
13411	Del sdn 2d, V8	3,010	2,339	—
13435	Del wgn 4d, V8	3,320	2,674	—
13469	Del sdn 4d, V8	3,050	2,377	—
Chevelle Malibu (wb 115.0) 152,200* built				
13535	wgn 4d, L6	3,225	2,647	—
13537	htp cpe, L6	2,930	2,377	—
13567	conv cpe, L6	3,025	2,588	—
13569	sdn 4d, L6	2,945	2,250	—
13635	wgn 4d, V8	3,355	2,755	—
13637	htp cpe, V8	3,065	2,485	—
13667	conv cpe, V8	3,160	2,696	—
13669	sdn 4d, V8	3,080	2,458	—

Chevelle Malibu SS (wb 115.0)—101,577 built (201 SS 396)		Wght	Price	Prod
13737	htp cpe, L6	2,980	2,539	—
13767	conv cpe, L6	3,075	2,750	—
13837	htp cpe, V8	3,115	2,647	—
13867	conv cpe, V8	3,210	2,858	—
Biscayne (wb 119.0)				
15311	sdn 2d, L6	3,305	2,363	
15335	wgn 4d, L6	3,765	2,764	107,700*
15369	sdn 4d, L6	3,365	2,417	
15411	sdn 2d, V8	3,455	2,470	
15435	wgn 4d, V8	3,900	2,871	37,600*
15469	sdn 4d, V8	3,515	2,524	
Bel Air (wb 119.0)				
15511	sdn 2d, L6	3,310	2,465	
15535	wgn 4d, L6	3,765	2,828	107,800*
15545	wgn 4d, 9P, L6	3,810	2,931	
15569	sdn 4d, L6	3,380	2,519	
15611	sdn 2d, V8	3,460	2,573	
15635	wgn 4d, V8	3,905	2,936	
15645	wgn 4d, 9P, V8	3,950	3,039	163,600*
15669	sdn 4d, V8	3,530	2,626	
Impala (wb 119.0)—803,400* built (includes Caprice pkg)				
16335	wgn 4d, L6	3,825	2,970	
16337	htp cpe, L6	3,385	2,678	
16339	htp sdn, L6	3,490	2,742	
16345	wgn 4d, 9P, L6	3,865	3,073	56,600*
16367	conv cpe, L6	3,470	2,943	
16369	sdn 4d, L6	3,460	2,672	
16435	wgn 4d, V8	3,960	3,078	
16437	htp cpe, V8	3,525	2,785	
16439	htp sdn, V8	3,630	2,850	
16445	wgn 4d, 9P, V8	4,005	3,181	746,800*
16467	conv cpe, V8	3,605	3,051	
16469	sdn 4d, V8	3,595	2,779	

1966 Caprice hardtop sedan

Impala SS (wb 119.0)—243,114 built		Wght	Price	Prod
16537	htp cpe, L6	3,435	2,839	—
16567	conv cpe, L6	3,505	3,104	—
16637	htp cpe, V8	3,570	2,947	—
16667	conv cpe, V8	3,655	3,212	—

*To nearest 100; does not include wagons. Wagon production: Chevy II 21,500; Chevelle 37,600; others 184,400. Convertible production: Malibu 19,765; Impala SS 27,842.

1965 Engines	bore×stroke	bhp	availability
L4, 153.0	3.88×3.25	90	S-Chevy II 100
L6, 194.0	3.56×3.25	120	S-Chevy II, Chevelle
L6. 230.0	3.87×3.25	140	S-Chevrolet; O-others
L6, 250.0	3.87×3.53	150	O-Chevrolet
V8, 283.0	3.88×3.00	195	S-Chevrolet, Chevelle; O-Chevy II
V8, 283.0	3.88×3.00	220	O-all
V8, 327.0	4.00×3.25	250/300	O-all
V8, 327.0	4.00×3.25	350	O-Chevelle
V8, 396.0	4.09×3.75	325-425	O-Chevrolet, Chevelle
V8, 409.0	4.31×3.50	340/400	O-Chevrolet

1966

Chevy II 100 (wb 110.0)		Wght	Price	Prod
11111	sdn 2d, L4	2,520	2,028	44,500*
11169	sdn 4d, L4	2,535	2,065	
11311	sdn 2d, L6	2,620	2,090	
11335	wgn 4d, L6	2,855	2,430	
11369	sdn 4d, L6	2,635	2,127	
11411	sdn 2d, V8	2,775	2,197	2,500*
11435	wgn 4d, V8	2,990	2,536	
11469	sdn 4d, V8	2,790	2,234	
Chevy II Nova (wb 110.0)				
11535	wgn 4d, L6	2,885	2,518	54,300*
11537	htp cpe, L6	2,675	2,271	
11569	sdn 4d, L6	2,640	2,245	
11635	wgn 4d, V8	3,010	2,623	19,600*
11637	htp cpe, V8	2,830	2,377	
11669	sdn 4d, V8	2,800	2,351	
Chevy II Nova SS (wb 110.0)				
11737	htp cpe, L6	2,740	2,430	6,700*
11837	htp cpe, V8	2,870	2,535	16,300*
Chevelle 300 (wb 115.0)				
13111	sdn 2d, L6	2,895	2,156	23,300*
13169	sdn 4d, L6	2,935	2,202	
13211	sdn 2d, V8	3,040	2,271	5,300*
13269	sdn 4d, V8	3,080	2,308	
13311	Del sdn 2d, L6	2,910	2,239	37,600*
13335	Del wgn 4d, L6	3,210	2,575	
13369	Del sdn 4d, L6	2,945	2,276	
13411	Del sdn 2d, V8	3,060	2,345	
13435	Del wgn 4d, V8	3,350	2,681	
13469	Del sdn 4d, V8	3,095	2,382	

1966 Chevy II Nova SS hardtop coupe

Chevelle Malibu (wb 115.0)—241,600* built		Wght	Price	Prod
13517	htp cpe, L6	2,935	2,378	—
13535	wgn 4d, L6	3,235	2,651	—
13539	htp sdn, L6	3,035	2,458	—
13567	conv cpe, L6	3,030	2,588	—
13569	sdn 4d, L6	2,960	2,352	—
13617	htp cpe, V8	3,075	2,484	—
13635	wgn 4d, V8	3,375	2,766	—
13639	htp sdn, V8	3,180	2,564	—
13667	conv cpe, V8	3,175	2,693	—
13669	sdn 4d, V8	3,110	2,456	—
Chevelle Malibu SS, V8 (wb 115.0)-72,300* built				
13817	htp cpe	3,375	2,776	—
13867	conv cpe, V8	3,470	2,984	—
Biscayne (wb 119.0)				
15311	sdn 2d, L6	3,310	2,379	
15335	wgn 4d, L6	3,770	2,772	83,200*
15369	sdn 4d, L6	3,375	2,431	
15411	sdn 2d, V8	3,445	2,484	
15435	wgn 4d, V8	3,895	2,877	39,200*
15469	sdn 4d, V8	3,519	2,537	
Bel Air (wb 119.0)				
15511	sdn 2d, L6	3,315	2,479	
15535	wgn 4d, 2S, L6	3,770	2,835	72,100*
15545	wgn 4d, 3S, L6	3,815	2,948	
15569	sdn 4d, L6	3,390	2,531	
15611	sdn 2d, V8	3,445	2,584	
15635	wgn 4d, 2S, V8	3,895	2,940	
15645	wgn 4d, 9P, V8	3,940	3,053	164,500*
15669	sdn 4d, V8	3,525	2,636	
Impala (wb 119.0)				
16335	wgn 4d, 2S, L6	3,805	2,971	
16337	htp cpe, L6	3,430	2,684	
16339	htp sdn, L6	3,525	2,747	
16345	wgn 4d, 3S, L6	3,860	3,083	33,100*
16367	conv cpe, L6	3,484	2,935	
16369	sdn 4d, L6	3,435	2,678	
16435	wgn 4d, 2S, V8	3,990	3,076	
16437	htp cpe, V8	3,555	2,789	
16439	htp sdn, V8	3,650	2,852	
16445	wgn 4d, 3S, V8	4,005	3,189	621,800*
16467	conv cpe, V8	3,610	3,041	
16469	sdn 4d, V8	3,565	2,783	
Impala SS (wb 119.0)—119,314 built				
16737	htp cpe, L6	3,460	2,842	—
16767	conv cpe, L6	3,505	3,093	—
16837	htp cpe, V8	3,585	2,947	—
16867	conv cpe, V8	3,630	3,199	—
Caprice, V8 (wb 119.0)—181,000* built				
16635	wgn 4d, 2S	3,970	3,234	—
16639	htp sdn	3,675	3,063	—
16645	wgn 4d, 3S	4,020	3,347	—
16647	htp cpe	3,600	3,000	—

*To nearest 100; does not include wagons. Wagon production: Chevy II 21,400; Chevelle 31,900; others 185,500. Impala SS convertible cpe 15,872.

1966 Engines	bore×stroke	bhp	availability
L4, 153.0	3.88×3.25	90	S-Chevy II 100
L6, 194.0	3.56×3.25	120	S-Chevy II, Chevelle
L6, 230.0	3.87×3.25	140	O-Chevy II, Chevelle
L6, 250.0	3.87×3.53	155	S-Chevrolet O-Chevy II
V8, 283.0	3.88×3.00	195	S-Chevelle, Chevrolet;
V8, 283.0	3.88×3.00	220	O-Chevrolet
V8, 327.0	4.00×3.25	275/300	O-all
V8, 327.0	4.00×3.25	350	O-Chevelle,Chevy II
V8, 396.0	4.09×3.76	325	S-Chvlle 396; O-Chvrlet, Chvlle
V8, 396.0	4.09×3.76	360/375	O-Chevelle

1967

Chevy II 100 (wb 110.0)		Wght	Price	Prod
11111	sdn 2d, L4	2,555	2,090	
11169	sdn 4d, L4	2,560	2,120	
11311	sdn 2d, L6	2,640	2,152	34,200*
11335	wgn 4d, L6	2,865	2,478	
11369	sdn 4d, L6	2,650	2,182	
11411	sdn 2d, V8	2,770	2,258	
11435	wgn 4d, V8	2,985	2,583	1,700*
11469	sdn 4d, V8	2,780	2,287	
Chevy II Nova (wb 110.0)				
11535	wgn 4d, L6	2,890	2,566	
11537	htp cpe, L6	2,660	2,330	34,400*
11569	sdn 4d, L6	2,660	2,298	
11635	wgn 4d, V8	3,015	2,671	
11637	htp cpe, V8	2,790	2,435	13,200*
11669	sdn 4d, V8	2,790	2,403	
Chevy II Nova SS (wb 110.0)				
11737	htp cpe, L6	2,690	2,487	1,900*
11837	htp cpe, V8	2,820	2,590	8,200*
Camaro (wb 108.1) (includes 602 Z-28s)				
12337	htp cpe, L6	2,770	2,466	
12367	conv cpe, L6	3,025	2,704	58,808
12437	htp cpe, V8	2,920	2,572	
12467	conv cpe, V8	3,180	2,809	162,109
Chevelle 300 (wb 115.0)				
13111	sdn 2d, L6	2,935	2,221	
13169	sdn 4d, L6	2,955	2,250	19,900*
13211	sdn 2d, V8	3,070	2,326	
13269	sdn 4d, V8	3,090	2,356	4,800*
13311	Del sdn 2d, L6	2,955	2,295	
13335	Del wgn 4d, L6	3,230	2,619	19,300*
13369	Del sdn 4d, L6	2,980	2,324	
13411	Del sdn 2d, V8	3,090	2,400	
13435	Del wgn 4d, V8	3,360	2,725	7,000*
13469	Del sdn 4d, V8	3,110	2,430	
Chevelle Malibu (wb 115.0)				
13517	htp cpe, L6	2,980	2,434	
13535	wgn 4d, L6	3,260	2,695	
13539	htp sdn, L6	3,065	2,506	40,600*
13567	conv cpe, L6	3,050	2,637	
13569	sdn 4d, L6	3,000	2,400	
13617	htp cpe, V8	3,115	2,540	
13635	wgn 4d, V8	3,390	2,801	
13639	htp sdn, V8	3,200	2,611	187,200*
13667	conv cpe, V8	3,185	2,743	
13669	sdn 4d, V8	3,130	2,506	

1967 Impala hardtop coupe

1967 Camaro SS 350 convertible coupe

1968 Impala SS 427 convertible coupe

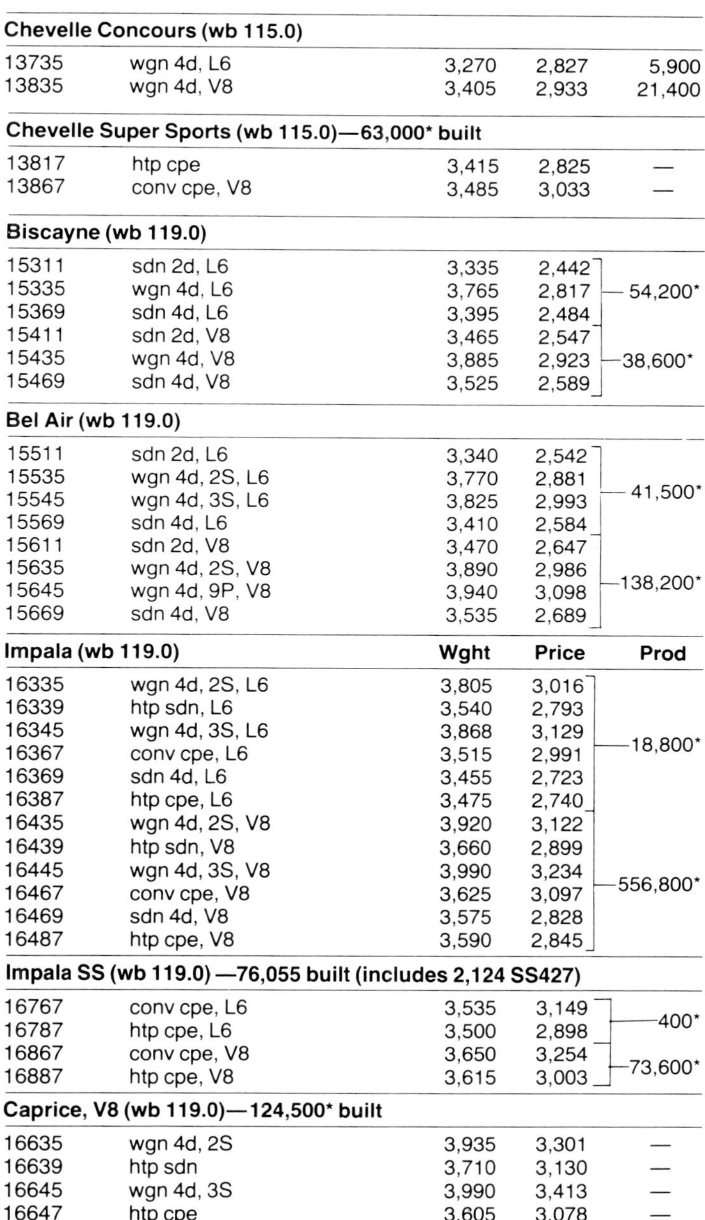

Chevelle Concours (wb 115.0)				
13735	wgn 4d, L6	3,270	2,827	5,900
13835	wgn 4d, V8	3,405	2,933	21,400
Chevelle Super Sports (wb 115.0)—63,000* built				
13817	htp cpe	3,415	2,825	—
13867	conv cpe, V8	3,485	3,033	—
Biscayne (wb 119.0)				
15311	sdn 2d, L6	3,335	2,442	
15335	wgn 4d, L6	3,765	2,817	54,200*
15369	sdn 4d, L6	3,395	2,484	
15411	sdn 2d, V8	3,465	2,547	
15435	wgn 4d, V8	3,885	2,923	38,600*
15469	sdn 4d, V8	3,525	2,589	
Bel Air (wb 119.0)				
15511	sdn 2d, L6	3,340	2,542	
15535	wgn 4d, 2S, L6	3,770	2,881	
15545	wgn 4d, 3S, L6	3,825	2,993	41,500*
15569	sdn 4d, L6	3,410	2,584	
15611	sdn 2d, V8	3,470	2,647	
15635	wgn 4d, 2S, V8	3,890	2,986	
15645	wgn 4d, 9P, V8	3,940	3,098	138,200*
15669	sdn 4d, V8	3,535	2,689	
Impala (wb 119.0)		**Wght**	**Price**	**Prod**
16335	wgn 4d, 2S, L6	3,805	3,016	
16339	htp sdn, L6	3,540	2,793	
16345	wgn 4d, 3S, L6	3,868	3,129	
16367	conv cpe, L6	3,515	2,991	18,800*
16369	sdn 4d, L6	3,455	2,723	
16387	htp cpe, L6	3,475	2,740	
16435	wgn 4d, 2S, V8	3,920	3,122	
16439	htp sdn, V8	3,660	2,899	
16445	wgn 4d, 3S, V8	3,990	3,234	
16467	conv cpe, V8	3,625	3,097	556,800*
16469	sdn 4d, V8	3,575	2,828	
16487	htp cpe, V8	3,590	2,845	
Impala SS (wb 119.0) —76,055 built (includes 2,124 SS427)				
16767	conv cpe, L6	3,535	3,149	400*
16787	htp cpe, L6	3,500	2,898	
16867	conv cpe, V8	3,650	3,254	
16887	htp cpe, V8	3,615	3,003	73,600*
Caprice, V8 (wb 119.0)—124,500* built				
16635	wgn 4d, 2S	3,935	3,301	—
16639	htp sdn	3,710	3,130	—
16645	wgn 4d, 3S	3,990	3,413	—
16647	htp cpe	3,605	3,078	—

*To nearest 100; does not include wagons. Wagon production: Chevy II 12,900; Chevelle 27,300; others 155,100. Convertible production: Camaro 25,141; Impala SS 9,545.

1967 Engines	bore×stroke	bhp	availability
L4, 153.0	3.88×3.25	90	S-Chevy II 100 sdns
L6, 194.0	3.56×3.25	120	S-Chevy II,Chevelle
L6, 230.0	3.88×3.25	140	S-Camaro
L6, 250.0	3.88×3.53	155	S-Chevrolet exc Caprice; O-others
V8, 283.0	3.88×3.00	195	S-all exc Camaro
V8, 302.0	4.00×3.00	290	O-Camaro (Z-28)
V8, 327.0	4.00×3.25	210	O-Camaro
V8, 327.0	4.00×3.25	275	O-all
V8, 327.0	4.00×3.25	325	O-Chevelle
V8, 350.0	4.00×3.48	295	O-Camaro
V8, 396.0	4.09×3.76	325	S-Chevelle 396; O-Cam,Chevrlt
V8, 396.0	4.09×3.76	350	O-Chevelle 396
V8, 427.0	4.25×3.76	385	O-Chevrolet

1968

Chevy II Nova (wb 111.0) —201,000* built (includes 6,571 SS cpes)				
11127	cpe L4	2,760	2,222	—
11169	sdn 4d, L4	2,790	2,252	—
11327	cpe L6	2,860	2,284	—
11369	sdn 4d, L6	2,890	2,314	—
11427	cpe, V8	2,995	2,390	—
11469	sdn 4d, V8	3,025	2,419	—
Camaro (wb 108.1) (includes 7,199 Z-28s)				
12337	htp cpe, L6	2,810	2,588	50,937
12367	conv cpe, L6	3,110	2,802	
12437	htp cpe, V8	2,955	2,694	
12467	conv cpe, V8	3,245	2,908	184,178
Chevelle 300 (wb 112.0; 4d-116.0)				
13127	cpe, L6	3,020	2,341	
13135	Nomad wgn 4d, L6	3,370	2,625	2,900*
13227	cpe, V8	3,155	2,447	
13235	Nomad wgn 4d, V8	3,500	2,731	9,700*
13327	Del cpe, L6	3,035	2,415	
13335	Cus Nomad wgn 4d, L6	3,415	2,736	25,500*
13337	Del htp cpe, L6	3,050	2,479	
13369	Del sdn 4d, L6	3,105	2,445	
13427	Del cpe, V8	3,170	2,521	
13435	Cus Nomad wgn 4d, V8	3,545	2,841	
13437	Del htp cpe, V8	3,185	2,584	17,700*
13469	Del sdn 4d, V8	3,240	2,550	
Chevelle Malibu (wb 112.0; 4d-116.0)		**Wght**	**Price**	**Prod**
13535	wgn 4d, L6	3,440	2,846	
13537	htp cpe, L6	3,070	2,558	
13539	htp sdn, L6	3,185	2,629	33,100*
13567	conv cpe, L6	3,135	2,757	
13569	sdn 4d, L6	3,125	2,524	
13635	wgn 4d, V8	3,575	2,951	
13637	htp cpe, V8	3,204	2,663	
13639	htp sdn, V8	3,315	2,735	233,200*
13667	conv cpe, V8	3,260	2,863	
13669	sdn 4d, V8	3,255	2,629	

Chevelle Concours (wb 116.0)				
13735	wgn 4d, L6	3,450	2,978	—
13835	wgn 4d, V8	3,580	3,083	—

Chevelle SS 396 (wb 112.0)				
13837	htp cpe	3,550	2,899	60,499
13867	conv cpe	3,570	3,102	2,286

Biscayne (wb 119.0)				
15311	sdn 2d, L6	3,400	2,581	
15335	wgn 4d, L6	3,790	2,957	44,500*
15369	sdn 4d, L6	3,465	2,623	
15411	sdn 2d, V8	3,520	2,686	
15435	wgn 4d, V8	3,900	3,062	37,600*
15469	sdn 4d, V8	3,585	2,728	

Bel Air (wb 119.0)				
15511	sdn 2d, L6	3,405	2,681	
15535	wgn 4d, 2S, L6	3,800	3,020	28,800*
15545	wgn 4d, 3S, L6	3,845	3,133	
15569	sdn 4d, L6	3,470	2,723	
15611	sdn 2d, V8	3,525	2,786	
15635	wgn 4d, 2S, V8	3,910	3,125	123,400*
15645	wgn 4d, 3S, V8	3,955	3,238	
15669	sdn 4d, V8	3,590	2,828	

Impala (wb 119.0)—38,210 SS built (includes 1,778 SS427)				
16339	hpt sdn, L6	3,605	2,917	
16369	sdn 4d, L6	3,520	2,846	11,400*
16387	htp cpe, L6	3,250	2,863	
16435	wgn 4d, 2S, V8	3,940	3,245	
16439	htp sdn, V8	3,715	3,022	
16445	wgn 4d, 3S, V8	3,905	3,358	
16447	Cus htp cpe, V8	3,645	3,021	699,500*
16467	conv cpe, V8	3,680	3,197	
16469	sdn 4d, V8	3,630	2,951	
16487	htp cpe, V8	3,630	2,968	

Caprice (wb 119.0)—115,500* built				
16635	wgn 4d, 2S	3,950	3,458	—
16639	htp sdn	3,755	3,271	—
16645	wgn 4d, 3S	4,005	3,570	—
16647	htp cpe	3,660	3,219	—

*To nearest 100; does not include wagons. Wagon production: Chevelle 45,500; others 175,600. Camaro convertible cpe 20,440.

1968 Engines	bore×stroke	bhp	availability
L4, 153.0	3.88×3.25	90	S-Chevy II
L6, 230.0	3.88×3.25	140	S-Chevy II, Camaro, Chevelle
L6, 250.0	3.88×3.53	155	S-Chevrolet; O-Camaro, Chevelle
V8, 302.0	4.00×3.00	290	O-Camaro (Z-28)
V8, 307.0	3.88×3.25	200	S-Chevy II, Chevelle, Chevrolet
V8, 327.0	4.00×3.25	210	S-Camaro
V8, 327.0	4.00×3.25	250	O-Chevelle,Chevrolet
V8, 327.0	4.00×3.25	275	O-all
V8, 327.0	4.00×3.25	325	O-Chevelle
V8, 350.0	4.00×3.48	295	O-Chevy II, Camaro
V8, 396.0	4.09×3.76	325	S-Chevelle 396; O-Camaro, Chevr
V8, 396.0	4.00×3.00	350/375	O-Camaro, Chevelle
V8, 427.0	4.25×3.76	385/425	O-Chevrolet

1969

Chevy II Nova (wb 111.0) —17,564 SS cpes built		Wght	Price	Prod
11127	cpe, L4	2,785	2,237	6,100*
11169	sdn 4d, L4	2,810	2,267	
11327	cpe L6	2,895	2,315	10,200*
11369	sdn 4d, L6	2,920	2,345	
11427	cpe, V8	3,035	2,405	89,900*
11469	sdn 4d, V8	3,065	2,434	

Camaro (wb 108.1) (includes 19,014 Z-28s)				
12337	htp cpe, L6	3,040	2,638	65,008**
12367	conv cpe, L6	3,160	2,852	
12437	htp cpe, V8	3,050	2,726	178,087**
12467	conv cpe, V8	3,295	2,940	

Note: wagon designation "CT" refers to conventional tailgate, opening from top. Most wagons had dual-action tailgates, opening from top or from side, from 1969 onward.

Chevelle Nomad (wb 116.0)				
13135	wgn 4d, CT, L6	3,390	2,668	—
13136	wgn 4d, L6	3,475	2,710	—
13235	wgn 4d, CT, V8	3,515	2,758	—
13236	wgn 4d, V8	3,600	2,800	—

Chevelle 300 Del (wb 112.0; 4d-116.0)				
13327	cpe, L6	3,035	2,458	
13337	htp cpe, L6	3,075	2,521	11,000*
13369	sdn 4d, L6	3,100	2,488	

1969 Chevelle SS 396 convertible coupe

1970 Chevelle SS 396 hardtop coupe

		Wght	Price	Prod
13427	cpe, V8	3,165	2,548	31,000*
13437	htp cpe, V8	3,205	2,611	
13469	sdn 4d, V8	3,230	2,577	
Chevelle Greenbrier (wb 116.0)				
13335	wgn 4d, CT, L6	3,445	2,779	7,400*
13336	wgn 4d, L6	3,530	2,821	
13435	wgn 4d, CT, V8	3,585	2,869	38,500*
13436	wgn 4d, 2S, V8	3,665	2,911	
13446	wgn 4d, 3S, V8	3,740	3,020	
Chevelle Malibu (wb 112.0; 4d-116.0)				
13537	htp cpe, L6	3,095	2,601	23,500*
13539	htp sdn, L6	3,205	2,672	
13567	conv cpe, L6	3,175	2,800	
13569	sdn 4d, L6	3,130	2,567	
13637	htp cpe, V8	3,230	2,690	343,600*
13639	htp sdn, V8	3,340	2,762	
13667	conv cpe, V8	3,300	2,889	
13669	sdn 4d, V8	3,265	2,657	
Chevelle Concours (wb 116.0)				
13536	wgn 4d, L6	3,545	2,931	—
13636	wgn 4d, 2S, V8	3,685	3,021	—
13646	wgn 4d, 3S, V8	3,755	3,141	—
13836	del wgn 4d, 2S, V8	3,680	3,153	—
13846	del wgn 4d, 3S, V8	3,730	3,266	—
Biscayne (wb 119.0)				
15311	sdn 2d, L6	3,530	2,645	27,400*
15336	wgn 4d, L6	4,045	3,064	
15369	sdn 4d, L6	3,590	2,687	
15411	sdn 2d, V8	3,670	2,751	41,300*
15436	wgn 4d, V8	4,170	3,169	
15469	sdn 4d, V8	3,725	2,793	
Bel Air (wb 119.0)				
15511	sdn 2d, L6	3,540	2,745	17,000*
15536	wgn 4d, 2S, L6	4,045	3,127	
15546	wgn 4d, 3S, L6	4,100	3,240	
15569	sdn 4d, L6	3,590	2,787	
15611	sdn 2d, V8	3,675	2,851	139,700*
15636	wgn 4d, 2S, V8	4,175	3,232	
15646	wgn 4d, 3S, V8	4,230	3,345	
15669	sdn 4d, V8	3,725	2,893	
Impala (wb 119.0) —2,455 SS427 built				
16337	htp cpe, L6	3,650	2,927	8,700*
16339	htp sdn, L6	3,735	2,981	
16369	sdn 4d, L6	3,640	2,911	
16436	wgn 4d, 2S, V8	3,725	3,352	768,300*
16437	htp cpe, V8	3,775	3,033	
16439	htp sdn, V8	3,855	3,056	
16446	wgn 4d, 3S, V8	4,285	3,465	
16447	Cus htp cpe, V8	3,800	3,085	
16467	conv cpe, V8	3,835	3,261	
16469	sdn 4d, V8	3,760	3,016	
Caprice, V8 (wb 119.0)—166,900* built				
16636	wgn 4d, 2S	4,245	3,565	—
16639	htp sdn	3,895	3,346	—
16646	wgn 4d, 3S	4,300	3,678	—
16647	htp cpe	3,815	3,294	—

*To nearest 100; does not include wagons.
**Includes 1970 extension of 1969 model. Wagon production: Chevelle 45,900; others 59,300. Camaro convertible cpe 17,573.

1969 Engines	bore×stroke	bhp	availability
L4, 153.0	3.88×3.25	90	S-Chevy II
L6, 230.0	3.88×3.25	140	S-Chevelle,Chevy II,Camaro
L6, 250.0	3.88×3.53	155	S-Chvr; O-Chvl,Chev II,Cam
V8, 302.0	4.00×3.00	350	O-Camaro (Z-28)
V8, 307.0	3.88×3.25	200	S-Chevy II, Chevelle
V8, 327.0	4.00×3.25	210	S-Camaro
V8, 327.0	4.00×3.25	235	S-Chevrolet
V8, 350.0	4.00×3.48	255	O-all
V8, 350.0	4.00×3.48	300	O-Chevr, Chevl, II SS, Cam SS
V8, 396.0	4.09×3.76	265	S-Chevelle 396; O-Chevrolet
V8, 396.0	4.09×3.76	325	O-Chevelle 396, Camaro SS
V8, 396.0	4.09×3.76	350/375	O-Chevelle/Nova/Camaro SS
V8, 427.0	4.25×3.76	335-425	O-Chevrolet

Note: Station wagon engines—for wb 116 read Chevelle; for wb 119 read Chevrolet.

1970

		Wght	Price	Prod
Nova (wb 111.0)—254,242* built (inc. 19,558 SS models)				
11127	htp cpe, L4	2,820	2,335	—
11169	sdn 4d, L4	2,843	2,365	—
11327	cpe, L6	2,919	2,414	—
11369	sdn 4d, L6	2,942	2,443	—
11427	cpe, V8	3,048	2,503	—
11469	sdn 4d, V8	3,071	2,533	—
Camaro (wb 108.1) (includes 8,733 Z-28s)				
12387	spt cpe, L6	3,076	2,749	12,566
12487	spt cpe, V8	3,190	2,839	112,323
Chevelle (wb 112.0; 4d-116.0)—354,855 built (including Malibu)				
13337	htp cpe, L6	3,142	2,620	—
13369	sdn 4d, L6	3,196	2,585	—
13437	htp cpe, V8	3,260	2,710	—
13469	sdn 4d, V8	3,312	2,679	-
Chev Malibu (wb 112.0; 4d 116.0) (53,599 SS; 3,733 w/454 V8)				
13537	htp cpe, L6	3,197	2,719	—
13539	htp sdn, L6	3,302	2,790	—
13567	conv cpe, L6	3,243	2,919	—
13569	sdn 4d, L6	3,221	2,685	—
13637	htp cpe, V8	3,307	2,809	—
13639	htp sdn, V8	3,409	2,881	—
13667	conv cpe, V8	3,352	3,009	—
13669	sdn 4d, V8	3,330	2,775	
Station Wagon (wb 116.0)				
13136	Nomad 4d, 2S, L6	3,615	2,835	—
13236	Nomad 4d, 2S, V8	3,718	2,925	—
13336	Greenbrier 4d, 2S, L6	3,644	2,946	—
13436	Greenbrier 4d, 2S, V8	3,748	3,100	—

		Wght	Price	Prod
13446	Greenbrier 4d, 3S, V8	3,794	3,213	—
13536	Concours 4d, 2S, L6	3,687	3,056	—
13636	Concours 4d, 2S, V8	3,794	3,210	—
13646	Concours 4d, 3S, V8	3,836	3,323	—
13836	Concours del wgn 4d, 2S, V8	3,821	3,342	—
13846	Concours del wgn 4d, 3S, V8	3,880	3,455	—
Biscayne (wb 119.0)				
15369	sdn 4d, L6	3,600	2,787	12,300*
15469	sdn 4d, V8	3,759	2,898	23,100*
Bel Air (wb 119.0)				
15569	sdn 4d, L6	3,604	2,887	9,000*
15669	sdn 4d, V8	3,763	2,998	66,800*
Impala (wb 119.0)—495,909 built exc 16467				
16337	htp cpe, L6	3,641	3,038	—
16369	sdn 4d, L6	3,655	3,021	—
16437	htp cpe, V8	3,788	3,149	—
16439	htp sdn, V8	3,871	3,203	—
16447	Cus htp cpe, V8	3,801	3,266	—
16467	conv cpe, V8	3,843	3,377	9,562
16469	sdn 4d, V8	3,802	3,132	—
Caprice (wb 119.0)				
16639	htp sdn	3,905	3,527	92,000*
16647	htp cpe	3,821	3,474	
Monte Carlo (wb 116.0) (inc. 3,823 w/SS454 pkg.)				
13857	htp cpe	3,460	3,123	130,657
Station Wagon (wb 119.0)				
15436	Brookwood 4d, 2S	4,204	3,294	—
15636	Townsman 4d, 2S	4,208	3,357	—
15646	Townsman 4d, 3S	4,263	3,469	—
16436	Kingswood 4d, 2S	4,269	3,477	—
16446	Kingswood 4d, 3S	4,329	3,589	—
16636	Kingswood del 4d, 2S	4,295	3,753	—
16646	Kingswood del 4d, 3S	4,361	3,886	—

*Includes 19,558 SS coupes.

1970 Engines	bore×stroke	bhp	availability
L4, 153.0	3.88×3.25	90	S-Nova
L6, 230.0	3.88×3.25	140	S-Camaro; O-Nova
L6, 250.0	3.88×3.53	155	S-Chevrolet exc Caprice & Impala cpe, Chevelle; O-Nova, Camaro
V8, 307.0	3.88×3.25	200	S-Nova, Camaro; O-Chevelle
V8, 350.0	4.00×3.48	250	S-Chevr, MC; O-others
V8, 350.0	4.00×3.48	300	O-Chevr, MC, Chevl, Cam, Nova SS
V8, 350.0	4.00×3.48	360	O-Camaro (Z-28)
V8, 402.0*	4.13×3.76	375	O-Camaro, Chevelle
V8, 402.0*	4.13×3.76	350	O-Camaro, Chevelle
V8, 400.0	4.12×3.75	265	O-Chevrolet, Monte Carlo
V8, 400.0	4.12×3.75	330	O-Monte Carlo, Chevelle
V8, 454.0	4.25×4.00	345	O-Chevrolet
V8, 454.0	4.25×4.00	360	O-Monte Carlo
V8, 454.0	4.25×4.00	390	O-Chevrolet

Note: Station wagon engines—for wb 116 read Chevelle; for wb 119 read Chevrolet. *Commonly known as "396," actual displacement 402 cid.

1971

Vega (wb 97.0)		Wght	Price	Prod
14111	sdn 2d	2,146	2,090	58,804
14177	htchbk cpe 3d	2,190	2,196	168,308
14115	Kammback wgn 3d	2,230	2,328	42,793
Nova (wb 111.0)				
11327	cpe 2d L6	2,952	2,376	65,891

1971 Monte Carlo hardtop coupe

		Wght	Price	Prod
11369	sdn 4d L6	2,976	2,405	29,037
11427	cpe 2d V8	3,084	2,471	77,344
11469	sdn 4d V8	3,108	2,501	22,606
Camaro (wb 108.1; incl. 4,862 Z/28s)				
12387	spt cpe L6	3,094	2,921	11,178
12487	spt cpe V8	3,218	3,016	103,452
Chevelle (wb 112.0; 4d-116.0)				
11337	htp cpe L6	3,166	2,712	6,660
11369	sdn 4d L6	3,210	2,677	6,621
13437	htp cpe V8	3,296	2,807	17,117
13469	sdn 4d V8	3,338	2,773	9,042
13537	Malibu htp cpe L6	3,212	2,885	6,220
13569	Malibu sdn 4d L6	3,250	2,851	4,241
13637	Malibu htp cpe V8	3,342	2,980	180,117
13639	Malibu htp sdn V8	3,450	3,052	20,775
13667	Malibu conv V8	3,390	3,260	5,089
13669	Malibu sdn 4d V8	3,380	2,947	37,385
Chevelle Wagon (wb 116.0)				
13136	Nomad 4d 2S L6	3,632	2,997	2,801
13236	Nomad 4d 2S V8	3,746	3,097	6,528
13436	Greenbrier 4d 2S V8	3,820	3,228	6,128
13446	Greenbrier 4d 3S V8	3,882	3,340	2,129
13636	Concours 4d 2S V8	3,864	3,337	12,716
13646	Concours 4d 3S V8	3,908	3,450	4,276
13836	Concours Estate 4d 2S V8	3,892	3,514	4,502
13846	Concours Estate 4d 3S V8	3,944	3,626	3,219
Biscayne (wb 121.5)				
15369	sdn 4d L6	3,732	3,096	5,846
15469	sdn 4d V8	3,888	3,448	16,463
Bel Air (wb 121.5)				
15569	sdn 4d L6	3,732	3,233	3,452
15669	sdn 4d V8	3,888	3,585	38,534
Impala (wb 121.5)				
16357	htp cpe L6	3,742	3,408	939
16369	sdn 4d L6	3,760	3,391	1,606
16439	htp sdn V8	3,978	3,813	140,300
16447	Custom htp cpe V8	3,912	3,826	139,437
16457	htp cpe V8	3,896	3,759	52,952
16467	conv V8	3,960	4,021	4,576
16469	sdn 4d V8	3,914	3,742	135,334
Caprice (wb 121.5)				
16639	htp sdn 4d	4,040	4,134	64,093
16647	htp cpe	3,964	4,081	46,404

1971 Impala hardtop coupe

1972 Nova two-door coupe

Monte Carlo (wb 116.0)		Wght	Price	Prod
13857	htp cpe	3,488	3,416	128,600
Chevrolet Wagon (wb 125.0)				
15435	Brookwood 4d 2S	4,542	3,929	5,314
15635	Townsman 4d 2S	4,544	4,020	12,951
15645	Townsman 4d 3S	4,598	4,135	6,870
16435	Kingswood 4d 2S	4,588	4,112	26,638
16445	Kingswood 4d 3S	4,648	4,227	32,311
16635	Kingswood Estate 4d 2S	4,678	4,384	11,913
16645	Kingswood Estate 4d 3S	4,738	4,498	19,010

1971 Engines	bore×stroke	bhp	availability
L4, 140.0	3.50×3.63	90	S-Vega
L4, 140.0	3.50×3.63	110	O-Vega
L6, 250.0	3.88×3.53	145	S-Nova,Chevl,Cam,Chevr
V8, 307.0	3.88×3.25	200	S-Nova,Chevl,Cam
V8, 350.0	4.00×3.48	245	S-MC,Chevr exc K/Est & Cap O-Nova,Chevl,Cam
V8, 350.0	4.00×3.48	270	O-Chevl,Cam,MC,Chevr
V8, 350.0	4.00×3.48	330	O-Camaro (Z-28)
V8, 400.0	4.12×3.75	255	S-Chevr K/Est & Cap; O-Chevr
V8, 402.0**	4.13×3.76	300	O-Chevl,Cam,MC,Chevr
V8, 454.0	4.25×4.00	365	O-Chevl,MC,Chevr
V8, 454.0	4.25×4.00	425	O-Chevl,MC

*"Chevr" for 1971-80 means full-size Chevrolets. In above context, this includes Biscayne, Bel Air, Impala, Caprice and full-size (125-in. wb) station wagons. **Commonly known as "396", actual displacement 402 cid.

1972

Vega (wb 97.0)		Wght	Price	Prod
1V11	sdn 2d	2,158	2,060	55,839
1V15	wgn 3d	2,333	2,285	71,957
1V77	htchbk cpe 3d	2,294	2,160	262,682
Nova (wb 111.0)				
1X27	cpe 2d L6	2,949	2,351	96,740
1X27	cpe 2d V8	3,083	2,441	163,475
1X69	sdn 4d L6	2,982	2,379	43,029
1X69	sdn 4d V8	3,116	2,469	46,489
Camaro (wb 108.1; includes 2,575 Z/28s)				
1Q87	spt cpe L6	3,121	2,730	4,824
1Q87	spt cpe V8	3,248	2,820	63,832
Chevelle (wb 112.0; 4d-116.0)				
1C37	htp cpe L6	3,172	2,669	6,993
1C37	htp cpe V8	3,300	2,759	22,714
1C69	sdn 4d L6	3,204	2,636	6,764
1C69	sdn 4d V8	3,332	2,726	12,881

		Wght	Price	Prod
1D37	Malibu htp cpe L6	3,194	2,833	4,790
1D37	Malibu htp cpe V8	3,327	2,923	207,598
1D39	Malibu htp sdn V8	3,438	2,991	24,192
1D67	Malibu conv V8	3,379	3,187	4,853
1D69	Malibu sdn 4d L6	3,240	2,801	3,562
1D69	Malibu sdn 4d V8	3,371	2,891	45,013
Chevelle Wagon (wb 116.0)				
1B36	Nomad 4d 2S L6	3,605	2,926	2,956
1B36	Nomad 4d 2S V8	3,732	3,016	7,768
1C36	Greenbrier 4d 2S V8	3,814	3,140	6,975
1C46	Greenbrier 4d 3S V8	3,870	3,247	2,370
1D36	Concours 4d 2S V8	3,857	3,244	17,968
1D46	Concours 4d 3S V8	3,909	3,351	6,560
1H36	Concours Estate 4d 2S V8	3,887	3,431	5,331
1H46	Concours Estate 4d 3S V8	3,943	3,538	4,407
Chevrolet (wb 122.0)				
1K69	Biscayne sdn 4d L6	3.857	3,074	1,504
1K59	Biscayne sdn 4d V8	4,045	3,408	19,034
1L69	Bel Air sdn 4d L6	3,854	3,204	868
1L69	Bel Air sdn 4d V8	4,042	3,538	41,020
1M39	Impala htp sdn V8	4,150	3,771	170,304
1M47	Impala Custom htp cpe V8	4,053	3,787	183,493
1M57	Impala htp cpe L6	3,864	3,385	289
1M57	Impala htp cpe V8	4,049	3,720	52,403
1M67	Impala conv V8	4,125	3,979	6,456
1M69	Impala sdn 4d L6	3,928	3,369	1,235
1M69	Impala sdn 4d V8	4,113	3,708	183,361
1N39	Caprice htp sdn V8	4,203	4,076	78,768
1N47	Caprice htp cpe V8	4,102	4,026	65,513
1N69	Caprice sdn 4d	4,166	4,009	34,174
Chevrolet Station Wagon (wb 125.0)				
1K35	Brookwood 4d 2S	4,686	3,882	8,150
1L35	Townsman 4d 2S	4,687	3,969	16,482
1L45	Townsman 4d 3S	4,769	4,078	8,667
1M35	Kingswood 4d 2S	4,734	4,056	43,152
1M45	Kingswood 4d 3S	4,817	4,165	40,248
1N35	Kingswood Estate 4d 2S	4,798	4,314	20,281
1N45	Kingswood Estate 4d 3S	4,883	4,423	34,723
Monte Carlo (wb 116.0)				
1H57	htp cpe V8	3,506	3,362	180,819

1972 Engines	bore×stroke	bhp	availability
L4, 140.0	3.50×3.63	80	S-Vega
L4, 140.0	3.50×3.63	90	O-Vega
L6, 250.0	3.88×3.53	110	S-Nova,Chevl,Cam,Chevr exc Cap & K/Est
V8, 307.0	3.88×3.25	130	S-Nova,Chevl, & Cam exc Cal

	bore×stroke	bhp	availability
V8, 350.0	4.00×3.48	165	S-Chevl & Cam in Cal. O-Nova, Chevl, Chevr
V8, 350.0	4.00×3.48	175	O-Chevl, MC
V8, 350.0	4.00×3.48	200	O-Cam,Chevr
V8, 350.0	4.00×3.48	255	O-Camaro (Z/28)
V8, 400.0	4.12×3.75	170	S-Chevr Cap & K/Est; O-Chevr
V8, 402.0	4.13×3.76	210	O-Chevr
V8, 402.0	4.13×3.76	240	O-Chevl,Cam, MC
V8, 454.0	4.25×4.00	270	O-Chevl, MC, Chevr

1973

Vega (wb 97.0)		Wght	Price	Prod
V11	sdn 2d	2,219	2,087	58,425
V15	wgn 3d	2,317	2,323	102,751
V77	htchbk cpe 3d	2,313	2,192	266,124
Nova (wb 111.0)				
X17	htchbk cpe 3d L6	3,145	2,528	11,005
X17	htchbk cpe 3d V8	3,274	2,618	33,949
X27	cpe L6	3,033	2,377	54,140
X27	cpe V8	3,162	2,467	81,679
X69	sdn 4d L6	3,065	2,407	27,440
X69	sdn 4d V8	3,194	2,497	32,843
Y17	Custom htchbk cpe 3d L6	3,152	2,701	3,172
Y17	Custom htchbk cpe 3d V8	3,281	2,792	42,886
Y27	Custom cpe L6	3,073	2,551	6,336
Y27	Custom cpe V8	3,202	2,741	52,042
Y69	Custom sdn 4d L6	3,105	2,580	4,344
Y69	Custom sdn 4d V8	3,234	2,671	19,673
Camaro (wb 108.1; incl. 11,574 Z/28s)				
Q87	spt cpe L6	3,119	2,781	3,614
Q87	spt cpe V8	3,238	2,872	60,810
S87	Type LT spt cpe V8	3,349	3,268	32,327
Chevelle (wb 112.0; 4d-116.0)				
C29	Deluxe Colonnade sdn 4d L6	3,435	2,719	5,253
C29	Deluxe Colonnade sdn 4d V8	3,585	2,835	15,502
C37	Deluxe Colonnade cpe L6	3,423	2,743	6,332
C37	Deluxe Colonnade cpe V8	3,580	2,860	15,045
D29	Malibu Colonnade sdn 4d L6	3,477	2,871	2,536
D29	Malibu Colonnade sdn 4d V8	3,627	2,987	58,143
D37	Malibu Colonnade cpe L6	3,430	2,894	3,157
D37	Malibu Colonnade cpe V8	3,580	3,010	165,627
E29	Laguna Colonnade sdn 4d V8	3,627	3,179	13,095
E37	Laguna Colonnade cpe V8	3,678	3,203	42,941
Chevelle Wagon (wb 116.0)				
C35	Deluxe 5d 2S L6	3,849	3,106	1,870
C35	Deluxe 5d 3S V8	4,054	3,331	1,316
C37	Deluxe 5d 2S V8	4,006	3,198	7,754
D37	Malibu 5d 3S V8	4,075	3,423	5,961
D35	Malibu 5d 2S V8	4,027	3,290	18,592
G35	Malibu Estate 5d 3S V8	4,080	3,608	4,099
G35	Malibu Estate 5d 2S V8	4,032	3,475	5,527
E35	Laguna 5d 3S V8	4,158	3,616	2,200
E35	Laguna 5d 2S V8	4,110	3,483	4,419
H35	Laguna Estate 5d 3S V8	4,189	3,795	3,709
H35	Laguna Estate 5d 2S V8	4,141	3,662	3,661
Chevrolet (wb 121.5)				
K69	Bel Air sdn 4d L6	3,895	3,247	1,394
K69	Bel Air sdn 4d V8	4,087	3,595	40,438
L39	Impala htp sdn V8	4,162	3,822	139,143
L47	Impala Custom cpe V8	4,110	3,836	176,824
L57	Impala cpe V8	4,096	3,769	42,979
L69	Impala sdn 4d	4,138	3,752	190,536
N39	Caprice Classic htp sdn V8	4,208	4,134	70,155
N47	Caprice Classic htp cpe V8	4,103	4,082	77,134
N67	Caprice Classic conv cpe V8	4,191	4,345	7,339
N69	Caprice Classic sdn 4d V8	4,176	4,064	58,126
Chevrolet Station Wagon (wb 125.0)				
K47	Bel Air 4d 3S	4,770	4,136	6,321
K35	Bel Air 4d 2S	4,717	4,022	14,549
L35	Impala 4d 2S	4,742	4,119	46,940
L45	Impala 4d 3S	4,807	4,233	43,664
N35	Caprice Estate 4d 2S	4,779	4,382	22,969
N45	Caprice Estate 4d 3S	4,858	4,496	39,535
Monte Carlo (wb 116.0)				
H57	spt cpe	3,713	3,415	4,960
H57	S spt cpe	3,720	3,562	177,963
H57	Landau spt cpe	3,722	3,806	107,770

1973 Engines	bore×stroke	bhp	availability
L6, 140.0	3.50×3.63	72	S-Vega
L4, 140.0	3.50×3.63	85	O-Vega
L6, 250.0	3.88×3.53	100	S-Nova,Chevl,Cam exc LTChevr

1974 Impala "Spirit of America" two-door coupe

	bore×stroke	bhp	availability
V8, 307.0	3.88×3.25	115	S-Nova,Chevl exc Lag,Cam exc LT
V8, 350.0	4.00×3.48	145	S-Lag,CamLT,MC, Chevr exc Cap O-Nova,Chevl, exc Lag, Cam exc LT, Chevr exc Cap.
V8, 350.0	4.00×3.48	175	O-Nova, Chevl, Cam, MC
V8, 350.0	4.00×3.48	245	O-Camaro (Z/28)
V8, 400.0	4.12×3.75	150	O-Chevr
V8, 454.0	4.25×4.00	215	O-Caprice
V8, 454.0	4.25×4.00	245	O-Chevl,MC,Cap

1974

Vega (wb 97.0)		Wght	Price	Prod
V11	sdn 2d	2,369	2,505	58,724
V11	LX sdn 2d	—	2,833	5,996
V15	wgn 3d 2S	2,514	2,748	88,248
V15	Estate wgn 3d 2S	—	2,976	27,089
V77	hatchback cpe 3d	—	—	276,028
Nova (wb 111.0)				
X17	htchbk cpe 3d L6	3,260	2,935	13,722
X17	htchbk cpe 3d V8	3,398	3,034	20,627
X27	cpe L6	3,150	2,811	87,399
X27	cpe V8	3,288	2,919	72,558
X69	sdn 4d L6	3,192	2,841	42,105
X69	sdn 4d V8	3,330	2,949	32,017
Y17	Custom htchbk cpe 3d L6	3,299	3,108	9,631
Y17	Custom htchbk cpe 3d V8	3,437	3,217	36,653
Y27	Custom cpe L6	3,206	2,985	11,115
Y27	Custom cpe V8	3,344	3,093	39,912
Y69	Custom sdn 4d L6	3,233	3,014	7,458
Y69	Custom sdn 4d V8	3,371	3,123	17,340
Camaro (wb 108.1; incl 13,802 Z/28s)				
Q87	spt cpe L6	3,309	3,162	22,210
Q87	spt cpe V8	3,450	3,366	79,835
S87	Type LT spt cpe V8	3,566	3,713	48,963
Chevelle (wb 112.0; 4d-116.0)				
C29	Malibu sdn Colonnade 4d L6	3,638	3,049	11,399
C29	Malibu sdn Colonnade 4d V8	3,788	3,340	26,841
C37	Malibu Colonnade cpe L6	3,573	3,054	15,790
C37	Malibu Colonnade cpe V8	3,723	3,345	37,583
D29	Malibu Classic Colonnade sdn 4d L6	3,695	3,304	4,457
D29	Malibu Classic Colonnade sdn 4d V8	3,845	3,595	51,468
D37	Malibu Classic Colonnade cpe L6	3,609	3,307	4,132
D37	Malibu Classic Colonnade cpe V8	3,759	3,598	116,962
D37	Malibu Classic Colonnade Landau cpe L6	—	3,518	351
D37	Malibu Classic Colonnade Landau cpe V8	—	3,800	27,490
E37	Laguna S3 Colonnade cpe V8	3,951	3,723	15,792
Chevelle Wagon (wb 116.0) (all V8)				
C35	Malibu 5d 3S	4,223	3,834	2,583
C37	Malibu 5d 2S	4,191	3,701	12,408
D35	Malibu Classic 5d 3S	4,315	4,251	4,909
D35	Malibu Classic 5d 2S	4,283	4,118	13,986
G35	Malibu Classic Estate 5d 3S	4,338	4,424	4,742
G35	Malibu Classic Estate 5d 2S	4,306	4,291	5,480
Chevrolet (wb 121.5)				
K69	Bel Air sdn 4d	4,148	3,960	24,778
L39	Impala spt sdn 4d	4,256	4,215	76,492
L47	Impala Custom cpe	4,169	4,229	98,062
L57	Impala spt cpe	4,167	4,162	50,036

1974 Nova "Spirit of America" hatchback coupe

		Wght	Price	Prod
L69	Impala sdn 4d	4,205	4,135	133,164
N39	Caprice Classic spt sdn 4d	4,344	4,534	48,387
N47	Caprice Classic Custom cpe	4,245	4,483	59,484
N67	Caprice Classic conv cpe	4,308	4,745	4,670
N69	Caprice Classic sdn 4d	4,294	4,465	43,367
Chevrolet Wagon (wb 125.0)				
K35	Bel Air 4d 2S	4,829	4,464	6,437
K45	Bel Air 4d 3S	4,884	4,578	2,913
L35	Impala 4d 2S	4,891	4,561	23,455
L45	Impala 4d 3S	4,936	4,675	23,259
N35	Caprice Estate 4d 2S	4,960	4,800	12,280
N45	Caprice Estate 4d 3S	5,004	4,914	23,063
Monte Carlo (wb 116.0)				
H57	S spt cpe	3,926	3,885	184,873
H57	Landau spt cpe	3,928	4,129	127,344

1974 Engines	bore×stroke	bhp	availability
L4, 140.0	3.50×3.63	75	S-Vega
L4, 140.0	3.50×3.63	85	O-Vega
L6, 250.0	3.88×3.53	100	S-Nova,Chevl,Cam
V8, 350.0	4.00×3.48	145	S-Nova,Chevl,Cam,MC, Chevr exc Cap
V8, 350.0	4.00×3.48	160	O-as above
V8, 350.0	4.00×3.48	185	O-Nova,Camaro
V8, 350.0	4.00×3.48	245	O-Camaro (Z/28)
V8, 400.0	4.12×3.75	150	S-Caprice exc wgns
V8, 400.0	4.12×3.75	180	S-wgns; O-Chevl, MC
V8, 454.0	4.25×4.00	235	O-Chevl,MC,Cap

1974 Vega "Spirit of America" hatchback coupe

1975 Caprice Classic four-door hardtop

1975

Vega (wb 97.0)		Wght	Price	Prod
V11	sdn 2d	2,415	2,786	33,878
V11	LX sdn 2d	—	3,119	1,255
V15	wgn 3d 2S	2,531	3,016	47,474
V15	Estate wgn 3d 2S	—	3,244	8,659
V77	htchbk cpe 3d	2,478	2,899	112,912
V77	Cosworth htchbk cpe 3d	—	5,916	2,061
Monza (wb 97.0)				
M27	Towne cpe	2,675	3,570	69,238
R07	S htchbk cpe 3d	—	3,648	9,795
R07	2+2 htchbk cpe 3d	2,753	3,953	57,170
Nova (wb 111.0)				
X17	htchbk cpe 3d L6	3,391	3,347	7,952
X17	htchbk cpe 3d V8	3,493	3,422	8,421
X27	cpe L6	3,276	3,205	48,103
X27	S cpe L6	—	3.099	16,655
X27	cpe V8	3,378	3,280	33,921
X27	S cpe V8	—	3,174	5,070
X69	sdn 4d L6	3,306	3,209	43,760
X69	sdn 4d V8	3,408	3,284	22,587
Y17	Custom htchbk cpe 3d L6	3,421	3,541	3,812
Y17	Custom htchbk cpe 3d V8	3,523	3,616	11,438
Y27	Custom cpe L6	3,335	3,402	7,214
Y27	LN Cpe L6	—	3,782	1,138
Y27	Custom cpe V8	3,437	3,477	19,074
Y27	LN cpe V8	—	3,857	11,395
Y69	Custom sdn 4d L6	3,367	3,415	8,959
Y69	LN sdn 4d L6	—	3,795	1,286
Y69	Custom sdn 4d V8	3,469	3,490	13,221
Y69	LN sdn 4d V8	—	3,870	8,976
Camaro (wb 108.1)				
Q87	spt cpe L6	3,421	3,540	29,749
Q87	spt cpe V8	3,532	3,685	76,178
S87	Type LT spt cpe V8	3,616	4,057	39,843

Chevelle (wb 112.0; 4d-116.0)		Wght	Price	Prod
C29	Malibu sdn 4d L6	3,713	3,402	12,873
C29	Malibu sdn 4d V8	3,833	3,652	24,989
C37	Malibu cpe L6	3,642	3,407	13,292
C37	Malibu cpe V8	3,762	3,657	23,708
D29	Malibu Classic sdn 4d L6	3,778	3,695	1
D29	Malibu Classic sdn 4d V8	3,898	3,945	51,070
D37	Malibu Classic cpe L6	3,681	3,698	4,330
D37	Malibu Classic cpe V8	3,801	3,948	76,607
D37	Malibu Classic Landau cpe L6	—	3,930	378
D37	Malibu Classic Landau cpe V8	—	4,180	22,691
E37	Lagunna S3 cpe V8	3,908	4,113	—
Chevelle Malibu Wagon (wb 116.0)				
C35	5d 3S	4,237	4,463	2,377
C35	5d 2S	4,207	4,318	11,600
D36	Classic 5d 3S	4,305	4,701	6,394
D36	Classic 5d 2S	4,275	4,556	15,974
G35	Classic Estate 5d 3S	4,331	4,893	4,600
G35	Classic Estate 5d 2S	4,301	4,748	4,637
Chevrolet (wb 121.5)				
K69	Bel Air sdn 4d	4,179	4,345	15,871
L39	Impala spt sdn 4d	4,265	4,631	47,125
L47	Impala Custom cpe	4,190	4,626	49,455
L47	Impala Landau cpe	—	4,901	2,465
L57	Impala spt cpe	4,207	4.575	21,333
L69	Impala sdn 4d	4,218	4,548	91,330
N39	Caprice Classic spt sdn 4d	4,360	4,891	40,482
N47	Caprice Classic cpe	4,275	4,837	36,041
N47	Caprice Classic Landau cpe	—	5,075	3,752
N67	Caprice Classic conv cpe	4,343	5,113	8,349
N69	Caprice Classic sdn 4d	4,311	4,819	33,715
Chevrolet Wagon (wb 125.0)				
K35	Bel Air 4d 2S	4,856	4,878	4,032
K45	Bel Air 4d 3S	4,913	4,998	2,386
L35	Impala 4d 2S	4,910	5,001	17,998

		Wght	Price	Prod
L45	Impala 4d 3S	4,959	5,121	19,445
N35	Caprice Estate 4d 2S	4,978	5,231	9,047
N45	Caprice Estate 4d 3S	5,036	5,351	18,858
Monte Carlo (wb 116.0)				
H57	S spt cpe	3,927	4,249	148,529
H57	Landau spt cpe	3,930	4,519	110,380

1975 Engines	bore×stroke	bhp	availability
L4, 122.0	3.50×3.16	111	S-Cosworth Vega
L4, 140.0	3.50×3.63	78	S-Vega,Monza exc 2+2
L4, 140.0	3.50×3.63	87	S-Monza 2+2; O-Vega
L6, 250.0	3.88×3.53	105	S-Nova,Chevl,Cam
V8, 262.0	3.67×3.10	110	O-Nova, Monza
V8, 350.0	4.00×3.48	125	O-Monza
V8, 350.0	4.00×3.48	145	S-Nova,Chevl,Cam,MC, Chevr exc wgns
V8, 350.0	4.00×3.48	155	O-Nova,Chevl,Cam,MC, Chev
V8, 400.0	4.12×3.75	175	S-Chevr wgns; O-Chevl, MC, Chevr
V8, 454.0	4.25×4.00	235	O-Chevl, MC, Chevr

1976

Chevette (wb 94.3)		Wght	Price	Prod
B08	htchbk sdn 3d	1,927	3,098	178,007
J08	Scooter htchbk sdn 3d	1,870	2,899	9,810
Vega (wb 97.0)				
V11	sdn 2d	2,443	2,984	27,619
V15	wgn 3d 2S	2,578	3,227	46,114
V15	Estate wgn 3d 2S	—	3,450	7,935
V77	htchbk cpe 3d	2,534	3,099	77,409
V77	Cosworth htchbk cpe 3d	—	6,066	1,447
Monza (wb 97.0)				
M27	Towne cpe	2,625	3,359	46,735
RO7	2+2 htchbk cpe 3d	2,668	3,727	34,170

Nova (wb 111.0)		Wght	Price	Prod
X17	htchbk cpe 3d L6	3,391	3,417	10,853
X17	htchbk cpe 3d V8	3,475	3,579	7,866
X27	cpe L6	3,188	3,248	87,438
X27	cpe V8	3,272	3,413	44,421
X69	sdn 4d L6	3,221	3,283	86,600
X69	sdn 4d V8	3,305	3,448	37,167
Y17	Concours htchbk cpe 3d L6	3,401	3,972	2,088
Y17	Concours htchbk cpe 3d V8	3,485	4,134	5,486
Y27	Concours cpe L6	3,324	3,795	6,568
Y27	Concours cpe V8	3,408	3,960	15,730
Y69	Concours sdn 4d L6	3,367	3,830	10,151
Y69	Concours sdn 4d V8	3,451	3,995	20,360
Camaro (wb 108.1)				
Q87	spt cpe L6	3,421	3,762	38,047
Q87	spt cpe V8	3,511	3,927	92,491
S87	Type LT spt cpe V8	3,576	4,320	52,421
Chevelle (wb 112.0; 4d-116.0)				
C29	Malibu sdn 4d L6	3,729	3,671	13,116
C29	Malibu sdn 4d V8	3,834	4,201	25,353
C37	Malibu cpe L6	3,650	3,636	12,616
C37	Malibu cpe V8	3,755	4,166	17,976
D29	Malibu Classic sdn 4d L6	3,827	4,196	4,253
D29	Malibu Classic sdn 4d V8	3,932	4,490	73,307
D37	Malibu Classic cpe L6	3,688	3,926	5,791
D37	Malibu Classic cpe V8	3,793	4,455	76,843
D37	Malibu Classic Landau cpe L6	—	4,124	672
D37	Malibu Classic Landau cpe V8	—	4,640	29,495
E37	Laguna S3 cpe V8	3,978	4,621	9,100
Chevelle Malibu Wagon (wb 116.0)				
C35	5d 3S	4,268	4,686	2,984
C35	5d 2S	4,238	4,543	13,581
D35	Classic 5d 3S	4,330	4,919	11,617
D35	Classic 5d 2S	4,300	4,776	24,635
G35	Malibu Classic Estate 5d 3S	4,356	5,114	6,386
G35	Malibu Classic Estate 5d 2S	4,326	4,971	5,518
Chevrolet (wb 121.5)				
L39	Impala spt sdn 4d	4,245	4,798	39,849
L47	Impala Custom cpe	4,175	4,763	43,219

1976 Monza Towne Coupe

		Wght	Price	Prod
L47	Impala Landau cpe	—	5.058	10,841
L69	Impala S spt sdn 4d	—	4,507	18,265
L69	Impala sdn 4d	4,222	4,706	86,057
N39	Caprice Classic spt sdn 4d	4,314	5,078	55,308
N47	Caprice Classic cpe	4,244	5,043	28,161
N47	Caprice Classic Landau cpe	—	5,284	21,926
N69	Caprice Classic sdn 4d	4,285	5,013	47,411
Chevrolet Wagon (wb 125.0)				
L35	Impala 4d 2S	4,912	5,166	19,657
L45	Impala 4d 3S	4,972	5,283	21,329
N35	Caprice Estate 4d 2S	4,948	5,429	10,029
N45	Caprice Estate 4d 3S	5,007	5,546	21,804
Monte Carlo (wb 116.0)				
H57	S spt cpe	3,907	4,673	191,370
H57	Landau spt cpe	—	4,966	161,902

1976 Engines	bore×stroke	bhp	availability
L4, 85.0	3.23×2.61	52	S-Chevt
L4, 97.6	3.23×2.98	60	O-Chevt
L4, 122.0	3.50×3.15	111	S-Cosworth Vega
L4, 140.0	3.50×3.63	70	S-Vega, Monza
L4, 140.0	3.50×3.63	84	O-Vega, Monza
L6, 250.0	3.88×3.53	105	S-Nova, Chevl, Cam
V8, 262.0	3.67×3.10	110	O-Monza
V8, 305.0	3.74×3.48	140	S-Nova,Chevl,Cam,MC; O-Monza
V8, 305.0	3.74×3.48	145	S-Chevl wgn,Chevr; O-MC
V8, 350.0	4.00×3.48	165	O-Nova,Chevl,Cam,MC, Chevr
V8, 400.0	4.12×3.75	175	S-Chevr wgn; O-Chevl,MC, Chevr
V8, 454.0	4.25×4.00	225	O-Chevr

1977

Chevette (wb 94.3)		Wght	Price	Prod
B08	htchbk sdn 3d	1,958	3,225	120,278
J08	Scooter htchbk sdn 3d	1,898	2,999	13,191
Vega (wb 97.0)				
V11	sdn 2d	2,459	3,249	12,365
V15	wgn 3d 2S	2,571	3,522	25,181
V15	Estate wgn 3d 2S	—	3,745	3,461
V77	htchbk cpe 3d	2,522	3,359	37,395

Monza (wb 97.0)		Wght	Price	Prod
M27	Town cpe	2,580	3,560	34,133
RO7	2+2 htchbk cpe 3d	2,671	3,840	39,215
Nova (wb 111.0)				
X17	htchbk cpe 3d L6	3,217	3,646	18,048
X17	htchbk cpe 3d V8	3,335	3,766	
X27	cpe L6	3,139	3,482	132,833
X27	cpe V8	3,257	3,602	
X69	sdn 4d L6	3,174	3,532	141,028
X69	sdn 4d V8	3,292	3,652	
Y17	Concours htchbk cpe 3d L6	3,378	4,154	5,481
Y17	Concours htchbk cpe 3d V8	3,486	4,274	
Y27	Concours cpe L6	3,283	3,991	28,602
Y27	Concours cpe V8	3,391	4,111	
Y69	Concours sdn 4d L6	3,329	4,066	39,272
Y69	Concours sdn 4d V8	3,437	4,186	
Camaro (wb 108.1)				
Q87	spt cpe	3,369	4,113	131,717
S87	Type LT spt cpe	3,422	4,478	72,787
Q87	Z/28 spt cpe V8	—	5,170	14,349
Chevelle Malibu (wb 112.0; 4d-116.0)				
C29	sdn 4d L6	3,628	3,935	39,064
C29	sdn 4d V8	3,727	4,055	
C37	cpe L6	3,551	3,885	28,793
C37	cpe V8	3,650	4,005	
D29	Classic sdn 4d L6	3,725	4,475	76,776
D29	Classic sdn 4d V8	3,824	4,595	
D37	Classic cpe L6	3,599	4,125	73,739
D37	Classic cpe V8	3,698	4,245	
D37	Classic Landau cpe L6	—	4,353	37,215
D37	Classic Landau cpe V8	—	4,473	
Chevelle Malibu Wagon (wb 116.0)				
C35	5d 3S	4,169	4,877	4,014
C35	5d 2S	4,139	4,734	18,023
D35	Classic 5d 3S	4,263	5,208	19,053
D35	Classic 5d 2S	4,233	5,065	31,539
Chevrolet (wb 116.0)				
L35	Impala wgn 4d 3S V8	4,072	5,406	28,255
L35	Impala wgn 4d 2S V8	4,042	5,289	37,108
L47	Impala Custom cpe L6	3,533	4,876	55,347
L47	Impala Custom cpe V8	3,628	4,996	
L47	Impala Landau cpe	—	—	2,745

1977 Monte Carlo Landau sport coupe

		Wght	Price	Prod
L69	Impala sdn 4d L6	3,564	4,901	196,824
L69	Impala sdn 4d V8	3,659	5,021	
N35	Caprice Classic wgn 4d 3S V8	4,118	5,734	33,639
N35	Caprice Classic wgn 4d 2S V8	4,088	5,617	22,930
N47	Caprice Classic cpe L6	3,571	5,187	62,366
N47	Caprice Classic cpe V8	3,666	5,307	
N69	Caprice Classic sdn 4d L6	3,606	5,237	212,840
N69	Caprice Classic sdn 4d V8	3,701	5,357	
N69	Caprice Landau cpe	—	—	9,607
Monte Carlo (wb 116.0)				
H57	S spt cpe	3,852	4,968	224,327
H57	Landau spt cpe	—	5,298	186,711

1977 Engines	bore×stroke	bhp	availability
L4, 85.0	3.23×2.61	57	S-Chevt
L4, 97.6	3.23×2.98	63	O-Chevt
L4, 140.0	3.50×3.15	84	S-Vega, Monza
L6, 250.0	3.88×3.53	110	S-Nova,Chevl,Cam,Chevr
V8, 305.0	3.74×3.48	145	S-Nova,Chevl exc Clsc wgn, Cam, MC,Chevr; O-Monza
V8, 350.0	4.00×3.48	170	S-Chevl Clsc wgn; O-Nova, Chevl,Cam,MC,Chevr

1978

Chevette (wb 94.3; 5d-97.3)		Wght	Price	Prod
B08	htchbk sdn 3d	1,965	3,644	118,375
B68	hthcbk sdn 5d	2,035	3,764	167,769
J08	Scooter htchbk sdn 3d	1,932	3,149	12,829
Monza (wb 97.0)				
M07	2+2 htchbk cpe 3d	2,732	3,779	36,227
M15	wgn 3d	2,723	3,868	24,255
M15	Estate wgn 3d	—	4,102	2,478
M27	cpe	2,688	3,622	37,878
M77	S htchbk cpe 3d	2,643	3,697	2,326
R07	2+2 htchbk cpe 3d	2,777	4,247	28,845
R27	spt cpe	2,730	4,100	6,823
Nova (wb 111.0)				
X17	htchbk cpe 3d L6	3,258	3,866	12,665
X17	htchbk cpe 3d V8	3,403	4,051	
X27	cpe L6	3,132	3,702	101,858
X27	cpe V8	3,277	3,887	
X69	sdn 4d L6	3,173	3,777	123,158
X69	sdn 4d V8	3,318	3,962	
Y27	Custom cpe L6	3,261	3,960	23,953
Y27	Custom cpe V8	3,396	4,145	
Y69	Custom sdn 4d L6	3,298	4,035	26,475
Y69	Custom sdn 4d V8	3,443	4,220	
Camaro (wb 108.1)				
Q87	spt cpe	3,300	4,414	134,491
Q87	Rally sport cpe	—	4,784	11,902
S87	Type LT spt cpe	3,352	4,814	65,635
S87	Type LT Rally sport cpe	—	5,065	5,696
Q87	Z/28 spt cpe V8	—	5,604	54,907
Malibu (wb 108.1)				
T19	sdn 4d V6	3,006	4,276	44,426
T19	sdn 4d V8	3,143	4,469	
T27	cpe V6	3,001	4,204	27,089
T27	cpe V8	3,138	4,394	
T35	wgn 4d 2S V6	3,169	4,516	30,850
T35	wgn 4d 2S V8	3,550	4,706	
W19	Classic sdn 4d V6	3,039	4,561	102,967
W19	Classic sdn 4d V8	3,175	4,751	
W27	Classic spt cpe V6	3,031	4,461	60,992
W27	Classic spt cpe V8	3,167	4,651	
W27	Classic Landau cpe V6	—	4,684	29,160
W27	Classic Landau cpe V8	—	4,874	

1978 Caprice Classic four-door sedan

1978 Monza 2+2 hatchback coupe

		Wght	Price	Prod
W35	Classic wgn 4d 2S V6	3,196	4,714	63,152
W35	Classic wgn 4d 2S V8	3,377	4,904	
Chevrolet (wb 116.0)				
L35	Impala wgn 4d 3S V8	4,071	5,904	28,518
L35	Impala wgn 4d 2S V8	4,037	5,777	40,423
L47	Impala cpe L6	3,511	5,208	33,990
L47	Impala cpe V8	3,619	5,393	
L47	Impala Landau cpe L6	—	5,598	4,652
L47	Impala Landau cpe V8	—	5,783	
L69	Impala sdn 4d L6	3,530	5,283	183,161
L69	Impala sdn 4d V8	3,638	5,468	
N35	Caprice Classic wgn 4d 3S V8	4,109	6,151	32,952
N35	Caprice Clasic wgn 4d 2S V8	4,079	6,012	24,792
N47	Caprice Classic cpe L6	3,548	5,526	37,301
N47	Caprice Classic cpe V8	3,656	5,711	
N47	Caprice Landau cpe L6	—	5,830	22,771
N47	Caprice Landau cpe V8	—	6,015	
N69	Caprice Classic sdn 4d L6	3,578	5,628	203,837
N69	Caprice Classic snd 4d V8	3,686	5,811	
Monte Carlo (wb 108.1)				
Z37	spt cpe V6	3,040	4,785	216,730
Z37	spt cpe V8	3,175	4,935	
Z37	Landau spt cpe V6	—	5,678	141,461
Z37	Landau spt cpe V8	—	5,828	

1978 Engines	bore×stroke	bhp	availability
L4, 97.6	3.23×2.98	63	S-Chevt
L4, 97.6	3.23×2.98	68	O-Chevt
L4, 151.0	4.00×3.00	85	S-Monza

	bore×stroke	bhp	availability
V6, 196.0	3.50×3.40	90	O-Monza
V6, 200.0	3.50×3.48	95	S-Malibu
V6, 231.0	3.80×3.40	105	S-MC; O-Malibu,Monza
L6, 250.0	3.88×3.53	110	S-Nova,Cam exc Z/28,Chevr
V8, 305.0	3.74×3.48	145	S-Nova,Mal,Cam exc Z/28, MC, Chevr; O-Monza
V8, 350.0	4.00×3.48	170	O-Nova, Mal wgns, Cam, Chevr
V8, 350.0	4.00×3.48	185	S-Camaro Z/28

1979

Chevette (wb 94.3; 5d-97.3)		Wght	Price	Prod
B08	htchbk sdn 3d	1,978	3,948	136,145
B68	htchbk sdn 5d	2,057	4,072	208,865
J08	Scooter htchbk sdn 3d	1,929	3,437	24,099
Monza (wb 97.0)				
M07	2+2 htchbk cpe 3d	2,630	4,161	56,871
M15	wgn 3d	2,631	4,167	15,190
M27	cpe	2,577	3,850	61,110
R07	2+2 htchbk cpe 3d	2,676	4,624	30,662
Nova (wb 111.0)				
X17	htchbk cpe 3d L6	3,264	4,118	4,819
X17	htchbk cpe 3d V8	3,394	4,353	
X27	cpe L6	3,135	3,955	36,800
X27	cpe V8	3,265	4,190	
X69	sdn 4d L6	3,179	4,055	40,883
X69	sdn 4d V8	3,309	4,290	
Y27	Custom cpe L6	3,194	4,164	7,529
Y27	Custom cpe V8	3,324	4,399	
Y69	Custom sdn 4d L6	3,228	4,264	7,690
Y69	Custom sdn 4d V8	3,358	4,499	
Camaro (wb 108.0)				
Q87	spt cpe	3,305	5,163	111,357
Q87	Rally sport cpe	—	5,572	19,101
S87	Berlinetta cpe	3,358	5,906	67,236
Q87	Z/28 spt cpe V8	—	6,748	84,877
Malibu (wb 108.1)				
T19	sdn 4d V6	2,988	4,915	59,674
T19	sdn 4d V8	3,116	5,180	
T27	cpe V6	2,983	4,812	41,848
T27	cpe V8	3,111	5,077	
T35	wgn 2d 2S V6	3,155	5,078	50,344
T35	wgn 2d 2S V8	3,297	5,343	
W19	Classic sdn 4d V6	3,024	5,215	104,222
W19	Classic sdn 4d V8	3,152	5,480	
W27	Classic cpe V6	3,017	5,087	60,751
W27	Classic cpe V8	3,145	5,352	
W27	Classic Landau cpe V6	—	5,335	25,213
W27	Classic Landau cpe V8	—	5,600	
W35	Classic wgn 4d V6	3,183	5,300	70,095
W35	Classic wgn 4d V8	3,325	5,565	
Chevrolet (wb 116.0)				
L35	Impala wgn 4d 3S V8	4,045	6,636	28,710
L35	Impala wgn 4d 2S V8	4,013	6,497	39,644
L47	Impala cpe V6	3,495	5,828	26,589
L47	Impala cpe V8	3,606	6,138	
L47	Impala Landau cpe L6	—	6,314	3,247
L47	Impala Landau cpe V8	—	6,624	
L69	Impala sdn 4d L6	3,513	5,928	172,717
L69	Impala sdn 4d V8	3,624	6,238	
N35	Caprice Classic wgn 4d 3S V8	4,088	6,960	32,693
N35	Caprice Classic wgn 4d 2S V8	4,056	6,800	23,568
N37	Caprice Classic cpe L6	3,538	6,198	36,629
N37	Caprice Classic cpe V8	3,649	6,508	
N47	Caprice Classic Landau cpe L6	—	6,617	21,824
N47	Caprice Classic Landau cpe V8	—	6,927	
N69	Caprice Classic sdn 4d L6	3,564	6,323	203,017
N69	Caprice Classic sdn 4d V8	3,675	6,633	
Monte Carlo (wb 108.1)				
Z37	spt cpe V6	3,039	5,333	225,073
Z37	spt cpe V8	3,169	5,598	
Z37	Landau spt cpe V6	—	6,183	91,850
Z37	Landau spt cpe V8	—	6,448	

1979 Engines	bore×stroke	bhp	availability
L4, 97.6	3.23×2.98	70	S-Chevt
L4, 97.6	3.23×2.98	74	O-Chevt
L4, 151.0	4.00×3.00	90	S-Monza 4s
V6, 196.0	3.50×3.40	105	S-Monza 6s
V6, 200.0	3.50×3.48	94	S-Malibu, MC
V6, 231.0	3.80×3.40	115	O-Mal, Monza, MC
L6, 250.0	3.88×3.53	115	S-Nova,Cam exc Z/28, Chevr exc wgns
V8, 267.0	3.50×3.48	125	S-Malibu, MC
V8, 305.0	3.74×3.48	130	S-Nova, Cam exc Z/28, Chevr; O-Monza
V8, 305.0	3.74×3.48	160	O-Monte Carlo,Chevelle
V8, 350.0	4.00×3.48	170	O-Nova,Mal,Chevrolet
V8, 350.0	4.00×3.48	175	S-Camaro Z/28; O-Camaro

1980

Chevette (wb 94.3; 5d-97.3)		Wght	Price	Prod
B08	htchbk sdn 3d	1,989	4,601	148,686
B68	htchbk sdn 5d	2,048	4,736	261,477
J08	Scooter htchbk	1,935	4,057	40,998
Monza (wb 97.0)				
M07	2+2 htchbk cpe 3d	2,672	4,746	53,415
M27	cpe	2,617	4,433	95,469
R07	Sport 2+2 htchbk cpe 3d	2,729	5,186	20,534
Citation (wb 104.9)*				
H11	cpe L4	2,391	4,800	42,909
H11	cpe V6	2,428	4,925	
X08	htchbk sdn 3d L4	2,417	5,422	210,258
X08	htchbk sdn 3d V6	2,454	5,547	

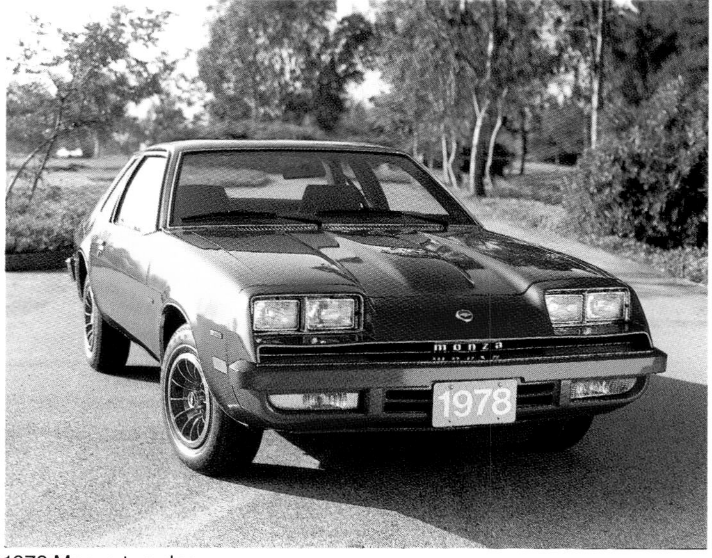

1978 Monza two-door coupe

1981 Monte Carlo two-door coupe

		Wght	Price	Prod
X11	club cpe L4	2,397	5,214	100,340
X11	club cpe V6	2,434	5,339	
X68	htchbk sdn 5d L4	2,437	5,552	458,033
X68	htchbk 5d V6	2,474	5,677	
Camaro (wb 108.1)				
P87	spt cpe	3,218	5,843	68,174
P87/Z85	RS cpe	—	6,086	12,015
S87	Berlinetta cpe	3,253	6,606	26,679
P87	Z/28 spt cpe V8	—	7,363	45,137
Malibu (wb 108.1)				
T19	sdn 4d V6	3,001	5,617	67,696
T19	sdn 4d V8	3,122	5,697	
T27	spt cpe V6	2,996	5,502	28,425
T27	spt cpe V8	3,117	5,582	
T35	wgn 4d 2S V6	3,141	5,778	30,794
T35	wgn 4d 2S V8	3,261	5,858	
W19	Classic sdn 4d V6	3,031	5,951	77,938
W19	Classic sdn 4d V8	3,152	6,031	
W27	Classic spt cpe V6	3,027	5,816	28,425
W27	Classic spt cpe V8	3,148	5,896	
W27/Z03	Classic Landau cpe V6	—	6,009	9,342
W27/Z03	Classic Landau cpe V8	—	6,149	
W35	Classic wgn 4d 2S V6	3,167	6,035	35,730
W35	Classic wgn 4d 2S V8	3,307	6,115	
Full-size Chevrolet (wb 116.0)				
L35	Impala wgn 4d 3S V8	3,924	7,186	6,767
L35	Impala wgn 4d 2S V8	3,892	7,041	11,203
L47	Impala spt cpe V6	3,344	6,535	10,756
L47	Impala spt cpe V8	3,452	6,615	
L69	Impala sdn 4d V6	3,360	6,650	70,801
L69	Impala sdn 4d V8	3,468	6,730	
N35	Caprice Clsc wgn 4d 3S V8	3,962	7,536	13,431
N35	Caprice Clsc wgn 4d 2S V8	3,930	7,369	9,873
N47	Caprice Clsc cpe V6	3,376	6,946	13,919
N47	Caprice Clsc cpe V8	3,484	7,026	
N47/Z03	Cap Clsc Lndu cpe V6	—	7,400	8,857
N47/Z03	Cap Clsc Lndu cpe V8	—	7,480	
N69	Caprice Classic sdn 4d V6/V8	—	—	91,208

Monte Carlo (wb 108.1)		Wght	Price	Prod
Z37	spt cpe V6	3,104	6,524	116,580
Z37	spt cpe V8	3,219	6,604	
Z37/Z03	Landau cpe V6	—	6,772	32,262
Z37/Z03	Landau cpe V8	—	6,852	

1980 Engines	bore×stroke	bhp	availability
L4, 97.6	3.23×2.98	70	S-Chevt
L4, 97.6	3.23×2.98	74	O-Chevt
L4, 151.0	4.00×3.00	86	S-Monza
L4, 151.0	4.00×3.00	90	S-Citation
V6, 173.0	3.50×3.00	115	S-Citation
V6, 229.0	3.74×3.48	115	S-Mal,Cam,MC,Chevr exc wgn
V6, 231.0	3.80×3.40	110	O-Cam, Monza, MC, Chevr exc wgn
V6T, 231.0	3.80×3.40	170	O-MC
V8, 267.0	3.50×3.48	120	S-Mal,Cam,MC,Chevr
V8, 305.0	3.74×3.48	155	O-Mal,Cam,MC,Chevr
V8, 350.0	4.00×3.48	190	S-Camaro Z/28; O-other Cam
V8D, 350.0	4.06×3.39	105	O-Chevr wgn

1981

Chevette (wb 94.3; 5d-97.3)		Wght	Price	Prod
B08	htchbk sdn 3d	2,000	5,255	114,621
B68	htchbk sdn 5d	2,063	5,394	250,616
J08	Scooter htchbk 3d	1,945	4,695	55,211
B08	Diesel htchbk sdn 3d	—	—	4,252
B68	Diesel htchbk sdn 5d	—	—	8,900
Citation (wb 104.9)				
X08	htchbk sdn 3d L4	2,404	6,270	113,983
X08	htchbk sdn 3d V6	2,459	6,395	
X68	htchbk sdn 5d L4	2,432	6,404	299,396
X68	htchbk sdn 5d V6	2,487	6,529	
Camaro (wb 108.0)				
P87	spt cpe V6	3,222	6,780	62,614
P87	spt cpe V8	3,392	6,830	

		Wght	Price	Prod
S87	Berlinetta cpe V6	3,275	7,576	20,253
S87	Berlinetta cpe V8	3,445	7,626	
P87	Z28 spt cpe V8	—	8,263	43,272
Malibu (wb 108.1)				
T69	sdn 4d V6	3,028	6,614	60,643
T69	sdn 4d V8	3,194	6,664	
T27	spt cpe V6	3,037	6,498	15,834
T27	spt cpe V8	3,199	6,548	
T35	wgn 4d 2S V6	3,201	6,792	29,387
T35	wgn 4d 2S V8	3,369	6,842	
W69	Classic sdn 4d V6	3,059	6,961	80,908
W69	Classic sdn 4d V8	3,225	7,011	
W27	Classic spt cpe V6	3,065	6,828	14,255
W27	Classic spt cpe V8	3,227	6,878	
W27/Z03	Classic Landau cpe V6	—	7,092	4,622
W27/Z03	Classic Landau cpe V8	—	7,142	
W35	Classic wgn 4d 2S V6	3,222	7,069	36,798
W35	Classic wgn 4d 2S V8	3,390	7,119	
Full-size Chevrolet (wb 116.0)				
L35/AQ4	Impala wgn 4d 3S V8	—	7,765	8,462
L35	Impala wgn 4d 2S V8	3,897	7,624	11,345
L47	Impala spt cpe V6	3,326	7,129	6,067
L47	Impala spt cpe V8	3,458	7,179	
L69	Impala sdn 4d V6	3,354	7,241	60,090
L69	Impala sdn 4d V8	3,486	7,291	
N35/AQ4	Caprice Clsc wgn 4d 3S V8	—	8,112	16,348
N35	Caprice Clsc wgn 4d 2S V8	3,940	7,948	11,184
N47	Caprice Clsc cpe V6	3,363	7,534	9,741
N47	Caprice Clsc cpe V8	3,495	7,584	
N47/Z03	Caprice Clsc Landau cpe V6	—	7,990	6,615
N47/Z03	Caprice Clsc Landau cpe V8	—	8,040	
N69	Caprice Classic sdn 4d V6	3,400	7,667	89,573
N69	Caprice Classic sdn 4d V8	3,532	7,717	
Monte Carlo (wb 108.1)				
Z37	spt cpe V6	3,102	7,299	149,659
Z37	spt cpe V8	3,228	7,349	
Z37/Z03	Landau cpe V6	—	8,006	38,191
Z37/Z03	Landau cpe V8	—	8,056	

1981 Engines	bore × stroke	bhp	availability
L4, 97.6	3.23 × 2.98	70	S-Chevette
L4D, 111.0	3.31 × 3.23	51	O-late Chevette
L4, 151.0	4.00 × 3.00	84	S-Citation
V6, 173.0	3.50 × 2.99	110	O-Citation
V6, 173.0	3.50 × 2.99	135	O-Citation
V6, 229.0	3.74 × 3.48	110	S-Cam, Mal, MC, Chevr cpe/sdn
V6, 231.0	3.80 × 3.40	110	S-Calif. Cam, Mal, MC, Chevr cpe/sdn
V6T, 231.0	3.80 × 3.40	170	O-Monte Carlo
V8, 267.0	3.50 × 3.48	115	O-Cam, Mal, MC, Chevr
V8, 305.0	3.74 × 3.48	150	S-Chevr wgn; O-Cam, Mal, MC, Chevrolet
V8, 305.0	3.74 × 3.48	165	S-Camaro Z28
V8, 350.0	4.00 × 3.48	175	O-Camaro Z28
V8D, 350.0	4.06 × 3.39	105	O-Chevrolet

1982

Chevette (wb 94.3; 5d-97.3)		Wght	Price	Prod
B08	htchbk sdn 3d	2,004	5,513	51,431
B68	htchbk sdn 5d	2,064	5,660	111,661
J08	Scooter htchbk 3d	1,959	4,997	31,281
J68	Scooter htchbk 5d	2,006	5,238	21,742
B08/Z90	Diesel sdn 3d	—	6,579	4,874
B68/Z90	Diesel sdn 5d	—	6,727	11,819
Cavalier (wb 101.2)				
D27	cpe	2,318	6,966	30,245
E77	htchbk cpe 3d	2,389	7,199	22,114
D69	sdn 4d	2,372	7,137	52,941
D35	wgn 5d	2,432	7,354	30,853
D27/Z11	Cadet cpe	—	6,278	2,281
D69/Z11	Cadet sdn 4d	—	6,433	9,511
D35/Z11	Cadet wgn 5d	—	6,704	4,754
D27/Z12	CL cpe	2,315	7,944	6,063
E77/Z12	CL htchbk cpe 3d	2,381	8,281	12,792
D69/Z12	CL sdn 4d	2,362	8,137	15,916
D35/Z12	CL wgn 5d	2,422	8,452	7,587
Citation (wb 104.9)				
H11	cpe L4	—	6,297	9,102
H11	cpe V6	—	6,515	
X08	htchbk sdn 3d L4	2,442	6,754	29,613
X08	htchbk sdn 3d V6	—	6,972	
X68	htchbk sdn 5d L4	2,409	6,899	126,932
X68	htchbk sdn 5d V6	—	7,024	
Camaro (wb 101.0)				
P87	spt cpe L4	—	7,631	78,761
P87	spt cpe V6	—	7,755	
P87	spt cpe V8	—	7,925	

1981 Citation X-11 three-door hatchback sedan

1982 Malibu Classic four-door sedan

		Wght	Price	Prod
S87	Berlinetta cpe V6	2,940	9,266	39,744
S87	Berlinetta cpe V8	—	9,436	
P87	Z28 spt cpe V8	2,870	9,700	63,563
Celebrity (wb 104.9)				
W27	cpe L4	2,691	8,313	19,629
W27	cpe V6	2,751	8,438	
W19	sdn 4d L4	2,734	8,463	72,701
W19	sdn 4d V6	2,794	8,588	
Malibu (wb 108.1)				
W69	Classic sdn 4d V6	3,091	8,137	70,793
W69	Classic sdn 4d V8	—	8,207	
W35	Classic wgn 4d 2S V6	3,240	8,265	45,332
W35	Classic wgn 4d 2S V8	—	8,335	
Full-size Chevrolet (wb 116.0)				
L35/AQ4	Impala wgn 4d 3S V8	4,050	8,670	6,245
L35	Impala wgn 4d 2S V8	3,930	8,516	10,654
L69	Impala sdn 4d V6	3,361	7,918	47,780
L69	Impala sdn 4d V8	—	7,988	
N35/AQ4	Caprice Clsc wgn 4d 3S V8	4,010	9,051	25,385
N47	Caprice Clsc spt cpe V6	3,373	8,221	11,999
N47	Caprice Clsc spt cpe V8	—	8,291	
N69	Caprice Classic sdn 4d V6	3,410	8,367	86,126
N69	Caprice Classic sdn 4d V8	—	8,437	
Monte Carlo (wb 108.1)				
Z37	spt cpe V6	3,190	8,177	92,392
Z37	spt cpe V8	—	8,247	

1982 Engines	bore × stroke	bhp	availability
L4, 97.6	3.23 × 2.98	65	S-Chevette
L4D, 111.0	3.36 × 3.28	51	O-Chevette
L4, 112.0	3.50 × 2.91	88	S-Cavalier
L4, 151.0	4.00 × 3.00	90	S-Cit, Camaro, Celebrity
V6, 173..0	3.50 × 2.99	102	S-Cam Berlinetta; O-Camaro
V6, 173.0	3.50 × 2.99	112	O-Citation, Celebrity
V6, 173.0	3.50 × 2.99	135	O-Citation
V6, 229.0	3.74 × 3.48	110	S-Mal, MC, Chevr cpe/sdn
V6, 231.0	3.80 × 3.40	110	S-Calif. Chevrolet
V6D, 262.0	4.06 × 3.39	85	O-Malibu, Monte Carlo
V8, 267.0	3.50 × 3.48	115	S-Chevr wag; O-Mal, MC, Chevrolet
V8, 305.0	3.74 × 3.48	145	S-Cam Z28; O-Cam, Mal, MC, Chevrolet
V8, 305.0	3.74 × 3.48	165	O-Camaro Z28
V8D, 350.0	4.06 × 3.39	105	O-Chevr, Malibu, MC

1983

Chevette (wb 94.3; 5d-97.3)		Wght	Price	Prod
B08	htchbk sdn 3d	2,088	5,469	37,537
B68	htchbk sdn 5d	2,148	5,616	81,297
J08	Scooter htchbk 3d	2,029	4,997	33,488
J68	Scooter htchbk 5d	2,098	5,333	15,303
B08/Z90	Diesel sdn 3d	—	6,535	439
B68/Z90	Diesel sdn 5d	—	6,683	1,501
Cavalier (wb 101.2)				
C27	cpe	2,384	5,888	23,028
C69	sdn 4d	2,403	5,999	33,333
C35	wgn 5d	2,464	6,141	27,922
D27	CS cpe	2,374	6,363	22,172
E77	CS htchbk cpe 3d	2,440	6,549	25,869
D69	CS sdn 4d	2,425	6,484	52,802
D35	CS wgn 5d	2,486	6,633	32,834
D27/Z08	CS conv cpe	—	10,990	627
Citation (wb 104.9)				
H11	cpe L4	2,471	6,333	6,456

1983 Citation three-door hatchback sedan

		Wght	Price	Prod
H11	cpe V6	2,526	6,483	
X08	htchbk sdn 3d L4	2,463	6,788	14,323
X08	htchbk sdn 3d V6	2,518	6,938	
X68	htchbk sdn 5d L4	2,511	6,934	71,405
X68	htchbk sdn 5d V6	2,566	7,084	
Camaro (wb 101.0)				
P87	spt cpe L4	—	8,036	63,806
P87	spt cpe V6	2,959	8,186	
P87	spt cpe V8	3,116	8,386	
S87	Berlinetta cpe V6	2,944	9,881	27,925
S87	Berlinetta cpe V8	3,136	10,106	
P87	Z28 spt cpe V8	3,061	10,336	62,100
Celebrity (wb 104.9)				
W27	cpe L4	2,710	8,059	19,221
W27	cpe V6	2,770	8,209	
W19	sdn 4d L4	2,730	8,209	120,608
W19	sdn 4d V6	2,790	8,359	
Malibu (wb 108.1)				
W69	Classic sdn 4d V6	3,199	8,084	61,534
W69	Classic sdn 4d V8	3,307	8,309	
W35	Classic wgn 4d 2S V6	3,343	8,217	55,892
W35	Classic wgn 4d 2S V8	3,470	8,442	
Full-size Chevrolet (wb 116.0)				
L69	Impala sdn 4d V6	3,490	8,331	45,154
L69	Impala sdn 4d V8	3,594	8,556	
N35	Caprice Clsc wgn 4d 3S V8	4,092	9,518	53,028
N69	Caprice Classic sdn 4d V6	3,537	8,802	122,613
N69	Caprice Classic sdn 4d V8	3,641	9,027	
Monte Carlo (wb 108.1)				
Z37	spt cpe V6	3,220	8,552	91,605
Z37	spt cpe V8	3,328	8,777	
Z37/Z65	SS spt cpe V8	—	10,474	4,714

1983 Engines	bore × stroke	bhp	availability
L4, 97.6	3.23 × 2.98	65	S-Chevette
L4D, 111.0	3.31 × 3.23	51	O-Chevette
L4, 121.0	3.50 × 3.15	88	S-Cavalier
L4, 151.0	4.00 × 3.00	92	S-Cit, Cam, Celeb
V6, 173.0	3.50 × 2.99	112	S-Cam Berlinetta; O-Cam, Citation, Celebrity
V6, 173.0	3.50 × 2.99	135	O-Citation
V6, 229.0	3.74 × 3.48	110	S-Mal, MC, Chevr cpe/sdn
V6, 231.0	3.80 × 3.40	110	S-Calif. Chevrolet
V6D, 262.0	4.06 × 3.39	85	O-Malibu, MC, Celebrity
V8, 305.0	3.74 × 3.48	50	S-Cam Z28, Chevr wgn; O-Cam, Malibu, MC, Chevr
V8, 305.0	3.74 × 3.48	175	S-MC SS; O-Camaro
V8D, 350.0	4.06 × 3.39	105	O-Chevr, Malibu, MC

1984 Caprice Classic coupe

1984

Chevette (wb 94.3; 5d-97.3)		Wght	Price	Prod
J08	htchbk sdn 3d	1,999	4,997	66,446
J68	htchbk sdn 5d	2,051	5,333	28,466
B08	CS htchbk 3d	2,038	5,489	47,032
B68	CS htchbk 5d	2,102	5,636	94,897
J08/Z90	Diesel sdn 3d	—	5,500	1,495
J68/Z90	Diesel sdn 5d	—	5,851	1,180
B08/Z90	CS diesel sdn 3d	2,261	5,999	1,000
B68/Z90	CS diesel sdn 5d	2,320	6,161	3,384
Cavalier (wb 101.2)				
C69	sdn 4d	2,386	6,222	90,023
C35	wgn 5d	2,455	6,375	50,718
D69	CS sdn 4d	2,398	6,666	110,295
D35	CS wgn 5d	2,468	6,821	58,739
E27	Type 10 cpe	2,367	6,477	103,204
E77	Type 10 htchbk cpe 3d	2,418	6,654	44,146
E27/Z08	Type 10 conv cpe	2,583	11,299	5,486
Citation II (wb 104.9)				
H11	cpe L4	2,454	6,445	4,936
H11	cpe V6	2,529	6,695	
X08	htchbk sdn 3d L4	2,494	6,900	8,783
X08	htchbk sdn 3d V6	2,569	7,150	
X68	htchbk sdn 5d L4	2,506	7,046	83,486
X68	htchbk sdn 5d V6	2,581	7,296	
Camaro (wb 101.0)				
P87	spt cpe L4	2,899	7,995	127,292
P87	spt cpe V6	2,932	8,245	
P87	spt cpe V8	3,112	8,545	
S87	Berlinetta cpe V6	2,944	10,895	33,400
S87	Berlinetta cpe V8	3,126	11,270	
P87	Z28 spt cpe V8	3,135	10,620	100,416
Celebrity (wb 104.9)				
W27	cpe L4	2,663	7,711	29,191
W27	cpe V6	2,781	7,961	
W19	sdn 4d L4	2,703	7,890	200,259
W19	wdn 4d V6	2,816	8,140	
W35	wgn 5d 2S L4	2,857	8,214	48,295
W35	wgn 5d 2S V6	2,964	8,464	
W35/AQ4	wgn 5d 3S L4	—	8,429	31,543
W35/AQ4	wgn 5d 3S V6	—	8,679	
Full-size Chevrolet (wb 116.0)				
L69	Impala sdn 4d V6	3,489	8,895	55,296
L69	Impala sdn 4d V8	3,628	9,270	
N35	Caprice Clsc wgn 4d 3S V8	4,053	10,210	65,688
N47	Caprice Clsc spt cpe V6	3,633	9,253	19,541
N47	Caprice Clsc spt cpe V8	3,834	9,628	
N69	Caprice Classic sdn 4d V6	3,532	9,400	135,970
N69	Caprice Classic sdn 4d V8	3,662	9,775	
Monte Carlo (wb 108.1)				
Z37	spt cpe V6	3,176	8,936	112,730
Z37	spt cpe V8	3,292	9,311	
Z37/Z65	SS spt cpe V8	3,434	10,700	24,050

1984 Engines	bore × stroke	bhp	availability
L4, 97.6	3.23 × 2.98	65	S-Chevette
L4D, 111.0	3.31 × 3.23	51	O-Chevette

1984 Citation II two-door coupe

	bore×stroke	bhp	availability
L4, 121.0	3.50×3.15	88	S-Cavalier
L4, 151.0	4.00×3.00	92	S-Citation, Camaro, Celeb
V6, 173.0	3.50×2.99	107	S-Cam Berlinetta; O-Cam
V6, 173.0	3.50×2.99	112	O-Citation, Celeb
V6, 173.0	3.50×2.99	130/135	O-Citation, Celeb
V6, 229.0	3.74×3.48	110	S-MC, Chevr cpe/sdn
V6, 231.0	3.80×3.40	110	S-Calif. Chevr
V6D, 262.0	4.06×3.39	85	O-Celebrity
V8, 305.0	3.74×3.48	150	S-Cam Z28, Chevr wgn; O-Cam, Monte Carlo, Chevrolet
V8, 305.0	3.74×3.48	180	S-Monte Carlo SS
V8, 305.0	3.74×3.48	190	O-Camaro Z28
V8D, 350.0	4.06×3.39	105	O-Chevr, MC

1985

Chevette (wb 94.3; 5d-97.3)		Wght	Price	Prod
B08	CS htchbk 3d	2,085	5,340	57,706
B68	CS htchbk 5d	2,145	5,690	65,128
B08/Z90	CS diesel sdn 3d	2,261	5,850	203
B68/Z90	CS diesel sdn 5d	2,320	6,215	462
Cavalier (wb 101.2)				
C69	sdn 4d	2,339	6,477	86,597
C35	wgn 5d	2,409	6,633	34,581
D69	CS sdn 4d	2,352	6,900	93,386
D35	CS wgn 5d	2,420	7,066	33,551
E27	Type 10 cpe	2,320	6,737	106,021
E77	Type 10 htchbk cpe 3d	2,382	6,919	25,508
E27/Z08	Type 10 conv cpe	2,458	11,693	4,108
Citation II (wb 104.9)				
X08	htchbk sdn 3d L4	2,499	6,940	7,443
X08	htchbk sdn 3d V6	2,568	7,200	
X68	htchbk sdn 5d L4	2,535	7,090	55,279
X68	htchbk sdn 5d V6	2,603	7,350	
Camaro (wb 101.0)				
P87	spt cpe L4	2,881	8,363	97,966
P87	spt cpe V6	2,977	8,698	
P87	spt cpe V8	3,177	8,998	
S87	Berlinetta cpe V6	3,056	11,060	13,649
S87	Berlinetta cpe V8	3,221	11,360	
P87/Z28	Z28 spt cpe V8	3,251	11,060	47,022
P87/B4Z	IROC-Z spt cpe V8	3,319	11,739	21,177
Celebrity (wb 104.9)				
W27	cpe L4	2,689	8,102	29,010
W27	cpe V6	2,790	8,362	
W19	sdn 4d L4	2,722	8,288	239,763
W19	sdn 4d V6	2,827	8,548	

		Wght	Price	Prod
W35	wgn 5d 2S L4	2,857	8,479	45,602
W35	wgn 5d 2S V6	2,953	8,739	
W35/AQ4	wgn 5d 3S L4	—	8,699	40,547
W35/AQ4	wgn 5d 3S V6	—	8,959	
Full-size Chevrolet (wb 116.0)				
L69	Impala sdn 4d V6	3,508	9,519	53,438
L69	Impala sdn 4d V8	3,634	9,759	
N35	Caprice Clsc wgn 4d 3S V8	4,083	10,714	55,886
N47	Caprice Classic cpe V6	3,525	9,888	16,229
N47	Caprice Classic cpe V8	3,651	10,128	
N69	Caprice Classic sdn 4d V6	3,549	10,038	139,240
N69	Caprice Classic sdn 4d V8	3,674	10,278	
Monte Carlo (wb 108.0)				
Z37	spt cpe V6	3,139	9,540	83,573
Z37	spt cpe V8	3,245	9,780	
Z37/Z65	SS spt cpe V8	3,385	11,380	35,484

1985 Engines	bore×stroke	bhp	availability
L4, 97.6	3.23×2.98	65	S-Chevette
L4D, 111.0	3.31×3.23	51	O-Chevette
L4, 121.0	3.50×3.15	85	S-Cavalier
L4, 151.0	4.00×3.00	88/92	S-Cit, Camaro, Celeb
V6, 173.0	3.50×2.99	112	O-Citation, Celeb
V6, 173.0	3.50×2.99	125/135	S-Cam Berlinetta; O-late Cav, Cit, Camaro, Cele[1]
V6, 262.0	4.00×3.48	130	S-MC, Chevrolet
V6D, 262.0	4.06×3.39	85	O-Celeb
V8, 305.0	3.74×3.48	150/165	S-Cam Z28, Capr wgn; O-Cam, MC, Chevrolet
V8, 305.0	3.74×3.48	180	S-Monte Carlo SS
V8, 305.0	3.74×3.48	190	O-Camaro IROC-Z
V8, 305.0	3.74×3.48	215	O-Camaro Z28/IROC-Z
V8D, 350.0	4.06×3.39	105	O-Chevr

1986

Chevette (wb 94.3; 5d-97.3)		Wght	Price	Prod
B08	CS htchbk 3d	2,080	5,645	48,756
B68	CS htchbk 5d	2,140	5,959	54,164
B08/Z90	CS diesel sdn 3d	2,261	6,152	124
B68/Z90	CS diesel sdn 5d	2,320	6,487	200
Nova (wb 95.7)				
K19	sdn 4d	2,163	7,435	124,961*
K68	htchbk sdn 5d	2,205	7,669	42,788*

*27,945 additional Novas were built late in the 1985 model year.

Cavalier (wb 101.2)		Wght	Price	Prod
C27	cpe 2d L4	2,299	6,706	57,370

1985 Camaro Z28 sport coupe

1986 Celebrity Classic four-door sedan

		Wght	Price	Prod
C27	cpe 2d V6	—	7,316	
C69	sdn 4d L4	2,342	6,888	86,492
C69	sdn 4d V6	—	7,498	
C35	wgn 5d L4	2,412	7,047	30,490
C35	wgn 5d V6	—	7,657	
D77	CS htchbk cpe L4	2,375	7,373	8,046
D77	CS htchbk cpe V6	—	7,983	
D69	CS sdn 4d L4	2,355	7,350	89,168
D69	CS sdn 4d V6	—	7,960	
D35	CS wgn 5d L4	2,423	7,525	23,101
D35	CS wgn 5d V6	—	8,135	
E27	RS cpe L4	2,325	7,640	53,941
E27	RS cpe V6	—	8,250	
E77	RS htchbk cpe 3d L4	2,387	7,830	7,504
E77	RS htchbk cpe 3d V6	—	8,440	
E69	RS sdn 4d L4	2,367	7,811	17,361
E69	RS sdn 4d V6	—	8,451	
E35	RS wgn 5d L4	2,440	7,979	6,252
E35	RS wgn 5d V6	—	8,589	
E67	RS conv cpe L4	2,444	12,530	5,785
E67	RS conv cpe V6	2,642	13,140	
F27	Z24 spt cpe V6	2,519	8,878	36,365
F77	Z24 htchbk cpe 3d V6	2,581	9,068	10,226
Camaro (wb 101.0)				
P87	spt cpe L4	2,900	8,935	99,517
P87	spt cpe V6	2,994	9,285	
P87	spt cpe V8	3,116	9,685	
S87	Berlinetta cpe V6	3,063	11,902	4,479
S87	Berlinetta cpe V8	3,116	12,302	
P87/Z28	Z28 spt cpe V8	3,201	11,902	38,547
P87/B4Z	IROC-Z spt cpe V8	3,278	12,561	49,585
Celebrity (wb 104.9)				
W27	cpe L4	2,689	8,735	29,223
W27	cpe V6	2,794	9,170	
W19	sdn 4d L4	2,719	8,931	291,760
W19	sdn 4d V6	2,824	9,366	
W35	wgn 5d 2S L4	2,847	9,081	36,655
W35	wgn 5d 2S V6	2,912	9,516	
W35/AQ4	wgn 5d 3S L4	2,850	9,313	47,245
W35/AQ4	wgn 5d 3S V6	—	9,748	
Caprice (wb 116.0)				
L69	sdn 4d V6	3,535	10,243	50,751
L69	sdn 4d V8	3,628	10,633	
N35	Classic wgn 4d 3S V8	4,095	11,511	45,183
N47	Classic spt cpe V6	3,546	10,635	9,869
N47	Classic spt cpe V8	3,638	11,025	
N69	Classic sdn 4d V6	3,564	10,795	67,772
N69	Classic sdn 4d V8	3,656	11,185	
N69/B45	Classic Brgm sdn 4d V6	3,574	11,429	69,320
N69/B45	Classic Brgm sdn 4d V8	3,667	11,819	
N69/B45	Classic LS Brgm sdn 4d V6	—	—	2,117
N69/B45	Classic LS Brgm sdn 4d V8	—	—	
Monte Carlo (wb 108.0)				
Z37	spt cpe V6	3,138	10,241	50,418
Z37	spt cpe V8	3,244	10,631	
Z37/Z09	LS cpe V6	3,138	10,451	27,428
Z37/Z09	LS cpe V8	—	10,841	
Z37/Z65	SS spt cpe V8	3,387	12,466	41,164
Z37/Z65	SS aerocoupe V8	3,440	14,191	200

1986 Engines	bore×stroke	bhp	availability
L4, 97.0	3.19×3.03	74	S-Nova
L4, 97.6	3.23×2.98	65	S-Chevette
L4D, 111.0	3.31×3.23	51	O-Chevette
L4, 121.0	3.50×3.15	85	S-Cavalier
L4, 151.0	4.00×3.00	88/92	S-Camaro, Celebrity
V6, 173.0	3.50×2.99	112	O-Celebrity
V6, 173.0	3.50×2.99	120/135	S-Cam Berlinetta, Cav Z24; O-Cav, Camaro, Celebrity
V6, 262.0	4.00×3.48	140	S-MC, Caprice
V8, 305.0	3.74×3.48	150/155	S-Cam Z28, Capr wgn;
		165	O-Cam, Monte Carlo, Caprice
V8, 305.0	3.74×3.48	180	S-Monte Carlo SS
V8, 305.0	3.74×3.48	190	O-Camaro IROC-Z
V8, 305.0	3.74×3.48	215	O-Camaro Z28/IROC-Z

1987

Chevette (wb 94.3; 5d-97.3)		Wght	Price	Prod
B08	CS htchbk 3d	2,078	4,995	26,135
B68	CS htchbk 5d	2,137	5,495	20,073
Nova (wb 95.7)				
K19	sdn 4d	2,206	8,258	123,782
K68	htchbk sdn 5d	2,253	8,510	26,224
Cavalier (wb 101.2)				
C27	cpe 2d L4	2,300	7,255	53,678
C27	cpe 2d V6	—	7,915	
E27	RS cpe L4	2,360	8,318	36,353
E27	RS cpe V6	—	8,978	
F27	Z24 spt cpe V6	2,511	9,913	42,890
D77	CS htchbk cpe L4	2,359	7,978	3,480
D77	CS htchbk cpe V6	—	8,638	
E77	RS htchbk cpe 3d L4	2,408	8,520	2,818
E77	RS htchbk cpe 3d V6	—	9,180	
F77	Z24 htchbk cpe 3d V6	2,560	10,115	4,517
C69	sdn 4d L4	2,345	7,449	84,445
C69	sdn 4d V6	—	8,109	
D69	CS sdn 4d L4	2,355	7,953	50,625
D69	CS sdn 4d V6	—	8,613	
E69	RS sdn 4d L4	2,397	8,499	15,482
E69	RS sdn 4d V6	—	9,159	
C35	wgn 5d L4	2,401	7,615	25,542
C35	wgn 5d V6	—	8,275	
D35	CS wgn 5d L4	2,411	8,140	15,023
D35	CS wgn 5d V6	—	8,800	
E35	RS wgn 5d L4	2,460	8,677	5,575
E35	RS wgn 5d V6	—	9,337	
E67	RS conv cpe L4	2,519	13,446	5,826
E67	RS conv cpe V6	—	14,106	
Camaro (wb 101.0)				
P87	spt cpe V6	3,062	9,995	83,890
P87	spt cpe V8	3,181	10,395	
P87	LT cpe V6	—	11,517	—
P87	LT cpe V8	—	11,917	—
P87/Z28	Z28 spt cpe V8	3,228	12,819	52,863
P87/Z28	IROC-Z spt cpe V8	—	13,488	
P67	conv cpe V8	—	14,794	263
P67/Z28	Z28 conv cpe V8	—	17,218	744
P67/Z28	IROC-Z conv cpe V8	—	17,917	
Corsica (wb 103.4)				
T69	sdn 4d L4	2,491	8,995	8,973
T69	sdn 4d V6	2,609	9,655	
Beretta (wb 103.4)				
V37	cpe L4	2,550	9,555	8,072
V37	cpe V6	2,648	10,215	
Celebrity (wb 104.9)				
W27	cpe L4	2,685	9,995	18,198
W27	cpe V6	2,769	10,605	
W19	sdn 4d L4	2,715	10,265	273,864
W19	sdn 4d V6	2,799	10,875	
W35	wgn 5d 2S L4	2,847	10,425	33,894
W35	wgn 5d 2S V6	2,931	11,035	
W35/AQ4	wgn 5d 3S L4	—	10,672	36,568
W35/AQ4	wgn 5d 3S V6	—	11,382	

1987 Camaro Z28 sport coupe

Caprice (wb 116.0)		Wght	Price	Prod
L35	wgn 4d 3S V8	4,114	11,995	11,953
N35	Classic wgn 4d 3S V8	4,125	12,586	28,387
N47	Classic cpe V6	3,512	11,392	3,110
N47	Classic cpe V8	3,605	11,802	
L69	sdn 4d V6	3,510	10,995	56,266
L69	sdn 4d V8	3,603	11,435	
N69	Classic sdn 4d V6	3,527	11,560	53,802
N69	Classic sdn 4d V8	3,620	12,000	
U69	Classic Brgm sdn 4d V6	3,576	12,549	51,341
U69	Classic Brgm sdn 4d V8	3,669	12,989	
U69/B6N	Classic LS Brgm sdn 4d V6	—	13,805	23,641
U69/B6N	Classic LS Brgm sdn 4d V8	—	14,245	
Monte Carlo (wb 108.0)				
Z37	LS cpe V6	3,283	11,306	72,993
Z37	LS cpe V8	3,389	11,746	
Z37/Z65	SS spt cpe V8	3,473	13,463	
Z37/Z16	SS aerocoupe V8	3,526	14,838	6,052

1987 Engines	bore × stroke	bhp	availability
L4, 97.0	3.19 × 3.03	74	S-Nova
L4, 97.6	3.23 × 2.98	65	S-Chevette
L4, 121.0	3.50 × 3.15	90	S-Cav, Corsica, Beretta
L4, 151.0	4.00 × 3.00	98	S-Celeb
V6, 173.0	3.50 × 2.99	120/135	S-Camaro, Cav Z24; O-Cav, Celebrity, Cors, Beretta
V6, 262.0	4.00 × 3.48	140/145	S-MC, Caprice cpe/sdn
V8, 305.0	3.74 × 3.48	150/170	S-Cam Z28; O-Cam, MC, Caprice
V8, 305.0	3.74 × 3.48	180	S-Monte Carlo SS
V8, 305.0	3.74 × 3.48	215	O-Camaro Z28/IROC-Z
V8, 307.0	3.80 × 3.38	140	S-Capr wgn
V8, 350.0	4.00 × 3.48	225	O-Camaro IROC-Z

Note: Corsica and Beretta were actually early 1988 models, introduced during the 1987 model year.

1988

Nova (wb 95.7)		Wght	Price	Prod
K19	sdn 4d	2,211	8,795	87,263
K68	htchbk sdn 5d	2,257	9,050	18,570
L19	Twin-cam sdn 4d	—	11,395	3,300
Cavalier (wb 101.2)				
C37	cpe 2d L4	2,359	8,120	34,470
C69	sdn 4d L4	2,363	8,195	107,438
C35	wgn 5d L4	2,413	8,490	29,806
C35	wgn 5d V6	—	9,150	
C37/WV9	VL cpe	—	6,995	43,611
E37	RS cpe L4	2,371	9,175	24,359
E69	RS sdn 4d L4	2,414	9,385	18,852
F37	Z24 cpe V6	2,558	10,725	55,658
F67	Z24 conv cpe V6	2,665	15,990	8,745
Camaro (wb 101.0)				
P87	spt cpe V6	3,054	10,995	66,605
P87	spt cpe V8	3,228	11,395	
P87/Z28	IROC-Z spt cpe V8	3,229	13,490	24,050
P87/Z08	conv cpe V8	3,350	16,255	1,859
P87/Z08	IROC-Z conv cpe V8	3,352	18,015	3,761
Corsica (wb 103.4)				
T69	sdn 4d L4	2,589	9,555	291,163
T69	sdn 4d V6	2,688	10,215	
Beretta (wb 103.4)				
V37	cpe L4	2,608	10,135	275,098
V37	cpe V6	2,707	10,795	
Celebrity (wb 104.9)				
W27	cpe L4	2,727	10,585	11,909
W27	cpe V6	2,793	11,195	
W19	sdn 4d L4	2,765	11,025	195,205
W19	sdn 4d V6	2,833	11,025	
W35/B5E	wgn 5d 2S L4	2,903	11,350	23,759

1988 Beretta GT coupe

1989 Corsica LTZ four-door sedan

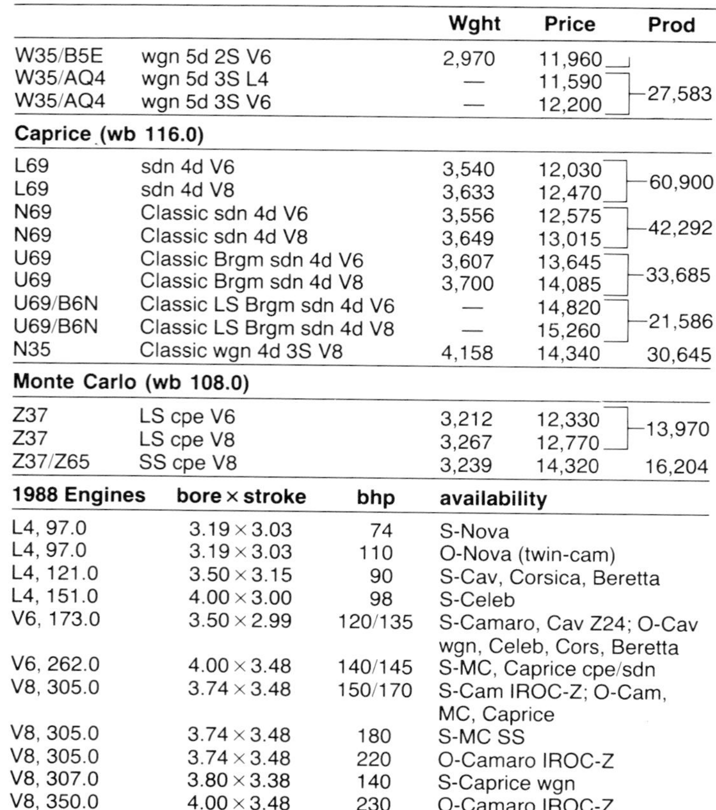

		Wght	Price	Prod
W35/B5E	wgn 5d 2S V6	2,970	11,960	
W35/AQ4	wgn 5d 3S L4	—	11,590	27,583
W35/AQ4	wgn 5d 3S V6	—	12,200	
Caprice (wb 116.0)				
L69	sdn 4d V6	3,540	12,030	60,900
L69	sdn 4d V8	3,633	12,470	
N69	Classic sdn 4d V6	3,556	12,575	42,292
N69	Classic sdn 4d V8	3,649	13,015	
U69	Classic Brgm sdn 4d V6	3,607	13,645	33,685
U69	Classic Brgm sdn 4d V8	3,700	14,085	
U69/B6N	Classic LS Brgm sdn 4d V6	—	14,820	21,586
U69/B6N	Classic LS Brgm sdn 4d V8	—	15,260	
N35	Classic wgn 4d 3S V8	4,158	14,340	30,645
Monte Carlo (wb 108.0)				
Z37	LS cpe V6	3,212	12,330	13,970
Z37	LS cpe V8	3,267	12,770	
Z37/Z65	SS cpe V8	3,239	14,320	16,204

1988 Engines	bore × stroke	bhp	availability
L4, 97.0	3.19 × 3.03	74	S-Nova
L4, 97.0	3.19 × 3.03	110	O-Nova (twin-cam)
L4, 121.0	3.50 × 3.15	90	S-Cav, Corsica, Beretta
L4, 151.0	4.00 × 3.00	98	S-Celeb
V6, 173.0	3.50 × 2.99	120/135	S-Camaro, Cav Z24; O-Cav wgn, Celeb, Cors, Beretta
V6, 262.0	4.00 × 3.48	140/145	S-MC, Caprice cpe/sdn
V8, 305.0	3.74 × 3.48	150/170	S-Cam IROC-Z; O-Cam, MC, Caprice
V8, 305.0	3.74 × 3.48	180	S-MC SS
V8, 305.0	3.74 × 3.48	220	O-Camaro IROC-Z
V8, 307.0	3.80 × 3.38	140	S-Caprice wgn
V8, 350.0	4.00 × 3.48	230	O-Camaro IROC-Z

1989

Cavalier (wb 101.2)		Wght	Price	Prod
C37	cpe 2d L4	2,418	8,395	
C69	sdn 4d L4	2,423	8,595	
C35	wgn 5d L4	2,478	8,975	
C35	wgn 5d V6	2,566	9,635	
C37/WV9	VL cpe L4	—	7,375	
F37	Z24 cpe V6	—	11,325	
F67	Z24 conv cpe V6	2,729	16,615	
Camaro (wb 101.0)				
P87	RS htchbk cpe 3d V6	3,082	11,495	
P87	RS htchbk cpe 3d V8	3,285	11,895	
P87/Z28	IROC-Z cpe V8	3,264	14,145	
P67	RS conv cpe V8	3,116	16,995	
P67/Z28	IROC-Z conv cpe V8	—	18,945	
Corsica (wb 103.4)				
T69	sdn 4d L4	2,595	9,985	

		Wght	Price	Prod
T69	sdn 4d V6	2,690	10,645	
T68	htchbk sdn 5d L4	2,648	10,375	
T68	htchbk sdn 5d V6	—	11,035	
Z69	LTZ sdn 4d V6	—	12,825	
Beretta (wb 103.4)				
V37	cpe L4	2,631	10,575	
V37	cpe V6	2,727	11,235	
W37	GT cpe V6	—	12,685	
W37	GTU cpe V6	—	—	
Celebrity (wb 104.9)				
W19	sdn 4d L4	2,751	11,495	
W19	sdn 4d V6	2,819	12,280	
W35/B5E	wgn 5d 2S L4	2,888	11,925	
W35/B5E	wgn 5d 2S V6	2,928	12,710	
W35/AQ4	wgn 5d 3S L4	—	12,175	
W35/AQ4	wgn 5d 3S V6	—	12,960	
Caprice (wb 116.0)				
L69	sdn 4d V8	3,693	13,865	
N69	Classic sdn 4d V8	—	14,445	
U69	Classic Brgm sdn 4d V8	—	15,615	
U69/B6N	Classic LS Brgm sdn 4d V8	—	16,835	
N35	Classic wgn 5d 3S V8	4,192	15,025	

1989 Engines	bore × stroke	bhp	availability
L4, 121.0	3.50 × 3.15	90	S-Cav, Corsica, Beretta
L4, 151.0	4.00 × 3.00	98	S-Celebrity
V6, 173.0	3.50 × 2.99	125/135	S-Cam RS, Cav Z24; O-Cav wgn, Celeb, Cors, Beretta
V8, 305.0	3.74 × 3.48	170	S-Cam RS conv, IROC-Z, Caprice; O-Camaro RS
V8, 305.0	3.74 × 3.48	220/230	O-Camaro IROC-Z
V8, 307.0	3.80 × 3.38	140	S-Caprice wgn
V8, 350.0	4.00 × 3.48	230/240	O-Camaro IROC-Z

1989 Cavalier Z24 convertible coupe

CHEVROLET CORVAIR

1960

500 (wb 108.0)		Wght	Price	Prod
0527	cpe	2,270	1,984	14,628
0569	sdn 4d	2,305	2,038	47,683
700 (wb 108.0)				
0727	cpe	2,290	2,049	36,562
0769	sdn 4d	2,315	2,103	139,208
900 Monza (wb 108.0)				
0927	cpe	2,280	2,238	11,926

1960 Engines	bore×stroke	bhp	availability
flat 6, 140.0	3.38×2.60	80	S-all
flat 6, 140.0	3.38×2.60	95	O-all

1961

500 (wb 108.0)		Wght	Price	Prod
0527	cpe	2,320	1,920	16,857
0535	Lakewood wgn 4d	2,530	2,266	5,591
0569	sdn 4d	2,355	1,974	18,752
700 (wb 108.0)				
0727	cpe	2,350	1,985	24,786
0735	Lakewood wgn 4d	2,555	2,331	20,451
0769	sdn 4d	2,380	2,039	51,948
900 Monza (wb 108.0)				
0927	cpe	2,395	2,201	109,945
0969	sdn 4d	2,420	2,201	33,745

1961 Engines	bore×stroke	bhp	availability
flat 6, 145.0	3.44×2.60	80	S-all
flat 6, 145.0	3.44×2.60	98	O-all

1962

500 (wb 108.0)		Wght	Price	Prod
0527	cpe	2,350	1,992	16,245
700 (wb 108.0)				
0727	cpe	2,390	2,057	18,474
0735	wgn 4d	2,590	2,407	3,716
0769	sdn 4d	2,410	2,111	35,368
900 Monza (wb 108.0)		**Wght**	**Price**	**Prod**
0927	cpe	2,440	2,273	144,844
0927	Spyder cpe	2,465	2,636	6,894
0935	wgn 4d	2,590	2,569	2,362
0967	conv cpe	2,625	2,483	13,995
0967	Spyder conv cpe	2,650	2,846	2,574
0969	sdn 4d	2,455	2,273	48,059

1962 Engines	bore×stroke	bhp	availability
flat 6, 145.0	3.44×2.60	80	S-all exc Spyder
flat 6, 145.0	3.44×2.60	102	O-all exc Spyder
flat 6, 145.0	3.44×2.60	150	S-Monza Spyder

1963

500 (wb 108.0)		Wght	Price	Prod
0527	cpe	2,330	1,992	16,680
700 (wb 108.0)		**Wght**	**Price**	**Prod**
0727	cpe	2,355	2,056	12,378
0769	sdn 4d	2,385	2,110	20,684
900 Monza (wb 108.0)				
0927	cpe	2,415	2,272	117,917
0927	Spyder cpe	2,440	2,589	11,627
0967	conv cpe	2,525	2,481	36,693
0967	Spyder conv cpe	2,550	2,798	7,472
0969	sdn 4d	2,450	2,326	31,120

1963 Engines	bore×stroke	bhp	availability
flat 6, 145.0	3.44×2.60	80	S-all exc Spyder
flat 6, 145.0	3.44×2.60	102	O-all exc Spyder
flat 6, 145.0	3.44×2.60	150	S-Monza Spyder

1964

500 (wb 108.0)		Wght	Price	Prod
0527	cpe	2,365	2,000	22,968
600 Monza Spyder (wb 108.0)				
0627	cpe	2,470	2,599	6,480
0667	conv cpe	2,580	2,811	4,761
700 (wb 108.0)				
0769	sdn 4d	2,415	2,119	16,295
900 Monza (wb 108.0)				
0927	cpe	2,445	2,281	88,440
0967	conv cpe	2,555	2,492	31,045
0969	sdn 4d	2,470	2,335	21,926

1964 Engines	bore×stroke	bhp	availability
flat 6, 164.0	3.44×2.94	95	S-all exc 600
flat 6, 164.0	3.44×2.94	110	O-all exc 600
flat 6, 164.0	3.44×2.94	150	S-600

1965

500 (wb 108.0)		Wght	Price	Prod
10137	htp cpe	2,385	2,066	36,747
10139	htp sdn	2,405	2,142	17,560
Monza (wb 108.0)				
10537	htp cpe	2,440	2,347	88,954
10539	htp sdn	2,465	2,422	37,157
10567	conv cpe	2,675	2,493	26,466
Corsa (wb 108.0)				
10737	htp cpe	2,475	2,519	20,291
10767	conv cpe	2,710	2,665	8,353

1964 Corvair 700 four-door sedan

1965 Engines	bore×stroke	bhp	availability
flat 6, 164.0	3.44×2.94	95	S-all exc Corsa
flat 6, 164.0	3.44×2.94	110	O-all exc Corsa
flat 6, 164.0	3.44×2.94	140	S-Corsa; O-others
flat 6, 164.0	3.44×2.94	180	O-Corsa

1966

500 (wb 108.0)		Wght	Price	Prod
10137	htp cpe	2,400	2,083	24,045
10139	htp sdn	2,445	2,157	8,779
Monza (wb 108.0)				
10537	htp cpe	2,445	2,350	37,605
10539	htp sdn	2,495	2,424	12,497
10567	conv cpe	2,675	2,493	10,345
Corsa (wb 108.0)				
10737	htp cpe	2,485	2,519	7,330
10767	conv cpe	2,720	2,662	3,142

1966 Engines	bore×stroke	bhp	availability
flat 6, 164.0	3.44×2.94	95	S-all exc Corsa
flat 6, 164.0	3.44×2.94	110	O-all exc Corsa
flat 6, 164.0	3.44×2.94	140	S-Corsa; O-others
flat 6, 164.0	3.44×2.94	180	O-Corsa

1967

500 (wb 108.0)		Wght	Price	Prod
10137	htp cpe	2,435	2,128	9,257
10139	htp sdn	2,470	2,194	2,959
Monza (wb 108.0)				
10537	htp cpe	2,465	2,398	9,771
10539	htp sdn	2,515	2,464	3,157
10567	conv cpe	2,695	2,540	2,109

1967 Engines	bore×stroke	bhp	availability
flat 6, 164.0	3.44×2.94	95	S-all
flat 6, 164.0	3.44×2.94	110/140	O-all

1968

500 (wb 108.0)		Wght	Price	Prod
10137	htp cpe	2,470	2,243	7,206
Monza (wb 108.0)				
10537	htp cpe	2,500	2,507	6,807
10567	conv cpe	2,725	2,626	1,386

1968 Corvair Monza hardtop coupe

1968 Engines	bore×stroke	bhp	availability
flat 6, 164.0	3.44×2.94	95	S-all
flat 6, 164.0	3.44×2.94	110	O-all

1969

500 (wb 108.0)		Wght	Price	Prod
10137	htp cpe	2,515	2,528	2,762
Monza (wb 108.0)				
10537	htp cpe	2,545	2,522	2,717
10567	conv cpe	2,770	2,641	521

1969 Engines	bore×stroke	bhp	availability
flat 6, 164.0	3.44×2.94	95	S-all
flat 6, 164.0	3.44×2.94	110	O-all

CHEVROLET CORVETTE

1953

290 (wb 102.0)		Wght	Price	Prod
2934	conv rdstr	2,705	3,513	315

1953 Engine	bore×stroke	bhp	availability
L6, 235.5	3.56×3.94	150	S-all

1954

290 (wb 102.0)		Wght	Price	Prod
2934	conv rdstr	2,705	3,523	3,640

1954 Engine	bore×stroke	bhp	availability
L6, 235.5	3.56×3.94	150	S-all

1955

290 (wb 102.0)		Wght	Price	Prod
2934	conv rdstr	2,650	2,934	674

1955 Engines	bore×stroke	bhp	availability
L6, 235.5	3.56×3.94	155	S-all
V8, 265.0	3.75×3.00	195	O-all

1956

290 (wb 102.0)		Wght	Price	Prod
2934	conv rdstr	2,764	3,149	3,467

1956 Engine	bore×stroke	bhp	availability
V8, 265.0	3.75×3.00	210/225	S-all

1957

290 (wb 102.0)		Wght	Price	Prod
2934	conv rdstr	2,730	3,465	6,339

1957 Engines	bore×stroke	bhp	availability
V8, 283.0	3.88×3.00	220	S-all
V8, 283.0	3.88×3.00	245/270	O-all
V8, 283.0	3.88×3.00	250/283	O-all (FI)

1958

(wb 102.0)		Wght	Price	Prod
867	conv rdstr	2,793	3,631	9,168

1958 Engines	bore×stroke	bhp	availability
V8, 283.0	3.88×3.00	230	S-all
V8, 283.0	3.88×3.00	245/270	O-all
V8, 283.0	3.88×3.00	250/290	O-all (FI)

1959

(wb 102.0)		Wght	Price	Prod
867	conv rdstr	2,840	3,875	9,670

1959 Engines	bore×stroke	bhp	availability
V8, 283.0	3.88×3.00	230	S-all
V8, 283.0	3.88×3.00	245/270	O-all
V8, 283.0	3.88×3.00	250/290	O-all (FI)

1960

(wb 102.0)		Wght	Price	Prod
0867	conv rdstr	2,840	3,872	10,261

1960 Engines	bore×stroke	bhp	availability
V8, 283.0	3.88×3.00	230	S-all
V8, 283.0	3.88×3.00	245/270	O-all
V8, 283.0	3.88×3.00	275/315	O-all (FI)

1961

(wb 102.0)		Wght	Price	Prod
0867	conv rdstr	2,905	3,934	10,939

1961 Engines	bore×stroke	bhp	availability
V8, 283.0	3.88×3.00	230	S-all
V8, 283.0	3.88×3.00	245/270	O-all
V8, 283.0	3.88×3.00	275/315	O-all (FI)

1962

(wb 102.0)		Wght	Price	Prod
0867	conv rdstr	2,925	4,038	14,531

1962 Engines	bore×stroke	bhp	availability
V8, 327.0	4.00×3.25	250	S-all
V8, 327.0	4.00×3.25	300/340	O-all
V8, 327.0	4.00×3.25	360	O-all (FI)

1963

Sting Ray (wb 98.0)		Wght	Price	Prod
0837	cpe	2,859	4,252	10,594
0867	conv rdstr	2,881	4,037	10,919

1963 Engines	bore×stroke	bhp	availability
V8, 327.0	4.00×3.25	250	S-all
V8, 327.0	4.00×3.25	300/340	O-all
V8, 327.0	4.00×3.25	360	O-all (FI)

1960 Corvette convertible roadster

1964

Sting Ray (wb 98.0)		Wght	Price	Prod
0837	cpe	2,960	4,252	8,304
0867	conv rdstr	2,945	4,037	13,925

1964 Engines	bore×stroke	bhp	availability
V8, 327.0	4.00×3.25	250	S-all
V8, 327.0	4.00×3.25	300-365	O-all
V8, 327.0	4.00×3.25	395	O-all (FI)

1965

Sting Ray (wb 98.0)		Wght	Price	Prod
19437	cpe	2,975	4,321	8,186
19467	conv rdstr	2,985	4,106	15,376

1965 Engines	bore×stroke	bhp	availability
V8, 327.0	4.00×3.25	250	S-all
V8, 327.0	4.00×3.25	300-365	O-all
V8, 327.0	4.00×3.25	395	O-all (FI)
V8, 396.0	4.09×3.75	425	O-all

1966 Corvette Sting Ray coupe

1966

Sting Ray (wb 98.0)		Wght	Price	Prod
19437	cpe	2,985	4,295	9,958
19467	conv rdstr	3,005	4,084	17,762

1966 Engines	bore×stroke	bhp	availability
V8, 327.0	4.00×3.25	300	S-all
V8, 327.0	4.00×3.25	350	O-all
V8, 427.0	4.25×3.76	390/425	O-all

1967

Sting Ray (wb 98.0)		Wght	Price	Prod
19437	cpe	3,000	4,353	8,504
19467	conv rdstr	3,020	4,141	14,436

1967 Engines	bore×stroke	bhp	availability
V8, 327.0	4.00×3.25	300	S-all
V8, 327.0	4.00×3.25	350	O-all
V8, 427.0	4.25×3.76	390–435	O-all

1968

(wb 98.0)		Wght	Price	Prod
19437	cpe	3,055	4,663	9,936
19467	conv rdstr	3,065	4,320	18,630

1968 Engines	bore×stroke	bhp	availability
V8, 327.0	4.00 × 3.25	300	S-all
V8, 327.0	4.00 × 3.25	350	O-all
V8, 427.0	4.25 × 3.76	390-435	O-all

1969

Stingray (wb 98.0)		Wght	Price	Prod
19437	cpe	3,140	4,781	22,154
19467	conv rdstr	3,145	4,438	16,608

1969 Engines	bore×stroke	bhp	availability
V8, 350.0	4.00×3.48	300	S-all
V8, 350.0	4.00×3.48	350	O-all
V8, 427.0	4.25×3.76	390–435	O-all

1970

Stingray (wb 98.0)		Wght	Price	Prod
19437	cpe	3,184	5,192	10,668
19467	conv rdstr	3,196	4,849	6,648

1970 Engines	bore×stroke	bhp	availability
V8, 350.0	4.00×3.48	300	S-all
V8, 350.0	4.00×3.48	350/370	O-all
V8, 454.0	4.25 × 4.00	390/465	O-all

Note: 1967-70 racing engines not listed.

1971

Stingray (wb 98.0)		Wght	Price	Prod
19437	cpe	3,202	5,533	14,680
19467	conv rdstr	3,216	5,296	7,121

1971 Engines	bore×stroke	bhp	availability
V8, 350.0	4.00×3.48	270	S-all
V8, 350.0	4.00×3.48	330	O-all
V8, 454.0	4.25×4.00	365/425	O-all

1972

Stingray (wb 98.0)		Wght	Price	Prod
1Z37	cpe	3,215	5,472	20,486
1Z67	conv rdstr	3,216	5,246	6,508

1972 Engines	bore×stroke	bhp	availability
V8, 350.0	4.00×3.48	200	S-all
V8, 350.0	4.00×3.48	255	O-all
V8, 454.0	4.25×4.00	270	O-all

1973—30,465 built

Stingray (wb 98.0)		Wght	Price	Prod
Z37	cpe	3,326	5,635	24,372*
Z67	conv rdstr	3,333	5,399	6,093*
Z67	above, two tops	3,387	5,676	

1973 Engines	bore×stroke	bhp	availability
V8, 350.0	4.00×3.48	190	S-all
V8, 350.0	4.00×3.48	250	O-all
V8, 454.0	4.25×4.00	275	O-all

*estimates; proportioned from total

1974 Corvette Stingray convertible roadster

1974

Stingray (wb 98.0)		Wght	Price	Prod
Z37	cpe	3,309	6,082	32,028
Z67	conv rdstr	3,315	5,846	5,474

1974 Engines	bore×stroke	bhp	availability
V8, 350.0	4.00×3.48	195	S-all
V8, 350.0	4.00×3.48	250	O-all
V8, 454.0	4.25×4.00	270	O-all

1975

Stingray (wb 98.0)		Wght	Price	Prod
Z37	cpe	3,433	6,797	33,836
Z67	conv rdstr	3,446	6,537	4,629

1975 Engines	bore×stroke	bhp	availability
V8, 350.0	4.00×3.48	165	S-all
V8, 350.0	4.00×3.48	205	O-all

1976

Stingray (wb 98.0)		Wght	Price	Prod
Z37	cpe	3,445	7,605	46,558

1976 Engines	bore×stroke	bhp	availability
V8, 350.0	4.00×3.48	180	S-all
V8, 350.0	4.00×3.48	210	O-all

1977

Stingray (wb 98.0)		Wght	Price	Prod
Z37	cpe	3,448	8,648	49,213

1977 Engines	bore×stroke	bhp	availability
V8, 350.0	4.00×3.48	180	S-all
V8, 350.0	4.00×3.48	210	O-all

1978

(wb 98.0)		Wght	Price	Prod
Z87	cpe	3,401	9,645	41,467*
Z87/Z78	Pace Car Replica cpe	3,450	13,653	6,200

*includes 2,500 Silver Anniversary editions

1978 Engines	bore×stroke	bhp	availability
V8, 350.0	4.00×3.48	185	S-all
V8, 350.0	4.00×3.48	220	O-all

1979

(wb 98.0)		Wght	Price	Prod
Z87	cpe	3,372	12,313	53,807

1979 Engines	bore×stroke	bhp	availability
V8, 350.0	4.00×3.48	195	S-all
V8, 350.0	4.00×3.48	225	O-all

1980

(wb 98.0)		Wght	Price	Prod
Z87	cpe	3,206	13,965	40,614

1980 Engines	bore×stroke	bhp	availability
V8, 350.0	4.00×3.48	190	S-all
V8, 350.0	4.00×3.48	230	O-all
V8, 305.0	3.74×3.48	180	O-all

1981

(wb 98.0)		Wght	Price	Prod
Y87	cpe	3,179	15,248	40,606

1981 Engine	bore × stroke	bhp	availability
V8, 350.0	4.00 × 3.48	190	S-all

1982

(wb 98.0)		Wght	Price	Prod
Y87	cpe	3,232	18,290	18,648
Y07	Collector Ed htchbk cpe	3,233	22,537	6,759

1982 Engine	bore × stroke	bhp	availability
V8, 350.0	4.00 × 3.48	200	S-all

1983

No 1983 Corvette model was produced.

1984

(wb 96.2)		Wght	Price	Prod
Y07	cpe	3,087	21,800	51,547

1984 Engine	bore × stroke	bhp	availability
V8, 350.0	4.00 × 3.48	205	S-all

1985

(wb 96.2)		Wght	Price	Prod
Y07	cpe 3d	3,191	24,873	39,729

1985 Engine	bore × stroke	bhp	availability
V8, 350.0	4.00 × 3.48	230	S-all

1986

(wb 96.2)		Wght	Price	Prod
Y07	cpe 3d	3,239	27,027	27,794
Y67	conv cpe 2d	—	32,032	7,315

1986 Engine	bore × stroke	bhp	availability
V8, 350.0	4.00 × 3.48	230	S-all

1988 Corvette coupe

1987

(wb 96.2)		Wght	Price	Prod
Y07	htchbk cpe 3d	3,216	27,999	20,007
Y67	conv cpe 2d	3,279	33,172	10,625

1987 Engine	bore × stroke	bhp	availability
V8, 350.0	4.00 × 3.48	240	S-all

1988

(wb 96.2)		Wght	Price	Prod
Y07	htchbk cpe 3d	3,229	29,480	15,382
Y67	conv cpe 2d	3,299	34,820	7,407

1988 Engine	bore × stroke	bhp	availability
V8, 350.0	4.00 × 3.48	245	S-all

1989

(wb 96.2)		Wght	Price	Prod
Y07	htchbk cpe 3d	3,229	31,545	
Y67	conv cpe 2d	3,269	36,785	
NA	ZR1 cpe	—	—	

1989 Engines	bore × stroke	bhp	availability
V8, 350.0	4.00 × 3.48	240/245	S-base models
V8, 350.0	NA	385	S-ZR1

CHRYSLER

1939

C-22 Royal (wb 119.0; lwb-136.0)	Wght	Price	Prod
cpe 2P	3,120	918	4,780
Windsor cpe 2P	3,130	983	
Victoria cpe 4P	3,160	970	239
Windsor Victoria cpe 4P	3,165	1,065	
brougham 5P	3,200	975	4,838
sdn 4d	3,265	1,010	45,955
Windsor sdn 4d	3,275	1,075	
Windsor club cpe 5P	3,245	1,185	2,983
lwb sdn 7P	3,520	1,235	621
lwb sdn limo 7P	3,625	1,325	191
chassis	—	—	394
C-23 Imperial/New Yorker/Saratoga (wb 125.0)			
Imperial bus cpe 2P	3,520	1,123	492
Imperial Victoria cpe 4P	3,555	1,160	35
Imperial brougham 5P	3,610	1,165	185
Imperial sdn 4d	3,640	1,198	10,536
New Yorker sdn 4d	3,695	1,298	
Saratoga sdn 4d	3,720	1,443	
New Yorker Victoria cpe 4P	3,665	1,395	99
New Yorker bus cpe 2P	3,540	1,223	606
New Yorker club cpe 5P	3,550	1,260	
Saratoga club cpe 5P	3,665	1,495	134
chassis	—	—	48
C-24 Custom Imperial (wb 144.0)			
sdn 5P	4,590	2,595	88
sdn 7P	4,620	2,595	95
sdn limo 7P	4,665	2,695	117
chassis	—	—	7

1939 Engines	bore×stroke	bhp	availability
L6, 241.5	3.38×4.50	100	S-C22
L6, 241.5	3.38×4.50	107	O-C22
L8, 323.5	3.25×4.88	130	S-C23
L8, 323.5	3.25×4.88	132	S-C24
L8, 323.5	3.25×4.88	138	O-C24

1940

Series C-25 (wb 122.5; 8P-139.5)	Wght	Price	Prod
Royal sdn 4d	3,175	995	23,274
Windsor sdn 4d	3,210	1,025	28,477
Royal sdn 2d	3,150	960	9,851
Windsor sdn 2d	3,175	995	
Royal bus cpe	3,075	895	5,117
Windsor bus cpe	3,095	935	
Royal cpe	3,110	960	4,315
Windsor cpe	3,135	995	
Windsor Highlander cpe	3,135	1,020	2,275
Windsor conv cpe	3,360	1,160	
Windsor Highlander conv cpe	3,360	1,185	
Royal sdn 4d, 8P	3,550	1,235	439
Windsor sdn 4d, 8P	3,575	1,275	
Royal limo	3,640	1,310	98
Windsor limo	3,660	1,350	
chassis	—	—	152
Series C-26 (wb 128.5)			
Traveler sdn 4d	3,590	1,180	14,603
New Yorker sdn 4d	3,635	1,260	
Saratoga sdn 4d	3,790	1,375	
Traveler cpe	3,525	1,150	1,117
New Yorker cpe	3,570	1,230	
New Yorker Highlander cpe	3,570	1,255	
Traveler bus cpe	3,475	1,095	731
New Yorker bus cpe	3,490	1,175	
Traveler sdn 2d	3,555	1,150	275
New Yorker sdn 2d	3,610	1,230	
New Yorker conv cpe	3,775	1,375	845
New Yorker Highlndr conv cpe	3,775	1,400	
Series C-27 Crown Imperial (wb 145.5)			
sdn 4d	4,340	2,245	355
sdn 4d, 8P	4,330	2,345	284
limo, 8P	4,365	2,445	210
chassis	—	—	1

1940 engines	bore×stroke	bhp	availability
L6, 241.5	3.38×4.50	108	S-Royal, Windsor
L6, 241.5	3.38×4.50	112	O-Royal, Windsor
L8, 323.5	3.25×4.88	135	S-Traveler, NY, Saratoga
L8, 323.5	3.25×4.88	143	O-Traveler, NY, Saratoga
L8, 323.5	3.25×4.88	132	S-Crown Imperial
L8, 323.5	3.25×4.88	143	O-Crown Imperial

1941

Series C-28S Royal (wb 121.5; 8P-139.5)	Wght	Price	Prod
sdn 4d	3,300	1,091	51,378
club cpe	3,260	1,085	10,830
luxury brougham 2d	3,270	1,066	8,006
bus cpe	3,170	995	6,846
town sdn 4d	3,320	1,136	1,277
sdn 4d, 8P	3,650	1,345	297
limo 8P	3,695	1,415	31
chassis	—	—	3
C-28W Windsor (wb 121.5; 8P-139.5)	**Wght**	**Price**	**Prod**
sdn 4d	3,300	1,165	36,396
club cpe	3,260	1,142	8,513
conv cpe	3,470	1,315	4,432
luxury brougham 2d	3,270	1,128	2,898

1940 Royal coupe

	Wght	Price	Prod
town sdn 4d	3,315	1,198	2,704
bus cpe	3,170	1,045	1,921
Town & Country wgn 4d, 9P	3,595	1,492	797
Town & Country wgn 4d, 6P	3,540	1,412	200
sdn 4d, 8P	3,575	1,410	116
limo, 8P	3,660	1,487	54
C-30K/30N (wb 127.5)			
Saratoga sdn 4d	3,755	1,320	15,868
New Yorker sdn 4d	3,775	1,389	
Saratoga club cpe	3,685	1,299	2,845
New Yorker club cpe	3,690	1,369	
Saratoga town sdn 4d	3,750	1,350	2,326
New Yorker town sdn 4d	3,785	1,399	
Saratoga bus cpe	3,600	1,245	771
New Yorker bus cpe	3,635	1,325	
Saratoga luxury brougham 2d	3,715	1,293	293
New Yorker luxury brougham 2d	3,745	1,369	
New Yorker conv cpe	3,945	1,548	1,295
Town & Country wgn 4d	exp	proto	1
chassis	—	—	9
C-33 Crown Imperial (wb 145.5)			
sdn 4d	4,435	2,595	179
sdn 4d, 8P	4,495	2,696	205
limo 8P	4,560	2,795	316
special town sdn 4d*	3,900	1,760	894
chassis	—	—	1

*C-30 body and chassis, C-33 engine and nameplates.

1941 Engines	bore×stroke	bhp	availability
L6, 241.5	3.38×4.50	108/112	S-Royal, Windsor
L6, 241.5	3.38×4.50	115	O-Royal, Windsor
L8, 323.5	3.25×4.88	137	S-Saratoga, NY
L8, 323.5	3.25×4.88	140	O-Saratoga, NY
L8, 323.5	3.25×4.88	143	S-Crown Imperial

1942

Series C-34S Royal (wb 121.5; 8P-139.5)	Wght	Price	Prod
bus cpe	3,331	1,075	479
club cpe	3,406	1,168	779
brougham 2d	3,431	1,154	709
sdn 4d	3,476	1,177	7,424
town sdn 4d	3,481	1,222	73
sdn 4d, 8P	3,854	1,535	79
limo 8P	3,895	1,605	21
C-34W Windsor (wb 121.5; 8P-139.5)			
bus cpe	3,351	1,140	250
club cpe	3,426	1,228	1,713
conv cpe	3,661	1,420	574
brougham 2d	3,441	1,220	317
sdn 4d	3,496	1,255	10,054
town sdn, 4d	3,506	1,295	479
Town & Country wgn 4d, 6P	3,614	1,595	150
Town & Country wgn 4d, 9P	3,699	1,685	849
sdn 4d, 8P	3,879	1,605	29
limo 8P	3,900	1,685	12
C-36K Saratoga (wb 127.5)			
bus cpe	3,703	1,325	80
club cpe	3,788	1,380	193
brougham 2d	3,798	1,365	36
sdn 4d	3,833	1,405	1,239
town sdn 4d	3,843	1,450	46
chassis	—	—	2
C-36N New Yorker (wb 127.5)			
bus cpe	3,728	1,385	158
club cpe	3,783	1,450	1,234
conv cpe	4,033	1,640	401
brougham 2d	3,798	1,440	62
Town & Country wgn 4d, 9P	—	proto	1
sdn 4d	3,873	1,475	7,045
town sdn 4d	3,893	1,520	1,648
C-33 Crown Imperial (wb 145.5)			
sdn 4d	4,565	2,815	81
sdn 4d, 8P	4,620	2,915	152
limo 8P	4,685	3,065	215
chassis	—	—	2

1942 Engines	bore×stroke	bhp	availability
L6, 250.6	3.44×4.50	120	S-Royal, Windsor
L8, 323.5	3.25×4.88	140	S-others

1946

Series C-38S Royal (wb 121.5; 8P-139.5)*	Wght	Price	Prod
sdn 4d	3,523	1,561	—
sdn 2d	3,458	1,526	—
club cpe	3,443	1,551	—
bus cpe	3,373	1,431	—
sdn 4d, 8P	3,997	1,943	—
limo 8P	4,022	2,063	—
chassis	—	—	—
C-38W Windsor (wb 121.5; 8P-139.5)*			
sdn 4d	3,528	1,611	—
sdn 2d	3,468	1,591	—
club cpe	3,448	1,601	—
bus cpe	3,383	1,481	—
conv cpe	3,693	1,861	—
sdn 4d, 8P	3,977	1,993	—
limo 8P	4,052	2,113	—
Traveler sdn 4d	3,610	1,746	—
C-39K Saratoga (wb 127.5)*			
sdn 4d	3,972	1,863	—
sdn 2d	3,932	1,838	—
club cpe	3,892	1,848	—
bus cpe	3,817	1,753	—
C-39N New Yorker (wb 127.5)*			
sdn 4d	3,973	1,963	—
sdn 2d	3,932	1,938	—
club cpe	3,897	1,948	—
bus cpe	3,837	1,853	—
conv cpe	4,132	2,193	—
chassis	—	—	—

C-38/39 Town & Country (wb 121.5; L8-127.5)*	Wght	Price	Prod
sdn 4d, L6	3,917	2,366	124
brougham 2d, L6	—	proto	1
conv cpe, L6	—	proto	1
sdn 4d, L8	4,300	2,718	100
conv cpe, L8	4,332	2,743	1,935
htp cpe, L8	—	proto	7
C-40 Crown Imperial (wb 145.5)*			
limo 8P	4,814	3,875	—

1946 Engines	bore×stroke	bhp	availability
L6, 250.6	3.44×4.50	114	S-Royal, Windsor, T&C six
L8, 323.5	3.25×4.88	135	S-others

1947

Series C-38S Royal (wb 121.5; 8P-139.5)*	Wght	Price	Prod
sdn 4d	3,523	1,661	—
sdn 2d	3,458	1,626	—
club cpe	3,443	1,651	—
bus cpe	3,373	1,561	—
sdn 4d, 8P	3,997	2,043	—
limo 8P	4,022	2,163	—
C-38W Windsor (wb 121.5; 8P-139.5)*			
sdn 4d	3,528	1,711	—
Traveler sdn 4d	3,610	1,846	—
sdn 2d	3,468	1,691	—
club cpe	3,448	1,701	—
bus cpe	3,383	1,611	—
conv cpe	3,693	2,075	—
sdn 4d, 8P	3,977	2,093	—
limo 8P	4,052	2,213	—
C-39K Saratoga (wb 127.5)*			
sdn 4d	3,972	1,973	—
sdn 2d	3,900	1,948	—
club cpe	3,930	1,958	—
bus cpe	3,817	1,873	—
C-39N New Yorker (wb 127.5)*			
sdn 4d	3,987	2,073	—
sdn 2d	3,932	2,048	—
club cpe	3,940	2,058	—
bus cpe	3,837	1,973	—
conv cpe	4,132	2,447	—
C-38/39 Town & Country (wb 121.5; L8-127.5)			
sdn 4d, L6	3,955	2,713	2,651
conv cpe, L8	4,332	2,998	3,136
C-40 Crown Imperial (wb 145.5)*			
sdn 4d, 8P	4,865	4,205	—
limo 8P	4,875	4,305	—

1947 Engines	bore×stroke	bhp	availability
L6, 250.6	3.44×4.50	114	S-Royal, Windsor, T&C six
L8, 323.5	3.25×4.88	135	S-others

1948–1949 First Series

Series C-38S Royal (wb 121.5; 8P-139.5)*	Wght	Price	Prod
sdn 4d	3,523	1,955	—
sdn 2d	3,485	1,908	—
club cpe	3,475	1,934	—
bus cpe	3,395	1,819	—
sdn 4d, 8P	3,925	2,380	—
limo 8P	4,022	2,506	—
C-38W Windsor (wb 121.5; 8P-139.5)*			
sdn 4d	3,528	2,021	—
Traveler sdn 4d	3,610	2,163	—
sdn 2d	3,510	1,989	—
club cpe	3,475	2,000	—
bus cpe	3,395	1,884	—
conv cpe	3,693	2,414	—
sdn 4d, 8P	3,935	2,434	—
limo 8P	4,035	2,561	—
C-39K Saratoga (wb 127.5)*			
sdn 4d	3,972	2,291	—
sdn 2d	3,900	2,254	—
club cpe	3,930	2,265	—
bus cpe	3,817	2,165	—
C-39N New Yorker (wb 127.5)*			
sdn 4d	3,987	2,411	—
sdn 2d	3,932	2,374	—
club cpe	3,940	2,385	—
bus cpe	3,837	2,285	—
conv cpe	4,132	2,815	—
C-38/39 Town & Country (wb 121.5; L8-127.5)			
sdn 4d, L6	3,955	2,860	1,175
conv cpe, L8	4,332	3,420	3,309
C-40 Crown Imperial (wb 145.5)*			
sdn 4d, 8P	4,865	4,662	—
limo 8P	4,875	4,767	—

1948 Engines	bore×stroke	bhp	availability
L6, 250.6	3.44×4.50	114	S-Royal, Windsor, T&C six
L8, 323.5	3.25×4.88	135	S-others

Note: First Series 1949 models sold December 1948 through March 1949 identical in weight and price to 1948 models and comprised about 15% of total production.

*Factory combined production figures for 1946 through 1949 first series and breakdowns are not available from Chrysler archives. However, since the Town & Country figures have been obtained (by historian Donald Narus), it is very likely that breakdowns exist for other models.

Combined 1946–1949 First Series Production:

C-38S Royal (wb 121.5; 8P-139.5)	Prod
sdn 4d	24,279
sdn 2d	1,117
club cpe	4,318
bus cpe	1,221
sdn 4d, 8P	626
limo 8P	169
chassis	1
C-38W Windsor (wb 121.5; 8P-139.5)	
sdn 4d	161,139
Traveler sdn 4d	4,182
sdn 2d	4,034
club cpe	26,482
bus cpe	1,980
conv cpe	11,200
sdn 4d, 8P	4,390
limo 8P	1,496
C-39K Saratoga (wb 127.5)	
sdn 4d	4,611
sdn 2d	155
club cpe	765
bus cpe	74
C-39N New Yorker (wb 127.5)	
sdn 4d	52,036
sdn 2d	545
club cpe	10,735

	Wght	Price	Prod
bus cpe			701
conv cpe			3,000
chassis			2
C-38/39 Town & Country (wb 121.5; L8-127.5)			
sdn 4d, L6			4,049
brougham 2d, L6 (proto)			1
conv cpe, L6 (proto)			1
sdn 4d, L8			100
conv cpe, L8			8,368
htp cpe, L8 (proto)			7
C-40 Crown Imperial (wb 145.5)			
sdn 4d, 8P			650
limo 8P			750

1949 Second Series

C-45-1 Royal (wb 125.5; 8P-139.5)	Wght	Price	Prod
sdn 4d	3,550	2,134	13,192
club cpe	3,495	2,114	4,849
wgn 4d, 9P	4,060	3,121	850
sdn 4d, 8P	4,200	2,823	185
C-45-2 Windsor (wb 125.5; 8P-139.5)			
sdn 4d	3,681	2,329	55,879
club cpe	3,631	2,308	17,732
conv cpe	3,845	2,741	3,234
sdn 4d, 8P	4,290	3,017	373
limo 8P	4,430	3,144	73
C-46-1 Saratoga (wb 131.5)			
sdn 4d	4,103	3,610	1,810
club cpe	4,037	2,585	465
C-46-2 New Yorker (wb 131.5)			
sdn 4d	4,113	2,726	18,779
club cpe	4,048	2,700	4,524
conv cpe	4,277	3,206	1,137
chassis	—	—	1
C-46-2 Town & Country (wb 131.5)			
conv cpe	4,630	3,970	1,000
C-46-2 Imperial (wb 131.5)			
sdn 4d	4,300	4,665	50
C-47 Crown Imperial (wb 145.5)			
sdn 4d, 8P	5,250	5,229	40
limo 8P	5,295	5,334	45

1949 Engines	bore×stroke	bhp	availability
L6, 250.6	3.44×4.50	116	S-Royal, Windsor
L8, 323.5	3.25×4.88	135	S-others

1950

C-48-1 Royal (wb 125.5; 8P-139.5)	Wght	Price	Prod
sdn 4d	3,610	2,134	17,713
club cpe	3,540	2,114	5,900
Town & Country wgn 4d, wood	4,055	3,163	599
Town & Country wgn 4d, steel	3,964	2,735	100
sdn 4d, 8P	4,190	2,855	375
C-48-2 Windsor (wb 125.5; 8P-139.5)			
sdn 4d	3,765	2,329	78,199
Traveler sdn 4d	3,830	2,560	900
club cpe	3,670	2,308	20,050
Newport htp cpe	3,875	2,637	9,925
conv cpe	3,905	2,741	2,201
sdn 4d, 8P	4,295	3,050	763
limo 8P	4,400	3,176	174

	Wght	Price	Prod
chassis	—	—	1
C-49-1 Saratoga (wb 131.5)	**Wght**	**Price**	**Prod**
sdn 4d	4,170	2,642	1,000
club cpe	4,110	2,616	300
C-49-2 New Yorker (wb 131.5)			
sdn 4d	4,190	2,758	22,633
club cpe	4,110	2,732	3,000
Newport htp cpe	4,370	3,133	2,800
conv cpe	4,360	3,232	899
wgn 4d, wood	—	proto	1
chassis	—	—	2
C-49-2 Town & Country (wb 131.5)			
Newport htp cpe	4,670	4,003	700
C-49-2 Imperial (wb 131.5)			
sdn 4d	4,245	3,055	9,500
Deluxe sdn 4d	4,250	3,176	1,150
C-50 Crown Imperial (wb 145.5)			
sdn 4d, 8P	5,235	5,229	209
limo 8P	5,305	5,334	205
chassis	—	—	1

1950 Engines	bore×stroke	bhp	availability
L6, 250.6	3.44×4.50	116	S-Royal, Windsor
L8, 323.5	3.25×4.88	135	S-others

1951

C-51W Windsor (wb 125.5; 8P-139.5)	Wght	Price	Prod
sdn 4d	3,527	2,390	10,151*
club cpe	3,570	2,368	4,243*
Town & Country wgn 4d	3,965	3,063	1,239*
sdn 4d, 8P	4,145	3,197	399*
ambulance (sp. order)	—	—	153
Deluxe sdn 4d	3,775	2,608	47,573*
Deluxe Traveler sdn 4d	3,890	2,867	850
Deluxe club cpe	3,700	2,585	8,365
Deluxe Newport htp cpe	3,855	2,953	6,426*
Deluxe conv cpe	3,945	3,071	2,646*
Deluxe sdn 4d, 8P	4,295	3,416	720
Deluxe limo 8P	4,415	3,557	152
C-55 Saratoga (wb 125.5; 8P-139.5)			
sdn 4d	4,018	3,016	22,375*
club cpe	3,948	2,989	5,355*
Newport htp cpe	—	proto	1
Town & Country wgn 4d	4,310	3,681	818*
sdn 4d, 8P	4,465	3,912	115*
ambulance (sp. order)	—	—	1
C-52 New Yorker (wb 131.5)			
sdn 4d	4,260	3,378	25,461*
club cpe	4,145	3,348	3,533
Newport htp cpe	4,330	3,798	3,654*
conv cpe	4,460	3,916	1,386*
Town & Country wgn 4d (4 C51s)	4,455	4,026	251
chassis	—	—	1
C-54 Imperial (wb 131.5)			
sdn 4d	4,350	3,674	13,678*
club cpe	4,230	3,661	2,226*
Newport htp cpe	4,380	4,042	749*
conv cpe	4,570	4,402	650
C-53 Crown Imperial (wb 145.5)			
sdn 4d, 8P	5,360	6,573	227*
limo 8P	5,450	6,690	213*
chassis	—	—	2

1951 Engines	bore×stroke	bhp	availability
L6, 250.6	3.44×4.50	116	S-Windsor
V8, 331.1	3.81×3.63	180	S-others

1952

C-51W Windsor (wb 125.5; 8P-139.5)	Wght	Price	Prod
sdn 4d	3,640	2,498	5,961*
club cpe	3,550	2,475	2,492*
Town & Country wgn 4d	4,015	3,200	728*
sdn 4d, 8P	4,145	3,342	234*
Deluxe sdn 4d	3,775	2,727	27,940*
Deluxe Newport htp cpe	3,855	3,087	3,774*
Deluxe conv cpe	3,990	3,210	1,554*
C-55 Saratoga (wb 125.5; 8P-139.5)			
sdn 4d	4,010	3,215	13,141*
club cpe	3,935	3,187	3,145*
Town & Country wgn 4d, 8P	4,345	3,925	481*
sdn 4d, 8P	4,510	4,172	68*
C-52 New Yorker (wb 131.5)			
sdn 4d	4,205	3,530	14,954*
Newport htp cpe	4,325	3,969	2,146*
conv cpe	4,450	4,093	814*
C-54 Imperial (wb 131.5)			
sdn 4d	4,315	3,839	8,033*
club cpe	4,220	3,826	1,307*
Newport htp cpe	4,365	4,224	440*
C-53 Crown Imperial (wb 145.5)			
sdn 4d, 8P	5,395	6,872	133*
limo 8P	5,430	6,994	125*

1952 Engines	bore×stroke	bhp	availability
L6, 264.5	3.44×4.75	119	S-Windsor
V8, 331.1	3.81×3.63	180	S-others

*As with other corporate makes, Chrysler combined model year production for 1951–52. However, production figures are known for several 1951-only body styles, making production estimates of remaining body styles (spanning both years) more accurate. In the above cases (*), estimates are based on the known percentages of the two-year run: 63% in 1951 and 37% in 1952.

1953

C-60-1 Windsor (wb 125.5; 8P-139.5)	Wght	Price	Prod
sdn 4d	3,660	2,462	18,879
club cpe	3,600	2,442	11,646
Town & Country wgn 4d	3,960	3,259	1,242
sdn 4d, 8P	4,170	3,403	425
C-60-2 Windsor Deluxe (wb 125.5)			
sdn 4d	3,775	2,691	45,385
Newport htp cpe	3,775	2,995	5,642
conv cpe	4,005	3,217	1,250
C-56-1 New Yorker (wb 125.5; 8P-139.5)			
sdn 4d	4,005	3,150	37,540
club cpe	3,925	3,121	7,749
Newport htp cpe	4,020	3,487	2,525
Town & Country wgn 4d	4,265	3,898	1,399
sdn 4d, 8P	4,510	4,334	100
C-56-2 New Yorker Deluxe (wb 125.5)			
sdn 4d	4,025	3,293	20,585
club cpe	3,925	3,264	1,934
Newport htp cpe	4,025	3,653	3,715
conv cpe	4,295	3,945	950
chassis	—	—	21
C-58 Custom Imperial (wb 133.5; htp cpe-131.5)			
sdn 4d	4,305	4,225	7,793
town limo 6P	4,525	4,762	243
Newport htp cpe	4,290	4,525	823
C-59 Crown Imperial (wb 145.5)			
sdn 4d, 8P	5,235	6,872	48
limo 8P	5,275	6,994	111
chassis	—	—	1

1953 Engines	bore×stroke	bhp	availability
L6, 264.5	3.44×4.75	119	S-Windsor
V8, 331.1	3.81×3.63	180	S-others

1954

C-62 Windsor Del (wb 125.5; 8P-139.5)	Wght	Price	Prod
sdn 4d	3,655	2,562	33,563
club cpe	3,565	2,541	5,659
Newport htp cpe	3,685	2,831	3,655
conv cpe	3,915	3,046	500
Town & Country wgn 4d	3,955	3,321	650
sdn 4d, 8P	4,185	3,492	500
C-63-1 New Yorker (wb 125.5; 8P-139.5)			
sdn 4d	3,970	3,229	15,788
club cpe	3,910	3,202	2,079
Newport htp cpe	4,005	3,503	1,312
Town & Country wgn 4d	4,245	4,024	1,100
sdn 4d, 8P	4,450	4,368	140
C-63-2 New Yorker Deluxe (wb 125.5)			
sdn 4d	4,065	3,433	26,907
club cpe	4,005	3,406	1,861
Newport htp cpe	4,095	3,707	4,814
conv cpe	4,265	3,938	724
chassis	—	—	17
C-64 Custom Imperial (wb 133.5)			
sdn 4d	4,355	4,260	4,324
town limo 6P	4,465	4,797	83
special town limo 6P	4,475	—	2
Newport htp cpe	4,345	4,560	1,249
conv cpe	—	proto	1
chassis	—	—	2
C-66 Crown Imperial (wb 145.5)			
sdn 4d, 8P	5,220	6,922	23
limo 8P	5,295	7,044	77

1954 Engines	bore×stroke	bhp	availability
L6, 264.5	3.44×4.75	119	S-Windsor Deluxe
V8, 331.1	3.81×3.63	195	S-NY
V8, 331.1	3.81×3.63	235	S-others

1955

C-67 Windsor Deluxe (wb 126.0)	Wght	Price	Prod
sdn 4d	3,925	2,660	63,896
Nassau htp cpe	3,930	2,703	18,474
Newport htp cpe	3,925	2,818	13,126
conv cpe	4,075	3,090	1,395
Town & Country wgn 4d	4,295	3,332	1,983
C-68 New Yorker Deluxe (wb 126.0)			
sdn 4d	4,160	3,494	33,342
Newport htp cpe	4,140	3,652	5,777
St. Regis htp cpe	4,125	3,690	11,076
conv cpe	4,285	3,924	946
Town & Country wgn 4d	4,430	4,209	1,036
chassis	—	—	1

C-68 300 (wb 126.0)		Wght	Price	Prod
	htp cpe	4,005	4,110	1,725

1955 Engines	bore×stroke	bhp	availability
V8, 301.0	3.63×3.63	188	S-Windsor Deluxe
V8, 331.1	3.81×3.63	250	S-NY Deluxe
V8, 331.1	3.81×3.63	300	S-300

1956

C-71 Windsor (wb 126.0)		Wght	Price	Prod
	sdn 4d	3,900	2,870	53,119
	Newport htp sdn	3,990	3,128	7,050
	Nassau htp cpe	3,910	2,905	11,400
	Newport htp cpe	3,920	3,041	10,800
	conv cpe	4,100	3,336	1,011
	Town & Country wgn 4d	4,290	3,598	2,700
C-72 New Yorker (wb 126.0)				
	sdn 4d	4,110	3,779	24,749
	Newport htp sdn	4,220	4,102	3,599
	Newport htp cpe	4,175	3,951	4,115
	St. Regis htp cpe	4,175	3,995	6,686
	conv cpe	4,360	4,243	921
	Town & Country wgn 4d	4,460	4,523	1,070
C-72 300B (wb 126.0)				
	htp cpe	4,145	4,419	1,102

1956 Engines	bore×stroke	bhp	availability
V8, 331.1	3.81×3.63	225	S-Windsor
V8, 331.1	3.81×3.63	250	O-Windsor
V8, 354.0	3.94×3.63	280	S-NY
V8, 354.0	3.94×3.63	340	S-300B
V8, 354.0	3.94×3.63	355	O-300B

1957

C-75-1 Windsor (wb 126.0)		Wght	Price	Prod
	sdn 4d	3,995	3,088	17,639
	htp sdn	4,030	3,217	14,354
	htp cpe	3,925	3,153	14,027
	Town & Country wgn 4d	4,210	3,575	2,035
C-75-2 Saratoga (wb 126.0)				
	sdn 4d	4,165	3,718	14,977
	htp sdn	4,195	3,832	11,586
	htp cpe	4,075	3,754	10,633
C-76 New Yorker (wb 126.0)				
	sdn 4d	4,315	4,173	12,369
	htp sdn	4,330	4,259	10,948
	htp cpe	4,220	4,202	8,863
	conv cpe	4,365	4,638	1,049
	Town & Country wgn 4d	4,490	4,746	1,391
C-76 300C (wb 126.0)				
	htp cpe	4,235	4,929	1,918
	conv cpe	4,390	5,359	484

1957 Engines	bore×stroke	bhp	availability
V8, 354.0	3.94×3.63	285	S-Windsor
V8, 354.0	3.94×3.63	295	S-Saratoga
V8, 392.0	4.00×3.90	325	S-NY
V8, 392.0	4.00×3.90	375	S-300C
V8, 392.0	4.00×3.90	390	O-300C

1958

LC-1-L Windsor (wb 122.0)		Wght	Price	Prod
	sdn 4d	3,895	3,129	12,861
	htp sdn	3,915	3,279	6,254
	htp cpe	3,860	3,214	6,205
	Town & Country wgn 4d, 9P	4,245	3,803	862
	Town & Country wgn 4d, 6P	4,155	3,616	791
	conv cpe	—	—	2
LC-2-M Saratoga (wb 126.0)				
	sdn 4d	4,120	3,818	8,698
	htp sdn	4,145	3,955	5,322
	htp cpe	4,045	3,878	4,466
LC-3-H New Yorker (wb 126.0)				
	sdn 4d	4,195	4,295	7,110
	htp sdn	4,240	4,404	5,227
	htp cpe	4,205	4,347	3,205
	conv cpe	4,350	4,761	666
	Town & Country wgn 4d, 9P	4,445	5,083	775
	Town & Country wgn 4d, 6P	4,435	4,868	428
LC-3-S 300D (wb 126.0)				
	htp cpe	4,305	5,173	618
	conv cpe	4,475	5,603	191

1958 Engines	bore×stroke	bhp	availability
V8, 354.0	3.94×3.63	290	S-Windsor
V8, 354.0	3.94×3.63	310	S-Saratoga
V8, 392.0	4.00×3.90	345	S-NY
V8, 392.0	4.00×3.90	380	S-300D
V8, 392.0	4.00×3.90	390	O-300D

1959

MC-1-L Windsor (wb 122.0)		Wght	Price	Prod
512	htp cpe	3,830	3,289	6,775
513	sdn 4d	3,800	3,204	19,910
514	htp sdn	3,735	3,353	6,084
515	conv cpe	3,950	3,620	961
576	Town & Country wgn 4d, 6P	4,045	3,691	751
577	Town & Country wgn 4d, 9P	4,070	3,878	992
MC-2-M Saratoga (wb 126.0)				
532	htp cpe	3,970	4,026	3,753
533	sdn 4d	4,010	3,966	8,783
534	htp sdn	4,035	4,104	4,943
MC-3-H New Yorker (wb 126.0)				
552	htp cpe	4,080	4,476	2,435
553	sdn 4d	4,120	4,424	7,792
554	htp sdn	4,165	4,533	4,805
555	conv cpe	4,270	4,890	286
578	Town & Country wgn 6P	4,295	4,997	444
579	Town & Country wgn 9P	4,360	5,212	564
—	chassis	—	—	3
MC-3-H 300E (wb 126.0)				
592	htp cpe	4,290	5,319	550
595	conv cpe	4,350	5,749	140

1959 Engines	bore×stroke	bhp	availability
V8, 383.0	4.03×3.75	305	S-Windsor
V8, 383.0	4.03×3.75	325	S-Saratoga
V8, 413.0	4.18×3.75	350	S-NY
V8, 413.0	4.18×3.75	380	S-300E

1960

PC-1-L Windsor (wb 122.0)		Wght	Price	Prod
23	htp cpe	3,855	3,279	6,496
27	conv cpe	3,855	3,623	1,467

		Wght	Price	Prod
41	sdn 4d	3,815	3,194	25,152
43	htp sdn	3,850	3,343	5,897
46	Town & Country wgn 4d, 6P	4,235	3,733	1,120
46	Town & Country wgn 4d, 9P	4,390	3,814	1,026
PC-2-M Saratoga (wb 126.0)				
23	htp cpe	4,030	3,989	2,963
41	sdn 4d	4,010	3,929	8,463
43	htp sdn	4,035	4,067	4,099
PC-3-H New Yorker (wb 126.0)				
23	htp cpe	4,175	4,461	2,835
27	conv cpe	4,185	4,875	556
41	sdn 4d	4,145	4,409	9,079
43	htp sdn	4,175	4,518	5,625
46	Town & Country wgn 6P	4,515	5,022	624
46	Town & Country wgn 9P	4,535	5,131	671
PC-3-H 300F (wb 126.0)				
23	htp cpe	4,270	5,411	964
27	conv cpe	4,310	5,841	248

1960 Engines	bore×stroke	bhp	availability
V8, 383.0	4.03×3.75	305	S-Windsor
V8, 383.0	4.03×3.75	325	S-Saratoga
V8, 413.0	4.18×3.75	350	S-NY
V8, 413.0	4.18×3.75	375	S-300F
V8, 413.0	4.18×3.75	400	O-300F

1961

RC-1-L Newport (wb 122.0)		Wght	Price	Prod
812	htp cpe	3,690	3,025	9,405
813	sdn 4d	3,710	2,964	34,370
814	htp sdn	3,730	3,104	7,789
815	conv cpe	3,760	3,442	2,135
858	Town & Country wgn 4d, 6P	4,070	3,541	1,832
859	Town & Country wgn 4d, 9P	4,155	3,622	1,571
RC-2-M Windsor (wb 122.0)				
822	htp cpe	3,710	3,303	2,941
823	sdn 4d	3,730	3,218	10,239
824	htp sdn	3,765	3,367	4,156
RC-3-H New Yorker (wb 126.0)				
832	htp cpe	4,065	4,175	2,541
833	sdn 4d	4,055	4,123	9,984
834	htp sdn	4,100	4,261	5,862
835	conv cpe	4,070	4,592	576
878	Town & Country wgn 4d, 6P	4,425	4,764	676
879	Town & Country wgn 4d, 9P	4,455	4,871	760
RC-4-P 300G (wb 126.0)				
842	htp cpe	4,260	5,411	1,280
845	conv cpe	4,315	5,841	337

1961 Engines	bore×stroke	bhp	availability
V8, 361.0	4.12×3.38	265	S-Newport
V8, 383.0	4.25×3.38	305	S-Windsor
V8, 413.0	4.18×3.75	350	S-NY
V8, 413.0	4.18×3.75	375	S-300G
V8, 413.0	4.18×3.75	400	O-300G

1962

SC1-L Newport (wb 122.0)		Wght	Price	Prod
812	htp cpe	3,650	3,027	11,910
813	sdn 4d	3,690	2,964	54,813
814	htp sdn	3,715	3,106	8,712

		Wght	Price	Prod
815	conv cpe	3,740	3,399	2,051
858	Town & Country wgn 4d, 6P	4,060	3,478	3,271
859	Town & Country wgn 4d, 9P	4,090	3,586	2,363
SC2-M 300 (wb 122.0)				
822	htp cpe	3,750	3,323	11,341
823	sdn 4d	—	—	1,801
824	htp sdn	3,760	3,400	10,030
825	conv cpe	3,815	3,883	1,848
SC3-H New Yorker (wb 126.0)				
833	sdn 4d	3,925	4,125	12,056
834	htp sdn	4,005	4,263	6,646
878	Town & Country wgn 4d, 6P	4,225	4,766	728
879	Town & Country wgn 4d, 9P	4,455	4,873	793
SC2-M 300H (wb 122.0)				
842	htp cpe	4,010	5,090	435
845	conv cpe	4,080	5,461	123

1962 Engines	bore×stroke	bhp	availability
V8, 361.0	4.12×3.38	265	S-Newport
V8, 383.0	4.25×3.38	305	S-300
V8, 413.0	4.18×3.75	340	S-NY
V8, 413.0	4.18×3.75	380	S-300H
V8, 413.0	4.18×3.75	405	O-300H

1963

TC1-L Newport (wb 122.0)		Wght	Price	Prod
812	htp cpe	3,760	3,027	9,809
813	sdn 4d	3,770	2,964	49,067
814	htp sdn	3,800	3,106	8,437
815	conv cpe	3,825	3,399	2,093
858	Town & Country wgn 4d, 6P	4,200	3,478	3,618
859	Town & Country wgn 4d, 9P	4,215	3,586	2,948
TC2-M 300 (wb 122.0)				
802	Pace Setter htp cpe	3,790	3,769	306
822	htp cpe	3,790	3,430	9,423
805	Pace Setter conv cpe	3,840	4,129	1,861
825	conv cpe	3,845	3,790	1,535
823	sdn 4d	3,790	—	1,625
824	htp sdn	3,815	3,400	9,915
TC3-H New Yorker (wb 122.0)				
833	sdn 4d	3,910	4,981	14,884
834	htp sdn	3,950	4,118	10,289
884	Salon htp sdn	4,290	5,860	593
878	Town & Country wgn 4d, 6P	4,350	4,708	950
879	Town & Country wgn 4d, 9P	4,370	4,815	1,244
TC2-M 300J (wb 122.0)				
842	htp cpe	4,000	5,184	400

1963 Engines	bore×stroke	bhp	availability
V8, 361.0	4.12×3.38	265	S-Newport
V8, 383.0	4.25×3.38	305	S-300
V8, 413.0	4.19×3.75	340	S-NY
V8, 413.0	4.19×3.75	360	O-300
V8, 413.0	4.19×3.75	390	S-300J

1964

VC1-L Newport (wb 122.0)		Wght	Price	Prod
812	htp cpe	3,760	2,962	10,579
813	sdn 4d	3,805	2,901	55,957
814	htp sdn	3,795	3,042	9,710

		Wght	Price	Prod
815	conv cpe	3,810	3,334	2,176
858	Town & Country wgn 4d, 6P	4,175	3,414	3,720
859	Town & Country wgn 4d, 9P	4,200	3,521	3,041
VC2-M 300 (wb 122.0)*				
822	htp cpe	3,850	3,443	18,379
824	htp sdn	3,865	3,521	11,460
823	sdn 4d	—	—	2,078
825	conv cpe	4,120	3,803	1,401
VC3-H New Yorker (wb 122.0)				
832	htp cpe	—	—	300
833	sdn 4d	4,015	3,994	15,443
834	htp sdn	4,035	4,131	10,887
878	Town & Country wgn 4d, 6P	4,385	4,721	1,190
879	Town & Country wgn 4d, 9P	4,395	4,828	1,603
884	Salon htp sdn	4,280	5,860	1,621
VC2-M 300K (wb 122.0)*				
842	htp cpe	3,965	4,056	3,022
845	conv cpe	3,995	4,522	625

*Silver 300 models: 300—2,152; 300K series—255.

1964 Engines	bore×stroke	bhp	availability
V8, 361.0	4.12×3.38	265	S-Newport
V8, 383.0	4.25×3.38	305	S-300
V8, 413.0	4.19×3.75	340	S-NY; O-300
V8, 413.0	4.19×3.75	360	S-300K; O-300
V8, 413.0	4.19×3.75	390	O-300K

1965

AC1-L Newport (wb 124.0; wgns-121.0)		Wght	Price	Prod
C12	htp cpe	4,035	3,070	23,655
C13	sdn 4d, 4W	4,045	3,009	61,054
C14	htp sdn	4,050	3,149	17,062
C15	conv cpe	4,025	3,442	3,192
C18	town sdn 4d, 6W	4,000	3,146	12,411
C56	Town & Country wgn 4d, 6P	4,360	3,521	4,683
C57	Town & Country wgn 4d, 9P	4,455	3,629	3,738
AC2-M 300 (wb 124.0)				
C22	htp cpe	4,085	3,551	11,621
C24	htp sdn 4W	4,150	3,628	12,452
C25	conv cpe	4,140	3,911	1,418
C28	htp town sdn 6W	—	—	2,187
AC3-H New Yorker (wb 124.0; wgns-121.0)				
C32	htp cpe	4,270	4,161	9,357
C34	htp sdn	4,295	4,238	21,110
C38	town sdn 4d, 6W	4,265	4,104	16,339
C76	Town & Country wgn 4d, 6P	4,650	4,827	1,368
C77	Town & Country wgn 4d, 9P	4,745	4,935	1,697
AC2-P 300L (wb 124.0)				
C42	htp cpe	4,245	4,153	2,405
C45	conv cpe	4,170	4,618	440

1965 Engines	bore×stroke	bhp	availability
V8, 383.0	4.25×3.38	270	S-Newport; O-300
V8, 383.0	4.25×3.38	315	S-300; O-Newport
V8, 413.0	4.19×3.75	340	S-NY
V8, 413.0	4.19×3.75	360	S-300L; O-300, NY

1966

BC1-L Newport (wb 124.0; wgns-121.0)		Wght	Price	Prod
23	htp cpe	3,920	3,112	37,622
27	conv cpe	4,020	3,476	3,085
41	sdn 4d, 4W	3,875	3,052	74,964
42	sdn 4d, 6W	3,910	3,183	9,432
43	htp sdn	4,010	3,190	24,966
45	wgn 4d, 6P	4,370	4,086	9,035
46	wgn 4d, 9P	4,550	4,192	8,567
BC2-M 300 (wb 124.0)				
23	htp cpe	3,940	3,583	24,103
27	conv cpe	4,015	3,936	2,500
41	sdn 4d	3,895	3,523	2,353
43	htp sdn	4,000	3,659	20,642
BC3-H New Yorker (wb 124.0)				
23	htp cpe	4,095	4,157	7,955
42	sdn 4d	4,100	4,101	13,025
43	htp sdn	4,140	4,233	26,599

1966 Engines	bore×stroke	bhp	availability
V8, 383.0	4.25×3.38	270	S-Newport
V8, 383.0	4.25×3.38	325	S-300; O-Newport
V8, 440.0	4.32×3.75	350	S-NY

1967

CC1-E Newport (wb 124.0; wgns-122.0)		Wght	Price	Prod
23	htp cpe	3,920	3,219	26,583
27	conv cpe	3,970	3,583	2,891
41	sdn 4d	3,955	3,159	48,945
43	htp sdn	3,980	3,296	14,247
45	wgn 4d, 6P	4,495	4,264	7,183
46	wgn 4d, 9P	4,550	4,369	7,520
CC1-L Newport Custom (wb 124.0)				
23	htp cpe	3,935	3,407	14,193
41	sdn 4d	3,975	3,347	23,101
43	htp sdn	3,995	3,485	12,728
CC2-M 300 (wb 124.0)				
23	htp cpe	4,070	3,936	11,556
27	conv cpe	4,105	4,289	1,594
43	htp sdn	4,135	4,012	8,744
CC3-H New Yorker (wb 124.0)				
23	htp cpe	4,170	4,264	6,885
41	sdn 4d	4,185	4,208	10,907
43	htp sdn	4,240	4,339	21,665

1967 Engines	bore×stroke	bhp	availability
V8, 383.0	4.25×3.38	270	S-Newport
V8, 383.0	4.25×3.38	325	O-Newport
V8, 440.0	4.32×3.75	350	S-300, NY; O-wgns
V8, 440.0	4.32×3.75	375	O-all exc wgns

1968

DC1-E Newport (wb 124.0; wgns-122.0)		Wght	Price	Prod
CE23	htp cpe*	3,840	3,366	36,768
CE27	conv cpe*	3,910	3,704	2,847
CE41	sdn 4d	3,850	3,306	61,436
CE43	htp sdn	3,865	3,444	20,191
CE45	Town & Country wgn 4d, 6P	4,340	4,418	9,908
CE46	Town & Country wgn 4d, 9P	4,410	4,523	12,233
DC1-L Newport Custom (wb 124.0)				
CL23	htp cpe	3,890	3,552	10,341
CL41	sdn 4d	3,855	3,493	16,915
CL43	htp sdn	3,860	3,631	11,460
DC2-M 300 (wb 124.0)				
CM23	htp cpe	3,985	4,010	16,953

1967 New Yorker hardtop coupe

1970 300 Hurst hardtop coupe

		Wght	Price	Prod
CM27	conv cpe	4,050	4,337	2,161
CM43	htp sdn	4,015	4,086	15,507
DC3-H New Yorker (wb 124.0)				
CH23	htp cpe	4,060	4,424	8,060
CH41	sdn 4d	4,055	4,367	13,092
CH43	htp sdn	4,090	4,500	26,991

*Sportsgrain models: htp cpe 965; conv cpe 175.

1968 Engines	bore×stroke	bhp	availability
V8, 383.0	4.25×3.38	290	S-Newport, T&C
V8, 383.0	4.25×3.38	330	O-Newport, T&C
V8, 440.0	4.32×3.75	350	S-300, NY; O-T&C
V8, 440.0	4.32×3.75	375	O-all exc T&C

1969

EC-E Newport (wb 124.0)*		Wght	Price	Prod
CE23	htp cpe	3,891	3,485	33,639
CE27	conv cpe	4,026	3,823	2,169
CE41	sdn 4d	3,941	3,414	55,083
CE43	htp sdn	4,156	3,549	20,608
EC-L Newport Custom (wb 124.0)				
CL23	htp cpe	3,891	3,652	10,955
CL41	sdn 4d	3,951	3,580	18,401
CL43	htp sdn	3,971	3,730	15,981
EC-P Town & Country (wb 122.0)				
CP45	wgn 4d, 6P	4,435	4,583	10,108
CP46	wgn 4d, 9P	4,485	4,669	14,408
EC-M 300 (wb 124.0)				
CM23	htp cpe	3,965	4,104	16,075
CM27	conv cpe	4,095	4,450	1,933
CM43	htp sdn	4,045	4,183	14,464
EC-H New Yorker (wb 124.0)				
CH23	htp cpe	4,070	4,539	7,537
CH41	sdn 4d	4,135	4,487	12,253
CH43	htp sdn	4,165	4,615	27,157

*Sportsgrain models 195.

1969 Engines	bore×stroke	bhp	availability
V8, 383.0	4.25×3.38	290	S-Newport, T&C
V8, 383.0	4.25×3.38	330	O-Newport, T&C
V8, 440.0	4.32×3.75	350	S-300, NY; O-T&C
V8, 440.0	4.32×3.75	375	O-all exc T&C

1970

FC-E Newport (wb 124.0)		Wght	Price	Prod
CE23	htp cpe*	4,030	3,589	21,664
CE27	conv cpe	4,085	3,925	1,124
CE41	sdn 4d	4,080	3,514	39,285
CE43	htp sdn*	4,110	3,652	16,940
FC-L Newport Custom (wb 124.0)				
CL23	htp cpe	4,035	3,781	6,639
CL41	sdn 4d	4,091	3,710	13,767
CL43	htp sdn	4,125	3,861	10,873
FC-P Town & Country (wb 122.0)				
CP45	wgn 4d, 6P	4,490	4,738	5,686
CP46	wgn 4d, 9P	4,555	4,824	9,583
FC-M 300 (wb 124.0)				
CM23	htp cpe*	4,135	4,234	10,084
CM27	conv cpe	4,175	4,580	1,077
CM43	htp sdn	4,220	4,313	9,846
FC-H New Yorker (wb 124.0)				
CH23	htp cpe	4,235	4,681	4,917
CH41	sdn 4d	4,310	4,630	9,389
CH43	htp sdn	4,335	4,761	19,903

*CE23 includes 1,868 Cordoba htp cpes; CE43 includes 1,873 Cordoba htp sdns; CM23 includes 501 300-H "Hurst" htp cpes.

1970 Engines	bore×stroke	bhp	availability
V8, 383.0	4.25×3.38	290	S-Newport, T&C
V8, 383.0	4.25×3.38	330	O-Newport auto, T&C
V8, 440.0	4.32×3.75	350	S-NY, 300; O-T&C
V8, 440.0	4.32×3.75	375	O-all exc T&C

1971

CE Newport (wb 124.0)		Wght	Price	Prod
23	Royal htp cpe	4,121	4,153	8,500
23	htp cpe	4,121	4,265	13,549
41	Royal sdn 4d	4,171	4,078	19,662
41	sdn 4d	4,171	4,190	24,834
43	Royal htp sdn	4,191	4,216	5,188
43	htp sdn	4,191	4,265	10,800
CP Town & Country (wb 122.0)				
45	wgn 4d 2S	4,525	4,951	5,697
46	wgn 4d 3S	4,580	5,037	10,993
CL Newport Custom (wb 124.0)				
23	htp cpe	4,126	4,391	5,527

		Wght	Price	Prod
41	sdn 4d	4,181	4,319	11,254
43	htp sdn	4,211	4,471	10,207
CS 300 (wb 124.0)				
23	htp cpe	4,246	4,608	7,256
43	htp sdn	4,321	4,687	6,683
CH New Yorker (wb 124.0)				
23	htp cpe	4,250	4,961	4,485
41	sdn 4d	4,335	4,910	9,850
43	htp sdn	4,355	5,041	20,633

1971 Engines	bore×stroke	bhp	availability
V8, 360.0	4.00×3.58	255	S-CE, Royal
V8, 383.0	4.25×3.38	275	S-CL,CP; O-CE Royal
V8, 383.0	4.25×3.38	300	O-CL,CP,CE Royal
V8, 440.0	4.32×3.75	335	O-CE,CL,CP;S-CS,CH
V8, 440.0	4.32×3.75	370	O-CE,CL,CP,CS,CH

1972

CL Newport Royal (wb 124.0)		Wght	Price	Prod
23	htp cpe	4,035	4,124	22,622
41	sdn 4d	4,095	4,051	47,437
43	htp sdn	4,100	4,186	15,185
CM Newport Custom (wb 124.0)				
23	htp cpe	4,130	4,357	10,326
41	sdn 4d	4,185	4,435	19,278
43	htp sdn	4,195	4,435	15,457
CP Town & Country (wb 122.0)				
45	wgn 4d 2S	4,610	5,055	6,473
46	wgn 4d 3S	4,665	5,139	14,116
CH New Yorker (wb 124.0)				
23	htp cpe	4,270	4,915	5,567
41	sdn 4d	4,335	4,865	7,296
43	htp sdn	4,365	4,993	10,013
CS New Yorker Brougham (wb 124.0)				
23	htp cpe	4,270	5,271	4,635
41	sdn 4d	4,335	5,222	5,971
43	htp sdn	4,365	5,350	20,328

1972 Engines	bore×stroke	bhp	availability
V8, 360.0	4.00×3.58	175	S-CL
V8, 400.0	4.34×3.38	190	S-CM,CP; O-CL
V8, 440.0	4.32×3.75	225	S-CH,CS;O-CL,CM,CP

1973

CL Newport (wb 124.0)		Wght	Price	Prod
23	htp cpe	4,160	4,254	27,456
41	sdn 4d	4,200	4,181	54,147
43	htp sdn	4,210	4,316	20,175
CM Newport Custom (wb 124.0)				
23	htp cpe	4,145	4,484	12,293
41	sdn 4d	4,200	4,419	20,092
43	htp sdn	4,225	4,567	20,050
CP Town & Country (wb 122.0)				
45	wgn 4d 2S	4,670	5,241	5,353
46	wgn 4d 3S	4,725	5,266	14,687
CH New Yorker (wb 124.0)				
41	sdn 4d	4,355	4,997	7,991
43	htp sdn	4,375	5,125	7,619
CS New Yorker Brougham (wb 124.0)				
23	htp cpe	4,335	5,413	9,190
41	sdn 4d	4,425	5,364	8,541
43	htp sdn	4,440	5,492	26,635

1973 Engines	bore×stroke	bhp	availability
V8, 400.0	4.34×3.38	185	S-CL,CM
V8, 440.0	4.32×3.75	215	S-CP,CH,CS; O-CL,CM

1974

CL Newport (wb 124.0)		Wght	Price	Prod
23	htp cpe	4,380	4,752	13,784
41	sdn 4d	4,430	4,677	26,944
43	htp sdn	4,440	4,816	8,968
CM Newport Custom (wb 124.0)				
23	htp cpe	4,430	5,105	7,206
41	sdn 4d	4,480	5,038	10,569
43	htp sdn	4,500	5,190	9,892
CP Town & Country (wb 124.0)				
45	wgn 4d 2S	4,915	5,767	2,236
46	wgn 4d 3S	4,970	5,896	5,958
CH New Yorker (wb 124.0)				
41	sdn 4d	4,560	5,554	3,072
43	htp sdn	4,595	5,686	3,066
CS New Yorker Brougham (wb 124.0)				
23	htp cpe	4,540	5,982	7,980
41	sdn 4d	4,640	5,931	4,533
43	htp sdn	4,655	6,063	13,165

1974 Engines	bore×stroke	bhp	availability
V8, 400.0	4.34×3.38	185	S-CL,CM
V8, 400.0	4.34×3.38	205	O-CL,CM
V8, 440.0	4.32×3.75	230	S-CP,CH,CS; O-CL,CM
V8, 440.0	4.32×3.75	275	O-CH,CS

1975

SS Cordoba (wb 115.0)		Wght	Price	Prod
22	cpe	3,975	5,072	150,105
CL Newport (wb 124.0)				
23	htp cpe	4,395	4,937	10,485
41	sdn 4d	4,440	4,854	24,339
43	htp sdn	4,475	5,008	6,846
CM Newport Custom (wb 124.0)				
23	htp cpe	4,450	5,329	5,831
41	sdn 4d	4,500	5,254	9,623
43	htp sdn	4,520	5,423	11,626
CP Town & Country (wb 124.0)				
45	wgn 4d 2S	5,015	6,099	1,891
46	wgn 4d 3S	5,050	6,244	4,764
CS New Yorker Brougham (wb 124.0)				
23	htp cpe	4,650	6,334	7,567
		Wght	Price	Prod
41	sdn 4d	4,630	6,277	5,698
43	htp sdn	4,690	6,424	12,774

1975 Engines	bore×stroke	bhp	availability
V8, 318.0	3.91×3.31	150	O-SS
V8, 360.0	4.00×3.58	180	S-SS; O-CL,CM
V8, 360.0	4.00×3.58	190	O-CL,CM
V8, 400.0	4.34×3.38	165	O-SS
V8, 400.0	4.34×3.38	175	S-CL,CM; O-CS
V8, 400.0	4.34×3.38	190	O-SS
V8, 400.0	4.34×3.38	195	O-CL,CM,CS

1976 Cordoba coupe

			Wght	Price	Prod
V8, 400.0	4.34×3.38	235	O-SS		
V8, 440.0	4.32×3.75	215	S-CP,CS; O-others		
V8, 440.0	4.32×3.75	260	O-CP		

1976

SS Cordoba (wb 115.0)		Wght	Price	Prod
22	cpe	4,130	5,392	120,462
CL Newport (wb 124.0)				
23	htp cpe	4,455	5,076	6,109
41	sdn 4d	4,490	4,993	16,370
43	htp sdn	4,525	5,147	5,908
CM Newport Custom (wb 124.0)				
23	htp cpe	4,530	5,479	6,448
41	sdn 4d	4,565	5,407	11,587
43	htp sdn	4,585	5,576	9,893
CP Town & Country (wb 124.0)				
45	wgn 5d 2S	5,045	6,084	1,770
46	wgn 5d 3S	5,075	6,244	3,769
CS New Yorker Brougham (wb 124.0)				
23	htp cpe	4,865	6,641	11,510
43	htp sdn	4,950	6,737	28,327

1976 Engines	bore×stroke	bhp	availability
V8, 318.0	3.91×3.31	150	O-SS
V8, 360.0	4.00×3.58	170/175	O-SS,CL,CM
V8, 400.0	4.34×3.38	175	S-SS,CL,CM; O-CS
V8, 400.0	4.34×3.38	210	O-all
V8, 400.0	4.34×3.38	240	O-SS
V8, 440.0	4.32×3.75	205	S-CP,CS; O-CL,CM

1977

FH LeBaron (wb 112.7)—54,851 built (incl. FP)		Wght	Price	Prod
22	cpe	3,510	5,066	—
41	sdn 4d	3,560	5,224	—
FP LeBaron Medallion (wb 112.7)		**Wght**	**Price**	**Prod**
22	cpe	3,615	5,436	—
41	sdn 4d	3,675	5,594	—
Cordoba (wb 115.0)				
SP22	cpe	NA	5,368	183,146 (SP22 + SS22)
SS22	cpe	4,045	5,418	
CL Newport (wb 124.0)				
23	htp cpe	4,400	5,374	16,227
41	sdn 4d	4,455	5,280	39,424
43	htp sdn	4,485	5,433	20,738
CP Town & Country (wb 124.0)				
45	wgn 5d 2S	5,025	6,461	2,488
46	wgn 5d 3S	5,060	6,647	6,081
CS New Yorker Brougham (wb 124.0)				
23	htp cpe	4,685	7,090	19,732
43	htp sdn	4,770	7,215	56,610

1977 Engines	bore×stroke	bhp	availability
V8, 318.0	3.91×3.31	135	O-Cordoba
V8, 318.0	3.91×3.31	145	S-LeB; O-Crdba
V8, 360.0	4.00×3.58	155	O-Crdba,Nwpt
V8, 360.0	4.00×3.58	170	O-Crdba
V8, 400.0	4.34×3.38	190	S-Crdba,Nwpt; O-T&C,NY
V8, 440.0	4.32×3.75	195	S-T&C,NY; O-Nwpt

1978

LeBaron (wb 112.7)		Wght	Price	Prod
FM22	"S" cpe L6	3,335	4,894	NA
FM22	"S" cpe V8	3,415	5,080	NA
FM41	"S" sdn 4d L6	3,400	5,060	NA
FM41	"S" sdn 4d V8	3,485	5,246	NA
FH22	cpe L6	3,420	5,144	16,273 (FH22 L6 + V8)
FH22	cpe V8	3,505	5,330	
FH41	sdn 4d L6	3,465	5,310	22,732 (FH41 L6 + V8)
FH41	sdn 4d V8	3,550	5,496	
FP22	Medallion cpe L6	3,495	5,526	37,138 (FP22 L6 + V8)
FP22	Medallion cpe V8	3,580	5,712	

		Wght	Price	Prod
FP41	Medallion sdn 4d L6	3,550	5,692	44,291
FP41	Medallion sdn 4d V8	3,635	5,878	
FH45	Town & Country wgn 5d 2S L6	3,600	5,724	25,256
FH45	Town & Country wgn 5d 2S V8	3,685	5,910	
Cordoba (wb 114.9)				
SS22	cpe	4,020	5,811	124,825
SS22	S cpe	NA	5,611	
Newport (wb 123.9)				
CL23	htp cpe	4,395	5,804	8,877
CL43	htp sdn	4,460	5,888	30,078
New Yorker Brougham (wb 123.9)				
CS23	htp cpe	4,620	7,702	11,469
CS43	htp sdn	4,670	7,831	33,090

1978 Engines	bore×stroke	bhp	availability
L6, 225.0	3.40×4.12	90	O-LeBaron
L6, 225.0	3.40×4.12	110	S-LeBaron
V8, 318.0	3.91×3.31	140	S-LeB; O-Crdba
V8, 318.0	3.91×3.31	155	O-LeB; Crdba
V8, 360.0	4.00×3.58	155	S-Crdba S; O-others
V8, 360.0	4.00×3.58	170	O-all
V8, 400.0	4.34×3.38	190	S-Crdba,Nwpt,NY; O-Crdba S
V8, 440.0	4.32×3.75	185/195	O-Nwpt,NY

1979

LeBaron (wb 112.7)		Wght	Price	Prod
FM22	cpe L6	3,270	5,381	10,987
FM22	cpe V8	3,365	5,692	
FM41	sdn 4d L6	3,330	5,479	14,297
FM41	sdn 4d V8	3,425	5,790	
FH22	Salon cpe L6	3,285	5,623	17,637
FH22	Salon cpe V8	3,385	5,934	
FH41	Salon sdn 4d L6	3,350	5,851	18,843
FH41	Salon sdn 4d V8	3,450	6,162	
FP22	Medallion cpe L6	3,345	6,017	21,762
FP22	Medallion cpe V8	3,440	6,328	
FP41	Medallion sdn 4d L6	3,425	6,425	25,041
FP41	Medallion sdn 4d V8	3,520	6,556	
FH45	Town & Country wgn 4d 2S L6	3,585	6,331	19,932
FH45	Town & Country wgn 4d 2S V8	3,675	6,642	
Cordoba (wb 114.9)				
SS22	cpe	3,680	6,337	88,015
SP22	"300" cpe	3,880	8,034	
Newport (wb 118.5)				
TH42	sdn 4d L6	3,530	6,405	78,296
TH42	sdn 4d V8	3,605	6,720	
New Yorker (wb 118.5)				
TP42	sdn 4d	3,800	10,026	54,640

1979 Engines	bore×stroke	bhp	availability
L6, 225.0	3.40×4.12	100	S-LeBaron
L6, 225.0	3.40×4.12	110	S-Nwpt; O-LeB
V8, 318.0	3.91×3.31	135	S-LeB,Crdba,Nwpt; O-NY
V8, 360.0	4.00×3.58	150	S-NY; O-others
V8, 360.0	4.00×3.58	195	S-"300"; O-others

1980

LeBaron (wb 112.7; cpe 108.7)		Wght	Price	Prod
FL41	Special sdn 4d L6	3,260	5,995	—
FM22	cpe L6	3,220	6,362	8,181
FM22	cpe V8	3,300	6,457	
FM41	sdn 4d L6	3,300	6,518	8,470
FM41	sdn 4d V8	3,385	6,613	
FM45	wgn 4d 2S L6	3,455	6,723	1,887
FM45	wgn 4d 2S V8	3,535	6,818	
FH22	Salon cpe L6	3,230	6,643	18,538
FH22	Salon cpe V8	3,310	6,738	
FH41	Salon sdn 4d L6	3,325	6,764	10,762
FH41	Salon sdn 4d V8	3,405	6,859	
FP22	Medallion cpe L6	3,285	7,185	10,448
FP22	Medallion cpe V8	3,360	7,280	
FP41	Medallion sdn 4d L6	3,400	7,329	13,079
FP41	Medallion sdn 4d V8	3,485	7,424	
FH45	Town & Country wgn 5d 2S L6	3,525	7,324	11,100
FH45	Town & Country wgn 5d 2S V8	3,610	7,419	
Cordoba (wb 112.7)				
SH22	cpe L6	3,270	6,978	31,238
SH22	cpe V8	3,355	7,073	
SP22	Crown cpe L6	3,320	7,428	22,233
SP22	Crown cpe V8	3,400	7,523	
SS22	LS cpe L6	3,270	6,745	
SP22	LS cpe V8	3,365	6,840	
SP22	"300" cpe V8	NA	NA	
Newport (wb 118.5)				
TH42	sdn 4d L6	3,545	7,247	15,061
TH42	sdn 4d V8	3,630	7,343	
New Yorker (wb 118.5)				
TP42	sdn 4d	3,810	10,872	13,513

1979 Cordoba coupe

1981 Cordoba coupe

1980 Engines	bore×stroke	bhp	availability
L6, 225.0	3.40×4.12	90	S-all sixes
V8, 318.0	3.91×3.31	120	S-all V8s exc "300"
V8, 360.0	4.00×3.58	130	O-Nwpt,NY
V8, 360.0	4.00×3.58	185	S-Crdba "300"

Note: Chrysler production through 1980 includes export models, which makes figures in this book somewhat higher than those quoted elsewhere.

1981

LeBaron (wb 112.7; cpe-108.7)		Wght	Price	Prod
FL45	Special cpe L6	—	6,672	11,890
FL45	Special cpe V8	—	6,734	
FL41	Special sdn 4d L6	3,275	6,495	
FL41	Special sdn 4d V8	—	6,557	
FM45	sdn 4d L6	3,470	7,346	2,136
FH22	Salon cpe L6	3,200	7,263	17,485
FH22	Salon cpe V8	3,325	7,325	
FH41	Salon sdn 4d L6	3,305	7,413	
FH41	Salon sdn 4d V8	3,430	7,475	
FP22	Medallion cpe L6	3,255	7,768	7,635
FP22	Medallion cpe V8	3,380	7,830	
FP41	Medallion sdn L6	3,365	7,917	
FP41	Medallion sdn V8	3,490	7,979	
FH45	Town & Country wgn 5d 2S L6	3,545	8,008	3,987
FH45	Town & Country wgn 5d 2S V8	3,665	8,070	
Cordoba (wb 112.7)				
SP22	cpe L6	3,355	7,969	12,978
SP22	cpe V8	3,495	8,033	
SS22	LS cpe L6	3,300	7,199	7,315
SS22	LS cpe V8	3,420	7,263	
Newport (wb 118.5)				
TH42	sdn 4d L6	3,515	7,805	3,622
TH42	sdn 4d V8	3,635	7,869	
New Yorker (wb 118.5)				
TP42	sdn 4d V8	3,805	10,463	6,548

1981 Engines	bore×stroke	bhp	availability
L6, 225.0	3.40×4.12	85	S-all sixes
V8, 318.0	3.91×3.31	130	S-all V8s
V8, 318.0	3.91×3.31	165	O-Nwpt, NY

1982

LeBaron (wb 99.9)		Wght	Price	Prod
CH22	cpe	2,470	8,143	14,295
CH41	sdn 4d	2,455	8,237	19,619
CH27	conv cpe	2,485	11,698	3,045
CP22	Medallion cpe	2,475	8,408	12,856
CP41	Medallion sdn	2,465	8,502	22,915
CP27	Medallion conv cpe	2,660	13,998	9,780
CP45	Town & Country wgn 5d 2S	2,660	9,425	7,809
Cordoba (wb 112.7)				
SP22	cpe L6	3,370	9,197	11,762
SP22	cpe V8	3,520	9,267	
SS22	LS cpe L6	3,315	8,258	3,136
SS22	LS cpe V8	3,465	8,328	
New Yorker (wb 112.7)				
FS41	sdn 4d L6	3,510	10,781	50,509
FS41	sdn 4d V8	3,655	10,851	

1982 Engines	bore×stroke	bhp	availability
L4, 135.0	3.44×3.62	84	S-LeBaron
L4, 156.0	3.59×3.86	92	S-LeB T&C; O-LeBaron
L6, 225.0	3.40×4.12	90	S-Cordoba, NY six
V8, 318.0	3.91×3.31	130	S-Cordoba, NY V8s
V8, 318.0	3.91×3.31	165	S-Calif. Cordoba, NY V8

1983

LeBaron (wb 100.3)		Wght	Price	Prod
CP22	cpe	2,464	8,514	18,331
CP41	sdn 4d	2,531	8,790	30,869
CP27	conv cpe	2,532	12,800	9,891
CP27	Mark Cross conv cpe	—	14,595	
CP27	Mark Cross T&C conv cpe	—	15,595	
CP45	Town & Country wgn 5d 2S	2,656	9,731	10,994
E Class (wb 103.3)				
TH41	sdn 4d	2,583	9,341	39,258
New Yorker (wb 103.3)				
TP41	sdn 4d	2,580	10,950	33,832
Cordoba (wb 112.7)				
SP22	cpe L6	3,467	9,580	13,471
SP22	cpe V8	3,605	9,805	
New Yorker Fifth Avenue (wb 112.7)				
FS41	sdn 4d L6	3,631	12,487	83,501
FS41	sdn 4d V8	3,781	12,712	
Executive (wb 124.0; limo 131.0)				
CP48	sdn 4d	—	18,900	—
CP49	limo 4d	—	21,900	—

1983 Engines	bore×stroke	bhp	availability
L4, 135.0	3.44×3.62	94	S-LeBaron, E Class, NY
L4, 156.0	3.59×3.86	93	O-LeB, E Class, NY
L6, 225.0	3.40×4.12	90	S-Cordoba, Fifth Ave six
V8, 318.0	3.91×3.31	130	S-Cordoba, Fifth Ave V8

1984

Laser (wb 97.0)		Wght	Price	Prod
GCH24	htchbk cpe 3d	2,525	8,648	33,976
GCP24	XE htchbk cpe 3d	2,545	10,546	25,882
LeBaron (wb 100.3)				
KCP22	cpe	2,445	8,783	24,963
KCP41	sdn 4d	2,495	9,067	47,664
KCP27	conv cpe	2,530	11,595	6,828
KCP27	Mark Cross conv cpe	—	15,495	8,275
KCP27	Mark Cross T&C conv cpe	—	16,495	1,105
KCP45	Town & Country wgn 5d 2S	2,665	9,856	11,578

1984 Laser hatchback coupe

1986 LeBaron four-door sedan

E Class (wb 103.3)		Wght	Price	Prod
ETH41	sdn 4d	2,530	9,565	32,237
New Yorker (wb 103.3)				
ETP41	sdn 4d	2,675	12,179	60,501
Fifth Avenue (wb 112.7)				
MFS41	sdn 4d	3,660	13,990	79,441
Executive (wb 124.0; limo 131.0)				
KCP48	sdn 4d	2,945	18,975	196
KCP49	limo 4d	—	21,975	594

1984 Engines	bore × stroke	bhp	availability
L4, 135.0	3.44 × 3.62	99	S-Laser, LeB, E Class, NY
L4T, 135.0	3.44 × 3.62	142	O-Laser, LeB, E Class, NY
L4, 156.0	3.59 × 3.86	101	S-Exec; O-LeB, E Class, NY
V8, 318.0	3.91 × 3.31	130	S-Fifth Ave

1985

Laser (wb 97.0)		Wght	Price	Prod
GCH24	htchbk cpe 3d	2,613	8,854	32,673
GCP24	XE htchbk cpe 3d	2,665	10,776	18,193
LeBaron (wb 100.3)				
KCP22	cpe	2,533	9,460	24,970
KCP41	sdn 4d	2,559	9,309	43,659
KCP27	conv cpe	2,616	11,889	9,196
KCP27	Mark Cross conv cpe	—	15,994	6,684
KCP27	Mark Cross T&C conv cpe	—	16,994	595
KCP45	Town & Country wgn 5d 2S	2,721	10,363	7,711
LeBaron GTS (wb 103.1)				
HCH44	spt sdn 5d	2,660	9,024	33,176
HCP44	LS spt sdn 5d	2,706	9,970	27,607
New Yorker (wb 103.3)				
ETP41	sdn 4d	2,583	12,865	60,700
Fifth Avenue (wb 112.7)				
MFS41	sdn 4d	3,741	13,978	109,971
Limousine (wb 131.3)				
KCP49	limo 4d	3,206	26,318	759

1985 Engines	bore × stroke	bhp	availability
L4, 135.0	3.44 × 3.62	99	S-Laser, LeBaron, GTS
L4T, 135.0	3.44 × 3.62	146	O-Laser, LeB, GTS, NY
L4, 156.0	3.59 × 3.86	101	S-NY, limo; O-LeBaron
V8, 318.0	3.91 × 3.31	140	S-Fifth Ave

1986

Laser (wb 97.0)		Wght	Price	Prod
GCH24	htchbk cpe 3d	2,547	9,364	21,123
GCP24	XE htchbk cpe 3d	2,599	11,501	8,560
GCP24/AGB	XT htchbk cpe 3d	2,695	11,854	6,989
LeBaron (wb 100.3)				
KCP22	cpe	2,525	9,977	24,761
KCP41	sdn 4d	2,559	10,127	40,116
KCP27	conv cpe	2,625	12,695	12,578
KCP27	Mark Cross conv cpe	2,751	16,595	6,905
KCP27	Mark Cross T&C conv cpe	2,774	17,595	501
KCP45	Town & Country wgn 5d 2S	2,702	11,370	6,493
LeBaron GTS (wb 103.1)				
HCH44	spt sdn 5d	2,601	9,754	42,841
HCP44	Premium spt sdn 5d	2,647	11,437	30,716

1987 LeBaron five-door sport sedan

New Yorker (wb 103.3)		Wght	Price	Prod
ETP41	sdn 4d	2,655	13,409	51,099
Fifth Avenue (wb 112.7)				
MFS41	sdn 4d	3,740	14,910	104,744
Limousine (wb 131.3)				
KCP49	limo 4d	3,206	27,495	138

1986 Engines	bore × stroke	bhp	availability
L4, 135.0	3.44 × 3.62	97	S-Laser, LeBaron, GTS
L4T, 135.0	3.44 × 3.62	146	S-limo; O-Laser, LeBaron, GTS, NY
L4, 153.0	3.44 × 4.09	100	S-Laser XE, LeB T&C wgn, NY; O-Laser, LeBaron, GTS
V8, 318.0	3.91 × 3.31	140	S-Fifth Ave

1988 New Yorker Landau four-door sedan

1989 LeBaron coupe

1987

LeBaron (wb 100.3)		Wght	Price	Prod
JCH21	cpe	2,690	11,295	44,124
JCP21	Premium cpe	2,731	12,288	31,291
JCP27	conv cpe	2,786	13,974	8,025
KCP41	sdn 4d	2,582	10,707	54,678
KCP45	Town & Country wgn 5d 2S	2,759	12,019	5,880
LeBaron GTS (wb 103.1)				
HCH44	spt sdn 5d	2,641	9,774	23,772
HCP44	Premium spt sdn 5d	2,709	11,389	15,278
New Yorker (wb 103.3)				
ETP41	sdn 4d	2,757	14,193	68,279
Fifth Avenue (wb 112.7)				
MFS41	sdn 4d	3,741	15,422	70,579

1987 Engines	bore × stroke	bhp	availability
L4, 135.0	3.44 × 3.62	97	S-LeBaron sdn, GTS
L4T, 135.0	3.44 × 3.62	146	S-limo; O-LeB, GTS, NY
L4, 153.0	3.44 × 4.09	100	S-LeBaron cpe/conv/wgn, NY; O-GTS
V8, 318.0	3.91 × 3.31	140	S-Fifth Ave

1988

LeBaron (wb 100.3)		Wght	Price	Prod
JCH21	cpe	2,769	11,473	38,733
JCP21	Premium cpe	2,875	13,830	9,938
JCH27	conv cpe	2,860	13,959	23,150
JCP27	Premium conv cpe	2,964	18,079	15,037
KCP41	sdn 4d	2,559	11,286	24,452
KCP45	Town & Country wgn 5d 2S	2,702	12,889	2,136
LeBaron GTS (wb 103.1)				
HCH44	spt sdn 5d	2,641	10,798	9,607
HCP44	Premium spt sdn 5d	2,709	12,971	4,604
New Yorker Turbo (103.3)				
ETP41	sdn 4d	2,826	17,373	8,805
New Yorker (wb 104.3)				
CCH41	sdn 4d	3,214	17,416	23,568
CCS41	Landau sdn 4d	3,276	19,509	47,400
Fifth Avenue (wb 112.6)				
MFS41	sdn 4d	3,759	17,243	43,486

1988 Engines	bore × stroke	bhp	availability
L4, 135.0	3.44 × 3.62	97	S-LeBaron sdn, GTS
L4T, 135.0	3.44 × 3.62	146	S-NY turbo; O-LeB, GTS
L4, 153.0	3.44 × 4.09	100	S-LeBaron cpe/conv/wgn
L4, 153.0	3.44 × 4.09	96	S-GTS prem; O-GTS
V6, 181.0	3.59 × 3.99	136	S-NY
V8, 318.0	3.91 × 3.31	140	S-Fifth Ave

1989

LeBaron (wb 100.3)		Wght	Price	Prod
JCH21	Highline cpe	2,810	11,495	
JCP21	Premium cpe	2,945	14,695	
JCH27	conv cpe	2,929	13,995	
JCP27	Premium conv cpe	3,038	18,195	
JCH21	GT cpe	—	14,795	
JCH27	GT conv cpe	—	17,195	
JCH21	GTC turbo cpe	—	17,435	
JCH27	GTC turbo conv cpe	—	19,666	
LeBaron Sedan (wb 103.1)				
HCH44	htchbk spt sdn 5d	2,714	11,495	
HCP44	Premium htchbk spt sdn 5d	2,827	13,495	
HCX44	GTS turbo htchbk spt sdn 5d	2,926	17,095	
New Yorker (wb 104.3)				
CCH41	sdn 4d	3,214	17,416	
CCS41	Landau sdn 4d	3,276	19,509	
Fifth Avenue (wb 112.6)				
MFS41	sdn 4d	3,741	18,345	

1989 Engines	bore × stroke	bhp	availability
L4, 135.0	3.44 × 3.62	93	S-LeBaron sdn
L4T, 135.0	3.44 × 3.62	174	S-LeBaron GTC, GTS
L4, 153.0	3.44 × 4.09	100	S-LeB cpe/conv, prem sdn; O-LeBaron sdn
L4T, 153.0	3.44 × 4.09	150	O-LeBaron GTC/GTS
V6, 181.4	3.59 × 3.99	140	S-NY
V8, 318.0	3.91 × 3.31	140	S-Fifth Ave

CLIPPER

(also see Packard)

1956

5640 Deluxe-Super (wb 122.0)		Wght	Price	Prod
5622	Deluxe sdn 4d	3,745	2,731	5,715
5642	Super sdn 4d	3,800	2,866	5,173
5647	Super htp cpe	3,825	2,916	3,999
5660 Custom (wb 122.0)				
5662	sdn 4d	3,860	3,069	2,129
5667	Constellation htp cpe	3,860	3,164	1,466

1956 Engines	bore×stroke	bhp	availability
V8, 352.0	4.00×3.50	240	S-Deluxe, Super
V8, 352.0	4.00×3.50	275	S-Custom

CONTINENTAL

1956

Mark II (wb 126.0)		Wght	Price	Prod
60A	htp cpe	4,825	9,695	1,325

1956 Engine	bore×stroke	bhp	availability
V8, 368.0	4.00×3.66	285	S-all

1957

Mark II (wb 126.0)		Wght	Price	Prod
60A	htp cpe	4,800	9,966	444

1957 Engine	bore×stroke	bhp	availability
V8, 368.0	4.00×3.66	300	S-all

1958

Mark III (wb 131.0)		Wght	Price	Prod
54A	sdn 4d	4,800	6,072	1,283
65A	htp cpe	4,865	5,825	2,328
68A	conv cpe	5,040	6,283	3,048
75A	Landau htp sdn	4,965	6,072	5,891

1958 Engine	bore×stroke	bhp	availability
V8, 430.0	4.30×3.70	375	S-all

CROSLEY

1939

Series 1A (wb 80.0)—2,017 built	Wght	Price	Prod
conv cpe, 2P	925	325	—
conv sdn, 4P	925	350	—

1956 Continental Mark II coupe

1958 Continental Mark III convertible coupe

1939 Engine	bore×stroke	bhp	availability
L2, 38.9	3.00×2.75	13.5	S-all

1940

Series 2A (wb 80.0)—422 built	Wght	Price	Prod
sdn 2d	975	349	—
Deluxe sdn 2d	975	359	—
conv cpe	950	299	—
covered wgn 2d	1,125	399	—
wgn 2d	1,160	450	—

1940 Engine	bore×stroke	bhp	availability
L2, 38.9	3.00×2.75	13.5	S-all

1941

Series CB41 (wb 80.0)—2,289 built	Wght	Price	Prod
sdn 2d	975	390	—
Deluxe sdn 2d	975	400	—
conv cpe	950	339	—
covered wgn 2d	1,125	441	—
wgn 2d	1,160	496	—

1941 Engine	bore×stroke	bhp	availability
L2, 38.9	3.00×2.75	13.5	S-all

1942

Series CB42 (wb 80.0)—1,029 built	Wght	Price	Prod
sdn 2d	975	468	—

	Wght	Price	Prod
Deluxe sdn 2d	1,050	516	—
conv cpe	975	413	—
wgn 2d	1,105	582	—

1942 Engine	bore×stroke	bhp	availability
L2, 38.9	3.00×2.75	13.5	S-all

1946

CC Four (wb 80.0)	Wght	Price	Prod
sdn 2d	1,145	905	4,987
conv cpe	1,150	proto	12

1946 Engine	bore×stroke	bhp	availability
L4, 44.0	2.50×2.25	26.5	S-all; O-cast-iron block

1947

CC Four (wb 80.0)	Wght	Price	Prod
sdn 2d	1,155	888	14,090
conv cpe	1,150	949	4,005
wgn 2d	1,305	929	1,249

1947 Engine	bore×stroke	bhp	availability
L4, 44.0	2.50×2.25	26.5	S-all; O-cast-iron block

1948

CC Four (wb 80.0)	Wght	Price	Prod
sdn 2d	1,280	869	2,760
Sport Utility sdn 2d	1,160	799	
conv cpe	1,210	899	2,485
wgn 2d	1,305	929	23,489

1948 Engine	bore×stroke	bhp	availability
L4, 44.0	2.50×2.25	26.5	S-all; O-cast-iron block

1949

CD Four (wb 80.0; rdstr-85.0)	Wght	Price	Prod
DeLuxe sdn 2d	1,363	866	2,231
conv cpe	1,320	866	645
wgn 4d	1,403	894	3,803
Hotshot rdstr	1,175	849	752

1949 Engine	bore×stroke	bhp	availability
L4, 44.0	2.50×2.25	26.5	S-all; O-cast-iron block

1947 convertible coupe

1950

CD Four (wb 80.0; rdstr-85.0)	Wght	Price	Prod
sdn 2d	1,363	882	1,367
Super sdn 2d	1,363	951	
conv cpe	1,320	882	478
Super conv cpe	1,320	954	
wgn 2d	1,403	916	4,205
Super wgn 2d	1,403	984	
Hotshot rdstr	1,175	872	742
Super Sports rdstr	1,175	925	

1950 Engine	bore×stroke	bhp	availability
L4, 44.0	2.50×2.25	26.5	S-all

1951

CD Four (wb 80.0; rdstr-85.0)	Wght	Price	Prod
bus cpe	1,355	943	1,077
Super sdn 2d	1,370	1,033	
wgn 2d	1,420	1,002	4,500
Super wgn 2d	1,450	1,077	
Super conv cpe	1,310	1,035	391
Hotshot rdstr	1,180	952	646
Super Sports rdstr	1,180	1,029	

1951 Engine	bore×stroke	bhp	availability
L4, 44.0	2.50×2.25	26.5	S-all

1952

CD Four (wb 80.0; rdstr-85.0)	Wght	Price	Prod
Standard bus cpe	1,355	943	216
Super sdn 2d	1,400	1,033	
Standard wgn 2d	1,430	1,002	1,355
Super wgn 2d	1,480	1,077	
Super conv cpe	1,400	1,035	146
Hotshot rdstr	1,240	952	358
Super Sports rdstr	1,240	1,029	

1952 Engine	bore×stroke	bhp	availability
L4, 44.0	2.50×2.25	25.5	S-all

DeSOTO

1939

S6 DeLuxe (wb 119.0; lwb-136.0)	Wght	Price	Prod
bus cpe 2P	3,064	870	5,176
cpe A/S 2-4P	3,089	925	2,124
touring sdn 2d 5P	3,129	930	7,472
touring sdn 4d 5P	3,174	970	31,513
lwb touring sdn 7P	3,454	1,195	425
sdn limo 7P	3,549	1,285	84
chassis	—	—	154
S6 Custom (wb 119.0; lwb-136.0)			
cpe 2P	3,069	923	498
cpe A/S 2-4P	3,094	978	287
club cpe 4P	3,164	1,145	264
touring sdn 2d 5P	3,134	983	424
touring sdn 4d 5P	3,179	1,023	5,993
lwb touring sdn 7P	3,459	1,248	30
sdn limo 7P	3,554	1,338	5

1939 Engines	bore×stroke	bhp	availability
L6, 228.1	3.38×4.25	93	S-all
L6, 228.1	3.38×4.25	100	O-all

1940

S-7S DeLuxe (wb 122.5; 7P-139.5)	Wght	Price	Prod
bus cpe	3,001	845	3,650
cpe, A/S	3,026	905	2,098
sdn 2d	3,066	905	7,072
sdn 4d	3,086	945	18,666
sdn 4d, 7P	3,490	1,175	142
S-7C Custom (wb 122.5; 7P-139.5)			
bus cpe	3,024	885	1,898
cpe, A/S	3,044	945	2,234
conv cpe	3,329	1,095	1,085
sdn 2d	3,084	945	3,109
sdn 4d	3,104	985	25,221
sdn 4d, 7P	3,490	1,215	206
limo 7P	3,550	1,290	34
chassis	—	—	52

1940 Engines	bore×stroke	bhp	availability
L6, 228.1	3.38×4.25	100	S-all
L6, 228.1	3.38×4.25	105	O-all

1941

S-8S DeLuxe (wb 121.5; 7P-139.5)	Wght	Price	Prod
bus cpe	3,134	945	4,449
club cpe	3,219	1,025	5,603
sdn 2d	3,224	1,008	9,228
sdn 4d	3,254	1,035	26,417
sdn 4d, 7P	3,629	1,270	101
S-8C Custom (wb 121.5; 7P-139.5)			
bus cpe	3,144	982	2,033
club cpe	3,239	1,080	6,726
conv cpe	3,494	1,240	2,937
brougham 2d	3,264	1,060	4,609
sdn 4d	3,269	1,085	30,876
town sdn	3,329	1,133	4,362
sdn 4d, 7P	3,649	1,310	120
limo 7P	3,700	1,390	35
chassis	—	—	1

1941 Engine	bore×stroke	bhp	availability
L6, 228.1	3.38×4.25	105	S-all

1942

S-10S DeLuxe (wb 121.5; 7P-139.5)	Wght	Price	Prod
bus cpe	3,190	1,010	469
club cpe	3,270	1,092	1,968
conv cpe	3,500	1,250	79
sdn 2d	3,270	1,075	1,781
sdn 4d	3,315	1,103	6,463
town sdn	3,335	1,147	291
sdn 4d, 7P	3,705	1,455	49
S-10C Custom (wb 121.5; 7P-139.5)			
bus cpe	3,205	1,046	120
club cpe	3,270	1,142	2,236
conv cpe	3,510	1,317	489
sdn 2d	3,305	1,142	913
sdn 4d	3,330	1,152	7,974
town sdn	3,365	1,196	1,084
sdn 4d, 7P	3,725	1,504	79
limo 7P	3,820	1,580	20

1942 Custom convertible coupe

1946 Custom convertible coupe

1942 Engine	bore×stroke	bhp	availability
L6, 236.6	3.44×4.25	115	S-all

1946

S-11S DeLuxe (wb 121.5)*	Wght	Price	Prod
bus cpe	3,302	1,331	—
club cpe	3,392	1,451	—
sdn 2d	3,397	1,426	—
sdn 4d	3,427	1,461	—
S-11C Custom (wb 121.5; 7–8P-139.5)*			
club cpe	3,378	1,501	—
conv cpe	3,618	1,761	—
sdn 2d	3,423	1,491	—
sdn 4d	3,433	1,511	—
sdn 4d, 7P	3,837	1,893	—
limo 8P	3,937	2,013	—
Suburban sdn 4d, 8P	4,012	2,093	—

1946 Engine	bore×stroke	bhp	availability
L6, 236.6	3.44×4.25	109	S-all

1947

S-11S DeLuxe (wb 121.5)*	Wght	Price	Prod
bus cpe	3,323	1,451	—
club cpe	3,413	1,541	—
sdn 2d	3,418	1,516	—
sdn 4d	3,448	1,551	—

S-11C Custom (wb 121.5; 7–8P-139.5)*	Wght	Price	Prod
club cpe	3,398	1,591	—
conv cpe	3,618	1,965	—
sdn 2d	3,443	1,581	—
sdn 4d	3,453	1,601	—
sdn 4d, 7P	3,837	1,983	—
limo 7P	3,995	2,013	—
Suburban sdn 4d, 8P	4,012	2,283	—

1947 Engine	bore×stroke	bhp	availability
L6, 236.6	3.44×4.25	109	S-all

1948

S-11S DeLuxe (wb 121.5)*	Wght	Price	Prod
bus cpe	3,285	1,699	—
club cpe	3,385	1,815	—
sdn 2d	3,375	1,788	—
sdn 4d	3,435	1,825	—
S-11C Custom (wb 121.5; 7–9P-139.5)*			
club cpe	3,389	1,874	—
conv cpe	3,599	2,296	—
sdn 2d	3,399	1,860	—
sdn 4d	3,439	1,892	—
sdn 4d, 7P	3,819	2,315	—
limo 7P	3,995	2,442	—
Suburban sdn 4d, 9P	3,974	2,631	—

1948 Engine	bore×stroke	bhp	availability
L6, 236.6	3.44×4.25	109	S-all

1949 First Series

S-11S DeLuxe (wb 121.5)*	Wght	Price	Prod
bus cpe	3,285	1,699	—
club cpe	3,385	1,815	—
sdn 2d	3,375	1,788	—
sdn 4d	3,435	1,825	—
S-11C Custom (wb 121.5; 7–9P-139.5)*			
club cpe	3,389	1,874	—
conv cpe	3,599	2,296	—
sdn 2d	3,399	1,860	—
sdn 4d	3,439	1,892	—
sdn 4d, 7P	3,819	2,315	—
limo 7P	3,995	2,442	—
Suburban sdn 4d, 9P	3,974	2,631	—

1949(1) Engine	bore×stroke	bhp	availability
L6, 236.6	3.44×4.25	109	S-all

*Factory combined production figures for 1946 through 1949 First Series.

Combined 1946–1949 First Series Production:

S-11S DeLuxe (wb 121.5)	Prod
bus cpe	1,950
club cpe	8,580
sdn 2d	12,751
sdn 4d	32,213
S-11C Custom (wb 121.5; 7–9P-139.5)	
club cpe	38,720
conv cpe	8,100
sdn 2d	1,600
sdn 4d	126,226
sdn 4d, 7P	3,530
limo 7P	120
Suburban 4d, 8–9P	7,500
chassis	105

1948 DeLuxe four-door sedan

1949 Second Series

S-13-1 DeLuxe (wb 125.5)	Wght	Price	Prod
club cpe	3,455	1,976	6,807
sdn 4d	3,520	1,986	13,148
Carry-All sdn 4d, 6P	3,565	2,191	2,690
wgn 4d, 9P	3,915	2,959	850
S-13-2 Custom (wb 125.5; 8–9P-139.5)			
club cpe	3,585	2,156	18,431
conv cpe	3,785	2,578	3,385
sdn 4d	3,645	2,174	48,589
sdn 4d, 8P	4,200	2,863	342
Suburban 4d, 9P	4,410	3,179	129

1949(2) Engine	bore×stroke	bhp	availability
L6, 236.6	3.44×4.25	112	S-all

1950

S-14-1 DeLuxe (wb 125.5; 8P-139.5)	Wght	Price	Prod
club cpe	3,450	1,976	10,704
sdn 4d	3,525	1,986	18,489
Carry-All sdn 4d, 5P	3,600	2,191	3,900
sdn 4d, 8P	3,995	2,676	235
chassis	—	—	1
S-14-2 Custom (wb 125.5; 8–9P-139.5)			
club cpe	3,575	2,156	18,302
Sportsman htp cpe	3,735	2,489	4,600
conv cpe	3,815	2,578	2,900
sdn 4d	3,640	2,174	72,664
wgn 4d (wood)	4,035	3,093	600
wgn 4d (steel)	3,900	2,717	100
sdn 4d, 8P	4,115	2,863	734
Suburban 4d, 9P	4,400	3,179	623
chassis	—	—	2

1950 Engine	bore×stroke	bhp	availability
L6, 236.6	3.44×4.25	112	S-all

1951

S-15-1 DeLuxe (wb 125.5; 8P-139.5)*	Wght	Price	Prod
club cpe	3,475	2,215	—
sdn 4d	3,570	2,227	—
Carry-All sdn 4d	3,685	2,457	—
sdn 4d, 8P	4,045	3,001	—
S-15-2 Custom (wb 125.5; 8–9P-139.5)*	**Wght**	**Price**	**Prod**
club cpe	3,585	2,418	—
Sportsman htp cpe	3,760	2,761	—
conv cpe	2,862	2,840	—
sdn 4d	3,685	2,438	—
wgn 4d	3,960	3,047	—
sdn 4d, 8P	4,122	3,211	—
Suburban 4d, 9P	4,395	3,566	—

1951 Engine	bore×stroke	bhp	availability
L6, 250.6	3.44×4.50	116	S-all

1952

S-15-1 DeLuxe (wb 125.5; 8P-139.5)*	Wght	Price	Prod
club cpe	3,435	2,319	—
sdn 4d	3,540	2,333	—
Carry-All sdn 4d	3,650	2,572	—
sdn 4d, 8P	4,035	3,142	—
S-15-2 Custom (wb 125.5; 8–9P-139.5)*	**Wght**	**Price**	**Prod**
club cpe	3,565	2,531	—
Sportsman htp cpe	3,720	2,890	—
conv cpe	3,865	2,996	—
sdn 4d	3,660	2,552	—
wgn 4d	4,020	3,189	—
sdn 4d, 8P	4,155	3,362	—
Suburban 4d, 9P	4,370	3,734	—
S-17 Firedome (wb 125.5; 8P-139.5)			
club cpe	3,675	2,718	5,699
Sportsman htp cpe	3,850	3,078	3,000
conv cpe	3,950	3,183	850
sdn 4d	3,760	2,740	35,651
wgn 4d	4,080	3,377	550
sdn 4d, 8P	4,325	3,547	50

1952 Engines	bore×stroke	bhp	availability
L6, 250.6	3.44×4.50	116	S-Deluxe, Custom
V8, 276.1	3.63×3.34	160	S-Firedome

*Factory combined 1951–1952 Deluxe and Custom production figures.

1951–1952 Deluxe and Custom Production:

S-15-1 DeLuxe (wb 125.5; 8P-139.5)	Prod
club cpe	6,100
sdn 4d	13,506
Carry-All sdn 4d	1,700
sdn 4d, 8P	343
S-15-2 Custom (wb 125.5; 8–9P-139.5)	
club cpe	19,000
Sportsman htp cpe	8,750
conv cpe	3,950
sdn 4d	88,491
wgn 4d	1,440
sdn 4d, 8P	769
Suburban 4d, 9P	600

1949 Custom club coupe

1953 Firedome eight-passenger four-door sedan

1953

S-18 Powermaster (wb 125.5; 8P-139.5)	Wght	Price	Prod
club cpe	3,480	2,334	8,063
Sportsman htp cpe	3,585	2,604	1,470
sdn 4d	3,535	2,356	33,644
wgn 4d	3,845	3,078	500
sdn 4d, 8P	4,080	3,251	225

S-16 Firedome (wb 125.5; 8P-139.5)	Wght	Price	Prod
club cpe	3,655	2,622	14,591
Sportsman htp cpe	3,740	2,893	4,700
conv cpe	3,990	3,114	1,700
sdn 4d	3,720	2,643	64,211
wgn 4d	3,995	3,351	1,100
sdn 4d, 8P	4,270	3,529	200

1953 Engines	bore×stroke	bhp	availability
L6, 250.6	3.44×4.50	116	S-Powermaster
V8, 276.1	3.63×3.34	160	S-Firedome

1954

S-20 Powermaster (wb 125.5; 8P-139.5)	Wght	Price	Prod
club cpe	3,505	2,364	3,499
Sportsman htp cpe (discont'd.)	3,590	2,635	250
sdn 4d	3,570	2,386	14,967
wgn 4d	3,855	3,108	225
sdn 4d, 8P	4,100	3,281	263

S-19 Firedome (wb 125.5; 8P-139.5)	Wght	Price	Prod
club cpe	3,735	2,652	5,762
Sportsman htp cpe	3,815	2,923	4,382
conv cpe	4,015	3,144	1,025
sdn 4d	3,790	2,673	45,095
wgn 4d	4,045	3,381	946
sdn 4d, 8P	4,305	3,559	165
chassis	—	—	1

1954 Engines	bore×stroke	bhp	availability
L6, 250.6	3.44×4.50	116	S-Powermaster
V8, 276.1	3.63×3.34	170	S-Firedome

1955

S-22 Firedome (wb 126.0)	Wght	Price	Prod
Special htp cpe	3,801	2,541	28,944 (Special and Sportsman combined)
Sportsman htp cpe	3,805	2,654	
conv cpe	4,010	2,824	625
sdn 4d	3,870	2,498	46,388
wgn 4d	4,185	3,170	1,803

S-21 Fireflite (wb 126.0)	Wght	Price	Prod
Sportsman htp cpe	3,890	2,939	10,313
conv cpe	4,115	3,151	775
sdn 4d (inc. Coronado)	3,940	2,727	26,637

1955 Engines	bore×stroke	bhp	availability
V8, 291.0	3.72×3.34	185	S-Firedome
V8, 291.0	3.72×3.34	200	S-Fireflite

1956

S-23 Firedome (wb 126.0)	Wght	Price	Prod
Seville htp cpe	3,800	2,684	19,136
Seville htp sdn	3,920	2,833	4,030
Sportsman htp cpe	3,835	2,854	4,589
Sportsman htp sdn	3,945	2,953	1,645
conv cpe	4,080	3,081	646
sdn 4d	3,780	2,678	44,909
wgn 4d	4,095	3,371	2,950

S-24 Fireflite (wb 126.0)	Wght	Price	Prod
Sportsman htp cpe	3,905	3,346	8,475
Sportsman htp sdn	3,970	3,431	3,350
conv cpe	4,075	3,544	1,385*
Pacesetter conv cpe	4,070	3,615	100*
sdn 4d	3,860	3,119	18,207
Adventurer htp cpe	3,870	3,728	996

*Estimated; total conv cpes 1,485.

1956 Engines	bore×stroke	bhp	availability
V8, 330.4	3.72×3.80	230	S-Firedome
V8, 330.4	3.72×3.80	255	S-Fireflite exc Adventurer
V8, 341.4	3.78×3.80	320	S-Adventurer

1955 Fireflite Sportsman hardtop coupe

1956 Fireflite Sportsman hardtop coupe

1957

S-27 Firesweep (wb 122.0)	Wght	Price	Prod
Sportsman htp cpe	3,645	2,836	13,333
Sportsman htp sdn	3,720	2,912	7,168
sdn 4d	3,675	2,777	17,300
Shopper wgn 4d, 6P	3,965	3,169	2,270
Explorer wgn 4d, 9P	3,970	3,310	1,198
S-25 Firedome (wb 126.0)			
Sportsman htp cpe	3,910	3,085	12,179
Sportsman htp sdn	3,960	3,142	9,050
conv cpe	4,065	3,361	1,297
sdn 4d	3,955	2,958	23,339
S-26 Fireflite (wb 126.0)			
Sportsman htp cpe	4,000	3,614	7,217
Sportsman htp sdn	4,125	3,671	6,726
conv cpe	4,085	3,890	1,151
sdn 4d	4,025	3,487	11,565
Shopper wgn 4d, 6P	4,290	3,982	837
Explorer wgn 4d, 9P	4,250	4,124	934
S-26A Adventurer (wb 126.0)			
htp cpe	4,040	3,997	1,650
conv cpe	4,235	4,272	300

1957 Engines	bore×stroke	bhp	availability
V8, 325.0	3.69×3.80	245	S-Firesweep
V8, 325.0	3.69×3.80	260	O-Firesweep
V8, 341.0	3.78×3.80	270	S-Firedome
V8, 341.0	3.78×3.80	295	S-Fireflite
V8, 345.0	3.80×3.80	345	S-Adventurer

1958

	LS1-L Firesweep (wb 122.0)	Wght	Price	Prod
23	Sportsman htp cpe	3,660	2,890	5,635
27	conv cpe	3,850	3,219	700
41	sdn 4d	3,660	2,819	7,646
43	Sportsman htp sdn	3,720	2,953	3,003
45A	Shopper wgn 4d, 6P	3,955	3,266	1,305
45B	Explorer wgn 4d, 9P	3,980	3,408	1,125
LS2-M Firedome (wb 126.0)				
23	Sportsman htp cpe	3,825	3,178	4,325
27	conv cpe	4,065	3,489	519
41	sdn 4d	3,855	3,085	9,505
43	Sportsman htp sdn	3,920	3,235	3,130
LS3-H Fireflite (wb 126.0)				
23	Sportsman htp cpe	3,920	3,675	3,284
27	conv cpe	4,105	3,972	474
41	sdn 4d	3,990	3,583	4,192
43	Sportsman htp sdn	3,980	3,731	3,243
45A	Shopper wgn 4d, 6P	4,225	4,030	318
45B	Explorer wgn 4d, 9P	4,295	4,172	609
LS3-S Adventurer (wb 126.0)				
23	htp cpe	4,000	4,071	350
27	conv cpe	4,180	4,369	82

1958 Engines	bore×stroke	bhp	availability
V8, 350.0	4.06×3.38	280	S-Firesweep
V8, 350.0	4.06×3.38	295	O-Firesweep
V8, 361.0	4.13×3.38	295	S-Firedome
V8, 361.0	4.13×3.38	305	S-Fireflite; O-Firedome
V8, 361.0	4.13×3.38	345	S-Adventurer
V8, 361.0	4.13×3.38	355	O-Adventurer

1959

	MS1-L Firesweep (wb 122.0)	Wght	Price	Prod
23	Sportsman htp cpe	3,625	2,967	5,481
27	conv cpe	3,840	3,315	596
41	sdn 4d	3,670	2,904	9,649
43	Sportsman htp sdn	3,700	3,038	2,875
45A	Shopper wgn 4d, 6P	3,950	3,366	1,054
45B	Explorer wgn 4d, 9P	3,980	3,508	1,179

1958 Fireflite convertible coupe

MS2-M Firedome (wb 126.0)		Wght	Price	Prod
23	Sportsman htp cpe	3,795	3,341	2,862*
27	conv cpe	4,015	3,653	299*
41	sdn 4d	3,840	3,234	9,171*
43	Sportsman htp sdn	3,895	3,398	2,744*
MS3-H Fireflite (wb 126.0)				
23	Sportsman htp cpe	3,910	3,831	1,393
27	conv cpe	4,105	4,152	186
41	sdn 4d	3,920	3,763	4,480
43	Sportsman htp sdn	3,950	3,888	2,364
45A	Shopper wgn 4d, 6P	4,170	4,216	271
45B	Explorer wgn 4d, 9P	4,205	4,358	433
MS3-S Adventurer (wb 126.0)				
23	htp cpe	3,980	4,427	590
27	conv cpe	4,120	4,749	97

*Includes Seville htp cpe, conv cpe, sdn 4d, and htp sdn, trim variation introduced in Spring 1959 to mark DeSoto's 30th anniversary.

1959 Engines	bore×stroke	bhp	availability
V8, 361.0	4.13×3.38	295	S-Firesweep
V8, 383.0	4.25×3.38	305	S-Firedome
V8, 383.0	4.25×3.38	325	S-Fireflite
V8, 383.0	4.25×3.38	350	S-Adventurer; O-others

1960

PS1-L Fireflite (wb 122.0)		Wght	Price	Prod
23	htp cpe	3,885	3,102	3,494
41	sdn 4d	3,865	3,017	9,032
43	htp sdn	3,865	3,167	1,958
PS3-M Adventurer (wb 122.0)				
23	htp cpe	3,945	3,663	3,092
41	sdn 4d	3,895	3,579	5,746
43	htp sdn	3,940	3,727	2,759

1960 Engines	bore×stroke	bhp	availability
V8, 361.0	4.13×3.38	295	S-Fireflite
V8, 383.0	4.25×3.38	305	S-Adventurer

1961

RS1-L (wb 122.0)		Wght	Price	Prod
612	htp cpe	3,760	3,102	911
614	htp sdn	3,820	3,167	2,123

1961 Engine	bore×stroke	bhp	availability
V8, 361.0	4.13×3.38	265	S-all

DODGE

1939

D11 Luxury Liner Special (wb 117.0)	Wght	Price	Prod
bus cpe 2P	2,905	756	12,300
sdn 2d	2,955	815	26,700
sdn 4d	2,995	855	32,000
D11 Luxury Liner DeLuxe (wb 117.0)			
bus cpe 2P	2,940	803	630
fstbk sdn 2d	3,010	865	270
sdn T/B 2d	2,990	895	1,585
fstbk sdn 4d	3,045	905	270
sdn T/B 4d	3,035	915	5,545
Town cpe 5P	3,075	1,055	300*

1939 Engine	bore×stroke	bhp	availability
L6, 217.8	3.25×4.38	87	S-all

*Estimated from total of 1000 built by Hayes for Dodge, Chrysler and Plymouth.

Note: Many sources also list a 2-4 passenger rumble-seat coupe (2,985 lbs/$860), and a 134-inch wheelbase 7-passenger sedan (3,440 lbs/$1,095) and limousine (3,545 lbs/$1,185). However, Dodge gives no production figures for these models, and their production in 1939 is in doubt.

1940

D-17 Special (wb 119.5)	Wght	Price	Prod
bus cpe	2,867	755	12,001
sdn 2d	2,942	815	27,700
sdn 4d	2,997	855	26,803
D-14 DeLuxe (wb 119.5; 7P-139.5)			
bus cpe	2,905	803	12,750
cpe, A/S	2,973	855	8,028
conv cpe	3,190	1,030	2,100
sdn 2d	2,990	860	19,838
sdn 4d	3,028	905	84,976
sdn 4d, 7P	3,460	1,095	932
limo 7P	3,500	1,170	79
chassis	—	—	298

1940 Engine	bore×stroke	bhp	availability
L6, 217.8	3.25×4.38	87	S-all

1941

D-19 DeLuxe (wb 119.5)	Wght	Price	Prod
bus cpe	3,034	862	22,318
sdn 2d	3,109	915	34,566
sdn 4d	3,149	954	49,579
D-19 Custom (wb 119.5; 7P-137.5)			
club cpe	3,154	995	18,024
conv cpe	3,384	1,162	3,554
brougham 2d	3,169	962	20,146
sdn 4d	3,194	999	72,067
town sdn	3,234	1,062	16,074
sdn 4d, 7P	3,579	1,195	601
limo 7P	3,669	1,262	50
chassis	—	—	20

1941 Engine	bore×stroke	bhp	availability
L6, 217.8	3.25×4.38	91	S-all

1942

D-22 DeLuxe (wb 119.5)	Wght	Price	Prod
bus cpe	3,056	895	5,257
club cpe	3,131	995	3,314
sdn 2d	3,131	958	9,767
sdn 4d	3,171	998	13,343
D-22 Custom (wb 119.5; 7P-137.5)			
club cpe	3,171	1,045	4,659
conv cpe	3,476	1,245	1,185
brougham 2d	3,171	1,008	4,685
sdn 4d	3,206	1,048	22,055
town sdn	3,256	1,105	4,047
sdn 4d, 7P	3,693	1,395	201
limo 7P	3,768	1,475	9

1942 Custom convertible coupe

1942 Engine	bore×stroke	bhp	availability
L6, 230.2	3.25×4.63	105	S-all

1946

D-24S DeLuxe (wb 119.5)*	Wght	Price	Prod
bus cpe	3,146	1,229	—
sdn 2d	3,236	1,299	—
sdn 4d	3,256	1,339	—
D-24C Custom (wb 119.5; 7P-137.5)*			
club cpe	3,241	1,384	—
conv cpe	3,461	1,649	—
sdn 4d	3,281	1,389	—
town sdn	3,331	1,444	—
sdn 4d, 7P	3,757	1,743	—

1946 Engine	bore×stroke	bhp	availability
L6, 230.2	3.25×4.63	102	S-all

1947

D-24S DeLuxe (wb 119.5)*	Wght	Price	Prod
bus cpe	3,147	1,347	—
sdn 2d	3,236	1,417	—
sdn 4d	3,256	1,457	—
D-24C Custom (wb 119.5; 7P-137.5)*			
club cpe	3,241	1,502	—
conv cpe	3,461	1,871	—
sdn 4d	3,281	1,507	—
town sdn	3,331	1,577	—
sdn 4d, 7P	3,757	1,861	—

1947 Engine	bore×stroke	bhp	availability
L6, 230.2	3.25×4.63	102	S-all

1948

D-24S DeLuxe (wb 119.5)*	Wght	Price	Prod
bus cpe	3,146	1,587	—
sdn 2d	3,236	1,676	—
sdn 4d	3,256	1,718	—
D-24C Custom (wb 119.5; 7P-137.5)*			
club cpe	3,241	1,774	—
conv cpe	3,461	2,189	—
sdn 4d	3,281	1,788	—
town sdn	3,331	1,872	—
sdn 4d, 7P	3,757	2,179	—

1948 Engine	bore×stroke	bhp	availability
L6, 230.2	3.25×4.63	102	S-all

1949 First Series

D-24S DeLuxe (wb 119.5)*	Wght	Price	Prod
bus cpe	3,146	1,587	—

1948 Custom four-door sedan

	Wght	Price	Prod
sdn 2d	3,236	1,676	—
sdn 4d	3,256	1,718	—
D-24C Custom (wb 119.5; 7P-137.5)*			
club cpe	3,241	1,774	—
conv cpe	3,461	2,189	—
sdn 4d	3,281	1,788	—
town sdn	3,331	1,872	—
sdn 4d, 7P	3,757	2,179	—

1949(1) Engine	bore×stroke	bhp	availability
L6, 230.2	3.25×4.63	102	S-all

*Factory combined production figures for 1946 through 1949 First Series.

Combined 1946–1949 First Series Production:

D-24S DeLuxe (wb 119.5)	Prod
bus cpe	27,600
sdn 2d	81,399
sdn 4d	61,987
D-24C Custom (wb 119.5; 7P-137.5)	
club cpe	103,800
conv cpe	9,500
sdn 4d	333,911
town sdn	27,800
sdn 4d, 7P	3,698
limo 7P (proto)	2
chassis	302

1949 Second Series

D-29 Wayfarer (wb 115.0)	Wght	Price	Prod
cpe	3,065	1,611	9,342
sdn 2d	3,180	1,738	49,054
rdstr	3,145	1,727	5,420
D-30 (wb 123.5; 8P-137.5)			
Meadowbrook sdn 4d	3,355	1,848	144,390
Coronet sdn 4d	3,380	1,927	
Coronet club cpe	3,325	1,914	45,435
Coronet conv cpe	3,570	2,329	2,411
Coronet wgn 4d, 9P	3,830	2,865	800
chassis	—	—	1

1949(2) Engine	bore×stroke	bhp	availability
L6, 230.2	3.25 × 4.63	103	S-all

1950

D-33 Wayfarer (wb 115.0)	Wght	Price	Prod
bus cpe	3,095	1,611	7,500
sdn 2d	3,200	1,738	65,000
Sportabout rdstr	3,155	1,727	2,903
D-34 (wb 123.5; 8P-137.5)			
Meadowbrook sdn 4d	3,395	1,848	221,791
Coronet sdn 4d	3,405	1,927	
Coronet club cpe	3,340	1,914	38,502
Coronet conv cpe	3,590	2,329	1,800
Coronet Diplomat htp cpe	3,515	2,233	3,600
Coronet wgn 4d (wood)	3,850	2,865	600
Coronet Sierra wgn 4d (steel)	3,726	2,485	100
chassis	—	—	1

1950 Engine	bore×stroke	bhp	availability
L6, 230.2	3.25×4.63	103	S-all

1950 Wayfarer Sportabout roadster

1951

D-41 Wayfarer (wb 115.0)	Wght	Price	Prod
bus cpe	3,125	1,795	*
sdn 2d	3,210	1,936	*
Sportabout rdstr	3,175	1,924	1,002
D-42 (wb 123.5; 8P-137.5)*			
Meadowbrook sdn 4d	3,415	2,059	—
Coronet sdn 4d	3,415	2,148	—
Coronet club cpe	3,320	2,132	—
Coronet Diplomat htp cpe	3,515	2,478	—
Coronet conv cpe	3,575	2,568	—
Coronet Sierra wgn 4d	3,750	2,768	—
Coronet sdn 4d, 8P	3,935	2,916	—

1951 Engine	bore×stroke	bhp	availability
L6, 230.2	3.25×4.63	103	S-all

1952

D-41 Wayfarer (wb 115.0)*	Wght	Price	Prod
bus cpe	3,053	1,886	—
sdn 2d	3,140	2,034	—
D-42 (wb 123.5; 8P-137.5)*			
Meadowbrook sdn 4d	3,355	2,164	—
Coronet sdn 4d	3,385	2,256	—
Coronet club cpe	3,290	2,240	—
Coronet conv cpe	3,520	2,698	—
Coronet Diplomat htp cpe	3,475	2,602	—
Coronet Sierra wgn 4d	3,735	2,908	—
Coronet sdn 4d, 8P	3,935	3,064	—

1952 Engine	bore×stroke	bhp	availability
L6, 230.2	3.25×4.63	103	S-all

*Factory combined 1951–1952 production.

Combined 1951–1952 production:

D-41 Wayfarer (wb 115.0)	Prod
bus cpe	6,702
sdn 2d	70,700
Sportabout rdstr (1951 only)	1,002
D-42 (wb 123.5; 8P-137.5)	
Meadowbrook-Coronet sdn 4d	329,202
Coronet club cpe	56,103
Coronet conv cpe	5,550
Coronet Diplomat htp cpe	21,600
Coronet Sierra wgn 4d	4,000
Coronet sdn 4d, 8P	1,150

1953

D-46 (wb 119.0)	Wght	Price	Prod
Meadowbrook Special cpe	3,100	1,958	
Meadowbrook cpe	3,085	1,958	36,766
Coronet cpe	3,155	2,084	
Meadowbrook Special sdn 4d	3,195	2,000	
Meadowbrook sdn 4d	3,175	2,000	84,158
Coronet sdn 4d	3,220	2,111	
D-47 Meadowbrook Suburban (wb 114.0)			
wgn 2d	3,190	2,176	15,751
D-44 Coronet Eight (wb 119.0)			
club cpe	3,325	2,198	32,439
sdn 4d	3,385	2,220	124,059
D-48 Coronet Eight (wb 114.0)			
conv cpe	3,438	2,494	4,100
Diplomat htp cpe	3,310	2,361	17,334
Sierra wgn 2d	3,425	2,503	5,400
chassis	—	—	1

1953 Engines	bore×stroke	bhp	availability
L6, 230.2	3.25×4.63	103	S-D-46, D-47
V8, 241.3	3.44×3.25	140	S-D-44, D-48

1954

D51-1 Meadowbrook L6 (wb 119.0)	Wght	Price	Prod
club cpe	3,120	1,983	3,501
sdn 4d	3,195	2,025	7,894
D50-1 Meadowbrook V8 (wb 119.0)			
club cpe	3,335	2,154	750
sdn 4d	3,390	2,176	3,299
D51-2 Coronet L6 (wb 119.0)			
club cpe	3,165	2,109	4,501
sdn 4d	3,235	2,136	14,900
D52 Coronet L6 (wb 119.0; 2d-114.0)			
Suburban wgn 2d	3,185	2,229	6,389
Sierra wgn 4d, 6P	3,430	2,719	312
Sierra wgn 4d, 8P	3,435	2,790	
D50-2 Coronet V8 (wb 119.0)			
club cpe	3,345	2,223	7,998
sdn 4d	3,405	2,245	36,063
D53-2 Coronet V8 (wb 114.0; 4d-119.0)			
Sport htp cpe	3,310	2,380	100
conv cpe	3,505	2,514	50

	Wght	Price	Prod
Suburban wgn 2d	3,400	2,517	3,100
Sierra wgn 4d, 6P	3,605	2,960	988
Sierra wgn 4d, 8P	3,660	3,031	
D50-3 Royal V8 (wb 119.0)			
club cpe	3,365	2,349	8,900
sdn 4d	3,425	2,373	50,050
D53-3 Royal V8 (wb 114.0)			
Sport htp cpe	3,355	2,503	3,852
conv cpe (prod inc 701 model 500)	3,575	2,632	2,000
chassis	—	—	1

1954 Engines	bore×stroke	bhp	availability
L6, 230.2	3.25×4.63	110	S-all 6s
V8, 241.3	3.44×3.25	140	S-Meadowbrook V8
V8, 241.3	3.44×3.25	150	S-others (Offenhauser manifold available)

1955

D56-1 Coronet L6 (wb 120.0)	Wght	Price	Prod
sdn 2d	3,235	2,013	13,277
sdn 4d	3,295	2,093	15,976
Suburban wgn 2d	3,410	2,349	3,248
Suburban wgn 4d, 6P	3,480	2,463	1,311
Suburban wgn 4d, 8P	3,595	2,565	
D55-1 Coronet V8 (wb 120.0)			
sdn 2d	3,360	2,116	10,827
club sdn 2d	3,235	2,124	
sdn 4d	3,395	2,196	30,098
Lancer htp cpe	3,375	2,281	26,727
Suburban wgn 2d	3,550	2,452	4,867
Suburban wgn 4d, 6P	3,590	2,566	4,641
Suburban wgn 4d, 8P	3,695	2,668	
D55-2 Royal V8 (wb 120.0)			
sdn 4d	3,425	2,310	45,323
Lancer htp cpe	3,425	2,395	25,831
Sierra wgn 4d, 6P	3,655	2,659	5,506
Sierra wgn 4d, 8P	3,730	2,761	
D55-3 Custom Royal V8 (wb 120.0)			
sdn 4d	3,485	2,473	55,503
Lancer sdn 4d	3,505	2,516	
Lancer htp cpe	3,480	2,543	30,499
Lancer conv cpe	3,610	2,748	3,302

1955 Engines	bore×stroke	bhp	availability
L6, 230.2	3.25×4.63	123	S-all 6s

1954 Royal 500 convertible coupe

1955 Custom Royal Lancer convertible coupe

	bore×stroke	bhp	availability
V8, 270.1	3.63×3.25	175	S-all V8s exc Custom Royal
V8, 270.1	3.63×3.25	183	S-Custom Royal
V8, 270.1	3.63×3.25	193	O-Custom Royal

1956

D62 Coronet L6 (wb 120.0)—142,613 built (includes D63-1)	Wght	Price	Prod
sdn 2d	3,250	2,194	—
sdn 4d	3,295	2,267	—
Suburban wgn 2d	3,455	2,491	—
D63-1 Coronet V8 (wb 120.0)			
club sdn 2d	3,380	2,302	—
sdn 4d	3,435	2,375	—
Lancer htp sdn	3,560	2,552	—
Lancer htp cpe	3,430	2,438	—
conv cpe	3,600	2,678	—
Sierra wgn 4d, 6P	3,600	2,716	—
Sierra wgn 4d, 8P	3,715	2,822	—
Suburban wgn 2d	3,605	2,599	—
D63-2 Royal V8 (wb 120.0)—48,780 built			
sdn 4d	3,475	2,513	—
Lancer htp sdn	3,625	2,697	—
Lancer htp cpe	3,505	2,583	—
Sierra wgn 4d, 6P	3,710	2,869	—
Sierra wgn 4d, 8P	3,800	2,974	—
Suburban wgn 2d	3,620	2,729	—
D63-3 Custom Royal V8 (wb 120.0)—49,293 built			
sdn 4d	3,520	2,623	—
Lancer htp sdn	3,675	2,807	—
Lancer htp cpe	3,505	2,693	—
conv cpe	3,630	2,913	—

1956 Engines	bore×stroke	bhp	availability
L6, 230.2	3.25×4.63	131	S-all 6s
V8, 270.0	3.63×3.25	189	S-Coronet V8
V8, 315.0	3.63×3.80	218	S-Royal, Custom Royal
V8, 315.0	3.63×3.80	230/260	O-all

1957

D72 Coronet L6 (wb 122.0)—160,979 built (includes D66 and D501)	Wght	Price	Prod
club sdn 2d	3,400	2,370	—
sdn 4d	3,470	2,451	—
D66 Coronet V8 (wb 122.0)			
club sdn 2d	3,530	2,478	—
sdn 4d	3,620	2,559	—
Lancer htp sdn	3,665	2,665	—
Lancer htp cpe	3,570	2,580	—
conv cpe	3,815	2,842	—
D501 Coronet D-500 V8 (wb 122.0)			
club sdn 2d	3,885	3,314	—
conv cpe	3,975	3,670	—
D67-1 Royal V8 (wb 122.0)—40,999 built			
sdn 4d	3,620	2,712	—
Lancer htp sdn	3,690	2,818	—
Lancer htp cpe	3,585	2,769	—
D67-2 Custom Royal V8 (wb 122.0)—55,149 built			
sdn 4d	3,690	2,881	—
Lancer htp sdn	3,750	2,991	—
Lancer htp cpe	3,670	2,920	—
conv cpe	3,810	3,146	—
D70 Station Wagon V8 (wb 122.0)—30,481 built (includes D71)			
Sierra wgn 4d, 6P	3,930	2,946	—
Sierra wgn 4d, 9P	4,015	3,073	—
Suburban wgn 2d	3,830	2,861	—
D71 Custom Station Wgn V8 (wb 122.0)			
Sierra wgn 4d, 6P	3,960	3,087	—
Sierra wgn 4d, 9P	4,030	3,215	—

1957 Engines	bore×stroke	bhp	availability
L6, 230.2	3.25×4.63	138	S-D72
V8, 325.0	3.69×3.80	245	S-all exc D72, D67-2, D501
V8, 325.0	3.69×3.80	260	S-D67-2
V8, 325.0	3.69×3.80	285/310	O-all (D-500)
V8, 354.0	3.94×3.63	340	O-all (D-500)

1956 Royal Lancer hardtop coupe

1957 Coronet convertible coupe

1958 Coronet Lancer hardtop coupe

1958

LD-1 Coronet L6 (wb 122.0)—77,388 built (includes LD-2 Coronet)	Wght	Price	Prod
club sdn 2d	3,360	2,449	—
sdn 4d	3,410	2,530	—
Lancer htp cpe	3,400	2,572	—
LD-2 Coronet V8 (wb 122.0)			
club sdn 2d	3,505	2,556	—
sdn 4d	3,555	2,637	—
Lancer htp sdn	3,605	2,764	—
Lancer htp cpe	3,540	2,679	—
conv cpe	3,725	2,942	—
LD-2 Royal V8 (wb 122.0)—15,165 built			
sdn 4d	3,570	2,797	—
Lancer htp sdn 4d	3,640	2,915	—
Lancer htp cpe	3,565	2,854	—
LD-3 Custom Royal V8 (wb 122.0)			
sdn 4d	3,640	3,030	
Lancer htp sdn	3,670	3,142	23,949
Lancer htp cpe	3,610	3,071	
conv cpe	3,785	3,298	
Regal Lancer htp cpe	3,650	3,245	1,163
LD-3 Station Wagon V8 (wb 122.0)–20,196 built			
Sierra wgn 4d, 6P	3,930	3,035	—
Sierra wgn 4d, 9P	3,990	3,176	—
Suburban wgn 2d	3,875	2,970	—
Custom Sierra wgn 4d, 6P	3,955	3,212	—
Custom Sierra wgn 4d, 9P	4,035	3,354	—

1958 Engines	bore×stroke	bhp	availability
L6, 230.2	3.25×4.63	138	S-Coronet 6
V8, 325.0	3.69×3.80	252	S-Coronet V8
V8, 325.0	3.69×3.80	265	S-Royal V8
V8, 350.0	4.06×3.38	285	S-Cus Royal, wgns
V8, 361.0	4.12×3.38	305/333	O-all (D-500)

1959

MD1-L Coronet L6 (wb 122.0)—96,782 built (includes MD2-L)		Wght	Price	Prod
21	club sdn 2d	3,375	2,516	—
23	Lancer htp cpe	3,395	2,644	—
41	sdn 4d	3,425	2,587	—
MD2-L Coronet V8 (wb 122.0)				
21	club sdn 2d	3,565	2,636	—
23	Lancer htp cpe	3,590	2,764	—
27	conv cpe	3,775	3,089	—
41	sdn 4d	3,615	2,707	—
43	Lancer htp sdn	3,620	2,842	—
MD3-M Royal V8 (wb 122.0)—14,807 built		**Wght**	**Price**	**Prod**
23	Lancer htp cpe	3,625	2,990	—
41	sdn 4d	3,640	2,934	—
43	Lancer htp sdn	3,690	3,069	—
MD3-H Custom Royal V8 (wb 122.0)—21,206 built				
23	Lancer htp cpe	3,675	3,201	—
27	conv cpe	3,820	3,422	—
41	sdn 4d	3,660	3,145	—
43	Lancer htp sdn	3,745	3,270	—
MD3-L Sierra V8 (wb 122.0)–23,590 built (includes Customs)				
45A	wgn 4d, 6P	3,940	3,103	—
45B	Sierra wgn 4d, 9P	4,015	3,224	—
MD3-H Custom V8 (wb 122.0)				
45A	wgn 4d, 6P	3,980	3,318	—
45B	wgn 4d, 9P	4,020	3,439	—

1959 Engines	bore×stroke	bhp	availability
L6, 230.2	3.25×4.63	138	S-Coronet 6
V8, 326.0	3.95×3.31	255	S-Coronet V8
V8, 361.0	4.12×3.38	295/305	S-all exc Coronet
V8, 383.0	4.25×3.38	320/345	O-all (D-500, Super D-500)

1960

PD3 Dart L6 (wb 118.0; wgns-122.0)		Wght	Price	Prod
L21	Seneca sdn 2d	3,385	2,278	
L41	Seneca sdn 4d	3,420	2,330	93,167
L45	Seneca wgn 4d	3,805	2,695	
M21	Pioneer sdn 2d	3,375	2,410	
M23	Pioneer htp cpe	3,410	2,488	
M41	Pioneer sdn 4d	3,430	2,459	36,434
M45A	Pioneer wgn 4d, 6P	3,820	2,787	
M45B	Pioneer wgn 4d, 9P	3,875	2,892	
H23	Phoenix htp cpe	3,410	2,618	
H27	Phoenix conv cpe	3,460	2,868	6,567
H41	Phoenix sdn 4d	3,420	2,595	
H43	Phoenix htp sdn	3,460	2,677	
PD4 Dart V8 (wb 118.0; wgns-122.0)				
L21	Seneca sdn 2d	3,530	2,397	
L41	Seneca sdn 4d	3,600	2,449	45,737
L45	Seneca wgn 4d	3,975	2,815	
M21	Pioneer sdn 2d	3,540	2,530	
M23	Pioneer htp cpe	3,610	2,607	
M41	Pioneer sdn 4d	3,610	2,578	74,655
M45A	Pioneer wgn 4d, 6P	4,000	2,906	
M45B	Pioneer wgn 4d, 9P	4,065	3,011	
H23	Phoenix htp cpe	3,605	2,737	
H27	Phoenix conv cpe	3,690	2,988	66,608
H41	Phoenix sdn 4d	3,610	2,715	
H43	Phoenix htp sdn	3,655	2,796	

PD1-L Matador (wb 122.0)—27,908 built		Wght	Price	Prod
23	htp cpe	3,705	2,996	—
41	sdn 4d	3,725	2,930	—
43	htp sdn	3,820	3,075	—
45A	wgn 4d, 6P	4,045	3,239	—
45B	wgn 4d, 9P	4,120	3,354	—
PD2-H Polara (wb 122.0)—16,728 built				
23	htp cpe	3,740	3,196	—
27	conv cpe	3,765	3,416	—
41	sdn 4d	3,735	3,141	—
43	htp sdn	3,815	3,275	—
45A	wgn 4d, 6P	4,085	3,506	—
45B	wgn 4d, 9P	4,220	3,621	—

1960 Engines	bore×stroke	bhp	availability
L6, 225.0	3.40×4.13	145	S-Dart 6
V8, 318.0	3.91×3.31	230	S-Seneca, Pioneer V8
V8, 318.0	3.91×3.31	255	S-Phoenix V8
V8, 361.0	4.12×3.38	295	S-Matador; O-Pioneer, Phoenix
V8, 383.0	4.25×3.38	325	S-Polara; O-Matador, Phoenix
V8, 383.0	4.25×3.38	330	O-Polara, Matador, Phoenix

1961

RW1-L Lancer 170 (wb 106.5)—25,508 built		Wght	Price	Prod
711	sdn 2d	2,585	1,979	—
713	sdn 4d	2,595	2,041	—
756	wgn 4d	2,760	2,354	—
RW1-H Lancer 770 (wb 106.5)—49,268 built				
723	htp cpe	2,595	2,164	—
731	spt cpe	2,643	2,075	—
733	sdn 4d	2,605	2,137	—
776	wgn 4d	2,775	2,449	—
RD3 Dart L6 (wb 118.0; wgns-122.0)				
L411	Seneca sdn 2d	3,290	2,278	60,527
L413	Seneca sdn 4d	3,335	2,330	
L456	Seneca wgn 4d	3,740	2,695	
M421	Pioneer sdn 2d	3,290	2,410	18,214
M422	Pioneer htp cpe	3,335	2,488	
M423	Pioneer sdn 4d	3,335	2,459	
M466	Pioneer wgn 4d, 6P	3,740	2,787	
M467	Pioneer wgn 4d, 9P	3,825	2,892	

		Wght	Price	Prod
H432	Phoenix htp cpe	3,325	2,618	4,273
H433	Phoenix sdn 4d	3,350	2,595	
H434	Phoenix htp sdn	3,385	2,677	
RD4 Dart V8 (wb 118.0; wgns-122.0)				
L511	Seneca sdn 2d	3,470	2,397	27,174
L513	Seneca sdn 4d	3,515	2,449	
L556	Seneca wgn 4d	3,920	2,815	
M521	Pioneer sdn 2d	3,460	2,530	39,054
M522	Pioneer htp cpe	3,500	2,607	
M523	Pioneer sdn 4d	3,510	2,578	
M566	Pioneer wgn 4d, 6P	3,940	2,906	
M567	Pioneer wgn 4d, 9P	4,005	3,011	
H532	Phoenix htp cpe	3,520	2,737	34,319
H533	Phoenix sdn 4d	3,535	2,715	
H534	Phoenix htp sdn	3,555	2,796	
H535	Phoenix conv cpe	3,580	2,988	
RD1-L Polara (wb 122.0)—14,032 built				
542	htp cpe	3,690	3,032	—
543	sdn 4d	3,700	2,966	—
544	htp sdn	3,740	3,110	—
545	conv cpe	3,765	3,252	—
578	wgn 4d, 6P	4,115	3,294	—
579	wgn 4d, 9P	4,125	3,409	—

1961 Engines	bore×stroke	bhp	availability
L6, 170.0	3.40×3.13	101	S-Lancer
L6, 225.0	3.40×4.13	145	S-Dart 6; O-Lancer
V8, 318.0	3.91×3.31	230	S-Dart V8
V8, 318.0	3.91×3.31	260	O-Dart V8
V8, 361.0	4.12×3.38	265	S-Polara
V8, 361.0	4.12×3.38	305	O-Dart V8 (D-500)
V8, 383.0	4.25 × 3.38	325	O-Polara (D-500), Dart V8
V8, 383.0	4.25 × 3.38	330	O-Polara, Dart V8 (ram ind)
V8, 413.0	4.19 × 3.75	350/375	O-Dart

1962

SL1-L Lancer 170 (wb 106.5)—19,780 built		Wght	Price	Prod
711	sdn 2d	2,495	1,951	—
713	sdn 4d	2,525	2,011	—
756	wgn 4d	2,685	2,306	—

1962 Polara 500 hardtop coupe

SL1-H Lancer 770 (wb 106.5)—30,888 built		Wght	Price	Prod
731	sdn 2d	2,520	2,052	—
733	sdn 4d	2,540	2,114	—
776	wgn 4d	2,705	2,408	—

SL1-P Lancer GT (wb 106.5)				
742	htp cpe	2,560	2,257	13,683

SD1 Dart L6 (wb 116.0)				
L401	Fleet Special sdn 2d	2,965	2,158	
L403	Fleet Special sdn 4d	2,995	2,214	
L411	sdn 2d	2,970	2,241	43,927
L413	sdn 4d	3,000	2,297	
L456	wgn 4d	3,270	2,644	
M421	330 sdn 2d	2,965	2,375	
M422	330 htp cpe	2,985	2,463	
M423	330 sdn 4d	3,000	2,432	11,606
M466	330 wgn 4d	3,275	2,739	
H432	440 htp cpe	3,025	2,606	
H433	440 sdn 4d	3,045	2,584	3,942

SD2 Dart V8 (wb 116.0)				
L501	Fleet Special sdn 2d	3,130	2,316	
L503	Fleet Special sdn 4d	3,165	2,372	
L511	sdn 2d	3,135	2,348	17,981
L513	sdn 4d	3,170	2,404	
L556	wgn 4d	3,435	2,751	
M521	330 sdn 2d	3,135	2,482	
M522	330 htp cpe	3,155	2,570	
M523	330 sdn 4d	3,170	2,540	26,544
M566	330 wgn 4d, 6P	3,435	2,848	
M567	330 wgn 4d, 9P	3,500	2,949	
H532	440 htp cpe	3,185	2,713	
H533	440 sdn 4d	3,205	2,691	
H534	440 htp sdn	3,260	2,763	
H535	440 conv cpe	3,285	2,945	42,360
H576	440 wgn 4d, 6P	3,460	2,989	
H577	440 wgn 4d, 9P	3,530	3,092	

SD2-P Polara 500 (wb 116.0)—12,268 built				
542	htp cpe	3,315	3,019	—
544	htp sdn	3,360	2,960	—
545	conv cpe	3,430	3,268	—

SD3-L Custom 880 (wb 122.0)—17,505 built				
612	htp cpe	3,615	3,030	—
613	sdn 4d	3,655	2,964	—
614	htp sdn	3,680	3,109	—
615	conv cpe	3,705	3,251	—
658	wgn 4d, 6P	4,025	3,292	—
659	wgn 4d, 9P	4,055	3,407	—

1962 Engines	bore×stroke	bhp	availability
L6, 170.0	3.40×3.13	101	S-Lancer
L6, 225.0	3.40×4.13	145	S-Dart 6; O-Lancer
V8, 318.0	3.91×3.31	230	S-Dart V8
V8, 318.0	3.91×3.31	260	O-Dart V8
V8, 361.0	4.12×3.38	265	S-Custom 880
V8, 361.0	4.12×3.38	305	S-Polara 500; O-Dart V8
V8, 413.0	4.19×3.75	410/420	O-Dart, Polara

1963

TL1-L Dart 170 (wb 111.0; wgns-106.0)—58,536 built		Wght	Price	Prod
711	sdn 2d	2,605	1,983	—
713	sdn 4d	2,625	2,041	—
756	wgn 4d	2,710	2,309	—

TL1-H Dart 270 (wb 111.0; wgns 106.0)—61,159 built				
731	sdn 2d	2,610	2,079	—
733	sdn 4d	2,635	2,135	—
735	conv cpe	2,740	2,385	—
776	wgn 4d	2,735	2,433	—

1963 440 four-door sedan

TL1-P Dart GT (wb 111.0)—34,227 built		Wght	Price	Prod
742	htp cpe	2,690	2,289	—
745	conv cpe	2,765	2,512	—

TD1-L 330 L6 (wb 119.0; wgns-116.0)—51,761 built				
401	Fleet Special sdn 2d	3,040	2,205	—
403	Fleet Special sdn 4d	3,065	2,261	—
411	sdn 2d	3,050	2,245	—
413	sdn 4d	3,070	2,301	—
456	wgn 4d, 2S	3,320	2,648	—
457	wgn 4d, 3S	3,380	2,749	—

TD1-M 440 L6 (wb 119.0; wgns-116.0)—13,146 built				
421	sdn 2d	3,050	2,381	—
422	htp cpe	3,050	2,470	—
423	sdn 4d	3,075	2,438	—

TD1-H Polara L6 (wb 119.0)—68,262 built				
432	htp cpe	3,105	2,624	—
433	sdn 4d	3,105	2,602	—

TD2-L 330 V8 (wb 119.0; wgns 116.0)—33,602 built				
601	Fleet Special sdn 2d	3,310	2,313	—
603	Fleet Special sdn 4d	3,335	2,369	—
611	sdn 2d	3,220	2,352	—
613	sdn 4d	3,245	2,408	—
656	wgn 4d, 2S	3,490	2,756	—
657	wgn 4d, 3S	3,550	2,857	—

TD2-M 440 V8 (wb 119.0; wgns 116.0)—49,591 built				
621	sdn 2d	3,215	2,489	—
622	htp cpe	3,245	2,577	—
623	sdn 4d	3,250	2,546	—
666	wgn 4d, 2S	3,495	2,854	—
667	wgn 4d, 3S	3,555	2,956	—

TD2-H Polara V8 (wb 119.0)—40,323 built				
632	htp cpe	3,255	2,732	—
633	sdn 4d	3,275	2,709	—
634	htp sdn	3,330	2,781	—
635	conv cpe	3,340	2,963	—

TD2-P Polara 500 V8 (wb 119.0)—7,256 built				
642	htp cpe	3,375	2,965	—
645	conv cpe	3,455	3,196	—

TA3 880 V8 (wb 122.0)				
E503	sdn 4d	3,800	2,815	
E556	wgn 4d, 6P	4,145	3,142	9,831
E557	wgn 4d, 9P	4,175	3,257	
L512	Custom htp cpe	3,825	3,030	
L513	Custom sdn 4d	3,815	2,964	
L514	Custom htp sdn	3,840	3,109	
L515	Custom conv cpe	3,845	3,251	18,435

		Wght	Price	Prod
L558	Custom htp wgn 4d, 2S	4,160	3,292	
L559	Custom htp wgn 4d, 3S	4,186	3,407	

1963 Engines	bore×stroke	bhp	availability
L6, 170.0	3.40×3.13	101	S-Dart
L6, 225.0	3.40×4.13	145	S-330/440/Polara 6; O-Dart
V8, 318.0	3.91×3.31	230	S-330, 440, Polara V8
V8, 361.0	4.13×3.38	265	S-880, Custom 880
V8, 383.0	4.25×3.38	305	S-Polara 500; O-others exc Dart
V8, 383.0	4.25×3.38	330	O-all exc Dart
V8, 413.0	4.19×3.75	360	O-880, Custom 880
V8, 426.0	4.25×3.75	415/425	O-all exc Dart (ram ind)

1964

VL1-L Dart 170 (wb 111.0; wgns-106.0)		Wght	Price	Prod
711	sdn 2d	2,615	1,988	L6: 74,625
713	sdn 4d	2,640	2,053	V8: 2,509
756	wgn 4d, 2S	2,740	2,315	
VL1-H Dart 270 (wb 111.0; wgns-106.0)				
731	sdn 2d	2,625	2,094	L6: 58,972
733	sdn 4d	2,645	2,160	V8: 7,097
735	conv cpe	2,735	2,389	
776	wgn 4d, 2S	2,745	2,414	
VL1-P Dart GT (wb 111.0)				
742	htp cpe	2,670	2,318	L6: 37,660
745	conv cpe	2,770	2,536	V8: 12,170
VD1-L 330 L6 (wb 119.0; wgns-116.0)—57,957 built				
411	sdn 2d	3,115	2,264	—
413	sdn 4d	3,145	2,317	—
456	wgn 4d, 2S	3,400	2,654	—
457	wgn 4d, 3S	3,475	2,755	—
VD1-M 440 L6 (wb 119.0)—15,147 built				
421	sdn 2d	3,110	2,401	—
422	htp cpe	3,120	2,483	—
423	sdn 4d	3,145	2,454	—
VD1-H Polara L6 (wb 119.0)—3,810 built				
432	htp cpe	3,135	2,637	—
433	sdn 4d	3,170	2,615	—
VD2-L 330 V8 (wb 119.0; wgns-116.0)—46,438 built				
611	sdn 2d	3,285	2,372	—
613	sdn 4d	3,325	2,424	—
656	wgn 4d, 2S	3,570	2,762	—
657	wgn 4d, 3S	3,620	2,863	—
VD2-M 440 V8 (wb 119.0; wgns-116.0)—68,861 built				
621	sdn 2d	3,280	2,508	—
622	htp cpe	3,295	2,590	—
623	sdn 4d	3,330	2,562	—
666	wgn 4d, 2S	3,585	2,861	—
667	wgn 4d, 3S	3,640	2,962	—
VD2-H Polara V8 (wb 119.0)—66,988 built				
632	htp cpe	3,320	2,745	—
633	sdn 4d	3,365	2,722	—
634	htp sdn	3,395	2,794	—
645	conv cpe	3,435	2,994	—
VD2-P Polara 500 V8 (wb 119.0)—17,787 built				
642	htp cpe	3,340	2,978	—
644	htp sdn	3,360	2,960	—
645	conv cpe	3,550	3,227	—
VA3 880 V8 (wb 122.0)				
E513	sdn 4d	3,795	2,826	10,526
E556	wgn 4d, 6P	4,165	3,155	
E557	wgn 4d, 9P	4,185	3,270	

		Wght	Price	Prod
L522	Custom htp cpe	3,765	3,043	21,234
L523	Custom sdn 4d	3,825	2,977	
L524	Custom htp sdn	3,860	3,122	
L525	Custom conv cpe	3,850	3,264	
L568	Custom htp wgn 4d, 2S	4,155	3,305	
L569	Custom htp wgn 4d, 3S	4,185	3,420	

1964 Engines	bore×stroke	bhp	availability
L6, 170.0	3.40×3.13	101	S-Dart
L6, 225.0	3.40×4.13	145	S-330/440/Polara 6;O-Dart
V8, 273.5	3.63×3.31	180	O-Dart
V8, 318.0	3.91×3.31	230	S-330, 440, Polara V8
V8, 361.0	4.13×3.38	265	S-880, Custom 880
V8, 383.0	4.25×3.38	305/330	O-all exc Dart
V8, 426.0	4.25×3.75	365	O-all exc Dart
V8, 426.0	4.25×3.75	415/425	O-all exc Dart (ram ind)

1965

AL1-L Dart 170 (wb 111.0; wgns-106.0)—86,013 built		Wght	Price	Prod
L11	sdn 2d	2,645	2,074	—
L13	sdn 4d	2,660	2,139	—
L56	wgn 4d	2,770	2,407	—
AL1-H Dart 270 (wb 111.0; wgns 106.0)—78,245 built				
L31	sdn 2d	2,650	2,180	—
L32	htp cpe	2,675	2,274	—
L33	sdn 4d	2,670	2,247	—
L35	conv cpe	2,765	2,481	—
L76	wgn 4d	2,770	2,506	—
AL1-P Dart GT (wb 111.0)—45,118 built				
L42	htp cpe	2,715	2,404	—
L45	conv cpe	2,795	2,628	—
AW1-L Coronet L6 (wb 117.0; wgns-116.0)*				
W11	Deluxe sdn 2d	3,090	2,257	—
W13	Deluxe sdn 4d	3,140	2,296	—
W21	sdn 2d	3,070	2,217	—
W23	sdn 4d	3,095	2,256	—
W56	Deluxe wgn 4d	3,390	2,592	—
AW1-H Coronet 440 L6 (wb 117.0; wgns-116.0)*				
W32	htp cpe	3,100	2,403	—
W33	sdn 4d	3,125	2,377	—
W35	conv cpe	3,230	2,622	—
W76	wgn 4d	3,395	2,674	—

1965 Dart GT convertible coupe

AW2-L Coronet V8 (wb 117.0; wgns-116.0)*		Wght	Price	Prod
W01	Hemi-Charger sdn 2d	3,165	—	—
W11	Deluxe sdn 2d	3,160	2,353	—
W13	Deluxe sdn 4d	3,210	2,392	—
W21	sdn 2d	3,145	2,313	—
W23	sdn 4d	3,195	2,352	—
W56	Deluxe wgn 4d	3,470	2,688	—
AW2-H Coronet 440 V8 (wb 117.0; wgns-116.0)*				
W32	htp cpe	3,180	2,499	—
W33	sdn 4d	3,230	2,473	—
W35	conv cpe	3,295	2,718	—
W76	wgn 4d, 6P	3,490	2,770	—
W77	wgn 4d, 9P	3,560	2,868	—
AW2-P Coronet 500 V8 (wb 117.0)—32,745 built				
W42	htp cpe	3,255	2,674	—
W45	conv cpe	3,340	2,894	—
AW2-L Polara V8 (wb 121.0)—12,705 built				
D12	htp cpe	3,850	2,837	—
D13	sdn 4d	3,905	2,806	—
D14	htp sdn	3,965	2,913	—
D15	conv cpe	3,940	3,131	—
D23	sdn 4d (318)	3,847	2,730	—
D56	wgn 4d, 6P	4,220	3,153	—
D57	wgn 4d, 9P	4,255	3,259	—
AD2-H Custom 880 V8 (wb 121.0)—44,496 built				
D32	htp cpe	3,945	3,085	—
D34	htp sdn	4,155	3,150	—
D35	conv cpe	3,965	3,335	—
D38	sdn 4d	3,915	3,010	—
D76	wgn 4d, 6P	4,270	3,422	—
D77	wgn 4d, 9P	4,355	3,527	—
AD2-P Monaco V8 (wb 121.0)				
D42	htp cpe	4,000	3,355	13,096

*Combined L6 and V8 production: Coronet 71,880; Coronet 440 104,767.

1965 Engines	bore×stroke	bhp	availability
L6, 170.0	3.40×3.13	101	S-Dart
L6, 225.0	3.40×4.13	145	S-Coronet/440 6; O-Dart
V8, 273.5	3.63×3.31	180	S-Coronet/440/500 V8s; O-Dart
V8, 273.5	3.63×3.31	235	O-Coronet/440/500 V8s, Dart
V8, 318.0	3.91×3.31	230	O-Coronet/440/500 V8s
V8, 361.0	4.12×3.38	265	O-Coronet/440/500 V8s
V8, 383.0	4.25×3.38	315	S-Monaco; O-Coronets
V8, 383.0	4.25×3.38	270	S-Polara, Custom 880
V8, 383.0	4.25×3.38	330	O-Coronet, 440, 500 V8s
V8, 413.0	4.19×3.75	340	O-Polara, Custom 880, Monaco
V8, 426.0	4.25×3.75	365	S-Hemi-Charger; O-others
V8, 426.0	4.25×3.75	425	S-Hemi-Charger 425

1966

BLL Dart (wb 111.0; wgns-106.0)—75,990 built		Wght	Price	Prod
1-21	sdn 2d, L6	2,670	2,094	—
2-21	sdn 2d, V8	2,860	2,222	—
1-41	sdn 4d, L6	2,695	2,158	—
2-41	sdn 4d, V8	2,895	2,286	—
1-45	wgn 4d, L6	2,780	2,436	—
2-45	wgn 4d, V8	2,990	2,564	—
BLH Dart 270 (wb 111.0; wgns 106.0)—69,996 built				
1-23	htp cpe, L6	2,720	2,307	—
2-23	htp cpe, V8	2,890	2,435	—
1-27	conv cpe, L6	2,805	2,570	—
2-27	conv cpe, V8	2,995	2,698	—
1-21	sdn 2d, L6	2,665	2,214	—
2-21	sdn 2d, V8	2,860	2,342	—

1966 Coronet 500 426 Hemi hardtop coupe

		Wght	Price	Prod
1-41	sdn 4d, L6	2,680	2,280	—
2-41	sdn 4d, V8	2,895	2,408	—
1-45	wgn 4d, L6	2,795	2,533	—
2-45	wgn 4d, V8	3,020	2,661	—
BLP Dart GT (wb 111.0)—30,041 built				
1-23	htp cpe, L6	2,735	2,417	—
2-23	htp cpe, V8	2,915	2,545	—
1-27	conv cpe, L6	2,830	2,700	—
2-27	conv cpe, V8	2,995	2,828	—
BWL Coronet (wb 117.0)—66,161 built				
1-21	sdn 2d, L6	3,055	2,264	—
2-21	sdn 2d, V8	3,215	2,358	—
1-41	sdn 4d, L6	3,077	2,306	—
2-41	sdn 4d, V8	3,245	2,396	—
1-21	Deluxe sdn 2d, L6	3,050	2,303	—
2-21	Deluxe sdn 2d, V8	3,215	2,391	—
1-41	Deluxe sdn 4d, L6	3,075	2,341	—
2-41	Deluxe sdn 4d, V8	3,240	2,435	—
1-45	Deluxe wgn 2d, L6	3,480	2,631	—
2-45	Deluxe wgn 2d, V8	3,595	2,725	—
BWH Coronet 440 (wb 117.0)—128,998 built				
1-23	htp cpe, L6	3,075	2,457	—
2-23	htp cpe, V8	3,235	2,551	—
1-27	conv cpe, L6	3,185	2,672	—
2-27	conv cpe, V8	3,310	2,766	—
1-41	sdn 4d, L6	3,095	2,432	—
2-41	sdn 4d, V8	3,220	2,526	—
1-45	wgn 4d, L6	3,515	2,722	—
2-45	wgn 4d, 2S, V8	3,585	2,816	—
2-46	wgn 4d, 3S, V8	3,680	2,926	—
BWP Coronet 500 (wb 117.0)—55,683 built				
1-23	htp cpe, L6	3,115	2,611	—
2-23	htp cpe, V8	3,275	2,705	—
1-27	conv cpe, L6	3,180	2,827	—
2-27	conv cpe, V8	3,345	2,921	—
1-41	sdn 4d, L6	3,120	2,586	—
2-41	sdn 4d, V8	3,280	2,680	—
BX2-P Charger (wb 117.0)				
29	htp cpe 4P	3,499	3,122	37,344
BD2-L Polara (wb 121.0)—107,832 built				
23	htp cpe	3,820	2,874	—
27	conv cpe	3,885	3,161	—
41	sdn 4d	3,860	2,838	—
41	sdn 4d (318)	3,765	2,763	—
43	htp sdn	3,880	2,948	—

		Wght	Price	Prod
45	wgn 4d, 2S	4,265	3,183	—
46	wgn 4d, 3S	4,295	3,286	—
BD2-H Monaco (wb 121.0)—49,773 built				
23	htp cpe	3,855	3,107	—
41	sdn 4d	3,890	3,033	—
43	htp sdn	4,835	3,170	—
45	wgn 4d, 2S	4,270	3,436	—
46	wgn 4d, 3S	4,315	3,539	—
BD2-P Monaco 500 (wb 121.0)				
23	htp cpe	3,895	3,604	10,840

1966 Engines	bore×stroke	bhp	availability
L6, 170.0	3.40×3.13	101	S-Dart 6s
L6, 225.0	3.40×4.13	145	S-Coronet 6; O-Dart 6
V8, 273.5	3.63×3.31	180	S-Coronet V8, Dart V8
V8, 273.5	3.63×3.31	235	O-Dart V8
V8, 318.0	3.91×3.31	230	S-Chrgr; O-Cor V8, Pol 318 sdn 4d
V8, 361.0	4.13×3.38	265	O-Charger, Coronet V8
V8, 383.0	4.25×3.38	270	S-Pol, Pol 500, Mon; O-Mon 500
V8, 383.0	4.25×3.38	325	S-Monaco 500; O-all exc Dart
V8, 426.0	4.25×3.75	425	O-Charger (max perf cam avail)
V8, 440.0	4.32×3.75	350	O-Pol, Pol 500, Mon, Mon 500

1967

CLL Dart (wb 111.0)—53,043 built		Wght	Price	Prod
1-21	sdn 2d, L6	2,710	2,187	—
2-21	sdn 2d, V8	2,895	2,315	—
1-41	sdn 4d, L6	2,725	2,224	—
2-41	sdn 4d, V8	2,910	2,352	—
CLH Dart 270 (wb 111.0)—63,227 built				
1-23	htp cpe, L6	2,725	2,388	—
2-23	htp cpe, V8	2,910	2,516	—
1-41	sdn 4d, L6	2,735	2,362	—
2-41	sdn 4d, V8	2,915	2,490	—
CLP Dart GT (wb 111.0)—38,225 built				
1-23	htp cpe, L6	2,750	2,499	—
2-23	htp cpe, V8	2,930	2,627	—
1-27	conv cpe, L6	2,850	2,732	—
2-27	conv cpe, V8	3,030	2,860	—
CWE Coronet (wb 117.0)—4,933 built				
1-45	wgn 4d, L6	3,485	2,622	—
2-45	wgn 4d, V8	3,650	2,716	—
CWL Coronet Deluxe (wb 117.0)—29,022 built				
1-21	sdn 2d, L6	3,045	2,359	—
2-21	sdn 2d, V8	3,210	2,453	—

		Wght	Price	Prod
1-41	sdn 4d, L6	3,070	2,397	—
2-41	sdn 4d, V8	3,235	2,491	—
1-45	wgn 2d, L6	3,495	2,693	—
2-45	wgn 2d, V8	3,625	2,787	—
CWH Coronet 440 (wb 117.0)—106,368 built				
1-23	htp cpe, L6	3,065	2,500	—
2-23	htp cpe, V8	3,235	2,594	—
1-27	conv cpe, L6	3,140	2,740	—
2-27	conv cpe, V8	3,305	2,834	—
1-41	sdn 4d, L6	3,060	2,475	—
2-41	sdn 4d, V8	3,225	2,569	—
1-45	wgn 4d, L6	3,495	2,771	—
2-45	wgn 4d, 2S, V8	3,605	2,865	—
2-46	wgn 4d, 3S, V8	3,705	2,975	—
CWP Coronet 500 (wb 117.0)—39,260 built (includes R/T)				
1-23	htp cpe, L6	3,115	2,679	—
2-23	htp cpe, V8	3,280	2,773	—
1-27	conv cpe, L6	3,190	2,919	—
2-27	conv cpe, V8	3,355	3,013	—
1-41	sdn 4d, L6	3,075	2,654	—
2-41	sdn 4d, V8	3,235	2,748	—
CW2-P Coronet R/T (wb 117.0)				
23	htp cpe, V8	3,565	3,199	—
27	conv cpe, V8	3,640	3,438	—
CW2-P Charger (wb 117.0)				
29	htp cpe 4P, V8	3,480	3,128	15,788
CD2-L Polara (wb 122.0)—69,798 built				
23	htp cpe	3,870	2,953	—
27	conv cpe	3,930	3,241	—
41	sdn 4d	3,885	2,915	—
41	sdn 4d (318)	3,765	2,843	—
43	htp sdn	3,920	3,028	—
45	wgn 4d, 2S	4,440	3,265	—
46	wgn 4d, 3S	4,450	3,368	—
CD2-M Polara 500 (wb 122.0)—5,606 built				
23	htp cpe	3,880	3,155	—
27	conv cpe	3,940	3,443	—
CD2-H Monaco (wb 122.0)—35,225 built				
23	htp cpe	3,885	3,213	—
41	sdn 4d	3,895	3,138	—
43	htp sdn	3,945	3,275	—
45	wgn 4d, 2S	4,425	3,543	—
46	wgn 4d, 3S	4,475	3,646	—
CD2-P Monaco 500 (wb 122.0)				
23	htp cpe	3,970	3,712	5,237

1966 Charger hardtop coupe

1968 Coronet 500 convertible coupe

1967 Engines	bore×stroke	bhp	availability
L6, 170.0	3.40×3.13	115	S-Dart 6
L6, 225.0	3.40×4.13	145	S-Coronet 6; O-Dart 6
V8, 273.5	3.63×3.31	180	S-Dart V8, Coronet V8
V8, 273.5	3.63×3.31	235	O-Dart V8
V8, 318.0	3.91×3.31	230	S-Chrgr, Polara 318; O-Cor V8
V8, 383.0	4.25×3.38	270	S-Polara, Monaco; O-Cor, Mon 500
V8, 383.0	4.25×3.38	325	S-Mon 500; O-Cor, Chrgr, Pol, Mon
V8, 426.0	4.25×3.75	425	O-Coronet R/T, Charger
V8, 440.0	4.32×3.75	350	O-Polara, Monaco
V8, 440.0	4.32×3.75	375	S-Cor R/T; O-Chrgr, Pol, Mon

1968

DLL Dart (wb 111.0)—60,250 built		Wght	Price	Prod
1-21	sdn 2d, L6	2,705	2,323	—
2-21	sdn 2d, V8	2,875	2,451	—
1-41	sdn 4d, L6	2,725	2,360	—
2-41	sdn 4d, V8	2,900	2,488	—
DLH Dart 270 (wb 111.0)—76,497 built				
1-23	htp cpe, L6	2,725	2,525	—
2-23	htp cpe, V8	2,885	2,653	—
1-41	sdn 4d, L6	2,710	2,499	—
2-41	sdn 4d, V8	2,900	2,627	—
DLP Dart GT (wb 111.0)—26,280 built				
1-23	htp cpe, L6	2,715	2,637	—
2-23	htp cpe, V8	2,895	2,675	—
1-27	conv cpe, L6	2,790	2,831	—
2-27	conv cpe, V8	2,970	2,959	—
DL2-S Dart GTS (wb 110.0)—8,745 built				
23	htp cpe, V8	3,065	3,189	—
27	conv cpe, V8	3,150	3,383	—
DWL Coronet Deluxe (wb 117.0)—46,299 built				
1-21	cpe, L6	3,015	2,487	—
2-21	cpe, V8	3,200	2,581	—
1-41	sdn 4d, L6	3,035	2,525	—
2-41	sdn 4d, V8	3,220	2,619	—
1-45	wgn 4d, L6	3,455	2,816	—
2-45	wgn 4d, V8	3,590	2,910	—
DWH Coronet 440 (wb 117.0)—116,348 built (includes Super Bee)				
1-21	cpe, L6	3,015	2,565	—
2-21	cpe, V8	3,200	2,671	—
1-23	htp cpe, L6	3,040	2,627	—
2-23	htp cpe, V8	3,225	2,733	—
1-41	sdn 4d, L6	3,035	2,603	—
2-41	sdn 4d, V8	3,320	2,709	—
1-45	wgn 4d, L6	3,450	2,924	—
2-45	wgn 4d, 2S, V8	3,585	3,030	—
2-46	wgn 4d, 3S, V8	3,680	3,140	—
DWH Coronet Super Bee (wb 117.0)				
M-21	cpe, V8	3,395	3,027	—
DW2-P Coronet 500 (wb 117.0)—40,139 built				
23	htp cpe, V8	3,260	2,879	—
27	conv cpe, V8	3,360	3,036	—
41	sdn 4d, V8	3,240	2,912	—
45	wgn 4d, 2S, V8	3,610	3,212	—
46	wgn 4d, 3S, V8	3,700	3,322	—
DW2-S Coronet R/T (wb 117.0)—10,849 built				
23	htp cpe, V8	3,530	3,379	—
27	conv cpe, V8	3,630	3,613	—
DX1-S Charger (wb 117.0)—96,108 built				
1P-29	htp cpe 4P, L6	3,100	2,934	—
2P-29	htp cpe 4P, V8	3,305	3,040	—
2X-29	R/T htp cpe, 4P, V8	3,575	3,506	—

DD2-L Polara (wb 122.0)—99,055 built		Wght	Price	Prod
23	htp cpe	3,700	3,027	—
27	conv cpe	3,755	3,288	—
41	sdn 4d	3,735	3,005	—
43	htp sdn	3,755	3,100	—
45	wgn 4d, 2S	4,155	3,388	—
46	wgn 4d, 3S	4,210	3,454	—
DD2-M Polara 500 (wb 122.0)—4,983 built				
23	htp cpe	3,740	3,226	—
27	conv cpe	3,780	3,487	—
DD2-H Monaco (wb 122.0)—37,412 built				
23	htp cpe	3,845	3,369	—
41	sdn 4d	3,885	3,294	—
43	htp sdn	3,910	3,432	—
45	wgn 4d, 2S	4,295	3,702	—
46	wgn 4d, 3S	4,360	3,835	—
DD2-P Monaco 500 (wb 122.0)				
23	htp cpe	3,885	3,869	4,568

1968 Engines	bore×stroke	bhp	availability
L6, 170.0	3.40×3.13	115	S-Dart 6
L6, 225.0	3.40×4.13	145	S-Coronet 6; O-Dart 6
V8, 273.5	3.63×3.31	190	S-Dart V8, Coronet V8
V8, 318.0	3.91×3.31	230	S-Chrgr, Pol; O-Dart V8, Cor V8
V8, 340.0	4.04×3.31	275	S-Dart GTS
V8, 383.0	4.25×3.38	300	O-Dart GTS
V8, 383.0	4.25×3.38	290	S-Mon; O-Cor V8, Chrgr, Pol
V8, 383.0	4.25×3.38	330	O-Cor V8, Chrgr, Pol, Mon
V8, 383.0	4.25×3.38	335	S-Coronet Super Bee
V8, 426.0	4.25×3.75	425	O-Cor R/T, Chrgr R/T; S-Chrgr Dayt
V8, 440.0	4.32×3.75	350	O-Polara & Monaco wgns
V8, 440.0	4.32×3.75	375	S-Cor R/T, Chrgr R/T; O-Pol, Mon

1969

LL Dart (wb 111.0)—106,329 built (includes Swinger 340)		Wght	Price	Prod
23	Swinger htp cpe	2,795	2,400	—
41	sdn 4d	2,810	2,413	—
LM Dart Swinger 340 (wb 111.0)				
23	htp cpe	3,097	2,836	—
LH Dart Custom (wb 110.0)—63,740 built				
23	htp cpe	2,795	2,577	—
41	sdn 4d	2,810	2,550	—
LP Dart GT (wb 111.0)—20,914 built				
23	htp cpe	2,800	2,672	—
27	conv cpe	2,905	2,865	—

1969 Charger R/T hardtop coupe

LS Dart GTS V8 (wb 110.0)—6,702 built		Wght	Price	Prod
23	htp cpe	3,105	3,226	—
27	conv cpe	3,210	3,419	—
WL Coronet Deluxe (wb 117.0)—23,988 built				
21	cpe	3,067	2,554	—
41	sdn 4d	3,097	2,589	—
45	wgn 4d	3,552	2,922	—
WH Coronet 440 (wb 117.0)—105,882 built				
21	cpe	3,067	2,630	—
23	htp cpe	3,097	2,692	—
41	sdn 4d	3,102	2,670	—
45	wgn 4d, 2S	3,557	3,033	—
46	wgn 4d, 3S, V8 only	3,676	3,246	—
WM Coronet Super Bee V8 (wb 117.0)—27,846 built				
21	cpe	3,440	3,076	—
23	htp cpe	3,470	3,138	—
WP Coronet 500 V8 (wb 117.0)—32,050 built				
23	htp cpe	3,171	2,929	—
27	conv cpe	3,306	3,069	—
41	sdn 4d	3,206	2,963	—
45	wgn 4d, 2S	3,611	3,280	—
46	wgn 4d, 3S	3,676	3,392	—
WS Coronet R/T (wb 117.0)—7,238 built				
23	htp cpe	3,601	3,442	—
27	conv cpe	3,721	3,660	—
XP/XS Charger (wb 117.0)				
XP29	htp cpe, L6	3,103	3,020	69,142
XP29	htp cpe, V8	3,256	3,126	
XS29	R/T htp cpe, V8	3,646	3,592	20,057
—	Daytona htp cpe, V8	—	4,000	505
XX Charger 500 V8 (wb 117.0)*				
XX29	htp cpe	3,671	3,860	—
DL Polara (wb 122.0)—83,122 built				
23	htp cpe	3,646	3,117	—
27	conv cpe	3,791	3,377	—
41	sdn 4d	3,701	3,095	—
43	htp sdn	3,731	3,188	—
45	wgn 4d, 2S	4,161	3,522	—
46	wgn 4d, 3S	4,211	3,629	—

DM Polara 500 (wb 122.0)—5,564 built		Wght	Price	Prod
23	htp cpe	3,681	3,314	—
27	conv cpe	3,801	3,576	—
DH Monaco (wb 122.0)—38,566 built				
23	htp cpe	3,811	3,528	—
41	sdn 4d	3,846	3,452	—
43	htp sdn	3,891	3,591	—
45	wgn 4d, 2S	4,306	3,917	—
46	wgn 4d, 3S	4,361	4,046	—

*Production included with XP 29 models

1969 Engines	bore×stroke	bhp	availability
L6, 170.0	3.40×3.13	115	S-Dart
L6, 225.0	3.40×4.13	145	S-Coronet Del/440; O-Dart
V8, 273.5	3.63×3.31	190	S-Dart V8
V8, 318.0	3.91×3.31	230	S-Cor Del/440/500, Chrgr, Pol; O-Dart
V8, 340.0	4.04×3.31	275	S-GTS, Swinger 340
V8, 383.0	4.25×3.38	290	S-Monaco; O-Polara, Chrgr, Coronet
V8, 383.0	4.25×3.38	330	O-GTS, Cor V8, Mon, Pol, Chrgr
V8, 383.0	4.25×3.38	335	S-Coronet Super Bee
V8, 426.0	4.25×3.75	425	O-Coronet R/T, Charger R/T, Daytona
V8, 440.0	4.32×3.75	350	O-Monaco & Polara wgns
V8, 440.0	4.32×3.75	375	S-Cor R/T, Chgr R/T, Daytona; O-Pol, Mon exc wagons
V8, 440.0	4.32×3.75	390	O-Coronet Super Bee

1970

LL Dart (wb 111.0)		Wght	Price	Prod
23	Swinger htp cpe	2,903	2,261	119,883
41	sdn 4d	2,900	2,308	35,499
LH Dart Custom (wb 111.0)				
23	htp cpe	2,898	2,463	17,208
41	sdn 4d	2,905	2,467	23,779
LM Dart Swinger 340 (wb 111.0)				
23	htp cpe	3,130	2,631	13,785
JH Challenger (wb 110.0)				
23	htp cpe	3,028	2,851	53,337
27	conv cpe	3,103	3,120	3,173
29	S.E. htp cpe	3,053	3,083	6,584

1970 Challenger R/T hardtop coupe

JS Challenger R/T (wb 110.0)		Wght	Price	Prod
23	htp cpe (inc T/A)	3,405	3,226	14,889
27	conv cpe	3,470	3,535	1,070
29	S.E. htp cpe	3,440	3,498	3,979
WL Coronet Deluxe (wb 117.0)				
21	cpe	3,150	2,669	2,978
41	sdn 4d	3,188	2,704	7,894
45	wgn 4d	3,675	3,048	3,694
WH Coronet 440 (wb 117.0)				
21	cpe	3,170	2,743	1,236
23	htp cpe	3,185	2,805	24,341
41	sdn 4d	3,190	2,783	33,258
45	wgn 4d	3,673	3,156	3,964
46	wgn 4d	3,775	3,368	3,772
WM Coronet Super Bee (wb 117.0)				
21	cpe	3,500	3,012	3,966
23	htp cpe	3,535	3,074	11,540
WP Coronet 500 (wb 117.0)				
23	htp cpe	3,235	3,048	8,247
27	conv cpe	3,345	3,188	924
41	sdn 4d	3,255	3,082	2,890
45	wgn 4d, 2S	3,715	3,404	1,657
46	wgn 4d, 3S	3,785	3,514	1,779
WS Coronet R/T (wb 117.0)				
23	htp cpe	3,545	3,569	2,319
27	conv cpe	3,610	3,785	296
XH/XP Charger (wb 117.0)				
XH29	htp cpe	3,293	3,001	39,431 (combined)
XP29	500 htp cpe	3,293	3,139	
XS/XX Charger R/T (wb 117.0)				
XS29	htp cpe	3,610	3,711	10,337 (combined)
XX29	Daytona htp cpe	3,710	3,993	
DE Polara (wb 122.0)*				
41	sdn 4d, L6	3,775	2,960	—
45	wgn 4d, 2S, V8	4,180	3,513	—
46	wgn 4d, 3S, V8	4,235	3,621	—
DL Polara "Deluxe" V8 (wb 122.0)				
23	htp cpe	3,770	3,224	*
27	conv cpe	3,830	3,527	842
41	sdn 4d	3,805	3,222	*
43	htp sdn	3,850	3,316	*
45	wgn 4d, 2S	4,180	3,670	*
46	wgn 4d, 3S	4,235	3,778	*
DM Polara Custom V8 (wb 122.0)*				
23	htp cpe	4,005	3,458	—
41	sdn 4d	3,975	3,426	—
43	htp sdn	3,925	3,528	—
DH Monaco (wb 122.0)				
23	htp cpe	3,950	3,679	3,522
41	sdn 4d	4,010	3,604	4,721
43	htp sdn	4,045	3,743	10,974
45	wgn 4d, 2S	4,420	4,110	2,211
46	wgn 4d, 3S	4,475	4,242	3,264

***Dodge combined production figures for most Polara models. Available figures are:**

		Prod
23	htp cpe (DL, DM)	15,243
27	conv cpe (DL)	842
41	sdn 4d (DE, DL, DM)	18,740
43	htp sdn (DL, DM)	19,223
45	wgn 4d, 2S (DE, DL)	3,074
46	wgn 4d, 3s (DE, DL)	3,546

1970 Engines	bore×stroke	bhp	availability
L6, 198.0	3.40×3.64	125	S-Dart
L6, 225.0	3.40×4.13	145	S-Chal/Cor/Chrgr/Polara 6s; O-Dart
V8, 318.0	3.91×3.31	230	S-Dart exc Swngr 340, Chal, Cor, Chrgr, Pol
V8, 340.0	4.04×3.31	275	S-Swngr 340; O-Chal
V8, 383.0	4.25×3.38	290	S-Mon, Pol Cus; O-Chal/Cor/Chrgr/Polara V8s
V8, 383.0	4.25×3.38	330	O-Chal, Cor, Pol, Pol Cus, Monaco
V8, 383.0	4.25×3.38	335	S-Super Bee, Chal R/T; O-Chal, Chrgr R/T
V8, 426.0	4.25×3.75	425	O-Chal, Super Bee, Cor/Chrgr R/Ts
V8, 440.0	4.32×3.75	350	O-Monaco, Polara, Polara Custom
V8, 440.0	4.32×3.75	375	S-Chrgr/Coronet/Challenger R/Ts
V8, 440.0	4.32×3.75	390	O-Chrgr/Cor/Chal R/Ts, Super Bee

1971

Dart (wb 111.0; fstbk cpes-108.0)		Wght	Price	Prod
LL29	Demon fstbk cpe	2,845	2,343	69,861
LL23	Swinger Special htp cpe	2,900	2,402	13,485
LL41	sdn 4d	2,900	2,450	32,711
LH23	Swinger htp cpe	2,900	2,561	102,480
LH41	Custom sdn 4d	2,900	2,609	21,785
LM29	Demon fstbk 340 cpe V8	3,165	2,721	10,098
Challenger (wb 110.0)				
JL23	cpe	3,050	2,727	23,088 (combined)
JH23	htp cpe	3,092	2,848	
JH27	conv cpe	3,180	3,105	2,165
JS23	R/T htp cpe V8	3,495	3,273	4,630

1971 Challenger R/T hardtop coupe

1972 Polara Custom hardtop sedan

Coronet (wb 118.0)		Wght	Price	Prod
WL41	sdn 4d	3,302	2,777	11,794
WL45	wgn 4d 2S	3,778	3,101	5,470
WH41	Custom sdn 4d	3,308	2,951	37,817
WH45	Custom wgn 4d 2S	3,812	3,196	5,365
WH46	Custom wgn 4d 3S V8	3,890	3,454	5,717
WP41	Brougham sdn 4d V8	3,475	3,232	4,700
WP45	Crestwood wgn 4d 2S V8	3,845	3,601	2,884
WP46	Crestwood wgn 4d 3S V8	3,900	3,682	3,981
Charger (wb 115.0)				
WL21	cpe	3,270	2,707	46,183
WH23	htp cpe	3,138	2,975	
WP23	500 htp cpe V8	3,350	3,223	11,948
WM23	Super Bee htp cpe V8	3,640	3,271	5,054
WP29	SE htp cpe V8	3,375	3,422	15,811
WS23	R/T htp cpe V8	3,685	3,777	3,118
Polara (wb 122.0)				
DE41	sdn 4d	3,788	3,298	16,444
DE23	htp cpe	3,755	3,319	11,500
DE43	htp sdn V8	3,875	3,497	2,487
DL41	Custom sdn 4d V8	3,835	3,593	13,850
DL43	Custom htp sdn V8	3,875	3,681	17,458
DL23	Custom htp cpe V8	3,805	3,614	9,682
DL45	Custom wgn 4d 2S V8	4,280	3,992	9,682
DL46	Custom wgn 4d 3S V8	4,335	4,098	
DM43	Brougham htp sdn V8	4,035	3,884	2,570
DM23	Brougham htp cpe V8	3,965	3,818	2,024
Monaco (wb 122.0)				
DH41	sdn 4d	4,050	4,223	16,900
DH43	htp sdn	4,080	4,362	
DH23	htp cpe	4,000	4,298	3,195
DH45	wgn 4d 2S	4,525	4,689	5,449
DH46	wgn 4d 3S	4,585	4,821	

1971 Engines	bore×stroke	bhp	availability
L6, 198.0	3.40×3.64	125	S-Dart,Chal JL
L6, 225.0	3.40×4.13	145	S-Chal JH,Cor,Chrgr,Pol; O-Dart,Chal JL
V8, 318.0	3.91×3.31	230	S-Chal,Cor,Chrgr,Pol; O-Dart
V8, 340.0	4.04×3.31	275	S-Demon 340; O-Chal
V8, 360.0	4.00×3.58	255	O-Polara
V8, 383.0	4.25×3.38	275	S-Chal RT,Chrgr SuperBee, Pol B'ham, Mon; O-Chal, Cor, Chrgr, Pol
V8, 383.0	4.25×3.38	300	O-Chal,Cor,Chrgr,Pol,Mon
V8, 426.0	4.25×3.75	335	O-Polara, Monaco
V8, 426.0	4.25×3.75	425	O-Charger,Challenger
V8, 440.0	4.32×3.75	335	O-Polara,Monaco
V8, 440.0	4.32×3.75	370	S-Charger RT; O-Charger
V8, 440.0	4.32×3.75	385	O-Challenger, Charger

1972

Dart (wb 111.0; fstbk cpes 108.0)		Wght	Price	Prod
LL29	Demon fstbk cpe	2,800	2,316	39,880
LL23	Swinger Special htp cpe	2,845	2,373	19,210
LL41	sdn 4d	2,855	2,420	26,019
LH23	Swinger htp cpe	2,835	2,528	119,618
LH41	Custom sdn 4d	2,855	2,574	49,941
LM29	Demon 340 fstbk cpe V8	3,125	2,759	8,750
Challenger (wb 110.0)				
JH23	cpe	3,098	2,790	18,535
JS23	Rallye htp cpe V8	3,225	3,082	8,123

Coronet (wb 118.0)		Wght	Price	Prod
WL41	sdn 4d	3,362	2,721	11,293
WL45	wgn 4d 2S V8	3,795	3,209	
WH45	Custom wgn 4d 2S V8	3,800	3,382	5,452
WH46	Custom wgn 4d 3S V8	3,840	3,460	
WH41	Custom sdn 4d	3,370	2,998	43,132
WP45	Crestwood wgn 4d 2S V8	3,810	3,604	6,471
WP46	Crestwood wgn 4d 3S V8	3,850	3,683	
Charger (wb 115.0)				
WL21	cpe	3,278	2,652	7,803
WH23	htp cpe	3,292	2,913	45,361
WP29	SE htp cpe V8	3,390	3,249	22,430
Polara (wb 122.0)				
DL41	sdn 4d	3,835	3,618	25,187
DL43	htp sdn	3,875	3,709	8,212
DL23	htp cpe	3,800	3,641	7,000
DM41	Custom sdn 4d	3,845	3,808	19,739
DM43	Custom htp sdn	3,890	3,898	22,505
DM23	Custom htp cpe	3,815	3,830	15,039
DM45	Custom wgn 4d 2S	4,320	4,262	3,497
DM46	Custom wgn 4d 3S	4,370	4,371	7,660
Monaco (wb 122.0)				
DP41	sdn 4d	3,980	4,095	6,474
DP43	htp sdn	4,030	4,216	15,039
DP23	htp cpe	3,960	4,153	7,786
DP45	wgn 4d 2S	4,445	4,627	2,569
DP46	wgn 4d 3S	4,490	4,756	5,145

1972 Engines	bore×stroke	bhp	availability
L6, 198.0	3.40×3.64	100	S-Dart
L6, 225.0	3.40×4.13	100	O-Dart
L6, 225.0	3.40×4.13	110	S-Chal,Cor,Chrgr; O-Dart
V8, 318.0	3.91×3.31	150	S-Chal,Cor,Chrgr,Pol; O-Dart
V8, 340.0	4.04×3.31	240	S-Demon 340; O-Dart, Chal,Chrgr
V8, 360.0	4.00×3.58	175	S-Mon; O-Pol
V8, 400.0	4.34×3.38	190	O-Chrgr,Pol,Mon
V8, 400.0	4.34×3.38	250	O-Pol,Mon
V8, 400.0	4.34×3.38	255	O-Charger
V8, 440.0	4.32×3.75	230	O-Monaco
V8, 440.0	4.32×3.75	235	O-Polara
V8, 440.0	4.32×3.75	280	O-Monaco
V8, 440.0	4.32 × 3.75	285	O-Pol, Mon
V8, 440.0	4.32 × 3.75	330	O-Cor, Chrgr

1973

Dart (wb 111.0; fstbk cpes-108.0)		Wght	Price	Prod
LL29	Sport fstbk cpe	2,850	2,424	68,113
LL23	Swinger Special htp cpe	2,895	2,462	17,480

1975 Coronet Brougham hardtop coupe

		Wght	Price	Prod
LL41	sdn 4d	2,910	2,504	21,539
LH23	Swinger htp cpe	2,890	2,617	107,619
LH41	Custom sdn 4d	2,910	2,658	62,626
LM29	340 fstbk cpe V8	3,205	2,853	11,315
Challenger (wb 110.0)				
JH23	htp cpe V8	3,155	3,011	32,596
Coronet (wb 118.0)				
WL41	sdn 4d	3,472	2,867	14,395
WL45	wgn 4d 2S V8	3,955	3,314	4,874
WH41	Custom sdn 4d	3,962	3,017	46,491
WH45	Custom wgn 4d 2S V8	3,955	3,442	
WH46	Custom wgn 4d 3S V8	4,000	3,560	13,018 (WH45, WH46)
WP45	Crestwood wgn 4d 2S V8	3,970	3,671	
WP46	Crestwood wgn 4d 3S V8	4,005	3,791	8,755 (WP45, WP46)
Charger (wb 115.0)				
WL21	cpe	3,428	2,810	11,995
WH23	htp cpe	3,465	3,060	45,415
WP29	SE htp cpe V8	3,540	3,375	61,908
Polara (wb 122.0)				
DL41	sdn 4d	3,865	3,729	15,015
DL23	htp cpe	3,835	3,752	6,432
DL45	wgn 4d 2S	4,420	4,186	3,327
DM41	Custom sdn 4d	3,870	3,911	23,939
DM43	Custom htp sdn	3,905	4,001	29,341
DM23	Custom htp cpe	3,835	3,928	17,406
DM45	Custom wgn 4d 2S	4,440	4,370	3,702
DM46	Custom wgn 4d 3S	4,485	4,494	8,839
Monaco (wb 122.0)				
DP41	sdn 4d	4,020	4,218	6,316
DP43	htp sdn	4,060	4,339	9,031
DP23	htp cpe	3,985	4,276	6,133
DP45	wgn 4d 2S	4,470	4,730	2,337
DP46	wgn 4d 3S	4,515	4,859	5,579

1973 Engines	bore×stroke	bhp	availability
L6, 198.0	3.40×3.64	95	S-Dart
L6, 225.0	3.40×4.13	105	S-Cor,Chrgr; O-Dart
V8, 318.0	3.91×3.31	150	S-Chal,Cor,Chrgr, Pol exc wgns; O-Dart
V8, 340.0	4.04×3.31	240	S-Dart Sport 340; O-Chal,Cor,Chrgr
V8, 360.0	4.00×3.58	170	S-Pol wgns, Mon; O-Pol
V8, 400.0	4.34×3.38	175	O-Coronet, Charger
V8, 400.0	4.34×3.38	185	S-Mon wgns; O-Pol, Mon
V8, 400.0	4.34×3.38	220	O-Polara, Monaco
V8, 400.0	4.34×3.38	260	O-Coronet, Charger
V8, 440.0	4.32×3.75	220	O-Polara, Monaco
V8, 440.0	4.32×3.75	280	O-Coronet, Charger

1974

Dart (wb 111.0; fstbk cpes-108.0)		Wght	Price	Prod
LL29	Sport fstbk cpe	2,990	2,878	59,567
LL23	Swinger Special htp cpe	3,035	2,918	16,155
LH23	Swinger htp cpe	3,030	3,077	89,242
LL41	sdn 4d	3,055	2,961	
LH41	Custom sdn 4d	3,055	3,119	78,216 (LL41, LH41)
LM29	360 fstbk cpe V8	3,330	3,320	3,951
LP41	Special Edition sdn 4d	3,641	3,837	
LP23	Special Edition htp cpe	3,599	3,794	12,385 (LP41, LP23)
Challenger (wb 110.0)				
JH23	htp cpe V8	3,225	3,143	16,437
Coronet (wb 118.0)				
WL41	sdn 4d	3,548	3,271	8,752
WL45	wgn 4d 2S V8	4,085	3,699	2,968
WH41	Custom sdn 4d	3,538	3,374	36,021
WH45	Custom wgn 4d 2S V8	4,090	3,882	2,975
WH46	Custom wgn 4d 3S V8	4,130	4,196	4,950
WP45	Crestwood wgn 4d 2S V8	4,100	4,117	1,916
Wp46	Crestwood wgn 4d 3S V8	4,135	4,433	3,146
Charger (wb 115.0)				
WL21	cpe	3,510	3,212	8,876
WH23	htp cpe	3,528	3,412	29,101
WP29	SE htp cpe V8	3,625	3,742	36,399
Monaco (wb 122.0; wgns-124.0)				
DM41	sdn 4d	4,170	4,259	9,101
DM23	htp cpe	4,150	4,283	3,347
DM45	wgn 4d 2S	4,760	4,706	1,583
DH41	Custom sdn 4d	4,175	4,446	12,655
DH43	Custom htp sdn	4,205	4,539	10,585
DH23	Custom htp cpe	4,155	4,464	6,649
DH45	Custom wgn 4d 2S	4,770	4,839	1,253
DH46	Custom wgn 4d 3S	4,815	4,956	3,272
DP41	Brougham sdn 4d	4,410	4,891	3,954
DP43	Brougham htp sdn	4,445	4,999	5,649
DP23	Brougham htp cpe	4,370	4,951	4,863
DP45	Brougham wgn 4d 2S	4,860	5,360	1,042
DP46	Brougham wgn 4d 3S	4,905	5,477	2,718

1974 Engines	bore×stroke	bhp	availability
L6, 198.0	3.40×3.64	95	S-Dart exc SE
L6, 225.0	3.40×4.13	105	S-Dart SE, Cor; O-Dart
V8, 318.0	3.91×3.31	150	S-Chal,Cor,Chrgr; O-Dart
V8, 360.0	4.00×3.58	180	S-Mon exc B'ham/wgns; O-Chrgr
V8, 360.0	4.00×3.58	200	O-Cor,Chrgr,Mon exc B'ham,wgn
V8, 360.0	4.00×3.58	245	S-Dart 360; O-Chal,Chrgr
V8, 400.0	4.34×3.38	185	S-Mon B'ham,wgns; O-Cor,Chrgr
V8, 400.0	4.34×3.38	205	O-Coronet, Charger
V8, 400.0	4.34×3.38	240	O-Monaco exc wagons
V8, 400.0	4.34×3.38	250	O-Coronet, Charger
V8, 440.0	4.32×3.75	230	O-Monaco exc wagons
V8, 440.0	4.32×3.75	250	O-Monaco wagons
V8, 440.0	4.32×3.75	275	O-Coronet, Charger

1975

Dart (wb 111.0; fstbk cpes-108.0)		Wght	Price	Prod
LL29	Sport fstbk cpe	2,980	3,297	50,312
LM29	360 fstbk cpe V8	3,335	4,014	1,043
LL23	Swinger Special htp cpe	3,045	3,341	9,304
LL41	sdn 4d	3,060	3,269	24,193
LH23	Swinger htp cpe	3,035	3,518	45,495
LH41	Custom sdn 4d	3,060	3,444	60,818
LP23	Special Edition htp cpe	3,260	4,232	5,680
LP41	Special Edition sdn 4d	3,280	4,159	13,194
Coronet (wb 117.5; htps-115.0)				
WL41	sdn 4d	3,652	3,641	8,138
WL21	htp cpe	3,620	3,591	6,058
WL45	wgn 4d 2S V8	4,185	4,358	2,852
WH41	Custom sdn 4d	3,692	3,754	26,219
WH23	Custom htp cpe	3,702	3,777	18,513
WH45	Custom wgn 4d 2S V8	4,240	4,560	2,623
WH46	Custom wgn 4d 3S V8	4,290	4,674	5,052
WP23	Brougham htp cpe V8	3,800	4,154	10,292
WP45	Crestwood wgn 4d 2S V8	4,230	4,826	1,784
WP46	Crestwood wgn 4d 3S V8	4,290	4,918	2,967
Charger (wb 115.0)				
XS22	SE htp cpe	3,950	4,903	30,812

Monaco (wb 121.5; wgns-124.0)		Wght	Price	Prod
DM41	sdn 4d	4,280	4,605	7,097
DM23	htp cpe	4,225	4,631	2,116
DH41	Royal sdn 4d	4,285	4,848	10,126
DH43	Royal htp sdn	4,310	4,951	8,117
DH23	Royal htp cpe	4,240	4,868	4,001
DP41	Royal Brougham sdn 4d	4,455	5,262	5,126
DP43	Royal Brougham htp sdn	4,485	5,382	5,964
DP29	Royal Brougham htp cpe	4,370	5,460	
DM45	wgn 4d 2S	4,885	5,109	1,547
DH45	Royal wgn 4d 2S	4,905	5,292	1,279
DH46	Royal wgn 4d 3S	4,945	5,415	2,666
DP45	Royal Brougham wgn 4d 2S	4,980	5,779	1,165
DP46	Royal Brougham wgn 4d 3S	5,025	5,905	2,909

1975 Engines	bore×stroke	bhp	availability
L6, 225.0	3.40×4.13	95	S-Dart, Coronet
V8, 318.0	3.91×3.31	135	O-Charger
V8, 318.0	3.91×3.31	145	O-Dart
V8, 318.0	3.91×3.31	150	S-Cor;O-Chrgr, Monaco
V8, 360.0	4.00×3.58	180	S-Chrgr,Mon exc B'ham wgns; O-Cor, Ryl Monaco B'ham
V8, 360.0	4.00×3.58	190	O-Chrgr,Ryl Monaco B'ham
V8, 360.0	4.00×3.58	230	S-Dart 360
V8, 400.0	4.34×3.38	165/190/235	O-Coronet, Charger
V8, 400.0	4.34×3.38	175	S-Ryl Mon B'ham; O-Mon
V8, 400.0	4.34×3.38	185	O-Charger
V8, 400.0	4.34×3.38	195	O-Monaco
V8, 440.0	4.32×3.75	195	O-Monaco exc Ryl B'ham
V8, 440.0	4.32×3.75	215	O-all Monaco

1976

Dart (wb 111.0; fstbk cpe-108.0)		Wght	Price	Prod
LL29	Sport fstbk cpe	2,990	3,258	18,873
LL23	Swinger Special htp cpe	3,050	3,337	3,916
LL41	sdn 4d	3,070	3,295	34,864
LH23	Swinger htp cpe	3,035	3,510	10,885
Aspen (wb 112.7; cpes-108.7)				
NL41	sdn 4d	3,252	3,371	17,573
NL29	cpe	3,222	3,336	27,730
NL45	wgn 5d 2S	3,605	3,658	37,642
NH41	Custom sdn 4d	3,240	3,553	32,163
NH29	Custom cpe	3,232	3,518	23,782
NP41	SE sdn 4d	3,470	4,440	24,378
NP29	SE cpe	3,432	4,413	21,564
NH45	SE wgn 5d 2S	3,630	3,988	34,617

Coronet (wb 117.5; htps-115.0)		Wght	Price	Prod
WL41	sdn 4d	3,742	3,770	15,658
WL45	wgn 4d 2S V8	4,285	4,634	2,632
WL46	wgn 4d 3S V8	4,350	4,776	3,336
WH41	Brougham sdn 4d	3,760	4,059	15,215
WH45	Crestwood wgn 4d 2S V8	4,285	5,023	1,725
WH46	Crestwood wgn 4d 3S V8	4,360	5,165	2,597
Charger (wb 115.0)				
WL23	htp cpe	3,712	3,736	9,906
WH23	cpe	3,718	4,025	13,826
XS22	SE htp cpe V8	3,945	4,763	42,168
Monaco (wb 121.5; wgns-124.0)				
DM41	sdn 4d	4,160	4,388	6,221
DM45	wgn 4d 2S	4,910	4,948	1,116
DH41	Royal sdn 4d	4,325	4,763	11,320
DH23	Royal htp cpe	4,280	4,778	2,915
DH45	Royal wgn 4d 2S	4,915	5,241	923
DH46	Royal wgn 4d 3S	4,950	5,364	1,429
DP41	Royal Brougham sdn 4d	4,520	5,211	5,111
DP29	Royal Brougham htp cpe	4,430	5,382	4,076
DP46	Royal Brougham wgn 4d 3S	4,995	5,869	2,480

1976 Engines	bore×stroke	bhp	availability
L6, 225.0	3.40×4.13	100	S-all sixes
V8, 318.0	3.91×3.31	150	S-Asp,Cor exc wgns,Chrgr, Mon exc Wgns/Ryl; O-Dart
V8, 360.0	4.00×3.58	170	S-Cor wgns, Ryl Mon; O-Asp,Cor,Chrgr,Ryl Mon B'ham
V8, 360.0	4.00×3.58	175	O-Coronet, Charger
V8, 360.0	4.00×3.58	220	O-Dart, Coronet
V8, 400.0	4.34×3.38	175	S-Mon wgns/Ryl B'hams; O-Cor,Chrgr,Monaco
V8, 400.0	4.34×3.38	185/240	O-Coronet, Charger
V8, 400.0	4.34×3.38	210	O-Monaco
V8, 400.0	4.34×3.38	255	O-Coronet
V8, 440.0	4.32×3.75	205	O-Monaco

1977

Aspen (wb 112.7; cpes-108.7)		Wght	Price	Prod
NL41	sdn 4d	3,290	3,631	32,662
NL29	cpe	3,235	3,582	33,102
NL45	wgn 5d 2S	3,492	3,953	67,294
NH41	Custom sdn 4d	3,295	3,813	45,697
NH29	Custom cpe	3,240	3,764	29,946
NP41	SE sdn 4d	3,492	4,366	25,949
NP29	SE cpe	3,428	4,317	19,985

1976 Aspen Special Edition four-door sedan

1977 Aspen R/T coupe

		Wght	Price	Prod
NH45	SE wgn 5d 2S	3,518	4,283	58,011
Charger (wb 115.0)				
XS22	SE htp cpe V8	3,895	5,098	42,542
Monaco (wb 117.4; htps-115.0)				
WL41	sdn 4d	3,772	3,988	20,633
WL23	htp cpe	3,630	3,911	14,054
WS23	Special htp cpe	NA	3,995	NA
WL45	wgn 4d 2S V8	4,335	4,724	3,896
WL46	wgn 4d 3S V8	4,395	4,867	4,594
WH41	Brougham sdn 4d	3,782	4,217	17,224
WH23	Brougham htp cpe	3,752	4,146	14,430
WH45	Crestwood wgn 4d 2S V8	4,330	5,224	1,948
WH46	Crestwood wgn 4d 3S V8	4,405	5,367	3,301
Diplomat (wb 112.7)				
GH41	sdn 4d	3,560	5,101	9,647
GH22	cpe	3,510	4,943	14,023
GP41	Medallion sdn 4d	3,675	5,471	4,667
GP22	Medallion cpe	3,615	5,313	9,215
Royal Monaco (wb 121.5; wgns-124.0)				
DM41	sdn 4d	4,125	4,716	12,646
DM23	htp cpe	4,050	4,731	3,360
DM45	wgn 4d 2S	4,905	5,353	2,010
DH41	Brougham sdn 4d	4,270	4,996	21,440
DH23	Brougham htp cpe	4,205	5,011	8,309
DH45	Brougham wgn 4d 2S	4,900	5,607	1,418
DH46	Brougham wgn 4d 3S	4,935	5,730	4,251

1977 Engines	bore×stroke	bhp	availability
L6, 225.0	3.40×4.13	100	S-Aspen exc wgns
L6, 225.0	3.40×4.13	110	S-Asp wgns, Mon; O-Aspen
V8, 318.0	3.91×3.31	145	S-Asp,Dip,Mon exc wgns, Chrgr, Ryl Mon
V8, 318.0	3.91×3.31	135	O-Mon,Chrgr
V8, 360.0	4.00×3.58	155	S-Mon wgns,Ryl Mon B'ham;O-Asp,Mon,Chrgr,Ryl Mon
V8, 360.0	4.00×3.58	160	O-Monaco, Charger
V8, 360.0	4.00×3.58	175	O-Aspen
V8, 400.0	4.34×3.38	190	S-Ryl Mon wgns; O-Mon, Chrgr, Ryl Mon
V8, 440.0	4.32×3.75	195	O-Ryl Mon

1978

Omni (wb 99.2)		Wght	Price	Prod
ZL44	htchbk sdn 5d	2,145	3,976	81,611
Aspen (wb 112.7; cpe-108.7)				
NL41	sdn 4d	3,235	3,911	60,191
NL29	cpe	3,195	3,783	75,599
NL45	wgn 5d 2S	3,448	4,253	61,917
Charger/Magnum (wb 114.9)				
XP22	Charger SE htp cpe V8	3,895	5,368	2,800
XS22	Magnum XE htp cpe V8	3,895	5,509	55,431
Monaco (wb 117.4; cpes-114.9)				
WL41	sdn 4d	3,760	4,344	20,292
SL23	htp cpe	3,738	4,254	10,291
WL45	wgn 4d 2S V8	4,310	5,103	2,376
WL46	wgn 4d 3S V8	4,375	5,246	2,944
WH41	Brougham sdn 4d	3,775	4,568	8,665
WH23	Brougham htp cpe	3,742	4,507	6,842
WH45	Crestwood wgn 4d 2S V8	4,305	5,549	1,329
WH46	Crestwood wgn 4d 3S V8	4,380	5,692	2,112
Diplomat (wb 112.7)				
GM41	S sdn 4d	3,438	4,937	1,667
GM22	S cpe	3,358	4,771	1,655
GH41	sdn 4d	3,508	5,187	21,094
GH22	cpe	3,462	5,021	19,000
GH45	wgn 5d 2S	3,598	5,538	11,226
GP41	Medallion sdn 4d	3,592	5,569	11,628
GP22	Medallion cpe	3,538	5,403	12,372

1978 Engines	bore×stroke	bhp	availability
L4, 104.7	3.13×3.40	70/75	S-Omni
L6, 225.0	3.40×4.13	90	O-Asp exc wgns, Dip
L6, 225.0	3.40×4.13	100	S-Aspen exc wgns
L6, 225.0	3.40×4.13	110	S-Asp wgns; O-Asp,Dip,Mon
V8, 318.0	3.91×3.31	140	S-Asp,Dip,Mag,Mon exc wgns
V8, 318.0	3.91×3.31	150	S-Charger
V8, 318.0	3.91×3.31	155	O-Asp,Dip,Mag,Mon
V8, 360.0	4.00×3.58	155	S-Mon wgns; O-Asp,Dip, Mag,Mon
V8, 360.0	4.00×3.58	165	O-Aspen
V8, 360.0	4.00×3.58	170	O-Dip,Mag,Mon,Chrgr
V8, 360.0	4.00×3.58	175	O-Aspen,Chrgr
V8, 400.0	4.34×3.38	190	O-Magnum, Monaco
V8, 400.0	4.34×3.38	175/185/ 240	O-Charger

1979

Omni (wb 99.2; 024-96.7)		Wght	Price	Prod
ZL44	htchbk sdn 5d	2,135	4,469	84,093
ZL24	024 htchbk cpe 3d	2,195	4,864	57,384
Aspen (wb 112.7; cpe-108.7)				
NL41	sdn 4d	3,175	4,516	62,568
NL29	cpe	3,110	4,399	42,833
NL45	wgn 5d 2S	3,380	4,838	38,183
Magnum (wb 114.9)				
XS22	XE htp cpe V8	3,675	6,039	30,354
Diplomat (wb 112.7)				
GM41	sdn 4d	3,378	5,336	10,675
GM22	cpe	3,318	5,234	8,733
GH41	Salon sdn 4d	3,400	5,714	5,479
GH22	Salon cpe	3,335	5,482	6,849
GH45	Salon wgn 5d 2S	3,588	6,127	9,511
GP41	Medallion sdn 4d	3,472	6,198	5,995
GP22	Medallion cpe	3,392	5,966	6,637
St. Regis (wb 118.5)				
EH42	sdn 4d	3,602	6,532	34,972

1978 Magnum XE hardtop coupe

1979 Engines	bore×stroke	bhp	availability
L4, 104.7	3.13×3.40	70	S-Omni
L6, 225.0	3.40×4.13	100	S-Aspen, Diplomat
L6, 225.0	3.40×4.13	110	S-St. Regis; O-Asp, Dip
V8, 318.0	3.91×3.31	135	S-Asp,Dip,St. Regis, Mag
V8, 360.0	4.00×3.58	150	O-Dip,St.Regis,Magnum
V8, 360.0	4.00×3.58	195	O-Asp,Dip,St.Regis, Magnum

1980

Omni (wb 99.2; 2dr 96.7)		Wght	Price	Prod
ZL44	htchbk sdn 5d	2,095	5,681	76,505
ZL24	024 htchbk cpe 3d	2,135	5,526	61,650
Aspen (wb 112.7; cpe-108.7)				
NE41	Special sdn 4d L6	3,210	5,151	19,225
NE29	Special cpe L6	3,155	5,151	13,166
NL41	sdn 4d L6/V8	3,242	5,162	26,239
NL29	cpe L6/V8	3,185	5,045	11,895
NL45	wgn 5d 2S L6/V8	3,410	5,434	14,944
Diplomat (wb 112.7; cpes 108.7)				
GL22	Special spt cpe L6	3,130	5,995	NA
GM41	sdn 4d	3,342	6,202	7,941
GM22	spt cpe	3,260	6,048	5,884
GM45	wgn 4d 2S	3,495	6,346	2,093
GH41	Salon sdn 4d	3,205	6,501	5,479
GH22	Salon cpe	3,270	6,372	6,849
GH45	Salon wgn 5d 2S	3,525	7,041	2,664
GP41	Medallion sdn 4d	3,442	7,078	2,159
GP22	Medallion cpe	3,322	6,931	2,131
Mirada (wb 112.7)				
XS22	S htp cpe	3,328	6,645	32,746
XH22	htp cpe	3,230	6,850	
St. Regis (wb 118.5)				
EH42	sdn 4d	3,608	7,129	17,068

1980 Engines	bore×stroke	bhp	availability
L4, 104.7	3.13×3.40	65	S-Omni
L6, 225.0	3.40×4.13	90	S-Asp,Dip,St.Regis,Mirada
V8, 318.0	3.91×3.31	120	S-Asp exc Spcls, Dip,St.Regis,Mirada
V8, 360.0	4.00×3.58	130/185	O-St.Regis,Mirada

Note: Dodge production through 1980 includes export models, which makes figures in this book somewhat higher than those reported elsewhere.

1981

Omni (wb 99.1; 024 96.6)		Wght	Price	Prod
ZL44	htchbk sdn 5d	2,130	5,690	41,056
ZE44	Miser htchbk sdn 5d	2,060	5,299	
ZL24	024 htchbk cpe 3d	2,205	6,149	35,983
ZE24	Miser 024 htchbk cpe 3d	2,137	5,299	
Aries (wb 99.6)				
DL41	sdn 4d	2,300	5,980	47,679
DL21	sdn 2d	2,305	5,880	
DH41	Custom sdn 4d	2,310	6,448	46,792
DH21	Custom sdn 2d	2,315	6,315	
DH45	Custom wgn 5d	2,375	6,721	31,380
DP41	SE sdn 4d	2,340	6,933	20,160
DP21	SE sdn 2d	2,340	6,789	
DP45	SE wgn 5d	2,390	7,254	9,770
Diplomat (wb 112.7; cpe 108.7)				
GL41	sdn 4d	3,337	6,672	4,608
GL22	spt cpe	3,272	6,495	
GM45	wgn 5d 2S	3,530	7,089	1,806
GH41	Salon sdn 4d	3,367	7,268	15,023
GH22	Salon cpe	3,262	7,134	
GH45	Salon wgn 5d 2S	3,565	7,670	1,206
GP41	Medallion sdn 4d	3,427	7,777	1,527
GP22	Medallion cpe	3,317	7,645	
Mirada (wb 112.7)				
XS22	htp cpe	3,350	7,700	11,899
St. Regis (wb 118.5)				
EH42	sdn 4d	3,587	7,674	5,388

1981 Engines	bore×stroke	bhp	availability
L4, 104.7	3.13×3.40	63	S-Omni
L4, 135.0	3.44×3.62	84	S-Aries; O-Omni
L4, 156.0	3.59×3.86	92	O-Aries
L6, 225.0	3.40×4.12	85	S-Dip, Mirada, St. Regis
V8, 318.0	3.91×3.31	130	O-Dip, Mirada, St. Regis
V8, 318.0	3.91×3.31	165	O-St. Regis

1982

Omni (wb 99.1; 024 96.6)		Wght	Price	Prod
ZH44	Custom htchbk sdn 5d	2,175	5,927	14,466
ZE44	Miser htchbk sdn 5d	2,110	5,499	16,105
ZP44	Euro-sedan 5d	2,180	6,636	639
ZH24	024 htchbk cpe 3d	2,205	6,421	11,287
ZE24	Miser 024 htchbk cpe 3d	2,180	5,799	14,947
ZP24	Charger 2.2 htchbk cpe 3d	2,315	7,115	14,420
Aries (wb 99.9)				
DL41	sdn 4d	2,310	6,131	28,561
DL21	sdn 2d	2,315	5,990	10,286
DH41	Custom sdn 4d	2,320	7,053	19,438
DH21	Custom sdn 2d	2,320	6,898	8,127
DH45	Custom wgn 5d	2,395	7,334	26,233
DP41	SE sdn 4d	2,385	7,736	4,269
DP21	SE sdn 2d	2,365	7,575	1,374
DP45	SE wgn 5d	2,470	8,101	6,375
400 (wb 99.9)				
VH41	sdn 4d	2,423	8,137	3,595
VH22	cpe 2d	2,470	8,043	12,716
VH27	conv cpe	2,485	12,300	5,541
VP41	LS sdn 4d	2,438	8,402	2,870
VP22	LS cpe 2d	2,475	8,308	6,727
Diplomat (wb 112.7)				
GL41	Salon sdn 4d	3,345	7,750	19,773
GH41	Medallion sdn 4d	3,375	8,799	3,373
Mirada (wb 112.7)				
XS22	htp cpe	3,380	8,619	6,818

1982 Engines	bore×stroke	bhp	availability
L4, 104.7	3.13×3.40	63	S-Omni
L4, 135.0	3.44×3.62	84	S-Aries, 400; O-Omni
L4, 156.0	3.59×3.86	92	O-Aries, 400
L6, 225.0	3.40×4.12	90	S-Diplomat, Mirada
V8, 318.0	3.91×3.31	130	O-Diplomat, Mirada

1983

Omni (wb 99.1)		Wght	Price	Prod
ZE44	htchbk sdn 5d	2,093	5,841	33,264
ZH44	Custom htchbk sdn 5d	2,124	6,071	9,290
Charger (wb 96.6)				
ZH24	htchbk cpe 3d	2,137	6,379	22,535
ZP24	2.2 htchbk cpe 3d	2,194	7,303	10,448
ZS24	Shelby htchbk cpe 3d	2,330	8,290	8,251

1984 Daytona Turbo hatchback coupe

Aries (wb 100.1)		Wght	Price	Prod
DL41	sdn 4d	2,263	6,718	51,783
DL21	sdn 2d	2,257	6,577	14,218
DH45	Custom wgn 5d	2,372	7,636	29,228
DH41	SE sdn 4d	2,300	7,417	8,962
DH21	SE sdn 2d	2,273	7,260	4,325
DP45	SE wgn 5d	2,424	8,186	4,023
400 (wb 100.3)				
VP41	sdn 4d	2,482	8,490	9,560
VP22	cpe 2d	2,404	8,014	11,504
VP27	conv cpe	2,473	12,500	4,888
600 (wb 103.1)				
EH41	sdn 4d	2,524	8,841	21,065
ES41	ES sdn 4d	2,504	9,372	12,423
Diplomat (wb 112.7)				
GL41	Salon sdn 4d	3,387	8,248	21,368
GH41	Medallion sdn 4d	3,458	9,369	3,076
Mirada (wb 112.7)				
XS22	htp cpe	3,378	9,011	5,597

1983 Engines	bore × stroke	bhp	availability
L4, 104.7	3.13 × 3.40	63	S-Omni, Charger
L4, 97.3	3.17 × 3.07	62	S-late Omni, Charger
L4, 135.0	3.44 × 3.62	94	S-Chgr 2.2, Aries, 400, 600; O-Omni, Charger
L4, 135.0	3.44 × 3.62	107	S-Shelby Charger
L4, 156.0	3.59 × 3.86	93	O-Aries, 400, 600
L6, 225.0	3.40 × 4.12	90	S-Diplomat, Mirada
V8, 318.0	3.91 × 3.31	130	O-Diplomat, Mirada

1984

Omni (wb 99.1)		Wght	Price	Prod
ZE44	htchbk sdn 5d	2,181	5,830	54,584
ZH44	Custom htchbk sdn 5d	2,249	6,148	13,486
ZE44/AGB	GLH sdn 5d	—	7,350	—
Charger (wb 96.6)				
ZH24	htchbk cpe 3d	2,222	6,494	34,763
ZP24	2.2 htchbk cpe 3d	2,360	7,288	11,949
ZS24	Shelby htchbk cpe 3d	2,388	8,541	7,552

Daytona (wb 97.0)		Wght	Price	Prod
VH24	htchbk cpe 3d	2,528	8,308	21,916
VS24	Turbo htchbk cpe 3d	2,596	10,227	27,431
VS24/AGS	Turbo Z htchbk cpe 3d	2,646	11,494	—
Aries (wb 100.3)				
DL41	sdn 4d	2,323	6,949	55,331
DL21	sdn 2d	2,317	6,837	11,921
DH45	Custom wgn 5d	2,432	7,736	31,421
DH41	SE sdn 4d	2,360	7,589	12,314
DH21	SE sdn 2d	2,333	7,463	4,231
DP45	SE wgn 5d	2,484	8,195	4,814
600 (wb 100.3)				
VP22	cpe 2d	2,465	8,376	13,296
VP27	conv cpe	2,533	10,595	10,960
VP27/AGT	Turbo conv cpe	—	12,895	—
600 sedan (wb 103.3)				
EH41	sdn 4d	2,564	8,903	28,646
ES41	ES sdn 4d	2,564	9,525	8,735
Diplomat (wb 112.7)				
GL41	Salon sdn 4d	3,454	9,180	16,261
GP41	SE sdn 4d	3,584	9,828	5,902

1984 600 convertible coupe

1984 Engines	bore × stroke	bhp	availability
L4, 97.3	3.17 × 3.07	64	S-Omni, Charger
L4, 135.0	3.44 × 3.62	96	S-Chgr 2.2, Aries, 600; O-Omni, Charger
L4, 135.0	3.44 × 3.62	99	S-Daytona, 600 sdn
L4, 135.0	3.44 × 3.62	110	S-Shelby; O-Omni, Chgr
L4T, 135.0	3.44 × 3.62	142	S-Dayt turbo; O-Dayt, 600
L4, 156.0	3.59 × 3.86	101	O-Aries, 600
V8, 318.0	3.91 × 3.31	130	S-Diplomat

1985 Engines	bore × stroke	bhp	availability
L4, 97.3	3.17 × 3.07	64	S-Omni, Charger
L4, 135.0	3.44 × 3.62	96	S-Aries; O-Omni, Charger
L4, 135.0	3.44 × 3.62	99	S-Dayt, Lncr, 600; O-Aries
L4, 135.0	3.44 × 3.62	110	S-Omni GLH, Chgr 2.2; O-Omni, Charger
L4T, 135.0	3.44 × 3.62	146	S-Shelby; O-Omni GLH, Dayt, Lancer, 600
L4, 156.0	3.59 × 3.86	101	O-Aries, 600
V8, 318.0	3.91 × 3.31	140	S-Diplomat

1985

Omni (wb 99.1)		Wght	Price	Prod
LZE44	htchbk sdn 5d	2,174	5,977	54,229
LZH44	SE htchbk sdn 5d	2,154	6,298	13,385
LZE44/AGB	GLH htchbk sdn 5d	2,222	7,620	6,513
Charger (wb 96.5)				
LZH24	htchbk cpe 3d	2,215	6,584	38,203
LZP24	2.2 htchbk cpe 3d	2,366	7,515	10,645
LZS24	Shelby htchbk cpe 3d	2,457	9,553	7,709
Daytona (wb 97.0)				
GVH24	htchbk cpe 3d	2,611	8,505	29,987
GVS24	Turbo htchbk cpe 3d	2,688	10,286	9,509
GVS24/AGS	Turbo Z htchek cpe 3d	2,744	11,620	8,023
Aries (wb 100.3)				
KDL41	sdn 4d	2,393	7,039	39,580
KDL21	sdn 2d	2,375	6,924	9,428
KDM41	SE sdn 4d	2,424	7,439	23,920
KDM21	SE sdn 2d	2,390	7,321	7,937
KDH45	SE wgn 5d	2,514	7,909	22,953
KDH41	LE sdn 4d	2,446	7,792	5,932
KDH21	LE sdn 2d	2,414	7,659	3,706
KDP45	LE wgn 5d	2,546	8,348	4,519
Lancer (wb 103.1)				
HDH44	spt sdn 5d	2,659	8,713	30,567
HDS44	ES sdn 5d	2,726	9,690	15,286
600 (wb 100.3; sdn 103.3)				
KVP22	cpe 2d	2,539	9,060	12,670
KVP27	conv cpe	2,601	10,889	8,188
KVP27/AGT	ES turbo conv cpe	—	13,995	5,621
EEH41	sdn 4d	2,591	8,953	32,368
Diplomat (wb 112.7)				
MGL41	Salon sdn 4d	3,558	9,399	25,398
MGP41	SE sdn 4d	3,628	10,418	13,767

1985 Lancer ES five-door sedan

1986

Omni (wb 99.1)		Wght	Price	Prod
LZE44	htchbk sdn 5d	2,154	6,209	61,812
LZH44	SE htchbk sdn 5d	2,174	6,558	8,139
LZE44/AGB	GLH htchbk sdn 5d	2,341	7,918	3,629
Charger (wb 96.5)				
LZH24	htchbk cpe 3d	2,215	6,787	38,172
LZP24	2.2 htchbk cpe 3d	2,366	7,732	4,814
LZS24	Shelby htchbk cpe 3d	2,382	9,361	7,669
Daytona (wb 97.0)				
GVH24	htchbk cpe 3d	2,546	9,013	26,771
GVS24	Turbo Z htchbk cpe 3d	NA	11,301	17,595
Aries (wb 100.3)				
KDL41	sdn 4d	2,402	7,301	14,445
KDL21	sdn 2d	2,395	7,184	2,437
KDM41	SE sdn 4d	2,429	7,759	40,254
KDM21	SE sdn 2d	2,412	7,639	9,084
KDM45	SE wgn 5d	2,513	8,186	17,757
KDH41	LE sdn 4d	2,444	8,207	5,638
KDH21	LE sdn 2d	2,427	8,087	2,475
KDH45	LE wgn 5d	2,549	8,936	5,278
Lancer (wb 103.1)				
HDH44	spt sdn 5d	2,650	9,426	34,009
HDS44	ES sdn 5d	2,702	10,332	17,888
600 (wb 100.3; sdn 103.3)				
KVP22	cpe 2d	2,523	9,577	11,714
KVP27	conv cpe	2,594	11,695	11,678
KVP27/AGT	ES turbo conv cpe	2,648	14,856	4,759
EEM41	sdn 4d	2,593	9,370	16,235
EEH41	SE sdn 4d	2,593	10,028	15,291
Diplomat (wb 112.7)				
MGL41	Salon sdn 4d	3,555	10,086	15,469
MGP41	SE sdn 4d	3,624	11,166	11,484

1986 Engines	bore × stroke	bhp	availability
L4, 97.3	3.17 × 3.07	64	S-Omni, Charger
L4, 135.0	3.44 × 3.62	96	O-Omni, Charger
L4, 135.0	3.44 × 3.62	97	S-Aries, Dayt, Lancer, 600
L4, 135.0	3.44 × 3.62	110	S-Omni GLH, Chgr 2.2; O-Omni, Chgr
L4T, 135.0	3.44 × 3.62	146	S-Shelby, Dayt Turbo; O-Omni GLH, Dayt, Lncr, 600
L4, 153.0	3.44 × 4.09	100	O-Aries, Dayt, Lancer, 600
V8, 318.0	3.91 × 3.31	140	S-Diplomat

1987

Omni (wb 99.1)		Wght	Price	Prod
LZE44	America htchbk sdn 5d	2,237	5,499	66,907
Charger (wb 96.5)				
LZH24	htchbk cpe 3d	2,290	6,999	24,275
LZS24	Shelby htchbk cpe 3d	2,483	9,840	2,011

Daytona (wb 97.0)		Wght	Price	Prod
GVH24	htchbk cpe 3d	2,676	9,799	18,485
GVP24	Pacifica htchbk cpe 3d	2,862	13,912	7,467
GVS24	Shelby Z htchbk cpe 3d	2,812	12,749	7,152
Shadow (wb 97.0)				
PDH44	htchbk sdn 5d	2,494	7,699	37,559
PDH24	htchbk sdn 3d	2,459	7,499	38,497
Aries (wb 100.3)				
KDL41	sdn 4d	2,415	7,655	4,710
KDM41	SE sdn 4d	2,484	8,134	66,506
KDL21	sdn 2d	2,409	7,655	204
KDM21	SE sdn 2d	2,468	8,134	7,517
KDM45	SE wgn 5d	2,588	8,579	20,362
Lancer (wb 103.1)				
HDH44	sdn 5d	2,645	9,474	17,040
HDS44	ES sdn 5d	2,692	10,428	9,579
600 (wb 103.3)				
EEM41	sdn 4d	2,594	9,891	20,074
EEH41	SE sdn 4d	2,601	10,553	20,317
Diplomat (wb 112.6)				
MGL41	Salon sdn 4d	3,566	10,598	11,256
MGP41	SE sdn 4d	3,627	11,678	9,371

1987 Engines	bore × stroke	bhp	availability
L4, 135.0	3.44 × 3.62	96	S-Omni, Charger
L4, 135.0	3.44 × 3.62	97	S-Aries, Shadow, Lncr, 600
L4T, 135.0	3.44 × 3.62	146	S-Shelby, Dayt Pacifica; O-Dayt, Shadow, Lncr, 600
L4T, 135.0	3.44 × 3.62	174	S-Daytona Shelby Z
L4, 153.0	3.44 × 4.09	100	S-Dayt; O-Aries, Lancer, 600
V8, 318.0	3.91 × 3.31	140	S-Diplomat

1988

Omni (wb 99.1)		Wght	Price	Prod
LZE44	America htchbk sdn 5d	2,225	5,999	59,867
Daytona (wb 97.0)				
GVH24	htchbk cpe 3d	2,676	10,025	54,075
GVP24	Pacifica htchbk cpe 3d	2,862	14,513	4,752
GVS24	Shelby Z htchbk cpe 3d	2,812	13,394	7,580
Shadow (wb 97.0)				
PDH44	htchbk sdn 5d	2,544	8,075	55,857
PDH24	htchbk sdn 3d	2,513	7,875	36,452

1988 Daytona hatchback coupe

1989 Lancer Shelby five-door sedan

Aries America (wb 100.3)		Wght	Price	Prod
KDH41	sdn 4d	2,485	6,995	85,613
KDH21	sdn 2d	2,459	6,995	6,578
KDH45	wgn 5d	2,537	7,695	19,172
Lancer (wb 103.1)				
HDH44	sdn 5d	2,646	10,482	6,580
HDS44	ES sdn 5d	2,702	12,715	2,484
DS44/AFP	Shelby sdn 5d	—	—	279
600 (wb 103.3)				
EEM41	sdn 4d	2,595	10,659	10,305
EEH41	SE sdn 4d	2,633	11,628	6,785
Dynasty (wb 104.3)				
CDH41	sdn 4d	2,956	11,666	26,653
CDP41	Premium sdn 4d	2,966	12,226	28,897
Diplomat (wb 112.6)				
MGE41	sdn 4d	3,584	12,127	444
MGL41	Salon sdn 4d	3,567	11,407	12,992
MGP41	SE sdn 4d	3,634	14,221	5,737

1988 Engines	bore × stroke	bhp	availability
L4, 135.0	3.44 × 3.62	93	S-Omni, Aries, Shadow, Lncr, 600
L4T, 135.0	3.44 × 3.62	146	S-Daytona Pacifica; O-Dayt, Shadow, Lncr, 600
L4T, 135.0	3.44 × 3.62	174	S-Dayt Shelby Z, Lncr Shelby
L4, 153.0	3.44 × 4.09	96	S-Dayt, Dynasty, Lancer ES; O-Aries, Shadow, Lncr, 600
V6, 181.4	3.59 × 2.99	136	O-Dynasty
V8, 318.0	3.91 × 3.31	140	S-Diplomat

1989

Omni (wb 99.1)		Wght	Price	Prod
LZE44	America htchbk sdn 5d	2,237	6,595	
Daytona (wb 97.0)				
GVL24	htchbk cpe 3d	2,751	9,295	
GVH24	ES htchbk cpe 3d	2,822	10,395	
GVS24	ES turbo cpe 3d	2,936	11,995	
GVX24	Shelby htchbk cpe 3d	2,951	13,295	
Shadow (wb 97.0)				
PDH44	htchbk sdn 5d	2,558	8,595	
PDH24	htchbk cpe 3d	2,520	8,395	
Aries America (wb 100.3)				
KDH41	sdn 4d	2,323	7,595	
KDH21	sdn 2d	2,317	7,595	

Lancer (wb 103.1)		Wght	Price	Prod
HDH44	spt sdn 5d	2,646	11,195	
HDS44	ES sdn 5d	2,702	13,695	
HDX44	Shelby sdn 5d	2,838	17,395	
Spirit (wb 103.3)				
ADH41	sdn 4d	2,765	—	
ADP41	ES sdn 4d	2,842	—	
ADX41	LE sdn 4d	2,901	—	
Dynasty (wb 104.3)				
CDH41	sdn 4d	2,992	12,295	
CDP41	LE sdn 4d	3,066	13,595	
Diplomat (wb 112.7)				
MGL41	Salon sdn 4d	3,582	11,995	
MGP41	SE sdn 4d	3,732	14,795	

1989 Engines	bore × stroke	bhp	availability
L4, 135.0	3.44 × 3.62	93	S-Omni, Aries, Shdw, Lncr
L4T, 135.0	3.44 × 3.62	174	S-Dayt/Lncr Shelby
L4, 153.0	3.44 × 4.09	100	S-Dayt, Dynasty, Spirit; O-Aries, Shadow, Lancer
L4T, 153.0	3.44 × 4.09	150	S-Spirit ES, Lncr ES; O-Dayt, Lncr, Shadow ES, Sprt
V6, 181.4	3.59 × 2.99	141	S-Dyna LE; O-Dyna, Sprt ES
V8, 318.0	3.91 × 3.31	140	S-Diplomat

Note: The Mitsubishi-built Dodge Colt (1971-up), Dodge Challenger (starting 1974) and other captive imports are not included in the above tables.

EDSEL

1958

Ranger (wb 118.0; wgns-116.0)		Wght	Price	Prod
21	sdn 2d	3,729	2,519	4,615
22	sdn 4d	3,805	2,592	6,576
23	htp cpe	3,724	2,593	5,546
24	htp sdn	3,796	2,678	3,077
26	Roundup wgn 2d	3,761	2,876	963
27	Villager wgn 4d, 6P	3,827	2,933	2,294
28	Villager wgn 4d, 9P	3,900	2,990	978
Pacer (wb 118.0; wgns-116.0)				
42	sdn 4d	3,826	2,735	6,083
43	htp cpe	3,773	2,805	6,139

1958 Citation convertible coupe

1959 Corsair convertible coupe

		Wght	Price	Prod
44	htp sdn	3,857	2,863	4,959
45	conv cpe	3,909	3,028	1,876
47	Bermuda wgn 4d, 6P	3,853	3,190	1,456
48	Bermuda wgn 4d, 9P	3,919	3,247	779
Corsair (wb 124.0)				
63	htp cpe	4,134	3,346	3,312
64	htp sdn	4,235	3,425	5,880
Citation (wb 124.0)				
83	htp cpe	4,136	3,535	2,535
84	htp sdn	4,230	3,615	5,112
85	conv cpe	4,311	3,801	930

1958 Engines	bore×stroke	bhp	availability
V8, 361.0	4.05×3.50	303	S-Ranger, Pacer
V8, 410.0	4.20×3.70	345	S-Corsair, Citation

1959

Ranger (wb 120.0)		Wght	Price	Prod
57F	htp sdn	3,682	2,756	2,352
58D	sdn 4d	3,774	2,684	12,814
63F	htp cpe	3,591	2,691	5,474
64C	sdn 2d	3,547	2,629	7,778
Corsair (wb 120.0)				
57B	htp sdn	3,709	2,885	1,694
58B	sdn 4d	3,696	2,812	3,301
63B	htp cpe	3,778	2,819	2,315
76E	conv cpe	3,790	3,072	1,343
Station Wagon (wb 120.0)				
71E	Villager wgn 4d, 9P	3,930	3,055	2,133
71F	Villager wgn 4d, 6P	3,842	2,971	5,687

1959 Engines	bore×stroke	bhp	availability
L6, 223.0	3.62×3.60	145	O-Ranger, Station Wagon
V8, 292.0	3.75×3.30	200	S-Ranger, Station Wagon
V8, 332.0	4.00×3.30	225	S-Corsair; O-others
V8, 361.0	4.05×3.50	303	O-all

1960

Ranger (wb 120.0)		Wght	Price	Prod
57A	htp sdn	3,718	2,770	135
58A	sdn 4d	3,700	2,697	1,288
63A	htp cpe	3,641	2,705	295
64A	sdn 2d	3,601	2,643	777
76B	conv cpe	3,836	3,000	76

Station Wagon (wb 120.0)		Wght	Price	Prod
71E	Villager wgn 4d, 9P	4,046	3,072	59
71F	Villager wgn 4d, 6P	4,029	2,989	216

1960 Engines	bore×stroke	bhp	availability
L6, 223.0	3.62×3.50	145	O-all
V8, 292.0	3.75×3.30	185	S-all
V8, 352.0	4.00×3.50	300	O-all

EXCALIBUR

1965

Series I (wb 109.0)*	Wght	Price	Prod
SSK rdstr	2,100	7,250	56

1965 Engine	bore×stroke	bhp	availability
V8, 289.0	3.56×3.62	290	S-all

1966

Series I (wb 109.0)*	Wght	Price	Prod
SSK rdstr	2,100	7,250	87 (SSK rdstr and rdstr)
rdstr	2,500	8,000	
phtn	2,500	7,950	3

1966 Engine	bore×stroke	bhp	availability
V8, 327.0	4.00×3.25	300	S-all

1967

Series I (wb 109.0)*	Wght	Price	Prod
SSK rdstr	2,100	8,000	38 (SSK rdstr and rdstr)
rdstr	2,500	8,500	
phtn	2,600	8,250	33

1967 Engines	bore×stroke	bhp	availability
V8, 327.0	4.00×3.25	300	S-all
V8, 327.0	4.00×3.25	400	O-all

1968

Series I (wb 109.0)*	Wght	Price	Prod
SSK rdstr	2,300	8,650	37 (SSK rdstr and rdstr)
rdstr	2,500	8,650	
phtn	2,600	9,850	20

1968 Engines	bore×stroke	bhp	availability
V8, 327.0	4.00×3.25	300	S-all
V8, 327.0	4.00×3.25	435	O-all

1969

Series I (wb 109.0)*	Wght	Price	Prod
SSK rdstr	2,400	9,000	47 (SSK rdstr and rdstr)
rdstr	2,550	9,000	
phtn	2,650	10,000	44

1969 Engines	bore×stroke	bhp	availability
V8, 327.0	4.00×3.25	300	S-all
V8, 327.0	4.00×3.25	435	O-all

*Production 1965-69; SSK 168; rdstr 59; phtn 89.

1970

Series II (wb 111.0)	Wght	Price	Prod
SSK rdstr	2,750	12,000	11 (SSK rdstr and SS rdstr)
SS rdstr	2,900	12,500	
SS phtn	3,000	12,900	26

1970 Engine	bore×stroke	bhp	availability
V8, 350.0	4.00×3.48	300	S-all

1971

Excalibur records show no 1971 model production.

1972

Series II (wb 111.0)	Wght	Price	Prod
SS rdstr	2,900	12,500	13
SS phtn	3,000	13,500	52

1970-74 Series II roadster

1972 Engine	bore×stroke	bhp	availability
V8, 454.0	4.25×4.00	NA	S-all

1973

Series II (wb 111.0)	Wght	Price	Prod
SS rdstr	2,900	13,500	22
SS phtn	3,000	16,000	100

1973 Engine	bore×stroke	bhp	availability
V8, 454.0	4.25×4.00	270	S-all

1974

Series II (wb 111.0)	Wght	Price	Prod
SS rdstr	2,900	17,000	26
SS phtn	3,000	17,000	92

1974 Engine	bore×stroke	bhp	availability
V8, 454.0	4.25×4.00	275	S-all

1975

Series III (wb 112.0)	Wght	Price	Prod
SS rdstr	4,350	18,900	8
SS phtn	4,350	18,900	82

1975 Engine	bore×stroke	bhp	availability
V8, 454.0	4.25×4.00	215	S-all

1976

Series III (wb 112.0)	Wght	Price	Prod
SS rdstr	4,350	21,500	11
SS phtn	4,350	21,500	173

1976 Engine	bore×stroke	bhp	availability
V8, 454.0	4.25×4.00	215	S-all

1977

Series III (wb 112.0)	Wght	Price	Prod
SS rdstr	4,350	23,600	15
SS phtn	4,350	23,600	222

1977 Engine	bore×stroke	bhp	availability
V8, 454.0	4.25×4.00	215	S-all

1980-84 Series IV phaeton

1978

Series III (wb 112.0)	Wght	Price	Prod
SS rdstr	4,350	25,600	15
SS phtn	4,350	25,600	248

1978 Engine	bore×stroke	bhp	availability
V8, 454.0	4.25×4.00	215	S-all

1979

Series III (wb 112.0)	Wght	Price	Prod
SS rdstr	4,350	28,600	27
SS phtn	4,350	28,600	340

1979 Engine	bore×stroke	bhp	availability
V8, 350.0	4.00×3.48	180	S-all

1980

Series IV (wb 125.0)	Wght	Price	Prod
SS rdstr	4,300	NA	0
SS phtn	4,300	37,700	93

1980 Engine	bore×stroke	bhp	availability
V8, 305.0	3.74×3.48	155	S-all

1981

Series IV (wb 125.0)	Wght	Price	Prod
rdstr	4,400	50,000	36
phtn	4,400	46,500	199

1981 Engines	bore×stroke	bhp	availability
V8, 305.0	3.74×3.48	155	S-all

1982

Series IV (wb 125.0)	Wght	Price	Prod
rdstr	4,400	57,500	60
phtn	4,400	52,000	152

1982 Engines	bore×stroke	bhp	availability
V8, 305.0	3.74×3.48	155	S-all

1983

Series IV (wb 125.0)	Wght	Price	Prod
rdstr	4,400	59,500	—
phtn	4,400	55,500	—

1983 Engines	bore×stroke	bhp	availability
V8, 305.0	3.74×3.48	155	S-all

1984

Series IV (wb 125.0)	Wght	Price	Prod
rdstr	4,400	59,500	—
phtn	4,400	57,000	—

1984 Engines	bore×stroke	bhp	availability
V8, 305.0	3.74×3.48	155	S-all

1985

Signature Series (wb 125.0)	Wght	Price	Prod
rdstr	4,400	62,000	—
phtn	4,400	59,500	—

1985 Engines	bore × stroke	bhp	availability
V8, 305.0	3.74 × 3.48	155	S-all

1986

Series V (wb 125.0)	Wght	Price	Prod
rdstr	—	65,000	*
phtn	—	65,000	*

1986 Engines	bore × stroke	bhp	availability
V8, 305.0	3.74 × 3.48	155	S-all

*Specifications and prices were announced for 1986, but the Excalibur Company went into bankruptcy. Production resumed in December 1986 with the 1987 models.

1987

(wb 124.0)	Wght	Price	Prod
rdstr	4,400	—	—
phtn	4,400	—	—

1987 Engines	bore × stroke	bhp	availability
V8, 305.0	3.74 × 3.48	170	S-all

1988

(wb 124.0; Touring Sdn 144.0)	Wght	Price	Prod
rdstr 2d	4,400	—	—
phtn 2d	4,400	—	—
touring sdn 4d	4,400	65,650	—

1988 Engines	bore × stroke	bhp	availability
V8, 305.0	3.74 × 3.48	170	S-all
V8, 350.0	4.00 × 3.48	NA	O-all

1989

(wb 124.0; Touring Sdn 144.0)	Wght	Price	Prod
rdstr 2d	4,400	71,865	—
phtn 2d	4,400	71,865	—
touring sdn 4d	4,400	72,325	—

1989 Engines	bore × stroke	bhp	availability
V8, 305.0	3.74 × 3.48	170	S-all
V8, 350.0	4.00 × 3.48	NA	O-all

1980-84 Series IV roadster

FORD

1939

Model 92A (wb 112.0)	Wght	Price	Prod
cpe 5W 2P	2,463	599	*
Tudor sdn 5P	2,608	640	*
Fordor sdn 5P	2,623	686	*
Model 91A (wb 112.0)			
cpe 5W 2P	2,710	640	*
Tudor sdn 5P	2,830	681	*
Fordor sdn 5P	2,850	727	*
wgn 4d	3,080	840	3,277
DeLuxe cpe 5W 2P	2,752	702	37,326
DeLuxe conv cpe 2-4P	2,840	788	10,422
DeLuxe Tudor sdn 5P	2,867	742	144,333
DeLuxe Fordor sdn 5P	2,898	788	90,551
DeLuxe conv sdn 5P	2,935	921	3,561
DeLuxe wgn 4d	3,095	916	6,155
DeLuxe sdn 7P	—	—	192

1939 Engines	bore×stroke	bhp	availability
V8, 136.0	2.60×3.20	60	S-92A
V8, 221.0	3.06×3.75	85	S-91A

*Production combined by body style as follows:

coupe	38,197
Tudor sdn	124,866
Fordor sdn	28,151

1940—541,896 built

01A V8/85 (wb 112.0)	Wght	Price	Prod
cpe	2,763	660	—
bus cpe	2,801	681	—
Tudor sdn	2,909	701	—
Fordor sdn	2,936	747	—
wgn 4d	3,249	875	—
DeLuxe cpe	2,791	722	27,919
DeLuxe bus cpe	2,831	742	20,183
DeLuxe conv cpe	2,956	849	23,704
DeLuxe Tudor sdn	2,927	762	171,368
DeLuxe Fordor sdn	2,966	808	91,756
DeLuxe wgn 4d	3,262	947	8,730
02A V8/60 (wb 112.0)			
cpe	2,519	619	—
bus cpe	2,549	640	—
Tudor sdn	2,669	660	—
Fordor sdn	2,696	706	—

1940 Engines	bore×stroke	bhp	availability
V8, 136.0	2.60×3.20	60	S-V8/60
V8, 221.0	3.06×3.75	85	S-V8/85

1941—691,896 built

1GA Six (wb 114.0)	Wght	Price	Prod
Special cpe	2,870	684	—
Special Tudor sdn	2,975	720	—
Special Fordor sdn	3,020	761	—
Deluxe cpe	2,947	715	—
DeLuxe cpe, A/S	2,970	746	—
DeLuxe Tudor sdn	3,065	756	—
DeLuxe Fordor sdn	3,100	797	—
DeLuxe wgn 4d	3,395	946	—
Super DeLuxe cpe	2,934	761	—
Super DeLuxe cpe, A/S	2,974	792	—

1940 DeLuxe convertible coupe

1942 DeLuxe Fordor V8 sedan

		Wght	Price	Prod
	Super DeLuxe sdn cpe	3,030	833	—
	Super DeLuxe conv cpe	3,145	931	—
	Super DeLuxe Tudor sdn	3,096	802	—
	Super DeLuxe Fordor sdn	3,131	843	—
	Super DeLuxe wgn 4d	3,400	998	—
11A V8 (wb 114.0)				
	Special cpe	2,878	700	—
	Special Tudor sdn	2,983	736	—
	Special Fordor sdn	3,033	777	—
	Deluxe cpe	2,953	730	—
	DeLuxe cpe, A/S	2,981	761	—
	DeLuxe Tudor sdn	3,095	772	—
	DeLuxe Fordor sdn	3,121	813	—
	DeLuxe wgn 4d	3,412	962	—
	Super DeLuxe cpe	2,969	777	—
	Super DeLuxe cpe, A/S	3,001	807	—
	Super DeLuxe sdn cpe	3,052	849	—
	Super DeLuxe conv cpe	3,187	946	—
	Super DeLuxe Tudor sdn	3,110	818	—
	Super DeLuxe Fordor sdn	3,146	859	—
	Super DeLuxe wgn 4d	3,419	1,013	—

1941 Engines	bore×stroke	bhp	availability
L6, 226.0	3.30×4.40	90	S-Six
V8, 221.0	3.06×3.75	85	S-V8

1942—160,432 built

2GA Six (wb 114.0)		Wght	Price	Prod
70C	Special Tudor sdn	3,053	815	—
73C	Special Fordor sdn	3,093	850	—
77C	Special cpe	2,910	780	—
70A	DeLuxe Tudor sdn	3,122	840	—
72A	DeLuxe sdn cpe	3,045	865	—
73A	DeLuxe Fordor sdn	3,141	875	—
77A	DeLuxe cpe	2,958	805	—
79A	DeLuxe wgn 4d, 8P	3,405	1,035	—
70B	Super DeLuxe Tudor sdn	3,136	885	—
72B	Super DeLuxe sdn cpe	3,109	910	—
73B	Super DeLuxe Fordor sdn	3,179	920	—
76	Super DeLuxe conv cpe	3,218	1,080	—
77B	Super DeLuxe cpe	3,030	850	—
79B	Super DeLuxe wgn 4d, 8P	3,453	1,115	—
21A V8 (wb 114.0)				
70A	DeLuxe Tudor sdn	3,141	850	—
72A	DeLuxe sdn cpe	3,065	875	—
73A	DeLuxe Fordor sdn	3,161	885	—
77A	DeLuxe cpe	2,978	815	—
79A	DeLuxe wgn 4d	3,420	1,090	—
70B	Super DeLuxe Tudor sdn	3,159	895	—
72B	Super DeLuxe sdn cpe	3,120	920	—
73B	Super DeLuxe Fordor sdn	3,200	930	—
76	Super DeLuxe conv cpe	3,238	1,090	—
77B	Super DeLuxe cpe	3,050	860	—
79B	Super DeLuxe wgn 4d, 8P	3,468	1,125	—

1942 Engines	bore×stroke	bhp	availability
L6, 226.0	3.30×4.40	90	S-Six
V8, 221.0	3.06×3.75	90	S-V8

1946

6GA Six (wb 114.0)*		Wght	Price	Prod
70A	DeLuxe Tudor sdn	3,157	1,136	—
73A	DeLuxe Fordor sdn	3,187	1,198	—
77A	DeLuxe cpe	3,007	1,074	—
70B	Super DeLuxe Tudor sdn	3,157	1,211	—
72B	Super DeLuxe cpe sdn	3,107	1,257	—
73B	Super DeLuxe Fordor sdn	3,207	1,273	—
77B	Super DeLuxe cpe	3,007	1,148	—
79B	Super DeLuxe wgn 4d	3,457	1,504	—
69A V8 (wb 114.0)*				
70A	DeLuxe Tudor sdn	3,190	1,185	—
73A	DeLuxe Fordor sdn	3,220	1,248	—
77A	DeLuxe cpe	3,040	1,123	—
70B	Super DeLuxe Tudor sdn	3,190	1,260	—
71	Super DeLuxe Sprtsmn conv	3,340	1,982	1,209
72B	Super DeLuxe cpe sdn	3,140	1,307	—
73B	Super DeLuxe Fordor sdn	3,240	1,322	—
76	Super DeLuxe conv cpe	3,240	1,488	—
77B	Super DeLuxe cpe	3,040	1,197	—
79B	Super DeLuxe wgn 4d, 8P	3,490	1,533	—

***Model Year Production by Body Style (Six/V8):**

DeLuxe (wb 114.0)	
Tudor sdn	74,954
Fordor sdn	9,246
cpe	10,670
chassis	86
Super DeLuxe (wb 114.0)	
Tudor sdn	163,370
Fordor sdn	92,056

				Prod
	sdn cpe			70,826
	conv cpe			16,359
	cpe			12,249
	wgn 4d			16,960
	chassis			37

1946 Engines	bore×stroke	bhp	availability
L6, 226.0	3.30×4.40	90	S-Six
V8, 239.4	3.19×3.75	100	S-V8

1947

7GA Six (wb 114.0)*	Wght	Price	Prod
DeLuxe Fordor sdn	3,213	1,270	—
DeLuxe Tudor sdn	3,183	1,212	—
Deluxe cpe	3,033	1,154	—
Super DeLuxe Fordor sdn	3,233	1,372	—
Super DeLuxe Tudor sdn	3,183	1,309	—
Super DeLuxe cpe sdn	3,133	1,330	—
Super DeLuxe cpe	3,033	1,251	—
Super DeLuxe wgn 4d, 8P	3,487	1,893	—
79A V8 (wb 114.0)*			
DeLuxe Fordor sdn	3,246	1,346	—
DeLuxe Tudor sdn	3,216	1,288	—
DeLuxe cpe	3,066	1,230	—
Super DeLuxe Fordor sdn	3,266	1,440	—
Super DeLuxe Tudor sdn	3,216	1,382	—
Super DeLuxe cpe sdn	3,166	1,409	—
Super DeLuxe conv cpe	3,266	1,740	22,159
Super DeLuxe Sprtsmn conv	3,366	2,282	2,250
Super DeLuxe wgn 4d, 8P	3,520	1,972	—

***Model Year Production by Body Style (Six/V8):**

DeLuxe (wb 114.0)		Prod
	Tudor sdn	44,523
	Fordor sdn	20
	cpe	10,872
	chassis	23
Super DeLuxe (wb 114.0)		
	Tudor sdn	136,126
	Fordor sdn	116,744
	cpe sdn	80,830
	wgn 4d, 8P	16,104
	chassis	23

1947 Engines	bore×stroke	bhp	availability
L6, 226.0	3.30×4.40	90	S-Six
V8, 239.4	3.19×3.75	100	S-V8

1948

87HA Six (wb 114.0)*		Wght	Price	Prod
70A	DeLuxe Tudor sdn	3,183	1,212	—
77A	Deluxe cpe	3,033	1,154	—
70B	Super DeLuxe Tudor sdn	3,183	1,309	—
72B	Super DeLuxe cpe sdn	3,133	1,330	—
73B	Super DeLuxe Fordor sdn	3,233	1,372	—
79B	Super DeLuxe wgn 4d, 8P	3,487	1,893	—
89A V8 (wb 114.0)*				
70A	DeLuxe Tudor sdn	3,216	1,288	—
77A	DeLuxe cpe	3,066	1,230	—
70B	Super DeLuxe Tudor sdn	3,216	1,382	—
71B	Super DeLuxe Sprtsmn conv	3,366	2,282	28
72B	Super DeLuxe cpe sdn	3,166	1,409	—
73B	Super DeLuxe Fordor sdn	3,266	1,440	—

1940 Sportsman convertible coupe

		Wght	Price	Prod
76B	Super DeLuxe conv cpe	3,266	1,740	12,033
79B	Super DeLuxe wgn 4d, 8P	3,520	1,972	—
***Model Year Production by Body Style (Six/V8):**				
DeLuxe (wb 114.0)				
	Tudor sdn			23,356
	cpe			5,048
Super DeLuxe (wb 114.0)				
	Tudor sdn			82,161
	Fordor sdn			71,358
	cpe sdn			44,826
	wgn 4d, 8P			8,912

1948 Engines	bore×stroke	bhp	availability
L6, 226.0	3.30×4.40	95	S-Six
V8, 239.4	3.19×3.75	100	S-V8

1949

Standard (wb 114.0)		Wght	Price	Prod
70A	Tudor sdn	2,965	1,425	126,770
72A	club cpe	2,945	1,415	4,170
72C	bus cpe	2,891	1,333	28,946
73A	Fordor sdn	3,010	1,472	44,563
—	chassis	—	—	1
Custom V8 (wb 114.0)				
70B	Tudor sdn	2,968	1,511	433,316
72B	club cpe	2,948	1,511	150,254
73B	Fordor sdn	3,013	1,559	248,176
76	conv cpe	3,254	1,886	51,133
79	wgn 2d, 8P	3,543	2,119	31,412
—	chassis	—	—	18

1949 Engines	bore×stroke	bhp	availability
L6, 226.0	3.30×4.40	95	S-Six
V8, 239.4	3.19×3.75	100	O-V8

1950

DeLuxe (wb 114.0)		Wght	Price	Prod
D70	Tudor sdn	3,007	1,424	275,360
D72C	bus cpe	2,949	1,333	35,120
D73	Fordor sdn	3,064	1,472	77,888
Custom (wb 114.0)				
C70	Tudor sdn	3,015	1,511	398,060
C70C	Crestliner sdn 2d	3,050	1,711	17,601
C72	club cpe	2,981	1,511	85,111
C73	Fordor sdn	3,078	1,558	247,181
C76	conv cpe	3,263	1,948	50,299
C79	Country Squire wgn 2d	3,511	2,028	22,929

1950 Custom Crestliner Tudor sedan

1951 Country Squire two-door wagon

1950 Engines	bore×stroke	bhp	availability
L6, 226.0	3.30×4.40	95	S-all exc C70C, C76
V8, 239.4	3.19×3.75	100	S-C70C, C76; O-others

1951

DeLuxe (wb 114.0)		Wght	Price	Prod
70	Tudor sdn	3,043	1,417	146,010
72C	bus cpe	2,979	1,324	20,343
73	Fordor sdn	3,102	1,465	54,265
Custom (wb 114.0)				
60	Victoria htp cpe	3,188	1,925	110,286
70	Tudor sdn	3,043	1,505	317,869
70C	Crestliner sdn 2d	3,065	1,595	8,703
72	club cpe	3,015	1,505	53,263
73	Fordor sdn	3,102	1,553	232,691
76	conv cpe	3,268	1,949	40,934
79	Country Squire wgn 2d	3,530	2,029	29,017

1951 Engines	bore×stroke	bhp	availability
L6, 226.0	3.30×4.40	95	S-all exc 60, 70C, 76
V8, 239.4	3.19×3.75	100	S-60, 70C, 76; O-others

1952

Mainline (wb 115.0)		Wght	Price	Prod
59A	Ranch Wagon 2d	3,212	1,832	32,566
70A	sdn 2d	3,111	1,485	79,931
72C	bus cpe	3,035	1,389	10,137
73A	sdn 4d	3,190	1,530	41,227
Customline (wb 115.0)				
70B	sdn 2d	3,111	1,570	175,762
72B	club cpe	3,116	1,579	26,550
73B	sdn 4d	3,190	1,615	188,303
79C	Country Sedan wgn 4d, 6P	3,617	2,060	11,927
Crestline (wb 115.0)				
60B	Victoria htp cpe	3,274	1,925	77,320
76B	Sunliner conv cpe	3,339	2,027	22,534
79B	Country Squire wgn 4d, 8P	3,640	2,186	5,426

1952 Engines	bore×stroke	bhp	availability
L6, 215.3	3.56×3.60	101	S-all exc 79C, Crestline (ohv)
V8, 239.4	3.19×3.75	110	S-79C, Crestline; O-others

1953

Mainline (wb 115.0)		Wght	Price	Prod
59A	Ranch Wagon 2d	3,406	1,917	66,976
70A	sdn 2d	3,092	1,497	152,995
72C	bus cpe	3,018	1,400	16,280
73A	sdn 4d	3,138	1,542	69,463
Customline (wb 115.0)				
70B	sdn 2d	3,100	1,582	305,433
72B	club cpe	3,084	1,591	43,999
73B	sdn 4d	3,154	1,628	374,487
79B	Country Sedan wgn 4d, 6P	3,539	2,076	37,743
Crestline (wb 115.0)				
60B	Victoria htp cpe	3,250	1,941	128,302
76B	Sunliner conv cpe	3,334	2,043	40,861
79C	Country Squire wgn 4d, 8P	3,609	2,203	11,001
—	chassis	—	—	2

1953 Engines	bore×stroke	bhp	availability
L6, 215.3	3.56×3.60	101	S-all exc 79B, Crestline
V8, 239.4	3.19×3.75	110	S-79B, Crestline; O-others

1954

Mainline (wb 115.5)		Wght	Price	Prod
59A	Ranch Wagon 2d	3,399	2,029	44,315
70A	sdn 2d	3,147	1,651	123,329
72C	bus cpe	3,082	1,548	10,665
73A	sdn 4d	3,203	1,701	55,371
Customline (wb 115.5)				
59B	Ranch Wagon 2d	3,405	2,122	36,086
70B	sdn 2d	3,160	1,744	293,375
72B	club cpe	3,141	1,753	33,951
73B	sdn 4d	3,216	1,793	262,499
79B	Country Sedan wgn 4d, 6P	3,574	2,202	48,384
Crestline (wb 115.5)				
60B	Victoria htp cpe	3,245	2,055	95,464
60F	Skyliner htp cpe	3,265	2,164	13,344
73C	sdn 4d	3,220	1,898	99,677
76B	Sunliner conv cpe	3,292	2,164	36,685
79C	Country Squire wgn 4d, 8P	3,624	2,339	12,797

1954 Engines	bore×stroke	bhp	availability
L6, 223.0	3.62×3.60	115	S-all exc 79B
V8, 239.4	3.50×3.10	130	S-79B; O-others (ohv)

1955

Mainline (wb 115.5)		Wght	Price	Prod
70A	sdn 2d	3,119	1,707	76,698
70D	bus cpe	3,081	1,606	8,809
73A	sdn 4d	3,161	1,753	41,794
Customline (wb 115.5)				
70B	sdn 2d	3,139	1,801	236,575
73B	sdn 4d	3,181	1,845	235,417
Fairlane (wb 115.5)				
60B	Victoria htp cpe	3,251	2,095	113,372
64A	Crown Victoria htp cpe	3,313	2,202	33,165
64B	Crown Vic htp cpe, glass top	3,321	2,272	1,999
70C	club sdn 2d	3,155	1,914	173,311
73C	Town Sedan	3,201	1,960	254,437
76B	Sunliner conv cpe	3,315	2,224	49,966
Station Wagon (wb 115.5)				
59A	Ranch 2d, 6P	3,376	2,043	40,493
59B	Custom Ranch 2d, 6P	3,394	2,109	43,671
79B	Country Sedan 4d, 8P	3,536	2,287	53,209
79C	Country Squire 4d, 8P	3,538	2,392	19,011
79D	Country Sedan 4d, 6P	3,460	2,156	53,075

1953 Crestline Victoria hardtop coupe

1955 Fairlane Club Sedan

1956 Fairlane Victoria hardtop sedan

1955 Engines	bore×stroke	bhp	availability
L6, 223.0	3.62×3.60	120	S-all
V8, 272.0	3.62×3.30	162	O-all
V8, 272.0	3.62×3.30	182	O-all

1956

Mainline (wb 115.5)		Wght	Price	Prod
70A	sdn 2d	3,143	1,850	106,974
70D	bus sdn 2d	3,088	1,748	8,020
73A	sdn 4d	3,183	1,895	49,448
Customline (wb 115.5)				
64D	Victoria htp cpe	3,202	1,985	33,130
70B	sdn 2d	3,163	1,939	164,828
73B	sdn 4d	3,203	1,985	170,695

1956 Customline Victoria hardtop coupe

Fairlane (wb 115.5)		Wght	Price	Prod
57A	Victoria htp sdn	3,369	2,249	32,111
64A	Crown Victoria htp cpe	3,289	2,337	9,209
64B	Crown Vic htp cpe, glass top	3,299	2,407	603
64C	Victoria htp cpe	3,274	2,194	177,735
70C	club sdn 2d	3,179	2,047	142,629
73C	Town Sedan	3,219	2,093	224,872
76B	Sunliner conv cpe	3,384	2,359	58,147
Station Wagon (wb 115.5)				
59A	Ranch 2d, 6P	3,402	2,185	48,348
59B	Custom Ranch 2d, 6P	3,417	2,249	42,317
59C	Parklane 2d	3,432	2,428	15,186
79B	Country Sedan 4d, 8P	3,555	2,428	85,374
79C	Country Squire 4d, 8P	3,566	2,533	23,221

1956 Engines	bore×stroke	bhp	availability
L6, 223.0	3.62×3.60	137	S-all
V8, 272.0	3.62×3.30	173	O-Mainline, Customline
V8, 292.0	3.75×3.30	200	O-Fairlane wgn, (202 bhp w/auto)
V8, 312.0	3.80×3.44	215	O-all (225 bhp w/auto)

1957

Custom (wb 116.0)		Wght	Price	Prod
70A	sdn 2d	3,211	1,991	116,963
70D	bus sdn 2d	3,202	1,879	6,888
73A	sdn 4d	3,254	2,042	68,924
Custom 300 (wb 116.0)				
70B	sdn 2d	3,224	2,105	160,360
73B	sdn 4d	3,269	2,157	194,877
Fairlane (wb 118.0)				
57B	Victoria htp sdn	3,411	2,357	12,695
58A	Town Sedan 4d	3,376	2,286	52,060
63B	Victoria htp cpe	3,366	2,293	44,127
64A	club sdn 2d	3,331	2,235	39,843
Fairlane 500 (wb 118.0)				
51A	Skyliner retrac conv cpe	3,916	2,942	20,766
57A	Victoria htp sdn	3,426	2,404	68,550
58B	Town Sedan 4d	3,384	2,286	193,162
63A	Victoria htp cpe	3,381	2,339	183,202
64B	club sdn 2d	3,346	2,281	93,756
76B	Sunliner conv cpe	3,536	2,505	77,726
Station Wagon (wb 116.0)				
59A	Ranch 2d, 6P	3,455	2,301	60,486
59B	Del Rio 2d, 6P	3,462	2,397	46,105
79C	Country Sedan 4d, 9P	3,614	2,556	49,638
79D	Country Sedan 4d, 6P	3,525	2,451	137,251
79E	Country Squire 4d, 9P	3,628	2,684	27,690

1957 Engines	bore×stroke	bhp	availability
L6, 223.0	3.62×3.60	144	S-all exc 51A
V8, 272.0	3.62×3.30	190	S-51A; O-others
V8, 292.0	3.75×3.30	212	O-Fairlane, Fairlane 500, wgns
V8, 312.0	3.80×3.44	245	O-all

1958

Custom (wb 116.0)		Wght	Price	Prod
70A	sdn 2d	3,250	2,055	36,272
70D	bus sdn	3,227	1,967	4,062
73A	sdn 4d	3,278	2,109	27,811
Custom 300 (wb 116.0)				
70B	sdn 2d	3,300	2,305	137,169
73B	sdn 4d	3,328	2,159	135,557
Fairlane (wb 118.0)				
57B	Victoria htp sdn	3,450	2,419	5,868
58A	Town Sedan 4d	3,427	2,275	57,490
63B	Victoria htp cpe	3,373	2,354	16,416
64A	club sdn 2d	3,375	2,221	38,366
Fairlane 500 (wb 118.0)				
51A	Skyliner retrac conv cpe	4,069	3,163	14,713
57A	Victoria htp sdn	3,488	2,499	36,509
58B	sdn 4d	3,452	2,428	105,698

1957 Fairlane 500 Victoria hardtop sedan

		Wght	Price	Prod
63A	Victoria htp cpe	3,390	2,435	80,439
64B	club sdn 2d	3,380	2,374	34,041
76B	Sunliner conv	3,556	2,650	35,029
Station Wagon (wb 116.0)				
59A	Ranch 2d, 6P	3,552	2,397	34,578
59B	Del Rio 2d, 6P	3,734	2,503	12,687
79A	Ranch 4d, 6P	3,608	2,451	32,854
79C	Country Sedan 4d, 9P	3,682	2,664	20,702
79D	Country Sedan 4d, 6P	3,614	2,557	68,772
79E	Country Squire 4d, 9P	3,718	2,794	15,020

1958 Engines	bore×stroke	bhp	availability
L6, 223.0	3.62×3.60	145	S-all exc 51A
V8, 292.0	3.75×3.30	205	S-51A; O-others
V8, 332.0	4.00×3.30	240	O-wgns (265 bhp w/auto)
V8, 332.0	4.00×3.30	265	O-all
V8, 352.0	4.00×3.50	300	O-all

1959

Custom 300 (wb 118.0)		Wght	Price	Prod
58E	sdn 4d	3,436	2,273	249,553
64F	sdn 2d	3,360	2,219	228,576
64G	bus sdn	3,334	2,132	4,084
Fairlane (wb 118.0)				
58A	Town Sedan 4d	3,466	2,411	64,663
64A	club sdn 2d	3,382	2,357	35,126
Fairlane 500 (wb 118.0)				
57A	Victoria htp sdn	3,502	2,602	9,308
58B	sdn 4d	3,468	2,530	35,670
63A	Victoria htp cpe	3,416	2,537	23,892
64B	club sdn 2d	3,388	2,476	10,141
Galaxie (wb 118.0)				
51A	Skyliner retrac htp cpe	4,064	3,346	12,915
54A	sdn 4d	3,456	2,582	183,108

		Wght	Price	Prod
64H	club sdn 2d	3,388	2,528	52,848
65A	Victoria htp cpe	3,428	2,589	121,869
75A	Victoria htp sdn	3,544	2,654	47,728
76B	Sunliner conv cpe	3,578	2,839	45,868
Station Wagon (wb 118.0)				
59C	Ranch 2d, 6P	3,640	2,567	45,588
59D	Del Rio 2d, 6P	3,664	2,678	8,663
71E	Country Sedan 4d, 9P	3,818	2,829	28,811
71F	Country Sedan 4d, 6P	3,768	2,745	94,601
71G	Country Squire 4d, 9P	3,808	2,958	24,336
71H	Ranch 4d, 6P	3,736	2,634	67,339

1959 Engines	bore×stroke	bhp	availability
L6, 223.0	3.62×3.60	145	S-all exc 51A
V8, 292.0	3.75×3.30	200	S-51A; O-others
V8, 332.0	4.00×3.30	225	O-all
V8, 352.0	4.00×3.50	300	O-all

1958 Fairlane 500 Victoria hardtop coupe

1960

Falcon (wb 109.5)		Wght	Price	Prod
58A	sdn 4d	2,288	1,974	167,896
59A	wgn 2d	2,540	2,225	27,552
64A	sdn 2d	2,259	1,912	193,470
71A	wgn 4d	2,575	2,287	46.758
Custom 300 (wb 119.0)				
58F	sdn 4d	3,576	2,284	572
64H	sdn 2d	3,465	2,230	302
Fairlane (wb 119.0)				
58E	sdn 4d	3,656	2,311	109,801
64F	sdn 2d	3,582	2,257	93,256
64G	bus sdn	3,555	2,170	1,733
Fairlane 500 (wb 119.0)				
58A	Town Sedan 4d	3,663	2,388	153,234
64A	club sdn 2d	3,586	2,334	91,041
Galaxie (wb 119.0)				
54A	Town Sedan 4d	3,684	2,603	104,784
62A	club sdn 2d	3,603	2,549	31,866
63A	Starliner htp cpe	3,617	2,610	68,461
75A	Victoria htp sdn	3,692	2,675	39,215
76B	Sunliner conv cpe	3,791	2,860	44,762
Station Wagon (wb 119.0)				
59C	Ranch 2d, 6P	3,881	2,586	27,136
71E	Country Sedan 4d, 9P	4,058	2,837	19,277
71F	Country Sedan 4d, 6P	4,012	2,752	59,302
71G	Country Squire 4d, 9P	4,072	2,967	22,237
71H	Ranch 4d, 6P	3,998	2,656	43,872

1960 Engines	bore×stroke	bhp	availability
L6, 144.3	3.50×2.50	90	S-Falcon only
L6, 223.0	3.62×3.60	145	S-all exc Falcon
V8, 292.0	3.75×3.30	185	O-all exc Falcon
V8, 352.0	4.00×3.50	235	O-all exc Falcon
V8, 352.0	4.00×3.50	300/360	O-all exc Falcon

1961

Falcon (wb 109.5)		Wght	Price	Prod
58A	sdn 4d	2,289	1,976	159,761
59A	wgn 2d	2,525	2,227	32,045
62A	Futura cpe	2,322	2,162	44,470
64A	sdn 2d (inc 50 Economy sdns)	2,254	1,914	150,032
71A	wgn 4d	2,558	2,270	87,933
Custom 300 (wb 119.0)				
58F	sdn 4d	3,516	—	303
64H	sdn 2d	3,405	—	49
Fairlane (wb 119.0)				
58E	sdn 4d	3,634	2,317	96,602
64F	sdn 2d	3,536	2,263	66,875
Fairlane 500 (wb 119.0)				
58A	sdn 4d	3,642	2,432	98,917
64A	sdn 2d	3,551	2,378	42,468
Galaxie (wb 119.0)				
54A	sdn 4d	3,619	2,592	141,823
62A	sdn 2d	3,537	2,538	27,780
63A	Starliner htp cpe	3,566	2,599	29,669
65A	Victoria htp cpe	3,594	2,599	75,437
75A	Victoria htp sdn	3,637	2,664	30,342
76B	Sunliner conv cpe	3,743	2,849	44,614
Station Wagon (wb 119.0)				
59C	Ranch 2d, 6P	3,865	2,588	12,042
71E	Country Sedan 4d, 9P	4,011	2,858	16,356
71F	Country Sedan 4d, 6P	3,983	2,754	46,311
71G	Country Squire 4d, 9P	4,015	3,013	14,657
71H	Ranch 4d, 6P	3,960	2,658	30,292
71J	Country Squire 4d, 6P	3,969	2,943	16,961

1961 Engines	bore×stroke	bhp	availability
L6, 144.3	3.50×2.50	85	S-Falcon
L6, 170.0	3.50×2.94	101	O-Falcon
L6, 223.0	3.62×3.30	135	S-all exc Falcon
V8, 292.0	3.75×3.30	175	S-all exc Falcon
V8, 352.0	4.00×3.50	220	O-all exc Falcon
V8, 390.0	4.05×3.78	300	O-all exc Falcon
V8, 390.0	4.05×3.78	375/401	O-all exc Falcon (limited)

1962

Falcon (wb 109.5)		Wght	Price	Prod
58A	sdn 4d	2,279	2,047	126,041
58B	Deluxe sdn 4d	2,285	2,133	
59A	wgn 2d	2,539	2,298	20,025
59B	Deluxe wgn 2d	2,545	2,384	
62C	Futura cpe	2,343	2,273	17,011
64A	sdn 2d	2,243	1,985	143,650
64B	Deluxe sdn 2d	2,249	2,071	
71A	wgn 4d	2,575	2,341	66,819
71B	Deluxe wgn 4d	2,581	2,427	
71C	Squire wgn 4d	2,591	2,603	22,583
Fairlane (wb 115.5)				
54A	sdn 4d	2,848	2,216	45,342
62A	sdn 2d	2,815	2,154	34,264
54B	500 sdn 4d	2,865	2,304	129,258
62B	500 sdn 2d	2,832	2,242	68,624
62C	500 spt cpe	2,928	2,403	19,628

1961 Galaxie Sunliner convertible coupe

1963 Galaxie 500 XL hardtop coupe

Galaxie (wb 119.0)		Wght	Price	Prod
54B	sdn 4d	3,636	2,507	115,594
62B	sdn 2d	3,554	2,453	54,930
Galaxie 500 (wb 119.0)				
54A	sdn 4d	3,650	2,667	174,195
62A	sdn 2d	3,568	2,613	27,824
65A	Victoria htp cpe	3,568	2,674	87,562
65B	XL Victoria htp cpe	3,672	2,268	28,412
75A	Victoria htp sdn	3,640	2,739	30,778
76A	Sunliner conv cpe	3,730	2,924	42,646
76B	XL Sunliner conv cpe	3,831	3,518	13,183
Station Wagon (wb 119.0)				
71A	Country Squire 4d, 9P	4,022	3,088	15,666
71B	Country Sedan 4d, 6P	3,992	2,829	47,635
71C	Country Sedan 4d, 9P	4,010	2,933	16,562
71D	Ranch 4d, 6P	3,968	2,733	33,674
71E	Country Squire 4d, 6P	4,006	3,018	16,114

1962 Engines	bore×stroke	bhp	availability
L6, 144.3	3.50×2.50	85	S-Falcon
L6, 170.0	3.50×2.94	101	O-Falcon
L6, 223.0	3.62×3.60	138	S-all exc Falcon
V8, 221.0	3.50×2.87	145	O-Fairlane
V8, 260.0	3.80×2.87	164	O-Fairlane
V8, 292.0	3.75×3.30	170	S-76B; O-all exc Falc, Fair
V8, 352.0	4.00×3.50	220	O-all exc Falcon, Fairlane
V8, 390.0	4.05×3.78	300/340	O-all exc Falcon, Fairlane
V8, 390.0	4.05×3.78	375/401	O-all exc Falcon, Fairlane
V8, 406.0	4.13×3.78	385/405	O-all exc Falcon, Fairlane

1963

Series 0 Falcon (wb 109.5)		Wght	Price	Prod
54A	sdn 4d	2,337	2,047	62,365
62A	sdn 2d	2,300	1,985	70,630
Series 10 Falcon Futura (wb 109.5)				
54B	sdn 4d	2,345	2,161	31,736
62B	sdn 2d	2,308	2,116	27,018
63B	htp cpe	2,438	2,198	28,496
63C	Sprint htp cpe	2,438	2,320	10,479
76A	conv cpe	2,645	2,470	31,192
76B	Sprint conv cpe	2,645	2,600	4,602
Series 20 Falcon Wagon (wb 109.5)				
59A	wgn 2d	2,580	2,298	7,322
59B	Deluxe wgn 2d	2,586	2,384	4,269
71A	wgn 4d	2,617	2,341	18,484
71B	Deluxe wgn 4d	2,623	2,427	23,477
71C	Squire wgn 4d	2,639	2,603	8,269
Series 30 Fairlane (wb 115.5)				
54A	sdn 4d	2,930	2,216	44,454
62A	sdn 2d	2,890	2,154	28,984
71B	Cus Ranch Wagon 4d	3,298	2,613	29,612
71D	Ranch Wagon 4d	3,281	2,525	24,006
71E	Squire Wagon 4d	3,295	2,781	7,983
Series 40 Fairlane 500 (wb 115.5)				
54B	sdn 4d	2,945	2,304	104,175
62B	sdn 2d	2,905	2,242	34,764
65A	htp cpe	2,923	2,324	41,641
65B	htp cpe, bkt sts	2,923	2,504	28,268
Series 50 300 (wb 119.0)				
54E	sdn 4d	3,627	2,378	44,142
62E	sdn 2d	3,547	2,324	26,010
Series 50 Galaxie (wb 119.0)				
54B	sdn 4d	3,647	2,507	82,419
62B	sdn 2d	3,567	2,453	30,335

1963 Fairlane 500 hardtop coupe

1964 Falcon Sprint convertible coupe

Series 60 Galaxie 500 (wb 119.0)		Wght	Price	Prod
54A	sdn 4d	3,667	2,667	205,722
62A	sdn 2d	3,587	2,613	21,137
63B	XL htp cpe, fstbk	3,772	2,674	134,370
65A	htp cpe	3,599	2,674	49,733
75A	htp sdn	3,679	2,739	39,154
76A	Sunliner conv cpe	3,757	2,924	29,713
Series 70 Station Wagon (wb 119.0)				
71A	Country Squire 4d, 9P	4,003	3,088	19,567
71B	Country Sedan 4d, 6P	3,977	2,829	64,954
71C	Country Sedan 4d, 9P	3,989	2,933	22,250
71E	Country Squire 4d, 6P	3,991	3,018	20,359

1963 Engines	bore×stroke	bhp	availability
L6, 144.3	3.50×2.50	85	S-Falcon
L6, 170.0	3.50×2.94	101	O-Falcon
L6, 200.0	3.68×3.13	116	S-Fairlane
L6, 223.0	3.62×3.60	138	S-all exc Falcon, Fairlane
V8, 221.0	3.50×2.87	145	O-Fairlane
V8, 260.0	3.80×2.87	164	S-Falcon Sprint; O-others
V8, 289.0	4.00×2.87	271	O-Fairlane
V8, 352.0	4.00×3.50	220	O-all exc Falcon, Fairlane
V8, 390.0	4.05×3.78	300/330	O-all exc Falcon, Fairlane
V8, 406.0	4.13×3.78	385/405	O-all exc Falcon, Fairlane
V8, 427.0	4.23×3.78	410/425	O-all exc Falcon, Fairlaine

1964

Series 0 Falcon (wb 109.5)		Wght	Price	Prod
01	sdn 4d	2,365	1,996	36,441
01	Deluxe sdn 2d	2,380	2,096	28,411
02	sdn 4d	2,400	2,058	27,722

		Wght	Price	Prod
02	Deluxe sdn 4d	2,420	2,158	26,532
Series 10 Falcon Futura (wb 109.5)				
11	htp cpe, bkt seats	2,545	2,325	8,607
12	conv cpe, bkt seats	2,735	2,597	2,980
13	Sprint htp cpe	2,813	2,436	13.830
14	Sprint conv cpe	3,008	2,671	4,278
15	conv cpe	2,710	2,481	13,220
16	sdn 4d	2,410	2,176	38,032
17	htp cpe	2,515	2,209	32,608
19	sdn 2d	2,375	2,127	16,833
Series 20 Falcon Wagon (wb 109.5)				
21	wgn 2d	2,660	2,326	6,034
22	wgn 4d	2,695	2,360	17,779
24	Deluxe wgn 4d	2,715	2,446	20,697
26	Squire wgn 4d	2,720	2,622	6,766
Series 30 Fairlane (wb 115.5)				
31	sdn 2d	2,855	2,194	20,421
32	sdn 4d	2,895	2,235	36,693
38	Ranch wgn 4d	3,290	2,531	20,980
Series 40 Fairlane 500 (wb 115.5)				
41	sdn 2d	2,863	2,276	23,447
42	sdn 4d	2,910	2,317	86,919
43	htp cpe	2,925	2,341	42,733
47	htp cpe, bkt sts	2,945	2,502	21,431
48	Ranch Cus wgn 4d	3,310	2,612	24,962
Series 50 Custom (wb 119.0)				
51	500 sdn 2d	3,559	2,464	20,619
52	500 sdn 4d	3,659	2,518	68,828
53	sdn 2d	3,529	2,361	41,359
54	sdn 4d	3,619	2,415	57,964
Series 60 Galaxie 500 (wb 119.0)				
60	XL htp sdn	3,722	3,298	14,661
61	sdn 2d	3,574	2,624	13,041
62	sdn 4d	3,674	2,678	198,805
64	htp sdn	3,689	2,750	49,242
66	htp cpe	3,584	2,685	206,998
65	Sunliner conv cpe	3,759	2,947	37,311
68	XL htp cpe	3,622	3,233	58,306
69	XL conv cpe	3,687	3,495	15,169

Series 70 Station Wagon (wb 119.0)		Wght	Price	Prod
72	Country Sedan 4d, 6P	3,973	2,840	68,578
74	Country Sedan 4d, 9P	3,983	2,944	25,661
76	Country Squire 4d, 6P	3,988	3,029	23,570
78	Country Squire 4d, 9P	3,998	3,099	23,120

1964 Engines	bore×stroke	bhp	availability
L6, 144.3	3.50×2.50	85	S-Flcn exc conv, Sprnt, Del wgns
L6, 170.0	3.50×2.94	101	S-Flcn conv, Sprnt, Del wgn; O-other Flcn
L6, 200.0	3.68×3.13	116	S-Fairlane; O-Falcon
L6, 223.0	3.62×3.60	138	S-all exc Fairlane, Falcon
V8, 260.0	3.80×2.87	164	S-Flcn Sprnt, Fairlane; O-Flcn
V8, 289.0	4.00×2.87	195/271	S-60, 68, 69; O-all exc Flcn
V8, 352.0	4.00×3.50	250	O-all exc Falcon, Fairlane
V8, 390.0	4.05×3.78	300/330	O-all exc Falcon, Fairlane
V8, 427.0	4.23×3.78	410/425	O-all exc Falcon, Fairlane

1965

Series 0 Falcon (wb 109.5)		Wght	Price	Prod
01	sdn 4d	2,366	2,020	35,858
01	Deluxe sdn 2d	2,381	2,120	13,824
02	sdn 4d	2,406	2,082	30,186
02	Deluxe sdn 4d	2,426	2,182	13,850
Series 10 Falcon Futura (wb 109.5)				
13	Sprint htp cpe	2,749	2,337	2,806
14	Sprint conv cpe	2,971	2,671	300
15	conv cpe	2,673	2,481	6,315
16	sdn 4d	2,413	2,192	33,985
17	htp cpe	2,491	2,226	25,754
19	sdn 2d	2,373	2,144	11,670
Series 20 Falcon Wagon (wb 109.5)				
21	wgn 2d	2,611	2,333	4,891
22	wgn 4d	2,651	2,367	14,911
24	Deluxe wgn 4d (Futura)	2,667	2,506	12,548
26	Squire wgn 4d	2,669	2,665	6,703
Series 30 Fairlane (wb 115.5)				
31	sdn 2d	2,902	2,230	13,685
32	sdn 4d	2,954	2,271	25,378
38	wgn 4d	3,279	2,567	13,911

1966 Fairlane 500 XL hardtop coupe

Series 40 Fairlane 500 (wb 115.5)		Wght	Price	Prod
41	sdn 2d	2,901	2,312	16,092
42	sdn 4d	2,959	2,353	77,836
43	htp cpe	2,973	2,377	41,405
47	htp cpe, bkt sts	2,984	2,538	15,141
48	wgn 4d	3,316	2,648	20,506
Series 50 Custom (wb 119.0)				
51	sdn 2d	3,336	2,464	49,034
52	sdn 4d	3,408	2,518	96,393
53	500 sdn 2d	3,306	2,361	19,603
54	500 sdn 4d	3,378	2,415	71,727
Series 60 Galaxie 500 (wb 119.0)				
60	LTD htp sdn	3,578	3,313	68,038
62	sdn 4d	3,440	2,678	181,183
64	htp sdn	3,480	2,765	49,982
65	conv cpe	3,592	2,950	31,930
66	htp cpe	3,380	2,685	157,284
67	LTD htp cpe	3,486	3,233	37,691
68	XL htp cpe	3,497	3,233	28,141
69	XL conv cpe	3,665	3,498	9,849
Series 70 Station Wagon (wb 119.0)				
71	Ranch 4d, 6P	3,869	2,763	30,817
72	Country Sedan 4d, 6P	3,879	2,855	59,693
74	Country Sedan 4d, 9P	3,893	2,959	32,344
76	Country Squire 4d, 6P	3,925	3,104	24,308
78	Country Squire 4d, 9P	3,937	3,174	30,502

1965 Engines	bore×stroke	bhp	availability
L6, 170.0	3.50×2.94	101	S-Flcn exc Futura, Squire until 9/25/64
L6, 200.0	3.68×3.13	120	S-Futura/Squire, Fairlane; O-Flcn
L6, 240.0	4.00×3.18	150	S-all exc Flcn, Fairlane, LTD, XL
V8, 289.0	4.00×2.87	200–271	S-LTD, XL;O-others
V8, 352.0	4.00×3.50	250	O-all exc Falcon, Fairlane
V8, 390.0	4.05×3.78	300/330	O-all exc Falcon, Fairlane
V8, 427.0	4.23×3.78	425	O-all exc Falcon, Fairlane

1966

Series O Falcon (wb 110.9; wgn-113.0)		Wght	Price	Prod
01	club cpe	2,519	2,060	41,432
02	sdn 4d	2,559	2,114	34,685
06	wgn 4d	3,037	2,442	16,653
Series 10 Falcon Futura (wb 110.9; wgn-113.0)				
11	club cpe	2,527	2,183	21,997
12	sdn 4d	2,567	2,237	34,039
13	spt cpe	2,597	2,328	20,289
16	wgn 4d	3,045	2,553	13,574
Series 30 Fairlane (wb 116; wgn 113.0)				
31	club cpe	2,832	2,240	13,498
32	sdn 4d	2,877	2,280	26,170
38	wgn 4d	3,267	2,589	12,379
Series 40 Fairlane 500 (wb 116; wgn-113.0)				
40	XL GT htp cpe, V8	3,493	2,843	33,015
41	club cpe	2,839	3,317	14,118
42	sdn 4d	2,884	2,357	68,635
43	htp cpe	2,941	2,378	75,947
44	XL GT conv cpe	3,070	3,068	4,327
45	conv cpe	3,169	2,603	9,299
46	XL conv cpe	3,184	2,768	4,560
47	XL htp cpe	2,969	2,533	23,942
48	Deluxe wgn 4d	3,277	2,665	19,826
49	Squire wgn 4d	3,285	2,796	11,558
Series 50 Custom (wb 119.0)				
51	500 sdn 2d	3,397	2,481	28,789
52	500 sdn 4d	3,466	2,533	109,449

		Wght	Price	Prod
53	sdn 2d	3,355	2,380	32,292
54	sdn 4d	3,455	2,432	72,245
Series 60 Galaxie 500 (wb 119.0)				
60	LTD htp sdn	3,649	3,278	69,400
61	7 Litre htp cpe	3,914	3,621	8,705
62	sdn 4d	3,478	2,677	171,886
63	7 Litre conv cpe, V8	4,059	3,872	2,368
64	htp sdn	3,548	2,762	54,884
65	conv cpe	3,655	2,934	27,454
66	htp cpe	3,459	2,685	198,532
67	LTD htp cpe	3,601	3,201	31,696
68	XL htp cpe	3,616	3,231	25,715
69	XL conv cpe	3,761	3,480	6,360
Series 70 Station Wagon (wb 119.0)				
71	Ranch 4d	3,941	2,793	33,306
72	Country Sedan 4d, 6P	3,956	2,882	55,616
74	Country Sedan 4d, 9P	3,997	2,999	36,633
76	Country Squire 4d, 6P	4,026	3,182	27,645
78	Country Squire 4d, 9P	4,040	3,265	41,953

1966 Engines	bore×stroke	bhp	availability
L6, 170.0	3.50×2.94	105	S-Falcon
L6, 200.0	3.68×3.13	120	S-Flcn Futura/wgn, Fair exc GT, GTA; O-Flcn
L6, 240.0	4.00×3.18	150	S-all exc Flcn, Fair; O-Flcn wgns
V8, 289.0	4.00×2.87	200/225	S-XL, LTD; O-Flcn, Fair exc GT, GTA; 50, 60, 70 exc 7L
V8, 352.0	4.00×3.50	250	O-all exc 7L, Fairlane, Falcon
V8, 390.0	4.05×3.78	265	O-all exc 7L, Fair GT/GTA, Flcn
V8, 390.0	4.05×3.78	315	O-all exc 7L, Fairlane, Falcon
V8, 390.0	4.05×3.78	335	S-Fair GT/GTA; O-other Fair
V8, 427.0	4.23×3.78	410/425	O-all exc 7L, 70, Fairlane, Flcn
V8, 428.0	4.13×3.98	345	S-7L; O-others exc Fairlane, Flcn

1967

Falcon (wb 110.9; wgn-113.0)		Wght	Price	Prod
10	sdn 2d	2,520	2,118	16,082
11	sdn 4d	2,551	2,167	13,554
12	wgn 4d	3,030	2,497	5,553
Falcon Futura (wb 110.9; wgns-113.0)				
20	club cpe	2,528	2,280	6,287
21	sdn 4d	2,559	2,322	11,254
22	spt cpe	3,062	2,437	7,053
23	Squire wgn 4d	2,556	2,609	4,552

1966 Galaxie 500 7 Litre convertible coupe

Fairlane (wb 116.0; wgns-113.0)		Wght	Price	Prod
30	sdn 2d	2,832	2,297	10,628
31	sdn 4d	2,867	2,339	19,740
32	Ranch wgn 4d	3,283	2,643	10,881
33	500 club cpe	2,840	2,377	8,473
34	500 sdn 4d	2,887	2,417	51,522
35	500 htp cpe	2,927	2,439	70,135
36	500 conv cpe	3,244	2,664	5,428
37	Deluxe wgn 4d	3,291	2,718	15,902
38	Country Squire wgn 4d	3,302	2,902	8,348
Fairlane 500XL (wb 116.0)				
40	htp cpe	2,955	2,724	14,871
41	conv cpe	3,272	2,950	1,943
42	GT htp cpe	3,301	2,839	18,670
43	GT conv cpe	3,607	3,064	2,117
Series 50 Custom (wb 119.0)				
50	sdn 2d	3,430	2,441	18,107
51	sdn 4d	3,488	2,496	41,417
52	500 sdn 2d	3,482	2,553	18,146
53	500 sdn 4d	3,490	2,595	83,260
Galaxie 500 (wb 119.0)				
54	sdn 4d	3,500	2,732	130,063
55	htp cpe	3,503	2,755	197,388
56	htp sdn	3,571	2,808	57,087
57	conv cpe	3,682	3,003	19,068
58	XL htp sdn	3,594	3,243	18,174
59	XL conv cpe	3,794	3,493	5,161
LTD (wb 119.0)				
62	htp cpe	3,626	3,362	46,036
64	sdn 4d	3,795	3,298	12,491
66	htp sdn	3,676	3,363	51,978
Station Wagon (wb 119.0)				
70	Ranch 4d, 6P	3,930	2,836	23,932
71	Country Sedan 4d, 6P	3,943	2,935	50,818
72	Country Sedan 4d, 9P	4,023	3,061	34,377
73	Country Squire 4d, 6P	3,990	3,234	25,600
74	Country Squire 4d, 9P	4,030	3,359	44,024

1967 Engines	bore×stroke	bhp	availability
L6, 170.0	3.50×2.94	105	S-Falcon exc Futura, wagons
L6, 200.0	3.68×3.13	120	S-Flcn Futura/wgns, Fair exc GTs
L6, 240.0	4.00×3.18	150	S-all exc Falcon, Fairlane
V8, 289.0	4.00×2.87	200	S-Fair GT, 500XL, LTD; O-others
V8, 289.0	4.00×2.87	225	O-Falcon
V8, 390.0	4.05×3.78	270	O-Fairlane
V8, 390.0	4.05×3.78	315	O-Cus, Gal, LTD, Station Wgn
V8, 390.0	4.05×3.78	320	O-Fairlane
V8, 427.0	4.23×3.78	410/425	O-all exc Falcon
V8, 428.0	4.13×3.98	345	O-all exc Falcon, Fairlane

1968

Falcon (wb 110.9; wgn-113.0)		Wght	Price	Prod
10	sdn 2d	2,680	2,252	29,166
11	sdn 4d	2,714	2,301	36,443
12	wgn 4d	3,123	2,617	15,576
Falcon Futura (wb 110.9; wgn-113.0)				
20	sdn 2d	2,685	2,415	10,633
21	sdn 4d	2,719	2,456	18,733
22	spt cpe	2,713	2,541	10,077
23	wgn 4d	3,123	2,728	10,761
Fairlane (wb 116.0; wgn-113.0)				
30	htp cpe	3,028	2,456	44,683
31	sdn 4d	2,986	2,464	18,146
32	wgn 4d	3,333	2,770	14,800
33	500 htp cpe	3,066	2,591	33,282

1967 Fairlane 500 XL hardtop coupe

		Wght	Price	Prod
34	500 sdn 4d	3,024	2,543	42,930
35	500 fstbk htp cpe	3,080	2,566	32,452
36	500 conv cpe	3,226	2,822	3,761
37	500 wgn 4d	3,377	2,880	10,190
Torino (wb 116.0; wgn-113.0)				
38	Squire wgn 4d	3,425	3,032	14,773
40	htp cpe	3,098	2,710	35,964
41	sdn 4d	3,062	2,688	17,962
42	GT fstbk htp cpe	3,208	2,747	74,135
43	GT conv cpe	3,352	3,001	5,310
44	GT htp cpe	3,194	2,772	23,939
Custom (wb 119.0)				
50	sdn 2d	3,471	3,584	18,485
51	sdn 4d	3,498	2,642	45,980
52	500 sdn 2d	3,460	2,699	8,983
53	500 sdn 4d	3,511	2,741	49,398
Galaxie 500 (wb 119.0)				
54	sdn 4d	3,516	2,864	117,877
55	fstbk htp cpe	3,534	2,881	69,760
56	htp sdn	3,562	2,936	55,461
57	conv cpe	3,679	3,108	11,832
58	htp cpe	3,540	2,916	84,332
60	XL fstbk htp cpe	3,588	2,985	50,048
61	XL conv cpe	3,745	3,214	6,066
LTD (wb 119.0)				
62	htp cpe	3,679	3,153	54,163
64	sdn 4d	3,596	3,135	22,834
66	htp sdn	3,642	3,206	61,755
Station Wagon (wb 119.0)				
70	Ranch 4d, 6P	3,925	3,000	18,237
71	Ranch 500 4d, 6P	3,935	3,063	18,181
72	Ranch 500 4d, 9P	3,981	3,176	13,421
73	Country Sedan 4d, 6P	3,944	3,184	39,335
74	Country Sedan 4d, 9P	4,001	3,295	29,374
75	Country Squire 4d, 6P	4,013	3,539	33,994
76	Country Squire 4d, 9P	4,059	3,619	57,776

1968 Engines	bore×stroke	bhp	availability
L6, 170.0	3.50×2.94	100	S-base Falcon cpes, sdns
L6, 200.0	3.68×3.13	115	S-Fair, Tor, Flcn Fut wgn; O-Flcn
L6, 240.0	4.00×3.18	150	S-all exc Futura, Tor GT, LTD
V8, 289.0	4.00×2.87	195	O-Falcon
V8, 302.0	4.00×3.00	210	S-LTD, Tor GT; O-all
V8, 302.0	4.00×3.00	230	O-Falcon, Fairlane, Torino
V8, 390.0	4.05×3.78	265	O-all exc Falcon
V8, 390.0	4.05×3.78	315	O-all exc Falcon, Fairlane
V8, 390.0	4.05×3.78	335	O-Fairlane
V8, 427.0	4.23×3.78	390	O-Fairlane/Torino htps
V8, 428.0	4.13×3.98	340	O-all exc Falcon, Fairlane

1969

Falcon (wb 110.9; wgn-113.0)		Wght	Price	Prod
10	sdn 2d	2,700	2,283	29,262
11	sdn 4d	2,735	2,333	22,719
12	wgn 4d	3,100	2,660	11,568
Falcon Futura (wb 110.9; wgn-113.0)				
20	sdn 2d	2,715	2,461	6,482
21	sdn 4d	2,748	2,498	11,850
22	spt cpe	2,738	2,598	5,931
23	wgn 4d	3,120	2,771	7,203
Fairlane (wb 116.0; wgn-113.0)				
30	htp cpe	3,079	2,499	85,630
31	sdn 4d	3,065	2,488	27,296
32	wgn 4d	3,441	2,841	10,882
33	500 htp cpe	3,090	2,626	28,179
34	500 sdn 4d	3,082	2,568	40,888
35	500 fstbk htp cpe	3,137	2,601	29,849
36	500 conv cpe	3,278	2,851	2,264
37	500 wgn 4d	3,469	2,951	12,869
Torino (wb 116.0; wgn-113.0)				
38	Squire wgn 4d	3,503	3,107	14,472
40	htp cpe	3,143	2,754	20,789
41	sdn 4d	3,128	2,733	11,971
42	GT fstbk htp cpe	3,220	2,840	61,319
43	GT conv cpe	3,356	3,090	2,552
44	GT htp cpe	3,173	2,865	17,951
45	Cobra htp cpe	3,490	3,164	—
46	Cobra fstbk htp cpe	3,537	3,189	—
Custom (wb 121.0)				
50	sdn 2d	3,605	2,649	15,439
51	sdn 4d	3,628	2,691	45,653
52	500 sdn 2d	3,590	2,748	7,585
53	500 sdn 4d	3,640	2,790	45,761
70	Ranch wgn 4d	4,089	3,091	17,489
71	500 wgn 4d, 6P	4,102	3,155	16,432
72	500 wgn 4d, 9P	4,152	3,268	11,563
Galaxie 500 (wb 121.0)				
54	sdn 4d	3,690	2,914	104,606
55	fstbk htp cpe	3,700	2,930	63,921
56	htp sdn	3,725	2,983	64,031
57	conv cpe	3,860	3,159	6,910
58	htp cpe	3,655	2,982	71,920
73	Country Sedan wgn 4d, 6P	4,087	3,274	36,387
74	Country Sedan wgn 4d, 9P	4,112	3,390	27,517
XL (wb 121.0)				
60	fstbk htp cpe	3,805	3,069	54,557
61	conv cpe	3,955	3,297	7,402
LTD (wb 121.0)				
62	htp cpe	3,745	3,251	111,565
64	sdn 4d	3,745	3,209	63,709
66	htp sdn	3,840	3,278	113,168
75	Country Squire wgn 4d, 6P	4,202	3,661	46,445
76	Country Squire wgn 4d, 9P	4,227	3,738	82,790

1969 Engines	bore×stroke	bhp	availability
L6, 170.0	3.50×2.94	100	S-Falcon exc Futura
L6, 200.0	3.68×3.13	115	S-Futura
L6, 240.0	4.00×3.18	150	S-all exc Flcn, Fair, Tor GT, LTD
L6, 250.0	3.68×3.91	155	S-Fairlane, Tor exc GT, Cobra
V8, 302.0	4.00×3.00	220	S-LTD, Tor GT; O-others
V8, 351.0	4.00×3.50	250	O-Fairlane, Tor exc Cobra
V8, 351.0	4.00×3.50	290	O-Fairlane, Tor exc Cobra
V8, 390.0	4.05×3.78	265	O-full-size
V8, 390.0	4.05×3.78	320	O-Fairlane, Tor exc Cobra
V8, 428.0	4.13×3.98	335*	S-Tor Cobra; O-Fairlane
V8, 429.0	4.36×3.59	320/360	O-full-size

1968 Galaxie 500 XL Sport Roof hardtop coupe

1969 Torino Talladega Sport Roof hardtop coupe

*Available in standard and Ram Air versions.

1970

Maverick (wb 103.0)		Wght	Price	Prod
91	sdn 2d	2,411	1,995	578,914
Falcon (wb 110.9, wgn-113.0)				
10	sdn 2d	2,708	2,390	4,373
11	sdn 4d	2,753	2,438	5,301
12	wgn 4d	3,155	2,767	1,624
Falcon Futura (wb 110.9; wgn-113.0)				
20	sdn 2d	2,727	2,542	1,129
21	sdn 4d	2,764	2,579	2,262
23	wgn 4d	3,191	2,878	1,005
"1970½" Falcon (wb 117.0)				
26	sdn 2d	3,100	2,460	26,071
27	sdn 4d	3,116	2,500	30,443
40	wgn 4d	3,483	2,801	10,539
Fairlane 500 (wb 117.0; wgn-114.0)				
28	sdn 4d	3,166	2,627	25,780
29	htp cpe	3,178	2,660	70,636
41	wgn 4d	3,558	2,957	13,613
Torino (wb 117.0; wgn-114.0)				
30	htp cpe	3,223	2,722	49,826
31	sdn 4d	3,208	2,689	30,117
32	htp sdn	3,239	2,795	14,312
33	Brougham htp cpe	3,293	3,006	16,911
34	fstbk htp cpe	3,261	2,899	12,490
35	GT htp cpe	3,366	3,105	56,819
36	Brougham htp sdn	3,309	3,078	14,543
37	GT conv cpe	3,490	3,212	3,939
38	Cobra fstbk htp cpe	3,774	3,270	7,675
42	wgn 4d	3,603	3,164	10,613
43	Squire wgn 4d	3,673	3,379	13,166

Custom (wb 121.0)		Wght	Price	Prod
51	sdn 4d	3,545	2,850	42,849
52	500 htp cpe	3,510	2,918	2,677
53	500 sdn 4d	3,585	2,872	41,261
70	Ranch wgn 4d	4,079	3,305	15,086
71	500 wgn 4d, 6P	4,049	3,368	15,304
72	500 wgn 4d, 9P	4,137	3,481	9,943
Galaxie 500 (wb 121.0)				
54	sdn 4d	3,601	3,026	101,784
55	fstbk htp cpe	3,610	3,043	50,825
56	htp sdn	3,672	3,096	53,817
58	htp cpe	3,611	3,094	57,059
73	Country Sedan wgn 4d, 6P	4,089	3,488	32,209
74	Country Sedan wgn 4d, 9P	4,112	3,600	22,645
XL (wb 121.0)				
60	fstbk htp cpe	3,750	3,293	27,251
61	conv cpe	3,983	3,501	6,348
LTD (wb 121.0)				
62	htp cpe	3,727	3,356	96,324
62	Brougham htp cpe	3,855	3,537	
64	sdn 4d	3,701	3,307	78,306
64	Brougham sdn	3,829	3,502	
66	htp sdn	3,771	3,385	90,390
66	Brougham htp sdn	4,029	3,579	
75	Country Squire wgn 4d, 6P	4,139	3,832	39,837
76	Country Squire wgn 4d, 9P	4,185	3,909	69,077

1970 Engines	bore×stroke	bhp	availability
L6, 170.0	3.50×2.94	105	S-Maverick
L6, 200.0	3.68×3.13	120	S-Falcon; O-Maverick
L6, 240.0	4.00×3.18	150	S-full-size exc XL, LTD
L6, 250.0	3.68×3.91	155	S-Tor exc GT, Brghm, Squire, Cobra
V8, 302.0	4.00×3.00	220	S-Tor GT/Brghm/Squire, Cobra; O-others
V8, 351.0	4.00×3.50	250	S-XL, LTD, big wgns; O-all exc Flcn, Cobra
V8, 351.0	4.00×3.50	300	O-Torino exc Cobra
V8, 390.0	4.05×3.78	265	O-all full-size
V8, 429.0	4.36×3.59	320	O-all full-size
V8, 429.0	4.36×3.59	360	S-Tor Cobra; O-Ford, Torino
V8, 429.0	4.36×3.59	370*	O-Torino exc wgns
V8, 429.0	4.36×3.59	375	O-Torino, Cobra

*Available in standard and Ram Air versions.

1970½ Engines	bore×stroke	bhp	availability
L6, 250.0	3.68×3.91	155	S-Falcon
V8, 302.0	4.00×3.00	220	O-Falcon
V8, 351.0	4.00×3.50	250/300	O-Falcon
V8, 429.0	4.36×3.59	360	O-Falcon
V8, 429.0	4.36×3.59	370	O-Falcon (w/o Ram Air)

1971

Pinto (wb 94.2)		Wght	Price	Prod
10	fstbk sdn 2d	1,949	1,919	288,606
11	Runabout htchbk sdn 3d	1,993	2,062	63,796
Maverick (wb 103.0; 4d-109.9)				
91	fstbk sdn 2d	2,546	2,175	159,726
92	sdn 4d	2,641	2,234	73,208
93	Grabber fstbk sdn 2d	2,601	2,354	38,963
Torino (wb 117.0; wgns-114.0)				
25	formal htp cpe	3,168	2,706	37,518
27	sdn 4d	3,163	2,672	29,501
40	wgn 5d	3,514	3,023	21,570
30	500 formal htp cpe	3,170	2,887	89,966
31	500 sdn 4d	3,160	2,855	35,650

1968 Torino GT Pace Car convertible coupe

1970 Torino GT Sports Roof hardtop coupe

		Wght	Price	Prod
32	500 htp sdn	3,196	2,959	12,724
34	500 fstbk htp cpe	3,179	2,943	11,150
42	500 wgn 5d	3,514	3,170	23,270
33	Brougham formal htp cpe V8	3,209	3,175	8,593
36	Brougham formal htp sdn V8	3,256	3,248	4,408
43	Squire wgn 5d V8	3,583	3,560	15,805
35	GT fstbk htp cpe V8	3,287	3,150	31,641
37	GT conv V8	3,428	3,408	1,613
38	Cobra fstbk htp cpe	3,525	3,295	3,054
Ford (wb 121.0)				
51	Custom sdn 4d	3,700	3,288	41,062
70	Custom Ranch Wagon 4d V8	4,222	3,890	16,696
53	Custom 500 sdn 4d	3,705	3,426	33,765
72	Custom 500 Ranch Wagon 5d 2S V8	4,231	3,982	25,957
72	Custom 500 Ranch Wagon 5d 3S V8	4,281	4,097	
54	Galaxie 500 sdn 4d	3,782	3,594	98,130
56	Galaxie 500 htp sdn	3,838	3,665	46,595
58	Galaxie 500 htp cpe	3,783	3,628	117,139
74	G500 Ctry Sdn wgn 5d 2S V8	4,246	4,074	60,487
74	G500 Ctry Sdn wgn 5d 3S V8	4,296	4,188	
61	LTD conv V8	4,053	4,094	5,750
62	LTD htp cpe V8	3,919	3,923	103,896
63	LTD sdn 4d V8	3,981	3,931	92,260
64	LTD htp sdn V8	3,976	3,969	48,166
76	Country Squire wgn 5d 2S V8	4,306	4,380	130,644
76	Country Squire wgn 5d 3S V8	4,356	4,496	
66	LTD Brougham sdn 4d V8	4,111	4,094	26,186
67	LTD Brougham htp sdn V8	4,016	4,140	27,820
68	LTD Brougham htp cpe V8	3,945	4,097	43,303

1971 Engines	bore×stroke	bhp	availability
L4, 98.6	3.19×3.06	75	S-Pinto

	bore×stroke	bhp	availability
L4, 122.0	3.58×3.03	100	0-Pinto
L6, 170.0	3.50×2.94	100	S-Maverick
L6, 200.00	3.68×3.13	115	0-Maverick
L6, 240.0	4.00×3.18	140	S-Ford
L6, 250.0	3.68×3.91	145	S-Tor exc Cobra; O-Mav
V8, 302.0	4.00×3.00	210	S-Mav, Ford Cus, Tor exc Cobra
V8, 351.0	4.00×3.50	240	S-Ford exc Cus
V8, 351.0	4.00×3.50	285	S-Tor Cobra; O-Torino
V8, 400.0	4.00×4.00	260	O-Ford
V8, 429.0	4.36×3.59	320/360	O-Ford
V8, 429.0	4.36×3.59	370	O-Torino

1972

Pinto (wb 94.2)		Wght	Price	Prod
10	fstbk sdn 2d	2,061	1,960	181,002
11	Runabout htchbk sdn 3d	2,099	2,078	197,290
12	wgn 3d	2,283	2,265	101,483
Maverick (wb 103.0; 4d-109.9)				
91	fstbk sdn 2d	2,654	2,140	145,931
92	sdn 4d	2,751	2,195	73,686
93	Grabber fstbk sdn 2d	2,708	2,309	35,347
Torino (wb 118.0; 2d-114.0)				
25	formal htp cpe	3,374	2,673	33,530
27	sdn 4d	3,442	2,641	33,486
40	wgn 5d	3,840	2,955	22,204
30	Gran Torino Formal htp cpe	3,410	2,878	132,284
31	Gran Torino sdn 4d	3,484	2,856	102,300
42	Gran Torino wgn 5d	3,874	3,096	45,212
35	GT Sport fstbk htp cpe V8	3,470	3,094	60,794
38	Gran Torino form htp cpe V8	3,466	3,094	31,239
43	Squire wgn 5d V8	3,938	3,486	35,595
Ford (wb 121.0)				
51	Custom sdn 4d	3,742	3,246	33,014
70	Custom Ranch wgn 5d V8	4,304	3,852	13,064
53	Custom 500 sdn 4d	3,808	3,377	24,870
72	C 500 Ranch Wagon 5d 2S V8	4,314	3,941	16,834
72	C 500 Ranch Wagon 5d 3S V8	4,364	4,051	
54	Galaxie 500 sdn 4d	3,848	3,537	104,167
56	Galaxie 500 htp sdn	3,910	3,604	28,939
58	Galaxie 500 htp cpe	3,852	3,572	80,855
74	G500 Ctry Sdn wgn 5d 2S V8	4,349	4,028	55,238
74	G500 Ctry Sdn wgn 5d 3S V8	4,399	4,136	
62	LTD htp cpe V8	3,999	3,882	101,048
63	LTD sdn 4d V8	4,065	3,890	104,167
64	LTD htp sdn V8	4,060	3,925	33,742
61	LTD conv V8	4,165	4,057	4,234
76	LTD Ctry Squire wgn 5d 2S V8	4,393	4,318	121,419
76	LTD Ctry Squire wgn 5d 3S V8	4,443	4,430	
66	LTD Brougham sdn 4d V8	4,095	4,031	36,909
67	LTD Brougham htp sdn V8	4,090	4,074	23,364
68	LTD B'ham formal htp cpe V8	4,031	4,034	50,409

1972 Engines	bore×stroke	bhp	availability
L4, 98.6	3.19×3.06	54	S-Pinto exc wgn
L4, 122.0	3.58×3.03	86	S-Pinto wgn; O-Pinto
L6, 170.0	3.50×2.94	82	S-Maverick
L6, 200.0	3.68×3.13	91	O-Maverick
L6, 240.0	4.00×3.18	103	S-Ford
L6, 250.0	3.68×3.91	95	S-Torino
L6, 250.0	3.68×3.91	98	O-Maverick
V8, 302.0	4.00×3.00	140	S-Torino, Ford Cus V8
V8, 302.0	4.00×3.00	143	S-Maverick
V8, 351.0	4.00×3.50	153	S-Ford wgn; O-Ford
V8, 351.0	4.00×3.50	161	O-Torino
V8, 351.0	4.00×3.50	248	O-Torino
V8, 400.0	4.00×4.00	168	O-Torino
V8, 400.0	4.00×4.00	172	O-Ford

1970 Maverick two-door sedan

	bore×stroke	bhp	availability
V8, 429.0	4.36×3.59	205	O-Torino
V8, 429.0	4.36×3.59	208	O-Ford

1973

Pinto (wb 94.2)		Wght	Price	Prod
10	fstbk sdn2d	2,115	2,021	116,146
11	Runabout htchbk sdn 3d	2,145	2,144	150,603
12	wgn 3d	2,386	2,343	217,763
Maverick (wb 103.0; 4d-109.9)				
91	fstbk sdn 2d	2,730	2,248	148,943
92	sdn 4d	2,844	2,305	110,382
93	Grabber fstbk sdn 2d	2,770	2,427	32,350
Torino (wb 118.0; 2d-114.0)				
25	htp cpe	3,548	2,732	28,005
27	sdn 4d	3,620	2,701	37,524
40	wgn 5d V8	4,063	3,198	23,982
30	Gran Torino htp cpe	3,591	2,921	138,962
30	Gran Torino B'ham htp cpe	3,598	3,071	
31	Gran Torino sdn 4d	3,675	2,890	98,404
31	Gran Torino B'ham sdn 4d	3,690	3,051	
42	Gran Torino wgn 5d V8	4,097	3,344	60,738
43	Gran Torino Squire wgn 5d V8	4,129	3,559	40,023
35	Gran Torino Sport fstbk htp cpe V8	3,664	3,154	51,853
38	Gran Torino formal htp cpe V8	3,650	3,154	17,090
Ford (wb 121.0)				
53	Custom 500 sdn 4d	4,059	3,606	42,549
72	C 500 Ranch Wagon 5d 2S	4,529	4,050	22,432
72	C 500 Ranch Wagon 5d 3S	4,579	4,164	
54	Galaxie 500 sdn 4d	4,086	3,771	85,654
56	Galaxie 500 htp sdn	4,102	3,833	25,802
58	Galaxie 500 htp cpe	4,034	3,778	70,808
74	G500 Country Sdn Wgn 5d 2S	4,555	4,146	51,290
74	G500 Country Sdn wgn 5d 3S	4,605	4,260	
62	LTD htp cpe	4,059	3,950	120,864
63	LTD sdn 4d	4,107	3,958	122,851
64	LTD htp sdn	4,123	4,001	28,606
76	LTD Coutnry Squire wgn 5d 2S	4,579	4,401	142,983
76	LTD Country Squire wgn 5d 3S	4,629	4,515	
66	LTD Brougham sdn 4d	4,130	4,113	49,553
67	LTD Brougham htp sdn	4,148	4,157	22,268
68	LTD Brougham htp cpe	4,077	4,107	68,901

1973 Engines	bore×stroke	bhp	availability
L4, 98.6	3.19×3.06	54	S-Pinto exc wgn
L4, 122.0	3.58×3.03	83	S-Pinto wgn; O-Pinto

1972 Gran Torino Formal hardtop coupe

1973 Gran Torino hardtop coupe

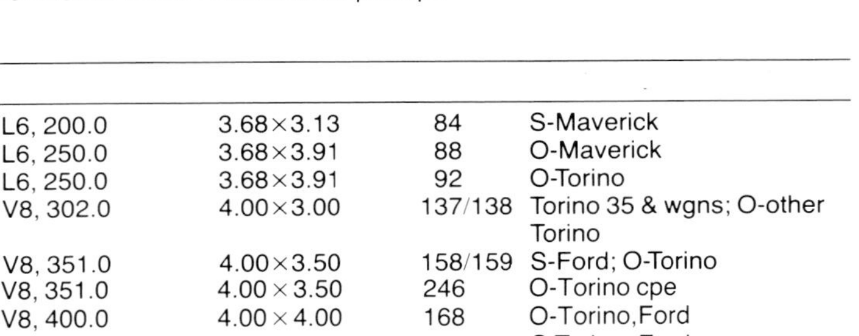

L6, 200.0	3.68×3.13	84	S-Maverick
L6, 250.0	3.68×3.91	88	O-Maverick
L6, 250.0	3.68×3.91	92	O-Torino
V8, 302.0	4.00×3.00	137/138	Torino 35 & wgns; O-other Torino
V8, 351.0	4.00×3.50	158/159	S-Ford; O-Torino
V8, 351.0	4.00 × 3.50	246	O-Torino cpe
V8, 400.0	4.00 × 4.00	168	O-Torino,Ford
V8, 429.0	4.36×3.59	201	O-Torino, Ford
V8, 460.0	4.36×3.85	202	O-Ford

1974

Pinto (wb 94.2)		Wght	Price	Prod
10	fstbk sdn 2d	2,372	2,527	132,061
11	Runabout htchbk sdn 3d	2,406	2,676	174,754
12	wgn 3d	2,576	2,771	237,394
Maverick (wb 103.0; 4d-109.9)				
91	fstbk sdn 2d	2,739	2,790	139,818
92	sdn 4d	2,932	2,824	137,728
93	Grabber fstbk sdn 2d	2,868	2,923	23,502
Torino (wb 118.0; 2d-114.0)				
25	htp cpe	3,709	3,236	22,738
27	sdn 4d	3,793	3,239	31,161
40	wgn 5d	4,175	3,818	15,393
30	Gran Torino htp cpe	3,742	3,411	76,290
31	Gran Torino sdn 4d	3,847	3,454	72,728
42	Gran Torino wgn 5d	4,209	4,017	29,866
32	Gran Torino Brougham htp cpe	3,794	3,975	26,402
33	Gran Torino Brougham sdn 4d	3,887	3,966	11,464
43	Gran Torino Squire wgn 5d	4,250	4,300	22,837
38	Gran Torino Sport htp cpe	3,771	3,824	23,142
21	Gran Torino Elite htp cpe	NA	4,437	96,604
Ford (wb 121.0)				
53	Custom 500 sdn 4d	4,180	3,982	28,941
72	C 500 Ranch Wagon 5d 2S	4,654	4,488	12,104
72	C 500 Ranch Wagon 5d 3S	4,687	4,608	
54	Galaxie 500 sdn 4d	4,196	4,164	49,661
56	Galaxie 500 htp sdn	4,212	4,237	11,526
58	Galaxie 500 htp cpe 5d	4,157	4,211	34,214
74	G500 Country Sdn wgn 5d 2S	4,690	4,584	22,400
74	G500 Country Sdn wgn 5d 3S	4,722	4,704	
62	LTD htp cpe	4,215	4,389	73,296
63	LTD sdn 4d	4,262	4,370	72,251
64	LTD htp sdn	4,277	4,438	12,375
76	LTD Cntry Squire wgn 5d 2S*	4,752	4,898	64,047
76	LTD Cntry Squire wgn 5d 3S*	4,785	5,018	
66	LTD Brougham sdn 4d	4,292	4,647	30,203
67	LTD Brougham htp sdn	4,310	4,717	11,371
68	LTD Brough htp cpe	4,247	4,669	39,084

*Prices with optional woodgrain bodyside trim. Non-woodgrain version $136 less.

1974 Engines	bore×stroke	bhp	availability
L4, 122.0	3.58×3.03	80	S-Pinto
L4, 140.0	3.78×3.13	82	O-Pinto
L6, 200.0	3.68×3.13	84	S-Maverick
L6, 250.0	3.68×3.91	91	O-Maverick, Torino
V8, 302.0	4.00×3.00	140	S-Maverick, Torino
V8, 351.0	4.00×3.50	162	S-Ford exc 76; O-Tor
V8, 400.0	4.00×4.00	170	S-Ford 76; O-Tor, Ford
V8, 460.0	4.36×3.85	220	O-Torino, Ford

1975

Pinto (wb 94.4; wgns-94.7)		Wght	Price	Prod
10	fstbk sdn 2d	2,495	2,769	64,081
11	Runabout htchbk sdn 3d	2,528	2,984	68,919
12	wgn 3d	2,692	3,153	90,763
Maverick (wb 103.0; 4d 109.9				
91	fstbk sdn 2d	2,896	3,025	90,695
92	sdn 4d	3,018	3,061	63,404
93	Grabber fstbk sdn 2d	2,903	3,282	8,473
Granada (wb 109.9)				
81	sdn 4d	3,279	3,756	118,168
82	sdn 2d	3,230	3,698	100,810
83	Ghia sdn 4d	3,392	4,283	43,652
84	Ghia sdn 2d	3,342	4,225	40,028
Torino (wb 118.0; 2d-114.0)				
25	htp cpe	3,981	3,954	13,394
27	sdn 4d	4,053	3,957	22,928
40	wgn 4d	4,406	4,336	13,291
30	Gran Torino htp cpe	3,992	4,314	35,324
31	Gran Torino sdn 4d	4,084	4,338	53,161
42	Gran Torino wgn 5d	4,450	4,673	23,951
43	Gran Torino Squire wgn 5d	4,490	4,952	
32	Gran Torino Brougham htp cpe	4,081	4,805	4,849
33	Gran Torino Brougham sdn 4d	4,157	4,837	5,929
38	Gran Torino Sport htp cpe	4,038	4,790	5,126
21	Elite htp cpe	4,154	4,767	123,372

1975 Torino Elite hardtop coupe

1977 LTD II Brougham hardtop coupe

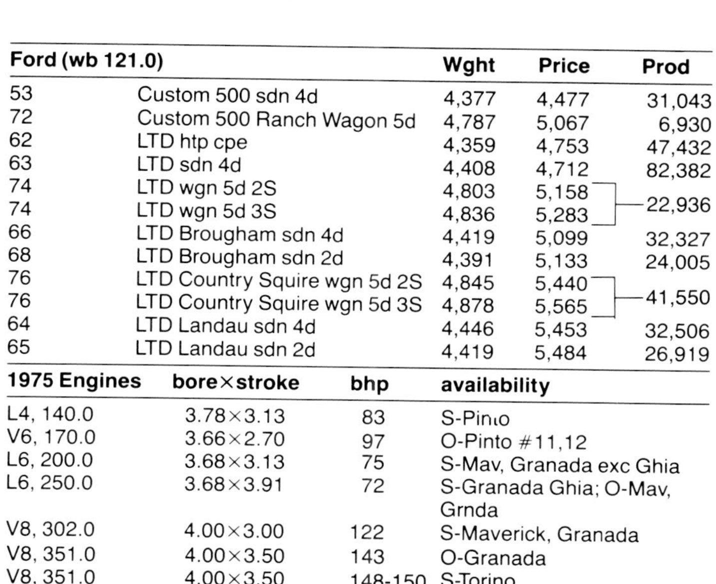

Ford (wb 121.0)		Wght	Price	Prod
53	Custom 500 sdn 4d	4,377	4,477	31,043
72	Custom 500 Ranch Wagon 5d	4,787	5,067	6,930
62	LTD htp cpe	4,359	4,753	47,432
63	LTD sdn 4d	4,408	4,712	82,382
74	LTD wgn 5d 2S	4,803	5,158	22,936
74	LTD wgn 5d 3S	4,836	5,283	
66	LTD Brougham sdn 4d	4,419	5,099	32,327
68	LTD Brougham sdn 2d	4,391	5,133	24,005
76	LTD Country Squire wgn 5d 2S	4,845	5,440	41,550
76	LTD Country Squire wgn 5d 3S	4,878	5,565	
64	LTD Landau sdn 4d	4,446	5,453	32,506
65	LTD Landau sdn 2d	4,419	5,484	26,919

1975 Engines	bore×stroke	bhp	availability
L4, 140.0	3.78×3.13	83	S-Pinto
V6, 170.0	3.66×2.70	97	O-Pinto #11,12
L6, 200.0	3.68×3.13	75	S-Mav, Granada exc Ghia
L6, 250.0	3.68×3.91	72	S-Granada Ghia; O-Mav, Grnda
V8, 302.0	4.00×3.00	122	S-Maverick, Granada
V8, 351.0	4.00×3.50	143	O-Granada
V8, 351.0	4.00×3.50	148-150	S-Torino
V8, 400.0	4.00×4.00	144/158	S-Ford 74,76; O-Torino, other Ford
V8, 460.0	4.36×3.85	216	O-Torino, Ford

1976

Pinto (wb 94.4; wgns-94.7)		Wght	Price	Prod
10	Pony MPG fstbk sdn 2d L4	2,450	2,895	92,264
10	MPG fstbk sdn 2d L4	2,452	3,025	
10	sdn 2d V6	2,590	3,472	
11	MPG htchbk sdn 3d L4	2,482	3,200	92,540
11	Squire MPG htchbk sdn 3d L4	2,518	3,505	
11	Runabout htchbk sdn 3d V6	2,620	3,647	
11	Squire htchbk sdn 3d V6	2,656	3,952	
12	MPG wgn 3d L4	2,635	3,365	105,328
12	Squire MPG wgn 3d L4	2,672	3,671	
12	wgn 3d V6	2,773	3,865	
12	Squire wgn 3d V6	2,810	4,171	
Maverick (wb 109.9; 2d-103.0)				
91	fstbk sdn 2d	2,846	3,117	60,611
92	sdn 4d	2,956	3,189	79,076
Granada (wb 109.9)				
81	sdn 4d	3,222	3,798	187,923
82	sdn 2d	3,172	3,707	161,618

		Wght	Price	Prod
83	Ghia sdn 4d	3,392	4,355	52,457
84	Ghia sdn 2d	3,334	4,265	46,786
Torino (wb 118.0; 2d-114.0)				
25	htp cpe	3,976	4,172	34,518
27	sdn 4d	4,061	4,206	17,394
30	Gran Torino htp cpe	3,999	4,461	23,939
31	Gran Torino sdn 4d	4,081	4,495	40,568
32	Gran Torino Brougham htp cpe	4,063	4,883	3,183
33	Gran Torino Brougham sdn 4d	4,144	4,915	4,473
40	wgn 5d	4,409	4,521	17,281
42	Gran Torino wgn 5d	4,428	4,769	30,596
43	Gran Torino Squire wgn 5d	4,454	5,083	21,144
Elite (wb 114.0)				
21	htp cpe	4,169	4,879	146,475
Ford (wb 121.0)				
52	Custom 500 sdn 2d	—	—	7,037
53	Custom 500 sdn 4d	4,298	4,493	23,447
72	Custom 500 Ranch Wagon 5d	4,737	4,918	4,633
62	LTD sdn 2d	4,257	4,780	62,844
63	LTD sdn 4d	4,303	4,752	108,168
74	LTD wgn 5d 2S	4,752	5,207	30,237
74	LTD wgn 5d 3S	4,780	5,333	
66	LTD Brougham sdn 4d	4,332	5,245	32,917
68	LTD Brougham sdn 2d	4,299	5,299	20,863
76	LTD Country Squire wgn 5d 2S	4,809	5,523	47,379
76	LTD Country Squire wgn 5d 3S	4,837	5,649	
64	LTD Landau sdn 4d	4,394	5,560	35,663
65	LTD Landau sdn 2d	4,346	5,613	29,673

1977 Granada two-door sedan

1976 Engines	bore×stroke	bhp	availability
L4, 140.0	3.78×3.13	92	S-Pinto
V6, 170.8	3.66×2.70	103	O-Pinto
L6, 200.0	3.68×3.13	81	S-Mav, Gran exc Ghia
L6, 250.0	3.68×3.91	90	S-Gran Ghia; O-Mav, Gran
V8, 302.0	4.00×3.00	134/138	S-Granada, Maverick
V8, 351.0	4.00×3.50	152/154	S-Tor, Elite, Ford exc wgns; O-Granada
V8, 400.0	4.00×4.00	180	S-Ford wgns; O-Tor, Ford, Elite
V8, 460.0	4.36×3.85	202	O-Torino, Elite, Ford

1977

Pinto (wb 94.4; wgns-94.7)		Wght	Price	Prod
10	Pony sdn 2d L4	2,313	3,099	48,863*
10	sdn 2d	2,376	3,237	
11	Runabout htchbk sdn 3d	2,412	3,353	74,237*
12	wgn 3d	2,576	3,548	79,449*
12	Squire wgn 3d	2,614	3,891	
Maverick (wb 109.9; 2d-103.0)				
91	fstbk sdn 2d	2,864	3,322	40,086
92	sdn 4d	2,970	3,395	58,420
Granada (wb 109.9)				
81	sdn 4d	3,222	4,118	163,071
82	sdn 2d	3,172	4,022	157,612
83	Ghia sdn 4d	3,276	4,548	35,730
84	Ghia sdn 2d	3,222	4,452	34,166
LTD II (wb 118.0; 2d-114.0)				
25	S htp cpe	3,789	4,528	9,531
27	S sdn 4d	3,894	4,579	18,775
30	htp cpe	3,789	4,785	57,449
31	sdn 4d	3,904	4,870	56,704
32	Brougham htp cpe	3,898	5,121	20,979
33	Brougham sdn 4d	3,930	5,206	18,851
40	S wgn 5d 2S	4,393	4,806	9,636
40	S wgn 5d 3S	4,410	4,906	
42	wgn 5d 2S	4,404	5,064	23,237
42	wgn 5d 3S	4,421	5,164	
43	Squire wgn 5d 3S	4,430	5,335	17,162
43	Squire wgn 5d 3S	4,447	5,435	
LTD (wb 121.0)				
52	Custom 500 sdn 2d	—	—	4,139
53	Custom 500 sdn 4d	—	—	5,582
62	LTD sdn 2d	4,190	5,128	73,637
63	LTD sdn 4d	4,240	5,152	160,255
64	LTD Landau sdn 4d	4,319	5,742	65,030
65	LTD Landau sdn 2d	4,270	5,717	44,396
72	Custom 500 Ranch Wagon 5d	—	—	1,406
74	LTD wgn 5d 2S	4,635	5,415	90,711
74	LTD wgn 5d 3S	4,679	5,541	
74	Country Squire wgn 5d 2S	4,674	5,866	
74	Country Squire wgn 5d 3S	4,718	5,992	

1977 Engines	bore×stroke	bhp	availability
L4, 140.0	3.78×3.13	89	S-Pinto
V6, 170.8	3.66×2.70	93	O-Pinto, exc. Pony
L6, 200.0	3.68×3.13	96	S-Maverick, Granada
L6, 250.0	3.68×3.91	98	S-Gran Ghia; O-Mav, Gran
V8, 302.0	4.00×3.00	122	O-Granada
V8, 302.0	4.00×3.00	130	S-LTD II exc wgns
V8, 302.0	4.00×3.00	137	O-Maverick
V8, 351.0	4.00×3.50	135	O-Granada
V8, 351.0	4.00×3.50	149	S-LTD II wgns; O-LTD II
V8, 351.0	4.00×3.50	161	S-LTD exc wgns; O-LTD II wgns
V8, 400.0	4.00×4.00	173	S-LTD wgns; O-LTD II, LTD
V8, 460.0	4.36×3.85	197	O-LTD

*incl. some units produced as 1978 models but sold as 1977 models.

1978

Pinto (wb 94.4; wgns-94.7)		Wght	Price	Prod
10	Pony sdn 2d L4	2,321	3,139	62,317
10	sdn 2d	2,400	3,629	
11	Runabout htchbk sdn 3d	2,444	3,744	74,313
12	wgn 3d	2,579	4,028	52,269
12	Squire wgn 3d	2,614	4,343	
Fairmont (wb 105.5)				
91	sdn 2d	2,590	3,624	78,776
92	sdn 4d	2,632	3,710	136,849
93	Futura cpe	2,626	4,103	116,966
94	wgn 5d	2,740	4,063	128,390
94	Squire wgn 5d	2,748	4,428	
Granada (wb 109.9)				
81	sdn 2d	3,132	4,300	110,481
81	Ghia sdn 2d	3,192	4,685	
81	ESS sdn 2d	3,190	4,872	
82	sdn 4d	3,167	4,390	139,305
82	Ghia sdn 4d	3,275	4,776	
82	ESS sdn 4d	3,225	4,962	

1978 Granada Ghia two-door sedan

1978 Pinto Runabout three-door hatchback

LTD II (wb 118.0; 2d-114.0)		Wght	Price	Prod
25	S htp cpe	3,746	4,850	9,004
27	S sdn 4d	3,836	4,935	21,122
30	htp cpe	3,773	5,112	76,285
30	Brougham htp cpe	3,791	5,448	
31	sdn 4d	3,872	5,222	64,133
31	Brougham sdn 4d	3,901	5,558	

LTD (wb 121.0)		Wght	Price	Prod
62	LTD htp cpe	3,972	5,398	57,466
63	LTD sdn 4d	4,032	5,483	112,392
64	LTD Landau htp cpe	4,029	5,970	27,305
65	LTD Landau sdn 4d	4,081	6,055	39,836
74	LTD wgn 5d 2S	4,532	5,885	71,285
74	LTD wgn 5d 3S	4,567	6,028	
74	Country Squire wgn 5d 2S	4,576	6,304	
74	Country Squire wgn 5d 3S	4,601	6,447	

Note: Fiesta not included (import).

1978 Engines	bore×stroke	bhp	availability
L4, 140.0	3.78×3.13	88	S-Pinto, Fairmont
V6, 170.0	3.66×2.70	90	O-Pinto, exc Pony
L6, 200.0	3.68×3.13	85	S-Fairmont
L6, 250.0	3.68×3.91	97	S-Granada
V8, 302.0	4.00×3.00	134	S-LTD II,LTD exc wgns
V8, 302.0	4.00×3.00	139	S-Granada;O-Fairmont
V8, 351.0	4.00×3.50	144/145	S-LTD wgns;O-LTD II, LTD
V8, 351.0	4.00×3.50	152	O-LTD II
V8, 400.0	4.00×4.00	166	O-LTD II, LTD
V8, 460.0	4.36×3.85	202	O-LTD

1979

Pinto (wb 94.4; wgns-94.7)		Wght	Price	Prod
10	Pony fstbk sdn 2d L4	2,329	3,434	75,789
10	fstbk sdn 2d	2,396	3,939	
11	Runabout htchbk sdn 3d	2,442	4,055	69,383
12	Pony wgn 3d L4	NA	3,899	53,846
12	wgn 3d	2,571	4,338	
12	Squire wgn 3d	2,607	4,654	

Fairmont (wb 105.5)		Wght	Price	Prod
91	sdn 2d	2,524	4,102	54,798
92	sdn 4d	2,578	4,220	133,813
93	Futura cpe	2,580	4,463	106,065
94	wgn 5d	2,708	4,497	100,691
94	Squire wgn 5d	NA	4,856	

Granada (wb 109.9)		Wght	Price	Prod
81	sdn 2d	3,088	4,678	76,850
81	Ghia sdn 2d	3,124	5,051	
81	ESS sdn 2d	3,140	5,211	
82	sdn 4d	3,134	4,782	105,526
82	Ghia sdn 4d	3,168	5,157	
82	ESS sdn 4d	3,210	5,317	

LTD II (wb 118.0; 2d-114.0)		Wght	Price	Prod
25	S htp cpe	3,781	5,561	834
27	S sdn 4d	3,844	5,661	9,649
30	htp cpe	3,797	5,799	18,300
30	Brougham htp cpe	3,815	6,135	
31	sdn 4d	3,860	5,924	19,781
31	Brougham sdn 4d	3,889	6,259	

LTD (wb 114.3)		Wght	Price	Prod
62	LTD sdn 2d	3,421	6,184	54,005
63	LTD sdn 4d	3,463	6,284	117,730
64	LTD Landau sdn 2d	3,472	6,686	42,314
65	LTD Landau sdn 4d	3,527	6,811	74,599
74	LTD wgn 5d 2S	3,678	6,550	37,955
74	LTD wgn 5d 3S	—	6,699	
76	Country Squire wgn 5d 2S	3,719	7,006	29,932
76	Country Squire wgn 5d 3S	—	7,155	

1979 LTD Landau four-door sedan

1979 Engines	bore×stroke	bhp	availability
L4, 140.0	3.78×3.13	88	S-Pinto, Fairmont
V6, 170.0	3.66×2.70	102	O-Pinto exc Pony
L6, 200.0	3.68×3.13	85	O-Fairmont
L6, 250.0	3.68×3.91	97	S-Granada
V8, 302.0	4.00×3.00	129	S-LTD
V8, 302.0	4.00×3.00	133	S-LTD II
V8, 302.0	4.00×3.00	137	O-Granada
V8, 302.0	4.00×3.00	140	O-Fairmont
V8, 351.0	4.00×3.50	142	O-LTD
V8, 351.0	4.00×3.50	151	O-LTD II, LTD

1980

Pinto (wb 94.4; wgns-94.7)		Wght	Price	Prod
10	Pony fstbk sdn 2d	2,377	4,117	84,053
10	fstbk sdn 2d	2,385	4,605	
11	Runabout htchbk sdn 3d	2,426	4,717	61,842
12	Pony wgn 2d	2,545	4,627	39,159
12	wgn 3d	2,553	5,004	
12/604	Squire wgn 3d	2,590	5,320	

Fairmont (wb 105.5)		Wght	Price	Prod
91	sdn 2d	2,576	4,894	45,074
92	sdn 4d	2,610	5,011	137,812
92	Futura sdn 4d	—	5,390	5,306
93	Futura cpe	2,623	5,325	51,878
94	wgn 5d	2,735	5,215	77,035

Granada (wb 109.9)		Wght	Price	Prod
81	sdn 2d	3,135	5,541	60,872
81/602	Ghia sdn 2d	3,168	5,942	
81/933	ESS sdn 2d	3,199	6,031	
82	sdn 4d	3,168	5,664	29,557
82/602	Ghia sdn 4d	3,209	6,065	
82/933	ESS sdn 4d	3,240	6,154	

LTD (wb 114.3)		Wght	Price	Prod
	S sdn 2d	—	—	553
61	S sdn 4d	3,464	6,875	19,283
62	sdn 2d	3,447	7,003	15,333
63	sdn 4d	3,475	7,117	51,630
64	Crown Victoria sdn 2d	3,482	7,628	7,725
65	Crown Victoria sdn 4d	3,524	7,763	21,962
72	S wgn 5d 2S	3,707	7,198	3,490
72	S wgn 5d 3S	3,748	7,344	
74	wgn 5d 2S	3,717	7,463	11,718
74	wgn 5d 3S	3,758	7,609	
76	Crown Victoria wgn 5d 2S	3,743	7,891	9,868
76	Crown Victoria wgn 5d 3S	3,784	8,042	

1980 Engines	bore×stroke	bhp	availability
L4, 140.0	3.78×3.13	88	S-Pinto, Fairmont
L6, 200.0	3.68×3.13	91	O-Fairmont
L6, 250.0	3.68×3.91	90	S-Granada

1981 LTD Country Squire station wagon

1981 Escort three-door hatchback

	bore×stroke	bhp	availability
V8, 255.0	3.68×3.00	119	O-Fairmont, Granada
V8, 302.0	4.00×3.00	130	S-LTD
V8, 302.0	4.00×3.00	134	O-Granada
V8, 351.0	4.00×3.50	140	O-LTD

1981

Escort (wb 94.2)		Wght	Price	Prod
05	htchbk sdn 3d	1,962	5,158	
05/60Q	L htchbk sdn 3d	1,964	5,494	
05/60Z	GL htchbk sdn 3d	1,987	5,838	192,554
05/602	GLX htchbk sdn 3d	2,029	6,476	
05/936	SS htchbk sdn 3d	2,004	6,139	
08	liftbk sdn 4d	2,074	5,731	
08/60Q	L liftbk sdn 4d	2,075	5,814	
08/60Z	GL liftbk sdn 4d	2,094	6,178	128,173
08/602	GLX liftbk sdn 4d	2,137	6,799	
08/936	SS liftbk sdn 4d	2,114	6,464	
Fair mont (wb 105.5)				
20	S sdn 2d	NA	5,701	—
20	sdn 2d	2,590	6,032	23,066
21	sdn 4d	2,640	6,151	104,883
21/605	Futura sdn 4d	2,674	6,361	
22	Futura cpe	2,645	6,347	24,197
23	wgn 5d	2,754	6,384	59,154
23/605	Futura wgn 5d	2,788	6,616	
Granada (wb 105.5)				
26	L sdn 2d	2,752	6,474	
26/602	GL sdn 2d	2,773	6,875	35,057
26/933	GLX sdn 2d	2,777	6,988	
27	L sdn 4d	2,795	6,633	
27/602	GL sdn 4d	2,822	7,035	86,284
27/933	GLX sdn 4d	2,829	7,148	
LTD (wb 114.3)				
31	S sdn 4d	3,490	7,527	17,490
32	sdn 2d	3,496	7,607	6,279
33	sdn 4d	3,538	7,718	35,932
34	Crown Victoria sdn 2d	3,496	8,251	11,061
35	Crown Victoria sdn 4d	3,538	8,384	39,139
37	S wgn 5d 2S	3,717	7,942	2,465
38	wgn 5d 2S	3,719	8,180	10,554
39	Country Squire wgn 5d 2S	3,737	8,640	9,443

1981 Engines	bore × stroke	bhp	availability
L4, 97.6	3.15×3.13	65	S-Escort
L4, 140.0	3.78×3.13	88	S-Fairmont, Granada
L6, 200.0	3.68×3.13	88	O-Fairmont, Granada
V8, 255.0	3.68×3.00	115/120	S-LTD; O-Fmont, Gran
V8, 302.0	4.00×3.00	130	O-LTD
V8, 351.0	4.00×3.50	145	O-LTD

1982

Escort (wb 94.2)		Wght	Price	Prod
05	htchbk sdn 3d	1,920	5,462	
05	L htchbk sdn 3d	1,926	6,046	
05	GL htchbk sdn 3d	1,948	6,406	165,660
05	GLX htchbk sdn 3d	1,987	7,086	
05	GT htchbk sdn 3d	1,963	6,706	
06	htchbk sdn 5d	1,926	5,668	
06	L htckbk sdn 5d	2,003	6,263	130,473
06	GL htchbk sdn 5d	2,025	6,622	
06	GLX htchbk sdn 5d	2,064	7,302	
08	L wgn 5d	2,023	6,461	
08	GL wgn 5d	2,043	6,841	88,999
08	GLX wgn 5d	2,079	7,475	
EXP (wb 94.2)				
01	htchbk cpe 3d	2,146	7,387	98,256
Fairmont Futura (wb 105.5)				
20	sdn 2d	2,616	5,985	8,222
21	sdn 4d	2,664	6,419	101,666
22	spt cpe	2,640	6,517	17,851
Granada (wb 105.5)				
26	L sdn 2d	2,732	7,126	
26	GL sdn 2d	2,758	7,543	12,802
26	GLX sdn 2d	2,776	7,666	
27	L sdn 4d	2,764	7,301	
27	GL sdn 4d	2,794	7,718	62,339
27	GLX sdn 4d	2,812	7,840	
28	L wgn 5d L6	2,965	7,983	45,182
28	GL wgn 5d L6	2,995	8,399	
LTD (wb 114.3)				
31	S sdn 4d	3,522	8,312	22,182
32	sdn 2d	3,496	8,455	3,510
33	sdn 4d	3,526	8,574	29,776
34	Crown Victoria sdn 2d	3,523	9,149	9,287
35	Crown Victoria sdn 4d	3,567	9,294	41,405
37	S wgn 5d 2S	3,725	8,783	2,973
38	wgn 5d 2S	3,741	9,073	9,294
39	Country Squire wgn 5d 2S	3,741	9,580	9,626

1982 Engines	bore × stroke	bhp	availability
L4, 97.6	3.15×3.13	70	S-Escort, EXP
L4, 97.6	3.15×3.13	80	O-late Escort, EXP
L4, 140.0	3.78×3.13	86	S-Fairmont, Granada

	bore×stroke	bhp	availability
L6, 200.0	3.68×3.13	87	S-Gran wgn; O-Fmont, Gran
V6, 232.0	3.80×3.40	112	O-Granada
V8, 255.0	3.68×3.00	122	S-LTD; O-Fmont (police)
V8, 302.0	4.00×3.00	132	S-LTD wgn; O-LTD
V8, 351.0	4.00×3.50	165	S-LTD (police only)

1983

Escort (wb 94.2)		Wght	Price	Prod
04	L htchbk sdn 3d	2,016	5,639	
05	GL htchbk sdn 3d	1,959	6,384	151,386
06	GLX htchbk sdn 3d	1,993	6,771	
07	GT htchbk sdn 3d	2,020	7,339	
13	L htckbk sdn 5d	2,078	5,846	
14	GL htchbk sdn 5d	2,025	6,601	84,649
15	GLX htchbk sdn 5d	2,059	6,988	
09	L wgn 5d	2,117	6,052	
10	GL wgn 5d	2,052	6,779	79,335
11	GLX wgn 5d	2,083	7,150	
EXP (wb 94.2)				
01	htchbk cpe 3d	2,156	6,426	
01/301B	HO htchbk cpe 3d	—	7,004	
01/302B	HO spt htchbk cpe 3d	—	7,794	19,697
01/303B	Luxury htchbk cpe 3d	—	8,225	
01/304B	GT htchbk cpe 3d	—	8,739	
Fairmont Futura (wb 105.5)				
35	sdn 2d	2,890	6,444	3,664
35/41K	S sdn 2d	2,628	5,985	
36	sdn 4d	2,933	6,590	69,287
36/41K	S sdn 4d	2,672	6,125	
37	spt cpe	2,908	6,666	7,882
LTD (wb 105.5)				
39	L sdn 4d	2,912	7,777	111,813
39/60H	Brougham sdn 4d	2,845	8,165	
40	wgn 5d L6	3,092	8,577	43,945
LTD Crown Victoria (wb 114.3)				
43	sdn 4d	3,748	10,094	81,859
43/41K	S sdn 4d	3,732	9,130	
42	sdn 2d	3,732	10,094	11,414
44	Country Squire wgn 5d 2S	3,901	10,253	
44/41E	wgn 5d 2S	3,895	10,003	20,343
44/41K	S wgn 5d 2S	3,891	9,444	

1983 Engines	bore × stroke	bhp	availability
L4, 97.6	3.15×3.13	70	S-Escort, EXP
L4, 97.6	3.15×3.13	80	O-Escort, EXP
L4, 97.6	3.15×3.13	88	S-Escort GT; O-Escort, EXP
L4, 140.0	3.78×3.13	90	S-Fairmont, LTD
L4P, 140.0	3.78×3.13	—	O-LTD (propane)
L6, 200.0	3.68×3.13	92	S-LTD wgn; O-Fmont, LTD
V6, 232.0	3.80×3.40	110	O-LTD
V8, 302.0	4.00×3.00	130	S-Crown Vic; O-LTD
V8, 302.0	4.00×3.00	145	O-Crown Vic
V8, 351.0	4.00×3.50	165	S-Crown Vic (police only)

1984

Escort (wb 94.2)		Wght	Price	Prod
04	htchbk sdn 3d	2,016	5,629	
04	L htchbk sdn 3d	2,080	5,885	
05	GL htchbk sdn 3d	2,122	6,382	184,323
07	GT htchbk sdn 3d	2,170	7,593	
07/935	GT turbo htchbk sdn 3d	—	8,680	
13	htchbk sdn 5d	2,078	5,835	
13	L htckbk sdn 5d	2,146	6,099	99,444
14	GL htchbk sdn 5d	2,188	6,596	
15	LX htchbk sdn 5d	2,222	7,848	
09	L wgn 5d	2,176	6,313	
10	GL wgn 5d	2,216	6,773	88,756
11	LX wgn 5d	2,249	7,939	
EXP (wb 94.2)				
01/A80	htchbk cpe 3d	2,212	6,653	
01/A81	Luxury cpe 3d	2,235	7,539	23,016
01/A82	Turbo cpe 3d	2,243	9,942	
Tempo (wb 99.9)				
18	L sdn 2d	2,286	6,936	
19	GL sdn 2d	—	7,159	107,065
20	GLX sdn 2d	—	7,621	
21	L sdn 4d	2,348	6,936	
22	GL sdn 4d	—	7,159	295,149
23	GLX sdn 4d	—	7,621	
LTD (wb 105.6)				
39	sdn 4d	2,830	8,605	154,173
39/60H	Brougham sdn 4d	—	9,980	
39/93B	LX sdn 4d V8	—	11,098	**
40	wgn 5d L6	3,123	9,102	59,569

1983 Fairmont Futura four-door sedan

LTD Crown Victoria (wb 114.3)		Wght	Price	Prod
43	sdn 4d	3,730	10,954	130,164
43/41K	S sdn 4d	3,728	9,826	
42	sdn 2d	3,689	10,954	12,522
44	Country Squire wgn 5d 2S	3,936	11,111	
44/41E	wgn 5d 2S	3,931	10,861	30,803
44/41K	S wgn 5d 2S	3,880	10,136	

1984 Engines	bore × stroke	bhp	availability
L4, 97.6	3.15 × 3.13	70	S-Escort
L4, 97.6	3.15 × 3.13	80	S-EXP; O-Escort
L4, 97.6	3.15 × 3.13	84	S-Escort LX, GT; O-Esc, EXP
L4T, 97.6	3.15 × 3.13	120	S-Escort GT, EXP turbo
L4D, 121.0	3.39 × 3.39	52	O-Escort, Tempo
L4, 140.0	3.70 × 3.30	84	S-Tempo
L4, 140.0	3.78 × 3.13	88	S-LTD
L4P, 140.0	3.78 × 3.13	—	O-LTD (propane)
V6, 232.0	3.80 × 3.40	120	S-LTD wgn; O-LTD
V8, 302.0	4.00 × 3.00	140	S-Crown Vic
V8, 302.0	4.00 × 3.00	155	S-Crown Vic wgn
V8, 351.0	4.00 × 3.50	180	S-Crown Vic (police only)

**3,260 LTD LX models built in 1984-85 model years combined.

1985

Escort (wb 94.2)		Wght	Price	Prod
04/41P	htchbk sdn 3d	1,990	5,620	
04	L htchbk sdn 3d	1,979	5,876	
05	GL htchbk sdn 3d	2,047	6,374	112,406*
07	GT htchbk sdn 3d	2,140	7,585	
07/935	GT turbo htchbk sdn 3d	2,172	8,680	
13	htchbk sdn 5d	2,078	5,835	
13/41P	L htckbk sdn 5d	2,055	5,827	62,709*
14	GL htchbk sdn 5d	2,114	6,588	
15	LX htchbk sdn 5d	2,175	7,840	
09	L wgn 5d	2,071	6,305	
10	GL wgn 5d	2,139	6,765	45,740*
11	LX wgn 5d	2,198	7,931	

*Estimated totals.

Escort Second Series 1985.5 (wb 94.2)		Wght	Price	Prod
31	sdn 3d	2,142	5,856	
31	L sdn 3d	—	6,127	100,554
32	GL sdn 3d	—	6,642	
36	L sdn 5d	2,195	6,341	48,676
37	GL sdn 5d	—	6,855	
34	L wgn 5d	2,223	6,622	36,998
35	GL wgn 5d	—	7,137	

EXP (wb 94.2)		Wght	Price	Prod
01/A80	htchbk cpe 3d	2,098	6,697	
01/A81	Luxury cpe 3d	2,124	7,585	26,462
01/A82	Turbo cpe 3d	2,232	9,997	
Tempo (wb 99.9)				
18	L sdn 2d	2,271	7,052	
19	GL sdn 2d	2,302	7,160	72,311
20	GLX sdn 2d	2,372	8,253	
21	L sdn 4d	2,328	7,052	
22	GL sdn 4d	2,358	7,160	266,776
23	GLX sdn 4d	2,428	8,302	
LTD (wb 105.6)				
39	sdn 4d L4/V6	2,852	8,874	
39/60H	Brougham sdn 4dL4/V6	2,857	9,262	162,884
39/938	LX sdn 4d V8	2,904	11,421	
40	wgn 5d V6	2,990	9,384	42,642
LTD Crown Victoria (wb 114.3)				
43	sdn 4d	3,588	11,627	154,612
43/41K	S sdn 4d	3,709	10,609	
42	sdn 2d	3,552	11,627	
44	Country Squire wgn 5d 2S	3,763	11,809	
44/41E	wgn 5d 2S	3,758	11,559	30,825
44/41K	S wgn 5d 2S	3,883	10,956	

1985 Engines	bore × stroke	bhp	availability
L4, 97.6	3.15 × 3.13	70	S-Escort
L4, 97.6	3.15 × 3.13	80	S-EXP; O-Escort
L4, 97.6	3.15 × 3.13	84	S-Escort LX, GT; O-Escort
L4T, 97.6	3.15 × 3.13	120	S-Escort, EXP turbo
L4, 113.5	3.23 × 3.46	86	S-late Escort
L4D, 121.0	3.39 × 3.39	52	O-Escort, Tempo
L4, 140.0	3.70 × 3.30	86	S-Tempo
L4, 140.0	3.70 × 3.30	100	O-Tempo
L4, 140.0	3.78 × 3.13	88	S-LTD
L4P, 140.0	3.78 × 3.13	—	O-LTD (propane)
V6, 232.0	3.80 × 3.40	120	S-LTD wgn; O-LTD
V8, 302.0	4.00 × 3.00	140	S-Crown Vic
V8, 302.0	4.00 × 3.00	155	O-Crown Vic
V8, 302.0	4.00 × 3.00	165	S-LTD LX
V8, 351.0	4.00 × 3.50	180	S-Crown Vic (police only)

1986

Escort (wb 94.2)		Wght	Price	Prod
31/41P	Pony sdn 3d	2,159	6,052	
31	L sdn 3d	2,153	6,327	228,013
32	LX sdn 3d	2,238	7,234	

1984 EXP Turbo coupe

1985 LTD Crown Victoria four-door sedan

1986 Tempo Sport GL two-door sedan

		Wght	Price	Prod
33	GT sdn 3d	2,364	8,112	
36	L sdn 5d	2,201	6,541	117,300
37	LX sdn 5d	2,281	7,448	
34	L wgn 5d	2,233	6,822	84,740
35	LX wgn 5d	2,311	7,729	
EXP (wb 94.2)				
01	cpe 3d	2,311	7,186	30,978
01/931	Luxury cpe 3d	2,413	8,235	
Tempo (wb 99.9)				
19	GL sdn 2d	2,339	7,358	69,101
20	GLX sdn 2d	2,461	8,578	
22	GL sdn 4d	2,398	7,508	208,570
23	GLX sdn 4d	2,522	8,777	
Taurus (wb 106.0)				
29	L sdn 4d L4/V6	2,979	9,645	
29/934	MT5 sdn 4d L4	2,878	10,276	178,737
29/60D	GL sdn 4d V6	3,009	11,322	
29/60H	LX sdn 4d V6	3,109	13,351	
30	L wgn 5d V6	3,184	10,763	
30/934	MT5 wgn 5d L4	3,076	10,741	
30/60D	GL wgn 5d V6	3,214	11,790	57,625
30/60H	LX wgn 5d V6	3,306	13,860	
LTD (wb 105.6)				
39	sdn 4d V6	3,001	10,032	58,270
39/60H	Brougham sdn 4d V6	3,009	10,420	
40	wgn 5d V6	3,108	10,132	14,213
LTD Crown Victoria (wb 114.3)				
43	sdn 4d	3,748	12,562	
43/60H	LX sdn 4d	3,781	13,784	97,314
43/41K	S sdn 4d	3,715	12,188	
42	sdn 2d	3,708	13,022	6,559
42/60H	LX sdn 2d	3,754	13,752	
44	Country Squire wgn 5d 2S	3,937	12,655	
44/60H	LX Country Squire wgn 5d 2S	3,829	13,817	
44/41E	wgn 5d 2S	3,930	12,405	20,164
44/41E	LX wgn 5d 2S	3,821	13,567	
44/41K	S wgn 5d 2S	3,921	12,468	

1986 Engines	bore×stroke	bhp	availability
L4, 113.5	3.23×3.46	86	S-Escort, EXP
L4, 113.5	3.23×3.46	108	S-Escort GT; O-Escort
L4D, 121.0	3.39×3.39	52	O-Escort, Tempo
L4, 140.0	3.70×3.30	86	S-Tempo
L4, 140.0	3.70×3.30	100	O-Tempo
L4, 153.0	3.70×3.60	88	S-late Taurus
V6, 182.0	3.50×3.15	140	S-Taurus LX, wgn; O-Taurus
V6, 232.0	3.80×3.40	120	S-LTD
V8, 302.0	4.00×3.00	150	S-Crown Vic
V8, 351.0	4.00×3.50	180	S-Crown Vic (police only)

1987

Escort (wb 94.2)		Wght	Price	Prod
20	Pony sdn 3d	2,180	6,436	
21	GL sdn 3d	2,187	6,801	206,729
23	GT sdn 3d	2,516	8,724	
25	GL sdn 5d	2,222	7,022	102,187
28	GL wgn 5d	2,274	7,312	65,849
EXP (wb 94.2)				
18	spt cpe 3d	2,388	8,831	25,888
17	Luxury cpe 3d	2,291	7,622	
Tempo (wb 99.9)				
31	GL sdn 2d	2,462	8,043	
32	LX sdn 2d	2,562	9,238	70,164
33	Spt GL sdn 2d	2,667	8,888	
34	AWD (4WD) sdn 2d	2,667	9,984	
36	GL sdn 4d	2,515	8,198	
37	LX sdn 4d	2,617	9,444	212,468
38	Spt GL sdn 4d	2,720	9,043	
39	AWD (4WD) sdn 4d	2,720	10,138	
Taurus (wb 106.0)				
50	L sdn 4d L4/V6	2,982	10,491	
51	MT5 sdn 4d L4	2,886	11,966	278,562
52	GL sdn 4d L4/V6	3,045	11,498	
53	LX sdn 4d V6	3,113	14,613	
55	L wgn 5d V6	3,186	11,722	
56	MT5 wgn 5d L4	3,083	12,534	96,201
57	GL wgn 5d V6	3,242	12,688	
58	LX wgn 5d V6	3,309	15,213	
LTD Crown Victoria (wb 114.3)				
73	sdn 4d	3,741	14,355	
72	S sdn 4d	3,708	13,860	105,789
74	LX sdn 4d	3,788	15,454	

		Wght	Price	Prod
70	cpe 2d	3,724	14,727	5,527
71	LX cpe 2d	3,735	15,421	
78	Country Squire wgn 5d	3,920	14,507	
76	wgn 5d	3,920	14,235	
75	S wgn 5d	3,894	14,228	17,562
79	LX Country Squire wgn 5d	4,000	15,723	
77	LX wgn 5d	4,000	15,450	

1987 Engines	bore × stroke	bhp	availability
L4, 113.5	3.23 × 3.46	90	S-Escort, EXP
L4, 113.5	3.23 × 3.46	115	S-Esc GT, EXP spt; O-Esc
L4D, 121.0	3.39 × 3.39	58	O-Escort
L4, 140.0	3.70 × 3.30	86	S-Tempo
L4, 140.0	3.70 × 3.30	94	S-Tempo AWD; O-Tempo
L4, 153.0	3.70 × 3.60	90	S-Taurus exc LX/wgn
V6, 182.0	3.50 × 3.15	140	S-Taurus LX, wgn; O-Taurus
V8, 302.0	4.00 × 3.00	150	S-Crown Vic
V8, 351.0	4.00 × 3.50	180	S-Crown Vic (police only)

1987 Escort GT three-door hatchback

1988

Escort (wb 94.2)		Wght	Price	Prod
20	Pony sdn 3d	2,180	6,632	
21	GL sdn 3d	2,187	6,949	
23	GT sdn 3d	2,516	9,055	
25	GL sdn 5d	2,222	7,355	
28	GL wgn 5d	2,274	7,938	
Escort Second Series 1988.5 (wb 94.2)				
90	Pony sdn 3d	—	6,747	
91	LX sdn 3d	2,258	7,127	
93	GT sdn 3d	—	9,093	
95	LX sdn 5d	2,295	7,457	
98	LX wgn 5d	2,307	8,058	
EXP (wb 94.2)				
17	Luxury cpe 3d	2,291	8,037	
EXP Second Series 1988.5 (wb 94.2)				
88	Luxury cpe 3d	2,359	8,201	

Tempo (wb 99.9)		Wght	Price	Prod
31	GL sdn 2d	2,536	8,658	
33	GLS sdn 2d	2,552	9,249	
36	GL sdn 4d	2,585	8,808	163,409
37	LX sdn 4d	2,626	9,737	
38	GLS sdn 4d	2,601	9,400	
39	AWD (4WD) sdn 4d	2,799	10,413	
Taurus (wb 106.0)				
50	L sdn 4d L4/V6	3,005	11,699	
51	MT5 sdn 4d L4	2,882	12,835	
52	GL sdn 4d L4/V6	3,049	12,200	
53	LX sdn 4d V6	3,119	15,295	387,577
55	L wgn 5d V6	3,182	12,884	
57	GL wgn 5d V6	3,215	13,380	
58	LX wgn 5d V6	3,288	15,905	
LTD Crown Victoria (wb 114.3)				
73	sdn 4d	3,779	15,218	
72	S sdn 4d	3,742	14,653	
74	LX sdn 4d	3,820	16,134	

1988 LTD Crown Victoria

		Wght	Price	Prod
78	Country Squire wgn 5d	3,998	15,613	
76	wgn 5d	3,991	15,180	
79	LX Country Squire wgn 5d	4,070	16,643	
77	LX wgn 5d	3,972	16,210	

1988 Engines	bore × stroke	bhp	availability
L4, 113.5	3.23 × 3.46	90	S-Escort, EXP
L4, 113.5	3.23 × 3.46	115	S-Escort GT
L4, 140.0	3.70 × 3.30	98	S-Tempo
L4, 140.0	3.70 × 3.30	100	S-Tempo AWD, GLS
L4, 153.0	3.70 × 3.60	90	S-Taurus exc LX/wgn
V6, 182.0	3.50 × 3.15	140	S-Taurus LX, wgn; O-Taurus
V6, 232.0	3.80 × 3.40	140	O-Taurus
V8, 302.0	4.00 × 3.00	150	S-Crown Vic
V8, 351.0	4.00 × 3.50	180	S-Crown Vic (police only)

1989

Escort (wb 94.2)		Wght	Price	Prod
90	Pony sdn 3d	2,235	6,964	
91	LX sdn 3d	2,242	7,349	
93	GT sdn 3d	2,442	9,315	
95	LX sdn 5d	2,313	7,679	
98	LX wgn 5d	2,312	8,280	
Probe (wb 99.0)				
20	GL htchbk 3d	2,715	10,660	
21	LX htchbk 3d	2,715	11,644	
22	GT htchbk 3d	2,870	13,794	
Tempo (wb 99.9)				
31	GL sdn 2d	2,529	9,057	
33	GLS sdn 2d	2,545	9,697	
36	GL sdn 4d	2,587	9,207	
37	LX sdn 4d	2,628	10,156	
38	GLS sdn 4d	2,603	9,848	
39	AWD (4WD) sdn 4d	2,787	10,860	
Taurus (wb 106.0)				
50	L sdn 4d L4/V6	3,001	11,778	
52	GL sdn 4d L4/V6	3,046	12,202	
53	LX sdn 4d V6	3,076	15,282	
—	SHO sdn 4d V6	3,078	19,739	
55	L wgn 5d V6	3,172	13,143	
57	GL wgn 5d V6	3,189	13,544	
58	LX wgn 5d V6	3,220	16,524	
LTD Crown Victoria (wb 114.3)				
73	sdn 4d	3,730	15,851	
74	LX sdn 4d	3,770	16,767	
78	Country Squire wgn 5d	3,935	16,527	
76	wgn 5d	3,941	16,209	
79	LX Country Squire wgn 5d	4,013	17,556	
77	LX wgn 5d	3,915	17,238	

1989 Engines	bore × stroke	bhp	availability
L4, 113.5	3.23 × 3.46	90	S-Escort
L4, 113.5	3.23 × 3.46	115	S-Escort GT
L4, 133.0	3.39 × 3.70	110	S-Probe GL/LX
L4T, 133.0	3.39 × 3.70	145	S-Probe GT
L4, 140.0	3.70 × 3.30	98	S-Tempo
L4, 140.0	3.70 × 3.30	100	S-Tempo AWD, GLS
L4, 153.0	3.70 × 3.60	90	S-Taurus exc LX/wgn
V6, 182.0	3.50 × 3.15	140	S-Taur LX sdn, wgn; O-Taur
V6, 182.0	3.50 × 3.15	220	S-Taurus SHO
V6, 232.0	3.80 × 3.40	140	S-Taurus LX wgn; O-Taurus
V8, 302.0	4.00 × 3.00	150	S-Crown Vic
V8, 351.0	4.00 × 3.50	180	S-Crown Vic (police only)

Note: Full-size (Crown Victoria) station wagons in the 1980s could have an optional dual-facing rear seat. Base prices of 1983-87 Escort and Tempo diesel models were higher than amounts shown.

FORD MUSTANG

1965

(wb 108.0)		Wght	Price	Prod
07	htp cpe	2,583	2,372	501,965
08	conv cpe	2,789	2,614	101,945
09	fstbk cpe	2,633	2,589	77,079

1965 Engines	bore×stroke	bhp	availability
L6, 170.0	3.50×2.94	101	S-all through 9/24/64
L6, 200.0	3.68×3.13	120	S-all after 9/25/64
V8, 260.0	3.80×2.87	164	O-all through 9/25/64
V8, 289.0	4.00×2.87	200	O-all after 9/25/64
V8, 289.0	4.00×2.87	225/271	O-all

Note: 1965 production totals include 121,538 early (1964½) models.

1966

(wb 108.0)		Wght	Price	Prod
01	htp cpe	2,488	2,416	499,751
02	fstbk cpe	2,519	2,607	35,698
03	conv cpe	2,650	2,653	72,119

1966 Engines	bore×stroke	bhp	availability
L6, 200.0	3.68×3.13	120	S-all
V8, 289.0	4.00×2.87	200	O-all
V8, 289.0	4.00×2.87	225/271	O-all

1965 Mustang convertible coupe

1966 Mustang GT convertible coupe

1967

(wb 108.0)		Wght	Price	Prod
01	htp cpe	2,568	2,461	356,271
02	fstbk cpe	2,605	2,592	71,042
03	conv cpe	2,738	2,698	44,808

1967 Engines	bore×stroke	bhp	availability
L6, 200.0	3.68×3.13	120	S-all
V8, 289.0	4.00×2.87	200	O-all
V8, 289.0	4.00×2.87	225/271	O-all
V8, 390.0	4.05×3.78	320	O-all

1968

(wb 108.0)		Wght	Price	Prod
01	htp cpe	2,635	2,602	249,447
02	fstbk cpe	2,659	2,712	42,581
03	conv cpe	2,745	2,814	25,376

1968 Engines	bore×stroke	bhp	availability
L6, 200.0	3.68×3.13	115	S-all
L6, 250.0	3.68×3.91	155	O-all (late)
V8, 289.0	4.00×2.87	195	O-all
V8, 302.0	4.00×3.00	220	O-all
V8, 390.0	4.05×3.78	335	O-all
V8, 427.0	4.23×3.78	390	O-all
V8, 428.0	4.13×3.98	335	O-all (late)

1969

(wb 108.0)		Wght	Price	Prod
01	htp cpe	2,798	2,635	128,458
02	fstbk cpe	2,822	2,635	60,046
02	Boss 302 fstbk cpe, V8	3,210	3,588	1,934
02	Boss 429 fstbk cpe, V8	—	4,798	858
03	conv cpe	2,908	2,849	14,746
04	Grande htp cpe	2,873	2,866	22,182
05	Mach I fstbk cpe	3,175	3,139	72,458

1969 Engines	bore×stroke	bhp	availability
L6, 200.0	3.68×3.13	115	S-all exc Mach I, Boss
L6, 250.0	3.68×3.91	155	O-all exc Mach I, Boss
V8, 302.0	4.00×3.00	220	O-all exc Mach I, Boss
V8, 302.0	4.00×3.00	290	S-Boss 302
V8, 351.0	4.00×3.50	250	S-Mach I;O-others exc Boss
V8, 351.0	4.00×3.50	290	O-all
V8, 390.0	4.05×3.78	320	O-all
V8, 428.0	4.13×3.98	335	O-Mach I (Ram Air avail)
V8, 429.0	4.36×3.59	360/375	S-Boss 429

1970

(wb 108.0)		Wght	Price	Prod
01	htp cpe	2,822	2,721	82,569
02	fstbk cpe	2,846	2,771	39,316
02	Boss 302 fstbk cpe, V8	3,227	3,720	6,319
02	Boss 429 fstbk cpe, V8	—	4,798	498
03	conv cpe	2,932	3,025	7,673
04	Grande htp cpe	2,907	2,926	13,581
05	Mach I cpe	3,240	3,271	40,970

1970 Engines	bore×stroke	bhp	availability
L6, 200.0	3.68×3.13	115	S-all exc Mach I, Boss 302
L6, 250.0	3.68×3.91	155	O-all exc Mach I, Boss 302
V8, 302.0	4.00×3.00	220	O-all exc Mach I, Boss 302
V8, 302.0	4.00×3.00	290	S-Boss 302
V8, 351.0	4.00×3.50	250	S-Mach I; O-others exc Boss 302
V8, 351.0	4.00×3.50	300	O-all
V8, 428.0	4.13×3.98	335	O-Mach I (Ram Air avail)
V8, 429.0	4.36×3.59	375	O-Mach 1, Boss

1971

(wb 109.0)		Wght	Price	Prod
01	htp cpe	2,982	2,911	65,696
02	fstbk cpe	2,950	2,973	23,956
02	Boss 351 fstbk cpe V8	3,281	4,124	
03	conv	3,102	3,227	6,121
04	Grandé htp cpe	3,006	3,117	17,406
05	Mach 1 fstbk cpe V8	3,220	3,268	36,499

1967 Mustang GTA hardtop coupe

1971 Engines	bore×stroke	bhp	availability
L6, 250.0	3.68×3.91	145	S-all exc Mach 1, Boss 351
V8, 302.0	4.00×3.00	210	O-all exc Mach 1, Boss 351
V8, 351.0	4.00×3.50	240	O-all exc Boss 351
V8, 351.0	4.00×3.50	285	O-all exc Boss 351
V8, 351.0	4.00×3.50	330	S-Boss 351; O-others
V8, 429.0	4.36×3.59	370	O-all

1972

(wb 109.0)		Wght	Price	Prod
01	htp cpe	2,983	2,729	57,350
02	fstbk cpe	2,952	2,786	15,622
03	conv	3,099	3,015	6,401
04	Grandé htp cpe	3,008	2,915	18,045
05	Mach 1 fstbk cpe V8	3,046	3,053	27,675

1972 Engines	bore×stroke	bhp	availability
L6, 250.0	3.68×3.91	99	S-all exc Mach I
V8, 302.0	4.00×3.00	141	S-Mach 1; O-others
V8, 351.0	4.00×3.50	177/266 /275	O-all

1973

(wb 109.0)		Wght	Price	Prod
01	htp cpe	3,040	2,760	51,480
02	fstbk cpe	3,053	2,820	10,820
03	conv	3,171	3,102	11,853
04	Grandé htp cpe	3,059	2,946	25,274
05	Mach 1 fstbk cpe V8	3,115	3,088	35,440

1973 Engines	bore×stroke	bhp	availability
L6, 250.0	3.68×3.91	95	S-all exc Mach 1
V8, 302.0	4.00×3.00	136	S-Mach 1; 0-others
V8, 351.0	4.00×3.50	154/156	O-all

1974

II (wb 96.2)		Wght	Price	Prod
02	cpe 2d	2,654	3,134	177,671
03	htchbk cpe 3d	2,734	3,328	74,799
04	Ghia cpe 2d	2,820	3,480	89,477
05	Mach 1 htchbk cpe 3d V6	2,778	3,674	44,046

1974 Engines	bore×stroke	bhp	availability
L4, 140.0	3.78×3.13	88	S-all exc Mach 1
V6, 170.0	3.66×2.70	105	S-Mach 1; O-others

1975

II (wb 96.2)		Wght	Price	Prod
02	cpe 2d	2,718	3,529	85,155
03	htchbk cpe 3d	2,754	3,818	30,038
04	Ghia cpe 2d	2,762	3,938	52,320
05	Mach 1 htchbk cpe 3d V6	2,879	4,188	21,062

1975 Engines	bore×stroke	bhp	availability
L4, 140.0	3.78×3.13	83	S-all exc Mach 1
V6, 170.0	3.66×2.70	97	S-Mach 1; O-others
V8, 302.0	4.00×3.00	122	O-all

1976

II (wb 96.2)		Wght	Price	Prod
02	cpe 2d	2,717	3,525	78,508
03	htchbk cpe 3d	2,745	3,781	62,312
04	Ghia cpe 2d	2,768	3,859	37,515
05	Mach 1 htchbk cpe V6 3d	2,822	4,209	9,232

1970 Mustang fastback coupe

1971 Mustang Mach I fastback coupe

1976 Engines	bore×stroke	bhp	availability
L4, 140.0	3.78×3.13	92	S-all exc Mach 1
V6, 170.0	3.66×2.70	103	S-Mach 1; O-others
V8, 302.0	4.00×3.00	134	O-all

1977

II (wb 96.2)		Wght	Price	Prod
02	cpe 2d	2,688	3,702	67,783
03	htchbk cpe 3d	2,734	3,901	49,161
04	Ghia cpe 2d	2,728	4,119	29,510
05	Mach 1 htchbk cpe V6 3d	2,785	4,332	6,719

1977 Engines	bore×stroke	bhp	availability
L4, 140.0	3.78×3.13	89	S-all exc Mach 1
V6, 170.0	3.66×2.70	93	S-Mach 1; 0-others
V8, 302.0	4.00×3.00	139	O-all

1978

II (wb 96.2)		Wght	Price	Prod
02	cpe 2d	2,656	3,555	81,304
03	htchbk cpe 3d	2,702	3,798	68,408
04	Ghia cpe 2d	2,694	3,972	34,730
05	Mach 1 htchbk cpe V6 3d	2,733	4,253	7,968

1978 Engines	bore×stroke	bhp	availability
L4, 140.0	3.78×3.13	88	S-all exc Mach 1
V6, 170.0	3.66×2.70	90	S-Mach 1; O-others
V8, 302.0	4.00×3.00	139	O-all

1979

(wb 100.4)		Wght	Price	Prod
02	cpe 2d	2,471	4,071	156,666
03	htchbk cpe 3d	2,491	4,436	120,535
04	Ghia cpe 2d	2,579	4,642	56,351
05	Ghia htchbk cpe 3d	2,588	4,824	36,384

1979 Engines	bore×stroke	bhp	availability
L4, 140.0	3.78×3.13	88	S-all
L4T, 140.0	3.78×3.13	140	O-all
V6, 170.0	3.66×2.70	109	O-all
L6, 200.0	3.68×3.13	91	O-all (late)
V8, 302.0	4.00×3.00	140	O-all

1980

(wb 100.4)		Wght	Price	Prod
02	cpe 2d	2,514	4,884	128,893
03	htchbk cpe 3d	2,548	5,194	98,497
04	Ghia cpe 2d	2,582	5,369	23,647
05	Ghia htchbk cpe 3d	2,606	5,512	20,285

1980 Engines	bore×stroke	bhp	availability
L4, 140.0	3.78×3.13	88	S-all
L4T, 140.0	3.78×3.13	140	O-all
L6, 200.0	3.68×3.13	91	O-all
V8, 255.0	2.68×3.00	118	O-all

1981

(wb 100.4)		Wght	Price	Prod
10	cpe 2d	2,537	6,171	77,458
15	htchbk cpe 3d	2,557	6,408	77,399
12	Ghia cpe 2d	2,571	6,645	13,422
13	Ghia htchbk cpe 3d	2,606	6,729	14,273

1981 Engines	bore × stroke	bhp	availability
L4, 140.0	3.78 × 3.13	88	S-all
L4T, 140.0	3.78 × 3.13	140	O-all
L6, 200.0	3.68 × 3.13	88/94	O-all
V8, 255.0	3.68 × 3.00	115	O-all

1982

(wb 100.4)		Wght	Price	Prod
10	L cpe 2d	2,568	6,345	45,316
10	GL cpe 2d	2,585	6,844	
16	GL htchbk cpe 3d	2,622	6,979	45,901
16	GT htchbk cpe 3d V8	2,597	8,308	23,447
12	GLX cpe 2d	2,600	6,980	5,828
13	GLX htchbk cpe 3d	2,636	7,101	9,926

1982 Engines	bore × stroke	bhp	availability
L4, 140.0	3.78 × 3.13	88	S-all
L6, 200.0	3.68 × 3.13	88	O-all
V8, 255.0	3.68 × 3.00	120	O-all
V8, 302.0	4.00 × 3.00	157	S-GT; O-all

1983

(wb 100.4)		Wght	Price	Prod
26	L cpe 2d	2,684	6,727	
26/60C	GL cpe 2d	2,743	7,264	33,201
26/602	GLX cpe 2d	2,760	7,398	
28/60C	GL htchbk cpe 3d	2,788	7,439	
28/602	GLX htchbk cpe 3d	2,801	7,557	64,234
28/932	GT htchbk cpe 3d V8	2,969	9,328	
28/932	Turbo GT htchbk cpe 3d	—	9,714	
27/602	GLX conv cpe V6	2,807	12,467	23,438
27/932	GT conv cpe V8	—	13,479	

1978 Mustang II King Cobra hatchback coupe

1983 Engines	bore × stroke	bhp	availability
L4, 140.0	3.78 × 3.13	90	S-all exc conv/GT
L4T, 140.0	3.78 × 3.13	142	S-Turbo GT
V6, 232.0	3.80 × 3.40	112	S-conv; O-all exc GT
V8, 302.0	4.00 × 3.00	175	S-GT; O-others

1984

(wb 100.4)		Wght	Price	Prod
26	L cpe 2d	2,736	7,098	37,780
26/602	LX cpe 2d	2,757	7,290	
28	L htchbk cpe 3d	2,782	7,269	
28/602	LX htchbk cpe 3d	2,807	7,496	
28/932	GT htchbk cpe 3d V8	3,013	9,578	86,200
28/932	Turbo GT htchbk cpe 3d	2,869	9,762	
28/939	SVO turbo htchbk cpe 3d	2,992	15,596	
27/602	LX conv cpe V6	3,020	11,849	
27/932	GT conv cpe V8	3,124	13,051	17,600
27/932	Turbo GT conv cpe	3,004	13,245	

1984 Engines	bore × stroke	bhp	availability
L4, 140.0	3.78 × 3.13	88	S-all exc conv/GT
L4T, 140.0	3.78 × 3.13	145	S-Turbo GT
L4T, 140.0	3.78 × 3.13	175	S-SVO
V6, 232.0	3.80 × 3.40	120	S-conv; O-all exc GT
V8, 302.0	4.00 × 3.00	165	O-all
V8, 302.0	4.00 × 3.00	175	S-GT

1985

(wb 100.4)		Wght	Price	Prod
26/602	LX cpe 2d	2,657	6,885	56,781
28/602	LX htchbk cpe 3d	2,729	7,345	

1983 Mustang GT hatchback coupe

		Wght	Price	Prod
28/932	GT htchbk cpe 3d V8	3,063	9,885	84,623
28/939	SVO turbo htchbk cpe 3d	2,991	14,521	
27/602	LX conv cpe V6	2,907	11,985	15,110
27/932	GT conv cpe V8	3,165	13,585	

1985 Engines	bore × stroke	bhp	availability
L4, 140.0	3.78 × 3.13	88	S-all exc conv/GT
L4T, 140.0	3.78 × 3.13	175	S-SVO
V6, 232.0	3.80 × 3.40	120	S-conv; O-all exc GT
V8, 302.0	4.00 × 3.00	180	O-all
V8, 302.0	4.00 × 3.00	210	S-GT

1986

(wb 100.4)		Wght	Price	Prod
26	LX cpe 2d	2,795	7,189	
27	LX conv cpe V6	3,044	12,821	106,720
27	GT conv cpe V8	3,269	14,523	
28	LX htchbk cpe 3d	2,853	7,744	
28	GT htchbk cpe V8	3,139	10,691	117,690
28/937	SVO turbo htchbk cpe 3d	3,140	15,272	

1986 Engines	bore × stroke	bhp	availability
L4, 140.0	3.78 × 3.13	88	S-all exc conv/GT
L4T, 140.0	3.78 × 3.18	200	S-SVO
V6, 232.0	3.80 × 3.40	120	S-conv; O-all exc GT
V8, 302.0	4.00 × 3.00	200	S-GT

1987

(wb 100.5)—159,145 built		Wght	Price	Prod
40	LX cpe 2d L4/V8	2,862	8,043	
44	LX conv cpe L4/V8	3,059	12,840	64,704*
45	GT conv cpe V8	3,214	15,724	
41	LX htchbk cpe 3d L4/V8	2,920	8,474	94,441*
42	GT htchbk cpe V8	3,080	11,835	

1987 Engines	bore × stroke	bhp	availability
L4, 140.0	3.78 × 3.13	90	S-LX
V8, 302.0	4.00 × 3.00	225	S-GT; O-LX

*Some industry sources state that 58,100 two-doors, 80,717 hatchbacks and 20,328 convertibles were built.

1988

(wb 100.4)		Wght	Price	Prod
40	LX cpe 2d L4/V8	2,894	8,726	
44	LX conv cpe L4/V8	3,081	13,702	
45	GT conv cpe V8	3,341	16,610	211,225
41	LX htchbk cpe 3d L4/V8	2,961	9,221	
42	GT htchbk cpe V8	3,193	12,745	

1985 Mustang SVO hatchback coupe

1988 Engines	bore × stroke	bhp	availability
L4, 140.0	3.78 × 3.13	90	S-LX
V8, 302.0	4.00 × 3.00	225	S-GT; O-LX

1989

(wb 100.4)		Wght	Price	Prod
40	LX cpe 2d L4	2,754	9,050	
40	LX 5.0L spt cpe 2d V8	3,045	11,410	
44	LX conv cpe L4	2,966	14,140	
44	LX 5.0L conv cpe V8	3,257	17,001	
45	GT conv cpe V8	3,333	17,512	
41	LX htchbk cpe 3d L4	2,819	9,556	
41	LX 5.0L spt htchbk 3d V8	3,110	12,265	
42	GT htchbk cpe V8	3,194	13,272	

1989 Engines	bore × stroke	bhp	availability
L4, 140.0	3.78 × 3.13	90	S-LX
V8, 302.0	4.00 × 3.00	225	S-GT; O-LX

FORD THUNDERBIRD

1955

(wb 102.0)		Wght	Price	Prod
40A	conv 2S	2,980	2,944	16,155

1955 Engines	bore×stroke	bhp	availability
V8, 292.0	3.75×3.30	193	S-stickshift
V8, 292.0	3.75×3.30	198	S-automatic

1956

(wb 102.0)		Wght	Price	Prod
40A	conv 2S	3,038	3,151	15,631

1956 Engines	bore×stroke	bhp	availability
V8, 292.0	3.75×3.30	202	S-3-speed trans
V8, 312.0	3.80×3.44	215	S-overdrive
V8, 312.0	3.80×3.44	225	S-automatic

1957

(wb 102.0)		Wght	Price	Prod
40	conv 2S	3,145	3,408	21,380

1957 Engines	bore×stroke	bhp	availability
V8, 292.0	3.75×3.30	212	S-3-speed trans
V8, 312.0	3.80×3.44	245	S-overdrive, automatic
V8, 312.0	3.80×3.44	270/285	O-all (3-speed briefly)
V8, 312.0	3.80×3.44	300	O-auto; few od/3sp (superchgd)

1958

(wb 113.0)		Wght	Price	Prod
63A	htp cpe	3,876	3,631	35,758
76A	conv cpe	3,944	3,929	2,134

1958 Engines	bore×stroke	bhp	availability
V8,352.0	4.00×3.50	300	S-all
V8, 430.0	4.30×3.70	350	O-prod questionable

1959 Thunderbird convertible coupe

1959

(wb 113.0)		Wght	Price	Prod
63A	htp cpe	3,813	3,696	57,195
76A	conv cpe	3,903	3,979	10,261

1959 Engines	bore×stroke	bhp	availability
V8, 352.0	4.00×3.50	300	S-all
V8, 430.0	4.30×3.70	350	O-all

1960

(wb 113.0)		Wght	Price	Prod
63A	htp cpe	3,799	3,755	76,447
63B	htp cpe, gold top	3,799	3,900*	2,536
76A	conv cpe	3,897	4,222	11,860

1960 Engines	bore×stroke	bhp	availability
V8, 352.0	4.00×3.50	300	S-all
V8, 430.0	4.30×3.70	350	O-all

*Estimated.

1961

(wb 113.0)		Wght	Price	Prod
63A	htp cpe	3,958	4,172	62,535
76A	conv cpe	4,130	4,639	10,516

1961 Engine	bore×stroke	bhp	availability
V8, 390.0	4.05×3.78	300	S-all

1962

(wb 113.0)		Wght	Price	Prod
63A	htp cpe	4,132	4,321	69,554*
63B	Landau htp cpe	4,144	4,398	
76A	conv cpe	4,370	4,788	7,030*
76B	Sports Roadster conv cpe	4,471	5,439	1,427*

*Some sources list total of 68,127 hardtops/Landaus and 9,884 convertibles.

1962 Engines	bore×stroke	bhp	availability
V8, 390.0	4.05×3.78	300	S-all
V8, 390.0	4.05×3.78	340	O-all

1963

Series 80 (wb 113.0)		Wght	Price	Prod
63A	htp cpe	4,195	4,445	42,806*
63B	Landau htp cpe	4,203	4,548	14,139*
76A	conv cpe	4,322	4,912	5,913*
76B	Sports Roadster conv cpe	4,396	5,563	455*

*Some sources list total of 59,000 hardtops/Landaus and 5,457 convertibles. Model 63B includes 2,000 Limited Edition Landaus with special trim; model 76B includes 37 units with 340-bhp engine.

1963 Engines	bore×stroke	bhp	availability
V8, 390.0	4.05×3.78	300	S-all
V8, 390.0	4.05×3.78	340	O-all

1964

Series 80 (wb 113.2)		Wght	Price	Prod
83	htp cpe	4,431	4,486	60,552
85	conv cpe	4,586	4,953	9,198
87	Landau htp cpe	4,441	4,589	22,715

1964 Engine	bore×stroke	bhp	availability
V8, 390.0	4.05×3.78	300	S-all

1965

Series 80 (wb 113.2)		Wght	Price	Prod
83	htp cpe	4,470	4,486	42,652
85	conv cpe	4,588	4,953	6,846
87	Landau htp cpe	4,478	4,589	20,974

1962 Thunderbird Sports Roadster convertible coupe

1963 Thunderbird Sports Roadster convertible coupe

1966 Thunderbird convertible coupe

		Wght	Price	Prod
87	Limited Ed Special Landau	4,500	4,639	4,500

1965 Engine	bore×stroke	bhp	availability
V8, 390.0	4.00×3.78	300	S-all

1966

Series 80 (wb 113.2)		Wght	Price	Prod
81	Town Hardtop cpe	4,359	4,483	15,633
83	htp cpe	4,386	4,426	13,389
85	conv cpe	4,496	4,879	5,049
87	Landau htp cpe	4,367	4,584	35,105

1966 Engines	bore×stroke	bhp	availability
V8, 390.0	4.00×3.78	315	S-all
V8, 428.0	4.13×3.98	345	O-all

1967

Series 80 (wb 114.7; 4d-117.2)		Wght	Price	Prod
81	htp cpe	4,248	4,603	15,567
82	Landau htp cpe	4,256	4,704	37,422
84	Landau sdn 4d	4,348	4,825	24,967

1964 Thunderbird hardtop coupe

1967 Engines	bore×stroke	bhp	availability
V8, 390.0	4.00×3.78	315	S-all
V8, 428.0	4.13×3.98	345	O-all

1968

Series 80 (wb 114.7; 4d-117.2)		Wght	Price	Prod
83	htp cpe	4,366	4,716	9,977
84	Landau htp cpe	4,372	4,845	33,029
87	Landau sdn 4d	4,458	4,924	21,925

1968 Engines	bore×stroke	bhp	availability
V8, 390.0	4.00×3.78	315	S-all
V8, 429.0	4.36×3.59	360	O-all

1969

Series 80 (wb 114.7; 4d-117.2)		Wght	Price	Prod
83	htp cpe	4,348	4,824	5,913
84	Landau htp cpe	4,360	4,964	27,664
87	Landau sdn 4d	4,460	5,043	15,695

1969 Engine	bore×stroke	bhp	availability
V8, 429.0	4.36×3.59	360	S-all

1970

Series 80 (wb 114.7; 4d-117.2)		Wght	Price	Prod
83	htp cpe	4,354	4,961	5,116
84	Landau htp cpe	4,630	5,104	36,847
87	Landau sdn 4d	4,464	5,182	8,401

1970 Engine	bore×stroke	bhp	availability
V8, 429.0	4.36×3.59	360	S-all

1971

Series 80 (wb 115.0, 4d 118.0)		Wght	Price	Prod
83	htp cpe	4,389	5,295	9,146
84	Landau htp cpe	4,360	5,438	20,356
87	Landau sdn 4d	4,496	5,516	6,553

1971 Engine	bore×stroke	bhp	availability
V8, 429.0	4.36×3.59	360	S-all

1972

Series 80 (wb 120.4)		Wght	Price	Prod
87	htp cpe	4,373	5,293	57,814

1972 Engines	bore×stroke	bhp	availability
V8, 429.0	4.36×3.59	212	S-all
V8, 460.0	4.36×3.85	224	O-all

1973

Series 80 (wb 120.4)		Wght	Price	Prod
87	htp cpe	4,505	6,437	87,269

1973 Engines	bore×stroke	bhp	availability
V8, 429.0	4.36×3.59	208	S-all
V8, 460.0	4.36×3.85	219	O-all

1974

Series 80 (wb 120.4)		Wght	Price	Prod
87	htp cpe	4,825	7,330	58,443

1974 Engine	bore×stroke	bhp	availability
V8, 460.0	4.36×3.85	220	S-all

1975

Series 80 (wb 120.4)		Wght	Price	Prod
87	htp cpe	4,893	7,701	42,685

1975 Engine	bore×stroke	bhp	availability
V8, 460.0	4.36×3.85	194	S-all

1976

Series 80 (wb 120.4)		Wght	Price	Prod
87	htp cpe	4,808	7,790	52,935*

1976 Engine	bore×stroke	bhp	availability
V8, 460.0	4.36×3.85	202	S-all

*includes 30 commemorative editions.

1977

(wb 114.0)		Wght	Price	Prod
87	htp cpe	3,907	5,063	318,140
87	Town Landau cpe	4,104	7,990	

1977 Engines	bore×stroke	bhp	availability
V8, 302.0	4.00×3.00	130	S-all
V8, 351.0	4.00×3.50	135	S-in Calif.; O-all
V8, 400.0	4.00×4.00	173	O-all

1978

(wb 114.0)		Wght	Price	Prod
87	htp cpe	3,907	5,411	333,757
87	Town Landau cpe	4,104	8,420	
87	Diamond Jubilee cpe	4,200	10,106	18,994

1980 Thunderbird two-door coupe

1983 Thunderbird two-door coupe

1985 Thunderbird Turbo Coupe

1978 Engines	bore×stroke	bhp	availability
V8, 302.0	4.00×3.00	134	S-all
V8, 351.0	4.00×3.50	152	O-all
V8, 400.0	4.00×4.00	166	O-all

1979—284,141 built

(wb 114.0)		Wght	Price	Prod
87	cpe	3,893	5,877	—
87/607	Town Landau cpe	4,284	8,866	—
87/603	Heritage cpe	4,178	10,687	—

1979 Engines	bore×stroke	bhp	availability
V8, 302.0	4.00×3.00	133	S-all
V8, 351.0	4.00×3.50	135/151	O-all

1980—156,803 built

(wb 108.4)		Wght	Price	Prod
87	cpe	3,118	6,432	—
87/607	Town Landau cpe	3,357	10,036	—
87/603	Silver Anniversary cpe	3,225	11,679	—

1980 Engines	bore×stroke	bhp	availability
V8, 255.0	3.68×3.00	115	S-all
V8, 302.0	4.00×3.00	131	S-Sil.Ann.; O-others

1981—86,693 built

(wb 108.4)		Wght	Price	Prod
42	cpe	3,064	7,551	—
42/60T	Town Landau cpe	3,127	8,689	—
42/607	Heritage cpe V8	3,303	11,355	—

1981 Engines	bore × stroke	bhp	availability
L6, 200.0	3.68 × 3.13	88	S-all exc Heritage
V8, 255.0	3.68 × 3.00	115	S-Heritage; O-others
V8, 302.0	4.00 × 3.00	130	O-all

1982—45,142 built

(wb 108.4)		Wght	Price	Prod
42	cpe L6/V8	3,068	8,492	—
42/60T	Town Landau cpe L6/V8	3,131	9,703	—
42/607	Heritage cpe V6/V8	3,303	12,742	—

1982 Engines	bore × stroke	bhp	availability
L6, 200.0	3.68 × 3.13	88	S-all exc Heritage
V6, 232.0	3.80 × 3.40	112	O-all exc Heritage
V8, 255.0	3.68 × 3.00	120	S-Heritage; O-others

1983—121,999 built

(wb 104.0)		Wght	Price	Prod
46	cpe V6/V8	3,076	9,197	—
46/607	Heritage cpe V6/V8	3,076	12,228	—
46/934	Turbo cpe L4T	—	11,790	—

1983 Engines	bore × stroke	bhp	availability
L4T, 140.0	3.78 × 3.13	142	S-turbo cpe
V6, 232.0	3.80 × 3.40	110	S-all exc turbo cpe
V8, 302.0	4.00 × 3.00	130	O-all exc turbo cpe

1984—170,533 built

(wb 104.0)		Wght	Price	Prod
46	cpe V6/V8	3,155	9,633	—
46/607	elan cpe V6/V8	3,221	12,661	—
46/606	Fila cpe V6/V8	3,326	14,471	—
46/934	Turbo cpe L4T	3,073	12,330	—

1984 Engines	bore × stroke	bhp	availability
L4T, 140.0	3.78 × 3.13	145	S-turbo cpe
V6, 232.0	3.80 × 3.40	120	S-all exc turbo cpe
V8, 302.0	4.00 × 3.00	140	O-all exc turbo cpe

1985—151,851 built

(wb 104.0)		Wght	Price	Prod
46	cpe V6/V8	3,004	10,249	—
46/607	elan cpe V6/V8	3,041	11,916	—
46/606	Fila cpe V6/V8	3,108	14,974	—
46/934	Turbo cpe L4T	2,990	13,365	—

1985 Engines	bore × stroke	bhp	availability
L4T, 140.0	3.78 × 3.13	155	S-turbo cpe
V6, 232.0	3.80 × 3.40	120	S-all exc turbo cpe
V8, 302.0	4.00 × 3.00	140	O-all exc turbo cpe

1986—163,965 built

(wb 104.0)		Wght	Price	Prod
46	cpe V6/V8	3,182	11,020	—
46	elan cpe V6/V8	3,238	12,554	—
46	Turbo cpe L4T	3,172	14,143	—

1986 Engines	bore × stroke	bhp	availability
L4T, 140.0	3.78 × 3.13	145/155	S-turbo cpe

1987 Thunderbird two-door coupe

1989 Thunderbird Super Coupe

	bore × stroke	bhp	availability
V6, 232.0	3.80 × 3.40	120	S-all exc turbo cpe
V8, 302.0	4.00 × 3.00	150	O-all exc turbo cpe

1987—128,135 built

(wb 104.2)—128,135 built		Wght	Price	Prod
60	cpe V6/V8	3,202	12,972	
61	spt cpe V8	3,346	15,079	
62	LX cpe V6/V8	3,245	15,383	
64	Turbo cpe L4T	3,380	16,805	

1987 Engines	bore × stroke	bhp	availability
L4T, 140.0	3.78 × 3.13	190	S-turbo cpe
L4T, 140.0	3.78 × 3.13	150	S-turbo cpe (automatic)
V6, 232.0	3.80 × 3.40	120	S-all exc turbo cpe
V8, 302.0	4.00 × 3.00	150	O-all exc turbo cpe

1988 —147,243 built

(wb 104.2)		Wght	Price	Prod
60	cpe V6/V8	3,280	13,599	
61	spt cpe V8	3,450	16,030	
62	LX cpe V6/V8	3,324	15,585	
64	Turbo cpe L4T	3,415	17,250	

1988 Engines	bore × stroke	bhp	availability
L4T, 140.0	3.78 × 3.13	190	S-turbo cpe
L4T, 140.0	3.78 × 3.13	150	S-turbo cpe (automatic)
V6, 232.0	3.80 × 3.40	140	S-all exc turbo cpe
V8, 302.0	4.00 × 3.00	155	S-spt; O-all exc turbo cpe

1989

(wb 113.0)		Wght	Price	Prod
—	cpe V6	3,542	—	
—	LX cpe V6	3,554	—	
—	Super cpe S/C V6	3,701	—	

1989 Engines	bore × stroke	bhp	availability
V6, 232.0	3.80 × 3.40	140	S-all exc super cpe
V6S/C, 232.0	3.80 × 3.40	210	O-super cpe (superchgd)

FRAZER

1947

Standard (wb 123.5)		Wght	Price	Prod
F47	sdn 4d	3,340	2,295	36,120
Manhattan (wb 123.5)				
F47C	sdn 4d	3,375	2,712	32,655

1947 Engines	bore × stroke	bhp	availability
L6, 226.2	3.31 × 4.38	100	S-all
L6, 226.2	3.31 × 4.38	112	O-Manhattan

1948

F485 Standard (wb 123.5)		Wght	Price	Prod
4851	sdn 4d	3,340	2,483	29,480
F486 Manhattan (wb 123.5)				
4861	sdn 4d	3,375	2,746	18,591

1951 Vagabond utility sedan

1948 Engines	bore×stroke	bhp	availability
L6, 226.2	3.31×4.38	100	S-all
L6, 226.2	3.31×4.38	112	O-Manhattan

1949-50

F495/505 Standard (wb 123.5)		Wght	Price	Prod
4951/5051	sdn 4d	3,386	2,395	14,700*
F496/506 Manhattan (wb 123.5)				
4961/5051	sdn 4d	3,391	2,595	9,950*
4962/5052	conv sdn	3,726	3,295	70*

*Estimated: actual total 24,923. Years were combined by factory; estimated breakdown 85% 1949, 15% 1950.

1949-50 Engine	bore×stroke	bhp	availability
L6, 226.2	3.31×4.38	112	S-all

1951

F515 Standard (wb 123.5)		Wght	Price	Prod
5151	sdn 4d	3,456	2,359	6,900*
5155	Vagabond util sdn 4d	3,556	2,399	3,000*
F516 Manhattan (wb 123.5)				
5161	htp sdn	3,771	3,075	152
5162	conv sdn	3,941	3,075	131

*Estimated from actual total of 9,931.

1951 Engines	bore×stroke	bhp	availability
L6, 226.2	3.31×4.38	115	S-all

GRAHAM

1939

96 Special (wb 120.0)—2,913 built*	Wght	Price	Prod
Combination cpe 5P	3,185	940	—
sdn 2d T/B	3,230	940	—
sdn 4d T/B	3,240	965	—
Custom Combination cpe 5P	3,200	1,070	—
Custom sdn 2d T/B	3,245	1,070	—
Custom sdn 4d T/B	3,255	1,095	—
97 Supercharged (wb 120.0)—2,479 built*			
Combination cpe 5P	3,260	1,070	—
sdn 2d T/B	3,285	1,070	—
sdn 4d T/B	3,295	1,095	—
Custom Combination cpe 5P	3,290	1,200	—
Custom sdn 2d T/B	3,315	1,200	—
Custom sdn 4d T/B	3,325	1,225	—

1939 Engines	bore×stroke	bhp	availability
L6, 217.8	3.25×4.38	90	S-96
L6, 217.8	3.25×4.38	116	S-97; O-96 Custom

*Production totals based on published serial number spans. Total calendar year production: 3,876.

1940

107 Supercharged (wb 120.0)—est. 1,000 built (includes Standard)	Wght	Price	Prod
Deluxe cpe	3,245	1,160	—
Deluxe sdn 2d	3,250	1,135	—
Deluxe sdn 4d	3,250	1,160	—
Custom cpe	3,370	1,295	—
Custom sdn 2d	3,365	1,265	—
Custom sdn 4d	3,370	1,295	—

1939 Graham Supercharger "combination" coupe

108 Standard (wb 120.0)	Wght	Price	Prod
Deluxe cpe	3,190	1,020	—
Deluxe sdn 2d	3,195	995	—
Deluxe sdn 4d	3,195	1,015	—
Custom cpe	3,315	1,160	—
Custom sdn 2d	3,315	1,135	—
Custom sdn 4d	3,320	1,160	—
Hollywood Custom Super (wb. 115.0)			
sdn 4d	2,965	1,250	*
conv cpe (prototype)	3,075	—	1-2

1940 Engines	bore×stroke	bhp	availability
L6, 217.8	3.25×4.38	93	S-unsupercharged
L6, 217.8	3.25×4.38	120	S-supercharged

1941

109 Custom Hollywood Schgd (wb 115.0)	Wght	Price	Prod
sdn 4d	2,965	1,065	*
113 Custom Hollywood (wb 115.0)			
sdn 4d	2,915	968	*

1941 Engines	bore×stroke	bhp	availability
L6, 217.8	3.25×4.38	95	S-unsupercharged
L6, 217.8	3.25×4.38	124	S-supercharged

*Total 1940-41 Hollywood production: 1,859 (some sources claim 1,597).

HENRY J

1951

K513 Standard (wb 100.0)		Wght	Price	Prod
5134	sdn 2d	2,293	1,363	38,500*
K514 DeLuxe (wb 100.0)				
5144	sdn 2d	2,341	1,499	43,400*

1951 Engines	bore×stroke	bhp	availability
L4, 134.2	3.13×4.38	68	S-K513
L6, 161.0	3.13×3.50	80	S-K514

1952 Vagabond two-door sedan

1952

K523 Vagabond (wb 100.0)		Wght	Price	Prod
5234	sdn 2d	2,365	1,407	3,000*
K524 Vagabond DeLuxe (wb 100.0)				
5244	sdn 2d	2,385	1,552	4,000*
K523 Corsair (wb 100.0)				
5234	sdn 2d	2,370	1,517	7,600*
K524 Corsair DeLuxe (wb 100.0)				
5244	sdn 2d	2,405	1,664	8,900*

1952 Engines	bore×stroke	bhp	availability
L4, 134.2	3.13×4.38	68	S-K523
L6, 161.0	3.13×3.50	80	S-K524

1953

K533 Corsair (wb 100.0)		Wght	Price	Prod
5334	sdn 2d	2,395	1,399	8,500*
K534 Corsair DeLuxe (wb 100.0)				
5344	sdn 2d	2,445	1,561	8,100*

1953 Engines	bore×stroke	bhp	availability
L4, 134.2	3.13×4.38	68	S-K533
L6, 161.0	3.13×3.50	80	S-K534

1954

K543 Corsair (wb 100.0)		Wght	Price	Prod
5434	sdn 2d	2,405	1,404	800*
K544 Corsair DeLuxe (wb 100.0)				
5444	sdn 2d	2,455	1,566	300*

1954 Engines	bore×stroke	bhp	availability
L4, 134.2	3.13×4.38	68	S-K543
L6, 161.0	3.13×3.50	80	S-K544

***Estimates based on highest serial numbers found. Total model year production:**

1951 all	81,942
1952 Vagabond	7,017
1952 Corsair	23,568
1953 all	16,672
1954 all	1,123

HUDSON

1939*

90 "112" Deluxe Six (wb 112.0)		Wght	Price	Prod
	Traveler cpe 3P	2,544	695	—
	cpe 3P	2,587	745	—
	victoria cpe 4P	2,622	791	—
	conv cpe 3P	2,627	886	—
	touring brougham 6P	2,682	775	—
	conv brougham 6P	2,732	936	—
	touring sdn 4d	2,712	806	—
	Utility coach 6P	2,634	725	—
	Utility cpe 3P	2,714	750	—
	Utility wgn 4d	2,880	931	—
91 Pacemaker Six (wb 118.0)				
	cpe 3P	2,717	793	—
	victoria cpe 5P	2,752	844	—
	touring brougham 6P	2,832	823	—
	touring sdn 4d	2,867	854	—
92 Six (wb 118.0)				
	cpe 3P	2,757	833	—
	victoria cpe 5P	2,787	879	—
	conv cpe 3P	2,782	982	—
	touring brougham 6P	2,847	866	—
	conv brougham 6P	2,892	1,042	—
	touring sdn 4d	2,897	908	—
93 Country Club Six (wb 122.0)				
	cpe 3P	2,848	919	—
	victoria cpe 5P	2,893	967	—
	conv cpe 3P	2,898	1,052	—
	touring brougham 6P	2,968	960	—
	conv brougham 6P	2,983	1,115	—
	touring sdn 4d	3,023	995	—
98 Big Boy Six (wb 119.0)				
	sdn 4d	2,909	884	—
	sdn 7P	3,022	1,114	—
95/97 Country Club Eight (wb 122.0; lwb-129.0)				
95	cpe 3P	3,003	1,009	—
95	victoria cpe 5P	3,053	1,051	—
95	conv cpe 3P	3,033	1,138	—
95	touring brougham 6P	3,138	1,049	—
95	conv brougham 6P	3,123	1,201	—
95	touring sdn 4d	3,193	1,079	—
97	lwb touring sdn 4d	3,268	1,174	—
97	lwb sdn 7P	3,378	1,430	—

1939 Engines	bore×stroke	bhp	availability
L6, 175.0	3.00×4.13	86	S-90, 98 sdn 4d
L6, 212.0	3.00×5.00	96/101	S-91, 92, 93, 98 sdn 7P
L8, 254.4	3.00×4.50	122	S-95, 97

*Total calendar year production: 81,521.

1940

40-T Traveler (wb 113.0)*		Wght	Price	Prod
	cpe 3P	2,800	670	—
	Victoria cpe 4P	2,830	750	—
	sdn 2d	2,895	735	—
	sdn 4d	2,940	763	—
40-P Deluxe (wb 113.0)*				
	cpe 3P	2,840	745	—
	Victoria cpe 4P	2,865	791	—
	conv cpe	2,860	930	—

	Wght	Price	Prod
sdn 2d	2,930	775	—
sdn 4d	2,965	808	—
conv sdn	2,920	955	—
41 Super (wb 118.0)*			
cpe 3P	2,950	809	—
Victoria cpe 4P	2,980	860	—
conv cpe	2,980	995	—
sdn 2d	3,020	839	—
sdn 4d	3,050	870	—
conv sdn	3,020	1,030	—
43 Country Club (wb 125.0)*			
sdn 4d	3,240	1,018	—
Special sdn 4d	3,240	1,044	—
sdn 4d, 7P	3,355	1,230	—
44 Eight (wb 118.0)*			
cpe 3P	3,040	860	—
Victoria cpe 4P	3,075	942	—
conv cpe	3,065	1,087	—
sdn 2d	3,140	918	—
sdn 4d	3,185	952	—
conv sdn	3,130	1,122	—
47 Country Club Eight (wb 125.0)*			
sdn 4d	3,285	1,118	—
Special sdn 4d	3,285	1,144	—
sdn 4d, 7P	3,400	1,330	—
48 Big Boy (wb 125.0)*			
Carry-all sdn 4d	3,245	989	—
sdn 4d, 7P	3,140	1,095	—

*Total model year production: 87,915; Sixes: 77,295; Eights: 10,620.

1940 Engines	bore×stroke	bhp	availability
L6, 175.0	3.00×4.13	92	S-40
L6, 212.0	3.00×5.00	98	S-48
L6, 212.0	3.00×5.00	102	S-41, 43
L8, 254.0	3.00×4.50	128	S-44, 47

1941

10-T Traveler (wb 116.0)*	Wght	Price	Prod
cpe 3P	2,765	754	—
club cpe 4P	2,835	847	—
sdn 2d	2,870	824	—
sdn 4d	2,900	852	—
10-P Deluxe (wb 116.0)*			
cpe 3P	2,840	870	—
club cpe 4P	2,880	917	—
sdn 2d	2,905	891	—
sdn 4d	2,945	925	—
conv sdn	3,085	1,132	140 est
11 Super (wb 121.0)*			
cpe 3P	2,925	956	—
club cpe 4P	2,995	1,011	—
sdn 2d	3,005	976	—
sdn 4d	3,040	1,007	—
conv sdn	3,145	1,230	300 est
wgn 4d	3,315	1,298	100 est
12 Commodore Six (wb 121.0)*			
cpe 3P	2,970	1,028	—
club cpe 4P	3,045	1,090	—
sdn 2d	3,070	1,059	—
sdn 4d	3,135	1,087	—
conv sdn	3,160	1,297	200 est

14 Commodore Eight (wb 121.0)*	Wght	Price	Prod
cpe 3P	3,110	1,071	—
club cpe 4P	3,195	1,133	—
sdn 2d	3,200	1,096	—
sdn 4d	3,250	1,132	—
conv sdn	3,350	1,347	200 est
wgn 4d	3,400	1,384	80 est
15-17 Commodore Eight (wb 121–128)*			
cpe 3P, wb 121.0	3,185	1,162	—
club cpe 4P, wb 121.0	3,235	1,225	—
sdn 4d, wb 128.0	3,370	1,330	—
sdn 4d, 7P, wb 128.0	3,440	1,537	—
18 Big Boy (wb 128.0)*			
sdn 4d, 7P	3,155	1,223	—

*Total model year production: 91,769; Sixes: 82,051; Eights: 9,718.

1941 Engines	bore×stroke	bhp	availability
L6, 175.0	3.00×4.13	92	S-10
L6, 212.0	3.00×5.00	98	S-18
L6, 212.0	3.00×5.00	102	S-11, 12
L8, 254.0	3.00×4.50	128	S-14, 15, 17

1942

20T Traveler (wb 116.0)*	Wght	Price	Prod
cpe 3P	2,795	828	—
club cpe 4P	2,845	897	—
sdn 2d	2,895	878	—
sdn 4d	2,940	905	—
20P Deluxe (wb 116.0)*			
cpe 3P	2,845	916	—
club cpe 4P	2,900	967	—
sdn 2d	2,935	946	—
sdn 4d	2,971	978	—
conv sdn	3,140	1,212	—
21 Super (wb 121.0)*			
cpe 3P	2,950	1,036	—
club cpe 4P	3,010	1,090	—
sdn 2d	3,035	1,065	—
sdn 4d	3,080	1,093	—
conv sdn	3,200	1,332	—
wgn 4d	3,315	1,412	—
22 Commodore Six (wb 121.0)*			
cpe 3P	2,995	1,115	—
club cpe 5P	3,090	1,175	—
sdn 2d	3,090	1,152	—
sdn 4d	3,145	1,182	—
conv sdn	3,280	1,402	—
24 Commodore Eight (wb 121.0)*			
cpe 3P	3,130	1,156	—
club cpe 5P	3,205	1,215	—
sdn 2d	3,230	1,187	—
sdn 4d	3,280	1,224	—
conv sdn	3,400	1,451	—
25 Commodore Custom Eight (wb 121.0)*			
club cpe 4P	3,235	1,311	—
27 Commodore Custom Eight (wb 128.0)*			
sdn 4d, 6P	3,395	1,430	—

*Total model year production: 40,661; Sixes: 34,069; Eights: 6,592.

1942 Engines	bore×stroke	bhp	availability
L6, 175.0	3.00×4.13	92	S-20
L6, 212.0	3.00×5.00	102	S-21, 22
L8, 254.0	3.00×4.50	128	S-24, 25, 27

1946

51 Super Six (wb 121.0)—61,787 built	Wght	Price	Prod
sdn 4d	3,085	1,555	—
Brougham sdn 2d	3,030	1,511	—
club cpe	3,015	1,553	—
cpe 3P	2,950	1,481	—
Brougham conv cpe	3,195	1,879	1035*
52 Commodore Six (wb 121.0)—17,685 built			
sdn 4d	3,150	1,699	—
club cpe	3,065	1,693	—
53 Super Eight (wb 121.0)—3,961 built			
sdn 4d	3,235	1,668	—
club cpe	3,185	1,664	—
54 Commodore Eight (wb 121.0)—8,193 built			
sdn 4d	3,305	1,774	—
club cpe	3,235	1,760	—
Brougham conv cpe	3,410	2,050	140*

*Estimated; total convertibles 1,177.

1946 Engines	bore×stroke	bhp	availability
L6, 212.0	3.00×5.00	102	S-51, 52
L8, 254.0	3.00×4.50	128	S-53, 54

1947

171 Super Six (wb 121.0)—49,276 built	Wght	Price	Prod
sdn 4d	3,110	1,749	—
Brougham sdn 2d	3,055	1,704	—
club cpe	3,040	1,744	—
cpe 3P	2,975	1,628	—
Brougham conv cpe	3,220	2,021	1,460*
172 Commodore Six (wb 121.0)—25,138 built			
sdn 4d	3,175	1,896	—
club cpe	3,090	1,887	—
173 Super Eight (wb 121.0)—5,076 built			
sdn 4d	3,260	1,862	—
club cpe	3,210	1,855	—
174 Commodore Eight (wb 121.0)—12,593 built			
sdn 4d	3,330	1,972	—
club cpe	3,260	1,955	—
Brougham conv cpe	3,435	2,196	360*

*Estimated; total convertibles 1,823.

1947 Engines	bore×stroke	bhp	availability
L6, 212.0	3.00×5.00	102	S-171, 172
L8, 254.0	3.00×4.50	128	S-173, 174

1948

481 Super Six (wb 124.0)—49,388 built	Wght	Price	Prod
sdn 4d	3,500	2,222	—
Brougham sdn 2d	3,470	2,172	—
club cpe	3,480	2,219	—
cpe 3P	3,460	2,069	—
Brougham conv cpe	3,750	2,836	88*
482 Commodore Six (wb 124.0)—27,159 built			
sdn 4d	3,540	2,399	—
club cpe	3,550	2,374	—
Brougham conv cpe	3,780	3,057	48*
483 Super Eight (wb 124.0)—5,338 built			
sdn 4d	3,525	2,343	—
club cpe	3,495	2,340	—
484 Commodore Eight (wb 124.0)—35,315 built			
sdn 4d	3,600	2,514	—
club cpe	3,570	2,490	—
Brougham conv cpe	3,800	3,138	64*

1949 Commodore Six convertible coupe

1951 Hornet Hollywood hardtop coupe

*Estimated; total convertibles 200.

1948 Engines	bore×stroke	bhp	availability
L6, 262.0	3.56×4.38	121	S-481, 482
L8, 254.0	3.00×4.50	128	S-483, 484

1949

491 Super Six (wb 124.0)—91,333 built	Wght	Price	Prod
sdn 4d	3,555	2,207	—
Brougham sdn 2d	3,515	2,156	—
club cpe	3,480	2,203	—
cpe 3P	3,485	2,053	—
Brougham conv cpe	3,750	2,799	1,870*
492 Commodore Six (wb 124.0)—32,715 built			
sdn 4d	3,625	2,383	—
club cpe	3,585	2,359	—
Brougham conv cpe	3,780	2,952	655*
493 Super Eight (wb 124.0)—6,365 built			
sdn 4d	3,565	2,296	—
Brougham sdn 2d	3,545	2,245	—
club cpe	3,550	2,292	—

494 Commodore Eight (wb 124.0)—28,687 built	Wght	Price	Prod
sdn 4d	3,650	2,472	—
club cpe	3,600	2,448	—
Brougham conv cpe	3,800	3,041	595*

*Estimated; total convertibles 3,119.

1949 Engines	bore×stroke	bhp	availability
L6, 262.0	3.56×4.38	121	S-491, 492
L8, 254.0	3.00×4.50	128	S-493, 494

1950

500 Pacemaker (wb 119.0)—39,455 built	Wght	Price	Prod
sdn 4d	3,510	1,933	—
Brougham sdn 2d	3,475	1,912	—
club cpe	3,460	1,933	—
cpe 3P	3,445	1,807	—
Brougham conv cpe	3,655	2,428	1,100*
50A Pacemaker Deluxe (wb 119.0)—22,297 built			
sdn 4d	3,520	1,959	—
Brougham sdn 2d	3,485	1,928	—
club cpe	3,470	1,959	—
Brougham conv cpe	3,665	2,444	630*
501 Super Six (wb 124.0)—17,246 built			
sdn 4d	3,590	2,105	—
Brougham sdn 2d	3,565	2,068	—
club cpe	3,555	2,102	—
Brougham conv cpe	3,750	2,629	465*
502 Commodore Six (wb 124.0)—24,605 built			
sdn 4d	3,655	2,282	—
club cpe	3,640	2,257	—
Brougham conv cpe	3,840	2,809	700*
503 Super Eight (wb 124.0)—1,074 built			
sdn 4d	3,605	2,189	—
Brougham sdn 2d	3,575	2,152	—
club cpe	3,560	2,186	—

504 Commodore Eight (wb 124.0)—16,731 built	Wght	Price	Prod
sdn 4d	3,675	2,366	—
club cpe	3,655	2,341	—
Brougham conv cpe	3,865	2,893	425*

*Estimated; total convertibles 3,322.

1950 Engines	bore×stroke	bhp	availability
L6, 232.0	3.56×3.88	112	S-500
L6, 262.0	3.56×4.38	123	S-50A, 501, 502
L8, 254.0	3.00×4.50	128	S-503, 504

1951

4A Pacemaker Custom (wb 119.0)—34,495 built	Wght	Price	Prod
sdn 4d	3,460	2,145	—
Brougham sdn 2d	3,430	2,102	—
club cpe	3,410	2,145	—
cpe 3P	3,380	1,965	—
Brougham conv cpe	3,600	2,642	430*
5A Super Six Custom (wb 124.0)—22,532 built			
sdn 4d	3,565	2,287	—
Brougham sdn 2d	3,535	2,238	—
club cpe	3,525	2,287	—
Hollywood htp cpe	3,590	2,605	1,100*
Brougham conv cpe	3,720	2,827	280*
6A Commodore Six Custom (wb 124.0)—16,979 built			
sdn 4d	3,600	2,480	—
club cpe	3,585	2,455	—
Hollywood htp cpe	3,640	2,780	820*
Brougham conv cpe	3,785	3,011	210*
7A Hornet (wb 124.0)—43,656 built			
sdn 4d	3,600	2,568	—
club cpe	3,580	2,543	—
Hollywood htp cpe	3,630	2,869	2,100*
Brougham conv cpe	3,780	3,099	550*

1955 Wasp Custom four-door sedan

8A Commodore Eight Custom (wb 124.0)—14,243 built	Wght	Price	Prod
sdn 4d	3,620	2,568	—
club cpe	3,600	2,543	—
Hollywood htp cpe	3,650	2,869	670*
Brougham conv cpe	3,800	3,099	180*

*Estimated; total convertibles 1,651; total hardtops 4,689.

1951 Engines	bore×stroke	bhp	availability
L6, 232.0	3.56×3.88	112	S-Pacemaker
L6, 262.0	3.56×4.38	123	S-Super & Commodore Six
L6, 308.0	3.81×4.50	145	S-Hornet
L8, 254.0	3.00×4.50	128	S-Commodore Eight

1952

4B Pacemaker (wb 119.0)—7,486 built	Wght	Price	Prod
sdn 4d	3,390	2,311	—
Brougham sdn 2d	3,355	2,264	—
club cpe	3,335	2,311	—
cpe 3P	3,305	2,116	—
5B Wasp (wb 119.0)—21,876 built			
sdn 4d	3,485	2,466	—
Brougham sdn 2d	3,470	2,413	—
club cpe	3,435	2,466	—
Hollywood htp cpe	3,525	2,812	1,320*
Brougham conv cpe	3,635	3,048	220*
6B Commodore Six (wb 124.0)—1,592 built			
sdn 4d	3,595	2,674	—
club cpe	3,550	2,647	—
Hollywood htp cpe	3,625	3,000	100*
Brougham conv cpe	3,750	3,247	20*
7B Hornet (wb 124.0)—35,921 built			
sdn 4d	3,600	2,769	—
club cpe	3,550	2,742	—
Hollywood htp cpe	3,630	3,095	2,160*
Brougham conv cpe	3,750	3,342	360*
8B Commodore Eight (wb 124.0)—3,125 built			
sdn 4d	3,630	2,769	—
club cpe	3,580	2,742	—
Hollywood htp cpe	3,660	3,095	190*
Brougham conv cpe	3,770	3,342	30*

*Estimated; total convertibles 636; total hardtops 3,777.

1952 Engines	bore×stroke	bhp	availability
L6, 232.0	3.56×3.88	112	S-Pacemaker
L6, 262.0	3.56×4.38	127	S-Wasp, Commodore Six
L6, 308.0	3.81×4.50	145	S-Hornet
L8, 254.0	3.00×4.50	128	S-Commodore Eight

1953

1C Jet (wb 105.0)—21,143 built (includes Super Jet)	Wght	Price	Prod
sdn 4d	2,650	1,858	—
2C Super Jet (wb 105.0)			
sdn 4d	2,700	1,954	—
sdn 2d	2,695	1,933	—
4C Wasp (wb 119.0)—17,792 built (includes Super Wasp)			
sdn 4d	3,380	2,311	—
sdn 4d	3,350	2,264	—
club cpe	3,340	2,311	—
5C Super Wasp (wb 119.0)			
sdn 4d	3,480	2,466	—
sdn 2d	3,460	2,413	—
club cpe	3,455	2,466	—
Hollywood htp cpe	3,525	2,812	590*
Brougham conv cpe	3,655	3,048	50*
7C Hornet (wb 124.0)—27,208 built			
sdn 4d	3,570	2,769	—
club cpe	3,530	2,742	—
Hollywood htp cpe	3,610	3,095	910*
Brougham conv cpe	3,760	3,342	—

*Estimated; total hardtops 1,501.

1953 Engines	bore×stroke	bhp	availability
L6, 202.0	3.00×4.75	104	S-Jet
L6, 202.0	3.00×4.75	106/114	O-Jet
L6, 232.0	3.56×3.88	127	S-Wasp
L6, 308.0	3.81×4.50	145	S-Hornet
L6, 308.0	3.81×4.50	160	O-Hornet
L6, 308.0	3.81×4.50	170	O-Hornet (7-X)

1954

1D Jet (wb 105.0)—14,224 built (includes Super Jet and Jet-Liner)	Wght	Price	Prod
sdn 4d	2,675	1,858	—
Utility sdn 2d	2,715	1,837	—
Family Club sdn 2d	2,635	1,621	—
2D Super Jet (wb 105.0)			
sdn 4d	2,725	1,954	—
club sdn 2d	2,710	1,933	—
3D Jet-Liner (wb 105.0)			
sdn 4d	2,760	2,057	—
club sdn 2d	2,740	2,046	—
4D Wasp (wb 119.0)—11,603 built (includes Super Wasp)			
sdn 4d	2,256	3,440	—
club sdn 2d	2,209	3,375	—
club cpe	2,256	3,360	—
5D Super Wasp (wb 119.0)			
sdn 4d	3,525	2,466	—
club sdn 2d	3,490	2,413	—
club cpe	3,475	2,466	—
Hollywood htp cpe	3,570	2,704	—
Brougham conv cpe	3,680	3,004	—

1957 Hornet Hollywood hardtop coupe

1956 Hornet Custom four-door sedan

6D Hornet Special (wb 124.0)—24,833 built (includes Hornet)		Wght	Price	Prod
	sdn 4d	3,560	2,619	—
	club sdn 2d	3,515	2,571	—
	club cpe	3,505	2,619	—
7D Hornet (wb 124.0)				
	sdn 4d	3,620	2,769	—
	club cpe	3,570	2,742	—
	Hollywood htp cpe	3,655	2,988	—
	Brougham conv cpe	3,800	3,288	—
Italia (wb 105.0)				
	cpe	2,710	4,800	20

1954 Engines	bore×stroke	bhp	availability
L6, 202.0	3.00×4.75	104	S-Jet
L6, 202.0	3.00×4.75	106/114	S-Italia; O-Jet
L6, 232.0	3.56×3.88	126	S-Wasp
L6, 262.0	3.56×4.38	140	S-Super Wasp
L6, 308.0	3.81×4.50	160	S-Hornet
L6, 308.0	3.81×4.50	170	O-Hornet (7-X)

1955

54 Metropolitan (wb 85.0)—3,000* built		Wght	Price	Prod
1	conv cpe 3P	1,803	1,469	—
2	htp cpe	1,843	1,445	—
55 Rambler (wb 100.0)				
12	Deluxe bus sdn	2,400	1,457	34
14-1	Super Suburban wgn 2d	2,532	1,869	1,335
16-1	Super club sdn	2,450	1,683	2,970
17-2	Custom Cntry Club htp cpe	2,518	2,098	1,601
55 Rambler (wb 108.0)				
15	Deluxe sdn 4d	2,567	1,695	
15-1	Super sdn 4d	2,570	1,798	7,210 (15, 15-1, 15-2)
15-2	Custom sdn 4d	2,606	1,989	
18-1	Super Cross Cntry wgn 4d	2,675	1,975	12,023 (18-1, 18-2)
18-2	Custom Cross Cntry wgn 4d	2,685	1,995	
3554 Wasp (wb 114.3)				
5-1	Super sdn 4d	3,254	2,290	5,551 (5-1, 5-2)
5-2	Custom sdn 4d	3,347	2,460	
7-2	Custom Hollywood htp cpe	3,362	2,570	1,640
3556 Hornet 6 (wb 121.3)				
5-1	Super sdn 4d	3,495	2,565	5,357 (5-1, 5-2)
5-2	Custom sdn 4d	3,562	2,760	
7-2	Custom Hollywood htp cpe	3,587	2,880	1,554
3558 Hornet V8 (wb 121.3)				
5-1	Super sdn 4d	3,806	2,825	4,449 (5-1, 5-2)
5-2	Custom sdn 4d	3,846	3,015	
7-2	Custom Hollywood htp cpe	3,878	3,145	1,770
Italia (wb 105.0)				
	cpe	2,710	4,800	5

*Estimated; total Nash & Hudson, 3,849.

1955 Engines	bore×stroke	bhp	availability
L4, 73.2	2.56×3.50	42	S-Metropolitan
L6, 195.6	3.13×4.25	90	S-Rambler
L6, 195.6	3.13×4.25	100	S-Rambler fleet model
L6, 202.0	3.00×4.75	110	S-Wasp
L6, 202.0	3.00×4.75	114	S-Italia
L6, 202.0	3.00×4.75	120	O-Wasp
L6, 308.0	3.81×4.50	160	S-Hornet 6
L6, 308.0	3.81×4.50	170	O-Hornet 6 (Twin-H)
V8, 320.0	3.81×3.50	208	S-Hornet V8

1956

54 Metropolitan (wb 85.0)—3,000* built		Wght	Price	Prod
1	conv cpe 3P	1,803	1,469	—
2	htp cpe 3P	1,843	1,445	—
56 Rambler DeLuxe (wb 108.0)—5,000 built (includes Super and Custom)				
15	sdn 4d	2,891	1,829	—
56 Rambler Super (wb 108.0)				
15-1	sdn 4d	2,096	1,939	—
18-1	Cross Cntry wgn 4d	2,992	2,233	—
56 Rambler Custom (wb 108.0)				
13-2	Cross Cntry htp wgn 4d	3,095	2,494	—
15-2	sdn 4d	2,929	2,059	—
18-2	Cross Cntry wgn 4d	3,110	2,329	—
19-2	htp sdn	2,990	2,224	—

3564 Wasp (wb 114.3)		Wght	Price	Prod
5-1	sdn 4d	3,264	2,214	2,519
3565 Hornet Special (wb 121.3)				
5-1	sdn 4d	3,467	2,405	1,528
7-1	Hollywood htp cpe	3,488	2,512	229
3566 Hornet 6 (wb 121.3)				
5-1	Super sdn 4d	3,545	2,544	3,022
5-2	Custom sdn 4d	3,636	2,777	
7-2	Hollywood htp cpe	3,646	2,888	358
3568 Hornet V8 (wb 121.3)				
5-2	sdn 4d	3,826	3,026	1,962
7-2	Hollywood htp cpe	3,026	3,159	1,053

*Estimated; total Nash & Hudson 7,645.

1956 Engines	bore×stroke	bhp	availability
L4, 73.2	2.56×3.50	42	S-Metropolitan
L6, 195.6	3.13×4.25	120	S-Rambler
L6, 202.0	3.00×4.75	120	S-Wasp
L6, 202.0	3.00×4 75	130	O-Wasp (Twin-H)
L6, 308.0	3.81 × 4.50	165	S-Hornet 6
L6, 308.0	3.81 × 4.50	175	O-Hornet 6 (Twin-H)
V8, 352.0	4.00 × 3.50	220	S-Hornet V8 (through 3/56)
V8, 250.0	3.50×3.25	190	S-Hornet Special (3/56 on)

1957—3,876 built

357-1 Hornet Super (wb 121.3)	Wght	Price	Prod
sdn 4d	3,631	2,821	—
Hollywood htp cpe	3,655	2,911	—
357-2 Hornet Custom (wb 121.3)			
sdn 4d	3,678	3,011	—
Hollywood htp cpe	3,693	3,101	—

1957 Engine	bore×stroke	bhp	availability
V8, 327.0	4.00×3.25	255	S-all

HUPMOBILE

1939

E "922" Senior Six (wb 122.0)—800 built		Wght	Price	Prod
EQ	DeLuxe touring sdn 4d	3,400	995	—
EQD	Custom touring sdn 4d	3,440	1,095	—
H "925" Senior Eight (wb 125.0)—200 built				
HQ	DeLuxe touring sdn 4d	4,085	1,145	—
HQD	Custom touring sdn 4d	4,215	1,245	—
Skylark (wb 115.0)				
	Custom sdn 4d	3,000	1,145	35*

*handbuilt prototypes

1939 Engines	bore × stroke	bhp	availability
L6, 245.3	3.50 × 4.25	101	S-922, Skylark
L8, 303.2	3.19 × 4.75	120	S-925 Eight

Note: 1939 production estimates are based on published serial number spans. Total calendar year production: 1,400.

1940

R-015 Skylark Custom (wb 115.0)		Wght	Price	Prod
RQK	sdn 4d	3,000	1,145	—

1940 Engine	bore×stroke	bhp	availability
L6, 245.0	3.50×4.25	101	S-all

1941

R-115 Skylark Custom (wb 115.0)		Wght	Price	Prod
RQK	sdn 4d	3,000	1,095	—

1941 Engine	bore×stroke	bhp	availability
L6, 245.0	3.50×4.25	101	S-all

Note: Total 1940-41 Skylark production: 319. Total registrations: 211 in 1940, 103 in 1941.

IMPERIAL

1955

C69 (wb 130.0)	Wght	Price	Prod
sdn 4d	4,565	4,483	7,840
Newport htp cpe	4,490	4,720	3,418
conv cpe (proto)	4,600	—	1
chassis	—	—	1
C70 Crown Imperial (wb 149.5)			
sdn 4d, 8P	5,180	6,973	45
limo	5,230	7,095	127

1955 Engine	bore×stroke	bhp	availability
V8, 331.0	3.81×3.63	250	S-all

1956

C73 (wb 133.0)	Wght	Price	Prod
sdn 4d	4,575	4,832	6,821
Southampton htp sdn	4,680	5,225	1,543
Southampton htp cpe	4,555	5,094	2,094
C70 Crown Imperial (wb 149.5)			
sdn 4d, 8P	5,145	7,603	51
limo	5,205	7,737	175

1956 Engine	bore×stroke	bhp	availability
V8, 354.0	3.94×3.63	280	S-all

1957

IM1-1 (wb 129.0)	Wght	Price	Prod
sdn 4d	4,640	4,838	5,654
Southampton htp sdn	4,780	4,838	7,527
Southampton htp cpe	4,640	4,736	4,885
IM1-2 Crown (wb 129.0)			
sdn 4d	4,740	5,406	3,642
Southampton htp sdn	4,920	5,406	7,843
Southampton htp cpe	4,755	5,269	4,199
conv cpe	4,830	5,598	1,167
IM1-4 LeBaron (wb 129.0)			
sdn 4d	4,765	5,743	1,729
Southampton htp sdn	4,900	5,743	911
Crown Imperial (wb 149.5)			
limo	5,960	15,075	36

1956 Imperial four-door sedan

1957 Engine	bore×stroke	bhp	availability
V8, 392.0	4.00×3.90	325	S-all

1958

LY1-L (wb 129.0)		Wght	Price	Prod
23	Southampton htp cpe	4,640	4,839	1,801
41	sdn 4d	4,590	4,945	1,926
43	Southampton htp sdn	4,795	4,945	3,336
LY1-M Crown (wb 129.0)				
23	Southampton htp cpe	4,730	5,388	1,939
27	conv cpe	4,820	5,729	675
41	sdn 4d	4,755	5,632	1,240
43	Southampton htp sdn	4,915	5,632	4,146
LY1-H LeBaron (wb 129.0)				
41	sdn 4d	4,780	5,969	501
43	Southampton htp sdn	4,940	5,969	538
Crown Imperial (wb 149.5)				
	limo	5,960	15,075	31

1958 Engines	bore×stroke	bhp	availability
V8, 392.0	4.00×3.90	345	S-all exc Crown Imperial
V8, 392.0	4.00×3.90	325	S-Crown Imperial

1959

MY1-L (wb 129.0)		Wght	Price	Prod
612	Southampton htp cpe	4,675	4,910	1,743
613	sdn 4d	4,735	5,016	2,071
614	Southampton htp sdn	4,745	5,016	3,984
MY1-M Crown (wb 129.0)				
632	Southampton htp cpe	4,810	5,403	1,728
633	sdn 4d	4,830	5,647	1,335
634	Southampton htp sdn	4,840	5,647	4,714
635	conv cpe	4,850	5,774	555
MY1-H LeBaron (wb 129.0)				
653	sdn 4d	4,865	6,103	510
654	Southampton htp sdn	4,875	6,103	622
Crown Imperial (wb 149.5)				
	limo	5,960	15,075	7

1959 Engines	bore×stroke	bhp	availability
V8, 413.0	4.18×3.75	350	S-all exc Crown Imperial
V8, 392.0	4.00×3.90	325	S-Crown Imperial

1959 Southampton hardtop coupe

1960

PY1-L Custom (wb 129.0)		Wght	Price	Prod
912	Southampton htp cpe	4,655	4,923	1,498
913	sdn 4d	4,700	5,029	2,335
914	Southampton htp sdn	4,760	5,029	3,953
PY1-M Crown (wb 129.0)				
922	Southampton htp cpe	4,720	5,403	1,504
923	sdn 4d	4,770	5,647	1,594
924	Southampton htp sdn	4,765	5,647	4,510
925	conv cpe	4,820	5,774	618
PY1-H LeBaron (wb 129.0)				
933	sdn 4d	4,860	6,318	692
934	Southampton htp sdn	4,835	6,318	999
Crown Imperial (wb 149.5)				
	limo	5,960	16,500	16

1960 Engine	bore×stroke	bhp	availability
V8, 413.0	4.18×3.75	350	S-all

1961

RY1-L Custom (wb 129.0)		Wght	Price	Prod
912	Southampton htp cpe	4,715	4,923	889
914	Southampton htp sdn	4,740	5,109	4,129
RY1-M Crown (wb 129.0)				
922	Southampton htp cpe	4,790	5,403	1,007
924	Southampton htp sdn	4,855	5,647	4,769
925	conv cpe	4,865	5,774	429
RY1-H LeBaron (wb 129.0)				
934	Southampton htp sdn	4,875	6,426	1,026
Crown Imperial (wb 149.5)				
	limo	5,960	16,500	9

1961 Engine	bore×stroke	bhp	availability
V8, 413.0	4.18×3.75	350	S-all

1962

SY1-L Custom (wb 129.0)		Wght	Price	Prod
912	Southampton htp cpe	4,540	4,920	826
914	Southampton htp sdn	4,620	5,106	3,587
SY1-M Crown (wb 129.0)				
922	Southampton htp cpe	4,650	5,400	1,010
924	Southampton htp sdn	4,680	5,644	6,911
925	conv cpe	4,765	5,770	554
SY1-H LeBaron (wb 129.0)				
934	Southampton htp sdn	4,725	6,422	1,449

1962 Engine	bore×stroke	bhp	availability
V8, 413.0	4.18×3.75	340	S-all

1963

TY1-L Custom (wb 129.0)		Wght	Price	Prod
912	Southampton htp cpe	4,640	5,058	749
914	Southampton htp sdn	4,690	5,243	3,264
TY1-M Crown (wb 129.0)				
922	Southampton htp cpe	4,720	5,412	1,067
924	Southampton htp sdn	4,740	5,656	6,960
925	conv cpe	4,795	5,782	531
TY1-H LeBaron (wb 129.0)				
934	Southampton htp sdn	4,830	6,434	1,537
Crown Imperial (wb 149.5)				
	limo	6,100	18,500	13

1963 Engine	bore×stroke	bhp	availability
V8, 413.0	4.18×3.75	340	S-all

1964

VY1-M Crown (wb 129.0)		Wght	Price	Prod
922	htp cpe	4,950	5,739	5,233
924	htp sdn	4,970	5,581	14,181
925	conv cpe	5,185	6,003	922
VY1-H LeBaron (wb 129.0)				
934	htp sdn	5,005	6,455	2,949
Crown Imperial (wb 149.5)				
	limo	6,100	18,500	10

1964 Engine	bore×stroke	bhp	availability
V8, 413.0	4.18×3.75	340	S-all

1965

AY1-M Crown (wb 129.0)		Wght	Price	Prod
922	htp cpe	5,075	5,930	3,974
924	htp sdn	5,015	5,772	11,628
925	conv cpe	5,345	6,194	633
AY1-H LeBaron (wb 129.0)				
934	htp sdn	5,080	6,596	2,164

1960 Crown four-door sedan

1962 LeBaron Southampton four-door hardtop

Crown Imperial (wb 149.5)			Wght	Price	Prod
	limo		6,100	18,500	10
1965 Engine	**bore×stroke**	**bhp**	**availability**		
V8, 413.0	4.18×3.75	340	S-all		

1966

BY3-M Crown (wb 129.0)			Wght	Price	Prod
23	htp cpe		5,000	5,887	2,373
27	conv cpe		5,315	6,164	514
43	htp sdn		4,990	5,733	8,977
BY3-H LeBaron (wb 129.0)					
43	htp sdn		5,090	6,540	1,878
1966 Engine	**bore×stroke**	**bhp**	**availability**		
V8, 440.0	4.32×3.75	350	S-all		

1967

CY1-M (wb 127.0)			Wght	Price	Prod
23	Crown htp cpe		4,780	6,011	3,235
27	conv cpe		4,815	6,244	577
41	sdn 4d		4,830	5,374	2,193
43	Crown htp sdn		4,860	5,836	9,415
CY1-H LeBaron (wb 127.0)					
43	htp sdn		4,970	6,661	2,194
LeBaron, Stageway body (wb 163.0)					
	limo		6,300	15,000	6
1967 Engine	**bore×stroke**	**bhp**	**availability**		
V8, 440.0	4.32×3.75	350	S-all		

1968

YM Crown (wb 127.0)			Wght	Price	Prod
23	htp cpe		4,660	5,722	2,656
27	conv cpe		4,795	6,497	474
41	sdn 4d		4,685	5,654	1,887
43	htp sdn		4,715	6,115	8,492
YH LeBaron (wb 127.0)					
43	htp sdn		4,815	6,940	1,852
LeBaron, Stageway body (wb 163.0)					
	limo		6,300	15,000	6
1968 Engines	**bore×stroke**	**bhp**	**availability**		
V8, 440.0	4.32×3.75	350	S-all		
V8, 440.0	4.32×3.75	360	O-all (dual exhaust)		

1969

Crown (wb 127.0)			Wght	Price	Prod
YL23	htp cpe		4,555	5,592	224
YL43	htp sdn		4,690	5,770	823
YM41	sdn 4d		4,620	5,770	1,617
LeBaron (wb 127.0)					
YM23	htp cpe		4,610	5,898	4,592
YM43	htp sdn		4,710	6,131	14,821
LeBaron, Stageway body (wb 163.0)					
	limo		6,300	16,000	6 est
1969 Engine	**bore×stroke**	**bhp**	**availability**		
V8, 440.0	4.32×3.75	350	S-all		

1970

YL Crown (wb 127.0)			Wght	Price	Prod
23	htp cpe		4,610	5,779	254
43	htp sdn		4,735	5,956	1,333
YM LeBaron (wb 127.0)					
23	htp cpe		4,660	6,095	1,803
43	htp sdn		4,805	6,328	8,426
LeBaron, Stageway body (wb 163.0)					
	limo		6,500	16,500	6 est
1970 Engine	**bore×stroke**	**bhp**	**availability**		
V8, 440.0	4.32×3.75	350	S-all		

1971

YM LeBaron (wb 127.0)			Wght	Price	Prod
23	htp cpe		4,800	6,632	1,442
43	htp sdn		4,950	6,864	10,116
1971 Engine	**bore×stroke**	**bhp**	**availability**		
V8, 440.0	4.32×3.75	335	S-all		

1972

YM LeBaron (wb 127.0)			Wght	Price	Prod
23	htp cpe		4,790	6,550	2,322
43	htp sdn		4,955	6,778	13,472
1972 Engine	**bore×stroke**	**bhp**	**availability**		
V8, 440.0	4.32×3.75	225	S-all		

1965 Crown Coupe

1969 LeBaron two-door hardtop

1973

YM LeBaron (wb 127.0)		Wght	Price	Prod
23	htp cpe	4,905	6,829	2,563
43	htp sdn	5,035	7,057	14,166

1973 Engine	bore×stroke	bhp	availability
V8, 440.0	4.32×3.75	215	S-all

1974

YM LeBaron (wb 124.0)		Wght	Price	Prod
23	htp cpe	4,825	7,673	3,850
43	htp sdn	4,965	7,804	10,576

1974 Engine	bore×stroke	bhp	availability
V8, 440.0	4.32×3.75	230	S-all

1975

YM LeBaron (wb 124.0)		Wght	Price	Prod
23	htp cpe	4,965	8,698	2,728
43	htp sdn	5,065	8,844	6,102

1975 Engine	bore × stroke	bhp	availability
V8, 440.0	4.32 × 3.75	215	S-all

Note: Chrysler built no cars under the Imperial name from 1975 to 1980.

1981—7,225 built

(wb 112.7)		Wght	Price	Prod
YS22	cpe	3,968	18,311	—

1981 Engine	bore × stroke	bhp	availability
V8, 318.0	3.91 × 3.31	140	S-all

1982—2,329 built

(wb 112.7)		Wght	Price	Prod
YS22	cpe	3,945	20,988	—

1982 Engine	bore × stroke	bhp	availability
V8, 318.0	3.91 × 3.31	140	S-all

1983—1,427 built

(wb 112.7)		Wght	Price	Prod
YS22	cpe	4,019	18,688	—

1983 Engine	bore × stroke	bhp	availability
V8, 318.0	3.91 × 3.31	140	S-all

KAISER

1947

K100 Special (wb 123.5)		Wght	Price	Prod
1005	sdn 4d	3,295	2,104	65,062
K101 Custom (wb 123.5)				
1015	sdn 4d	3,295	2,456	5,412

1947 Engines	bore×stroke	bhp	availability
L6, 226.2	3.31×4.38	100	S-all
L6, 226.2	3.31×4.38	112	O-Custom

1948

K481 Special (wb 123.5)		Wght	Price	Prod
4815	sdn 4d	3,295	2,244	90,588
K482 Custom (wb 123.5)				
4825	sdn 4d	3,295	2,466	1,263

1948 Engines	bore×stroke	bhp	availability
L6, 226.2	3.31×4.38	100	S-all
L6, 226.2	3.31×4.38	112	O-Custom

1949-50

K491 Special (wb 123.5)		Wght	Price	Prod
4911	sdn 4d	3,311	1,995	29,000*
4915	Traveler util sdn 4d	3,456	2,088	22,000*
K492 Deluxe (wb 123.5)				
4921	sdn 4d	3,341	2,195	38,250*
4922	conv sdn	3,726	3,195	54*
4923	Virginian htp sdn	3,541	2,995	946*
4925	Vagabond util sdn 4d	3,501	2,288	4,500*

*1949-50 production combined by factory; approximate breakdown 84 percent 1949, 16 percent 1950. Estimates for body styles based on body numbers in extant vehicles. Actual 1949-50 production: 95,175.

1949-50 Engines	bore×stroke	bhp	availability
L6, 226.2	3.31×4.38	100	S-Special
L6, 226.2	3.31×4.38	112	S-Deluxe

1951

K511 Special (wb 118.5)		Wght	Price	Prod
5110	Traveler util sdn 2d	3,210	2,265	1,500*

1982 Imperial two-door coupe

1953 Kaiser "Hardtop" Dragon four-door sedan

		Wght	Price	Prod
5111	sdn 4d	3,126	2,212	43,500*
5113	bus cpe	3,061	1,992	1,500*
5114	sdn 2d	3,106	2,160	10,000*
5115	Traveler util sdn 4d	3,270	2,317	2,000*
5117	club cpe	3,066	2,058	1,500*
K512 Deluxe (wb 118.5)				
5120	Traveler util sdn 2d	3,285	2,380	1,000*
5121	sdn 4d	3,171	2,328	70,000*
5124	sdn 2d	3,151	2,275	11,000*
5125	Traveler util sdn 4d	3,345	2,433	1,000*
5127	club cpe	3,111	2,296	6,000*

*Estimates based on extant vehicles. Actual total model year production: 139,452.

1951 Engine	bore×stroke	bhp	availability
L6, 226.2	3.31×4.38	115	S-all

1952

K521 Virginian Special (wb 118.5)*		Wght	Price	Prod
5110	Traveler util sdn 2d	3,210	2,085	—
5111	sdn 4d	3,126	2,036	—
5113	bus cpe	3,061	1,832	—
5114	sdn 2d	3,106	1,988	—
5115	Traveler util sdn 4d	3,270	2,134	—
K522 Virginian Deluxe (wb 118.5)*				
5120	Traveler util sdn 2d	3,285	2,192	—
5121	sdn 4d	3,171	2,143	—
5124	sdn 2d	3,151	2,095	—
5125	Traveler util sdn 4d	3,345	2,241	—
5127	club cpe	3,111	2,114	—
K521 Deluxe (wb 118.5)				
5211	sdn 4d	3,195	2,537	5,000**
5214	sdn 2d	3,145	2,484	2,000**
5215	Traveler util sdn 4d	3,369	2,643	***
5217	club cpe	3,045	2,296	500**
K522 Manhattan (wb 118.5)				
5221	sdn 4d	3,220	2,654	16,500**
5224	sdn 2d	3,185	2,601	2,000**
5227	club cpe	3,185	2,622	500**

*Total Virginian production: 5,579
**Estimates based on extant vehicles. Total Deluxe/Manhattan production: 26,552.
***Actual production questionable.

1952 Engine	bore×stroke	bhp	availability
L6, 226.2	3.31×4.38	115	S-all

1953

K530 "Hardtop" Dragon (wb 118.5)		Wght	Price	Prod
5301	sdn 4d	3,320	3,924	1,277
K531 Deluxe (wb 118.5)				
5311	sdn 4d	3,200	2,513	5,800*
5314	sdn 2d	3,150	2,459	1,500*
5315	Traveler util sdn 4d	3,315	2,619	1,000*
K532 Manhattan (wb 118.5)				
5321	sdn 4d	3,265	2,650	15,450*
5324	sdn 2d	3,235	2,597	2,500*
5325	Traveler util sdn 4d	3,371	2,755	**
K538 Carolina (wb 118.5)				
5381	sdn 4d	3,185	2,373	1,400*
5384	sdn 2d	3,135	2,313	400*

1953 Engine	bore×stroke	bhp	availability
L6, 226.2	3.31×4.38	118	S-all

***Estimates based on extant vehicles. Model year production:**

K531	Deluxe	7,883
K532	Manhattan	17,957
K538	Carolina	1,182

**One example found; volume production questionable.

1954

161 Darrin (wb 100.0)		Wght	Price	Prod
161	rdstr	2,175	3,668	435
K542 Manhattan (wb 118.5)				
5421	sdn 4d	3,375	2,670	3,860*
5424	sdn 2d	3,265	2,334	250*
K545 Special (wb 118.5)**				
5451	sdn 4d	3,265	2,389	3,000*
5454	sdn 2d	3,235	2,334	500*
K545 Special, late (wb 118.5)				
5451	sdn 4d	3,305	2,389	800*
5454	sdn 2d	3,265	2,334	125*

1954 Engines	bore×stroke	bhp	availability
L6, 161.0	3.13×3.50	90	S-Darrin
L6, 226.2	3.31×4.38	118	S-Special
L6, 226.2	3.31×4.38	140	S-Manhattan

***Estimates based on extant vehicles. Model year production:**

K542	Manhattan	4,110
K545	Special**	3,500
K545	Special, late	929

**Converted leftover 1953 Manhattans.

1955

Manhattan (wb 118.5)		Wght	Price	Prod
51363	sdn 4d (export)	3,350	—	1,021
51367	sdn 4d	3,375	2,670	226
51467	sdn 2d	3,335	2,617	44

1955 Engine	bore×stroke	bhp	availability
L6, 226.2	3.31×4.38	140	S-all

1954 Kaiser-Darrin two-door roadster

LaSALLE

1939

Series 50 (wb 120.0)		Wght	Price	Prod
5011	sdn 2d T/B	3,710	1,280	977
5011A	Sunroof sdn 2d T/B	3,780	1,320	23
5019	sdn 4d T/B	3,740	1,320	15,928
5019A	Sunroof sdn 4d T/B	3,810	1,380	404
5027	cpe 2-4P, opt. seats	3,635	1,240	2,525
5029	conv sdn 5P	3,780	1,800	185
5067	conv cpe 2-4P	3,715	1,395	1,056
	chassis	—	—	29

1939 Engine	bore×stroke	bhp	availability
V8, 322.0	3.38×4.50	125	S-all

1940

40-50 (wb 123.0)		Wght	Price	Prod
5011	sdn 2d	3,760	1,280	375
5019	sdn 4d	3,790	1,320	6,722
5027	cpe, A/S	3,700	1,240	1,527
5029	conv sdn	4,000	1,800	125
5067	conv cpe	3,805	1,395	599
50	chassis	—	—	1,032
40-52 Special (wb 123.0)				
5219	sdn 4d	3,900	1,440	10,250
5227	cpe	3,810	1,380	3,000
5229	conv sdn	4,110	1,895	75
5267	conv cpe	3,915	1,535	425

1940 Engine	bore×stroke	bhp	availability
V8, 322.0	3.38×4.50	130	S-all

LINCOLN

1939

Series 96H Zephyr (wb 125.0)		Wght	Price	Prod
700	cpe sdn	3,600	1,369	800
720	cpe 3P	3,520	1,358	2,500
730	sdn 4d	3,620	1,399	16,663
737	Town limo	3,670	1,747	95
740	conv sdn 5P	3,900	1,839	302
760B	conv cpe 2-4P	3,790	1,747	640
Model K (wb 136.0; lwb-145.0)				
403	Willoughby lwb touring 7P	5,870	5,932	1
404A	sdn 5P 2W	5,735	4,905	2
404B	sdn 5P 3W	5,740	4,905	12
406	Willoughby cpe 5P	5,615	5,926	1
407A	lwb sdn 7P	5,880	5,109	25
407B	limo 7P (lwb)	5,970	5,211	58
408	Brunn conv vic 5P	5,530	5,926	2
409A	Brunn lwb cab 5P	6,010	6,947	1
409B	Brunn lwb cab 5P semi-clpsble	6,030	7,049	1
410	LeBaron conv rdstr 2-4P	5,050	5,313	2
411	Brunn lwb brougham 7P	6,120	7,049	2
412	LeBaron cpe 2P	5,435	5,313	4
413A	LeBaron lwb conv sdn	5,670	5,828	3
413B	LeBaron conv sdn/partition (lwb)	5,780	6,028	6
415	Judkins sdn limo 7P (lwb)	5,950	6,334	2
417A	Judkins lwb berline 5P 2W	5,770	6,028	2
417B	Judkins lwb berline 5P 3W	5,840	6,130	1
419	Willoughby limo 7P (lwb)	6,140	6,232	4
421	Willoughby lwb spt sdn 5P	6,300	7,049	1
423	Willoughby panel brougham 7P (lwb)	NA	NA	1
425	Brunn lwb touring cab 5P	5,870	7,253	2

1939 Engines	bore×stroke	bhp	availability
V12, 267.3	2.75×3.75	110	S-Zephyr
V12, 414.0	3.13×4.50	150	S-Model K

1940

06H Zephyr (wb 125.0)		Wght	Price	Prod
56	Continental conv cpe	3,740	2,916	54
57	Continental club cpe	3,850	2,783	350
72A	cpe 3P	3,500	1,399	1,256
72A	cpe 3P, Custom interior	3,500	1,506	
72B	cpe, A/S	3,480	1,429	316
73	sdn 4d	3,660	1,439	15,764
73	sdn 4d, Custom interior	3,660	1,547	
76	conv cpe	3,760	1,818	700
77	club cpe	3,590	1,439	3,500
77	club cpe, Custom interior	3,590	1,547	
22	Custom Town Limousine	3,700	1,787	4
26	Custom Town Car	3,650	1,750	4
K Series (wb 136.0)*				
404A	sdn 4d	5,735	4,905	—
406	cpe, Willoughby	5,615	5,926	—
408	conv Victoria, Brunn	5,530	5,926	—
410	rdstr, LeBaron	5,505	5,313	—
412	stationary cpe, LeBaron	5,415	5,313	—
K Series (wb 145.0)*				
407A	sdn 4d, 7P	5,880	5,109	—
407B	limo	5,970	5,211	—
409	cabriolet, Brunn	6,010	6,947	—
411	brougham 7P, Brunn	6,120	7,049	—
413	conv sdn, LeBaron	5,670	5,823	—
415	sdn limo 7P, Judkins	5,950	6,334	—
417A	berline 2W, Judkins	5,770	6,028	—
417B	berline 3W, Judkins	5,840	6,130	—
419	limo, Willoughby	6,140	6,232	—
421	spt sdn, Willoughby	6,300	7,049	—
425	cabriolet 2P, Brunn	5,870	7,253	—

*Total K Series model year production: 133.

1940 Engines	bore×stroke	bhp	availability
V12, 292.0	2.88×3.75	120	S-Zephyr
V12, 414.0	3.13×4.50	150	S-K Series

1942 Zephyr convertible coupe

1941

16H Zephyr (wb 125.0)		Wght	Price	Prod
72A	cpe 3P	3,560	1,478	972
72A	cpe 3P, Custom interior	3,560	1,557	
72B	cpe 5P	3,580	1,464	178
73	sdn 4d	3,710	1,541	14,469
73	sdn 4d, Custom interior	3,710	1,641	
76	conv cpe	3,840	1,858	725
77	club cpe	3,640	1,541	3,750
77	club cpe, Custom interior	3,640	1,541	
16H Continental (wb 125.0)				
56	conv cpe ("cabriolet")	3,860	2,865	400
57	club cpe	3,890	2,812	850
168H Custom (wb 138.0)				
31	sdn 4d, 8P	4,250	2,704	355
32	limo	4,270	2,836	295

1941 Engine	bore×stroke	bhp	availability
V12, 292.0	2.88×3.75	120	S-all

1942

26H Zephyr (wb 125.0)		Wght	Price	Prod
72A	cpe 3P	3,730	1,650	1,236
72A	cpe 3P, Custom interior	3,730	1,735	
73	sdn 4d	3,920	1,700	4,418
73	sdn 4d, Custom interior	3,920	1,795	
76	conv cpe	4,130	2,150	191
77	club cpe	3,810	1,700	253
77	club cpe, Custom interior	3,810	1,795	
26H Continental (wb 125.0)				
56	conv cpe ("cabriolet")	4,020	3,000	136
57	club cpe	4,000	3,000	200
268H Custom (wb 138.0)				
31	sdn 4d, 8P	4,380	2,950	47
32	limo	4,400	3,075	66

1942 Engine	bore×stroke	bhp	availability
V12, 305.0	2.94×3.75	130	S-all

1946

66H (wb 125.0)—16,179 built		Wght	Price	Prod
73	sdn 4d	3,980	2,337	—
73	sdn 4d, Custom interior	3,980	2,486	—
76	conv cpe	4,210	2,883	—
77	club cpe	3,380	2,318	—
77	club cpe, Custom interior	3,380	2,467	
66H Continental (wb 125.0)		**Wght**	**Price**	**Prod**
56	conv cpe ("cabriolet")	4,090	4,474	201
57	club cpe	4,100	4,392	265

1946 Engine	bore×stroke	bhp	availability
V12, 292.0	2.88×3.75	125	S-all

1947 Lincoln four-door sedan

1947

76H (wb 125.0)—19,891 built		Wght	Price	Prod
73	sdn 4d	4,015	2,554	—
73	sdn 4d, Custom interior	4,015	2,722	—
76	conv cpe	4,245	3,142	—
77	club cpe	3,915	2,533	—
77	club cpe, Custom interior	3,915	2,701	—
76H Continental (wb 125.0)				
56	conv cpe ("cabriolet")	4,135	4,746	738
57	club cpe	4,125	4,662	831

1947 Engine	bore×stroke	bhp	availability
V12, 292.0	2.88×3.75	125	S-all

1948

876H (wb 125.0)—6,470 built		Wght	Price	Prod
73	sdn 4d	4,015	2,554	—
73	sdn 4d, Custom interior	4,015	2,722	—
76	conv cpe	4,245	3,142	—
77	club cpe	3,915	2,533	—
77	club cpe, Custom interior	3,915	2,701	—
876H Continental (wb 125.0)				
56	conv cpe ("cabriolet")	4,135	4,746	452
57	club cpe	4,125	4,662	847

1948 Engine	bore×stroke	bhp	availability
V12, 292.0	2.88×3.75	125	S-all

1949

9EL (wb 121.0)—38,384 built		Wght	Price	Prod
	cpe	3,959	2,527	—
	Sport Sedan 4d	4,009	2,575	—
	conv cpe	4,224	3,116	—
9EH Cosmopolitan (wb 125.0)—35,123 built				
	cpe	4,194	3,186	—
	Sport Sedan 4d	4,259	3,238	—
	Town sdn 4d	4,274	3,238	—
	conv cpe	4,419	3,948	—

1949 Engine	bore×stroke	bhp	availability
V8, 336.7	3.50×4.38	152	S-all

1950

0EL (wb 121.0)		Wght	Price	Prod
L-72	cpe	4,090	2,529	5,748
L-72C	Lido cpe	4,145	2,721	
L-74	Sport Sedan 4d	4,115	2,576	11,741
0EH Cosmopolitan (wb 125.0)				
H-72	cpe	4,375	3,187	1,824
H-72C	Capri cpe	4,385	3,406	
H-74	Sport Sedan 4d	4,410	3,240	8,341
H-76	conv cpe	4,640	3,950	536

1950 Engine	bore×stroke	bhp	availability
V8, 336.7	3.50×4.38	152	S-all

1951

1EL (wb 121.0)		Wght	Price	Prod
L-72B	cpe	4,065	2,505	4,482
L-72C	Lido cpe	4,100	2,702	
L-74	Sport Sedan 4d	4,130	2,553	12,279
1EH Cosmopolitan (wb 125.0)				
H-72B	cpe	4,340	3,129	2,727
H-72C	Capri cpe	4,360	3,350	
H-74	Sport Sedan 4d	4,415	3,182	12,229
H-76	conv cpe	4,615	3,891	857

1951 Engine	bore×stroke	bhp	availability
V8, 336.7	3.50×4.38	154	S-all

1952

2H Cosmopolitan (wb 123.0)		Wght	Price	Prod
60C	Spt htp cpe	4,155	3,293	4,545
73A	sdn 4d	4,125	3,198	*
2H Capri (wb 123.0)				
60A	htp cpe	4,235	3,518	5,681
73B	sdn 4d	4,140	3,331	*
76A	conv cpe	4,350	3,665	1,191

*Combined sedan production: 15,854.

1952 Engine	bore×stroke	bhp	availability
V8, 317.5	3.80×3.50	160	S-all

1953

8H Cosmopolitan (wb 123.0)		Wght	Price	Prod
60C	Sport htp cpe	4,155	3,322	6,562
73A	sdn 4d	4,135	3,226	7,560
8H Capri (wb 123.0)				
60A	htp cpe	4,165	3,549	12,916
73B	sdn 4d	4,150	3,453	11,352
76A	conv cpe	4,310	3,699	2,372

1953 Engine	bore×stroke	bhp	availability
V8, 317.5	3.80×3.50	205	S-all

1954

Cosmopolitan (wb 123.0)		Wght	Price	Prod
60C	Sport htp cpe	4,155	3,625	2,994
73A	sdn 4d	4,135	3,522	4,447
Capri (wb 123.0)				
60A	htp cpe	4,250	3,869	14,003
73B	sdn 4d	4,245	3,711	13,598
76A	conv cpe	4,310	4,031	1,951

1954 Engine	bore×stroke	bhp	availability
V8, 317.5	3.80×3.50	205	S-all

1955

Custom (wb 123.0)		Wght	Price	Prod
60C	Sport htp cpe	4,185	3,666	1,362
73A	sdn 4d	4,235	3,563	2,187
Capri (wb 123.0)				
60A	htp cpe	4,305	3,910	11,462
73B	sdn 4d	4,245	3,752	10,724
76A	conv cpe	4,415	4,072	1,487

1955 Engine	bore×stroke	bhp	availability
V8, 341.0	3.94×3.50	225	S-all

1956

Capri (wb 126.0)		Wght	Price	Prod
60E	Sport htp cpe	4,305	4,119	4,355
73A	sdn 4d	4,315	4,212	4,436
Premiere (wb 126.0)				
60B	htp cpe	4,357	4,601	19,619
73B	sdn 4d	4,347	4,601	19,465
76B	conv cpe	4,452	4,747	2,447

1956 Engine	bore×stroke	bhp	availability
V8, 368.0	4.00×3.66	285	S-all

1957

Capri (wb 126.0)		Wght	Price	Prod
57A	Landau htp sdn	4,460	4,794	1,451
58A	sdn 4d	4,349	4,794	1,476
60A	htp cpe	4,373	4,649	2,973
Premiere (wb 126.0)				
57B	Landau htp sdn	4,538	5,294	11,223
58B	sdn 4d	4,527	5,294	5,139
60B	htp cpe	4,451	5,149	15,185
76B	conv cpe	4,676	5,381	3,676

1957 Engine	bore×stroke	bhp	availability
V8, 368.0	4.00×3.66	300	S-all

1958

Capri (wb 131.0)		Wght	Price	Prod
53A	sdn 4d	4,799	4,951	1,184
57A	Landau htp sdn	4,810	4,951	3,084
63A	htp cpe	4,735	4,803	2,591
Premiere (wb 131.0)				
53B	sdn 4d	4,802	5,505	1,660
57B	htp sdn	4,798	5,505	5,572
63B	htp cpe	4,734	5,318	3,043

1958 Engine	bore×stroke	bhp	availability
V8, 430.0	4.30×3.70	375	S-all

1959

Capri (wb 131.0)		Wght	Price	Prod
53A	sdn 4d	4,823	5,090	1,312
57A	htp sdn	4,824	5,090	4,417
63A	htp cpe	4,741	4,902	2,200

1957 Premiere hardtop coupe

Premiere (wb 131.0)		Wght	Price	Prod
53B	sdn 4d	4,887	5,594	1,282
57B	htp sdn	4,880	5,594	4,606
63B	htp cpe	4,798	5,347	1,963
Continental Mark IV (wb 131.0)				
23A	limo	5,061	10,230	49
23B	form sdn	5,190	9,208	78
54A	sdn 4d	5,061	6,845	955
65A	htp cpe	4,967	6,598	1,703
68A	conv cpe	5,076	7,056	2,195
75A	htp sdn	5,050	6,845	6,146

1959 Engine	bore×stroke	bhp	availability
V8, 430.0	4.30×3.70	350	S-all

1960

(wb 131.0)		Wght	Price	Prod
53A	sdn 4d	5,016	5,441	1,093
57A	Landau htp sdn	5,012	5,441	4,397
63A	htp cpe	4,917	5,253	1,670
Premiere (wb 131.0)				
53B	sdn 4d	5,064	5,945	1,010
57B	Landau htp sdn	5,060	5,945	4,200
63B	htp cpe	4,965	5,696	1,365
Continental Mark V (wb 131.0)				
23A	limo	5,481	10,230	34
23B	form sdn	5,272	9,208	136
54A	sdn 4d	5,143	6,845	807
65A	htp cpe	5,044	6,598	1,461
68A	conv cpe	5,180	7,056	2,044
75A	htp sdn	5,139	6,845	6,604

1960 Engine	bore×stroke	bhp	availability
V8, 430.0	4.30×3.70	315	S-all

1961

Continental (wb 123.0)		Wght	Price	Prod
53A	htp sdn	4,927	6,067	22,303
57C	htp sdn, special model	—	—	4
74A	conv sdn	5,215	6,713	2,857

1961 Engine	bore×stroke	bhp	availability
V8, 430.0	4.30×3.70	300	S-all

1962

Continental (wb 123.0)		Wght	Price	Prod
53A	htp sdn	4,966	6,074	27,849
74A	conv sdn	5,370	6,720	3,212

1962 Engine	bore×stroke	bhp	availability
V8, 430.0	4.30×3.70	300	S-all

1963

Continental (wb 123.0)		Wght	Price	Prod
53A	htp sdn	4,936	6,270	28,095
74A	conv sdn	5,340	6,916	3,138

1963 Engine	bore×stroke	bhp	availability
V8, 430.0	4.30×3.70	320	S-all

1964

Continental (wb 126.0)		Wght	Price	Prod
82	htp sdn	5,055	6,292	32,969
86	conv sdn	5,393	6,938	3,328

1964 Engine	bore×stroke	bhp	availability
V8, 430.0	4.30×3.70	320	S-all

1965

Continental (wb 126.0)		Wght	Price	Prod
82	htp sdn	5,075	6,292	36,824
86	conv sdn	5,475	6,938	3,356

1965 Engine	bore×stroke	bhp	availability
V8, 430.0	4.30×3.70	320	S-all

1966

Continental (wb 126.0)		Wght	Price	Prod
82	sdn 4d	5,085	5,750	35,809
86	conv sdn	5,480	6,383	3,180
89	htp cpe	4,985	5,485	15,766

1966 Engine	bore×stroke	bhp	availability
V8, 462.0	4.38×3.83	340	S-all

1967

Continental (wb 126.0)		Wght	Price	Prod
82	sdn 4d	5,049	5,795	33,331
86	conv sdn	5,505	6,449	2,276
89	htp cpe	4,940	5,553	11,060

1967 Engine	bore×stroke	bhp	availability
V8, 462.0	4.38×3.83	340	S-all

1968

Continental (wb 126.0)		Wght	Price	Prod
81	htp cpe	4,883	5,736	9,415
82	sdn 4d	4,978	5,970	29,719
Continental Mark III (wb 117.2)				
89	htp cpe	4,739	6,585	7,770

1968 Engine	bore×stroke	bhp	availability
V8, 460.0	4.36×3.75	365	S-all

1969

Continental (wb 126.0)		Wght	Price	Prod
81	htp cpe	4,910	5,830	9,032
82	sdn 4d	5,005	6,063	29,258
Continental Mark III (wb 117.2)				
89	htp cpe	4,762	6,758	23,088

1962 Continental convertible sedan

1969 Engine	bore×stroke	bhp	availability
V8, 460.0	4.36×3.85	365	S-all

1970

Continental (wb 126.0)		Wght	Price	Prod
81	htp cpe	4,669	5,976	9,073
82	sdn 4d	4,719	6,211	28,622
Continental Mark III (wb 117.2)				
89	htp cpe	4,675	7,281	21,432

1970 Engine	bore×stroke	bhp	availability
V8, 460.0	4.36×3.85	365	S-all

1971

Continental (wb 127.0)		Wght	Price	Prod
81	htp cpe	5,032	7,172	8,205
82	sdn 4d	5,072	7,419	27,346
Continental Mark III (wb 117.2)				
89	htp cpe	5,003	8,813	27,091

1971 Engine	bore×stroke	bhp	availability
V8,460.0	4.36×3.85	365	S-all

1972

Continental (wb 127.0)		Wght	Price	Prod
81	htp cpe	4,906	7,068	10,408
82	sdn 4d	4,958	7,302	35,561
Continental Mark IV (wb 120.4)				
89	htp cpe	4,792	8,640	48,591

1972 Engines	bore×stroke	bhp	availability
V8,460.0	4.36×3.85	224	S-81,82
V8, 460.0	4.36×3.85	212	S-89

1973

Continental (wb 127.0)		Wght	Price	Prod
81	htp cpe	5,016	7,230	13,348
82	sdn 4d	5,049	7,474	45,288
Continental Mark IV (wb 120.4)				
89	htp cpe	4,908	8,984	69,437

1973 Engines	bore×stroke	bhp	availability
V8, 460.0	4.36×3.85	219	S-81,82
V8, 460.0	4.36×3.85	208	S-89

1974

Continental (wb 127.2)		Wght	Price	Prod
81	htp cpe	5,366	8,053	7,318
82	sdn 4d	5,361	8,238	29,351
Continental Mark IV (wb 120.4)				
89	htp cpe	5,362	10,194	57,316

1974 Engines	bore×stroke	bhp	availability
V8, 460.0	4.36×3.85	215	S-81,82
V8, 460.0	4.36×3.85	220	S-89

1975

Continental (wb 127.2)		Wght	Price	Prod
81	cpe	5,219	9,214	21,185
82	sdn 4d	5,229	9,656	33,513
Continental Mark IV (wb 120.4)				
89	htp cpe	5,145	11,082	47,145

1975 Engines	bore×stroke	bhp	availability
V8, 460.0	4.36×3.85	206	S-81,82
V8, 460.0	4.36×3.85	194	S-89

1976

Continental (wb 127.2)		Wght	Price	Prod
81	cpe	5,035	9,142	24,663
82	sdn 4d	5,083	9,293	43,983
Continental Mark IV (wb 120.4)				
89	htp cpe	5,051	11,060	56,110

1976 Engine	bore×stroke	bhp	availability
V8, 460.0	4.36×3.85	202	S-all

1977

Versailles (wb 109.9)		Wght	Price	Prod
84	sdn 4d	3,800	11,500	15,434
Continental (wb 127.2)				
81	cpe	4,836	9,474	27,440
82	sdn 4d	4,880	9,636	68,160
Continental Mark V (wb 120.4)				
89	htp cpe	4,652	11,396	80,321

1977 Engines	bore×stroke	bhp	availability
V8, 351.0	4.00×3.50	135	S-Versailles
V8, 400.0	4.00×4.00	179	S-81,82,89
V8, 460.0	4.36×3.85	208	O-81,82,89

1978

Versailles (wb 109.9)		Wght	Price	Prod
84	sdn 4d	3,759	12,529	8,931
Continental (wb 127.2)				
81	cpe	4,659	9,974	20,977
82	sdn 4d	4,660	10,166	67,110
Continental Mark V (wb 120.4)				
89	htp cpe	4,567	12,099	72,602

1978 Engines	bore×stroke	bhp	availability
V8, 302.0	4.00×3.00	133	S-Versailles
V8, 400.0	4.00×4.00	166	S-81,82,89
V8, 460.0	4.36×3.85	210	O-81,82,89

1971 Continental hardtop coupe

1977 Versailles four-door sedan

1979

Versailles (wb 109.9)		Wght	Price	Prod
84	sdn 4d	3,684	12,939	21,007
Continental (wb 127.2)				
81	cpe	4,639	10,985	16,142
82	sdn 4d	4,649	11,200	76,458
Continental Mark V (wb 120.4)				
89	htp cpe	4,589	13,067	75,939

1979 Engines	bore×stroke	bhp	availability
V8, 302.0	4.00×3.00	130	S-Versailles
V8, 400.0	4.00×4.00	159	S-81,82,89

1980

Versailles (wb 109.9)		Wght	Price	Prod
84	4d	3,661	14,674	4,784
Continental (wb 117.3)				
81	cpe	3,843	12,555	7,177
82	sdn 4d	3,919	12,884	24,056
Continental Mark VI (wb 117.3)				
89	sdn 2d	3,892	15,424	38,891
90	sdn 4d	3,988	15,824	
96	Signature sdn 2d	3,896	20,940	
96	Signature sdn 4d	3,993	21,309	

1980 Engines	bore×stroke	bhp	availability
V8, 302.0	4.00×3.00	132	S-Versailles
V8,302.0	4.00×3.00	129	S-Contl,Mk VI
V8,351.0	4.00×3.50	140	O-Contl,Mk VI

1981

Town Car (wb 117.3)		Wght	Price	Prod
93	sdn 2d	3,884	13,707	4,935
94	sdn 4d	3,958	14,068	27,904
Continental Mark VI (wb 117.3; 2d 114.3)				
95	cpe 2d	3,899	16,858	18,740
95	Signature cpe 2d	3,990	22,463	
96	sdn 4d	3,944	17,303	17,958
96	Signature sdn 4d	4,035	22,838	

1981 Engines	bore x stroke	bhp	availability
V8, 302.0	4.00×3.00	130	S-all

1982

Continental (wb 108.7)		Wght	Price	Prod
98	sdn 4d V6/V8	3,512	21,302	23,908
98/603	Signature sdn 4d V6/V8	3,610	24,456	
98/60H	Givenchy sdn 4d V6/V8	3,610	24,803	
Mark VI (wb 114.3; 4d 117.3)				
95	cpe 2d	3,879	19,452	11,532
95/603	Signature cpe 2d	3,888	22,252	
95/60M	Givenchy cpe 2d	3,910	22,722	
95/60N	Bill Blass cpe 2d	3,910	23,594	
96	sdn 4d	3,976	19,924	14,804
96/603	Signature sdn 4d	3,985	22,720	
96/60P	Pucci sdn 4d	3,970	23,465	
Town Car (wb 117.3)				
94	sdn 4d	3,936	16,100	35,069
94/60U	Signature sdn 4d	3,952	17,394	
94/605	Cartier sdn 4d	3,944	18,415	

1982 Engines	bore x stroke	bhp	availability
V6, 232.0	3.80×3.40	112	S-Continental

1980 Continental Mark VI Signature Series four-door sedan

	bore×stroke	bhp	availability
V8, 302.0	4.00×3.00	131	S-Continental
V8, 302.0	4.00×3.00	134	S-Mark, Town

1983

Continental (wb 108.6)		Wght	Price	Prod
97	sdn 4d	3,719	20,985	
98/60R	Valentino sdn 4d	3,757	22,576	16,831
97/60M	Givenchy sdn 4d	3,757	22,576	
Mark VI (wb 114.3; 4d 117.3)				
98	cpe 2d	4,004	20,229	
98/603	Signature cpe 2d	4,013	23,124	12,743
98/60N	Bill Blass cpe 2d	4,035	24,533	
98/60P	Pucci cpe 2d	—	24,345	
99	sdn 4d	4,105	20,717	
99/603	Signature sdn 4d	4,114	23,612	18,113
99/60P	Pucci sdn 4d	4,099	24,407	
Town Car (wb 117.3)				
96	sdn 4d	4,062	16,923	
96/60U	Signature sdn 4d	4,078	18,265	53,381
96/605	Cartier sdn 4d	4,070	19,601	

1983 Engines	bore×stroke	bhp	availability
V8, 302.0	4.00×3.00	130	S-all
V8, 302.0	4.00×3.00	145	O-Mark

1984

Continental (wb 108.6)		Wght	Price	Prod
97	sdn 4d	3,750	21,769	
97/60R	Valentino sdn 4d	—	24,217	30,468
97/60M	Givenchy sdn 4d	—	24,242	
Mark VII (wb 108.6)				
98	cpe 2d	3,625	21,707	
98/938	LSC cpe 2d	—	23,706	33,344
98/60N	Bill Blass cpe 2d	—	24,807	
98/60P	Versace cpe 2d	—	24,406	
Town Car (wb 117.3)				
96	sdn 4d	4,062	18,071	
96/60U	Signature sdn 4d	4,078	20,040	93,622
96/605	Cartier sdn 4d	4,070	21,706	

1984 Engines	bore×stroke	bhp	availability
V6TD, 149.0	3.15×3.19	115	O-Cont, Mark VII
V8, 302.0	4.00×3.00	140	S-all
V8, 302.0	4.00×3.00	155	O-Town Car

1985

Continental (wb 108.5)		Wght	Price	Prod
97/850A	sdn 4d	3,790	22,573	
97/865A	Valentino sdn 4d	—	26,078	28,253
97/860A	Givenchy sdn 4d	—	25,783	
Mark VII (wb 108.5)				
98/800A	cpe 2d	3,615	22,399	
98/805A	LSC cpe 2d	—	24,332	18,355
98/810A	Bill Blass cpe 2d	—	26,659	
98/815A	Versace cpe 2d	—	26,578	
Town Car (wb 117.3)				
96/700A	sdn 4d	4,027	19,047	
96/705A	Signature sdn 4d	—	22,130	119,878
96/710A	Cartier sdn 4d	—	23,637	

1985 Engines	bore×stroke	bhp	availability
V6TD, 149.0	3.15×3.19	115	O-Cont, Mark VII
V8, 302.0	4.00×3.00	140	S-all exc LSC
V8, 302.0	4.00×3.00	155	O-Town Car
V8, 302.0	4.00×3.00	180	S-Mark VII LSC

Note: 1984-85 Lincolns with turbodiesel V-6 were priced higher than amounts shown.

1986

Continental (wb 108.5)		Wght	Price	Prod
97/850A	sdn 4d	3,778	24,556	19,012
97/860A	Givenchy sdn 4d	3,808	26,837	
Mark VII (wb 108.5)				
98/800A	cpe 2d	3,667	22,399	
98/805B	LSC cpe 2d	3,718	23,857	20,056
98/810B	Bill Blass cpe 2d	3,732	23,857	
Town Car (wb 117.3)				
96/700B	sdn 4d	4,038	20,764	
96/705B	Signature sdn 4d	4,121	23,972	117,771
96/710B	Cartier sdn 4d	4,093	25,235	

1986 Engines	bore×stroke	bhp	availability
V8, 302.0	4.00×3.00	150	S-all exc LSC
V8, 302.0	4.00×3.00	200	S-Mark VII LSC

1987

Continental (wb 108.5)		Wght	Price	Prod
97	sdn 4d	3,799	26,402	17,597
98	Givenchy sdn 4d	3,826	28,902	
Mark VII (wb 108.5)				
91	cpe 2d	3,722	24,216	
93	LSC cpe 2d	3,772	25,863	15,286
92	Bill Blass cpe 2d	3,747	25,863	
Town Car (wb 117.3)				
81	sdn 4d	4,051	22,549	
82	Signature sdn 4d	4,106	25,541	76,483
83	Cartier sdn 4d	4,086	26,868	

1987 Engines	bore×stroke	bhp	availability
V8, 302.0	4.00×3.00	150	S-all exc LSC
V8, 302.0	4.00×3.00	200	S-Mark VII LSC

Continental (wb 109.0)		Wght	Price	Prod
97	sdn 4d	3,628	26,078	41,287
98	Signature sdn 4d	3,618	27,944	

1988 Continental four-door sedan

Mark VII (wb 108.5)		Wght	Price	Prod
93	LSC cpe 2d	3,772	25,016	38,259
92	Bill Blass cpe 2d	3,747	25,016	
Town Car (wb 117.3)				
81	sdn 4d	4,093	23,126	201,113
82	Signature sdn 4d	4,119	25,990	
83	Cartier sdn 4d	4,107	27,273	

1988 Engines	bore × stroke	bhp	availability
V6, 232.0	3.80 × 3.40	140	S-Continental
V8, 302.0	4.00 × 3.00	150	S-Town Car
V8, 302.0	4.00 × 3.00	225	S-Mark VII

1989

Continental (wb 109.0)		Wght	Price	Prod
97	sdn 4d	3,635	27,468	
98	Signature sdn 4d	3,633	29,334	
Mark VII (wb 108.5)				
93	LSC cpe 2d	3,743	27,218	
92	Bill Blass cpe 2d	3,783	27,218	
Town Car (wb 117.3)				
81	sdn 4d	4,044	25,205	
82	Signature sdn 4d	4,070	28,206	
83	Cartier sdn 4d	4,059	29,352	
—	Gucci sdn 4d	4,059	—	

1989 Engines	bore × stroke	bhp	availability
V6, 232.0	3.80 × 3.40	140	S-Continental
V8, 302.0	4.00 × 3.00	150	S-Town Car
V8, 302.0	4.00 × 3.00	225	S-Mark VII

MERCURY

1939—75,000 built*

*estimated

Series 99A (wb 116.0)		Wght	Price	Prod
	conv club cpe 5P	2,995	1,018	—
	sdn 2d 5P	2,997	916	—
	cpe sdn 2d 5P	3,000	957	—
	Town Sedan 4d 5P	3,013	957	—

1939 Engine	bore×stroke	bhp	availability
V8, 239.4	3.19×3.75	95	S-all

1940

Series 09A (wb 116.0)—81,128* built		Wght	Price	Prod
	conv cpe	3,107	1,079	—
	sdn 2d	3,068	946	—
	cpe-sdn 2d	3,030	978	—
	Town Sedan 4d	3,103	987	—
	conv sdn	3,249	1,212	—

*Estimate (see note below 1942).

1940 Engine	bore × stroke	bhp	availability
V8, 239.4	3.19 × 3.75	95	S-all

1941

Series 19A (wb 118.0)—82,391* built		Wght	Price	Prod
67	cpe, A/S	3,049	936	—
70	Tudor sdn	3,184	946	—
72	cpe-sdn 2d	3,118	977	—
73	Town Sedan 4d	3,221	987	—
76	conv cpe	3,222	1,100	—
77	cpe, 2P	3,008	910	—
79	wgn, 4d	3,468	1,141	—

*Estimate (see note below 1942).

1941 Engine	bore × stroke	bhp	availability
V8, 239.4	3.19 × 3.75	95	S-all

1942

Series 29A (wb 118.0)—22,816* built		Wght	Price	Prod
70	Tudor sdn	3,228	1,030	—
72	cpe-sdn 2d	3,148	1,055	—
73	Town Sedan 4d	3,263	1,065	—
76	conv cpe	3,288	1,215	—
77	cpe, 3P	3,073	995	—
79	wgn, 4d, 8P	3,528	1,260	—

*Estimate (see below).

Note: Factory records provide only calendar year production during 1940-41. Estimates are calculated by adding 25% of previous year's calendar production to 75% of current year's production. Model year production began in October each year.

1942 Engine	bore × stroke	bhp	availability
V8, 239.4	3.19 × 3.75	100	S-all

1946

Series 69M (wb 118.0)		Wght	Price	Prod
70	sdn 2d	3,240	1,448	13,108
71	Sportsman conv cpe	3,407	2,209	200
72	cpe-sdn 2d	3,190	1,495	24,163
73	Town Sedan 4d	3,270	1,509	40,280
76	conv cpe	3,340	1,711	6,044
79	wgn 4d	3,540	1,729	2,797
—	chassis	—	—	11

1946 Engine	bore × stroke	bhp	availability
V8, 239.4	3.19 × 3.75	100	S-all

1947

Series 79M (wb 118.0)		Wght	Price	Prod
70	sdn 2d	3,268	1,592	34
72	cpe-sdn 2d	3,218	1,645	29,284
73	Town Sedan 4d	3,298	1,660	43,281
76	conv cpe	3,368	2,002	10,221
79	wgn 4d	3,571	2,207	3,558
—	chassis	—	—	5

1940 Sedan-Coupe

1947 Engine	bore × stroke	bhp	availability
V8, 239.4	3.19 × 3.75	100	S-all

1948

Series 89M (wb 118.0)		Wght	Price	Prod
72	cpe-sdn 2d	3,218	1,645	16,476
73	Town Sedan 4d	3,298	1,660	24,283
76	conv cpe	3,368	2,002	7,586
79	wgn 4d	3,571	2,207	1,889
—	chassis	—	—	34

1948 Engine	bore × stroke	bhp	availability
V8, 239.4	3.19 × 3.75	100	S-all

1949

Series 9CM (wb 118.0)		Wght	Price	Prod
72	cpe	3,321	1,979	120,616
74	Sport Sedan 4d	3,386	2,031	155,882
76	conv cpe	3,591	2,410	16,765
79	wgn 2d, 8P	3,626	2,716	8,044
—	chassis	—	—	12

1949 Engine	bore × stroke	bhp	availability
V8, 255.4	3.19 × 4.00	110	S-all

1950

Series OCM (wb 118.0)		Wght	Price	Prod
M-72A	cpe (economy)	3,345	1,875	151,489 (M-72A through M-72C)
M-72B	club cpe	3,430	1,980	
M-72C	Monterey cpe, canvas top	3,480	2,146	
M-72C	Monterey cpe, vinyl top	3,480	2,157	
M-74	Sport Sedan 4d	3,470	2,032	132,082
M-76	conv cpe	3,710	2,412	8,341
M-79	wgn 2d, 8P	3,755	2,561	1,746

1950 Engine	bore × stroke	bhp	availability
V8, 255.4	3.19 × 4.00	110	S-all

1951

Series 1CM (wb 118.0)		Wght	Price	Prod
M-72B	cpe	3,485	1,947	142,168 (M-72B through M-72C)
M-72C	Monterey cpe, canvas top	3,485	2,116	
M-72C	Monterey cpe, vinyl top	3,485	2,127	
M-74	Sport Sedan 4d	3,550	2,000	157,648
M-76	conv cpe	3,760	2,380	6,759
M-79	wgn 2d, 8P	3,800	2,530	3,812

1953 Monterey two-door hardtop

1951 Engine	bore × stroke	bhp	availability
V8, 255.4	3.19 × 4.00	112	S-all

1952

Series 2M (wb 118.0)		Wght	Price	Prod
60B	Monterey htp cpe	3,520	2,225	24,453
60E	Sport Coupe	3,435	2,100	30,599
70B	sdn 2d	3,335	1,987	25,812
73B	sdn 4d	3,390	2,040	83,475 (73B and 73C)
73C	Monterey sdn 4d	3,375	2,115	
76B	Monterey conv cpe	3,635	2,370	5,261
79B	wgn 4d, 6P	3,795	2,525	2,487 (79B and 79D)
79D	wgn 4d, 8P	3,795	2,570	

1952 Engine	bore × stroke	bhp	availability
V8, 255.4	3.19 × 4.00	125	S-all

1953

3M Custom (wb 118.0)		Wght	Price	Prod
60E	Sport Coupe	3,465	2,117	39,547
70B	sdn 2d	3,405	2,004	50,183
73B	sdn 4d	3,450	2,057	59,794
3M Monterey (wb 118.0)				
60B	htp cpe	3,465	2,244	76,119
73C	sdn 4d	3,425	2,133	64,038
76B	conv cpe	3,585	2,390	8,463
79B	wgn 4d, 8P	3,765	2,591	7,719

1953 Engine	bore × stroke	bhp	availability
V8, 255.4	3.19 × 4.00	125	S-all

1954

Custom (wb 118.0)		Wght	Price	Prod
60E	Sport htp cpe	3,485	2,315	15,234
70B	sdn 2d	3,435	2,194	37,146
73B	sdn 4d	3,480	2,251	32,687
Monterey (wb 118.0)				
60B	htp cpe	3,520	2,452	79,533
60F	Sun Valley htp cpe	3,535	2,582	9,761
73C	sdn 4d	3,515	2,333	65,995
76B	conv cpe	3,620	2,610	7,293
79B	wgn 4d, 8P	3,735	2,776	11,656

1954 Engine	bore × stroke	bhp	availability
V8, 256.0	3.62 × 3.10	161	S-all

1955

Custom (wb 119.0; wgn-118.0)		Wght	Price	Prod
60E	htp cpe	3,480	2,341	7,040
70B	sdn 2d	3,395	2,218	31,295
73B	sdn 4d	3,450	2,277	21,219
79B	wgn 4d	3,780	2,686	14,134
Monterey (wb 119.0; wgn-118.0)				
60B	htp cpe	3,510	2,465	69,093
73C	sdn 4d	3,500	2,400	70,392
79C	wgn 4d	3,770	2,844	11,968
Montclair (wb 119.0)				
58A	sdn 4d	3,600	2,685	20,624
64A	htp cpe	3,490	2,631	71,588
64B	Sun Valley htp cpe	3,560	2,712	1,787
76B	conv cpe	3,685	2,712	10,668

1955 Montclair two-door hardtop

1955 Engines	bore × stroke	bhp	availability
V8, 292.0	3.75×3.30	188	S-Custom, Monterey
V8, 292.0	3.75×3.30	198	S-Montclair; O-others

1956

Medalist (wb 119.0)		Wght	Price	Prod
57D	Phaeton htp sdn	3,530	2,458	6,685
64E	Sport htp cpe	3,545	2,389	11,892
70C	sdn 2d	3,430	2,254	20,582
73D	sdn 4d	3,500	2,313	6,653
Custom (wb 119.0; wgn-118.0)				
57C	Phaeton htp sdn	3,550	2,555	12,187
64D	Sport htp cpe	3,560	2,485	20,857
70B	sdn 2d	3,505	2,351	16,343
73B	sdn 4d	3,520	2,410	15,860
76A	conv cpe	3,665	2,712	2,311
79B	wgn 4d, 8P	3,860	2,819	9,292
79D	wgn 4d, 6P	3,790	2,722	8,478
Monterey (wb 119.0;wgn-118.0)				
57B	Phaeton htp sdn	3,800	2,700	10,726
58B	Sport Sedan 4d	3,550	2,652	11,765
64C	Sport htp cpe	3,590	2,630	42,863
73C	sdn 4d	3,570	2,555	26,735
79C	wgn 4d, 8P	3,885	2,977	13,280
Montclair (wb 119.0)				
57A	Phaeton htp sdn	3,640	2,835	23,493
58A	Sport Sedan 4d	3,610	2,786	9,617
64A	Sport htp cpe	3,620	2,765	50,562
76B	conv cpe	3,725	2,900	7,762

1956 Engines	bore × stroke	bhp	availability
V8, 312.0	3.80×3.44	210	S-Medalist, Custom 3spd
V8, 312.0	3.80×3.44	225	S-Medalist, Custom auto, Mntclr
V8, 312.0	3.80×3.44	235	S-Montclair; Monterey auto

1957

Monterey (wb 122.0)		Wght	Price	Prod
57A	Phaeton htp sdn	3,915	2,763	22,475
58A	sdn 4d	3,890	2,645	53,839
63A	Phaeton htp cpe	3,870	2,693	42,199
64A	sdn 2d	3,875	2,576	33,982
76A	Phaeton conv cpe	4,035	3,005	5,033
Montclair (wb 122.0)				
57B	Phaeton htp sdn	3,925	3,317	21,567
58B	sdn 4d	3,905	3,188	19,836
63B	Phaeton htp cpe	3,900	3,236	30,111
76B	Phaeton conv cpe	4,010	3,430	4,248
Turnpike Cruiser (wb 122.0)		**Wght**	**Price**	**Prod**
65A	htp cpe	4,005	3,758	7,291
75A	htp sdn	4,015	3,849	8,305
76S	conv cpe	4,125	4,103	1,265
Station Wagon (wb 122.0)				
56A	Commuter 2d, 6P	4,115	2,903	4,885
56B	Voyager 2d, 6P	4,240	3,403	2,283
77A	Commuter 4d, 6P	4,195	2,973	11,990
77B	Colony Park 4d, 9P	4,165	3,677	7,386
77C	Commuter 4d, 9P	4,155	3,070	5,752
77D	Voyager 4d, 9P	4,280	3,570	3,716

1957 Engines	bore × stroke	bhp	availability
V8, 312.0	3.80×3.44	255	S-all exc Turnpike Cruiser
V8, 368.0	4.00×3.66	290	S-Turnpike Cruiser; O-others

1958

Medalist (wb 122.0)		Wght	Price	Prod
58C	sdn 4d	3,875	2,617	10,982
64B	sdn 2d	3,790	2,547	7,750
Monterey (wb 122.0)				
57A	Phaeton htp sdn	4,150	2,840	6,909
58A	sdn 4d	4,160	2,721	28,892
63A	Phaeton htp cpe	4,075	2,769	13,693
64A	sdn 2d	4,080	2,652	10,526
76A	conv cpe	4,225	3,081	2,292
Montclair (wb 122.0)				
57B	Phaeton tp sdn	4,165	3,365	3,609
58B	sdn 4d	4,155	3,236	4,801
63B	Phaeton htp cpe	4,085	3,284	5,012
65A	Turnpike Cruiser htp cpe	4,150	3,498	2,864
75A	Turnpike Cruiser htp sdn	4,230	3,577	3,543
76B	conv cpe	4,295	3,536	844

Park Lane (wb 125.0)		Wght	Price	Prod
57C	Phaeton htp sdn	4,390	3,944	5,241
63C	Phaeton htp cpe	4,280	3,867	3,158
76C	conv cpe	4,405	4,118	853
Station Wagon (wb 122.0)				
56A	Commuter 2d, 6P	4,400	3,035	1,912
56B	Voyager 2d, 6P	4,435	3,535	568
77A	Commuter 4d, 6P	4,485	3,105	8,601
77B	Colony Park 4d, 6-9P	4,605	3,775	4,474
77C	Commuter 4d, 9P	4,525	3,201	4,227
77D	Voyager 4d, 6-9P	4,540	3,635	2,520

1958 Engines	bore × stroke	bhp	availability
V8, 312.0	3.80×3.44	235	S-Medalist only
V8, 383.0	4.30×3.30	312	S-Monterey, Commuter
V8, 383.0	4.30×3.30	330	S-Montclair, Voyager, Col Park
V8, 430.0	4.30×3.70	360	S-Park Lane; O-others
V8, 430.0	4.30×3.70	400	O-all

1959

Monterey (wb 126.0)		Wght	Price	Prod
57A	htp sdn	4,013	2,918	11,355
58A	sdn 4d	3,985	2,832	43,570
63A	htp cpe	3,932	2,854	17,232
64A	sdn 2d	3,914	2,768	12,694
76A	conv cpe	4,074	3,150	4,426
Montclair (wb 126.0)				
57B	htp sdn	4,234	3,437	6,713
58B	sdn 4d	4,205	3,308	9,514
63B	htp cpe	4,146	3,357	7,375
Park Lane (wb 128.0)				
57C	htp sdn	4,386	4,031	7,206
63C	htp cpe	4,311	3,955	4,060
76C	conv cpe	4,455	4,206	1,257
Station Wagon (wb 126.0)				
56A	Commuter 2d, 6P	4,334	3,145	1,051
77A	Commuter 4d, 6P	4,405	3,215	15,122
77B	Colony Park 4d, 6P	4,535	3,932	5,929
77D	Voyager 4d, 6P	4,483	3,793	2,496

1959 Engines	bore × stroke	bhp	availability
V8, 312.0	3.80×3.44	210	S-Monterey
V8, 383.0	4.30×3.30	280	S-commuter;O-Monterey
V8, 383.0	4.30×3.30	322	S-Montclair,Voyager,Col Park
V8, 430.0	4.30×3.70	345	S-Park Lane

1960

Comet (wb 114.0; wgn—109.5)		Wght	Price	Prod
54A	sdn 4d	2,432	2,053	47,416
59A	wgn 2d	2,548	2,310	5,115
62A	sdn 2d	2,399	1,998	45,374
71A	wgn 4d	2,581	2,365	18,426
Monterey (wb 126.0)				
57A	Cruiser htp sdn	4,011	2,845	9,536
58A	sdn 4d	3,981	2,730	49,594
63A	Cruiser htp cpe	3,931	2,781	15,790
64A	sdn 2d	3,901	2,631	21,557
76A	conv cpe	4,131	3,077	6,062
Monclair (wb 126.0)				
57B	Cruiser htp sdn	4,285	3,394	5,548
58B	sdn 4d	4,255	3,280	8,510
63B	Cruiser htp cpe	4,205	3,331	5,756
Park Lane (wb 126.0)				
57F	Cruiser htp sdn	4,380	3,858	5,788
63F	Cruiser htp cpe	4,300	3,794	2,974
76D	conv cpe	4,500	4,018	1,525
Station Wagon (wb 126.0)				
77A	Commuter 4d, 6–9P	4,301	3,127	14,949
77B	Colony Park 4d, 9P	4,558	3,837	7,411

1960 Engines	bore × stroke	bhp	availability
L6, 144.3	3.50×2.50	90	S-Comet
V8, 312.0	3.80×3.44	205	S-Monterey, Commuter
V8, 383.0	4.30×3.30	280	O-Monterey, Commuter
V8, 430.0	4.30×3.70	310	S-Montclair, P Lane, Col Park

1961

Comet (wb 114.0; wgn-109.5)		Wght	Price	Prod
54A	sdn 4d	2,411	2,055	85,332
59A	wgn 2d	2,548	2,312	4,199
62A	sdn 2d	2,376	2,000	71,563
62C	S-22 sdn 2d	2,441	2,284	14,004
71A	wgn 4d	2,581	2,355	22,165
Meteor (wb 120.0)				
58A	600 sdn 4d	3,714	2,589	18,117 (58A, 64A)
64A	600 sdn 2d	3,647	2,535	
54A	800 sdn 4d	3,762	2,767	35,005 (54A, 62A, 65A, 75A)
62A	800 sdn 2d	3,680	2,713	
65A	800 htp cpe	3,694	2,774	
75A	800 htp sdn	3,780	2,839	

1957 Turnpike Cruiser four-door hardtop

1959 Park Lane two-door hardtop

Monterey (wb 120.0)		Wght	Price	Prod
54B	sdn 4d	3,777	2,871	22,881
65B	htp cpe	3,709	2,878	10,942
75B	htp sdn	3,795	2,943	9,252
76A	conv cpe	3,872	3,128	7,053
Station Wagon (wb 120.0)				
71A	Commuter 4d, 6P	4,115	2,924	8,945
71B	Colony Park 4d, 6P	4,131	3,120	7,887
71B	Colony Park 4d, 9P	4,171	3,191	
71C	Commuter 4d, 9P	4,155	2,994	6

1961 Engines	bore×stroke	bhp	availability
L6, 144.3	3.50×2.50	85	S-Comet
L6, 170.0	3.50×2.94	101	O-Comet
L6, 223.0	3.62×3.60	135	O-Meteor 600/800, Commuter
V8, 292.0	3.75×3.30	175	S-all exc Comet
V8, 352.0	4.00×3.50	220	O-all exc Comet
V8, 390.0	4.05×3.78	300	O-all exc Comet
V8, 390.0	4.05×3.78	330	O-Meteor

1962

Comet (wb 114.0; wgn-109.5)		Wght	Price	Prod
54A	sdn 4d	2,457	2,139	70,227
54B	Custom sdn 4d	2,648	2,226	
59A	wgn 2d	2,626	2,396	2,121
59B	Custom wgn 2d	2,642	2,483	
62A	sdn 2d	2,420	2,084	73,880
62B	Custom sdn 2d	2,431	2,170	
62C	S-22 sdn 2d	2,458	2,368	
71A	wgn 4d	2,662	2,439	16,759
71B	Custom wgn 4d	2,679	2,526	
71C	Villager wgn 4d	2,712	2,710	2,318
Meteor (wb 116.5)				
54A	sdn 4d	2,956	2,340	18,708
54B	Custom sdn 4d	2,964	2,428	23,484
62A	sdn 2d	2,922	2,278	11,550
62B	Custom sdn 2d	2,930	2,366	9,410
62C	S-33 sdn 2d	2,960	2,509	5,900
Monterey (wb 120.0)				
54A	sdn 4d	3,772	2,726	18,975
62A	sdn 4d	3,695	2,672	5,117
65A	htp cpe	3,712	2,733	5,328
75A	htp sdn	3,781	2,798	2,691
Monterey Custom (wb 120.0)				
54B	sdn 4d	3,836	2,965	27,591
65B	htp cpe	3,772	2,972	10,814
65C	S-55 htp cpe	4,802	3,488	2,772
75B	htp sdn	3,851	3,037	8,932
76A	conv cpe	3,938	3,222	5,489
76B	S-55 conv cpe	3,968	3,738	1,315
Station Wagon (wb 120.0)				
71A	Commuter 4d, 6P	4,120	2,920	8,389
71C	Commuter 4d, 9P	4,132	2,990	
71B	Colony Park 4d, 6P	4,186	3,219	9,596
71D	Colony Park 4d, 9P	4,198	3,289	

1962 Engines	bore×stroke	bhp	availability
L6, 144.3	3.50×2.50	85	S-Comet
L6, 170.0	3.50×2.94	101	S-Meteor; O-Comet
L6, 223.0	3.62×3.60	138	S-Monterey, Commuter
V8, 221.0	3.50×2.87	145	O-Meteor
V8, 260.0	3.80×2.87	164	O-Meteor
V8, 292.0	3.75×3.30	170	S-Custom, Col Park; O-Mntry, Cmmtr
V8, 352.0	4.00×3.50	220	O-all except Comet, Meteor
V8, 390.0	4.05×3.78	300	S-S55; O-all exc Comet,Meteor
V8, 390.0	4.05×3.78	330	O-all exc Comet, Meteor
V8, 406.0	4.13×3.78	385	O-all exc Comet, Meteor

1963

Comet (wb 114.0; wgn-109.5)		Wght	Price	Prod
54A	sdn 4d	2,499	2,139	24,230
54B	Custom sdn 4d	2,508	2,206	27,498
59A	wgn 2d	2,644	2,440	623
59B	Custom wgn 2d	2,659	2,527	272
62A	sdn 2d	2,462	2,084	24,351
62B	Custom sdn 2d	2,471	2,171	11,897
62C	S-22 sdn 2d	2,512	2,368	6,303
63B	Custom htp cpe	2,572	2,605	9,432
63C	S-22 htp cpe	2,613	2,635	5,807
71A	wgn 4d	2,681	2,483	4,419
71B	Custom wgn 4d	2,696	2,570	5,151
71C	Villager wgn 4d	2,736	2,754	1,529
76A	Custom conv cpe	2,784	2,557	7,354
76B	S-22 conv cpe	2,825	2,710	5,757
Meteor (wb 116.5; wgn-115.5)				
54A	sdn 4d	3,025	2,340	9,183
54B	Custom sdn 4d	3,031	2,428	14,498
62A	sdn 2d	2,986	2,278	3,935
62B	Custom sdn 2d	2,992	2,366	2,704
65A	Custom htp cpe	3,010	2,448	7,565
65B	S-33 htp cpe	3,030	2,628	4,865
71B	wgn 4d, 6P	3,303	2,631	2,904
71D	Cus Cruiser wgn 4d, 6-9P	3,319	2,886	1,485
71E	Custom wgn 4d, 6-9P	3,311	2,719	3,636
Monterey (120.0)				
54A	sdn 4d	3,944	2,887	18,177
62A	sdn 2d	3,854	2,834	4,640
65A	htp cpe	3,869	2,930	3,879
75A	htp sdn	3,959	2,995	1,692
Monterey Custom (wb 120.0)				
54B	sdn 4d	3,956	3,075	39,542
63B	Marauder fstbk htp cpe	3,887	3,083	7,298
63C	S-55 Marauder fstbk htp cpe	3,900	3,650	2,319
65B	htp cpe	3,881	3,083	10,693
65C	S-55 htp cpe	3,894	3,650	3,863
75B	htp sdn	3,971	3,148	8,604
75C	S-55 htp sdn	3,984	3,715	1,203
76A	conv cpe	4,043	3,333	3,783
76B	S-55 conv cpe	4,049	3,900	1,379
Station Wagon (wb 120.0)				
71B	Colony Park 4d, 6P	4,306	3,295	6,447
71D	Colony Park 4d, 9P	4,318	3,365	7,529

1963 Engines	bore×stroke	bhp	availability
L6, 144.3	3.50×2.50	85	S-Comet sdns
L6, 170.0	3.50×2.94	101	S-other Comet, Meteor
V8, 221.0	3.50×2.87	145	O-Comet, Meteor
V8, 260.0	3.80×2.87	164	O-Meteor/Cus, S-33, Comet

1961 Monterey convertible coupe

	bore×stroke	bhp	availability
V8, 390.0	4.05×3.78	250	S-Monterey, Monterey Custom
V8, 390.0	4.05×3.78	300	S-S-55; O-other Monterey
V8, 390.0	4.05×3.78	330	O-Montereys, wagons
V8, 406.0	4.13×3.78	385	O-Monterey, Monterey Custom
V8, 406.0	4.13×3.78	405	O-Monterey, Monterey Custom
V8, 427.0	4.23×3.78	410	O-late Monterey, Mont Custom

1964

Comet 202 (wb 114.0)		Wght	Price	Prod
01	sdn 2d	2,539	2,126	33,824
02	sdn 4d	2,580	2,182	29,147
32	wgn 4d	2,727	2,463	5,504
Comet 404 (wb 114.0)				
11	sdn 2d	2,551	2,213	12,512
12	sdn 4d	2,588	2,269	25,136
34	Custom wgn 4d	2,741	2,550	6,918
36	Villager wgn 4d	2,745	2,734	1,980
Comet Caliente (wb 114.0)				
22	sdn 4d	2,668	2,350	27,218
23	htp cpe	2,688	2,375	31,204
25	conv cpe	2,861	2,636	9,039
Comet Cyclone (wb 114.0)				
27	htp cpe	2,860	2,655	7,454
Monterey (wb 120.0)				
41	sdn 2d	3,895	2,819	3,932
42	sdn 4d	3,985	2,892	20,234
43	htp cpe	3,910	2,884	2,926
45	conv cpe	4,027	3,226	2,592
47	Marauder fstbk htp cpe	3,916	2,884	8,760
48	Marauder fstbk htp sdn	3,914	2,957	4,143
Montclair (wb 120.0)				
52	sdn 4d	3,996	3,116	15,520
53	htp cpe	3,921	3,127	2,329
57	Marauder fstbk htp cpe	3,927	3,127	6,459
58	Marauder fstbk htp sdn	4,017	3,181	8,655
Park Lane (wb 120.0)				
62	sdn 4d	4,035	3,348	6,230
63	htp cpe	3,960	3,359	1,786
64	htp sdn	4,050	3,413	2,402
65	conv cpe	4,066	3,549	1,967
67	Marauder fstbk htp cpe	3,966	3,359	1,052
68	Marauder fstbk htp sdn	4,056	3,413	4,505
Station Wagon (wb 120.0)				
72	Commuter 4d, 6P	4,259	3,236	3,484
72	Commuter 4d, 9P	4,271	3,306	1,839
76	Colony Park 4d, 6P	4,275	3,434	4,234
76	Colony Park 4d, 9P	4,287	3,504	5,624

1964 Engines	bore×stroke	bhp	availability
L6, 170.0	3.50×2.94	101	S-Comet
L6, 200.0	3.68×3.15	116	O-Comet
V8, 260.0	3.80×2.87	164	O-Comet
V8, 289.0	4.00×2.87	210	S-Cyclone; O-other Comets
V8, 390.0	4.05×3.78	250	S-all exc Comet, Park Lane
V8, 390.0	4.05×3.78	266	O-all exc Comet, Park Lane
V8, 390.0	4.05×3.78	300	S-Park Lane
V8, 390.0	4.05×3.78	330	O-Park Lane
V8, 427.0	4.23×3.78	410	O-Monterey, Montclair, P Lane
V8, 427.0	4.23×3.78	425	O-Monterey, Montclair, P Lane

1965

Comet 202 (wb 114.0)		Wght	Price	Prod
01	sdn 2d	2,584	2,154	32,425
02	sdn 4d	2,624	2,210	23,501
32	wgn 4d	2,784	2,491	4,814
Comet 404 (wb 114.0)				
11	sdn 2d	2,594	2,241	10,900
12	sdn 4d	2,629	2,294	18,628
34	Custom wgn 4d	2,789	2,578	5,226
36	Villager wgn 4d	2,789	2,762	1,592
Comet Caliente (wb 114.0)				
22	sdn 4d	2,659	2,378	20,337
23	htp cpe	2,684	2,403	29,247
25	conv cpe	2,869	2,664	6,035
Comet Cyclone (wb 114.0)				
27	htp cpe	2,994	2,683	12,347
Monterey (wb 123.0)				
42	Breezeway sdn 4d	3,898	2,904	19,569
43	sdn 2d	3,788	2,767	5,775

1962 Monterey Custom S-55 convertible coupe

1963 Meteor Custom hardtop coupe

		Wght	Price	Prod
44	sdn 4d	3,853	2,839	23,363
45	conv cpe	3,928	3,230	4,762
47	htp cpe	3,823	2,902	16,857
48	htp sdn	3,893	2,978	10,047
Montclair (wb 123.0)				
52	Breezeway sdn 4d	3,933	3,137	18,924
57	htp cpe	3,848	3,135	9,645
58	htp sdn	3,928	3,210	16,977
Park Lane (wb 123.0)				
62	Breezeway sdn 4d	3,988	3,369	8,335
65	conv cpe	4,013	3,599	3,006
67	htp cpe	3,908	3,367	6,853
68	htp sdn	3,983	3,442	14,211
Station Wagon (wb 119.0)				
72	Commuter 4d, 6P	4,178	3,235	5,453
72	Commuter 4d, 9P	4,213	3,312	2,628
76	Colony Park 4d, 6P	4,228	3,434	6,910
76	Colony Park 4d, 9P	4,263	3,511	8,384

1965 Engines	bore × stroke	bhp	availability
L6, 200.0	3.68×3.15	120	S-Comet
V8, 289.0	4.00×2.87	200	S-Cyclone; O-other Comet
V8, 289.0	4.00×2.87	225	O-Comet
V8, 390.0	4.05×3.78	250	S-Monterey, Commuter
V8, 390.0	4.05×3.78	266	S-Montclair, Colony Park
V8, 390.0	4.05×3.78	300	S-Park Lane; O-all exc Comet
V8, 390.0	4.05×3.78	330	O-all exc Comet
V8, 427.0	4.23×3.78	425	O-all exc Comet

1966

Comet 202 (wb 116.0; wgn-113.0)		Wght	Price	Prod
01	sdn 2d	2,864	2,206	35,964
02	sdn 4d	2,908	2,263	20,440
06	Voyager wgn 4d	3,282	2,553	7,595
Comet Capri (wb 116.0; wgn-113.0)				
12	sdn 4d	2,928	2,378	15,635
13	htp cpe	2,960	2,400	15,031
16	Villager wgn 4d	3,319	2,790	3,880
Comet Caliente (wb 116.0)				
22	sdn 4d	2,930	2,453	17,933
23	htp cpe	2,966	2,475	25,862
25	conv cpe	3,228	2,735	3,922
Comet Cyclone (wb 116.0)				
27	htp cpe	3,078	2,700	6,889
27	GT htp cpe	3,315	2,891	13,812
29	conv cpe	3,321	2,961	1,305
29	GT conv cpe	3,595	3,152	2,158
Monterey (wb 123.0)				
42	Breezeway sdn 4d	3,966	2,917	14,174
43	sdn 2d	3,835	2,783	2,487
44	sdn 4d	3,903	2,854	18,998
45	conv cpe	4,039	3,237	3,279
47	fstbk htp cpe	3,885	2,915	19,103
48	fstbk htp sdn	3,928	2,990	7,647
S-55 (wb 123.0)				
46	conv cpe	4,148	3,614	669
49	fstbk htp cpe	4,031	3,292	2,916
Montclair (wb 123.0)				
54	sdn 4d	3,921	3,087	11,856
57	fstbk htp cpe	3,887	3,144	11,290
58	fstbk htp sdn	3,971	3,217	15,767
Park Lane (wb 123.0)				
62	Breezeway sdn 4d	4,051	3,389	8,696
65	conv cpe	4,148	3,608	2,546
67	fstbk htp cpe	3,971	3,387	8,354
68	fstbk htp sdn	4,070	3,460	19,204
Station Wagon (wb 119.0)				
72	Commuter 4d, 6P	4,280	3,240	3,970
72	Commuter 4d, 9P	4,331	3,336	2,877
76	Colony Park 4d, 6P	4,332	3,502	7,190
76	Colony Park 4d, 9P	4,383	3,598	11,704

1966 Engines	bore × stroke	bhp	availability
L6, 200.0	3.68×3.15	120	S-Comet exc Cyclone
V8, 289.0	4.00×2.87	200	S-Cyclone; O-other Comet
V8, 390.0	4.05×3.78	265	S-Cyclone GT, full-size w/man
V8, 390.0	4.05×3.78	275	S-full-size w/auto;O-Cyclone GT
V8, 390.0	4.05×3.78	335	O-Cyclone GT
V8, 410.0	4.05×3.98	330	S-Park Lane; O-other full-size
V8, 428.0	4.13×3.98	345	S-S-55; O-other full-size

1967

Comet 202 (wb 116.0)		Wght	Price	Prod
01	sdn 2d	2,868	2,284	14,251
02	sdn 4d	2,906	2,336	10,281
Comet Capri (wb 116.0)				
06	sdn 4d	2,940	2,436	9,292
07	htp cpe	2,970	2,459	11,671
Comet Caliente (wb 116.0)				
10	sdn 4d	2,952	2,535	9,153
11	htp cpe	2,982	2,558	9,966
12	conv cpe	3,250	2,818	1,539
Comet Station Wagon (wb 113.0)				
03	Voyager 4d	3,310	2,604	4,930
08	Villager 4d	3,332	2,841	3,140
Comet Cyclone (wb 116.0)				
15	htp cpe	3,075	2,737	2,682
15	GT htp cpe	3,090	3,034	3,419
16	conv cpe	3,339	2,997	431
16	GT conv cpe	3,350	3,294	378
Cougar (wb 111.0)				
91	htp cpe	2,988	2,851	116,260
91	GT htp cpe	3,000	3,175	7,412
93	XR7 htp cpe	3,015	3,081	27,221
Monterey (wb 123.0)				
44	sdn 4d	3,798	2,904	15,177
44	Breezeway sdn 4d	3,847	2,967	5,910
45	conv cpe	3,943	3,314	2,673
46	S-55 conv cpe	3,960	3,837	145
47	htp cpe	3,820	2,985	16,910

		Wght	Price	Prod
48	htp sdn	3,858	3,059	8,013
49	S-55 fstbk htp cpe	3,837	3,511	570
Montclair (wb 123.0)				
54	sdn 4d	3,863	3,187	5,783
54	Breezeway sdn 4d	3,881	3,250	4,151
57	htp cpe	3,848	3,244	4,118
58	htp sdn	3,943	3,316	5,870
Park Lane (wb 123.0)				
61	Brougham Breezeway sdn 4d	3,980	3,896	3,325
62	Brougham htp sdn	4,000	3,986	4,189
64	Breezeway sdn 4d	4,011	3,736	4,163
65	conv cpe	4,114	3,984	1,191
67	htp cpe	3,947	3,752	2,196
68	htp sdn	3,992	3,826	5,412
Marquis (wb 123.0)				
69	htp cpe	3,995	3,989	6,510
Station Wagon (wb 119.0)				
72	Commuter 4d, 6P	4,178	3,289	3,447
72	Commuter 4d, 9P	4,297	3,384	4,451
76	Colony Park 4d, 6P	4,258	3,657	5,775
76	Colony Park 4d, 9P	4,294	3,752	12,915

1967 Engines	bore × stroke	bhp	availability
L6, 200.0	3.68×3.15	120	S-Comet exc Cyclone
V8, 289.0	4.00×2.87	200	S-Cougar, Cycl; O-other Comet
V8, 289.0	4.00×2.87	225	O-Cougar
V8, 390.0	4.05×3.78	270	S-Mntry,Mntclr,S Wgn;O-Comet
V8, 390.0	4.05×3.78	320	S-Cycl/Cougar GT;O-other Cougar
V8, 410.0	4.05×3.98	330	S-P Lane, Brghm, Marquis; O-Monterey, Montclair
V8, 427.0	4.23×3.78	410	O-Comet htps and 2d sedans
V8, 427.0	4.23×3.78	425	O-Comet htps and 2d sedans
V8, 428.0	4.13×3.98	345	S-S-55; O-other full-size

1968

Comet (wb 116.0)		Wght	Price	Prod
01	htp cpe	3,166	2,477	16,693
Montego (wb 116.0; wgn-113.0)				
06	sdn 4d	3,062	2,504	18,492
07	htp cpe	3,138	2,552	15,002
08	MX wgn 4d	3,460	2,876	9,328
10	MX sdn 4d*	3,088	2,657	18,413
11	MX htp cpe*	3,162	2,676	25,827
12	MX conv cpe	3,374	2,935	3,248
Cyclone (wb 116.0)				
15	fstbk htp cpe	3,407	2,768	6,165
15	GT fstbk htp cpe	3,430	2,936	6,105
17	htp cpe	3,361	2,768	1,034
17	GT htp cpe	3,380	2,936	334
Cougar (wb 111.0)**				
91	htp cpe	3,134	2,933	81,014
93	XR7 htp cpe	3,174	3,232	32,712
Monterey (wb 123.0)				
44	sdn 4d	3,895	3,052	30,727
45	conv cpe	3,977	3,436	1,515
47	htp cpe	3,854	3,133	15,845
48	htp sdn	3,892	3,207	8,927
Montclair (wb 123.0)				
54	sdn 4d	3,897	3,331	7,255
57	htp cpe	3,882	3,387	3,497
58	htp sdn	3,907	3,459	4,008
Park Lane (wb 123.0)				
64	sdn 4d*	4,019	3,552	6,408
65	conv cpe	4,122	3,822	1,112
67	htp cpe	3,955	3,575	2,584
68	htp sdn*	4,000	3,647	10,390
Marquis (wb 123.0)				
69	htp cpe	3,987	3,685	3,965
Station Wagon (wb 119.0)				
72	Commuter 4d, 6P	4,212	3,441	3,497
72	Commuter 4d, 9P	4,331	3,569	5,191
76	Colony Park 4d, 6P	4,259	3,460	5,674
76	Colony Park 4d, 6P	4,295	3,888	15,505

*Includes cars with Brougham trim option
**Includes cars with GT and GTE package options.

1968 Park Lane convertible coupe

1968 Engines	bore × stroke	bhp	availability
L6, 200.0	3.68×3.15	115	S-Comet, Montego
V8, 289.0	4.00×2.87	195	S-base Cougars; O-Comet
V8, 302.0	4.00×3.00	210	S-Cougar Cyclone, O-Montego
V8, 302.0	4.00×3.00	230	O-Cougar, Montego
V8, 390.0	4.05×3.78	265	S-full-size w/man; O-Montego, Cyclone
V8, 390.0	4.05×3.78	280	S-full-size w/auto; O-Cougar
V8, 390.0	4.05×3.78	315	S-P Lane, Brghm, Marquis; O-other full-size
V8, 390.0	4.05×3.78	325	S-Cougar GT; O-Montego exc MX wgn, Cyclone, Cougar, XR7
V8, 390.0	4.05×3.78	335	O-Montego exc wgn, Cyclone
V8, 427.0	4.23×3.78	390	S-CgrGTE; O-Cycln, Mntgo htps
V8, 428.0	4.13×3.98	335	O-Montego, Cyclone, Cougar
V8, 428.0	4.13×3.98	340	O-full-size only

1969

Comet (wb 116.0)		Wght	Price	Prod
01	htp cpe	3,175	2,532	14,104
Montego (wb 116.0; wgn-113.0)				
06	sdn 4d	3,140	2,556	21,950
07	htp cpe	3,154	2,605	17,785
08	MX wgn 4d	3,504	2,979	10,590
10	MX sdn 4d	3,174	2,718	16,148
10	MX Brougham sdn 4d	3,198	2,808	1,590
11	MX htp cpe	3,186	2,736	23,160
11	MX Brougham htp cpe	3,210	2,826	1,226
12	MX conv cpe	3,356	2,979	1,725
Cyclone (wb 116.0)				
15	fstbk htp cpe	3,273	2,771	5,882
16	CJ fstbk htp cpe	3,634	3,224	3,261

Cougar (wb 111.0)		Wght	Price	Prod
91	htp cpe	3,219	3,016	66,331
92	conv cpe	3,343	3,382	5,796
93	XR7 htp cpe	3,221	3,315	23,918
94	XR7 conv cpe	3,343	3,595	4,024
Monterey (wb 124.0, wgn 121.0)				
44	sdn 4d	3,948	3,158	23,009
45	conv cpe	4,093	3,540	1,297
46	htp cpe	3,970	3,237	9,865
48	htp sdn	4,008	3,313	6,066
72	wgn 4d, 6–9P	4,277	3,536	5,844
Monterey Custom (wb 124.0; wgn-121.0)				
54	sdn 4d	4,013	3,377	7,103
56	htp cpe	3,998	3,459	2,898
58	htp sdn	4,023	3,533	2,827
74	wgn 4d, 6–9P	4,342	3,757	1,920
Marauder (wb 121.0)				
60	htp cpe	4,044	3,368	9,031
61	X-100 htp cpe	4,191	4,091	5,635
Marquis (wb 124.0; wgn-121.0)				
63	sdn 4d	4,226	3,857	16,787
63	Brougham sdn 4d	4,195	4,129	14,601
65	conv cpe	4,359	4,124	2,319
66	htp cpe	4,192	3,919	9,907
66	Brougham htp cpe	4,215	4,191	8,395
68	htp sdn	4,237	3,990	14,423
68	Brougham htp sdn	4,436	4,262	14,966
76	Colony Park wgn 4d, 6–9P	4,376	3,895	25,604

1969 Engines	bore × stroke	bhp	availability
L6, 250.0	3.68×3.91	155	S-Comet, Montego
V8, 302.0	4.00×3.00	220	S-Cyclone; O-Comet, Montego
V8, 302.0	4.00×3.00	290	O-Cougar (Boss)
V8, 351.0	4.00×3.50	250	S-Coug; O-Montego, Comet, Cyc
V8, 351.0	4.00×3.50	290	O-Coug, Comet, Cyc, Montego
V8, 390.0	4.05×3.78	265	S-Mntry, Mrdr, SW w/man
V8, 390.0	4.05×3.78	280	O-Mntry, Mrdr, SW w/man
V8, 390.0	4.05×3.78	320	O-Coug, Montego, Cyc, Comet
V8, 428.0	4.13×3.98	335	S-CJ; O-Cougar; Montego exc Brghm, SW, conv/sdns with 4spd
V8, 428.0	4.13×3.98	335	O-Coug, Cyc, Cyc CJ (ram air)
V8, 429.0	4.36×3.59	320	S-Marquis; O-other full-size
V8, 429.0	4.36×3.59	360	S- X-100; O-other full-size

1970

Montego (wb 117.0; wgn-114.0)		Wght	Price	Prod
01	htp cpe	2,859	2,645	21,298
02	sdn 4d	3,208	2,631	13,988
06	MX sdn 4d	3,215	2,728	16,708
07	MX htp cpe	3,228	2,740	15,533
08	MX wgn 4d, 6P	3,653	3,091	5,094
10	MX Brougham sdn 4d	3,238	2,896	3,315
11	MX Brougham htp cpe	3,248	2,915	8,074
12	MX Brougham htp sdn	3,268	3,037	3,685
18	MX Brghm wgn 4d, 6P	3,668	3,304	2,682
Cyclone (wb 117.0)				
15	htp cpe	3,721	3,238	1,695
16	GT htp cpe	3,462	3,226	10,170
17	Spoiler htp cpe	3,773	3,759	1,631
Cougar (wb 111.1)				
91	htp cpe	3,285	3,114	49,479
92	conv cpe	3,382	3,480	2,322
93	XR7 htp cpe	3,311	3,413	18,565
94	XR7 conv cpe	3,408	3,692	1,977
Monterey (wb 124.0; wgn-121.0)				
44	sdn 4d	3,926	3,248	29,432
45	conv cpe	4,071	3,668	581
46	htp cpe	3,890	3,329	9,359
48	htp sdn	3,961	3,406	5,032
72	wgn 4d, 6P	4,235	3,682	1,657
72	wgn 4d, 9P	4,327	3,774	3,507
Monterey Custom (wb 124.0)				
54	sdn 4d	3,931	3,520	4,823
56	htp cpe	3,922	3,600	1,357
58	htp sdn	3,973	3,676	1,194
Marauder (wb 121.0)				
60	htp cpe	3,972	3,503	3,397
61	X-100 htp cpe	4,128	4,136	2,646

1970 Cougar XR 7 convertible coupe

Marquis (wb 124.0; wgn-121.0)		Wght	Price	Prod
62	Brougham sdn 4d	4,166	4,367	14,920
63	sdn 4d	4,121	4,052	14,394
64	Brougham htp cpe	4,119	4,428	7,113
65	conv cpe	4,337	4,318	1,233
66	htp cpe	4,072	4,113	6,229
67	Brougham htp sdn	4,182	4,500	11,623
68	htp sdn	4,141	4,185	8,411
74	wgn 4d, 6P	4,347	3,930	959
74	wgn 4d, 9P	4,393	4,022	1,429
76	Colony Park wgn 4d, 6P	4,442	4,123	4,655
76	Colony Park wgn 4d, 9P	4,488	4,215	14,549

1970 Engines	bore × stroke	bhp	availability
L6, 250.0	3.68×3.91	155	S-Montego
V8, 302.0	4.00×3.00	220	O-Montego
V8, 302.0	4.00×3.00	290	O-Cougar Eliminator
V8, 351.0	4.00×3.50	250	S-Cyclone, Cougar; O-Montego
V8, 351.0	4.00×3.50	300	S-Cgr Elmntr; O-Coug, Montego
V8, 390.0	4.05×3.78	265	S-Monterey, Marauder, C. Park w/man
V8, 390.0	4.05×3.78	280	S-above models w/auto
V8, 428.0	4.13×3.98	335	O-Cougar
V8, 429.0	4.36×3.59	320	S-Marquis exc Colony Park
V8, 429.0	4.36×3.59	360	S-Cyc exc Spoiler, Mrdr X-100; O-Mntg, Mntry, Mrdr, C Park
V8, 429.0	4.36×3.59	370	S-Spoiler; O-Cyclone, GT*
V8, 429.0	4.36×3.59	375	O-all Cyclone
V8, 429.0	4.36×3.59	375	O-all Cyclone,Cougar ("Boss")

*Available in Ram-Air and non-Ram-Air versions.

1971

Comet (wb 109.9; 2d-103.0)		Wght	Price	Prod
30	sdn 4d	2,789	2,446	28,116
31	fstbk sdn 2d	2,700	2,387	54,884
Montego (wb 117.0; wgns-114.0)				
01	hdtp cpe	3,229	2,893	9,623
02	sdn 4d	3,228	2,888	5,718
06	MX sdn 4d	3,235	2,994	13,559
07	MX hdtp cpe	3,236	3,007	13,719
08	MX wgn 5d	3,651	3,331	3,698
10	MX Brougham sdn 4d	3,258	3,189	1,565
11	MX Brougham hdtp cpe	3,275	3,201	2,851
12	MX Brougham hdtp sdn	3,302	3,273	1,156
18	MX Villager wgn 5d	3,666	3,572	2,121
Cyclone (wb 117.0)				
15	fstbk hdtp cpe	3,595	3,369	444
16	GT fstbk hdtp cpe	3,492	3,680	2,287
17	Spoiler fstbk hdtp cpe	3,585	3,801	353
Cougar (wb 113.0)				
91	hdtp cpe	3,331	3,289	34,008
92	conv	3,461	3,681	1,723
93	XR7 hdtp cpe	3,360	3,629	25,416
94	XR7 conv	3,480	3,877	1,717
Monterey (wb 124.0; wgns-121.0)				
44	sdn 4d	4,029	3,858	22,744
46	hdtp cpe	3,959	3,900	9,099
48	hdtp sdn	4,024	3,968	2,483
72	wgn 5d 3S	4,451	4,410	4,160 (3S and 2S combined)
72	wgn 5d 2S	4,401	4,283	
54	Custom sdn 4d	4,144	4,030	12,411
56	Custom hdtp cpe	4,074	4,113	4,508
58	Custom hdtp sdn	4,140	4,185	1,397
Marquis (wb 124.0; wgns-121.0)				
63	sdn 4d	4,346	4,474	16,030
66	hdtp cpe	4,276	4,557	7,726
68	hdtp sdn	4,341	4,624	5,491
74	wgn 5d 3S	4,501	4,674	2,158 (3S and 2S combined)
74	wgn 5d 2S	4,451	4,547	
62	Brougham sdn 4d	4,346	4,880	25,790
64	Brougham hdtp cpe	4,276	4,963	14,570
67	Brougham hdtp sdn	4,341	5,033	13,781
76	Colony Park wgn 5d 3S	4,562	4,933	20,004 (3S and 2S combined)
76	Colony Park wgn 5d 2S	4,512	4,806	

1971 Engines	bore×stroke	bhp	availability
L6, 170.0	3.50x2.94	100	S-Comet
L6, 200.0	3.68x3.13	115	O-Comet
L6, 250.0	3.68×3.91	145	S-Montego; O-Comet
V8, 302.0	4.00×3.00	210	O-Montego, Comet
V8, 351.0	4.00×3.50	240	S-Cyc GT, Cgr, Mntry exc Cus & wgn
V8, 351.0	4.00×3.50	285	S-Cyc exc GT; O-Cougar
V8, 400.0	4.00×4.00	260	S-Mntry Cus,wgns;O-Mntry
V8, 429.0	4.36×3.59	320/360	S-Marquis; O-Mntry
V8, 429.0	4.36×3.59	370	O-Cyclone, Cougar

1972

Comet (wb 109.9; 2d-103.0)		Wght	Price	Prod
30	sdn 4d	2,674	2,398	29,092
31	fstbk sdn 2d	2,579	2,342	53,267
Montego (wb 118.0; 2d-114.0)				
02	sdn 4d	3,454	2,843	8,658
03	hdtp cpe	3,390	2,848	9,963
04	MX sdn 4d	3,485	2,951	23,387
07	MX hdtp cpe	3,407	2,971	25,802
08	MX wgn 5d	3,884	3,264	6,268
10	MX Brougham sdn 4d	3,512	3,127	17,540
11	MX Brougham hdtp cpe	3,433	3,137	28,417
18	MX Villager wgn 5d	3,907	3,438	9,237
16	GT fstbk hdtp cpe	3,517	3,346	5,820
Cougar (wb 112.1)				
91	hdtp cpe	3,282	3,016	23,731
92	conv	3,412	3,370	1,240
93	XR7 hdtp cpe	3,298	3,323	26,802
94	XR7 conv	3,451	3,547	1,929
Monterey (wb 124.0; wgns-121.0)				
44	sdn 4d	4,136	3,793	19,012
46	hdtp cpe	4,086	3,832	6,731
48	hdtp sdn	4,141	3,896	1,416
72	wgn 5d 3S	4,545	4,334	4,644 (3S and 2S combined)
72	wgn 5d 2S	4,495	4,212	
54	Custom sdn 4d	4,225	3,956	16,879

1970 Cyclone Spoiler hardtop coupe

		Wght	Price	Prod
56	Custom hdtp cpe	4,175	4,035	5,910
58	Custom hdtp sdn	4,230	4,103	1,583
Marquis (wb 124.0; wgns-121.0)				
63	sdn 4d	4,386	4,493	14,122
66	hdtp cpe	4,236	4,572	5,507
68	hdtp sdn	4,391	4,637	1,583
74	wgn 5d 3S	4,589	4,567	2,085
74	wgn 5d 2S	4,539	4,445	
62	Brougham sdn 4d	4,436	4,890	38,242
64	Brougham hdtp cpe	4,386	4,969	20,064
67	Brougham hdtp sdn	4,441	5,034	12,841
76	Colony Park wgn 5d 3S	4,629	4,672	20,192
76	Colony Park wgn 5d 2S	4,579	4,550	

1972 Engines	bore×stroke	bhp	availability
L6, 170.0	3.50×2.94	82	S-Comet
L6, 200.0	3.68×3.13	91	O-Comet
L6, 250.0	3.68×3.91	95	O-Montego
L6, 250.0	3.68×3.91	98	O-Comet
V8, 302.0	4.00×3.00	140	S-Montego
V8, 302.0	4.00×3.00	143	S-Comet
V8, 351.0	4.00×3.50	161	O-Montego
V8, 351.0	4.00×3.50	163	S-Mntry exc Cus wgn
V8, 351.0	4.00×3.50	164	S-Cougar
V8, 351.0	4.00×3.50	262/266	O-Cougar
V8, 400.0	4.00×4.00	168	O-Montego
V8, 400.0	4.00×4.00	172	S-Mntry Cus & Marq wgns
V8, 429.0	4.36×3.59	205	O-Montego
V8, 429.0	4.36×3.59	208	S-Marquis exc wgn
V8, 460.0	4.36×3.85	224	O-Monterey, Marquis

1973

Comet (wb 109.9; 2d-103.0)		Wght	Price	Prod
30	sdn 4d	2,904	2,489	28,984
31	fstbk sdn 2d	2,813	2,432	55,707
Montego (wb 118.0; 2d-114.0)				
02	sdn 4d	3,719	2,916	7,459
03	hdtp cpe	3,653	2,926	7,082
04	MX sdn 4d	3,772	3,009	25,300
07	MX hdtp cpe	3,683	3,041	27,812
08	MX wgn 5d	4,124	3,417	7,012
10	MX Brougham sdn 4d	3,813	3,189	24,329
11	MX Brougham hdtp cpe	3,706	3,209	40,951
18	MX Villager wgn 5d	4,167	3,606	12,396
16	GT fstbk hdtp cpe	3,662	3,413	4,464
Cougar (wb 113.0)				
91	hdtp cpe	3,396	3,372	21,069
92	conv	3,524	3,726	1,284
93	XR7 hdtp cpe	3,416	3,679	35,110
94	XR7 conv	3,530	3,903	3,165
Monterey (wb 124.0; wgns 121.0)				
44	sdn 4d	4,225	3,961	16,622
46	hdtp cpe	4,167	4,004	6,452
72	wgn 5d 3S	4,673	4,501	4,275
72	wgn 5d 2S	4,623	4,379	
54	Custom sdn 4d	4,295	4,124	20,873
56	Custom hdtp cpe	4,239	4,207	6,962
Marquis (wb 124.0; wgns-121.0)				
63	sdn 4d	4,477	4,648	15,250
66	hdtp cpe	4,411	4,727	5,973
68	hdtp sdn	4,453	4,782	2,185
74	wgn 5d 3S	4,745	4,730	2,464
74	wgn 5d 2S	4,695	4,608	
62	Brougham sdn 4d	4,547	5,072	46,624
64	Brougham hdtp cpe	4,475	5,151	22,770
67	Brougham hdtp sdn	4,565	5,206	10,613
76	Colony Park wgn 5d 3S	4,780	4,835	23,283
76	Colony Park wgn 5d 2S	4,730	4,713	

1973 Engines	bore×stroke	bhp	availability
L6, 200.0	3.68×3.13	84	S-Comet 6
L6, 250.0	3.68×3.91	88	O-Comet 6
L6, 250.0	3.68×3.91	92	O-Montego
V8, 302.0	4.00×3.00	137/138	S-Montego/Comet
V8, 351.0	4.00×3.50	159/161	S-Mntry exc Cus/wgn; O-Mntgo
V8, 351.0	4.00×3.50	168	S-Cougar
V8, 351.0	4.00×3.50	246	O-Montego cpes
V8, 351.0	4.00×3.50	264	O-Cougar (CJ option)
V8, 400.0	4.00×4.00	168/171	S-Mntry Cus/wgn; O-Mntgo
V8, 429.0	4.36×3.59	171	S-Marquis exc wgn; O-Marquis wgn
V8, 429.0	4.36×3.59	198/200	O-Monterey,Montego
V8, 460.0	4.36×3.85	202/267	O-Monterey, Marquis

1974

Comet (wb 109.9; 2d-103.0)		Wght	Price	Prod
30	sdn 4d	2,969	3,042	60,944
31	fstbk sdn 2d	2,861	3,008	64,751
Montego (wb 118.0; 2d-114.0)				
02	sdn 4d	4,062	3,360	5,674
03	hdtp cpe	3,977	3,327	7,645
04	MX sdn 4d	4,092	3,478	19,446
07	MX hdtp cpe	3,990	3,443	20,957
08	MX wgn 5d	4,426	4,083	4,085
10	MX Brougham sdn 4d	4,143	3,680	13,467
11	MX Brougham hdtp cpe	4,010	3,646	20,511
18	MX Villager wgn 5d	4,463	4,307	6,234
Cougar (wb 114.0)				
93	XR7 hdtp cpe	4,255	4,706	91,670
Monterey (wb 124.0; wgns-121.0)				
44	sdn 4d	4,559	4,367	6,185
46	hdtp cpe	4,506	4,410	2,003
72	wgn 5d 3S	4,966	4,853	1,669
72	wgn 5d 2S	4,916	4,731	
54	Custom sdn 4d	4,561	4,480	13,113
56	Custom hdtp cpe	4,504	4,523	4,510
Marquis (wb 124.0; wgns-121.0)				
63	sdn 4d	4,757	5,080	6,910
66	hdtp cpe	4,698	5,080	2,633

1973 Marquis Brougham hardtop coupe

		Wght	Price	Prod
68	hdtp sdn	4,753	5,080	784
74	wgn 5d 3S	5,023	5,082	1,111
74	wgn 5d 2S	4,973	4,960	
62	Brougham sdn 4d	4,833	5,519	24,477
64	Brougham hdtp cpe	4,762	5,519	10,207
67	Brougham hdtp sdn	4,853	5,519	4,189
76	Colony Park wgn 5d 3S	5,056	5,188	10,802
76	Colony Park wgn 5d 2S	5,006	5,066	

1974 Engines	bore×stroke	bhp	availability
L6, 200.0	3.68×3.13	84	S-Comet
L6, 250.0	3.68×3.91	91	O-Comet
V8, 302.0	4.00×3.00	140	S-Comet, Montego
V8, 351.0	4.00×3.50	162	S-Cougar; O-Montego
V8, 351.0	4.00×3.50	246/264	O-Montego, Cougar (CJ)
V8, 400.0	4.00×4.00	170	S-Mntry; O-Mntgo, Cgr
V8, 460.0	4.36×3.85	195	S-Marquis; O-Mntgo, Mntry
V8, 460.0	4.36×3.85	220	O-Cougar
V8, 460.0	4.36×3.85	275	O-Monterey, Marquis

1975

Bobcat (wb 94.5; wgn-94.8)		Wght	Price	Prod
20	Runabout htchbk sdn 3d	2,535	3,189	20,651
22	Villager wgn 3d	2,668	3,481	13,583
Comet (wb 109.9; 2d-103.0)				
30	sdn 4d	3,193	3,270	31,080
31	fstbk sdn 2d	3,070	3,236	22,768
Monarch (wb 109.9)				
34	sdn 4d	3,195	3,822	34,307
35	sdn 2d	3,142	3,764	29,151
37	Ghia sdn 4d	3,281	4,349	22,723
37	Grand sdn 4d	3,432	5,375	
38	Ghia sdn 2d	3,231	4,291	17,755
Montego (wb 118.0; 2d-114.0)				
02	sdn 4d	4,066	4,128	4,142
03	hdtp cpe	4,003	4,092	4,051
04	MX sdn 4d	4,111	4,328	16,033
07	MX hdtp cpe	4,030	4,304	13,666
08	MX wgn 5d	4,464	4,674	4,508
10	MX Brougham sdn 4d	4,130	4,498	8,235
11	MX Brougham hdtp cpe	4,054	4,453	8,791
18	MX Villager wgn 5d	4,522	4,909	5,754
Cougar (wb 114.0)				
93	XR7 hdtp cpe	4,108	5,218	62,987
Marquis (wb 124.0; wgns-121.0)				
63	sdn 4d	4,513	5,115	20,058
66	hdtp cpe	4,470	5,049	6,807
74	wgn 5d 3S	4,930	5,538	1,904
74	wgn 5d 2S	4,880	5,411	
62	Brougham sdn 4d	4,799	6,037	19,667
64	Brougham hdtp cpe	4,747	5,972	7,125
60	Grand Marquis sdn 4d	4,815	6,469	12,307
61	Grand Marquis hdtp cpe	4,762	6,403	4,945
76	Colony Park wgn 5d 2S	5,003	5,725	11,652
76	Colony Park wgn 5d 2S	4,953	5,598	

1975 Engines	bore×stroke	bhp	availability
L4, 140.0	3.78×3.13	83	S-Bobcat
V6, 170.8	3.66×2.70	97	O-Bobcat
L6, 200.0	3.68×3.13	75	S-Mnrch exc Ghia; O-Comet
L6, 250.0	3.68×3.91	72	S-Mnrch Ghia; O-Cmt, Mntry
V8, 302.0	4.00×3.00	122	S-Comet
V8, 302.0	4.00×3.00	129	S-Monarch
V8, 351.0	4.00×3.50	148/150	S-Cougar,Montego
V8, 351.0	4.00×3.50	154	O-Monarch

1978 Grand Marquis four-door sedan

	bore×stroke	bhp	availability
V8, 400.0	4.00×4.00	158	S-Marq exc wgn & Bham; O-Mntgo, Cgr
V8, 460.0	4.36×3.85	216	S-Grand Marq, wgn & Marq Brghm; O-Mntgo, Cgr, Marq

1976

Bobcat (wb 94.5; wgn-94.8)		Wght	Price	Prod
20	MPG Runabout htchbk sdn 3d	2,535	3,338	28,905
22	MPG Villager wgn 3d	2,668	3,643	18,731
Comet (wb 109.9; 2d-103.0)				
30	sdn 4d	3,058	3,465	21,006
31	fstbk sdn 2d	2,952	3,398	15,068
Monarch (wb 109.9)				
34	sdn 4d	3,195	3,864	56,351
35	sdn 2d	3,142	3,773	47,466
37	Ghia sdn 4d	3,218	4,422	27,056
37	Grand sdn 4d	3,432	5,740	
38	Ghia sdn 2d	3,231	4,331	14,950
Montego (wb 118.0; 2d-114.0)				
02	sdn 4d	4,133	4,343	3,403
03	hdtp cpe	4,057	4,299	2,287
04	MX sdn 4d	4,133	4,498	12,666
07	MX hdtp cpe	4,085	4,465	12,367
08	MX wgn 5d	4,451	4,778	5,012
10	MX Brougham sdn 4d	4,150	4,670	5,043
11	MX Brougham hdtp cpe	4,097	4,621	3,905
18	MX Villager wgn 5d	4,478	5,065	6,412
Cougar (wb 114.0)				
93	XR7 hdtp cpe	4,168	5,125	83,765
Marquis (wb 124.0; wgns-121.0)				
63	sdn 4d	4,460	5,063	28,212
66	hdtp cpe	4,436	5,063	10,450
62	Brougham sdn 4d	4,693	6,035	22,411
64	Brougham hdtp cpe	4,652	5,955	10,431
60	Grand Marquis sdn 4d	4,723	6,528	17,650
61	Grand Marquis hdtp cpe	4,679	6,439	9,207
74	wgn 5d 3S	4,824	5,401	2,493
74	wgn 5d 2S	4,796	5,275	
76	Colony Park wgn 5d 3S	4,906	5,716	15,114
76	Colony Park wgn 5d 2S	4,878	5,590	

1976 Engines	bore×stroke	bhp	availability
L4, 140.0	3.78×3.13	92	S-Bobcat
V6, 170.8	3.66×2.70	100	O-Bobcat
L6, 200.0	3.68×3.13	81	S-Mnrch exc Ghia; O-Comet
L6, 250.0	3.68×3.91	90	S-Mnrch Ghia; O-Cmt, Mnrch
V8, 302.0	4.00×3.00	134	S-Monarch
V8, 302.0	4.00×3.00	138	S-Comet
V8, 351.0	4.00×3.50	154	S-Montego exc wgn

	bore×stroke	bhp	availability
V8, 351.0	4.00×3.50	152	S-Mntgo wgn, Cgr; O-Mnrch
V8, 400.0	4.00×4.00	180	S-Marq; O-Mntgo, Cgr
V8, 460.0	4.36×3.85	202	O-Mntgo, Cgr, Marquis

1977

Bobcat (wb 94.5; wgn-94.8)		Wght	Price	Prod
20	Runabout htchbk sdn 3d	2,369	3,438	18,405*
22	wgn 3d	2,505	3,629	13,047*
22	Villager wgn 3d	—	3,771	
Comet (wb 109.9; 2d-103.0)				
30	sdn 4d	3,065	3,617	12,436
31	fstbk sdn 2d	2,960	3,544	9,109
Monarch (wb 109.9)				
34	sdn 4d	3,250	4,154	55,952
35	sdn 2d	3,200	4,076	44,509
37	Ghia sdn 4d	3,382	4,722	16,545
38	Ghia sdn 2d	3,321	4,643	11,051
Cougar (wb 118.0; 2d-114.0)				
90	sdn 4d	3,893	4,832	15,256
91	hdtp cpe	3,811	4,700	15,910
92	wgn 5d	4,434	5,104	4,951
93	XR7 hdtp cpe	3,909	5,274	124,799
94	Brougham sdn 4d	3,946	5,230	16,946
95	Brougham hdtp cpe	3,852	4,990	8,392
96	Villager wgn 5d	4,482	5,363	8,569
Marquis (wb 124.0; wgns-121.0)				
63	sdn 4d	4,326	5,496	36,103
66	hdtp cpe	4,293	5,496	13,242
62	Brougham sdn 4d	4,408	6,324	29,411
64	Brougham hdtp cpe	4,350	6,229	12,237
60	Grand Marquis hdtp sdn	4,572	6,975	31,231
61	Grand Marquis hdtp cpe	4,516	6,880	13,445
74	wgn 5d 3S	4,678	5,794	20,363
74	wgn 5d 2S	4,628	5,631	

1977 Engines	bore×stroke	bhp	availability
L4, 140.0	3.78×3.13	89	S-Bobcat
V6, 170.8	3.66×2.70	93	O-Bobcat
L6, 200.0	3.68×3.13	96	S-Monarch exc Ghia; O-Cmt
L6, 250.0	3.68×3.91	98	S-Mnrch Ghia; O-Mnrch, Cmt
V8, 302.0	4.00×3.00	122	S-Monarch
V8, 302.0	4.00×3.00	130	S-Cougar exc wgn
V8, 302.0	4.00×3.00	137	S-Comet
V8, 351.0	4.00×3.50	149	O-Cougar exc wgn
V8, 351.0	4.00×3.50	161	S-Cgr wgn; O-Monarch
V8, 400.0	4.00×4.00	173	S-Marq exc Grand; O-Cgr
V8, 460.0	4.36×3.85	197	S-Grand Marquis; O-Marquis

*includes some cars built as 1978 models but sold as 1977 models.

1978

Bobcat (wb 94.5; wgn-94.8)		Wght	Price	Prod
20	Runabout htchbk sdn 3d	2,389	3,830	23,428
22	wgn 3d	2,532	4,112	8,840
22	Villager wgn 3d	—	4,244	
Zephyr (wb 105.5)				
31	sdn 2d L4/V6	2,594	3,777	27,673
32	sdn 4d L4/V6	2,636	3,863	47,334
35	Z-7 spt cpe L4/V6	2,630	4,154	44,569
36	wgn 5d L4/V6	2,744	4,216	32,596
Monarch (wb 109.9)				
33	sdn 2d L6/V8	3,094	4,366	38,939
34	sdn 4d L6/V8	3,138	4,457	52,775
Cougar (wb 118.0; 2d-114.0)				
91	hdtp cpe	3,761	5,052	21,398
92	sdn 4d	3,848	5,179	25,364
93	XR7 hdtp cpe	3,865	5,720	166,508
Marquis (wb 124.0; wgns-121.0)				
61	hdtp cpe	4,296	5,897	27,793
62	sdn 4d	4,328	5,949	11,176
63	Brougham hdtp cpe	4,317	6,525	10,368
64	Brougham sdn 4d	4,346	6,638	26,030
65	Grand Marquis hdtp cpe	4,342	7,290	15,624
66	Grand Marquis sdn 4d	4,414	7,399	37,753

1978 Cougar XR 7 two-door coupe

			Wght	Price	Prod
74	wgn 5d 3S		4,606	6,292	16,883
74	wgn 5d 2S		4,578	6,106	

1978 Engines	bore×stroke	bhp	availability
L4, 140.0	3.78×3.13	88	S-Bobcat, Zephyr
V6, 170.6	3.66×2.70	90	O-Bobcat
L6, 200.0	3.68×3.13	85	O-Zephyr
L6, 250.0	3.68×3.91	97	S-Monarch
V8, 302.0	4.00×3.00	134	S-Cougar
V8, 302.0	4.00×3.00	139	S-Monarch, O-Zephyr
V8, 351.0	4.00×3.50	144/145	O-Cougar,S-Marquis
V8, 351.0	4.00×3.50	152	O-Cougar
V8, 400.0	4.00×4.00	160	O-Marquis
V8, 400.0	4.00×4.00	166	O-Cougar
V8, 460.0	4.36×3.85	202	O-Marquis

1978 Bobcat Villager station wagon

1979

Bobcat (wb 94.5; wgn-94.8)		Wght	Price	Prod
20	Runabout htchbk sdn 3d	2,424	4,104	35,667
22	wgn 3d	2,565	4,410	9,119
22	Villager wgn 3d	—	4,523	
Capri (wb 100.4)				
14	htchbk cpe 3d	2,548	4,872	92,432
16	Ghia htchbk cpe 3d	2,645	5,237	17,712
Zephyr (wb 105.5)				
31	sdn 2d	2,518	4,253	15,920
32	sdn 4d	2,582	4,370	41,316
35	Z-7 spt cpe	2,553	4,504	42,923
36	wgn 5d	2,683	4,647	25,218
Monarch (wb 109.9)				
33	sdn 2d	3,110	4,735	28,285
34	sdn 4d L6/V8	3,151	4,841	47,594
Cougar (wb 118.0; 2d 114.0)				
91	hdtp cpe	3,792	5,379	2,831
92	sdn 4d	3,843	5,524	5,605
93	XR7 hdtp cpe	3,883	6,430	163,716

Marquis (wb 114.3)		Wght	Price	Prod
61	hdtp cpe	3,507	6,292	10,035
62	sdn 4d	3,557	6,387	32,289
63	Brougham hdtp cpe	3,540	6,986	10,627
64	Brougham sdn 4d	3,605	7,176	24,682
65	Grand Marquis hdtp cpe	3,592	7,721	11,066
66	Grand Marquis sdn 4d	3,659	7,909	32,349
74	wgn 5d 3S	3,825	6,894	5,994
74	wgn 5d 2S	3,775	6,701	
76	Colony Park wgn 5d 3S	3,850	7,688	13,758
76	Colony Park wgn 5d 2S	3,800	7,495	

1979 Engines	bore×stroke	bhp	availability
L4, 140.0	3.78×3.13	88	S-Bobcat, Zephyr, Capri
L4T, 140.0	3.78×3.13	140	O-Capri
V6, 170.6	3.66×2.70	102	O-Bobcat
V6, 170.6	3.66×2.70	109	O-Capri
L6, 200.0	3.68×3.13	85	O-Zephyr
L6, 250.0	3.68×3.91	97	S-Monarch
V8, 302.0	4.00×3.00	129/133	S-Marquis/Cougar

1979 Grand Marquis four-door sedan

	bore×stroke	bhp	availability
V8, 302.0	4.00×3.00	137	S-Monarch
V8, 302.0	4.00×3.00	140	O-Capri, Zephyr
V8, 351.0	4.00×3.50	135	S-Cougar XR7
V8, 351.0	4.00×3.50	138	O-Marquis
V8, 351.0	4.00×3.50	151	O-Cougar

1980

Bobcat (wb 94.5; wgn-94.8)		Wght	Price	Prod
20	Runabout htchbk sdn 3d	2,445	4,764	28,103
22	wgn 3d	2,573	5,070	5,547
22	Villager wgn 3d	—	5,183	
Capri (wb 100.4)				
14	htchbk cpe 3d	2,566	5,672	72,009
16	Ghia htchbk cpe 3d	2,651	5,968	7,975
Zephyr (wb 105.5)				
31	sdn 2d	2,607	5,041	10,977
32	sdn 4d	2,649	5,158	40,399
35	Z-7 spt cpe	2,646	5,335	19,486
36	wgn 5d	2,771	5,364	20,341
Monarch (wb 109.9)				
33	sdn 2d L6/V8	3,126	5,628	8,772
34	sdn 4d L6/V8	3,180	5,751	21,746
Cougar (wb 108.4)				
93	XR7 cpe	3,191	7,045	58,028
Marquis (wb 114.3)				
61	sdn 2d	3,450	7,075	2,521
62	sdn 4d	3,488	7,185	13,018
63	Brougham sdn 2d	3,476	7,860	2,353
64	Brougham sdn 4d	3,528	8,057	8,819
65	Grand Marquis sdn 2d	3,504	8,631	3,434
66	Grand Marquis sdn 4d	3,519	8,824	15,995
74	wgn 5d 3S	3,747	7,782	2,407
74	wgn 5d 2S	3,697	7,583	
76	Colony Park wgn 5d 3S	3,793	8,676	5,781
76	Colony Park wgn 5d 2S	3,743	8,477	

1980 Engines	bore×stroke	bhp	availability
L4, 140.0	3.78×3.13	88	S-Bobcat, Zphyr, Capri
L4T, 140.0	3.78×3.13	140	O-Capri, Zephyr*
L6, 200.0	3.68×3.13	91	O-Capri, Zephyr
L6, 250.0	3.68×3.91	90	S-Monarch
V8, 255.0	3.68×3.00	115	S-Cougar
V8, 255.0	3.68×3.00	118/119	O-Capri/Zephyr, Monarch
V8, 302.0	4.00×3.00	130/131	S-Marquis/O-Cougar
V8, 302.0	4.00×3.00	134	O-Monarch
V8, 351.0	4.00×3.50	140	O-Marquis

*withdrawn for Zephyr after announcement; production doubtful

1981

Lynx (wb 94.2)		Wght	Price	Prod
63	htchbk sdn 3d	—	5,603	
63	L htchbk sdn 3d	1,935	5,665	
63/60Z	GL htchbk sdn 3d	1,957	5,903	72,786
63/602	GS htchbk sdn 3d	1,996	6,642	
63/603	LS htchbk sdn 3d	2,004	7,127	
63/936	RS htchbk sdn 3d	1,980	6,223	
65	liftbk 4d	—	5,931	
65	L liftbk 4d	2,059	6,070	
65/60Z	GL liftbk 4d	2,074	6,235	39,192
65/602	GS liftbk 4d	2,114	6,914	
65/936	RS liftbk 4d	2,098	6,563	
Capri (wb 100.4)				
67	htchbk cpe 3d	2,589	6,685	51,786
68	GS htchbk cpe 3d	2,636	6,867	7,160
Zephyr (wb 105.5)				
70	sdn 2d	2,558	6,103	5,814
—	S sdn 2d	—	5,769	—
71	sdn 4d	2,623	6,222	34,334
73	wgn 5d	2,698	6,458	16,283
72	Z-7 cpe	2,610	6,252	10,078
Cougar (wb 105.5; XR7 108.4)				
76	sdn 2d L4/V6	2,727	6,535	10,793
77	sdn 4d L4/V6	2,771	6,694	42,860

1981 Cougar GS two-door sedan

1981 Grand Marquis four-door sedan

		Wght	Price	Prod
90	XR7 cpe L6/V8	3,068	7,799	37,275
Marquis (wb 114.3)				
81	sdn 4d	3,493	7,811	10,392
82	Brougham sdn 2d	3,513	8,601	2,942
83	Brougham sdn 4d	3,564	8,800	11,744
84	Grand Marquis sdn 2d	3,533	9,228	4,268
85	Grand Marquis sdn 4d	3,564	9,459	23,780
87	wgn 5d 2S	3,745	8,309	2,219
88	Colony Park wgn 5d 2S	3,800	9,304	6,293

1981 Engines	bore × stroke	bhp	availability
L4, 97.6	3.15 × 3.13	65	S-Lynx
L4, 140.0	3.78 × 3.13	88	S-Capri, Zephyr, Cougar
L4T, 140.0	3.78 × 3.13	—	O-Capri
L6, 200.0	3.68 × 3.13	88/95	S-XR7; O-Capri, Zphyr, Cgr
V8, 255.0	3.68 × 3.00	115/120	S-Marq; O-Capri, Zphyr, Cgr
V8, 302.0	4.00 × 3.00	130	O-Cougar XR7, Marquis
8, 351.0	4.00 × 3.50	145	O-Marquis
V8, 351.0	4.00 × 3.50	165	S-Marquis (police only)

1982

Lynx (wb 94.2)		Wght	Price	Prod
63	htchbk sdn 3d	1,924	5,502	54,611
63	L htchbk sdn 3d	1,927	6,159	
63/60Z	GL htchbk sdn 3d	1,950	6,471	
63/602	GS htchbk sdn 3d	1,987	7,257	
63/603	LS htchbk sdn 3d	1,952	7,762	
63/936	RS htchbk sdn 3d	1,961	6,790	
64	htchbk sdn 5d	1,984	5,709	40,713
64	L htchbk sdn 5d	1,989	6,376	
64/60Z	GL htchbk sdn 5d	2,012	6,688	
64/602	GS htchbk sdn 5d	2,049	7,474	
64/603	LS htchbk sdn 5d	2,014	7,978	
65	L wgn 5d	2,028	6,581	23,835
65/60Z	GL wgn 5d	2,049	6,899	
65/602	GS wgn 5d	2,087	7,594	
65/603	LS wgn 5d	2,052	8,099	
LN7 (wb 94.2)				
61	htchbk cpe 3d	2,059	7,787	35,147

Capri (wb 100.4)		Wght	Price	Prod
67	htchbk cpe 3d	2,554	6,711	36,134
67	L htchbk cpe 3d	2,627	7,245	
67	Black Magic cpe 3d	—	7,946	
67	RS htchbk cpe 3d V8	—	8,107	
68	GS htchbk cpe 3d	2,637	7,432	
Zephyr (wb 105.5)				
71	sdn 4d	2,690	6,411	31,698
71/602	GS sdn 4d	2,703	6,734	
72 Z-7	spt cpe	2,687	6,309	7,394
72/602	Z-7 GS spt cpe	2,697	6,670	
Cougar (wb 105.5)				
76	GS sdn 2d L4/V6	2,939	7,983	6,984
76	LS sdn 2d L4/V6	2,974	8,415	
77	GS sdn 4d L4/V6	2,981	8,158	30,672
77	LS sdn 4d L4/V6	3,023	8,587	
78	GS wgn 5d L4/V6	3,114	8,216	19,294
Cougar XR-7 (wb 108.4)				
90	GS cpe L6/V8	3,220	9,094	16,867
90/60H	LS cpe L6/V8	3,229	9,606	

1982 Lynx hatchback sedan

Marquis (wb 114.3)		Wght	Price	Prod
81	sdn 4d	3,734	8,674	9,454
82	Brougham sdn 2d	3,693	9,490	2,833
83	Brougham sdn 4d	3,776	9,767	15,312
84	Grand Marquis sdn 2d	3,724	10,188	6,149
85	Grand Marquis sdn 4d	3,809	10,456	32,918
87	wgn 5d 2S	3,880	9,198	2,487
88	Colony Park wgn 5d 2S	3,890	10,252	8,004

1982 Engines	bore × stroke	bhp	availability
L4, 97.6	3.15 × 3.13	70	S-Lynx
L4, 140.0	3.78 × 3.13	88	S-Capri, Zephyr
L6, 200.0	3.68 × 3.13	87	S-Cgr, XR7; O-Capri, Zphyr
V6, 232.0	3.80 × 3.40	112	O-Cougar, XR7
V8, 255.0	3.68 × 3.00	111-122	S-Marquis; O-Capri, XR7
V8, 302.0	4.00 × 3.00	132	S-Marq B'ham, Grand Marquis 4d; O-Marquis
V8, 302.0	4.00 × 3.00	157	O-Capri
V8, 351.0	4.00 × 3.50	165	S-Marquis (police only)

1983

Lynx (wb 94.2)		Wght	Price	Prod
54	L htchbk sdn 3d	1,922	5,751	
55	GS htchbk sdn 3d	1,948	6,476	40,142
58	LS htchbk sdn 3d	1,950	7,529	
57	RS htchbk sdn 3d	1,997	7,370	
55	L htchbk sdn 5d	1,984	5,958	
66	GS htchbk sdn 5d	2,010	6,693	28,461
68	LS htchbk sdn 5d	2,012	7,746	
65/934	LTS htchbk sdn 5d	1,920	7,334	
60	L wgn 5d	2,026	6,166	
61	GS wgn 5d	2,050	6,872	19,192
63	LS wgn 5d	2,050	7,909	
LN7 (wb 94.2)				
51/A80	htchbk cpe 3d	2,076	7,398	
51/A8C	RS htchbk cpe 3d	—	8,765	4,528
51/A8A	Sport htchbk cpe 3d	—	8,084	
51/ABB	Grand Sport cpe 3d	—	8,465	
Capri (wb 100.4)				
79/41P	htchbk cpe 3d	2,643	7,156	
79	L htchbk cpe 3d	2,669	7,711	
79	Black Magic cpe 3d	2,651	8,629	25,376
79	Crimson Cat cpe 3d	—	8,525	
79/602	GS htchbk cpe 3d	—	7,914	
79	RS htchbk cpe 3d	—	9,241	
Cougar (wb 104.0)				
92	cpe 2d	2,997	9,521	75,743
92/603	LS cpe 2d	2,911	10,850	

Zephyr (wb 105.5)		Wght	Price	Prod
86	sdn 4d	2,690	6,545	21,732
86/602	GS sdn 4d	2,756	7,311	
87	Z-7 spt cpe	2,687	6,442	3,471
87/602	Z-7 GS spt cpe	2,750	7,247	
Marquis (wb 105.5)				
89	sdn 4d	2,778	7,893	50,169
89	Brougham sdn 4d	—	8,202	
90	wgn 5d L6	2,978	8,693	17,189
90	Brougham wgn 5d L6	—	8,974	
Grand Marquis (wb 114.3)				
93	sdn 2d	3,607	10,654	11,117
93/60H	LS sdn 2d	3,607	11,209	
95	sdn 4d	3,761	10,718	72,207
95/60H	LS sdn 4d	3,761	11,273	
94	Colony Park wgn 5d 2S	3,788	10,896	12,394

1983 Engines	bore × stroke	bhp	availability
L4, 97.6	3.15 × 3.13	70	S-Lynx, LN7
L4, 97.6	3.15 × 3.13	80	O-Lynx, LN7
L4, 97.6	3.15 × 3.13	88	O-Lynx, LN7
L4, 140.0	3.78 × 3.13	90	S-Capri, Zephyr, Marquis
L4T, 140.0	3.78 × 3.13	142	O-Capri
L4P, 140.0	3.78 × 3.13	—	O-Marquis (propane)
L6, 200.0	3.68 × 3.13	92	O-Zephyr, Marquis
V6, 232.0	3.80 × 3.40	110-112	S-Cougar; O-Capri, Marq
V8, 302.0	4.00 × 3.00	130	S-Grand Marq; O-Cougar
V8, 302.0	4.00 × 3.00	145	O-Grand Marquis
V8, 302.0	4.00 × 3.00	175	O-Capri
V8, 351.0	4.00 × 3.50	165	S-Grand Marq (police only)

1984

Lynx (wb 94.2)		Wght	Price	Prod
54	htchbk sdn 3d	2,176	5,758	
54	L htchbk sdn 3d	2,087	6,019	
55	GS htchbk sdn 3d	2,128	6,495	38,208
57	RS htchbk sdn 3d	2,177	7,641	
57	Turbo RS htchbk sdn 3d	1,997	8,728	
65	htchbk sdn 5d	2,241	5,965	
65	L htchbk sdn 5d	2,152	6,233	21,090
66	GS htchbk sdn 5d	2,193	6,709	
68/934	LTS htchbk sdn 5d	—	7,879	
60	L wgn 5d	2,181	6,448	16,142
61	GS wgn 5d	2,220	6,887	
Topaz (wb 99.9)				
72	GS sdn 2d	2,357	7,477	32,749
73	LS sdn 2d	—	7,880	
75	GS sdn 4d	2,415	7,477	96,505
76	LS sdn 4d	2,447	7,880	

1983 LN7 three-door hatchback coupe

1984 Topaz two-door sedan

Capri (wb 100.5)		Wght	Price	Prod
79	GS htchbk cpe 3d L4/V6	2,827	7,758	20,642
79	RS htchbk cpe 3d V8	—	9,638	
79	RS Turbo htchbk cpe 3d L4T	2,775	9,822	
Cougar (wb 104.0)				
92	cpe 2d	3,151	9,978	131,190
92/603	LS cpe 2d	3,180	11,265	
92/934	XR7 cpe 2d L4T	3,053	13,065	
Marquis (wb 105.6)				
89	sdn 4d	2,966	8,727	91,808
89	Brougham sdn 4d	—	9,030	
90	wgn 5d V6	3,128	9,224	16,004
90	Brougham wgn 5d V6	—	9,498	
Grand Marquis (wb 114.3)				
93	sdn 2d	3,734	11,576	13,657
93/60H	LS sdn 2d	—	12,131	
95	sdn 4d	3,780	11,640	117,739
95/60H	LS sdn 4d	—	12,195	
94	Colony Park wgn 5d 2S	3,981	11,816	17,421

1984 Engines	bore × stroke	bhp	availability
L4, 97.6	3.15 × 3.13	70	S-Lynx
L4, 97.6	3.15 × 3.13	80	O-Lynx
L4, 97.6	3.15 × 3.13	88	S-Lynx RS; O-Lynx
L4D, 121.0	3.39 × 3.39	52	O-Lynx, Topaz
L4, 140.0	3.70 × 3.30	84	S-Topaz
L4, 140.0	3.78 × 3.13	88	S-Capri GS, Marquis
L4T, 140.0	3.78 × 3.13	145	S-Cougar XR7
L4T, 140.0	3.78 × 3.13	175	O-Capri
L4P, 140.0	3.78 × 3.13	—	O-Marquis (propane)
V6, 232.0	3.80 × 3.40	120	S-Cougar, Marq wgn; O-Capri, Marq
V8, 302.0	4.00 × 3.00	140	S-Grand Marq; O-Cougar
V8, 302.0	4.00 × 3.00	155	O-Grand Marquis
V8, 302.0	4.00 × 3.00	165/175	O-Capri
V8, 351.0	4.00 × 3.50	180	S-Grand Marq (police only)

1985

Lynx (wb 94.2)		Wght	Price	Prod
54/41P	htchbk sdn 3d	1,980	5,750	26,653*
54	L htchbk sdn 3d	2,000	6,170	
55	GS htchbk sdn 3d	2,070	6,707	
65	L htchbk sdn 5d	2,060	6,384	11,658*
66	GS htchbk sdn 5d	2,125	6,921	
60	L wgn 5d	2,080	6,508	7,948*
61	GS wgn 5d	2,155	6,973	

*Estimated totals for First Series.

Lynx Second Series 1985.5 (wb 94.2)		Wght	Price	Prod
51	htchbk sdn 3d	2,158	5,986	20,515
51	L htchbk sdn 3d	—	6,272	
52	GS htchbk sdn 3d	—	6,962	
63	L htchbk sdn 5d	2,206	6,486	11,297
64	GS htchbk sdn 5d	—	7,176	
58	L wgn 5d	—	6,767	6,721
59	GS wgn 5d	—	7,457	
Topaz (wb 99.9)				
72	GS sdn 2d	2,395	7,767	18,990
73	LS sdn 2d	2,445	8,931	
75	GS sdn 4d	2,450	7,767	82,366
76	LS sdn 4d	2,500	8,980	
Capri (wb 100.5)				
79	GS htchbk cpe 3d L4/V6	2,885	7,944	18,657
79	RS/5.0L htchbk cpe 3d V8	3,290	10,223	
Cougar (wb 104.0)				
92	cpe 2d	3,010	10,650	117,274
92/603	LS cpe 2d	3,040	11,850	
92/934	XR7 cpe 2d L4T	2,978	13,599	
Marquis (wb 105.6)				
89	sdn 4d	2,915	8,996	91,465
89/60H	Brougham sdn 4d	2,923	9,323	
90	wgn 5d V6	2,993	9,506	12,733
90/60H	Brougham wgn 5d V6	3,000	9,805	
Grand Marquis (wb 114.3)				
93	sdn 2d	3,619	12,240	10,900
93/60H	LS sdn 2d	—	12,789	
95	sdn 4d	3,657	12,305	136,239
95/60H	LS sdn 4d	—	12,854	
94	Colony Park wgn 5d 2S	3,828	12,511	14,119

1985 Engines	bore × stroke	bhp	availability
L4, 97.6	3.15 × 3.13	70	S-Lynx
L4, 97.6	3.15 × 3.13	80	S-Lynx GS; O-Lynx
L4, 113.0	3.23 × 3.46	86	S-late Lynx
L4D, 121.0	3.39 × 3.39	52	O-Lynx, Topaz
L4, 140.0	3.70 × 3.30	86	S-Topaz
L4, 140.0	3.70 × 3.30	100	O-Topaz
L4, 140.0	3.78 × 3.13	88	S-Capri, Marquis

1985 Cougar XR7 two-door coupe

1986 Sable LS four-door sedan

1987 Grand Marquis LS four-door sedan

	bore×stroke	bhp	availability
L4T, 140.0	3.78×3.13	155	S-Cougar XR7
V6, 232.0	3.80×3.40	120	S-Cougar; O-Capri, Marq
V8, 302.0	4.00×3.00	140	S-Grand Marq; O-Cougar
V8, 302.0	4.00×3.00	155	O-Grand Marquis
V8, 302.0	4.00×3.00	180	O-Capri
V8, 302.0	4.00×3.00	210	S-Capri RS; O-Capri GS

1986

Lynx (wb 94.2)		Wght	Price	Prod
51	htchbk sdn 3d	2,156	6,182	45,880
51	L htchbk sdn 3d	2,158	6,472	
52	GS htchbk sdn 3d	2,246	7,162	
53	XR3 htchbk sdn 3d	2,374	8,193	
63	L htchbk sdn 5d	2,206	6,686	26,512
64	GS htchbk sdn 5d	2,289	7,376	
58	L wgn 5d	2,238	6,967	13,580
59	GS wgn 5d	2,312	7,657	
Topaz (wb 99.9)				
72	GS sdn 2d	2,377	8,085	15,757
73	LS sdn 2d	2,464	9,224	
75	GS sdn 4d	2,440	8,235	62,640
76	LS sdn 4d	2,531	9,494	
Capri (wb 100.5)				
79	GS htchbk cpe 3d L4/V6	2,877	8,331	20,869
79	5.0L htchbk cpe 3d V8	3,183	10,950	
Cougar (wb 104.0)				
92	GS cpe 2d	3,178	11,421	135,909
92	LS cpe 2d	3,214	12,757	
92	XR7 cpe 2d L4T	3,158	14,377	
Marquis (wb 105.6)				
89	sdn 4d	2,969	9,660	24,121
89/60H	Brougham sdn 4d	2,994	10,048	
90	wgn 5d V6	3,112	10,254	4,461
90/60H	Brougham wgn 5d V6	3,139	10,613	
Sable (wb 106.0)				
87	GS sdn 4d L4/V6	2,983	10,700	71,707
87	LS sdn 4d V6	3,135	12,574	
88	GS wgn 5d V6	3,210	11,776	23,931
88	LS wgn 5d V6	3,225	13,068	

Grand Marquis (wb 114.3)		Wght	Price	Prod
93	sdn 2d	3,782	13,480	5,610
93/60H	LS sdn 2d	3,782	13,929	
95	sdn 4d	3,818	13,504	93,919
95/60H	LS sdn 4d	3,818	13,952	
94	Colony Park wgn 5d 2S	3,993	13,724	9,891

1986 Engines	bore×stroke	bhp	availability
L4, 113.5	3.23×3.46	86	S-Lynx
L4, 113.5	3.23×3.46	108	S-Lynx XR3; O-Lynx
L4D, 121.0	3.39×3.39	52	O-Lynx, Topaz
L4, 140.0	3.70×3.30	86	S-Topaz
L4, 140.0	3.70×3.30	100	O-Topaz
L4, 140.0	3.78×3.13	88	S-Capri, Marquis
L4T, 140.0	3.78×3.13	145/155	S-Cougar XR7
L4, 153.0	3.70×3.60	88	S-late Sable GS sdn
V6, 182.0	3.50×3.15	140	S-Sable LS/wgn; O-Sable
V6, 232.0	3.80×3.40	120	S-Cougar, Marq wgn; O-Capri,Marquis
V8, 302.0	4.00×3.00	150	S-Grand Marq; O-Cougar
V8, 302.0	4.00×3.00	200	S-Capri 5.0L

1987

Lynx (wb 94.2)		Wght	Price	Prod
20	L htchbk sdn 3d	2,183	6,569	20,930
21	GS htchbk sdn 3d	2,202	6,951	
23	XR3 htchbk sdn 3d	2,396	8,808	
25	GS htchbk sdn 5d	2,258	7,172	12,124
28	GS wgn 5d	2,277	7,462	6,985
Topaz (wb 99.9)				
31	GS sdn 2d	2,503	8,562	19,738
33	GS spt sdn 2d	2,565	9,308	
36	GS sdn 4d	2,557	8,716	78,692
38	GS spt sdn 4d	2,621	9,463	
76	LS sdn 4d	2,631	10,213	
Cougar (wb 104.2)				
60	LS cpe 2d	3,202	13,595	104,526
62	XR7 cpe 2d V8	3,355	15,832	
Sable (wb 106.0)				
50	GS sdn 4d V6	3,054	12,240	91,001
53	LS sdn 4d V6	3,138	14,522	

		Wght	Price	Prod
55	GS wgn 5d V6	3,228	12,793	30,312
58	LS wgn 5d V6	3,311	15,054	
Grand Marquis (wb 114.3)				
72	LS sdn 2d	3,764	15,323	4,904
74	GS sdn 4d	3,794	15,198	115,599
75	LS sdn 4d	3,803	15,672	
78	Colony Park GS wgn 5d 2S	3,975	15,462	10,691
79	Colony Park LS wgn 5d 2S	4,015	16,010	

1987 Engines	bore × stroke	bhp	availability
L4, 113.5	3.23 × 3.46	90	S-Lynx
L4, 113.5	3.23 × 3.46	115	S-Lynx XR3
L4D, 121.0	3.39 × 3.39	58	O-Lynx
L4, 140.0	3.70 × 3.30	86	S-Topaz
L4, 140.0	3.70 × 3.30	94	O-Topaz
V6, 182.0	3.50 × 3.15	140	S-Sable
V6, 232.0	3.80 × 3.40	120	S-Cougar
V8, 302.0	4.00 × 3.00	150/155	S-XR7, Grand Marq; O-Cougar

1988

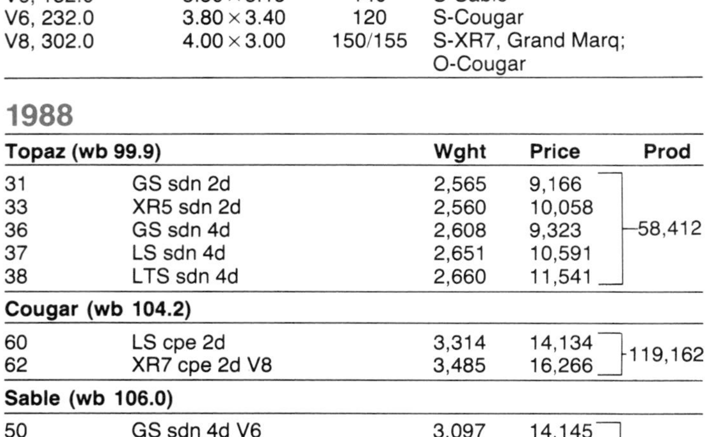

Topaz (wb 99.9)		Wght	Price	Prod
31	GS sdn 2d	2,565	9,166	58,412
33	XR5 sdn 2d	2,560	10,058	
36	GS sdn 4d	2,608	9,323	
37	LS sdn 4d	2,651	10,591	
38	LTS sdn 4d	2,660	11,541	
Cougar (wb 104.2)				
60	LS cpe 2d	3,314	14,134	119,162
62	XR7 cpe 2d V8	3,485	16,266	
Sable (wb 106.0)				
50	GS sdn 4d V6	3,097	14,145	121,285
53	LS sdn 4d V6	3,165	15,138	
55	GS wgn 5d V6	3,208	14,665	
58	LS wgn 5d V6	3,268	15,683	

1988 Topaz GS four-door sedan

Grand Marquis (wb 114.3)		Wght	Price	Prod
74	GS sdn 4d	3,828	16,100	
75	LS sdn 4d	3,839	16,612	
78	Colony Park GS wgn 5d 2S	4,019	16,341	
79	Colony Park LS wgn 5d 2S	4,025	16,926	

1988X Engines	bore × stroke	bhp	availability
L4, 140.0	3.70 × 3.30	98/100	S-Topaz
V6, 182.0	3.50 × 3.15	140	S-Sable
V6, 232.0	3.80 × 3.40	140	S-Cougar; O-Sable
V8, 302.0	4.00 × 3.00	150/155	S-XR7, Grand Marq; O-Cougar

1989

Topaz (wb 99.9)		Wght	Price	Prod
31	GS sdn 2d	2,567	9,577	
33	XR5 sdn 2d	2,544	10,498	

1989 Cougar XR7 two-door coupe

		Wght	Price	Prod
36	GS sdn 4d	2,606	9,734	
37	LS sdn 4d	2,647	11,030	
38	LTS sdn 4d	2,706	11,980	
Sable (wb 106.0)				
50	GS sdn 4d V6	3,054	14,101	
53	LS sdn 4d V6	3,168	15,094	
55	GS wgn 5d V6	3,228	14,804	
58	LS wgn 5d V6	3,252	15,872	
Cougar (wb 113.0)				
60	LS cpe	3,553	—	
60	XR7 cpe	3,710	—	
Grand Marquis (wb 114.3)				
74	GS sdn 4d	3,763	16,701	
75	LS sdn 4d	3,774	17,213	
	50th anniversary sdn 4d	3,887	—	
78	Colony Park GS wgn 5d 2S	3,995	17,338	
79	Colony Park LS wgn 5d 2S	3,913	17,922	

1989 Engines	bore × stroke	bhp	availability
L4, 140.0	3.70 × 3.30	98/100	S-Topaz
V6, 182.0	3.50 × 3.15	140	S-Sable
V6, 232.0	3.80 × 3.40	140	S-Cougar; O-Sable
V6S/C, 232.0	3.80 × 3.40	210	S-Cougar XR7 (superchgd)
V8, 302.0	4.00 × 3.00	150	S-Grand Marquis

Note: 1981-89 Colony Park wagons could have optional dual-facing rear seats.
Base prices of 1984-87 Lynx and Tempo models with diesel engines were higher than figures shown above.

NASH

1939

3910 Lafayette (wb 117.0)—37,302 built*		Wght	Price	Prod
3910	Deluxe sdn 4d T/B	3,350	885	—
3911	Deluxe All-Purpose cab 5P	3,340	950	—
3912	Deluxe All-Purpose cpe 5P	3,260	860	—
3913	Deluxe sdn 2d	3,320	855	—
3914	Deluxe bus cpe 3P	3,270	825	—
3915	Special bus cpe 3P	3,200	770	—
3916	Special sdn 2d	3,250	810	—
3917	Special sdn 4d	3,290	840	—
3918	Deluxe sdn 4d	3,350	855	—
3919	Special sdn 4d T/B	3,285	840	—
3920 Ambassador Six (wb 121.0)—8,500 built*				
3920	sdn 4d T/B	3,470	985	—
3921	All-Purpose cab 5P	3,430	1,050	—
3922	All-Purpose cpe 5P	3,360	960	—
3923	sdn 2d	3,420	955	—
3925	bus cpe 3P	3,370	925	—
3928	sdn 4d	3,450	985	—
3980 Ambassador Eight (wb 125.0)—17,052 built*				
3980	sdn 4d T/B	3,820	1,235	—
3981	All-Purpose cab 5P	3,740	1,295	—
3982	All-Purpose cpe 5P	3,710	1,210	—
3983	sdn 2d	3,770	1,205	—
3985	bus cpe 3P	3,720	1,175	—
3988	sdn 4d	3,800	1,235	—

1939 Engines	bore×stroke	bhp	availability
L6, 234.8	3.38×4.38	99	S-3910
L6, 234.8	3.38×4.38	105	S-3920
L8, 260.8	3.13×4.25	115	S-3980 (Twin Ign.)

*Maximum possible production, derived from published serial number spans.

1939 Ambassador Six business coupe

1940—62,131 built

Lafayette (wb 117.0)		Wght	Price	Prod
4010	T/B sdn 4d	3,280	875	—
4011	All-Purpose cabriolet	3,310	975	—
4012	All-Purpose cpe	3,190	850	—
4013	fstbk sdn 2d	3,235	845	—
4014	bus cpe	3,190	795	—
4018	fstbk sdn 4d	3,275	875	—
Ambassador Six (wb 121.0)				
4020	T/B sdn 4d	3,385	985	—
4021	All-Purpose cabriolet	3,410	1,085	—
4022	All-Purpose cpe	3,295	960	—
4023	fstbk sdn 2d	3,350	955	—
4025	bus cpe	3,290	925	—
4028	fstbk sdn 4d	3,380	985	—
Ambassador Eight (wb 125.0)				
4080	T/B sdn 4d	3,660	1,195	—
4081	All-Purpose cabriolet	3,640	1,295	—
4082	All-Purpose cpe	3,575	1,170	—
4083	fstbk sdn 2d	3,260	1,165	—
4085	bus cpe	3,555	1,135	—
4088	fstbk sdn 4d	3,655	1,195	—

1940 Engines	bore × stroke	bhp	availability
L6, 234.8	3.38 × 4.38	99	S-Lafayette
L6, 234.8	3.38 × 4.38	105	S-Ambassador Six
L8, 260.8	3.13 × 4.25	115	S-Ambassador Eight

1941—84,007 built

600 (wb 112.0)		Wght	Price	Prod
4140	DeLuxe T/B sdn 4d	2,655	880	—
4142	DeLuxe bus cpe	2,500	772	—
4143	DeLuxe Brougham 2d	2,575	835	—
4145	Special bus cpe	2,490	730	—
4146	Special fstbk cpe	2,630	765	—
4147	Special fstbk sdn 4d	2,615	805	—
4148	DeLuxe fstbk sdn 4d	2,630	837	—
4149	DeLuxe fstbk sdn 2d	2,640	797	—

Ambassador Six (wb 121.0)		Wght	Price	Prod
4160	T/B sdn 4d	3,300	1,065	—
4161	All-Purpose cabriolet	3,430	1,130	—
4162	bus cpe	3,180	940	—
4163	Brougham 2d	3,235	1,009	—
4165	Special bus cpe	3,310	890	—
4167	Special fstbk sdn 4d	3,300	970	—
4168	fstbk sdn 4d	3,300	1,020	—
4169	Special sdn 2d	3,320	933	—
Ambassador Eight (wb 121.0)				
4180	T/B sdn 4d	3,475	1,186	—
4181	All-Purpose cabriolet	3,580	1,250	—
4183	DeLuxe Brougham 2d	3,400	1,116	—
4187	Special fstbk sdn 4d	3,465	1,091	—
4188	DeLuxe fstbk sdn 4d	3,455	1,141	—

1941 Engines	bore × stroke	bhp	availability
L6, 172.6	3.13 × 3.75	75	S-600
L6, 234.8	3.38 × 4.38	105	S-Ambassador Six
L8, 260.8	3.13 × 4.25	115	S-Ambassador Eight

1942—31,780 built

600 (wb 112.0)		Wght	Price	Prod
4240	T/B sdn 4d	2,655	918	—
4242	bus cpe	2,540	843	—
4243	Brougham 2d	2,580	883	—
4248	fstbk sdn 4d	2,650	893	—
4249	sdn 2d	2,605	873	—
Ambassador Six (wb 121.0)				
4260	T/B sdn 4d	3,335	1,069	—
4262	bus cpe	3,200	994	—
4263	Brougham 2d	3,230	1,034	—
4268	fstbk sdn 4d	3,335	1,044	—
4269	sdn 2d	3,285	1,024	—

1942 600 four-door sedan

Ambassador Eight (wb 121.0)		Wght	Price	Prod
4280	T/B sdn 4d	3,485	1,119	—
4282	bus cpe	3,350	1,035	—
4283	Brougham 2d	3,385	1,084	—
4288	fstbk sdn 4d	3,485	1,094	—
4289	fstbk sdn 2d	3,485	1,065	—

1942 Engines	bore × stroke	bhp	availability
L6, 172.6	3.13 × 3.75	75	S-600
L6, 234.8	3.38 × 4.38	105	S-Ambassador Six
L8, 260.8	3.13 × 4.25	115	S-Ambassador Eight

1946—94,000 built

600 (wb 112.0)		Wght	Price	Prod
4640	T/B sdn 4d	2,740	1,342	—
4643	Brougham 2d	2,685	1,293	—
4648	fstbk sdn 4d	2,780	1,298	—

1942 Ambassador four-door sedan

Ambassador (wb 121.0)		Wght	Price	Prod
4660	T/B sdn 4d	3,335	1,511	—
4663	Brougham 2d	3,260	1,453	—
4664	Suburban sdn 4d	3,470	1,929	272
4668	fstbk sdn 4d	3,360	1,469	—

1946 Engines	bore × stroke	bhp	availability
L6, 172.6	3.13 × 3.75	82	S-600
L6, 234.8	3.38 × 4.38	112	S-Ambassador

1947—101,000 built

600 (wb 112.0)		Wght	Price	Prod
4740	T/B sdn 4d	2,740	1,464	—
4743	Brougham 2d	2,685	1,415	—
4748	fstbk sdn 4d	2,780	1,420	—
Ambassador (wb 121.0)				
4760	T/B sdn 4d	3,335	1,809	—
4763	Brougham 2d	3,260	1,751	—
4764	Suburban sdn 4d	4,664	2,227	595
4788	fstbk sdn 4d	3,360	1,767	—

1947 Engines	bore × stroke	bhp	availability
L6, 172.6	3.13 × 3.75	82	S-600
L6, 234.8	3.38 × 4.38	112	S-Ambassador

1948*

600 (wb 112.0)		Wght	Price	Prod
4840	Super T/B sdn 4d	2,786	1,587	—
4842	DeLuxe bus cpe	2,635	1,478	—
4843	Super Brougham 2d	2,731	1,538	—
4848	Super fstbk sdn 4d	2,826	1,543	—
4850	Custom T/B sdn 4d	2,786	1,776	—
4853	Custom Brougham 2d	2,731	1,727	—
4858	Custom fstbk sdn 4d	2,826	1,732	—

Ambassador (wb 121.0)		Wght	Price	Prod
4860	Super T/B sdn 4d	3,387	1,916	—
4863	Super Brougham 2d	3,312	1,858	—
4864	Super Suburban sdn 4d	3,522	2,239	130
4868	Super fstbk sdn 4d	3,412	1,874	—
4870	Custom T/B sdn 4d	3,387	2,105	—
4871	Custom cabriolet (conv)	3,465	2,345	1,000
4873	Custom Brougham 2d	3,312	2,047	—
4878	Custom fstbk sdn 4d	3,412	2,063	—

*Model year registrations: 110,000.

1948 Engines	bore × stroke	bhp	availability
L6, 172.6	3.13 × 3.75	82	S-600
L6, 234.8	3.38 × 4.38	112	S-Ambassador

1949*

600 (wb 112.0)		Wght	Price	Prod
4923	Super Special Brougham 2d	2,960	1,846	—
4928	Super Special sdn 4d	2,950	1,849	—
4929	Super Special sdn 2d	2,935	1,824	—
4943	Super Brougham 2d	2,960	1,808	—
4948	Super sdn 4d	2,950	1,811	—
4949	Super sdn 2d	2,935	1,786	—
4953	Custom Brougham 2d	2,970	1,997	—
4958	Custom sdn 4d	2,985	2,000	—
4959	Custom sdn 2d	2,985	1,975	—
Ambassador (wb 121.0)				
4963	Super Brougham 2d	3,390	2,191	—
4968	Super sdn 4d	3,385	2,195	—
4969	Super sdn 2d	3,365	2,170	—
4973	Custom Brougham 2d	3,415	2,359	—
4978	Custom sdn 4d	3,415	2,363	—
4979	Custom sdn 2d	3,400	2,338	—
4993	Super Special Brougham 2d	3,390	2,239	—
4998	Super Special sdn 4d	3,385	2,243	—

1948 Ambassador Custom Cabriolet

1949 Ambassador four-door sedan

		Wght	Price	Prod
4999	Super Special sdn 2d	3,365	2,218	—

*Model year registrations: 135,328.

1949 Engines	bore × stroke	bhp	availability
L6, 172.6	3.13×3.75	82	S-600
L6, 234.8	3.38×4.38	112	S-Ambassador

1950*

Rambler (wb 100.0)		Wght	Price	Prod
5021	Custom Landau conv cpe	2,430	1,808	—
5024	Custom wgn 2d	2,515	1,808	—
Statesman (wb 112.0)				
5032	DeLuxe bus cpe	2,830	1,633	—
5043	Super club cpe	2,940	1,735	—
5048	Super sdn 4d	2,965	1,738	—
5049	Super sdn 2d	2,930	1,713	—
5053	Custom club cpe	2,965	1,894	—
5058	Custom sdn 4d	2,990	1,897	—
5059	Custom sdn 2d	2,950	1,872	—
Ambassador (wb 121.0)				
5063	Super club cpe	3,335	2,060	—
5068	Super sdn 4d	3,350	2,064	—
5069	Super sdn 2d	3,325	2,039	—
5073	Custom club cpe	3,385	2,219	—
5078	Custom sdn 4d	3,390	2,223	—
5079	Custom sdn 2d	3,365	2,198	—

*Model year registrations: 171,782.

1950 Engines	bore × stroke	bhp	availability
L6, 172.6	3.13×3.75	82	S-Rambler
L6, 184.0	3.13×4.00	82	S-Statesman
L6, 234.8	3.38×4.38	112	S-Ambassador

1951*

Rambler (wb 100.0)		Wght	Price	Prod
5114	Super Suburban wgn 2d	2,515	1,885	—
5121	Custom conv cpe	2,430	1,993	—
5124	Custom wgn 2d	2,515	1,993	—
5127	Custom Cntry Club htp cpe	2,420	1,968	—
Statesman (wb 112.0)				
5132	DeLuxe bus cpe	2,835	1,841	—
5143	Super club cpe	2,935	1,952	—
5148	Super sdn 4d	2,970	1,955	—
5149	Super sdn 2d	2,930	1,928	—
5153	Custom club cpe	2,950	2,122	—
5158	Custom sdn 4d	2,990	2,125	—
5159	Custom sdn 2d	2,940	2,099	—
Ambassador (wb 121.0)				
5163	Super club cpe	3,370	2,326	—
5168	Super sdn 4d	3,410	2,330	—
5169	Super sdn 2d	3,370	2,304	—
5173	Custom club cpe	3,395	2,496	—
5178	Custom sdn 4d	3,445	2,501	—
5179	Custom sdn 2d	3,380	2,474	—

*Model year registrations: 205,307.

1951 Engines	bore × stroke	bhp	availability
L6, 172.6	3.13×3.75	82	S-Rambler
L6, 184.0	3.13×4.00	85	S-Statesman
L6, 234.8	3.38×4.38	115	S-Ambassador

1952*

Rambler (wb 100.0)		Wght	Price	Prod
5214	Super Suburban wgn 2d	2,515	2,003	—
5221	Custom conv cpe	2,430	2,119	—
5224	Custom wgn 2d	2,515	2,119	—
5227	Custom Cntry Club htp cpe	2,420	2,094	—

Statesman (wb 114.3)		Wght	Price	Prod
5245	Super sdn 4d	3,045	2,178	—
5246	Super sdn 2d	3,025	2,144	—
5255	Custom sdn 4d	3,070	2,332	—
5256	Custom sdn 2d	3,050	2,310	—
5257	Custom Cntry Club htp cpe	3,095	2,433	—
Ambassador (wb 121.3)				
5265	Super sdn 4d	3,430	2,557	—
5266	Super sdn 2d	3,410	2,521	—
5275	Custom sdn 4d	3,480	2,716	—
5276	Custom sdn 2d	3,450	2,695	—
5277	Custom Cntry Club htp cpe	3,550	2,829	—

*Model year registrations: 154,291.

1952 Engines	bore×stroke	bhp	availability
L6, 172.6	3.13×3.75	82	S-Rambler
L6, 195.6	3.13×4.25	88	S-Statesman
L6, 252.6	3.50×4.38	120	S-Ambassador

1953*

Rambler (wb 100.0)		Wght	Price	Prod
5314	Super Suburban wgn 2d	2,555	2,003	—
5321	Custom conv cpe	2,590	2,150	—
5324	Custom wgn 2d	2,570	2,119	—
5327	Custom Cntry Club htp cpe	2,550	2,125	—
Statesman (wb 114.3)				
5345	Super sdn 4d	3,045	2,178	—
5346	Super sdn 2d	3,025	2,143	—
5355	Custom sdn 4d	3,070	2,332	—
5356	Custom sdn 2d	3,050	2,310	—
5357	Custom Cntry Club htp cpe	3,095	2,433	—
Ambassador (wb 121.3)				
5365	Super sdn 4d	3,430	2,557	—
5366	Super sdn 2d	3,410	2,521	—
5375	Custom sdn 4d	3,480	2,716	—
5376	Custom sdn 2d	3,450	2,695	—
5377	Custom Cntry Club htp cpe	3,550	2,829	—

*Model year registrations: 121,793.

1953 Engines	bore×stroke	bhp	availability
L6, 184.0	3.13×4.00	85	S-Rambler manual
L6, 195.6	3.13×4.25	90	S-Rambler automatic
L6, 195.6	3.13×4.25	100	S-Statesman
L6, 252.6	3.50×4.38	120	S-Ambassador
L6, 252.6	3.50×4.38	140	O-Ambassador

1952 Statesman Super four-door sedan

1954*

Rambler (wb 100.0, 4d-108.0)		Wght	Price	Prod
5406	DeLuxe sdn 2d	2,425	1,550	—
5414	Super Suburban wgn 2d	2,520	1,800	—
5415	Super sdn 4d	2,570	1,795	—
5416	Super sdn 2d	2,425	1,700	—
5417	Super Cntry Club htp cpe	2,465	1,800	—
5421	Custom conv cpe	2,555	1,980	—
5424	Custom wgn 2d	2,535	1,950	—
5425	Custom sdn 4d	2,630	1,965	—
5427	Custom Cntry Club htp cpe	2,515	1,950	—
5428	Custom Cross Cntry wgn 4d	2,715	2,050	—
Statesman (wb 114.3)				
5445	Super sdn 4d	3,045	2,158	—
5446	Super sdn 2d	3,025	2,110	—
5455	Custom sdn 4d	3,095	2,332	—
5457	Custom Cntry Club htp cpe	3,120	2,423	—
Ambassador (wb 121.3)				
5465	Super sdn 4d	3,430	2,417	—
5466	Super sdn 2d	3,410	2,365	—
5475	Custom sdn 4d	3,505	2,600	—
5477	Custom Cntry Club htp cpe	3,575	2,735	—

*Model year registrations: 91,121.

1954 Engines	bore×stroke	bhp	availability
L6, 184.0	3.13×4.00	85	S-Rambler 2dr manual
L6, 195.6	3.13×4.25	90	S-Rambler 4dr, 2dr automatic
L6, 195.6	3.13×4.25	110	S-Statesman
L6, 252.6	3.50×4.38	130	S-Ambassador
L6, 252.6	3.50×4.38	140	O-Ambassador

1955*

Rambler (wb 100.0, 4d-108.0)		Wght	Price	Prod
5512	Fleet bus sdn 2d	2,400	—	—
5514	DeLuxe Suburban wgn 2d	2,528	1,771	—
5514-1	Super Suburban wgn 2d	2,532	1,869	—
5515	DeLuxe sdn 4d	2,567	1,695	—
5515-1	Super sdn 4d	2,570	1,798	—
5515-2	Custom sdn 4d	2,606	1,989	—
5516	DeLuxe sdn 2d	2,432	1,585	—
5516-1	Super sdn 2d	2,450	1,683	—
5517-2	Custom Cntry Club htp cpe	2,518	1,995	—
5518-1	Fleet Cross Cntry wgn 4d	2,675	—	—
5518-2	Cus Cross Cntry wgn 4d	2,685	2,098	—
2504	Fleet util wgn 2d	2,500	—	—
Statesman (wb 114.5)				
5545-1	Super sdn 4d	3,134	2,215	—
5545-2	Custom sdn 4d	3,204	2,385	—
5547-2	Custom Cntry Club htp cpe	3,220	2,495	—
Ambassador Six (wb 121.3)				
5565-1	Super sdn 4d	3,538	2,480	—
5565-2	Custom sdn 4d	3,576	2,675	—
5567-2	Cus Cntry Club htp cpe	3,593	2,795	—
Ambassador Eight (wb 121.3)				
5585-1	Super sdn 4d	3,795	2,775	—
5585-2	Custom sdn 4d	3,827	2,965	—
5587-2	Custom Cntry Club htp cpe	3,839	3,095	—

*Model year registrations: 121,261.

1955 Engines	bore×stroke	bhp	availability
L6, 195.6	3.13×4.25	90	S-Rambler exc Fleet
L6, 195.6	3.13×4.25	100	S-Rambler Fleet, Statesman man
L6, 195.6	3.13×4.25	110	S-Statesman auto
L6, 252.6	3.50×4.38	130	S-Ambassador Six

1956 Ambassador Eight Custom Country Club hardtop coupe

	bore×stroke	bhp	availability
L6, 252.6	3.50×4.38	140	O-Ambassador Six
V8, 320.0	3.81×3.50	208	S-Ambassador Eight

1956

Rambler (wb 108.0)*		Wght	Price	Prod
5613-2	Cus Cross Cntry htp wgn 4d	3,095	2,494	—
5615	DeLuxe sdn 4d	2,891	1,829	—
5615-1	Super sdn 4d	2,906	1,939	—
5615-2	Custom sdn 4d	2,929	2,059	—
5618-1	Super Cross Cntry wgn 4d	2,992	2,233	—
5618-2	Cus Cross Cntry wgn 4d	3,110	2,329	—
5619-2	Custom htp sdn	2,990	2,224	—
Statesman (wb 114.5)*				
5645-1	Super sdn 4d	3,134	2,139	—

Ambassador Special (wb 121.3)—4,145 built*		Wght	Price	Prod
5657-1	sdn 4d	3,397	2,355	—
5657-2	Country Club htp cpe	3,418	2,462	—
5657-3	Custom sdn 4d	3,567	2,541	—
Ambassador Six (wb 121.3)*				
5665-1	Super sdn 4d	3,555	2,425	—
Ambassador Eight (wb 121.3)*				
5685-1	Super sdn 4d	3,748	2,716	—
5685-2	Custom sdn 4d	3,846	2,939	—
5687-2	Cus Cntry Club htp cpe	3,854	3,072	—

*Estimated Rambler production 10,000; total Statesman/Ambassador 14,352.

1956 Engines	bore×stroke	bhp	availability
L6, 195.6	3.13×4.25	120	S-Rambler, Statesman
L6, 252.6	3.50×4.38	130	S-Ambassador Six

1956 Ambassador Special Custom four-door sedan

1957 Ambassador Custom four-door sedan

	bore×stroke	bhp	availability
L6, 252.6	3.50×4.38	140	O-Ambassador Six
V8, 250.0	3.50×3.25	190	S-Ambassador Special
V8, 352.0	4.00×3.33	200	S-Ambassador Eight

1957*

Ambassador Super (wb 121.3)		Wght	Price	Prod
5785-1	sdn 4d	3,639	2,586	—
5787-1	Country Club htp cpe	3,655	2,670	—
Ambassador Custom (wb 121.3)				
5785-2	sdn 4d	3,701	2,763	—
5787-2	Country Club htp cpe	3,722	2,847	—

*Approximate model year production: 5,000.

1957 Engine	bore×stroke	bhp	availability
V8, 327.0	4.00×3.25	255	S-all

Note: See Rambler listing for 1957 and later models.

NASH METROPOLITAN

1954

Series 54 (wb 85.0)—13,095* built		Wght	Price	Prod
541	conv cpe 3P	1,803	1,469	—
542	cpe 3P	1,843	1,445	—

*Includes 743 shipments in 1953. All production figures are calendar year shipments, including some destined for Canada.

1954 Engine	bore×stroke	bhp	availability
L4, 73.8	2.56×3.50	42	S-all

1955

Series 54 (wb 85.0)—6,096 built		Wght	Price	Prod
541	conv 3P	1,803	1,469	—
542	cpe 3P	1,843	1,445	—

1955 Engine	bore×stroke	bhp	availability
L4, 73.8	2.56×3.50	42	S-all

1956—9,068 built

Series 54 (wb 85.0)		Wght	Price	Prod
541	conv 3P	1,803	1,469	—
542	cpe 3P	1,843	1,445	—
Series 56 "1500" (wb 85.0)				
561	conv 3P	1,803	1,551	—
562	cpe 3P	1,843	1,527	—

1956 Engines	bore×stroke	bhp	availability
L4, 73.8	2.56×3.50	42	S-Series 54 (1200)
L4, 90.9	2.88×3.50	52	S-Series 56 (1500)

1957

Series 56 "1500" (wb 85.0)—15,317 built		Wght	Price	Prod
561	conv 3P	1,803	1,591	—
562	cpe 3P	1,843	1,567	—

1957 Engine	bore×stroke	bhp	availability
L4, 90.9	2.88×3.50	52	S-all

1954 Series 54 coupe

1958

Series 56 "1500" (wb 85.0)—13,128 built		Wght	Price	Prod
561	conv 3P	1,835	1,650	—
562	cpe 3P	1,875	1,626	—

1958 Engine	bore×stroke	bhp	availability
L4, 90.9	2.88×3.50	52	S-all

1959

Series 56 "1500" (wb 85.0)—22,309 built		Wght	Price	Prod
561	conv 3P	1,835	1,650	—
562	cpe 3P	1,875	1,626	—

1959 Engine	bore×stroke	bhp	availability
L4, 90.9	2.88×3.50	52	S-all

1960

Series 56 "1500" (wb 85.0)—13,103 built		Wght	Price	Prod
561	conv 3P	1,850	1,697	—
562	cpe 3P	1,890	1,673	—

1960 Engine	bore×stroke	bhp	availability
L4, 90.9	2.88×3.50	52	S-all

1961

Series 56 "1500" (wb 85.0)—853 built		Wght	Price	Prod
561	conv 3P	1,850	1,697	—
562	cpe 3P	1,890	1,673	—

1961 Engine	bore×stroke	bhp	availability
L4, 90.9	2.88×3.50	52	S-all

1962

Series 56 "1500" (wb 85.0)—412 built		Wght	Price	Prod
561	conv 3P	1,850	1,697	—
562	cpe 3P	1,890	1,673	—

1962 Engine	bore×stroke	bhp	availability
L4, 90.9	2.88×3.50	52	S-all

Note: Metropolitans were built in England but marketed by American Motors. See 1955-57 Hudson listing for additional Metropolitan models.

OLDSMOBILE

1939

F-39 Series 60 (wb 115.0)	Wght	Price	Prod
bus cpe 2P	2,870	777	5,575
club cpe 2-4P	2,915	833	2,273
sdn 2d	2,965	838	16,910
sdn 4d	3,000	889	15,958
G-39 Series 70 (wb 120.0)			
bus cpe 2P	3,040	840	5,211
club cpe 2-4P	3,080	891	4,795
conv cpe 2-4P	3,230	1,045	1,714
sdn 2d (incl. 17 Sun sdns)	3,140	901	19,442
sdn 4d (incl. 81 Sun sdns)	3,180	952	38,224
L-39 Series 80 (wb 120.0)			
bus cpe 2P	3,190	920	738
club cpe 2-4P	3,230	971	1,147
conv cpe 2-4P	3,390	1,119	472
sdn 2d (incl. 7 Sun sdns)	3,290	992	1,571
sdn 4d (incl. 85 Sun sdns)	3,340	1,043	13,197

1939 Engines	bore×stroke	bhp	availability
L6, 216.0	3.44×3.87	90	S-60
L6, 229.7	3.44×4.19	95	S-70
L8, 257.1	3.25×3.88	110	S-90

1940

F-40 Series 60 (wb 116.0)	Wght	Price	Prod
bus cpe	3,030	807	2,752
club cpe	3,015	848	7,664
conv cpe	3,110	1,021	1,347
sdn 2d	3,065	853	27,220
sdn 4d	3,100	899	24,422
wgn 4d	3,255	1,042	633
G-40 Series 70 (wb 120.0)			
bus cpe	3,100	865	4,337
club cpe	3,105	901	8,505
conv cpe	3,240	1,045	1,070
sdn 2d	3,170	912	21,486
sdn 4d	3,220	963	41,467
L-40 Series 90 (wb 124.0)			
club cpe	3,440	1,069	10,836
conv cpe	3,590	1,222	290
sdn 4d	3,555	1,131	33,075
conv phaeton 4d	3,750	1,570	50

1940 Engines	bore×stroke	bhp	availability
L6, 229.7	3.44×4.13	95	S-60, 70
L8, 257.1	3.25×3.88	110	S-90

1941

66 Special 6 (wb 119.0)	Wght	Price	Prod
bus cpe	3,145	852	6,433
club cpe	3,185	893	23,796
conv cpe	3,355	1,048	2,814
sdn 2d	3,190	898	30,475
sdn 4d	3,230	945	25,899
Town Sedan 4d	3,220	945	11,921
wgn 4d	3,565	1,176	604
68 Special 8 (wb 119.0)			
bus cpe	3,260	893	188
club cpe	3,300	935	2,684
conv cpe	3,455	1,089	776
sdn 2d	3,305	940	499
sdn 4d	3,360	987	3,831
Town Sedan 4d	3,345	987	2,188
wgn 4d	3,660	1,217	95
76 Dynamic Cruiser 6 (wb 125.0)			
bus cpe	3,260	908	353
club sdn	3,325	954	46,885
sdn 4d	3,390	1,010	40,719

1940 Series 90 four-door sedan

78 Dynamic Cruiser 8 (wb 125.0)	Wght	Price	Prod
bus cpe	3,360	944	51
club sdn	3,420	989	13,598
sdn 4d	3,500	1,045	15,580
96 Custom Cruiser 6 (wb 125.0)			
club cpe	3,320	1,043	2,176
conv cpe	3,525	1,191	325
sdn 4d	3,410	1,099	4,196
98 Custom Cruiser 8 (wb 125.0)			
club cpe	3,430	1,079	6,305
conv cpe	3,620	1,227	1,263
conv phaeton 4d	3,790	1,575	119
sdn 4d	3,500	1,135	22,081

1941 Engines	bore × stroke	bhp	availability
L6, 238.1	3.50×4.13	100	S-66, 76, 96
L8, 257.1	3.25×3.88	110	S-68, 78, 98

1942

66 "Sixty" 6 (wb 119.0)	Wght	Price	Prod
bus cpe	3,230	915	1,026*
club cpe	3,265	955	3,762*
conv cpe	3,560	1,185	746*
club sdn	3,270	970	9,744*
sdn 2d	3,280	960	3,245*
sdn 4d	3,315	1,005	7,086*
Town Sedan 4d	3,320	1,005	3,421*
wgn 4d	3,735	1,280	700*
68 "Sixty" 8 (wb 119.0)			
bus cpe	3,365	955	140*
club cpe	3,405	995	501*
conv cpe	3,715	1,225	102*
club sdn	3,405	1,010	1,022*
sdn 2d	3,410	1,000	443*
sdn 4d	3,455	1,045	967*
Town Sedan 4d	3,445	1,045	467*
wgn 4d	3,890	1,320	95*
76 "Seventy" 6 (wb 125.0)			
club sdn	3,395	1,010	7,481*
Deluxe club sdn	3,460	1,095	2,247*
sdn 4d	3,465	1,065	6,507*
Deluxe sdn 4d	3,510	1,150	2,414*
78 "Seventy" 8 (wb 125.0)			
club sdn	3,520	1,050	3,055*
Deluxe club sdn	3,570	1,135	918*
sdn 4d	3,580	1,105	2,659*
Deluxe sdn 4d	3,640	1,190	986*
98 "Ninety" 8 (wb 127.0)			
conv cpe	3,955	1,450	216
club sdn	3,635	1,220	1,771
sdn 4d	3,715	1,275	4,672

*Estimates based on percentage distribution of known production of 66 (30,219), 68 (4,089), 76 (19,013) and 78 (7,803).

1942 Engines	bore × stroke	bhp	availability
L6, 238.1	3.50×4.13	100	S-66, 76
L8, 257.1	3.25×3.88	110	S-68, 78, 98

1946

F-46 Special 66 (wb 119.0)	Wght	Price	Prod
conv cpe	3,605	1,681	1,409
club cpe	3,315	1,407	4,537
club sdn 2d	3,330	1,433	11,721
sdn 4d	3,350	1,471	11,053
wgn 4d	3,750	2,089	140
G-46 Dynamic Cruiser 76 (wb 125.0)			
club sdn 2d	3,460	1,497	30,929
Deluxe club sdn 2d	3,505	1,610	1,923
sdn 4d	3,510	1,568	18,425
Deluxe sdn 4d	3,555	1,678	2,179
J-46 Dynamic Cruiser 78 (wb 125.0)			
club sdn 2d	3,600	1,554	8,723
Deluxe club sdn 2d	3,630	1,666	2,188
sdn 4d	3,640	1,624	7,103
Deluxe sdn 4d	3,670	1,733	2,939
L-46 Custom Cruiser 98 (wb 127.0)			
club sdn 2d	3,680	1,762	2,459
conv cpe	4,025	2,040	874
sdn 4d	3,775	1,812	11,031

1946 Engines	bore × stroke	bhp	availability
L6, 238.1	3.50×4.13	100	S-66, 76
L8, 257.1	3.25×3.88	110	S-78, 98

1947

F-47 Special 66 (wb 119.0)	Wght	Price	Prod
club sdn 2d	3,330	1,513	21,366*
club cpe	3,325	1,488	10,723*
conv cpe	3,605	1,845	3,949
sdn 4d	3,355	1,556	16,995*
wgn 4d	3,770	2,456	968
E-47 Special 68 (wb 119.0)			
club sdn 2d	3,430	1,572	7,122*
club cpe	3,420	1,546	3,574*
conv cpe	3,710	1,903	2,579
sdn 4d	3,460	1,614	5,665*
wgn 4d	3,885	2,514	492
G-47 Dynamic Cruiser 76 (wb 125.0)			
club sdn 2d	3,470	1,584	22,509*
Deluxe club sdn 2d	3,515	1,705	3,951*
sdn 4d	3,525	1,659	18,196*
Deluxe sdn 4d	3,590	1,773	4,710*
J-47 Dynamic Cruiser 78 (wb 125.0)			
club sdn 2d	3,590	1,643	15,643*
Deluxe club sdn 2d	3,650	1,762	2,476*
sdn 4d	3,655	1,717	12,645*
Deluxe sdn 4d	3,705	1,830	3,184*
L-47 Custom Cruiser 98 (wb 127.0)			
club sdn	3,715	1,865	8,475
conv cpe	4,075	2,307	3,940
sdn 4d	3,795	1,917	24,733

*Estimates based on percentage distribution of known production of 66 (55,610), 68 (17,956), 76 (49,711) and 78 (33,963).

1947 Engines	bore × stroke	bhp	availability
L6, 238.1	3.50×4.13	100	S-66, 76
L8, 257.1	3.25×3.88	110	S-68, 78, 98

1948

Dynamic 66 (wb 119.0)	Wght	Price	Prod
club sdn 2d	3,285	1,634	15,071*
Deluxe club sdn 2d	3,300	1,776	2,016*
club cpe	3,240	1,609	5,923*
Deluxe club cpe	3,255	1,749	792*
conv cpe	3,550	2,003	1,801
sdn 4d	3,320	1,677	11,406*

	Wght	Price	Prod
Deluxe sdn 4d	3,335	1,818	1,656*
wgn 4d	3,620	2,614	840
Deluxe wgn 4d	3,635	2,739	553
Dynamic 68 (wb 119.0)			
club sdn 2d	3,420	1,693	5,861*
Deluxe club sdn 2d	3,435	1,834	784*
club cpe	3,355	1,667	2,303*
Deluxe club cpe	3,370	1,808	308*
conv cpe	3,660	2,061	2,091
sdn 4d	3,445	1,735	4,436*
Deluxe sdn 4d	3,460	1,876	644*
wgn 4d	3,770	2,672	760
Deluxe wgn 4d	3,785	2,797	554
Dynamic 76 (wb 125.0)			
club sdn 2d	3,425	1,726	9,984*
Deluxe club sdn 2d	3,445	1,873	4,866*
sdn 4d	3,500	1,801	7,342*
Deluxe sdn 4d	3,535	1,947	7.199*
Dynamic 78 (wb 125.0)			
club sdn 2d	3,545	1,785	6,939*
Deluxe club sdn 2d	3,590	1,931	3,383*
sdn 4d	3,625	1,859	5,102*
Deluxe sdn 4d	3,665	2,005	5,003*
Dynamic/Futuramic 98 (wb 127.0/125.0)**			
club sdn 2d	3,645	2,078	2,311
Deluxe club sdn 2d	3,685	2,182	11,949
sdn 4d	3,705	2,151	5,605
Deluxe sdn 4d	3,745	2,256	32,456
Deluxe conv cpe	4,035	2,624	12,914

*Estimates based on percentage distribution of known production of 66 (41,993), 68 (16,614), 76 (29,167) and 78 (20,651).
**Futuramic 98 introduced early 1948; weights and prices are for Futuramic, 98 production figures are for total Dynamic and Futuramic production.

1949 Futuramic 98 Deluxe four-door sedan

1948 Engines	bore × stroke	bhp	availability
L6, 238.1	3.50 × 4.13	100	S-66, 76
L8, 257.1	3.25 × 3.88	110	S-68, 78
L8, 257.1	3.25 × 3.88	115	S-98

1949

Futuramic 76 (wb 119.5)	Wght	Price	Prod
club sdn 2d	3,290	1,758	23,059
Deluxe club sdn 2d	3,355	1,900	8,960
club cpe	3,260	1,732	9,403
Deluxe club cpe	3,315	1,873	3,280
conv cpe	3,580	2,148	5,338

1949 Futuramic 98 four-door sedan

	Wght	Price	Prod
Town Sedan 4d	3,335	1,821	3,741
Deluxe Town Sedan 4d	3,400	1,963	2,725
sdn 4d	3,340	1,832	23,631
Deluxe sdn 4d	3,375	1,974	13,874
Deluxe wgn 4d	3,680	2,895	1,545
Futuramic 88 (wb 119.5)			
club sdn 2d	3,585	2,170	16,887
Deluxe club sdn 2d	3,615	2,301	11,820
club cpe	3,550	2,143	6,562
Deluxe club cpe	3,590	2,274	4,999
conv cpe	3,845	2,559	5,434
Town Sedan 4d	3,625	2,233	2,859
Deluxe Town Sedan 4d	3,665	2,364	2,974
sdn 4d	3,615	2,244	23,342
Deluxe sdn 4d	3,645	2,375	23,044
Deluxe wgn 4d	3,945	3,296	1,355
Futuramic 98 (wb 125.0)			
club sdn	3,835	2,426	3,849
Deluxe club sdn	3,840	2,520	16,200
sdn 4d	3,890	2,500	8,820
Deluxe sdn 4d	3,925	2,594	49,001
Deluxe Holiday htp cpe	4,000	2,973	3,006
Deluxe conv cpe	4,200	2,973	12,602

1949 Engines	bore × stroke	bhp	availability
L6, 257.1	3.53×4.38	105	S-76
V8, 303.7	3.75×3.44	135	S-88, 98

1950

Futuramic 76 (wb 119.5)	Wght	Price	Prod
club sdn 2d	3,280	1,745	3,186
Deluxe club sdn 2d	3,285	1,813	1,919
club cpe	3,260	1,719	2,238
Deluxe club cpe	3,280	1,787	1,126

1950 Futuramic 76 club coupe

	Wght	Price	Prod
conv cpe	3,585	2,135	973
Holiday htp cpe	3,335	2,003	144
Deluxe Holiday htp cpe	3,385	2,108	394
sdn 4d	3,320	1,819	7,396
Deluxe sdn 4d	3,340	1,887	9,159
sdn 2d	3,290	1,761	3,865
Deluxe sdn 2d	3,295	1,829	2,489
wgn 4d	3,610	2,362	121
Deluxe wgn 4d	3,615	2,504	247
Futuramic 88 (wb 119.5)			
club sdn 2d	3,475	1,904	14,705
Deluxe club sdn 2d	3,486	1,982	16,388
club cpe	3,435	1,878	10,684
Deluxe club cpe	3,455	1,956	10,772

1950 Futuramic 88 Holiday hardtop coupe

	Wght	Price	Prod
conv cpe	3,745	2,294	9,127
Holiday htp cpe	3,510	2,162	1,366
Deluxe Holiday htp cpe	3,565	2,267	11,316
sdn 4d	3,515	1,978	40,301
Deluxe sdn 4d	3,520	2,056	100,810
sdn 2d	3,485	1,920	23,889
Deluxe sdn 2d	3,500	1,998	26,672
wgn 4d	3,775	2,520	1,830
Deluxe wgn 4d	3,780	2,662	552
Futuramic 98 (wb 122.0)			
club sdn 2d	3,685	2,225	2,270
Deluxe club sdn 2d	3,705	2,319	9,719
Deluxe conv cpe	4,150	2,772	3,925
Holiday htp cpe	3,775	2,383	317
Deluxe Holiday htp cpe	3,840	2,641	7,946
Town Sedan 4d	3,710	2,267	255
Deluxe Town Sedan 4d	3,755	2,361	1,523
sdn 4d	3,765	2,299	7,499
Deluxe sdn 4d	3,775	2,393	72,766

1950 Engines	bore × stroke	bhp	availability
L6, 257.1	3.53×4.38	105	S-76
V8, 303.7	3.75×3.44	135	S-88, 98

1951

88 (wb 119.5)	Wght	Price	Prod
sdn 4d	3,542	2,111	22,848
sdn 2d	3,507	2,049	11,792
Super 88 (wb 120.0)			
club cpe	3,557	2,219	7,328
sdn 4d	3,636	2,328	90,131
sdn 2d	3,579	2,265	34,963
conv cpe	3,831	2,673	3,854
Holiday htp cpe	3,743	2,558	14,180
98 (wb 122.0)			
Deluxe sdn 4d	3,787	2,610	78,122
Holiday htp cpe	3,762	2,545	3,917
Deluxe Holiday htp cpe	3,857	2,882	14,012
Deluxe conv cpe	4,107	3,025	4,468

1951 Engine	bore × stroke	bhp	availability
V8, 303.7	3.75×3.44	135	S-all

1951 98 Holiday hardtop coupe

1953 Super 88 two-door sedan

1952

88 Deluxe (wb 120.0)	Wght	Price	Prod
sdn 4d	3,608	2,327	12,215
sdn 2d	3,565	2,262	6,402
Super 88 (wb 120.0)			
club cpe	3,597	2,345	2,050
sdn 4d	3,649	2,462	70,606
sdn 2d	3,603	2,395	24,963
conv cpe	3,867	2,853	5,162
Holiday htp cpe	3,640	2,673	15,777
98 (wb 124.0)			
sdn 4d	3,765	2,786	58,550
conv cpe	4,111	3,229	3,544
Holiday htp cpe	3,874	3,022	14,150

1952 Engines	bore × stroke	bhp	availability
V8, 303.7	3.75×3.44	145	S-88
V8, 303.7	3.75×3.44	160	S-Super 88, 98

1953

88 Deluxe (wb 120.0)	Wght	Price	Prod
sdn 4d	3,642	2,327	20,400
sdn 2d	3,603	2,262	12,400
Super 88 (wb 120.0)			
sdn 4d	3,673	2,462	119,317
sdn 2d	3,628	2,395	36,824
conv cpe	3,905	2,853	8,310
Holiday htp cpe	3,661	2,673	36,881
98 (wb 124.0)			
sdn 4d	3,779	2,786	64,431
conv cpe	4,119	3,229	7,521
Holiday htp cpe	3,893	3,022	27,920
Fiesta conv cpe	4,453	5,717	458

1953 Engines	bore × stroke	bhp	availability
V8, 303.7	3.75×3.44	150	S-88
V8, 303.7	3.75×3.44	165	S-Super 88, 98
V8, 303.7	3.75×3.44	170	S-Fiesta

1954

88 (wb 122.0)	Wght	Price	Prod
sdn 4d	3,719	2,337	29,028
sdn 2d	3,699	2,272	18,013
Holiday htp cpe	3,721	2,449	25,820

Super 88 (wb 122.0)	Wght	Price	Prod
sdn 4d	3,780	2,477	111,326
sdn 2d	3,729	2,410	27,882
conv cpe	4,003	2,868	6,452
Deluxe Holiday htp cpe	3,775	2,688	42,155
98 (wb 126.0)			
Deluxe sdn 4d	3,895	2,806	47,972
Holiday htp cpe	3,851	2,826	8,865
Deluxe Holiday htp cpe	3,938	3,042	29,688
Starfire conv cpe	4,193	3,249	6,800

1954 Engines	bore × stroke	bhp	availability
V8, 324.3	3.88 × 3.44	170	S-88
V8, 324.3	3.88 × 3.44	185	S-Super 88, 98

1955

88 (wb 122.0)	Wght	Price	Prod
sdn 4d	3,707	2,362	57,777
sdn 2d	3,688	2,297	37,507
Holiday htp sdn	3,768	2,548	41,310
Holiday htp cpe	3,707	2,474	85,767
Super 88 (wb 122.0)			
sdn 4d	3,762	2,503	111,316
sdn 2d	3,720	2,436	11,950
conv cpe	3,983	2,894	9,007
Deluxe Holiday htp sdn	3,825	2,788	47,385
Deluxe Holiday htp cpe	3,765	2,714	62,534
98 (wb 126.0)			
sdn 4d	3,864	2,833	39,847
Starfire conv cpe	4,159	3,276	9,149
Deluxe Holiday htp sdn	3,976	3,140	31,267
Deluxe Holiday htp cpe	3,924	3,069	38,363

1955 Engines	bore × stroke	bhp	availability
V8, 324.3	3.88 × 3.44	185	S-88
V8, 324.3	3.88 × 3.44	202	S-Super 88, 98; O-88

1956

88 (wb 122.0)	Wght	Price	Prod
sdn 4d	3,748	2,487	57,092
sdn 2d	3,691	2,422	31,949
Holiday htp sdn	3,797	2,671	52,239
Holiday htp cpe	3,741	2,599	74,739
Super 88 (wb 122.0)			
sdn 4d	3,768	2,640	59,728
sdn 2d	3,717	2,574	5,465
Holiday htp sdn	3,869	2,881	61,192
Holiday htp cpe	3,771	2,808	43,054
conv cpe	4,033	3,031	9,561
98 (wb 126.0)			
sdn 4d	4,028	3,298	20,105
Holiday htp sdn	4,167	3,551	42,320
Holiday htp cpe	4,080	3,480	19,433
Starfire conv cpe	4,325	3,740	8,581

1956 Engines	bore × stroke	bhp	availability
V8, 324.3	3.88 × 3.44	230	S-88
V8, 324.3	3.88 × 3.44	240	S-Super 88, 98; O-88

1957

Golden Rocket 88 (wb 122.0)		Wght	Price	Prod
3611	sdn 2d	3,942	2,733	18,477
3637	Holiday htp cpe	3,963	2,854	49,187
3639	Holiday htp sdn	4,052	2,932	33,830
3667TX	conv cpe	4,232	3,182	6,423
3669	sdn 4d	4,000	2,798	53,923
3693	Fiesta wgn 4d	4,281	3,202	5,052
3695	Fiesta htp wgn 4d	4,314	3,313	5,767
Golden Rocket Super 88 (wb 122.0)				
3637SD	Holiday htp cpe	4,010	3,180	31,155
3639SD	Holiday htp sdn	4,117	3,257	39,162
3667DTX	conv cpe	4,283	3,447	7,128
3669D	sdn 4d	4,044	3,030	42,629

1955 Super 88 convertible coupe

1956 Super 88 convertible coupe

		Wght	Price	Prod
3695SD	Fiesta htp wgn 4d	4,364	3,541	8,981
3611D	sdn 2d	4,001	2,968	2,983
Starfire 98 (wb 126.0)				
3037SDX	Holiday htp cpe	4,296	3,937	17,791
3039SDX	Holiday htp sdn	4,385	4,013	32,099
3067DX	conv cpe	4,572	4,217	8,278
3069D	sdn 4d	4,322	3,741	21,525

1957 Engines	bore×stroke	bhp	availability
V8, 371.1	4.00×3.69	277	S-all
V8, 371.1	4.00×3.69	300	O-all (J-2)

1958

Dynamic 88 (wb 122.5)		Wght	Price	Prod
3611	sdn 2d	3,961	2,772	11,833
3637	Holiday htp cpe	3,972	2,893	35,036
3639	Holiday htp sdn	4,035	2,971	28,241
3667TX	conv cpe	3,987	3,221	4,456
3669	sdn 4d	3,985	2,837	60,429
3693	Fiesta wgn 4d	4,258	3,284	3,249
3695	Fiesta htp wgn 4d	4,297	3,395	3,323
Super 88 (wb 122.5)				
3637SD	Holiday htp cpe	4,000	3,262	18,653
3639SD	Holiday htp sdn	4,073	3,339	27,521
3667DTX	conv cpe	4,010	3,529	3,799
3669D	sdn 4d	4,008	3,112	33,844
3695SD	Fiesta htp wgn 4d	4,334	3,623	5,175
98 (wb 126.5)				
3037SDX	Holiday htp cpe	4,329	4,020	11,012
3039SDX	Holiday htp sdn	4,391	4,096	27,603
3067DX	conv cpe	4,318	4,300	5,605
3069D	sdn 4d	4,316	3,824	16,595

1958 Engines	bore×stroke	bhp	availability
V8, 371.1	4.00×3.69	265	S-88
V8, 371.1	4.00×3.69	305	S-Super 88, 98
V8, 371.1	4.00×3.69	312	O-Super 88, 98

1959

Dynamic 88 (wb 123.0)		Wght	Price	Prod
3211	sdn 2d	4,040	2,837	16,123
3219	Celebrity sdn 4d	4,130	2,902	70,995
3235	Fiesta wgn 4d	4,465	3,365	11,298
3237	Scenic htp cpe	4,085	2,958	38,488
3239	Holiday htp sdn	4,165	3,036	48,707
3267	conv cpe	4,120	3,286	8,491
Super 88 (wb 123.0)				
3519	Celebrity sdn 4d	4,135	3,178	37,024
3535	Fiesta wgn 4d	4,485	3,669	7,015
3537	Scenic htp cpe	4,090	3,328	20,259
3539	Holiday htp sdn	4,185	3,405	38,467

1957 Golden Rocket Super 88 Holiday hardtop coupe

		Wght	Price	Prod
3567	conv cpe	4,135	3,595	4,895
98 (wb 126.3)				
3819	Celebrity sdn 4d	4,390	3,890	23,106
3837	Scenic htp cpe	4,360	4,086	13,669
3839	Holiday htp sdn	4,450	4,162	36,813
3867	conv cpe	4,360	4,366	7,514

1959 Engines	bore × stroke	bhp	availability
V8, 371.1	4.00×3.69	270	S-88
V8, 371.1	4.00×3.69	300	O-88
V8, 394.0	4.13×3.69	315	S-Super 88, 98

1960

Dynamic 88 (wb 123.0)		Wght	Price	Prod
3211	sdn 2d	4,026	2,835	13,545
3219	Celebrity sdn 4d	4,091	2,900	76,377
3235	Fiesta wgn 4d, 6P	4,449	3,363	8,834
3237	Sceni-Coupe htp	4,049	2,956	29,368
3239	Holiday htp sdn	4,139	3,034	43,761
3245	Fiesta wgn 4d, 8P	4,470	3,471	5,708
3267	conv cpe	4,101	3,284	12,271
Super 88 (wb 123.0)				
3519	Celebrity sdn 4d	4,128	3,176	35,094
3535	Fiesta wgn 4d, 6P	4,483	3,665	3,765
3537	Sceni-Coupe htp	4,086	3,325	16,464
3539	Holiday htp sdn	4,182	3,402	33,285
3545	Fiesta wgn 4d, 8P	4,506	3,773	3,475
3567	conv cpe	4,134	3,592	5,830
98 (wb 126.3)				
3819	Celebrity sdn 4d	4,360	3,887	17,188
3837	Sceni-Coupe htp	4,322	4,083	7,635
3839	Holiday htp sdn	4,431	4,159	27,257
3867	conv cpe	4,349	4,362	7,284

1960 Engines	bore × stroke	bhp	availability
V8, 371.1	4.00×3.69	240	S-88
V8, 371.1	4.00×3.69	260	O-88
V8, 394.0	4.13×3.69	315	S-Super 88, 98

1961

F-85 (wb 112.0)		Wght	Price	Prod
3019	sdn 4d	2,541	2,384	19,765
3027	club cpe	2,549	2,330	2,336
3035	wgn 4d, 6P	2,716	2,681	6,677
3045	wgn 4d, 8P	2,800	2,762	10,087
F-85 Deluxe (wb 112.0)				
3117	Cutlass spt cpe	2,664	2,621	9,935
3119	sdn 4d	2,547	2,519	26,311
3135	wgn 4d, 6P	2,731	2,816	526
3145	wgn 4d, 8P	2,822	2,897	757
Dynamic 88 (wb 123.0)				
3211	sdn 2d	3,966	2,835	4,920
3235	wgn 4d, 6P	4,354	3,363	5,374
3237	Holiday htp cpe	3,981	2,956	19,878
3239	Holiday htp sdn	4,074	3,034	51,562
3245	wgn 4d, 8P	4,428	3,471	4,013
3267	conv cpe	4,068	3,284	9,049
3269	Celebrity sdn 4d	4,031	2,900	42,584
Super 88 (wb 123.0)				
3535	wgn 4d, 6P	4,382	3,665	2,761
3537	Holiday htp cpe	4,024	3,325	7,009
3539	Holiday htp sdn	4,099	3,402	23,272
3545	wgn 4d, 8P	4,445	3,773	2,170
3567	conv cpe	4,099	3,592	2,624
3569	Celebrity sdn 4d	4,065	3,176	15,328
3667	Starfire conv cpe	4,330	4,647	7,600
98 (wb 126.3)				
3819	Town sdn 4d	4,208	3,887	9,087
3829	Holiday htp sdn	4,269	4,021	13,331
3837	Holiday htp cpe	4,187	4,083	4,445
3839	Sport Sedan (htp)	4,319	4,159	12,343
3867	conv cpe	4,225	4,362	3,804

1961 Engines	bore × stroke	bhp	availability
V8, 215.0	3.50×2.80	155	S-F-85
V8, 394.0	4.13×3.69	250	S-88
V8, 394.0	4.13×3.69	325	S-Super 88, 98; O-88
V8, 394.0	4.13×3.69	330	S-Starfire

1962 Starfire Holiday hardtop coupe

1961 Super 88 Holiday hardtop coupe

1962 F-85 Deluxe Jetfire convertible coupe

1962

F-85 (wb 112.0)		Wght	Price	Prod
3019	sdn 4d	2,599	2,457	8,074
3027	club cpe	2,607	2,403	7,909
3035	wgn 4d, 6P	2,780	2,754	3,204
3045	wgn 4d, 8P	2,852	2,835	1,887
3067	conv cpe	2,790	2,760	3,660
F-85 Deluxe (wb 112.0)				
3117	Cutlass spt cpe	2,651	2,694	32,461
3119	sdn 4d	2,634	2,592	18,736
3135	wgn 4d, 6P	2,812	2,889	4,974
3167	Cutlass conv cpe	2,830	2,971	9,893
3147	Jetfire spt cpe	2,739	3,049	3,765
Dynamic 88 (wb 123.0)				
3235	wgn 4d, 6P	4,392	3,460	8,527
3239	Holiday htp sdn	4,080	3,131	53,438
3245	wgn 4d, 8P	4,428	3,568	6,417
3247	Holiday htp cpe	3,992	3,054	39,676
3267	conv cpe	4,104	3,381	12,212
3269	Celebrity sdn 4d	4,038	2,997	68,467
Super 88 (wb 123.0)				
3535	Fiesta wgn 4d	4,412	3,762	3,837
3539	Holiday htp sdn	4,117	3,499	21,175
3547	Holiday htp cpe	4,022	3,422	9,010
3569	Celebrity sdn 4d	4,069	3,273	24,125
Starfire (wb 123.0)				
3647	htp cpe	4,213	4,131	34,839
3667	conv cpe	4,334	4,744	7,149
98 (wb 126.0)				
3819	Town Sedan 4d	4,258	3,984	12,167
3829	Holiday htp sdn	4,306	4,118	7,653
3839	Sport Sedan (htp)	4,337	4,256	33,095
3847	Holiday htp cpe	4,231	4,180	7,546
3867	conv cpe	4,298	4,459	3,693

1962 Engines	bore×stroke	bhp	availability
V8, 215.0	3.50×2.80	155	S-F-85 exc Cutlass/Jetfire
V8, 215.0	3.50×2.80	185	S-F-85 Cutlass; O-F-85
V8T, 215.0	3.50×2.80	215	S-F-85 Jetfire
V8, 394.0	4.13×3.69	260	O-88
V8, 394.0	4.13×3.69	280	S-88
V8, 394.0	4.13×3.69	330	S-Super 88, 98
V8, 394.0	4.13×3.69	345	S-Starfire

1963

F-85 (wb 112.0)		Wght	Price	Prod
3019	sdn 4d	2,629	2,457	8,937
3027	club cpe	2,599	2,403	11,276
3035	wgn 4d	2,812	2,754	3,348
F-85 Deluxe (wb 112.0)				
3117	Cutlass club cpe	2,679	2,694	41,343
3119	sdn 4d	2,659	2,592	29,269
3135	wgn 4d	2,833	2,889	6,647
3147	Jetfire htp cpe	2,774	3,048	5,842
3167	Cutlass conv cpe	2,858	2,971	12,149
Dynamic 88 (wb 123.0)				
3235	wgn 4d, 6P	4,322	3,459	9,615
3239	Holiday htp sdn	4,059	3,130	62,351
3245	wgn 4d, 8P	4,354	3,566	7,116
3247	Holiday htp cpe	3,839	3,052	39,071
3267	conv cpe	4,039	3,379	12,551
3269	Celebrity sdn 4d	3,998	2,995	68,611
Super 88 (wb 123.0)				
3535	Fiesta wgn 4d	4,347	3,748	3,878
3539	Holiday htp sdn	4,083	3,473	25,387
3547	Holiday htp cpe	3,966	3,408	8,930
3569	Celebrity sdn 4d	4,027	3,246	24,575
Starfire (wb 123.0)				
3657	htp cpe	4,172	4,129	21,148
3667	conv cpe	4,293	4,742	4,401
98 (wb 126.0)				
3819	Town Sedan 4d	4,240	3,982	11,053
3829	Luxury htp sdn	4,362	4,332	19,252
3839	Sport Sedan (htp)	4,347	4,258	23,330
3847	Holiday htp cpe	4,215	4,178	4,984
3867	conv cpe	4,272	4,457	4,267
3947	Custom htp cpe	4,285	4,381	7,422

1963 Engines	bore×stroke	bhp	availability
V8, 215.0	3.50×2.80	155	S-F-85 exc Cutlass/Jetfire
V8, 215.0	3.50×2.80	185	S-F-85 Cutlass; 0-F-85
V8, 215.0	3.50×2.80	215	S-F-85 Jetfire
V8, 394.0	4.13×3.69	260	O-88
V8, 394.0	4.13×3.69	280	S-88
V8, 394.0	4.13×3.69	330	S-Super 88, 98 exc Custom
V8, 394.0	4.13×3.69	345	S-Starfire, 98 Custom

1964

F-85 (wb 115.0; Vista Crsr-120.0)		Wght	Price	Prod
3027	club cpe	2,980	2,343	16,298
3035	wgn 4d	3,274	2,689	4,047
3055	Vista Cruiser wgn 4d, 2S	3,652	2,938	1,305
3065	Vista Cruiser wgn 4d, 3S	3,729	3,072	2,089
3069	sdn 4d	3,025	2,397	12,106
3127	Del Sports Coupe	2,824	2,537	6,594
3135	Del wgn 4d	3,304	2,797	909
3169	Del sdn 4d	3,055	2,505	7,428
Cutlass (wb 115.0)				
3227	Sports Coupe	3,141	2,644	15,440
3237	Holiday htp cpe	3,180	2,784	36,153
3255	Custom wgn 4d 2S	3,714	3,146	3,320
3265	Custom Wgn 4d, 3S	3,781	3,270	7,286
3267	conv cpe	3,263	2,984	12,822
Jetstar 88 (wb 123.0)				
3339	Holiday htp sdn	3,783	3,069	19,325
3347	Holiday htp cpe	3,701	2,992	14,663
3367	conv cpe	3,754	3,318	3,903
3369	Celebrity sdn 4d	3,729	2,935	24,614
Dynamic 88 (123.0)				
3435	wgn 4d, 2S	4,286	3,468	10,747
3439	Holiday htp sdn	4,012	3,139	50,327
3445	wgn 4d, 3S	4,324	3,576	6,599
3447	Holiday htp cpe	3,924	3,062	32,369
3457	Jetstar I spt cpe	4,019	3,603	16,084
3467	conv cpe	3,996	3,389	10,042
3469	Celebrity sdn 4d	3,966	3,005	57,590
Super 88 (wb 123.0)				
3539	Holiday htp sdn	4,069	3,486	17,778
3569	Celebrity sdn 4d	4,009	3,256	19,736
Starfire (wb 123.0)				
3657	htp cpe	4,167	4,138	13,753
3667	conv cpe	4,253	4,753	2,410
98 (wb 126.0)				
3819	Town Sedan 4d	4,234	3,993	11,380
3829	Luxury sdn 4d	4,337	4,342	17,346
3839	Sport Sedan (htp)	4,323	4,265	24,791
3847	htp cpe	4,205	4,118	6,139

1964 98 hardtop coupe

		Wght	Price	Prod
3867	conv cpe	4,255	4,468	4,004
3947	Custom htp cpe	4,271	4,391	4,594

1964 Engines	bore × stroke	bhp	availability
V6, 225.0	3.75×3.40	155	S-F-85
V8, 330.0	3.94×3.38	230	S-Vista Crsr; O-F-85, Jetstar 88
V8, 330.0	3.94×3.38	245	S-Jetstar 88
V8, 330.0	3.94×3.38	290	S-Cutlass; O-F-85, Jetstar 88
V8, 330.0	3.94×3.38	310	O-F-85 V8 (4-4-2 pkg.)
V8, 394.0	4.13×3.69	280	S-88
V8, 394.0	4.13×3.69	330	S-Super 88, 98; 0-88
V8, 394.0	4.13×3.69	345	S-Jetstar I, Starfire, 98 Custom; O-Super 88, 98

1965

F-85 (wb 115.0; Vista Crsr-120.0)		Wght	Price	Prod
3327	club cpe, V6	2,940	2,344	5,289
3335	wgn 4d, V6	3,252	2,689	714
3369	sdn 4d, V6	2,991	2,398	3,089
3427	club cpe, V8	3,146	2,415	7,720
3435	wgn 4d, V8	3,457	2,760	2,496
3455	Vista Crsr. wgn, 6P, V8	3,732	2,937	2,110
3465	Vista Crsr. wgn, 8P, V8	3,809	3,072	3,335
3469	sdn 4d, V8	3,174	2,469	5,661
F-85 Deluxe (wb 115.0; Cus-120.0)				
3527	Sports Coupe, V6	2,980	2,538	6,141
3535	wgn 4d, V6	3,262	2,797	659
3569	sdn 4d, V6	3,016	2,505	4,989
3635	wgn 4d, V8	3,459	2,868	10,365
3669	sdn 4d, V8	3,218	2,576	47,767
3855	Cus wgn 4d, 6P, V8	3,762	3,146	9,335

		Wght	Price	Prod
3865	Cus wgn 4d, 8P, V8	3,864	3,270	17,205
Cutlass (wb 115.0)				
3827	Sports Coupe, V8	3,221	2,643	26,441
3837	Holiday htp cpe, V8	3,245	2,784	46,138
3867	conv cpe, V8	3,338	2,983	12,628
Jetstar 88 (wb 123.0)				
5237	Holiday htp cpe	3,688	2,995	13,911
5239	Holiday htp sdn	3,775	3,072	15,922
5267	conv cpe	3,741	3,337	2,879
5269	Celebrity sdn 4d	3,726	2,938	22,725
Jetstar I (wb 123.0)				
5457	Sports Coupe	3,982	3,602	6,552
Dynamic 88 (wb 123.0)				
5637	Holiday htp cpe	3,873	3,065	24,746
5639	Holiday htp sdn	3,961	3,143	38,889
5667	conv cpe	3,946	3,408	8,832
5669	Celebrity sdn 4d	3,908	3,008	47,030
Delta 88 (wb 123.0)				
5837	htp cpe	3,924	3,253	23,194
5839	htp sdn	4,010	3,330	37,358
5869	Celebrity sdn 4d	3,940	3,158	29,915
Starfire (wb 123.0)				
6657	htp cpe	4,152	4,138	13,024
6667	conv cpe	4,247	4,778	2,236
98 (wb 126.0)				
8437	htp cpe	4,178	4,197	12,166
8439	htp sdn	4,286	4,273	28,480

		Wght	Price	Prod
8467	conv cpe	4,250	4,493	4,903
8469	Town Sedan 4d	4,186	4,001	13,266
8669	Luxury sdn 4d	4,285	4,351	33,591

1965 Engines	bore × stroke	bhp	availability
V6, 225.0	3.75×3.40	155	S-F-85 6
V8, 330.0	3.94×3.38	250/260	S-F-85 V8 exc Cutlass/Jetstar 88
V8, 330.0	3.94×3.38	315	S-Cutlass
V8, 400.0	4.00×3.98	320	O-Cutlass
V8, 400.0	4.00×3.98	345	O-F-85 (4-4-2 pkg.)
V8, 425.0	4.13×3.98	310	S-Delta 88, Dynamic 88; 0-98
V8, 425.0	4.13×3.98	360	S-98; O-other full-size
V8, 425.0	4.13×3.98	370	S-Jetstar I, Starfire; O-full-size

1966

F-85 (wb 115.0)		Wght	Price	Prod
33307	cpe, L6	2,951	2,348	6,341
33335	wgn 4d, L6	3,246	2,695	508
33369	sdn 4d, L6	3,001	2,401	2,862
33407	cpe, V8	3,153	2,418	4,923*
33435	wgn 4d, V8	3,431	2,764	1,652
33469	sdn 4d, V8	3,187	2,471	3,754
F-85 Deluxe (wb 115.0)				
33517	Holiday htp cpe, L6	2,990	2,513	2,974
33535	wgn 4d, L6	3,273	2,793	434
33539	Holiday htp sdn, L6	3,077	2,629	1,002
33569	sdn 4d, L6	3,023	2,497	3,568
33617	Holiday htp cpe, V8	3,196	2,583	13,141*
33635	wgn 4d, V8	3,453	2,862	8,058
33639	Holiday htp sdn, V8	3,272	2,699	6,911
33669	sdn 4d, V8	3,210	2,567	27,452
Cutlass (wb 115.0)				
33807	Sports Coupe	3,219	2,633	13,518*
33817	Holiday htp cpe	3,243	2,770	34,580*
33839	Supreme htp sdn	3,296	2,846	30,871
33867	conv cpe	3,349	2,965	9,410*
33869	Celebrity sdn 4d	3,240	2,673	9,017
Vista Cruiser (wb 120.0)				
33455	wgn 4d, 2S	3,735	2,935	1,660
33465	wgn 4d, 3S	3,806	3,087	1,869
33855	Custom wgn 4d, 2S	3,765	3,137	8,910
33865	Custom wgn 4d, 3S	3,861	3,278	14,167

4-4-2 (wb 115.0)		Wght	Price	Prod
33407	cpe	3,454	2,604	1,430*
33617	htp cpe	3,502	2,769	3,827*
33807	spt cpe	3,506	2,786	3,937*
33817	Holiday htp cpe	3,523	2,923	10,053*
33867	conv cpe	3,629	3,118	2,750*
Jetstar 88 (wb 123.0)				
35237	Holiday htp cpe	3,727	2,983	8,575
35239	Holiday htp sdn	3,823	3,059	7,938
35269	Celebrity sdn 4d	3,776	2,927	13,734
Dynamic 88 (wb 123.0)				
35637	Holiday htp cpe	3,899	3,069	20,768
35639	Holiday htp sdn	3,982	3,144	30,784
35667	conv cpe	3,971	3,404	5,540
35669	Celebrity sdn 4d	3,930	3,013	38,742
Delta 88 (wb 123.0)				
35837	Holiday htp cpe	3,944	3,253	20,857
35839	Holiday htp sdn	4,026	3,328	33,326
35867	conv cpe	4,010	3,588	4,303
35869	Celebrity sdn 4d	3,963	3,160	30,140
Starfire (wb 123.0)				
35457	htp cpe	4,013	3,564	13,019
98 (wb 126.0)				
38437	Holiday htp cpe	4,165	4,158	11,488
38439	Holiday htp sdn	4,266	4,233	23,048
38467	conv cpe	4,233	4,443	4,568
38469	Town Sedan 4d	4,177	3,966	10,892
38669	Luxury Sedan 4d	4,271	4,308	38,123
Toronado (wb 119.0)				
39487	htp cpe	4,311	4,617	6,333
39687	Deluxe htp cpe	4,366	4,812	34,630

*Production combined; numbers given are proportional to production of same models in F-85 and Cutlass lines. Total 4-4-2 production: 21,997.

1966 Engines	bore × stroke	bhp	availability
L6, 250.0	3.88×3.53	155	S-F-85 6
V8, 330.0	3.94×3.38	250	S-F-85 V8, Vista Crsr; O-Jetstar 88
V8, 330.0	3.94×3.38	260	S-Jetstar 88
V8, 330.0	3.94×3.38	310	O-Cutlass, F-85, Vista Crsr
V8, 330.0	3.94×3.38	320	S-Cutlass; O-Jetstar 88, F-85, Vst. Crsr
V8, 400.0	4.00×3.98	350	S-442

1966 Toronado hardtop coupe

	bore×stroke	bhp	availability
V8, 425.0	4.13×3.98	300	O-Delta 88, Dynamic 88
V8, 425.0	4.13×3.98	310	S-Delta 88, Dynamic 88
V8, 425.0	4.13×3.98	365	S-98; O-Delta 88, Dynamic 88
V8, 425.0	4.13×3.98	375	S-Starfire; 0-98, Delta 88
V8, 425.0	4.13×3.98	385	S-Toronado

1967

F-85 (wb 115.0)		Wght	Price	Prod
33307	club cpe, L6	3,014	2,410	5,349
33335	wgn 4d, L6	3,295	2,749	2,749
33369	Town Sedan 4d, L6	3,031	2,457	2,458
33407	club cpe, V8	3,184	2,480	6,700
33435	wgn 4d, V8	3,463	2,818	1,625
33469	Town Sedan 4d, V8	3,469	2,527	5,126
Cutlass (wb 115.0)				
33517	Holiday htp cpe, L6	3,033	2,574	2,564
33535	wgn 4d, L6	3,308	2,848	365
33539	Holiday htp sdn, L6	3,125	2,683	644
33567	conv cpe, L6	3,125	2,770	567
33569	Town Sedan 4d, L6	3,055	2,552	2,219
33617	Holiday htp cpe, V8	3,216	2,644	29,799
33635	wgn 4d, V8	3,473	2,917	8,130
33639	Holiday htp sdn, V8	3,292	2,753	7,344
33667	conv cpe, V8	3,306	2,839	3,777
33669	Town Sedan 4d, V8	3,223	2,622	29,062
Cutlass Supreme (wb 115.0)				
33807	Sports Coupe	3,238	2,694	13,041*
33817	Holiday htp cpe	3,262	2,831	41,344*
33839	Holiday htp sdn	3,346	2,900	22,571
33867	conv cpe	3,867	3,026	7,793*
33869	Town Sedan 4d	3,258	2,726	8,346
4-4-2 (wb 115.0)				
33807	Sports Coupe	3,540	2,788	5,215*
33817	Holiday htp cpe	3,568	3,015	16,514*
33867	conv cpe	4,047	3,210	3,104*
Vista Cruiser (wb 120.0)				
33465	wgn 4d, 3S	3,836	3,136	2,748
33855	Custom wgn 4d, 2S	3,796	3,228	9,513
33865	Custom wgn 4d, 3S	3,907	3,369	15,293
Delmont 88 "330" (wb 123.0)				
35239	Holiday htp sdn	3,932	3,139	10,600
35269	Town Sedan 4d	3,867	3,008	15,076
35287	Holiday htp cpe	3,819	3,063	10,786
Delmont 88 "425" (wb 123.0)				
35639	Holiday htp sdn	4,007	3,202	22,980
35667	conv cpe	4,010	3,462	3,525
35669	Town Sedan 4d	3,968	3,071	28,690
35687	Holiday htp cpe	3,914	3,126	16,699
Delta 88 (wb 123.0)				
35839	Holiday htp sdn	4,053	3,386	21,909
35867	conv cpe	4,039	3,646	2,447
35869	Town Sedan 4d	3,986	3,218	22,770
35887	Holiday htp cpe	3,956	3,310	14,471
Delta 88 Custom (wb 123.0)				
35439	Holiday htp sdn	4,081	3,582	14,306
35487	Holiday htp cpe	3,994	3,522	12,192
98 (wb 126.0)				
38439	Holiday htp sdn	4,323	4,276	17,533
38457	Holiday htp cpe	4,221	4,214	10,476
38467	conv cpe	4,271	4,498	3,769
38469	Town Sedan 4d	4,242	4,009	8,900
38669	Luxury Sedan 4d	4,309	4,351	35,511

1966 Cutlass Holiday hardtop coupe

1970 4-4-2 Holiday hardtop coupe

Toronado (wb 119.0)		Wght	Price	Prod
39487	htp cpe	4,310	4,674	1,770
39687	Deluxe htp cpe	4,362	4,869	20,020

*Production combined; numbers given are proportional to production of same models in Cutlass Supreme line. Total 4-4-2 production: 24,833.

1967 Engines	bore×stroke	bhp	availability
L6, 250.0	3.88×3.53	155	S-F-85 6, Cutlass 6
V8, 330.0	3.94×3.38	250	S-F-85 V8, Cutlass V8, Vst. Crsr, Delm 88 man; O-Delm auto
V8, 330.0	3.94×3.38	260	S-Delmont 88 w/auto
V8, 330.0	3.94×3.38	310	O-Supreme, Cutls, F-85, VC
V8, 330.0	3.94×3.38	320	S-Sprme; O-Delm, VC, F-85,Cutls
V8, 400.0	4.00×3.98	300	O-Sprme cpe & conv
V8, 400.0	4.00×3.98	350	S-442; O-Sprme cpe & conv
V8, 425.0	4.13×3.98	300	S-all 88 man; O-all 88 auto
V8, 425.0	4.13×3.98	310	S-all 88 automatic
V8, 425.0	4.13×3.98	365	S-98; O-Delta 88, Delmont 425
V8, 425.0	4.13×3.98	375	O-98, Delta 88, Delmont 425
V8, 425.0	4.13×3.98	385	S-Toronado

1968

F-85 (wb 116.0; 2d-112.0)		Wght	Price	Prod
33169	Town Sedan 4d, L6	3,108	2,560	1,847
33177	club cpe, L6	3,062	2,512	4,052
33269	Town Sedan 4d, V8	3,304	2,665	3,984
33277	club cpe, V8	3,255	2,618	5,426
Cutlass (wb 116.0; 2d-112.0)				
33535	wgn 4d, 2S, L6	3,473	2,969	354
33539	Holiday htp sdn, L6	3,193	2,804	265
33567	conv cpe, L6	3,161	2,949	410

		Wght	Price	Prod
33569	Town Sedan 4d, L6	3,143	2,674	1,305
33577	Sports Coupe, L6	3,064	2,632	1,181
33587	Holiday htp cpe, L6	3,108	2,696	1,492
33635	wgn 4d, 2S, V8	3,649	3,075	9,291
33639	Holiday htp sdn, V8	3,374	2,910	7,839
33667	conv cpe, V8	3,342	3,055	13,667
33669	Town Sedan 4d, V8	3,325	2,779	25,994
33677	Sport Coupe, V8	3,271	2,738	14,586
33687	Holiday htp cpe, V8	3,282	2,801	59,577
Cutlass Supreme (wb 116.0; 2d-112.0)				
34239	Holiday htp sdn	3,421	3,057	15,067
34269	Town Sedan 4d	3,372	2,884	5,524
34287	Holiday htp cpe	3,312	2,982	33,518
4-4-2 (wb 112.0)*				
34467	conv cpe	3,580	3,341	5,142
34477	Sports Coupe	3,502	3,087	4,282
34487	Holiday htp cpe	3,512	3,150	24,183
Vista Cruiser (wb 121.0)				
34855	Custom wgn 4d, 2S	3,917	3,367	13,375
34865	Custom wgn 4d, 3S	4,027	3,508	22,768
Delmont 88 (wb 123.0)**				
35439	Holiday htp sdn	3,928	3,278	21,056
35467	conv cpe	3,916	3,515	2,812
35469	Town Sedan 4d	3,873	3,146	24,365
35487	Holiday htp cpe	3,844	3,202	18,391
Delta 88 (wb 123.0)**				
36439	Holiday htp sdn	4,038	3,525	30,048
36469	Town Sedan 4d	3,979	3,357	33,689
36487	Holiday htp cpe	3,950	3,449	18,501
36639	Custom Holiday htp sdn	4,059	3,721	10,727
36687	Custom Holiday htp cpe	3,982	3,661	9,540
98 (wb 126.0)				
38439	Holiday htp sdn	4,278	4,422	21,147
38457	Holiday htp cpe	4,185	4,360	15,319
38467	conv cpe	4,264	4,618	3,942
38469	Town Sedan 4d	4,197	4,155	10,584
38669	Luxury Sedan 4d	4,273	4,497	40,755
Toronado (wb 119.0)				
39487	htp cpe	4,322	4,750	3,957
39687	Custom htp cpe	4,374	4,945	22,497

*4-4-2 production includes 515 Hurst/Olds models.
**Factory records also indicate 54,794 Dynamic 88s, although other sources do not include these models.

1970 4-4-2 convertible coupe

1968 Engines	bore × stroke	bhp	availability
L6, 250.0	3.88 × 3.53	155	S-F-85 6, Cutlass 6
V8, 350.0	4.06 × 3.38	250	S-Dlmnt88, VstCrsr; O-Ctls, F-85
V8, 350.0	4.06 × 3.38	310	S-Supreme; O-F-85, Cutls, Vista Cruiser, Delmont 88 auto
V8, 400.0	4.00 × 3.98	290	O-442 auto, Vista Cruiser auto
V8, 400.0	4.00 × 3.98	325	S-442 auto; O-Vista Cruiser auto
V8, 400.0	4.00 × 3.98	350	S-442 manual
V8, 400.0	4.00 × 3.98	360	O-442 all
V8, 455.0	4.13 × 4.25	310	S-Delta 88 & Custom; O-Delm
V8, 455.0	4.13 × 4.25	320	0-above models w/automatic
V8, 455.0	4.13 × 4.25	365	S-98; O-all 88 w/automatic
V8, 455.0	4.13 × 4.25	375	S-Toronado
V8, 455.0	4.13 × 4.25	390	O-442 (Hurst/Olds)
V8, 455.0	4.13 × 4.25	400	O-Toronado

1969

F-85 (wb 116.0; 2d-112.0)		Wght	Price	Prod
33177	Sports Coupe, L6	3,082	2,561	2,899
33277	Sports Coupe, V8	3,281	2,672	5,541
Cutlass (wb 116.0; 2d-112.0)				
33535	wgn 4d, 2S, L6	3,537	3,055	180
33539	Holiday htp sdn, L6	3,212	2,853	236
33567	S conv cpe, L6	3,188	2,998	236
33569	Town Sedan 4d, L6	3,155	2,722	137
33577	S Sports Coupe, L6	3,093	2,681	483
33587	S Holiday htp cpe, L6	3,118	2,745	566
33635	wgn 4d, 2S, V8	3,736	3,165	8,559
33639	Holiday htp sdn, V8	3,407	2,964	7,046
33667	S conv cpe, V8	3,386	3,109	13,498
33669	Town Sedan 4d, V8	3,356	2,833	24,521
33677	S Sports Coupe, V8	3,293	2,792	10,682
33687	S Holiday htp cpe, V8	3,316	2,855	66,495
Cutlass Supreme (wb 116; 2d-112.0)				
34239	Holiday htp sdn	3,421	3,111	8,714
34269	Town Sedan 4d	3,361	2,938	4,522
34287	Holiday htp cpe	3,331	3,036	24,193
4-4-2 (wb 112.0)*				
34467	conv cpe	3,580	3,395	4,295
34477	Sports Coupe	3,502	3,141	2,475
34487	Holiday htp cpe	3,512	3,204	19,587
*4-4-2 production includes 914 Hurst/Olds models (2 convertibles).				
Vista Cruiser (wb 121.0)				
34855	wgn 4d, 2S	3,952	3,457	11,879
34865	wgn 4d, 3S	4,052	3,600	21,508
Delta 88 (wb 124.0)				
35437	Holiday htp cpe	3,812	3,277	41,947
35439	Holiday htp sdn	3,901	3,353	42,690
35467	conv cpe	3,892	3,590	5,294
35469	Town Sedan 4d	3,859	3,222	49,995
36437	Custom Holiday htp cpe	3,927	3,525	22,083
36439	Custom Holiday htp sdn	4,009	3,600	36,502
36469	Custom Town Sedan 4d	3,962	3,432	31,012
36647	Royale Holiday htp cpe	3,935	3,836	22,564
98 (wb 127.0)				
38439	Holiday htp sdn	4,260	4,523	17,294
38457	Holiday htp cpe	4,150	4,461	27,041
38467	conv cpe	4,223	4,719	4,288
38469	Town Sedan 4d	4,150	4,255	11,169
38639	Luxury Sedan (htp)	4,288	4,692	25,973
38669	Luxury Sedan 4d	4,245	4,598	30,643
Toronado (wb 119.0)				
39487	htp cpe	4,316	4,835	3,421
39687	Custom htp cpe	4,368	5,030	25,073

1971 4-4-2 convertible coupe

1972 Hurst/Olds Cutlass convertible coupe

1969 Engines	bore×stroke	bhp	availability
L6, 250.0	3.88×3.53	155	S- F-85, Cutlass
V8, 350.0	4.06×3.38	250	S-Cutlass S/sdns/wgns, F-85, Delta 88, Vst Crsr; O-Supreme
V8, 350.0	4.06×3.38	310	S-Supreme; O-Cutlass, Vst Crsr, F-85
V8, 350.0	4.06×3.38	325	O-Cutlass S, F-85
V8, 400.0	4.00×3.98	325	S-442 auto, Vista Cruiser auto
V8, 400.0	4.00×3.98	350	S-442 manual
V8, 400.0	4.00×3.98	360	O-442
V8, 455.0	4.13×4.25	310	S-Dlta 88 Cus/Royale; O-Delta
V8, 455.0	4.13×4.25	365	S-98; O-all Delta 88
V8, 455.0	4.13×4.25	375	S-Toronado
V8, 455.0	4.13×4.25	380	O-442 (Hurst/Olds)
V8, 455.0	4.13×4.25	390	O-all Delta 88
V8, 455.0	4.13×4.25	400	O-Toronado

1970

F-85 (wb 116.0; 2d-112.0)		Wght	Price	Prod
33177	Sports Coupe, L6	3,190	2,676	2,836
33277	Sports Coupe, V8	3,401	2,787	8,274
Cutlass (wb 116.0; 2d-112.0)				
33535	wgn 4d, 2S, L6	3,630	3,234	85
33539	Holiday htp sdn, L6	3,326	2,968	238
33569	Town Sedan 4d, L6	3,257	2,837	1,171
33577	S Sports Coupe, L6	3,201	2,796	484
33587	S Holiday htp cpe, L6	3,238	2,859	729
33635	wgn 4d, 2S, V8	3,837	3,344	7,686
33639	Holiday htp sdn, V8	3,523	3,079	9,427
33669	Town Sedan, V8	3,468	2,948	35,239
33677	S Sports Coupe, V8	3,416	2,907	10,677
33687	S Holiday htp cpe, V8	3,452	2,970	88,578
Cutlass Supreme (wb 116; 2d-112.0)				
34239	Holiday htp sdn	3,558	3,226	10,762
34257	Holiday htp cpe	3,471	3,151	68,309
34267	conv cpe	3,510	3,335	11,354
4-4-2 (wb 112.0)				
34467	conv cpe	3,740	3,567	2,933
34477	Sports Coupe	3,667	3,312	1,688
34487	Holiday htp cpe	3,713	3,376	14,709
Vista Cruiser (wb 121.0)				
34855	wgn 4d, 2S	4,064	3,636	10,758
34865	wgn 4d, 3S	4,166	3,778	23,336
Delta 88 (wb 124.0)				
35437	Holiday htp cpe	3,900	3,590	33,017
35439	Holiday htp sdn	3,986	3,666	37,695
35467	conv cpe	3,985	3,903	3,095
35469	Town Sedan 4d	3,944	3,534	47,067
36437	Custom Holiday htp cpe	3,999	3,848	16,149
36439	Custom Holiday htp sdn	4,087	3,924	28,432
36469	Custom Town Sedan 4d	4,040	3,755	24,727
36647	Royale Holiday htp cpe	4,002	4,159	13,249
98 (wb 127.0)				
38439	Holiday htp sdn	4,329	4,582	14,098
38457	Holiday htp cpe	4,257	4,656	21,111
38467	conv cpe	4,289	4,914	3,161
38469	Town Sedan 4d	4,263	4,451	9,092
38639	Luxury htp sdn	4,400	4,888	19,377
38669	Luxury sdn 4d	4,356	4,793	29,005
Toronado (wb 119.0)				
39487	htp cpe	4,331	5,023	2,351
39687	Custom htp cpe	4,386	5,216	23,082

1970 Engines	bore×stroke	bhp	availability
L6, 250.0	3.88×3.53	155	S- F-85, Cutlass
V8, 350.0	4.06×3.38	250	S- F-85/Cutlass V8, Vst Crsr; O-Supreme
V8, 350.0	4.06×3.38	310	S-Supreme; O-Vst Crsr, F-85, Cutlass
V8, 350.0	4.06×3.38	325	O-F-85, Cutlass S auto or 4 spd
V8, 455.0	4.13×4.25	310	S-Delta 88 manual
V8, 455.0	4.13×4.25	320	O-Cutlass w/automatic
V8, 455.0	4.13×4.25	365	S-442, 98; O-Supreme, 88/Vst Crsr manual
V8, 455.0	4.13×4.25	370	O-442 w/auto or close-ratio 4spd
V8, 455.0	4.13×4.25	375	S-Toronado
V8, 455.0	4.13×4.25	390	O-Delta 88
V8, 455.0	4.13×4.25	400	O-Toronado

1971

F-85 (wb 116.0)		Wght	Price	Prod
33169	Town sdn 4d L6	3,226	2,885	769
33269	Town sdn 4d V8	3,424	3,006	3,650
Cutlass (wb 116.0; 2d-112.0)				
33187	Holiday htp cpe L6	3,292	2,901	1,345
33536	wgn 4d 2S L6	3,732	3,454	47
33569	Town sdn 4d L6	3,252	2,999	618
33287	Holiday htp cpe V8	3,398	3,022	32,278
33636	wgn 4d 2S V8	3,927	3,575	6,742
33669	Town sdn 4d V8	3,438	3,120	31,904
33577	S spt cpe L6	3,196	2,958	113
33587	S Holiday htp cpe L6	3,228	3,021	169
33677	S spt cpe V8	3,392	3,079	4,339

		Wght	Price	Prod
33687	S Holiday htp cpe V8	3,398	3,142	63,145
Cutlass Supreme (wb 116.0; 2d-112.0)				
34239	Holiday htp sdn	3,541	3,398	10,458
34257	Holiday htp cpe	3,429	3,323	60,599
34267	conv	3,513	3,507	10,255
4-4-2 (wb 112.0)				
34467	conv cpe	3,731	3,743	1,304
34487	Holiday cpe	3,688	3,552	6,285
Vista Cruiser (wb 121.0)				
34856	wgn 4d 2S	4,163	3,866	5,980
34866	wgn 4d 3S	4,251	4,008	20,566
Delta 88 (wb 124.0; wgns-127.0)				
35439	Holiday sdn 4d	4,202	4,103	31,420
35457	Holiday htp cpe	4,122	4,041	27,031
35469	Town sdn 4d	4,150	3,985	38,298
36439	Custom Holiday htp sdn 4d	4,237	4,366	26,593
36457	Custom Holiday cpe	4,179	4,291	24,251
36469	Custom Town sdn 4d	4,202	4,198	22,209
36647	Royale Holiday htp cpe	4,221	4,549	8,397
36667	Royale conv	4,296	4,557	2,883
36835	Custom Cruiser wgn 4d 2S	4,880	4,776	4,049
36845	Custom Cruiser wgn 4d 3S	5,000	4,917	9,932
Ninety-Eight (wb 127.0)				
38437	Holiday htp cpe	4,382	4,790	8,335
38439	Holiday htp sdn	4,467	4,852	15,025
38637	Luxury htp cpe	4,418	5,065	14,876
38639	Luxury htp sdn	4,504	5,159	45,055
Toronado (wb 123.0)				
39657	htp cpe	4,522	5,457	28,980

1971 Engines	bore×stroke	bhp	availability
L6, 250.0	3.88×3.53	145	S-F-85, Cutlass
V8, 350.0	4.06×3.38	240	S-F-85, Cutlass, Delta, VC
V8, 350.0	4.06×3.38	260	S-Supreme, O-F-85, Cutlass, VC
V8, 455.0	4.13×4.25	280	O-Delta
V8, 455.0	4.13×4.25	320	S-98; O-442, F-85, Ctls, VC, DLta
V8, 455.0	4.13×4.25	340	S-442; O-F-85, Cutlass, VC
V8, 455.0	4.13×4.25	350	S-Toronado

1972

F-85 (wb 116.0)		Wght	Price	Prod
3D69	sdn 4d	3,420	2,958	3,792
Cutlass (wb 116.0; 2d-112.0)				
3F87	cpe	3,379	2,973	37,790
3G36	Cruiser wgn 4d 2S	3,919	3,498	7,979
3G69	Town sdn 4d	3,443	3,066	38,893
3G77	S spt cpe	3,387	3,027	4,141
3G87	S Holiday htp cpe	3,404	3,087	78,461
3J39	Supreme Holiday htp sdn	3,530	3,329	14,955
3J57	Supreme Holiday htp cpe	3,395	3,258	105,087
3J67	Supreme conv	3,528	3,433	11,571
Vista Cruiser (wb 121.0)				
3K56	wgn 4d 2S	4,150	3,774	10,573
3K66	wgn 4d 3S	4,241	3,908	21,340
Delta 88 (wb 124.0)				
3L39	Holiday sdn 4d	4,235	4,060	35,538
3L57	Holiday htp cpe	4,133	4,001	32,036
3L69	Town sdn 4d	4,187	3,948	46,092
3N39	Royale Holiday sdn 4d	4,263	4,238	42,606
3N57	Royale Holiday htp cpe	4,184	4,179	34,345
3N67	Royale conv	4,257	4,387	3,900
3N69	Royale Town sdn 4d	4,198	4,101	34,150
3R35	Custom Cruiser wgn 4d 2S	4,947	4,700	6,907
3R45	Custom Cruiser wgn 4d 3S	5,040	4,834	18,087
Ninety-Eight (wb 127.0)				
3U37	Holiday htp cpe	4,372	4,748	13,111
3U39	htp sdn	4,448	4,807	17,572
3V37	Luxury htp cpe	4,428	5,009	24,453
3V39	Luxury htp sdn	4,533	5,098	69,920
Toronado (wb 122.0)				
3Y57	Custom htp cpe	4,544	5,341	48,900

1973 Cutlass Supreme Colonnade hardtop coupe

1972 Engines	bore×stroke	bhp	availability
V8, 350.0	4.06×3.38	160	S-F-85,Ctls,Dlta exc wgns
V8, 350.0	4.06×3.38	180	S-Supreme; O-Ctls,F-85, VC Delta exc wgn
V8, 455.0	4.13×4.25	225	S-Dlta wgn, 98; O-Dlta
V8, 455.0	4.13×4.25	250	S-Toro; O-Delta, 98
V8, 455.0	4.13×4.25	270/300	O-Ctls cpe/conv(Hurst/Olds)

Note: A total of 629 Hurst/Olds packages were installed on Cutlass models.

1973

Omega (wb 111.0)		Wght	Price	Prod
B17	htchbk cpe 3d	3,329	2,762	21,433
B27	cpe	3,217	2,613	26,126
B69	sdn 4d	3,280	2,641	12,804
Cutlass (wb 116.0; 2d-112.0)				
G29	Colonnade sdn 4d	3,786	3,137	35,578
F37	Colonnade sdn 2d	3,713	3,049	22,022
G37	Colonnade S sdn 2d	3,721	3,159	77,558
J29	Supreme Colonnade sdn 4d	3,808	3,395	26,099
J57	Supreme Colonnade sdn 2d	3,694	3,324	219,857
Vista Cruiser (wb 121.0)				
J35	wgn 5d 2S	4,240	3,789	10,894
J45	wgn 5d 3S	4,290	3,902	13,531
Delta 88 (wb 124.0)				
L39	htp sdn	4,270	4,108	27,986
L57	htp cpe	4,192	4,047	27,096
L69	Town sdn 4d	4,243	3,991	42,476
N39	Royale htp sdn	4,296	4,293	49,145
N57	Royale htp cpe	4,206	4,221	27,096
N67	Royale conv	4,298	4,442	7,088
N69	Royale Town sdn 4d	4,255	4,156	42,672
Q35	wgn 4d 2S	4,997	4,630	5,275
Q45	wgn 4d 3S	5,061	4,769	7,341
R35	Royale wgn 4d 2S	4,999	4,785	7,142
R45	Royale wgn 4d 3S	5,063	4,924	19,163
Ninety-Eight (wb 127.0)				
T37	htp cpe	4,435	4,799	7,850
T39	htp sdn	4,522	4,860	13,989
V37	Luxury htp cpe	4,471	5,071	26,925
V39	Luxury htp sdn	4,560	5,164	55,695
X39	Regency htp sdn	4,594	5,418	34,009
Toronado (wb 122.0)				
Y57	htp cpe	4,654	5,441	55,921

1973 Engines	bore×stroke	bhp	availability
L6, 250.0	3.88×3.53	100	S-Omega
V8, 350.0	4.06×3.38	160	S-Delta exc wgns
V8, 350.0	4.06×3.38	180	S-Omega, Cutlass, VC
V8, 455.0	4.13×4.25	225	S-Dlta wgns; 98; O-Dlta
V8, 455.0	4.13×4.25	250	S-Toronado, O-Cutlass,VC

1974

Omega (wb 111.0)		Wght	Price	Prod
B17	htchbk cpe 3d	3,423	3,166	12,449
B27	cpe	3,319	3,043	27,075
B69	sdn 4d	3,367	3,071	10,756
Cutlass (wb 116.0; 2d-112.0)				
F37	Colonnade sdn 2d	3,868	3,793	16,063
G29	Colonnade sdn 4d	3,924	3,868	25,718
G37	Colonnade S sdn 2d	3,883	3,890	50,860
J29	Supreme Colonnade sdn 4d	3,969	4,142	12,525
J57	Supreme Colonnade sdn 2d	3,872	4,085	172,360
H35	Supreme Cruiser wgn 5d 2S	4,369	4,289	3,437
H45	Supreme Cruiser wgn 5d 3S	4,406	4,402	3,101
Vista Cruiser (wb 121.0)				
J35	wgn 4d 2S	4,380	4,499	4,191
J45	wgn 4d 3S	4,417	4,612	7,013
Delta 88 (wb 124.0)				
L39	htp sdn	4,428	4,490	11,941
L57	htp cpe	4,375	4,429	11,615
L69	Town sdn 4d	4,396	4,373	17,939
N39	Royale htp sdn	4,462	4,650	26,363
N57	Royale htp cpe	4,397	4,584	27,515
N67	Royale conv	4,454	4,799	3,716
N69	Royale Town sdn 4d	4,414	4,513	22,504
Q35	Custom Cruiser wgn 4d 2S	5,120	4,981	1,481
Q45	Custom Cruiser wgn 4d 3S	5,182	5,120	2,528
R35	Royale wgn 4d 2S	5,123	5,136	2,960
R45	Royale wgn 4d 3S	5,184	5,275	8,947
Ninety-Eight (wb 127.0)				
T39	htp sdn	4,699	5,303	4,395
V37	Luxury cpe	4,638	5,514	9,236
V39	Luxury htp sdn 4d	4,730	5,607	21,896
X37	Regency cpe	4,664	5,776	10,719
X39	Regency htp sdn 4d	4,759	5,869	24,310
Toronado (wb 122.0)				
Y57	htp cpe	4,698	5,933	27,582

1974 Engines	bore×stroke	bhp	availability
L6, 250.0	3.88×3.53	100	S-Omega
V8, 350.0	4.06×3.38	180	S-Omega,Ctls,VC,Delta exc wgns
V8, 350.0	4.06×3.38	200	O-Ctls,VC,Delta exc wgns
V8, 455.0	4.13×4.25	210	S-Delta wgns, 98; O-Delta
V8, 455.0	4.13×4.25	230	S-Toro; O-all exc Omega
V8, 455.0	4.13×4.25	275	O-Cutlass, VC

1975

Starfire (wb 97.0)		Wght	Price	Prod
D37	htchbk cpe 3d	2,914	4,144	31,081
T07	htchbk cpe 3d	2,889	3,873	
Omega (wb 111.0)				
S27	F-85 htchbk cpe 3d	3,250	3,203	15,979
B27	cpe	3,390	3,422	
B17	htchbk cpe	3,482	3,546	6,287
B69	sdn 4d	3,436	3,450	13,971
C17	Salon htchbk cpe 3d	3,566	4,298	1,694
C27	Salon cpe	3,476	4,148	2,176

1977 Cutlass Supreme coupe

		Wght	Price	Prod
C69	Salon sdn 4d	3,526	4,192	1,758
Cutlass (wb 116.0; 2d-112.0)				
F37	Colonnade sdn 2d	3,684	3,742	12,797
G29	Colonnade sdn 4d	3,806	3,818	30,144
G37	Colonnade S sdn 2d	3,740	3,840	42,921
J29	Supreme Colonnade sdn 4d	3,852	4,092	15,517
J57	Supreme Colonnade sdn 2d	3,754	4,035	150,874
K29	Salon Colonnade sdn 4d V8	4,008	4,713	5,810
K57	Salon Colonnade sdn 2d V8	3,915	4,641	39,050
H35	Supreme Cruiser wgn 5d 2S V8	4,376	4,665	8,329
H45	Supreme Cruiser wgn 5d 3S V8	4,413	4,778	3,096
J35	Vista Cruiser wgn 5d 2S V8	4,380	4,875	7,089
J45	Vista Cruiser wgn 5d 3S V8	4,417	4,988	7,101
Delta 88 (wb 124.0)				
L39	htp sdn	4,404	4,891	9,283
L57	htp cpe	4,343	4,830	8,522
L69	Town sdn 4d	4,356	4,778	16,112
N39	Royale htp sdn	4,454	5,051	32,481
N57	Royale htp cpe	4,386	4,985	23,465
N67	Royale conv	4,455	5,200	21,038
N69	Royale Town sdn 4d	4,385	4,914	7,181
Q35	Custom Cruiser wgn 4d 2S	5,095	5,413	6,008
R35	Royale wgn 4d 2S	5,107	5,568	
Q45	Custom Cruiser wgn 4d 3S	5,146	5,552	10,060
R45	Royale wgn 4d 3S	5,161	5,707	
Ninety-Eight (wb 127.0)				
V37	Luxury cpe	4,591	5,950	8,798
V39	Luxury htp sdn 4d	4,743	6,091	18,091
X37	Regency cpe	4,621	6,212	16,697
X39	Regency htp sdn 4d	4,755	6,353	35,264
Toronado (wb 122.0)				
Y57	Custom htp cpe	4,647	6,523	4,419
Z57	Brougham htp cpe	4,691	6,753	18,882

1975 Engines	bore×stroke	bhp	availability
V6, 231.0	3.80×3.40	110	S-Starfire
L6, 250.0	3.88×3.53	105	S-Omega,Ctls exc wgns
V8, 260.0	3.50×3.39	110	S-Omega,Ctls exc wgns
V8, 350.0	4.06×3.38	145	O-Omega
V8, 350.0	4.06×3.38	165	O-Omega
V8, 350.0	4.06×3.38	170	S-Ctls wgns, Delta exc Cust Crsr; O-Ctls
V8, 400.0	4.12×3.75	185	O-Delta, 98
V8, 455.0	4.13×4.25	190	S-Delta Cus Crsr, 98; O-Ctls, other Delta
V8, 455.0	4.13×4.25	215	S-Toronado

1976

Starfire (wb 97.0)		Wght	Price	Prod
D07	SX htchbk cpe 3d	2,864	4,062	20,854
T07	htchbk cpe 3d	2,857	3,882	8,305
Omega (wb 111.0)				
S27	F-85 cpe	3,246	3,390	3,918
B17	htchbk cpe 3d	3,322	3,627	4,497
B27	cpe	3,248	3,485	15,347
B69	sdn 4d	3,270	3,514	20,221
E17	Brougham htchbk cpe 3d	3,332	3,817	1,235
E27	Brougham cpe	3,252	3,675	5,363
E69	Brougham sdn 4d	3,286	3,704	7,587
Cutlass (wb 116.0; 2d-112.0)				
G29	S Colonnade sdn 4d	3,772	4,033	34,994
G37	S Colonnade sdn 2d	3,690	3,999	59,179
J29	Supreme Colonnade sdn 4d	3,812	4,415	37,112
J57	Supreme Colonnade cpe 2d	3,718	4,291	186,647
M57	Supreme Brougham cpe	3,750	4,580	91,312
K29	Salon Colonnade sdn 4d V8	3,949	4,965	7,921
K57	Salon Colonnade cpe 2d V8	3,829	4,890	48,440
H35	Sprme Cruiser wgn 5d 2S V8	4,298	4,923	13,964
H35	Sprme Cruiser wgn 5d 3S V8	4,350	5,056	
J35	Vista Cruiser wgn 5d 2S V8	4,304	5,041	20,560
J35	Vista Cruiser wgn 5d 3S V8	4,350	5,174	
Delta 88 (wb 124.0; wgns 127.0)				
L39	sdn 4d	4,336	5,038	9,759
L57	cpe 2d	4,243	4,975	7,204
L69	Town sdn 4d	4,279	4,918	17,115
N39	Royale sdn 4d	4,268	5,217	52,103
N57	Royale cpe 2d	4,263	5,146	33,364
N69	Royale Town sdn 4d	4,294	5,078	33,268
Q35	Custom Cruiser wgn 4d 2S	4,987	5,563	2,572
Q45	Custom Cruiser wgn 4d 3S	5,060	5,705	3,626
R35	Custom Cruiser wgn 4d 2S (woodgrain)	5,009	5,719	3,849
R45	Custom Cruiser wgn 4d 3S (woodgrain)	5,071	5,861	12,269
Ninety-Eight (wb 127.0)				
V37	Luxury cpe 2d	4,501	6,271	6,056
V39	Luxury htp sdn 4d	4,633	6,419	16,802
X37	Regency cpe 2d	4,535	6,544	26,282
X39	Regency htp sdn 4d	4,673	6,691	55,339
Toronado (wb 122.0)				
Y57	Custom htp cpe	4,694	6,891	2,555
Z57	Brougham htp cpe	4,729	7,137	21,749

1976 Engines	bore×stroke	bhp	availability
V6, 231.0	3.80×3.40	105	S-Starfire
L6, 250.0	3.88×3.53	105	S-Omega,Ctls exc Salon
V8, 260.0	3.50×3.39	110	S-Omega,Ctls Salon; O-Ctls
V8, 350.0	3.80×3.85	140/155	O-Omega
V8, 350.0	4.06×3.38	170	S-Ctls exc Salon; Delta exc wgn; O-Ctls, Salon
V8, 455.0	4.13×4.25	190	S-Delta wgn, 98; O-Ctls, other Delta
V8, 455.0	4.13×4.25	215	S-Toronado

1977

Starfire (wb 97.0)		Wght	Price	Prod
D07	SX htchbk cpe 3d	2,836	4,140	14,181
T07	htchbk cpe 3d	2,808	3,942	4,910
Omega (wb 111.0)				
S27	F-85 cpe	3,184	3,653	2,241
B17	htchbk cpe 3d	3,270	3,905	4,739
B27	cpe	3,202	3,740	18,611
B69	sdn 4d	3,236	3,797	21,723
E17	Brougham htchbk cpe 3d	3,302	4,105	1,189
E27	Brougham cpe	3,226	3,934	6,478
E67	Brougham sdn 4d	3,262	3,994	9,003
Cutlass (wb 116.0; 2d 112.0)				
G29	S sdn 4d	3,690	4,387	42,923
G37	S cpe 2d	3,608	4,351	70,155
J29	Supreme sdn 4d	3,438	4,734	37,929
J57	Supreme cpe 2d	3,638	4,670	242,874
M29	Supreme Brougham sdn 4d	3,764	5,033	16,738
M57	Supreme Brougham cpe 2d	3,656	4,969	124,712
K57	Salon cpe 2d V8	3,787	5,269	56,757
H35	Supreme Cruiser wgn 5d V8	4,218	5,243	14,838
H35	Vista Cruiser wgn 5d V8	4,255	5,395	25,816
Delta (wb 116.0)				
L37	cpe	3,496	5,145	8,788
L69	Town sdn 4d	3,537	5,205	26,084
N37	Royale cpe	3,505	5,363	61,138

		Wght	Price	Prod
N69	Royale Town sdn 4d	3,561	5,433	117,571
Q35	Custom Cruiser wgn 4d 2S V8	4,064	5,923	32,827
Q35	Custom Cruiser wgn 4d 3S V8	4,095	6,098	
Ninety-Eight (wb 119.0)				
V37	Luxury cpe	3,753	6,609	5,058
V69	Luxury sdn 4d	3,807	6,786	14,323
X37	Regency cpe	3,767	6,949	32,072
X69	Regency sdn 4d	3,840	7,133	87,970
Toronado (wb 122.0)				
W57	XS/XSR htp cpe	4,688	11,132	2,714
Z57	Brougham htp cpe	4,634	8,134	31,371

1977 Engines	bore×stroke	bhp	availability
L4, 140.0	3.50×3.63	84	S-Starfire
V6, 231.0	3.80×3.40	105	S-Omega,Ctls,Delta; O-Strfre
V8, 260.0:	3.50×3.39	110	S-Ctls Salon; O-Omega, Cutlass, Delta
V8, 305.0	3.74×3.48	145	O-Omega
V8, 350.0	4.06×3.38	160	O-Delta
V8, 350.0	4.06×3.38	170	S-Omega,Ctls exc Salon, Delta, 98; O-Ctls Salon
V8, 403.0	4.35×3.38	185	O-Cutlass, Delta, 98
V8, 403.0	4.35×3.38	200	S-Toronado

1978

Starfire (wb 97.0)		Wght	Price	Prod
D07	SX htchbk cpe 3d	2,790	4,306	9,265
T07	htchbk cpe 3d	2,786	4,095	8,056

Omega (wb 111.0)		Wght	Price	Prod
B17	htchbk cpe 3d	3,250	4,173	4,084
B27	cpe	3,184	4,009	15,632
B69	sdn 4d	3,236	4,094	19,478
E27	Brougham cpe	3,204	4,215	3,798
E69	Brougham sdn 4d	3,246	4,300	7,125
Cutlass (wb 108.1)				
G09	Salon sdn 4d	3,136	4,543	29,509
G87	Salon cpe	3,122	4,433	21,198
J09	Salon Brougham sdn 4d	3,186	4,828	21,902
J87	Salon Brougham cpe	3,082	4,717	10,741
R47	Supreme cpe	3,228	4,873	240,917
K47	Calais cpe	3,212	5,231	40,842
M47	Supreme Brougham cpe	3,204	5,287	117,880
H35	Cruiser wgn 4d 2S	3,308	5,287	44,617
Delta 88 (wb 116.0)				
L37	cpe	3,496	5,549	17,469
L67	sdn 4d	3,541	5,634	25,322
N37	Royale cpe	3,507	5,778	68,469
N69	Royale sdn 4d	3,569	5,888	131,430
Q35	Custom Cruiser wgn 4d 2S V8	4,045	6,419	34,491
Q35	Custom Cruiser wgn 4d 3S V8	4,075	6,605	
Ninety-Eight (wb 119.0)				
V37	Luxury cpe	3,753	7,170	2,956
V69	Luxury sdn 4d	3,805	7,351	9,136
X37	Regency cpe	3,767	7,538	28,573
X69	Regency sdn 4d	3,836	7,726	78,100
Toronado (wb 122.0)				
Z57	Brougham cpe	4,624	9,412	22,362
W57	XSC cpe	4,627	—	2,453

1977 Delta 88 Royale Town Sedan

1978 Engines	bore×stroke	bhp	availability
L4, 151.0	4.00×3.00	85	S-Starfire
V6, 231.0	3.80×3.40	105	S-Omega,Ctls,Delta; O-Starfre
V8, 260.0	3.50×3.39	110	S-Cutlass; O-Delta
V8, 305.0	3.74×3.48	145	O-Starfire,Omega,Cutlass
V8, 305.0	3.74×3.48	165	O-Cutlass
V8, 350.0dsl	4.06×3.38	120	O-Delta, 98
V8, 350.0	4.06×3.38	170	S-Delta, 98; O-Omega, Ctls
V8, 403.0	4.35×3.38	185/190	S-Toro; O-Delta, 98

1979

Starfire (wb 97.0)		Wght	Price	Prod
D07	SX htchbk cpe 3d	2,703	4,475	7,155
T07	htchbk cpe 3d	2,690	4,275	13,144
Omega (wb 111.0)				
B17	htchbk cpe 3d	3,222	4,345	956
B27	cpe	3,145	4,181	4,806
B69	sdn 4d	3,183	4,281	5,826
E27	Brougham cpe	3,156	4,387	1,078
E69	Brougham sdn 4d	3,214	4,487	2,145
Cutlass (wb 108.1)				
G09	Salon sdn 4d	3,138	5,038	20,266
G87	Salon cpe	3,118	4,938	8,399
J09	Salon Brougham sdn 4d	3,185	5,352	18,714
J87	Salon Brougham cpe	3,158	5,227	3,617
R47	Supreme cpe	3,148	5,390	277,944
K47	Calais cpe	3,180	5,828	43,780
M47	Supreme Brougham cpe	3,174	5,829	137,323
G35	Cruiser wgn 4d 2S	3,281	5,223	10,755
H35	Cruiser B'ham wgn 4d 2S	3,325	5,775	42,953
Delta 88 (wb 116.0)				
L37	cpe	3,550	6,112	16,202
L69	sdn 4d	3,576	6,212	25,424
N37	Royale cpe	3,560	6,399	60,687
N69	Royale sdn 4d	3,602	6,524	152,526
Q35	Custom Cruiser wgn 4d 2S V8	4,042	7,201	36,648
Q35	Custom Cruiser wgn 4d 3S V8	4,092	7,394	
Ninety-Eight (wb 119.0)				
V37	Luxury cpe	3,806	8,614	2,104
V69	Luxury sdn 4d	3,850	8,795	6,720
X37	Regency cpe	3,810	9,236	29,965
X69	Regency sdn 4d	3,885	9,424	91,962
Toronado (wb 114.0)				
Z57	Brougham cpe	3,731	10,709	50,056

1979 Engines	bore×stroke	bhp	availability
L4, 151.0	4.00×3.00	85	O-Starfire
L4, 151.0	4.00×3.00	90	S-Starfire
V6, 231.0	3.80×3.40	115	S-Omega,Ctls,Dlta; O-Strfre
V8D, 260.0	3.50×3.39	90	O-Cutlass
V8, 260.0	3.50×3.39	105	S-Ctls, Delta exc wgn
V8, 301.0	4.00×3.00	135	O-Delta exc wgn
V8, 305.0	3.74×3.48	130	S-Omega; O-Starfire
V8, 305.0	3.74×3.48	160	O-Cutlass
V8, 350.0	4.06×3.38	160	S-Delta wagons
V8D, 350.0	4.06×3.38	125	O-Ctls, Delta, 98, Toronado
V8, 350.0	4.06×3.38	160	S-98
V8, 350.0	4.06×3.38	165	S-Toro; O-Omega, Ctls wgn
V8, 403.0	4.35×3.38	175	O-Delta wgns, 98

1980

Starfire (wb 97.0)		Wght	Price	Prod
D07	SX htchbk cpe 3d	2,668	4,950	8,237
T07	htchbk cpe 3d	2,656	4,750	
Omega (wb 104.9)				
B37	cpe	2,420	5,501	28,267
B69	sdn 4d	2,446	5,672	42,172
E37	Brougham cpe	2,452	5,858	21,595
E69	Brougham sdn 4d	2,478	6,013	42,289
Cutlass (wb 108.1)				
G69	sdn 4d	3,144	6,124	36,923
G87	Salon cpe	3,140	5,764	3,429
J87	Salon Brougham cpe	3,140	6,054	965
R47	Supreme cpe	3,264	6,655	169,597
R69	LS sdn 4d	3,254	6,780	86,868
K47	Calais cpe	3,276	7,119	26,269
M47	Supreme Brougham cpe	3,276	7,094	77,875
M69	Supreme Brougham sdn 4d	3,280	7,219	52,462
G35	Cruiser wgn 4d 2S	3,343	6,572	7,815
H35	Cruiser Brougham wgn 4d 2S	3,380	6,809	22,791
Delta 88 (wb 116.0)				
L37	cpe	3,395	6,808	6,845
L69	sdn 4d	3,428	6,905	15,285
N37	Royale cpe	3,403	7,076	39,303
N69	Royale sdn 4d	3,406	7,228	87,178

1979 Starfire hatchback coupe with Firenza option

1979 Delta 88 Custom Cruiser four-door wagon

1980 Delta 88 Royale two-door coupe

		Wght	Price	Prod
P35	Custom Cruiser wgn 4d 2S V8	3,910	7,820	17,067
P35	Custom Cruiser wgn 4d 3S V8	3,940	8,028	
Ninety-Eight (wb 119.0)				
V69	Luxury sdn 4d	3,789	9,517	2,640
X37	Regency cpe	3,811	10,035	12,391
X69	Regency sdn 4d	3,832	10,159	58,603
Toronado (wb 114.0)				
Z57	cpe	3,627	11,934	43,440

1980 Engines	bore×stroke	bhp	availability
L4, 151.0	4.00×3.00	85/90	S-Starfire, Omega
V6, 173.0	3.50×3.00	115	O-Omega
V6, 231.0	3.80×3.40	110	S-Ctls,Delta exc wgns; O-Starfire
V8, 260.0	3.50×3.39	105	S-Cutlass
V8, 265.0	3.75×3.00	120	S-Delta exc wgns
V8, 305.0	3.74×3.48	155	O-Cutlass
V8, 307.0	3.80×3.38	150	S-Delta wgns, 98, Toro;O-Delta
V8, 350.0dsl	4.06×3.38	105	O-Ctls,Delta,98,Toro
V8, 350.0	4.06×3.38	160	O-Ctls,Delta,98,Toro

1981

Omega (wb 104.9)		Wght	Price	Prod
B37	cpe 2d	2,439	6,343	27,323
B69	sdn 4d	2,469	6,514	51,715
E37	Brougham cpe 2d	2,462	6,700	19,260
E69	Brougham sdn 4d	2,499	6,855	49,620
Cutlass (wb 108.1)				
G69	sdn 4d	3,205	6,955	25,580
R47	Supreme cpe	3,213	7,484	187,875
R69	LS sdn 4d	3,236	7,652	84,272
K47	Calais cpe	3,227	8,004	4,105
M47	Supreme Brougham cpe	3,238	7,969	93,855
M69	Supreme Brougham sdn 4d	3,242	8,100	53,952
G35	Cruiser wgn 4d 2S	3,369	7,418	31,926
H35	Cruiser Brougham wgn 4d 2S	3,367	7,725	
Delta 88 (wb 116.0)				
L37	cpe	3,485	7,429	3,330
L69	sdn 4d	3,501	7,524	10,806
N37	Royale cpe	3,489	7,693	41,682
Y37	Royale Brougham cpe	3,519	8,058	
N69	Royale sdn 4d	3,530	7,842	104,124
Y69	Royale Brougham sdn 4d	3,564	8,141	
P35	Custom Cruiser wgn 4d 2S V8	3,950	8,452	18,956

Ninety-Eight (wb 119.0)		Wght	Price	Prod
V69	Luxury sdn 4d	3,741	9,951	1,957
X37	Regency cpe	3,735	10,440	13,696
X69	Regency sdn 4d	3,794	10,558	74,017
Toronado (wb 114.0)				
Z57	cpe	3,631	12,148	42,604

1981 Engines	bore×stroke	bhp	availability
L4, 151.0	4.00×3.00	90	S-Omega
V6, 173.0	3.50×3.00	110	O-Omega
V6, 231.0	3.80×3.40	110	S-Cutlass, Delta exc wgns
V6, 252.0	3.97×3.40	125	S-98, Toronado
V8, 260.0	3.50×3.39	105	O-Cutlass, Delta 88
V8, 307.0	3.80×3.39	140	S-Delta wgn; O-Cutlass wgn, Delta, 98, Toro
V8D, 350.0	4.06×3.39	105	O-Ctls, Delta, 98, Toro

1982

Firenza (wb 101.2)		Wght	Price	Prod
C77	S cpe	2,344	7,413	8,894
C69	sdn 4d	2,345	7,448	9,256
D77	SX cpe	2,379	8,159	6,017
D69	LX sdn 4d	2,370	8,080	5,941
Omega (wb 104.9)				
B37	cpe	2,506	7,388	12,140
B69	sdn 4d	2,538	7,574	29,548

1981 Toronado coupe

		Wght	Price	Prod
E37	Brougham cpe	2,529	7,722	9,430
E69	Brougham sdn 4d	2,569	7,891	26,351
Cutlass Ciera (wb 104.9)				
G27	cpe	2,618	8,847	5,185
G19	sdn 4d	2,637	8,997	9,717
J27	LS cpe	2,618	8,968	10,702
J19	LS sdn 4d	2,624	9,157	29,322
M27	Brougham cpe	2,620	9,397	12,518
M19	Brougham sdn 4d	2,626	9,599	33,876
Cutlass (wb 108.1)				
R47	Supreme cpe	3,231	8,588	89,617
R69	sdn 4d	3,292	8,712	60,053
K47	Calais cpe	3,304	9,379	17,109
M47	Supreme Brougham cpe	3,258	9,160	59,592
M69	Supreme Brougham sdn 4d	3,317	9,255	34,717
H35	Cruiser wgn 4d 2S	3,433	8,905	20,363
Delta 88 (wb 116.0)				
L69	sdn 4d	3,557	8,603	8,278
N37	Royale cpe	3,534	8,733	41,382
Y37	Royale Brougham cpe	3,572	9,202	
N69	Royale sdn 4d	3,572	8,894	105,184
Y69	Royale Brougham sdn 4d	3,608	9,293	
P35	Custom Cruiser wgn 4d 2S V8	4,026	9,614	19,367
Ninety-Eight (wb 119.0)				
X37	Regency cpe	3,785	12,117	11,832
X69	Regency sdn 4d	3,842	12,294	79,135
W69	Regency Brougham sdn 4d	3,890	13,344	
Toronado (wb 114.0)				
Z57	Brougham cpe	3,695	14,462	33,928

1982 Engines	bore × stroke	bhp	availability
L4, 112.0	3.50 × 2.91	88	S-Firenza
L4, 121.0	3.50 × 3.15	90	O-Firenza
L4, 151.0	4.00 × 3.00	90	S-Omega, Ctls Ciera
V6, 173.0	3.50 × 3.00	112	O-Omega
V6, 173.0	3.50 × 3.00	130	O-Omega
V6, 181.0	3.80 × 2.66	110	O-Cutlass Ciera
V6, 231.0	3.80 × 3.40	110	S-Ctls Supreme, Delta
V6, 252.0	3.97 × 3.40	125	S-98, Toronado
V8, 260.0	3.50 × 3.39	100	O-Ctls Supreme, Delta
V6D, 262.0	4.06 × 3.39	85	O-Cutlass Ciera, Supreme
V8, 307.0	3.80 × 3.39	140	S-Delta wgn; O-Ctls Supreme, Delta, 98, Toro
V8D, 350.0	4.06 × 3.39	105	O-Supreme, Delta, 98, Toro

1983

Omega (wb 104.9)		Wght	Price	Prod
C77	S cpe 3d	2,440	7,007	8,208
C69	sdn 4d	2,418	7,094	11,278
D77	SX cpe 3d	2,478	7,750	3,767
D69	LX sdn 4d	2,438	7,646	5,067
C35	Cruiser wgn 5d	2,496	7,314	7,460
D35	LX Cruiser wgn 5d	2,520	7,866	4,972
Omega (wb 104.9)				
B37	cpe	2,531	7,478	6,448
B69	sdn 4d	2,569	7,676	24,287
E37	Brougham cpe	2,562	7,767	5,177
E69	Brougham sdn 4d	2,594	7,948	18,014
Cutlass Ciera (wb 104.9)				
J27	LS cpe	2,732	8,703	12,612
J19	LS sdn 4d	2,765	8,892	66,731
M27	Brougham cpe	2,754	9,183	17,088
M19	Brougham sdn 4d	2,789	9,385	73,219

1982 Cutlass Cruiser four-door wagon

Cutlass (wb 108.1)		Wght	Price	Prod
R47	Supreme cpe	3,340	8,950	107,946
R69	sdn 4d	3,382	9,103	56,347
M47	Supreme Brougham cpe	3,377	9,589	60,025
M69	Supreme Brougham sdn 4d	3,416	9,719	28,451
K47	Calais cpe	3,357	9,848	16,660
K47/W40	Calais Hurst/Olds cpe V8	—	12,069	3,000
H35	Cruiser wgn 4d 2S	3,529	9,381	22,037
Delta 88 (wb 116.0)				
L69	sdn 4d	3,644	9,084	8,297
N37	Royale cpe	3,632	9,202	54,771
Y37	Royale Brougham cpe	3,648	9,671	
N69	Royale sdn 4d	3,679	9,363	132,683
Y69	Royale Brougham sdn 4d	3,689	9,762	
P35	Custom Cruiser wgn 5d 2S V8	4,202	10,083	25,243
Ninety-Eight (wb 119.0)				
X37	Regency cpe	3,910	12,943	13,816
X69	Regency sdn 4d	3,964	13,120	105,948
W69	Regency Brougham sdn 4d	4,006	14,170	
Toronado (wb 114.0)				
Z57	Brougham cpe	3,816	15,252	39,605

1983 Engines	bore × stroke	bhp	availability
L4, 112.0	3.34 × 3.13	84	O-Firenza
L4, 121.0	3.50 × 3.15	86	S-Firenza
L4, 151.0	4.00 × 3.00	90	S-Omega, Ctls Ciera
V6, 173.0	3.50 × 3.00	112	O-Omega
V6, 173.0	3.50 × 3.00	130	O-Omega

1983 Firenza SX hatchback coupe

V6, 181.0	3.80 × 2.66	110	O-Cutlass Ciera
V6, 231.0	3.80 × 3.40	110	S-Ctls Supreme, Delta
V6, 252.0	3.97 × 3.40	125	S-98, Toronado
V6D, 262.0	4.06 × 3.39	85	O-Cutlass Ciera, Supreme
V8, 307.0	3.80 × 3.39	140	S-Delta wgn; O-Ctls Supreme, Delta, 98, Toro
V8, 307.0	3.80 × 3.39	180	S-Calais Hurst/Olds
V8D, 350.0	4.06 × 3.39	105	O-Supreme, Delta, 98, Toro

1984

Firenza (wb 101.2)		Wght	Price	Prod
C77	S cpe 3d	2,457	7,214	13,811
C69	sdn 4d	2,461	7,301	34,564
D77	SX cpe 3d	2,505	7,957	4,179
D69	LX sdn 4d	2,505	7,853	11,761
C35	Cruiser wgn 5d	2,507	7,521	12,389
D35	LX Cruiser wgn 5d	2,525	8,073	5,771
Omega (wb 104.9)				
B37	cpe	2,539	7,634	5,242
B69	sdn 4d	2,572	7,832	21,571
E37	Brougham cpe	2,556	7,923	5,870
E69	Brougham sdn 4d	2,593	8,104	20,303
Cutlass Ciera (wb 104.9)				
J27	LS cpe	2,742	9,014	14,887
J19	LS sdn 4d	2,762	9,203	99,182
M27	Brougham cpe	2,768	9,519	22,687
M19	Brougham sdn 4d	2,788	9,721	102,667
J35	LS Cruiser wgn 5d	2,957	9,551	41,816
Cutlass (wb 108.1)*				
R47	Supreme cpe	3,301	9,376	132,913
R69	sdn 4d	3,344	9,529	62,136
M47	Supreme Brougham cpe	3,340	10,015	87,207
M69	Supreme Brougham sdn 4d	3,374	10,145	37,406
K47	Calais cpe	3,377	10,274	21,393
K47/W40	Calais Hurst/Olds cpe V8	—	12,644	3,500

*Cutlass totals include Canadian production for the U.S. market.

Delta 88 (wb 115.9)		Wght	Price	Prod
N37	Royale cpe	3,585	9,939	23,387
Y37	Royale Brougham cpe	3,619	10,408	41,913
N69	Royale sdn 4d	3,624	10,051	87,993
Y69	Royale Brougham sdn 4d	3,654	10,499	89,450
V69	Royale B'ham LS sdn 4d V8	3,853	13,854	17,064
P35	Custom Cruiser wgn 5d 2S V8	4,128	10,839	34,061
Ninety-Eight (wb 119.0)				
G37	Regency cpe	4,090	13,974	7,855
G69	Regency sdn 4d	4,126	14,151	26,919
H69	Regency brougham sdn 4d	4,177	15,201	42,059
Toronado (wb 114.0)				
Z57	Brougham cpe	3,795	16,107	48,100

1984 Engines	bore × stroke	bhp	availability
L4, 112.0	3.34 × 3.13	82	O-Firenza
L4, 121.0	3.50 × 3.15	88	S-Firenza
L4, 151.0	4.00 × 3.00	92	S-Omega, Ctls Ciera
V6, 173.0	3.50 × 3.00	112	O-Omega
V6, 173.0	3.50 × 3.00	130	O-Omega
V6, 181.0	3.80 × 2.66	110	O-Cutlass Ciera
V6, 231.0	3.80 × 3.40	110	S-Ctls Supreme, Delta
V6, 252.0	3.97 × 3.40	125	S-Toronado
V6D, 262.0	4.06 × 3.39	85	O-Cutlass Ciera, Supreme
V8, 307.0	3.80 × 3.39	140	S-Delta wgn, 98; O-Ctls Supreme, Delta, Toro
V8 307.0	3.80 × 3.39	180	S-Calais Hurst/Olds
V8D, 350.0	4.06 × 3.39	105	O-Supreme, Delta, 98, Toro

1985

Firenza (wb 101.2)		Wght	Price	Prod
C77	S cpe 3d	2,388	7,588	5,842
C69	sdn 4d	2,385	7,679	25,066
D77	SX cpe 3d	2,438	8,395	1,842
D69	LX sdn 4d	2,441	8,255	7,563
C35	Cruiser wgn 5d	2,450	7,898	6,291
D35	LX Cruiser wgn 5d	2,487	8,492	2,436
Calais (wb 103.4)				
F27	cpe	2,545	8,499	49,545
T27	Supreme cpe	2,547	8,844	56,695
Cutlass Ciera (wb 104.9)				
J27	LS cpe	2,763	9,307	13,396
J19	LS sdn 4d	2,802	9,497	118,575
M27	Brougham cpe	2,784	9,787	20,476
M19	Brougham sdn 4d	2,825	9,998	112,441
J35	LS Cruiser wgn 5d	2,962	9,858	38,225
Cutlass (wb 108.1)				
R47	Supreme cpe	3,277	9,797	75,045
R69	sdn 4d	3,321	9,961	43,085
M47	Supreme Brougham cpe	3,308	10,468	58,869
M69	Supreme Brougham sdn 4d	3,341	10,602	28,741
K47	Salon cpe	3,308	10,770	14,512
K47/W42	Salon 4-4-2 cpe V8	—	12,435	3,500
Delta 88 (wb 115.9)				
N37	Royale cpe	3,584	10,488	15,002
Y37	Royale Brougham cpe	3,584	10,968	31,891
N69	Royale sdn 4d	3,616	10,596	69,641
Y69	Royale Brougham sdn 4d	3,616	11,062	72,103
V69	Royale B'ham LS sdn 4d V8	3,515	14,331	30,239
P35	Custom Cruiser wgn 5d 2S V8	4,085	11,627	22,889
Ninety-Eight (wb 110.8)				
X11	Regency cpe	3,261	14,725	4,734
X69	Regency sdn 4d	3,297	14,665	43,697
W11	Regency Brougham cpe	3,261	15,932	9,704
W69	Regency Brougham sdn 4d	3,297	15,864	111,297
Toronado (wb 114.0)				
Z57	Brougham cpe	3,853	16,798	42,185

198X Engines	bore × stroke	bhp	availability
L4, 112.0	3.34 × 3.13	82	O-Firenza
L4, 121.0	3.50 × 3.15	88	S-Firenza
L4, 151.0	4.00 × 3.00	92	S-Calais, Ctls Ciera
V6, 173.0	3.50 × 3.00	130	O-Firenza
V6, 181.0	3.80 × 2.66	110	S-98; O-Cutlass Ciera

1984 Delta 88 Royale coupe

	bore×stroke	bhp	availability
V6, 181.0	3.80×2.66	125	O-Calais
V6, 231.0	3.80×3.40	110	S-Ctls Supreme, Delta
V6, 231.0	3.80×3.40	125	S-98 B'ham; O-Ciera, 98
V6D, 262.0	4.06×3.39	85	O-Ciera, Supreme, 98
V8, 307.0	3.80×3.39	140	S-Delta LS/wgn, Toro; O-Ctls Supreme, Delta
V8, 307.0	3.80×3.39	180	S-Calais 4-4-2
V8D, 350.0	4.06×3.39	105	O-Supreme, Delta, Toronado

1986

Firenza (wb 101.2)		Wght	Price	Prod
C27	cpe 2d	2,344	7,782	12,003
D27	LC cpe 2d	2,396	8,611	2,867
C77	S cpe 3d	2,396	7,941	2,531
D77	GT cpe 3d V6	2,445	9,774	1,032
C69	sdn 4d	2,397	8,035	18,437
D69	LX sdn 4d	2,428	8,626	4,415
C35	Cruiser wgn 4d	2,454	8,259	5,416
Calais (wb 103.4)				
F27	cpe	2,531	9,283	52,726
F69	sdn 4d	2,598	9,478	40,393
T27	Supreme cpe	2,542	9,668	33,060
T69	Supreme sdn 4d	2,601	9,863	25,128
Cutlass Ciera (wb 104.9)				
J27	LS cpe	2,761	10,153	9,233
J37	S cpe	2,757	10,619	16,281
J19	LS sdn 4d	2,805	10,354	144,466
M27	Brougham cpe	2,778	10,645	11,534
M37	Brougham SL cpe	2,800	11,154	12,525
M19	Brougham sdn 4d	2,834	10,868	123,027
J35	LS Cruiser wgn 5d	2,964	10,734	35,890
Cutlass (wb 108.1)				
R47	Supreme cpe	3,277	10,698	79,654
R69	sdn 4d	3,320	10,872	41,973
M47	Supreme Brougham cpe	3,307	11,408	55,275
M69	Supreme Brougham sdn 4d	3,341	11,551	24,646
K47	Salon cpe	3,340	11,728	9,608
K47/W42	Salon 4-4-2 cpe V8	—	14,343	
Delta 88 (wb 110.8)				
N37	Royale cpe	3,141	12,760	13,696
N69	Royale sdn 4d	3,186	12,760	88,564
Y37	Royale Brougham cpe	3,170	13,461	23,697
Y69	Royale Brougham sdn 4d	3,211	13,461	108,344
Custom Cruiser (wb 115.9)				
P35	wgn 5d 2S V8	4,085	13,416	21,073
Ninety-Eight (wb 110.8)				
X11	Regency cpe	3,268	16,062	803
X69	Regency sdn 4d	3,304	15,989	23,717
W11	Regency Brougham cpe	3,285	17,052	5,007
W69	Regency Brougham sdn 4d	3,320	16,979	95,045
Toronado (wb 108.0)				
Z57	cpe	3,304	19,418	15,924

1986 Engines	bore×stroke	bhp	availability
L4, 112.0	3.34×3.13	84	O-Firenza
L4, 121.0	3.50×3.15	88	S-Firenza
L4, 151.0	4.00×3.00	92	S-Calais, Ctls Ciera
V6, 173.0	3.50×3.00	112	O-Cutlass Ciera
V6, 173.0	3.50×3.00	130	S-Firenza GT
V6, 181.0	3.80×2.66	125	S-Delta; O-Calais
V6, 231.0	3.80×3.40	110	S-Ctls Supreme
V6, 231.0	3.80×3.40	140	S-98, Toronado
V6, 231.0	3.80×3.40	150	O-Ciera, Delta
V8, 307.0	3.80×3.39	140	S-Cust Cruiser; O-Supreme
V8, 307.0	3.80×3.39	180	S-Calais 4-4-2

1987

Omega (wb 104.9)		Wght	Price	Prod
C27	cpe 2d	2,327	8,541	5,335
D27	LC cpe 2d	2,379	9,639	874
C77	S hatch cpe 3d	2,380	8,976	991
D77	GT cpe 3d V6	2,576	11,034	783
C69	sdn 4d	2,381	8,499	12,597
D69	LX sdn 4d	2,412	9,407	2,388
C35	Cruiser wgn 5d	2,438	9,146	2,860
Calais (wb 103.4)				
F27	cpe	2,516	9,741	52,286
F69	sdn 4d	2,584	9,741	35,169
T27	Supreme cpe	2,529	10,397	17,883
T69	Supreme sdn 4d	2,595	10,397	11,676
Cutlass Ciera (wb 104.9)				
J37	S cpe	2,811	10,940	21,904

1985 Delta 88 Royale Brougham LS four-door sedan

1986 Delta 88 two-door coupe

1987 Calais coupe with GT package

1988 Cutlass Supreme International Series coupe

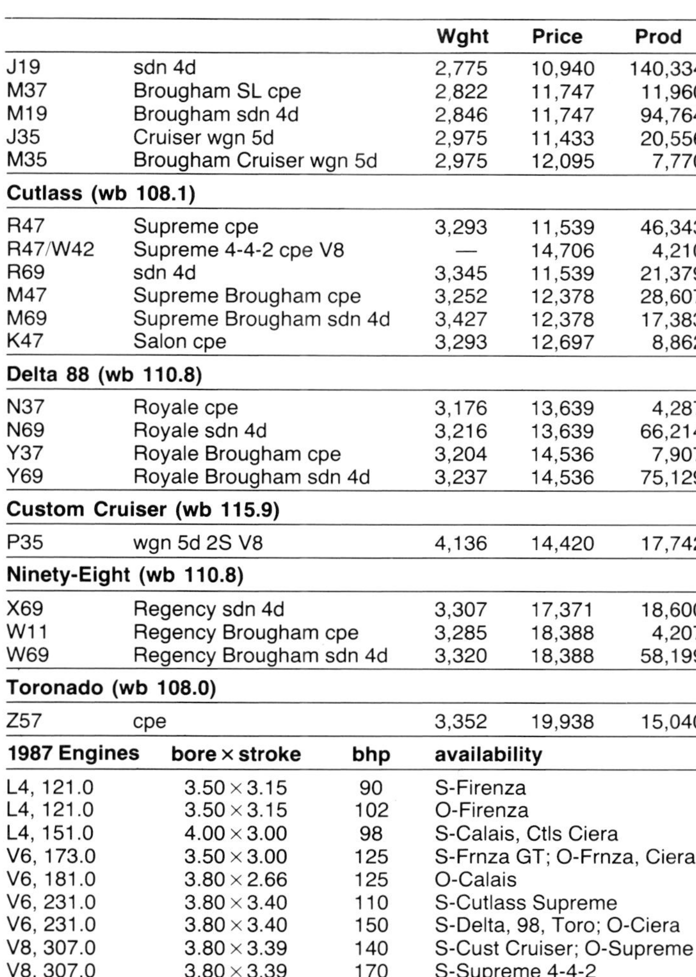

		Wght	Price	Prod
J19	sdn 4d	2,775	10,940	140,334
M37	Brougham SL cpe	2,822	11,747	11,960
M19	Brougham sdn 4d	2,846	11,747	94,764
J35	Cruiser wgn 5d	2,975	11,433	20,556
M35	Brougham Cruiser wgn 5d	2,975	12,095	7,770
Cutlass (wb 108.1)				
R47	Supreme cpe	3,293	11,539	46,343
R47/W42	Supreme 4-4-2 cpe V8	—	14,706	4,210
R69	sdn 4d	3,345	11,539	21,379
M47	Supreme Brougham cpe	3,252	12,378	28,607
M69	Supreme Brougham sdn 4d	3,427	12,378	17,383
K47	Salon cpe	3,293	12,697	8,862
Delta 88 (wb 110.8)				
N37	Royale cpe	3,176	13,639	4,287
N69	Royale sdn 4d	3,216	13,639	66,214
Y37	Royale Brougham cpe	3,204	14,536	7,907
Y69	Royale Brougham sdn 4d	3,237	14,536	75,129
Custom Cruiser (wb 115.9)				
P35	wgn 5d 2S V8	4,136	14,420	17,742
Ninety-Eight (wb 110.8)				
X69	Regency sdn 4d	3,307	17,371	18,600
W11	Regency Brougham cpe	3,285	18,388	4,207
W69	Regency Brougham sdn 4d	3,320	18,388	58,199
Toronado (wb 108.0)				
Z57	cpe	3,352	19,938	15,040

1987 Engines	bore × stroke	bhp	availability
L4, 121.0	3.50 × 3.15	90	S-Firenza
L4, 121.0	3.50 × 3.15	102	O-Firenza
L4, 151.0	4.00 × 3.00	98	S-Calais, Ctls Ciera
V6, 173.0	3.50 × 3.00	125	S-Frnza GT; O-Frnza, Ciera
V6, 181.0	3.80 × 2.66	125	O-Calais
V6, 231.0	3.80 × 3.40	110	S-Cutlass Supreme
V6, 231.0	3.80 × 3.40	150	S-Delta, 98, Toro; O-Ciera
V8, 307.0	3.80 × 3.39	140	S-Cust Cruiser; O-Supreme
V8, 307.0	3.80 × 3.39	170	S-Supreme 4-4-2

1988

Firenza (wb 101.2)		Wght	Price	Prod
C27	cpe 2d	2,327	9,295	
C69	sdn 4d	2,381	9,295	12,260
C35	Cruiser wgn 5d	2,438	9,995	

Calais (wb 103.4)		Wght	Price	Prod
F27	cpe	2,500	10,320	
F69	sdn 4d	2,571	10,320	
T27	SL cpe	2,518	11,195	110,276
T69	SL sdn 4d	2,583	11,195	
K27	International cpe L4	2,757	13,695	
K69	International sdn 4d L4	2,830	13,695	
Cutlass Ciera (wb 104.9)				
J37	cpe	2,805	10,995	
J19	sdn 4d	2,769	11,656	
M37	Brougham SL cpe	2,816	11,845	
M19	Brougham sdn 4d	2,840	12,625	21,620
S37	International cpe V6	2,958	14,995	
S19	International sdn 4d V6	1,913	15,825	
J35	Cruiser wgn 5d	2,968	12,320	
M35	Brougham Cruiser wgn 5d	3,039	12,995	
Cutlass Supreme FWD (wb 107.5)				
H47	cpe	2,958	12,846	
S47	SL cpe	—	13,495	94,723
R47	International cpe	—	15,644	
Cutlass Supreme Classic RWD (wb 108.1)				
R47	cpe	3,180	13,163	27,678
M47	Brougham cpe	3,233	13,995	
Delta 88 (wb 110.8)				
N37	Royale cpe	3,172	14,498	
N69	Royale sdn 4d	3,216	14,498	160,913
Y37	Royale Brougham cpe	3,187	15,451	
Y69	Royale Brougham sdn 4d	3,220	15,451	
Custom Cruiser RWD (wb 115.9)				
P35	wgn 5d 2S V8	4,136	15,655	11,114
Ninety-Eight (wb 110.8)				
X69	Regency sdn 4d	3,300	17,995	
W69	Regency Brougham sdn 4d	3,316	19,371	79,935
V69	Touring sdn 4d	3,421	24,470	
Toronado (wb 108.0)				
Z57	cpe	3,364	20,598	16,496
V57	Trofeo cpe	3,426	22,695	

1988 Engines	bore × stroke	bhp	availability
L4, 121.0	3.50 × 3.15	90	S-Firenza
L4, 121.0	3.50 × 3.15	96	O-Firenza
L4, 138.0	3.62 × 3.35	150	S-Calais Int'l; O-Calais
L4, 151.0	4.00 × 3.00	98	S-Calais, Ctls Ciera

1988 Cutlass Cruiser Brougham wagon

	bore×stroke	bhp	availability
V6, 173.0	3.50×3.00	125	S-Ctls Supreme; O-Ciera
V6, 181.0	3.80×2.66	125	O-Calais
V6, 231.0	3.80×3.40	150	S-Ciera Intl, Delta; O-Ciera
V6, 231.0	3.80×3.40	165	S-98, Toro; O-Delta
V8, 307.0	3.80×3.39	140	S-Cust Crsr; O-Supr Classic

1989

Cutlass Calais (wb 103.4)		Wght	Price	Prod
L27	VL cpe	2,512	9,995	
L69	VL sdn 4d	2,573	9,995	
F27	S cpe	2,512	10,895	
F69	S sdn 4d	2,573	10,995	
T27	SL cpe	2,538	11,895	
T69	SL sdn 4d	2,597	11,995	
K27	International cpe L4	2,740	14,395	
K69	International sdn 4d L4	2,804	14,495	
Cutlass Ciera (wb 104.9)				
J37	cpe	2,736	11,695	
J69	sdn 4d	2,764	12,195	
M37	SL cpe	2,767	12,695	
M69	SL sdn 4d	2,791	13,495	
S37	International cpe V6	—	15,995	
S69	International sdn 4d V6	—	16,795	
J35	Cruiser wgn 5d	2,913	12,995	
M35	Brougham Cruiser wgn 5d	2,938	13,995	
Cutlass Supreme (wb 107.7)				
H47	cpe	3,084	14,295	
S47	SL cpe	—	15,195	
R47	International cpe	—	16,995	
88 (wb 110.8)				
N37	Royale cpe	3,215	15,195	
N69	Royale sdn 4d	3,265	15,295	
Y37	Royale Brougham cpe	3,236	16,295	
Y69	Royale Brougham sdn 4d	3,285	16,395	
Custom Cruiser RWD (wb 115.9)				
P35	wgn 5d 2S V8	4,221	16,795	

Ninety-Eight (wb 110.8)		Wght	Price	Prod
X69	Regency sdn 4d	3,329	19,295	
W69	Regency Brougham sdn 4d	3,353	20,495	
V69	Touring sdn 4d	3,494	25,995	
Toronado (wb 108.0)				
Z57	cpe	3,361	21,995	
V57	Trofeo cpe	3,428	24,995	

1989 Engines	bore×stroke	bhp	availability
L4, 138.0	3.62×3.35	150	S-Calais Int'l; O-Calais
L4, 138.0	3.62×3.35	185	O-late Calais
L4, 151.0	4.00×3.00	110	S-Calais, Cutlass Ciera
V6, 173.0	3.50×3.00	125	O-Cutlass Ciera
V6, 173.0	3.50×3.00	130	S-Ctls Supreme
V6, 189.0	3.50×3.27	138	O-late Cutlass Supreme
V6, 204.0	3.70×3.16	160	S-Ciera Intl; O-Cal, Ciera
V6, 231.0	3.80×3.40	165	S-88, 98, Toronado
V8, 307.0	3.80×3.39	140	S-Custom Cruiser

1989 88 Royale Brougham four-door sedan

PACKARD

1939

1700 Six (wb 122.0)—24,350 built		Wght	Price	Prod
1282	touring sdn 4d	3,400	1,095	—
1283	wgn 4d 7P	3,652	1,404	—
1285	club cpe 2-4P	3,365	1,045	—
1284	touring sdn 2d	3,390	1,065	—
1288	bus cpe 2P	3,295	1,000	—
1289	conv cpe 2-4P	3,385	1,092	—
1701 One Twenty (wb 127.0)*				
1292	touring sdn 4d	3,605	1,295	—
1293	wgn 4d 7P	3,850	1,636	—
1294	touring sdn 2d	3,595	1,265	—
1295	club cpe 2-4P	3,535	1,245	—
1297	conv sdn 5P	3,780	1,700	—
1298	bus cpe 2P	3,490	1,200	—
1299	conv cpe 2-4P	3,545	1,390	—
1702 One Twenty (wb 148.0)*				
1290	touring limo 7P	4,185	1,955	—
1291	touring sdn 7P	4,100	1,805	—
1703 Super Eight (wb 127.0)**				
1272	touring sdn 4d	3,930	1,732	—
1275	club cpe 2-4P	3,860	1,650	—
1277	conv sdn 5P	4,005	2,130	—
1279	conv cpe 2-4P	3,870	1,875	—
1705 Super Eight (wb 148.0)**				
1270	touring limo 7P	4,510	2,294	—
1271	touring sdn 7P	4,425	2,156	—
1707 Twelve (wb 134.0)				
594	Rollston A/W cab 7P	4,950	6,730	—
1227	victoria 5P	5,570	5,230	—
1232	formal sdn 5P	5,745	4,865	—
1233	touring sdn 4d	5,670	4,155	—
1236	club cpe 5P	5,590	4,255	—
1237	cpe 5P	5,425	4,185	—
1238	cpe 2-4P	5,400	4,185	—
1239	conv cpe 2-4P	5,540	4,375	—
1708 Twelve (wb 139.0)***				
595	Rollston A/W town car 7P	5,075	6,880	—
1234	touring sdn 7P	5,750	4,485	—
1235	touring limo 7P	5,825	4,690	—
1253	conv sdn 5P	5,890	5,395	—
4086	Brunn touring cabriolet 5P	5,845	8,355	—
4087	Brunn A/W cabriolet 6P	5,845	8,355	—

1939 One Twenty convertible sedan

*Total One Twenty production: 17,647
**Total Super Eight production: 3,962
***Total Twelve production: 446

1939 Engines	bore×stroke	bhp	availability
L6, 245.0	3.50×4.25	100	S-Six
L8, 282.0	3.25×4.25	120	S-One Twenty
L8, 320.0	3.19×5.00	130	S-Super Eight
V12, 473.0	3.44×4.25	175	S-Twelve

1940

1800 One Ten (wb 122.0) — 62,300 built		Wght	Price	Prod
1382	sdn 4d	3,200	996	—
1383	wgn 4d, 8P	3,380	1,200	—
1384	sdn 2d	3,190	964	—
1385	club cpe	3,165	940	—
1388	bus cpe	3,120	867	—
1389	conv cpe	3,200	1,104	—
1801 One Twenty (wb 127.0) — 28,138 built				
700	conv vic by Darrin	3,826	3,819	—
1392	sdn 4d	3,520	1,166	—
1393	wgn 4d, 8P	3,590	1,404	—
1394	sdn 2d	3,510	1,135	—
1395	club cpe	3,450	1,111	—
1396	club sdn	3,520	1,239	—
1397	conv sdn	3,710	1,573	—
1398	bus cpe	3,340	1,038	—
1399	conv cpe	3,540	1,277	—
DE1392	Deluxe sdn 4d	3,495	1,246	—
DE1395	Deluxe club cpe	3,400	1,161	—
DE1396	Deluxe club sdn	3,480	1,314	—
DE1399	Deluxe conv cpe	3,470	1,318	—
1803 Super Eight One Sixty (wb 127.0) — 5,662 built (includes all One Sixtys)				
1372	sdn 4d	3,855	1,655	—
1375	club cpe	3,760	1,614	—
1376	club sdn	3,855	1,740	—
1377	conv sdn	4,000	2,075	—
1378	bus cpe	3,735	1,524	—
1379	conv cpe	3,825	1,797	—
1804 Super Eight One Sixty (wb 138.0)				
1362	sdn 4d	4,165	1,919	—
1805 Super Eight One Sixty (wb 148.0)				
1370	limo 7P	4,500	2,179	—
1371	sdn 4d, 7P	4,425	2,051	—
1806 Custom Super Eight One Eighty (wb 127.0) — 1,900 built (includes all One Eightys)				
700	conv vic by Darrin	4,121	4,593	—
1356	club sdn	3,900	2,243	—
1807 Custom Super Eight One Eighty (wb 138.0)				
694	A/W cabriolet by Rollston	4,050	4,473	—
710	conv sdn by Darrin	4,050	6,332	—
1332	form sdn	4,210	2,855	—
1342	sdn 4d	4,210	2,422	—
1808 Custom Super Eight One Eighty (wb 148.0)				
695	A/W town car by Rollston	4,175	4,599	—
1350	limo 7P	4,585	2,683	—
1351	sdn 4d, 7P	4,510	2,554	—

1940 convertible sedan by Darrin

1940 Engines	bore × stroke	bhp	availability
L6, 245.3	3.50×4.25	100	S-One Ten
L8, 282.0	3.25×4.25	120	S-One Twenty
L8, 356.0	3.50×4.63	160	S-Super/Custom Super Eights

1941

1900 One Ten (wb 122.0) — 34,700 built		Wght	Price	Prod
1482	sdn 4d	3,260	1,076	—
1483	wgn 4d, 8P	3,460	1,251	—
1484	sdn 2d	3,250	1,010	—
1485	club cpe	3,230	1,020	—
1488	bus cpe	3,190	927	—
1489	conv cpe	3,260	1,195	—
1463DE	Deluxe wgn 4d, 8P	3,470	1,236	—
1482DE	Deluxe sdn 4d	3,280	1,136	—
1484DE	Deluxe sdn 2d	3,270	1,070	—
1485DE	Deluxe club cpe	3,250	1,058	—
1489DE	Deluxe conv cpe	3,280	1,229	—
1901 One Twenty (wb 127.0) — 17,000 built				
1473	Deluxe wgn 4d, 8P	3,730	1,541	—
1492	sdn 4d	3,535	1,291	—
1493	wgn 4d, 8P	3,720	1,466	—
1494	sdn 2d	3,525	1,260	—
1495	club cpe	3,470	1,235	—
1497	conv sdn	3,725	1,753	—
1498	bus cpe	3,360	1,142	—
1499	conv cpe	3,570	1,407	—
1951 Clipper (wb 127.0)				
1401	sdn 4d	3,725	1,420	16,600
1903 Super Eight One Sixty (wb 127.0) — 3,525 built (includes all One Sixtys)				
1472	sdn 4d	3,995	1,795	—
1475	club cpe	3,900	1,754	—
1477	conv sdn	4,140	2,225	—
1478	bus cpe	3,875	1,639	—
1479	conv cpe	3,965	1,937	—
1477DE	Deluxe conv sdn	4,160	2,450	—
1479DE	Deluxe conv cpe	3,985	2,112	—
1904 Super Eight One Sixty (wb 138.0)				
1462	sdn 4d	4,305	2,054	—
1905 Super Eight One Sixty (wb 148.0)				
1470	limo 7P	4,570	2,334	—
1471	sdn 4d 7P	4,495	2,206	—
1906 Custom Super Eight One Eighty (wb 127.0) — 930 built (inc all One Eightys)				
1429	conv vic by Darrin	4,040	4,595	—
1907 Custom Super Eight One Eighty (wb 138.0)				
794	A/W cabriolet by Rollston	4,075	4,695	—
1422	spt sdn by Darrin	4,490	4,795	—

1941 One Twenty convertible coupe

		Wght	Price	Prod
1432	form sdn	4,350	3,090	—
1442	sdn 4d	4,350	2,632	—
1452	Sport Brougham by LeBaron	4,450	3,545	—

1908 Custom Super Eight One Eighty (wb 148.0)				
795	A/W town car by Rollston	4,200	4,820	—
1420	limo 7P by LeBaron	4,850	5,595	—
1421	sdn 4d, 7P by LeBaron	4,740	5,345	—
1450	limo 7P	4,650	2,913	—
1451	sdn 4d, 7P	4,590	2,769	—

1941 Engines	bore × stroke	bhp	availability
L6, 245.3	3.50 × 4.25	100	S-One Ten
L8, 282.0	3.25 × 4.25	120	S-One Twenty
L8, 282.0	3.25 × 4.25	125	S-Clipper
L8, 356.0	3.50 × 4.63	160	S-One Sixty, One Eighty

1942

2000 Clipper 110 Special (wb 120.0) — 11,325 built (includes all 110s)		Wght	Price	Prod
1582	sdn 4d	3,435	1,232	—
1585	club sdn	3,415	1,199	—
1588	bus cpe	3,365	1,166	—
2010 Clipper 110 Custom (wb 120.0)				
1502	sdn 4d	3,460	1,299	—
1505	club sdn	3,440	1,266	—
2020 Clipper 110 (wb 122.0)				
1589	conv cpe	3,315	1,375	—
2001 Clipper 120 Special (wb 120.0) — 19,199 built (includes all 120s)				
1592	sdn 4d	3,560	1,275	—
1595	club sdn	3,540	1,241	—
1598	bus cpe	3,490	1,208	—
2011 Clipper 120 Custom (wb 120.0)				
1512	sdn 4d	3,585	1,341	—
1515	club sdn	3,565	1,308	—
2021 Clipper 120 (wb 127.0)				
1599	conv cpe	3,585	1,469	—
2003 Clipper One Sixty (wb 127.0) — 2,580 built (includes all One Sixtys)				
1572	sdn 4d	4,005	1,688	—
1575	club sdn	3,985	1,630	—
2023 Clipper One Sixty (wb 127.0)				
1579	conv cpe	3,905	1,786	—
2004 Clipper One Sixty (wb 138.0)				
1562	sdn 4d	4,090	1,893	—
2005 Clipper One Sixty (wb 148.0)				
1570	limo 7P	4,445	2,156	—
1571	sdn 4d, 7P	4,325	2,034	—
2055 Clipper One Sixty (wb 148.0)				
1590	bus limo 7P	4,435	2,010	—
1591	bus sdn 4d, 7P	4,315	1,888	—
2006 Clipper One Eighty (wb 127.0) — 672 built (includes all One Eightys)				
1522	sdn 4d	4,030	2,196	—
1525	club sdn	4,010	2,099	—
1529	conv vic by Darrin	3,920	4,519	—
2007 Clipper One Eighty (wb 138.0)				
894	A/W cabriolet by Rollston	4,075	4,792	—
1532	form sdn	4,390	3,011	
1542	sdn 4d	4,280	2,440	—
2008 Clipper One Eighty (wb 148.0)				
895	A/W town car by Rollston	4,200	4,889	—
1520	limo 7P by LeBaron	4,850	5,690	—
1521	sdn 4d, 7P by LeBaron	4,740	5,446	—
1550	limo 7P	4,540	2,645	—
1551	sdn 4d, 7P	4,525	2,523	—

1942 Engines	bore × stroke	bhp	availability
L6, 245.3	3.50 × 4.25	105	S-Clipper 110
L8, 282.0	3.25 × 4.25	125	S-Clipper 120
L8, 356.0	3.50 × 4.63	165	S-Clipper One Sixty, One Eighty

1946

2100 Clipper Six (wb 120.0) — 15,892 built		Wght	Price	Prod
1682	sdn 4d	3,495	1,730	—
1685	club sdn	3,450	1,680	—
2101 Clipper Eight (wb 120.0)				
1692	sdn 4d	3,630	1,802	1,500
2111 Clipper Deluxe Eight (wb 120.0) — 5,714 built				
1612	sdn 4d	3,670	1,869	—
1615	club sdn	3,625	1,817	—
2103 Super Clipper (wb 127.0) — 4,924 built				
1672	sdn 4d	3,995	2,290	—
1675	club sdn	3,950	2,241	—
2106 Custom Super Clipper (wb 127.0)				
1622	sdn 4d	4,060	3,047	1,472 (1622 and 1625)
1625	club sdn	4,000	2,913	
2126 Custom Super Clipper (wb 148.0)				
1650	limo 7P	4,900	4,496	1,291 (1650 and 1651)
1651	sdn 4d, 7P	4,870	4,332	

1946 Engines	bore × stroke	bhp	availability
L6, 245.3	3.50 × 4.25	105	S-Clipper Six
L8, 282.0	3.25 × 4.25	125	S-Clipper Eight/DeLuxe Eight
L8, 356.0	3.50 × 4.63	165	S-Super/Custom Super Clipper

1947

2100 Clipper Six (wb 120.0) — 14,949 built		Wght	Price	Prod
2182	sdn 4d	3,520	1,937	—
2185	club sdn	3,475	1,912	—
2111 Clipper DeLuxe Eight (wb 120.0) — 23,855 built				
2112	sdn 4d	3,695	2,149	—
2115	club sdn	3,650	2,124	—

1946 Custom Super Clipper four-door sedan

2103 Super Clipper (wb 127.0) — 4,802 built		Wght	Price	Prod
2172	sdn 4d	4,025	2,772	—
2175	club sdn	3,980	2,747	—
2106 Custom Super Clipper (wb 127.0) — 7,480 built (includes 148 wb)				
2122	sdn 4d	4,090	3,449	—
2125	club sdn	3,384	2,125	—
2126 Custom Super Clipper (wb 148.0)				
2150	limo 7P	4,920	4,668	—
2151	sdn 4d, 7P	4,890	4,504	—

1947 Engines	bore × stroke	bhp	availability
L6, 245.3	3.50×4.25	105	S-Clipper Six
L8, 282.0	3.25×4.25	125	S-Clipper Eight/DeLuxe Eight
L8, 356.0	3.50×4.63	165	S-Super/Custom Super Clipper

1948

2201 Eight (wb 120.0) — 12,782* built		Wght	Price	Prod
2292	sdn 4d	3,815	2,275	—
2293	Station Sedan wgn 4d	4,075	3,425	—
2295	club sdn	3,755	2,250	—
2211 DeLuxe Eight (wb 120.0) — 47,807 built				
2262	sdn 4d	3,840	2,543	—
2265	club sdn	3,770	2,517	—
2202 Super Eight (wb 120.0) — 12,921 built				
2272	sdn 4d	3,855	2,827	—
2275	club sdn	3,790	2,802	—
2222 Super Eight (wb 141.0) — 1,766 built				
2270	DeLuxe limo 7P	4,610	4,000	—
2271	DeLuxe sdn 4d, 7P	4,590	3,850	—
2276	limo 7P	4,525	3,650	—
2277	sdn 4d, 7P	4,460	3,500	—
2232 Super Eight (wb 120.0)				
2279	conv cpe	4,025	3,250	7,763
2206 Custom Eight (wb 127.0) — 5,936 built				
2252	sdn 4d	4,175	3,750	—
2255	club sdn	4,110	3,700	—
2226 Custom Eight (wb 148.0) — 230 built				
2250	limo 7P	4,880	4,868	—
2251	sdn 4d, 7P	4,860	4,704	—

1953 Patrician four-door sedan

2313 Custom Eight (wb 148.0)		Wght	Price	Prod
—	chassis	—	—	1,941
2233 Custom Eight (wb 127.0)				
2259	conv cpe	4,380	4,295	1,105

1948 Engines	bore × stroke	bhp	availability
L8, 288.0	3.50×3.75	130	S-Eight, DeLuxe Eight
L8, 327.0	3.50×4.25	145	S-Super Eight
L8, 356.0	3.50×4.63	160	S-Custom Eight

1949 First Series

2201 Eight (wb 120.0) — 13,553* built		Wght	Price	Prod
2292-9	sdn 4d	3,815	2,275	—
2293-9	Station Sedan wgn 4d	4,075	3,425	—
2295-9	club sdn	3,755	2,250	—
2211 DeLuxe Eight (wb 120.0) — 27,422 built				
2262-9	sdn 4d	3,840	2,543	—
2265-9	club sdn	3,770	2,517	—
2202 Super Eight (wb 120.0) — 5,879 built				
2272-9	sdn 4d	3,855	2,827	—
2275-9	club sdn	3,790	2,802	—
2222 Super Eight (wb 141.0) — 867 built				
2270-9	DeLuxe limo 7P	4,610	4,000	—
2271-9	DeLuxe sdn 4d, 7P	4,590	3,850	—
2276-9	limo 7P	4,525	3,650	—
2277-9	sdn 4d, 7P	4,460	3,500	—
2232 Super Eight (wb 120.0)				
2279-9	conv cpe	4,025	3,250	1,237
2206 Custom Eight (wb 127.0) — 2,990 built				
2252-9	sdn 4d	4,175	3,750	—
2255-9	club sdn	4,110	3,700	—
2226 Custom Eight (wb 148.0) — 50 built				
2250-9	limo 7P	4,880	4,868	—
2251-9	sdn 4d, 7P	4,860	4,704	—
2213 Custom Eight (wb 148.0)				
—	chassis	—	—	220
2233 Custom Eight (wb 127.0)				
2259-9	conv cpe	4,380	4,295	213

1949 Second Series

2301 Eight (wb 120.0) — 53,168* built		Wght	Price	Prod
2362	DeLuxe sdn 4d	3,840	2,383	—
2365	DeLuxe club sdn	3,770	2,358	—
2392	sdn 4d	3,815	2,249	—
2393	Station Sedan wgn 4d	4,075	3,449	—
2395	club sdn	3,740	2,224	—
2302 Super Eight (wb 127.0) — 8,759 built				
2372	DeLuxe sdn 4d	3,925	2,919	—
2375	DeLuxe club sdn	3,855	2,894	—
2382	sdn 4d	3,870	2,633	—
2385	club sdn	3,800	2,608	—
2322 Super Eight (wb 141.0) — 4 built				
2370	DeLuxe limo 7P	4,620	4,100	—
2371	DeLuxe sdn 4d, 7P	4,600	3,950	—
2332 Super Eight (wb 127.0)				
2332	DeLuxe conv cpe	4,260	3,350	685

2306 Custom Eight (wb 127.0)		Wght	Price	Prod
2352	sdn 4d	4,310	3,750	973
2313 Custom Eight (wb 148.0)				
—	chassis	—	—	160
2333 Custom Eight (wb 127.0)				
2359	conv cpe	4,530	4,295	68

1949 Engines	bore × stroke	bhp	availability
L8, 288.0	3.50×3.75	135	S-Eight, DeLuxe Eight
L8, 327.0	3.50×4.25	150	S-Super/Super DeLuxe Eight
L8, 356.0	3.50×4.63	160	S-Custom Eight

1950

2301 Eight (wb 120.0) — 36,471* built		Wght	Price	Prod
2362-5	DeLuxe sdn 4d	3,840	2,383	—
2365-5	DeLuxe club sdn	3,770	2,358	—
2392-5	sdn 4d	3,815	2,249	—
2393-5	Station Sedan wgn 4d	4,075	3,449	—
2395-5	club sdn	3,740	2,224	—
2302 Super Eight (wb 127.0) — 4,528 built				
2372-5	DeLuxe sdn 4d	3,925	2,919	—
2375-5	club sdn	3,855	2,894	—
2382-5	sdn 4d	3,870	2,633	—
2385-5	club sdn	3,800	2,608	—
2332 Super Eight (wb 127.0)				
2379-5	conv cpe	4,110	3,350	600
2306 Custom Eight (wb 127.0)				
2352-5	sdn 4d	4,310	3,975	707
2313 Custom Eight (wb 148.0)				
—	chassis	—	—	244
2333 Custom Eight (wb 127.0)				
2359-5	conv cpe	4,530	4,520	77

1950 Engines	bore × stroke	bhp	availability
L8, 288.0	3.50×3.75	135	S-Eight, DeLuxe Eight
L8, 327.0	3.50×4.25	150	S-Super/Super DeLuxe Eight
L8, 356.0	3.50×4.63	160	S-Custom Eight

*Although Packard did not break down model year production by body style, some calendar year figures exist for the Station Sedan. These are: 126 in 1947, 3,266 in 1948, and 472 in 1949, for a total of 3,864. An estimated 75 percent were 1948 models.

1951

2401 200 (wb 122.0)		Wght	Price	Prod
2462	DeLuxe sdn 4d	3,660	2,616	47,052
2465	DeLuxe club sdn	3,605	2,563	
2492	sdn 4d	3,665	2,469	24,310
2495	club sdn	3,600	2,416	
2498	bus cpe	3,550	2,302	
2401 250 (wb 122.0) — 4,640 built				
2467	Mayfair htp cpe	3,820	3,234	—
2469	conv cpe	4,040	3,391	—
2402 300 (wb 127.0)				
2472	sdn 4d	3,875	3,034	15,309
2413 300 (wb 127.0)				
—	chassis	—	—	401
2406 Patrician 400 (wb 127.0)				
2452	sdn 4d	4,115	3,662	9,001

1951 Engines	bore × stroke	bhp	availability
L8, 288.0	3.50×3.75	135	S-Eight, DeLuxe Eight
L8, 327.0	3.50×4.25	150	S-250/300 manual
L8, 327.0	3.50×4.25	155	S-Patrician 400, 250/300 auto

1952

2501 200 (wb 122.0)—46,720 built		Wght	Price	Prod
2562	DeLuxe sdn 4d	3,685	2,695	—
2565	DeLuxe club sdn	3,660	2,641	—
2592	sdn 4d	3,680	2,548	—
2595	club sdn	3,640	2,494	—
2531 250 (wb 122.0)—5,201 built				
2577	Mayfair htp cpe	3,805	3,318	—
2579	conv cpe	4,000	3,476	—
2502 300 (wb 127.0)				
2572	sdn 4d	3,380	3,116	6,705
2513 300 (127.0)				
—	chassis	—	—	320
2506 Patrician 400 (wb 127.0)				
2552	sdn 4d	4,100	3,797	3,975

1952 Engines	bore × stroke	bhp	availability
L8, 288.0	3.50×3.75	135	S-Eight, DeLuxe Eight
L8, 327.0	3.50×4.25	150	S-250/300 manual
L8, 327.0	3.50×4.25	155	S-Patrician 400, 250/300 auto

1953

2601 Clipper (wb 122.0)		Wght	Price	Prod
2692	sdn 4d	3,730	2,598	23,126
2695	club sdn	3,700	2,544	6,370
2697	Sportster cpe	3,720	2,805	3,672
—	chassis	—	—	1
2611 Clipper DeLuxe (wb 122.0)				
2662	sdn 4d	3,760	2,745	26,037
2665	club sdn	3,720	2,691	4,678
2633 Clipper commercial (wb 122.0)				
—	chassis (Henney bodies)	—	—	380
2631 (wb 122.0)				
2677	Mayfair htp cpe	3,905	3,278	5,150
2678	Caribbean conv cpe	4,265	5,210	750
2679	conv cpe	4,125	3,486	1,518
2602 Cavalier (wb 127.0)				
2672	sdn 4d	3,975	3,244	10,799
2613 Packard commercial (wb 127.0)				
—	chassis (Henney bodies)	—	—	166
2606 Patrician (wb 127.0)				
2652	sdn 4d	4,190	3,740	7,456
2653	form sdn by Derham	4,335	6,531	25*
2626 (wb 149.0)				
2650	Corporation limo 8P	4,720	7,100	50
2651	Executive sdn 4d, 8P	4,650	6,900	100
2602-2606-2631				
—	chassis	—	—	9

*Constructed from finished Patricians.

1953 Engines	bore × stroke	bhp	availability
L8, 288.0	3.50×3.75	150	S-2601

1953 Caribbean convertible coupe

1956 Executive hardtop coupe

	bore×stroke	bhp	availability
L8, 327.0	3.50×4.25	160	S-2611
L8, 327.0	3.50×4.25	180	S-2602, 2631 (5 main bearing)
L8, 327.0	3.50×4.25	180	S-2606, 2626 (9 main bearing)

1954

5400 Clipper Special (wb 122.0)		Wght	Price	Prod
5482	sdn 4d	3,650	2,594	970
5485	club sdn	3,585	2,544	912
5401 Clipper DeLuxe (wb 122.0)				
5492	sdn 4d	3,660	2,695	7,610
5495	club sdn	3,650	2,645	1,470
5497	Sportster cpe	3,595	2,830	1,336
5411 Clipper Super (wb 122.0)				
5462	sdn 4d	3,695	2,815	6,270
5465	club sdn	3,610	2,765	887
5467	Panama htp cpe	3,765	3,125	3,618
5433 Clipper commercial (wb 122.0)				
—	chassis (Henney bodies)	—	—	120
5402 Cavalier (wb 127.0)				
5472	sdn 4d	3,955	3,344	2,580
5413 Packard commercial (wb 127.0)				
—	chassis (Henney bodies)	—	—	205
5431 (wb 122.0)				
5477	Pacific htp cpe	4,065	3,827	1,189

1955 Caribbean convertible coupe

		Wght	Price	Prod
5478	Caribbean conv cpe	4,660	6,100	400
5479	convertible cpe	4,290	3,935	863
—	chassis	—	—	1
5406 Patrician (wb 127.0)				
5452	sdn 4d	4,190	3,890	2.760
5426 (wb 149.0)				
5450	Corporation limo 8P	4,720	5,960	35
5451	Executive sdn 4d, 8P	4,650	5,610	65

1954 Engines	bore×stroke	bhp	availability
L8, 288.0	3.50×3.75	150	S-5400
L8, 327.0	3.50×4.25	165	S-5401, 5411
L8, 327.0	3.50×4.25	185	S-5402
L8, 359.0	3.56×4.50	212	S-5406, 5426, 5431 (9 mains)

1955

5540 Clipper (wb 122.0)		Wght	Price	Prod
5522	DeLuxe sdn 4d	3,680	2,586	8,309
5542	Super sdn 4d	3,670	2,686	7,979
5547	Super Panama htp cpe	3,700	2,776	7,016
5560 Clipper Custom (wb 122.0)				
5562	sdn 4d	3,885	2,926	8,708
5567	Constellation htp cpe	3,865	3,076	6,672
5580 (wb 127.0)				
5582	Patrician sdn 4d	4,275	3,890	9,127
5587	Four Hundred htp cpe	4,250	3,930	7,206
5588	Caribbean conv cpe	4,755	5,932	500*

*A very few 1955 Caribbean hardtops have been discovered.

1955 Engines	bore×stroke	bhp	availability
V8, 320.0	3.81×3.50	225	S-Clipper DeLuxe/Super
V8, 352.0	4.00×3.50	245	S-Clipper Custom
V8, 352.0	4.00×3.50	260	S-Packard exc Caribbean
V8, 352.0	4.00×3.50	275	S-Caribbean

1956

5670 Executive (wb 122.0)		Wght	Price	Prod
5672	sdn 4d	4,185	3,465	1,784
5677	htp cpe	4,185	3,560	1,031
5680 (wb 127.0)				
5682	Patrician sdn 4d	4,045	4,160	3,775
5687	Four Hundred htp cpe	4,080	4,190	3,224

5688 Caribbean (wb 127.0)		Wght	Price	Prod
5697	htp cpe	4,590	5,495	263
5699	conv cpe	4,960	5,995	276

1956 Engines	bore × stroke	bhp	availability
V8, 352.0	4.00×3.50	275	S-Executive
V8, 374.0	4.13×3.50	290	S-Patrician, Four Hundred
V8, 374.0	4.13×3.50	310	S-Caribbean

Note: Clipper was marketed as a separate make for 1956 only, and is listed separately in this book.

1957 Clipper

57L (wb 120.5; wgn-116.5)		Wght	Price	Prod
Y8	Town Sedan 4d	3,570	3,212	3,940
P8	Country Sedan wgn 4d	3,650	3,384	869

1957 Engine	bore × stroke	bhp	availability
V8, 289.0	3.56×3.63	275	S-all (supercharged)

1958

58L (wb 120.5; wgn/htp-116.5)		Wght	Price	Prod
J8	sdn 4d	3,505	3,212	1,200
J8	htp cpe	3,480	3,262	675
K9	Hawk htp cpe	3,470	3,995	588
P8	wgn 4d	3,555	3,384	159

1958 Engines	bore × stroke	bhp	availability
V8, 289.0	3.56×3.63	275	S-Hawk (supercharged)
V8. 289.0	3.56×3.63	210	S-Others

Note: Final (1957-58) Packards were based on Studebaker models, following the merger of the two companies.

PLYMOUTH

1939

P7 Roadking (wb 114.0)	Wght	Price	Prod
cpe 2P	2,724	645	22,537
cpe 2-4P	2,784	695	222
sdn 2d	2,824	685	7,499
touring sdn 2d T/B	2,824	699	42,186
sdn 4d	2,839	726	2,553
touring sdn 4d T/B	2,829	740	23,047
util sdn 2d	2,844	685	341
commercial sdn	—	—	2,270
Suburban wgn 4d	—	—	97
chassis	—	—	1,616

P8 DeLuxe (wb 114.0; lwb-134.0)	Wght	Price	Prod
cpe 2P	2,789	725	41,924
cpe 2-4P	2,874	755	1,332
conv cpe 2-4P	3,044	895	5,976
sdn 2d	2,889	761	2,653
touring sdn 2d T/B	2,894	775	80,981
sdn 4d	2,909	791	2,279
touring sdn 4d T/B	2,919	885	175,054
Suburban wgn 4d 8P (side curtains)	3,089	930	1,680
Suburban wgn 4d 8P (glass encl.)	3,189	970	
util sd 2d	—	—	13
lwb sdn 7P T/B	3,374	1,005	1,837
sdn limo 7P (lwb)	3,440	1,095	98
chassis and taxicabs	—	—	947

P8 DeLuxe (wb 117.0)	Wght	Price	Prod
conv sdn T/B 5P	3,209	1,150	387

1939 Deluxe two-door coupe

1939 Engine	bore×stroke	bhp	availability
L6, 201.3	3.13×4.38	82	S-all

1940

P9 Roadking (wb 117.0)	Wght	Price	Prod
bus cpe	2,769	645	26,745
sdn 2d	2,834	699	55,092
sdn 4d	2,869	740	20,076
util sdn	2,769	699	589
club cpe	2,814	699	360
wgn 4d	3,089	925	80
chassis	—	—	907

P10 DeLuxe (wb 117.0; 7P-137.0)	Wght	Price	Prod
bus cpe	2,804	725	32,244
sdn 2d	2,889	775	76,781
sdn 4d	2,924	805	173,351
util sdn	2,824	775	4
club cpe	2,849	770	22,174
conv cpe	3,049	950	6,986
wgn 4d	3,144	970	3,126

P10 DeLuxe (wb 117.0; 7P-137.0)	Wght	Price	Prod
sdn 4d 7P	3,359	1,005	1,179
limo 7P	3,409	1,080	68
chassis	—	—	503

1940 Engine	bore×stroke	bhp	availability
L6, 201.3	3.13×4.38	84	S-all

1941

P11 DeLuxe (wb 117.0)	Wght	Price	Prod
bus cpe	2,809	720	23,754
sdn 2d	2,859	769	46,646
sdn 4d	2,889	800	21,175
util sdn	2,794	760	468
club cpe	2,819	764	994
wgn 4d	3,139	1,006	217
DeLuxe bus cpe	2,839	760	15,862
DeLuxe sdn 2d	2,899	809	46,138
DeLuxe sdn 4d	2,924	845	32,336
DeLuxe club cpe	2,859	804	204
DeLuxe util sdn	—	proto	1
chassis	—	—	676

P12 Special DeLuxe (wb 117.0; 7P-137.0)	Wght	Price	Prod
bus cpe	2,859	795	23,851
sdn 2d	2,934	845	84,810
sdn 4d	2,959	877	190,513

1941 Special Deluxe convertible coupe

	Wght	Price	Prod
util sdn	—	proto	2
club cpe	2,934	842	37,352
conv cpe	3,166	1,007	10,545
wgn 4d	3,194	1,031	5,594
sdn 4d, 7P	3,379	1,078	1,127
limo, 7P	3,429	1,153	24
chassis	—	—	321

1941 Engine	bore×stroke	bhp	availability
L6, 201.3	3.13×4.38	87	S-all

1942

P14S DeLuxe (wb 117.0)	Wght	Price	Prod
bus cpe	2,906	812	3,783
sdn 2d	2,961	850	9,350
sdn 4d	3,001	889	11,973
util sdn	2,906	842	80
club cpe	2,966	885	2,458
chassis	—	—	1
P14C Special DeLuxe (wb 117.0)			
bus cpe	2,931	855	7,258
sdn 2d	2,996	895	24,142
sdn 4d	3,036	935	68,924
Town Sedan	3,061	980	5,821
club cpe	3,011	928	14,685
conv cpe	3,231	1,078	2,806
wgn 4d	3,371	1,145	1,136
chassis	—	—	10

1942 Engine	bore×stroke	bhp	availability
L6, 217.8	3.25×4.38	95	S-all

1946*

P15S DeLuxe (wb 117.0)	Wght	Price	Prod
bus cpe	2,977	1,089	—
sdn 2d	3,047	1,124	—
sdn 4d	3,082	1,164	—
club cpe	3,037	1,159	—
chassis	—	—	—

P15C Special DeLuxe (wb 117.0)	Wght	Price	Prod
bus cpe	2,982	1,159	—
sdn 2d	3,062	1,199	—
sdn 4d	3,107	1,239	—
club cpe	3,057	1,234	—
conv cpe	3,282	1,439	—
wgn 4d	3,402	1,539	—
chassis	—	—	—

1946 Engine	bore×stroke	bhp	availability
L6, 217.8	3.25×4.38	95	S-all

1947*

P15S DeLuxe (wb 117.0)	Wght	Price	Prod
bus cpe	2,977	1,139	—
sdn 2d	3,047	1,164	—
sdn 4d	3,082	1,214	—
club cpe	3,037	1,189	—
chassis	—	—	—
P15C Special DeLuxe (wb 117.0)			
bus cpe	2,982	1,209	—
sdn 2d	3,062	1,239	—
sdn 4d	3,107	1,289	—
club cpe	3,057	1,264	—
conv cpe	3,282	1,565	—
wgn 4d	3,402	1,765	—
chassis	—	—	—

1947 Engine	bore×stroke	bhp	availability
L6, 217.8	3.25×4.38	95	S-all

1948*

P15S DeLuxe (wb 117.0)	Wght	Price	Prod
bus cpe	2,955	1,346	—
sdn 2d	2,995	1,383	—
sdn 4d	3,030	1,441	—
club cpe	3,005	1,409	—
chassis	—	—	—

P15C Special DeLuxe (wb 117.0)	Wght	Price	Prod
bus cpe	2,950	1,440	—
sdn 2d	3,030	1,471	—
sdn 4d	3,045	1,529	—
club cpe	3,020	1,503	—
conv cpe	3,225	1,857	—
wgn 4d	3,320	2,068	—
chassis	—	—	—

1948 Engine	bore×stroke	bhp	availability
L6, 217.8	3.25×4.38	95	S-all

1949 First Series*

P15S DeLuxe (wb 117.0)	Wght	Price	Prod
bus cpe	2,955	1,346	—
sdn 2d	2,995	1,383	—
sdn 4d	3,030	1,441	—
club cpe	3,005	1,409	—
chassis	—	—	—
P15C Special DeLuxe (wb 117.0)			
bus cpe	2,950	1,440	—
sdn 2d	3,030	1,471	—
sdn 4d	3,045	1,529	—
club cpe	3,020	1,503	—
conv cpe	3,225	1,857	—
wgn 4d	3,320	2,068	—
chassis	—	—	—

1949(1) Engine	bore×stroke	bhp	availability
L6, 217.8	3.25×4.38	95	S-all

*Factory combined production figures for 1946 through 1949 First Series.

Combined 1946–1949 First Series Production:

P15S DeLuxe (wb 117.0)	Prod
bus cpe	16,117
sdn 2d	49,918
sdn 4d	120,757
club cpe	10,400
chassis	10
P15C Special DeLuxe (wb 117.0)	
bus cpe	31,399
sdn 2d	125,704
sdn 4d	514,986
club cpe	156,629
conv cpe	15,295
wgn 4d	12,913
chassis	5,361

1949 Second Series

P17 DeLuxe (wb 111.0)	Wght	Price	Prod
bus cpe	2,825	1,371	13,715
sdn 2d	2,951	1,492	28,516
Suburban wgn 2d	3,105	1,840	19,220
chassis	—	—	4
P18 DeLuxe (wb 118.5)			
sdn 4d	3,059	1,551	61,021
club cpe	3,034	1,519	25,687
P18 Special DeLuxe (wb 118.5)			
sdn 4d	3,079	1,629	252,878
club cpe	3,046	1,603	99,680
conv cpe	3,323	1,982	15,240
wgn 4d	3,341	2,372	3,443
chassis	—	—	981

1949(2) Engine	bore×stroke	bhp	availability
L6, 217.8	3.25×4.38	97	S-all

1950

P19 DeLuxe (wb 111.0)	Wght	Price	Prod
bus cpe	2,872	1,371	16,861
sdn 2d	2,946	1,492	67,584
Suburban wgn 2d	3,116	1,840	34,457
Suburban Special wgn 2d	3,155	1,946	
chassis	—	—	1
P20 DeLuxe (wb 118.5)			
sdn 4d	3,068	1,551	87,871
club cpe	3,040	1,519	53,890
P20 Special DeLuxe (wb 118.5)			
sdn 4d	3,072	1,629	234,084
club cpe	3,041	1,603	99,361
conv cpe	3,295	1,982	12,697
wgn 4d	3,353	2,372	2,057
chassis	—	—	2,091

1950 Engine	bore×stroke	bhp	availability
L6, 217.8	3.25×4.38	97	S-all

1951*

P22 Concord (wb 111.0)	Wght	Price	Prod
bus cpe	2,919	1,537	—
sdn 2d	2,969	1,673	—
Savoy wgn 2d	3,184	2,182	—
Suburban wgn 2d	3,124	2,064	—

1948 Special Deluxe four-door sedan

1951 Cranbrook Belvedere hardtop coupe

P23 Cambridge (wb 118.5)	Wght	Price	Prod
sdn 4d	3,104	1,739	—
club cpe	3,059	1,703	—
P23 Cranbrook (wb 118.5)			
sdn 4d	3,109	1,826	—
club cpe	3,074	1,796	—
conv cpe	3,294	2,222	—
Belvedere htp cpe	3,182	2,114	—

1951 Engine	bore×stroke	bhp	availability
L6, 217.8	3.25×4.38	97	S-all

1952*

P22 Concord (wb 111.0)	Wght	Price	Prod
bus cpe	2,893	1,610	—
sdn 2d	2,959	1,753	—
Savoy wgn 2d	3,165	2,287	—
Suburban wgn 2d	3,145	2,163	—
P23 Cambridge (wb 118.5)			
sdn 4d	3,068	1,822	—
club cpe	3,030	1,784	—
P23 Cranbrook (wb 118.5)			
sdn 4d	3,088	1,914	—
club cpe	3,046	1,883	—
conv cpe	3,256	2,329	—
Belvedere htp cpe	3,105	2,216	—

1952 Engine	bore×stroke	bhp	availability
L6, 217.8	3.25×4.38	97	S-all

*Factory combined 1951 and 1952 production figures.

Combined 1951–1952 Production:

P22 Concord (wb 111.0)	Prod
bus cpe	14,255
sdn 2d	49,139
Savoy/Suburban wgn 2d	76,520
P23 Cambridge (wb 118.5)	
sdn 4d	179,417
club cpe	101,784
P23 Cranbrook (wb 118.5)	
sdn 4d	388,785
club cpe	126,725
Belvedere htp cpe	51,266
conv cpe	15,650
chassis	4,171

1953

P24-1 Cambridge (wb 114.0)	Wght	Price	Prod
bus cpe	2,888	1,618	6,975
sdn 2d	2,943	1,727	56,800
sdn 4d	2,983	1,765	93,585
club cpe	2,950	1,725	1,050
Suburban wgn 2d	3,129	2,064	43,545
P24-2 Cranbrook (wb 114.0)			
sdn 4d	3,023	1,873	298,976
club cpe	2,971	1,843	92,102
Belvedere htp cpe	3,027	2,064	35,185
conv cpe	3,193	2,220	6,301
Savoy wgn 2d	3,170	2,207	12,089
chassis	—	—	843

1953 Engine	bore×stroke	bhp	availability
L6, 217.8	3.25×4.38	100	S-all

1954

P25-1 Plaza (wb 114.0)	Wght	Price	Prod
bus cpe	2,889	1,618	5,000
club cpe	2,950*	1,700*	1,275
sdn 4d	3,004	1,765	43,077
sdn 2d	2,943	1,727	27,976
Suburban wgn 2d	3,122	2,064	35,937

1953 Cranbrook convertible coupe

	Wght	Price	Prod
chassis	—	—	1
P25-2 Savoy (wb 114.0)			
club cpe	2,982	1,843	30,700
sdn 4d	3,036	1,873	139,383
sdn 2d	2,986	1,835	25,396
Suburban wgn 2d	3,165*	2,172*	450
chassis	—	—	3,588
P25-3 Belvedere (wb 114.0)			
sdn 4d	3,050	1,953	106,601
Sport Coupe htp	3,038	2,145	25,592
conv cpe	3,273	2,301	6,900
Suburban wgn 2d	3,186	2,288	9,241
chassis	—	—	2,031

*Estimated.

1954 Engines	bore×stroke	bhp	availability
L6, 217.8	3.25×4.38	100	S-all to engine #P25-243000
L6, 230.2	3.25×4.63	110	S-all from engine #P25-243001

1955

P26-1 Plaza, L6 (wb 115.0)	Wght	Price	Prod
sdn 4d	3,129	1,781	68,826
club cpe	3,089	1,738	45,561
Suburban wgn 2d	3,261	2,077	23,319
Suburban wgn 4d	3,282	2,158	10,594
bus cpe	3,025	1,639	4,882
P27-1 Plaza, V8 (wb 115.0)			
sdn 4d	3,246	1,884	15,330
club cpe	3,202	1,841	8,049
Suburban wgn 2d	3,389	2,180	8,469
Suburban wgn 4d	3,408	2,262	4,828
P26-3 Savoy, L6 (wb 115.0)			
sdn 4d	3,154	1,880	93,716
club cpe	3,109	1,837	45,438

	Wght	Price	Prod
chassis	—	—	1
P27-3 Savoy, V8 (wb 115.0)			
sdn 4d	3,265	1,983	69,025
club cpe	3,224	1,940	29,442
P26-2 Belvedere, L6 (wb 115.0)			
sdn 4d	3,159	1,979	69,128
club cpe	3,129	1,936	19,471
Sport Coupe htp	3,330	2,113	13,942
Suburban wgn 4d	3,312	2,322	6,197
P27-2 Belvedere V8 (wb 115.0)			
sdn 4d	3,262	2,082	91,856
club cpe	3,228	2,039	22,174
Sport Coupe htp	3,261	2,217	33,433
conv cpe	3,409	2,351	8,473
Suburban wgn 4d	3,475	2,425	12,291

1955 Engines	bore×stroke	bhp	availability
L6, 230.2	3.25×4.63	117	S-all Sixes
V8, 241.0	3.44×3.25	157	O-all V8
V8, 260.0	3.56×3.25	167	S-all V8
V8, 260.0	3.56×3.25	177	O-all V8

1956

P28/29-1 Plaza (wb 115.0)	Wght	Price	Prod
bus cpe	3,100	1,784	3,728
sdn 4d	3,210	1,926	60,197
club sdn	3,175	1,883	43,022
P28/29-2 Savoy (wb 115.0)			
sdn 4d	3,228	2,025	151,762
club sdn	3,190	1,982	57,927
Sport Coupe htp	3,200	2,130	16,473
P28/29-3 Belvedere (wb 115.0)			
sdn 4d	3,248	2,109	84.218

1955 Belvedere V8 convertible coupe

1956 Belvedere Sport Coupe hardtop

	Wght	Price	Prod
club sdn 2d	3,285	2,170	19,057
Sport Sedan htp	3,343	2,281	17,515
Sport Coupe htp	3,243	2,214	24,723
conv cpe	3,435	2,478	6,735
P28/29 Suburban (wb 115.0)			
DeLuxe wgn 2d	3,373	2,196	23,866
Custom wgn 2d	3,418	2,267	9,489
Custom wgn 4d	3,470	2,314	33,333
Sport wgn 4d	3,513	2,484	15,104
P29-3 Fury (wb 115.0)			
htp cpe	3,650	2,866	4,485

1956 Engines	bore×stroke	bhp	availability
L6, 230.2	3.25×4.38	125	S-all exc Fury, Belv conv
L6, 230.2	3.25×4.38	131	O-all exc Fury, Belv conv
V8, 270.0	3.63×3.26	180	O-Plaza, Savoy, Belvedere
V8, 277.0	3.75×3.13	187	S-Belv conv; O-Belv, Savoy, Plaza
V8, 277.0	3.75×3.13	200	O-all exc Fury
V8, 303.0	3.82×3.31	240	S-Fury

1957

P30/31-1 Plaza (wb 118.0)	Wght	Price	Prod
bus cpe	3,235	1,899	2,874
sdn 4d	3,333	2,050	70,248
sdn 2d	3,245	2,009	49,137
P30/31-2 Savoy (wb 118.0)			
sdn 4d	3,340	2,194	153,093
Sport Sedan htp	3,428	2,317	7,601
sdn 2d	3,263	2,147	55,590
Sport Coupe htp	3,335	2,229	31,373
P30/31-3 Belvedere (wb 118.0)			
sdn 4d	3,373	2,310	110,414
Sport Sedan htp	3,428	2,419	37,446
sdn 2d	3,288	2,264	55,590

	Wght	Price	Prod
Sport Coupe htp	3,348	2,349	67,268
conv cpe	3,585	2,638	9,866
P30/31 Suburban (wb 122.0)			
DeLuxe wgn 2d	3,620	2,330	20,111
Custom wgn 2d	3,668	2,440	11,196
Custom wgn 4d, 6P	3,753	2,494	40,227
Custom wgn 4d, 9P	3,800	2,649	9,357
Sport wgn 4d, 6P	3,748	2,622	15,414
Sport wgn 4d, 9P	3,795	2,777	7,988
P31 Fury (wb 118.0)			
htp cpe	3,595	2,925	7,438

1957 Engines	bore×stroke	bhp	availability
L6, 230.2	3.25×4.63	132	S-all exc Fury, Belv conv
V8, 277.0	3.75×3.13	197	S-Plaza
V8, 277.0	3.75×3.13	235	O-Plaza
V8, 301.0	3.91×3.13	215	S-Savoy, Belv V8; O-Plaza
V8, 301.0	3.91×3.13	235	O-all exc Fury
V8, 318.0	3.91×3.31	290	S-Fury

1957 Fury hardtop coupe

1958

LP1/2-L Plaza (wb 118.0)		Wght	Price	Prod
21	club sdn	3,253	2,118	39,062
22	bus cpe	3,245	2,028	1,472
41	sdn 4d	3,335	2,169	54,194
LP1/2-M Savoy (wb 118.0)				
21	club sdn	3,290	2,254	17,624
23	Sport Coupe htp	3,320	2,329	19,500
41	sdn 4d	3,310	2,305	67,933
43	Sport Sedan htp	3,393	2,400	5,060
LP1/2-H Belvedere (wb 118.0)				
21	club sdn	3,305	2,389	4,229
23	Sport Coupe htp	3,325	2,457	36,043
27	conv cpe	3,545	2,762	9,941
41	sdn 4d	3,343	2,440	49,124
43	Sport Sedan htp	3,425	2,528	18,194
LP1/2 Suburban (wb 122.0)				
—	Deluxe wgn 4d	3,660	2,486	15,535
25	DeLuxe wgn 2d	3,560	2,432	15,625
25	Custom wgn 2d	3,630	2,553	5,925
45A	Custom wgn 4d, 6P	3,665	2,607	38,707
45B	Custom wgn 4d, 9P	3,763	2,747	17,158
45A	Sport wgn 4d, 6P	3,680	2,760	10,785
45B	Sport wgn 4d, 9P	3,758	2,900	12,385
LP2-H Fury (wb 118.0)				
23	htp cpe	3,510	3,067	5,303

1958 Engines	bore×stroke	bhp	availability
L6, 230.2	3.25×4.63	132	S-all exc Fury, Belv conv
V8, 318.0	3.91×3.31	225	O-all exc Fury
V8, 318.0	3.91×3.31	250	O-all exc Fury
V8, 318.0	3.91×3.31	290	S-Fury
V8, 350.0	4.06×3.38	305	O-all
V8, 350.0	4.06×3.38	315	O-all (fuel injection)

1959

MP1/2-L Savoy (wb 118.0)		Wght	Price	Prod
21	club sdn	3,333	2,222	46,979
22	bus cpe	3,130	2,143	1,051
41	sdn 4d	3,333	2,283	84,272
MP1/2-M Belvedere (wb 118.0)				
21	club sdn	3,310	2,389	13,816
23	htp cpe	3,318	2,461	23,469
27	conv cpe	3,580	2,814	5,063
41	sdn 4d	3,353	2,440	67,980
43	htp sdn 4d	3,335	2,525	5,713
MP2-H Fury (wb 118.0)				
23	htp cpe	3,435	2,714	21,494
41	sdn 4d	3,455	2,691	30,149
43	htp sdn	3,505	2,771	13,614
MP2-P Sport Fury (wb 118.0)				
23	htp cpe	3,475	2,927	17,867
27	conv cpe	3,670	3,125	5,990
MP1/2 Suburban (wb 122.0)				
25	DeLuxe wgn 2d	3,625	2,694	15,074
25	Custom wgn 2d, 6P	3,690	2,814	1,852
45A	DeLuxe wgn 4d	3,675	2,761	35,086
45A	Custom wgn 4d, 6P	3,678	3,881	35,024
45B	Custom wgn 4d, 9P	3,775	2,991	16,993
45A	Sport wgn 4d, 6P	3,760	3,021	7,224
45B	Sport wgn 4d, 9P	3,805	3,131	9,549

1959 Engines	bore×stroke	bhp	availability
L6, 230.2	3.25×4.63	132	S-Savoy, Belvedere, Suburb exc Cus 9P, Sports
V8, 318.0	3.91×3.31	230	S-Fury; O-other exc Sport Fury
V8, 318.0	3.91×3.31	260	S-Sport Fury; O-others
V8, 361.0	4.12×3.38	305	O-all

1958 Belvedere Sport Sedan four-door hardtop

1959 Sport Fury convertible coupe

1960

V100 Valiant (wb 106.5)		Wght	Price	Prod
110	sdn 4d	2,635	2,053	52,788
140	wgn 4d, 6P	2,815	2,365	12,018
—	wgn 4d, 9P	2,845	2,488	1,928
V200 Valiant (wb 106.5)				
130	sdn 4d	2,655	2,130	106,515
170	wgn 4d, 6P	2,855	2,443	16,368
—	wgn 4d, 9P	2,860	2,566	4,675
PP1/2-L Savoy (wb 118.0)				
21	club sdn	3,410	2,260	26,820
41	sdn 4d	3,433	2,310	51,384
PP1/2-M Belvedere (wb 118.0)				
21	club sdn	3,423	2,389	6,529
23	htp cpe	3,438	2,641	14,085
41	sdn 4d	3,448	2,439	42,130
PP1/2-H Fury (wb 118.0)				
23	htp cpe	3,465	2,599	18,079
27	conv cpe	3,630	2,967	7,080
41	sdn 4d	3,475	2,575	21,292
43	htp sdn	3,528	2,656	9,036

1960 Suburban Sport four-door wagon

PP1/2 Suburban (wb 122.0)		Wght	Price	Prod
25	DeLuxe wgn 2d	3,375	2,721	5,503
45	DeLuxe wgn 4d	3,815	2,787	18,484
45	Custom wgn 4d, 6P	3,890	2,880	17,308
45	Custom wgn 4d, 9P	3,875	2,990	8,116
45	Sport wgn 4d, 6P	3,895	3,024	3,333
45	Sport wgn 4d, 9P	4,020	3,134	4,253

1960 Engines	bore×stroke	bhp	availability
L6, 170.0	3.40×3.13	101	S-Valiant
L6, 170.0	3.40×3.13	148	O-Valiant only
L6, 225.0	3.40×4.13	145	S-full-size only
V8, 318.0	3.91×3.31	230	S-full-size V8 (PP2)
V8, 361.0	4.12×3.38	305	O-all full-size
V8, 383.0	4.25×3.38	310/330	O-full-size

1961

V100 Valiant (wb 106.5)		Wght	Price	Prod
111	sdn 2d	2,565	1,955	22,230
113	sdn 4d	2,590	2,014	25,695
156	wgn 4d	2,745	2,327	6,717
V200 Valiant (wb 106.5)				
132	htp cpe	2,605	2,137	18,586
133	sdn 4d	2,600	2,110	59,056
176	wgn 4d	2,770	2,423	10,794
RP1/2-L Savoy (2b 118.0)				
211	sdn 2d, L6	3,300	2,260	18,729
311	sdn 2d, V8	3,440	2,379	
213	sdn 4d, L6	3,310	2,310	44,913
313	sdn 4d, V8	3,465	2,430	
RP1/2-M Belvedere (wb 118.0)				
221	sdn 2d, L6	3,300	2,389	4,740
321	sdn 2d, V8	3,450	2,508	
222	htp cpe, L6	3,320	2,461	9,591
322	htp cpe, V8	3,460	2,580	
223	sdn 4d, L6	3,315	2,439	40,090
323	sdn 4d, V8	3,470	2,559	
RP1/2-H Fury (wb 118.0)				
232	htp cpe, L6	3,330	2,599	16,141
332	htp cpe, V8	3,520	2,718	
233	sdn 4d, L6	3,350	2,575	22,619
333	sdn 4d, V8	3,515	2,694	
234	htp sdn, L6	3,390	2,656	8,507
334	htp sdn, V8	3,555	2,775	
335	conv cpe, V8	3,535	2,967	6,948

RP1/2 Suburban (wb 122.0)		Wght	Price	Prod
255	DeLuxe wgn 2d, L6	3,675	2,602	2,464
355	DeLuxe wgn 2d, V8	3,845	2,721	
256	DeLuxe wgn 4d, L6	3,715	2,668	12,980
356	DeLuxe wgn 4d, V8	3,885	2,788	
266	Custom wgn 4d, L6	3,730	2,761	13,553
366	Custom wgn 4d, V8	3,885	2,880	
367	Custom wgn 4d, 9P, V8	3,985	2,990	
376	Sport wgn 4d, 6P, V8	3,890	3,024	2,844
377	Sport wgn 4d, 9P, V8	3,995	3,134	3,088

1961 Engines	bore×stroke	bhp	availability
L6, 170.0	3.40×3.13	101	S-Valiant
L6, 170.0	3.40×3.13	148	O-Valiant only
L6, 225.0	3.40×4.13	145	S-full-size only
V8, 318.0	3.91×3.31	230	S-full-size eights (RP2)
V8, 318.0	3.91×3.31	260	O-full-size with TorqueFlite
V8, 361.0	4.12×3.38	305	O-full-size exc PowerFlite or air cond
V8, 383.0	4.25×3.38	330	O-full-size exc PowerFlite or air cond
V8, 413.0	4.19×3.75	350/375	O-full-size

1962

SV1-L Valiant V100 (wb 106.5)		Wght	Price	Prod
111	sdn 2d	2,480	1,930	19,679
113	sdn 4d	2,500	1,991	33,769
156	wgn 4d	2,660	2,285	5,932
SV1-H Valiant V200 (wb 106.5)				
131	sdn 2d	2,500	2,026	8,484
133	sdn 4d	2,510	2,087	55,789
176	wgn 4d	2,690	2,381	8,055
SV1-P Valiant Signet (wb 106.5)				
142	htp cpe	2,515	2,230	25,586
SP1/2-L Savoy (wb 115.0)				
211	sdn 2d, L6	2,930	2,206	18,825
311	sdn 2d, V8	3,080	2,313	
213	sdn 4d, L6	2,960	2,262	49,777
313	sdn 4d, V8	3,115	2,369	
SP1/2-M Belvedere (wb 116.0)				
221	sdn 2d, L6	2,930	2,342	3,128
321	sdn 2d, V8	3,070	2,450	
222	htp cpe, L6	2,945	2,431	5,086
322	htp cpe, V8	3,075	2,538	
223	sdn 4d, L6	2,960	2,399	31,263
323	sdn 4d, V8	3,095	2,507	
SP1/2-H Fury (wb 116.0)				
232	htp cpe, L6	2,960	2,585	9,589
332	htp cpe, V8	3,105	2,693	

1960 Fury hardtop coupe

1961 Suburban Sport four-door wagon

		Wght	Price	Prod
233	sdn 4d, L6	2,990	2,563	17,531
333	sdn 4d, V8	3,125	2,670	
334	htp sdn, V8	3,190	2,742	5,995
335	conv cpe, V8	3,210	2,924	4,349
SP2-P Sport Fury (wb 116.0)				
342	htp cpe, V8	3,195	2,851	4,039
345	conv cpe, V8	3,295	3,082	1,516
SP1/2 Suburban (wb 116.0)*				
256	Savoy wgn 4d, L6	3,225	2,609	12,710
356	Savoy wgn 4d, V8	3,390	2,717	
266	Belvedere wgn 4d, 6P, L6	3,245	2,708	9,781
366	Belvedere wgn 4d, 6P, V8	3,390	2,815	
367	Belvedere wgn 4d, 9P, V8	3,440	2,917	4,168
376	Fury wgn 4d, 6P, V8	3,395	2,968	2,352
377	Fury wgn 4d, 9P, V8	3,455	3,071	2,411

*Due to factory numbering in 1962, model names such as "Savoy" were listed as body style names. This practice occurred in 1962 only.

1962 Engines	bore×stroke	bhp	availability
L6, 170.0	3.40×3.13	101	S-Valiant
L6, 225.0	3.40×4.13	145	S-SP1; O-Valiant
V8, 318.0	3.91×3.31	230	S-all SP2 exc Sport Fury
V8, 318.0	3.91×3.31	260	O-all SP2 exc Sport Fury
V8, 361.0	4.12×3.38	305	S-Sport Fury; O-other SP2 exc w/PowerFlite or AC
V8, 383.0	4.25×3.38	335	O-SP2
V8, 413.0	4.19×3.75	410	O-Sport Fury

1963

TV1-L Valiant V100 (wb 106.0)		Wght	Price	Prod
111	sdn 2d	2,515	1,910	32,761
113	sdn 4d	2,535	1,973	54,617
156	wgn 4d	2,700	2,268	11,864
TV1-H Valiant V200 (wb 106.0)				
131	sdn 2d	2,515	2,035	10,605
133	sdn 4d	2,555	2,097	57,029
135	conv cpe	2,640	2,340	7,122
176	wgn 4d	2,715	2,392	11,147
TV1-P Valiant Signet 200 (wb 106.0)				
142	htp cpe	2,570	2,230	30,857
145	conv cpe	2,675	2,454	9,154
TP1/2-L Savoy (wb 116.0)				
211	sdn 2d, L6	2,980	2,206	20,281
311	sdn 2d, V8	3,200	2,313	
213	sdn 4d, L6	3,020	2,262	56,313
313	sdn 4d, V8	3,220	2,369	
256	wgn 4d, 6P, L6	3,325	2,609	12,874
356	wgn 4d, 6P, V8	3,475	2,717	
257	wgn 4d, 9P, L6	3,375	2,710	4,342
357	wgn 4d, 9P, V8	3,560	2,818	
TP1/2-M Belvedere (wb 116.0)				
221	sdn 2d, L6	3,000	2,342	6,218
321	sdn 2d, V8	3,215	2,450	
222	htp cpe, L6	3,025	2,431	9,204
322	htp cpe, V8	3,190	2,538	
223	sdn 4d, L6	3,020	2,399	54,929
323	sdn 4d, V8	3,235	2,507	
366	wgn 4d, 6P, V8	3,490	2,815	10,297
367	wgn 4d, 9P, V8	3,585	2,917	4,012
TP1/2-H Fury (wb 116.0)				
232	htp cpe, L6	3,030	2,585	13,832
332	htp cpe, V8	3,215	2,693	
233	sdn 4d, L6	3,075	2,563	31,891
333	sdn 4d, V8	3,265	2,670	

1963 Sport Fury hardtop coupe

1964 Sport Fury hardtop coupe

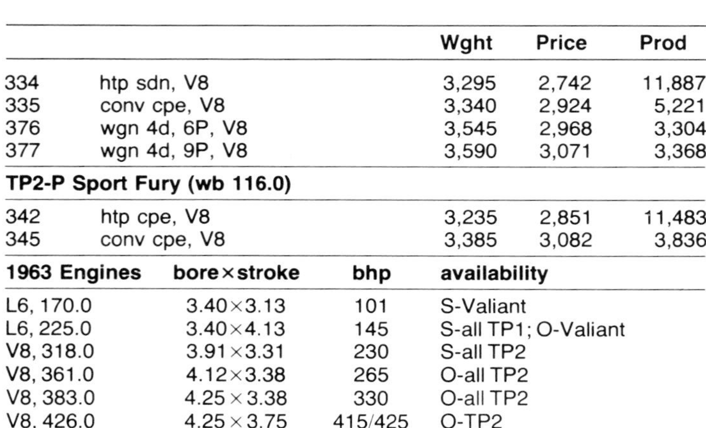

		Wght	Price	Prod
334	htp sdn, V8	3,295	2,742	11,887
335	conv cpe, V8	3,340	2,924	5,221
376	wgn 4d, 6P, V8	3,545	2,968	3,304
377	wgn 4d, 9P, V8	3,590	3,071	3,368
TP2-P Sport Fury (wb 116.0)				
342	htp cpe, V8	3,235	2,851	11,483
345	conv cpe, V8	3,385	3,082	3,836

1963 Engines	bore×stroke	bhp	availability
L6, 170.0	3.40×3.13	101	S-Valiant
L6, 225.0	3.40×4.13	145	S-all TP1; O-Valiant
V8, 318.0	3.91×3.31	230	S-all TP2
V8, 361.0	4.12×3.38	265	O-all TP2
V8, 383.0	4.25×3.38	330	O-all TP2
V8, 426.0	4.25×3.75	415/425	O-TP2

1964

VV1-L Valiant V100 (wb 106.0)		Wght	Price	Prod
111	sdn 2d	2,540	1,921	35,403
113	sdn 4d	2,575	1,992	44,208
156	wgn 4d	2,725	2,273	10,759
VV1-H Valiant V200 (wb 106.0)				
131	sdn 2d	2,545	2,044	11,013
133	sdn 4d	2,570	2,112	63,828
135	conv cpe	2,670	2,349	5,856
176	wgn 4d	2,730	2,388	11,146
VV1-P Valiant Signet 200 (wb 106.0)				
142	htp cpe	2,600	2,256	37,736
145	conv cpe	2,690	2,473	7,636
149	Barracuda htp cpe	2,740	2,365	23,443
VP1/2-L Savoy (wb 116.0)				
211	sdn 2d, L6	2,990	2,224	21,326 (211 & 311)
311	sdn 2d, V8	3,205	2,332	
213	sdn 4d, L6	3,040	2,280	51,024 (213 & 313)
313	sdn 4d, V8	3,210	2,388	
256	wgn 4d, 6P, L6	3,345	2,620	12,401 (256 & 356)
356	wgn 4d, 6P, V8	3,495	2,728	
257	wgn 4d, 9P, L6	3,400	2,721	3,242 (257 & 357)
357	wgn 4d, 9P, V8	3,600	2,829	
VP1/2-M Belvedere (wb 116.0)				
221	sdn 2d, L6	3,000	2,359	5,364 (221 & 321)
321	sdn 2d, V8	3,210	2,466	
222	htp cpe, L6	3,010	2,444	16,334 (222 & 322)
322	htp cpe, V8	3,190	2,551	

		Wght	Price	Prod
223	sdn 4d, L6	3,065	2,417	57,307 (223 & 323)
323	sdn 4d, V8	3,225	2,524	
366	wgn 4d, 6P, V8	3,510	2,826	10,317
367	wgn 4d, 9P, V8	3,605	2,928	4,207
VP1/2-H Fury (wb 116.0)				
232	htp cpe, L6	3,040	2,598	26,303 (232 & 332)
332	htp cpe, V8	3,212	2,706	
233	sdn 4d, L6	3,045	2,573	34,901 (233 & 333)
333	sdn 4d, V8	3,230	2,680	
334	htp sdn, V8	3,300	2,752	13,713
335	conv cpe, V8	3,345	2,937	5,173
376	wgn 4d, 6P, V8	3,530	2,981	3,646
377	wgn 4d, 9P, V8	3,630	3,084	4,482
VP2-P Sport Fury (wb 116.0)				
342	htp cpe, V8	3,270	2,864	23,695
345	conv cpe, V8	3,405	3,095	3,858

1964 Engines	bore×stroke	bhp	availability
L6, 170.0	3.40×3.13	101	S-Valiant
L6, 225.0	3.40×4.13	145	S-VP1; O-Valiant
V8, 273.0	3.62×3.31	180	O-Valiant
V8, 318.0	3.91×3.31	230	S-all VP2
V8, 361.0	4.12×3.38	265	O-all exc Valiant
V8, 383.0	4.25×3.38	330	O-all exc Valiant
V8, 426.0	4.25×3.75	365	O-all exc Valiant
V8, 426.0	4.25×3.75	400-425	O-VP2 (Super Stock/Street)

1965

AV1-L Valiant 100 (wb 106.0)*		Wght	Price	Prod
V11	sdn 2d	2,560	2,004	40,434
V13	sdn 4d	2,590	2,075	42,857
V56	wgn 4d	2,750	2,361	10,822
AV1-H Valiant 200 (wb 106.0)*				
V31	sdn 2d	2,570	2,127	8,919
V33	sdn 4d	2,605	2,195	41,642
V35	conv cpe	2,695	2,437	2,769
V78	wgn 4d	2,755	2,476	6,133
AV-1P Valiant Signet (wb 106.0)*				
V42	htp cpe	2,620	2,340	10,999
V45	conv cpe	2,725	2,561	2,578
AV1-P Barracuda (wb 106.0)*				
V89	htp cpe	2,725	2,487	64,596
Belvedere I (wb 116.0; SS-115.0)				
R01	Super Stock htp cpe	3,170	4,671	—

		Wght	Price	Prod
R11	sdn 2d	3,088	2,226	12,536
R13	sdn 4d	3,153	2,265	35,968
R56	wgn 4d	3,423	2,562	8,338
Belvedere II (wb 116.0)				
R32	htp cpe	3,123	2,378	24,924
R33	sdn 4d	3,128	2,352	41,445
R35	conv cpe	3,230	2,597	1,921
R76	wgn 4d, 6P	3,425	2,649	5,908
R77	wgn 4d, 9P	3,488	2,747	3,294
Satellite (wb 116.0)				
R42	htp cpe	3,220	2,649	23,341
R45	conv cpe	3,325	2,869	1,860
Fury I (wb 119.0; wgns-121.0)				
P11	sdn 2d	3,518	2,376	17,294
P13	sdn 4d	3,573	2,430	48,575
P56	wgn 4d	4,030	2,776	13,360
Fury II (wb 119.0; wgn-121.0)				
P21	sdn 2d	3,525	2,478	4,109
P23	sdn 4d	3,573	2,532	43,350
P66	wgn 4d, 6P	4,135	2,948	12,853
P67	wgn 4d, 9P	4,160	3,051	6,445
Fury III (wb 119.0; wgns-121.0)				
P32	htp cpe	3,563	2,691	43,251
P33	sdn 4d	3,595	2,684	50,725
P34	htp sdn	3,690	2,863	21,367
P35	conv cpe	3,710	3,048	5,524
P76	wgn 4d, 6P	4,140	3,090	8,931
P77	wgn 4d, 9P	4,200	3,193	9,546
Sport Fury (wb 119.0)				
P42	htp cpe	3,715	2,960	38,348
P45	conv cpe	3,755	3,209	6,272

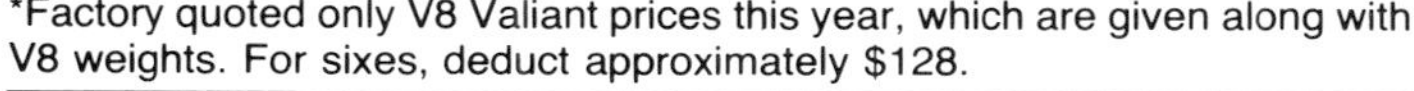
*Factory quoted only V8 Valiant prices this year, which are given along with V8 weights. For sixes, deduct approximately $128.

1965 Engines	bore×stroke	bhp	availability
L6, 170.0	3.40×3.13	101	S-Valiant
L6, 225.0	3.40×4.13	145	S-Barracuda, Furys, Belv; O-Valiant
V8, 273.0	3.62×3.31	180	S-Satellite; O-Valiant, Barracuda, Belvedere
V8, 273.0	3.62×3.31	235	O-Valiant, Barracuda
V8, 318.0	3.91×3.31	230	S-Furys; O-Belvedere, Satellite
V8, 361.0	4.12×3.38	265	O-Belvedere, Satellite
V8, 383.0	4.25×3.38	270	O-Belv, Satellite, Furys
V8, 383.0	4.25×3.38	330	O-Belv, Satellite, Furys
V8, 426.0	4.25×3.75	365	S-Belv I SS; O-Belvedere, Satellite, Furys
V8, 426.0	4.25×3.75	425	O-Belvedere I Super Stock

1966 Valiant Signet hardtop coupe

1966

BV1/2-L Valiant 100 (wb 106.0)		Wght	Price	Prod
21	sdn 2d	2,700	2,025	35,787
41	sdn 4d	2,725	2,095	36,031
45	wgn 4d	2,648	2,387	6,838
BV1/2-H Valiant 200 (wb 106.0)				
41	sdn 4d	2,728	2,226	39,392

1967 Barracuda convertible coupe

		Wght	Price	Prod
45	wgn 4d	2,883	2,502	4,537
BV1/2-H Valiant Signet (wb 106.0)				
23	htp cpe	2,735	2,261	13,045
27	conv cpe	2,830	2,527	2,507
BV1/2-P Barracuda (wb 106.0)				
29	htp cpe	2,865	2,556	38,029
BR1/2-L Belvedere I (wb 116.0; wgn-117.0)				
21	sdn 2d	3,095	2,277	9,381
41	sdn 4d	3,125	2,315	31,063
45	wgn 4d	3,523	2,605	8,200
BR1/2-H Belvedere II (wb 116.0; wgn-117.0)				
23	htp cpe	3,123	2,430	36,644
27	conv cpe	3,200	2,644	2,502
41	sdn 4d	3,115	2,405	49,941
45	wgn 4d, 6P	3,525	2,695	8,667
46	wgn 4d, 9P	3,618	2,804	4,726
BR2-P Satellite (wb 116.0)				
23	htp cpe	3,255	2,695	35,399
27	conv cpe	3,320	2,910	2,759
BP1/2-L Fury I (wb 119.0; wgn-121.0)				
21	sdn 2d	3,518	2,426	12,538
41	sdn 4d	3,570	2,479	39,698
45	wgn 4d	4,048	2,836	9,690
BP1/2-M Fury II (wb 119.0; wgn-121.0)				
21	sdn 2d	3,530	2,526	2,503
41	sdn 4d	3,573	2,579	55,016
45	wgn 4d, 6P	4,145	2,986	10,718
46	wgn 4d, 9P	4,175	3,087	5,580
BP1/2-H Fury III (wb 119.0; wgn-121.0)				
23	htp cpe	3,578	2,724	41,869
27	conv cpe	3,720	3,074	4,326
41	sdn 4d	3,217	2,718	46,505
43	htp sdn	3,730	2,893	33,922
45	wgn 4d, 6P	4,155	3,115	9,239
46	wgn 4d, 9P	4,165	3,216	10,886

BP2-P Sport Fury (wb 119.0)		Wght	Price	Prod
23	htp cpe	3,730	3,006	32,523
27	conv cpe	3,755	3,251	3,418
VP2-H VIP (wb 119.0)*				
23	htp cpe	3,700	3,069	—
43	htp sdn	3,780	3,133	—

*Included with Fury III.

1966 Engines	bore×stroke	bhp	availability
L6, 170.0	3.40×3.13	101	S-Valiant
L6, 225.0	3.40×4.13	145	S-Brcda, Belv exc Satellite, Fury sdns/wgns, Fury III 43; O-Val
V8, 273.0	3.62×3.31	180	S-Sat; O-Belv, Brcda, Val
V8, 273.0	3.62×3.31	235	O-Brcda, Valiant exc wgns
V8, 318.0	3.91×3.31	230	S-VIP, Spt Fury, Fury II wgns, Fury III conv/htp/wgn; O-Fury, Belv
V8, 361.0	4.12×3.38	265	O-Belvedere, Satellite
V8, 383.0	4.25×3.38	325	O-VIP, Furys, Belv, Sat
V8, 426.0	4.25×3.75	425	O-Belv, Sat exc wgns
V8, 440.0	4.32×3.75	365	O-VIP, Furys

1967

CV1/2-L Valiant 100 (wb 108.0)		Wght	Price	Prod
21	sdn 2d	2,738	2,117	29,093
41	sdn 4d	2,753	2,163	46,638
CV1/2-H Valiant Signet (wb 108.0)				
21	sdn 2d	2,765	2,262	6,843
41	sdn 4d	2,750	2,308	26,395
CV1/2-P Barracuda (wb 108.0)				
23	htp cpe	2,793	2,449	28,196
27	conv cpe	2,903	2,779	4,228
29	fstbk cpe	2,878	2,639	30,110
CR1/2-E Belvedere (wb 117.0)				
45	wgn 4d	3,543	2,579	5,477

1968 Barracuda convertible coupe

1969 Sport Fury hardtop coupe

1970 Road Runner Superbird hardtop coupe

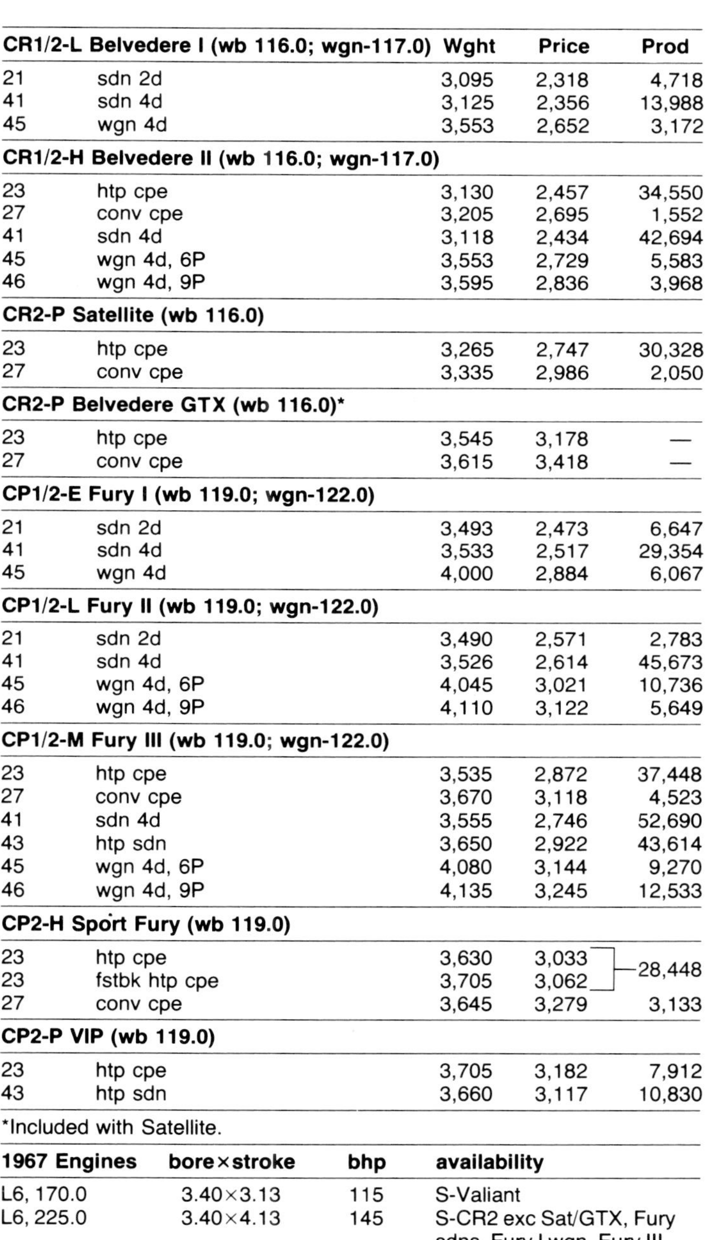

CR1/2-L Belvedere I (wb 116.0; wgn-117.0)		Wght	Price	Prod
21	sdn 2d	3,095	2,318	4,718
41	sdn 4d	3,125	2,356	13,988
45	wgn 4d	3,553	2,652	3,172
CR1/2-H Belvedere II (wb 116.0; wgn-117.0)				
23	htp cpe	3,130	2,457	34,550
27	conv cpe	3,205	2,695	1,552
41	sdn 4d	3,118	2,434	42,694
45	wgn 4d, 6P	3,553	2,729	5,583
46	wgn 4d, 9P	3,595	2,836	3,968
CR2-P Satellite (wb 116.0)				
23	htp cpe	3,265	2,747	30,328
27	conv cpe	3,335	2,986	2,050
CR2-P Belvedere GTX (wb 116.0)*				
23	htp cpe	3,545	3,178	—
27	conv cpe	3,615	3,418	—
CP1/2-E Fury I (wb 119.0; wgn-122.0)				
21	sdn 2d	3,493	2,473	6,647
41	sdn 4d	3,533	2,517	29,354
45	wgn 4d	4,000	2,884	6,067
CP1/2-L Fury II (wb 119.0; wgn-122.0)				
21	sdn 2d	3,490	2,571	2,783
41	sdn 4d	3,526	2,614	45,673
45	wgn 4d, 6P	4,045	3,021	10,736
46	wgn 4d, 9P	4,110	3,122	5,649
CP1/2-M Fury III (wb 119.0; wgn-122.0)				
23	htp cpe	3,535	2,872	37,448
27	conv cpe	3,670	3,118	4,523
41	sdn 4d	3,555	2,746	52,690
43	htp sdn	3,650	2,922	43,614
45	wgn 4d, 6P	4,080	3,144	9,270
46	wgn 4d, 9P	4,135	3,245	12,533
CP2-H Sport Fury (wb 119.0)				
23	htp cpe	3,630	3,033	28,448
23	fstbk htp cpe	3,705	3,062	
27	conv cpe	3,645	3,279	3,133
CP2-P VIP (wb 119.0)				
23	htp cpe	3,705	3,182	7,912
43	htp sdn	3,660	3,117	10,830

*Included with Satellite.

1967 Engines	bore×stroke	bhp	availability
L6, 170.0	3.40×3.13	115	S-Valiant
L6, 225.0	3.40×4.13	145	S-CR2 exc Sat/GTX, Fury sdns, Fury I wgn, Fury III htp, Brcda; O-Val

	bore × stock	bhp	availability
V8, 273.0	3.62×3.31	180	S-CR2 exc GTX, Brcda, Val
V8, 273.0	3.62×3.31	235	O-Valiant, Barracuda
V8, 318.0	3.91×3.31	230	S-Furys; O-Belv exc GTX
V8, 383.0	4.25×3.38	270	O-Furys; Belv exc GTX
V8, 383.0	4.25×3.38	280	O-Barracuda
V8, 383.0	4.25×3.38	325	O-Brcda, Furys, Belv exc GTX
V8, 426.0	4.25×3.75	425	O-Belvedere GTX
V8, 440.0	4.32×3.75	350	O-Fury wgns
V8, 440.0	4.32×3.75	375	S-GTX; O-Furys exc wgns

1968

VL Valiant 100 (wb 108.0)*		Wght	Price	Prod
21	sdn 2d	2,733	2,254	31,178
41	sdn 4d	2,763	2,301	49,446
VH Valiant Signet (wb 108.0)				
21	sdn 2d	2,745	2,400	6,265
41	sdn 4d	2,768	2,447	23,906
VH Barracuda (wb 108.0)				
23	htp cpe	2,810	2,605	19,997
27	conv cpe	2,923	2,907	2,840
29	fstbk cpe	2,895	2,762	22,575
RL Belvedere (wb 116.0; wgn-117.0)				
21	cpe	3,050	2,444	15,702
41	sdn 4d	3,080	2,483	17,214
45	wgn 4d	3,553	2,773	8,982
RH Satellite (wb 116.0; wgn-117.0)				
23	htp cpe	3,070	2,594	46,539
27	conv cpe	3,188	2,824	1,771
41	sdn 4d	3,080	2,572	42,309
45	wgn 4d, 6P	3,605	2,891	12,097
46	wgn 4d, 9P	3,625	2,998	10,883
RP Sport Satellite (wb 116.0; wgn-117.0)				
23	htp cpe	3,155	2,822	21,014
27	conv cpe	3,285	3,036	1,523
45	wgn 4d, 6P	3,610	3,131	**
46	wgn 4d, 9P	3,685	3,239	**
RM Road Runner (wb 116.0)				
21	cpe	3,440	2,896	29,240
23	htp cpe	3,455	3,034	15,359
RS GTX (wb 116.0)				
23	htp cpe	3,470	3,355	17,914
27	conv cpe	3,595	3,590	1,026

PE Fury I (wb 119.0)		Wght	Price	Prod
21	sdn 2d	3,480	2,617	5,788
41	sdn 4d	3,653	2,660	23,208
PL Fury II (wb 119.0)				
21	sdn 2d	3,488	2,715	3,112
41	sdn 4d	3,533	2,757	49,423
PM Fury III (wb 119.0)				
23	htp cpe	3,538	2,912	60,472
23	fstbk htp cpe "PX"	3,528	2,932	
27	conv cpe	3,680	3,236	4,483
41	sdn 4d	3,545	2,890	57,899
43	htp sdn	3,635	3,067	45,147
PH Sport Fury (wb 119.0)				
23	htp cpe	3,620	3,206	6,642
23	fstbk htp cpe "PS"	3,615	3,225	17,073
27	conv cpe	3,710	3,425	2,489
PP VIP (wb 119.0)				
23	fstbk htp cpe	3,615	3,260	6,768
43	htp sdn	3,655	3,326	10,745
DP Suburban (wb 122.0)				
45	wgn 4d	3,990	3,048	6,749
45	Custom wgn 4d, 6P	4,045	3,252	17,078
46	Custom wgn 4d, 9P	4,090	3,353	9,954
45	Sport wgn 4d, 6P	4,055	3,442	9,203
46	Sport wgn 4d, 9P	4,100	3,543	13,224

*Includes "Valiant 200" trim option.
**Sport Satellite wagon included with Satellite wagon.

1968 Engines	bore×stroke	bhp	availability
L6, 170.0	3.40×3.13	115	S-Valiant
L6, 225.0	3.40×4.13	145	S-Brcda, Belv, Sat, FI/II, FIII sdn, htps, Suburban; O-Val
V8, 273.0	3.62×3.31	190	O-Val, Belv, Sat, Spt Sat wgn
V8, 318.0	3.91×3.31	230	S-Spt Sat, Fury III; O-Val, Brcda, Belv, Sat, Spt Sat wgn
V8, 340.0	4.04×3.31	275	S-Barracuda Formula S
V8, 383.0	4.25×3.38	290	O-Belv, Sat, Spt Sat, Furys
V8, 383.0	4.25×3.38	300	O-Barracuda Formula S
V8, 383.0	4.25×3.38	330	O-Belv, Satellite, Furys, Suburbans
V8, 383.0	4.25×3.38	335	S-Road Runner
V8, 426.0	4.25×3.75	425	O-Road Runner, GTX
V8, 440.0	4.32×3.75	375	S-GTX; O-Fury exc DP
V8, 440.0	4.32×3.75	350	O-Suburban

1969

VL Valiant 100 (wb 108.0)*		Wght	Price	Prod
21	sdn 2d	2,740	2,094	29,672
41	sdn 4d	2,760	2,154	49,409
VH Valiant Signet (wb 108.0)				
21	sdn 2d	2,740	2,253	6,645
41	sdn 4d	2,760	2,313	21,492
VH Barracuda (wb 108.0)				
23	htp cpe	2,815	2,780	12,757
27	conv cpe	2,940	3,082	1,442
29	fstbk htp cpe	2,902	2,813	17,788
RL Belvedere (wb 116.0; wgn-117.0)				
21	cpe	3,052	2,509	7,063
41	sdn rd	3,082	2,548	12,914
45	wgn 4d	3,540	2,879	7,038
RH Satellite (wb 116.0; wgn-117.0)				
23	htp cpe	3,080	2,659	38,323
27	conv cpe	3,200	2,875	1,137
41	sdn 4d	3,087	2,635	35,296
45	wgn 4d, 6P	3,540	2,997	5,837
46	wgn 4d, 9P	3,612	3,106	4,730
RP Sport Satellite (wb 116.0; wgn-117.0)				
23	htp cpe	3,156	2,883	15,807
27	conv cpe	3,276	3,081	818
41	sdn 4d	3,196	2,911	5,836
45	wgn 4d, 6P	3,596	3,241	3,221
45	wgn 4d, 9P	3,666	3,350	3,152
RM Road Runner (wb 116.0)				
21	cpe	3,435	2,945	33,743
23	htp cpe	3,450	3,083	48,549
27	conv cpe	3,790	3,313	2,128
RS GTX (wb 116.0)				
23	htp cpe	3,465	3,416	14,902
27	conv cpe	3,590	3,635	700
PE Fury I (wb 120.0)				
21	sdn 2d	3,501	2,701	4,971
41	sdn 4d	3,533	2,744	18,771
PL Fury II (wb 120.0)				
21	sdn 2d	3,506	2,813	3,268
41	sdn 4d	3,536	2,841	41,047
PM Fury III (wb 120.0)				
23	htp cpe	3,516	3,000	44,168
27	conv cpe	3,704	3,324	4,129
29	form htp cpe	3,601	3,020	22,738
41	sdn 4d	3,541	2,979	72,747
43	htp sdn	3,643	3,155	68,818
PH Sport Fury (wb 120.0)				
23	htp cpe	3,603	3,283	14,120
27	conv cpe	3,729	3,502	1,579
29	form htp cpe	3,678	3,303	2,169
PP VIP (wb 120.0)				
23	htp cpe	3,583	3,382	4,740
29	form htp cpe	3,668	3,382	1,059
43	htp sdn	3,663	3,433	7,982
EP Suburban (wb 122.0)				
45	wgn 4d	4,056	3,231	6,424
45	Custom wgn 4d, 6P	4,103	3,436	15,976
46	Custom wgn 4d, 9P	4,148	3,527	10,216
45	Sport wgn 4d, 6P	4,123	3,651	8,201
46	Sport wgn 4d, 9P	4,173	3,718	13,502

*Includes "Valiant 200" trim option.

1969 Engines	bore×stroke	bhp	availability
L6, 170.0	3.40×3.13	115	S-Valiant
L6, 225.0	3.40×4.13	145	S-Brcda, Belv, Sat, Fury I/II; O-Valiant
V8, 273.0	3.62×3.31	190	O-Valiant
V8, 318.0	3.91×3.31	230	S-Breda, SptSat, FuryIII, Spt Fury, VIP, Suburban
V8, 340.0	4.04×3.31	275	O-Barracuda
V8, 383.0	4.25×3.38	290	O-Belv, Sat, Spt Sat, Furys, VIP
V8, 383.0	4.25×3.38	330	O-Brcda, Belv, Sat, Spt Sat, Furys, VIP
V8, 383.0	4.25×3.38	335	S-Road Runner
V8, 426.0	4.25×3.75	425	O-Road Runner, GTX
V8, 440.0	4.32×3.75	375	S-GTX; O-Furys exc EP
V8, 440.0	4.32×3.75	350	O-Suburban

1970

VL Valiant (wb 108.0)		Wght	Price	Prod
29	Duster fstbk cpe	2,830	2,172	192,375
41	sdn 4d	2,835	2,250	50,810
VS Valiant Duster 340 (wb 108.0)				
29	htp cpe	3,110	2,547	24,817
BH Barracuda (wb 108.0)				
23	htp cpe	2,905	2,764	25,651
27	conv cpe	3,071	3,034	1,554
BP Barracuda Gran Coupe (wb 108.0)				
23	htp cpe	3,015	2,934	8,183
27	conv cpe	3,090	3,160	596
BS 'Cuda (wb 108.0)				
23	htp cpe	3,395	3,164	18,880
27	conv cpe	3,480	3,433	635
RL Belvedere (wb 116.0; wgn-117.0)				
21	cpe	3,095	2,603	4,717
41	sdn 4d	3,130	2,641	13,945
45	wgn 4d	3,655	3,075	5,584
RH Satellite (wb 116.0; wgn-117.0)				
23	htp cpe	3,105	2,765	28,200
27	conv cpe	3,225	3,006	701
41	sdn 4d	3,125	2,741	30,377
45	wgn 4d, 6P	3,637	3,101	4,204
46	wgn 4d, 9P	3,747	3,211	3,277
RP Sport Satellite (wb 116.0; wgn-117.0)				
23	htp cpe	3,170	2,988	8,749
41	sdn 4d	3,205	3,017	3,010
45	wgn 4d, 6P	3,675	3,345	1,975
46	wgn 4d, 9P	3,750	3,455	2,161
RM Road Runner (wb 116.0)				
21	cpe	3,450	2,896	15,716
23	htp cpe	3,475	3,034	24,944
23	Superbird htp cpe	3,785	4,298	1,920
27	conv cpe	3,550	3,289	824
RS GTX (wb 116.0)				
23	htp cpe	3,515	3,535	7,748
PE Fury I (wb 120.0)				
21	sdn 2d	3,603	2,790	2,353
41	sdn 4d	3,640	2,825	14,813
PL Fury II (wb 120.0)				
21	sdn 2d	3,583	2,903	21,316
41	sdn 4d	3,643	2,922	27,694
PM Fury III (wb 120.0)				
23	htp cpe	3,610	3,091	21,373
27	conv cpe	3,770	3,415	1,952
29	form htp cpe	3,645	3,333	12,367
41	sdn 4d	3,645	3,069	50,876
43	htp sdn	3,690	3,246	47,879
PH Sport Fury (wb 120.0)				
23	htp cpe	3,630	3,313	8,018 (combined with next two)
23	S/23 htp cpe "PS"	3,660	3,379	
23	GT htp cpe "PP"	3,925	3,898	
29	form htp cpe	3,645	3,333	5,688
41	sdn 4d	3,680	3,291	5,135
43	htp sdn	3,705	3,363	6,854
PL Fury Gran Coupe (wb 120.0)				
21	cpe	3,864	3,833	*
FP Suburban (wb 122.0)				
45	wgn 4d, 6P	4,125	3,303	5,300
46	wgn 4d, 9P	4,205	3,518	2,250
45	Custom wgn 4d, 6P	4,155	3,527	8,898
46	Custom wgn 4d, 9P	4,215	3,603	6,792
45	Sport wgn 4d, 6P	4,200	3,725	4,403
46	Sport wgn 4d, 9P	4,260	3,804	9,170

*Included with Fury II sdn 2d.

1970 Engines	bore×stroke	bhp	availability
L6, 198.0	3.40×3.64	125	S-Valiant, Duster
L6, 225.0	3.40×4.13	145	S-Brcda, Belv, Sat, Fury I/II; O-Valiant, Duster
V8, 318.0	3.91×3.31	230	S-Spt Sat, Fury III, Spt Fury, Gran Coupe, Suburban
V8, 340.0	4.04×3.31	275	S-Duster 340; O-'Cuda
V8, 383.0	4.25×3.38	290	O-all exc Valiant
V8, 383.0	4.25×3.38	330	O-all exc Valiant
V8, 383.0	4.25×3.38	335	S-Road Runner, 'Cuda
V8, 426.0	4.25×3.75	425	O-RR, 'Cuda, GTX
V8, 440.0	4.32×3.75	350	S-Spt Fury GT; O-other Fury
V8, 440.0	4.32×3.75	375	S-GTX; O-'Cuda
V8, 440.0	4.32×3.75	390	O-'Cuda, RR, GTX, PH23

1971

Valiant (wb 108.0; Scamp-111.0)		Wght	Price	Prod
VL29	Duster fstbk cpe	2,825	2,313	173,592
VL41	sdn 4d	2,831	2,392	42,660
VH23	Scamp htp cpe	2,900	2,561	48,253
VS29	Duster 340 fstbk cpe	3,140	2,703	12,886
Barracuda (wb 108.0)				
VH21	cpe 2d	3,040	2,654	9,459 (combined with next)
VH23	htp cpe	3,075	2,766	
VH27	conv	3,145	3,023	1,014
VP23	Gran Coupe htp cpe V8	3,105	3,029	1,615
VS23	'Cuda htp cpe V8	3,475	3,155	6,228
VS27	'Cuda conv cpe V8	3,550	3,412	374
Satellite (wb 117.0; 2d-115.0)				
RL41	sdn 4d	3,294	2,734	11,059
RL21	cpe	3,230	2,663	46,807 (combined with next)
RH23	Sebring htp cpe	3,256	2,931	
RL45	wgn 4d 2S	3,770	3,058	7,138
RH41	Custom sdn 4d	3,286	2,908	30,773
RH45	Custom wgn 4d 2S	3,776	3,235	5,045
RH46	Custom wgn 4d 3S	3,846	3,315	4,626
RM23	Road Runner htp cpe V8	3,640	3,147	14,218
RP23	Sebring Plus htp cpe V8	3,300	3,179	16,253
RP41	Brougham sdn 4d V8	3,330	3,189	3,020
RP45	Regent wgn 4d 2S V8	3,815	3,558	2,161
RP46	Regent wgn 4d 3S V8	3,885	3,638	2,985
RS23	GTX htp cpe V8	3,675	3,733	2,942
Fury (wb 120.0; wgn-122.0)				
PE41	I sdn 4d	3,742	3,163	16,395 (combined with next)
PE41	I Custom sdn 4d	3,742	3,241	
PE21	I sdn 2d	3,708	3,113	5,152 (combined with next)
PE21	I Custom sdn 2d	3,708	3,208	
PL23	II htp cpe	3,710	3,283	7,859
PL41	II sdn 4d	3,746	3,262	20,098
PL45	II Suburban wgn 4d 2S V8	4,245	3,758	4,877
PL46	II Suburban wgn 4d 3S V8	4,290	3,869	2,662
PM23	III htp cpe	3,716	3,458	21,319
PM41	III sdn 4d	3,752	3,437	44,244
PM29	III formal htp cpe V8	3,750	3,600	24,465
PM43	III htp sdn V8	3,820	3,612	55,356
PM45	III Cus Suburban wgn 4d 2S V8	4,240	3,854	10,874
PM46	III Cus Suburban wgn 4d 3S V8	4,300	3,930	11,702

1971 Valiant Duster 340 fastback coupe

Sport Fury (wb 120.0; wgn-122.0)		Wght	Price	Prod
PH23	htp cpe V8	3,805	3,677	3,912
PH29	formal htp cpe V8	3,810	3,710	3,957
PH41	sdn 4d V8	3,845	3,656	2,823
PH43	htp sdn V8	3,865	3,724	4,813
PH45	Sport Suburban wgn 4d 2S V8	4,290	4,071	5,103
PH46	Sport Suburban wgn 4d 3S V8	4,370	4,146	13,021
PP23	GT htp cpe V8	4,090	4,111	375

1971 Engines	bore×stroke	bhp	availability
L6, 198.0	3.40×3.64	125	S-Val,Brcda cpe
L6, 225.0	3.40×4.13	145	S-Brcda exc cpe, Sat,Fury; O-Val,Brcda cpe
V8, 318.0	3.91×3.31	230	S-Sat,Fury; O-Val,Brcda
V8, 340.0	4.04×3.31	275	S-Dstr 340,Cuda; O-Brcda
V8, 360.0	4.00×3.58	255	O-Fury
V8, 383.0	4.25×3.38	275	O-Brcda,Rd Runner,Fury
V8, 383.0	4.25×3.38	300	S-Cuda,Rd Runner; O-Barracuda,Fury
V8, 426.0	4.25×3.75	425	O-Barracuda
V8, 440.0	4.32×3.75	335	O-Fury
V8, 440.0	4.32×3.75	370	S-GTX, Fury GT; O-Fury
V8, 440.0	4.32×3.75	385	O-Barracuda

1972

Valiant (wb 108.0; Scamp-111.0)		Wght	Price	Prod
VL29	Duster fstbk cpe	2,780	2,287	212,331
VL41	sdn 4d	2,800	2,363	52,911
VH23	Scamp htp cpe	2,825	2,528	49,470
VS29	Duster 340 fstbk cpe	3,100	2,742	15,681
Barracuda (wb 108.0)				
VH23	htp cpe	3,185	2,710	10,622
VS23	'Cuda htp cpe V8	3,195	3,029	7,828
Satellite (wb 117.0; 2d-115.0)				
RL21	cpe	3,272	2,609	10,507
RL41	sdn 4d	3,312	2,678	12,794
RL45	wgn 4d 2S V8	3,785	3,167	7,377
RH23	Sebring htp cpe	3,282	2,871	34,353
RH41	Custom sdn 4d	3,318	2,848	34,973
RH45	Custom wgn 4d 2S V8	3,825	3,340	5,485
RH46	Custom wgn 4d 3S V8	3,780	3,418	5,637
RP23	Sebring Plus htp cpe V8	3,320	3,127	21,399
RP45	Regent wgn 4d 2S V8	3,790	3,562	1,893
RP46	Regent wgn 4d 3S V8	3,830	3,640	2,907
RM23	Road Runner htp cpe V8	3,495	3,095	7,628
Fury (wb 120.0; wgn-122.0)				
PL41	I sdn 4d	3,840	3,464	14,006
PM23	II htp cpe	3,790	3,605	7,515
PM41	II sdn 4d	3,830	3,583	20,051
PM45	II Suburban wgn 4d 2S	4,315	4,024	5,268
PM46	II Suburban wgn 4d 3S	4,360	4,139	2,773
PH23	III htp cpe	3,790	3,785	21,204
PH29	III formal htp cpe	3,790	3,818	9,036
PH41	III sdn 4d	3,830	3,763	46,731
PH43	III htp sdn	3,855	3,829	48,618
PH45	III Cus Suburban wgn 4d 2S	4,315	4,123	11,067
PH46	III Cus Suburban wgn 4d 3S	4,365	4,201	14,041
PP23	Gran Fury htp cpe	3,735	3,941	15,840
PP29	Gran Fury formal htp cpe	3,805	3,974	8,509
PP43	Gran Fury htp sdn	3,865	3,987	17,551
PP45	Sport Suburban wgn 4d 2S	4,335	4,389	4,971
PP46	Sport Suburban wgn 4d 3S	4,395	4,466	15,628

1972 Engines	bore×stroke	bhp	availability
L6, 198.0	3.40×3.64	100	S-Valiant
L6, 225.0	3.40×4.13	110	S-Brcda,Sat; O-Valiant
V8, 318.0	3.91×3.31	150	S-Sat,Fury; O-Val,Brcda
V8, 340.0	4.04×3.31	240	S-Duster 340,Cuda, Rd Runner; O-Barracuda
V8, 360.0	4.00×3.58	170	O-Fury
V8, 400.0	4.34×3.38	190/250	O-Fury
V8, 440.0	4.32×3.75	230/285	O-Fury

1973

Valiant (wb 108.0; Scamp-111.0)		Wght	Price	Prod
VL29	Duster fstbk cpe	2,830	2,376	249,243
VL41	sdn 4d	2,865	2,447	61,826
VH23	Scamp htp cpe	2,885	2,617	53,792

		Wght	Price	Prod
VS29	Duster 340 fstbk cpe	3,175	2,822	15,731
Barracuda (wb 108.0)				
VH23	htp cpe	3,140	2,935	11,587
VS23	'Cuda htp cpe	3,235	3,120	10,626
Satellite (wb 117.0; 2d-115.0)				
RL21	cpe	3,408	2,755	13,570
RL41	sdn 4d	3,482	2,824	14,716
RL45	wgn 4d 2S V8	3,950	3,272	6,906
RH23	Sebring htp cpe	3,425	2,997	51,575
RH41	Custom sdn 4d	3,478	2,974	46,748
RH45	Custom wgn 4d 2S V8	3,945	3,400	6,733
RH46	Custom wgn 4d 3S V8	3,990	3,518	7,705
RP23	Sebring Plus htp cpe V8	3,455	3,258	43,628
RP45	Regent wgn 4d 2S V8	3,950	3,621	2,781
RP46	Regent wgn 4d 3S V8	4,010	3,740	4,786
RM21	Road Runner cpe V8	3,525	3,115	19,056
Fury (wb 120.0; wgn-122.0)				
PL41	I sdn 4d	3,865	3,575	17,365
PM41	II sdn 4d	3,845	3,694	21,646
PM45	II Suburban wgn 4d 2S	4,410	4,150	5,206
PH23	III htp cpe	3,815	3,883	34,963
PH41	III sdn 4d	3,860	3,866	51,742
PH43	III htp sdn	3,880	3,932	51,215
PH45	III Cus Suburban wgn 4d 2S	4,420	4,246	9,888
PH46	III Cus Suburban wgn 4d 3S	4,465	4,354	15,671
PP23	Gran Fury htp cpe	3,845	4,064	18,127
PP43	Gran Fury htp sdn	3,890	4,110	14,852
PP45	Sport Suburban wgn 4d 2S	4,435	4,497	4,832
PP46	Sport Suburban wgn 4d 3S	4,495	4,599	15,680

1973 Engines	bore×stroke	bhp	availability
L6, 198.0	3.40×3.64	100	S-Valiant
L6, 225.0	3.40×4.13	110	S-Brcda,Sat; O-Valiant
V8, 318.0	3.91×3.31	150	S-Sat,Fury; O-Val,Brcda
V8, 340.0	4.04×3.31	240	S-Duster 340,Cuda,Rd Runner; O-Barracuda
V8, 360.0	4.00×3.58	175	O-Fury
V8, 400.0	4.34×3.38	190/250	O-Fury
V8, 440.0	4.32×3.75	230/285	O-Fury

1972 Satellite Road Runner hardtop coupe

1974

Valiant (wb 111.0; fstbk-108.0)		Wght	Price	Prod
VL29	Duster fstbk cpe	2,975	2,829	277,409
VS29	Duster 360 fstbk cpe	3,315	3,288	
VL41	sdn 4d	3,035	2,942	127,430
VP41	Brougham sdn 4d	3,195	3,819	
VP23	Brougham htp cpe	3,180	3,794	2,545
VH23	Scamp htp cpe	3,010	3,077	51,699
Barracuda (wb 108.0)				
VH23	htp cpe	3,210	3,067	6,745
VS23	'Cuda htp cpe	3,300	3,252	4,989
Satellite (wb 117.0; 2d-115.0)				
RL21	cpe	3,470	3,155	10,634
RL41	sdn 4d	3,555	3,226	12,726
RL45	wgn 4d 2S V8	4,065	3,654	4,622
RH23	Sebring htp cpe	3,490	3,353	31,980
RH41	Custom sdn 4d	3,550	3,329	45,863

1972 Valiant four-door sedan

		Wght	Price	Prod
RH45	Custom wgn 4d 2S V8	4,065	3,839	4,354
RH46	Custom wgn 4d 3S V8	4,110	4,152	5,591
RP45	Regent wgn 4d 2S V8	4,065	4,066	2,026
RP46	Regent wgn 4d 3S V8	4,130	4,381	3,132
RP23	Sebring Plus htp cpe V8	3,555	3,621	18,480
RM21	Road Runner cpe V8	3,615	3,545	11,555
Fury (wb 120.0; wgn-124.0)				
PL41	I sdn 4d	4,185	4,101	8,162
PM41	II sdn 4d	4,165	4,223	11,649
PM45	II Suburban wgn 4d 2S	4,745	4,669	2,490
PH23	III htp cpe	4,125	4,418	14,167
PH41	III sdn 4d	4,180	4,400	27,965
PH43	III htp sdn	4,205	4,268	18,778
PH45	III Cus Suburban wgn 4d 2S	4,755	4,767	3,877
PH46	III Cus Suburban wgn 4d 3S	4,800	4,878	5,628
PP23	Gran Fury htp cpe	4,300	4,627	9,617
PP43	Gran Fury htp sdn	4,370	4,675	8,191
PP45	Sport Suburban wgn 4d 2S	4,795	5,025	1,712
PP46	Sport Suburban wgn 4d 3S	4,850	5,130	6,047

1974 Engines	bore×stroke	bhp	availability
L6, 198.0	3.40×3.64	95	S-Valiant exc B'ham
L6, 225.0	3.40×4.13	105	S-Val,B'ham,Sat; O-Val
V8, 318.0	3.91×3.31	150	S-Brcda,Sat; O-Valiant
V8, 318.0	3.91×3.31	170	S-Road Runner
V8, 360.0	4.00×3.58	180	S-Fury exc wgn/Gran Fury
V8, 360.0	4.00×3.58	200	O-Sat, Fury exc wgn/G.Fury
V8, 360.0	4.00×3.58	245	S-Duster 360; O-Valiant
V8, 400.0	4.34×3.38	185	S-G.Fury,Fury wgns; O-Fury
V8, 400.0	4.34×3.38	205	O-Satellite, Fury
V8, 400.0	4.34×3.38	240	O-Fury
V8, 400.0	4.34×3.38	250	O-Satellite
V8, 440.0	4.32×3.75	230/250	O-Fury
V8, 440.0	4.32×3.75	275	O-Satellite

1975

Valiant (wb 111.0; fstbk-108.0)		Wght	Price	Prod
VL29	fstbk cpe	2,970	3,243	79,384
VH29	Duster Custom fstbk cpe	2,970	3,418	38,826
VL41	sdn 4d	3,040	3,247	44,471
VH41	Custom sdn 4d	3,040	3,422	56,258
VH23	Scamp htp cpe	3,020	3,518	23,581
VS29	Duster 360 fstbk cpe V8	3,315	3,979	1,421
VP23	Brougham htp cpe	3,240	4,232	5,781
VP41	Brougham sdn 4d	3,250	4,139	17,803
Fury (wb 117.5; 2d-115.0)				
RL21	cpe	3,612	3,542	8,398
RL41	sdn 4d	3,642	3,591	11,432
RL45	wgn 4d V8	4,180	4,309	4,468
RH23	Custom cpe	3,692	3,711	27,486
RH41	Custom sdn 4d	3,692	3,704	31,080
RH45	Custom wgn 4d 2S V8	4,230	4,512	3,890
RH46	Custom wgn 4d 3S V8	4,285	4,632	4,285
RP23	Sport htp cpe V8	3,790	4,105	17,782
RP45	Sport Suburban wgn 4d 2S V8	4,230	4,770	1,851
RP46	Sport Suburban wgn 4d 3S V8	4,295	4,867	3,107
Gran Fury (wb 121.5; wgn-124.0)				
PM41	sdn 4d	4,260	4,565	8,185
PM45	wgn 4d 2S	4,855	5,067	2,295
PH23	Custom htp cpe	4,205	4,781	6,041
PH41	Custom sdn 4d	4,260	4,761	19,043
PH43	Custom htp sdn	4,290	4,837	11,292
PH45	Custom wgn 4d 2S	4,870	5,176	3,155
PH46	Custom wgn 4d 3S	4,915	5,294	4,500
PP29	Brougham htp cpe	4,310	5,146	6,521
PP43	Brougham htp sdn	4,400	5,067	5,521
PP45	Sport Suburban wgn 4d 2S	4,885	5,455	1,508
PP46	Sport Suburban wgn 4d 3S	4,930	5,573	4,740

1975 Engines	bore×stroke	bhp	availability
L6, 225.0	3.40×4.13	90	S-Valiant
L6, 225.0	3.40×4.13	95	S-Fury
V8, 318.0	3.91×3.31	135	O-Fury, Valiant
V8, 318.0	3.91×3.31	150	S-Fury; O-G. Fury exc wgn/B'ham
V8, 360.0	4.00×3.58	180	S-G.F. exc wgn/B'ham; O-Fury, G.F. wgn/B'ham
V8, 360.0	4.00×3.58	190	O-Fury, Gran Fury
V8, 360.0	4.00×3.58	230	S-Duster 360
V8, 400.0	4.34×3.38	165/185	O-Fury
V8, 400.0	4.34×3.38	175	S-G.F. B'ham wgn; O-other
V8, 400.0	4.34×3.38	190/235	O-Fury
V8, 400.0	4.34×3.38	195	O-Gran Fury
V8, 440.0	4.32×3.75	215	O-Gran Fury

1976

Valiant (wb 111.0; fstbk-108.0)		Wght	Price	Prod
VL23	Scamp Special htp cpe	3,020	3,337	4,018
VL29	Duster fstbk cpe	2,975	3,241	34,681
VL41	sdn 4d	3,050	3,276	40,079
VH23	Scamp htp cpe	3,020	3,510	6,908
Volare (wb 112.5; cpe-108.5)				
HL29	spt cpe	3,222	3,324	37,024
HL41	sdn 4d	3,252	3,359	23,058
HL45	wgn 5d	3,622	3,646	46,065
HH29	Custom spt cpe	3,232	3,506	31,252
HH41	Custom sdn 4d	3,262	3,541	36,407
HP29	Premier cpe	3,438	4,402	31,475
HP41	Premier sdn 4d	3,472	4,389	37,131
HH45	Premier wgn 5d	3,628	3,976	49,507
Fury (wb 117.5; 2d-115.0)				
RL23	htp cpe	3,708	3,699	16,415
RL41	sdn 4d	3,742	3,733	22,654
RL45	wgn 4d 2S V8	4,285	4,597	4,624
RL46	wgn 4d 3S V8	4,350	4,739	4,412
RH23	Sport htp cpe	3,712	3,988	28,851
RH41	Salon sdn 4d	3,762	4,022	20,234
RH45	Sport Suburban wgn 2S V8	4,285	4,986	2,175
RH46	Sport Suburban wgn 3S V8	4,360	5,128	3,482
Gran Fury (wb 121.5; wgn-124.0)				
PM41	sdn 4d	4,140	4,349	8,928
PM45	wgn 4d 2S	4,880	4,909	1,587
PH23	Custom htp cpe	4,265	4,730	2,733
PH41	Custom sdn 4d	4,305	4,715	14,738
PH45	Custom Suburban wgn 4d 2S	4,895	5,193	1,433
PH46	Custom Suburban wgn 4d 3S	4,940	5,316	1,998
PP29	Brougham htp cpe	4,400	5,334	2,619
PP41	Brougham sdn 4d	4,435	5,162	2,990
PP46	Sport Suburban wgn 4d 3S	4,975	5,761	2,484

1977 Fury Sport hardtop coupe

1976 Engines	bore×stroke	bhp	availability
L6, 225.0	3.40×4.13	100	S-Val,Vol,Fury exc wgn
V8, 318.0	3.91×3.31	150	S-Vol,Fury exc wgn, GF sdn; O-Valiant
V8, 360.0	4.00×3.58	170	S-Fury wgn, G.Fury Cus; O-Val,Vol,Fury, G.F. exc Cus/B'ham
V8, 360.0	4.00×3.58	220	O-Valiant
V8, 400.0	4.34×3.38	175	S-GF wgn/B'ham; O-Fury
V8, 400.0	4.34×3.38	200/240	O-Gran Fury
V8, 440.0	4.32×3.75	205	O-Gran Fury

1977

Volare (wb 112.7; cpe-108.7)		Wght	Price	Prod
HL29	spt cpe	3,235	3,570	42,455
HL41	sdn 4d	3,290	3,619	44,550
HL45	wgn 4d	3,500	3,941	80,180
HH29	Custom spt cpe	3,240	3,752	34,196
HH41	Custom sdn 4d	3,295	3,801	50,859
HP29	Premier spt cpe	3,430	4,305	21,979
HP41	Premier sdn 4d	3,496	4,354	31,443
HH45	Premier wgn 5d	3,505	4,271	76,756
Fury (wb 117.5; 2d-115.0)				
RL23	htp cpe	3,742	3,893	16,410
RL41	sdn 4d	3,772	3,944	25,172
RL45	Suburban wgn 4d 2S V8	4,335	4,687	6,765
RL46	Suburban wgn 4d 3S V8	4,390	4,830	5,556
RH23	Sport htp cpe	3,748	4,132	30,075
RH41	Salon sdn 4d	3,782	4,185	25,617
RH45	Sport Suburban wgn 4d 2S V8	4,330	5,192	2,502
RH46	Sport Suburban wgn 4d 3S V8	4,400	5,335	4,065
Gran Fury (wb 121.5; wgn-124.0)				
PM23	cpe	4,070	4,692	2,772
PM41	sdn 4d	4,145	4,677	14,242
PM45	Suburban wgn 4d 2S	4,885	5,315	2,055
PH23	Brougham cpe	4,190	4,963	4,846
PH41	Brougham sdn 4d	4,250	4,948	17,687
PH45	Sport Suburban wgn 4d 2S	4,880	5,558	1,631
PH46	Sport Suburban wgn 4d 3S	4,925	5,681	4,319

1977 Engines	bore×stroke	bhp	availability
L6, 225.0	3.40×4.13	100	S-Volare exc wgns
L6, 225.0	3.40×4.13	110	S-Vol wgns; Fury exc wgns
V8, 318.0	3.91×3.31	145	S-Vol,Fury exc wgns, Gran Fury exc B'ham wgn
V8, 360.0	4.00×3.58	155	S-Fury wgns, GF B'ham; O-Volare,Fury, Gran Fury
V8, 360.0	4.00×3.58	170	O-Fury, Gran Fury
V8, 400.0	4.34×3.38	190	S-GF wgns; O-Fury, GF
V8, 440.0	4.32×3.75	185/195	O-Gran Fury

1978

Horizon (wb 99.2)		Wght	Price	Prod
ML44	htchbk sdn 5d	2,145	3,976	106,772
Volare (wb 112.7; cpe-108.7)				
HL29	spt cpe	3,200	3,771	74,818
HL41	sdn 4d	3,235	3,899	100,718
HL45	wgn 5d	3,465	4,241	81,242
Fury (wb 117.5; 2d-115.0)				
RL23	htp cpe	3,725	4,236	13,276
RL41	sdn 4d	3,760	4,326	83,649
RL45	Suburban wgn 4d 2S V8	4,310	5,084	4,522
RL46	Suburban wgn 4d 3S V8	4,370	5,227	3,889
RH23	Sport htp cpe	3,735	4,483	13,031
RH41	Salon sdn 4d	3,770	4,568	14,964
RH45	Sport Suburban wgn 4d 2S V8	4,300	5,545	1,720
RH46	Sport Suburban wgn 4d 3S V8	4,375	5,688	2,528

1981 Reliant SE four-door wagon

1978 Engines	bore×stroke	bhp	availability
L4, 104.7	3.13×3.40	70	S-Horizon
L6, 225.0	3.40×4.13	90	O-Volare exc wgn
L6, 225.0	3.40×4.13	100	S-Volare exc wgn
L6, 225.0	3.40×4.13	110	S-Volare wgn, Fury
V8, 318.0	3.91×3.31	140	S-Volare, Fury exc wgns
V8, 318.0	3.91×3.31	155	O-Volare, Fury exc wgns
V8, 360.0	4.00×3.58	155	S-Fury wgns; O-Vol, Fury
V8, 360.0	4.00×3.58	165/175	O-Volare
V8, 360.0	4.00×3.58	170	O-Fury
V8, 400.0	4.34×3.38	190	O-Fury

1979

Horizon (wb 99.2; TC3-96.7)		Wght	Price	Prod
ML24	TC3 htchbk cpe 3d	2,195	4,864	63,715
ML44	htchbk sdn 5d	2,135	4,469	99,048
Volare (wb 112.7; cpe-108.7)				
HL29	spt cpe	3,110	4,387	63,620
HL41	sdn 4d	3,175	4,504	95,383
HL45	wgn 5d 2S	3,435	5,110	50,683

1979 Engines	bore×stroke	bhp	availability
L4, 104.7	3.13×3.40	70	S-Horizon
L6, 225.0	3.40×4.13	100	S-Volare
L6, 225.0	3.40×4.13	110	O-Volare
V8, 318.0	3.91×3.31	135	S-Volare
V8, 360.0	4.00×3.58	195	O-Volare

1980

Horizon (wb 99.2; TC3-96.7)		Wght	Price	Prod
ML24	TC3 htchbk cpe 3d	2,135	5,681	67,738
ML44	htchbk sdn 5d	2,095	5,526	94,740
Volare (wb 112.7; cpes 108.7)				
HE29	Special cpe L6	3,155	5,151	16,475
HE41	Special sdn 4d L6	3,210	5,151	25,509
HL29	cpe	3,170	5,033	17,781
HL41	sdn 4d	3,225	5,150	30,097
HL45	wgn 5d 2S	3,540	5,422	19,910
Gran Fury (wb 118.5)				
JL42	sdn 4d	3,562	6,741	15,469
JH42	Salon sdn 4d	3,438	7,116	3,255

1980 Engines	bore×stroke	bhp	availability
L4, 104.7	3.13×3.40	65	S-Horizon
L6, 225.0	3.40×4.13	90	S-Volare, Gran Fury

	bore×stroke	bhp	availability
V8, 318.0	3.91×3.31	120	S-Volare exc Spcl, G. Fury
V8, 360.0	4.00×3.58	130	O-Gran Fury

Note: Plymouth production totals through 1980 include export models, which makes figures in this book higher than some quoted elsewhere.

1981

Horizon (wb 99.1; TC3-96.6)		Wght	Price	Prod
ML24	TC3 htchbk cpe 3d	2,205	6,149	36,312
ME24	Miser TC3 htchbk cpe 3d	2,137	5,299	
ML44	htchbk sdn 5d	2,130	5,690	58,547
ME44	Miser htchbk sdn 5d	2,060	5,299	
Reliant (wb 99.6)				
PL21	sdn 2d	2,305	5,880	58,093
PL41	sdn 4d	2,300	5,980	
PH21	Custom sdn 2d	2,315	6,315	13,587
PH41	Custom sdn 4d	2,310	6,448	
PH45	Custom wgn 5d	2,375	6,721	40,830
PP21	SE sdn 2d	2,340	6,789	28,457
PP41	SE sdn 4d	2,340	6,933	
PP45	SE wgn 5d	2,390	7,254	10,670
Gran Fury (wb 118.5)				
L42	sdn 4d	3,547	7,387	7,719

1981 Engines	bore×stroke	bhp	availability
L4, 104.7	3.13×3.40	63	S-Horizon
L4, 135.0	3.44×3.62	84	S-Relnt, late TC3; O-Horiz
L4, 156.0	3.59×3.86	92	O-Reliant
L6, 225.0	3.40×4.12	85	S-Gran Fury
V8, 318.0	3.91×3.31	130	O-Gran Fury
V8, 318.0	3.91×3.31	165	O-Gran Fury (Calif.)

1982

TC3 (wb 96.6)		Wght	Price	Prod
MH24	Custom htchbk cpe 3d	2,205	6,421	12,889
ME24	Miser htchbk cpe 3d	2,180	5,799	18,359
MP24	Turismo htchbk cpe 3d	2,285	7,115	6,608
Horizon (wb 99.1)				
MH44	htchbk sdn 5d	2,175	5,927	17,315
ME44	Miser htchbk sdn 5d	2,110	5,499	19,102
MP44	Euro-Sedan sdn 5d	2,285	6,636	779
Reliant (wb 99.6)				
PL21	sdn 2d	2,315	5,990	12,026
PL41	sdn 4d	2,310	6,131	37,488
PH21	Custom sdn 2d	2,320	6,898	12,403
PH41	Custom sdn 4d	2,320	7,053	29,980
PH45	Custom wgn 5d	2,395	7,334	32,501
PP21	SE sdn 2d	2,365	7,575	2,536
PP41	SE sdn 4d	2,385	7,736	4,578
PP45	SE wgn 5d	2,470	8,101	7,711
Gran Fury (wb 112.7)				
BL41	sdn 4d	3,345	7,750	18,111

1982 Engines	bore×stroke	bhp	availability
L4, 104.7	3.13×3.40	63	S-TC3, Horizon
L4, 135.0	3.44×3.62	84	S-Reliant, TC3 Turismo; O-TC3, Horizon
L4, 156.0	3.59×3.86	92	O-Reliant
L6, 225.0	3.40×4.12	90	S-Gran Fury
V8, 318.0	3.91×3.31	130	O-Gran Fury
V8, 318.0	3.91×3.31	165	O-Gran Fury (Calif.)

1983

Turismo (wb 96.6)		Wght	Price	Prod
MH	htchbk cpe 3d	2,226	6,379	22,527
MP	2.2 htchbk cpe 3d	2,363	7,303	9,538
Horizon (wb 99.1)				
ME44	htchbk sdn 5d	2,175	5,841	35,796
MH	Custom htchbk sdn 5d	2,206	6,071	10,675
Reliant (wb 100.1)				
PL21	sdn 2d	2,317	6,577	16,109
PL41	sdn 4d	2,323	6,718	69,112
PH45	Custom wgn 5d	2,372	7,636	38,264
PH21	SE sdn 2d	2,333	7,260	5,852
PH41	SE sdn 4d	2,360	7,417	13,434
PP45	SE wgn 5d	2,432	8,186	3,791
Gran Fury (wb 112.7)				
BL41	Salon sdn 4d	3,478	8,248	15,739

1983 Reliant SE two-door sedan

1983 Engines	bore × stroke	bhp	availability
L4, 97.3	3.17 × 3.07	62	S-late Turismo, Horizon
L4, 104.7	3.13 × 3.40	63	S-early Turismo, Horizon
L4, 135.0	3.44 × 3.62	94	S-Reliant, Turismo 2.2; 0-Turismo, Horizon
L4, 156.0	3.59 × 3.86	93	O-Reliant
L6, 225.0	3.40 × 4.12	90	S-Gran Fury
V8, 318.0	3.91 × 3.31	130	O-Gran Fury

1984

Turismo (wb 96.6)		Wght	Price	Prod
MH24	htchbk cpe 3d	2,220	6,494	38,835
MP24	2.2 htchbk cpe 3d	2,327	7,288	10,881
Horizon (wb 99.1)				
ME44	htchbk sdn 5d	2,151	5,830	62,903
MH44	SE htchbk sdn 5d	2,180	6,148	15,661
Reliant (wb 100.3)				
PL21	sdn 2d	2,354	6,837	14,533
PL41	sdn 4d	2,361	6,949	72,595
PH45	Custom wgn 5d	2,450	7,736	39,207
PH21	SE sdn 2d	2,364	7,463	5,287
PH41	SE sdn 4d	2,394	7,589	16,223
PP45	SE wgn 5d	2,501	8,195	4,338
Gran Fury (wb 112.7)				
BL41	Salon sdn 4d	3,558	9,180	14,516

1984 Engines	bore × stroke	bhp	availability
L4, 97.3	3.17 × 3.07	64	S-Turismo, Horizon
L4, 135.0	3.44 × 3.62	96	S-Reliant; O-Trsmo, Horizon
L4, 135.0	3.44 × 3.62	101	S-Turismo 2.2
L4, 135.0	3.44 × 3.62	110	O-Turismo, Horizon
L4, 156.0	3.59 × 3.86	101	O-Reliant
V8, 318.0	3.91 × 3.31	130	S-Gran Fury

1985

Turismo (wb 96.6)		Wght	Price	Prod
LMH24	htchbk cpe 3d	2,215	6,584	44,377
LMP24	2.2 htchbk cpe 3d	2,366	7,515	7,785
Horizon (wb 99.1)				
LME44	htchbk sdn 5d	2,154	5,977	71,846
LMH44	SE htchbk sdn 5d	2,174	6,342	16,165
Reliant (wb 100.3)				
KPL21	sdn 2d	2,375	6,924	11,317
KPL41	sdn 4d	2,393	7,039	46,972
KPM21	SE sdn 2d	2,390	7,321	9,530
KPM41	SE sdn 4d	2,424	7,439	27,231
KPH45	SE wgn 5d	2,514	7,909	27,489
KPH21	LE sdn 2d	2,414	7,659	4,110
KPH41	LE sdn 4d	2,446	7,792	7,072
KPP45	LE wgn 5d	2,546	8,348	4,017
Caravelle (wb 103.3)				
EJH41	SE sdn 4d	2,593	9,007	39,971
Gran Fury (wb 112.7)				
MBL41	Salon sdn 4d	3,553	9,658	19,102

1985 Engines	bore × stroke	bhp	availability
L4, 97.3	3.17 × 3.07	64	S-Turismo, Horizon
L4, 135.0	3.44 × 3.62	96	S-Reliant; O-Trsmo, Hrzn
L4, 135.0	3.44 × 3.62	99	S-Caravelle
L4, 135.0	3.44 × 3.62	110	S-Turismo 2.2
L4T, 135.0	3.44 × 3.62	146	O-Caravelle
L4, 156.0	3.59 × 3.86	101	O-Reliant, Caravelle
V8, 318.0	3.91 × 3.31	140	S-Gran Fury

1985 Gran Fury Salon four-door sedan

1986

Turismo (wb 96.6)		Wght	Price	Prod
LMH24	htchbk cpe 3d	2,215	6,787	41,899
LMP24	2.2 htchbk cpe 3d	2,366	7,732	4,488
Horizon (wb 99.1)				
LME44	htchbk sdn 5d	2,154	6,209	76,458
LMH44	SE htchbk sdn 5d	2,174	6,558	8,050
Reliant (wb 100.3)				
KPL21	sdn 2d	2,395	7,184	2,573
KPL41	sdn 4d	2,402	7,301	26,220
KPM21	SE sdn 2d	2,412	7,639	10,707
KPM41	SE sdn 4d	2,429	7,759	47,827
KPM45	SE wgn 5d	2,513	8,186	22,154
KPH21	LE sdn 2d	2,427	8,087	2,482
KPH41	LE sdn 4d	2,444	8,207	5,941
KPH45	LE wgn 5d	2,549	8,936	5,101
Caravelle (wb 103.3)				
EJM41	sdn 4d	2,589	9,241	18,968
EJH41	SE sdn 4d	2,589	9,810	15,654
Gran Fury (wb 112.7)				
MBL41	Salon sdn 4d	3,550	9,947	14,761

1986 Engines	bore × stroke	bhp	availability
L4, 97.3	3.17 × 3.07	64	S-Turismo, Horizon

1986 Turismo Duster hatchback coupe

1933 Engines	bore×stroke	bhp	availability
L4, 135.0	3.44×3.62	96	O-Turismo, Horizon
L4, 135.0	3.44×3.62	97	S-Reliant, Caravelle
L4, 135.0	3.44×3.62	110	S-Turismo 2.2
L4T, 135.0	3.44×3.62	146	O-Caravelle
L4, 153.0	3.44×4.09	100	O-Reliant, Caravelle
V8, 318.0	3.91×3.31	140	S-Gran Fury

1987

Turismo (wb 96.6)		Wght	Price	Prod
LMH24	htchbk cpe 3d	2,290	7,199	24,104
Horizon (wb 99.1)				
LME44	htchbk sdn 5d	2,237	5,799	79,449
Sundance (wb 97.0)				
PPH24	htchbk sdn 3d	2,527	7,599	35,719
PPH44	htchbk sdn 5d	2,565	7,799	39,960
Reliant (wb 100.3)				
KPL21	sdn 2d	2,409	7,655	204
KPL41	sdn 4d	2,415	7,655	5,142
KPM21	LE sdn 2d	2,468	8,134	9,127
KPM41	LE sdn 4d	2,484	8,134	66,575
KPM45	LE wgn 5d	2,588	8,579	22,905
Caravelle (wb 103.3)				
EJM41	sdn 4d	2,589	9,762	23,132
EJH41	SE sdn 4d	2,596	10,355	19,333
Gran Fury (wb 112.7)				
MBL41	Salon sdn 4d	3,599	10,598	10,377

1987 Engines	bore×stroke	bhp	availability
L4, 135.0	3.44×3.62	96	O-Turismo, Horizon
L4, 135.0	3.44×3.62	97	S-Sundance, Reliant, Carav
L4T, 135.0	3.44×3.62	146	O-Sundance, Caravelle
L4, 153.0	3.44×4.09	100	O-Reliant, Caravelle
V8, 318.0	3.91×3.31	140	S-Gran Fury

1988

Horizon (wb 99.1)		Wght	Price	Prod
LME44	America htchbk sdn 5d	2,225	5,999	61,715
Sundance (wb 97.0)				
PPH24	htchbk sdn 3d	2,513	7,975	34,827
PPH44	htchbk sdn 5d	2,544	8,175	53,521
Reliant (wb 100.3)				
KPH21	America sdn 2d	2,459	6,995	8,543
KPH41	America sdn 4d	2,485	6,995	95,551
KPH45	America wgn 5d	2,537	7,695	21,213
Caravelle (wb 103.3)				
EJM41	sdn 4d	2,594	10,659	9,718
EJH41	SE sdn 4d	2,632	11,628	7,171
Gran Fury (wb 112.7)				
MBE41	sdn 4d	3,576	12,127	238
MBL41	Salon sdn 4d	3,588	11,407	11,183

1988 Engines	bore×stroke	bhp	availability
L4, 135.0	3.44×3.62	93	O-Hrzn, Sndnce, Rlnt, Carav
L4T, 135.0	3.44×3.62	146	O-Sundance, Caravelle
L4, 153.0	3.44×4.09	96	O-Sndnce, Reliant, Caravelle
V8, 318.0	3.91×3.31	140	S-Gran Fury

1989

Horizon (wb 99.1)		Wght	Price	Prod
LME44	htchbk sdn 5d	2,237	6,595	
Sundance (wb 97.0)				
PPH24	htchbk sdn 3d	2,520	8,395	
PPH44	htchbk sdn 5d	2,558	8,595	
Reliant (wb 100.3)				
KPH21	America sdn 2d	2,317	7,595	
KPH41	America sdn 4d	2,323	7,595	
Acclaim (wb 103.3)				
APJ41	sdn 4d	2,753	—	
APP41	LE sdn 4d	2,827	—	
APX41	LX sdn 4d	2,968		
Gran Fury (wb 112.7)				
MBL41	Salon sdn 4d	3,599	11,995	

1989 Engines	bore×stroke	bhp	availability
L4, 135.0	3.44×3.62	93	O-Horizon, Sndnce, Reliant
L4, 153.0	3.44×4.09	100	S-Acclaim; Sundnce, Rlnt
L4T, 153.0	3.44×4.09	150	O-Sundance, Acclaim
V6, 181.0	3.59×2.99	141	S-Acclaim LX
V8, 318.0	3.91×3.31	140	S-Gran Fury

Note: The Mitsubishi-built Colt, Sapporo and other Plymouth captive imports are not included in the above tables.

1988 Reliant America four-door wagon

1989 Acclaim LX four-door sedan

PONTIAC

1939

6EA Quality DeLuxe (wb 115.0)—55,736 built	Wght	Price	Prod
cpe 3P	2,875	758	—
spt cpe 5P	2,920	809	—
touring sdn 2d T/B	2,965	820	—
touring sdn 4d T/B	3,000	866	—
wgn 4d	3,175	990	—
6EB DeLuxe 120 (wb 120.0)—53,830 built			
cpe 3P	3,020	814	—
spt cpe 5P	3,055	865	—
conv cpe 5P	3,155	993	—
touring sdn 2d T/B	3,115	871	—
touring sdn 4d T/B	3,165	922	—
8EA DeLuxe Eight (wb 120.0)—34,774 built			
cpe 3P	3,105	862	—
spt cpe 5P	3,165	913	—
conv cpe 5P	3,250	1,046	—
touring sdn 2d T/B	3,225	919	—
touring sdn 4d T/B	3,265	970	—

1939 Engines	bore×stroke	bhp	availability
L6, 222.7	3.44×4.00	85	S-6EA,6EB
L8, 248.9	3.25×3.75	100	S-Eight

1940

25HA Special Six (wb 117.0)—106,892 built	Wght	Price	Prod
cpe 3P	3,060	783	—
spt cpe 4P	3,045	819	—
sdn 2d	3,095	830	—
wgn 4d, 8P	3,295	1,015	—
sdn 4d	3,125	876	—
26HB DeLuxe Six (wb 120.0)—58,452 built			
cpe 3P	3,115	835	—
spt cpe 4P	3,105	876	—
cabriolet (conv)	3,190	1,003	—
sdn 2d	3,170	881	—
sdn 4d	3,210	932	—
28HA DeLuxe Eight (wb 120.0)—20,433 built			
cpe 3P	3,180	875	—
spt cpe 4P	3,195	913	—
cabriolet (conv)	3,280	1,046	—
sdn 2d	3,250	919	—
sdn 4d	3,300	970	—
29HB Torpedo Eight (wb 122.0)—31,224 built			
spt cpe 4P	3,390	1,016	—
sdn 4d	3,475	1,072	—

1939 Deluxe Eight convertible coupe

1940 Engines	bore×stroke	bhp	availability
L6, 222.7	3.44×4.00	87	S-Six
L8, 248.9	3.25×3.75	100	S-DeLuxe Eight
L8, 248.9	3.25×3.75	103	S-Torpedo Eight

1941

25JA DeLuxe Torpedo Six (wb 119.0)—117,976 built	Wght	Price	Prod
cpe 3P	3,145	828	—
sdn cpe	3,180	864	—
conv cpe	3,335	1,023	—
sdn 2d	3,190	874	—
sdn 4d	3,235	921	—
Metropolitan sdn 4d	3,230	921	—
26JB Streamliner Torpedo Six (wb 122.0)—82,527 built			
sdn cpe	3,305	923	—
Super sdn cpe	3,320	969	—
sdn 4d	3,365	980	—
Super sdn 4d	3,400	1,026	—
24JC Custom Torpedo Six (wb 122.0)—8,257 built			
sdn cpe	3,260	995	—
sdn 4d	3,355	1,052	—
wgn 4d, 8P	3,650	1,175	—
DeLuxe wgn 4d, 8P	3,665	1,225	—
27JA DeLuxe Torpedo Eight (wb 119.0)—37,823 built			
cpe 3P	3,220	853	—
sdn cpe	3,250	889	—
conv cpe	3,390	1,048	—
sdn 2d	3,250	899	—
sdn 4d	3,285	946	—
Metropolitan sdn 4d	3,295	946	—
28JB Streamliner Torpedo Eight (wb 122.0)—66,287 built			
sdn cpe	3,370	948	—
Super sdn cpe	3,385	994	—
sdn 4d	3,425	1,005	—
Super sdn 4d	3,460	1,051	—
29JC Custom Torpedo Eight (wb 122.0)—17,191 built			
sdn cpe	3,325	1,020	—
sdn 4d	3,430	1,077	—
wgn 4d, 8P	3,715	1,200	—
DeLuxe wgn 4d, 8P	3,730	1,250	—

1941 Engines	bore×stroke	bhp	availability
L6, 239.2	3.56×4.00	90	S-Six
L8, 248.9	3.25×3.75	103	S-Eight

1942

25KA Torpedo Six (wb 119.0)—29,886 built	Wght	Price	Prod
cpe 3P	3,210	895	—
sdn cpe	3,255	950	—

	Wght	Price	Prod
spt cpe	3,260	935	—
conv cpe	3,535	1,165	—
sdn 2d	3,265	940	—
sdn 4d	3,305	985	—
Metropolitan sdn 4d	3,295	985	—
26KB Streamliner Six (wb 122.0)			
sdn cpe	3,355	980	
sdn 4d	3,415	1,035	10,284
wgn 4d, 8P	3,810	1,265	
Chieftain sdn cpe	3,400	1,030	
Chieftain sdn 4d	3,460	1,085	2,458
Chieftain wgn 4d, 6P	3,785	1,315	
27KA Torpedo Eight (wb 119.0)—14,421 built			
cpe dP	3,270	920	—
sdn cpe	3,320	975	—
spt cpe	3,320	960	—
conv cpe	3,605	1,190	—
sdn 2d	3,325	965	—
sdn 4d	3,360	1,010	—
Metropolitan sdn 4d	3,355	1,010	—
28KB Streamliner Eight (wb 122.0)			
sdn cpe	3,430	1,005	
sdn 4d	3,485	1,060	15,465
wgn 4d, 8P	3,885	1,290	
Chieftain sdn cpe	3,460	1,055	
Chieftain sdn 4d	3,515	1,110	11,041
Chieftain wgn 4d, 6P	3,865	1,340	

1942 Engines	bore×stroke	bhp	availability
L6, 239.2	3.56×4.00	90	S-Six
L8, 248.9	3.25×3.75	103	S-Eight

1946

25LA Torpedo Six (wb 119.0)—26,636 built	Wght	Price	Prod
sdn 4d	3,361	1,427	—
sdn 2d	3,326	1,368	—
cpe sdn	3,326	1,399	—
spt cpe	3,311	1,353	—
cpe 3P	3,261	1,307	—
conv cpe	3,591	1,631	—
26LB Streamliner Six (wb 122.0)—43,430 built			
sdn 4d	3,490	1,510	—
cpe sdn	3,435	1,438	—
wgn 4d, 8P	3,790	1,942	—
DeLuxe wgn 4d, 8P	3,735	2,019	—
27LA Torpedo Eight (wb 119.0)—18,273 built			
sdn 4d	3,436	1,455	—
sdn 2d	3,396	1,395	—
cpe sdn	3,391	1,428	—
spt cpe	3,376	1,381	—
cpe 3P	3,331	1,335	—
conv cpe	3,651	1,658	—
28LB Streamliner Eight (wb 122.0)—49,301 built			
sdn 4d	3,550	1,538	—
cpe sdn	3,495	1,468	—
wgn 4d, 8P	3,870	1,970	—
DeLuxe wgn 4d, 8P	3,850	2,047	—

1946 Engines	bore×stroke	bhp	availability
L6, 239.2	3.56×4.00	90	S-Six
L8, 248.9	3.25×3.75	103	S-Eight

1947

6MA Torpedo Six (wb 119.0)—67,125 built	Wght	Price	Prod
sdn 4d	3,320	1,512	—
sdn 2d	3,295	1,453	—
cpe sdn	3,300	1,484	—
spt cpe	3,295	1,438	—
cpe 3P	3,245	1,387	—
conv cpe	3,560	1,811	—
DeLuxe conv cpe	3,560	1,853	—
6MB Streamliner Six (wb 122.0)—42,336 built			
sdn 4d	3,450	1,598	—
cpe sdn	3,400	1,547	—

1947 Torpedo Eight convertible coupe

1948 Streamliner Eight DeLuxe four-door sedan

1949 Chieftain Eight sedan coupe

	Wght	Price	Prod
wgn 4d, 8P	3,775	2,235	—
DeLuxe wgn 4d, 8P	3,715	2,312	—
8MA Torpedo Eight (wb 119.0)—34,815 built			
sdn 4d	3,405	1,559	—
sdn 2d	3,370	1,500	—
cpe sdn	3,370	1,531	—
spt cpe	3,360	1,485	—
cpe 3P	3,310	1,434	—
conv cpe	3,635	1,854	—
DeLuxe conv cpe	3,635	1,900	—
8MB Streamliner Eight (wb 122.0)—86,324 built			
sdn 4d	3,515	1,645	—
cpe sdn	3,455	1,595	—
wgn 4d, 8P	3,845	2,282	—
DeLuxe wgn 4d, 8P	3,790	2,359	—

1947 Engines	bore×stroke	bhp	availability
L6, 239.2	3.56×4.00	90	S-Six
L8, 248.9	3.25×3.75	103	S-Eight

1948

6PA Torpedo Six (wb 119.0)—39,262 built	Wght	Price	Prod
sdn 4d	3,320	1,641	—
sdn 2d	3,280	1,583	—
cpe sdn	3,275	1,614	—
spt cpe	3,220	1,552	—
bus cpe	3,230	1,500	—
DeLuxe sdn 4d	3,340	1,731	—
DeLuxe cpe sdn	3,275	1,704	—
DeLuxe spt cpe	3,230	1,641	—
DeLuxe conv cpe	3,525	2,025	—
6PB Streamliner Six (wb 122.0)—37,742 built			
sdn 4d	3,450	1,727	—
cpe sdn	3,365	1,677	—
wgn 4d, 8P	3,755	2,364	—
DeLuxe sdn 4d	3,455	1,817	—
DeLuxe cpe sdn	3,370	1,766	—
DeLuxe wgn 4d, 6P	3,695	2,442	—

8PA Torpedo Eight (wb 119.0)—35,300 built	Wght	Price	Prod
sdn 4d	3,395	1,689	—
sdn 2d	3,360	1,630	—
cpe scn	3,340	1,661	—
spt cpe	3,295	1,599	—
bus cpe	3,295	1,548	—
DeLuxe sdn 4d	3,395	1,778	—

	Wght	Price	Prod
DeLuxe cpe sdn	3,340	1,751	—
DeLuxe spt cpe	3,305	1,689	—
DeLuxe conv cpe	3,600	2,072	—
8PB Streamliner Eight (wb 122.0)—123,115 built			
sdn 4d	3,525	1,775	—
cpe sdn	3,425	1,724	—
wgn 4d, 8P	3,820	2,412	—
DeLuxe sdn 4d	3,530	1,864	—
DeLuxe cpe sdn	3,455	1,814	—
DeLuxe wgn 4d, 6P	3,765	2,490	—

1948 Engines	bore×stroke	bhp	availability
L6, 239.2	3.56×4.00	90	S-Six
L8, 248.9	3.25×3.75	104	S-Eight

1949

6R Streamliner Six (wb 120.0)—69,654 built (includes 6R Chieftain)	Wght	Price	Prod
sdn 4d	3,385	1,740	—
cpe sdn	3,360	1,689	—
wgn 4d, 8P wood body	3,745	2,543	—
wgn 4d, 8P metal body	3,650	2,543	—
DeLuxe sdn 4d	3,415	1,835	—
DeLuxe cpe sdn	3,375	1,784	—
DeLuxe wgn 4d, 6P wood body	3,730	2,622	—
DeLuxe wgn 4d, 6P metal body	3,580	2,622	—
6R Chieftain Six (wb 120.0)			
sdn 4d	3,385	1,761	—
sdn 2d	3,355	1,710	—
cpe sdn	3,330	1,710	—
bus cpe	3,280	1,587	—
DeLuxe sdn 4d	3,415	1,856	—
DeLuxe sdn 2d	3,360	1,805	—
DeLuxe cpe sdn	3,345	1,805	—
DeLuxe conv cpe	3,600	2,138	—
8R Streamliner Eight (wb 120.0)—235,165 built (inc 8R Chieftain)			
sdn 4d	3,470	1,808	—
cpe sdn	3,435	1,758	—
wgn 4d, 8P wood body	3,835	2,611	—
wgn 4d, 8P metal body	3,690	2,611	—
DeLuxe sdn 4d	3,500	1,903	—
DeLuxe cpe sdn	3,445	1,853	—
DeLuxe wgn 4d, 6P wood body	3,800	2,690	—
DeLuxe wgn 4d, 6P metal body	3,640	2,690	—
8R Chieftain Eight (wb 120.0)			
sdn 4d	3,475	1,829	—
sdn 2d	3,430	1,779	—

1949 Streamliner Six DeLuxe four-door sedan

	Wght	Price	Prod
cpe sdn	3,390	1,779	—
bus cpe	3,355	1,656	—
DeLuxe sdn 4d	3,480	1,924	—
DeLuxe sdn 2d	3,430	1,874	—
DeLuxe cpe sdn	3,415	1,874	—
DeLuxe conv cpe	3,670	2,206	—

1949 Engines	bore×stroke	bhp	availability
L6, 239.2	3.56×4.00	90	S-Six
L6, 239.2	3.56×4.00	93	O-Six
L8, 248.9	3.25×3.75	104	S-Eight
L8, 248.9	3.25×3.75	106	O-Eight

1950

6T Streamliner Six (wb 120.0)—115,542 built (includes 6T Chieftain)	Wght	Price	Prod
fstbk sdn 4d	3,414	1,724	—
fstbk cpe sdn	3,379	1,673	—
wgn 4d, 8P	3,714	2,264	—
DeLuxe fstbk sdn 4d	3,419	1,819	—
DeLuxe fstbk cpe sdn	3,399	1,768	—
DeLuxe wgn 4d, 6P	3,649	2,343	—
6T Chieftain Six (wb 120.0)			
sdn 4d	3,409	1,745	—
sdn 2d	3,384	1,694	—
cpe sdn	3,359	1,694	—
bus cpe	3,319	1,571	—
DeLuxe sdn 4d	3,414	1,840	—
DeLuxe sdn 2d	3,389	1,789	—
DeLuxe cpe sdn	3,364	1,789	—
DeLuxe Catalina htp cpe	3,469	2,000	—
DeLuxe conv cpe	3,624	2,122	—
Super Catalina htp cpe	3,469	2,058	—
8T Streamliner Eight (wb 120.0)—330,887 built (inc 8T Chieftain)			
fstbk sdn 4d	3,499	1,792	—
fstbk cpe sdn	3,464	1,742	—
wgn 4d, 8P	3,799	2,332	—
DeLuxe fstbk sdn 4d	3,509	1,887	—
DeLuxe fstbk cpe sdn	3,469	1,837	—
DeLuxe wgn 4d, 6P	3,739	2,411	—
8T Chieftain Eight (wb 120.0)			
sdn 4d	3,494	1,813	—
sdn 2d	3,454	1,763	—
cpe sdn	3,444	1,763	—
bus cpe	3,399	1,640	—
DeLuxe sdn 4d	3,499	1,908	—
DeLuxe sdn 2d	3,464	1,858	—
DeLuxe cpe sdn	3,454	1,858	—
DeLuxe Catalina htp cpe	3,549	2,069	—
DeLuxe conv cpe	3,704	2,190	—
Super Catalina htp cpe	3,549	2,127	—

1950 Engines	bore×stroke	bhp	availability
L6, 239.2	3.56×4.00	90	S-Six
L8, 268.4	3.38×3.75	108	S-Eight

1951

6U Streamliner Six (wb 120.0)—53,748 built (includes 6U Chieftain)	Wght	Price	Prod
fstbk cpe sdn	3,363	1,824	—
wgn 4d, 8P	3,718	2,470	—
DeLuxe fstbk cpe sdn	3,378	1,927	—
DeLuxe wgn 4d, 6P	3,638	2,556	—
6U Chieftain Six (wb 120.0)			
sdn 4d	3,388	1,903	—
sdn 2d	3,358	1,848	—
cpe sdn	3,338	1,848	—
bus cpe	3,308	1,713	—
DeLuxe sdn 4d	3,388	2,006	—
DeLuxe sdn 2d	3,358	1,951	—
DeLuxe cpe sdn	3,343	1,951	—
DeLuxe Catalina htp cpe	3,458	2,182	—

	Wght	Price	Prod
DeLuxe conv cpe	3,603	2,314	—
Super Catalina htp cpe	3,468	2,244	—
8U Streamliner Eight (wb 120.0)—316,411 built (inc 8U Chieftain)			
fstbk cpe sdn	3,458	1,900	—
wgn 4d, 8P	3,813	2,544	—
DeLuxe fstbk cpe sdn	3,463	2,003	—
DeLuxe wgn 4d, 6P	3,743	2,629	—
8U Chieftain Eight (wb 120.0)			
sdn 4d	3,478	1,977	—
sdn 2d	3,443	1,922	—
cpe sdn	3,418	1,922	—
bus cpe	3,388	1,787	—
DeLuxe sdn 4d	3,488	2,081	—
DeLuxe sdn 2d	3,448	2,026	—
DeLuxe cpe sdn	3,433	2,026	—
DeLuxe Catalina htp cpe	3,543	2,257	—
DeLuxe conv cpe	3,683	2,388	—
Super Catalina htp cpe	3,548	2,320	—

1951 Engines	bore×stroke	bhp	availability
L6, 239.2	3.56×4.00	96/100	S-Six
L8, 268.4	3.38×3.75	116/120	S-Eight

1952

6W Chieftain Six (wb 120.0)—19,809 built	Wght	Price	Prod
sdn 4d	3,403	2,014	—
sdn 2d	3,378	1,956	—
wgn 4d, 8P	3,718	2,615	—
DeLuxe sdn 4d	3,403	2,119	—
DeLuxe sdn 2d	3,378	2,060	—
DeLuxe Catalina htp cpe	3,483	2,304	—
DeLuxe conv cpe	3,603	2,444	—
DeLuxe wgn 4d, 6P	3,653	2,699	—
Super Catalina htp cpe	3,493	2,370	—
8W Chieftain Eight (wb 120.0)—251,564 built			
sdn 4d	3,503	2,090	—
sdn 2d	3,458	2,031	—
wgn 4d, 8P	3,813	2,689	—
DeLuxe sdn 4d	3,503	2,194	—
DeLuxe sdn 2d	3,458	2,136	—
DeLuxe Catalina htp cpe	3,568	2,380	—
DeLuxe conv cpe	3,683	2,518	—
DeLuxe wgn 4d, 6P	3,758	2,772	—
Super Catalina htp cpe	3,573	2,446	—

1952 Engines	bore×stroke	bhp	availability
L6, 239.2	3.56×4.00	100	S-Six man
L6, 239.2	3.56×4.00	102	S-Six auto
L8, 268.4	3.38×3.75	118	S-Eight man
L8, 268.4	3.38×3.75	122	S-Eight auto

1953

6X Chieftain Six (wb 122.0)—38,914 built	Wght	Price	Prod
sdn 4d	3,506	2,015	—
sdn 2d	3,466	1,956	—
wgn 4d, 6P	3,713	2,450	—
wgn 4d, 6P (woodgrain)	3,713	2,530	—
wgn 4d, 8P	3,791	2,505	—
wgn 4d, 8P (woodgrain)	3,791	2,585	—
DeLuxe sdn 4d	3,521	2,119	—
DeLuxe sdn 2d	3,481	2,060	—
DeLuxe Catalina htp cpe	3,546	2,304	—
DeLuxe conv cpe	3,696	2,444	—
DeLuxe wgn 4d, 6P	3,751	2,590	—
DeLuxe wgn 4d, 6P (woodgrain)	3,751	2,670	—
Custom Catalina htp cpe	3,546	2,370	—
8X Chieftain Eight (wb 122.0)—379,705 built			
sdn 4d	3,581	2,090	—
sdn 2d	3,546	2,031	—
wgn 4d, 6P	3,811	2,525	—
wgn 4d, 6P (woodgrain)	3,811	2,605	—
wgn 4d, 8P	3,881	2,580	—
wgn 4d, 8P (woodgrain)	3,881	2,660	—
DeLuxe sdn 4d	3,596	2,194	—
DeLuxe sdn 2d	3,561	2,136	—
DeLuxe Catalina htp cpe	3,621	2,380	—
DeLuxe conv cpe	3,751	2,518	—
DeLuxe wgn 4d, 6P	3,841	2,664	—
DeLuxe wgn 4d, 6P (woodgrain)	3,841	2,744	—
Custom Catalina htp cpe	3,621	2,446	—

1950 Chieftain Eight DeLuxe convertible coupe

1953 Engines	bore×stroke	bhp	availability
L6, 239.2	3.56×4.00	115	S-Six man
L6, 239.2	3.56×4.00	118	S-Six auto
L8, 268.4	3.38×3.75	118	S-Eight man
L8, 268.4	3.38×3.75	122	S-Eight auto

1954

6Z Chieftain Six (wb 122.0)—22,670 built	Wght	Price	Prod
Special sdn 4d	3,391	2,027	—
Special sdn 2d	3,331	1,968	—
Special wgn 4d, 8P	3,691	2,419	—
Special wgn 4d, 6P	3,601	2,364	—
DeLuxe sdn 4d	3,406	2,131	—
DeLuxe sdn 2d	3,351	2,072	—
DeLuxe Catalina htp cpe	3,421	2,316	—
DeLuxe wgn 4d, 6P	3,646	2,504	—
Custom Catalina htp cpe	3,421	2,382	—
8Z Chieftain Eight (wb 122.0)—149,986 built			
Special sdn 4d	3,451	2,102	—
Special sdn 2d	3,396	2,043	—
Special wgn 4d, 8P	3,771	2,494	—
Special wgn 4d, 6P	3,676	2,439	—
DeLuxe sdn 4d	3,466	2,206	—
DeLuxe Catalina htp cpe	3,491	2,392	—
DeLuxe wgn 4d, 6P	3,716	2,579	—
Custom Catalina htp cpe	3,491	2,458	—
8Z Star Chief (wb 124.0)—115,088 built			
DeLuxe sdn 4d	3,536	2,301	—
DeLuxe conv cpe	3,776	2,630	—
Custom sdn 4d	3,536	2,394	—
Custom Catalina htp cpe	3,551	2,557	—

1954 Engines	bore×stroke	bhp	availability
L6, 239.2	3.56×4.00	115	S-Chieftain Six man
L6, 239.2	3.56×4.00	118	S-Chieftain Six auto
L8, 268.4	3.38×3.75	122	S-Chftn 8/Star Chief man
L8, 268.4	3.38×3.75	127	S-Chftn 8/Star Chief auto

1955

860 Chieftain (wb 122.0)	Wght	Price	Prod
sdn 4d	3,511	2,164	65,155
sdn 2d	3,476	2,105	58,654
wgn 4d, 8P	3,686	2,518	6,091
wgn 2d, 6P	3,626	2,434	8,620
870 Chieftain (wb 122.0)			
sdn 4d	3,511	2,268	91,187
sdn 2d	3,476	2,209	28,950
Catalina htp cpe	3,521	2,335	72,608
wgn 4d, 6P	3,676	2,603	19,439
Custom Safari wgn 2d, 6P*	3,636	2,962	3,760
Star Chief (wb 124.0)			
sdn 4d	3,556	2,362	44,800
conv cpe	3,791	2,691	19,762
Custom sdn 4d	3,557	2,455	35,153
Custom Catalina htp cpe	3,566	2,499	99,629

*Star Chief wagon on 122 inch wheelbase.

1955 Engines	bore×stroke	bhp	availability
V8, 287.2	3.75×3.25	173	S-all (manual)
V8, 287.2	3.75×3.25	180	S-all (automatic)

1956

860 Chieftain (wb 122.0)	Wght	Price	Prod
sdn 4d	3,512	2,298	41,987
Catalina htp sdn	3,577	2,443	35,201
sdn 2d	3,452	2,240	41,908
Catalina htp cpe	3,512	2,370	46,335
wgn 4d, 9P	3,707	2,653	12,702
wgn 2d, 6P	3,612	2,569	6,099
870 Chieftain (wb 122.0)			
sdn 4d	3,512	2,413	22,082
Catalina htp sdn	3,577	2,534	25,372
Catalina htp cpe	3,512	2,840	24,744
wgn 4d, 6P	3,657	2,749	21,674
Custom Safari wgn 2d, 6P*	3,642	3,129	4,042
Star Chief (wb 124.0)			
sdn 4d	3,577	2,527	18,346
conv cpe	3,797	2,857	13,510
Custom Catalina htp sdn	3,647	2,735	48,035
Custom Catalina htp cpe	3,567	2,665	43,392

*Star Chief wagon on 122 inch wheelbase.

1956 Engines	bore×stroke	bhp	availability
V8, 316.6	3.94×3.25	192	O-Chieftain
V8, 316.6	3.94×3.25	205	S-Chieftain
V8, 316.6	3.94×3.25	216	O-Star Chief
V8, 316.6	3.94×3.25	227	S-Star Chief
V8, 316.6	3.94×3.25	285	O-all

1953 Chieftain Eight DeLuxe four-door wagon

1957

Chieftain (wb 122.0)	Wght	Price	Prod
sdn 4d	3,560	2,527	35,671
Catalina htp sdn	3,635	2,614	40,074
sdn 2d	3,515	2,463	21,343
Catalina htp cpe	3,555	2,529	51,017
Safari wgn 4d, 9P	3,835	2,898	11,536
Safari wgn 2d, 6P	3,690	2,841	2,934
Super Chief (wb 122.0)			
sdn 4d	3,585	2,664	15,153
Catalina htp sdn	3,640	2,793	19,758
Catalina htp cpe	3,570	2,735	15,494
Safari wgn 4d, 6P	3,765	3,021	14,095
Custom Safari wgn 2d, 6P*	3,750	3,481	1,292
Star Chief (wb 124.0; wgn-122.0)			
sdn 4d	3,630	2,839	3,774
conv cpe	3,860	3,105	12,789
Custom sdn 4d	3,645	2,896	8,874
Custom Catalina htp sdn	3,710	2,975	44,283
Custom Catalina htp cpe	3,640	2,901	32,862
Custom Safari wgn 4d, 6P	3,810	3,636	1,894
Bonneville (wb 124.0)			
conv cpe	4,285	5,782	630

*All Pontiac wagons were called Safaris in 1957. The model indicated is the hardtop-styled Safari, first offered in 1955 and discontinued after 1957. It was a Star Chief model, but on 122 inch wheelbase.

1957 Engines	bore×stroke	bhp	availability
V8, 347.0	3.94×3.56	227	S-Chieftain w/manual
V8, 347.0	3.94×3.56	252	S-Chieftain
V8, 347.0	3.94×3.56	244	S-Super, Star w/manual
V8, 347.0	3.94×3.56	270	S-Super Chief, Star Chief
V8, 347.0	3.94×3.56	290	O-all exc Bonneville
V8, 347.0	3.94×3.56	310	S-Bonneville (fuel injection)

1958

Chieftain (wb 122.0)		Wght	Price	Prod
2567	conv cpe	3,850	3,019	7,359
2731	Catalina htp cpe	3,650	2,707	26,003
2739	Catalina htp sdn	3,785	2,792	17,946
2741	sdn 2d	3,640	2,573	17,394
2749	sdn 4d	3,735	2,638	44,999
2793	Safari wgn 4d, 6P	4,025	3,019	9,701
2794	Safari wgn 4d, 9P	4,070	3,088	5,417
Super Chief (wb 124.0)				
2831D	Catalina htp cpe	3,690	2,880	7,236
2839D	Catalina htp sdn	3,810	2,961	7,886
2849D	sdn 4d	3,770	2,834	12,006
Star Chief Custom (wb 124.0)				
2793SC	Safari wgn 4d, 6P	4,065	3,350	2,905
2831SD	Catalina htp cpe	3,735	3,122	13,888
2839SD	Catalina htp sdn	3,850	3,210	21,455
2849SD	sdn 4d	3,825	3,071	10,547
Bonneville Custom (wb 122.0)				
2547SD	htp cpe	3,710	3,481	9,144
2567SD	conv cpe	3,925	3,586	3,096

1958 Engines	bore×stroke	bhp	availability
V8, 370.0	4.06×3.56	240	S-Chieftain/Super Chief man
V8, 370.0	4.06×3.56	255	S-Star Chief/Bonneville man
V8, 370.0	4.06×3.56	270	S-Chieftain/Super Chief auto
V8, 370.0	4.06×3.56	285	S-Star Chief/Bonneville auto
V8, 370.0	4.06×3.56	300	O-all (Tri-Power)
V8, 370.0	4.06×3.56	310	O-all (fuel injection)

1959

Catalina (wb 122.0)		Wght	Price	Prod
2111	Sport sdn 2d	3,870	2,633	26,102
2119	sdn 4d	3,955	2,704	72,377
2135	Safari wgn 4d, 6P	4,345	3,101	21,162
2137	Sport htp cpe	3,900	2,768	38,309
2139	Vista htp sdn	4,005	2,844	45,012
2145	Safari wgn 4d, 9P	4,405	3,209	14,084
2167	conv cpe	3,970	3,080	14,515
Star Chief (wb 124.0)				
2411	Sport sdn 2d	3,930	2,934	10,254
2419	sdn 4d	4,005	3,005	27,872
2439	Vista htp sdn	4,055	3,138	30,689
Bonneville (wb 124.0; wgn-122.0)				
2735	Custom Safari wgn 4d, 6P	4,370	3,532	4,673
2837	Sport htp cpe	3,985	3,257	27,769
2839	Vista htp sdn	4,085	3,333	38,696
2867	conv cpe	4,070	3,478	11,426

1959 Engines	bore×stroke	bhp	availability
V8, 389.0	4.06×3.75	215	O-all auto
V8, 389.0	4.06×3.75	245	S-Catalina/Star Chief man
V8, 389.0	4.06×3.75	260	S-Bonneville manual
V8, 389.0	4.06×3.75	280	S-Catalina/Star Chief auto
V8, 389.0	4.06×3.75	300	S-Bonneville auto

1956 Chieftain Custom Safari two-door wagon

1958 Bonneville Custom convertible coupe

1959 Bonneville Sport hardtop coupe

	bore×stroke	bhp	availability
V8, 389.0	4.06×3.75	300/330	O-all (4bbl)
V8, 389.0	4.06×3.75	315/345	O-all (Tri-Power)

1960

Catalina (wb 122.0)		Wght	Price	Prod
2111	Sport sdn 2d	3,835	2,631	25,504
2119	sdn 4d	3,935	2,702	72,650
2135	Safari wgn 4d, 6P	4,310	3,099	21,253
2137	Sport htp cpe	3,850	2,766	27,496
2139	Vista htp sdn	3,990	2,842	32,710
2145	Safari wgn 4d, 9P	4,365	3,207	14,149
2167	conv cpe	3,940	3,078	17,172
Ventura (wb 122.0)				
2337	Sport htp cpe	3,865	2,971	27,577
2339	Vista htp sdn	3,990	3,047	28,700
Star Chief (wb 124.0)				
2411	Sport sdn 2d	3,910	2,932	5,797
2419	sdn 4d	3,995	3,003	23,038
2439	Vista htp sdn	4,040	3,136	14,856
Bonneville (wb 124.0; wgn-122.0)				
2735	Custom Safari wgn 4d, 6P	4,360	3,530	5,163
2837	Sport htp cpe	3,965	3,255	24,015
2839	Vista htp sdn	4,065	3,331	39,037
2867	conv cpe	4,030	3,476	17,062

1960 Engines	bore×stroke	bhp	availability
V8, 389.0	4.06×3.75	215	O-all auto
V8, 389.0	4.06×3.75	245	S-Star Chief/Cat/Vent man
V8, 389.0	4.06×3.75	281	S-Bonneville man
V8, 389.0	4.06×3.75	283	S-Star Chief/Cat/Vent auto
V8, 389.0	4.06×3.75	303	S-Bonneville auto
V8, 389.0	4.06×3.75	318/348	O-all (Tri-Power)

1961

Tempest (wb 112.0)		Wght	Price	Prod
2117	Custom spt cpe	2,795	2,297	7,455
2119	sdn 4d	2,800	2,167	22,557
2120	Custom sdn 4d	2,810	2,351	40,082
2127	spt cpe	2,785	2,113	7,432
2135	wgn 4d	2,980	2,438	7,404
2136	Custom wgn 4d	2,990	2,622	15,853
Catalina (wb 119.0)				
2311	Sport sdn 2d	3,650	2,631	9,846
2335	Safari wgn 4d, 6P	4,135	3,099	12,595
2337	Sport htp cpe	3,680	2,766	14,524
2339	Vista htp sdn	3,785	2,842	17,589
2345	Safari wgn 4d, 9P	4,175	3,207	7,783
2367	conv cpe	3,805	3,078	12,379
2369	sdn 4d	3,725	2,702	38,638
Ventura (wb 119.0)				
2537	Sport htp cpe	3,685	2,971	13,297
2539	Vista htp sdn	3,795	3,047	13,912
Star Chief (wb 123.0)				
2639	Vista htp sdn	3,870	3,136	13,557
2669	sdn 4d	3,840	3,003	16,024
Bonneville (wb 123.0)				
2735	Custom Safari wgn 4d	4,185	3,530	3,323
2837	Sport htp cpe	3,810	3,255	16,906
2839	Vista htp sdn	3,895	3,331	30,830
2867	conv cpe	3,905	3,476	18,264

1961 Engines	bore×stroke	bhp	availability
L4, 194.5	4.06×3.75	110	S-Tempest man
L4, 194.5	4.06×3.75	130	S-Tempest auto
V8, 215.0	3.50×2.80	155	O-Tempest
V8, 389.0	4.06×3.75	215	S-Star Chief/Cat/Vent man
V8, 389.0	4.06×3.75	230	O-all auto exc Tempest
V8, 389.0	4.06×3.75	235	S-Bonneville man; O-other man
V8, 389.0	4.06×3.75	267	S-Catalina/Ventura auto
V8, 389.0	4.06×3.75	283	S-Star Chief auto
V8, 389.0	4.06×3.75	287	O-Catalina/Ventura auto
V8, 389.0	4.06×3.75	303	S-Bonneville auto; O-Star Chief auto
V8, 389.0	4.06×3.75	318/348	O-all exc Tempest (Tri-Power)
V8, 389.0	4.06 × 3.75	333	O-full-size (4bbl)
V8, 421.0	4.09 × 4.00	373	O-Catalina cpe

1962

Tempest (wb 112.0)*		Wght	Price	Prod
2117	spt cpe	2,800	2,294	51,981
2119	sdn 4d	2,815	2,240	37,430
2127	cpe	2,785	2,186	15,473
2135	Safari wgn 4d	2,995	2,511	17,674
2167	conv cpe	2,955	2,564	20,635
Catalina (wb 120.0; wgn-119.0)				
2311	Sport sdn 2d	3,705	2,725	14,263
2335	Safari wgn 4d, 6P	4,180	3,193	19,399
2339	Vista htp sdn	3,825	2,936	29,251
2345	Safari wgn 4d, 9P	4,220	3,301	10,716
2347	Sport htp cpe	3,730	2,860	46,024
2367	conv cpe	3,855	3,172	16,877
2369	sdn 4d	3,765	2,796	68,124
Star Chief (wb 123.0)				
2639	Vista htp sdn	3,925	3,230	13,882
2669	sdn 4d	3,875	3,097	27,760
Bonneville (wb 123.0)		**Wght**	**Price**	**Prod**
2735	Custom Safari wgn 4d	4,255	3,624	4,527
2839	Vista htp sdn	4,005	3,425	44,015
2847	Sport htp cpe	3,900	3,349	31,629
2867	conv cpe	4,005	3,570	21,582
Grand Prix (wb 120.0)				
2947	Sport htp cpe	3,835	3,490	30,195

***Tempest includes DeLuxe and LeMans trim options. Factory records include the following production breakdowns:**

	std	DeLuxe	LeMans
cpe	15,473	—	—
spt cpe	—	12,319	39,662
sdn 4d	16,057	21,373	—
wgn 4d	6,504	11,170	—
conv cpe	—	5,076	15,559

1962 Engines	bore×stroke	bhp	availability
L4, 194.5	4.06×3.75	110	S-Tempest man
L4, 194.5	4.06×3.75	115	S-Tempest auto
V8, 215.0	3.50×2.80	185	O-Tempest
V8, 389.0	4.06×3.75	215	S-Catalina/Star Chief man
V8, 389.0	4.06×3.75	230	O-all full-size
V8, 389.0	4.06×3.75	235	S-Bonn man; O-Cat/S Chf man
V8, 389.0	4.06×3.75	267	S-Catalina auto
V8, 389.0	4.06×3.75	283	S-Star Chief auto
V8, 389.0	4.06×3.75	303	S-Bonn auto, GP; O-others
V8, 389.0	4.06×3.75	318	O-all full-size (Tri-Power)
V8, 389.0	4.06×3.75	333	O-all full-size (4bbl)
V8, 389.0	4.06×3.75	348	O-all full-size (Tri-Power)
V8, 421.0	4.09×4.00	405	O-Catalina cpe

1963

Tempest (wb 112.0)		Wght	Price	Prod
2117	DeLuxe spt cpe	2,820	2,294	13,157
2119	sdn 4d (incl DeLuxe)	2,835	2,241	28,221
2127	cpe	2,810	2,188	13,307
2135	wgn 4d (incl DeLuxe)	2,995	2,512	10,135
2167	DeLuxe conv cpe	2,980	2,564	5,012
Tempest LeMans (wb 112.0)				
2217	spt cpe	2,865	2,418	45,701
2267	conv cpe	3,035	2,742	15,957
Catalina (wb 120.0, wgn-119.0)				
2311	Sport sdn 2d	3,685	2,725	14,091
2335	Safari wgn 4d, 6P	4,175	3,193	18,446
2339	Vista htp sdn	3,815	2,934	31,256
2345	Safari wgn 4d, 9P	4,230	3,300	11,751
2347	Sport htp cpe	3,725	2,859	60,795
2367	conv cpe	3,835	3,179	18,249
2369	sdn 4d	3,755	2,795	79,961
Star Chief (wb 123.0)				
2639	Vista htp sdn	3,915	3,229	12,448
2669	sdn 4d	3,885	3,096	28,309
Bonneville (wb 123.0; wgn-119.0)				
2835	Safari wgn 4d, 6P	4,245	3,623	5,156
2839	Vista htp sdn	3,985	3,423	49,929
2847	Sport htp cpe	3,895	3,348	30,995
2865	conv cpe	3,970	3,568	23,459
Grand Prix (wb 120.0)				
2957	Sport htp cpe	3,915	3,489	72,959

1963 Engines	bore×stroke	bhp	availability
L4, 194.5	4.06×3.75	115	S-Tempest
L4, 194.5	4.06×3.75	120	O-Tempest man
L4, 194.5	4.06×3.75	140	O-Tempest auto
L4, 194.5	4.06×3.75	166	O-Tempest
V8, 326.0	3.72×3.75	260	O-Tempest
V8, 389.0	4.06×3.75	215	S-Catalina/Star Chief man
V8, 389.0	4.06×3.75	230	O-all full-size auto
V8, 389.0	4.06×3.75	235	S-Bonn man; O-Cat/ Star Chief man
V8, 389.0	4.06×3.75	267	S-Catalina man
V8, 389.0	4.06×3.75	283	S-Star Chief man
V8, 389.0	4.06×3.75	303	S-GP, Bonn auto; O-SC/Cat auto
V8, 389.0	4.06×3.75	318	O-all full-size (Tri-Power)

	bore×stroke	bhp	availability
V8, 421.0	4.09×4.00	353	O-all full-size
V8, 421.0	4.09×4.00	370	O-all full-size
V8, 421.0	4.09×4.00	390/410	O-Catalina cpe

1964

Tempest (wb 115.0)		Wght	Price	Prod
2027	spt cpe	2,930	2,259	6,365
2035	Safari wgn 4d	3,245	2,605	6,834
2069	sdn 4d	2,970	2,313	19,427
2127	Custom spt cpe	2,955	2,345	25,833
2135	Custom Safari wgn 4d	3,260	2,691	10,696
2167	Custom conv cpe	3,075	2,641	7,987
2169	Custom sdn 4d	2,990	2,399	29,948
2227	LeMans spt cpe	2,975	2,491	31,317
2237	LeMans htp cpe	2,995	2,556	31,310
2267	LeMans conv cpe	3,125	2,796	17,559
Tempest G.T.O. (wb 115.0)				
2227	spt cpe	3,000	3,200	7,384
2237	htp cpe	3,020	3,250	18,422
2267	conv cpe	3,150	3,500	6,644
Catalina (wb 120.0; wgn-119.0)*				
2311	sdn 2d	3,695	2,735	12,480
2335	Safari wgn 4d, 6P	4,190	3,203	20,356
2339	Vista htp sdn	3,835	2,945	33,849
2345	Safari wgn 4d, 9P	4,235	3,311	13,140
2347	Sport htp cpe	3,750	2,869	74,793
2367	conv cpe	3,825	3,181	18,693
2369	sdn 4d	3,770	2,806	84,457
Star Chief (wb 123.0)				
2639	Vista htp sdn	3,945	3,239	11,200
2669	sdn 4d	3,885	3,107	26,453

1963 Grand Prix Sport hardtop coupe

1964 Tempest G.T.O. convertible coupe

Bonneville (wb 120.0; wgn-119.0)		Wght	Price	Prod
2835	Safari wgn 4d	4,275	3,633	5,844
2839	htp sdn	3,995	3,433	57,630
2847	htp cpe	3,920	3,358	34,769
2867	conv cpe	3,985	3,578	22,016
Grand Prix (wb 120.0)				
2957	Sport htp cpe	3,930	3,499	63,810

*Includes models equipped with 2+2 option package.

1964 Engines	bore×stroke	bhp	availability
L6, 215.0	3.75×3.25	140	S-Tempest exc GTO
V8, 326.0	3.72×3.75	250	O-Tempest
V8, 326.0	3.72×3.75	280	O-Tempest
V8, 389.0	4.06×3.75	230	O-all full-size auto
V8, 389.0	4.06×3.75	235	S-Catalina/Star Chf man
V8, 389.0	4.06×3.75	267	S-Catalina/Star Chf auto
V8, 389.0	4.06×3.75	283	S-Cat 2+2 option; O-Cat/SC auto
V8, 389.0	4.06×3.75	303	S-GP/Bonn auto; O-Cat/SC auto
V8, 389.0	4.06×3.75	306	S-GP/Bonn man; O-Cat/SC man
V8, 389.0	4.06×3.75	325	S-GTO; O-Tempest
V8, 389.0	4.06×3.75	330	O-full-size
V8, 389.0	4.06×3.75	348	O-GTO
V8, 421.0	4.09×4.00	320/350	O-full-size
V8, 421.0	4.09×4.00	370	O-full-size

1965

233 Tempest (wb 115.0)		Wght	Price	Prod
27	spt cpe	2,930	2,260	18,198
35	Safari wgn 4d	3,220	2,605	5,622
69	sdn 4d	2,975	2,313	15,705
235 Tempest Custom (wb 115.0)				
27	spt cpe	2,975	2,346	18,367
35	Safari wgn 4d	3,215	2,619	10,792
37	htp cpe	2,975	2,411	21,906
67	conv cpe	3,080	2,641	8,346
69	sdn 4d	2,980	2,400	25,242

237 Tempest LeMans (wb 115.0)		Wght	Price	Prod
27	spt cpe	3,020	2,491	18,881
27	G.T.O. spt cpe	3,468	2,751	8,319
37	htp cpe	3,030	2,556	60,548
37	G.T.O. htp cpe	3,478	2,816	55,722
67	conv cpe	3,115	2,797	13,897
67	G.T.O. conv cpe	3,563	3,057	11,311
69	sdn 4d	3,020	2,551	14,227
252 Catalina (wb 121.0)*				
11	sdn 2d	3,695	2,734	9,526
35	Safari wgn 4d, 6P	4,165	3,202	22,399
37	Sport htp cpe	3,750	2,868	92,009
39	Vista htp sdn	3,855	2,945	34,814
45	Safari wgn 4d, 9P	4,210	3,309	15,110
67	conv cpe	3,815	3,196	18,347
69	sdn 4d	3,750	2,805	78,853
256 Star Chief (wb 124.0)				
39	htp sdn	3,925	3,238	9,132
69	sdn 4d	3,860	3,106	22,183
262 Bonneville (wb 124.0; wgn-121.0)				
35	Safari wgn 4d	4,310	3,632	6,460
37	Sport htp cpe	3,890	3,357	44,030
39	htp sdn	3,990	3,433	62,480
67	conv cpe	3,950	3,594	21,050
266 Grand Prix (wb 121.0)				
57	Sport htp cpe	3,940	3,498	57,881

*Includes models equipped with 2+2 option package.

1965 Engines	bore×stroke	bhp	availability
L6, 215.0	3.75×3.25	140	S-Tempest exc GTO
V8, 326.0	3.72×3.75	250	O-Tempest
V8, 326.0	3.72×3.75	285	O-Tempest
V8, 389.0	4.06×3.75	256	S-Cat/SC man; O-other full-size
V8, 389.0	4.06×3.75	290	S-Catalina/Star Chf auto
V8, 389.0	4.06×3.75	325	S-Bonn/Grand Prix auto
V8, 389.0	4.06×3.75	333	S-Bonn/Grand Prix man
V8, 389.0	4.06×3.75	335	S-GTO
V8, 389.0	4.06×3.75	360	O-GTO

1965 Catalina 2+2 convertible coupe

	bore×stroke	bhp	availability
V8, 421.0	4.09×4.00	338	S-Cat 2+2; O-other full-size
V8, 421.0	4.09×4.00	356	O-all full-size
V8, 421.0	4.09×4.00	376	O-all full-size

1966

233 Tempest (wb 115.0)		Wght	Price	Prod
07	spt cpe	3,040	2,278	22,266
35	wgn 4d	3,340	2,624	4,095
69	sdn 4d	3,075	2,331	17,392
235 Tempest Custom (wb 115.0)				
07	spt cpe	3,060	2,362	17,182
17	htp cpe	3,075	2,426	31,322
35	wgn 4d	3,355	2,709	7,614
39	htp sdn	3,195	2,547	10,996
67	conv cpe	3,170	2,665	5,557
69	sdn 4d	3,100	2,415	23,988
237 LeMans (wb 115.0)				
07	spt cpe	3,090	2,505	16,654
17	htp cpe	3,125	2,568	78,109
39	htp sdn	3,195	2,701	13,897
67	conv cpe	3,220	2,806	13,080
242 Tempest G.T.O. (wb 115.0)				
07	spt cpe	3,445	2,783	10,363
17	htp cpe	3,465	2,847	73,785
67	conv cpe	3,555	3,082	12,798
252 Catalina (wb 121.0)				
11	sdn 2d	3,715	2,762	7,925
35	wgn 4d, 6P	4,250	3,217	21,082
37	htp cpe	3,835	2,893	79,013
39	htp sdn	3,910	2,968	38,005
45	wgn 4d, 9P	4,315	3,338	12,965
67	conv cpe	3,860	3,219	14,837
69	sdn 4d	3,785	2,831	80,483
254 2+2 (wb 121.0)*				
37	htp cpe	4,005	3,298	—
67	conv cpe	4,030	3,602	—
256 Star Chief Executive (wb 124.0)				
37	htp cpe	3,920	3,170	10,140
39	htp sdn	3,980	3,244	10,583
69	sdn 4d	3,920	3,114	24,489
262 Bonneville (wb 124.0; wgn-121.0)				
37	htp cpe	4,020	3,354	42,004
39	htp sdn	4,070	3,428	68,646
45	wgn 4d, 3S	4,390	3,747	8,452
67	conv cpe	4,015	3,586	16,299
266 Grand Prix (wb 121.0)				
57	htp cpe	4,015	3,492	36,757

*Included in Catalina production figures (6,383 built).

1966 Engines	bore×stroke	bhp	availability
L6, 230.0	3.88×3.25	165	S-Tempest, LeMans
L6, 230.0	3.88×3.25	207	O-Tempest, LeMans
V8, 326.0	3.72×3.75	250	O-Tempest, LeMans
V8, 326.0	3.72×3.75	285	O-Tempest, LeMans
V8, 389.0	4.06×3.75	256	S-Cat/SC man O-other full-size
V8, 389.0	4.06×3.75	290	O-Catalina, Star Chief
V8, 389.0	4.06×3.75	325	S-Bonn/GP auto; O-Cat, Star Chief
V8, 389.0	4.06×3.75	333	S-Bonn/GP man, GTO
V8, 389.0	4.06×3.75	360	O-GTO
V8, 421.0	4.09×4.00	338	S-2+2; O-other full-size

1966 Tempest G.T.O. convertible coupe

	bore×stroke	bhp	availability
V8, 421.0	4.09×4.00	356	O-all full-size
V8, 421.0	4.09×4.00	376	O-all full-size

1967

223 Firebird (wb 108.1)		Wght	Price	Prod
37	htp cpe	2,955	2,666	67,032
67	conv cpe	3,247	2,903	15,528
233 Tempest (wb 115.0)				
07	cpe	3,110	2,341	17,978
35	wgn 4d	3,370	2,666	3,495
69	sdn 4d	3,140	2,388	13,136
235 Tempest Custom (wb 115.0)				
07	cpe	3,130	2,437	12,469
17	htp cpe	3,140	2,494	30,512
35	wgn 4d	3,370	2,760	5,324
39	htp sdn	3,240	2,608	5,493
67	conv cpe	3,240	2,723	4,082
69	sdn 4d	3,145	2,482	17,445
237 LeMans (wb 115.0)				
07	cpe	3,155	2,586	10,693
17	htp cpe	3,155	2,648	75,965
39	htp sdn	3,265	2,771	8,424
67	conv cpe	3,250	2,881	9,820
239 Tempest Safari (wb 115.0)				
35	wgn 4d	3,390	2,936	4,511
242 Tempest G.T.O. (wb 115.0)				
07	cpe	3,425	2,871	7,029
17	htp cpe	3,430	2,935	65,176
67	conv cpe	3,515	3,165	9,517
252 Catalina (wb 121.0)*				
11	sdn 2d	3,735	2,807	5,633
35	wgn 4d, 6P	4,275	3,252	18,305
39	htp sdn	3,960	3,020	37,256
45	wgn 4d, 9P	4,340	3,374	11,040
67	conv cpe	3,910	3,276	10,033
69	sdn 4d	3,825	2,866	80,551
87	htp cpe	3,860	2,951	77,932
256 Executive (wb 124.0; wgn-121.0)				
35	wgn 4d, 6P	4,290	3,600	5,903
39	htp sdn	4,020	3,296	8,699
45	wgn 4d, 9P	4,370	3,722	5,593

		Wght	Price	Prod
87	htp cpe	3,925	3,227	6,931
262 Bonneville (wb 124.0; wgn-121.0)				
39	htp sdn	4,110	3,517	56,307
45	wgn 4d, 9P	4,415	3,819	6,771
67	conv cpe	4,010	3,680	8,902
87	htp cpe	3,975	3,448	31,016
266 Grand Prix (wb 121.0)				
57	htp cpe	4,005	3,549	37,125
67	conv cpe	4,040	3,813	5,856

*Includes models equipped with 2+2 option package.

1967 Engines	bore×stroke	bhp	availability
L6, 230.0	3.88×3.25	165	S-Firebird, LeMans,Temp exc GTO
L6, 230.0	3.88×3.25	215	O-Firebird, LeMans, Temp exc GTO
V8, 326.0	3.72×3.75	250	O-Firebird, LeMans, Temp exc GTO
V8, 326.0	3.72×3.75	285	O-Firebird, LeMans, Temp exc Tempest Safari wgn
V8, 400.0	4.12×3.75	255	O-GTO auto
V8, 400.0	4.12×3.75	265	S-Cat/Vent/Exec man; O-auto
V8, 400.0	4.12×3.75	290	S-Cat/Vent/Exec auto
V8, 400.0	4.12×3.75	325	S-Bonn auto, Firebird 400 O-Catalina, Ventura, Exec
V8, 400.0	4.12×3.75	333	S-Bonn man; O-Cat, Vent, Exec
V8, 400.0	4.12×3.75	335	S-GTO
V8, 400.0	4.12×3.75	350	S-Grand Prix
V8, 400.0	4.12×3.75	360	O-GTO
V8, 428.0	4.12×4.00	360	S-2+2; O-Cat, Exec, Bonn, Grand Prix
V8, 428.0	4.12×4.00	376	O-Catalina, Exec, Bonn, Grand Prix

1968

		Wght	Price	Prod
223 Firebird (wb 108.1)				
37	htp cpe	3,061	2,781	90,152
67	conv cpe	3,346	2,996	16,960
233 Tempest (wb 116.0; 2d-112.0)				
27	spt cpe	3,242	2,461	19,991
69	sdn 4d	3,309	2,509	11,590
235 Tempest Custom (wb 116.0; 2d-112.0)				
27	spt cpe	3,252	2,554	10,634
35	wgn 4d	3,667	2,906	8,253
37	htp cpe	3,277	2,614	40,574
39	htp sdn	3,384	2,728	6,147
67	conv cpe	3,337	2,839	3,518
69	sdn 4d	3,297	2,602	17,304
237 LeMans (wb 116.0; 2d-112.0)				
27	spt cpe	3,287	2,724	8,439
37	htp cpe	3,302	2,786	110,036
39	htp sdn	3,407	2,916	9,002
67	conv cpe	3,377	3,015	8,820
239 Tempest Safari (wb 116.0)				
35	wgn 4d	3,677	3,107	4,414
242 Tempest G.T.O. (wb 112.0)				
37	htp cpe	3,506	3,101	77,704
67	conv cpe	3,590	3,227	9,980
252 Catalina (wb 121.0)				
11	sdn 2d	3,839	2,945	5,247
35	wgn 4d, 6P	4,327	3,390	21,848
39	htp sdn	4,012	3,158	41,727
45	wgn 4d, 9P	4,408	3,537	13,363
67	conv cpe	3,980	3,391	7,339
69	sdn 4d	3,888	3,004	94,441
87	htp cpe	3,943	3,089	92,217
256 Executive (wb 124.0; wgn-121.0)				
35	wgn 4d, 6P	4,378	3,744	6,195
39	htp sdn	4,077	3,439	7,848
45	wgn 4d, 9P	4,453	3,890	5,843
69	sdn 4d	4,022	3,309	18,869
87	htp cpe	3,975	3,371	5,880
262 Bonneville (wb 124.0; wgn-121.0)				
39	htp sdn	4,171	3,660	57,055
45	wgn 4d, 9P	4,485	3,987	6,926
67	conv cpe	4,090	3,800	7,358
69	sdn 4d	4,122	3,530	3,499
87	htp cpe	4,054	3,592	29,598
266 Grand Prix (wb 121.0)				
57	htp cpe	4,075	3,697	31,711

1967 Catalina 2+2 hardtop coupe

1968 Engines	bore×stroke	bhp	availability
L6, 250.0	3.88×3.53	175	S-Firebird, LeMans, Tempest exc GTO
L6, 250.0	3.88×3.53	215	S-Frbrd Sprint; O-as above exc wgns
V8, 350.0	3.88×3.75	265	S-Frbrd 350; O-Tempest exc GTO, LeMans
V8, 350.0	3.88×3.75	320	S-Frbrd HO; O-Temp, LeM exc wgns
V8, 400.0	4.12×3.75	265	O-GTO, all full-size
V8, 400.0	4.12×3.75	290	S-Catalina, Ventura, Exec
V8, 400.0	4.12×3.75	330	S-Firebird 400
V8, 400.0	4.12×3.75	335	O-Firebird 400 (Ram-Air)
V8, 400.0	4.12×3.75	340	S-Bonn; O-Cat, Vent, Exec
V8, 400.0	4.12×3.75	350	S-Grand Prix, GTO
V8, 400.0	4.12×3.75	360	O-GTO
V8, 428.0	4.12×4.00	375	O-Cat, Vent, Exec, Bonn, GP
V8, 428.0	4.12×4.00	390	O-Cat, Vent, Exec, Bonn, GP

1969

		Wght	Price	Prod
223 Firebird (wb 108.0)*				
37	htp cpe	3,080	2,821	76,059
67	conv cpe	3,330	3,045	11,649
233 Tempest (wb 116.0; 2d-112.0)				
27	spt cpe	3,180	2,510	17,181
69	sdn 4d	3,250	2,557	9,741

235 Tempest Custom (wb 116.0; 2d-112.0)		Wght	Price	Prod
27	spt cpe	3,210	2,603	7,912
35	wgn 4d	3,595	2,956	6,963
37	htp cpe	3,220	2,663	46,886
39	htp sdn	3,315	2,777	3,918
67	conv cpe	3,265	2,888	2,379
69	sdn 4d	3,235	2,651	16,532
237 LeMans (wb 116.0; 2d-112.0)				
27	spt cpe	3,225	2,773	5,033
37	htp cpe	3,245	2,835	82,817
67	conv cpe	3,290	3,064	5,676
69	htp sdn	3,360	2,965	6,475
239 Tempest Safari (wb 116.0)				
36	wgn 4d	3,690	3,198	4,115
242 Tempest G.T.O. (wb 112.0)				
37	htp cpe	3,503	3,156	64,851
67	conv cpe	3,553	3,382	7,436
252 Catalina (wb 122.0)				
36	wgn 4d, 6P	4,455	3,519	20,352
37	htp cpe	3,925	3,174	84,006
39	htp sdn	4,005	3,244	38,819
46	wgn 4d, 9P	4,520	3,664	13,393
67	conv cpe	3,985	3,476	5,436
69	sdn 4d	3,945	3,090	84,590
256 Executive (wb 125.0; wgn-122.0)				
36	wgn 4d, 6P	4,475	3,872	6,411
37	htp cpe	3,970	3,456	4,492
39	htp sdn	4,065	3,525	6,522
46	wgn 4d, 9P	4,545	4,017	6,805
69	sdn 4d	4,045	3,394	14,831
262 Bonneville (wb 125.0; wgn-122.0)				
37	htp cpe	4,080	3,688	27,773
39	htp sdn	4,180	3,756	50,817
46	wgn 4d, 9P	4,600	4,104	7,428
67	conv cpe	4,130	3,896	5,438
69	sdn 4d	4,180	3,626	4,859
276 Grand Prix (wb 118.0)				
57	htp cpe	3,715	3,866	112,486

*Includes 697 Trans Am models (8 convertibles).

1969 Engines	bore×stroke	bhp	availability
L6, 250.0	3.88×3.53	175	S-Frbrd, LeMans, Tempest exc GTO
L6, 250.0	3.88×3.53	230	S-Frbrd Sprint; O-LeMans, Tempest exc GTO
V8, 350.0	3.88×3.75	265	S-Frbrd 350; O-Tempest, LeMans
V8, 350.0	3.88×3.75	325	S-Firebird 350 HO
V8, 350.0	3.88×3.75	330	O-Frbrd, Tpst, LeMans exc wgns/GTO
V8, 400.0	4.12×3.75	265	O-GTO/full-size auto
V8, 400.0	4.12×3.75	290	S-Catalina, Ventura, Exec
V8, 400.0	4.12×3.75	330	S-Firebird 400
V8, 400.0	4.12×3.75	335	O-Firebird 400 (Ram Air)
V8, 400.0	4.12×3.75	345	O-Firebird 400 (Ram Air)
V8, 400.0	4.12×3.75	350	S-GTO, Grand Prix
V8, 400.0	4.12×3.75	366	O-GTO (Ram Air)
V8, 400.0	4.12×3.75	370	O-GTO (Ram Air)

1970

223 Firebird (wb 108.0)		Wght	Price	Prod
87	htp cpe	3,140	2,875	18,874
87	Formula 400 htp cpe	3,470	3,370	7,708
87	Trans Am htp cpe	3,550	4,305	3,196
87	Esprit htp	3,435	3,241	18,961
233 Tempest (wb 116.0; 2d-112.0)				
27	cpe	3,225	2,623	11,977
37	htp cpe	3,250	2,683	20,883
69	sdn 4d	3,295	2,670	9,187
235 LeMans (wb 116.0, 2d-112.0)				
27	cpe	3,240	2,735	5,656
35	wgn 4d	3,585	3,092	7,165
37	htp cpe	3,265	2,795	52,304
39	htp sdn	3,385	2,921	3,872
69	sdn 4d	3,315	2,782	15,255
237 LeMans Sport (wb 116.0; 2d-112.0)				
27	cpe	3,265	2,891	1,673
36	wgn 4d	3,775	3,328	3,823
37	htp cpe	3,290	2,953	58,356
39	htp sdn	3,405	3,083	3,657
67	conv cpe	3,330	3,182	4,670
242 G.T.O. (112.0)*				
37	htp cpe	3,641	3,267	36,366
67	conv cpe	3,691	3,492	3,783
252 Catalina (wb 122.0)				
36	wgn 4d, 6P	4,517	3,646	16,944
37	htp cpe	3,952	3,249	70,350
39	htp sdn	4,042	3,319	35,155
46	wgn 4d, 9P	4,607	3,791	12,450
67	conv cpe	4,027	3,604	3,686
69	sdn 4d	3,997	3,164	84,795

1968 Bonneville hardtop coupe

1969 Tempest G.T.O. hardtop coupe with "The Judge" option package

256 Executive (wb 125.0; wgn-122.0)		Wght	Price	Prod
36	wgn 4d, 6P	4,552	4,015	4,861
37	htp cpe	4,042	3,600	3,499
39	htp sdn	4,132	3,669	5,376
46	wgn 4d, 9P	4,632	4,160	5,629
69	sdn 4d	4,087	3,538	13,061
262 Bonneville (wb 125.0; wgn-122.0)				
37	htp cpe	4,111	3,832	23,418
39	htp sdn	4,226	3,900	44,241
46	wgn 4d, 9P	4,686	4,247	7,033
67	conv cpe	4,161	4,040	3,537
69	sdn 4d	4,181	3,770	3,802
276 Grand Prix (wb 118.0)				
57	htp cpe	3,784	3,985	65,750

*Includes models equipped with "The Judge" option (3,629 coupes and 168 convertibles).

1970 Engines	bore×stroke	bhp	availability
L6, 250.0	3.88×3.53	155	S-Tempest, LeMans, Firebird
V8, 350.0	3.88×3.75	255	S-Firebird Esprit; O-above models, Cat exc conv and wgns
V8, 400.0	4.12×3.75	265	O-all auto exc GTO, Bonn
V8, 400.0	4.12×3.75	290	S-Cat conv/wgn, Exec; O-other Cat
V8, 400.0	4.12×3.75	330	S-Frbrd 400; O-Tpst/LeM/Cat/Exec auto
V8, 400.0	4.12×3.75	345	S-Frbrd Trans Am; O-Tpst/LeMans man
V8, 400.0	4.12×3.75	350	S-GTO, Grand Prix
V8, 400.0	4.12×3.75	366	S-GTO Judge; O-GTO (Ram Air)
V8, 400.0	4.12×3.75	370	O-GTO (Ram Air); O-GTO Judge
V8, 455.0	4.15×4.21	360	S-Bonn; O-Cat, Exec, GTO
V8, 455.0	4.15×4.21	370	S-Bonn wgn, Grand Prix SJ; O-GP J, Cat, Exec, Bonn

1971

Ventura II (wb 111.0)		Wght	Price	Prod
21327	cpe	3,010	2,458	34,681
21369	sdn 4d	3,050	2,488	13,803
Firebird (wb 108.0)				
22387	cpe	3,292	3,047	23,021
22487	Esprit cpe V8	3,423	3,416	20,185
22687	Formula 400 cpe V8	3,473	3,445	7,802
22887	Trans Am cpe V8	3,578	4,595	2,116
LeMans (wb 116.0; 2d 112.0)				
23327	T-37 cpe	3,317	2,747	7,184
23337	T-37 htp cpe	3,322	2,807	29,466
23369	T-37 sdn 4d	3,347	2,795	8,336
23527	cpe	3,327	2,877	2,374
23536	wgn 4d 2S	3,867	3,353	6,311
23537	htp cpe	3,327	2,938	40,966
23539	htp sdn	3,442	3,064	3,186
23546	wgn 4d 3S	3,917	3,465	4,363
23569	sdn 4d	3,357	2,925	11,979
23737	Sport htp cpe	3,327	3,125	34,625
23739	Sport htp sdn	3,442	3,255	2,451
23767	Sport conv	3,417	3,359	3,865
24237	GTO htp cpe V8	3,619	3,446	9,497
24237	GTO Judge htp cpe	3,650	3,840	357
24267	GTO conv	3,664	3,676	661
24267	GTO Judge conv	3,700	4,070	17
Catalina (wb 124.0; wgn-127.0)				
25235	Safari wgn 4d 2S	4,815	4,315	10,332
25239	htp sdn	4,107	3,939	22,333
25245	Safari wgn 4d 3S	4,905	4,462	9,283
25257	htp cpe	4,042	3,870	46,257
25267	conv	4,081	4,156	2,036
25269	sdn 4d	4,077	3,770	59,355
25839	Brougham htp sdn	4,179	4,154	9,001
25857	Brougham htp cpe	4,119	4,084	8,823
25869	Brougham sdn 4d	4,149	4,000	6,069
Bonneville (wb 126.0; wgn-127.0)				
26235	Grand Safari wgn 4d 2S	4,843	4,643	3,613
26239	htp sdn	4,273	4,340	16,393
26245	Grand Safari wgn 4d 3S	4,913	4,790	5,972
26257	htp cpe	4,188	4,272	8,778
26269	sdn 4d	4,213	4,210	6,513
Grand Ville (wb 126.0)				
26847	htp cpe	4,223	4,497	14,017
26849	htp sdn	4,303	4,566	30,524
26867	conv cpe	4,266	4,706	1,789
	chassis	—	—	194
Grand Prix (wb 118.0)				
27657	htp cpe	3,863	4,557	58,325

1971 Engines	bore×stroke	bhp	availability
L6, 250.0	3.88×3.53	145	S-LeM exc GTO; Fbd exc Formula & T/A
L6, 250.0	3.88×3.53	185	S-Ventura
V8, 307.0	3.88×3.25	235	S-Ventura
V8, 350.0	3.88×3.75	250	S-LeM exc GTP, Fbd exc T/A, Cat exc Br/Saf

1971 LeMans GTO convertible coupe

1972 Firebird Formula coupe

	bore×stroke	bhp	availability
V8, 400.0	4.12×3.75	265	S-Cat Br/Saf; O-Fbd exc Frmla & T/A, Catalina
V8, 400.0	4.12×3.75	300	S-GTO, Fbd Frmla, GP O-LeMans, Fbd Esprit
V8, 455.0	4.15×4.21	280	S-Bonn; O-Catalina
V8, 455.0	4.15×4.21	325	S-GV; O-LeM, Fbd T/A, Catalina, GP
V8, 455.0	4.15×4.21	335	S-Trans Am; O-LeMans

1972

Ventura II (wb 110.0)		Wght	Price	Prod
2Y27	cpe	3,019	2,426	51,203
2Y69	sdn 4d	3,054	2,454	21,584
Firebird (wb 108.0)				
2S87	cpe	3,263	2,828	12,000
2T87	Esprit cpe V8	3,359	3,194	11,415
2U87	Formula cpe V8	3,424	3,221	5,250
2V87	Trans Am cpe V8	3,564	4,256	1,286
LeMans (wb 116.0; 2d-112.0)*				
2D27	cpe	3,402	2,722	6,855
2D36	wgn 4d 2S	3,907	3,271	8,332
2D37	htp cpe	3,342	2,851	80,383
2D46	wgn 4d 3S	3,947	3,378	5,266
2D67	conv	3,392	3,228	3,438
2D69	sdn 4d	3,377	2,814	19,463
2G37	Luxury htp cpe V8	3,488	3,196	37,615
2G39	Luxury htp sdn V8	3,638	3,319	8,641
Catalina (wb 123.5; wgns 127.0)				
2L35	Safari wgn 4d 2S	4,743	4,232	14,536
2L39	htp sdn	4,879	3,874	28,010
2L45	Safari wgn 4d 3S	4,818	4,372	12,766
2L57	htp cpe	4,129	3,808	60,233
2L67	conv	4,204	4,080	2,399
2L69	sdn 4d	4,154	3,713	83,004
2M39	Brougham htp sdn	4,238	4,062	8,762
2M57	Brougham htp cpe	4,158	3,996	10,545
2M69	Brougham sdn 4d	4,188	3,916	8,007
Bonneville (wb 126.0; wgns 127.0)				
2N35	Grand Safari wgn 4d 2S	4,918	4,581	5,675
2N39	htp sdn	4,338	4,293	15,806
2N45	Grand Safari wgn 4d 3S	4,938	4,721	8,540
2N57	htp cpe	4,238	4,228	10,568
2N69	sdn 4d	4,288	4,169	9,704
Grand Ville (wb 126.0)				
2P47	htp cpe	4,262	4,442	19,852
2P49	htp sdn	4,378	4,507	41,346
2P67	conv cpe	4,333	4,640	2,213
	chassis	—	—	320
Grand Prix (wb 118.0)				
2K57	htp cpe	3,898	4,472	91,961

*Note: Sport ($164), GTO ($344) and GT ($231) were option packages. GTO production: 5,807.

1972 Engines	bore×stroke	bhp	availability
L6, 250.0	3.88×3.53	110	S-Vntra,LeM,Fbd exc T/A
V8, 307.0	3.88×3.25	130	S-Ventura exc Calif.
V8, 350.0	3.88×3.75	160	S-Vntra (Cal.), LeM, Fbd exc T/A, Cat exc Saf,Br
V8, 400.0	4.12×3.75	175	S-Cat Saf, Br; O-LeM,Cat,Firebird exc T/A
V8, 400.0	4.12×3.75	250	S-GP; O-Fbd exc T/A
V8, 455.0	4.15×4.21	185	S-Bonn, GV,GSaf; O-Cat
V8, 455.0	4.15×4.21	220	O-Bonn,GV,GSaf,Cat
V8, 455.0	4.15×4.21	230	O-LeMans
V8, 455.0	4.15×4.21	250	O-LeMans, Grand Prix

	bore×stroke	bhp	availability
V8, 455.0	4.15×4.21	300	S-Fbd T/A; O-LeM, Fbd

1973

Ventura (wb 111.0)		Wght	Price	Prod
Y17	htchbk cpe 3d	3,276	2,603	26,335
Z17	Custom htchbk cpe 3d	3,309	2,759	
Y27	cpe	3,170	2,452	49,153
Z27	Custom cpe	3,203	2,609	
Y69	sdn 4d	3,230	2,481	21,012
Z69	Custom sdn 4d	3,263	2,638	
Firebird (wb 108.0)				
S87	cpe	3,270	2,895	14,096
T87	Esprit cpe V8	3,309	3,249	17,249
U87	Formula cpe V8	3,318	3,276	10,166
V87	Trans Am cpe V8	3,504	4,204	4,802
LeMans (wb 116.0; 2d-112.0)				
D29	Colonnade sdn 4d	3,713	2,918	26,554
D35	Safari wgn 5d 2S	4,064	3,296	10,446
D37	Colonnade sdn 2d	3,687	2,920	68,230
D45	Safari wgn 5d 3S	4,101	3,429	6,127
F37	Sport Colonnade sdn 2d	3,702	3,008	50,999
G29	Luxury Colonnade sdn 4d V8	3,867	3,344	9,377
G37	Luxury Colonnade sdn 2d V8	3,799	3,274	33,916
Grand Am (wb 116.0; 2d-112.0)				
H29	Colonnade sdn 4d V8	4,018	4,353	8,691
H37	Colonnade sdn 2d V8	3,992	4,264	34,443
Catalina (wb 124.0; wgn-127.0)				
L35	Safari wgn 4d 2S	4,791	4,311	15,762
L39	htp sdn	4,270	3,938	31,663
L45	Safari wgn 4d 3S	4,873	4,457	14,654
L57	htp cpe	4,190	3,869	74,394
L69	sdn 4d	4,234	3,770	100,592
Bonneville (wb 124.0)				
N39	htp sdn	4,369	4,292	17,202
N57	htp cpe	4,292	4,225	13,866
N69	sdn 4d	4,333	4,163	15,830
Grand Ville/Grand Safari (wb 126.0/127.0)				
P35	Grand Safari wgn 4d 2S	4,823	4,674	6,894
P45	Grand Safari wgn 4d 3S	4,925	4,821	10,776
P47	Grand Ville htp cpe	4,321	4,524	23,963
P49	Grand Ville htp sdn	4,376	4,592	44,092
P67	Grand Ville conv	4,339	4,766	4,447
	chassis	—	—	240

1973 Firebird Trans Am coupe

Grand Prix (wb 116.0)		Wght	Price	Prod
K57	htp cpe	4,025	4,583	153,899

Note: GT ($246) and GTO ($368) were option packages. GTO production: 4,806.

1973 Engines	bore×stroke	bhp	availability
L6, 250.0	3.88×3.53	100	S-Vntra,LeM,Fbd exc T/A
V8, 350.0	3.88×3.75	150	S-Vntra,LeM,Fbd exc T/A,Cat exc wgn
V8, 350.0	3.88×3.75	175	O-Vntra,LeM,Fbd exc T/A
V8, 400.0	4.12×3.75	170	S-GA,Bonn,Cat wgn; O-LeMans, Catalina
V8, 400.0	4.12×3.75	185	O-GA,LeM,Bon,Cat
V8, 400.0	4.12×3.75	200	S-Grand Saf
V8, 400.0	4.12×3.75	230	S-GA,LeM,Fbd exc T/A, GSaf,Cat, Bonn
V8, 400.0	4.12×3.75	250	S-Grand Prix
V8, 455.0	4.15×4.21	215	S-GV; O-GSaf,Cat,Bonn
V8, 455.0	4.15×4.21	250	S-Fbd T/A; O-Fbd,GSaf,GV,Bonn,GP
V8, 455.0	4.15×4.21	310	O-Firebird

1974

Ventura (wb 111.1)		Wght	Price	Prod
Y17	htchbk cpe 3d	3,372	3,018	16,694
Z17	Custom htchbk cpe 3d	3,376	3,176	
Y27	cpe	3,262	2,892	47,782
Z27	Custom cpe	3,298	3,051	
Y69	sdn 4d	3,284	2,921	17,323
Z69	Custom sdn 4d	3,332	3,080	
Firebird (wb 108.0)				
S87	cpe	3,394	3,335	26,372
T87	Esprit cpe V8	3,540	3,687	22,583
U87	Formula cpe V8	3,548	3,659	14,519
V87	Trans Am cpe V8	3,655	4,446	10,255
LeMans (wb 116.0; 2d-112.0)				
D29	Colonnade sdn 4d	3,736	3,236	17,266
D37	Colonnade sdn 2d	3,660	3,216	37,061
D35	Safari wgn 5d 2S V8	4,333	4,052	4,743
D45	Safari wgn 5d 3S V8	4,371	4,186	3,004
F37	Sport Colonnade sdn 2d	3,688	3,300	37,955
G35	Luxury Safari wgn 5d 2S V8	4,363	4,326	952
G29	Luxury Colonnade sdn 4d V8	3,904	3,759	4,513
G37	Luxury Colonnade sdn 2d V8	3,808	3,703	25,882
G45	Luxury Safari wgn 5d 3S V8	4,401	4,459	1,178
Grand Am (wb 116.0; 2d-112.0)				
H29	Colonnade sdn 4d	4,073	4,623	3,122
H37	Colonnade sdn 2d	3,992	4,534	13,961
Catalina (wb 124.0; wgn-127.0)				
L35	Safari wgn 4d 2S	4,973	4,692	5,662
L39	htp sdn	4,352	4,347	11,769
L45	Safari wgn 4d 3S	5,037	4,834	6,486
L57	htp cpe	4,279	4,278	40,657
L69	sdn 4d	4,294	4,190	46,025
Bonneville (wb 124.0)				
N39	htp sdn	4,444	4,639	6,151
N57	htp cpe	4,356	4,572	7,639
N69	sdn 4d	4,384	4,510	6,770
Grand Ville/Safari (wb 124.0/127.0)				
P35	Grand Safari wgn 4d 2S	5,011	5,099	2,894
P45	Grand Safari wgn 4d 3S	5,112	5,256	5,255
P47	Grand Ville htp cpe	4,432	4,871	11,631
P49	Grand Ville htp sdn	4,515	4,939	21,714
P67	Grand Ville conv	4,476	5,113	3,000
	chassis	—	—	113

Grand Prix (wb 116.0)		Wght	Price	Prod
K57	htp cpe	4,096	4,936	99,117

Note: GTO ($195) was an option package for Ventura coupe only. GTO production: 7,058

1974 Engines	bore×stroke	bhp	availability
L6, 250.0	3.88×3.53	100	S-Vntra,LeM,Fbd S87
V8, 350.0	3.88×3.75	155	S-Vntra,LeM,Fbd S87/T87
V8, 350.0	3.88×3.75	170	S-Fbd U87; O-LeMans
V8, 350.0	3.88×3.75	200	O-LeMans
V8, 400.0	4.12×3.75	175	S-GA,Cat,Bonn,GSaf,GV
V8, 400.0	4.12×3.75	190	O-Grand Am
V8, 400.0	4.12×3.75	200	O-Cat,Bon,GSaf,GV
V8, 400.0	4.12×3.75	225	S-Fbd T/A,GP;O-GA,Fbd
V8, 455.0	4.15×4.21	215	S-GV; O-GA, Cat, Bonn
V8, 455.0	4.15×4.21	250	O-GA,Fbd T/A,GP
V8, 455.0	4.15×4.21	255	O-all full-size LNP
V8, 455.0	4.15×4.21	290	O-Fbd Formula/Trans Am

1975

Astre (wb 97.0)		Wght	Price	Prod
C11	S sdn 2d	2,416	2,841	8,339
C15	S Safari wgn 3d	2,519	3,071	
V15	Safari wgn 3d	2,545	3,175	15,322
X15	SJ Safari wgn 3d	2,602	3,686	
C77	S htchbk cpe 3d	2,487	2,954	
V77	htchbk cpe 3d	2,499	3,079	40,809
X77	SJ htchbk cpe 3d	2,558	3,610	
Ventura (wb 111.1)				
E27	S cpe	3,360	3,162	
Y27	cpe	3,382	3,293	34,023
Z27	Custom cpe	3,442	3,449	
B27	SJ cpe	3,424	3,829	
Y17	htchbk cpe	3,466	3,432	
Z17	Custom htchbk cpe 3d	3,482	3,593	10,463
B17	SJ htchbk cpe 3d	3,484	3,961	
Y69	sdn 4d	3,418	3,304	
Z69	Custom sdn 4d	3,462	3,464	22,068
B69	SJ sdn 4d	3,454	3,846	
Firebird (wb 108.0)				
S87	cpe	3,498	3,713	22,293
T87	Esprit cpe	3,543	3,958	20,826
U87	Formula cpe V8	3,631	4,349	13,670
W87	Trans Am cpe V8	3,716	4,740	27,274
LeMans (wb 116.0; 2d-112.0)				
D29	Colonnade sdn 4d	3,838	3,612	15,065

1974 Bonneville hardtop coupe

	bore×stroke	bhp	availability
V8, 350.0	3.80×3.85	160	O-Phoenix,Firebird
V8, 350.0	3.80×3.85	155/170	O-Catalina, Bonn
V8, 400.0	4.12×3.75	180	S-Fbd T/A; O-Fbd Fmla Cat, Bonn
V8, 403.0	4.36×3.38	185	O-Fbd,Cat,Bonn

1979

Sunbird (wb 97.0)		Wght	Price	Prod
M07	cpe	2,642	4,379	24,221
M15	Safari spt wgn 3d	2,651	4,321	2,902
M27	spt cpe	2,593	4,274	30,087
E27	htchbk cpe 3d	2,593	4,016	40,560
Phoenix (wb 111.1)				
Y17	htchbk cpe 3d	3,319	4,239	923
Y27	cpe	3,236	4,089	9,233
Y69	sdn 4d	3,286	4,189	10,565
Z27	LJ cpe	3,345	4,589	1,826
Z69	LJ sdn 4d	3,394	4,689	2,353
Firebird (wb 108.0)				
S87	cpe	3,294	5,260	38,642
T87	Esprit cpe	3,324	5,638	30,853
U87	Formula cpe V8	3,460	6,564	24,851
W87	Trans Am cpe V8	3,551	6,883	109,609
X87	T/A Limited Edition	3,551	10,620	7,500
LeMans (wb 108.1)				
D19	sdn 4d	3,082	5,134	26,958
D27	cpe	3,076	5,031	14,197
D35	Safari wgn	3,240	5,587	27,517
F19	Grand LeMans sdn 4d	3,126	5,430	28,577
F27	Grand LeMans cpe	3,098	5,302	13,020
F35	Grand LeM Safari wgn	3,274	5,931	20,783
G19	Grand Am sdn 4d	3,124	5,529	1,865
G27	Grand Am cpe	3,120	5,530	4,021
Catalina (wb 116.0)				
L35	wgn 4d 2S V8	3,997	6,681	13,353
L35	wgn 4d 3S V8	4,029	6,864	
L37	cpe	3,534	6,020	5,410
L69	sdn 4d	3,566	6,076	28,121
Bonneville (wb 116.0)				
N35	Safari wgn 4d 2S	4,022	7,050	16,925
N35	Safari wgn 4d 3S	4,054	7,233	
N37	cpe	3,616	6,593	34,127
Q37	Brougham cpe	3,659	7,395	39,094
N69	sdn 4d	3,672	6,718	71,906
Q69	Brougham sdn 4d	3,726	7,584	17,364

Grand Prix (wb 108.1)		Wght	Price	Prod
J37	cpe	3,166	5,454	124,815
K37	LJ cpe V8	3,285	6,555	61,175
H37	SJ cpe V8	3,349	6,814	24,060

1979 Engines	bore×stroke	bhp	availability
L4, 151.0	4.00×3.00	85	S-Sunbd; O-Phnx
V6, 231.0	3.74×3.48	115	S-all 6s; O-Sunbd
V8, 301.0	4.00×3.00	140	S-Phnx,LeM exc GA, Fbd,GP exc SJ
V8, 301.0	3.80×3.85	150	O-LeM GA, GP SJ
V8, 305.0	3.80×3.85	145	S-Phnx,LeM,Fbd S/T87; O-Sunbd, Lem GA, GP
V8, 350.0	3.88×3.75	160	O-Phnx, Fbd
V8, 350.0	3.88×3.75	155/170	O-Catalina, Bonn
V8, 400.0	4.12×3.75	180	S-Fbd T/A; O-Fbd Fml, Cat, Bonn
V8, 400.0	4.12×3.75	220	O-Fbd Formula, T/A
V8, 403.0	4.36×3.38	185	O-Fbd, Cat, Bonn

Note: Because 350 cid V8s from several GM divisions were used in the late 1970s, bore/stroke may differ from dimensions shown.

1980

Sunbird (wb 97.0)		Wght	Price	Prod
E07	htchbk cpe 3d	2,651	4,808	52,952
M07	spt cpe	2,657	4,996	135,027
E27	htchbk cpe 3d	2,603	4,623	
M27	spt cpe	2,609	4,885	
Phoenix (wb 104.9)				
Y37	cpe	2,516	5,465	49,485
Y67	htchbk sdn 5d	2,558	5,656	72,875
Z37	LJ cpe	2,550	5,936	23,674
Z68	LJ htchbk sdn 5d	2,610	6,127	32,257
Firebird (wb 108.0)				
S87	cpe	3,306	5,948	29,811
T87	Esprit cpe	3,360	6,311	17,277
V87	Formula cpe V8	3,410	7,256	9,356
W87	Trans Am cpe V8	3,429	7,480	50,896
LeMans (wb 108.0)				
D19	sdn 4d	3,080	5,758	20,485
D27	cpe	3,064	5,652	9,110
D35	Safari wgn 4d	3,296	6,257	12,912
F19	Grand LeMans sdn 4d	3,129	6,120	18,561
F27	Grand LeMans cpe	3,090	5,947	6,477
F35	Grand LeMans Safari wgn 4d	3,328	6,682	14,832
G27	Grand Am cpe V8	3,299	7,504	1,647
Catalina (wb 116.0)				
L35	Safari wgn 4d 2S V8	3,929	7,362	2,931
L35	Safari wgn 4d 3S V8	3,961	7,561	
L37	cpe	3,448	6,703	3,319
L69	sdn 4d	3,474	6,761	10,408
Bonneville (wb 116.0)				
N35	Safari wgn 4d 2S V8	3,939	7,958	5,309
N35	Safari wgn 4d 3S V8	3,981	8,157	
N37	cpe	3,486	7,034	16,771
R37	Brougham cpe	3,525	7,968	12,374
N69	sdn 4d	3,532	7,167	26,112
R69	Brougham sdn 4d	3,610	8,160	21,249
Grand Prix (wb 108.1)				
J37	cpe V6/V8	3,201	6,621	72,659
K37	LJ cpe V6/V8	3,342	7,000	34,968
H37	SJ cpe V8	3,291	7,597	7,087

| 1980 Engines | bore×stroke | bhp | availability |

	bore×stroke	bhp	availability
V6, 229.0	3.74×3.48	115	S-LeMans
V6, 231.0	3.80×3.40	110/115	S-Fbd,Cat,Bon,GP; O-Sbd
V8, 265.0	3.75×3.00	120	S-LeM,Fbd S/T, Cat, Bonn exc wgn, GP exc SJ
V8, 301.0	4.00×3.00	140	S-GA,Fbd V/W,Cat,Bonn wgn, GP SJ; O-LeM, Fbd, Cat,Bonn, GP
V8, 301.0 turbo	4.00×3.00	210	O-Fbd V/W
V8, 305.0	3.70×3.48	150	O-LeM, Fbd, GP
V8, 350.0 dsl	3.88×3.75	105	O-Cat,Bonn wgn/B'ham
V8, 350.0	4.06×3.39	155/160	O-Catalina, Bonn

1981

T1000 (wb 94.3; 5d-97.3)		Wght	Price	Prod
M08	htchbk sdn 3d	2,058	5,358	26,415
M68	htchbk sdn 5d	2,122	5,504	43,779
Phoenix (wb 104.9)				
Y37	cpe	2,477	6,307	31,829
Y68	htchbk sdn 5d	2,524	6,498	62,693
Z37	LJ cpe	2,519	6,778	11,975
Z68	LJ htchbk sdn 5d	2,579	6,969	21,372
Firebird (wb 108.2)				
S87	cpe	3,312	6,901	20,541
T87	Esprit cpe	—	7,645	10,938
V87	Formula cpe	—	7,854	5,927
W87	Trans Am cpe V8	—	8,322	33,493
X87	Trans Am turbo SE cpe	—	12,257	
LeMans (wb 108.1)				
D27	cpe	3,093	6,689	2,578
D69	sdn 4d	3,110	6,797	22,186
D69/Y83	LJ sdn 4d	—	7,100	
D35	Safari wgn 4d	3,313	7,316	13,358
F27	Grand LeMans cpe	3,121	6,976	1,819
F69	Grand LeMans sdn 4d	3,166	7,153	25,241
F35	Grand LeMans Safari wgn 4d	3,352	7,726	16,683

Catalina (wb 116.0)		Wght	Price	Prod
L35	Safari wgn 4d 2S V8	3,924	8,666	2,912
L37	cpe	3,480	7,367	1,074
L69	sdn 4d	3,488	7,471	6,456
Bonneville (wb 116.0)				
N35	Safari wgn 4d 2S V8	3,949	9,205	6,855
N37	cpe	3,502	7,649	14,940
R37	Brougham cpe	3,502	8,580	14,317
N69	sdn 4d	3,520	7,776	32,056
R69	Brougham sdn 4d	3,520	8,768	23,395
Grand Prix (wb 108.1)				
J37	cpe	3,226	7,424	74,786
K37	LJ cpe	3,255	7,803	46,842
P37	Brougham cpe	3,281	8,936	26,083

1981 Engines	bore×stroke	bhp	availability
L4, 97.6	3.23×2.98	70	S-T1000
L4, 151.0	4.00×3.00	84	S-Phoenix
V6, 173.0	3.50×3.00	110	O-Phoenix
V6, 231.0	3.80×3.40	110	S-Fbd, LeM, Cat, Bon, GP
V8, 265.0	3.75×3.00	120	S-Fbd Formula; O-Fbd, LeM, Cat, Bon, GP
V8, 301.0	4.00×3.00	135/150	O-Fbd, Cat, Bon, LeM wgn
V8T, 301.0	4.00×3.00	200	O-Fbd Formula, Trans Am
V8, 305.0	3.74×3.48	145	O-Fbd Formula, Trans Am
V8, 307.0	3.80×3.39	145	S-Bon/Cat wgn; O-Cat, Bon
V8D, 350.0	4.06×3.39	105	O-Cat, Bon, Safari, GP

1982

T1000 (wb 94.3; 5d-97.3)		Wght	Price	Prod
L08	htchbk sdn 3d	2,034	5,782	21,053
L68	htchbk sdn 5d	2,098	5,945	23,416
J2000 (wb 101.2)				
B27	cpe	2,295	6,999	15,865
B77	htchbk cpe 3d	2,353	7,275	21,219
B69	sdn 4d	2,347	7,203	29,920

		Wght	Price	Prod
B35	wgn 5d	2,418	7,448	16,014
E27	S cpe	2,295	6,734	2,722
E69	S sdn 4d	2,353	6,902	2,760
E35	S wgn 5d	2,355	7,208	1,245
C27	LE cpe	2,302	7,372	6,313
C69	LE sdn 4d	2,353	7,548	14,268
D77	SE htchbk cpe 3d	2,362	7,654	8,533
Firebird (wb 101.0)				
S87	cpe L4/V6	—	7,996	41,683
S87	cpe V8	—	8,291	
X87	S/E cpe V6/V8	—	9,624	21,719
W87	Trans Am cpe V8	—	9,658	52,960
Phoenix (wb 104.9)				
Y37	cpe	2,395	6,964	12,282
Y68	htchbk sdn 5d	2,503	7,172	24,026
Z37	LJ cpe	2,494	7,449	4,436
Z68	LJ htchbk sdn 5d	2,527	7,658	7,161
T37	SJ cpe V6	2,562	8,723	994
T68	SJ htchbk sdn 5d V6	2,612	8,884	268
6000 (wb 104.9)				
F27	cpe	2,531	8,729	6,505
F19	sdn 4d	2,676	8,890	17,751
G27	LE cpe	2,636	9,097	7,025
G19	LE sdn 4d	2,682	9,258	26,253
Bonneville G (wb 108.1)				
N69	sdn 4d	3,203	8,527	44,378
R69	Brougham sdn 4d	3,213	8,985	20,035
N35	wgn 4d	3,380	8,694	16,100
Grand Prix (wb 108.1)				
J37	cpe	3,226	8,333	37,672
K37	LJ cpe	3,248	8,788	29,726
P37	Brougham cpe	3,264	9,209	12,969

1982 Engines	bore × stroke	bhp	availability
L4, 97.6	3.23 × 2.98	70	S-T1000
L4, 112.0	3.50 × 2.91	88	S-J2000
L4, 151.0	4.00 × 3.00	90	S-Phoenix, Fbd, 6000
V6, 173.0	3.50 × 3.00	105	S-Fbd S/E; O-Firebird
V6, 173.0	3.50 × 3.00	112	O-Phoenix, 6000
V6, 173.0	3.50 × 3.00	135	O-Phoenix SJ
V6, 231.0	3.80 × 3.40	110	S-Bonneville, Grand Prix
V6, 252.0	3.96 × 3.40	125	O-Bonneville, Grand Prix
V6D, 262.0	4.06 × 3.39	85	O-6000, Bonneville
V8, 305.0	3.74 × 3.48	145	S-Fbd Trans Am; O-Firebird
V8, 305.0	3.74 × 3.48	165	O-Fbd Trans Am
V8D, 350.0	4.06 × 3.39	105	O-Bonneville, Grand Prix

1983

1000 (wb 94.3; 5d-97.3)		Wght	Price	Prod
L08	htchbk sdn 3d	2,081	5,582	13,171
L68	htchbk sdn 5d	2,130	5,785	12,806
2000 (wb 101.2)				
B27	cpe	2,353	6,499	22,063
B77	htchbk cpe 3d	2,413	6,809	7,331
B69	sdn 4d	2,412	6,621	24,833
B35	wgn 5d	2,487	6,926	10,214
C27	LE cpe	2,385	7,020	2,690
C67	LE conv cpe	—	—	626
C69	LE sdn 4d	2,436	7,194	6,957
C35	LE wgn 5d	2,517	7,497	1,780
D77	SE htchbk cpe 3d	2,470	8,393	1,835
Firebird (wb 101.0)				
S87	cpe L4/V6	2,937	8,399	32,020
S87	cpe V8	3,117	8,774	
X87	S/E cpe V6/V8	3,055	10,322	10,934
W87	Trans Am cpe V8	3,107	10,396	31,930
Phoenix (wb 104.9)				
Y37	cpe	2,512	6,942	7,205
Y68	htchbk sdn 5d	2,569	7,087	13,377
Z37	LJ cpe	2,553	7,489	2,251
Z68	LJ htchbk sdn 5d	2,601	7,698	3,635
T37	SJ cpe V6	2,581	8,861	853

1983 Phoenix SJ coupe

		Wght	Price	Prod
T68	SJ htchbk sdn 5d V6	2,642	8,948	172
6000 (wb 104.9)				
F27	cpe	2,719	8,399	3,524
F19	sdn 4d	2,757	8,569	20,267
G27	LE cpe	2,732	8,837	4,278
G19	LE sdn 4d	2,771	8,984	33,676
H19	STE sdn 4d V6	2,823	13,572	6,719
Bonneville (wb 108.1)				
N69	sdn 4d	3,252	8,899	47,003
R69	Brougham sdn 4d	3,248	9,399	19,335
N35	wgn 4d	3,313	9,112	17,551
Grand Prix (wb 108.1)				
J37	cpe	3,261	8,698	41,511
K37	LJ cpe	—	9,166	33,785
P37	Brougham cpe	—	9,781	10,502
Parisienne (wb 115.9)				
L69	sdn 4d	3,409	9,609	9,279
T69	Brougham sdn 4d	—	9,779	5,139
L35	wgn 4d V8	3,963	9,927	3,027

1983 Engines	bore × stroke	bhp	availability
L4, 97.6	3.23 × 2.98	65	S-1000
L4, 109.0	3.34 × 3.13	84	S-2000
L4D, 111.0	3.31 × 3.23	51	O-T1000 3d
L4, 121.0	3.50 × 3.15	88	O-2000
L4, 151.0	4.00 × 3.00	90	S-Phoenix, Fbd, 6000
V6, 173.0	3.50 × 3.00	107/112	O-Phoenix, Fbd, 6000
V6, 173.0	3.50 × 3.00	125-135	S-Phnx SJ, Fbd S/E, 6000 STE
V6, 231.0	3.80 × 3.40	110	S-Bon, GP, Parisienne
V6D, 262.0	4.06 × 3.39	85	O-6000
V8, 305.0	3.74 × 3.48	150	S-Trans Am; O-Fbd, Bon, GP
V8, 305.0	3.74 × 3.48	175	O-Firebird Trans Am
V8D, 350.0	4.06 × 3.39	105	O-Bon, GP, Parisienne

1984

Fiero (wb 94.4)		Wght	Price	Prod
E37	cpe	2,437	7,999	7,099
M37	spt cpe	2,465	8,499	62,070
F37	SE cpe	2,465	9,599	67,671
1000 (wb 94.3; 5d-97.3)				
L08	htchbk sdn 3d	2,078	5,621	19,628
L68	htchbk sdn 5d	2,138	5,824	17,118

2000 Sunbird (wb 101.2)		Wght	Price	Prod
B27	cpe	2,347	6,675	53,070
B77	htchbk cpe 3d	2,424	6,995	12,245
B69	sdn 4d	2,406	6,799	59,312
B35	wgn 5d	2,483	7,115	15,143
C27	LE cpe	2,384	7,333	5,189
C67	LE conv cpe	2,514	11,749	5,458
C69	LE sdn 4d	2,436	7,499	11,183
C35	LE wgn 5d	2,504	7,819	2,011
D27	SE cpe	2,469	9,019	2,141
D77	SE htchbk cpe 3d	2,477	9,489	2,165
D69	SE sdn 4d	2,528	9,185	1,373
Firebird (wb 101.0)				
S87	cpe L4/V6	2,955	8,349	62,621
S87	cpe V8	3,157	9,024	
X87	S/E cpe V6/V8	3,072	10,649	10,309
W87	Trans Am cpe V8	3,189	10,699	55,374
Phoenix (wb 104.9)				
Y37	cpe	2,518	7,090	7,461
Y68	htchbk sdn 5d	2,587	7,165	11,545
Z37	LE cpe	2,578	7,683	1,357
Z68	LE htchbk sdn 5d	2,615	7,816	1,783
T37	SE cpe V6	2,681	9,071	701
6000 (wb 104.9)				
F27	cpe	2,707	8,699	4,171
F19	sdn 4d	2,748	8,873	35,202
G27	LE cpe	2,731	9,142	4,731
G19	LE sdn 4d	2,772	9,292	41,218
F35	wgn 5d	2,909	9,221	8,423
G35	LE wgn 5d	2,924	9,612	9,211
H19	STE sdn 4d V6	2,990	14,437	19,236
Bonneville (wb 108.1)				
N69	sdn 4d	3,213	9,131	40,908
R69	Brougham sdn 4d	3,247	9,835	15,030
S69	LE sdn 4d	3,221	9,358	17,451
Grand Prix (wb 108.1)				
J37	cpe	3,258	9,145	36,893
K37	LE cpe	3,278	9,624	31,037
P37	Brougham cpe	3,319	10,299	9,514
Parisienne (wb 115.9)				
L69	sdn 4d	3,535	9,881	18,713
T69	Brougham sdn 4d	3,575	10,281	25,212
L35	wgn 4d V8	4,080	10,394	16,599

1984 Engines	bore × stroke	bhp	availability
L4, 97.6	3.23 × 2.98	65	S-1000

1984 Parisienne four-door sedan

1984 Fiero coupe

	bore×stroke	bhp	availability
L4, 109.0	3.34×3.13	84	S-2000
L4T, 109.0	3.34×3.13	150	O-2000
L4, 121.0	3.50×3.15	88	O-2000
L4, 151.0	4.00×3.00	92	S-Fiero, Phoenix, Fbd, 6000
V6, 173.0	3.50×3.00	107/112	O-Phoenix, Fbd, 6000
V6, 173.0	3.50×3.00	125-130	S-Phnx SE, Firebird S/E, 6000 STE; O-Phoenix
V6, 231.0	3.80×3.40	110	S-Bon, GP, Parisienne
V6D, 262.0	4.06×3.39	85	O-6000
V8, 305.0	3.74×3.48	150	S-Trans Am, Paris wgn; O-Fbd, Bon, GP, Parisienne
V8, 305.0	3.74×3.48	190	O-Firebird Trans Am
V8D, 350.0	4.06×3.39	105	O-Bon, GP, Parisienne

1986 6000 STE four-door sedan

1985

Fiero (wb 93.4)		Wght	Price	Prod
E37	cpe	2,454	8,495	5,280
M37	spt cpe	2,500	8,995	23,823
F37	SE cpe	2,525	9,995	24,734
G37	GT cpe	—	11,795	22,534
1000 (wb 94.3; 5d-97.3)				
L08	htchbk sdn 3d	2,083	5,445	8,647
L68	htchbk sdn 5d	2,142	5,695	8,216
Sunbird (wb 101.2)				
B27	cpe	2,316	6,875	39,721
B77	htchbk cpe 3d	2,392	7,215	5,235
B69	sdn 4d	2,372	6,995	44,553
B35	wgn 5d	2,446	7,335	7,371
C27	LE cpe	2,349	7,555	3,424
C67	LE conv cpe	2,534	12,035	2,114
C69	LE sdn 4d	2,435	7,725	6,287
C35	LE wgn 5d	2,468	8,055	1,036
D27	SE cpe L4T	2,422	9,295	965
D77	SE htchbk cpe 3d L4T	2,500	9,765	535
D69	SE sdn 4d L4T	2,479	9,455	658
Firebird (wb 101.0)				
S87	cpe L4/V6	2,933	8,763	46,644
S87	cpe V8	3,135	9,357	
X87	SE cpe V6/V8	3,124	11,063	5,208
W87	Trans Am cpe V8	3,213	11,113	44,028
Grand Am (wb 103.4)				
E27 cpe	2,575	7,995	40,275	
V27	LE cpe	2,595	8,485	42,269
6000 (wb 104.9)				
F27	cpe	2,766	8,899	4,493
F19	sdn 4d	2,809	9,079	54,424
G27	LE cpe	2,777	9,385	3,777
G19	LE sdn 4d	2,821	9,539	54,284
F35	wgn 5d	2,931	9,435	8,491
G35	LE wgn 5d	2,937	9,869	8,025
H19	STE sdn 4d V6	3,065	14,829	22,728
Bonneville (wb 108.1)				
N69	sdn 4d	3,267	9,549	34,466
R69	Brougham sdn 4d	3,308	10,280	8,425
S69	LE sdn 4d	3,281	9,789	10,503
Grand Prix (wb 108.1)				
J37	cpe	3,276	9,569	30,365
K37	LE cpe	3,296	10,049	21,195
P37	Brougham cpe	3,314	10,749	8,223
Parisienne (wb 116.0)				
L69	sdn 4d	3,573	10,395	25,638
T69	Brougham sdn 4d	3,586	11,125	38,831
L35	wgn 4d V8	4,095	10,945	17,638

1985 Engines	bore×stroke	bhp	availability
L4, 97.6	3.23×2.98	65	S-1000
L4, 109.0	3.34×3.13	82	S-Sunbird
L4T, 109.0	3.34×3.13	150	S-Sunbird SE
L4, 121.0	3.50×3.15	88	O-Sunbird
L4, 151.0	4.00×3.00	88/92	S-Fiero, G Am, Fbd, 6000
V6, 173.0	3.50×3.00	112	O-6000
V6, 173.0	3.50×3.00	125-135	S-Firebird S/E, 6000 STE; O-Fiero, Firebird, 6000
V6, 181.0	3.80×2.70	125	O-Grand Am
V6, 231.0	3.80×3.40	110	S-Bonneville, Grand Prix
V6, 262.0	4.00×3.48	130	S-Parisienne
V6D, 262.0	4.06×3.39	85	O-6000
V8, 305.0	3.74×3.48	165	S-Trans Am, Paris wgn; O-Fbd, Bon, GP, Parisienne
V8, 305.0	3.74×3.48	190/205	O-Firebird Trans Am
V8D, 350.0	4.06×3.39	105	O-Parisienne

1986

Fiero (wb 93.2)		Wght	Price	Prod
E37	cpe L4	2,490	8,949	9,143
M37	spt cpe L4	2,504	9,449	24,866
F37	SE cpe L4/V6	2,531	10,595	32,305
G97	GT cpe V6	2,696	12,875	17,660
1000 (wb 94.3; 5d-97.3)				
L08	htchbk sdn 3d	2,076	5,749	12,266
L68	htchbk sdn 5d	2,135	5,969	9,423
Sunbird (wb 101.2)				
B69	sdn 4d	2,383	7,495	60,080
B35	wgn 5d	2,456	7,879	7,445
D27	SE cpe	2,365	7,469	37,526
D77	SE htchbk cpe 3d	2,405	7,829	3,822
D67	SE conv cpe	2,549	12,779	1,598
U27	GT cpe	2,488	9,459	18,118
U67	GT conv cpe	2,645	14,399	1,268
U77	GT htchbk cpe 3d	2,564	9,819	2,442
U69	GT sdn 4d	2,540	9,499	2,802
Firebird (wb 101.0)				
S87	cpe L4/V6	2,909	9,279	59,334
S87	cpe V8	2,955	10,029	
X87	SE cpe V6/V8	2,991	11,995	2,259
W87	Trans Am cpe V8	3,227	12,395	48,870
Grand Am (wb 103.4)				
E27	cpe	2,529	8,549	69,545
E69	sdn 4d	2,605	8,749	49,166
V27	LE cpe	2,565	9,079	48,530
V69	LE sdn 4d	2,631	9,279	31,790

1986 6000 S/E four-door wagon

		Wght	Price	Prod
W27	SE cpe V6	2,686	11,499	15,506
W69	SE sdn 4d V6	2,756	11,749	8,957
6000 (wb 104.9)				
F27	cpe	2,781	9,549	4,739
F19	sdn 4d	2,817	9,729	81,531
G27	LE cpe	2,799	10,049	4,803
G19	LE sdn 4d	2,836	10,195	67,697
E19	SE sdn 4d V6	2,914	11,179	7,348
F35	wgn 5d	2,954	10,095	10,094
G35	LE wgn 5d	2,972	10,579	7,556
E35	SE wgn 5d V6	3,067	11,825	1,308
H19	STE sdn 4d V6	3,122	15,949	26,299
Bonneville (wb 108.1)				
N69	sdn 4d	3,276	10,249	27,801
R69	Brougham sdn 4d	3,305	11,079	5,941
S69	LE sdn 4d	3,285	10,529	7,179
Grand Prix (wb 108.1)				
J37	cpe	3,283	10,259	21,668
J37	2+2 cpe V8	3,530	18,214	200
K37	LE cpe	3,305	10,795	13,918
P37	Brougham cpe	3,328	11,579	4,798
Parisienne (wb 116.0)				
L69	sdn 4d	3,639	11,169	27,078
T69	Brougham sdn 4d	3,667	11,949	43,540
L35	wgn 4d V8	4,102	11,779	14,464

1986 Engines	bore × stroke	bhp	availability
L4, 97.6	3.23 × 2.98	65	S-1000
L4, 109.0	3.34 × 3.13	84	S-Sunbird
L4T, 109.0	3.34 × 3.13	150	S-Sunbird GT
L4, 151.0	4.00 × 3.00	88/92	S-Fiero, G Am, Fbd, 6000
V6, 173.0	3.50 × 3.00	112	O-6000
V6, 173.0	3.50 × 3.00	130-140	S-Firebird SE, 6000 STE; O-Fiero, Firebird
V6, 181.0	3.80 × 2.70	125	S-Grand Am SE; O-Grand Am
V6, 231.0	3.80 × 3.40	110	S-Bonneville, Grand Prix
V6, 262.0	4.00 × 3.48	130	S-Parisienne
V8, 305.0	3.74 × 3.48	150-165	S-Trans Am, Paris wgn; O-Fbd, Bon, GP, Parisienne
V8, 305.0	3.74 × 3.48	190/205	O-Firebird Trans Am

1987

Fiero (wb 93.4)		Wght	Price	Prod
E37	cpe L4	2,542	8,299	23,603
M37	spt cpe L4	2,546	9,989	3,135
F37	SE cpe L4/V6	2,567	11,239	3,875
G97	GT cpe V6	2,708	13,489	15,968
1000 (wb 94.3; 5d-97.3)				
L08	htchbk sdn 3d	2,114	5,959	3,246
L68	htchbk sdn 5d	2,173	6,099	2,382
Sunbird (wb 101.2)				
B69	sdn 4d	2,366	7,999	41,248
B35	wgn 5d	2,427	8,529	4,637
D27	SE cpe	2,339	7,979	41,825
D77	SE htchbk cpe 3d	2,385	8,499	1,069
D67	SE conv cpe	2,511	13,799	2,470
U27	GT cpe	2,412	10,299	12,060
U67	GT conv cpe	2,551	15,569	1,505
U77	GT htchbk cpe 3d	2,427	10,699	415
U69	GT sdn 4d	2,427	10,349	1,540
Firebird (wb 101.0)				
S87	cpe V6/V8	3,186	10,359	42,558
S87/W66	Formula cpe V8	3,350	11,829	13,164
W87	Trans Am cpe V8	3,274	13,259	32,890
W87/Y84	Trans Am GTA cpe V8	3,435	14,104	—

1987 Grand Am SE coupe

Grand Am (wb 103.4)		Wght	Price	Prod
E27	cpe	2,525	9,299	90,146
E69	sdn 4d	2,598	9,499	52,177
V27	LE cpe	2,561	9,999	47,414
V69	LE sdn 4d	2,623	10,199	21,196
W27	SE cpe	2,641	12,659	23,142
W69	SE sdn 4d	2,719	12,899	10,653
6000 (wb 104.9)				
F27	cpe	2,764	10,499	3,161
F19	sdn 4d	2,797	10,499	72,645
G19	LE sdn 4d	2,731	11,099	33,939
E19	S/E sdn 4d V6	2,986	12,089	6,649
F35	wgn 5d	2,943	10,095	7,740
G35	LE wgn 5d	2,867	11,499	3,797
E35	S/E wgn 5d V6	3,162	13,049	1,756
H19	STE sdn 4d V6	3,101	18,099	8,802
Grand Prix (wb 108.1)				
J37	cpe	3,286	11,069	8,599
K37	LE cpe	3,306	11,799	6,226
P37	Brougham cpe	3,308	12,519	1,717
Bonneville (wb 110.8)				
X69	sdn 4d	3,316	13,399	53,912
Z69	LE sdn 4d	3,355	14,866	69,904
Safari (wb 116.0)				
L35	Brougham wgn 4d V8	4,109	13,959	13,154

1987 Engines	bore×stroke	bhp	availability
L4, 97.6	3.23×2.98	65	S-1000
L4, 121.0	3.39×3.39	96	S-Sunbird
L4T, 121.0	3.39×3.39	165	O-Sunbird SE/GT, G Am SE
L4, 151.0	4.00×3.00	98	S-Fiero, Grand Am, 6000
V6, 173.0	3.50×3.00	125-135	S-Fiero GT, 6000 S/E, 6000 STE; O-Fiero, Firebird, 6000
V6, 181.0	3.80×2.70	125	S-Grand Am SE; O-Grand Am
V6, 231.0	3.80×3.40	110	S-Grand Prix
V6, 231.0	3.80×3.40	150	S-Bonneville
V6, 262.0	4.00×3.48	140	O-Grand Prix
V8, 305.0	3.74×3.48	140	S-Safari wgn
V8, 305.0	3.74×3.48	150	S-Grand Prix 2+2; OP
V8, 305.0	3.74×3.48	155	O-Firebird
V8, 305.0	3.74×3.48	165/205	O-Firebird Trans Am
V8, 350.0	4.00×3.48	210	S-Fbd GTA; O-Formula, T/A

1988

Fiero (wb 93.4)		Wght	Price	Prod
E37	cpe L4	2,597	8,999	⌉

1989 Bonneville SSE four-door sedan

1989 Firebird Formula coupe V8

		Wght	Price	Prod
E37/W66	Formula cpe V6	—	10,999	26,402
G97	GT cpe V6	2,783	13,999	
Sunbird (wb 101.2)				
B69	sdn 4d	2,366	8,499	93,694
D37	SE cpe	2,339	8,599	
D69	SE sdn 4d	2,427	8,799	
D35	SE wgn 5d	2,427	9,399	
U37	GT cpe L4T	2,412	10,899	
U67	GT conv cpe L4T	2,551	16,199	
Firebird (wb 101.0)				
S87	cpe V6/V8	3,102	10,999	62,467
S87/W66	Formula cpe V8	—	11,999	
W87	Trans Am cpe V8	3,355	13,999	
W87/Y84	Trans Am GTA cpe V8	—	19,299	
Grand Am (wb 103.4)				
E27	cpe	2,493	9,869	
E69	sdn 4d	2,568	10,069	

1989 Grand Am SE coupe

		Wght	Price	Prod
Y27	LE cpe	2,519	10,569	235,371
Y69	LE sdn 4d	2,591	10,769	
W27	SE cpe L4T	2,713	12,869	
W69	SE sdn 4d L4T	2,781	13,099	
6000 (wb 104.9)				
F19	sdn 4d	2,828	11,999	61,446
G19	LE sdn 4d	2,846	11,839	
E19	S/E sdn 4d V6	2,888	12,739	
F35	wgn 5d	2,964	11,639	
G35	LE wgn 5d	2,982	12,299	
E35	S/E wgn 5d V6	3,041	13,639	
H19	STE sdn 4d V6	3,109	18,699	
Grand Prix (wb 107.6)				
J37	cpe	3,038	12,539	86,357
K37	LE cpe	3,056	13,239	
P37	SE cpe	3,113	15,249	
Bonneville (wb 110.8)				
X69	LE sdn 4d	3,275	14,099	108,580
Z69	SE sdn 4d	3,341	16,299	
Y69	SSE sdn 4d	3,481	21,879	
Safari (wb 116.0)				
L35	wgn 4d V8	4,109	14,519	6,397

1988 Engines	bore × stroke	bhp	availability
L4, 121.0	3.39 × 3.39	96	S-Sunbird
L4T, 121.0	3.39 × 3.39	165	S-Sunbird GT, G Am SE
L4, 138.0	3.62 × 3.35	150	O-Grand Am (Quad 4)
L4, 151.0	4.00 × 3.00	98	S-Fiero, Grand Am, 6000
V6, 173.0	3.50 × 3.00	125/130	S-6000 S/E, STE, GP; O-6000
V6, 173.0	3.50 × 3.00	135	S-Fiero Formula/GT, Fbd
V6, 191.0	3.50 × 3.31	135	S-6000 STE AWD
V6, 231.0	3.80 × 3.40	150	S-Bonneville
V6, 231.0	3.00 × 3.40	165	S-Bonneville SE/SSE
V8, 305.0	3.74 × 3.48	140	S-Safari wgn
V8, 305.0	3.74 × 3.48	170	S-Trans Am/Formula; O-Fbd

1959 Ambassador Custom four-door sedan

Six (wb 108.0)		Wght	Price	Prod
5915	DeLuxe sdn 4d	2,934	2,098	—
5915-1	Super sdn 4d	2,951	2,268	—
5915-2	Custom sdn 4d	2,956	2,383	—
5918	DeLuxe Crss Cntry wgn 4d	3,047	2,427	—
5918-1	Super Crss Cntry wgn 4d	3,082	2,562	—
5918-2	Custom Crss Cntry wgn 4d	3,097	2,677	—
5919-1	Super Ctry Club htp sdn	2,961	2,343	—
Rebel V8 (wb 108.0)				
5925	DeLuxe sdn 4d	3,283	2,228	—
5925-1	Super sdn 4d	3,287	2,398	—
5925-2	Custom sdn 4d	3,295	2,513	—
5928-1	Super Crss Cntry wgn 4d	3,398	2,692	—
5928-2	Custom Crss Cntry wgn 4d	3,407	2,807	—
5929-2	Custom Ctry Club htp sdn	3,338	2,588	—
Ambassador (wb 117.0)				
5983-2	Custom htp wgn 4d	3,591	3,116	—
5985-1	Super sdn 4d	3,428	2,587	—
5985-2	Custom sdn 4d	3,437	2,732	—
5988-1	Super Crss Cntry wgn 4d	3,546	2,881	—
5988-2	Custom Crss Cntry wgn 4d	3,562	3,026	—
5989-2	Custom Ctry Club htp sdn	3,483	2,822	—

*Total model year registrations: 363,372.

1959 Engines	bore×stroke	bhp	availability
L6, 195.6	3.13×4.25	90	S-American
L6, 195.6	3.13×4.25	127	S-Six
L6, 195.6	3.13×4.25	138	O-Six
V8, 250.0	3.50×3.25	215	S-Rebel
V8, 327.0	4.00×3.25	270	S-Ambassador

		Wght	Price	Prod
6004-2	Custom wgn 2d	2,606	2,235	—
6005	DeLuxe sdn 4d	2,474	1,844	—
6005-1	Super sdn 4d	2,490	1,929	—
6005-2	Custom sdn 4d	2,551	2,059	—
6006	DeLuxe sdn 2d	2,451	1,795	—
6006-1	Super sdn 2d	2,462	1,880	—
6006-2	Custom sdn 2d	2,523	2,010	—
Six (wb 108.0)				
6015	DeLuxe sdn 4d	2,912	2,098	—
6015-1	Super sdn 4d	2,930	2,268	—
6015-2	Custom sdn 4d	2,929	2,383	—
6018	DeLuxe wgn 4d	3,051	2,427	—
6018-1	Super wgn 4d, 6P	3,054	2,562	—
6018-2	Custom wgn 4d, 6P	3,057	2,677	—
6018-3	Super wgn 4d, 8P	3,117	2,687	—
6018-4	Custom wgn 4d, 8P	3,137	2,802	—
6019-2	Custom htp sdn	2,981	2,458	—

Rebel V8 (wb 108.0)		Wght	Price	Prod
6025	DeLuxe sdn 4d	3,252	2,217	—
6025-1	Super sdn 4d	3,270	2,387	—
6025-2	Custom sdn 4d	3,278	2,502	—
6028-1	Super wgn 4d, 6P	3,391	2,681	—
6028-2	Custom wgn 4d, 6P	3,395	2,796	—
6028-3	Super wgn 4d, 8P	3,446	2,806	—
6028-4	Custom wgn 4d, 8P	3,447	2,921	—
6029-2	Custom htp sdn	3,319	2,577	—
Ambassador (wb 117.0)				
6083-2	Custom htp wgn 4d	3,583	3,116	—
6085	DeLuxe sdn 4d	3,384	2,395	—
6085-1	Super sdn 4d	3,395	2,587	—
6085-2	Custom sdn 4d	3,408	2,732	—
6088-1	Super wgn 4d, 6P	3,521	2,881	—
6088-2	Custom wgn 4d, 6P	3,538	3,026	—
6088-3	Super wgn 4d, 8P	3,581	3,006	—
6088-4	Custom wgn 4d, 8P	3,592	3,151	—
6089-2	Custom htp sdn	3,465	2,822	—

*Total model year registrations: 422,273.

1960 Engines	bore×stroke	bhp	availability
L6, 195.6	3.13×4.25	90	S-American
L6, 195.6	3.13×4.25	127	S-Six
L6, 195.6	3.13×4.25	138	O-Six
V8, 250.0	3.50×3.25	200	S-Rebel
V8, 250.0	3.50×3.25	215	O-Rebel
V8, 327.0	4.00×3.25	250	S-Ambassador
V8, 327.0	4.00×3.25	270	O-Ambassador

1961*

American (wb 100.00)		Wght	Price	Prod
6102	DeLuxe bus sdn 2d	2,454	1,831	—
6104	DeLuxe wgn 2d	2,549	2,080	—
6104-1	Super wgn 2d	2,556	2,165	—
6104-2	Custom wgn 2d	2,617	2,295	—
6105	DeLuxe sdn 4d	2,523	1,894	—
6105-1	Super sdn 4d	2,530	1,979	—
6105-2	Custom sdn 2d	2,557	2,060	—
6106	DeLuxe sdn 2d	2,490	1,845	—
6106-1	Super sdn 2d	2,499	1,930	—
6106-2	Custom sdn 2d	2,557	2,060	—
6107-2	Custom conv cpe	2,712	2,369	—
6108	DeLuxe wgn 4d	2,595	2,129	—
6108-1	Super wgn 4d	2,602	2,214	—
6108-2	Custom wgn 4d	2,660	2,344	—
Classic Six (wb 108.0)				
6115	DeLuxe sdn 4d	2,905	2,098	—
6115-1	Super sdn 4d	2,923	2,268	—
6115-2	Custom sdn 4d	2,863	2,413	—
6118	DeLuxe wgn 4d	3,037	2,437	—
6118-1	Super wgn 4d, 6P	3,046	2,572	—
6118-2	Custom wgn 4d, 6P	2,984	2,717	—
6118-3	Super wgn 4d, 8P	3,087	2,697	—
6118-4	Custom wgn 4d, 8P	3,023	2,842	—
Classic V8 (wb 108.0)				
6125	DeLuxe sdn 4d	3,237	2,227	—
6125-1	Super sdn 4d	3,255	2,397	—
6125-2	Custom sdn 4d	3,262	2,512	—
6128-1	Super wgn 4d, 6P	3,372	2,701	—
6128-2	Custom wgn 4d, 6P	3,378	2,816	—
6128-3	Super wgn 4d, 8P	3,408	2,826	—
6128-4	Custom wgn 4d, 8P	3,420	2,941	—
Ambassador (wb 117.0)				
6185	DeLuxe sdn 4d	3,343	2,395	—
6185-1	Super sdn 4d	3,361	2,537	—
6185-2	Custom sdn 4d	3,380	2,682	—
6188-1	Super wgn 4d, 6P	3,493	2,841	—
6188-2	Custom wgn 4d, 6P	3,495	2,986	—
6188-3	Super wgn 4d, 8P	3,560	2,966	—
6188-4	Custom wgn 4d, 8P	3,566	3,111	—

*Total model year registrations: 370,685.

1961 Engines	bore×stroke	bhp	availability
L6, 195.6	3.13×4.25	90	S-American exc Custom
L6, 195.6	3.13×4.25	125	S-American Custom
L6, 195.6	3.13×4.25	127	S-Classic Six
L6, 195.6	3.13×4.25	138	O-Classic Six
V8, 250.0	3.50×3.25	200	S-Classic V8

1963 Classic 770 four-door sedan

	bore×stroke	bhp	availability
V8, 250.0	3.50×3.25	215	O-Classic V8
V8, 327.0	4.00×3.25	250	S-Ambassador
V8, 327.0	4.00×3.25	270	O-Ambassador

1962*

American (wb 100.0)		Wght	Price	Prod
6202	DeLuxe bus sdn 2d	2,454	1,832	—
6204	DeLuxe wgn 2d	2,555	2,081	—
6204-2	Custom wgn 2d	2,565	2,141	—
6205	DeLuxe sdn 4d	2,500	1,895	—
6205-2	Custom sdn 4d	2,512	1,958	—
6205-5	400 sdn 4d	2,585	2,089	—
6206	DeLuxe sdn 2d	2,480	1,846	—
6206-2	Custom sdn 2d	2,492	1,909	—
6206-5	400 sdn 2d	2,558	2,040	—
6207-5	400 conv cpe	2,735	2,344	—
6208	DeLuxe wgn 4d	2,573	2,130	—
6208-2	Custom wgn 4d	2,600	2,190	—
6208-5	400 wgn 4d	2,692	2,320	—
Classic (wb 108.0)				
6215	DeLuxe sdn 4d	2,888	2,050	—
6215-2	Custom sdn 4d	2,898	2,200	—
6215-5	400 sdn 4d	2,853	2,349	—
6216	DeLuxe sdn 4d	2,866	2,000	—
6216-2	Custom sdn 2d	2,876	2,150	—
6216-5	400 sdn 2d	2,841	2,299	—
6218	DeLuxe wgn 4d, 6P	3,014	2,380	—
6218-2	Custom wgn 4d, 6P	3,024	2,492	—
6218-4	Custom wgn 4d, 8P	3,094	2,614	—
6218-5	400 wgn 4d	2,985	2,640	—
Ambassador (wb 108.0)				
6285	DeLuxe sdn 4d	3,249	2,336	—
6285-2	Custom sdn 4d	3,259	2,464	—
6285-5	400 sdn 4d	3,283	2,605	—
6286	DeLuxe sdn 2d	3,227	2,282	—
6286-2	Custom sdn 2d	3,237	2,410	—
6286-5	400 sdn 2d	3,261	2,551	—
6288	DeLuxe wgn 4d	3,375	2,648	—
6288-2	Custom wgn 4d	3,385	2,760	—
6288-5	400 wgn 4d, 6P	3,408	2,901	—
6288-6	400 wgn 4d, 8P	3,471	3,023	—

*Total model year registrations: 423,104.

1962 Engines	bore×stroke	bhp	availability
L6, 195.6	3.13×4.25	90	S-American
L6, 195.6	3.13×4.25	125	O-American
L6, 195.6	3.13×4.25	127	S-Classic
L6, 195.6	3.13×4.25	138	O-Classic
V8, 327.0	4.00×3.25	250	S-Ambassador
V8, 327.0	4.00×3.25	270	O-Ambassador

1963*

American (wb 100.0)		Wght	Price	Prod
6302	220 bus sdn 2d	2,446	1,832	—
6304	220 wgn 2d	2,528	2,081	—
6304-2	330 wgn 2d	2,539	2,141	—
6305	220 sdn 4d	2,485	1,895	—
6305-2	330 sdn 4d	2,500	1,958	—
6305-5	440 sdn 4d	2,575	2,089	—
6306	220 sdn 2d	2,472	1,846	—
6306-2	330 sdn 2d	2,484	1,909	—
6306-5	440 sdn 2d	2,556	2,040	—
6307-5	440 conv cpe	2,743	2,344	—
6308	220 wgn 4d	2,549	2,130	—
6308-2	330 wgn 4d	2,561	2,190	—
6308-5	440 wgn 4d	2,638	2,320	—
6309-5	440 htp cpe	2,550	2,136	—
6309-7	440H htp cpe 4P	2,567	2,281	—
Classic (wb 112.0)				
6315	550 sdn 4d	2,729	2,105	—
6315-2	660 sdn 4d	2,740	2,245	—
6315-5	770 sdn 4d	2,686	2,349	—

1963 American 440H hardtop coupe

1963 Ambassador 990 four-door sedan

		Wght	Price	Prod
6316	550 sdn 2d	2,720	2,055	—
6316-2	660 sdn 2d	2,725	2,195	—
6316-5	770 sdn 2d	2,663	2,299	—
6318	550 wgn 4d	2,893	2,435	—
6318-2	660 wgn 4d, 6P	2,890	2,537	—
6318-4	660 wgn 4d, 9P	2,885	2,609	—
6318-5	770 wgn 4d	2,828	2,640	—
Ambassador (wb 112.0)				
6385	800 sdn 4d	3,140	2,391	—
6385-2	880 sdn 4d	3,145	2,519	—
6385-5	990 sdn 4d	3,158	2,660	—
6386	800 sdn 2d	3,110	2,337	—
6386-2	880 sdn 2d	3,116	2,465	—
6386-5	990 sdn 2d	3,132	2,606	—
6388	800 wgn 4d	3,270	2,703	—
6388-2	880 wgn 4d	3,275	2,815	—
6388-5	990 wgn 4d, 6P	3,298	2,956	—
6388-6	990 wgn 4d, 9P	3,305	3,018	—

*Total model year registrations: 428,346.

1963 Engines	bore×stroke	bhp	availability
L6, 195.6	3.13×4.25	90	S-American 220/330; 0-440
L6, 195.6	3.13×4.25	125	S-American 440; 0-220/330
L6, 195.6	3.13×4.25	127	S-Classic
L6, 195.6	3.13×4.25	138	S-American 440H; O-Classic
V8, 287.0	3.75×3.25	198	O-Classic
V8, 327.0	4.00×3.25	250	S-Ambassador
V8, 327.0	4.00×3.25	270	O-Ambassador

1964*

American (wb 106.0)		Wght	Price	Prod
6405	220 sdn 4d	2,527	1,964	—
6405-2	330 sdn 4d	2,526	2,057	—
6405-5	440 sdn 4d	2,572	2,150	—
6406	220 sdn 2d	2,506	1,907	—
6406-2	330 sdn 2d	2,504	2,000	—
6407-5	440 conv cpe	2,752	2,346	—
6408	220 wgn 4d	2,661	2,240	—
6408-2	330 wgn 4d	2,675	2,324	—
6409-5	440 htp cpe	2,596	2,133	—
6409-7	440H htp cpe 5P	2,617	2,292	—
Classic (wb 112.0)				
6415	550 sdn 4d	2,755	2,116	—
6415-2	660 sdn 4d	2,758	2,256	—
6415-5	770 sdn 4d	2,763	2,360	—
6416	550 sdn 2d	2,732	2,066	—
6416-2	660 sdn 2d	2,736	2,206	—
6416-5	770 sdn 2d	2,740	2,310	—
6418	550 wgn 4d	2,915	2,446	—
6418-2	660 wgn 4d	2,916	2,548	—
6418-5	770 wgn 4d	2,921	2,651	—
6419-5	770 htp cpe	2,789	2,397	—
6419-7	Typhoon htp cpe	2,818	2,509	—
Ambassador 990 (wb 112.0)				
6485-5	sdn 4d	3,204	2,671	—
6488-5	wgn 4d	3,350	2,985	—

1964 American 440 four-door sedan

		Wght	Price	Prod
6489-5	htp cpe	3,213	2,736	—
6489-7	990H htp cpe	3,255	2,917	—

*Total model year registrations: 379,412.

1964 Engines	bore×stroke	bhp	availability
L6, 195.6	3.13×4.25	90	S-American 220/330; 0-440
L6, 195.6	3.13×4.25	125	S-American 440; 0-220/330
L6, 195.6	3.13×4.25	127	S-Classic
L6, 195.6	3.13×4.25	138	S-American 440H; O-Classic exc Typhoon
L6, 232.0	3.75×3.50	145	S-Typhoon; O-other Classic
V8, 287.0	3.75×3.25	198	O-Classic
V8, 327.0	4.00×3.25	250	S-Ambassador exc 990H
V8, 327.0	4.00×3.25	270	S-Amb 990H; O-Other Amb

1965 Ambassador 990H hardtop coupe

1965*

American (wb 106.0)		Wght	Price	Prod
6505	220 sdn 4d	2,518	2,036	—
6505-2	330 sdn 4d	2,522	2,129	—
6505-5	440 sdn 4d	2,580	2,222	—
6506	220 sdn 2d	2,492	1,979	—
6506-2	330 sdn 2d	2,490	2,072	—
6507-5	440 conv cpe	2,747	2,418	3,882
6508	220 wgn 4d	2,684	2,312	—
6508-2	330 wgn 4d	2,682	2,396	—
6509-5	440 htp cpe	2,596	2,205	—
6509-7	440H htp cpe	2,622	2,327	—
Classic (wb 112.0)				
6515	550 sdn 4d	2,987	2,192	—
6515-2	660 sdn 4d	—	—	—
Classic 550 (wb 112.0)				
6515	sdn 4d	2,987	2,192	—
6516	sdn 2d	2,963	2,142	—
6518	wgn 4d	3,134	2,522	—
Classic 660 (wb 112.0)				
6515-2	sdn 4d	3,016	2,332	—
6516-2	sdn 2d	2,991	2,282	—
6518-2	wgn 4d	3,155	2,624	—
Classic 770 (wb 112.0)				
6515-5	sdn 4d	3,029	2,436	—
6517-5	conv cpe	3,169	2,696	4,953
6518-5	wgn 4d	3,180	2,727	—
6519-5	htp cpe	3,063	2,436	—
6519-7	770H htp cpe	3,089	2,548	—

Marlin (wb 112.0)		Wght	Price	Prod
6559-7	htp cpe	3,234	3,100	10,327
Ambassador (wb 116.0)				
6585-2	880 sdn 4d	3,120	2,565	—
6585-5	990 sdn 4d	3,151	2,656	—
6586-2	880 sdn 2d	3,087	2,512	—
6587-5	990 conv cpe	3,265	2,955	3,499
6588-2	880 wgn 4d	3,247	2,879	—
6588-5	990 wgn 4d	3,268	2,970	—
6589-5	990 htp cpe	3,168	2,669	—
6589-7	990H htp cpe	3,198	2,837	—

*Total model year registrations: 324,669.

1965 Engines	bore×stroke	bhp	availability
L6, 195.6	3.13×4.25	90	S-American 220/330
L6, 195.6	3.13×4.25	125	S-American 440/440H
L6, 199.0	3.75×3.00	128	S-Classic 550
L6, 232.0	3.75×3.25	145	S-Classic 660/770/770H, Marlin; O-Amb, American
L6, 232.0	3.75×3.25	155	S-Amb; O-Classic
V8, 287.0	3.75×3.25	198	O-Classic, Marlin, Amb
V8, 327.0	4.00×3.25	270	O-Classic, Marlin, Amb

1966*

American 220 (wb 106.0)		Wght	Price	Prod
6605	sdn 4d	2,574	2,086	—
6606	sdn 2d	2,554	2,017	—

1964 American 440 convertible coupe

		Wght	Price	Prod
6608	wgn 4d	2,740	2,369	—
American 440 (wb 106.0)				
6605-5	sdn 4d	2,582	2,203	—
6606-5	sdn 2d	2,562	2,134	—
6607-5	conv cpe	2,782	2,486	—
6608-5	wgn 4d	2,745	2,477	—
6609-5	htp cpe	2,610	2,227	—
Rogue (wb 106.0)				
6609-7	htp cpe	2,630	2,370	—
Classic 550 (wb 112.0)				
6615	sdn 4d	2,885	2,238	—
6616	sdn 2d	2,860	2,189	—
6618	wgn 4d	3,070	2,542	—
Classic 770 (wb 112.0)				
6615-5	sdn 4d	2,905	2,337	—
6617-5	conv cpe	3,070	2,616	—
6618-5	wgn 4d	3,071	2,629	—
6619-5	htp cpe	2,935	2,363	—
Rebel (wb 112.0)				
6619-7	htp cpe	2,950	2,523	—

*Total model year registrations: 265,712.

1966 Engines	bore×stroke	bhp	availability
L6, 199.0	3.75×3.00	128	S-American, Rogue
L6, 232.0	3.75×3.50	145	S-Classic, Rebel
L6, 232.0	3.75×3.50	155	O-all
V8, 287.0	3.75×3.25	198	O-Classic, Rebel
V8, 327.0	4.00×3.25	250	O-Classic, Rebel
V8, 327.0	4.00×3.25	270	O-Classic, Rebel

1967*

American 220 (wb 106.0)		Wght	Price	Prod
6705	sdn 4d	2,621	2,142	—
6706	sdn 2d	2,591	2,073	—

1967 Rebel SST hardtop coupe

		Wght	Price	Prod
6708	wgn 4d	2,767	2,425	—
American 440 (wb 106.0)				
6705-5	sdn 4d	2,613	2,259	—
6706-5	sdn 2d	2,586	2,191	—
6708-5	wgn 4d	2,769	2,533	—
6709-5	htp cpe	2,643	2,283	—
American Rogue (wb 106.0)				
6707-7	conv cpe	2,821	2,611	—
6709-7	htp cpe	2,663	2,426	—
Rebel 550 (wb 114.0)				
6715	sdn 4d	3,055	2,319	—
6716	sdn 2d	3,089	2,294	—
6718	wgn 4d	3,287	2,623	—
Rebel 770 (wb 114.0)				
6715-5	sdn 4d	3,053	2,418	—
6718-5	wgn 4d	3,288	2,710	—
6719-5	htp cpe	3,092	2,443	—

1967 American 440 four-door sedan

1967 American 220 two-door sedan

1969 Rogue hardtop coupe

Rebel SST (wb 114.0)		Wght	Price	Prod
6717-7	conv cpe	3,180	2,872	—
6719-7	htp cpe	3,109	2,604	—

*Total model year registrations: 237,785.

1967 Engines	bore×stroke	bhp	availability
L6, 199.0	3.75×3.00	128	S-American
L6, 232.0	3.75×3.25	145	S-Rebel; O-American
L6, 232.0	3.75×3.25	155	O-American, Rebel
V8, 290.0	3.75×3.28	200	O-American, Rebel
V8, 290.0	3.75×3.28	225	O-American
V8, 343.0	4.08×3.28	235	O-Rebel
V8, 343.0	4.08×3.28	280	O-Rebel

1968*

American (wb 106.0)		Wght	Price	Prod
6805	sdn 4d	2,638	2,024	—
6806	sdn 2d	2,604	1,946	—
American 440 (wb 106.0)				
6805-5	sdn 4d	2,643	2,166	—
6808-5	wgn 4d	2,800	2,426	—
Rogue (wb 106.0)				
6809-7	htp cpe	2,678	2,244	—

*Total model year registrations: 259,346

1968 Engines	bore×stroke	bhp	availability
L6, 199.0	3.75×3.00	128	S-American
L6, 232.0	3.75×3.50	145	S-Rogue; O-American
V8, 290.0	3.75×3.28	225	O-American, Rogue

1969*

American (wb 106.0)		Wght	Price	Prod
6905	sdn 4d	2,638	2,076	—
6906	sdn 2d	2,604	1,998	—
American 440 (wb 106.0)				
6905-5	sdn 4d	2,643	2,218	—
6908-5	wgn 4d	2,800	2,478	—
Rogue (wb 106.0)				
6909-7	htp cpe	2,678	2,296	—
SC/Rambler-Hurst (wb 106.0)				
6909-7	htp cpe	3,160	2,998	1,512

*Total model year registrations: 239,937.

1969 Engines	bore×stroke	bhp	availability
L6, 199.0	3.75×3.00	128	S-American
L6, 232.0	3.75×3.50	145	S-Rogue; O-American
V8, 290.0	3.75×3.28	200	O-Rogue, American 440
V8, 290.0	3.75×3.28	225	O-Rogue
V8, 390.0	4.17×3.57	315	S-SC/Rambler-Hurst

Note: See Nash listing for Rambler models prior to 1957. See AMC listing for related 1966-69 models, and those built after 1969.

SHELBY

1965

GT-350 (wb 108.0)	Wght	Price	Prod
fstbk cpe	2,800	4,547	562

1965 Engine	bore×stroke	bhp	availability
V8, 289.0	4.00×2.87	306	S-all

1966

GT-350 (wb 108.0)	Wght	Price	Prod
fstbk cpe	2,800	4,600	2,380

1966 Engine	bore×stroke	bhp	availability
V8, 289.0	4.00×2.87	306	S-all

1966 GT-350 fastback coupe

1967

GT-350 (wb 108.0)	Wght	Price	Prod
fstbk cpe	2,800	3,995	1,175
GT500 (wb 108.0)			
fstbk cpe	3,000	4,195	2,050

1967 Engines	bore×stroke	bhp	availability
V8, 289.0	4.00×2.87	290	S-GT350
V8, 428.0	4.13×3.98	400*	S-GT500

*Estimated; advertised bhp lower.

1968

GT-350 (wb 108.0)	Wght	Price	Prod
fstbk cpe	3,000	4,117	1,253
conv cpe	3,100	4,238	404
GT-500 (wb 108.0)			
fstbk cpe	3,100	4,317	1,140
conv cpe	3,200	4,439	402
GT-500KR (wb 108.0)			
fstbk cpe	3,200	4,473	933
conv cpe	3,300	4,594	318

1968 Engines	bore×stroke	bhp	availability
V8, 302.0	4.00×3.00	250	S-GT350
V8, 302.0	4.00×3.00	350	O-GT350 (supercharged)
V8, 390.0	4.05×3.78	335	S-GT500
V8, 428.0	4.13×3.98	360	S-GT500
V8, 428.0	4.13×3.98	400*	S-GT500KR

*Estimated; advertised bhp lower.

1969

GT-350 (wb 108.0)	Wght	Price	Prod
fstbk cpe	3,000	4,434	1,085
conv cpe	3,100	4,753	194
GT-500 (wb 108.0)			
fstbk cpe	3,100	4,709	1,536
conv cpe	3,200	5,027	335

1968 GT-500KR fastback coupe

1987 Shelby CSX hatchback coupe

1969 Engines	bore×stroke	bhp	availability
V8, 351.0	4.00×3.50	290	S-GT350
V8, 428.0	4.13×3.98	400*	S-GT500

*Estimated; advertised bhp lower.

1970

GT-350 (wb 108.0)	Wght	Price	Prod
fstbk cpe	3,000	4,500*	350 (fstbk cpe and conv cpe combined)
conv cpe	3,100	4,800*	
GT-500 (wb 108.0)			
fstbk cpe	3,100	4,800*	286 (fstbk cpe and conv cpe combined)
conv cpe	3,200	5,100*	

*Estimated.

1970 Engines	bore×stroke	bhp	availability
V8, 351.0	4.00×3.50	290	S-GT350
V8, 428.0	4.13×3.98	375*	S-GT500

*Estimated; advertised bhp lower.

1986

Shelby GLH-S (wb 99.1)	Wght	Price	Prod
htchbk sdn 5d	2300	10,995	500

1986 Engines	bore × stroke	bhp	availability
I4T,135.0	3.44 × 3.62	175	S-Shelby GLH-S

1987

Shelby Charger GLH-S (wb 96.5)	Wght	Price	Prod
htchbk cpe 3d	2483	12,995	1,000
Shelby CSX (wb 97.0)			
htchbk cpe 3d	2690	13,495	750
Shelby Lancer (wb 103.1)			
htchbk sdn 5d	2895	16,950*	400

1987 Engines	bore × stroke	bhp	availability
I4T, 135.0	3.44 × 3.62	175	S-Shelby Charger GLH-S S-Shelby CSX S-Shelby Lancer

1988

Shelby CSX-T (wb 97.0)	Wght	Price	Prod
htchbk cpe 3d	2675	—**	1,000

1988 Engines	bore × stroke	bhp	availability
I4T, 135.0	3.44 × 3.62	146	S-Shelby CSX-T

1989

Shelby CSX (wb 97.0)	Wght	Price	Prod
htchbk cpe 3d	2790	15,000	500
Shelby Dakota (wb 112.0)			
pickup truck	3610	15,650	1500

1989 Engines	bore × stroke	bhp	availability
I4T, 135.0	3.22 × 3.62	175	S-Shelby CSX
V8, 318.0	3.91 × 3.31	175	S-Shelby Dakota

*5-speed manual transmission, cloth upholstery; $17,950, automatic transmission, leather upholstery.
**All were sold to Thrifty Car Rental at fleet prices.

	Wght	Price	Prod
DeLuxe Starlight cpe	2,695	1,868	—
Regal sdn 4d	2,745	1,949	—
Regal sdn 2d	2,715	1,917	—
Regal Starlight cpe	2,700	1,955	—
Regal Starliner htp cpe	2,760	2,116	—
4H Commander (wb 116.5; LC/cpes-120.5)—76,092 built			
DeLuxe sdn 4d	3,075	2,121	—
DeLuxe DeLuxe sdn 2d	3,055	2,089	—
DeLuxe Starlight cpe	3,040	2,127	—
Regal sdn 4d	3,095	2,208	—
Regal Starlight cpe	3,040	2,213	—
Regal Starliner htp cpe	3,120	2,374	—
Land Cruiser sdn 4d	3,180	2,316	—

1953 Engines	bore×stroke	bhp	availability
L6, 169.6	3.00×4.00	85	S-Champion
V8, 232.6	3.38×3.25	120	S-Commander

1954

15G Champion Six (wb 116.5; cpes-120.5)—51,431 built	Wght	Price	Prod
Custom sdn 4d	2,735	1,801	—
Custom sdn 2d	2,705	1,758	—
DeLuxe sdn 4d	2,765	1,918	—
DeLuxe sdn 2d	2,730	1,875	—
DeLuxe Starlight cpe	2,740	1,972	—
DeLuxe Conestoga wgn 2d	2,930	2,187	—
Regal sdn 4d	2,780	2,026	—
Regal sdn 2d	2,745	1,983	—
Regal Starlight cpe	2,750	2,080	—
Regal Starliner htp cpe	2,825	2,241	—
Regal Conestoga wgn 2d	2,950	2,295	—
5H Commander (wb 116.5; LC/cpes-120.5)—30,499 built			
DeLuxe sdn 4d	3,105	2,179	—
DeLuxe sdn 2d	3,075	2,136	—
DeLuxe Starlight cpe	3,085	2,233	—
DeLuxe Conestoga wgn 2d	3,265	2,448	—
Regal sdn 4d	3,120	2,287	—

1953 Commander Land Cruiser four-door sedan

	Wght	Price	Prod
Regal Starlight cpe	3,095	2,341	—
Regal Starliner htp cpe	3,175	2,502	—
Regal Conestoga wgn 2d	3,265	2,556	—
Land Cruiser sdn 4d	3,180	2,438	—

1954 Engines	bore×stroke	bhp	availability
L6, 169.6	3.00×4.00	85	S-Champion
V8, 232.6	3.38×3.25	120	S-Commander

1955

16G Champion (wb 116.5; cpes-120.5)—50,368 built	Wght	Price	Prod
Custom sdn 4d	2,790	1,783	—
Custom sdn 2d	2,740	1,741	—
DeLuxe sdn 4d	2,805	1,885	—
DeLuxe sdn 2d	2,780	1,841	—
DeLuxe cpe	2,790	1,875	—
DeLuxe wgn 2d	2,980	2,141	—

1954 Champion Regal Conestoga two-door wagon

1955 President Speedster hardtop coupe

	Wght	Price	Prod
Regal sdn 4d	2,815	1,993	—
Regal cpe	2,795	1,975	—
Regal htp cpe	2,865	2,125	—
Regal wgn 2d	2,985	2,312	—
6G Commander (wb 116.5; cpes-120.5)—58,792 built			
Custom sdn 4d	3,065	1,919	—
Custom sdn 2d	3,105	1,873	—
DeLuxe sdn 4d	3,075	2,014	—
DeLuxe sdn 2d	3,045	1,969	—
DeLuxe cpe	3,065	1,989	—
DeLuxe wgn 2d	3,265	2,274	—
Regal sdn 4d	3,080	2,127	—
Regal cpe	3,065	2,094	—
Regal htp cpe	3,150	2,282	—
Regal Conestoga wgn 2d	3,274	2,445	—

1956 President Classic four-door sedan

6H President (wb 120.5)	Wght	Price	Prod
DeLuxe sdn 4d	3,165	2,311	
State sdn 4d	3,220	2,381	22,451 (bracketed, DeLuxe sdn 4d–State htp cpe)
State cpe	3,210	2,270	
State htp cpe	3,175	2,456	
Speedster htp cpe	3,301	3,253	2,215

1955 Engines	bore×stroke	bhp	availability
L6, 185.6	3.00×4.38	101	S-Champion
V8, 224.3	3.56×2.81	140	S-early Commander
V8, 259.2	3.56×3.25	162	S-late Commander
V8, 259.2	3.56×3.25	175	S-early President
V8, 259.2	3.56×3.25	185	S-early Spdstr;O-late Pres

1956

56G Six (wb 116.5; Hawk-120.5)—28,918* built	Wght	Price	Prod
Champion sdn 4d	2,835	1,996	—
Champion sdn 2d	2,800	1,946	—
Champion sedanet	2,780	1,844	—
Pelham wgn 2d	3,000	2,232	—
Flight Hawk cpe	2,780	1,986	—
56B V8, 259 (wb 116.5; Hawk-120.5)—30,654* built			
Commander sdn 4d	3,140	2,125	—
Commander sdn 2d	3,110	2,076	—
Commander sedanet	3,085	1,974	—
Parkview wgn 2d	3,300	2,354	—
Power Hawk cpe	3,095	2,101	—
56H V8, 289 (wb 116.5; Classic/Hawk-120.5)			
President sdn 4d	3,210	2,235	
President sdn 2d	3,180	2,188	18,209 (bracketed, both)

	Wght	Price	Prod
President Classic sdn 4d	3,295	2,489	
Pinehurst wgn 2d	3,395	2,529	
Sky Hawk htp cpe	3,215	2,477	3,610
56J V8, 352 (wb 120.5)			
Golden Hawk htp cpe	3,360	3,061	4,071

*Includes 11,484 Flight Hawks and Power Hawks.

1956 Engines	bore×stroke	bhp	availability
L6, 185.6	3.00×4.38	101	S-Champion, Flight Hawk, Pelham
V8, 259.2	3.56×3.25	170	S-Commander, Power Hawk Parkview
V8, 259.2	3.56×3.25	185	O-Champ, Comm, Power/ Flight Hawk, Wgns
V8, 289.0	3.56×3.63	195	S-President, Pinehurst
V8, 289.0	3.56×3.63	210	S-Classic, Sky Hawk
V8, 289.0	3.56×3.63	225	O-Pres,Pinehurst,Sky Hawk
V8, 352.0	4.00×3.50	275	S-Golden Hawk

1957*

57G Six (wb 116.5; Hawk-120.5)	Wght	Price	Prod
Scotsman sdn 4d	2,725	1,826	—
Scotsman club sdn	2,680	1,776	—
Scotsman wgn 2d	2,875	1,995	—
Champion Custom sdn 4d	2,785	2,049	—
Champion Custom club sdn	2,755	2,001	—
Champion DeLuxe sdn 4d	2,810	2,171	—
Champion DeLuxe club sdn	2,780	2,123	—
Pelham wgn 2d	3,015	2,382	—
Silver Hawk cpe	2,790	2,142	**
57B V8, 259 (wb 116.5)			
Commander Custom sdn 4d	3,105	2,173	—
Commander Custom club sdn	3,075	2,124	—
Commander DeLuxe sdn 4d	3,140	2,295	—
Commander DeLuxe club sdn	3,100	2,246	—
Provincial wgn 4d	3,355	2,561	—
Parkview wgn 2d	3,310	2,505	—

1957 Broadmoor four-door wagon

57H V8, 289 (wb 116.5; Classic/Hawks-120.5)	Wght	Price	Prod
President Classic sdn 4d	3,270	2,539	—
President sdn 4d	3,205	2,407	—
President club sdn	3,170	2,358	—
Broadmoor wgn 4d	3,415	2,666	—
Silver Hawk cpe	3,185	2,263	**
Golden Hawk htp cpe	3,185	3,182	4,356

*Total 1957 production: 74,738.
**Silver Hawk only: 15,318.

1957 Engines	bore×stroke	bhp	availability
L6, 185.6	3.00×4.38	101	S-Scotsman, Champ, Silver Hawk, Pelham
V8, 259.2	3.56×3.25	180	S-Commander & 57B Wagons
V8, 259.2	3.56×3.25	195	O-Commander & 57B Wagons
V8, 289.0	3.56×3.63	210	S-President, Silver Hawk, 57H Wagons
V8, 289.0	3.56×3.63	225	S-President Classic; O-Silver Hawk, 57H Wgn
V8, 289.0	3.56×3.63	275	S-Golden Hawk

1957 Champion DeLuxe Club sedan

1959 Lark two-door wagon

1958

58G Six (wb 116.5; Hawk-120.5)	Wght	Price	Prod
Silver Hawk cpe	2,810	2,291	*
Scotsman sdn 4d	2,740	1,874	
Scotsman sdn 2d	2,695	1,795	20,870
Scotsman wgn 2d	2,870	2,055	
Champion sdn 4d	2,835	2,253	10,325
Champion sdn 2d	2,795	2,189	

58B V8, 259 (wb 116.5)—12,249 built	Wght	Price	Prod
Commander sdn 4d	3,185	2,378	—
Commander Starlight htp cpe	3,270	2,493	—
Provincial wgn 4d	3,420	2,664	—

58H V8, 289 (wb 120.5; Starlight htp-116.5)	Wght	Price	Prod
President sdn 4d	3,365	2,639	10,442
President Starlight htp cpe	3,355	2,695	
Silver Hawk cpe	3,210	2,352	*
Golden Hawk htp cpe	3,470	3,282	878

*Total Silver Hawk: 7,350.

1958 Engines	bore×stroke	bhp	availability
L6, 185.6	3.00×4.38	101	S-Scotsman, Champion, Silver Hawk
V8, 259.2	3.56×3.25	180	S-Commander, Provincial
V8, 289.0	3.56×3.63	210	O-Silver Hawk
V8, 289.0	3.56×3.63	225	S-President; O-Silver Hawk
V8, 289.0	3.56×3.63	275	S-Golden Hawk

1959

59S Lark VI (wb 108.5; Regal wgn-113.0)—98,744 built	Wght	Price	Prod
DeLuxe sdn 4d	2,605	1,995	—
DeLuxe sdn 2d	2,577	1,925	—
DeLuxe wgn 2d	2,805	2,295	—
Regal sdn 4d	2,600	2,175	—
Regal htp cpe	2,710	2,275	—
Regal wgn 2d	2,815	2,455	—

59V Lark VIII (wb 108.5; wgn-113.0)—32,334 built	Wght	Price	Prod
Regal sdn 4d	2,924	2,310	—
Regal htp cpe	3,034	2,411	—
Regal wgn 2d	3,148	2,590	—

59S/59V Silver Hawk (wb 120.5)	Wght	Price	Prod
cpe, L6	2,795	2,360	2,417
cpe, V8	3,140	2,495	5,371

1959 Engines	bore×stroke	bhp	availability
L6, 169.6	3.00×4.00	90	S-Lark VI, Silver Hawk 6
V8, 259.2	3.56×3.25	180	S-Lark VIII, Silver Hawk 8
V8, 259.2	3.56×3.25	195	O-Lark VIII, Silver Hawk 8

1960

60S Lark VI (wb 108.5; wgns-113.0)—70,153 built	Wght	Price	Prod
DeLuxe sdn 4d	2,592	2,046	—
DeLuxe sdn 2d	2,588	1,976	—
DeLuxe wgn 4d	2,792	2,441	—
DeLuxe wgn 2d	2,763	2,366	—
Regal sdn 4d	2,619	2,196	—
Regal htp cpe	2,697	2,296	—
Regal conv cpe	2,961	2,621	—
Regal wgn 4d	2,836	2,591	—

60V Lark VIII (wb 108.5; wgns-113.0)—57,562 built	Wght	Price	Prod
DeLuxe sdn 4d	2,941	2,181	—
DeLuxe sdn 2d	2,921	2,111	—
DeLuxe wgn 4d	3,161	2,576	—
DeLuxe wgn 2d	3,138	2,501	—
Regal sdn 4d	2,966	2,331	—
Regal htp cpe	3,033	2,431	—
Regal conv cpe	3,315	2,756	—
Regal wgn 4d	3,183	2,726	—

60S/60V Hawk (wb 120.5)—3,939 built	Wght	Price	Prod
cpe, L6	2,770	2,383	—
cpe, V8	3,207	2,650	—

1959 Lark Regal hardtop coupe

1960 Engines	bore×stroke	bhp	availability
L6, 169.6	3.00×4.00	90	S-Lark VI
V8, 259.2	3.56×3.25	180	S-Lark VIII
V8, 259.2	3.56×3.25	195	O-Lark VIII
V8, 289.0	3.56×3.63	210	S-Hawk
V8, 289.0	3.56×3.63	225	O-Hawk

1961

61S Lark VI (wb 108.5; wgns-113.0)—41,035 built	Wght	Price	Prod
DeLuxe sdn 4d	2,665	1,935	—
DeLuxe sdn 2d	2,661	2,005	—
DeLuxe wgn 4d	2,865	2,370	—
DeLuxe wgn 2d	2,836	2,290	—
Regal sdn 4d	2,692	2,155	—
Regal htp cpe	2,770	2,243	—
Regal conv cpe	3,034	2,554	—
Regal wgn 4d	2,836	2,520	—
61V Lark VIII (wb 108.5; Crsr/wgns-113.0)—25,934 built			
DeLuxe sdn 4d	2,941	2,140	—
DeLuxe sdn 2d	2,921	2,070	—
DeLuxe wgn 4d	3,183	2,505	—
DeLuxe wgn 2d	3,112	2,425	—
Regal sdn 4d	2,956	2,290	—
Regal htp cpe	3,074	2,378	—
Regal conv cpe	3,315	2,689	—
Regal wgn 4d	3,183	2,655	—
Cruiser sdn 4d	3,001	2,458	—
61V Hawk (wb 120.5)			
cpe	3,205	2,650	3,340

1961 Engines	bore×stroke	bhp	availability
L6, 169.6	3.00×4.00	112	S-Lark VI
V8, 259.2	3.56×3.25	180	S-Lark VIII
V8, 259.2	3.56×3.25	195	O-Lark VIII
V8, 289.0	3.56×3.63	210	S-Hawk
V8, 289.0	3.56×3.63	225	O-Hawk

1962

62S Lark Six (wb 113.0; 2d-109.0)—54,397 built	Wght	Price	Prod
DeLuxe sdn 4d	2,760	2,040	—
DeLuxe sdn 2d	2,655	1,935	—
DeLuxe wgn 4d	2,845	2,405	—

1960 Lark Regal convertible coupe

1961 Hawk coupe

	Wght	Price	Prod
Regal sdn 4d	2,770	2,190	—
Regal wgn 4d	2,875	2,555	—
Regal htp cpe	2,765	2,218	—
Regal conv cpe	3,075	2,589	—
Daytona htp cpe	2,765	2,308	—
Daytona conv cpe	3,075	2,679	—
62V Lark Eight (wb 113.0; 2d-109.0)—38,607 built			
DeLuxe sdn 4d	3,015	2,175	—
DeLuxe sdn 2d	2,925	2,070	—
DeLuxe wgn 4d	3,115	2,540	—
Regal sdn 4d	3,025	2,325	—
Regal wgn 4d	3,145	2,690	—

	Wght	Price	Prod
Regal htp cpe	3,015	2,353	—
Regal conv cpe	3,305	2,724	—
Daytona htp cpe	3,015	2,443	—
Daytona conv cpe	3,305	2,814	—
Cruiser sdn 4d	3,030	2,493	—
62V Gran Turismo Hawk (wb 120.5)			
htp cpe	3,230	3,095	8,388

1962 Engines	bore×stroke	bhp	availability
L6, 169.6	3.00×4.00	112	S-Lark Six
V8, 259.2	3.56×3.25	180	S-Lark Eight
V8, 259.2	3.56×3.25	195	O-Lark Eight
V8, 289.0	3.56×3.63	210	S-GT Hawk; O-Lark Cruiser
V8, 289.0	3.56×3.63	225	O-GT Hawk, Lark Cruiser

1963

63S Lark Six (wb 113.0; 2d-109.0)—74,201 built (includes 63V)	Wght	Price	Prod
Standard sdn 4d	2,775	2,040	—
Standard sdn 2d	2,650	1,935	—
Standard wgn 4d	3,285	2,430	—
Regal sdn 4d	2,790	2,160	—
Regal sdn 2d	2,665	2,055	—
Regal wgn 4d	3,200	2,550	—
Custom sdn 4d	2,800	2,285	—
Custom sdn 2d	2,680	2,180	—
Daytona wgn 4d	3,245	2,700	—
Daytona htp cpe	2,795	2,308	—

1962 Lark four-door sedan

1963 Daytona four-door wagon

	Wght	Price	Prod
Daytona conv cpe	3,045	2,679	—
63V Lark Eight (wb 113.0; 2d-109.0)			
Standard sdn 4d	2,985	2,175	—
Standard sdn 2d	2,910	2,070	—
Standard wgn 4d	3,435	2,565	—
Regal sdn 4d	3,000	2,295	—
Regal sdn 2d	2,925	2,190	—
Regal wgn 4d	3,450	2,685	—
Custom sdn 4d	3,010	2,420	—
Custom sdn 2d	2,940	2,315	—
Daytona wgn 4d	3,490	2,835	—
Daytona htp cpe	3,035	2,443	—

	Wght	Price	Prod
Daytona conv cpe	3,265	2,814	—
Cruiser sdn 4d	3,065	2,595	—
63V Gran Turismo Hawk (wb 120.5)			
htp cpe	3,280	3,095	4,634
63R Avanti (wb 109.0)			
spt cpe	3,140	4,445	3,834

1963 Engines	bore×stroke	bhp	availability
L6, 169.6	3.00×4.00	112	S-Lark 6
V8, 259.2	3.56×3.25	180	S-Lark V8
V8, 259.2	3.56×3.25	195	O-Lark V8
V8, 289.0	3.56×3.63	210	S-Hawk, Cruiser; O-Lark V8
V8, 289.0	3.56×3.63	225	O-Hawk, Lark V8, Cruiser
V8, 289.0	3.56×3.63	240	S-Avanti; O-Hawk, Lark V8 (R1)
V8, 289.0	3.56×3.63	290	O-Avanti, Hawk, Lark V8 (R2)

1964

64S Lark Six (wb 113.0; 2d-109.0)—44,184 built (includes 64V)	Wght	Price	Prod
Challenger sdn 4d	2,780	2,048	—
Challenger sdn 2d	2,660	1,943	—
Challenger wgn 4d	3,230	2,438	—
Commander sdn 4d	2,815	2,168	—
Commander sdn 2d	2,695	2,063	—
Commander Special sdn 2d	2,725	2,193	—

1963 Avanti sport coupe

1964 Avanti sport coupe

	Wght	Price	Prod
Commander wgn 4d	3,265	2,558	—
Daytona sdn 4d	2,790	2,318	—
Daytona conv cpe	3,040	2,670	—
Daytona wgn 4d	3,240	2,708	—
64V Lark Eight (wb 113.0; 2d-109.0)			
Challenger sdn 4d	3,010	2,183	—

	Wght	Price	Prod
Challenger sdn 2d	2,910	2,078	—
Challenger wgn 4d	3,480	2,573	—
Commander sdn 4d	3,045	2,303	—
Commander sdn 2d	2,945	2,198	—
Commander Special sdn 2d	2,975	2,328	—
Daytona sdn 4d	3,055	2,453	—
Daytona htp cpe	3,060	2,451	—

1964 Gran Turismo Hawk hardtop coupe

1964 Lark Eight Cruiser four-door sedan

			Wght	Price	Prod
Daytona conv cpe			3,320	2,805	—
Daytona wgn 4d			3,555	2,843	—
Cruiser sdn 4d			3,120	2,603	—
64V Gran Turismo Hawk (wb 120.5)					
htp cpe			3,120	2,966	1,767
64R Avanti (wb 109.0)					
spt cpe			3,195	4,445	809

1964 Engines	bore×stroke	bhp	availability
L6, 169.6	3.00×4.00	112	S-Challenger/Commander/ Daytona 6
V8, 259.2	3.56×3.25	180	S-Challenger/Commander/ Daytona 8
V8, 259.2	3.56×3.25	195	O-Challenger/Commander/ Daytona 8
V8, 289.0	3.56×3.63	210	S-Hawk,Cruiser; O-other V8
V8, 289.0	3.56×3.63	225	O-all V8 exc Avanti
V8, 289.0	3.56×3.63	240	S-Avanti; O-other V8 (R1)
V8, 289.0	3.56×3.63	290	O-all (R2)
V8, 304.5	3.65×3.63	335	O-all exc. Challenger (R3)
V8, 304.5	3.65×3.63	280	O-all exc. Challenger (R4)

1965—19,435 built

C-1 Six (wb 113.0; 2d-109.0)	Wght	Price	Prod
Commander sdn 4d	2,815	2,230	—
Commander sdn 2d	2,695	2,125	—
Commander wgn 4d	3,265	2,620	—
Cruiser sdn 4d	2,820	2,470	—

C-5 Eight (wb 113.0; 2d-109.0)	Wght	Price	Prod
Commander sdn 4d	2,995	2,370	—
Commander sdn 2d	2,895	2,265	—
Commander wgn 4d	3,465	2,760	—
Daytona Sport sdn 2d	2,970	2,565	—
Daytona wgn 4d	3,505	2,890	—
Cruiser sdn 4d	3,070	2,610	—

1965 Eight Daytona Sport two-door sedan

1966 Eight Daytona two-door sedan

1965 Engines	bore×stroke	bhp	availability
L6, 194.0	3.56×3.25	120	S-Commander 6, Cruiser 6
V8, 283.0	3.88×3.00	195	S-Commander/Cruiser V8, Daytona

1966—8,947 built

Six (wb 113.0; 2d-109.0)	Wght	Price	Prod
Commander sdn 4d	2,815	2,165	—
Commander sdn 2d	2,695	2,060	—
Wagonaire wgn 2d	3,246	2,555	—
Daytona sdn 2d	2,755	2,405	—
Cruiser sdn 4d	2,815	2,405	—
Eight (wb 113.0; 2d-109.0)			
Commander sdn 4d	2,991	2,305	—
Commander sdn 2d	2,891	2,200	—
Wagonaire wgn 2d	3,501	2,695	—
Daytona sdn 2d	3,006	2,500	—
Cruiser sdn 4d	3,066	2,545	—

1966 Engines	bore×stroke	bhp	availability
L6, 194.0	3.56×3.25	120	S-Commander/Cruiser/ Daytona 6
L6, 230.0	3.88×3.25	140	O-sixes
V8, 283.0	3.88×3.00	195	S-Commander/Cruiser/ Daytona V8

Postwar Studebaker production includes cars manufactured in South Bend and Hamilton, Ontario for U.S., Canadian, and export sale.
All 1965-66 Studebakers were built in Canada.

TUCKER

1947

(wb 128.0)		Wght	Price	Prod
Torpedo	sdn 4d	4,235	2,245	51

1947 Engines	bore×stroke	bhp	availability
flat 6, 335.0	4.50×3.50	166	S-all

1948 Torpedo four-door sedan

WILLYS

1939

38 (wb 100.0)*	Wght	Price	Prod
Standard cpe 2P	2,181	499	—
Standard sdn 2d	2,258	539	—
Standard sdn 4d	2,300	563	—
Deluxe cpe 2P	2,181	574	—
Deluxe sdn 2d	2,258	575	—
Deluxe sdn 4d	2,306	614	—
39 Overland (wb 102.0)—15,214 built			
Standard Speedway cpe 2P	2,137	596	—
Standard Speedway sdn 2d	2,217	616	—
Standard Speedway sdn 4d	2,249	631	—
Deluxe cpe 2P	2,193	646	—
Deluxe sdn 2d	2,262	667	—
Deluxe sdn 4d	2,306	689	—
Speedway Special cpe 2P	2,193	610	—
Speedway Special sdn 2d	2,262	631	—
Speedway Special sdn 4d	2,306	646	—
48 (wb 100.0)—2,625 built			
cpe 2P	2,181	524	—
sdn 2d	2,258	565	—
sdn 4d	2,300	586	—

*26,691 built in 1938-39.

1939 Engines	bore×stroke	bhp	availability
L4, 134.2	3.13×4.38	48	S-38,48

1941 pickup truck

	bore×stroke	bhp	availability
L4, 134.2	3.13×4.38	62	S-39

1940

440 (wb 102.0)—26,698 built	Wght	Price	Prod
Speedway cpe	2,146	529	—
Speedway sdn 4d	2,238	596	—
DeLuxe cpe	2,190	641	—
DeLuxe sdn 4d	2,255	672	—
DeLuxe wgn 4d	2,124	830	—

1940 Engine	bore×stroke	bhp	availability
L4, 134.2	3.13×4.38	61	S-all

1939 Overland four-door sedan

1941

441 Americar (wb 104.0)*	Wght	Price	Prod
Speedway cpe	2,116	634	—
Speedway sdn 4d	2,230	674	—
DeLuxe cpe	2,135	685	—
Deluxe sdn 4d	2,265	720	—
DeLuxe wgn 4d	2,483	916	—
Plainsman cpe	2,175	740	—
Plainsman sdn 4d	2,305	771	—

1941 Engine	bore×stroke	bhp	availability
L4, 134.2	3.13×4.38	63	S-all

1942

442 Americar (wb 104.0)*	Wght	Price	Prod
Speedway cpe	2,142	695	—
Speedway sdn 4d	2,261	745	—
DeLuxe cpe	2,184	769	—
DeLuxe sdn 4d	2,295	795	—
DeLuxe wgn 4d	2,512	978	—
Plainsman cpe	2,242	819	—
Plainsman sdn 4d	2,353	845	—

1942 Engine	bore×stroke	bhp	availability
L4, 134.2	3.13×4.38	63	S-all

*Total 1941-1942 Americar production: 28,935.

1948

463 Four (wb 104.0)	Wght	Price	Prod
Jeepster phtn conv	2,468	1,765	10,326

1948 Engine	bore×stroke	bhp	availability
L4, 134.3	3.13×4.38	63	S-all

1949

463 Four (wb 104.0)—2,307 built (includes VJ-3 Four)	Wght	Price	Prod
Jeepster phtn conv	2,468	1,495	—
VJ-3 Four (wb 104.5)			
Jeepster phtn conv	2,468	1,495	—

1941 Americar DeLuxe coupe

1949 Jeepster phaeton convertible

VJ-3 Six (wb 104.0)			Wght	Price	Prod
Jeepster phtn conv			2,392	1,530	653
1949 Engines	**bore×stroke**	**bhp**	**availability**		
L4, 134.3	3.13×4.38	63	S-463 Four		
L4, 134.3	3.13×4.38	72	S-VJ3 Four (F-head)		
L6, 148.5	3.00×3.50	72	S-Six		

1950

473 Four (wb 104.0)—4,066 built (includes VJ-3)			Wght	Price	Prod
Jeepster phtn conv			2,459	1,390	—
VJ-3 Four (wb 104.0)					
Jeepster phtn conv			2,468	1,495	—
673VJ Six (wb 104.0)					
Jeepster phtn conv			2,485	1,490	1,778
1950 Engines	**bore×stroke**	**bhp**	**availability**		
L4, 134.2	3.13×4.38	63	S-Four, 1st series, L-head		
L4, 134.2	3.13×4.38	72	S-Four, 2nd series, F-head		
L6, 148.5	3.00×3.50	72	S-Six, 1st series, L-head		
L6, 161.0	3.13×3.50	75	S-Six, 2nd series, F-head		

1951

473-VJ Four (wb 104.0)*			Wght	Price	Prod
Jeepster phtn conv			2,459	1,426	—
673-VJ Six (wb 104.0)*					
Jeepster phtn conv			2,485	1,529	—

*Combined with 1950 totals; includes 1950 leftovers sold as '51s.

1951 Engines	bore×stroke	bhp	availability
L4, 134.2	3.13×4.38	72	S-Four
L6, 161.0	3.13×3.50	75	S-Six

1952

652-K Aero-Lark (wb 108.0)	Wght	Price	Prod
KA2-675 sdn 2d	2,487	1,731	7,474

1950 Jeepster phaeton convertible

1952 Aero-Wing two-door sedan

652-L Aero-Wing (wb 108.0)	Wght	Price	Prod
LA1-685 sdn 2d	2,570	1,989	12,819
652-M Aero (wb 108.0)			
MA1-685 Ace sdn 2d	2,584	2,074	8,706
MC1-685 Eagle htp cpe	2,575	2,155	2,364

1952 Engines	bore×stroke	bhp	availability
L6, 161.0	3.13×3.50	75	S-Lark
L6, 161.0	3.13×3.50	90	S-Wing, Ace, Eagle

1953

653-K Aero-Lark (wb 108.0)	Wght	Price	Prod
KA1-675 sdn 2d	2,487	1,646	8,205
KB1-675 sdn 4d	2,509	1,732	7,692

1954 Ace DeLuxe four-door sedan

653-M Aero- (wb 108.0)	Wght	Price	Prod
MA1-685 Ace sdn 2d	2,584	1,963	4,988
MB1-685 Ace sdn 4d	2,735	2,038	7,475
MC1-685 Eagle htp cpe	2,575	2,157	7,018
653-P Aero-Falcon (wb 108.0)			
PA1-675 sdn 2d	2,507	1,760	3,054
PB1-675 sdn 4d	2,529	1,861	3,117

1953 Engines	bore×stroke	bhp	availability
L4, 134.2	3.13×4.38	72	S-Lark 4
L6, 161.0	3.13×3.50	75	S-Lark 6, Falcon
L6, 161.0	3.13×3.50	90	S-Ace, Eagle

1954

654-K Aero-Lark (wb 108.0)	Wght	Price	Prod
KA2 sdn 2d, (226)	2,740	—	59
KB2 sdn 4d, (226)	2,730	—	282
KA3-685 sdn 2d	2,623	1,737	1,370
KA3-685 Custom sdn 2d	2,678	1,798	1,132
KB3-685 sdn 4d	2,661	1,823	1,482
KB3-685 Custom sdn 4d	2,722	1,878	548
654-M Aero- (wb 108.0)			
MA1 Ace DeLuxe sdn 2d (226)	2,751	—	1,195
MA1 Ace DeLuxe Custom sdn 2d (226)	2,806	—	7
MB1 Ace DeLuxe sdn 4d (226)	2,778	—	1,498
MB1 Ace DeLuxe Custom sdn 4d (226)	2,833	—	9
MA2-685 Ace sdn 2d	2,682	1,892	2
MA2-685 Ace Custom sdn 2d	2,737	1,947	586
MB2-685 Ace sdn 4d	2,709	1,968	1,380
MB2-685 Ace Custom sdn 4d	2,764	2,023	611
MC1 Eagle htp cpe (226)	2,847	—	660
MC1 Eagle Custom htp cpe (226)	2,904	—	11
MC2 Eagle Special htp cpe (226)	—	—	302
MC3-685 Eagle DeLuxe htp cpe	—	2,222	84
MC3-685 Eagle DeLuxe Custom htp cpe	—	2,411	499

1954 Engines	bore×stroke	bhp	availability
L4, 134.2	3.13×4.38	72	S-Lark 4
L6, 161.0	3.13×3.50	90	S-Lark 6, Ace, Eagle
L6, 226.2	3.31×4.38	115	O-Lark 6, Ace, Eagle

1953 Aero-Lark DeLuxe two-door sedan

1955

522/6 Ace (wb 108.0)	Wght	Price	Prod
52367 sdn 4d (226)	—	—	659
523/4 Custom (wb 108.0)			
52367 sdn 4d (226)	2,778	1,795	2,822
52462 sdn 2d (161)	—	—	2
52467 sdn 2d (226)	2,751	1,725	288
525 Bermuda (wb 108.0)			
52527 htp cpe (161)	—	—	59
52567 htp cpe (226)	2,831	1,997	2,156

1955 Engines	bore×stroke	bhp	availability
L6, 161.0	3.13×3.50	90	S-Custom, Bermuda
L6, 226.2	3.31×4.38	115	S-Ace; O-Custom, Bermuda

Willys production does not include steel-bodied station wagons manufactured from 1946 through 1961, or Wagoneers (wagons) manufactured from 1960 onward. Aero production does not include export or taxi models. Production continued in Brazil through 1962.

1955 Bermuda hardtop coupe

BRICKLIN

1974

(wb 96.0)		Wght	Price	Prod
SV-1	cpe	NA	7,490	*

1974 Engines	bore × stroke	bhp	availability
V8, 360.0	4.08 × 3.44	175	S-all

1975

(wb 96.0)		Wght	Price	Prod
SV-1	cpe	NA	9,775	*

1975 Engines	bore × stroke	bhp	availability
V8, 351.0	4.00 × 3.50	162	S-all

*Total 1974-75 production, 2,897.

CUNNINGHAM

1951

(wb 105.0)		Wght	Price	Prod
	cpe	3,450	—	proto

1951 Engines	bore × stroke	bhp	availability
V8, 331.0	3.81 × 3.63	220	S-all

1951-52

(wb 105.0)		Wght	Price	Prod
C-2	cpe	3,200	9,000	—
C-2	conv cpe	—	8,000	—

1953 Cunningham C-3 coupe

1953 Muntz Jet hardtop coupe

51-52 Engines	bore × stroke	bhp	availability
V8, 331.0	3.81 × 3.63	220-270	S-all

1953-55

(wb 105.0)		Wght	Price	Prod
C-3	cpe	2,800	10,000	27
C-3	conv cpe	2,800	13,999*	

53-55 Engines	bore × stroke	bhp	availability
V8, 331.0	3.81 × 3.63	235	S-all

*1954 price.

MUNTZ

1950

(wb 113.0)		Wght	Price	Prod
	cpe	3,300	—	28

1950 Engines	bore × stroke	bhp	availability
V8, 331.0	3.81 × 3.63	160	S-all

1951-52

(wb 116.0)		Wght	Price	Prod
	cpe	3,780	4,450	230

51-52 Engines	bore × stroke	bhp	availability
V8, 337.0	3.50 × 4.38	154	S-all

1953-54

(wb 116.0)		Wght	Price	Prod
	cpe	3,560	5,515	136

53-54 Engines	bore × stroke	bhp	availability
V8, 337.0	3.50 × 4.38	218	S-all

INDEX

R

S

T

V

W

Y

Z